Children's Books in Children's Hands

An Introduction to Their Literature

Charles Temple
Hobart and William Smith Colleges

Miriam Martinez
University of Texas at San Antonio

Junko Yokota
National-Louis University

Alice Naylor
Appalachian State University

With Contributions by

Evelyn B. Freeman   **Joy Moss**
The Ohio State University   *University of Rochester*

Allyn and Bacon
Boston   London   Toronto   Sydney   Tokyo   Singapore

Sr. Editor: Virginia Lanigan
Editorial Assistant: Kris Lamarre
Sr. Marketing Manager: Kathy Hunter
Sr. Editorial Production Administrator: Susan McIntyre
Editorial Production Service: Jane Hoover/Lifland et al., Bookmakers
Composition and Prepress Buyer: Linda Cox
Manufacturing Buyer: Megan Cochran
Cover Administrator: Linda Knowles
Text Design: Barbara Libby; Quica Ostrander/Lifland et al., Bookmakers
Electronic Composition Manager: Tim Ries
Electronic Page Layout: Shelley Davidson
Color Separator: Eastern Rainbow

Copyright © 1998 by Allyn & Bacon
A Viacom Company
160 Gould Street
Needham Heights, MA 02194

Internet: www.abacon.com
American Online: keyword: College Online

Illustrations on pages vii–xxi, 2–3, 4, 5, 14, 27, 30, 31, 43, 52, 57, 58, 72, 77, 81, 82, 89, 114, 134–135, 136, 137, 144, 163, 170, 171, 204, 205, 225, 226, 227, 248, 257, 264, 265, 270, 293, 308, 313, 327, 335, 336, 346, 363, 376, 377, 379, 399, 410–411, 412, 413, 417, 441, 449, 450, 461, 472, 480, 481, 495, 500, 512, 534, 535, 538, 545, and 547 copyright © 1997 by Frané Lessac. Photo and text credits appear on pages 579 and 580, which constitute a continuation of the copyright page.

Library of Congress Cataloging-in-Publication Data

Children's books in children's hands : an introduction to their
  literature/Charles Temple . . . [et al.] ; with contributions by
  Evelyn Freeman, Joy Moss.
       p.   cm.
  Includes bibliographical references (p.   ) and index.
  ISBN 0-205-16995-3 (hc)
   1. Children's literature—History and criticism   2. Children's—
Books and reading.   I. Temple, Charles A.   II. Freeman,
Evelyn B. (Evelyn Blossom)   III. Moss, Joy F.
  PN1009.ALC5118   1997
  809' .89282—dc21
                                                                    97-9950
                                                                        CIP

Printed in the United States of America

10 9 8 7 6 5 4 3 2 1   VHP   04 03 02 01 00 99 98 97

To Anna Brooke, Jessie, and Tyler, and in memory of Frances

C.T.

To my parents for the stories they shared with me,
to David and Chris for the opportunities to share stories with them,
and to Cheo for the stories he shares each day

M.M.

To Alyssa and Jeremy, Mia and Reid

J.Y.

To my grandchildren: Armon, Arriane, and Kaveh Emdad;
Jennifer and Nathan Naylor; and Maya Losardo

A.N.

Brief Contents

Contents

✓2 Literary Elements of Children's Literature 30

3   The Child Reader Responds to Literature   57

4   Literature Representing Diverse Perspectives   81

6   Picture Books   170

7 Poetry for Children   225

8 Realistic Fiction   264

11   Informational Books and Biography   376

13 Encouraging Response to Literature: Literary Discussion   449

14 Literature Units in the Curriculum   480

Preface

S uppose there was a long-lived squadron of extraterrestrials that checked in on earth once every century over many thousands of years. Surely they would recognize, from their previous visits, what some of us earthlings are doing now, in the closing days of the twentieth century, as we read a book to a classroom of students. "Typical," they might say, "those earthlings are always sharing what they think is important with their children through stories."

The circumstances in which humans have shared stories have changed over time, true enough. The earliest stories were told as people huddled around campfires wrapped in animal skins. Later, stories were shared in a temple with camel skins spread on the floor or in a drafty cathedral packed with wide-eyed and bedraggled pilgrims. Sometimes people told stories in front of a fireplace, as the wind howled around a cottage way out on the prairie. Sometimes the stories were shared in the cold, heaving berth of a grimy steamer bound for Ellis Island. Sometimes grandparents or parents told children stories in order to pass on family history. And sometimes, today, children hear stories in a classroom, on a carpet at a teacher's feet. But, whatever the circumstances, the habit of delighting, enchanting, instructing, and challenging through the medium of story—through *literature*—has always been at the center of the way humans brought up their young. There are many reasons why.

Some say stories educate the imagination—fire the spirit with a sense of possibility. Though this is no doubt true, contemporary children's books also help children understand the pressing issues of their lives—from sibling rivalry to the pull of the peer group to the limiting viciousness of racism.

Some say sharing literature virtually makes childhood possible, by giving children a separate world of images and ideas that insulates them from everyday reality. Though this may be true, children's books also fascinate youngsters by explaining the workings of the real world—from desert ecosystems to the origins of napkins and forks to the structure of DNA.

Some say children's books pass on the truths and values that adults hold to be most important. Though this is often the case, many children's books and many teachers challenge children to think for themselves, to find their own truths.

And some say children's books pass on a cultural heritage and tell children who they are. Though this is often true, contemporary children's literature also acquaints children with many cultures other than their own and may thus help increase tolerance and cooperation in today's diverse society.

In this book, we seek to explain the vital importance of sharing ideas with the young through children's literature and to nurture a richer appreciation of the books themselves. We had several goals in writing this book:

- To help the adult reader recognize the many ways children benefit from literature at different times in their lives and appreciate what happens when a child is engaged by a book

- To acquaint the adult reader with the wealth of children's books that are available today and to enable that reader to make critical judgments about them
- To equip the reader with a range of proven strategies to bring children together with books productively and pleasurably

HOW THIS BOOK IS ORGANIZED

Part One of this book, "Understanding Literature and the Child Reader," orients the reader to the study of children's literature. Chapter 1, "Children's Books in Children's Hands," introduces the child reader and the reading process, focusing in turn on what is known about children's intellectual and personality development and on the nature of children's responses to literature. Chapter 2, "Literary Elements of Children's Literature," introduces a set of literary concepts with which to approach children's books, describing how plots are organized, how characters are drawn, and how themes are developed. Chapter 3, "The Child Reader Responds to Literature," discusses reader response theory and its implications for the study and sharing of children's literature. Chapter 4, "Literature Representing Diverse Perspectives," reflects this book's strong emphasis on multicultural literature. It investigates the ways various cultural groups are depicted in children's literature, highlights the progress that has been made in publishing children's books that represent various cultural groups more extensively and fairly, surveys the multicultural and international books that are available, and sets out guidelines for selecting high-quality multicultural books for children.

Part Two, "Exploring the Genres of Children's Literature," surveys children's books by genre. Each of the chapters in this part outlines the historical development of a particular genre, examines the literary qualities that distinguish the genre and the reading demands those qualities place on the child, reviews outstanding examples of works from the genre, and sets out criteria for selecting good works in the genre. Each chapter closes with an extensive annotated list of recommended books in the genre.

Chapter 5 "Traditional Literature," looks at folk literature from many times and cultures. Chapter 6, "Picture Books," focuses on how art and text combine to form unique works. Chapter 7, "Poetry for Children," surveys this genre from nursery rhymes to contemporary multicultural poetry for children. Chapter 8, "Realistic Fiction," looks at ways authors create believable books that are set in the "here and now" and that address the wide-ranging problems and delights of today's children. Books set in times that may be many generations removed from our own are discussed in Chapter 9, "Historical Fiction," which explains the origins of the current emphasis on meticulous accuracy in this genre. Many highly imaginative works are explored in Chapter 10, "Modern Fantasy and Science Fiction," which considers the artistry that enables readers to enter hypothetical worlds. Chapter 11, "Informational Books and Biography," surveys a growing area of children's literature, in which talented writers present the real world and its people to young readers in skillfully focused works that can be as riveting as fiction.

Part Three, "Creating the Literature-Based Classroom," was written for current and future teachers and librarians and anyone else who wants to share literature with children in ways that ensure that they will get the most from the encounters. Chapter 12, "Inviting Children into Literature," details how to entice children into literature through the creation of classroom libraries and through activities such as reading aloud, storytelling, readers theater, and journal writing. Conducting book discussions with children so that they are empowered to say what they feel and are encouraged to grow through the discussions is the topic of Chapter 13, "Encouraging Response to Literature: Literary Discussion." Constructing literature units and guiding children through them is the focus of Chapter 14, "Literature Units in the Curriculum." This chapter, like the others in this part, provides extensive lists of recommended books for use in the literature-based classroom.

The appendixes offer several lists of useful information: the recipients of major children's book awards, names and addresses of professional organizations, names and addresses of major children's book publishers, book selection aids, children's magazines, and useful web sites for and about children's literature.

PEDAGOGICAL AND ENRICHMENT FEATURES OF THIS BOOK

Each chapter includes an "Ask the Author" (or Editor or Illustrator) box, in which a prominent children's author, illustrator, or editor responds to a question related to the chapter content. Each chapter also features an "Issue to Consider" box, which presents a highly debated issue in children's literature related to that chapter's content.

Several useful features appear at the end of every chapter. "Teaching Ideas" provide valuable, practical lessons and activities for sharing literature with children in the classroom. "Experiences for Your Learning" are activities readers of this book can do to increase and deepen their own understanding of the chapter content. Finally, lists of Recommended Books offer publication data and a brief annotation and indicate interest level by age for every book listed.

ACKNOWLEDGMENTS

Frances Temple and Nancy Roser helped shape our thinking early in the project; we are grateful to both. We also wish to thank Nancy for suggesting the title of the book, which so aptly captures our mission as the authors. Bird Stasz and her students at Wells College used the book in manuscript form and tried out many of the exercises with the children at Peachtown School in Aurora, New York, where Bill Schara is head teacher. We thank all of these people for their encouragement and valuable feedback.

Joy Moss, a teacher educator at the University of Rochester (New York) and an elementary school literature teacher, contributed her expertise and enthusiasm about literature units in the curriculum by way of an outstanding Chapter 14. Joy also brought her considerable experiences in sharing literature with children to bear in reading and commenting on the entire book in its formative stages.

Thanks are due to Evelyn B. Freeman, who contributed Chapter 11 on informational books. Evie's delightful energy and enthusiasm for her field of specialty and her impressive bibliographic knowledge in that area resulted in what many reviewers deemed the most complete and authoritative discussion of informational books for children they've encountered in any survey text.

We have long admired the colorful and vibrant art of Frané Lessac; so we were honored when she agreed to create illustrations for this book—and delighted with the results.

Thanks to A. Waller Hastings, professor of children's literature at Northern State University in Aberdeen, South Dakota, for preparing the annotated list of web sites in Appendix F.

Thanks also go to the talented children's book authors, illustrators, and editors who so generously shared their thoughts and experiences for the "Ask the Author" features. In addition, several writer and illustrator friends gave us a look inside their craft: thanks to the Rochester Writers Group, especially Cynthia DeFelice, Ellen Stoll Walsh, M. J. Auch, Vivian Van de Veld, and Robin Pulver; and also to Barbara Seuling and Bill Hooks. Several children's book editors did much the same thing, and we wish to thank Matilda Welter, Refna Wilkin, Kent Brown, and Richard Jackson.

For their expert knowledge of children's books, our thanks go to Pat Farthing and Susan Golden, children's literature specialists of the Belk Library at Appalachian State University; to Lisa Neale of the Watauga County (North Carolina) Public Library; and to Marcia Kraut and Lucy Goldberg of Baker Demonstration School Library. For editorial help and valuable insights, thank you to Bill Teale, Celia Whitlock, Sarah Borders, Cheri Triplett, Dottie Black, and Jeanne Chaney. A special thank you goes to Kathleen Emdad and Maureen Doyle Endres for their unwavering support.

We had a fine team of reviewers, and we gratefully acknowledge their thoughtful and expert suggestions:

Alma Flor Ada, University of San Francisco

Peter Fisher, National-Louis University

M. Jean Greenlaw, University of North Texas

Dan Hade, Penn State University

Darwin L. Henderson, University of Cincinnati

Judith Hillman, St. Michael's College

Nancy J. Johnson, Western Washington University

Linda Leonard Lamme, University of Florida

Barbara A. Lehman, The Ohio State University

Susan Lehr, Skidmore College

Amy A. McClure, Ohio Wesleyan University

Dianne L. Monson, University of Minnesota

Sam Sebesta, University of Washington

Lesley Shapiro, National-Louis University

Elizabeth A. Smith, Otterbein College

The staff at Allyn and Bacon deserves much credit for helping us pull this off: Ann Greenberger, our developmental editor through the middle stage of the project; Nihad Farooq and Kris Lamarre, editorial assistants; and especially our editor, Virginia Lanigan, who provided good cheer and good sense from the very beginning.

About the Authors

The authors of this text were drawn together by a love of children's books and a fascination with the people who make them and by the hope that another generation of students, teachers, librarians, and parents could be inspired to take up the challenge of getting those works into the hands of children.

Charles Temple is a banjo-picking storyteller and teacher educator at Hobart and William Smith Colleges in Geneva, New York. He has written many books in the field of reading and language arts as well as several books for children. Active in the International Reading Association, Dr. Temple currently works on its behalf with teachers in Eastern Europe to develop interesting ways to discuss literature with their students, given the climate of increasing openness to the rest of the world since the fall of the Berlin Wall.

Miriam Martinez is a teacher educator at the University of Texas at San Antonio who loves nothing more than getting lost in good books, including children's books, of course! She served for seven years as the coeditor of "Bookalogues," a children's book review column in the journal *Language Arts*; she also served as a reviewer for the eleventh edition of *Adventuring with Books* (1998), published by the National Council of Teachers of English. Dr. Martinez coedited *Book Talk and Beyond: Children and Teachers Respond to Literature* (1995), published by the International Reading Association. The focus of her research and writing is on ways of bringing children and books together to foster students' literary and literacy development.

Junko Yokota is a teacher educator at National-Louis University in Evanston, Illinois. She was a classroom teacher and a school librarian during the first ten years of her career. She is currently the editor of *Kaleidoscope*, a publication of the National Council of Teachers of English that presents reviews of multicultural children's books. Dr. Yokota is a recipient of the Virginia Hamilton Award for Contribution to Multicultural Literature and was a member of the 1997 Caldecott Award Committee.

Alice Naylor is a teacher educator at Appalachian State University in Boone, North Carolina. She began her career as a librarian and storyteller and fell naturally into being a teacher of children's literature and storytelling. For five years, she hosted a weekly children's television program for the Milwaukee Public Library. She has served on many children's book award committees for the Association of Library Service to Children and the National Council of Teachers of English; she served twice on the John Newbery Medal Committee, once as chair, and was chair of the Batchelder Committee. She coauthored *Children Talking about Books* (Oryx, 1993) with a former student, Sarah Borders. Her passion is teaching teachers to value and love literature—and her efforts have been acknowledged by several outstanding teacher awards from her university.

Children's Books in Children's Hands

Part One

Understanding Literature and the Child Reader

1 Children's Books in Children's Hands

Wish I *could* let him make a little noise. It's not natural, I know, to keep an animal so quiet. But he's *happy*-quiet, not *scared*-quiet. I know that much.

I move my arms off my face after a while and let him rest his paws on my chest, and I'm lying there petting his head and he's got this happy dog-smile on his face. The breeze is blowing cool air in from the west, and I figure I'm about as happy right then as you can get in your whole life.

And then I hear someone say, "Marty." I look up, and there's Ma.

In an upstate New York classroom, Midge Burns is reading to her third graders. The book is Phyllis Reynolds Naylor's ***Shiloh*** (1991), which tells what happens when Marty, an Appalachian mountain boy, shelters a runaway beagle named Shiloh from its cruel and abusive owner, Judd Travers. Marty's action threatens the equilibrium of the close-knit rural community and brings stress to his family. The tension is reflected in the students' body language. They groan when Marty's secret is discovered by his mother—and cheer when she agrees to let Marty keep the dog a while longer.

"Who do you think was to blame for what happened in this story?" asks Mrs. Burns, when the book is finally closed. The ensuing conversation lasts an hour.

> . . . and they tucked him in bed
> all soft and warm
> and they held his paw
> and they sang him a song.

A four-year-old child in her mother's lap hears Margaret Wise Brown's ***Little Fur Family*** (1946) and is filled with a secure feeling of being a special child, very much loved. In the coming months, the child picks up the book every now and then, and that same feeling of warmth and security comes over her each time she does.

Illustration 1.1
Newbery Medal–winner *Shiloh* poses a thought-provoking ethical dilemma that pits animal rights—and a boy's love for a dog—against property rights. (*Shiloh* by Phyllis Reynolds Naylor. Illustration © Lynne Dennis.)

Illustration 1.2
Like a "security blanket," *Little Fur Family* has comforted thousands of children as they moved from close dependence on their parents to autonomy. (*The Little Fur Family* by Margaret Wise Brown. Copyright © 1946 by HarperCollins Publishers. Used by permission of HarperCollins Publishers.)

Brown Bear, Brown Bear, What Do You See? by Bill Martin Jr., with illustrations by Eric Carle, has helped countless young children get off to a confident start as readers.

A teacher reads aloud from George Ancona's picture book ***Pablo Remembers: The Fiesta of the Day of the Dead*** (1993). Miguel—quiet Miguel—suddenly comes to life: "*El día de los muertos,*" he exclaims. The other children listen with fascination as he gives the proper pronunciation to the Spanish words in the book. Miguel then carefully finds the English words to describe this old Mexican celebration, when the spirits of loved ones are felt to come near the living.

> Brown bear, brown bear, what do you see?
> I see a yellow duck looking at me.

In a first-grade classroom on the South Pacific island of Fiji, the teacher has created a hand-lettered enlarged version of Bill Martin Jr.'s ***Brown Bear, Brown Bear, What Do You See?*** (1983). She reads it to her assembled children, pointing with a ruler to each word. Even before she has finished the first reading, children are anticipating what she is going to say next. The second time through, the children, supported by the patterned text and the illustrations, are reading along with her. There are no bears on Fiji, though, and soon the children are writing their own book based on the pattern of Bill Martin's but featuring a mongoose, a cockatiel, a python, and other local animals. Martin's book has helped these children of Fiji learn to read and write.

> Trip-trap, trip-trap, trip-trap, trip-trap.
> "WHO'S THAT WALKING ON MY BRIDGE?" roared the Troll.
> "It is I, Little Billy Goat Gruff."

In a South Texas classroom, Jackie murmurs, "Oh, good," when Ms. Sloan sends her group to the library center—a favorite in the classroom. Some of her fellow students browse through the collection looking for particular books. Jackie says, "Let's do *The Three Billy Goats Gruff*." Four other children agree and cut short their search. Now the five children—three goats, one troll, and a narrator—are acting out this folktale that is so well known to them from their teacher's reading it aloud. And of course one performance will not do. Everyone wants a chance to be the troll!

Good books—like good paintings, plays, movies, sculptures, and other creative works—merit appreciation in their own right. But good books serve children in some specific ways. Good children's books can evoke strong feelings and come to stand for childhood emotions, much in the way a security blanket does. Good books can give children reference points for understanding their own experiences—lessons that may last a lifetime. Good books may validate for children their own culture and open windows onto other cultures. Good books may help children understand how they and their neighbors think through moral issues and give them important experiences in clarifying differences and building consensus. Good books, and the sharing of them, cultivate children's capacity for empathy and compassion. Good books educate the imagination—as children stretch to visualize what it would be like to walk in the shoes of a character in a book. Good books may give children much of the motivation and the wherewithal to learn to read and models that show them how to write. Good books offer children delight, mystery, charm, an experience of awe, and companionship. Good books may invite children to play with language. Good picture books cultivate children's visual literacy and their aesthetic sense. Good books of all kinds nurture children's appreciation of the author's craft.

WHAT ARE GOOD BOOKS FOR CHILDREN?

For the student of children's literature, there is a lot to understand. "What *are* good books for each child?" That is something all of us want to know—whether we are or are going to be parents, teachers, librarians, booksellers, book editors, authors, or just well-read citizens.

The answers to this question will be complex, because books aren't simply "good" in the abstract. A book may lead to a satisfying experience for a particular child or group of children; with particular interests, concerns, and backgrounds; in certain situations.

The answers will partly depend on an understanding of the ways readers respond to literature and how they differ in their responses at different ages.

The answers will be made still richer by an understanding of how reading books from different cultures affects children—whether a child from a particular cultural group is reading books about others in that culture, or another child is discovering through a book the particular ways people in varied cultures strive to get along.

To know what "good books" are for different children requires some intelligent way of talking about goodness and mediocrity in books—an accepted set of terms for looking at the literary features of children's books.

Identifying "good books"—especially in terms of an author or an illustrator's achievement—requires a sense of where children's books have come from. Children's books, indeed, have a history, and that history is intertwined with the history of the life-stage called childhood.

Having considered these background issues, you will be ready to look more closely at the books themselves: the kinds of books available, the evolution over the years of books of each kind (or genre), and exemplary writers and illustrators of children's books.

Finally, many of you will want answers to other questions: "What can I do to create a love of reading in every child, and how can I use books to expand children's knowledge?" Answers to those questions will range from ways of putting books into children's hands, to ways of engaging children in books, to ways of constructing instructional units that use children's literature. All of these topics are what this book is about.

WHAT IS CHILDREN'S LITERATURE?

Children's literature is the collection of books and book-based media that are read to and by children. That collection is enormous: There are more than fifty thousand English-language children's titles in print. It is still growing: Five thousand new titles are published every year in the United States alone. And it is old: The tradition of publishing literature for English-speaking children dates back 250 years, predating the founding of the American republic.

Children's literature spans the range from alphabet books and nursery rhyme collections for the very young through novels and informational books for adolescents (or "young adults," as they are called in the book trade)—in other words, from birth to about age fifteen.

Today, most children's books are written expressly for children, of course. But there are books written originally for adults that have become popular with children—from an earlier period, John Bunyan's **Pilgrim's Progress** (1678) and Daniel Defoe's **Robinson Crusoe** (1719), and more recently, **Platero and I** (**Platero y yo**) (1978), by Juan Ramon Jimenez. Other works—such as Charles Perrault's **Sleeping Beauty in the Woods** (1697) and Miguel de Cervantes' **Don Quijote** (1605)—were written for adults but have been adapted for children. And the oral tradition—myths, ballads, epics, and folktales—comprises a large body of material that was told to adults and children alike—including the well-known stories of "Jack and the Beanstalk," "Bo Rabbit and the Briar Patch," "Cucarachita Martina and Ratóncito Perez," and "Anansi the Spider."

Today, children's books are published by the juvenile books branches of large publishing houses, such as Random House and Houghton Mifflin, as well as by publishers that serve the children's market exclusively, such as Tambourine Books and Holiday House. Many publishers offer books published under *imprints*—which might, like Atheneum, be names of originally independent publishers that have been taken over by a larger house or, like Richard Jackson Books, Margaret K. McElderry Books, and Walter Lorraine Books, reflect arrangements by which publishers allow their most successful editors to publish books under their own names.

Sales of children's books have increased tremendously in recent years, to the point that publishing children's books is currently the most robust of many publishers' activities. As more families have gotten the message about the importance of having children's books in the home, sales of these books to individuals have at last surpassed sales to schools and libraries. Major newspapers now review books for children just as they review adult fare.

Qualities of Children's Literature

As teachers of college courses on children's literature, we sometimes catch ourselves smiling to see an adult student smuggling **Frog and Toad Are Friends** (1970) to class between a copy of *War and Peace* and a thick tome on organic chemistry. That image sometimes makes us stop to ask: What is the study of children's literature doing in a college curriculum—just how serious is the quality of children's books? There are several ways to answer that question.

First, it must be said that although children's books may appear deceptively simple, their simplicity is achieved through very hard work by talented writers. Many people try to produce books for children, but the percentage of manuscripts that are actually published is unbelievably small. In a recent year, one major house received five thousand unsolicited manuscripts and published two of them.

Award-winning author Katherine Paterson compares writing a children's book to composing music. She suggests that a good children's book is like a score for a chamber quartet, rather than a work for a full symphony. The work for the chamber quartet is less elaborate; but if its melodies are pleasing and its harmonies are apt, it will have no less quality than a full orchestral work. In the same way, a good children's book will have fewer layers of complexity than a good book for adults, but if it is created with great care, it can also have excellence.

Second, because children's literature grew out of the folktales from oral traditions, children's books contain many timeless stories that know no age boundaries. In *The Anatomy of Criticism* (1957), Northrop Frye wrote that all literature is one fabric, woven of many strands of plot, image, and theme that have been told over and over in stories around the world, throughout all time. The most basic stories—those that tell of virtue rewarded, of straying into danger and struggling to get back out, of learning to distinguish the things of lasting value, of finding one's true qualities and putting them to the service of others—are the materials out of which all literature is made. They are found in their purest form in myths and folktales from around the world, and in books for children.

Third, children's books are worthy of serious study because the education of children warrants society's best energies. Good books will help children by making them literate, giving them knowledge of the world and empathy for those with whom they share it, offering them stories and images to furnish their minds and nurture their imaginations, and kindling their appreciation for language well used. Given its worthy goals, such literature deserves attention and respect.

What makes a book a *children's* book? A children's book usually has these qualities:

- *A child protagonist and an issue that concerns children.* A children's book usually has a central character who is the age of the intended audience. Children identify more easily with "one of their own." Even when the central character is not a child—as in "Cinderella," for example—children need to feel that the central issues of a story concern them in some way.

- *A straightforward story line, with a linear and limited time sequence in a confined setting.* Books for younger children usually focus on one or two main characters, cover short time sequences (they are usually—but not always—told straight through from problem to solution, without flashbacks), and most often are set in one place. When writing for older children, authors gradually take more license with time sequences, being careful not to muddle their young readers' understanding, however.

- *Language that is concrete and vivid and not overly complex.* The words in children's books primarily name actors and actions—especially in picture books. Books without pictures have more description to help children visualize characters and settings. They use dialogue to move the story along. And they give glimpses of the characters' motives. In all these cases, readers see more of what characters do than of what they say, and certainly than of what they think.

Qualities of Outstanding Children's Literature

What makes a *good* children's book? Qualities that make outstanding children's books apply to excellent literature for any age. If a book satisfies these criteria, it is a good children's book:

- *Good books expand awareness.* Good books give children names for things in the world and for their own experiences. Good books take children inside other characters' perspectives and let children "walk two moons" in their shoes. They broaden children's understanding of the world and their capacity for empathy.

- *Good books provide an enjoyable read that doesn't overtly teach or moralize.* Many children's books turn out to be about something, and it is often possible to derive a lesson from them. But if a

ASK THE EDITOR... *Roger Sutton*

What are your standards for an excellent children's book?

I have no standards for "an excellent children's book." How could the same standards possibly apply to, for example, Paula Fox's *One Eyed Cat* (a quiet, intense novel about a boy who finds redemption) and Jonathan Etra and Stephanie Spinner's *Aliens for Breakfast* (a slapstick transitional reader about a boy who finds an extraterrestrial in his cereal)? The only thing those two books have in common is that I really, really like them a lot—hardly what you would call a "standard." You can't work from standards or checklists because the best books break the rules, while at the same time keeping true to their own promises. I've reviewed upwards of four thousand children's books in my career thus far, and the best advice I ever had was to take it "one book at a time."

Popularity and quality are not opposites. The first is measurable—sales figures, circulation data, discussion with young readers, and readers' choice awards can all help us get a grip on what books are "popular." Quality, though, is not only not measurable, it is not definable—my "great books" will not, and should not, be yours. Even in cases where critics universally acclaim a book, we're really only talking about a different kind of popularity.

Roger Sutton is the editor-in-chief of The Horn Book Magazine. *Formerly the editor of* The Bulletin of the Center for Children's Books, *he has also worked as a children's and young adult librarian. His articles about children's books and reading have appeared in several journals, and he is the author of a nonfiction book for young adults,* Hearing Us Out: Voices from the Gay and Lesbian Community *(1994).*

Favorite Books as a Child

Nobody Listens to Andrew
by Elizabeth Guilfoile

They Were Strong and Good
by Robert Lawson

Little Runner of the Long House
by Betty Baker

---

book seems too obviously contrived to teach a lesson, children (and critics) will not tolerate it.

- *Good books tell the truth.* Outstanding children's books usually deal with significant truths about the human experience. Moreover, the characters in them are true to life, and the insights the books imply are accurate, perhaps even wise.

- *Good books embody quality.* The words are precisely chosen, and often poetic in their sound and imagery; the plot is convincing, the characters believable, and the description telling.

- *Good books have integrity.* The genre, plot, language, characters, style, theme, and illustrations, if any, all come together to make a satisfying whole.

- *Good books show originality.* Excellent children's books introduce readers to unique characters or situations or show them the world from a unique viewpoint; they stretch the minds of readers, giving them new ways to think about the world and new possibilities to think about.

CHILDREN'S BOOKS AND CHILDHOOD

The criteria for excellence just outlined have not always held true. That is because the life-stage of childhood has changed throughout history, as adults changed their definition of it and their views of young people. Literature for children has changed, too, following the fortunes of childhood as a life-stage.

In the past six centuries, children in the West have, in turn, been treated in the following ways:

- They have been ignored.
- They have been suspected of harboring great evil.
- They have been felt to be in need of moral instruction and idealistic example.
- Sometimes, they have been understood as they were and given a good read.

Let's look at these phases in more detail.

Children Were Ignored

It has been said that until roughly five hundred years ago, childhood as we know it did not exist in the West (Aries, 1962). That is because up to the Renaissance, children's activities—the games they played and the stories they heard—were not separated from those of adults. Children drank alcoholic beverages, smoked tobacco, and used coarse language. After the age of seven, they were made to work in the kitchen, in the fields, or in shops.

It is not surprising, then, that books were not written expressly for children in those times. The few children who could read had no choice but to turn to adult fare. The ballad "Robin Hood," for example, was known as far back as 1360 AD, and three printed versions of the legend existed before 1534. Child readers, then as now, enjoyed and accepted the romantic concept of robbing the rich to help the poor. Other romantic stories circulating at the time were those about King Arthur and the Knights of the Round Table, and Bevis, a thirteenth-century hero who hacked his way out of dungeons and slew dragons.

In 1476, William Caxton established the first printing press in England, and in 1477, he published one of the earliest books expressly for children. Called **A Booke of Curteseye**, it was filled with do's and don'ts for an audience of aristocratic boys preparing for social engagements and military careers.

Children Were Suspected of Harboring Great Evil

By the seventeenth century, more works were being written for children, but most did not make for enjoyable reading. The Puritans, the stern religious exiles who established the English colonies in America, infused early American children's works with their certainty that the devil could enter young bodies. They even wrote poems exalting death at an early age—better to die innocent than grow corrupted. Given the didactic and fiery messages of Puritan authors, it

Texts written for children of Puritans often exalted a blameless early death as an ideal.

is not surprising that most of their works are no longer read. Here is an example of Puritan prose by one Thomas Parkhurst (1702):

> My dear Children, consider what comfort it will be unto you when you have come to dye, that when other children have been playing, you have been praying. The time will come, for ought you know very shortly, . . . when thou shalt be sick upon thy bed, and thou shalt be struggling for life, thy poor little body will be trembling, so that the very bed will shake under thee, thine eyestrings will break, and then thy heartstrings will break; . . . then, O then, the remembrance of thy holy life will give thee reassurance of the love of God.

Nonetheless, there were some bright moments. Books were generally instructional and religious in nature, but many writers did sugarcoat their instruction with rhymes, riddles, and good stories. Also, children continued to find adult fare to their liking. John Bunyan's *Pilgrim's Progress* was read for generations. What made it palatable to children was its portrayal of a sense of family. Children are presumed to have skipped over the lengthy religious commentary to savor the happy family life. Indeed, the story of Christian can still hold the imagination of children who read the adapted, abridged, and illustrated versions.

Children of the fifteenth to eighteenth centuries also turned to hornbooks and chapbooks for their reading fare. In both England and America, door-to-door salesmen traveled from town to town selling pots, pans, needles, medicine, and *hornbooks*—which looked like paddles, averaged two and a half by five inches, were usually made of wood, and often were attached to a leather thong so that children could hang them around the neck or wrist. The lesson sheet or story was pasted on the flat surface, then covered with "horn," a film of protective material similar to animal horn. Hornbooks were filled with lessons in religion, manners, the alphabet, and reading.

Those same traveling salesmen who peddled hornbooks inspired the invention of *chapbooks* ("chap" is derived from the word "cheap"). Chapbooks were made of folded sheets of paper and so were inexpensive to produce and light to carry. They contained popular stories of the day, such as "Jack, the Giant Killer," "The History of Sir Richard Whittington," and "St. George and the Dragon," and also large numbers of cautionary tales, those that inform of the do's and don'ts of childhood. Gail E. Haley has written and illustrated **The Dream Peddler** (1993) about a fictitious chapbook peddler who was proud of his profession because he gave children fairytales and adventures to cultivate their dreams.

Children Were Felt to Be in Need of Moral Instruction and Idealistic Example

In 1693, John Locke published *Some Thoughts Concerning Education*, which influenced childrearing practices on both sides of the Atlantic. The book's exhortation that "some easy pleasant book" be given to children was good for the circulation of children's books. Nonetheless, the books still promoted strict moralistic teachings, if in narrative form.

At the dawn of the eighteenth century, more playful and pleasurable literature began to emerge. The verses of Isaac Watts were popular, and although to a contemporary ear they sound overly moralistic and didactic, for their time they were less so than those of his predecessors. Mary Cooper published **The Child's**

Hornbooks, the reading fare of many early American children, usually contained an alphabet and a prayer or psalm.

In Adam's Fall
We sinned all.

Thy Life to mend,
This Book attend.

The Cat doth play,
And after slay.

A Dog will bite
A Thief at Night.

An Eagle' flight
Is out of fight.

The idle Fool
Is whipt at School.

The New England Primer combined an alphabet and a catechism—a summary of the rules a good Christian should follow.

Illustration 1.3
For more than two centuries, young readers have brushed past the adult satire and relished the colorful adventures in *Gulliver's Travels*. (*Gulliver's Adventures in Lilliput* retold by Ann Keay Beneduce. Illustration copyright © 1993 by Gennady Spirin. Used by permission of Philomel Books.)

New Plaything, Being a Spelling Book Intended to Make the Learning to Read a Diversion (1743). An American edition of the book came out in 1750 with even more "diversions," reflecting a change in how stories for children were perceived. *The New England Primer* (1790), which combined alphabet and catechism, was the most widely read book of the period—another indication of the "instructive mindset" of the eighteenth century.

During this period, children also continued to read books written for adults. Many of Daniel Defoe's works were popular with children. In fact, *The Life and Surprising Adventures of Robinson Crusoe of York, Marine* (1719), with its fearless optimism and high adventure, proved popular with children for the better part of two centuries. Jonathan Swift's *Gulliver's Travels* (1726) was another book published for adults but adopted by children. Although the book is filled with heavy satire, reflecting Swift's strong objections to the imperfections of humankind in general and Englishmen in particular, its language and plot are irresistible.

An innovative entrepreneur named John Newbery prepared the way for the blossoming of children's literature in the nineteenth and twentieth centuries. Newbery moved to London in 1744 and launched the first commercially successful company dedicated almost exclusively to publishing beautiful and pleasurable children's books. In his thirty-year career, Newbery published twenty titles for children in attractive, playful formats, including the "accordion" book, made of one long strip folded accordion-style to form "pages." He was the first to introduce illustrations by first-rate artists, and he published books in more permanent, attractive bindings than the popular, less expensive chapbooks. His books have been described as "homey" and clearly intended to appeal to children.

Newbery is believed also to have written some of the books he published, including *A Little Pretty Pocket Book* (1791) and *The History of Little Goody Two Shoes* (1765). Read for the better part of a century in England and the United States, *Little Goody Two Shoes* was the first bestseller written for children (and one of the longest-lasting). The book may not be familiar to you, but the phrase "goody two shoes" is still used to mean a person with overly perfect behavior.

More than a century after Newbery's death, Daniel Melcher of the Wilson Publishing Company made a donation to the American Library Association to establish an annual award for the most distinguished contribution to literature for children. The award was fittingly named after John Newbery. (A list of the award winners and the honor books over the past eight decades appears in Appendix A.)

Children Were Sometimes Understood as They Were and Given a Good Read

Darton (1966) defines books for children as "printed words produced ostensibly to give children spontaneous pleasure." It was in the nineteenth and the twentieth centuries that books truly fitting Darton's definition emerged. Nineteenth-century books for children have become today's classics. Books written in that century that still circulate briskly include Hans Christian Andersen's *The Ugly Duckling* and *The Little Mermaid* (English translations published in 1885), Carlo Collodi's *The Adventures of Pinocchio* (1892), Lewis Carroll's *Alice's Adventures in Wonderland* (1865), Louisa May Alcott's *Little Women*

Are librarians or teachers ever justified in censoring books for children?

Few people would defend putting gruesomely violent, racially demeaning, or sexually provocative material in school libraries or children's sections of public libraries. But there are books written by respected authors that some adults find unsuitable for children and demand to have removed from children's libraries. Here are some examples.

Maurice Sendak's picture book *In the Night Kitchen* (1970) features nude drawings of a young boy named Mickey. Several school librarians have removed the book from their shelves; others have taken marking pens and drawn a swimsuit or diaper on Mickey.

Jean de Brunhoff's "Babar the Elephant" is one of the most popular series of children's books of all time. Yet some articulate critics have charged that these stories defend European neo-colonialism in Africa.

The main character in Katherine Paterson's middle-grade novel *The Great Gilly Hopkins* (1978) is a tough girl who has bounced around many foster homes and sometimes resorts to four-letter words for emphasis. Some parents have insisted the book be kept out of children's hands. Richard Peck's *Are You in the House Alone?* (1977) describes the rape of a teenage girl, and for that reason some adults find the book unsuitable.

All of these books have defenders who believe they have literary merit. Yet many parents and school board members want to shelter children from such material. Children, they say, are exposed to far too many pernicious influences; school, at least, should be a place where children won't be exposed to materials parents wouldn't allow them to see at home.

All teachers and librarians must sometimes decide on matters of appropriateness—engaging in what some would call censorship. Librarians must decide whether to order books with literary merit but controversial content; teachers must decide whether to include such books in classroom libraries or use them in reading and discussion groups.

What do *you* think? Who *should* have final say in what books are available to children in classrooms and libraries? Why? And what criteria should be used in deciding what books—if any—are not appropriate for children to read?

Illustration 1.4
Cautious-minded librarians sometimes paint a bathing suit or diaper on Mickey, making this one of the most censored illustrations in children's literature. (*In the Night Kitchen* by Maurice Sendak. Copyright © 1970 by Maurice Sendak. Used by permission of HarperCollins Publishers.)

(1868), and Mark Twain's *The Adventures of Tom Sawyer* (1876) and *The Adventures of Huckleberry Finn* (1885). Nonetheless, though wonderful classics came out of the nineteenth century, there is simply nothing to compare with the rich diversity of children's literature in the twentieth century. The exciting changes in children's literature that have occurred over the past two centuries will be explored in depth in the genre chapters of this text (Chapters 6 through 11).

The history of children's literature does not really fit such a neat pattern as this presentation may suggest, of course. For one thing, the tendency to moralize and to socialize children through books is not entirely gone. Although more books than ever before are created with pure enjoyment as their goal, many adults still associate children's books with moral teaching, as the recent popularity of William Bennett's *The Children's Book of Virtues* (1996) clearly demonstrates. Indeed, any children's librarian can tell you of the tensions between those who want to restrict children's reading to the works they consider to be "wholesome" and others who struggle against what they see as the censorship of children's literature.

CHILDREN'S DEVELOPMENT AND RESPONSE TO LITERATURE

There is no doubt that books give children edification and delight. There is also no doubt that what children take from books changes in fairly systematic ways as they pass from age to age. This is the topic we take up now, paying special attention to children's intellectual, moral, and personality development.

Intellectual Development

The modern study of intellectual development has shown that children's minds grow not by passively absorbing information, but by acting on the world and learning from what happens. Similarly, intellectual growth is measured not only by how much children know, but also by changes in the way they think. Since both of these principles have bearing on the way children respond to literature, let's consider each in more detail.

The Processes of Intellectual Development. The influential Swiss psychologist Jean Piaget suggested that people's intellects grow through the twin activities of *assimilation* and *accommodation*. That is, each of us at any point in our lives has a set of *mental schemes,* or concepts about the world. We use a scheme to interpret something we encounter, and in the process of interpreting—recognizing something or dealing with it appropriately—we *assimilate* that thing to our scheme in order to make sense of it. (We see a particular bush with flowers and say it is a rhododendron; we call that violent man who opposes the hero the villain.) But if an experience is slightly different from the experiences we've had before, we have to modify the scheme somewhat, in order to *accommodate,* or adapt, the scheme to the experience. This slightly modified scheme makes us capable of making sense of an even broader range of experiences. Thus, by interpreting the world, we expand our capacity for making sense of what we encounter in the future. (We come to recognize, for instance, that some green bushes lack flowers in the winter but are still rhododendrons, and some men who behave nicely but ultimately harm the hero are still villains.)

Note that how we perceive the world is largely determined by the schemes we already have in our minds. That is to say, the world is what we can make of it—or *construct of it*—with the available schemes we have. One person's experience of a set of events (or story, or poem) will be somewhat different from another person's experience of the same events, because each is interpreting events through her or his particular schemes. Since we are all limited to our own individual set of schemes, the more opportunities we have to compare our meanings with those of others, the better we will understand other people's processes of construction—with the hoped-for result that we may all understand each other better (Piaget, 1955).

The Stages of Intellectual Development. Although the process of learning just described is the same at all times of life, according to Piaget, the kinds of schemes people develop change as they proceed from early childhood to adolescence. Piaget noted that these changes take each person through four basic periods: the *sensorimotor period*, the *preoperational period*, the *concrete operational period*, and the *formal operational period*.

Children are in the *sensorimotor period* from birth to about age two. This is a time when children discover the most basic physical concepts about the world: "The object is still there, even when I can't see it. I can make that bell ring by swatting it with my hand. I can make Mama come by crying. I can make her smile by smiling." Note, however, that children still don't have language to express these concepts. As soon as children can reliably use words, their thinking passes on to the next stage.

It's no wonder that books for very young children are often made of cloth or heavy cardboard: Children page through them roughly, delighting in making a favorite picture appear and disappear (What control! What mastery!). They stab triumphantly at a recognized animal. They may even try to gobble up an illustrated cookie.

The next stage, the *preoperational period*, begins at around age two and ends at around age seven. The rapid emergence of language makes children's thinking more versatile. Their memories improve as they learn names for more things and actions, and they can use their new concepts to interpret more experiences and construct still more concepts.

The preoperational period is famous, though, for its distortions of thought. Children can be empathetic, but they tend to be *egocentric*: That is, they are stuck in their own point of view. They can't easily keep secrets, because they don't realize that others don't know what they know. They can believe that the mountains were put there by powerful creatures or that the moon follows them around. Magic is possible—in fact, children make no clear distinction between magic and everyday events. Nor can they reliably distinguish between truth and fiction.

Children in the preoperational period look at one aspect of a thing at a time: If you push apart the pennies in a row, a child thinks there must be more pennies (because she or he focuses on their spread and ignores the sparsity). Through the preoperational period, children also tend to look at only one *level* of a problem at a time: They won't believe that you can be a Catholic *and* a Christian, or live in Kentucky *and* Louisville. In the same vein, they don't see that the statement "You got out of the wrong side of the bed this morning" can refer to both risings and bad moods or that the story "Hansel and Gretel" might symbolize the dangers of children being too dependent on their parents for too long.

Children between the ages of seven and eleven are in the *concrete operational period*. Their earlier distortions of thought begin to be replaced by concrete reasoning. Mountains are seen to be caused by slow collisions of the earth's crust. Seven pennies are seven pennies, regardless of how close together or spread out they are. Children come to accommodate other viewpoints besides their own. Children's art loses its magical expressiveness—and the details of this fascinating world-as-it-is begin to capture their attention. Santa Claus and Cinderella are gradually recognized as fictitious.

Around age eleven—that is, toward the end of true childhood and at the beginning of preadolescence—begins the last of Piaget's cognitive stages, the *formal operations period*. What has changed? As the name "concrete operational period" implies, children in that stage think through issues best when they have concrete referents. They don't do so well, however, with abstractions—ethical positions and the like. That limitation usually falls away in early adolescence—and the child who used to make fun of her older brother's campaigns in favor of environmental conservation suddenly finds herself a passionate partisan of Amnesty International.

Learning According to Vygotsky. Piaget's learning theory stresses children's own discoveries and holds that children discover (or "construct") concepts in concrete, nonverbal ways and only later attach words to them. The Russian psychologist Lev Vygotsky disagreed, at least about emphasis. Vygotsky worried that if children were left to discover concepts about the world through their exploration only, they would get things confused (Vygotsky, 1969). Through the centuries, cultures have carved the world up into concepts, given names to these concepts, and placed them in ordered relationships to each other. There is little chance that children will get all this right unless they learn in the presence of others who speak appropriately (for the culture) about the things of this world.

Fortunately, there is a dimension of children's thinking that opens them up to social influence. That is, when young children think, they tend to speak their ideas aloud. (Adults may still do this when trying to remember a telephone number or solve a complicated algebra problem.) While children's thinking is externalized in this way, adults can talk to them about what they are thinking, and the children can hear those thoughts and reorient their ideas as necessary. With later maturity, children internalize their thinking. It follows from Vygotsky's research that children—especially young children—should be given plenty of opportunities to express themselves. For them, thinking is talking (and moving, and singing, and drawing). Also, adults should talk with children often, because children need to hear more educated people verbalize their own understandings in proper terms in order to match those terms with the phenomena of the world.

Vygotsky would suggest that young children's most natural responses to books will be active and overt. And that is just what researchers have found (as we will see later in this chapter).

Vygotsky's ideas make a nice complement to Piaget's. We agree with Piaget that children's active discovery is necessary for them to learn, but we also agree with Vygotsky that children often learn best in social situations—where they voice their thoughts aloud and listen to others doing the same (Vygotsky, 1978).

Intellectual Development and Response to Literature. The trends of intellectual development just described suggest that children's thinking is first concerned with outward and concrete experience. With time, they devote themselves more to inward, psychological, and abstract experience. Also, children's thought at first considers only one aspect of a problem at a time, but later can take more than one perspective on an issue. These trends have been observed not only in studies of children's thinking, but also in their responses to literature.

Arthur Applebee's work (1975) suggested that prior to the onset of the concrete operational period (at about age seven or eight), children usually do not distinguish fiction from nonfiction. Most stories are thought to portray events that might have happened. When asked if they could go see Cinderella, for example, children younger than age seven or eight typically reply that they cannot; but if pressed, they will say it's because she lives too far away, or she's too busy cleaning up for her vain sisters to have time for a visit!

This is not to say that children cannot learn from stories, or even that they do not see that a story has a point or theme. In fact, Susan Lehr's research (1988) shows that even kindergarteners can recognize that two stories have the same theme—especially if they have rich experiences with literature. But it is still not likely to dawn on young children that a story can be an elaborate metaphor for a truth on a different plane. Piaget demonstrated this point by asking children the meaning of statements such as "When the cat's away, the mice will play." Children in the preoperational period thought the expression only referred to cats and mice; they didn't seem to get the connection to children's behavior when the teacher is out of the room (Piaget, 1955).

Janet Hickman (1992) observed children's natural response to stories. She found that young children (age five) tend to respond with their bodies—clapping, moving, and shouting refrains. Slightly older children are more attuned to plots—making predictions and showing obvious signs of suspense and relief. By nine and ten, children are freely discussing meanings and even the author's style.

It would be wrong to conclude from what we have said so far that younger children are oblivious to the meanings of stories. For one thing, they certainly have understandings that they cannot yet verbalize. For another thing, even if Piaget was correct in concluding that young children may not realize that the events in a story may stand for another level of truth, children may still take meaning from stories the same way they take meaning from life (see Chapter 3). (In fact, their difficulty in making a distinction between fact and fiction makes this supposition all the more likely.) Indeed, not only our own experiences as parents and teachers but the writings of thoughtful scholars such as Robert Coles (in *The Call of Stories*, 1989) and Gareth Matthews (in *Philosophy and the Young Child*, 1980, and *Dialogues with Children*, 1984) have persuaded us that young children can have surprisingly rich and interesting responses to stories.

Moral Development

Many books pose challenges to children's sense of fairness, to their moral reasoning. Of course, there are many moral issues and many stands a child may take on each one, but the *manner* in which children go about resolving an issue tends to go through a series of changes as they grow. That is, a six-year-old and a nine-year-old may both decide not to tell a lie, but their reasons for that decision may differ according to their respective stages of development.

The patterns of thinking described in the previous section affect the way children think through moral issues, too. For instance, Piaget's research (1932) has shown that children in the lower primary grades focus on certain aspects of moral questions:

- Their own interests and point of view
- One dimension of a problem at a time
- Consequences rather than motives
- Rules rather than the intentions behind the rules

For an example of young children's moral reasoning, consider a group of first graders who heard Norma Green's **The Hole in the Dike** (1993), about a

Dutch boy who saved Holland from a flood when he stuck his finger in a hole in the dike. Several were puzzled when, at the end of the book, the boy was called the Hero of Holland. "But he was naughty! He stayed out all night at the dike and he should have gone *straight* home!" said one. "He should be punished for breaking the rules . . . and making his mom worry!" said another. These children focused narrowly on one aspect of the problem—the rule infraction—rather than on the greater good the boy did.

Similarly, five-year-old Mirel is indignant when the vulnerable pig plays tricks on the wolf in Susan Meddaugh's hilarious picture book **Hog-Eye** (1995)—even though the wolf has kidnapped the pig and intends to eat it. Mirel seems to find actions more compelling than motives, just as Piaget's research predicts she will at this age.

A few years' growth—and the experience of hearing and discussing many more stories—makes a profound difference in children's thinking about moral issues. Children begin to consider motives. For example, when William Steig's **The Real Thief** (1974) was read aloud to third and fourth graders, most of them empathized with the mouse, Derek, who stole a number of items from the royal treasury: "He's not a real villain . . . he's not really bad . . . he just wanted to make his place nicer so he could feel more special . . . and important. . . ." "He didn't *mean* to get Gawain in trouble." "And anyway, he put it back later when Gawain got accused. I feel sorry for Derek. I'm glad the author let him get a second chance." A few still held to their earlier way of seeing moral issues: "He stole, and that's wrong, and he should be punished!" "I didn't like the ending because he didn't really get punished."

This exchange demonstrates the value of having open discussions of books that present children with moral dilemmas. As children who still think in less mature ways hear their more advanced classmates state their positions and their reasons for them, the less mature children are challenged to question their own thinking, and eventually they will advance to more sophisticated levels of moral reasoning.

William Damon's work (1977) suggests that between the ages of four and eleven, children grow through predictable stages in their thinking about fairness. For example, given the dilemma of how to divide rewards, children typically respond as follows: The youngest children (age four) respond egocentrically, stating unabashedly that *they* should receive the lion's share of whatever is being given out. Slightly older children (ages five and six) may make up pretenses to cover their egocentrism—"I should get more because I'm a boy"—but the result is still egocentric. Seven- and eight-year-olds apply one criterion: Everyone should get the same. Children of eight and nine apply a different single criterion: Those who worked hardest should get more, and those who worked least should be left out. By ten and eleven, though, children's judgments are trying to balance several competing criteria: The hungriest individuals are still deserving of rewards, because their hunger may have kept them from being productive. In other words, the children's reasoning reflects the real-world imperative to consider many factors at once.

Children's moral development through these stages is evident in their responses to books. For example, children in a second-grade class were asked to respond to Aesop's fable "Grasshopper and the Ant" and Leo Lionni's modern version, *Frederick* (1967). After listening to Aesop's fable, most of the children agreed that the ant was right to let the grasshopper starve because he didn't do the work to get food for the winter. However, after listening to **Frederick**, most of the children developed a new perspective. Frederick did not collect grain with the other, hard-working mice, but they tolerated his uniqueness and recognized his contribution as an artist. His poetry provided food for the mind and the imagination during the long, dark days of winter. The children contrasted the acceptance of individual differences in Lionni's fable with the harsh justice of the ant in Aesop's fable: "I liked *Frederick* better. Everybody's different, and you shouldn't punish someone just because they're different." "I think the Ant should have read *Frederick*. . . . I bet Grasshopper's music could have made the Ant happier during the winter."

Again, children's developing thought processes about morality resemble their cognitive development in general: Their perspectives start with egocentrism and gradually incorporate others' points of view. Also, their reasoning starts with a single criterion—at first a selfish one, and grows to include a more sophisticated mix of valid but competing criteria.

Personality Development

How do children's stories mesh with the problems children face at different times in their lives? Is there any general answer to that question that is worth having? Forty years ago, the late child psychologist Erik Erikson put together a scheme involving the major issues of childhood and adulthood and the stages of life at which these issues are most critical. His scheme is still believed to be a useful description of the stages children pass through from infancy to adolescence.

Erik Erikson on Childhood. Erik Erikson was one of the great psychologists of the twentieth century. Although he never graduated from college, he was a personal associate of Sigmund Freud, a therapist for children, and a Harvard professor for nearly half a century. He developed a widely respected scheme of personality development with eight stages. Here, only the first five—those that refer to childhood and adolescence—are relevant. Erikson described these stages in terms of major issues that arise and have to be resolved toward the end of each stage. Of course, the issues identified with one stage can come up again at a later time. Especially if an issue is not resolved adequately, it is likely to re-emerge as a problem later on.

First Stage: Basic Trust versus Basic Mistrust (Age One to Two). From birth through the first year of life, the major issue is establishing a trusting relationship with one or more parents—or what psychologists call the "primary caregivers." Children who are lucky to have someone who is engaged and reliable enough during their first year that they can become securely attached to that person have a secure base from which they may explore the curious sights in their surroundings, and, soon, other people, too. [Research shows that about two children out of three in the United States have such parents (Ainsworth, 1982). In poorer urban neighborhoods, however, it is estimated that only about half of the children do (Konner, 1994).] Erikson believed that in the long term, developing a sense of basic trust leads to a sense of optimism and confidence in oneself and others.

Children's books are important to the stage of basic trust in two ways. First, in many households, the give-and-take of reading aloud contributes to the building of trusting relationships between children and their parents. And read-aloud routines keep on offering the potential for building relationships of trust between children and their teachers. Second, children may be deeply affected by stories of belonging, of lost children finding their mothers. P. D. Eastman's *Are You My Mother?* (1960) and Robert McCloskey's *Make Way for Ducklings*

(1976) are written to this theme, and so is Rosemary Wells's *Hazel's Amazing Mother* (1985).

Second Stage: Autonomy versus Shame and Doubt (Age Two to Three). At age two (as any parent will tell you), children feel the urge to push away from their parents, to define themselves as separate people. Of course, the minute they do that, they may begin to doubt themselves. Some potential for shame and doubt is probably healthy, but children need to "stand on their own two feet" (is it a coincidence that this is the toddler stage?). And the issues of autonomy, how far to push it, and how to overcome the shame and doubt that go with it will concern children for some time.

This stage also relates to children's books in two ways: Books can be a vehicle for autonomy, and they can deal with that theme. For a child who is seeking to gain autonomy, a children's book may function like a baby blanket. It comes alive for a child during cozy read-alouds, and its soothing power is reinforced during many repeated readings. Later, as the child pages through the story without a parent around, the book may bring a piece of reassurance into her autonomous activities, so that she may feel secure at the same time as she ventures to experience some independence. When they function this way, books are serving as "transitional objects" (Winnicott, 1974), bridging the gap between the security of the parental presence and making it on one's own.

Books may inform children about autonomy and its consequences, too. A book that addresses the theme of autonomy is Maurice Sendak's *Where the Wild Things Are* (1964). Max roars defiance at his mother, travels to "Where the Wild Things Are," cavorts with beasts that are imaginative extensions of his drawings, and still finds his mother's love intact when he gets back. Peter Rabbit also seeks adventure and independence, but he returns home to his mother and a soothing cup of camomile tea.

Third Stage: Initiative versus Guilt (Age Three to Five or Six). In this stage, the child can not only walk but run, not only utter sentences but chatter on enthusiastically. This amazing flurry of development has its imaginative outlets in wonder stories of all sorts. Magic is at the height of possibility at this age, and stories of magical transformation abound, such as Robert D. San Souci's *The Talking Eggs* (1989), William Hooks's *Moss Gown* (1987), and the classic folk- and fairytales. This is also the beginning of an interest in adventure stories, especially those featuring an unsuspected hero, whose youth and small size disguise a capacity for great deeds.

For example, after hearing Jane Yolen's *The Emperor and the Kite* (1967), Elizabeth Hillman's *Min-Yo and the Moon Dragon* (1992), and Robert D. San Souci's *The Samurai's Daughter: A Japanese Legend* (1992), a group of first and second graders discussed the heroines in these tales: "I like stories about *girls* who go on adventures!" "Min-Yo and the emperor's daughter were so small . . . but they saved their kingdoms!" "Even though they were little . . . they did big things!" "And they didn't use magic . . . but they were very brave and smart." "The Samurai's daughter was a pearl diver . . . that's how she knew how to kill the sea monster. . . . She didn't need magic. . . . I bet her father was really surprised that she could do all that . . . even though she's a girl!"

Fourth Stage: Industry versus Inferiority (Age Six or Seven to Eleven or Twelve). In cultures all over the world, life takes a serious turn at the age of six or seven. In ancient Greece, Rome, and Israel, boys entered their tutorials, and girls began training in home economics. (There was nothing simple about this, though, since it amounted to managing the affairs of a complex enterprise including gardening, food preparation, cloth making, and more). In medieval England, children were sent out to work in the fields or committed to long apprenticeships at the age of seven. In tribal societies, children started their long training in weaving, hunting, gardening, and fishing at this age. In modern societies, they enter school.

What do all these paths have in common? Clearly, some deep shift in the functioning of the mind and the focusing of the personality occurs and makes possible the pursuit of more serious purposes. And because it does, children's goals—and their budding sense of self-worth—become set on mastering those skills that are important in their society.

For most American children, personal success is primarily defined as success in school. Of course, there's potential for serious injustice here, because a larger sense of self-worth can come down to how well a child can handle a small set of graphic scratchings that stand for ideas and quantities. Some children are much better prepared by their family background to read and count than others are. But no matter: It's skill in reading, writing, and math—rather than dribbling and shooting; or painting, singing, making friends; or telling imaginative stories or sailing a boat; or finding one's way through thick woods; or speaking more than one language and knowing one's way around more than one culture—that this society has picked as the chief measure of success in the school years. Children who fail to read and write well can feel themselves to be failures in general. Because this is true and realizing that society really doesn't have one child to lose, wise teachers and parents of elementary-age children go out of their way to make sure children are recognized—genuinely—for their abilities in many domains.

Erikson used terms such as "reality orientation" and "sense of industry and task orientation" to describe this developmental period. These terms describe many of the central characters in the survival stories that are so popular among children in this age group. These young readers are able to identify with characters who, like them, want to use their new skills and reasoning abilities to master real situations independently and to prove their own ability to cope and succeed without adult help. In the context of this stage, it is not difficult to understand the appeal of books such as Scott O'Dell's *Island of the Blue Dolphins* (1960), Felice Holman's *The Wild Children* (1983), Virginia Hamilton's *The Planet of Junior Brown* (1971), and *Daniel's Story*, by Carol Matas (1993).

Responding to *Island of the Blue Dolphins*, a fourth grader said, "Karan had to break a taboo of her tribe . . . that women weren't allowed to make weapons. At first she was so afraid she'd be punished by some supernatural power if she did. But then she thought carefully about what she *had* to do to survive on that island . . . so she made a weapon and nothing happened! So she was able to get rid of her fear."

A fifth-grade boy who had read both *The Wild Children* (about the homeless "wild children" who wandered around Russia following the Bolshevik Revolution) and *The Planet of Junior Brown* (about children who make their home in a school basement) commented: "All those kids were homeless and alone, but they learned how to help each other survive. . . . They formed their own family groups . . . but they all had to live in hiding. And, in both stories, the leaders set up a moral code so they *wouldn't* be 'wild.' They were more humane than the adults around them!"

Students who read *Daniel's Story* as part of a study of the Holocaust discussed the triumph of the human spirit in a setting of overwhelming evil and

Children's books give young readers models for understanding their own and others' feelings and can help provide a conceptual underpinning for a harmonious social life.

unspeakable horror: "This was like the other survival stories because it took courage and determination and all Daniel's skills to survive physically . . . but this story was different because he also had to struggle to survive as a human being." "Remember at the end his father said, 'We're not like them . . . if we get to be like them, they've won.'"

Books like these are essential vehicles to bring acts of struggle and triumph into the classroom for discussion and recognition.

Fifth Stage: Identity versus Role Confusion (Age Thirteen or Fourteen to Eighteen and Beyond). Adolescence is the time for finding who one really is. Traditional societies made this a certain business. You were a farmer, fisherman, mother-and-grower, or trader. On reaching puberty, you went through an initiation ceremony in which the whole community came together and acknowledged your transition to your adult role. Communist countries, too, offered some of this same sort of certainty. You were observed and tested during the school years and put on a track to this or that career in a guaranteed job at which you were bound to succeed. (Seeing the anxiety of young people in former communist countries reminds us of the uncertainty our own children face as they seek to define themselves.)

Erikson's formula for identity (which he adapted from Freud's teaching) was threefold: You are whom you are part of; you are what you can do; you are who you feel yourself to be. Piaget, the brilliant student of intelligence, added one more dimension: As an adolescent, you are aware of a higher plane of reality than before. You can recognize ideals, abstractions, and various "-isms," just as surely as you can a Mazda Miata.

These may be the underlying issues, but the problems of adolescence are legion. Young people may lose themselves in the group. They may die many deaths as they are rejected by this or that companion or by this or that cohort. They may yield to the ever-present temptation to sell themselves short—by falling into crime, or drugs, or materialism. Self-definition can mean identifying with a nationality different from that of one's parents or coming to grips once and for all with one's racial identity. It certainly means defining one's sexual orientation.

Books can help. Books reflect identities back to people. Whether biographies, essays, realistic fiction, or poetry, many books are about young people's struggle for self-definition, their struggle against the problems of adolescence, and their suddenly awakened recognition of justice and hypocrisy.

HOW DOES READING "WORK"?

How do children experience literature? How do they understand it? What does it do for them at different ages? The answers to these questions determine what teachers or parents do when they sit down with a child or group of children and a book. There are some surprises here.

Young children, researchers suggest, learn their very language at least in part from encounters with books. Children learn the words for things via the familiar lap-reading pattern: "What's that?" "Dog!" "Right! Dog. Now, what's that?" But being read to does more: Hearing the same words come from the same books over and over gives children the assurance that language, that evanescent medium, has some kind of substance. Knowing names for things and thinking of language as a substantial medium, capable of being represented in print, help children when it comes time to learn to read (Olson, 1984).

Learning to Read

Knowing the letters of the alphabet helps children learn to read (Walsh, Price, and Gillingham, 1988), but there are other important concepts about print that are critical to children's early success in reading. Being able to find one's way around in a book (Clay, 1985) and along a line of print (Morris, 1983) are enormously helpful when beginning to learn to read. Children can often absorb these concepts from playful and informal encounters with books, especially if they are given books of their own and encouraged to share them with others (McCormick and Mason, 1986).

The importance of early encounters with engaging books should not be missed. Most children who get off to a significantly slow start in reading do not catch up (Juel, 1989); yet giving children early and repeated encounters with engaging books has been shown to head off reading failure.

When children *are* learning to read, it helps if they are given books with predictable patterns in order to practice their growing skill. Even after reading ability begins to develop, children are still helped if, at the same time as adults are reading to them, they have interesting but simply written books they can read themselves. The mere provision of interesting and readable books has made an enormous improvement in children's learning to read, especially in literature-based reading programs now practiced around the world.

Once reading has begun in earnest, reading specialists often speak of component abilities in a child's reading skill. One of these is *word recognition*, the ability to read words. If children can read many words instantly—without having to sound them out or guess what they are—they have more of their attention left over for following the story line and pondering meanings. Beginning readers are taught the rudiments of word recognition, but there is little doubt that what really nourishes children's *sight vocabulary* (that is, the collection of all the words they have learned to recognize) is a great deal of reading.

A higher-order ability is *reading comprehension*. We have already said that rapid comprehension partly depends on word recognition, because children who struggle to puzzle out words won't have much attention left for understanding what they read. Comprehension is often defined as understanding new information in light of what is already known. Besides well-developed word recognition, three other things contribute to reading comprehension.

The first, as the definition of comprehension implies, is a background of knowledge: Even a little familiarity with the topic of a work or its style makes it possible to see the significance of what is read. Where does this "little familiarity" come from? Like as not, it comes from reading.

The second determiner of good comprehension is a familiarity with the structure, or organization, of the work. That is, readers who know how stories are organized, or limericks, or persuasive essays, are more likely to adjust their thoughts appropriately to those forms of writing. How will they learn to do this? Some teaching will surely help, but, again, the best teacher is reading.

The third aspect of reading comprehension is the habit of searching actively for meaning: asking questions, making predictions, taking note of surprises, and revising expectations. More than the other two aspects, the habit of searching for meaning is fostered by good teaching—or rather, by good book discussions. A few lucky children get opportunities for lively discussions of books at home, but the rest must depend on their teachers to organize and encourage such discussions.

Note how much good reading comprehension depends on children's having the habit of reading: Reading is the best teacher of reading. No wonder some observers of reading achievement say, "The rich get richer and the poor get poorer." Those children who can read, who like to read, who do read, find that reading only gets easier and more meaningful. Sadly, the process also works in reverse.

Same Book, Different Responses

Once they can read—or when they are read to—how do children of different ages respond to literature? Studies have shown a progression from overt and active responses to covert psychological ones. Kindergarteners respond with their bodies. They like to repeat chants, clap along, and act out scenes. In the lower elementary grades, children follow plots and can make predictions based on them. Children in the upper elementary grades can talk about thematic issues and can more readily discuss the artistry of a book (Hickman, 1992). Yet even kindergarteners show awareness of themes, especially if they have been read to often (Lehr, 1988).

Now that's an odd thought: The same book is eliciting different reactions from children of different ages. But such, it turns out, is the nature of literary response. What a book finally "means" to a reader is constructed by the reader, from the suggestions found on the page. The reader brings to the reading unique and personal understandings, expectations, fears, interests, and—especially— past reading experiences. The book offers words, arranged according to the author's plan. The author relies on conventions of plot, characterization, and theme to shape the reader's response, but the reader must bring visualizations and emotions to the encounter. It shouldn't be surprising that readers of different ages have different experiences from the same book. Same-age readers from different parts of town have different responses, too.

The dynamics of literary response cut many ways. Several critics have commented on the reader's influence on the text—the freedom to construct the meaning of the book according to the furniture of one's own imagination. But, of course, the influence works the other way, too. Books can take readers up out of their seats or their beds and make them imaginatively live other lives.

That is why, along with historical fiction, multicultural literature is such a promising development in children's literature in the United States. American children can get a glimpse of what it is like to flee from Vietnam in a boat, to undertake an arduous trek to Johannesburg to save a baby's life, to survive a hurricane on a small Caribbean island, or to be pushed out of the house by your mother's new companion in a Guatemalan village.

In the United States, barriers to intercultural understanding are abundant. Examples of the dangers of misunderstanding flare up in the newspapers almost daily. Children's literature is one of the few rich sources of insights into diverse people's lives.

GENRES OF CHILDREN'S LITERATURE

Authors rely on conventions of plot, characterization, and theme to shape readers' responses. They also work within an awareness of genre. *Genre* is a French word meaning "kind" or "type." Once readers know what genre they're

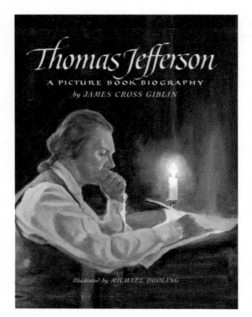

Illustration 1.5
James Cross Giblin is a master of the informational genre. Besides histories of chimney sweeps, windows, and table manners, he has written this illustrated biography of Thomas Jefferson.
(*Thomas Jefferson: A Picture Book Biography* by James Cross Giblin. Illustration copyright © 1994 by Mike Dooling. Used by permission of Scholastic Inc.)

reading, they know what to expect from a text: whether magic, or realism, or humor, or facts.

What are the recognized genres of children's books? These are *traditional literature* (including folktales and fairytales, myths, epics, and ballads), *poetry* of all kinds, *fantasy and science fiction*, *realistic fiction*, *historical fiction*, *informational books and biographies*, and *picture books* (a curious category, because picture books can fit into any of the other genres). We will devote the whole middle portion of this book to exploring children's books by genre. Traditional literature is covered in Chapter 5. Picture books are the subject of Chapter 6. Poetry is considered in Chapter 7. In Chapter 8, we consider realistic fiction. In Chapter 9, the topic is historical fiction. Fantasy and science fiction are covered in Chapter 10. And in Chapter 11, we look at informational books and biographies.

The idea of genre means that both author and reader are working within a set of expectations. Informational books describe things in the real world. Realistic fiction does not describe things in the real world, yet it does describe things that *could* happen there. If a book describes things that *couldn't* happen, it's probably a fairytale or a fantasy or a work of science fiction. In each of the chapters devoted to a genre, we include a section that explores what it means to write and read within the genre. We also trace the evolution of books in that genre and describe outstanding writers, past and present, who work within it.

RESOURCES FOR CHILDREN'S BOOKS

Studying children's literature in college differs in many ways from studying other literature, especially in this way: The focus is turned as much or more toward contemporary books for children as it is toward great works of the past. That is because—with the explosion in the number of books published for children, improvements in the technology of color reproduction, and a growing diversity in the range of people children need to know and care about—many of the very best books for contemporary children have appeared in the past twenty years. And they continue to be published every year. Thus, to be well-read in children's books, you must read backwards and forwards: Read the best of the books already published, and read the best of those coming out.

For the best books already published, you can count on the Recommended Books section at the end of each chapter (especially those in Chapters 5 through 11). The most important books in the development of each genre are discussed in each chapter in the section on historical development. If you want a historical perspective on children's literature, you should read those books as well. But what of the new books? How can you find your way to those that are best?

Several journals have emerged to review children's books and to promote the best ones. These journals, which include *The Horn Book Magazine, School Library Journal, Booklist, Bookbird,* and *The New Advocate*—as well as the book review sections of several professional magazines such as *The Reading Teacher* and *Language Arts*—have slightly different emphases and target audiences, so you should consider the information in Appendix E carefully.

Many organizations promote children's literature. Subscribing to their publications and attending their regional and national conferences is an excellent way to keep abreast of new children's books. Publishers display new books at the larger professional gatherings. Names and addresses of professional groups concerned with children's literature are listed in Appendix B.

BRINGING CHILDREN AND BOOKS TOGETHER

This text is mostly about children's books—their types and notable titles, their features, and their effects on readers. Nonetheless, teachers throughout North America are using children's books like never before in every part of the school day. Thus, the chapters that make up the last third of this book are devoted to ways of sharing books with children.

Negotiating the symbol system is a barrier to reading literature. So the first priority is to involve children in literature without having them struggle to read it. That means refining your skill at reading aloud, working on your storytelling (and involving children in storytelling, too), and engaging children in drama. Such activities engage children in the meaning and the beauty and the fascination of literature, without making an obstacle out of reading the words. Reading will come in due time—and even when it does, you can engage children in texts more elaborate and rewarding than the simple ones they can read themselves by reading aloud, storytelling, and engaging in drama. Chapter 12 (Inviting Children into Literature) lays out techniques for all these activities.

Encouraging children's voluntary reading is enormously important, too. We want children to love reading right from the first. And if they have had more television than bedtime stories in their early lives, this is all the more reason to entice them with free access to colorful books. Ways of setting up classroom libraries to invite exploring and free reading are also described in Chapter 12.

As solitary and cozy as reading can be, it is also a rewarding social activity. People who read enjoy talking to others about books. A good book chat deepens a reader's insights into a text and even provides a window into the ways other people think. Book talks that are open and informal have been shown to invite more thoughtful and satisfying participation from children than sessions that are dominated by the teacher's pedagogical purposes. That is why the emphasis in Chapter 13 (Encouraging Response to Literature: Literary Discussion) is on *book clubs*. More and more teachers use this name for discussions that are flexible and maximally open to children's ideas and feeling about books. That chapter describes several ways to arrange for such discussions.

As teachers discover the power of literature to teach about the world, children's books are being used across the curriculum. There is a logic that leads from this story to that nonfiction book to that interview to this art project. That logic is woven into the web of literature units. Chapter 14 (Literature Units in the Curriculum) discusses in detail several approaches to thematic teaching using literature.

 TEACHING IDEAS

Learning about the Books Children Like. Interview four children of different ages about their favorite books. Note carefully what they say. Is there a difference in what children of different ages admire in books? How do their criteria for good children's books compare with those set out in this chapter?

Finding Different Ways to Use Books with Children. Interview three teachers of the elementary grades. Ask them how many different ways they use children's books with their students. Compare their answers with the vignettes found on pages 5–6.

Investigating Ways Children's Books Have Changed over the Years. Find a school librarian or a children's librarian who has worked in the field for thirty years or more. Ask her or him to talk about the ways the books for children have changed, children's interests have changed, and parents' concerns about their children's reading have changed—and how these have remained the same. Prepare a two-column list of ways children's books have remained the same and ways they have changed. Share your list with your peers.

EXPERIENCES FOR YOUR LEARNING

1. Reread the vignettes on pages 5–6. See if you can think of books that served you in each of those ways when you were a child. Are there other ways that books appealed to you? Compare your answers with those of your classmates.

2. Pick a children's book. Evaluate it according to the criteria of a "good" children's book set out on pages 8–11. How does it fare? Are there other criteria of excellence that you would propose?

3. This chapter stated that many or most of the best books for children have been published in the past twenty years. Do you agree? Why do you think that claim is true—or false? What exceptions to that claim can you think of?

4. This chapter stated that children's books have changed throughout history, roughly as views of childhood changed. What trends do you see at work in society that may change children's literature in the next twenty years? What qualities or values would you expect to see remain the same in children's literature?

REFERENCES

Ainsworth, Mary D. S. "Attachment: Retrospect and Prospect." *The Place of Attachment in Human Behavior.* Eds. C. M. Parkes and J. Stevenson-Hinde. New York: Basic Books, 1982.

Applebee, Authur. *The Child's Concept of Stories.* Chicago: University of Chicago Press, 1975.

Aries, Phillippe. *Centuries of Childhood: A Social History of Family Life.* New York: Knopf, 1962.

Bennett, William. *The Child's Book of Virtues.* Illustrated by Michael Hague. New York: Simon & Schuster, 1995.

Clay, Marie M. *The Early Detection of Reading Difficulties.* 3rd ed. Portsmouth, NH: Heinemann, 1985.

Coles, Robert. *The Call of Stories: Teaching and the Moral Imagination.* Boston: Houghton Mifflin, 1989.

Damon, William. *The Social World of the Child.* San Francisco: Jossey-Bass, 1977.

Darton, F. J. Harvey. *Children's Books in England: Five Centuries of Social Life.* 2nd ed. London: Cambridge University Press, 1966.

Egan, Kieran. "Individual Development in Literacy." *Stories and Readers.* Eds. Charles Temple and Patrick Collins. Norwood, MA: Christopher-Gordon, 1992.

Erikson, Erik. *Identity: Youth and Crisis.* New York: Norton, 1968.

Frye, Northrop. *The Anatomy of Criticism.* Princeton: Princeton University Press, 1957.

Ginsburg, Herbert, and Sylvia Opper. *Piaget's Theory of Intellectual Development.* 2nd ed. Upper Saddle River, NJ: Prentice Hall, 1979.

Hamilton, Virginia. *The Planet of Junior Brown.* New York: Macmillan, 1971.

Hickman, Janet. "What Comes Naturally: Growth and Change in Children's Free Response to Literature." *Stories and Readers.* Eds. Charles Temple and Patrick Collins. Norwood, MA: Christopher-Gordon, 1992.

Holman, Felice. *The Wild Children.* New York: Scribner's, 1983.

Jiminez, Juan Ramon. Trans. Antonio T. Di Nicholas. *Platero and I: An Andalusian Elegy.* Boulder, CO: Shambhala/Random House, 1978.

Juel, Connie. "The Longitudinal Study of Reading Acquisition (grades 1 to 4)." Paper presented at the 39th annual meeting of the National Reading Conference, Austin, Texas, 1989.

Konner, Robert. *Becoming Attached.* New York: Warner, 1994.

Lehr, Susan. "The Child's Developing Sense of Theme as a Response to Literature." *Reading Research Quarterly* 23.3 (1988): 337–357.

Leonni, Leo. *Frederick*. New York: Pantheon, 1967.

Matas, Carol. *Daniel's Story*. New York: Scholastic, 1993.

Matthews, Gareth. *Dialogues with Children*. Cambridge, MA: Harvard University Press, 1984.

———. *Philosophy and the Young Child*. Cambridge, MA: Harvard University Press, 1980.

McCormick, Christine, and Jana Mason. "Intervention Procedures for Increasing Preschool Children's Interest and Knowledge About Reading." *Emergent Literacy*. Eds. William Teale and Elizabeth Sulzby. Norwood, NJ: Ablex, 1986.

Morris, Darrell. "Concept of Word and Phonemic Awareness in the Beginning Reader." *Research in the Teaching of English* 17 (1983): 359–73.

O'Dell, Scott. *Island of the Blue Dolphins*. Boston: Houghton Mifflin, 1960.

Olson, David. "'See! Jumping!' Some Oral Antecedents of Literacy." *Awakening to Literacy*. Eds. H. Goelman, A. Oberg, and F. Smith. Portsmouth, NH: Heinemann, 1984.

Perrault, Charles. *Cinderella*. Retold by Christine San José. Illustrated by Deborah Santini. Honesdale, PA: Boyds Mills Press, 1994.

Piaget, Jean. *The Language and Thought of the Child*. Cleveland: World, 1955.

———. *The Moral Judgement of the Child*. 1932. New York: Free Press, 1965.

Vygotsky, Lev. *Mind in Society: The Development of Higher Psychological Processes*. Cambridge, MA: Harvard University Press, 1978.

———. *Thought and Language*. Cambridge, MA: MIT Press, 1969.

Walsh, Daniel, Gary Price, and Mark Gillingham. "The Critical But Transitory Importance of Letter Naming." *Reading Research Quarterly* 23 (1988): 108–22.

Winnicott, D. W. *The Child, the Family, and the Outside World*. London: Pelican, 1974.

2 Literary Elements of Children's Literature

Once upon a time, far away in Japan, a poor young artist sat alone in his little house, waiting for his dinner. His housekeeper had gone to market, and he sat sighing to think of all the things he wished she would bring home. He expected her to hurry in at any minute, bowing and opening her little basket to show him how wisely she had spent their few pennies. He heard her step, and jumped up. He was very hungry!

But the housekeeper lingered by the door, and the basket stayed shut.

"Come," he cried. "What is in that basket?"

The housekeeper trembled, and held the basket tight in two hands. "It has seemed to me, sir," she said, "that we are very lonely here." Her wrinkled face looked humble and obstinate.

from The Cat Who Went to Heaven *(1958)*
by Elizabeth Coatsworth

THE ARTISTRY OF LITERARY ELEMENTS

Literature is a miracle. With words on a page, a writer can take readers to a place that never was, let them know people who never lived, and help them share adventures that never happened—and in spite of the artifice, create something truer than life itself.

Is it possible to look closely at the magic of literature without destroying its ability to amaze us? We think so. It may actually enhance your appreciation of a work to have a vocabulary and a set of concepts to help you admire its wonders or note the shortcomings of a less-than-satisfactory work.

In this chapter, we will describe the aspects of literary quality that critics and teachers most often refer to when they talk about texts. Knowing these will give you a vocabulary for evaluating texts and also for exploring the elements of them that move readers.

We will ground our discussion with numerous examples taken from a few key books: Phyllis Naylor's *Shiloh* (1991), Mildred Taylor's *Roll of Thunder, Hear My Cry* (1976), Natalie Babbitt's *Tuck Everlasting* (1975), and Alma Flor Ada's *The Gold Coin* (1991). Although it is not necessary for you to have read these books before you read this chapter, you will definitely get more out of the chapter if you do so.

The main elements of a literary work are the setting, the characterization, the plot, the themes, the stance of the implied reader, the point of view, and the author's style. Let's first take a closer look at each of these literary elements and then consider some special literary features of informational books and poetry.

SETTINGS: HOW DO AUTHORS CREATE TIMES AND PLACES?

The *setting* is the time and place in which the events of a story are imagined to have occurred. An important part of any author's task is to help the reader visualize the events being narrated and the people who are living them. Since whatever is visualized must be seen in time and space, the setting of the story is an important part of the reader's invitation into an imaginary experience.

How explicit the setting is varies with the genre. In a folktale, the setting may get scant mention, yet it can still have symbolic significance. In realistic fiction, the setting can be used to add *verisimilitude*, or lifelikeness, to the story and make it easier for readers to believe in the events. In a survival story, the setting plays the role of antagonist—almost as if it were a character. In historical fiction or in stories from other cultures, the setting may share center stage with the characters and events, since readers may be as curious about what life is or was like in that setting as they are about what happens in the story. The same can be said of science fiction or fantasy—genres in which the author is free to make up whole new worlds. Let's look, then, at how settings vary with some of these genres.

Settings in Folktales and Fairytales

The Grimms' story "The Frog Prince" (Grimm and Grimm, 1972) has this setting:

> In olden times when wishing still helped one, there lived a king whose daughters were all beautiful, but the youngest was so beautiful that the sun itself, which had seen so much, was astonished whenever it shone in her face. Close by the king's castle lay a dark forest, and under an old lime-tree in the forest was a well, and when the day was very warm, the King's child went out into the forest and sat down beside the cool fountain. . . . (p. 17)

The first sentence introduces this "no-particular-time" when magical things happened. Japanese folktales often begin just as simply: "Once long ago in the middle of the mountains. . . ." Native American tales often say: "Many lifetimes ago, in the days of the Ancient Ones. . . ." Arabic folktales sometimes begin: "There was, and there was not, in the fullness of time. . . ." Young children's first question about these tales, of course, is "Did that really happen?" The storyteller doesn't want to deny the ultimate truth of the story, so she or he finds a way of saying that these events were cast in a setting that is beyond the everyday, where things can be morally true, if not factually so.

Settings in folktales are briefly described. They represent everywhere and nowhere, but they often have particular associations. In European tales, *home* is where normal life is lived, securely. *The forest* is where one may be tested by sinister forces. *The country* is where simple but honest folk live, whereas *the city* is the place of sophisticated but possibly treacherous people. *A hovel* is a place one usually wants to rise above (but may have to learn to settle for), and *a palace* is the residence of those who were born privileged or who have had triumphant success.

Settings in Realistic Fiction

Settings in realistic fiction are usually described with greater detail to give readers a feeling for a particular place. Here are the opening lines of *Shiloh*:

> The day Shiloh come, we're having us a big Sunday dinner. Dara Lynn's dipping bread in her glass of cold tea, the way she likes, and Becky pushes her beans up over the edge of her plate in her rush to get 'em down. (p. 11)

These lines reveal the "country ways" of Marty's family, through their way of speech and their table manners. Knowing how people act and talk can provide one sort of clue to the setting. Two pages further into the book, Marty takes the reader for a walk around the physical setting:

> We live high up in the hills above Friendly, but hardly anybody knows where that is. Friendly's near Sistersville, which is halfway between Wheeling and Parkersburg. Used to be, Daddy told me, Sistersville was one of the best places you could live in the whole state. You ask *me* the best place to live, I'd say right where we are, a little four-room house with hills on three sides.
>
> Afternoon is my second-best time to go up in the hills, though; morning's the best, especially in summer. Early, *early* morning. One morning I saw three kinds of animals, not counting cats, dogs, frogs, cows, and horses. Saw a groundhog, saw a doe with two fawns, and saw a gray fox with a reddish head. Bet his daddy was a gray fox and his ma was a red one. (pp. 12–13)

More clues to the setting: Whatever happens in the story will have to be consistent with a Southern rural mountain environment. Good writers don't waste details, so the reader can expect the ways of nature and animals to figure in this story.

Settings as Important Features in Themselves

In some genres, settings can figure so strongly as to share attention with the characters in the story. The setting may produce challenges that characters must strive against. The grinding and desolate urban setting of Jerry Spinelli's **Maniac Magee** (1990) seems to have permeated people's attitudes with harshness, and Maniac must struggle against both in his quest for humanity.

The racist society of Mississippi during the depression of the 1930s, portrayed in Mildred Taylor's **Roll of Thunder, Hear My Cry,** shows readers what the Logan children must endure. The implications of racial antagonism affect everything that happens in the book.

In multicultural literature, details of the setting may seem commonplace to one group but be striking to another. For example, Alma Flor Ada's **My Name Is Maria Isabel** (1993) begins:

> Maria Isabel looked at the cup of coffee with milk and the buttered toast in front of her. But she couldn't bring herself to eat.
>
> Her mother said, "Maribel, *cariño*, hurry up."
>
> Her father added, "You don't want to be late on your first day, do you?" (p. 1)

Children who trace their origins to the Spanish-speaking Caribbean or to Central America will find that scene reassuringly familiar. But other readers may be surprised that a young girl would drink coffee for breakfast, moved at the mother's affectionate shortening of the girl's name, and impressed that the mother speaks to her daughter in two languages. In effect, the setting is functioning almost as a character in the story.

In a historical novel, the details of the setting may also go a long way to satisfy young readers' curiosity about a place that is far removed in time. The earthiness of English village life early in the fourteenth century is brought home in the first paragraph of Karen Cushman's **The Midwife's Apprentice** (1995):

> When animal droppings and garbage and spoiled straw are piled up in a great heap, the rotting and moiling give forth heat. Usually no

ASK THE EDITOR . . .

Richard W. Jackson

Richard W. Jackson

What was the best manuscript you ever received, and what qualities do you look for in an author?

The best manuscript I've received? *Ever?* You might have asked me to choose between my children! There are several bests. Paula Fox's *Maurice's Room*—she'd written only three chapters at the time I first saw it but I remember reading them aloud to my wife and saying, "This woman will win the Newbery Medal someday." And she did. Such vividness in the people, such kindness in the humor. And such a voice. Also a favorite—the text for *The Relatives Came* by Cynthia Rylant, for somewhat the same reasons. I believe we didn't change a word, though "best" for me doesn't mean word perfect. More important than immediate perfection is the breath of life in a piece. Frances Temple's *Taste of Salt* was another revelation— a "breathing" book about modern Haiti, about brave young people whose lives were, at the time, largely unimaginable by Americans (of any age). The book is written in two first-person teenage voices, and there is urgency in every word. For "I" stories, urgency is crucial.

Even "light" books, such as Avi's *S.O.R. Losers* or Judy Blume's *"Are You There God? It's Me, Margaret,"* depend on urgency for their success. In funny stories as well as serious, you need to sense the narrator's urge to bend your ear. *Toning the Sweep* by Angela Johnson is another unique example of urgent voice. It began as a collec-tion of quick scenes, poetic impres-sions, snippets of conversation about a girl witnessing her grandmother's struggle with cancer; it grew into a novel over several years. Thrilling years.

I look for long-term associations with writers or illustrators and rarely take on anyone published by many houses—for snobbish reasons, I sup-pose. I look for loyalty and for brains. For devotion to hard work and a cer-tain delicacy of touch. I listen for voice. Just this minute the phone rang and—speaking of voice—a cheery one said: "I've figured out how to do it, the whole book. It was our conver-sation yesterday that helped." The caller was Theresa Nelson, a superb novelist whose first book, *The 25-cent Miracle,* is another best. She's written four beauties since. My response to such calls has remained unchanging since 1962: gratitude and joy.

Richard W. Jackson is editor of Richard Jackson Books, an imprint of Orchard Books, which publishes some thirty new titles a year. His articles have appeared in The Horn Book Magazine, School Library Journal, *and* The New Advocate.

one gets close enough to notice because of the stench. But the girl noticed and, on that frosty night, burrowed deep into the warm, rotting muck, heedless of the smell. (p. 1)

Here again, although the characters also do much to impress themselves on readers, the setting of this historical novel continually surprises and informs them.

CHARACTERIZATION: HOW DO PEOPLE EMERGE FROM THE PAGE?

Characterization is the art of creating people out of words on the page. When a writer has done a good job of characterization, readers feel as if they have gotten to know another person. How does a writer achieve that?

Sigmund Freud suggested that we know people by three things: by what they do and how they do it, by the others they affiliate with and how they feel about each other, and by the way they feel about themselves. These same dynamics work in literature. In coming to know a character in a work of literature, though, readers are affected by one more variable—the role the character plays in the story. Let's look at each of these dimensions.

Characters Are Developed through Their Actions

In a guidebook for fiction writers, Anne Bernays and Pamela Painter (1995) remind us of a character in F. Scott Fitzgerald's *The Great Gatsby* who wore cufflinks made of human molars. Rather than saying "He was insensitive, domineering, and gross," Fitzgerald simply gave us that one detail—and that detail made readers see the character more clearly than descriptive words ever could have.

When readers meet Marty on the first page of ***Shiloh***, they hear this exchange:

> "I looked that rabbit over good, Marty, and you won't find any buckshot in that thigh," Dad says, buttering his bread. "I shot him in the neck."
>
> Somehow I wish he hadn't said that. I push the meat from one side of my plate to the other, through the sweet potatoes and back again.
>
> "Did it die right off?" I ask, knowing I can't eat at all unless it had. "Soon enough."
>
> "You shoot its head clean off?" Darlene asks. She's like that.
>
> Dad chews real slow before he answers. "Not quite," he says, and goes on eating.
>
> Which is when I leave the table. (pp. 11–12)

Here, too, readers get to know Marty by what he does and says, rather than by what the author says about him. Marty is the most sensitive member of a family that is used to earthy living, but he is trying to hang in there. Readers absorb that impression better because they infer it from the above exchange, rather than being told it directly.

Characters Are Developed through Their Relations with Others

Characters are also brought to life when readers see who "their people" are—and how they relate to them. Cassie in ***Roll of Thunder, Hear My Cry*** is an African American child, a member of a black community in segregationist

Mississippi during the Depression. Marty in *Shiloh* is a member of a hard-working and frugal family in rural Appalachia. Jason in *The Giver* (1993) lives in a deliberately wholesome family in a bland, engineered society.

Often, book characters are portrayed as being out of harmony with their group. In *Shiloh*, Marty is at home in the woods with a rifle in his hands—but unlike the rest of his family, he is sensitive to the suffering of animals. Jesse, in Katherine Paterson's *Bridge to Terabithia* (1975), is more sensitive than the rest of his farm family; his friend Lesley is more down-to-earth than her idealistic professional family. They are more like each other than like their own kin. Cassie, in *Roll of Thunder, Hear My Cry*, belongs to a family that refuses to accept second-class citizenship in a society harshly governed by whites. Cassie doesn't understand, however, as her parents do, the care and skill it takes for a black family to avoid disaster in that situation. Juan, the thief in Alma Flor Ada's *The Gold Coin*, doesn't belong to anybody. Yet as he pursues Doña Josefa through the countryside in order to rob her, his series of contacts with other working people eventually draws him into the human family.

In all of these cases, the characters come to life through a sort of comparison and contrast: A character is like the group in some ways, but strikingly different from it in some particular way.

Characters can also be drawn in opposition to other, contrasting characters. In *Shiloh*, Marty's ethics are starkly contrasted to those of the brutish Judd Travers, who lies, cheats, and abuses his animals. Marty also differs from his best friend, David Howard, who comes from better-off professional people living in town and who is not nearly as robust as Marty. In *The Gold Coin*, Juan the thief is starkly contrasted with Doña Josefa the healer: He wants nothing but to take; she wants nothing but to give.

In sum, it is often possible to find two characters in a story who are drawn as opposites, making the attributes of both clearer.

Characters Are Developed through Their Sense of Themselves

In *Roll of Thunder, Hear My Cry*, Cassie Logan can't imagine why she should step off the sidewalk when a white girl tells her to. She experiences horror and outrage when her grandmother, Big Ma, forces her to apologize to her offender. Readers know Cassie by her unquestioned sense of her own worth.

The central conflict in *Shiloh* comes about because Marty is keeping a dog away from its owner, in violation of the law and common behavior and against the wishes of his parents. The author shows how Marty experiences this conflict by having him utter this prayer:

> "Jesus," I whisper finally, "which you want me to do? Be one hundred percent honest and carry that dog back to Judd so that one of your creatures can be kicked and starved all over again, or keep him here and fatten him up to glorify your creation?"
>
> The question seemed to answer itself, and I'm pretty proud of that prayer. (p. 57)

Readers get to know Marty all the better through this expression of his thoughts. As characters get to know themselves, readers get to know them. By comparing their own experiences to those of the characters, readers get to know *themselves* a little better, too.

Characters Are Developed through the Roles They Play in the Plot

If a character in a story is cast in the role of the *protagonist*, or the hero, readers are inclined to be sympathetic. If the character is cast as the *antagonist*, the villain or the hero's rival, readers are disposed to "fill in the blanks" with bad qualities. This happens in real life, too: Just listen to what emotional sports fans say about players on the opposing team!

If the character is cast as the *helper*, readers may expect her or him to be loyal and generous, possibly amusing—but not more beautiful, brave, or admirable than the hero. If the character plays the role of *receiver*, the person whom the hero wants to rescue or otherwise help, readers expect that person to be deserving of that help (Souriau, 1955).

How much the plot influences the way we think of characters, though, depends on the genre of the story. In a folktale, readers can be told almost nothing about a character and yet be sympathetic or unsympathetic depending on whether he or she plays a hero or a villain. Readers pull for Jack—even though he's been presented as lazy and stupid—because he's cast as the hero of "Jack and the Beanstalk." Readers are not sorry when the giant meets a bad end, even though he's been robbed and then killed—because he opposes the hero, Jack.

In realistic fiction, the writer is obliged to go further and spell out the characters' motives and personal qualities. Even an antagonistic character's motives must be explained. In *Shiloh*, for example, the author leads readers to understand Judd Travers's insensitive manners by planting hints about his own harsh upbringing.

Taking us inside the motives of characters—whether they are sympathetic or not—is one of the great contributions literature makes to our understanding of other people. For centuries before the discipline of psychology was invented, people counted on literature for insights into what makes other people do what they do.

When a writer creates well-developed characters—those whose thoughts, feelings, and attitudes are evident through what they think, say, and do in the story—readers feel they are getting to know other people.

A *plot* is a meaningful ordering of events with their consequences, a "what happened to whom and why." A plot is the conveyor belt that pulls a reader through the text, getting to know characters and scenes along the way, before arriving at a cumulative insight.

Plots fascinate people. When you add up not just the literature people read, but also the films and videos they watch and the TV shows (don't forget the soap operas) they consume during so many hours each day, it is clear that most people consider plots a staple of life.

Ask a person to recount her day, and like as not she will weave a plot, starring herself as the main character—hero or victim. Critics have noted that we all depend on plots to give meaning to our lives. As critic Frank Kermode (1975) pointed out, our daily lives have no clear meaning without an answer to the question "What is it all adding up to?" We never really know what our lives are adding up to until they're over, so we crave a sense of an ending, which we find in the plots of stories, because only stories—and dead people's lives—ever end.

Thus, stories are frameworks that give meaning to events. Much as words and concepts give people the means to name and think about the phenomena that surround them, stories—plots—give them ways of finding meaning in the dynamic events and the ongoing processes of their lives. It's no wonder people are hungry for plots.

In this section, we look at the structures of plots, then at several variations of plots.

Plots: The Basics

Plots unfold when a character is drawn toward a significant goal. The goal is almost always related to *conflict,* either within the character, between the character and some rival person, between the character and nature, or between the character and the expectations of society.

The events in a plot are set in motion by a *complication,* in which the main character experiences a problem and explicitly or implicitly sets a goal. The plot continues with *rising action,* in which the character strives to reach the goal and solve the problem. Toward the end, the plot arrives at a *climax,* in which tension is at its height as the matter of the character's success or failure is about to be decided. And the plot culminates in the *resolution,* in which the problem is decided, for good or ill. Some plots close with a *denouement,* which is a brief display of the characters' state of affairs following the resolution.

Most folktales and other simple stories follow the linear plot pattern just described. In Alma Flor Ada's **The Gold Coin,** Juan's adventure begins when, approaching a hut he plans to rob, he spies an old woman inside holding a gold coin and saying, "I must be the richest person in the world." His conflict arises when he breaks into the hut after the woman leaves and finds no gold coin: Now he must follow her. Of course, his goal is to have the coin. Tensions mount (the rising action) throughout the story as Juan follows the old woman, Doña Josefa, to one farm after another—where he is told of a generous and helpful act she has just performed and given work to do to pass the time before the farmers can take him to his next destination. The climax is the surprising events that befall Juan when he catches up with Doña Josefa alone on the road. And the resolution

Illustration 2.1

An original book with the simplicity and moral clarity of a folktale, *The Gold Coin* has a linear story line that culminates in a surprise ending. (*The Gold Coin* by Alma Flor Ada. Illustration copyright © 1991 Neil Waldman. Used by permission of Atheneum Books for Young Readers, an imprint of Simon & Schuster Children's Publishing Division.)

follows when Juan realizes he has been transformed. The denouement in this story is tactfully left for the reader to imagine. How will Juan lead his life, now that he has learned the value of being trusted by others, of being generous?

Episodes: Stories within Stories

Many books, especially those for older children, are built around more complex patterns. Beverly Cleary's *Ramona and Her Father* (1978) begins with Mr. Quimby's losing his job. This is the main conflict of the story, and it won't be resolved until the last few pages. This main problem spawns several smaller problems—each with a story of its own (and each providing provisional closure when read in a single sitting). Some of the problems last through several chapters: For example, because Ramona and Beezus see more of their father, they grow concerned about his smoking, and they start a guerrilla campaign to make him stop. Some problems last only through a single chapter—like the antics that occur when Ramona imagines she might become a highly paid child actor in a TV advertisement, able to support her besieged family in lavish style.

Ramona and Her Father is an intricate pattern of connected plots: one main problem leading logically to several smaller problems that pull the child reader through one, two, or three chapters, each with its own closure, until the main conflict of the book is resolved.

The "Real" Story versus the Story as Revealed

In Virginia Hamilton's *The House of Dies Drear* (1968), an African American family goes to live in a small town in Ohio, where they move into a large house on the edge of town. After discovering a secret passage below the house, the son has an encounter with what seems to be a ghost. Readers' curiosity is aroused, and they are prompted to guess at many different explanations for events while paging through the book—so that the reading is an experience of curiosity, tension, excitement, and final satisfaction. When the truth about the mystery is revealed at the end of the book, readers find themselves looking back over the events and retelling the story to themselves in light of what they have learned.

In *The House of Dies Drear* and most other mystery stories, then, there are really two stories: the puzzling narrative that is fed to the reader page by page and the underlying story that the narrative points to (Barthes, 1974). Mystery and suspense are created as readers ask themselves, "What is really going on?"—that is, as they inquire about the deeper plot that underlies the incomplete plot full of hints that the author is parceling out to us.

Variations in Time

A simple story is told straight through, with events following one after another. But in some stories, the action is liberated from a straight time sequence. These stories use *flashbacks*, in which events that happened before are recalled into the time of the narration, like Dicey Tillerman's memories of going to see her mother, recalled during her travels in Cynthia Voigt's *The Homecoming* (1983).

Tuck Everlasting employs time shifts, too. Near the beginning of the book, Winnie Foster observes Jesse Tuck uncovering and drinking from the spring that magically stops one from aging. A short while later, readers learn that the Tuck family had drunk from the spring eighty-seven years before. Finally, in the epilogue to the book, set seventy years after the main action, the Tucks come upon Winnie's grave—and thus answer the lingering question of whether Winnie will drink from the spring and remain young forever.

Recurring Plots

Some plot forms are used again and again in stories. To lump them together by their common forms is to take nothing away from them—on the contrary, it may point out their larger psychic meaning and their contribution to our understanding of the human drama.

The Initiation Story. In traditional societies in which initiation rituals are still required of young people, a high price is exacted for reaching adulthood. In one anthropologist's account (Turnbull, 1982), initiates are commonly taken out of the tribe and into the woods, where they are exposed to extreme pain or danger. Their childhood is stripped from them as their old clothes and other possessions are confiscated and burned. They are taught weighty secrets and given new responsibilities, before finally being reintroduced to the tribe, where the community pays homage to them and recognizes their new state.

Children's literature is full of *initiation stories*, in which a young character is given some challenge to get through; having successfully met the challenge, she or he is recognized as being more mature or more worthy. "Jack and the Beanstalk" and "Hansel and Gretel" are initiation stories. *Nessa's Fish* (1990), written by Nancy Luenn and illustrated by Neil Waldman, is an initiation story that tells of a young Inuit girl's thoughtful and heroic efforts to save her incapacitated grandmother who is stranded out on the ice with a cache of fish. Gary Paulsen's *Hatchet* (1987) is an initiation story of a boy's survival in the woods; Katherine Paterson's *Lyddie* (1991) is an initiation story about a girl's learning to stand up for herself in the harsh environment of early industrial Lowell, Massachusetts. Mary Hoffman's *Amazing Grace* (1991) (illustrated by Caroline Binch) is an initiation story about an African American girl's efforts to transcend the limits of race and sex and play the part of Peter Pan in a first-grade play.

Becoming initiated sometimes implies trade-offs: The protagonist must trade innocence for experience. Hansel and Gretel lost their childhood and experienced horror before they could be reunited with their father, in what must have been an uneasy relationship. In Roald Dahl's *Danny the Champion of the World* (1982), Danny learns a terrible secret about his father and his father's family. The knowledge destroys his cozy domesticity with his father, but it also enables Danny to save his father from danger and eventually to become a family and community hero.

Growing up requires pain and struggle, embracing some things and giving up others—scary steps for a child. Initiation stories point the way—not by revealing the

Illustration 2.2
A sophisticated children's initiation story like *Amazing Grace* can make a first grader's struggle for success seem heroic and satisfying. (From *Amazing Grace* by Mary Hoffman. Illustrations by Caroline Binch. Copyright © 1991 by Mary Hoffman, text. Copyright © 1991 by Caroline Binch, illustrations. Used by permission of Dial Books for Young Readers, a division of Penguin Books USA Inc.)

particular path a child will take, because that is necessarily unique to each person, but by offering the hope and assurance that there is sunlight up above the clouds.

The Journey. Another metaphor for arduous progress and change is the journey. People all over the world have been motivated by deep urges to uproot themselves and travel long distances. As hunter-gatherers, humans ranged widely over the landscape, following animals or seeking greener habitats. In ancient times began the custom of making pilgrimages to religious places—to Rome, Canterbury, Mecca, Santiago de Compostela, Lourdes—a practice that survives today. Voyages of discovery, for trade, to make war or bring comfort to the suffering—all seem to follow some deep-seated human urge to go, to see, and to be changed along the way.

Cynthia Voigt's *The Homecoming* (1983) is an unforgettable example of the journey, as the children of the Tillerman family go in search of someone to raise them. Sharon Creech's *Walk Two Moons* (1994), another story of a child's journey in search of family, won the Newbery Medal in 1995. Frances Temple's *The Ramsay Scallop* (1994) goes to the roots of the tradition, as it recounts a young betrothed couple's pilgrimage from England to Spain, in the year 1299.

In all of these stories, the characters grow in their awareness of other people and of themselves with every challenge they meet along the way, and thus the journey itself ultimately means more than the destination. Surely there is a lesson in this for young readers.

Plot and Genre

The genre of a story determines the range of possible actions that can happen in it. In a folktale, it is acceptable if a cockroach marries a mouse, which is what happens in "Cucarchita Martina and Ratóncito Perez," or if a spider spins greedy plots, as Anansi does in "Anansi the Spider." On the other hand, it would be quite surprising if Brian Robeson, the reluctant survivor in *Hatchet*, were rescued from his wilderness isolation by a spaceship or if Lesley and Jesse encountered a talking animal on their island retreat in Katherine Paterson's Newbery Medal winner *The Bridge to Terabithia*.

Some stories, especially mysteries, create tension and suspense by keeping readers guessing not only about what will happen, but also about what genre of story they are reading—and thus, about what kinds of events, and causes for them, to expect (Todorov, 1973). In *The House of Dies Drear*, readers don't know until the very end if the story is dealing with natural or supernatural events, because Virginia Hamilton plants ambiguous clues that could point either way. Only in the last few pages is it clear which realm of possibility readers have been given and which genre of book—realistic fiction or fantasy—they have just read.

In Cynthia Rylant's Newbery Medal–winning novel *Missing May* (1992), readers are left wondering until the very end if a spiritualist can really help a bereft widower to contact his dead wife. When it doesn't work out, readers, like the characters in Rylant's touching book, are brought back to the conviction that people must make the best they can of life within the limits of their mortality—seeking small epiphanies in their relationships with others, perhaps, but not counting on breakthroughs to another world.

Jerry Spinelli played with genre in an interesting way in crafting *Maniac Magee*. By passing on the oral histories about Maniac before letting readers in on the story, he gave his book the cast of a legend. The story wavers between realistic fiction and legend—which has the effect of underscoring the legendary importance of someone's breaching the racial barrier in contemporary urban America, while showing the real-life innocence and vulnerability of the heroic kid who does the breaching.

THEMES: HOW DO STORIES GET MEANING?

A *theme* is an issue or a lesson that a story brings to a readers' consciousness. Beyond the question "What happened to whom and why?" readers sometimes ask, "What is this work really about?" "What does it mean?" or even "Why did the author write this work?" Answers to those questions are usually statements of theme.

Explicit and Implicit Themes

Themes may be stated explicitly or suggested implicitly by the text. A good example of an *explicit theme* is found in the Zuni story *The Dragonfly's Tale* (1992), retold and illustrated by Kristina Rodanas. A community that has long been blessed by bounteous crops suddenly experiences famine when the people squander their food and callously offend the two goddesses who have been responsible for their bounty. When the village goes off in search of something to eat, a thoughtful and generous boy and girl again win the favor of the goddesses. The theme of the story, the virtues of conservation and kindness, is made explicit in the closing lines of the book:

> From then on, the people were careful not to take the Corn Maidens' gifts for granted. They respected the boy and his sister, and learned their ways of kindness. The cornfields thrived, and all the Ashiwi prospered. (n.pag.)

An *implicit theme* is an idea that is strongly suggested but not explicitly stated. In Alma Flor Ada's *The Gold Coin*, there is no explicit mention of the lesson that giving is better than taking, or that the esteem of one's fellows is more valuable than gold. Readers have to infer those ideas from what happens in the story.

Especially in contemporary literature, stating themes is not always an easy or foolproof matter. Good writers rarely start with explicit themes in mind. Author Frances Temple (1994) explained her approach to themes this way: "At first, I'm just getting out the story. Once it's written down, I can go through and see what the story is adding up to—and then as I rewrite I can make sure that what stays in the book pulls more or less in the same direction."

Many authors express surprise, however, at the themes others find in their works. For instance, Charles Temple was surprised to read in a review of his *Shanty Boat* (1993) (illustrated by Melanie Hall) that the work was about the importance of respecting differences. Temple had thought it was just a rhyme about a quirky old guy who lived on a boat; he had created it as an exaggerated portrait of his own brother.

Themes and Images

Often, writers plant images in their works that come to stand for a central idea or theme. For example, Natalie Babbitt's *Tuck Everlasting* begins:

> The first week of August hangs at the very top of summer, the top of the live-long year, like the highest seat of a Ferris wheel when it pauses in its turning. (p. 3)

ISSUE TO CONSIDER

As we've mentioned, the theme of a contemporary literary work is more often implied than explicitly stated. Not surprisingly, the identification and interpretation of themes that are not explicitly stated give rise to lively debates. Critics argue not only about what the theme of a specific work really is, but also about whether the inherent difficulty in identifying implied themes makes it impossible to state *any* book's theme definitively. While some critics claim that skilled readers are adept at discovering themes that less skilled readers will miss, others (known as "deconstructionists" or "transactionalists" in the field of literary theory) insist that what a book means—its theme—lies entirely in the experience, background, and personality of each reader who encounters it.

These differing opinions certainly do not prevent literary critics, authors, and book lovers from discussing themes. Readers often have different ideas about the theme of a particular book. And authors sometimes even disagree with what the critics identify as the themes of their books!

What do you think? If you have read Natalie Babbitt's *Tuck Everlasting*, for example, what would you say the theme is? Do you agree with what the author says it is? With what your teacher or classmates think it is? How will you decide what the theme is?

Later in the book Tuck seems to state the theme of the book explicitly, again using the image of the wheel:

> Not now. Your time's not now. But dying's part of the wheel, right there next to being born. You can't pick out the pieces you like and leave the rest. Being part of the whole thing, that's the blessing. (p. 63)

Thus, Natalie Babbitt uses the image of the wheel to stand for the inevitability of the life cycle: birth, growth, decline, and death.

Reading against the Grain

The explicit and implicit themes described above were the sort many authors might have agreed were present in the work. But if we define a theme, as the critic Rebecca Lukens does, as a source of ". . . insight into people and how they think and feel" (Lukens, 1990), then there are other layers of themes that we must take into account. These are layers of themes that the authors probably did *not* intend.

Reading against the grain is a way to examine the unexamined, question the unquestioned, and hold up to scrutiny the unspoken assertions the text is making about the way lives are lived in society. Reading against the grain means asking: Is this book a true portrait of how people behave? Is it a portrait of how they *ought* to behave?

One fruitful way to read against the grain is to ask questions about differences in a text's portrayals of various characters:

- Males and females
- Old people and young people

- People of different social classes
- People of different races
- Americans and Third-World residents
- People who are differently abled

Another way to read against the grain is to list the characteristic actions taken by different people in the story and then to match those actions with the rewards the people receive. An examination of the story "Beauty and the Beast" to determine the ways males and females acted and the rewards or punishments they received revealed that males were rewarded for going after what they wanted—although they had to learn the hard way to be respectful of all sorts of people. Women, though, were rewarded for *not* going after what they wanted— for focusing on serving others and being pure (Temple, 1992).

Another way to examine the unexamined is to ask: What would have been different if these events had happened to another character? For example, what if Marty's father had found Shiloh, instead of Marty? Would he have tried to keep him? What would he have done differently? Why? What does this tell us about differences between ages?

What if Marty's little sister, Dara Lynn, had found Shiloh instead of Marty? Would her parents have taken her devotion to the dog as seriously? Would she have had the freedom to keep it secretly and arrange to give it food? What does this tell the reader about the range of activity boys and girls are permitted?

What if Marty's well-to-do friend, David Howard, had found Shiloh? Would he have gone to so much trouble not to confront Judd with his mistreatment of animals—or would he simply have called the authorities? Would he and his family have been so careful not to make an enemy of Judd?

A text is a piece of virtual experience that can be held up and examined from many angles. As the questions above make clear, readers can find interesting meanings to talk about in almost any text, whether an author intended those meanings or not.

THE STANCE OF THE IMPLIED READER

Besides the plot, the setting, the characters, and the theme, one more device is written into a work—the stance of the implied reader (Booth, 1961; Iser, 1974). The *implied reader* is the ideal interpreter of a work, as imagined by the author. The implied reader is not directly mentioned in the text, but his or her activity is essential. To say that events or characters in a text are exciting, funny, sad, suspenseful, heroic, blameworthy, or even understandable really means that the events or characters are perceived in those ways by some reader, because those qualities do not exist except as responses of a reader to a work. Thus, in constructing a piece of literature, the writer must consciously or unconsciously keep an ideal reader in mind and arrange the details of the work in such a way as to evoke the desired responses from that reader—or, more truthfully, from anyone willing or able to perceive the work in more or less the way the implied reader would.

As they begin to read a work, actual readers implicitly take the perspective of the implied reader and begin to have emotional and intellectual reactions to the work in ways the author has scripted for them. Or else they don't: If a book is too silly or too "hard" or too far outside their usual way of seeing things, they may not be willing or able to take the stance of the implied reader—and the book will not work for them.

There are at least three ways in which an actual reader can take the stance of the implied reader. The first is by *identifying with characters*. The second is by *taking a moral perspective on the story*. The third is by *filling in gaps to make the story "work."*

Identifying with Characters

When readers discover in **Shiloh** that Marty is eating only part of his supper and spiriting away the rest for his dog, they begin to feel—as Phyllis Naylor surely intended for them to feel—Marty's uneasiness and regret over having to disappoint his mother. When they read that Marty has sneaked up the hill after dinner to feed the dog the uneaten food he spirited away from the table—and when suddenly his mother walks up and confronts him—readers feel his shock, his embarrassment, and finally his relief at having his secret shared at last. They have identified with Marty; they have entered into his actions and reactions so that what happens to him is happening to them.

Identification is a powerful way of learning from a text: It puts readers in the shoes of a character, makes them suffer what he or she suffers, makes them face the dilemmas that character faces, and makes them feel the consequences of the choices they (the character and the readers) made.

Another striking example of the way an author fosters identification is found in Mildred Taylor's **Roll of Thunder, Hear My Cry**. In the very first scene of the book, readers are walking along in Depression-era Mississippi with the Logan children, following an unpaved road with steep banks on either side and skirting deep-red muddy pools. A school bus careens along behind them. But it doesn't stop to pick them up. Instead, the driver veers into a puddle and raises a wave of thick red ooze that douses their clothes, hair, and bodies. The driver grins wildly, and the young passengers laugh and jeer as the bus roars on. The children wring out their clothes and keep walking. The bus driver and the passengers are white. The Logan children—and, through identifying with them, the readers—are black.

For white students, the effect of reading that scene can be as transforming as Mildred Taylor intended it to be—but only if they accept the stance of the implied reader.

Taking the Intended Moral Stance

Another way the text influences readers is by inviting them to take a moral stance on the story—a stance the author has staked out as part of the construction of the work. As noted above, for a story to work, the author has to be able to count on readers to believe that some goals are worthwhile, that some events are exciting, that some things people say are funny or sad or shocking. If readers adopt these views—if only for the duration of the reading—the book will "come together" for them. If they don't, it won't. So far, so good.

But no readers hold precisely the orientations asked of them by all books. They occasionally have to stretch to accept a certain point of view, for the time that they participate in a certain book. This stretching has consequences. We all have had the experience of being told a joke that was so sexist or racist or otherwise mean-spirited that we had to decide whether to keep listening, scold the teller, or walk away. It's the times we didn't quite muster the energy to do either of the latter two that are most bothersome. If, for the sake of the humor, we temporarily agree to take the stance the joke requires of us, we may give a polite

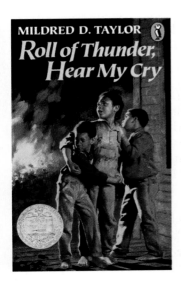

Illustration 2.3
As we allow ourselves to assume the role of the implied reader of *Roll of Thunder, Hear My Cry*, we may take on the emotional and intellectual perspective of those who have suffered painful racial oppression. (*Roll of Thunder, Hear My Cry* by Mildred D. Taylor. Illustration copyright © 1991 by Max Ginsburg. Used by permission of Puffin Books, a division of Penguin Books USA Inc.)

laugh, but feel compromised. That is because we have just agreed to live the life of a bigot, if only for two minutes.

Author Mildred Taylor challenges readers to take a moral stance early in **Roll of Thunder, Hear My Cry**. Following the muddy road incident, the Logans dig the bottom out of one of the puddles, so that when the driver again tries to douse them, he breaks the axle of the bus. Will readers go along with that? If they do, they will close ranks with the Logans for the duration of the book. If they don't, they have an uneasy reading experience ahead of them.

Filling in the Gaps

The implied reader functions in one last way. A writer friend of ours says, "You have to trust your readers to figure some things out for themselves. They'll feel more like they're with you if you let them have the fun of figuring things out. Telling them too much spoils the fun."

Writers leave gaps in their work to be filled in by the reader's realizations. In Maurice Sendak's **Where the Wild Things Are** (1964), for example, a visual clue is given early in the book as to where the Wild Things came from. (Can you find it?)

Illustration 2.4
It is left for the reader of *Miss Nelson Is Missing!* to guess that Viola Swamp was Miss Nelson in disguise; doing so draws the reader into a satisfying involvement with the book. (*Miss Nelson Is Missing!* by Harry Allard and James Marshall. Illustration copyright © 1977 by James Marshall. Used by permission of Houghton Mifflin Company. All rights reserved.)

In Harry Allard and James Marshall's **Miss Nelson Is Missing!** (1977), readers are never told where Miss Viola Swamp, the no-nonsense substitute teacher, came from—or, for that matter, where she went. But at the end of the story the reader sees Miss Nelson reading in bed, next to a closet with an ugly black dress hanging in it—just like the one Viola Swamp wore. And there's a box on the shelf marked in upside-down letters that spell WIG.

In **Shiloh**, Marty's mother tells him she's afraid that if she doesn't tell his father that Marty has been hiding the dog, he might wonder what other secrets she has been keeping from him. She doesn't come right out and say that she's afraid of creating suspicions of marital infidelity in her husband's mind. But that Marty's mother is thinking about sexual fidelity is strongly suggested by the very next scene. As she's washing dishes, she sings along as a singer on the country music station croons:

> It's you I wanna come home to,
> It's you to bake my bread,
> It's you to light my fire,
> It's you to share my bed. (p. 85)

She blushes slightly when Marty enters the kitchen and hears her singing.

POINT OF VIEW

Point of view is the perspective from which the events in a story are perceived and narrated. The choices of point of view are *first person* (in which one of the characters in the work narrates the story, using the first-person pronoun

"I") and *third person* (in which a narrator outside the story relates events that happened to those in it, using the third-person pronouns "her," "him," and "them"). When the author's knowledge of events shifts freely between different characters' points of view and the author describes events no one character could have known, he or she is writing from the point of view known as *third-person omniscient* ("all-knowing").

Stories in the First Person

Stories in the first person, like **Shiloh**, tell the tale through a character's voice. Narration in the first person lends an immediacy to the action and lets readers know what the character is feeling. But it also limits readers to that character's perspective.

Stories in the Third Person

Most of the time authors describe the action as happening to someone else—him, her, or them. This point of view is called third-person narration.

Writing in the third person gives the author a broader range of choices of what to show the reader. Writing in the third person doesn't excuse an author from keeping a unified point of view, though. Skilled writers narrate events as if from one character's point of view at a time. For example, in *Tuck Everlasting*, when Winnie and Tuck paddle out in a rowboat, Babbitt uses her narrator's voice to begin describing the scene, but soon she anchors the reader's perspective in Winnie's eyes:

> The rowboat had drifted at last to the end of the pond, but now its bow bumped into the rotting branches of a fallen tree that thrust its thick fingers into the water. . . . The water slipped past . . . and farther down Winnie could see that it hurried into a curve, around a leaning willow, and disappeared. . . . (pp. 62–63)

Then Tuck speaks and explains their predicament of "being stuck":

> That's what us Tucks are, Winnie. Stuck so's we can't move on. We ain't part of the wheel no more. Dropped off, Winnie. (p. 63)

And the reader gets an internal reaction from Winnie:

> Winnie blinked, and all at once her mind was flooded with the realization of what he was saying. . . . (p. 63)

Even though the story is narrated in the third person, there is only one perspective at a time. When Winnie is around, the perspective is hers. Readers see things through her eyes and experience her emotions. The fact that Winnie is the age of the likely readers of this book is no accident. Even though she is not the narrator, she is the readers' guide to the strange events of the story.

STYLE

Style is not what is said, but how it is said. When a book makes you hear a distinct voice in your head or when you find a passage so good you want to read it to a friend, chances are you're responding to style. Style is not the same thing as talent. A talented writer may write in different styles and may have a gift for matching a style with the content of each book she or he writes.

Illustration 2.5
Natalie Babbitt uses the image of a wheel in the text of *Tuck Everlasting* to remind the reader how important it is to accept that one is part of the life cycle. (*Tuck Everlasting* by Natalie Babbitt. Jacket design copyright © 1975 by Natalie Babbitt. Used by permission of Farrar, Straus & Giroux, Inc.)

When a book makes you hear a distinctive voice in your head or when you find a passage so compelling you have to share it with a friend, chances are you're responding to an author's style.

Illustration 2.6
Narrated in the voice of a twelve-year-old refugee, *Grab Hands and Run* uses simple syntax and vocabulary that nonetheless describe moving scenes and powerful events.
(*Grab Hands and Run* by Frances Temple. Illustration copyright © 1993 by Frances Nolting Temple. Used by permission of the Publisher, Orchard Books, New York.)

Some of the elements of style are *words, images, metaphors, sounds,* and *voice.* Let's look at each.

Words

The poet William Carlos Williams wrote: "Each object in nature and each idea has an exact name." Good writers behave as if that were true, and they strive to name experiences exactly. Twain wrote: "The difference between the right word, and almost the right word, is the difference between the lightning bug and the lightning."

But what makes a word "right"? Good word choices are concrete and vivid—they show, rather than sum up and judge. Or if they sum up and judge, they do so exactly. Good words create fresh images. Good writing crackles with insight.

Writing can be sparse or rich, as writers use few words or many to create impressions. Rich writing was more common in the nineteenth century and early in the twentieth. Note this passage from Kenneth Grahame's immortal ***The Wind in the Willows*** (1908/1953):

> Never in his life had he seen a river before—this sleek, sinuous, full-bodied animal, chasing and chuckling, gripping things with a gurgle and leaving them with a laugh, to fling itself on fresh playmates that shook themselves free, and were caught and held again. All was a-shake and a-shiver—glints and gleams and sparkles, rustle and swirl, chatter and bubble. (p. 3–4)

Grahame's language consists of long sentences awash with colorful adjectives, images, and metaphors.

Spare writing can also be powerful. Frances Temple told ***Grab Hands and Run*** (1993) in the voice of twelve-year-old Felipe, and so the words she chose are simple and direct. Here is a scene from a parsonage in Guatemala, where Salvadoran refugees find momentary protection:

> Another little girl comes in, a child with big dark eyes, younger than Romy. Father Ramon opens his arms to her and speaks gently, but at the sight of him she begins to scream and fastens herself around the leg of a table. Her screams are terrible, and no one can stop them.
>
> Father Ramon looks so upset that I follow him into the courtyard. "Why does she scream, *Padre*?" I ask him. "Can I help?"
>
> "Ask the soldiers why she screams, son," says Father Ramon. I have never heard anyone sound so sad. (p. 62)

Word choice doesn't depend on a fancy vocabulary—just on exact descriptions.

Images

Imagery is the art of making readers experience details as if through their five senses. Alexander Carmichael had a good phrase for it: "bringing the different characters before the mind as clearly as the sculptor brings the figure before the eye" (quoted in Briggs, 1977, p. 10). That's the art of imagery—whether they're characters, settings, or actions that are illuminated for the mind's eye. The trick may be no more than mentioning sensory details: The writer mentions, however offhandedly, how things smelled, felt, tasted, sounded, and looked. But the effect is of living the moments described, rather than hearing a summary of them. Here's a moment from ***Tuck Everlasting***:

Shifting his position, he turned his attention to a little pile of pebbles next to him. As Winnie watched, scarcely breathing, he moved the pile carefully to one side, pebble by pebble. Beneath the pile, the ground was shiny wet. The boy lifted a final stone and Winnie saw a low spurt of water, arching up and returning, like a fountain, into the ground. He bent and put his lips to the spurt, drinking noiselessly, and then he sat up again and drew his shirt sleeve across his mouth. As he did this, he turned his face in her direction—and their eyes met. (p. 26)

Read that passage again, and see how many senses it appeals to. You feel the shifts of posture in your body and the quiet breathing in your chest. You relish the many visual images—the ground shiny wet, the spurt of water arching and returning. You hear the silence of the stealthy motions. You almost taste the water and feel the rough swipe of the shirt sleeve across your lips. With her skillful use of imagery, Babbitt has not so much described this scene as enacted it.

Metaphors

To use a metaphor is to describe one thing in terms of something else. Technically, there is a distinction between a *simile*, which is an overt comparison that says "X *is like* Y"; a true *metaphor*, which talks about X *as if it were* Y; and *personification*, which ascribes human features, actions, or motives to something that isn't human.

Here's **Tuck Everlasting** again:

The road that led to Treegap had been trod out long before by a herd of cows who were, to say the least, relaxed. It wandered along in curves and easy angles, swayed off and up in a pleasant tangent to the top of a small hill, ambled down again between fringes of bee-hung clover, and then cut sidewise across a meadow. (p. 5)

This isn't quite personification: The road is described as if it were not a person, but a cow—wandering, swaying, and ambling. To describe the road this way is to enliven the writing with unobtrusive magic.

Sounds

Aristotle advised writers to get the sounds of language and the sense would take care of itself. In the voice of a good prose writer, the sounds of language speak almost as beautifully as they do in poetry.

You may think of poetry as rhyme and rhythm, but to catch the poetry of prose, you must widen your scope. Prose doesn't often rhyme, but its sounds speak to each other through *consonance* (a run of similar consonant sounds) and *assonance* (a run of similar vowel sounds). Prose doesn't scan into this meter or that, but there is a rhythm to the flow of the words: a sing-song cadence, a pell-mell dash, or a chant and refrain.

Listen to the sounds from a page of Patricia MacLachlan's prose text from her picture book **What You Know First** (1995):

We'll sleep in the hay with our eyes open
Until they drop shut.
Listening
    to the rain on the tin roof
    the wind rattling the windows

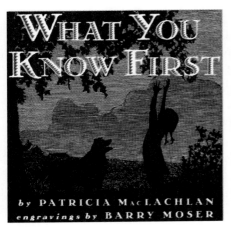

Illustration 2.7
The text of a fine picture book is much like poetry—efficient and powerful. In *What You Know First*, Patricia MacLachlan uses sounds with a poet's keen ear. (*What You Know First* by Patricia MacLachlan. Illustration copyright © 1995 by Barry Moser. Used by permission of HarperCollins Publishers.)

Waking when the rooster crows
In sunlight. (n.pag.)

Do you hear the r's and the w's echoing each other? That is consonance. Do you hear the words that begin with vowels, too ("eyes open"), as well as the similar vowel sounds ("windows" and "crows") speaking to each other? Both are examples of assonance. Read the passage aloud and listen for the rhythm. Hear the flow of the words until the abrupt "drop shut." See how those choppy words break the flow, just as closed eyes signal that the flow of consciousness has been interrupted by sleep.

More on rhythm—here is an excerpt from Bruce Brooks's *The Moves Make the Man* (1984):

> . . . cradling the ball and at the last minute pulling my left hand away like Oscar Robertson and snapping that lubricated right wrist and knowing, feeling it right straight through from the tips of the fingers that had let fly the ball and touched it all the way to the last, straight down the front edge of my body to my toes just before they hit the ground again, that the shot was true, feeling the swish and tickle of the net cords rushing quick down my nerves, and landing square and jaunty in time to watch, along with everybody else, as the ball popped through the net without a single bit of deceit, so clean it kicked the bottom of the cords back up and looped them over the rim, which is called a bottoms up and means you shot it perfect and some people even count them three points in street games. (p. 70)

One long sentence! The rhythm here is the breathless tumble of an athlete's thoughts, which find expression in the equally breathless patter of sportscasters.

Another sound device in Brooks's passage is *onomatopoeia*—using the sound of words themselves to convey a sound impression. Brooks does this in the phrase ". . . feeling the *swish* and *tickle* of the net cords rushing quick down my nerves. . . ."

Voice

Voice in literature has to do with the way the author comes across—from folksy to impersonal, from bold to timid, from expert to unreliable. Especially if the author writes in the first person, the voice of the piece may involve the narrator's dialect, personality, and "slant" on the world. Listen to Lucille Clifton's narrator in *Three Wishes*:

> My name is Zenobia, after somebody in the Bible. My name is Zenobia and everybody call me Nobie. Everybody but Victor. He call me Lena, after Lena Horne, and when I get grown I'm goin' to Hollywood and sing in the movies and Victorius is gonna go with me 'cause he's my best friend. That's his real name. (p. 1)

But even if a book is written in the third person, the narrator can come across as someone to be reckoned with. Natalie Babbitt begins *Tuck Everlasting* with these words:

> The first week of August hangs at the very top of summer, the top of the live-long year, like the highest seat of a Ferris wheel when it pauses in its turning. The weeks that come before only climb from balmy spring, and those that follow drop to the chill of autumn, but

Illustration 2.8
Few writers convey different personalities through their speech as compellingly as Bruce Brooks does in *The Moves Make the Man*. (*The Moves Make the Man* by Bruce Brooks. Copyright © 1984 by Bruce Brooks. Used by permission of HarperCollins Publishers.)

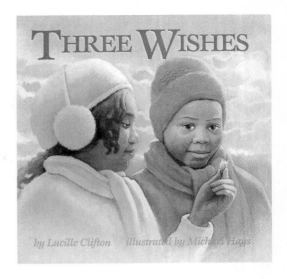

Illustration 2.9
Gifted poet and children's author Lucille Clifton captures the voice of an urban African American girl in *Three Wishes*.
(*Three Wishes* by Lucille Clifton. Illustration copyright © 1973 by Michael Hays. Used by permission of Delacorte Press, a division of Bantam Doubleday Dell Publishing Group, Inc.)

the first week of August is motionless, and hot. It is curiously silent, too, with blank white dawns and glaring noons, and sunsets smeared with too much color. Often at night there is lightning, but it quivers all alone. There is no thunder, no relieving rain. These are strange and breathless days, the dog days when people are led to do things they are sure to feel sorry for after. (p. 3)

Listen to the tone she takes. Authoritative, knowledgeable, impersonal—maybe even a little bossy. (The weather's not like that where *we* live.) This is the voice of a storyteller who is fully in charge.

Now listen to Roald Dahl's first words in **Matilda** (1988):

It's a funny thing about mothers and fathers. Even when their own child is the most disgusting little blister you could ever imagine, they still think that he or she is wonderful.

Some parents go further. They become so blinded by adoration they manage to convince themselves their child has qualities of genius.

Well, there is nothing very wrong with all this. It's the way of the world. It is only when the parents begin telling *us* about the brilliance of their own revolting offspring, that we start shouting, "Bring us a basin! We're going to be sick!" (p. 7)

Dahl's voice is outrageous, risqué, opinionated—but likely to be a lot of fun. Dahl seems to be out to undermine his own narrator's authority. Like as not, children will feel compelled to talk back to him.

LITERARY FEATURES OF INFORMATIONAL BOOKS

Traditionally, the study of literature has been devoted to fiction and poetry. But works in other genres have gained grudging recognition for their literary merit. In adult literature, Thucydides' *Peloponnesian Wars* and Gibbon's *The History of the Decline and Fall of the Roman Empire* have been singled out as much for the quality of their writing as for their treatment of the subject matter. Sigmund Freud distinguished himself for the energy and clarity with which he

wrote out his theory of psychoanalysis. Other stylists such as John McPhee, Annie Dillard, and Richard Rodriguez have been lauded for their skill with the language as well as for the force of their ideas. In children's literature, too, writers such as Patricia Lauber, Gail Gibbons, Jean Fritz, Joanna Cole, Seymour Simon, Milton Meltzer, Donald Carrick, and James Giblin have produced informational books that are as splendid for their skillful writing and presentation as for their content.

Writers of quality informational books face many challenges. They must be scrupulously accurate, they must arouse and sustain interest even about topics that are not obviously dramatic or humorous, and they must make complicated ideas accessible to young audiences without either trivializing the subject matter or overwhelming their readers. No wonder, then, that a handful of writers such as those just mentioned stand out as champions in the field of modern informational books.

Writers and illustrators of informational books can produce good literature. Their works may be distinguished by many of the matters of style surveyed earlier in this chapter: by vivid word choices, lively imagery, language that complements their topic, and a voice that engages readers while honoring the importance of the subject. We will discuss these elements of literary quality in informational books in Chapter 11.

A good informational book—like good literature of any genre—has the capacity to engage young readers through humor, vivid imagery, and engaging style, while making accurate information readily accessible to them.

LITERARY FEATURES OF POETRY

Poetry is more obviously literary than informational books are. Poetry is a form of writing in which sounds, images, meanings, metaphors, and word choices are condensed efficiently. Above all, poems convey emotion and insight. There is a detailed discussion of literary elements of poetry in Chapter 7.

 TEACHING IDEAS

Exploring Folktale Settings. How many folktales do children know with forests in them? Make a chart in which children describe things that happen in forests, the kinds of creatures the characters encounter, and the kinds of challenges they face. Later, during a writing workshop, children may want to write stories in which transforming things happen to characters in a forest.

Using Plot Structure to Guide Predictions. Choose a story to read aloud to a group of students. Write the parts of the story that conform to the plot structure described on pages 38–39 (complication, rising action, climax, resolution, and denouement) on separate pieces of tagboard. Before reading the story, ask the students to arrange the parts of the story in the order in which they think events might unfold. Then read the story. Finally, ask the students to go back and check the accuracy of their predictions.

Plotting the Story Journey. Students can make a kind of graph to plot a story journey. Drawing a line from left to right across a chart, they can make the line go up for events when morale is high and down for events when morale is low.

Above the line, they can write in what happened. Below the line, they can write in how a character felt or what she or he learned.

Discussing the Implied Reader. Introduce the idea of the implied reader (though not necessarily the term). After students have read or heard a simple story, such as "Jack and the Beanstalk," ask them: "Did you feel closer to one character out of all the characters in this story? If so, which character and why?" "Did you get the feeling the author wanted you to feel closer to and want to be more like one character? What was it about the way the story was written that made you feel closer to that character?"

More on the Implied Reader. To pursue children's growing awareness of the dynamics of the implied reader, ask them: "Were there times in the story when you felt that you really liked what was going on? When? What did you especially like about these times?" "Were there times in the story when you didn't especially like what was going on?" "Were there things in the story that you thought maybe the author felt were okay, but you didn't?"

EXPERIENCES FOR YOUR LEARNING

1. Think of two different characters in a book you've recently read—say, *The Gold Coin*. Prepare a Venn diagram, writing the features of personality and temperament the characters have in common in the overlapping area and those that separate them in the other parts of each circle. Compare your diagram with those of your classmates.

2. Make three columns on a piece of paper. In the left-hand column, list three male and three female characters in *Shiloh*. In the middle column, write two or three major actions these people took in the book. In the right-hand column, list the rewards or punishments they received at the end. Discuss these results. Can you formulate a statement that explains the pattern of who is rewarded and who is not in the story?

3. Choose a short but poignant scene from *Tuck Everlasting* (Chapter 12 will work nicely). Think through the scene from a different character's point of view—visualize the scene, for example, from Tuck's point of view rather than Winnie's. Which of Tuck's concerns come to the surface that do not in the scene as written? How does Winnie appear?

RECOMMENDED BOOKS

* indicates a picture book; I indicates interest level (P = preschool, YA = young adult)

Books with Striking Settings

Avi. *The True Confessions of Charlotte Doyle*. New York: Orchard, 1990. Life on an eighteenth-century merchant ship, with Charlotte living "before the mast." (I: 11–YA)

Cameron, Ann. *The Most Beautiful Place in the World*. New York: Knopf, 1988. What it's like to live as a peasant child in a Guatemalan village. (I: 8–10)

Cushman, Karen. *Catherine Called Birdy*. New York: Clarion, 1994. Diary of a fourteen-year-old recreates thirteenth-century English life. (I: 11–YA)

Naylor, Phyllis Reynolds. *Shiloh*. New York: Atheneum, 1990. Marty, an Appalachian mountain boy, shelters a runaway beagle named Shiloh from its cruel and abusive owner. (I: 8–11)

Paulsen, Gary. *Hatchet*. New York: Bradbury, 1987. The Canadian wilderness is the setting in which Paulsen's character struggles to survive. (I: 11–YA)

Soto, Gary. *Baseball in April and Other Stories*. New York: Harcourt, 1990. Young life among mostly poor Mexican Americans in contemporary Fresno, California. (I: 11–YA)

Taylor, Mildred D. *Roll of Thunder, Hear My Cry*. New York: Dial, 1976. The Logan family endures racism in Mississippi in the 1930s. (I: 11–YA)

* Williams, Shirley A. *Working Cotton*. Illustrated by Carole Byard. New York: Harcourt, 1992. spreads of cotton rows and the blank eyes of the young narrator reveal the dawn-to-dusk life of pickers in a California cotton field. (I: 5–9)

Books with Interesting Characterization

Ada, Alma Flor. *The Gold Coin*. New York: Macmillan, 1991. In this original story with folktale elements, the young thief Juan pursues Doña Josepha through the countryside to rob her of her gold coin, but learns trust and generosity along the way. (I: 9–11)

Cleary, Beverly. *Dear Mr. Henshaw*. New York: Morrow, 1983. Leigh Botts, the son of divorced parents, is portrayed through his correspondence with a children's author. (I: 9–11)

———. *Ramona Quimby, Age 8*. New York: Morrow, 1981. Any of Cleary's Ramona books are examples of excellent characterization. (I: 8–10)

* Cooney, Barbara. *Miss Rumphius*. New York: Viking, 1982. A remarkable turn-of-the-century New England lady comes to life in the eyes of a young friend. (I: 5–9)

Cushman, Karen. *The Midwife's Apprentice*. New York: Clarion, 1995. Alyce, a homeless waif taken in by a midwife, is given an opportunity to find an identity and make a place for herself in medieval England. (I: 11–YA)

Dahl, Roald. *The BFG*. New York: Farrar, 1982. The Big Friendly Giant comes across as a real person in this imaginative story. (I: 9–12)

———. *Danny the Champion of the World*. New York: Farrar, 1982. Danny's is perhaps the most remarkable of fathers. (I: 9–12)

Hamilton, Virginia. *M. C. Higgins the Great*. New York: Simon & Schuster, 1974. A dreamy rural African American hero emerges from the pages of this Newbery Medal–winning novel. (I: 11–YA)

* Houston, Gloria. *My Great-Aunt Arizona*. Illustrated by Susan Condie Lamb. New York: Harper, 1992. A portrait of a remarkable Appalachian school teacher at the turn of the century. (I: 6–10)

MacLachlan, Patricia. *Sarah, Plain and Tall*. New York: Harper, 1985. The story of the wooing of a mail-order bride from Maine by a lonely prairie family. (I: 8–12)

Meyers, Walter Dean. *The Mouse Rap*. New York: HarperCollins, 1990. The life and times of a thirteen-year-old resident of Harlem. (I: 9–12)

Paterson, Katherine. *The Great Gilly Hopkins*. New York: HarperCollins, 1978. A veteran of many foster homes comes to life in this novel. (I: 9–12)

Paulsen, Gary. *Sisters/Hermanas*. New York: Harcourt, 1993. In this bilingual (Spanish/English) book, the character of a young Mexican prostitute is compared with that of a young white Texas cheerleader. (I: 12–YA)

* Say, Allen. *Grandfather's Journey*. Boston: Houghton Mifflin, 1993. The story of a young man's immigration to the United States from Japan, how he fared, and why he went back. (I: 5–10)

Woodson, Jacqueline. *Last Summer with Maizon*. New York: Delacorte, 1992. Inside the thoughts of a contemporary African American girl from the city. (I: 12–YA)

Books with Interesting Plots

Babbitt, Natalie. *Tuck Everlasting*. New York: Farrar, 1975. Young Winnie encounters and befriends members of the Tuck family, who have been endowed with the burdensome gift of everlasting life. (I: 10–YA)

Barrett, Judi. *Cloudy with a Chance of Meatballs*. Illustrated by Ron Barrett. New York: Atheneum, 1978. Life is easy in the town of Chew and Swallow, where food comes from the sky—until the weather takes a turn for the worse. (I: 7–10)

Bunting, Eve. *The Hideout*. New York: Harcourt, 1991. Andy runs away from home and finds the key to a luxurious suite in a grand hotel. What he thinks is a lucky break turns out to be a terrifying experience. (I: 8–12)

Cleary, Beverly. *Ramona and Her Father*. New York: Morrow, 1978. The problem of the father's unemployment gives rise to smaller problems, whetting the reader's curiosity for the long term and the short term. (I: 7–10)

Coatsworth, Elizabeth. *The Cat Who Went to Heaven*. Illustrated by Lynd Ward. New York: Collier/Macmillan, 1958. A magical cat teaches an impoverished painter to be generous and patient. (I: 10–12)

Cole, Brock. *The Goats*. New York: Farrar, 1990. When they are left naked on a deserted island by their fellow campers, two preadolescents learn to stand up for themselves. (I: 11–YA)

* de Paola, Tomie. *Strega Nona*. New York: Simon & Schuster, 1979. The story of the witch Strega Nona and the fool Big Anthony has a straightforward plot, with an interesting contrast of characters. (I: 5–8)

Hahn, Mary Downing. *Stepping on Cracks*. New York: Clarion, 1991. In the midst of World War II, Elizabeth and her best friend discover a conscientious objector living in the woods near their home. (I: 11–12)

Hamilton, Virginia. *The House of Dies Drear*. New York: Simon & Schuster, 1968. As noted in this chapter, this African American historical mystery novel is a good example of a "surface story" slowly revealing an underlying story. (I: 11–13)

Hite, Sid. *An Even Break*. New York: Holt, 1995. When twelve-year-old Frisk gets a summer job managing a pool for kids fifteen and up, he has to work hard to prove he's the right person for the job. (I: 10–13)

* Kellogg, Steven. *Much Bigger than Martin*. New York: Dial, 1976. More than anything a boy wants to be as big as his older brother so he won't be left out of activities. (I: 5–8)

Paulsen, Gary. *The Voyage of The Frog*. New York: Orchard, 1989. A survival story of a perilous ocean crossing, in which a young boy proves what he's made of. (I: 11–YA)

* Steig, William. *The Amazing Bone*. New York: Farrar, 1976. This book, like Steig's *Sylvester and the Magic Pebble*, *Caleb and Kate*, and *Roland, the Minstrel Pig*, has a straightforward plot that follows the pattern described in this chapter: conflict, rising action, climax, resolution, denouement. (I: 5–10)

Temple, Frances. *Grab Hands and Run*. New York: Orchard, 1993. A journey story about the flight of a Salvadoran refugee family from their homeland through the United States to Canada. (I: 10–13)

Voigt, Cynthia. *The Homecoming*. New York: Atheneum, 1983. Determined to keep her family together after her mother disappears, Dicey leads her siblings on a secret journey to find a grandmother they have never known. (I: 12–YA)

Yarbrough, Camille. *The Shimmershine Queens*. New York: Putnam, 1989. Angie and her best friend struggle to maintain pride and self-respect in the midst of negative peer pressure. (I: 11–12)

Books with Interesting Themes

Ada, Alma Flor. *My Name Is Maria Isabel*. New York: Atheneum, 1993. What it's like to come into an urban American school from another place, where people speak another language. (I: 8–11)

* Barrett, Joyce Durham. *Willy's Not the Hugging Kind*. Illustrated by Pat Cummings. New York: Harper-Collins, 1989. Willie decides he's too big for hugs,

but he soon discovers how much he misses them. (I: 5–7)

* Bunting, Eve. *A Day's Work*. Illustrated by Ron Himler. New York: Clarion, 1994. Francisco learns a lesson about honesty and pride from his grandfather. (I: 6–8)

* Clifton, Lucille. *Everett Anderson's Goodbye*. Illustrated by Ann Grifalconi. New York: Holt, 1983. A boy goes through the grieving process after his father dies. (I: 4–7)

* ———. *Everett Anderson's Nine Month Long*. Illustrated by Ann Grifalconi. New York: Holt, 1978. While Everett Anderson waits for a new baby to be born, he works out the wrinkles in his relationship with his new stepfather. (I: 4–7)

* Demi. *The Empty Pot*. New York: Holt, 1990. A little boy is rewarded for his honesty. (I: 5–8)

* de Paola, Tomie. *The Legend of the Bluebonnet*. Putnam, 1983. A young girl sacrifices her most precious possession in order to save her people from drought. (I: 5–8)

* de Regniers, Beatrice Schenk. *May I Bring a Friend?* Illustrated by Beni Montresor. New York: Atheneum, 1980. When the king and queen invite a little boy to tea, he brings a host of animal friends and then reciprocates by inviting the king and queen to the zoo for tea. (I: 4–6)

* Hesse, Karen. *Lester's Dog*. Illustrated by Nancy Carpenter. New York: Crown, 1993. More than anything, a boy fears Lester's vicious dog, but his loyalty to his deaf friends helps him triumph over his fear. (I: 4–7)

* Hoffman, Mary. *Amazing Grace*. Illustrated by Caroline Binch. New York: Dial, 1991. Grace's grandmother helps her realize she can do anything she wants to. (I: 5–9)

MacLachlan, Patricia. *Journey*. New York: Delacorte, 1991. Having been deserted by his mother and father, Journey sets out to discover his past and learns that things can be good enough without being perfect. (I: 10–12)

* Ness, Evaline. *Sam, Bangs, and Moonshine*. New York: Holt, 1966. In an important step in growing up, Sam discovers that imagination cannot be allowed to get in the way of responsibility. (I: 6–10)

* Rodanas, Kristina. *The Dragonfly's Tale*. New York: Clarion, 1992. A Zuni legend with a conservationist theme. Most folktales and legends strongly emphasize themes. (I: 6–10)

Talbert, Marc. *A Sunburned Prayer*. New York: Simon & Schuster, 1995. Eloy determines to go alone on a pilgrimage to save his grandmother, who is dying of cancer. (I: 10–12)

Thesman, Jean. *Rachel Chance*. Boston: Houghton Mifflin, 1990. When Rachel's baby brother is kidnapped by a charismatic preacher, Rachel sets out to find him. (I: 11–YA)

* Williams, Vera B. *A Chair for My Mother*. New York: Mulberry, 1982. A little girl and her family pull together to make a new home when theirs is destroyed by fire. (I: 6–10)

RESOURCES

Egoff, Sheila, G. T. Stubbs, and L. F. Ashley. *Only Connect: Readings on Children's Literature*. 2nd ed. New York: Oxford Universtity Press, 1980.

Frye, Northrop. *The Educated Imagination*. Bloomington: Indiana University Press, 1964.

Hearne, Betsy, and Marilyn Kaye. *Celebrating Children's Literature*. Lothrop, Lee, & Shepard, 1981.

Hunt, Peter. *Children's Literature: The Development of Criticism*. New York: Routledge, 1990.

Lukens, Rebecca. *A Critical Handbook to Children's Literature*. 4th ed. New York: HarperCollins, 1990.

May, Jill. *Children's Literature and Critical Theory*. New York: Oxford University Press, 1995.

Nodleman, Perry, ed. *Touchstones: Reflections on the Best in Children's Literature*. West Bend, IN: Children's Literature Association, 1985.

Sale, Roger. *Fairy Tales and After: Snow White to E. B. White*. Cambridge, MA: Harvard University Press, 1978.

Scholes, Robert. *Structuralism in Literature*. New Haven, CT: Yale University Press, 1974.

Temple, Charles, and Patrick Collins, eds. *Stories and Readers*. Norwood, MA: Christopher-Gordon, 1992.

REFERENCES

Allard, Harry. *Miss Nelson Is Missing*! Illustrated by James Marshall. Boston: Houghton Mifflin, 1977.

Barthes, Roland. *S/Z*. Trans. Richard Miller. New York: Hill & Wang, 1974.

Bernays, Anne, and Pamela Painter. *Guide for Fiction Writers*. New York: HarperCollins, 1995.

Booth, Wayne. *The Rhetoric of Fiction*. Chicago: University of Chicago Press, 1961.

Briggs, Katherine. *British Folktales*. New York: Pantheon, 1977.

Coatsworth, Elizabeth. *The Cat Who Went to Heaven*. New York: Macmillan, 1931.

Cushman, Karen. *The Midwife's Apprentice*. New York: Clarion, 1995.

Grahame, Kenneth. *The Wind in the Willows*. 1908. New York: Scribner's, 1953.

Grimm, Jacob, and Wilhelm Grimm. *The Complete Grimms' Fairy Tales*. New York: Pantheon, 1972.

Iser, Wolfgang. *The Implied Reader: Patterns of Communication in Prose Fiction from Bunyan to Beckett*. Baltimore: Johns Hopkins University Press, 1974.

Kermode, Frank. *The Sense of an Ending*. Chicago: University of Chicago Press, 1975.

Lukens, Rebecca. *A Critical Handbook to Children's Literature*. 4th ed. New York: HarperCollins, 1990.

Rylant, Cynthia. *Missing May*. New York: Orchard, 1992.

Sendak, Maurice. *Where the Wild Things Are*. New York: Harper & Row, 1963.

Souriau, Etienne. *Les Deux Cent Milles Situations Dramatiques*. Paris: Flammarion, 1955.

Spinelli, Jerry. *Maniac Magee*. Boston: Little, Brown, 1990.

Temple, Charles. *Shanty Boat*. Illustrated by Melanie Hall. Boston: Houghton Mifflin, 1993.

Temple, Charles. "'What If *Beauty* Had Been Ugly?' Reading against the Grain of Gender Bias in Children's Books." *Language Arts* 70 (February 1993): 89–93.

Temple, Frances. Personal communication. 1994.

Todorov, Tzvetan. *The Fantastic: A Structural Approach to a Literary Genre*. Translated by Richard Howard. Cleveland: Case Western Reserve, 1973.

Turnbull, Colin. *The Human Cycle*. New York: HarperCollins, 1982.

3 The Child Reader Responds to Literature

In literature class Mr. Joseph was reading a book to us, a chapter at a time. It was called *The Year in San Fernando*, and it was the only thing that could make Marlon Peters and his gang pay attention. In fact, whenever it was time for *The Year in San Fernando*, Marlon Peters and Naushad Ali would pick up their chairs and move to the front of the class. There they sat, as still as statues, listening. If anyone made the slightest noise, the two of them would turn and glare at that person.

But nobody would willfully disturb Mr. Joseph when he was reading this story. The whole class was captivated. It was a story about *us*, and *our* world! We were surprised, and thrilled, that the ordinary, everyday things we took part in could find their way into a story! It meant that we were real, and had weight, like the people in stories.

From For the Life of Laetitia *(1993)*
by Merle Hodge

Teachers long to see the kind of reader involvement in books that author Merle Hodge describes in **For the Life of Laetitia**. Reading is commonly described as a reader/text interaction, and teachers who understand both the readers (the children who will be enthusiastically reading and listening to literature) and the texts (children's literature) are likely to be in a good position to nurture this type of engagement. Although the major thrust of this book is learning about the literature you'll be channeling into the hands of children, this chapter ventures into different territory. Here we consider what happens when readers read literature, how reading literature may differ from other types of reading, and what research reveals about how children in particular respond to literature. To explore these topics in more depth, we use many examples of readers' responses to Jerry Spinelli's Newbery Medal–winning book **Maniac Magee** (1990). You may want to read this book before reading the chapter.

LITERARY MEANING MAKING

What happens when a reader encounters a piece of literature? Based on the work of literary critics, we can identify at least five ways of reading: reading for content, reading to make aesthetic judgments, reading by textual structures, reading for social attitudes, and reading as a transaction (see Table 3.1).

Reading for Content

A reader may take in—or fail to take in—a series of impressions that the author has set out in a text. Looking at reading this way—as if knowledge resided solely in the text for all to see—can be called *reading for content*. All readers have had the experience of at first "not getting it" and then suddenly understanding some development in a story. That means there is something in the text for the reader to "get."

When teachers teach as if texts contain certain meanings that good readers get more of and poor readers less of, they ask students questions about "main ideas" and "supporting details" and try to guide them toward "comprehension." The practice of giving tests following a reading stems from the assumption that there are main ideas and details in a text for all to see.

Table 3.1 Five Ways of Reading

Way of Reading	Definition
Reading for content	Reading for knowledge that is assumed to be residing in the text
Reading to make aesthetic judgments	A tradition in which judgments are made about the literary worth of texts
Reading by textual structures	A study of the literary structures and literary devices used by writers
Reading for social attitudes	A study of the ways in which texts influence readers' social views
Reading as a transaction	A study of the ways in which readers connect their own experiences and feelings to texts

On the other hand, "getting the main ideas" and being tested on them are experiences that children have only in school. Real reading—what readers do with the books they buy or check out of the library—may begin with comprehension, but it is much more than that. It is more personal, more creative, more liberated, more social.

Reading to Make Aesthetic Judgments

The reader may appreciate the achievements of a work, may implicitly or explicitly rate it as a work of "good" literature, distinguishing it from inferior works. Experts who give awards to books for children read to make aesthetic judgments. So do teachers and librarians who write reviews for local or national publications. Editors read in this way when they choose a handful of manuscripts from the thousands that come across their desks, and also when they help authors refine those few chosen manuscripts.

In contrast to the experts, most readers may be only dimly aware that they are in the presence of beautiful or flat writing. If the text is "working" for them—if they are caught up in its power—they are probably not conscious of aesthetic issues, unless someone asks them to go back and comment on the author's craft.

Reading by Textual Structures

A reader may rely on implicit knowledge of text structures and other literary devices in order to bring the work to life and understand it. That is, the reader may intuitively assign people, things, and events to the roles of main character, antagonists, setting, goal, resolution, and so forth—much the way she or he understands spoken language by intuitively recognizing subject, verb, and object.

Being aware on some level of the structures that order texts surely affects a reader's understanding. But it is also clear that a satisfying reading experience is more than tracking information that unfolds in predictable patterns. Moreover, readers often "bust out of the code." That is, no set of rules or structures ultimately limits readers in what they choose to notice in a text. A reader may, for example, be intrigued by rich details of text or illustration that correspond to no identified literary structure.

Illustration 3.1
Stereotypical gender roles are turned topsy turvy in *The Paper Bag Princess*. (*The Paper Bag Princess* by Robert N. Munsch. Text copyright ©1980 by Robert N. Munsch. Illustration copyright ©1980 by Michael Martchenko. Used by permission of Annick Press Ltd.)

Reading for Social Attitudes

Readers may, without realizing it, be subtly influenced to accept or question a particular set of ideas about society—for example, about the roles of male and female, black and white, or rich and poor. When we examine the way a work of literature spotlights or influences readers' social views, we are reading for social attitudes.

Readers usually are not aware of social issues in a text, unless it differs from their usual experience. This is just what happens in ***The Paper Bag Princess*** (1980) by Robert Munsch. The author casts a princess in a liberated role that contrasts sharply with the stereotypically passive heroine usually found in traditional folktales. A book like ***The Paper Bag Princess*** tends to call into question the all-too-commonplace practice of assigning females to more passive roles. Of course, a classroom discussion about almost any piece of literature can serve the same purpose.

Reading as a Transaction

The reader's own memories, feelings, and thought associations may be evoked by a text—whether or not the author anticipated those reactions (and how would you know?). When we look at readers' personal responses during an encounter with a text, we are viewing reading as a transaction. This perspective on reading is also known as *reader response theory*.

Most of this chapter explores reading as a transaction. Bear in mind, though, that the other approaches to understanding what happens when readers and texts come together—reading for content, reading to make aesthetic judgments, reading by textual structures, and reading for social attitudes—all have their uses. We will refer to them from time to time in later chapters.

PERSPECTIVES ON READER RESPONSE

In recent years, reader response theory, which was first articulated by Louise Rosenblatt in 1938, has been having a huge impact in elementary classrooms. To understand reader response theory, you may find it helpful to reflect on your own reading experiences.

Think of a story you have really "gotten into" and try to describe what that experience was like. Perhaps you became so wrapped up in the book that you flew from page to page to discover how the twists and turns of the story line would unfold, and even though it was 2:00 AM, you simply could not stop reading. Maybe it was a different sort of book, one in which you found so much to ponder that you spent as much time reflecting and wondering as reading. Or perhaps it was a book in which a character's plight moved you to tears. Or was it a book whose language was so evocative that you read it aloud just to savor the author's words?

When a person becomes immersed in reading a piece of literature, she or he is engaged in what Louise Rosenblatt (1993) calls *aesthetic reading*. Rosenblatt describes the experience this way:

> In aesthetic reading . . . we draw on our reservoir of past experience with people and the world, our past inner linkage of words and things, our past encounters with spoken or written text. We listen to the sound of the words in the inner ear; we lend our sensations, our emotions, our sense of being alive, to the new experience which, we feel, correspond to the text. We participate in the story, we identify with the characters, we share their conflicts and their feeling. (p. 9)

Snuggled up in a favorite reading spot, a child can easily become lost in a good book.

According to Rosenblatt, aesthetic reading lies at one end of a reading continuum. What she has called *efferent reading* lies at the other end. When reading efferently, readers are intent on gaining information through their reading—on finding out when to take their medicine, how to put the bookshelves together, or what position a candidate takes on immigration. Earlier, we referred to this type of reading as reading for content. Readers who pick up particular texts move more toward one end or the other of the reading continuum, depending on their purposes for reading. But reading literature generally means moving toward the aesthetic end of the continuum.

The reader's role is of great importance in aesthetic reading, and because readers bring their own experiences, feelings, and perspectives to a text, the literary experience can be very personal. This is not to say, however, that the text is unimportant. In fact, Rosenblatt has described the text as a "blueprint" that guides the reader's work, though it is readers who construct literary meaning, drawing on both their own experiences and the text itself.

Of course, children can become totally caught up in the world of a story. However, in school settings this won't happen if children are only asked to read literature for information—to answer comprehension questions or to find five new words in the story. Yet if teachers are to succeed in nurturing committed, lifelong readers, it is essential that children discover the joys of reading literature. As you prepare to help students read literature aesthetically, we think you'll find it helpful to understand more about the reader/text transaction and how children respond to literature.

So far we have talked about the reader/text transaction as though it were a single type of interaction, but Richard Beach (1993) identifies five different

Table 3.2 Five Perspectives on Reader Response

Perspective	Definition
Experiential	A perspective that emphasizes the role of the reader's personal experiences and feelings in shaping response
Developmental	A perspective that recognizes that children in different stages of cognitive, moral, and social development respond to literature differently
Social	A perspective that recognizes that a reader's literary transaction can be shaped by the responses of other readers
Cultural	A perspective that recognizes that readers' cultural values, attitudes, and assumptions shape their transactions with texts
Textual	A perspective that recognizes that readers' responses are influenced by their knowledge of narrative conventions, literary elements, genre conventions, and other aspects of a text

perspectives on the transaction—experiential, developmental, social, cultural, and textual—each of which represents a different window onto the same response process. See Table 3.2 for definitions of each perspective.

Experiential Perspective on Reader Response

People who look at literary reading from an experiential perspective emphasize the reader in the reader/text transaction. Judith Langer (1990), a reading response theorist, has described aesthetic reading from an experiential perspective. "Envisionment building" is the term that Langer uses to describe literary meaning making. An *envisionment* is what a reader understands about a story, and as readers move through stories, their understanding grows and sometimes even changes dramatically. For example, one preservice teacher reported that she initially envisioned Jerry Spinelli's **Maniac Magee** as a book about homelessness, but as she read on, she began to envision it as being about racial divisiveness and conflict.

According to Langer, in creating their envisionments, readers may assume any one of four different stances (or different relationships with a text) as they read:

- *Being out and stepping in*: Readers make their initial contact with a book.
- *Being in and moving through*: Readers build a personal envisionment.
- *Being in and stepping out*: Readers reflect on the way(s) a book relates to their own life or the lives of others.
- *Stepping out and objectifying the experience*: Readers reflect on the story as a crafted object.

Being Out and Stepping In. Readers assume the stance of "being out and stepping in" as they make their initial contact with a book. They try to get enough information about the genre, setting, characters, and story line to begin to build an envisionment. They may even start this process before reading the

Young children begin to learn how to engage in "envisionment building" by participating in storybook reading with mature readers.

first page as they look at the dust jacket or book cover; and the process continues as they begin reading the story and make the acquaintance of characters and discover the basic story situation. For example, a reader picking up *Maniac Magee* might note from information on the dust jacket that Maniac became a legend and that he was best known for what he did for the kids from the East Side and the West Side of town. The book's introduction is especially intriguing as readers first learn that Maniac allegedly had a sofa spring for a heart, that he kept an eight-inch cockroach on a leash, and that there was a trick that would make him run as slowly as any kid. Taken together, all this early information that readers glean about Maniac contributes to an emerging envisionment of a tale about a legendary figure with a decidedly contemporary twist.

Even very young children assume this stance. When four-year-old Josh's mother announced she had a new alphabet book for him, Josh asked, "Do the letters have animals?" Josh's question signaled his familiarity with the alphabet genre, which he was trying to use to "step into" the world of the book.

Being In and Moving Through. When they are "in and moving through," readers become absorbed in the story world, using text information and their own store of information to build their envisionment. Readers who are "in and moving through" try to understand why characters behave as they do, why events are unfolding as they are, and what is likely to happen. When reading *Maniac Magee*, one reader reported her certainty that Grayson would adopt Maniac and give him the home he longed for. When Grayson died, the reader had to modify her envisionment to make it consistent with the text information. Four-year-old Maria Dolores also "moved through" a story world. She was listening to her father read Roger Duvoisin's *Petunia* (1950), a book about a silly goose who is convinced she has pearls of wisdom worth sharing with all the barnyard animals. This is what Maria Dolores said when her father read the scene in which Petunia is helping Noisy the dog, who has his head stuck in a rabbit hole:

STORY: And so, wise Petunia built a fire in the other end of the
            hole and fanned it well with the Book. Her trick worked

nicely. Noisy, choking with smoke, jerked his head out of the hole and ran off howling with pain. His nose was singed with the fire, and his ears were cut and bruised. Poor moaning dog.

MARIA DOLORES: I wouldn't do that to you or my horse!

FATHER: No?

MARIA DOLORES: Or my dog!

FATHER: Well, that's because you know more than the silly goose does.

MARIA DOLORES: Right. If my dog stuck his nose in the rabbit hole, I would just dig a bigger, bigger hole, bigger than his head, and I would pull his head out.

Maria Dolores's outrage at what Petunia did signals that she had "stepped into" the story world and was "moving through" it.

Being In and Stepping Out. When they are "in and stepping out," readers use the text as a basis for reflecting on their own lives, on the lives of others, or even on the human experience. When readers of *Maniac Magee* discuss the ethnic and racial divisions in their own community in light of the divisions they see in Two Mills, they are "stepping out" of their envisionment. Even young children can "step out" of the story world to reflect on how the story relates to their own experiences or to those of others. This is how a second grader, Daniel, responded when his teacher read Cynthia Rylant's *This Year's Garden* (1984): "I liked this story because it was very good. I felt like I was doing the work in my garden. Every year I help my granddad garden."

Stepping Out and Objectifying the Experience. Langer's final stance, "stepping out and objectifying the experience," is one in which readers distance themselves from the text world and talk about the work as a crafted object, about other texts the story reminds them of, or about their own responses to the story. The reader who wondered why Jerry Spinelli did not end his book with Maniac living with Grayson was "stepping out" of *Maniac Magee* to reflect on why the author had structured his work in a particular way. So were the readers who discussed the impact Spinelli achieved by weaving into his book so many diverse images of home. Children also "step out" of a story and objectify their literary experience when they focus on the ways an artist has illustrated a story. While reading William Steig's *Shrek!* (1990), eight-year-old David came to an illustration showing Shrek seeing his repeated reflection in the Hall of Mirrors. David "stepped out" of the story world to muse on the craft of the illustrator: "I wonder how the artist made this picture. I wonder if he made each picture [each mirrored image of Shrek] or if he just made this one [pointing to the first image] and then copied it over and over and pasted the others in and painted them."

These examples suggest that young children do engage in the envisionment building Judith Langer has described. Although researchers have not used Langer's model directly to describe how young children respond to literature, a number of researchers have

Illustration 3.2
Much of the humor in *Shrek!*, a contemporary fantasy, arises from the author's reliance on traditional folktale devices. (*Shrek!* by William Steig. Copyright ©1990 by William Steig. Used by permission of Farrar, Straus & Giroux, Inc.)

described children's literary meaning making. Marilyn Cochran-Smith (1982) is one of those researchers. Focusing on preschoolers' transactions with literature, she found that three- to five-year-olds engaged in two types of transactions: life-to-text and text-to-life transactions. In their life-to-text transactions, these young children made connections between the text and their personal experiences and real-world knowledge. They might, for example, talk about their own pets when listening to a story about a child and his pet. Cochran-Smith found that these preschoolers also engaged in text-to-life transactions, in which they extended or related story situations or information to their own life experiences. They often made these text-to-life connections long after hearing a story, as they played or worked in situations well removed from storybook reading.

In *Wally's Stories: Conversations in the Kindergarten* (1981), author and kindergarten teacher Vivian Paley includes many examples of text-to-life connections. In one instance, one of her kindergartners told about going to another child's house only to find that that child would not let him in. A classmate proposed a literature-inspired solution—going down the chimney of the house. A second classmate provided a caution (also inspired by "The Three Little Pigs")—going down the chimney just might result in getting boiled. It is evident that the story experience does not always end for young children when the reading is finished; a story can become a lens through which children attempt to understand their world.

Developmental Perspective on Reader Response

People who assume a developmental perspective on reader response realize that children in different stages of cognitive, moral, and social development think about the world in very different ways and that these differences are reflected in the ways they respond to stories. Arthur Applebee (1978) and Janet Hickman (1981) have conducted the most extensive studies of how children's responses to literature change across age levels. Applebee interviewed six-year-olds and nine-year-olds and asked thirteen-year-olds and seventeen-year-olds to write about literature. Hickman obtained her data by spending a full semester observing and recording children's spontaneous responses to literature in three combined-grade classrooms: kindergarten-first, second-third, and fourth-fifth. Both researchers found distinctive differences in the ways children of different ages respond to literature.

Applebee only looked at what children had to say about stories; Hickman, however, found that children spontaneously expressed their ideas, feelings, and understanding about stories in many different forms—not just by talking and writing. The children responded to literature through movement—by clapping, smiling, kissing the book covers. Their literature-based artwork, writing, and dramatic presentations were also vehicles for expressing responses. The younger children in Hickman's study were especially likely to rely on nonverbal ways of expressing their responses.

Both Hickman and Applebee found that younger children were likely to become caught up in the action of stories. Applebee studied this aspect of response at length and found that when young children (the six-year-olds in his study) were invited to talk about a favorite story, they did so by retelling the plot in great detail. (If you have ever made the mistake of asking a young child to tell you about a movie, you could probably have anticipated this finding!) However, nine-year-olds responded to the same invitation ("Tell about a favorite story") by briefly summarizing a story line.

When Applebee asked the six- and nine-year-olds to evaluate stories, the six-year-olds evaluated in very general terms, saying, for example, that a story was "good." If pressed as to the particulars that made a story good, they seized on minor details, saying, for example, that "Little Red Riding Hood" was a good story because Little Red Riding Hood had a basket. This is just the sort of thinking that Piaget described for children in the preoperational stage of development. The nine-year-olds in Applebee's study evaluated stories by placing them in categories: "It's funny." "It's a scary story." Once again, Piaget's work helps in understanding these responses, for children in the concrete operational period of development are able to think categorically and to reason in concrete terms.

To find out if young children were capable of interpretation, Applebee used a strategy originally used by Piaget. He asked children to interpret two familiar sayings: "When the cat's away, the mice will play" and "You must have gotten out of the wrong side of the bed this morning." Once again, the six- and nine-year-olds responded differently: The six-year-olds responded to both sayings literally, insisting, for example, that they had gotten out of bed on the right side. The nine-year-olds interpreted the sayings just as adults would.

Hickman looked at children's ability to interpret stories (not just familiar sayings). She found that the kindergartners and first graders could reduce stories to "lessons" when invited to interpret the meaning of a story. For example, in response to "The Little Red Hen," one child said, "When someone already baked a cake and you haven't helped, they're probably just gonna say no." This child expressed the story's lesson in the context of the story situation. The young children in Hickman's study clearly learned from stories, just as they learn from events in real life. By contrast, Hickman found that the fourth and fifth graders expressed their understanding of meaning using more abstract thematic statements not tied directly to the content of a story.

Applebee also included thirteen- and seventeen-year-olds in his study. None of the six- and nine-year-olds whom he interviewed analyzed or made generalizations about stories; in contrast, the thirteen- and seventeen-year-olds, with their more sophisticated cognitive abilities, typically analyzed the structures of stories and made generalizations about their meanings.

Hickman found still other differences in the responses from the younger (kindergarten-first) and older (fourth-fifth) children in her study. These differences are summarized in Table 3.3. However, the responses of the second and third graders in her study were much harder to characterize. At times, they responded much as the kindergartners and first graders did; at other times, their responses were more sophisticated, like those of the fourth and fifth graders. What set the second and third graders apart was their concern with becoming independent readers. They spent long periods of time reading and had much to say about the conventions of print.

Although the work of both Applebee and Hickman helps explain the developmental differences in children's responses, Hickman's work, which was done in a naturalistic classroom setting, also demonstrates how important it is to watch children closely if you want to understand how they interact with literature. Just asking children questions about stories doesn't give a complete picture; it may tell you about their story comprehension, but not necessarily about what they're thinking, feeling, and wondering. To learn about those things, it's important to observe students throughout the day—watching their body movements; seeing how they express their ideas about stories through art, writing, and drama; and listening to their spontaneously expressed ideas during storybook reading and literature discussion and at times when stories are not the focus of activity.

Table 3.3   Characteristic Responses of Children in Hickman's Study

Responses of Kindergartners and First Graders	Responses of Fourth and Fifth Graders
Relied on their bodies to express responses as they imitated movements in stories, acted out story elements to explain them, and incorporated story elements in their dramatic play	Expressed strong feelings for and against particular selections
"Collected" story elements in pictures rather than trying to present a cohesive story line through their artwork	Demonstrated extensive knowledge of story conventions and story structure in their literature-based writing, artwork, and skits
Spent time browsing in their independent contacts with books—that is, picked up a book, briefly flipped through its pages, and then moved on to the next book	Sustained their attention for long periods of time in their independent contacts with books
Were concerned with sorting out what was happening in stories and frequently used a retelling strategy when answering questions about stories	Had less need to focus on literal meanings in their verbal responses
Made personal statements loosely tied to the story	Often revealed connections between their own experiences and an interpreted story meaning
Expressed a concern with the reality of stories by talking about whether stories were "true" or "possible"	Relied on literary terminology in discussing the reality of stories
Could reduce stories to "lessons" when invited to interpret their meaning.	Expressed understandings of meaning using disembedded thematic statements
Expressed more interest in stories than in the authors of stories	Clearly recognized the role of author as the creator of a story

Both Applebee and Hickman relied on the work of Piaget to explain the differences they observed in children's responses at different ages. However, a word of caution is in order. Susan Lehr's (1988) work suggests that other factors (beyond developmental ones) also come into play in children's literary meaning making. There are dramatic differences in the extent of children's exposure to literature before they start school, and these differences influence children's literary meaning making. Lehr investigated the ability of kindergartners, second graders, and fourth graders to generate thematic statements for stories. She found that the older students were better able to do this, but even the kindergartners were able to devise statements of theme when they had rich prior experience with literature, though their statements were qualitatively different from those made by adults. These findings clearly indicate that teachers must ensure that their students have rich experiences with literature in order to prepare them to engage in thematic thinking about stories.

As the research described in this section suggests, children of different ages respond to literature in different (though equally interesting) ways. Thus, it is important for teachers to become attuned to how children of different ages think about literature. However, it is just as important to note that it is not age alone that prepares children to get the most out of books. Exposure to and experience with literature—factors that teachers can certainly influence—are equally important.

Social Perspective on Reader Response

Social factors also affect reader response, as do the context and temporal factors that are so integrally bound up with social factors in the classroom. Research in this area is especially important for educators because of the insights it yields into the creation of classrooms that nurture children's growth as responders to texts. Just as teachers can't simply wait for children to become better readers or to master increasingly complex math concepts, they shouldn't wait for children to respond more deeply to the literature they encounter. Instead, teachers need to take the necessary steps to see that such growth occurs. To do this, they must understand the social, contextual, and temporal factors that influence children's thinking about literature.

The Literature-Rich Classroom. Janet Hickman was the first person in the United States to study children's spontaneous responses to literature in a naturalistic setting, and she was also the first to notice the way context shapes children's responses. Because the classrooms in which she conducted her study were "literature-rich," Hickman knew it was important to describe what the teachers did that nurtured their students' growth as responders. She found that these teachers invited responses to literature through the physical context they created, the ways they used time, and the ways they encouraged response. In particular, Hickman (1981) recommended that teachers do the following:

- Build extensive book collections and fill the classroom with attractive displays of books.
- Select high-quality books and present them in related sets (for example, books about Halloween, African folktales, or friendship stories).
- Build in ample time for all children to interact with books daily.
- Share literature with children daily by reading aloud and by introducing new books before putting them on display in the classroom.
- Encourage students to share their thinking about literature.
- Support children's understanding of literary craft by providing them with critical terminology when they have an idea but need the words to talk about it more easily.
- Encourage children to explore books through art, writing, and drama, and support their efforts by providing time, space, materials and ideas for projects and by ensuring that they have opportunities to share their work with peers.
- Provide children with opportunities to revisit some books repeatedly.

Evolution of Response. Children's responses to stories can evolve over time, becoming deeper and more insightful. Reading stories repeatedly to children seems to be an effective vehicle for fostering such growth. Janet Hickman identified repeated readings of stories as one of the classroom factors that encourage rich response. A number of other investigators have looked specifically at what happens when children hear stories repeatedly. Miriam Martinez and Nancy Roser (1985) found that the story talk of preschoolers changed when parents and teachers read stories to them repeatedly. The children talked more about familiar stories than unfamiliar ones. Also, on a first reading of a story, the children tended to share fewer observations about the story and instead asked more

Children enjoy expressing their responses to literature through their artwork.

questions as they worked to sort out characters and story events. On subsequent readings, the children chose to explore different facets of the stories, which suggests that as they gained control over particular facets, they became able to shift their attention to others. However, if they did return to discuss a portion of a story they had previously talked about, the children showed more insightful thinking than they had initially. Leslie Morrow (1988) compared the responses of four-year-olds who heard stories read repeatedly to those of other four-year-olds who listened to different stories read only one time. The children who heard repeated readings made more comments than did the children who listened to different books, and they also shared a wider variety of responses and more complex interpretive responses.

So far we have talked about studies focusing on very young children. Researcher Amy McClure (1985) investigated responses to poetry in a combined fifth- and sixth-grade classroom. The teacher in this classroom frequently reread the same poems, and these rereadings enabled her students to move beyond hearing the words of the poem to really reflecting on meaning.

Other vehicles, in addition to repeated readings of literature, also encourage the deepening of children's responses over time. Janet Hickman (1981) found that when children worked on response activities (art projects, writing, and the like), they seemed to think more deeply about stories. Similarly, Joanne Golden and her colleagues (1992) and Lynda Weston (1993) found that children's responses to stories continued to grow as they engaged in drama, art, and writing activities based on literature. These activities are discussed in Chapters 12 and 13.

Literature Discussion. The actual reading of a text is a solitary experience, but Susan Hepler and Janet Hickman (1982) once observed that "the literary transaction, the one-to-one conversation between author and the audience, is frequently surrounded by other voices" (p. 279). In the elementary classroom, these "other voices" are those of the teacher and classmates. Ralph Peterson and Maryann Eeds (1995) believe that when readers come together to share their varied interpretations of a piece of literature, the "meaning potential of the text is expanded" (p. 21). For example, some fourth graders worked collaboratively to create meaning after listening to a chapter in **Castle in the Attic** (1985), a time-travel fantasy set primarily in medieval times. Just after William, the young protagonist of the story, confronts Alastor, the wicked wizard who turned much of the kingdom's populace into lead, Alastor disappears. The discussion begins in response to an entry Gavin wrote in his response journal:

GAVIN: I wonder what is going to happen to the lead people.

MRS. FRY: You're worried about all those lead people that are in there. What is your thought—what do you think might happen to the lead people?

GAVIN: I think maybe there's some kind of spell that can reverse it that they have to find.

MRS. FRY: Somehow or other they're going to have to find a spell that will reverse it. Okay—any guess, any ideas?

GINA: He could go into Alastor's room now that the wizard's gone.

CHRIS: I think he should, well when William turned Alastor into lead, well he has to find a way to turn him back because the token was on his neck, the one that restores you to normal size was on his neck.

MONICA: He grabbed it. He grabbed both.

CHRIS: Oh, I thought he just grabbed the lead.

MELISSA: I don't think they should go in Alastor's room because it didn't say where Alastor ended up. He's probably just like the Silver Knight. He went back in time probably.

MRS. FRY: So what you're worried about is if they go into the room, they might find him there.

TASHA: They turned him to lead. And last time when Alastor turned the Silver Knight to lead, he went back in time.

LAURA: I disagree with Melissa because remember, he said they grabbed the necklace when he was tumbling inside the gallery. And then he started doing something, and then Mrs. Calendar turned around and said something, and he turned to a lead person. So he's still in the gallery, and he can't move his hands.

ALLISON: It said that he vanished.

This is a wonderful example of the way children can better understand a story by talking and working together.

Chapter 13 examines literature discussion at length, with particular emphasis on how teachers can ensure that their students have the opportunity to share their insights into literature. To prepare you for that chapter, let's look briefly at what research has to say about literature discussions in elementary school.

Literature Discussions in Elementary Classrooms. How does participation in literature discussions enrich elementary students' literary experiences? Maryann Eeds and Deborah Wells (1989) studied fifth- and sixth-grade literature discussion groups that were facilitated by preservice teachers, who participated as group members with the students. Eeds and Wells found four ways in which participation in these groups enriched the students' literature experiences. First, when students were confused about characters or story events, their peers helped them sort out their confusions. A second way in which these fifth and sixth graders worked together to build meaning was by sharing personal stories related to the books they read. A personal story is a window onto a reader's interpreted meaning, and sharing personal stories gave the students insights into the interpretations of their peers. The students also worked collaboratively to build meaning by extending and enriching one another's predictions and hypotheses. Finally, the students critiqued stories together—commenting on each

Children gain new insights into a story by listening to what their peers and teachers say about it.

author's purpose and on issues related to the crafting of books.

Young Children and Literature Discussion. Eeds and Wells's study shows that children can engage in collaborative meaning making, but the participants in that study were fifth and sixth graders. Can younger children do the same? Lea McGee (1992) used Eeds's term "grand conversations" to describe the conversations in which the first-grade students in her study participated after listening to stories read aloud. They responded in rich and diverse ways to the stories—sharing personal reactions, interpretations, and evaluations as well as more text-focused responses related to textual structure and the techniques used by the author. Similarly, Jennifer Battle (1995) found that the bilingual kindergartners in her study engaged enthusiastically in literature discussion and grappled with and negotiated ideas collaboratively.

Teacher Roles in Literature Discussion Groups. Janice Almasi (1995) studied teacher-led and peer-led discussion groups in fourth-grade classrooms. In the teacher-led groups, the teachers assumed a traditional role in which they directed discussion by asking questions and evaluating students' answers. In the peer-led groups, teachers played minimal roles—scaffolding (or supporting) interaction and discussion only as necessary. Their ultimate goal was that students be able to conduct literature discussions without any teacher support. The differences between the two types of groups were remarkable. The students in the peer-led groups were far more reflective. When they had difficulty understanding or interpreting texts, they sought the group's help in working through the confusion. In the teacher-led groups, this type of student-initiated reflective thinking rarely occurred, because the teacher was typically in charge of initiating topics of discussion. In addition, students in peer-led groups talked almost twice as much as those in teacher-led groups. Students in peer-led groups heard more alternative story interpretations than did students in teacher-led groups, and they were more likely to establish the discussion agenda than were the students in teacher-led groups. Finally, in the peer-led groups, the students asked the questions instead of the teacher.

The teachers in the peer-led groups that Almasi studied played minimal roles in literature discussion, but other researchers have found that teachers can contribute to rich literature discussion when they assume somewhat more involved roles. Eeds and Wells (1989) found that the preservice teachers who were most successful in leading conversations about literature were highly encouraging, asked few questions, and responded to many opportunities to talk about literary elements. By watching for opportunities to discuss and label literary elements, the teachers added depth to discussions and helped the students acquire literary insights (and the language of literature).

Cultural Perspective on Reader Response

We are all cultural beings who belong to particular ethnic, class, and gender groups and, as members of these groups, share values, attitudes, assumptions, and knowledge with other group members. Patricia Enciso (1994) says that our cultural understandings are "everywhere and always a part of how we interpret

What is the role of personal stories when young children talk about literature?

ISSUE TO CONSIDER

Reader response theorists maintain that during the reader/text interaction, readers' personal memories, feelings, and thought associations are evoked by the stories they read. So when readers get together to talk about books, they often share some of those personal stories. Sharing of this nature can benefit all the participants in a literature discussion because personal associations and memories often reflect one's interpretation of the story, and readers can extend their own understanding of a story by listening to others' interpretations.

Yet for response to reach its richest potential, readers must move beyond personal stories to reflect on and return to the text to find support for their ideas, feelings, and emerging interpretations. In fact, Rosenblatt has pointed out that not all responses are equally valid; their value is determined by the extent to which readers and listeners make use of the text to defend and support their ideas (Farrell and Squire, 1990). Similarly, Britton (1968) has noted that growth in response becomes evident as readers learn to perceive ". . . more complex patterns of events, . . . pick . . . up clues more widely separated and more diverse in character, and . . . find . . . satisfaction in patterns of events less directly related to [their] expectations" (pp. 4–5).

In the classroom, children enjoy coming together to share their responses to stories, and certainly those responses include personal memories and personal stories. However, as any teacher of young children will tell you, the personal stories that children share after reading or listening to a story often seem only remotely connected to the story itself. For example, after listening to *Where the Wild Things Are* (1963), a child may remember a time when he went sailing in his uncle's boat. The next child, in turn, may want to tell about a time when her family vacationed at the ocean and saw a regatta in the bay. Before long, as children share more and more boat stories, Max's act of defiance toward his mother and his rumpus with the Wild Things seem far removed.

What should a teacher of young children do when they seem to go off on tangents during literature discussions? Should children always be given the opportunity to express their initial and pressing responses to a story, even if those responses seem only tangentially related to the story? Or, instead of inviting children to share their spontaneous responses to stories, should teachers of younger children rely more heavily on the use of questions to ensure that story discussion is story-related? What do you think?

the world and our place in it" (p. 532). So, of course, cultural understandings shape readers' transactions with texts, either by supporting or constraining them. A teacher's response to Sherley Anne Williams's **Working Cotton** (1992) reflected a cultural perspective. In this book, Williams documents a day that an African American child spends working in the cotton fields with her family, who are migrant workers. On first reading this book, the teacher observed how impressed she was by the beauty of the illustrations and the straightforward manner in which the story is narrated; nonetheless, she put the book aside, finding this

story about a child working in the fields from sunup to sundown too painful to share with children. Her initial response was constrained by cultural experiences. Only later when she realized that **Working Cotton** is a book with which migrant students can readily connect did it come down off her shelf.

Although we are becoming increasingly aware of the likely impact of culture on children's responses to literature, little research has been done in this area. One early study, done by Rudine Sims (1983), investigated the responses of a ten-year-old African American girl to books about African Americans. Sims interviewed the girl about the books she had read and discovered that she preferred books related to her own African American experiences and having characters with whom she could identify. In particular, she liked strong, active, female, black characters.

Ann Egan-Robertson (1993) asked four eighth graders of Puerto Rican descent to share culturally authentic stories about Puerto Rico with younger siblings and friends. The students responded enthusiastically to books they perceived as authentically representing their culture and very naturally brought their own cultural experiences and understandings to bear on the stories.

The research of Sims and Egan-Robertson underscores the importance of bringing into the classroom literature that authentically represents students' cultures. Finding the right books is likely to require an investment of time and energy, but the effort is worth making.

Coming together to talk about literature allows people with different perspectives (sometimes vastly different ones) to exchange ideas, to step into the shoes of others and thereby to calibrate their own judgments. For example, Mexican American students from rural backgrounds could help their peers better understand and appreciate Carmen Lomas Garza's **Family Pictures** (1990). Diane Lapp and her colleagues (1995) studied teachers from different ethnic groups who met in a book club to discuss multicultural literature and found that participants who were of the same ethnic background as the author of the book the group was discussing were able to share cultural insights that made the literary experience a richer one for the other participants. This also happened in a university class when a group of preservice teachers discussed **Maniac Magee**. The students, most of whom were white middle-class females, did not believe the book was realistic—especially the scenes set in the McNab home. In particular, they questioned the authenticity of the scene in which Maniac mistakes the roaches covering the floor for raisins and the scene in which the McNab twins jump through a hole in the ceiling from the second floor to the first. At this

Illustration 3.4
The richness of Mexican American life in South Texas emerges through the pages of *Family Pictures*. (*Family Pictures* by Carmen Lomas Garza. Used by permission of Children's Book Press, San Francisco, CA.)

point, a student who had sat quietly on the sidelines for most of the semester spoke up, explaining that she lived in a housing project and had firsthand experience with the kinds of living conditions Spinelli described. Her classmates listened intently and thereafter viewed both the book and their classmate's contributions to discussion in a different light.

Cultural differences often have a positive effect when students are encouraged to help their fellow students interpret a book by sharing their related cultural experiences. However, you also need to be aware that children's conversations about a book are sometimes constrained by their cultural perspectives—just as cross-cultural conversations about social issues are too often constrained. Researcher Patricia Enciso (1994) found this to be the case when she discussed **Maniac Magee** with fourth and fifth graders. She found that the white students and the African American students at times made different connections to the book, which stymied their discussions. When the students discussed the scene in which Maniac takes a bite of Mars Bar's candy bar, cultural miscommunication occurred. The white children were appalled that Maniac took a bite of the candy. However, they insisted that their reaction stemmed from a concern about germs. Yet when an African American student expressed sympathy toward Mars Bar, the other students were not willing to even discuss the boy's response to an African American character they viewed as an antagonist.

Teachers must be ever alert to cultural roadblocks that may arise and put a damper on literature discussion and must attempt to help students get around those roadblocks. Constructivist theory maintains that one's interpretation of an event, influenced as it is by one's unique culture-based experience, *is* the event. In light of this theory, it is important for teachers to encourage students to come together in literature study as diverse members of society and to consider actively the issues and experiences found in literature. The very act of considering literature will reveal how differently students think about things and will provide opportunities to understand others' points of view.

Like students, teachers also bring cultural perspectives to texts. These perspectives can have an effect on the kinds of literature a teacher selects. More importantly, how the teacher responds to and perceives the literature will influence how she or he guides the literature discussion. Teachers need to try to monitor their own culturally based responses to texts to ensure that they do not constrain students' responses.

Textual Perspective on Reader Response

Earlier we said that aesthetic reading is a reader/text transaction in which the reader brings to bear on the text his or her experience, knowledge, beliefs, and feelings. Knowledge about texts is one type of knowledge that readers bring to the transaction, and textual theorists place special emphasis on such knowledge. The more experience readers (or listeners) have had with literature, the greater their store of knowledge about how literature "works." This store may include knowledge of narrative conventions, genre conventions, literary elements, literary language, visual elements, and design.

Preschoolers who have been read to have already begun to build a store of literary knowledge, as evidenced by their use of "once upon a time" to begin

ASK THE AUTHOR... *Laurence Yep*

Laurence Yep

In what ways, if any, would you expect young Chinese Americans to respond to your work differently from other young readers?

Every Chinese American grows up in two cultures, and the two cultures couldn't be more disparate. Chinese culture emphasizes cooperation. American culture emphasizes competition. Chinese culture stresses community. American culture stresses the individual. It's like trying to ride two horses simultaneously, even though the two horses are pulling in opposite directions.

Chinese American children recognize their own unique conflicts in my stories and the sense of isolation that these contradictions create. I think I also reassure them that they are not monsters for feeling ambivalent about various issues—from the most basic things like their lunch snacks to the foundations of their identity.

> ### Favorite Books as a Child
>
> *Dorothy and the Wizard of Oz*
> by Frank Baum
>
> *Star Beast*
> by Robert Heinlein
>
> *Star Rangers*
> by Andre Norton

Laurence Yep has written many prize-winning books and has even had plays staged off-Broadway. He lives in central California with his wife, Joanne.

their own stories or by the concern they express when a wolf enters the scene as they are listening to a story—they know full well that this stock character is not to be trusted. You can sometimes even anticipate how textual knowledge is likely to influence children's transactions with particular books. Children who are familiar with spooky stories are likely to be caught up from the very beginning of Keith Moseley's *It Was a Dark and Stormy Night* (1991), for the opening line ("It was a dark and stormy night") signals that a mysterious and scary story is forthcoming. Children's delight in Jon Scieszka's *The Stinky Cheese Man and Other Fairly Stupid Tales* (1992) can be understood (at least in part) in light of a textual perspective on response. Scieszka's wonderfully mixed-up fantasy violates every imaginable book convention: The book begins with text, which is *followed* by the title page. Readers are invited to put their own name into the dedication (which happens to be written upside down). The table of contents is shown falling onto the characters in "Chicken Lichen." One of the characters (the Little Red Hen) insists on narrating her story at the most inopportune times. Children love this story—*if* they have already acquired an understanding of how stories work.

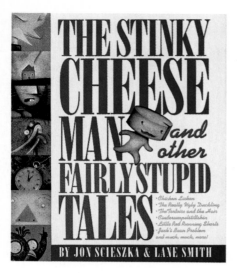

Illustration 3.5
Both the story lines of traditional tales and the features of typical book formats are humorously manipulated in *The Stinky Cheese Man and Other Fairly Stupid Tales* (a Caldecott Honor Book). (*The Stinky Cheese Man and Other Fairly Stupid Tales* by Jon Scieszka. Text copyright ©1992 by Jon Scieszka. Illustration copyright ©1992 by Lane Smith. Used by permission of Viking Penguin, a division of Penguin Books USA, Inc.)

Readers also bring knowledge of other texts to the reading of particular books, and reading a story in light of other stories can enrich readers' responses (Cairney, 1992). This was true in the case of the preservice teacher who connected Florence Parry Heide and Judith Heide Gilliland's *The Day of Ahmed's Secret* (1990) to Eve Bunting's *The Wednesday Surprise* (1989): "The story reminds me of *The Wednesday Surprise*. In that book it's the grandmother who learns to read, but it's the grandmother and the little girl who share the secret. And just like Ahmed, they can hardly wait to share the secret with their family."

Creating intertextuality, the process of bringing knowledge of one text to make meaning of another, is something mature readers do, and children can also be encouraged to read one story in light of another. In fact, part of the delight that children find in *The Stinky Cheese Man and Other Fairly Stupid Tales* can be explained with reference to intertextuality. The book is a collection of folktale spin-offs; for example, the title story, "The Stinky Cheese Man," is a spin-off of "The Gingerbread Man," "The Princess and the Bowling Ball" is a spin-off of "The Princess and the Pea," and "Jack's Bean Problem" is clearly related to "Jack and the Beanstalk." Children who know the original tales are the ones who most delight in Scieszka's work.

Researchers have not directly studied the ways in which text affects children's responses. However, there are reasons to believe that aspects of the text are likely to play a part when children read and respond to literature. First, there are many indications that children are sensitive to text features—whether they choose to talk about them or not. When children have been exposed to literature, they often use literary language and literary conventions in their dramatizations and their writing, and this is true of even very young children. Also, Georgia Green and Margaret Laff (1980) found that many five-year-olds, without any reference to illustrations, were able to discriminate among the diverse writing styles of Bill Peet, Virginia Kahl, Beatrix Potter, Dr. Seuss, and Margaret Wise Brown. They did so by matching stories written by the same author. Some of these young children were even able to explain the basis on which they matched stories.

In this chapter, we have looked at literary meaning making from various perspectives—experiential, developmental, social, cultural, and textual. These five windows onto literary meaning making complement one another. By under-

Illustration 3.6
The Day of Ahmed's Secret evokes shifting moods as the reader follows a young boy through the bustling streets of Cairo and joins him in reflective moments by an ancient wall. (*The Day of Ahmed's Secret* by Florence Parry Heide and Judith Heide Gilliland. Illustration Copyright ©1990 by Ted Lewin. Used by permission of Lothrop, Lee & Shepard Books, a division of William Morrow & Company, Inc.)

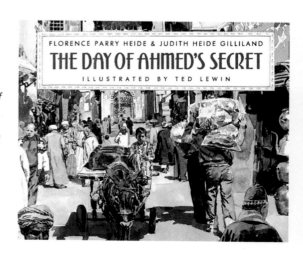

standing each perspective, you will be able to make better decisions as a teacher. By knowing, for example, that mature readers understand a text in light of others they have read, you will be more likely to encourage your students to make connections among stories. By realizing that readers understand stories in light of their own cultural experiences, you will recognize the importance of selecting multicultural titles for your students.

 ## TEACHING IDEAS

Helping Children "Step Into" Stories. Langer (1990) admits that sometimes it is difficult to "step into" a story. To help your students step into new stories, you can encourage them to adopt the habit of reading dust jackets and book covers. Also, to help with initial envisionment building, you might sometimes read the first chapter of a book aloud and then let students continue to read on their own.

Helping Children Talk about Literary Crafting. Langer says that readers often "step out and objectify a literary experience." In doing so, readers think about or talk about how a story is crafted. However, we have found that children generally do not choose to talk about the ways authors craft their works. One way of encouraging children to think about issues of crafting is to share distinctly crafted stories with them. For example, in *Two Bad Ants* (1988), Chris Van Allsburg repeatedly draws attention to perspective in his illustrations. Author Eric Carle frequently relies on repetition in his work. You are likely to find that as you share such distinctive works with children, they become more sensitive to how authors and illustrators craft their stories.

Helping Children Connect Life and Literature. Children come from families with very different literature traditions. Not all children are in a habit of making what Cochran-Smith (1982) called "text-to-life transactions." That is, not all children use stories as lenses through which to view the world. Teachers can encourage this type of response by modeling. Develop the habit of connecting children's literature to life experiences. For example, you might describe bad days as "Alexander days"—a reference to Judith Viorst's *Alexander and the Terrible, Horrible, No Good, Very Bad Day* (1972). And there is no better description for a mischievous child than "Curious George"—from H. A. Rey's *Curious George* (1941).

Reading a Story Repeatedly. One way of deciding which book to read repeatedly to younger students is to invite them to select a book they want to hear again. More likely than not, children will select a book they find both interesting and challenging. If you work with younger children, you want repeated readings to become routine in your classroom. One way of doing this is to designate a particular day of the week as the day on which you'll revisit an "old friend."

EXPERIENCES FOR YOUR LEARNING

1. Langer (1990) says that readers assume different stances (or different relationships to a text) as they read. Review the discussion on pages 62–65 of the four stances Langer describes: *being out and stepping in; being in and moving through; being in and stepping out;* and *stepping out and objectifying the experience.* Then select a book to read, perhaps *Maniac Magee*, and as you read,

keep a journal in which you record your responses to the book. After completing the book, go back and identify the different stances you assumed as you responded to the book.

2. Discuss a piece of multicultural literature such as **The Shimmershine Queens** (1989) with a group of peers from different cultural backgrounds. How, if at all, do your different cultural perspectives come into play in the discussion?

3. As children acquire experience with literature, their knowledge of how texts "work" increases. Read Jon Scieszka's **The Stinky Cheese Man and Other Fairly Stupid Tales** to children of different

ages. Describe how differences in the children's responses to the story might be understood in light of their textual knowledge.

4. Hickman (1981) identified physical features of classrooms that support rich literary responses. Visit two classrooms, and note which of the features listed on page 68 are present. What differences do you find in the two classrooms? Can you discern any differences in the richness of the children's responses to literature? To what extent might differences in the physical features of the classrooms account for the differences in children's responses?

RECOMMENDED BOOKS

* indicates a picture book; **I** indicates interest level (P = preschool, YA = young adult)

* Barrett, Judi. *Cloudy with a Chance of Meatballs.* Illustrated by Ron Barrett. New York: Atheneum, 1978. Life is easy in the town of Chew and Swallow, where food comes from the sky—until the weather takes a turn for the worse. (**I:** P–8)

* Bunting, Eve. *The Wednesday Surprise.* Illustrated by Donald Carrick. New York: Clarion, 1989. A little girl teaches her grandmother to read. (**I:** 6–9)

* Duvoisin, Roger. *Petunia.* New York: Knopf, 1950. Petunia the goose creates chaos in the barnyard as she spreads her "pearls of wisdom." (**I:** P–8)

* Garza, Carmen Lomas. *Family Pictures.* As told to Harriet Rohmer. Spanish version by Rosalma Zubizarreta. San Francisco: Children's Book Press, 1990. Artist Carmen Garza portrays scenes from her childhood in a Mexican American community in South Texas. (**I:** 6–10)

* Heide, Florence Parry, and Judith Heide Gilliland. *The Day of Ahmed's Secret.* Illustrated by Ted Lewin. New York: Lothrop, Lee & Shepard, 1990. As a boy moves through the streets of Cairo doing his work, he looks forward to the evening when he can share his secret with his family—he has learned to write his name. (**I:** 6–10)

Hodge, Merle. *For the Life of Laetitia.* New York: Farrar, 1993. A girl leaves behind her life with her extended family in a rural community to attend school in the city and live with her father's second family. (**I:** 11–YA)

* Moseley, Keith. *It Was a Dark and Stormy Night.* Design by L. Birkinshaw. New York: Dial, 1991. This pop-up

book, in which a parlor mystery unfolds, invites direct reader participation in solving the mystery. (**I:** P–8)

* Munsch, Robert N. *The Paper Bag Princess.* Illustrated by Michael Martchenko. Toronto: Annick Press, 1980. This modern-day fantasy turns the traditional roles of prince and princess topsy turvy. (**I:** P–8)

* Rey, H. A. *Curious George.* Boston: Houghton Mifflin, 1941. A little monkey has lots of adventures, all because of his curiosity. (**I:** P–7)

* Rylant, Cynthia. *This Year's Garden.* New York: Bradbury, 1984. This is a celebration of a family's garden. (**I:** P–8)

* Scieszka, Jon. *The Stinky Cheese Man and Other Fairly Stupid Tales.* Illustrated by Lane Smith. New York: Viking, 1992. A novel format is used in presenting humorous spin-offs of familiar European folktales and fairytales. (**I:** 6 and up)

* Sendak, Maurice. *Where the Wild Things Are.* New York: Harper, 1963. When sent to bed without his supper, a boy travels to "Where the Wild Things Are" and becomes their king. (**I:** P–8)

Spinelli, Jerry. *Maniac Magee.* Boston: Little, Brown, 1990. On his way to becoming a legend, a homeless boy brings together the two sides of a racially divided town. (**I:** 9–12)

* Steig, William. *Shrek!* New York: Farrar, 1990. Shrek the monster sets out to find his true love in this upside-down, contemporary fairytale. (**I:** P–8)

* Van Allsburg, Chris. *Two Bad Ants.* Boston: Houghton Mifflin, 1988. A visit to a house spells near disaster for two ants. (**I:** P–9)

* Viorst, Judith. *Alexander and the Terrible, Horrible, No Good, Very Bad Day.* Illustrated by Ray Cruz.

New York: Atheneum, 1972. Alexander tells about all the things that have gone wrong in a single day. (**I:** P–8)

* Williams, Sherley Anne. *Working Cotton*. Illustrated by Carole Byard. New York: Harcourt, 1992. A young girl describes a day spent in the fields with her migrant worker family. (**I:** P–8)

Winthrop, Elizabeth. *Castle in the Attic*. New York: Holiday House, 1985. A boy travels back in time to confront a wicked wizard and save a kingdom. (**I:** 6–10)

Yarbrough, Camille. *The Shimmershine Queens*. New York: Putnam, 1989. Angie loves to dream about her future, but her dreams begin to fade in the face of peer pressure. (**I:** 10–YA)

RESOURCES

Applebee, Arthur. *The Child's Concept of Story*. Chicago: University of Chicago Press, 1978.

Beach, Richard. *A Teacher's Introduction to Reader-Response Theories*. Urbana, IL: National Council of Teachers of English, 1993.

Langer, Judith A. *Literature Instruction: A Focus on Student Response*. Urbana, IL: National Council of Teachers of English, 1992.

Lehr, Susan. *The Child's Developing Sense of Theme: Responses to Literature*. New York: Columbia University Teachers College Press, 1990.

Martinez, Miriam G., and Nancy L. Roser. "Children's Responses to Literature." *Handbook of Research on Teaching the English Language Arts*. Eds. James Flood, Julie M. Jensen, Diane Lapp, and James R. Squire. New York: Macmillan, 1991. 643–654.

Roser, Nancy, and Miriam Martinez, eds. *Book Talk and Beyond: Children and Teachers Respond to Literature*. Newark, DE: International Reading Association, 1995.

REFERENCES

Almasi, Janice. "The Nature of Fourth Graders' Socio-cognitive Conflicts in Peer-led and Teacher-led Discussions of Literature." *Reading Research Quarterly* 30 (1995): 314–51.

Applebee, Arthur. *The Child's Concept of Story*. Chicago: University of Chicago Press, 1978.

Battle, Jennifer. "Collaborative Story Talk in a Bilingual Kindergarten." *Book Talk and Beyond: Children and Teachers Respond to Literature*. Eds. Nancy Roser and Miriam Martinez. Newark, DE: International Reading Association, 1995. 157–67.

Beach, Richard. *A Teacher's Introduction to Reader-Response Theories*. Urbana, IL: National Council of Teachers of English, 1993.

Britton, James. "Response to Literature." *Response to Literature*. Ed. James R. Squire. Urbana, IL: National Council of Teachers of English, 1968. 3–9.

Cairney, Trevor H. "Fostering and Building Students' Intertextual Histories." *Language Arts* 69 (1992): 502–7.

Cochran-Smith, Marilyn. "The Making of a Reader: A Case Study of Preschool Literary Socialization." Diss. University of Pennsylvania, 1982.

Eeds, Maryann, and Deborah Wells. "Grand Conversations: An Exploration of Meaning Construction in Literature Study Groups." *Research in the Teaching of English* 23 (1989): 4–29.

Egan-Robertson, Ann. "Puerto Rican Students Respond to Children's Books with Puerto Rican Themes." *Journeying: Children Responding to Literature*. Eds. Kathleen E. Holland, Rachael A. Hungerford, and Shirley B. Ernst. Portsmouth, NH: Heinemann, 1993. 204–18.

Enciso, Patricia E. "Cultural Identity and Response to Literature: Running Lessons from *Maniac Magee*." *Language Arts* 71 (1994): 524–33.

Farrell, Edmond J., and James R. Squire. *Transactions with Literature: A Fifty-Year Perspective*. Urbana, IL: National Council of Teachers of English, 1990.

Golden, Joanne M., Annyce Meiners, and Stanley Lewis. "The Growth of Story Meaning." *Language Arts* 69 (1992): 36–43.

Green, Georgia M., and Margaret O. Laff. "Five-Year-Olds' Recognition of Authorship by Literary Style." Technical Report No. 181. Urbana, IL: University of Illinois Center for the Study of Reading, 1980.

Hepler, Susan, and Janet Hickman. "'The Book Was Okay. I Love You'—Social Aspects of Response to Literature." *Theory into Practice* 21 (1982): 278–83.

Hickman, Janet. "A New Perspective on Response to Literature: Research in an Elementary School Setting." *Research in the Teaching of English* 15 (1981): 343–54.

Langer, Judith. "Understanding Literature." *Language Arts* 67 (1990): 812–16.

Lapp, Diane, James Flood, Carol Kibildis, Mary Ann Jones, and Juel Moore. "Teacher Book Clubs: Making Multicultural Connections." *Book Talk and Beyond: Children and Teachers Respond to Literature*. Eds.

Nancy Roser and Miriam Martinez. Newark, DE: International Reading Association, 1995. 42–49.

Lehr, Susan. "The Child's Developing Sense of Theme as a Response to Literature." *Reading Research Quarterly* 23 (1988): 337–57.

McClure, Amy A. "Children's Responses to Poetry in a Supportive Context." Diss. The Ohio State University, 1985.

McGee, Lea M. "An Exploration of Meaning Construction in First Graders' Grand Conversations." *Literacy Research, Theory, and Practice: Views from Many Perspectives*. Eds. Charles K. Kinzer and Donald J. Leu. Chicago: National Reading Conference, 1992. 177–86.

Martinez, Miriam, and Nancy Roser. "Read It Again: The Value of Repeated Readings during Storytime." *The Reading Teacher* 38 (1985): 782–86.

Morrow, Leslie M. "Young Children's Responses to One-to-One Story Readings in School Settings." *Reading Research Quarterly* 23 (1988): 89–107.

Paley, Vivian. *Wally's Stories: Conversations in the Kindergarten*. Cambridge, MA: Harvard University Press, 1981.

Peterson, Ralph, and Maryann Eeds. "More Compelling Questions in Reading Education." *Reading Today* (1995, June/July): 21.

Rosenblatt, Louise M. *Literature as Exploration*. 4th ed. New York: MLA, 1938.

———. "The Literary Transaction: Evocation and Response." *Journeying: Children Responding to Literature*. Eds. Kathleen E. Holland, Rachael A. Hungerford, and Shirley B. Ernst. Portsmouth, NH: Heinemann, 1993. 6–23.

Sims, Rudine. "Strong Black Girls: A Ten-Year-Old Responds to Fiction about Afro-Americans." *Journal of Research and Development in Education* 16 (1983): 21–28.

Weston, Lynda Hobson. "The Evolution of Response through Discussion, Drama, Writing, and Art in a Fourth Grade." *Journeying: Children Responding to Literature*. Eds. Kathleen E. Holland, Rachael A. Hungerford, and Shirley B. Ernst. Portsmouth, NH: Heinemann, 1993. 137–50.

4 Literature Representing Diverse Perspectives

"I'm a sophomore," Sheila said. "Three more years in this place."

"And you just got here, Maizon," Charli said, bouncing down next to me. She had more energy than Li'l Jay.

"Buckle your seat belt, girlfriend, 'cause you in for one heck of a ride."

"Charli. You're slipping," Marie said, frowning.

"Oh, chill out, Marie." Charli waved her hand and lay back on the bed. "We're among our own."

From Maizon at Blue Hill *(1992)*
by Jacqueline Woodson

In *Maizon at Blue Hill,* a girl enters a private academy and discovers that she is one of only five African American students there. Incidents throughout the book reveal how she feels in this situation, how she sees her place in this setting, and how she interacts with others. The passage above implies that people feel and act differently when they are able to say, "We're among our own." How does being among people whose perspectives are different from your own make you feel? Reading and discussing books such as *Maizon at Blue Hill* allows children to reflect on what it means to live in a diverse world and how issues of diversity affect them.

DIVERSE PERSPECTIVES IN THE UNITED STATES

Schools in the United States are seeing a tremendous increase in the cultural and ethnic diversity of the children they serve. According to the 1990 census, "people of color" comprise 25 percent of the U.S. population. It is believed that by 2020, nearly half of the students in U.S. schools will be "of color" (Pallas, Natriello, and McDill, 1989). That reality, along with the United States' expanding relationships with countries around the world, increases the need for children to see themselves as members of a multicultural global community. Since good literature reaches the minds and hearts of its readers, reading and discussing multicultural literature will broaden children's perpectives and increase their understanding in a way that affects—for the better, we hope—how people live in this pluralistic society.

Multicultural education theorists define pluralism as diversity in "ethnic, racial, linguistic, religious, economic, and gender [characteristics], among others" (Nieto, 1996). Nieto argues "that all students of all backgrounds, languages, and experiences need to be acknowledged, valued, and used as important sources of their education" (p. 8). This inclusive definition of pluralism correlates with beliefs about the need for diverse perspectives in education. Banks (1994) asks that multicultural education include voices that have been "marginalized" in the past but not ignore the achievements of Western civilization in doing so. The goal of multicultural education is *freedom*—allowing "students to develop the knowledge, attitudes, and skills to participate in a democratic and free society." Banks acknowledges that students should know their own culture before they can successfully participate in other cultures.

The United States is a diverse society, and this diversity has many sources. The obvious ways in which both the general and school populations are diverse are gender, culture, ethnic and racial background, language, and physical and mental abilities. Less often acknowledged are differences in social class. All of these differences can affect the ways people see themselves and others. And all must be taken into account in forging a working democracy or a harmonious classroom.

The Role of Schools in Presenting Multiple Perspectives

Schools face many demands in shaping the curriculum. Some of these demands are made by people who want the curriculum to be presented from one perspective—their own. Multiple viewpoints serve students best. If students are shown only male, white, able-bodied characters, then female students, children of color, students in wheelchairs, and children with learning exceptionalities are likely to feel that the school day is not planned with them in mind. They may even feel that their place in society in general is questionable. Schools can be instrumental in providing opportunities for students to read and discuss material from multiple viewpoints. Such discussions are important in developing attitudes of open-mindedness about diversity. This chapter (and this book) recommends books that offer multiple perspectives.

Literature's Role in Influencing the Reader's Perspective

What role does literature have in influencing children's understanding of diverse perspectives? Depending on their experiences, some children feel uncomfortable when presented with an opportunity to interact with someone who is different from themselves. How can children resolve their misunderstanding, lack of understanding, or fear? Developing a hypersensitivity that leads to avoidance is a serious mistake. "Many people have an inhibition about talking with someone in a wheelchair. They don't know quite what to say, so they don't say anything at all and ignore both the person and the chair" (Haldane, 1991, n.pag.). People may respond to any kind of diversity in this way. Although it is a vicarious experience, interacting with diverse people through literature can help. Literature that portrays diversity in natural ways can provide realistic images as well as spark discussion.

Fiction and informational books are powerful vehicles for helping students understand other cultures, because they offer cultural insights in natural ways. Such books should not be narrowly viewed as replacements for social studies textbooks, for too often students miss the richness of the writing if they read merely to locate cultural information. However, fiction and informational books can enhance children's understanding of cultures by involving them emotionally. Their narrower focus allows for deeper exploration of the thoughts, feelings, and experiences of people from diverse groups. Thus, through story, readers take an emotional stake in understanding how and why people live as they do.

Milton Meltzer (1989) believes that the writer has a "social responsibility" and that "writing about social issues need not depress and dispirit readers; it should provide them with courage. If they learn to confront life as it is, it may give them the heart to strive to make it better" (p. 157). Meltzer is saying that literature is a powerful vehicle when it treats issues honestly. But, as Jean Little (1990) points out, literature designed as object lessons, in which teachers point out the "good messages," appears self-righteous and rarely changes people's opinions. Well-written books that speak from the writer's vision pull readers into the characters' experiences and emotions and build compassion, thereby having a lasting effect on readers' understandings of the world in which they live.

Books depicting diverse perspectives are found in all genres of children's literature. In this chapter, we will examine the criteria for viewing multicultural and international issues, as well as issues of gender, social diversity, and exceptionality, in children's books. These criteria form a foundation for evaluating the literature you encounter in all the genre chapters that follow.

MULTICULTURAL LITERATURE DEFINED

Although there is general agreement that multicultural literature is about people who are not in the mainstream, there is no consensus as to what constitutes nonmainstream populations (Cai and Bishop, 1994). Some contend that multicultural literature is that by or about people of color in the United States. Many include literature about religious minorities (such as the Amish and Jews) or about people who live in specific regions of the United States (such as Appalachia). Some include literature about diverse lifestyles (such as families headed by same-sex parents or people with disabilities). Some include books about people in countries outside the United States. There is value in having an inclusive definition when considering issues of diversity; however, too broad a definition dilutes the focus.

We will define *multicultural literature* as literature that reflects the multitude of cultural groups within the United States. In order to address the issues of multiculturalism most salient to our study of children's literature, we will focus on literature that reflects ethnic and regional groups whose cultures historically have been less represented than European cultures. A related body of literature is international literature—literature that is about countries outside the United States or that was originally written and published in countries outside the United States. Literature that addresses many other kinds of diversities—social diversity, diversity in gender preference, and differences in ways of learning, to name a few—should also be included under the larger umbrella of "literature reflecting diverse perspectives."

One reason we focus on books about ethnic groups within the United States is that these books reflect experiences of the children in American schools today, since most were either born or raised in this country. Often, books of this type are classified as African American, Asian American, Latin American, or Native American. Virginia Hamilton's ***The House of Dies Drear*** (1968) is an example. In this mystery story set in Ohio, a professor and his son move into a house once used as a station of the Underground Railroad. They find that the spirits of those who passed through the house still maintain a presence there. This book and its sequel, ***The Mystery of Drear House*** (1987), include historic details about the Underground Railroad, an African American experience.

We use the term "multicultural" rather than "minority," with its implied reference to groups that have been historically "minor" in number compared to the "majority." Some groups that historically have been considered "minorities" are no longer numerically in the minority. Unfortunately, however, underrepresentation and misrepresentation of these groups continue. Virginia Hamilton's (1993) term "parallel cultures" has gained wide acceptance because it defines various cultures as parallel to the mainstream, rather than in a minority status. However, the ideal is not simply existence on parallel planes but an interaction between cultures that leads to interdependence.

The Value of Multicultural Literature

Why should children's books deliberately include the perspectives of people from many backgrounds? This is a legitimate question. Many people believe that the "melting pot" is the target that literature should strive for—it shouldn't accentuate ethnic and cultural differences, because that emphasizes the stresses tearing apart the fabric of society.

There are two compelling reasons for making sure children's literature includes the perspectives of people from many groups. First, students feel welcome in school to the extent that they find themselves and their experiences represented in the books and materials they find there. Second, students need to understand and empathize with people who are different from themselves. If books do not portray differences, students cannot learn to transcend them.

Rudine Sims Bishop (1990) uses the metaphor "mirrors and windows" to emphasize these two values of multicultural literature. Mirrors let readers see reflections of their own lives; windows let them see others' lives. Multicultural literature provides both types of experience. What value is there in seeing oneself represented in literature? Quite simply, it engenders a sense of pride. When readers encounter images of people they consider like themselves in a book, they take more interest in the book and feel a sense of involvement in the literary discussion that follows their reading.

Identifying Multicultural Books

All multicultural books depict people of diverse cultures, but the degree to which such books focus on cultural or social issues varies significantly. It is not enough to count the diverse faces in a book; the important thing is how the members of various cultures are portrayed. Rudine Sims Bishop (1992) identifies three kinds of books that depict people from nonmainstream cultures: culturally neutral, culturally generic, and culturally specific books. All three types include diversity; but they differ in the degree and the specificity of their emphasis, and, accordingly, in the cultural understandings that they offer to the reader.

Culturally Neutral Books. Culturally neutral books have themes that are not identifiable as an aspect of any particular culture (Sims Bishop, 1996). People of different cultures are deliberately included so that the illustrations appear visually diverse. The text does not require that characters be of a particular culture. Diversity is *incidentally* depicted. One example of a culturally neutral book is *How Much Is a Million?* (1985) by David M. Schwartz. Steven Kellogg's illustrations include children of various ethnicities, yet the book's focus is not at all on ethnic diversity—it is on a mathematical concept. Still, books that depict multicultural inclusiveness even when the focus is not on any aspect of diversity are important because they increase readers' exposure and awareness.

Culturally Generic Books. Culturally generic books purposefully and prominently feature multicultural characters but are otherwise "generically American" in theme and plot. An example of culturally generic books is the *Jamaica* series by Juanita Havill, illustrated by Anne Sibley O'Brien. In *Jamaica's Find* (1986), a little African American girl finds a stuffed dog at the playground. She struggles with her desire to keep the toy, but decides to turn it in to the lost-and-found office. Eventually, she is able to help the owner reclaim the missing toy. Jamaica's struggle is universal—one that children experience regardless of their culture.

Culturally Specific Books. Culturally specific books illuminate the experience of members of a particular cultural group (Sims Bishop, 1992). The nuances of daily life are captured accurately, reflecting language use, attitudes, values, and beliefs of members of the group portrayed. Such details add texture to the writing, making the stories more real and more believable and therefore making it more likely that readers will see the stories as authentic. An example of a culturally specific book is Mildred Taylor's ***Roll of Thunder, Hear My Cry*** (1976). Not only are the descriptions of situations and events historically accurate, but the character names, the forms of address, the dialogue, and the interactions are true to the culture of the people whose lives are reflected.

Although they differ in the depth of the cultural experiences they provide to readers, all three types of multicultural books contribute to readers' understandings of their own and others' cultures. Sometimes, readers see themselves and others as sharing universal experiences, and thus cultural group membership need not be explicitly discussed. But it is culturally specific books that offer the insights necessary to truly further readers' understanding of different cultures.

EVOLUTION OF MULTICULTURAL LITERATURE

From the time children's books were first published in this country until well after World War II, most of those books reflected mainstream characters, settings, values, and lifestyles. Most children learned to read from books that presented primarily European American lifestyles and values. People who did not resemble the so-called American ideal—people of African, Asian, Latin American, and Southern European origins, as well as Native Americans—were regularly singled out for discrimination. Likewise, early portrayals of nonmainstream characters tended to be highly stereotypical. Such characters were portrayed as "cute," "savage," "primitive," uncouth, untrustworthy, or underdeveloped. Since the late 1960s, increasing efforts have been made to include honest depictions of people from all cultural groups in children's books—not just to talk about them, but to narrate their perspectives and experiences through their eyes and in their voices.

Although several individuals (for example, Augusta Baker, Virginia Lacy, Charlamae Rollins) campaigned for inclusion of people of diversity in children's books prior to 1965, the "wake-up call" that made the U.S. public aware of the situation is usually considered to be Nancy Larrick's 1965 article in the *Saturday Review,* "The All-White World of Children's Books." In her study, Larrick found that only 6.7 percent of children's books published between 1962 and 1964 included any African Americans in illustrations or text, and just 0.9 percent depicted them in contemporary settings. Other cultural groups were represented even less. The decade that followed saw an increase in the number of books that included people of diversity. The Council for Interracial Books for Children was founded in 1966 to heighten public awareness of diversity issues related to children's books. The Coretta Scott King Award was established in 1969 to give recognition annually to an African American author and an African American illustrator who contributed the most distinguished work of the previous year.

Larrick's study was replicated a decade later in order to examine how things had changed (Chall, Radwin, French, and Hall, 1985). The percentages had more than doubled: 14.4 percent of all children's books published from 1973 to 1975 included African Americans in text or illustrations, and 4 percent showed them in contemporary settings. This increase was attributed, in part, to the rise of the civil rights movement, along with long overdue recognition of the inequities highlighted by Larrick and others. However, Rollock (1984) found that these increases were only temporary and that in the five years following the

Chall study, between 1979 and 1984, only 1.5 percent of newly published children's books included African Americans.

Limited data are available on representation in children's books of groups other than African Americans. But sources such as the Council on Interracial Books for Children (1975), Nieto (1983), Schon (1988), and Sims (1985) indicate that there has been even less representation of groups such as Asian Americans, Native Americans, and Latin Americans.

The beginning of the 1990s saw the largest surge to date in multicultural publishing in the children's book field. Bishop's (1991) note of optimism reflected a general increase in the level of awareness and understanding of the importance of multicultural literature. But despite the increase in numbers of multicultural publications, a study by Reimer (1992) revealed a lack of multicultural representation in popular booklists such as "Children's Choices" (International Reading Association, 1989), Jim Trelease's *The New Read Aloud Handbook* (1989), and former U.S. Secretary of Education William Bennett's list of recommended reading for elementary students (Bennett, 1988).

Other problems were highlighted in the early 1990s. Because of the predominance of European American writers and illustrators, multicultural literature was presented primarily from an "outside" perspective. Related to this problem was the fact that some Native Americans believed that mainstream authors had "stolen" their stories. Another problem was the grouping of related but distinctly separate cultures under one label (for example, labeling Mexican Americans, Puerto Rican Americans, and Cuban Americans as "Hispanic"). In addition, there was a lack of teacher awareness of the importance of including multiple cultural perspectives in the classroom (Harris, 1992; Reimer, 1992; and Sims Bishop, 1992).

Currently, authors, illustrators, publishers, and educators are paying more attention to the issues of "authenticity" that were raised in the early 1990s and before. Authors and illustrators from diverse cultures are accepting the call to create culturally authentic work. (Ironically, many had tried unsuccessfully to have their work published in earlier years. In many cases, it was the annual contest sponsored by the Council on Interracial Books for Children that led to the publication of books written by people from diverse cultures.) Today, publishers are seeking ways to ensure authenticity in the books they produce. Librarians and reviewers are recognizing authenticity as a critical criterion in evaluating multicultural books. And teachers are working to include authentic multicultural books as featured reading materials in their classrooms. However, they should also look critically at the books from years past still found in many school libraries and classrooms. Such books have value in specialized collections that allow people to see historic trends in the publication of multicultural books. However, teachers should be careful that young readers are not exposed to these books without some disussion of the damaging racist or stereotypical images they contain.

ISSUES RELATED TO MULTICULTURAL LITERATURE

To evaluate the influence of multicultural literature on children's understanding of the world around them and to establish criteria for good multicultural literature, we need to consider several issues: (1) whether a work presents cultural details authentically, (2) whether the author writes from an inside or an outside perspective, (3) whether a work promotes stereotypes, and (4) which cultural group is being described in the work. Consideration of these issues can guide teachers in selecting multicultural literature and facilitating discussions of such literature among their students.

Cultural Authenticity

When a book presents a theme that is true to a culture and is filled with specific details that are authentic, members of that culture who read it feel that their experiences have been reflected and illuminated for others to share. Culturally authentic books are written by authors who have developed a "culturally conscious" way to "provide exceptional aesthetic experiences: [to] entertain, educate, and inform; and . . . engender racial pride" (Harris, 1990, p. 551). However, when a book distorts or misrepresents information about a culture, such misinformation leads to misunderstandings of that culture by those in other cultures and creates feelings of betrayal in members of that culture.

Illustration 4.1

In *In My Family/En mi familia* (a companion book to *Family Pictures/ Cuadros de familia*), readers are introduced to more of Carmen Lomas Garza's descriptions and images of family events. (*In My Family* by Carmen Lomas Garza. Used by permission of Children's Book Press, San Francisco, CA.)

Examples of culturally authentic books are Carmen Lomas Garza's *In My Family/En mi familia* (1996) and her earlier book *Family Pictures/Cuadros de familia* (1990). Based on the author's life in South Texas, these books include various paintings that illustrate events in her childhood, accompanied by bilingual text. In *Family Pictures/Cuadros de familia*, the page entitled "Birthday Party/Cumpleaños" begins with "That's me hitting the piñata at my sixth birthday party." Following the English sentence is the Spanish translation: "Ésa soy yo, pegándole a la piñata en la fiesta que me dieron cuando cumplí seis años." Readers can identify specific details such as the framed picture of the Last Supper, the flamenco dancers on the calendar, and the assembling of the tamales, all of which are culturally authentic. Through illustrations and text, *In My Family/En mi familia* tells about the making of empañadas, birthday barbecue parties, and summer dance time. Mexican American readers can feel a sense of kinship with the creator of such books—a sense of shared experiences and understandings. Readers outside the culture can gain new insights from these authentic depictions of the culture.

When a book lacks authenticity, it is likely to convey misleading images of a culture. Sometimes, the text gives readers a stereotyped or dated image of a culture; other times, confused illustrations depict a culture in inappropriate ways. Readers outside the portrayed culture may not be able to discern what is authentic and what is not.

Perspective: Insider or Outsider

The perspective of the writer has become a major issue in multicultural literature: Does the author have an "inside" or an "outside" perspective on the culture being portrayed? An author with an inside perspective writes as a member of the culture and therefore is more likely to portray the cultural group authentically. An author with an outside perspective writes from a point of view of a nonmember of the group being portrayed. But even among those inside a culture, the range of cultural experiences and opinions regarding the depictions of the culture vary, showing the multidimensionality of any culture (Noll, 1995).

Members of the dominant culture have had multiple opportunities to see their world interpreted through eyes like their own. But they may not have had the experience of being wrongly portrayed, and therefore they may not know the

ISSUE
TO
CONSIDER

How much artistic license should be given to illustrators as they create images of a culture?

Some illustrators argue that demands for absolute accuracy of every detail rob the illustrator of the right to use imagination and individual style in portraying an image. They contend that unless the illustrations are photographs, the style of illustration will influence the degree of attention to detail.

Others argue that accurate details in illustrations create the overall sense of cultural authenticity. They point out that misconceptions may develop from incorrect images. In some cases, highly regarded illustrators whose work is exceptional from an artistic viewpoint have been criticized for creating images that "mix" cultures. Critics say that this mixing of cultures robs each culture of its distinction. Yet the illustrators express their desire to create unified images of cultures that sometimes share a common voice. One example is *Brother Eagle, Sister Sky: A Message from Chief Seattle* (1991) by Susan Jeffers. Controversy arose over the text because the words were based on a script for a 1971 television commercial decrying pollution. Controversy arose over the illustrations because they mixed images of various Native American cultures and contained inaccuracies of both history and culture. Jeffers defended her position by stating that the important point is that the book reflects a Native American philosophy (Noll, 1995).

How do you view this issue of authenticity versus artistic license in children's book illustrations? How will the type of illustrations affect child readers who do not intimately know the culture portrayed? How will the illustrations affect child readers whose own cultures are portrayed? What do you think?

feeling of betrayal at having their culture misrepresented. An outsider may miss the rhythm, accent, and flavor that make the ethnic experience live for the insider audience. An outsider's interpretation of an ethnic experience may be filled with details that are factually accurate, but the presentation may be bland and dry, lacking the cultural nuances that would make it come alive. A simple missed or misrepresented detail may be enough to negate authenticity for members of the culture being portrayed (Kaplan, 1995).

In his article "Can We Fly across Cultural Gaps on the Wings of Imagination? Ethnicity, Experience, and Cultural Authenticity," Cai (1995) compares a novel by Laurence Yep, an insider of the Chinese culture, to one by Vanya Oakes, an outsider. Through detailed comparisons, Cai clearly outlines the differences between the inside and outside perspectives. Can those born outside a culture produce authentic material about that culture? Some say no. Others, such as scholar Henry Louis Gates, Jr., W. E. B. Du Bois Professor of Literature at Harvard, believe that inside perspective *can* be gained by cultural outsiders. Gates believes that "no human culture is inaccessible to someone who makes the effort to understand, to learn, to inhabit another world" (cited in Sims Bishop, 1992, p. 42). Some, through their own life experiences and extensive research, have been able to create culturally authentic portrayals of a group different from that into which they were born. Many African Americans view Arnold Adoff's writing as having an inside perspective, yet he is not African American. Many of his books, such as *Black Is Brown Is Tan* (1973), speak from his biracial family's experiences. Similarly, Demi's picture books, such as *The Empty Pot* (1990) and *Chingis Khan* (1991), are set in China. Although she was not born Chinese, her thoroughness of research is evident, and readers who are Chinese find that her work reflects the perspective of insiders.

Clearly, the issue of insider versus outsider authorship is complex. However, books that present authentic voices and images—no matter who created them—offer a uniquely valuable contribution to literature about a culture. They allow readers within the culture to enjoy the sense of kinship and pride that come from having one's own experience accurately portrayed. They also broaden the perspective of readers from other cultures and offer them fresh insights about the cultural group depicted.

Stereotyping and Other Unacceptable Depictions of Cultural Groups

When a single set of attributes is assigned to an entire cultural group, diversity and individuality are overlooked, and stereotyping results. A stereotyped impression of a cultural group may be created by how characters are portrayed, how characters interact with one another, how a book's setting is described, how a theme is treated, or simply how information is conveyed.

In years past, literature often depicted nonmainstream cultures in patronizing and condescending ways. Stereotypes abounded in images created by mainstream writers and illustrators. Books such as *The Story of Little Black Sambo* (Bannerman, 1899) and *The Five Chinese Brothers* (Bishop, 1938) presented negative and stereotyped images of blacks and Asians, respectively. Although *The Story of Little Black Sambo* is set in India, the illustrations in the original edition depict stereotyped images of blacks. The story line of *The Five Chinese Brothers* requires that the brothers look alike; however, the book depicts all the Chinese people of the village as identical and with yellow skin. Some more recent books are also controversial because of their stereotyped images. Despite the explanations at the end of the book that document distinctions among ten of the tribes, some Native Americans belive that *Ten Little Rabbits* (Grossman and Long, 1991) is problematic. Too often, Native American characters are portrayed as animals or depicted as something to be "counted," perpetuating the myth that all Native American people are alike—in this case, "they just wear different blankets" (McCarty, 1995). Stereotyped images of Latin Americans include "Mexican men wearing wide-brimmed hats snoozing under a giant cactus" and images of "sarapes, piñatas, burros, bare feet, and broken English" (Council on Interracial Books for Children, 1974).

Many books that present stereotypical images of a cultural group are still in print and may be on the shelf of your local bookstore, school library, or public library. Sometimes, these books are purchased by adults who remember them from their childhood and want to share them with young children. However, having loved a book as a child is not in itself an adequate selection criterion, unless you are prepared to take advantage of this "teachable moment" to discuss stereotypes in older books that represent dominant cultural mores of those times. Ginny Moore Kruse, Director of the Cooperative Children's Book Center at the University of Wisconsin, Madison, cautions against the use of materials that contain "hurtful images" or perpetuate erroneous information about cultures (1991).

Certainly, not all books by mainstream writers and illustrators depicting diversity contain stereotypes. Good depictions can be found in the works of Ezra Jack Keats and Ann Grifalconi.

In recent years, efforts have been made to replace stereotyped images in old stories by publishing new versions. Sometimes, the original author/illustrator team creates the revised version, as in the case of a story set in Alaska and titled **On Mother's Lap** (1992), written by Ann Herbert Scott and illustrated by Glo Coalson. Margaret Mahy provided new text for **The Seven Chinese Brothers** (1990), which was illustrated by Jean and Mou-sien Tseng. Julius Lester and Jerry Pinkney collaborated in the creation of **Sam and the Tigers** (1996), a retelling of the Sambo story in the African American tradition. In **The Story of Little Babaji** (1996), Fred Marcellino reillustrated Helen Bannerman's original text for the Sambo story, renaming the characters with Indian names and depicting the setting in India, as the text indicates.

Identification of Cultural Groups

For some time, there has been ongoing discussion as to which groups should be included under the "multicultural literature" umbrella. African Americans, Asian Americans, Latin Americans, and Native Americans are always included. However, other groups outside the mainstream share some of the same problems of being underrepresented and misrepresented in children's literature and deserve attention as teachers and librarians evaluate and select multicultural literature.

Jewish Americans. Until recent years, there were not many books that reflected Jewish history, religion, and culture. Books such as **Number the Stars** (Lowry, 1989) share an important part of Jewish history with readers who may or may not be familiar with the Holocaust. The story is about a strong friendship and about people who help others facing unjust treatment. The specific circumstances focus on the Danish resistance to the Holocaust, but the themes are universal.

Some contemporary works are important in that they offer possibilities for understanding the lives of Jewish Americans today. In Sonia Levitin's **The Golem and the Dragon Girl** (1993), a Chinese American girl and a Jewish American boy find that there are parallels between their two cultures that make them feel less different from each other.

Patricia Polacco tells of her own family's heritage and traditions in **The Keeping Quilt** (1988). Passing on the traditions of her heritage is the important theme of this book, which is filled with such cultural markers as a babushka and a wedding huppa. By some definitions, this book would be identified as multicultural because it is about a Jewish family that emigrated from Russia; by other definitions, it would not be considered a multicultural book. However, books such as these help readers gain insights into a culture and a history that reading only "mainstream" literature cannot provide.

Appalachian Americans. Another group that has historically been underrepresented in children's literature is the people of the Appalachian region of the United States, who have a distinct culture and way of life. Books such as those by Cynthia Rylant, George Ella Lyon, and Gloria Houston authentically reflect this group's experiences. In **My Great-Aunt Arizona** (Houston, 1992), for example, details of the schoolhouse are accurately depicted. Also, the fact that five genera-

Illustration 4.2

In *The Keeping Quilt,* which won an award from the Association of Jewish Libraries, varied uses of an old quilt symbolize the passing on of family traditions and heritage. (*The Keeping Quilt* by Patricia Polacco. Copyright © 1988 Patricia Polacco. Used by permission of Simon & Schuster Books for Young Readers.)

Illustration 4.3
Cynthia Rylant's story about an Appalachian family evokes the universal experience that families share when relatives travel from afar for a reunion. (*The Relatives Came* by Cynthia Rylant. Illustrations copyright © 1985 Stephen Gammell. Used by permission of Simon & Schuster Books for Young Readers, an imprint of Simon & Schuster Children's Publishing Division.)

tions of the family in the book attended the same school and had Aunt Arizona as their teacher is typical of real-life Appalachian families of the era. *The Relatives Came* (Rylant, 1985) reflects the universal experience of family members coming together for a reunion. However, that experience takes on a special meaning from the fact that Appalachian people are separated from their neighbors by mountains and therefore often live in relative isolation. Both text and illustrations support the sense of distance traveled along small, mountain roads. But it is the activities of the family—"hugging and eating and breathing together"— that give readers vivid insight into the experience.

European Americans. Groups usually excluded from the multicultural umbrella are the European American cultures, because they make up the mainstream population in the United States and have generally been well represented in the literature of the past. However, Swedish Americans, Italian Americans, and the other European American groups all have rich and distinct cultural heritages. Because the literature of the past most frequently depicted a "generic" American experience, not much attention was given to any of these European American cultures separately. Therefore, although European American cultural groups do not need the corrective attention that other groups may need, teachers and librarians should not overlook books that give insight into their experiences.

MAJOR AUTHORS AND ILLUSTRATORS OF MULTICULTURAL LITERATURE

Most of the authors and illustrators we discuss in this section are insiders, born and raised within the cultures they depict in their works. But a good deal of what was available during the early years of multicultural publishing was written and illustrated by people outside of the cultures represented. As they played major roles in helping create and define the field, some of them are also included.

Verna Aardema

Verna Aardema's interest in writing was evident from the time she was a young child in New Era, Michigan. Encouraged by her mother, Aardema spent hours at the cedar swamp behind her house, thinking up stories to tell children. Later, she contributed to school newspapers, won writing contests, worked for her college publications office, and wrote for the local newspaper.

It was in the 1950s, during the arduous routine of cajoling her daughter, Paula, to eat, that Aardema started telling stories for children again. Each day, Paula would eat only if her mother told a story at mealtime. Aardema's interest in Africa led her to tell stories set on that continent. Although Aardema is not African American, her many African-themed books are a result of passionate interest in and careful research on African culture, customs, traditions, geography, and folklore. In 1960, she published a collection of retold stories, *Tales from the Story Hat,* which was based on years of studying the many distinct cultures of Africa.

Today, Aardema enjoys an established reputation as a modern reteller of traditional African tales. *Why Mosquitoes Buzz in People's Ears: A West African Tale* (1975) is a story about a chain of events set off when a mosquito tells a big lie; illustrated by Leo and Diane Dillon, it won the Caldecott Medal in 1976.

Another of her books illustrated by the Dillons is **Who's in Rabbit's House? A Masai Tale** (1977), in which Rabbit's friends try to get rid of a mysterious Long One. Jerry Pinkney illustrated Aardema's **Rabbit Makes a Monkey of Lion: A Swahili Tale** (1989), in which a little rabbit outwits a big lion.

Alma Flor Ada

Alma Flor Ada was born in Cuba, was educated in Spain and Peru, and now lives in San Francisco, where she is a professor at the University of San Francisco. Ada is active in the promotion of bilingualism, writing books in both Spanish and English, as well as translating books written by others.

As a child, Alma Flor Ada was fortunate to be surrounded by storytellers. Her grandmother and her uncle told many stories, and her father passed on his knowledge of the world by making up stories. Ada's books include retellings of traditional tales and a contemporary story set in a Latin American country, as well as a story about the cultural conflict experienced by a child who grows up in an ethnic community in the United States.

The Rooster Who Went to His Uncle's Wedding (1993) is a retelling of a traditional Latin American folktale. In cumulative style, it recounts a rooster's efforts to solicit help in cleaning his dirty beak before he goes to his uncle's wedding. The dilemma is solved with the help of the sun, which has always enjoyed the rooster's morning song. **The Gold Coin** (1991) tells the story of how a thief is transformed. A young thief follows Doña Josefa with the intent of taking her gold coin, but changes his mind as he meets the people whom Doña Josefa has helped. **My Name Is Maria Isabel/Me llamo María Isabel** (1993) is about a little girl who must find a way to express pride in her heritage amidst people who misunderstand her culture. **Jordi's Star** (1996) is an original tale in which a falling star inspires a shepherd to beautify his surroundings.

Arnold Adoff

Arnold Adoff was born in the Bronx and began his teaching career in Harlem. He was disturbed to find that the textbooks his students were using included very little literature that reflected their lives. After collecting poetry written by African Americans so that his students would hear the voices of people such as Langston Hughes and Gwendolyn Brooks, Adoff edited and published his first book, **I Am the Darker Brother: An Anthology of Modern Poems by Negro Americans** (1970). During the next decade, Adoff continued to anthologize poems that focused on the experiences of African Americans.

Adoff's own poetry often expresses ethnic pride and addresses issues of race relations. Adoff, of Jewish heritage, is married to African American writer Virginia Hamilton, and together they have two children. Adoff has written two books that focus on what it means to be of biracial heritage: **Black Is Brown Is Tan** (1973) and **All the Colors of the Race** (1982). His poetry has a rhythmic, unrhymed quality meant to be shared aloud and a visual playfulness meant to be seen on the page. His works are frequently on lists of notable books. In 1988, Adoff was honored with the National Council of Teachers of English Award for Excellence in Poetry for Children for his lifetime contribution.

Joseph Bruchac

Joseph Bruchac's rich cultural heritage includes Abenaki ancestry, and his writing is lauded for its authentic images of Native Americans. He has written novels, compiled poetry and folktales, and coauthored volumes of stories and

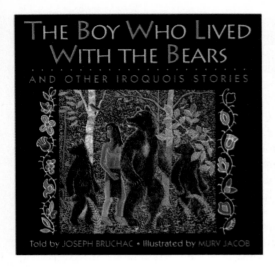

Illustration 4.4

Generations of Iroquois storytellers passed down the six stories in *The Boy Who Lived with the Bears* to teach lessons about the importance of caring and responsibility and the dangers of selfishness and pride. (*The Boy Who Lived with the Bears and Other Iroquois Stories* by Joseph Bruchac. Book jacket art and illustration copyright © 1995 Murv Jacob. Jacket design by Tom Starace. Used by permission of HarperCollins Publishers.)

activities. *Keepers of the Earth: Native American Stories and Environmental Activities for Children* (1988), *Keepers of the Animals: Native American Stories and Wildlife Activities for Children* (1991), and *Keepers of Life: Discovering Plants through Native American Stories and Earth Activities for Children* (1994) were coauthored with Michael J. Caduto. These books present stories about animals and other aspects of nature, followed by various activities for children, to be guided by teachers or other adults.

Bruchac has written poems and retold folktales that have been published as picture books. He and Jonathan London coauthored *Thirteen Moons on Turtle's Back: A Native American Year of Moons* (1992). The thirteen poems are based on the belief of many Native American groups that each of the thirteen moons in a year holds a story; each poem reflects a different Native American group. *The First Strawberries: A Cherokee Story* (1993) is a retelling of the legend of a couple whose quarrel was resolved when the Sun sent gifts of raspberries, blueberries, blackberries, and finally strawberries. *The Boy Who Lived with the Bears and Other Iroquois Stories* (1995) contains six animal tales first told around the central fire in Iroquois longhouses.

Ashley Bryan

Ashley Bryan says that he cannot remember a time when he wasn't a creator of books—even as early as kindergarten, he created hundreds of handmade books with the encouragement of his family. Bryan later pursued the formal study of art and has taught art to children and adults. He developed his own style based on the influences of the art of his African ancestors. Bryan has done block printing, painting that is reminiscent of woodcuts, and other painting styles.

Bryan is known for both writing and illustrating. *Beat the Story-Drum, Pum-Pum* (1980) and *What a Morning! The Christmas Story in Black Spirituals* (1988) were honored with the Coretta Scott King Award for illustration. *Lion and the Ostrich Chicks and Other African Folk Tales* (1986) was awarded the Coretta Scott King Award for writing. Another of the books for which he is well known is *The Dancing Granny* (1977), which was inspired by Bryan's grandmother's visit from the West Indies when she was in her seventies. She learned the latest dance steps and outdanced her great-grandchildren.

Bryan's interest in text, music, and art is evident in his books, as he combines these elements to create an overall effect. Bryan's text is influenced by his study of African American poets and his belief that poetry and stories are meant to be shared aloud. His dramatic storytelling style can be "heard" in his texts, which make readers feel as though they were listening to a storyteller. To research folktales, Bryan begins with the scholarly collections made in the nineteenth century by missionaries and anthropologists. He then relies on his own background knowledge and his storytelling ability to create an original version. In addition, he has published several collections of African American spirituals. Bryan's desire in sharing them is to bring the "musical genius" of these works to a wider audience.

Today, Bryan lives on an island off the coast of Maine, where he has spent summers painting for fifty years. He continues to produce books for children, entertain others with his storytelling, and collect materials on the beach for creating puppets.

Paul Goble

Although not of Native American heritage, Paul Goble has a rare authentic voice reflecting a culture he embraced and adopted. In return, he was adopted by the Sioux and Yakima tribes. Chief Edgar Red Cloud gave him the name "Wakinyan Chikala," which means "Little Thunder." Born and raised in England, Goble moved to the Black Hills of South Dakota as an adult. From early childhood, he was fascinated by Native Americans, reading and collecting anything he could find about them.

In the early years of multicultural publishing, Goble made the stories of the Plains Indians available to an audience that might not otherwise have had access to them. In all his books, the thoroughness of his research is evident. Goble's hope is that his books contribute to children's understanding of the natural world by depicting it differently than in the mass media and popular books. Rather than depicting animals as something to be feared or tamed, he casts them in their natural relationship to humans living on the same land. Goble challenges readers to see events of the past from a perspective they might not have considered before. For example, in *Death of the Iron Horse* (1987), Goble depicts a Native American attack on a railroad train as a defense of the land from the "iron horse" that the attackers feared would bind up "Mother Earth" with rails.

Most of Goble's work from the 1970s and 1980s is myths and legends, retold in Native American storytelling style and with illustrations styled like Native American art. Goble was awarded the Caldecott Medal for *The Girl Who Loved Wild Horses* (1978).

Eloise Greenfield

Eloise Greenfield has published many award-winning picture books, collections of poetry, and biographies during the last two decades. Among her most noted books is *Honey, I Love and Other Love Poems* (1978), illustrated by Leo and Diane Dillon. These poems speak to the goals that Greenfield hopes to achieve in her work: to provide young children with words to love and grow on and to portray African American children who have a good self-concept. Most of Greenfield's work depicts relationships among families and friends. In *Grandpa's Face* (1988), illustrated by Floyd Cooper, a girl's relationship with her grandfather is central to the story. Although most of the themes are universal, details such as language use give authenticity to the African American experiences portrayed. Greenfield's desire to give children information about their black heritage led her to produce a number of biographies of African Americans, such as *Rosa Parks* (1973) and *Mary McLeod Bethune* (1977).

Greenfield's numerous awards include the Coretta Scott King Award for *Africa Dreams* (1977); *Nathaniel Talking* (1988) and *Night on Neighborhood Street* (1991) were Coretta Scott King Honor Books. *Africa Dreams* tells the story of a young girl who dreams of someday visiting her granddaddy's village in Africa. Both *Nathaniel Talking* and *Night on Neighborhood Street* are poetry books featuring a young boy who narrates his experiences growing up in his neighborhood. They were illustrated by Jan Spivey Gilchrist, with whom Greenfield has also collaborated on a series of board books for the very young.

Virginia Hamilton

For thirty years, Virginia Hamilton has been publishing a wide variety of work that includes folktales, biographies, and stories about families. All are tied

ASK THE AUTHOR . . . *Julius Lester*

J. Leste

How do you feel about the argument that one has to be a member of a culture in order to write about it?

The issue is not whether one writes about his or her culture or another culture. The issue is what it has always been—that one write well, that one write with integrity, that one write as much of the truth as he or she is able to see and communicate.

No one has the power to say that you cannot write about his or her culture. Cultures are not pieces of property. Cultures cannot be owned or controlled, nor should they be. However, we live in an age in which some wish to turn cultures into idols to be worshipped and adored. This is a misuse of culture, an abuse of the mystery of human experience.

Culture is not the essence of human experience, though it appears there are those who would have us think so. Culture is merely the ways in which a given group of people express their humanness. This does not mean that I understand or approve of all the ways in which that humanness is expressed. I do not. This does not mean that I am comfortable with every culture. I am not. This does not mean that every aspect of a culture is accessible to me as an outsider. It isn't.

But there can be no limitation put on the imagination, that extraordinary faculty which permits one to live in times and places that do not exist physically, to live in times and places one will never have the opportunity to visit physically. Above all, the imagination enables me to be someone I am not—female, Russian, animal, or spirit. The imagination is the empathic bridge between cultures. Instead of placing barriers around a culture and denying others permission to enter, we should be thankful that someone from outside our culture is interested, is curious, wants to learn, wants to feel a sense of belonging with us. As long as the outsider respects the culture, there is no harm.

One can regard his or her culture as a private reserve or as an offering. It is my hope that the people will choose the latter.

Julius Lester is the author of twenty-five books, including fifteen books for children and young adults. His books have been recognized with such honors as the Boston Globe–Horn Book Award, the Newbery Medal, and the Caldecott Medal, among others. He lives in a small town in western Massachusetts with his wife, stepdaughter, cat, and four computers.

Favorite Books as a Child

When I was a child, I did not read children's books. I grew up in a violent neighborhood, and the children's books of my growing up years did not speak to my reality. I read tons of comic books, as well as murder magazines and mysteries. I also read numerous biographies, as well as books about native American history.

together in their focus on African American experiences. Hamilton says that she regards herself as a storyteller and believes that people tell stories in order to "keep their cultural heritage safe, to save the very language in which heritage is made symbolic through story" (Hamilton, 1995):

> I see my books and the language I use in them as empowering me to give utterance to my dreams and wishes and those of other African

Americans like myself. I see the imaginative use of language and ideas as a way to illuminate a human condition, lest we forget where we came from. All of us came from somewhere else.

My work, as a novelist, a biographer, and a creator and compiler of stories, has been to portray the essence of a people who are a parallel culture community in America. (p. 440)

Among Hamilton's many awards are the Newbery Medal for *M. C. Higgins, the Great* (1974); the Newbery Honor Book awards for *The Planet of Junior Brown* (1971), *Sweet Whispers, Brother Rush* (1982), and *In the Beginning: Creation Stories from Around the World* (1988); Coretta Scott King awards for *The People Could Fly: American Black Folktales* (1985), *Anthony Burns: The Defeat and Triumph of a Fugitive Slave* (1988), and *Her Stories* (1995); and the 1992 Hans Christian Andersen award, presented by the International Board on Books for Young People for the body of her work and the influence it has had on young readers around the world. Her books are widely translated.

Walter Dean Myers

Walter Dean Myers's writing career was launched in 1968 when he won the Council on Interracial Books for Children's picture book competition. A multi-

talented writer, Myers began his writing career with picture books and informational books. However, he is best known for his notable contribution to young adult literature reflecting the lives of contemporary African Americans. Many of his novels draw on his childhood experiences growing up in New York City's Harlem. *Fast Sam, Cool Clyde, and Stuff* (1975) and *Scorpions* (1988) are both stories of gang rivalry in an urban setting. *The Mouse Rap* (1990), tells the story of an urban youth called Mouse, who opens each chapter with rap verse.

Myers's recent publications reveal a shift in his creative focus. He won the 1991 Coretta Scott King Award for the informational book *Now Is Your Time! The African American Struggle for Freedom* (1990), and the biography *Malcolm X: By Any Means Necessary* (1993) was a 1993 Honor Book. For two volumes of poetry, *Brown Angels: An Album of Pictures and Verse* (1993) and *Glorious Angels* (1995), he collected old photographs and imagined the lives behind them. *The Glory Field* (1994) is historical fiction that traces 250 years of a family's history. *Shadow of the Red Moon* (1995) is a futuristic fantasy.

Myers's awards are numerous and varied. He has won the Coretta Scott King Award five times: for *The Young Landlords* (1979), for *Motown and Didi: A Love Story* (1984), for *Fallen Angels* (1988), for *Now Is Your Time! The African American Struggle for Freedom* (1990), and for *Slam!* (1996). *Scorpions* (1988) and *Somewhere in the Darkness* (1992) were Newbery Honor Books. In 1992, Walter Dean Myers was named the winner of the Margaret A. Edwards Award for Outstanding Contribution to Literature for Young Adults.

Allen Say

Born and raised in Japan, Allen Say emigrated to the United States when he was sixteen and is now a U.S. citizen. Say's books often have themes showing his love of both countries. His talent and interest in drawing led him, by age twelve,

Illustration 4.5
Through poetry, Walter Dean Myers imagines the lives of the children whose photographs he has collected. (*Brown Angels: An Album of Pictures and Verse* by Walter Dean Myers. Jacket copyright © 1993 by HarperCollins Publishers. Used by permission of HarperCollins Publishers.)

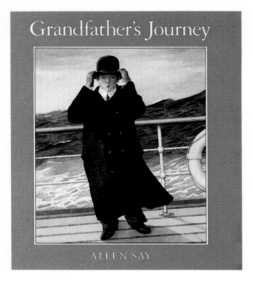

Illustration 4.6
Grandfather's Journey is an auto-biographical account that reflects the emotions of many immigrants whose strong love of "home" is aroused by two very different countries. (*Grandfather's Journey* by Allen Say. Copyright © 1993 by Allen Say. Used by permission of Houghton Mifflin Company. All rights reserved.)

to be apprenticed to a renowned cartoonist. In his autobiography, *The Ink-Keeper's Apprentice* (1979), Say recounts his early life and the start of his career as an artist.

A study of the pictures in Say's books makes it clear that the illustrator is from Japan, since most depict Japanese or Japanese American settings. His pictures are extremely effective in capturing the overall ambience of his settings and are painstakingly accurate in detail. For example, whereas the scissors used by the woman sewing in *The Boy of the Three-Year Nap* (Snyder, 1988) are Japanese sewing scissors, the scissors used by the mother in *Tree of Cranes* (1991) are the kind used in Japan for flower arranging and gardening. Although such details will not be noticeable to all, his attention to them confirms the overall impression of authenticity in Say's work.

Allen Say has received wide recognition for his work. *The Boy of the Three-Year Nap* was a 1989 Caldecott Honor Book. Say won the 1994 Caldecott Medal for *Grandfather's Journey* (1993). His recent books, including *Grandfather's Journey*, are autobiographical.

Gary Soto

It was not until 1990 that Gary Soto, author of books and poetry for adults, published his first juvenile work, *Baseball in April and Other Stories*. Since then, he has published other widely acclaimed collections of short stories and poetry, novels, and picture books. The details of Soto's writing reflect his Mexican American ancestry, as he recounts various experiences growing up in the industrial part of Fresno, California. Soto's childhood memories are revealed in his poems in *Neighborhood Odes* (1992). In "Ode to a Sprinkler," Soto reminisces about the sprinkler that provided many hours of water play in the summer. He recalls his love of competition and playground games, as well as hours of play with the discarded things in his neighborhood.

In *Taking Sides* (1991), Lincoln Mendoza moves from the barrio of his childhood to a suburban neighborhood where being Latino sets him apart from his basketball teammates. Readers can follow Lincoln's continuing search for his cultural identity as he goes abroad as a foreign exchange student in *Pacific Crossing* (1992). Soto has published a number of picture books, including *Too Many Tamales* (1993) and *Chato's Kitchen* (1995). *Too Many Tamales* tells of a little girl who secretly tries on her mother's ring while making tamales, then must talk her cousins into eating a mound of tamales in order to try and find the lost ring.

In addition to receiving other awards, Soto's *Baseball in April* was recognized as an honor book in the first year of the Pura Belpré Children's Book Award. This biannual award is sponsored jointly by Reforma (a national association to promote library services to Spanish speakers) and the American Library Association's Association of Library Services to Children.

John Steptoe

During his high school years, John Steptoe recognized a need for children's books containing authentic dialogue that black children could relate to, so he decided to write them himself. The publication of *Stevie*, in 1969, received much attention. To tell this story of a little boy who initially resents having to share his mother and his possessions with a younger boy who eventually becomes like a little brother, the nineteen-year-old author and illustrator used black dialect and depicted an urban setting. The numerous awards bestowed on this book were just precursors to the many others Steptoe would earn in his short life.

His two children influenced some of his work; they are featured in *Daddy Is a Monster . . . Sometimes* (1980), in which two boys discuss their father and realize that he's not mean all the time. Steptoe also illustrated the work of others, such as Arnold Adoff's *All the Colors of the Race* (1982).

Steptoe's last few books were particularly noteworthy. *The Story of Jumping Mouse: A Native American Legend* (1984) was a 1985 Caldecott Honor Book. Generosity is the virtue that is rewarded in this story, as Jumping Mouse sets off to see the far-off land. *Mufaro's Beautiful Daughters: An African Tale* (1987) both earned the Coretta Scott King Award for illustration and was named a Caldecott Honor Book. In this Cinderella-themed story, Mufaro has two beautiful daughters with very different personalities. Both vie to become the wife of the king, but it is the good-natured daughter who is rewarded for her kindness toward others. John Steptoe's final book, *Baby Says* (1988), was one of the first board books for babies that depicted an African American baby. Steptoe died in 1989 at the age of 38.

Mildred Taylor

Mildred Taylor's books allow readers to get a glimpse into the tragic history of injustice and violence against African Americans. Taylor relies on experiences she had growing up to provide the events in her books. Born in Mississippi, and raised in Ohio, she experienced many of the circumstances of the Logan family featured in her books. Taylor brings to life the injustices endured by African Americans living in the strictly segregated society of the South. Many members of the Logan family are based on her own family members, and the feelings of the main character, Cassie, resemble the author's.

As a child, Taylor realized that her people's stories were not found in the textbooks she encountered. Having had the good fortune to come from a family of storytellers, Taylor had heard many stories of African Americans and their heritage, and she, in turn, put these stories on paper. Taylor wrote *Song of the Trees* (1975) in four days, for a contest sponsored by the Council on Interracial Books for Children. This story won the contest in the African American category and introduced the Logan family.

Mildred Taylor's books have won many awards. *Roll of Thunder, Hear My Cry* (1976), her second book, won the 1977 Newbery Medal. The Logan family's story was continued in *Let the Circle Be Unbroken* (1981), the winner of the 1982 Coretta Scott King Award. Several other books about the Logan family followed: *The Friendship* (1987), *The Gold Cadillac* (1987), *The Road to Memphis* (1990), *Mississippi Bridge* (1990), and *The Well* (1995). Both *The Friendship* and *The Road to Memphis* won the Coretta Scott King Award.

Yoshiko Uchida

Yoshiko Uchida is best known for her historical novels, which give middle-grade readers a look into Japanese American heritage. Two of her books in particular are based on her own experiences during her teen and young adult years in U.S. internment camps for Japanese Americans in World War II. Uchida spent five months living in a horse stall at Tanforan Racetracks in California until her family was moved to Topaz, in the desert of Utah. *Journey to Topaz: A Story of the Japanese-American Evacuation* (1971) and its sequel, *Journey Home* (1978), tell the story of eleven-year-old Yuki Sakane and her family during the internment and the difficult years of readjustment that followed. It was Uchida's hope that sharing the pain of the experiences would prevent them from being repeated. Three novels, *A Jar of Dreams* (1981), *The Best Bad Thing* (1983), and *The Happiest Ending* (1985), depict eleven-year-old Rinko's life during the Depression years of the 1930s. All of the novels address the sensitive issue of struggling with one's heritage amidst prejudice. For many young readers, Uchida's books are an introduction to issues faced by Japanese Americans, seen through the eyes of a main character close to their own age.

Uchida also compiled and retold a number of Japanese folktales. Several of her short stories were published posthumously as picture books. *The Bracelet* (1993) tells of a Japanese American girl who receives a bracelet from a non-Japanese friend as she leaves for internment in a horse stall at Tanforan Racetracks.

Mildred Pitts Walter

Mildred Pitts Walter was an elementary school teacher in Los Angeles for nearly twenty years. As an activist during the years of the civil rights movement, Walter sought to improve the future for African Americans. During the 1960s, lamenting the scarcity of African Americans in books for children, a publisher encouraged her to fill that void. With the 1971 publication of two picture books about an African American girl in an urban setting, Walter began her career as a writer of books for children. But by then the sociopolitical climate had changed, and it was not easy to get books about African American experiences published. More than a decade later, however, the climate changed again; Walter's writing had developed, and her publishing career resumed. In 1980, she published *Ty's One-Man Band*, a story of a boy who meets a mysterious man who can make music with ordinary household things—a washboard, a wooden spoon, a tin pail, and a comb.

Family, nuclear and extended, and community are important to Walter's personal life and work. Although her childhood in rural Louisiana was filled with the hardships of poverty and racial prejudice, her family passed on the work ethic and gave her support as she developed her sense of self. Later, Walter realized that the community that had supported her in her early years was based on the traditions of the African village, her heritage. Those years were critical in establishing Walter's understanding of racial tensions in social settings as well as the strength-building bonds of family life, two themes commonly found in her writing. In *Justin and the Best Biscuits in the World* (1986), ten-year-old Justin, whose father died earlier, finds himself in search of a male role model. During a visit to his grandfather's ranch, Justin learns that cowboys must become self-sufficient by learning to do the jobs that Justin earlier deemed "women's work." This book won the 1987 Coretta Scott King Award.

In addition, Mildred Pitts Walter has written an original folktale, *Brother to the Wind* (1985), and an informational book taking a historical look at voting rights in Mississippi, *Mississippi Challenge* (1992). Other books such as *My Mama Needs Me* (1983), *Mariah Keeps Cool* (1990), and *Mariah Loves Rock* (1989) focus on contemporary African American family life.

Laurence Yep

Laurence Yep grew up in a black neighborhood, felt like an outsider at his school in Chinatown because he didn't speak Chinese, and attended a high school with mostly white students. He identifies writing as the activity that helped him clarify his own cultural identity. Six years of researching Chinese American history led to the writing of *Dragonwings* (1975), one of his most highly acclaimed books. Yep found extensive factual documentation of the work experiences of the Chinese men who immigrated to the United States during the nineteenth century, yet it required much imagination to portray the human emotions arising from the daily life experiences and the hardships these men suffered. *Dragonwings* was named a Newbery Honor Book, in addition to receiving numerous other prestigious awards. The inspiration for this story began when Yep read about a Chinese American, Fung Joe Guey, who built and flew "dragonwings" at about the same time the Wright brothers made their first flights. Another work of historical fiction reflecting the experiences of early Chinese immigrants is Yep's Newbery Honor Book *Dragon's Gate* (1993). This book recounts the involvement of the Chinese in building the transcontinental railroad.

Yep has written science fiction, fantasy, historical fiction, realistic fiction, and an autobiography and has retold folktales. He has edited Asian American short stories and poetry and published picture books and a number of shorter, realistic stories that reflect contemporary experiences of young Chinese Americans. In *Later, Gator* (1995), two brothers who usually do not get along at all collaborate on a scheme to hide a pet alligator.

CRITERIA FOR EVALUATING AND SELECTING MULTICULTURAL LITERATURE

With the growth in the number of multicultural books, it is important to select those of quality. Naturally, when judging the quality of multicultural books, a teacher should apply the criteria for evaluating the various genres of children's literature that are discussed throughout this text. However, in addition, there are specific questions to consider regarding multicultural books:

- Do the author and illustrator present insider perspectives?
- Is the culture portrayed multidimensionally?
- Are cultural details naturally integrated?
- Are details accurate and interpretation current?
- Is language used authentically?
- Is the collection balanced?

Do the Author and Illustrator Present Insider Perspectives?

The author should maintain an insider's mind-set and point of view when writing about a cultural group in order to portray it authentically. Voices such as Patricia Polacco's and Pat Mora's are inside voices because these authors write of experiences based on their own heritage. Polacco's *The Keeping Quilt* (1988) and Mora's *A Birthday Basket for Tia* (1992) both tell of the authors' personal lives. However, as discussed earlier in this chapter, the crucial issue is not heritage by fact of birth, but whether the author thinks as a member of the group or as an outsider looking in. Careful research and experience living within the culture contribute to Demi's inside voice in a book such as *Liang and the Magic Paintbrush* (1980).

Illustrations should be accurate, true to the time period portrayed, and culturally authentic. They must not stereotype, homogenize, or ridicule any cultural group. Racial groups should be depicted with a variety of physical features that are not overemphasized. Illustrations play a major role in transmitting cultural images, especially in picture books. Often, a book's cover illustration sends an immediate message about the book's perspective.

Is the Culture Portrayed Multidimensionally?

Cultural groups should be presented multidimensionally in order to help readers realize the depth and breadth of experiences within cultures. For example, *El Chino* (Say, 1990), a biography of Billy Wong, tells the story of a son of Chinese immigrants who became a bullfighter despite what was expected of him by others. To pursue his dream, he had to fight those expectations. Others said, "Who's ever heard of a Chinese athlete?" and "Only the Spaniards can become true matadors." But he remembered what his father said: "In America, you can be anything you want to be." Presenting a culture's multidimensionality means presenting the members of that culture in a range of ways.

Cultural groups should not be presented through images that could lead to stereotyping. There is no particular experience that is so universal as to be defined as "The _____ Experience." Rather, multiple dimensions of all cultures should be presented objectively, without bias. Roles of cultural members should also be varied, as in *Justin and the Best Biscuits in the World* (Walter, 1986), in which the African American grandfather, a rancher, serves as an important role model for his grandson.

Are Cultural Details Naturally Integrated?

The flow of the story should be maintained while the cultural details necessary to make it come alive are related. These details should be presented in context so that cumbersome explanations are not necessary. If longer explanations are needed, footnotes or endnotes can serve to clarify. Laurence Yep's *Dragon's Gate* (1993) is filled with cultural details. The hardships endured, the power relationships and the actions they lead to, the dialogues among the Chinese workers, and the dialogues between the Chinese workers and their white bosses are all described with a completeness that gives readers insight into the lives of the men who left their families behind in hopes of getting rich in a foreign land. These details are necessary for readers to develop deepened understanding and empathy.

Are Details Accurate and Interpretation Current?

Details must be accurate and true to the situation in which they are presented. Factual errors, omissions, and changes are sometimes indicative of sloppy research and presentation. Other times, these problems may actually reflect an attempt on the author's part to meet the expectations of a mainstream readership with preconceived notions of cultures. Series books that focus on children in various countries are sometimes guilty of such intentional errors. One book featuring a child in the Netherlands included all the preconceived images that mainstream readers might expect to find: a blond girl wakes up, puts on her wooden shoes, and passes a windmill and a field of tulips on her way to school!

There are also series books that are written according to a formula, such as books about other countries in which authors "fill in the blanks" of standardized formats. In many cases, these authors have no first-hand experience with the country they write about.

Currency of interpretation can sometimes be evaluated by considering recency of copyright and thoroughness of revision. Books that claim to cite "current" statistics should be carefully analyzed to determine whether the statistic reported is still appropriate, years after the book is published. Sometimes, the interpretation of factual information is more influential than the facts themselves. The author's understanding of the culture determines his or her choice of words, which in turn influences the readers' perceptions. For example, reference to a Japanese father as "honorable father" is a literal translation of the word *otoosan*. The "o" at the beginning of the word for father denotes the honoring of the person addressed. However, constantly referring to each adult as "honorable" may lead readers to an exaggerated, stereotypical view that is not in keeping with the literal translation of the word.

Is Language Used Authentically?

The language and dialect spoken by characters should authentically portray the kinds of interactions typical of those characters, and terminology that refers to aspects of culture should be acceptable by contemporary standards. For example, Gary Soto writes from the perspective of a Mexican American who grew up in California. Readers with a background similar to his sense a true voice of their experiences. In his book *Pacific Crossing* (1992), Soto portrays two teenage Mexican American boys as foreign exchange students in Japan. Soto uses terminology and phrases that Mexican Americans might use to communicate with each another. He also follows the Japanese language's very strict rules of verbal exchange, which take into consideration the gender, the age, and the familiarity of the speakers. Katherine Paterson's translations of Japanese folktales such as Momoko Ishii's *The Tongue-Cut Sparrow* (1987) and Sumiko Yagawa's *The Crane Wife* (1981) retain onomatopoeic words that echo the sounds of the Japanese language within the storytelling format.

Is the Collection Balanced?

A special consideration is the need to present children with a balanced collection of multicultural books. The term "collection" refers to the books available in a school, classroom, or public library, and also to the books selected to serve as teaching units within a classroom. Budget constraints, space limitations, and the need to present readers with the best possible choices make careful decisions regarding book collections a necessity. Readers need to be able to find recommended books readily—not buried under an avalanche of mediocre books. It is generally accepted that purchasing multiple copies of excellent books is better than including mediocre books simply to increase the size of the collection. Because a great number of quality multicultural books are available today, there is no need to include books simply to fulfill a quota.

To compile a balanced multicultural collection, a teacher or librarian should assess needs and match available quality books with those identified needs. In assessing needs, consideration should be given to (1) readers' preferences, (2) existing multicultural books in the collection, (3) curricular needs, (4) the availability of quality multicultural books, and (5) provision of a strong selection across genres. In addition, the compiler should ensure that adequate numbers of books are available for recreational reading, for teacher read-alouds, and for placement in the classroom library.

Consider Readers' Preferences. Both teachers and librarians need to acquire an understanding of the general background knowledge and the preferences of the readers for whom the particular collection is being developed, including the range of materials they enjoy and the types of books they choose. Often, children will be interested in reading books about their own cultural group, but that is not always the case. Some readers will voluntarily read books about other cultural groups; others may need to be introduced to and encouraged to select such books.

Survey Multicultural Books Already in the Collection. Multicultural books already in the collection form the core of the collection and help determine what is needed. Overselecting or underselecting certain types of books can be avoided by conducting a careful inventory of existing books in the collection. Is there an overabundance of folktales from various cultures? Are there enough contemporary stories about people of diversity? Are there books that show multiple perspectives? Familiarity with the existing collection also allows a teacher or librarian to weed out and discard books that are not culturally appropriate.

Assess Curricular Needs. It is important to assess curricular needs to determine what is needed to supplement units of study. Because of the current emphasis on literature-based curriculum, more and more quality books are being used in all curricular areas. As teachers and librarians work together to obtain books that fit the needs of the curriculum, they should attempt to include books that extend beyond the basic information and enhance multicultural understanding.

Determine Availability of Quality Multicultural Books. Determine the availability of quality multicultural books because no matter what the needs are, only high-quality books should be considered. Obtaining lower-quality books simply to fill a shelf is not recommended.

Provide a Strong Selection across Genres. Another goal in establishing a balanced collection of multicultural books is to provide a variety of different genres. For example, when creating a collection of books about Mexico, the teacher or librarian should make a point to include folklore, history, informational books, picture books, historical fiction, biography, poetry, and modern realistic fiction. There should be books set in Mexico as well as books about Mexican Americans. The books must represent a broad range of experiences and voices if readers are to understand the diverse nature of Mexico and its people.

INTERNATIONAL LITERATURE DEFINED

Another category of literature that can provide readers with diverse perspectives is international literature. Traditionally, the term "international literature" applied to books originally written and published outside the United States. If these books were originally written in a language other than English, they were translated for the U.S. audience. In recent years, an increasing number of books set entirely in foreign countries have been written and published in the United States. Both types of international books are discussed here.

Literature That Originates Outside of the United States

The first category of international literature is books written and published in countries outside the United States and translated into English if originally written in another language. Mem Fox's *Possum Magic* (1987) is an English-language book originally published in Australia. In this fantasy of a possum made invisible by magic, the possum's grandmother tries to remember how to make him visible once again. Along the way, readers hear the names of the Australian

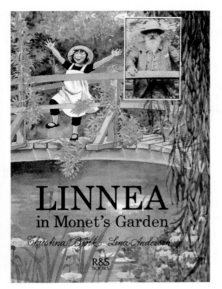

Illustration 4.7
Linnea in Monet's Garden is an example of a wonderful book originally published in a foreign country and now enjoyed by children around the world after being translated into English and other languages. (*Linnea in Monet's Garden* by Christina Bjork. Jacket design copyright © 1985 by Lena Anderson. Used by permission of Farrar, Straus & Giroux.)

cities to which Hush and Grandmother journey and the various Australian foods they eat at each stop. Christina Bjork's series about Linnea is another example of quality international literature. *Linnea in Monet's Garden* (1987) was originally written in Swedish and then was translated into English and made available to the U.S. audience. Importing books from abroad makes the works of the best authors and illustrators in the world available to children in the United States.

Literature about Other Countries, Written and Published in the United States

The second category of international literature is books set in a country other than the United States but written and published in the United States. These books are set in a "root country," or a country from which some American children's ancestors originally came. Although most children will not have lived long, if ever, in the country of their family's origin, they may feel a connection to it. Beverley Naidoo's *Journey to Jo'burg: A South African Story* (1986) tells of how Naledi travels to Jo'burg to deliver the news of her baby sister's near-death from an illness to her mother, who works and lives in the home of white people. The circumstances described in the story accurately reflect a recent period in South African history that is likely somewhat removed in immediacy from the lives of American children of South African ancestry.

The primary purpose for all international books is the same: to tell a compelling story. However, because international books that originate in the country portrayed and international books that are written and published in the United States have different intended audiences, they contribute to children's understanding of world cultures in different ways. Books originating in a foreign country allow U.S. readers to experience native perceptions of that country. International books written in the United States include information that may enlighten nonnative readers about a foreign country.

EVALUATING QUALITY IN INTERNATIONAL LITERATURE

With the exception of authenticity, the evaluation and selection issues previously discussed in connection with multicultural literature are also important for international literature originating outside the United States. Although many countries publish material that is about cultures outside their own, the books that get exported to other countries tend to be about native experiences. When one's own country is the setting, cultural authenticity is expected, as both author and illustrator have an inside perspective. Two crucial issues specific to international literature are the intended audience and the quality of the translation.

Intended Audience

An international book is originally written from the perspective of an author within the country, with readers in that country as the intended audience. Only later is the book taken abroad to other countries. When a book travels away from its intended audience, sometimes the new audience needs support in order to understand it. Teachers should consider these questions: Is the book geared specifically toward readers in the book's country of origin, or does it make the transition to a broader audience outside of that country? Who will be able to empathize and identify with the story? Books written in the United States and intended for American children tend to include explanations of things that readers native to the country portrayed take for granted. On the other hand, books originally written for readers in another country often assume understandings that only the original intended audience would have. Sometimes, misinterpretations may occur when details are not understood; other times, inability to pick up details doesn't detract from the reader's understanding of the story as a whole.

As an example, let's examine Akiko Hayashi's illustrations of the series of books about Anna. The pictures are laden with cultural details—mailboxes attached on the inside of the front door, slippers in the entry way, artificial flowers on the street light, a place where children wash their hands at the park. Even the way Anna steps on the back of her shoes shows she is rushing as she tries to discover the identity of her new friend in *Anna's Secret Friend* (Tsutsui, 1987). Japanese children would pick up these details because they are very natural to their understanding of home and community. American children may not take particular note of these details or may find them interesting but not different enough to interfere with an understanding of the story.

Sometimes, details in the original edition of a book, which would be innately understood by the original audience, are explained when the book is prepared in an international edition. Uri Orlev's Batchelder Award book *The Lady with the Hat* (1995) has two characters stopping for a meal while on a trip in a remote area of Palestine. Foods such as hummus, tahini, shashlik, kebab, baklava, and Turkish coffee are described for readers unfamiliar with them—for example, ". . . small cakes filled with pistachio nuts and honey that were called baklava."

Translation

An issue of critical concern with international books is translation. When a book was originally published in a language other than English, the translator who makes it available to English-language readers plays an important role in how the material is received by the new audience. The translator is as important as the author and illustrator in presenting the story. A skilled translator does not merely present the author's words in another language, but instead interprets the words, selecting ways to evoke images and emotions that reflect the author's original intent. The translator must consider several things:

- Creating a flow in the translated language, despite differences in the sentence structures of the two languages

- Balancing the amount of "foreign" information in order to maintain readability and reader attention yet retain the unique details that make the work authentic

- Explaining foreign situations unknown to readers while maintaining the pace of the original text

Even when a book is from another English-language country, some differences in language use are noticeable to American readers. Should these differences be changed? When comprehension may suffer, the answer is yes. But maintaining as much of the original language as possible is part of maintaining the authenticity of the book. In Mem Fox's book *Shoes from Grandpa* (1990), originally published in Australia, the family was enjoying a "barbie." A U.S. audience, unexposed to this name for a barbecue, might imagine the doll known as Barbie. The word was changed in this case. Yet, in another of Mem Fox's books, *Possum Magic* (1987), references to Australian foods such as "mornay, vegemite and pavlova" were

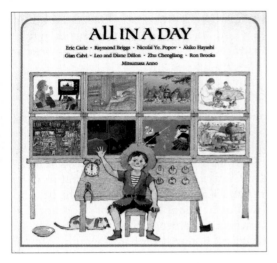

Illustration 4.8
Mitsumasa Anno created *All in a Day* because he believes that world understanding begins with children imagining the lives of other children around the world. (*All in a Day* by Mitsumasa Anno. Copyright © 1986 by Kuso-Kubo, Raymond Briggs, Ron Brooks, Gian Calvi, Eric Carle, Leo & Diane Dillon, Akiko Hayashi, Nicolai Ye. Popov & Zhu Chengliang. Used by permission of Philomel Books.)

maintained in the U.S. version. These words, although unknown to most American children, do not interfere with their understanding of the story. With the words left in, the story remains true to the original context of the Australian culture. A benefit of this approach is that U.S. children are introduced to vocabulary that expands their knowledge of another country.

It does require extra effort to make international books accessible to American audiences. But the benefits gained from including international books in children's repertoire make the extra effort worthwhile. One notable example of an international book is Mitsumasa Anno's ***All in a Day*** (1986). A young child is on a deserted island, somewhere near the international date line. Each double-page spread shows this child in the center section, with text to one side. Across the top and the bottom of the spread are depictions of what New Year's Day might be like for children in eight different countries; each picture is by an illustrator from that country. Each time the reader turns a page, three hours have passed. In the preface to the book, Anno asks readers to consider the fact that while some children sleep, others play, and while some swim, others build snowmen. He points out that differences exist around the world in homes, clothes, languages, and so on, but he also notes that there are some things that remain the same around the world, such as facial expressions, the sounds of laughing or crying, and the moon and the sun in the sky. Anno and his team of illustrators offer a note of optimism. Their hope—and ours as well—is that by the time the children of today grow up, the world will have become a better place. This book exemplifies a sense of world community from a child's point of view. Although the book was originally published in Japanese, the composition of the illustration team and the theme make this book truly international.

AWARDS FOR MULTICULTURAL AND INTERNATIONAL LITERATURE

Multicultural books qualify for all of the general awards that are given to children's literature, such as the Caldecott Medal and the Newbery Medal. Several multicultural books have been recipients of such awards. For example, Ed Young was presented the Caldecott Medal for ***Lon Po Po: A Red-Riding Hood Story from China*** (1989). However, some awards are designated specifically for multicultural and international literature. Some are given for a single book, and others for the author's or illustrator's entire body of work. The awards are intended to bring attention to various aspects of multicultural book publishing. The most prestigious of these awards are the Coretta Scott King Award, the Hans Christian Andersen Award, and the Mildred Batchelder Award. In addition, awards are sometimes given to previously unpublished authors and illustrators to encourage the writing and illustrating of

Illustration 4.9
Children can share in other countries' heritages by reading folktales from those cultures, such as *Lon Po Po*, the Chinese "Little Red Riding Hood." (*Lon Po Po* by Ed Young. Copyright © 1989 by Ed Young. Used by permission of Philomel Books and McIntosh and Otis, Inc.)

books on multicultural subjects. Sometimes, these awards have played important roles in launching the careers of authors and illustrators. Awards provide public recognition for a book, author, or illustrator and serve as selection and evaluation tools.

The Coretta Scott King Award

At an American Library Association conference in 1969, after lamenting the fact that a "minority" author or illustrator had never been awarded the Newbery or Caldecott Medal, school librarians Mabel McKissick and Glyndon Greer were encouraged by publisher John Carroll to launch a new award highlighting the accomplishments of African American authors and illustrators. The award was named in honor of Coretta Scott King to "commemorate the life and work of Martin Luther King, Jr." as well as to honor his wife for "courage and determination in continuing to work for peace and brotherhood" (Smith, 1994). Author Lillie Patterson was the first recipient, honored for her biography **Martin Luther King, Jr., Man of Peace** (1969). The illustrator award began in 1974, and George Ford was the first recipient for his illustrations in Sharon Bell Mathis's biography **Ray Charles** (1974).

Illustration 4.10
The story of *Tar Beach* (both a winner of the Coretta Scott King Award and a Caldecott Honor Book in 1992) originally appeared in the form of a "story quilt," with the text surrounding a central picture on a quilt. (*Tar Beach (Woman on a Beach Series #1)*, 1988 by Faith Ringgold. The Solomon R. Guggenheim Museum, New York, Gift, Mr. and Mrs. Gus and Judith Leiber. Photograph by David Heald © The Solomon R. Guggenheim Foundation, New York.)

The Coretta Scott King Award has been presented at the annual meeting of the American Library Association since 1972 and has been recognized as an official ALA award since 1982. Selection criteria for the award have evolved with the increase in the number of books from which to choose. At the beginning, any book reflecting some aspect of the black experience or embracing concepts of brotherhood was considered. In recent years, however, the criteria have become more stringent and now specify that "recipients are African American authors and illustrators whose distinguished books promote an understanding and appreciation of the culture and contribution of all people to the realization of the 'American dream.'" Refer to Appendix A for a list of past winners and honor books.

Since 1993, the Genesis Award certificate of recognition has been given to African American authors and illustrators who show significant promise in their work. Basic criteria for this award are the same as for the Coretta Scott King Award, but winners can have no more than three published works.

The Hans Christian Andersen Award

The International Board on Books for Young People (IBBY) established the Hans Christian Andersen Award in 1956. The purpose of this international award is to honor an author who has made a significant contribution to children's literature; an award for illustrators has been offered since 1966. The entire body of work by an author or an illustrator is considered, and national IBBY chapters nominate an author and an illustrator from their country. This award is given every two years at the IBBY World Congress, which is held in various locations throughout the world. Past U.S. winners include author Meindert DeJong in 1962, illustrator Maurice Sendak in 1970, author Scott O'Dell in 1972, author Paula Fox in 1978, and author Virginia Hamilton in 1992. Some winners from other countries have books published in the United States, among them Astrid Lindgren from Sweden, Svend Otto S. from Denmark, Suekichi Akaba and Mitsumasa Anno from Japan, Lygia Bojunga Nunes from Brazil, Patricia

Wrightson and Robert Ingpen from Australia, and Lisbeth Zwerger from Austria. A complete list of past winners can be found in Appendix A.

The Mildred Batchelder Award

The Mildred Batchelder Award was established in 1966 by the American Library Association's Association of Library Services to Children (ASLC) to promote international exchange of books for young people; it has been given to a U.S. publisher annually since 1968. The award is named in honor of a former executive director of the ASLC. Books originally published in a foreign language in a foreign country and translated and published in the United States in the year preceding the award are considered. The citation is given to publishers to recognize their commitment to bringing books from abroad and making them available to young people in this country. With the exception of a few picture books, including **Hiroshima No Pika** (Maruki, 1982) and **Rose Blanche** (Innocenti and Gallaz, 1986), most books are novels for older children. A complete list of past winners can be found in Appendix A.

Other International Book Awards

Many countries have book awards equivalent to the Caldecott and Newbery Medals. Great Britain has the Kate Greenaway Medal and the Carnegie Medal. Canada has the Amelia Frances Howard-Gibbon Medal and the Canadian Children's Book of the Year award. Australia has the Picture Book of the Year award and the Australian Children's Book of the Year for Young Readers award. The major book awards given by other English-language countries are included in Appendix A.

More multicultural books are being published today than in any previous decade, and an increasing number of international books are continuing to find their way onto bookstore and library shelves. Thus, teachers and parents have the opportunity and the responsibility to select high-quality multicultural and international books. In her book *Against Borders*, Hazel Rochman (1993) suggests that teachers and parents look for books that fight against the idea of borders that separate people and seek out books that help readers tear down those borders by beginning to understand people around the world.

LITERATURE PORTRAYING OTHER DIVERSE PERSPECTIVES

Literature plays a vital role in providing vicarious experience in interacting with others—whether those others are like ourselves or very different. In some cases, literature confirms a reader's first-hand experiences in interacting with people of differing perspectives; in other cases, literature substitutes for experiences the reader may not have had first-hand.

Literature Portraying Gender Equity and Gender Roles

Father leaves for the office carrying a briefcase and wearing a top coat and hat. Mother stays home and does housework, wearing a dress. Boys have adventures and are brave. Girls need protection and are passive. Images such as these abounded in children's books of the past and can still be found in some books today. The danger is that children who experience only books with these messages will come away with the idea that these images represent the norm of gender roles. Well-written gender-sensitive literature fights stereotypes by depicting the diversity and multidimensionality of men and women, girls and boys.

The following criteria should be used to evaluate the content of messages that are sent to readers regarding gender issues: Occupations should be gender-free, achievements should be judged without gender bias, both parents should share family responsibilities, and gender stereotyping based on physical description and behaviors should be avoided (Rudman, 1995). It is important to evaluate character portrayal, interactions among characters, and societal expectations of character roles. Sexist language is a sign of the writer's perspective on gender roles and therefore should be avoided at all times.

Gender Equity. Gender equity has different facets A book reflecting gender equity shows equal opportunities for both genders in the workplace and depicts multiple and diverse personal roles for individuals of both genders. Children begin receiving messages about their gender's places and roles in society from the time they are infants. These messages come from family, friends, books, media, and society in general. What are the messages found in books?

Let's examine a message from a book published in 1957. *Dear Garbage Man* (Zion, 1957) is still in print and available to children through book club order forms distributed in schools. In it, Stan the garbage man tries to "recycle" people's unwanted trash by redistributing it to others. The accompanying text reads: "After everyone had helped themselves, fathers went to work and mothers went back to the dishes." The next day, the new owners realize that these items are indeed trash and return them to the garbage man. At first, he is disappointed, but then a "big smile brighten[s] his face" as he says, "All this stuff will fill in lots and lots of swamps!" The driver responds, "Stan, you're a real garbage man now!" This books presents several gender stereotypes: Jobs involving physical labor are reserved for men; all garbage collectors are men; men go to work and women do dishes. And, of course, the ecological message of this book is troubling. Because books often reflect societal values and prejudices that prevail at the time of writing, some older books contain themes and messages that are not considered appropriate for children today.

Some books do a good job of portraying nontraditional gender roles in believable ways that are natural to the story. For example, *The King's Equal* (Paterson, 1992) depicts a prince who is searching for a princess who is "his equal," only to find that he must prove to be "her equal." Rachel Isadora's *Max* (1976) is about a boy who finds that taking dance class with his sister is a great way to warm up for his baseball games on Saturdays. Readers find a female not only having an adventure but *leading* many outrageous adventures when they read about Ms. Frizzle, a teacher who takes her class on field trips on the Magic School Bus.

It is a problem, though, when books try too hard—when they depict the opposites of the stereotyped gender roles in hard-to-believe ways or are didactic in presentation. *Piggybook* (Browne, 1986) addresses the problem of women who are enslaved to their families. The front cover shows the mother carrying her husband and two sons "piggyback." As the story unfolds, the illustrations show the males of the family (and their surroundings) turning more and more pig-like until finally the mother leaves them with a note stating, "You are pigs." When

Illustration 4.11
Max defies the stereotype that "boys don't dance" when he finds that dance lessons are a good warm-up to his afternoon baseball games. (*Max* by Rachel Isadora. Copyright © 1976 Rachel Isadora. Used by permission of Simon & Schuster.)

Illustration 4.12

Ms. Frizzle is an example of a woman who defies the stereotype of the passive female as she leads her students on magnificently adventuresome field trips in *The Magic School Bus* series. (*The Magic School Bus at the Waterworks* by Joanna Cole. Illustration © 1986 by Bruce Degen. Used by permission of Scholastic Inc. *The Magic School Bus* is a registered trademark of Scholastic Inc.)

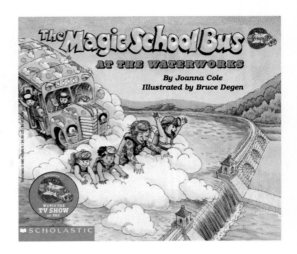

depicted washing dishes, vacuuming carpets, making beds, ironing, cooking, and washing clothes, in shadowy pictures without her face showing—now fixes the car! The story is humorous in many ways. But such a dramatic change in roles—especially one that requires the sudden acquisition of specific knowledge—is hardly believable and perhaps trivializes the importance of representing equal gender opportunities and roles.

Homosexuality and Alternative Family Structures. The school curriculum at the primary level is most often developed around the concept of a "nuclear" family composed of a mother, father, and their children. However, over the past decades, schools have become increasingly populated with children whose home life does not fit that model. Although people typically think of a nontraditional family as a single-parent family or one in which grandparents raise the children, many "variant" households are headed by lesbian or gay parents. When the New York State Board of Education required that first-grade curricula include the reading of **Daddy's Roommate** (Willhoite, 1990), much controversy surrounded the issue of alternative lifestyles. This picture book depicts a divorced father who lives with his homosexual partner. A book for older children, *From the Notebooks of Melanin Sun* (Woodson, 1995), is about a boy whose mother is in love with a woman. Books such as these portray what it means for the children when their parents have a partner of the same gender.

Literature Portraying Social Diversity

American society also shows its diversity in many ways besides the cultural identities of ethnicity, race, physical/mental ability, and gender. Poverty, low social class, homelessness, illiteracy, and "migrant" lifestyle, among other factors, just as significantly create an identifying "culture." Living and working under those circumstances affects the way people experience the world and the way the world views them. It is important to note that poverty, the most common of social diversities, is often found in conjunction with other types of social diversity, so children's books dealing with any form of social diversity may touch on poverty as well.

In choosing children's books depicting social diversity, of utmost importance is finding authentic, nonstereotyped portrayals that are believable. Eve Bunting has written several books that deal with sensitive issues of social diver-

sity. *The Wednesday Surprise* (1989) begins with seven-year-old Anna and her grandmother spending Wednesday nights together while Mom works late at the office and Dad is away on his truck. Every week, Grandma brings a bag of picture books to Anna's house and they "read the story together, out loud," book after book. The surprise is for Dad's birthday. When Grandma stands up and begins reading aloud, "Mom and Dad and Sam are all astonished." When did she learn to read? Grandma reveals that Anna taught her on Wednesday nights and then she took the books home and practiced. This family had urged Grandma to go to classes to learn to read; instead, she found that reading picture books with her granddaughter was a good incentive.

Eve Bunting's *A Day's Work* (1994) looks at the plight of new immigrants. A little boy and his non–English-speaking grandfather are hired off a street corner to pull weeds. Inadvertently, they pull up all the plants and leave all the weeds. The grandfather insists on redoing the job, and in an unexpected act of patience and understanding, the employer rehires the boy and his grandfather.

Readers of Frances Temple's *Grab Hands and Run* (1993) find themselves drawn into the story of a family escaping a threat on their lives in El Salvador. Through the eyes of the young narrator, Felipe, the story of the dangerous journey north to Canada is told. In *Journey of the Sparrows* (Buss, 1991), three siblings are smuggled into the United States nailed into crates. Once in the United States, they must hide from immigration officials, find work in order to have food and shelter, and save enough money to send for the rest of the family they have left behind. The rich details throughout both books fill in gaps in the experiences of most readers. Most of us can't imagine a life filled with constant hunger and fear of being found and returned to a land of certain death. Because of the array of human emotions that ring true, readers come to believe in the reality of the situations portrayed in these books.

Literature about People with Exceptionalities

Literature about people with exceptionalities or special needs portrays those with physical, mental, emotional, or learning disabilities, as well as gifted and talented children. Sometimes, an exceptionality is a life-threatening or debilitating illness that alters a person's ability to lead life in the same way a healthy child can.

There are many stereotyped views that distort children's understanding of exceptional learners and give rise to fear, pity, and misunderstandings of intellectual and social abilities. Exceptional children should be portrayed in books as individuals with many facets to their lives. They should not be considered "heroic" for learning to live with disabilities and differing abilities. Also important is how people with exceptionalities are treated by others. When a book portrays exceptional learners in unconventional ways, readers may feel betrayed or may be led to accept a mistaken image.

Illustration 4.14
Books such as *Helping Hands* deal directly with the lives of children with special needs and thus help all readers learn about their realities. (*Helping Hands* by Suzanne Haldane. Copyright © 1991 by Suzanne Haldane. Used by permission of Dutton Children's Books, a division of Penguin Books USA Inc.)

A number of informational books use photographs and narration to provide contemporary images of people with disabilities. *Helping Hands: How Monkeys Assist People Who Are Disabled* (Haldane, 1991) is the story of a teenager with quadriplegia and his helper monkey, a Capuchin named Willie. The text and accompanying photographs show how Willie is trained to assist—he can fetch a sandwich from the refrigerator, warm it in the microwave, and serve it on a tray. Such information can help children get a sense of one aspect of daily life for someone who is quadriplegic. In *Handtalk School* (Miller and Ancona, 1991), readers follow a day at a residential school for the deaf and see children communicating through American Sign Language (ASL) as well as with a telephone device for the deaf (TDD). The book shows signed messages with accompanying text so that readers can follow along.

Fictional books can depict exceptional children in ways that provide insight for readers. In Alfred Slote's *Hang Tough, Paul Mather* (1973), the protagonist is twelve-year-old Paul, who has leukemia. Paul's enthusiasm for baseball and his relationship with his teammates give readers a realistic glimpse of what it means to live with the illness and the accompanying treatments.

Biographies of both famous and ordinary people provide glimpses into the lives of exceptional learners. Author Jean Little's autobiography, *Little by Little: A Writer's Education* (1987), describes how her "bad eyes" led to a childhood full of ridicule and rejection until she found that her retreat into her imagination paved the way for her career as a writer.

TEACHERS' ROLES IN PRESENTING MULTIPLE AND DIVERSE PERSPECTIVES

It is important for teachers to read a wide variety of books. Personal reading of quality adult books depicting diverse perspectives enhances the teacher's understanding of the world. Professional reading offers teachers theories on why reading a broad range of books is helpful. Reading children's books allows teachers to identify books appropriate in content and level for the children with whom they will be shared.

Understanding Diverse Perspectives through Adult Literature

Reading is important both to enhance current understandings and to add new perspectives on the world. Teachers frequently seek out books that provide such reading experiences for their students. But it is also important for teachers to read adult books so that they can better understand diverse perspectives. A children's book offers a certain level of insight into diversity. A young adult book allows more space and time to reflect on issues. An adult book allows readers to think about these issues in even greater depth.

Research indicates that students frequently relate best to a teacher's messages when the students' cultural background is similar to the teacher's (Au, 1993; Delpit, 1988). Teachers understand the world from their own cultural perspectives, and it is impossible to share the background of each of their students. One way that teachers can try to build their background is by joining a discussion group that discusses adult books depicting diverse viewpoints; such discussions take the understandings gained from reading to a deeper level. By building their own background, teachers can enhance their ability to facilitate discussions of literature with their students.

Understanding Diverse Perspectives through Professional Literature

Teachers can choose from a variety of professional materials dealing with literature that reflects diversity. Such professional materials discuss the importance of reading multicultural literature, recommend criteria for evaluation and selection, and present methods for discussing and eliciting responses to the literature. Often, there are annotated bibliographies to help teachers identify books that may interest students. Reading professional materials improves understanding of the critical role teachers play in making multicultural literature accessible to children.

Helping Children Gain Diverse Perspectives

It is generally accepted that children's reading choices are often based on recommendations of peers and influential adults. Therefore, teachers, library media specialists, and other influential adults have a responsibility to be knowledgeable about books that offer a wide variety of perspectives.

Teachers can help to ensure that their students gain a variety of perspectives by keeping diversity in mind when they are selecting reading material for the whole class and when they are deciding what choices are offered to students in book clubs and are available to students for individual free choice. The importance of the school librarian or media specialist in acting as a consultant to the teacher and to individual students in choosing reading materials cannot be overlooked.

Even more important than the role teachers and librarians play in the selection of reading materials is their role in facilitating discussions and in providing opportunities for responding to literature. Chapter 13 details the critical role of the teacher in leading discussion. Chapter 14 describes the many ways teachers can provide opportunities for students to respond to literature.

 TEACHING IDEAS

Assess Gender Roles in Books Published in the Past. Begin discussion by having children list gender characteristics they believe to be true. Find some books (for example, **Dear Garbage Man**) that show outdated images of gender roles. Challenge the children to identify ways the books no longer reflect society. Lead a discussion that focuses on issues of gender equality. Compare comments made during the discussion with the gender characteristics identified earlier.

Focus Attention on International Books. Gather some international books mentioned in this chapter. First, identify the ones with which children are already familiar. See if they can identify the country of origin of each book. If they cannot, introduce the children to the fact that many books already familiar to them are international books and name the country of origin. When applicable, have the children cite details from the books that identify the country of origin.

Read a Social Issue Book and Follow Up with Social Action. After reading a book that focuses children's attention on a social issue, discuss the issue with children and generate ideas for how children can participate actively in making a difference. When possible, guide the children in following through with their plans for being activists.

Discuss Family Stories. All children have stories of family experiences. Locate and read several books about family reunions and gatherings—for example, *Bigmama's* (1991), by Donald Crews; *Family Pictures/Cuadros de familia* (1990), by Carmen Lomas Garza; and *The Relatives Came* (1985), by Cynthia Rylant. Encourage children to talk to their parents and other family members about family experiences. Have children write or tell their own family stories, accompanied by photographs or drawings.

Identify Cultural Markers. Cultural markers are found in culturally authentic books. They are the details that are true to a culture—artifacts, character behavior, language use, physical descriptions. Select a picture book that includes cultural markers and have children list all those they encounter in either the text or the illustrations.

Connect across Genres. Read several books from different genres that all depict one cultural group. For instance, select a picture book, a book of poetry, a novel, an informational book, and a biography that all relate to a particular culture. Use this opportunity to help children gain a well-rounded view of that culture.

EXPERIENCES FOR YOUR LEARNING

1. Storytelling is popular throughout the world. Many cultures have developed unique ways of telling stories. Select a story to tell, study the culture's storytelling style, and practice presenting the story to others. Resources that may be of help include Anne Pellowski's *Hidden Stories in Plants* (1990), *Family Story-telling Handbook* (1987), and *The Story Vine* (1984).

2. Select a universal theme and gather a number of books from various cultures related to that theme. Examples of themes are the search for freedom, immigrating to the United States, coming of age, friendships and peer relationships, and intergenerational relationships. Read the books and make a list of similarities and differences across cultural groups.

3. Locate several books with copyrights before 1970. Examine how various cultures are depicted. Decide whether the images portrayed in the text and illustrations are still acceptable or are stereotyped and unacceptable. One interesting comparison is of series books that were published over a number of decades and changed over the years. For example, look at two Nancy Drew books with the same title but copyrighted before and after 1950. What changes were made in the depiction of various cultures?

4. Survey the range of work of an author or illustrator of cultural diversity. Consult sources such as reference books, the encyclopedic series *Something about the Author,* biographies, brochures produced by publishers, and biographical information on end flaps of book jackets to obtain information about the person. Study the person's work to learn how he or she goes about creating texts or illustrations.

5. Survey several books popular with children and analyze the portrayals of gender roles. What traits do the males and females have? What characteristics are valued? What messages are communicated to readers about gender roles? If books portray diverse and multidimensional gender roles, consider whether the portrayals are believable or didactic.

6. Select a social issue and find several children's books about it. Compare and contrast the treatments of the issue. Do the books treat the issue in a believable way? Do they deal with the issue honestly? What messages are communicated to children?

7. Survey the multicultural books available in your public or school library and collect a representative sample. Look at the books in light of the issues discussed in this chapter. Are they written and illustrated from an inside or an outside perspective? Is there evidence of stereotyping or other unacceptable depictions of cultural groups? Are cultural details presented authentically? As a collection, what messages do these books send to readers regarding different cultures?

8. Collect a sampling of books that portray the lives of people with exceptionalities and analyze the ways the people are presented to readers. Are they portrayed as individuals with many facets to their lives? Do other characters treat them with fear or pity? Are they considered "heroic" because they can live with disabilities?

RECOMMENDED BOOKS

* indicates a picture book; I indicates interest level (P = preschool, YA = young adult)

African and African American

* Aardema, Verna. *Rabbit Makes a Monkey of Lion: A Swahili Tale.* Illustrated by Jerry Pinkney. New York: Dial, 1989. To "make a monkey" is to make one appear to be a fool, and this Swahili tale is about a little rabbit that outwits the big lion. (I: P–7)

* ———. *Who's in Rabbit's House? A Masai Tale.* Illustrated by Leo Dillon and Diane Dillon. New York: Dial, 1977. Rabbit's friends try to get rid of a mysterious Long One that is occupying Rabbit's House—and the solution is a surprising one. The illustrations portray this story as a play, acted out by Masai wearing masks. (I: P–8)

* ———. *Why Mosquitoes Buzz in People's Ears: A West African Tale.* Illustrated by Leo Dillon and Diane Dillon. New York: Dial, 1978. A chain of events is started when a mosquito tells a big lie. (I: P–8)

* Adoff, Arnold. *All the Colors of the Race.* Illustrated by John Steptoe. New York: Lothrop, Lee & Shepard,1982. The poems in this book deal with issues of race. (I: 8–11)

* ———. *In for Winter, Out for Spring.* Illustrated by Jerry Pinkney. San Diego, CA: Harcourt, 1991. Rebecca shares with her family special moments that the seasons bring throughout the year. (I: 6–11)

Adoff, Arnold, ed. *My Black Me: A Beginning Book of Black Poetry.* 1974. New York: Dutton, 1994. This anthology opens with Adoff's words "This book of Black is for you." Poets such as Langston Hughes, Lucille Clifton, Nikki Giovanni, and Imamu Amiri Baraka contributed to the anthology. (I: 9–YA)

Bryan, Ashley. *Beat the Story-Drum, Pum-Pum.* New York: Atheneum, 1980. This collection of retellings includes five Nigerian folktales. (I: 7–10)

* ———. *Sing to the Sun.* New York: Harper/Collins, 1992. This collection of original poetry and art by Ashley Bryan celebrates life and the emotions aroused by everyday occurrences (I: 6–10)

* ———. *The Story of Lightning and Thunder.* New York: Atheneum, 1993. Ram Lightning and his mother, Ma Sheep Thunder, could call down the rains whenever the people in West Africa needed it. But when Ram Lightning creates problems with his power, the two are forced to leave Earth for a new home. (I: 6–8)

* Caines, Jeannette. *I Need a Lunch Box.* Illustrated by Pat Cummings. New York: HarperCollins, 1988. A preschool boy longs for a lunch box like his school-age siblings have, so that he can store his treasures in it. (I: P–7).

* ———. *Just Us Women.* Illustrated by Pat Cummings. New York: Harper & Row, 1982. A young girl and her Aunt Martha take a car trip that allows "just us women" to do whatever they like along the way. (I: 6–9)

Clifton, Lucille. *The Lucky Stone.* Illustrated by Dale Payson. New York: Delacorte, 1979. Tee wishes she owned the lucky stone as she listens to her great-grandmother tell stories of how it has helped its owners for over a hundred years. (I: 7–9)

* ———. *Some of the Days of Everett Anderson.* Illustrated by Evaline Ness. New York: Holt, 1970. Everett Anderson, a black six-year-old who lives in Apt. 14A, tells how he spends his time. Related titles are *Everett Anderson's Friend* (1976), *Everett Anderson's Christmas Coming* (1971/1991), and *Everett Anderson's Goodbye* (1983). (I: P–7)

* Cooper, Floyd. *Coming Home: From the Life of Langston Hughes.* New York: Philomel, 1994. This picture book biography of the African American poet describes his childhood and his search for "home." (I: 7–10)

* Crews, Donald. *Bigmama's*. Greenwillow, 1991. This is an autobiographical story of visiting "Bigmama's" house and visiting with relatives in the summertimes during Donald Crews's youth. Also by Crews is *Shortcut* (1992). (**I:** P–8)

Curtis, Christopher Paul. *The Watsons Go to Birmingham—1963*. New York: Delacorte, 1995. The Watsons are an African American family from Flint, Michigan. Their 1963 summer visit to Grandmother in Alabama changes their lives dramatically. (**I:** 10–YA)

* Feelings, Tom. *Daydreamers*. Text by Eloise Greenfield. New York: Dial, 1981. Feelings's sensitive portraits of children and Greenfield's poetic text describe the dreamers these children may be. (**I:** 6–9)

* ———. *The Middle Passage*. New York: Dial, 1995. This wordless book dramatically depicts the hardships of the journey across the Atlantic Ocean made by Africans bound for slavery in America. (**I:** 10–YA)

* ———. *Soul Looks Back in Wonder*. New York: Dial, 1993. Feelings created the stunning art, which is acompanied by the voices of noted poets, including Maya Angelou, Langston Hughes, and Lucille Clifton, who write of their African American heritage. (**I:** 9–YA)

* Flournoy, Valerie. *The Patchwork Quilt*. Illustrated by Jerry Pinkney. New York: Dial, 1985. As Tanya helps her mother and grandmother create a quilt from the scraps of their family's clothes, she comes to realize the stories and memories the quilt holds. A sequel is *Tanya's Reunion* (1995). (**I:** 6–9)

* Fox, Mem. *Sophie*. Illustrated by Aminah Brenda Lynn Robinson. New York: Harcourt Brace, 1989. Sophie holds onto her grandfather's hand as she grows up. He holds onto hers as he gets smaller and older. (**I:** P–6)

* Giovanni, Nikki. *Spin a Soft Black Song*. 1971. Illustrated by George Martins. New York: Harper-Collins, 1985. This is a collection of poems reflecting African American children's everyday thoughts in their own voices. (**I:** 6–10)

* Greenfield, Eloise. *Africa Dreams*. 1977. Illustrated by Carole Byard. New York: Harper, 1989. A young African American girl dreams about what it would be like to visit her granddaddy's village. (**I:** P–8)

* ———. *Grandpa's Face*. Illustrated by Floyd Cooper. New York: Philomel, 1988. Tamika is afraid of losing her Grandpa's love when she notices him making mean faces as he practices his role as an actor. (**I:** 6–9)

* ———. *Honey, I Love and Other Love Poems*. Illustrated by Diane Dillon and Leo Dillon. New York: Harper, 1978. These poems, narrated by a young African American girl, tell of love and friendship. (**I:** 7–9)

* ———. *My Doll, Keshia*. Illustrated by Jan Spivey Gilchrist. Black Butterfly, 1991. A little girl's experience of playing with her doll is shown in this board book, which is one of a series. (**I:** P)

* ———. *Nathaniel Talking*. Illustrated by Jan Spivey Gilchrist. New York: Writers & Readers/Black Butterfly, 1988. Through various forms of poetry, Nathaniel talks about the happenings in his neighborhood from his eight-year-old perspective. A related title is *Night on Neighborhood Street* (Dial, 1991). (**I:** 7–9)

———. *Rosa Parks*. Illustrated by Eric Marlow. New York: Harper, 1973. This biography about Rosa Parks tells how her stance set off the Montgomery bus strike and the civil rights struggle that followed. (**I:** 7–9)

* ———. *She Come Bringing Me That Little Baby Girl*. Illustrated by John Steptoe. New York: Harper, 1974. Although he is at first disappointed at news of the birth of a baby sister (instead of the baby brother he had requested), Kevin takes pride in his role of big brother. (**I:** P–8)

* Grimes, Nikki. *Meet Danitra Brown*. Illustrated by Floyd Cooper. New York: Lothrop, Lee & Shepard, 1994. Through poetry, Zuri Jackson relates her feelings about her special friendship with a "splendiferous" girl, Danitra Brown. (**I:** 6–9)

* Hamilton, Virginia. *Drylongso*. Illustrated by Jerry Pinkney. San Diego, CA: Harcourt, 1992. Drylongso, a mysterious stranger, arrives just ahead of a dust storm to a drought-stricken farm that had been "dry so long." He uses a dowsing stick to find water and gives the family a sense of hope. (**I:** 9–11)

———. *Her Stories: African American Folktales, Fairy Tales, and True Tales*. Illustrated by Leo and Diane Dillon. New York: Scholastic, 1995. This collection of stories is about women in African American folktales, fairytales, animal stories, supernatural tales, legends, and biographical accounts. (**I:** 9–YA)

———. *The House of Dies Drear*. Illustrated by Eros Keith. New York: Simon & Schuster, 1968. When a history professor and his son move into a rented house, they find the spirits of the past—those who passed through the house when it was a station on the Underground Railroad. The sequel is *The Mystery of Drear House* (1987). (**I:** 10–YA)

———. *Many Thousand Gone: African Americans from Slavery to Freedom*. Illustrated by Leo and Diane Dillon. New York: Knopf, 1993. This book tells the stories of many slaves who made it to freedom through the Underground Railroad. (**I:** 10–YA)

———. *The People Could Fly: American Black Folktales*. Illustrated by Leo Dillon and Diane Dillon. New York: Knopf, 1985. This collection of 24 American black folktales includes a range from familiar to lesser known ones. (I: 9–13)

———. *Zeely*. Illustrated by Symeon Shimin. New York: Macmillan, 1967. Eleven-year-old Geeder learns to move from her dreams to reality as she acquires better self-understanding with the help of Zeely, a queen-like figure who is extraordinarily tall, beautiful, and kind. (I: 11–YA)

Haskins, Jim. *Get on Board: The Story of the Underground Railroad*. New York: Scholastic, 1993. This book explores the ways slaves escaped north to freedom, including the Underground Railroad, and the ways slave owners tried to keep the slaves from escaping. (I: 10–12)

* Havill, Juanita. *Jamaica's Find*. Illustrated by Anne Sibley O'Brien. Boston: Houghton Mifflin, 1986. Jamaica finds a stuffed dog at the playground and must cope with her desire to keep the toy. Sequels are *Jamaica Tag-Along* (1989) and *Jamaica and Brianna* (1993). (I: P–8)

* Hooks, William H. *Freedom's Fruit*. Illustrated by James Ransome. New York: Knopf, 1996. In order to gain freedom for Sheba and her beloved, Mama, a slave and a conjurer, casts a spell on her master's grapes. (I: 8–11)

* Hopkinson, Deborah. *Sweet Clara and the Freedom Quilt*. Illustrated by James Ransome. New York: Knopf, 1993. Clara is determined to be reunited with her mother and to find their way north to freedom. She uses her skills as a seamstress, listens to the conversations around her, and creates a quilt that maps the way to freedom. (I: 7–10)

* Howard, Elizabeth Fitzgerald. *Aunt Flossie's Hats (and Crab Cakes Later)*. Illustrated by James Ransome. New York: Clarion, 1991. For Sarah and Susan, visiting their great-great-aunt Flossie means sipping tea and eating cookies while trying on her many hats and listening to the stories associated with them. (I: 6–9)

* ———. *Chita's Christmas Tree*. Illustrated by Floyd Cooper. New York: Bradbury, 1989. Chita enjoys the many aspects of the Christmas holidays, but especially the trip with her Papa, from Baltimore deep into the woods to find their Christmas tree. A related title is *Papa Tells Chita a Story* (Simon & Schuster, 1995). (I: 6–9)

* Hudson, Wade, comp. *Pass It On: African-American Poetry for Children*. Illustrated by Floyd Cooper. New York: Scholastic, 1993. This book of poetry about African American experiences has contribu-tions by poets such as Langston Hughes, Nikki Giovanni, Eloise Greenfield, and Lucille Clifton. (I: 8–10)

* Hudson, Wade, and Cheryl Hudson, comps. *How Sweet the Sound: African-American Songs for Children*. Illustrated by Floyd Cooper. New York: Scholastic, 1995. Presented in picture book style, the words to various African American songs are accompanied by double-page illustrations that echo the emotions of the songs. Background information on each song and the musical notations for the melody of each one are included at the end of the book. (I: all ages)

* Johnson, Angela. *Do Like Kyla*. Illustrated by James E. Ransome. New York: Orchard, 1990. All day long, a little girl follows her big sister Kyla around, "doing like Kyla," but at the end of the day, "Kyla does just like me." (I: P–7)

* ———. *The Girl Who Wore Snakes*. Illustrated by James E. Ransome. New York: Orchard, 1993. Ali loves snakes so much that she wears them, and she is pleased when her aunt says the snakes remind her of the "sun and the earth and everything in between." (I: P–8)

* ———. *One of Three*. Illustrated by David Soman. New York: Orchard, 1991. The youngest of three sisters describes what it is like to be "one of three." (I: P–7)

* ———. *Tell Me a Story, Mama*. Illustrated by David Soman. New York: Orchard, 1989. At bedtime, a little girl asks, "Tell me a story, Mama, about when you were little." But then, she tells a story herself, with Mama only adding comments. (I: P–8)

* ———. *When I Am Old with You*. Illustrated by David Soman. New York: Orchard, 1990. A grandson imagines what it would be like to be old with Granddaddy and what activities they would enjoy together. (I: P–8)

* Lawrence, Jacob. *Harriet and the Promised Land*. New York: Simon & Schuster, 1968. The life of Harriet Tubman is described in verse, and the story of her commitment to helping fellow slaves to freedom is told. (I: 9–11)

Lester, Julius. *Long Journey Home: Stories from Black History*. 1972. New York: Dial, 1993. Six stories, based on the lives of real people, tell about the impact of escaping from slavery on the lives of individuals and families. (I: 11–YA)

* ———. *Sam and the Tigers*. Illustrated by Jerry Pinkney. New York: Dial, 1996. Based on the story "Little Black Sambo," this new version is told in Lester's "Southern black storytelling voice," with Pinkney's

illustrations setting the story in the mythical land of Sam-sam-sa-mara. (I: 6–9)

* Little, Lessie Jones. *Children of Long Ago*. Illustrated by Jan Spivey Gilchrist. New York: Philomel, 1988. This collection of poems reflects on the author's peaceful childhood experience of growing up in the early 1900s. (I: 7–9)

* Maddern, Eric. *The Fire Children: A West African Creation Tale*. Illustrated by Frané Lessac. New York: Dial, 1993. This is a retelling of the West African tale of the world's creation and how the different people came to be. (I: 9–12)

* Marzollo, Jean. *Happy Birthday, Martin Luther King*. Illustrated by J. Brian Pinkney. New York: Scholastic, 1993. Simple text explains why we celebrate the birthday of famous civil rights leader Dr. Martin Luther King, Jr. (I: 6–9)

Mathis, Sharon Bell. *The Hundred Penny Box*. Illustrated by Leo and Diane Dillon. New York: Puffin, 1975. Great-great-aunt Dew is a hundred years old and has a box with a penny in it for each of her birthdays. Michael loves to listen to the stories each penny holds and intercedes on her behalf when his mother wants to throw out the old "hundred penny box" and buy a new one. (I: 8–10)

Mattox, Cheryl Warren. *Shake It to the One That You Love the Best: Play Songs and Lullabies from Black Musical Traditions*. Illustrated by Varnette P. Honeywood and Brenda Joysmith. Sobrante, CA: Warren-Mattox, 1989. African American songs that accompany jumprope, hopscotch, and other games are featured in this collection. (I: P–9)

* McKissack, Patricia. *Flossie and the Fox*. Illustrated by Rachel Isadora. New York: Dial, 1986. A little girl meets a creature in the woods and insists upon his proof of identity as a fox before she will give up her eggs. (I: 7–9)

* Mollel, Tololwa M. *The King and the Tortoise*. Illustrated by Kathy Blankley. New York: Clarion, 1993. When the king challenges the animals of his kingdom to make him a robe of smoke to prove they are more clever than he is, only the tortoise is able to outsmart the king. (I: 7–10)

* ———. *The Orphan Boy*. Illustrated by Paul Morin. New York: Clarion, 1990. A mysterious arrival of an orphan boy delights a lonely old man. However, the old man's curiosity about the boy's magical powers leads to trouble. (I: 7–10)

* Myers, Walter Dean. *Brown Angels*. New York: HarperCollins, 1993. Photographs of African American children from the turn of the century provide inspiration for the poems written by Myers. Also by Myers is *Glorious Angels* (1995). (I: 7–9)

———. *Malcolm X: By Any Means Necessary*. New York: Scholastic, 1993. This is the story of the famous civil rights leader. (I: 9–11)

Naidoo, Beverley. *Journey to Jo'burg: A South African Story*. New York: Harper, 1986. Naledi travels from her South African village to Jo'burg to deliver news of her baby sister's near-death from an illness to her mother, who works and lives in the home of some white people. (I: 9–11)

* Onyefulu, Ifeoma. *A Is for Africa*. New York: Penguin/Cobblehill, 1993. Through text and photographs by a member of the Igbo tribe of Nigeria, the letters of the alphabet from A to Z are used to organize information about African peoples. (I: 6–9)

* Pinkney, Andrea Davis. *Dear Benjamin Banneker*. Illustrated by Brian Pinkney. San Diego, CA: Harcourt, 1994. Benjamin Banneker was an accomplished mathematician and astronomer and was the first black creator of an almanac. When he realized the injustice of the words in the Declaration of Independence proclaiming that "all men are created equal," he wrote to Secretary of State Thomas Jefferson. (I: 7–9)

* ———. *Seven Candles for Kwanzaa*. Illustrated by Brian Pinkney. New York: Dial, 1993. This book describes the seven-day festival of Kwanzaa, a holiday during which Americans of African descent celebrate their ancestral values. (I: 6–9)

* Pinkney, Brian. *JoJo's Flying Side Kick*. New York: Simon & Schuster, 1995. When JoJo is to be tested to earn her yellow belt in *tae kwon do* class, she gets a lot of advice from others. At the moment of the test, though, she realizes for herself how to perform the flying side kick and break the board. (I: P–8)

* ———. *Max Found Two Sticks*. New York: Simon & Schuster, 1994. Max doesn't feel like talking, but he uses two twigs to drum messages in response to others. (I: P–7)

* Pinkney, Gloria. *Back Home*. Illustrated by Jerry Pinkney. New York: Dial, 1992. Eight-year-old Ernestine takes a train trip to visit relatives at the North Carolina farm where she was born. The prequel is *The Sunday Outing* (1994). (I: 6–9)

* Raschka, Chris. *Charlie Parker Played Be Bop*. New York: Orchard, 1992. Lively words in rhythmic text seem like the be bop music of the famous jazz saxophonist. (I: P–8)

* Ringgold, Faith. *Tar Beach*. New York: Crown, 1991. A young girl remembers spending summer evenings on the "tar beach" on the roof of their apartment building, imagining that she could fly over Manhattan and claim all she saw for herself and her family. (I: 6–9)

* Schroeder, Alan. *Minty: A Story of Young Harriet Tubman*. Illustrated by Jerry Pinkney. New York: Dial, 1996. Harriet Tubman's "cradle" name was Araminta, and therefore she was nicknamed Minty. She was a slave on the Brodas plantation in the 1820s, and not only did she always long to escape, she prepared for it. (I: 7–9)

* ———. *Satchmo's Blues*. Illustrated by Floyd Cooper. Garden City, NY: Doubleday, 1996. This fictionalized account of Louis Armstrong's childhood in New Orleans describes how he worked and earned his first trumpet. (I: 6–10)

Sisulu, Elinor Batezat. *The Day Gogo Went to Vote: South Africa*. Illustrated by Sharon Wilson. Boston: Little, Brown, 1996. Thembi and her great-grandmother participate in the election on the historic day on which black South Africans were allowed to vote for the first time. (I: 7–10)

* Smalls-Hector, Irene. *Irene and the Big, Fine Nickel*. Illustrated by Tyrone Geter. Boston: Little, Brown, 1991. Irene and her friends enjoy a summer day in Harlem in the 1950s. When they find a nickel in the street, they are sure it's a special day. (I: 6–9)

* Steptoe, John. *Baby Says*. New York: Lothrop, Lee & Shepard, 1988. In this nearly wordless book, a baby and his big brother learn to play together. (I: P)

———. *Mufaro's Beautiful Daughters: An African Tale*. New York: Lothrop, Lee & Shepard, 1987. Mufaro's daughters are both beautiful, and both vie to be chosen as the new wife of the king. Nyasha's gentle and kind temperament contrasts with Manyara's greed and mean-spiritedness as they encounter various creatures along their separate journeys to the city. (I: P–7)

———. *Stevie*. New York: Harper, 1969. When Stevie's mother has to work and Stevie is left with Robert's family, Robert initially resents having to share his belongings and his mother. (I: P–7)

Taylor, Mildred. *The Friendship*. Illustrated by Max Ginsburg. New York: Dial, 1987. In 1930s rural Mississippi, the four Logan children witness a confrontation when Mr. Tom Bee, an elderly black man, calls a white storekeeper by his first name. Other titles about the Logans include *Road to Memphis* (1990) and *The Well* (1995). (I: 8–11)

———. *The Gold Cadillac*. Illustrated by Michael Hays. New York: Dial, 1987. Father brings home a new gold Cadillac, and 'Lois and Wilmato are proud to be riding in it. But driving south from Ohio to Mississippi to visit relatives, the family faces prejudice and racism and must temporarily trade the Cadillac for a less conspicuous car. (I: 8–11)

———. *Mississippi Bridge*. Illustrated by Max Ginsburg. New York: Dial, 1990. In the 1930s, amidst racial tension, black passengers are ordered off a bus to accommodate white passengers. Crossing the flooded river on a weak bridge, the bus is swept off and the passengers die. (I: 10–12)

———. *Roll of Thunder, Hear My Cry*. Illustrated by Jerry Pinkney. New York: Dial, 1976. The Logan family faces many problems associated with being black in the rural South during the Depression. The sequel is *Let the Circle Be Unbroken* (1981). (I: 11–13)

———. *Song of the Trees*. Illustrated by Jerry Pinkney. New York: Dial, 1975. Papa is away, working on the railroad, during the Depression. When white men cut down the old trees on the Logan farm, they find they must answer to Papa. (I: 9–12)

Towle, Wendy. *The Real McCoy: The Life of an African-American Inventor*. Illustrated by Wil Clay. New York: Scholastic, 1993. This biography of noted inventor Elijah McCoy explains why the term "the real McCoy" has come to mean "genuine." His invention of the automatic oil cup decreased the number of times trains had to stop for lubrication. (I: 7–9)

* Walter, Mildred Pitts. *Brother to the Wind*. Illustrated by Leo and Diane Dillon. New York: Lothrop, Lee & Shepard, 1985. A young African boy, Emeke, believes that the Good Snake can make his dream to fly come true. (I: 6–8)

* ———. *Justin and the Best Biscuits in the World*. Illustrated by Catherine Stock. New York: Lothrop, Lee & Shepard, 1986. Justin lives in a house full of women and considers cooking and cleaning to be "women's work." Spending time on his grandfather's ranch shows Justin a different view of work. (I: 9–11)

———. *Mariah Keeps Cool*. New York: Macmillan, 1990. Mariah's concerns center around swimming meets, but she finds that her world changes when a half-sister moves into her home. (I: 8–11)

* ———. *My Mama Needs Me*. Illustrated by Pat Cummings. New York: Lothrop, Lee & Shepard, 1983. Jason is so anxious to help his mother care for his new baby sister that he refuses to play with his friends or to leave the house. (I: P–7)

* ———. *Ty's One-Man Band*. 1980. Illustrated by Margot Tomes. New York: Macmillan, 1987. Ty's one-legged friend, Andro, can produce music with a washboard, wooden spoons, a comb, and a tin pail. (I: 6–8)

* Williams, Sherley Anne. *Working Cotton*. Illustrated by Carole Byard. San Diego, CA: Harcourt, 1992. A

little girl tells how her migrant family spends the day, from dawn to dusk, picking cotton in the fields of central California. (I: P–8)

* Wisniewski, David. *Sundiata: Lion King of Mali.* Photographs of David Wisniewski's cut-paper illustrations taken by Lee Salsbery. New York: Clarion, 1992. This is the story of Sundiata, son of the king of Mali, and how he was driven into exile eight hundred years ago, overcame physical problems, and returned to claim his throne. (I: 8—11)

Woodson, Jacqueline. *Last Summer with Maizon.* New York: Delacorte, 1992. Margaret knows that after the summer ends, her best friend, Maizon, will be leaving their neighborhood in Brooklyn to attend a boarding school where she has won a scholarship. The sequel is *Maizon at Blue Hill* (1992). (I: 11–YA)

* Young, Ruth. *Golden Bear.* Illustrated by Rachel Isadora. New York: Viking, 1992. A little boy and his "golden bear" are constant companions throughout the day. (I: P–6)

Asian and Asian American

* Aruego, Jose, and Ariane Aruego. *A Crocodile's Tale: A Philippine Folk Story.* New York: Scribner's, 1972. A boy saves a crocodile, only to be threatened with being eaten. He tries to find an arbitrator to define gratitude and what's right, and a clever monkey helps out. (I: P–7)

* Breckler, Rosemary K. *Hoang Breaks the Lucky Teapot.* Illustrated by Adrian Frankel. Boston: Houghton Mifflin, 1992. Hoang throws his ball at an imaginary dragon—and breaks the lucky teapot that his grandmother gave his family as they left Vietnam. Worried that Good Fortune will leave the house and Bad Fortune will come in, he tries to resolve the problem of the broken *gia truyen,* the lucky teapot. (I: 6–9)

* Chinn, Karen. *Sam and the Lucky Money.* Illustrated by Cornelius Van Wright and Ying-Hwa Hu. New York: Lee & Low, 1995. Chinese New Year means gifts of money in red envelopes for children. When he sees a homeless man, Sam struggles with the knowledge that he is free to spend his "lucky money" in any way he wishes. (I: 6–9)

* Choi, Sook Nyul. *Halmoni and the Picnic.* Illustrated by Karen M. Dugan. Boston: Houghton Mifflin, 1993. When the class plans a field trip, a classmate invites Yunmi's *halmoni* (grandmother) to serve as a chaperone. Yunmi worries about what her classmates will think of her grandmother's Korean ways and foods. (I: 6–9)

——. *Year of Impossible Goodbyes.* Boston: Houghton Mifflin, 1991. Ten-year-old Sookan and her family live under the cruelties of Japanese occupation of their homeland of Korea during the 1940s. When the Communists defeat the Japanese, Sookan and her family make a dangerous escape south. Sequels are *Echoes of the White Giraffe* (1993) and *My Brother My Sister and I* (1994). (I: 11–YA)

* Coerr, Eleanor. *Sadako and the Thousand Paper Cranes.* Illustrated by Ed Young. New York: Putnam, 1993. Believing in the Japanese tradition that folding a thousand origami cranes will restore her health, a little girl named Sadako tries to survive the leukemia that resulted from the bombing of Hiroshima. (I: 9–12)

* Demi. *The Artist and the Architect.* New York: Holt, 1991. The jealous artist plots to eliminate the talented architect, but is outwitted. The book illustrates the proverb "The small man harbors an envious spirit; the great man rejoices in the talents of others." (I: 6–9)

* ——. *Chingis Khan.* New York: Holt, 1991. This picture book presents a biography of the famous king of the Mongols. (I: 9–11)

* ——. *The Dragon's Tale and Other Animal Fables of the Chinese Zodiac.* New York: Holt, 1996. Twelve fables tell the stories of the animals of the Chinese zodiac. (I: 7–11)

* ——. *The Empty Pot.* New York: Holt, 1990. The Emperor distributes seeds to children across China, and the one who grows the best flower will inherit the kingdom. Ping finds that he must face the emperor honestly with his empty pot when springtime comes, as nothing has grown from the seed he was given. (I: 6–9)

* ——. *Liang and the Magic Paintbrush.* New York: Holt, 1980. A small boy in China is given a paintbrush, and everything he paints magically comes to life. (I: 6–9)

* ——. *The Magic Boat.* New York: Holt, 1990. Chang's helpful nature earns him a small dragon boat that magically changes from miniature to full size and back, allowing Chang to use it to help animals and people in need. When Ying, a tricky man, steals the boat, Chang must attempt to retrieve it. (I: 6–9)

* Hamanaka, Sheila. *The Journey.* New York: Orchard, 1990. A historical look at Japanese Americans is provided through closeup details of an actual mural, accompanied by text explaining the significance of each section. (I: 10–YA)

* ——. *Screen of Frogs.* New York: Orchard, 1993. A rich man's spending habits force him to sell off his land. When a frog appears to him in a dream, he realizes how much the animals depend on his land for their survival. A mysterious painting of frogs

appears on a blank screen following his change of heart. (I: 6–9)

* Han, Suzanne Crowder. *The Rabbit's Escape.* Illustrated by Yumi Heo. New York: Holt, 1995. The Dragon King of the East Sea's illness can be cured only by eating raw liver of a rabbit. Faithful Turtle returns from land with a rabbit, but Rabbit cleverly finds a way to be taken back there. Bilingual Korean/English text. (I: P–8)

Ho, Minfong. *The Clay Marble.* New York: Farrar, 1991. Rebuilding homes and lives in a camp near the Thai border, families struggle to survive the destruction of war. A marble made from clay serves as a toy and a gesture of friendship between children in this camp. (I: 12–YA)

* Hong, Lily Toy. *Two of Everything.* Morton Grove, IL: Whitman, 1993. While digging in his field, Mr. Haktak finds a big pot, and everything he puts in it comes out doubled. He faces a dilemma when his wife falls into the pot! (I: 6–9)

* Hoyt-Goldsmith, Diane. *Hoang Anh: A Vietnamese-American Boy.* Photographs by Lawrence Migdale. New York: Holiday House, 1992. Through colorful photographs and text narrated by Hoang Anh, this Vietnamese American boy describes his daily life with his family in California and how the traditional culture and customs exist alongside his life as a contemporary American boy. (I: 7–10)

Ishii, Momoko. *The Tongue-Cut Sparrow.* Illustrated by Suekichi Akaba. Translated by Katherine Paterson. New York: Dutton, 1987. When an old man and his wife care for a sparrow, each of them is rewarded according to their kindness or greediness. (I: 6–9)

* Lee, Jeanne M. *Toad Is the Uncle of Heaven.* New York: Holt, 1985. In this Vietnamese folktale, Toad leads a group of animals to ask the King of Heaven to send rain, and he ends up being treated with the utmost respect—symbolized by being called "Uncle." (I: P–8)

Lee, Marie G. *If It Hadn't Been for Yoon Jun.* Boston: Houghton Mifflin, 1993. Alice Larson was adopted as an infant and is now a seventh-grade cheerleader who runs with a popular crowd. She is reluctant when asked to help the new Korean boy, Yoon Jun, adjust to the American school. However, she develops an interest in her own Korean heritage. (I: 12–YA)

* Levinson, Riki. *Our Home Is the Sea.* Illustrated by Dennis Luzak. New York: Dutton, 1988. A young Chinese boy who lives on a houseboat in Hong Kong harbor looks forward to joining his father on his grandfather's big boat, knowing that he will someday become a fisherman. (I: P–7)

* Long, Jan Freeman. *The Bee and the Dream.* Illustrated by Kaoru Ono. New York: Dutton, 1996. Shin's friend Tasuke has a dream of finding riches. Shin buys the dream, borrows money, and goes to seek a fortune. His initial disappointment later turns into surprise. (I: 6–9)

* Mahy, Margaret. *The Seven Chinese Brothers.* Illustrated by Jean and Mou-sien Tseng. New York: Scholastic, 1990. When one brother is ordered executed, the seven brothers take turns escaping death by virtue of their extraordinary abilities. (I: 6–9)

Melmed, Laura Krauss. *The First Song Ever Sung.* Illustrated by Ed Young. New York: Lothrop, Lee & Shepard, 1993. A little boy asks family members and animals, "What was the first song ever sung?" They respond in ways that reflect individual perspectives. (I: 7–9)

* Mills, Claudia. *A Visit to Amy-Claire.* Illustrated by Sheila Hamanaka. New York: Macmillan, 1992. Through a visit with her older cousin, Amy-Claire, five-year-old Rachel begins to see the delights in being an older sister. (I: P–6)

* Mochizuki, Ken. *Baseball Saved Us.* Illustrated by Dom Lee. New York: Lee & Low, 1993. While forced to live in an internment camp for Japanese Americans during World War II, a young boy learns to play baseball. (I: 6–9)

* Morimoto, Junko. *My Hiroshima.* New York: Viking, 1987. The author recalls her childhood in Hiroshima and what happened on the day of the atomic bomb. (I: 9–12)

* Namioka, Lensey. *The Loyal Cat.* Illustrated by Aki Sogabe. San Diego, CA: Harcourt, 1995. Huku is a loyal cat with magical power. He helps the priest Tetsuzan just far enough out of poverty to make repairs to the modest temple and to eat again. (I: 7–9)

* Rappaport, Doreen. *The Journey of Meng.* Illustrated by Yang Ming-Yi. New York: Dial Books, 1991. In this well-known Chinese tale, Meng travels far to deliver warm clothes to her husband, a scholar, who has been forced into manual labor at the Great Wall. (I: 7–9)

* Rhee, Nami. *Magic Spring.* New York: Putnam, 1993. An elderly couple return to their youth after taking a sip of water from a magic spring, but their greedy neighbor ends up with unexpected results. (I: 6–9)

* Say, Allen. *El Chino.* Boston: Houghton Mifflin, 1990. This picture book biography of Bong Way "Bill" Wong tells how he became a famous Chinese American bullfighter in Spain. (I: 6–9)

* ———. *Grandfather's Journey.* Boston: Houghton Mifflin, 1993. A Japanese man emigrates to the

United States and learns to love his new home but misses his homeland. When visiting Japan, he finds that the war will keep him from returning to the United States. (I: 6–9)

* ———. *Tree of Cranes.* Boston: Houghton Mifflin, 1991. A Japanese mother brings a tree indoors at Christmas time and tells her son about her memories of Christmas in California. (I: 6–9)

* Shea, Pegi Deitz. *The Whispering Cloth: A Refugee's Story.* Illustrated by Anita Riggio. Stitched by You Yang. Honesdale, PA: Boyds Mills, 1995. Mai practices stitching borders in embroidered story cloths while in a Thai refugee camp with her grandmother. She finds a story within herself so that she, too, can stitch her own *pa'ndau.* (I: 7–10)

* Snyder, Dianne. *The Boy of the Three-Year Nap.* Illustrated by Allen Say. Boston: Houghton Mifflin, 1988. Taro is a lazy boy who sleeps so much that people say he would nap for three years if left alone. He schemes to get rich without doing any work, but his plan backfires when it proceeds further than he hoped. (I: 6–9)

* So, Meilo. *The Emperor and the Nightingale.* New York: Bradbury, 1992. The Emperor of China is moved to tears upon hearing the piercing beauty of the song of the nightingale. (I: 6–9)

* Turner, Ann. *Through Moon and Stars and Night Skies.* Illustrated by James Graham Hale. New York: Harper & Row, 1990. A little boy reminisces about how he came from far away and was adopted by his new family. (I: P–6)

* Uchida, Yoshiko. *The Bracelet.* Illustrated by Joanna Yardley. 1976. New York: Philomel, 1993. Emi and her family are sent to an internment camp during World War II. Emi loses the bracelet that was a gift from her best friend, but she comes to realize that she does not need the physical reminder of her friendship in order to remember. (I: 6–9)

———. *A Jar of Dreams.* New York: Macmillan, 1981. Faced with the prejudice against Japanese in the 1930s in California, Rinko wants to be as American as possible. When Aunt Waka visits from Japan, Rinko begins to understand the strength of her family and the Japanese American community. Related titles are *The Best Bad Thing* (1983) and *The Happiest Ending* (1985). (I: 9–11)

———. *Journey to Topaz: A Story of the Japanese–American Evacuation.* 1971. Illustrated by Donald Carick. Berkeley, CA: Creative Arts, 1984. Eleven-year-old Yuki and her family are sent to an internment camp in the desert, following the bombing of Pearl Harbor. A sequel is *Journey Home* (Macmillan, 1978). (I: 9–12)

Vuong, Lynette Dyer. *The Brocaded Slipper and Other Vietnamese Tales.* 1982. Illustrated by Vo-Dinh Mai. New York: Harper Trophy, 1992. This collection of five Vietnamese fairytales includes "The Brocaded Slipper," "Little Finger of the Watermelon Patch," "The Fairy Grotto," "Master Frog," and "The Lampstand Princess." (I: 8–11)

———. *The Golden Carp and Other Tales from Vietnam.* Illustrated by Manabu Saito. New York: Lothrop, Lee & Shepard, 1993. This collection of six tales of ancient Vietnam describes such virtues as courage, bravery, and honesty. (I: 8–11)

Watkins, Yoko Kawashima. *So Far From the Bamboo Grove.* New York: Lothrop, Lee & Shepard, 1986. The story of escaping Korea to return to Japan at the end of World War II is a fictionalized version of the author's life. (I: 10–12)

———. *Tales from the Bamboo Grove.* Illustrations by Jean and Mou-sien Tseng. New York: Bradbury, 1992. Six retellings of traditional Japanese tales are included in this collection: "Dragon Princess, Tatsuko"; "The Fox Wife"; "Why Is Seawater Salty?"; "Yayoi and the Spirit Tree"; "Monkey and Crab"; and "The Grandmother Who Became an Island." (I: 7–11)

* Xiong, Blia. *Nine-in-One, Grr! Grr! A Folktale from the Hmong People of Laos.* Adapted by Cathy Spagnoli. Illustrated by Nancy Hom. San Francisco: Children's Book Press, 1989. Tiger is promised nine cubs a year by the god, Shao. Bird fears that tigers will overtake the land and tries to think of a way to prevent that from happening. (I: 6–10)

* Yacowitz, Caryn. *The Jade Stone.* Illustrated by Ju-Hong Chen. New York: Holiday House, 1992. Although Chan Lo has been directed by the Great Emperor of All China to carve a dragon of wind and fire out of the perfect piece of jade, he discovers he must listen to the stone's spirit crying out to be something else. (I: 7–9)

Yagawa, Sumiko. *The Crane Wife.* Illustrated by Suekichi Akaba. Translated by Katherine Paterson. New York: Morrow, 1987. A lonely man's kindness is rewarded with the mysterious arrival of a wife. When his curiosity goes too far, he is punished by her departure. (I: 6–9)

* Yep, Laurence. *The Boy Who Swallowed Snakes.* Illustrated by Jean and Mou-Sien Tseng. New York: Scholastic, 1994. A poor boy's brave and unselfish act of swallowing a dangerous snake is rewarded differently than is a rich man's greedy act. (I: 6–9)

———. *Dragon's Gate.* New York: HarperCollins, 1993. In 1867, Chinese men came to the United States and found work digging and dynamiting tunnels through the rocks of the Sierra Mountains in order for the railroad to cross the nation. (I: 11–YA)

———. *Dragonwings.* New York: Harper, 1975. Moon Shadow leaves his remote Chinese village in 1903 to join his father, Windrider, in California. Together, they survive the 1906 earthquake and the hardships of life in the "Golden Mountain" as they work to realize their dream of building a dragon-like flying machine. (I: 10–12)

———. *Later, Gator.* New York: HarperCollins, 1995. Two brothers who usually do not get along find that they must cooperate with each other when they wind up with a pet alligator they know their parents will not approve of. (I: 8–10)

———. *The Star Fisher.* New York: Morrow, 1991. This fictionalized biography of Laurence Yep's grandmother tells of fifteen-year-old Joan Lee and her family's move from Ohio to West Virginia in the 1920s. Being the only Asians in the community, they face the problem of being "different" from their neighbors. (I: 11–YA)

* Young, Ed. *Cat and Rat: The Legend of the Chinese Zodiac.* New York: Holt, 1995. This is the story of how the twelve animals became part of the Chinese zodiac. (I: 7–10)

* ———. *Lon Po Po: A Red-Riding Hood Story from China.* New York: Philomel, 1989. When mother leaves the children at home, a wolf enters their house. The children must think quickly and come up with a plan to outsmart the wolf. (I: 7–10)

* ———. *Red Thread.* New York: Philomel, 1993. When a man from the spirit world shows Wei Gu the three-year-old girl who will become his future wife, Wei Gu tries to change his destiny. (I: 6–9)

Latin American

* Ada, Alma Flor. *Jordi's Star.* Illustrated by Susan Gaber. New York: Putnam, 1996. A lonely shepherd believes that a star has fallen into a pool, and his efforts to create a place of beauty for the star turn rocky slopes into green and vibrant hillsides. (I: 6–9)

* ———. *The Rooster Who Went to His Uncle's Wedding.* Illustrated by Kathleen Kuchera. New York: Putnam, 1993. Told in cumulative form, this folktale from Latin America is about how Rooster needs his beak cleaned in time to attend his uncle's wedding. It is the sun, who has long enjoyed the rooster's morning call, who sets off the chain of events that makes it possible. (I: 6–9)

* Ancona, George. *Pablo Remembers: The Fiesta of the Day of the Dead.* New York: Lothrop, Lee & Shepard, 1993. Pablo and his family prepare for the three-day fiesta of El Día de Los Muertos, a festival to honor the spirits of the dead. (I: 6–9)

* ———. *The Piñata Maker/El piñatero.* San Diego, CA: Harcourt, 1994. Don Ricardo is a craftsman in Ejutla de Crespo in southern Mexico. He makes piñatas for birthday parties and other fiestas. (I: 6–9)

* Cowley, Joy. *Gracias, the Thanksgiving Turkey.* Illustrated by Joe Cepeda. New York: Scholastic, 1996. Papa sends Miguel a turkey with instructions to fatten the bird for Thanksgiving dinner. When Miguel becomes attached to his new pet, he faces a problem. (I: 6–9)

* Czernecki, Stefan, and Timothy Rhodes. *The Hummingbirds' Gift.* Illustrated by Stefan Czernecki with straw weavings by Julianna Reyes de Silva and Juan Hilario Silva. New York: Hyperion, 1994. This story tells how the village of Tzintzuntzan, Mexico, was given the Tarascan Indian name for "the place of the hummingbirds." The illustrations combine woven straw figures called *panicuas* with gouache paintings. (I: 6–9)

* Delacre, Lulu. *Arroz con leche: Popular Songs and Rhymes from Latin America.* New York: Scholastic, 1989. The songs and rhymes in this bilingual collection are known throughout the Spanish-speaking countries. A related title is *Las Navidades: Popular Christmas Songs from Latin America* (1990). (I: P–8)

* ———. *Golden Tales: Myths, Legends and Folktales from Latin America.* New York: Scholastic, 1996. The twelve classic tales in this collection come from four cultures of Latin America—Taino, Zapotec, Muisca, Inca—and from many different countries. (I: 9–12)

* Dorros, Arthur. *Abuela.* Illustrated by Elisa Kleven. New York: Dutton, 1991. Rosalba imagines that she goes flying over New York City with her adventurous grandma, Abuela. Also by Dorros is *Isla* (1995). (I: P–8)

* Emberley, Rebecca. *My House/Mi casa: A Book in Two Languages.* Boston: Little, Brown, 1990. Things commonly found in a house are labeled throughout the illustrations in both English and Spanish. A related title is *Taking a Walk/Caminando: A Book in Two Languages* (1990). (I: P–7)

* Garza, Carmen Lomas. *Family Pictures/Cuadros de familia.* San Francisco: Children's Book Press, 1990. Bilingual text accompanies folk art illustrations depicting the author's experiences of growing up Mexican American in South Texas. Another book by Garza is *In My Family/En mi familia* (1996). (I: 6–10)

González, Lucía, M. *Señor Cat's Romance and Other Favorite Stories from Latin America.* Illustrated by Lulu Delacre. New York: Scholastic, 1997. Each of the six tales about outrageous Señor Cat, silly Juan Bobo, and others is followed by a note about the culture it comes from. (I: 6–9)

* Hurwitz, Johanna. *New Shoes for Silvia.* Illustrated by Jerry Pinkney. New York: Morrow, 1993. Silvia's Tía Rosita has sent new red shoes to her in the mail, "as red as the setting sun," "as red as the inside of a watermelon," and "the color of a rose." They are too big, but Silvia finds many uses for them until she grows into them. (I: P–7)

* Lauture, Denizé. *Running the Road to ABC.* Illustrated by Reynolds Ruffins. New York: Simon & Schuster, 1996. Haitian children run to school while it is still dark outside, anticipating learning their ABCs. (I: 6–9)

* Markun, Patricia Maloney. *The Little Painter of Sabana Grande.* Illustrated by Robert Casilla. New York: Bradbury, 1993. Fernando makes his paints the way the country people of Panama make theirs—out of charcoal from burned tree stumps, berries, dried grasses, and clay. His father realizes how hard it must be for Fernando not to have paints and allows him to paint on the exterior walls of the house. (I: 6–9)

* Martinez, Alejandro Cruz. *The Woman Who Outshone the Sun/La mujer que brillaba aún más que el sol.* Illustrated by Fernando Olivera. Story by Rosalma Zubizarreta, Harriet Rohmer, and David Schecter from a poem by Alejandro Cruz Martinez. San Francisco: Children's Book Press, 1991. This retelling of a Zapotec Indian legend from Mexico is the story of Llucia Zenteno, a beautiful woman who possesses magical powers. When she is sent away from a mountain village, she takes its water away in punishment. (I: 7–10)

Mohr, Nicholasa. *Felita.* 1979. New York: Bantam, 1990. Moving is always hard, but when Felita's family moves to an area where there aren't other Puerto Rican families speaking Spanish, the adjustment feels even more lonely. Also by Mohr is *Going Home* (1986). (I: 9–12)

* Mora, Pat. *A Birthday Basket for Tia.* Illustrated by Cecily Lan. New York: Macmillan, 1992. Cecila wants to find the perfect present for her great-aunt's ninetieth birthday. (I: P–6)

* ———. *The Desert Is My Mother/El desierto es mi madre.* Illustrated by Daniel Lechón. Houston, TX: Arte Público/Piñata, 1994. The desert is described by a young girl who poetically narrates how she interacts with nature. (I: P–6)

* Roe, Eileen. *Con mi hermano/With My Brother.* Illustrated by Robert Casilla. New York: Bradbury, 1991. In bilingual text, a little boy describes his big brother with admiration and looks forward to the day he will be like his big brother. (I: P–6)

Soto, Gary. *Baseball in April and Other Stories.* New York: Harcourt, 1990. The eleven short stories in this collection tell of experiences growing up Mexican American in Fresno, California. (I: 9–12)

* ———. *Chato's Kitchen.* New York: Putnam, 1995. Illustrated by Susan Guevara. Cool cat Chato is thrilled to see who has moved into the barrio—a family of tasty-looking mice. When they accept a dinner invitation, Chato is filled with anticipation as he prepares the frijoles, guacamole, arroz, tortillas, and more, but things go differently than he expects when the mice's friend shows up. (I: 7–9)

———. *Neighborhood Odes.* Illustrated by David Diaz. New York: Harcourt, 1992. These twenty-one poems describe various everyday joys of growing up in a Mexican American neighborhood. (I: 9–YA)

* ———. *The Old Man and His Door.* Illustrated by Joe Cepeda. New York: Putnam, 1996. The story is based on a Mexican song that goes "La puerta. El puerco. There's no difference to el viejo." Misunderstanding his wife's instructions on what to take to a party, an old man takes a door instead of a pig. But the door proves useful along the way, and the old man has many surprises for his wife. (I: P–8)

———. *Taking Sides.* New York: Harcourt, 1991. Lincoln Mendoza moves from his familiar neighborhood to the suburbs when his mother gets a better-paying job. When the basketball team of his new school plays against his former team, he realizes he needs to sort out his self-identity. (I: 10–12)

* ———. *Too Many Tamales.* Illustrated by Ed Martinez. New York: Putnam, 1993. While helping to make tamales, Maria slips her mother's diamond ring on her hand to admire it. Upon realizing that the ring is missing, she enlists the help of her cousins in eating the tamales until the ring is found. (I: 6–9)

* Torres, Leyla. *Saturday Sancocho.* New York: Mirasol/Farrar, 1995. María Líli's mother decides to make *sancocho* but needs a chicken; the two go to the marketplace to trade eggs for a series of items. (I: 6–9)

Native American

* Begay, Shonto. *Ma'ii and Cousin Horned Toad.* New York: Scholastic, 1992. This traditional Navajo story is about a coyote who is always hungry. Because he hates to work, he visits his cousin and tries to trick him out of food and farm. (I: 6–9)

* Bruchac, Joseph. *Between Earth and Sky: Legends of Native American Sacred Places.* Illustrated by Thomas Locker. San Diego, CA: Harcourt, 1996. A man teaches his nephew about the sacredness of living things. Various Native American legends tell of sacred places. (I: 10–13)

* ———. *The Boy Who Lived with the Bears and Other Iroquois Stories.* Illustrated by Murv Jacob. New York: HarperCollins, 1995. This is a collection of six Iroquois animal stories that have been passed down through generations of storytellers. (I: 8–11)

* ———. *Dog People: Native Dog Stories.* Illustrated by Murv Jacob. Golden, CO: Fulcrum, 1995. These six short stories, set in northern New England shortly after the glaciers receded northward, describe the special relationship between Abenaki children and their faithful friends, the dogs. (I: 9–12)

* ———. *The First Strawberries: A Cherokee Story.* Illustrated by Anna Vojtech. New York: Dial, 1993. This folktale tells how the first man's arrogance causes the first woman to leave when he becomes angry at her for spending time on flowers rather than on preparing dinner. (I: P–8)

* Bruchac, Joseph, and Jonathan London. *Thirteen Moons on Turtle's Back: A Native American Year of Moons.* Illustrated by Thomas Locker. New York: Philomel, 1992. Many Native American tribes relate the thirteen moons of the year to the pattern of thirteen large scales on the turtle's back. These poems, each based on a story from a different Native American nation such as the Cherokee, Cree, or Sioux, comprise the text for this book. (I: 8–10)

* Bunting, Eve. *Cheyenne Again.* Illustrated by Irving Toddy. New York: Clarion, 1995. Set in the late 1880s, this story is of a ten-year-old Cheyenne boy named Young Bull, who was taken away from his family and home and sent to a boarding school to learn the white man's ways. The illustrator experienced a similar situation in his own life. (I: 6–9)

Caduto, Michael J., and Joseph Bruchac. *Keepers of the Animals: Native American Stories and Wildlife Activities for Children.* Illustrated by John Kahionhes Fadden, David Kanietakeron Fadden, D. D. Tyler, and Carol Wood. Golden, CO: Fulcrum, 1991. Seventeen sets of stories about animals combine information about Native American heritage with environmental lessons, each followed by suggestions for cross-curriculum activities to increase understanding of animals and their needs. (I: 6–12)

———. *Keepers of the Earth: Native American Stories and Environmental Activities for Children.* Illustrated by John Kahionhes Fadden and Carol Wood. Golden, CO: Fulcrum, 1988. This book's purpose is to teach children about Native American cultures and the link between humans and nature through an interdisciplinary approach. Twenty-three sets of lessons each feature a story followed by suggested activities to enhance learning. (I: 6–12)

* Cohen, Caron Lee. *The Mud Pony.* Illustrated by Shonto Begay. New York: Scholastic, 1988. A poor boy creates a mud pony and cares for it as if it were real. He dreams that the pony comes alive, and he awakens to find that it will guide him through many ordeals. (I: 6–9)

* de Paola, Tomie. *The Legend of the Bluebonnet.* New York: Putnam, 1983. She-Who-Is-Alone gives up her most valued possession—her doll from her deceased parents—in order to stop the drought and save her people from a famine. The scattered ashes of her doll come up as the bluebonnet, the state flower of Texas. A related title is *The Legend of the Indian Paintbrush* (1983). (I: 6–9)

Dorris, Michael. *Guests.* New York: Hyperion, 1994. As his people prepare for an annual harvest feast that may be the first Thanksgiving, a Native American boy named Moss is caught between childhood and coming of age. (I: 8–10)

———. *Morning Girl.* New York: Hyperion, 1992. Morning Girl and her younger brother Star Boy describe their island life in alternating chapters. The story closes with the arrival of the first Europeans to her world. (I: 9–12)

* Ekoomiak, Normee. *Arctic Memories.* New York: Holt, 1988. Appliqued, stitched, and painted illustrations show everyday and special events in the lives of Inuits of the past. Through bilingual Inuktitut and English text, the author/illustrator describes his memories of his childhood in an Inuit community in northern Quebec. (I: 7–10)

* Esbensen, Barbara Juster. *The Star Maiden: An Ojibway Tale.* Illustrated by Helen K. Davie. Boston: Little, Brown, 1988. A star that wants to come to Earth considers what kind of flower to come as—a wild rose, a bluebonnet, or a water lily. (I: 8–10)

* Goble, Paul. *Death of the Iron Horse.* New York: Bradbury, 1987. Fearful of what will happen as the white men approach their territory, a group of Cheyenne braves derail a freight train in 1867, believing it to be an Iron Horse whose rails are binding Mother Earth. (I: 8–10)

* ———. *The Girl Who Loved Wild Horses.* New York: Macmillan, 1978. A girl's love of horses leads her to be among them, where her family finds her. She finds that she feels a sense of belonging when she is with the horses. (I: 6–8)

* Hoyt-Goldsmith, Diane. *Cherokee Summer.* Photographs by Lawrence Migdale. New York: Holiday

House, 1993. A young Cherokee girl describes contemporary life, telling of day-to-day experiences as well as a little about the Cherokee language, traditions, a legend, and a stomp dance. A related title is *Pueblo Storyteller* (1991), about a young Cochiti Indian girl. (**I:** 8–10)

* Martin, Rafe. *The Boy Who Lived with the Seals.* Illustrated by David Shannon. New York: Putnam, 1993. This story of a lost boy who grows up with seals is from Chinook Indian legend. Years later, his parents find him and reclaim him as their son, but the boy hears the seals calling and longs to rejoin them. (**I:** 6–9)

* Osofsky, Audrey. *Dreamcatcher.* Illustrated by Ed Young. New York: Orchard, 1992. While an Ojibway baby sleeps, the dream catcher snags bad dreams and lets only the good dreams through the center hole in the web. (**I:** 6—9)

* Ross, Gayle. *How Turtle's Back Was Cracked.* Illustrated by Murv Jacob. New York: Dial, 1995. Turtle is always boasting, and the wolves decide they've heard enough. This story tells how Turtle's shell ended up breaking into twelve pieces and why, even today, you can see the lines where it was put back together. (**I:** 6–9)

* Scott, Ann Herbert. *On Mother's Lap.* 1972. Illustrated by Glo Coalson. New York: Clarion, 1992. Michael enjoys rocking in Mother's lap—along with Dolly, Boat, reindeer blanket, and puppy—until Mother hears the baby crying. The illustrator created the original sketches while living in an Inuit village. (**I:** P—6)

* Sneve, Virginia Driving Hawk. *The Hopis.* Illustrated by Ronald Himler. New York: Holiday House, 1995. This book is part of the series *The First Americans* (which includes *The Sioux, The Navajos, The Seminoles, The Nez Perce, The Iroquois*). The creation story of the Hopis, their history, arts and crafts, life style, religion, and how they live today are discussed. (**I:** 7–10)

* Steptoe, John. *The Story of Jumping Mouse.* New York: Lothrop, Lee & Shepard, 1984. Jumping Mouse sets out to find the "far-off land." He finds that his generosity pays off as each of the animals he encounters bestows a gift to ensure his safe passage to his "far-off land." (**I:** 9–13)

* Yellow Robe, Rosebud. *Tonweya and the Eagles: And Other Lakota Tales.* Illustrated by Jerry Pinkney. New York: Dial, 1979. This collection of animal tales is based on the oral storytelling tradition of the Lakota Sioux. (**I:** 6–9)

* Yolen, Jane. *Encounter.* Illustrated by David Shannon. San Diego, CA: Harcourt, 1992. This story is narrated by a young Taino boy, who tells of the arrival of Columbus and his ships in 1492. (**I:** 7–11)

Other Cultures

* Burgie, Irving. *Caribbean Carnival: Songs of the West Indies.* Illustrated by Frané Lessac. New York: Morrow/Tambourine, 1992. This collection of Calypso classics and Caribbean folksongs includes the lyrics and musical notations for piano and guitar accompaniment. Lessac's primitive paintings depict the colorful island setting. (**I:** all ages)

* Houston, Gloria. *My Great-Aunt Arizona.* Illustrated by Susan Condie Lamb. New York: Harper, 1992. Arizona Houston Hughes was born in a log cabin in the Blue Ridge Mountains, and she grew up to become a teacher in the one-room school she had attended as a child. Generations of children are inspired by Arizona to imagine the faraway places they will someday visit. (**I:** 6–9)

Joseph, Lynn. *A Wave in Her Pocket: Stories from Trinidad.* Illustrated by Brian Pinkney. New York: Clarion, 1991. Tantie, the family storyteller, shares six stories that originated in Trinidad, West Africa, and in her imagination. A sequel is *The Mermaid's Twin Sister: More Stories from Trinidad* (1994). (**I:** 8–12)

Lowry, Lois. *Number the Stars.* Boston: Houghton Mifflin, 1989. When the Nazis come to find the Jews, ten-year-old Annemarie's family shelters a Jewish girl and participates as part of the Danish resistance in helping Jews escape to Sweden. (**I:** 10–13)

* Nye, Naomi Shihab. *Sitti's Secrets.* Illustrated by Nancy Carpenter. New York: Four Winds, 1994. An American girl can't speak Arabic, the language of her grandmother—her *sitti*—but she remembers that they learned to communicate during time they spent together in Palestine. (**I:** 6–9)

* Polacco, Patricia. *The Keeping Quilt.* New York: Simon & Schuster, 1988. A quilt made of scraps from clothes of family members left behind in Russia is passed down through the generations. The quilt serves a multitude of purposes: to welcome babies into the world, as a tent during play time, as a picnic cloth for a romantic date, and as a wedding huppa. (**I:** 7–10)

———. *Mrs. Katz and Tush.* New York: Bantam, 1992. A lonely Jewish widow gains companionship when an African American boy gives her a kitten. (**I:** 6–9)

* Rylant, Cynthia. *The Relatives Came.* Illustrated by Stephen Gammell. New York: Bradbury, 1985. This book celebrates a family reunion in the Appalachian mountains, where relatives must travel over winding mountain roads for a visit. (**I:** P–8)

* San Souci, Robert D. *The Faithful Friend*. Illustrated by Brian Pinkney. New York: Simon & Schuster, 1995. In this traditional tale from the French West Indies island of Martinique, Clemente and Hippolyte are friends who find love, strange zombies, and danger. (I: 7–10)

* ———. *Sukey and the Mermaid*. Illustrated by Brian Pinkney. New York: Four Winds, 1992. Sukey is unhappy with her life at home until she meets Mama Jo, a mermaid. (I: 7–10)

Multiple Cultures

* Adoff, Arnold. *Black Is Brown Is Tan*. Illustrated by Emily Arnold McCully. New York: Harper, 1973. Two children with a "chocolate momma," a "white" daddy, and "granny white and grandma black" share the joys of being a family. (I: 6–9)

* Dooley, Norah. *Everybody Cooks Rice*. Illustrated by Peter J. Thornton. Minneapolis, MN: Carolrhoda, 1991. It is dinner time and Carrie sets out to find her little brother. At each home, she finds that rice is part of the family's evening meal, but that it is prepared differently because of the various cultural backgrounds of the families. A related title is *Everybody Bakes Bread* (1996). (I: 6–9)

Jenness, Aylette. *Families: A Celebration of Diversity, Commitment, and Love*. Boston: Houghton Mifflin, 1990. Photographs and brief text introduce seventeen families of varying composition, including divorced parents, stepfamilies, gay parents, foster siblings, and extended families. (I: 7–10)

Levitin, Sonia. *The Golem and the Dragon Girl*. Illustrated by Ellen Thompson. New York: Dial, 1993. A Jewish American boy and a Chinese American girl find that their cultures have interesting parallels. (I: 10–14)

* Medearis, Angela. *Dancing with the Indians*. Illustrated by Samuel Byrd. New York: Holiday House, 1991. The author reflects on accounts from her own African American family history about watching and participating in an annual Seminole celebration dance. (I: 6–9)

Nelson, Vaunda Micheaux. *Mayfield Crossing*. Illustrated by Leonard Jenkins. New York: Putnam, 1993. When the school in Mayfield Crossing closes and its black students are sent to another school, they face racial and socioeconomic prejudices for the first time. (I: 8–12)

* Nikola-Lisa, W. *Bein' with You This Way*. Illustrated by Michael Bryant. New York: Lee & Low, 1994. Through upbeat rhythm, the text points out and celebrates people's physical similarities and differences. (I: P–8)

* Rosen, Michael. *Elijah's Angel: A Story for Chanukah and Christmas*. Illustrated by Aminah Brenda Lynn Robinson. San Diego, CA: Harcourt, 1992. This story is based on an actual friendship between a young Jewish boy and an elderly African American barber who is a Christian. A gift exchange of a carved angel and a menorah is symbolic of their friendship. (I: 9–12)

Rosenberg, Maxine. *Living in Two Worlds*. New York: Lothrop, Lee & Shepard, 1986. Five children, each of whom has parents of different ethnicities, describe their experiences growing up biracial. (I: 9–12)

Soto, Gary. *Pacific Crossing*. San Diego, CA: Harcourt, 1992. When two Mexican American boys go to Japan as foreign exchange students to study martial arts, they realize that the bonds of friendship with people in their host country outweight their cultural differences. (I: 10–14)

Spinelli, Jerry. *Maniac Magee*. Boston: Little, Brown, 1990. Twelve-year-old Jeffrey Lionel Magee earns the nickname "Maniac" in this tall tale because of the incredible feats he supposedly performs. Maniac crosses racial boundaries separating the East End and the West End. (I: 10–12)

Woodson, Jacqueline. *Maizon at Blue Hill*. New York: Delacorte, 1992. Maizon enters a private boarding school and learns to deal with being one of only five African American students. She spends much time reflecting on what it feels like to be different from most. (I: 11–YA)

World Cultures Compared

* Anno, Mitsumasa. *All in a Day*. New York: Philomel, 1986. The narrator, on a deserted island near the international date line, describes how children in eight countries celebrate New Year's Day. (I: 6–9)

* Lankford, Mary. *Hopscotch Around the World*. Illustrated by Karen Milone. New York: Morrow, 1992. This book gives general descriptions, historical significance, cultural notes, geographical notes, and language notes on nineteen versions of hopscotch played around the world. (I: 6–10)

* Lewin, Ted. *Market!* New York: Lothrop, Lee & Shepard, 1996. A look at marketplaces in Ecuador, Nepal, Ireland, Uganda, Morocco, and the United States, showing the various things people bring to sell or trade. (I: 6–9)

* Morris, Ann. *Houses and Homes*. Photography by Ken Heyman. New York: Lothrop, Lee & Shepard, 1992. Through photographs and simple text, readers are introduced to the varieties of homes in which people around the world live, ranging from

Buckingham Palace to houses on stilts, houses on boats, and straw huts. (I: 5–9)

Nye, Naomi Shihab, ed. *This Same Sky: A Collection of Poems from Around the World*. New York: Four Winds, 1992. The many forms of life under "this same sky"—human, animal, and nature—are reflected in poems written by 129 poets from 68 different countries. (I: 10–YA)

Social Issues

* Bunting, Eve. *A Day's Work*. New York: Clarion, 1994. A boy and his grandfather find work by the day, and when they misunderstand the directions and mistakenly perform the roadside job of pulling weeds all wrong, they make arrangements to correct their mistake the next day. (I: 6–8)

* ———. *Flyaway Home*. Illustrated by Ronald Himler. New York: Clarion, 1991. A homeless father and son pass the time in the airport. A trapped bird that is freed gives the little boy hope about his future. (I: 6–9)

* ———. *Smoky Night*. Illustrated by David Diaz. San Diego, CA: Harcourt, 1994. The Los Angeles riots are seen from the perspective of a little boy and his mother as they seek shelter from danger. (I: 9–11)

* ———. *The Wednesday Surprise*. Illustrated by Donald Carrick. New York: Clarion, 1989. Anna and her grandmother spend every Wednesday together, reading. The surprise comes on Anna's father's birthday when Grandma gets up and reads for the first time, having learned from her "smart" grandchild. (I: 6–9)

Buss, Fran Leeper. *Journey of the Sparrows*. New York: Penguin/Lodestar, 1991. Three siblings escape the war in El Salvador and head for the hope of new life, nailed into a crate on the back of a truck. (I: 12–YA)

Cleary, Beverly. *Dear Mr. Henshaw*. Illustrated by Paul Zelinsky. New York: Morrow, 1983. Lee first writes to an author as part of a school assignment. In the continued correspondence, Lee increasingly confides in Mr. Henshaw about various issues that concern him—his parents' divorce, relationships with peers, etc. (I: 9–11)

* Dugan, Barbara. *Loop the Loop*. Illustrated by James Stevenson. New York: Greenwillow, 1992. While playing outside, Anne encounters Mrs. Simpson, a woman who rides in a wheelchair, claims to be 969 years old, and performs fabulous tricks with a yo-yo. When Mrs. Simpson breaks her hip, Anne takes Mrs. Simpson's cat and a yo-yo to the hospital. (I: 6–9)

Hamilton, Virginia. *Plain City*. New York: Scholastic, 1993. Buhlaire, a child of mixed racial heritage, is ostracized by peers for her family's unusual habits.

Her mother sings in clubs and she thinks her father is Missing in Action—until one day a homeless man appears. (I: 11–YA)

* Hausherr, Rosemarie. *Celebrating Families*. New York: Scholastic, 1997. Color photos and accompanying text introduce children from single-parent families, adoptive families, extended families, and other types. (I: 6–9)

Jenness, Aylette. *Families: A Celebration of Diversity, Commitment, and Love*. Boston: Houghton Mifflin, 1990. Definitions of families today are diverse, as is family membership. Personal voices describe what it is like to be part of various family compositions. (I: 7–10)

Paterson, Katherine. *The Flip Flop Girl*. New York: Viking, 1994. Father's death is hard enough to cope with, but moving to a new place, living with grandmother, and dealing with poverty make life even more difficult. (I: 9–12)

———. *The Great Gilly Hopkins*. New York: Crowell, 1978. Gilly's attempts to be difficult and unlikable lead to her being moved from one foster home to another. Trotter, a foster mother, helps Gilly accept the love and security she craves. (I: 9–12)

* Pearson, Susan. *Happy Birthday, Grampie*. Illustrated by Ronald Himler. New York: Dial, 1987. Age has taken away Grampie's vision, and he has forgotten English and reverted to his mother tongue, Swedish. Martha makes Grampie a card he can "feel" and hopes it will communicate her birthday wishes. (I: 6–9)

* Sun, Chyng Feng. *Mama Bear*. Illustrated by Lolly Robinson. Boston: Houghton Mifflin, 1994. Mei-Mei wants a big toy bear she sees in a store window, but her mother needs money to fix the furnace so that they can keep warm this winter. (I: P–8)

Temple, Frances. *Grab Hands and Run*. New York: Orchard, 1993. Felipe and his family face threats to their lives at their home in El Salvador. He tells the story of their escape and the dangerous journey to Canada. (I: 12–YA)

———. *Tonight, by Sea*. New York: Orchard, 1995. Poverty and government brutality make life in Haiti unbearable, so Paulie and other villagers help her uncle build a boat so that they can secretly attempt to escape to the United States. (I: 12–YA)

Gender Issues

* Cole, Joanna. *The Magic School Bus at the Waterworks*. Illustrated by Bruce Degen. New York: Scholastic, 1986. In the *Magic School Bus* series, Ms. Frizzle, the teacher, leads the class on numerous adventuresome field trips. (I: 6–9)

* Hoffman, Mary. *Amazing Grace*. Illustrated by Caroline Binch. New York: Dial, 1991. When Grace is told by classmates that she can't be Peter Pan in the class play because she's black and a girl, she proves otherwise. (I: 6–8)

* Isadora, Rachel. *Max*. New York: Macmillan, 1976. Max finds that taking dance lessons with his sister is a nice warm-up to his afternoon baseball games. (I: 5–8)

Lasky, Kathryn. *Beyond the Divide*. New York: Macmillan, 1983. Meribah's father is shunned by his Amish community, loses touch with his family, and decides to go west for the gold rush. Meribah's choice to go with him is the first of many difficult choices she must make while heading west. (I: 11–YA)

* Merrill, Jean. *The Girl Who Loved Caterpillars*. Illustrated by Floyd Cooper. New York: Philomel, 1992. This is a retelling of a twelfth-century Japanese story of Izumi, a free-spirited girl who preferred studying caterpillars over learning the arts of the ancient court. (I: 7–10)

* Paterson, Katherine. *The King's Equal*. Illustrated by Vladimir Vagin. New York: HarperCollins, 1992. A prince in search of a princess to be his equal finds that he must prove to be her equal as well. (I: 7–10)

————. *Lyddie*. New York: Penguin/Lodestar, 1991. In the mid 1800s, Lyddie becomes a factory girl in the mill town of Lowell, Massachusetts, to earn wages in an attempt to save the family farm. (I: 11–YA)

* Willhoite, Michael. *Daddy's Roommate*. Boston: Alyson Wonderland, 1990. Following a divorce, Daddy lives with another man. (I: P–8)

Woodson, Jacqueline. *From the Notebooks of Melanin Sun*. New York: Scholastic/Blue Sky, 1995. Melanin Sun faces the everyday challenges of a thirteen-year-old growing up, but life is complicated when he hears rumors about his mother's love for a woman of a different race. (I: 12–YA)

* Zolotow, Charlotte. *William's Doll*. Illustrated by William P. duBois. New York: Harper, 1972. William participates in traditional activities for boys but also wants a doll. Despite objections from male characters, Grandmother gets William a doll so that he can prepare for when he will be a father. (I: P–8)

Exceptional Learners

Adler, C. S. *Good-bye Pink Pig*. New York: Putnam, 1985. Amanda escapes to a fantasy world of miniature animals as a way to cope with her relationship with a mother who presents herself as "perfect" but hides emotional problems. (I: 10–12)

* Barrett, Mary Brigid. *Sing to the Stars*. Illustrated by Sandra Speidel. Boston: Little, Brown, 1994. When an accident takes his daughter's life and leaves him blind, Mr. Washington stops playing the piano. Ephram plays his violin and convinces Mr. Washington to join him on the stage so that they can make music together. (I: 8–10)

* Booth, B. D. *Mandy*. Illustrated by Jim Lamarche. New York: Lothrop, Lee & Shepard, 1991. Mandy's musings about why she fears the dark and wonderings about the sounds of the world allow readers to get inside the thinking of a child with hearing loss. (I: 6–8)

* Brown, Tricia. *Someone Special Just Like You*. Photographs by Fran Ortiz. New York: Holt, 1982. Photographs and simple text addressed to the reader, show children with various disabilities engaged in activities in which all children participate. (I: P–6).

Byars, Betsy. *Summer of the Swans*. Illustrated by Ted CoConis. New York: Viking, 1970. Sara learns to cope with her feelings of resentment toward her younger brother who is developmentally delayed. (I: 10–13)

* Cohen, Miriam. *See You Tomorrow, Charles*. Illustrated by Lillian Hoban. New York: Greenwillow, 1983. In this book (part of a series), Charles is a child with vision loss in a class of first graders who learn with and from each other. (I: 5–7)

* Fanshawe, Elizabeth. *Rachel*. Illustrated by Michael Charlton. New York: Bradbury, 1975. Rachel uses a wheelchair to get around and participate in various activities. She attends school, goes to Brownies, goes on trips, and enjoys participating in everyday family life. (I: P–8)

* Fleming, Virginia. *Be Good to Eddie Lee*. Illustrated by Floyd Cooper. New York: Philomel, 1993. Christy learns to appreciate the sensitive heart of Eddie Lee, a child with Down syndrome, when he noisily tags along on a visit to the woods in search of frog eggs. (I: 7–9)

* Haldane, Suzanne. *Helping Hands: How Monkeys Assist People Who Are Disabled*. New York: Dutton, 1991. A teen boy with quadriplegia performs daily routines with the aid of a monkey. (I: 6–12)

Little, Jean. *Little by Little: A Writer's Education*. New York: Viking, 1987. A child who has visual impairment retreats into her imagination and discovers her talent as a writer. (I: 12–YA)

* Miller, Mary Beth, and George Ancona. *Handtalk School*. New York: Four Winds, 1991. A guide to a day in a boarding school for children with hearing loss shows through color photographs the use of American Sign Language to communicate. (I: all ages)

Philbrick, Rodman. *Freak the Mighty*. New York: Blue Sky Press/Scholastic, 1993. A boy with physical size and might and a boy with intellectual brilliance are the book's main characters. Separately, each lacks what the other has, but together they become "Freak the Mighty." (I: 10–14)

* Rankin, Laura. *The Handmade Alphabet*. New York: Dial, 1991. The alphabet is depicted in sign language letters, with a picture cue to accompany each hand sign. (I: P–9)

Rosenberg, Maxine B. *Finding a Way: Living with Exceptional Brothers and Sisters*. New York: Lothrop, Lee & Shepard, 1988. Three children describe what it is like to have siblings with physical disorders: diabetes, severe asthma, and spina bifida. (I: 7–9)

Slote, Alfred. *Hang Tough, Paul Mather*. Philadelphia: Lippincott, 1973. Twelve-year-old Paul's enthusiasm for baseball helps him through the difficulty of living with treatments for leukemia. (I: 9–11)

RESOURCES

Aoki, Elaine. "Turning the Page: Asian Pacific American Children's Literature." *Teaching Multicultural Literature in Grades K–8*. Ed. Violet Harris. Norwood, MA: Christopher-Gordon, 1992. 109–35.

Banks, James A. *An Introduction to Multicultural Education*. Boston: Allyn & Bacon, 1994.

———. *Multiethnic Education: Theory and Practice*. 3rd ed. Boston: Allyn & Bacon, 1994.

Barrera, Rosalinda B., Olga Ligouri, and Loretta Salas. "Ideas a Literature Can Grow On: Key Insights for Enriching and Expanding Children's Literature About the Mexican-American Experience." *Teaching Multicultural Literature in Grades K–8*. Ed. Violet Harris. Norwood, MA: Christopher-Gordon, 1992. 203–31.

Bello, Yahaya. "Caribbean Children's Literature." *Teaching Multicultural Literature in Grades K–8*. Ed. Violet Harris. Norwood, MA: Christopher-Gordon, 1992. 243–65.

Cai, Mingshui, and Rudine Sims Bishop. "Multicultural Literature for Children: Towards a Clarification of the Concept." *The Need for Story: Cultural Diversity in Classroom and Community*. Eds. A. H. Dyson and C. Genishi. Urbana, IL: National Council of Teachers of English, 1994.

Cooperative Children's Book Center. *The Multicolored Mirror: Cultural Substance in Literature for Children and Young Adults*. Ed. Merri V. Lindgren. Fort Atkinson, WI: Highsmith, 1991.

Friedberg, Joan Brest, June B. Mullins, and Adelaide Weir Sukiennik. *Portraying Persons with Disabilities: An Annotated Bibliography of Nonfiction for Children and Teenagers*. New Providence, NJ: Bowker, 1992.

Grossman, Herbert, and Suzanne H. Grossman. *Gender Issues in Education*. Boston: Allyn & Bacon, 1994.

Harris, Violet J. "African American Children's Literature: The First One Hundred Years." *Journal of Negro Education* 59 (1990): 540–55.

———. "Contemporary Griots: African-American Writers of Children's Literature." *Teaching Multicultural Literature in Grades K–8*. Ed. Violet Harris. Norwood, MA: Christopher-Gordon, 1992. 55–108.

———. "Have You Heard About an African Cinderella Story? The Hunt for Multiethnic Literature." *Publishing Research Quarterly* 7 (1991): 23–36.

Harris, Violet J., ed. *Teaching Multicultural Literature in Grades K–8*. Norwood, MA: Christopher-Gordon Publishers, 1992b.

Harris, Violet J., Junko Yokota, Georgia Johnson, and Oralia Garza de Cortes. "Bookalogues: Multicultural Literature." *Language Arts* 70 (1993): 215–44.

Jenkins, E., and M. Austin. *Literature for Children about Asians and Asian Americans: Analysis and Annotated Bibliography with Additional Readings for Adults*. Westport, CT: Greenwood, 1987.

Kruse, Ginny Moore, and Kathleen T. Horning. *Multicultural Literature for Children and Young Adults: A Selected Listing of Books 1980–1990 By and About People of Color*. 3rd ed. Madison, WI: Cooperative Children's Book Center, 1991.

MacCann, Donnarae. "Native Americans in Books for the Young." *Teaching Multicultural Literature in Grades K–8*. Ed. Violet Harris. Norwood, MA: Christopher-Gordon, 1992. 137–69.

Miller-Lachmann, Lyn. *Our Family, Our Friends, Our World*. New Providence, NJ: Bowker, 1992.

New York Public Library. *The Black Experience in Children's Books*. 3rd ed. New York: New York Public Library, 1989.

Nieto, Sonia. "We Have Stories to Tell: A Case Study of Puerto Ricans in Children's Books." *Teaching Multicultural Literature in Grades K–8*. Ed. Violet Harris. Norwood, MA: Christopher-Gordon, 1992. 171–201.

Robertson, Debra. *Portraying Persons with Disabilities: An Annotated Bibliography of Fiction for*

Children and Teenagers. New Providence, NJ: Bowker, 1992.

Rochman, Hazel. *Against Borders: Promoting Books for a Multicultural World.* Chicago: American Library Association, 1993.

Rudman, Masha Kabakow. *Children's Literature: An Issues Approach.* 3rd ed. White Plains, NY: Longman, 1995.

Schon, Isabel. *A Hispanic Heritage: A Guide to Juvenile Books about Hispanic People and Culture.* 3rd ed. Metuchen, NJ: Scarecrow, 1988.

Sims, Rudine. *Shadow and Substance: Afro-American Experience in Contemporary Children's Fiction.* 2nd ed. Chicago: National Council of Teachers of English/American Library Association, 1982.

Sims Bishop, Rudine, and the Multicultural Booklist Committee, eds. *Kaleidoscope.* Urbana, IL: National Council of Teachers of English, 1995.

———. "Multicultural Literature for Children: Making Informed Choices." *Teaching Multicultural Literature in Grades K–8.* Ed. Violet Harris. Norwood, MA: Christopher-Gordon, 1992. 37–54.

Slapin, Beverly, and Doris Seale. *Books without Bias: Through Indian Eyes.* Berkeley, CA: Oyate, 1988.

Smith, Henrietta M., ed. *The Coretta Scott King Awards Book: From Vision to Reality.* Chicago: American Library Association, 1994.

Stensland, A. L. *Literature By and About the American Indian.* Urbana, IL: National Council of Teachers of English, 1979.

Taxel, Joel. "The Politics of Children's Literature: Reflections on Multiculturalism, Political Correctness, and Christopher Columbus." *Teaching Multicultural Literature in Grades K–8.* Ed. Violet Harris. Norwood, MA: Christopher-Gordon, 1992. 1–36.

Yokota, Junko. "Asian and Asian American Literature for Children: Implications for Classroom Teachers and Librarians." *Multicultural Literature and Literacies: Making Space for Difference.* Eds. Suzanne Miller and Barbara McCaskill. Albany, NY: State University of New York Press, 1993. 229–46.

———. "Issues in Selecting Multicultural Children's Literature." *Language Arts* 70 (1993): 156–67.

REFERENCES

Adoff, Arnold. *I Am the Darker Brother: An Anthology of Modern Poems by Negro Americans.* New York: Macmillan, 1970.

Au, Kathryn H. *Literacy Instruction in Multicultural Settings.* Ft. Worth, TX: Harcourt, 1993.

Banks, James A. *An Introduction to Multicultural Education.* Boston: Allyn & Bacon, 1994.

Bannerman, Helen. *The Story of Little Black Sambo.* New York: HarperCollins, 1899.

Bennett, William. "Education Secretary Bennett's Suggested List for Elementary-School Pupils." *Chronicle of Higher Education* (1988, September 14): B3.

Bishop, Claire Huchet. *The Five Chinese Brothers.* Illustrated by Kurt Wiese. New York: Coward, 1938.

Browne, Anthony. *Piggybook.* New York: Knopf, 1986.

Cai, Mingshui. "Can We Fly across Cultural Gaps on the Wings of Imagination? Ethnicity, Experience, and Cultural Authenticity." *The New Advocate* 8.1 (1995): 1–16.

Cai, Mingshui, and Rudine Sims Bishop. "Multicultural Literature for Children: Towards a Clarification of the Concept." *The Need for Story: Cultural Diversity in Classroom and Community.* Eds. Anne Haas Dyson and Celia Genishi. Urbana, IL: National Council of Teachers of English, 1994.

Chall, J. S., E. Radwin, V. W. French, and C. R. Hall. "Blacks in the World of Children's Books." *The Black American in Books for Children.* 2nd ed. Eds. Donnarae MacCann and G. Woodard. Metuchen, NJ: Scarecrow, 1985. 211–21.

Council on Interracial Books for Children. Special issue on Puerto Rican materials. *Bulletin of the Council on Interracial Books for Children* 4 (1974).

———. Special issue on Chicano materials. *Bulletin of the Council on Interracial Books for Children* 5 (1975).

Delpit, Lisa D. "The Silenced Dialogue: Power and Pedagogy in Educating Other People's Children." *Harvard Educational Review* 58 (1988): 280–98.

Grossman, Virginia, and Sylvia Long. *Ten Little Rabbits.* New York: Chronicle, 1991.

Hamilton, Virginia. "Everything of Value: Moral Realism in Literature for Children" (May Hill Arbuthnot Lecture). *Journal of Youth Services in Libraries* 6 (Summer 1993): 363–77.

———. "Laura Ingalls Wilder Medal Acceptance." *Horn Book* 71.4 (July/August 1995): 436–41.

Harris, Violet J. "African American Children's Literature: The First One Hundred Years." *Journal of Negro Education* 59 (1990): 540–55.

Kaplan, Esther. Personal communication, December 1995.

Larrick, Nancy. "The All-White World of Children's Books." *Saturday Review* (1965, September 11): 63–65.

Little, Jean. *Little by Little: A Writer's Education.* New York: Penguin, 1987.

———. "A Writer's Social Responsibility." *The New Advocate* 3.2 (1990): 79–88.

McCarty, Teresa L. "What's Wrong with Ten Little Rabbits?" *The New Advocate* 8.2 (1995): 97–98.

Meltzer, Milton. "The Social Responsibility of the Writer." *The New Advocate* 2.3 (1989): 155–57.

Nieto, Sonia. "Puerto Ricans in Children's Literature and History Texts: A Ten-Year Update." *Bulletin of the Council on Interracial Books for Children* 14 (1983).

———. *Affirming Diversity.* 2nd ed. White Plains, NY: Longman, 1996.

Noll, Elizabeth. "Accuracy and Authenticity in American Indian Children's Literature: The Social Responsibility of Authors and Illustrators." *The New Advocate* 8.1 (1995): 29–43.

Pallas, A. M., G. Natriello, and E. L. McDill, "The Changing Nature of the Disadvantaged Population: Current Dimensions and Future Trends." *Educational Researcher* 18.5 (1989): 16–22.

Pellowski, Anne. *The Family Story-telling Handbook: How to Use Stories, Anecdotes, Rhymes, Handkerchiefs, Paper, and Other Objects to Enrich Your Family Traditions.* Illustrated by Lynn Sweat. New York: Macmillan, 1987.

———. *Hidden Stories in Plants: Unusual and Easy-to-Tell Stories from Around the World Together with Creative Things to Do While Telling Them.* New York: Macmillan, 1990.

———. *The Story Vine: A Source Book of Unusual and Easy-to-Tell Stories from Around the World.* Illustrated by Lynn Sweat. New York: Macmillan, 1984.

Reimer, K. M. "Multiethnic Literature: Holding Fast to Dreams." *Language Arts* 69 (1992): 14–21.

Rochman, Hazel. *Against Borders: Promoting Books for a Multicultural World.* Chicago: American Library Association, 1993.

Rollock, Barbara. *The Black Experience in Children's Books.* 2nd ed. New York: New York Public Library, 1984.

Rudman, Masha Kabakow. *Children's Literature: An Issues Approach.* 3rd ed. White Plains, NY: Longman, 1995.

Say, Allen. *The Ink-Keeper's Apprentice.* Boston: Houghton Mifflin, 1979.

Schon, Isabel. *A Hispanic Heritage: A Guide to Juvenile Books about Hispanic People and Culture.* 3rd ed. Metuchen, NJ: Scarecrow, 1988.

Schwartz, David M. *How Much Is a Million?* Illustrated by Steven Kellogg. New York: Lothrop, Lee & Shepard, 1985.

Sims, Rudine. "Children's Books about Blacks: A Mid-Eighties Status Report." *Children's Literature Review* 8 (1985): 9–13.

Sims Bishop, Rudine. "African American Literature for Children: Anchor, Compass, and Sail." *Perspectives* 7 (1991): ix–xii.

———. "Mirrors, Windows, and Sliding Glass Doors." *Perspectives* 6 (1990): ix–xi.

———. "Multicultural Literature for Children: Making Informed Choices." *Teaching Multicultural Literature in Grades K–8.* Ed. Violet Harris. Norwood, MA: Christopher-Gordon, 1992. 37–54.

———. Personal communication. October, 1996.

Steptoe, John. *Daddy Is a Monster . . . Sometimes.* New York: Harper, 1980.

Trelease, Jim. *The New Read-Aloud Handbook.* New York: Viking Penguin, 1989.

Zion, Gene. *Dear Garbage Man.* Illustrations by Margaret Bloy Graham. New York: Harper & Row, 1957.

Part Two

Exploring the Genres of Children's Literature

5 Traditional Literature

Beloved friend, my boon companion . . .
start now to sing with me, begin to recite together . . .
Let us clasp hand in hand, fingers in fingers,
so that we may sing fine things, give voice to the best things
for those dear ones to hear, for those desiring to know them
among the rising younger generation . . .

from The Kalevala *(1963)*
compiled by Elias Lonnrot

These words introduce the long collection of ancient Finnish poems called *The Kalevala*, twenty thousand lines of wisdom and magic that recount the exploits of heroes and common folk from Viking times. For well over a thousand years before they were written down, the verses that comprise *The Kalevala* were memorized by illiterate poets, who, huddled with their listeners around peat fires, could recite them for a whole week of evenings.

TRADITIONAL LITERATURE DEFINED

Traditional literature is the body of stories and poems that came to us by oral transmission and whose authors are unknown. "Literature" is something of a misnomer, since these works were told and heard long before they were written and read. Thus, the works that make up the body of traditional literature have met a standard that most other children's literature has not: Traditional works are so appealing and so memorable that they passed from generation to generation without the aid of writing. Even after having been written down, traditional works, because they are not considered the property of any one author, continue to inspire storytellers, writers, and artists (as well as choreographers and filmmakers and musicians) to produce new versions.

Besides having demonstrated a timeless popularity, traditional literature makes up a very important part of children's literature for three other reasons:

1. Traditional stories and poems had to have clear structures, plots, rhymes, or rhythms in order to be remembered. These features appeal to children.

2. Traditional literature invites participation: Listeners had to learn these stories and poems, or else they would have died out. Traditional literature still makes an active and exciting entry point into verbal texts.

3. When it comes to children's fare, oral traditions are still stronger than written ones in many cultures. Therefore, traditional literature is a vital part of multicultural literature.

THE EVOLUTION OF TRADITIONAL LITERATURE

Where did the literature in the oral tradition come from? And how did it develop into written material? Of course, we cannot know what the first stories were, but those opening words of *The Kalevala* offer a clue about their nature:

> Let us . . . give voice to the best things
> for those dear ones to hear, for those desiring to know them
> among the rising younger generation . . .

Stories surely arose because people wanted to remember the "best things" (and sometimes the worst) and pass them on. For young Iron Age Finns, the stories that comprise *The Kalevala* answered certain questions: Who are we? What should we believe? How should we behave? Most of the oldest stories offered answers to the important questions about the human experience and passed on a people's accumulated wisdom as to what the young should know, aspire to, and believe—forging a cultural identity in the process.

Whether we are speaking of *The Kalevala* or *The Odyssey* (the epic of the ancient Greek hero Odysseus) or *The Popol Vuh* (the legend of the Toltec emperor Quetzocuoatl), traditional works relied on strong plots, legendary characters, fantastic events, and the clear polarization of qualities like good and evil. They employed chants and refrains and poetic language—for these devices aid memory. They also relied on the economy of symbolism—though often short, the old stories could be understood on many levels and invited pondering for their truths and their applications to real life, long after the telling was done.

Where writing and formal education advanced, however, the oral tradition was pushed to the periphery. (Even by the fourth century BC, Plato wrote of his distrust for storytellers and mythmongers.) In Europe, formal schools such as those inspired by the German theologian Martin Luther (1483–1546) were established to teach people to read religious texts, and then other works. Science slowly matured, with theories to rival mythical accounts of the world. With the spread of education, culture slowly divided between written knowledge and everything else. Among the educated, "myth" and "old wive's tale" took on the connotations they still have in popular parlance—the unreliable lore of unsophisticated people.

But traditional lore still flourished, especially outside church and school. Folktales and legends drew their truths from the old myths and religious stories and continued to mix these with the people's own fantasies and fears. Folktales and legends came to constitute the unofficial lore of a culture. In church, the priest said "Thou shalt not steal" and urged the congregation to practice mercy and forgiveness; around the hearth, however, Jack still robbed fabulous riches from the giant, and Snow White still honeymooned while her wicked stepmother danced to hell in hot iron shoes. Teachers stressed book learning and the virtues of hard work, but in folktales, a simpleton like Juan Bobo was always more likely to succeed than someone more diligent and well prepared.

The Brothers Grimm and the Elevation of Folktales

In the early nineteenth century, two scholars of language built a bridge between the oral tradition and the written one. Jacob and Wilhelm Grimm, born in 1785 and 1786 in Hanau, Germany, were well known in their time as scholars of language. While studying law at Marburg, the Grimm brothers were fired by the poet and dramatist Clemens Brentano and the legal scholar Karl von Savigny with the conviction that the spirit and culture of the German people resided in the old tales and legends. Soon after, the Grimms began their quest for German folktales. The two hundred tales they gathered have been translated into seventy languages and have made a contribution to world literature that has been likened to that of the Bible.

Germany in the early nineteenth century was a loose federation of princi-palities, where landowners held most of the wealth and the peasants' lives were kept primitive. Roads were bad, communication was limited, and education was largely unavailable to the poor—conditions that made for hard lives but created fertile ground for storytelling. The Grimm brothers collected stories from many people, but their greatest source was a peasant woman named Frau Viehmannin living near Kassell.

As linguists, the Grimms wanted to keep the tales faithful to the original telling, and Frau Viehmannin, or "Gammer Grethel," as she was later called, learned to tell her tales slowly enough that the brothers could write them down almost verbatim. Still, some editing was inevitable, as they heard competing ver-sions of the same tales. For example, some tellers had a wolf, not a witch, occu-pying the house of sweets where Hansel and Gretel's misadventures took place.

The Grimms published their first volume of "Nursery and Household Tales" in 1812 and the second in 1815. The books received a cool critical recep-tion, but they sold briskly and were soon translated and read throughout Europe and the United States.

The Grimms introduced "Hansel and Gretel," "Snow White," "Little Red Riding Hood," and a host of other stories to a wide audience. Furthermore, the commercial success of their books aroused new interest in the few existing collec-tions of oral tales and inspired others to collect tales in their own countries.

Folktales from Everywhere

Inspired by the Grimms, Joseph Jacobs and Andrew Lang collected and published English folktales. There soon followed collections of folktales from Ireland and Scotland, from Russia, Italy, Spain, and Scandinavia.

In the United States, Joel Chandler Harris collected stories he learned on a plantation in Georgia from a former slave named Uncle Remus. The tales of "The Tar Baby" and "Brer Rabbit and Brer Fox," among others, were first written down by Harris (though versions more pleasing to the contemporary ear have become available since).

Native American stories were collected early in the twentieth century by anthropologists and linguists (although many stories that have never been "col-lected" are still being told by Native Americans today).

Many tall tales—especially of lumberjacks, cowboys, riverboat characters, and canal boat drivers—arose from the American experience and became famous all over the world (creating, to be sure, interesting stereotypes of what American life was like).

The 1930s saw a great harvest of American folktales. A New Deal program under the Works Progress Administration sent writers and anthropologists into the cabins of the rural South, ahead of power lines and telephones, collecting tales such as "Wiley and the Hairy Man," "Taily Po," and "Little Eight John." Richard Chase visited storytellers in Appalachia to collect *Jack Tales* (1943), American variants of European folktales reworked in a mountain setting. Further west, stories of ranch life and cattle drives were collected from men and women who experienced them and written up in many fine books by J. Frank Dobie and others. In New York State, stories of the Erie Canal were collected by Walter D. Edmonds, and they inspired his original works, including *The Matchlock Gun* (1941), which won the Newbery Medal in 1942.

Throughout the first decades of the twentieth century, folksong collector John Lomax collected cowboy songs throughout the Southwest. Later, his son

Alan Lomax, with the support of the Smithsonian Institute, continued collecting songs among African American workers and prisoners in the Southeast and from people in the mountain cabins of the Appalachians. The result of their work, *The Folksongs of North America* (1975), complements the collections by poet Carl Sandburg and balladeer John Jacob Nyles and offers amazing riches of song from the common folk of this country.

Folklore as a Field of Study

Folklore became the focus of serious academic study in the middle of the nineteenth century (the word "folklore" was coined in 1846 by W. J. Thoms). By the early twentieth century, so much folk material had been collected from all around the world that some way was needed to keep track of it.

Even a quick comparison of folktale collections shows intriguing similarities among tales from widely separate places. Grouping similar folktales, however, is not a simple matter. The story we know as "Cinderella," for example, has many variants. It originated long ago in China, where it was called "Yeh-Shen." In France, the tale was known as "Cendrillon"; in Germany, "Ashyputtel"; in England, "Ash Bottom"; and among the Algonquin people of North America, "The Rough-Face Girl." There are 650 variations in all, most having different names. How could you look up different versions of the same story, if each has a different name? And suppose it was not the whole story you want to compare, but a single detail—say, the prince's recognizing the true princess by fitting her with a shoe or a pumpkin that turns into a carriage?

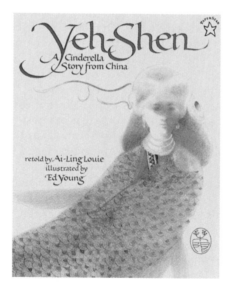

Illustration 5.1
Yeh-Shen, a Chinese version of the Cinderella story, is perhaps closest to the earliest version of the tale. (*Yeh-Shen: A Cinderella Story from China* by Ai-Ling Louie. Illustration copyright © 1982 by Ed Young. Used by permission of Philomel Books.)

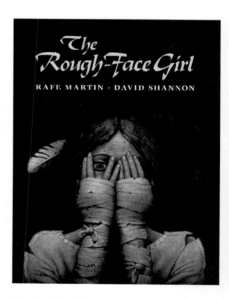

Illustration 5.2
The Rough-Face Girl, traditionally told among the Algonquin people, is less materialistic than European versions of the Cinderella story. (*The Rough-Face Girl* by Rafe Martin. Illustration copyright © 1992 by David Shannon. Used by permission of G. P. Putnam's Sons.)

It was to solve these problems that Antti Aarne and Stith Thompson compiled their six-volume work, *The Types of the Folktale*, published in Helsinki in 1961. In it, they distinguished between a *motif*, which is a strand or detail that makes up a story, and a *tale type*, which is a weaving together of many motifs to make a recognizable story pattern.

Fortunately for teachers and librarians, the gifted storyteller and folklore scholar Margaret Read MacDonald produced a one-volume simplification of the Aarne–Thompson index, called *The StoryTeller's Sourcebook: A Subject, Title, and Motif-Index to Folklore Collections for Children* (1982). After a few minutes' orientation, you can easily find your way around this work. Because MacDonald cites children's books among other materials, you can pull together, from those in your own library, books that constitute variations of the same tale or that use the same motifs.

CATEGORIES OF TRADITIONAL LITERATURE

The traditional literature that is available to children today consists of many sorts of narratives—including folktales, myths, fables, legends, and tall tales. There is poetry, too—from epics and ballads to folksongs to Mother Goose and skipping rhymes. Some also include riddles, jokes, and games. As we look more closely at these types of traditional literature, please bear in mind that some texts fit into more than one of the categories.

Myths and Religious Stories

Myths and religious stories are texts that try to explain the mysteries of the universe in terms that are understandable to the average person. As Carl Jung wrote, because people's certainty stops with the world they have at hand, myths use familiar images as symbols to point beyond what people can know directly (Jung, 1961).

Myths and religious stories offer answers to questions such as "How did the world come to be?" "Why are we here?" "What is a good person, and why does it matter if I am a good person?" and "What happens to us after we die?"

Sometimes mythical answers clash with scientific explanations. For example, both the account of the Creation offered by the Biblical story of Adam and Eve and the Native American tales of the world forming on Turtle's back clash with the scientific explanations of the "Big Bang" theory and the origins of life on earth (as arising from certain amino acids). Just as often, though, myths offer a different kind of truth from scientific explanations. The Greek myth of Dionysius, for example, warns us with gruesome examples that great unhappiness may result when men and women are too far polarized, with one gender supposed to be unfeeling, rigid, and punishing and the other limited to qualities of physical beauty, sensuality, and intuition. In a similar way, the Zuni myth that Kristina Rodanas retold and illustrated as **Dragonfly's Tale** (1992) warned that famine and unhappiness would surely come if the people took nature's bounty for granted. The truths of both these myths are arguably still relevant today.

Fables

Fables are short dramatic tales, often with animal characters, that point to a clear lesson. The lesson is often stated explicitly at the end, where it takes the form of a *proverb*: a short memorable statement of advice or an observation about human nature. "A bird in the hand is worth two in the bush" is a proverb that restates the theme of the fable "The Dog and His Shadow." A greedy dog carrying a piece of meat over a bridge across a brook sees its reflection in the water and snaps at the illusory meat, only to lose the piece it already had. "He who tries to please everybody pleases nobody" concludes the fable of "The Farmer, His Son, and the Ass," about a pair who try, ridiculously, to follow strangers' advice as they take their donkey to market.

The fables attributed to the Greek storyteller Aesop, who was said to have been a slave living around 600 years BC, have instructed children and their parents for thousands of years—though different generations have changed the morals to suit the mores of the day. Aesop's fables include "The Town Mouse and the Country Mouse," "The Fox and the Grapes," and "The Lion and the Mouse." The seventeenth-century French poet Jean de La Fontaine published several of Aesop's fable in verse form. A modern collection of fables written and illustrated by Arnold Lobel is fittingly entitled *Fables* (1980).

Folktales of Many Kinds

Folktales are stories that have been passed on by word of mouth and have unknown originators. They come in many forms.

Animal Stories. Many folktales ascribe human actions to animal characters. Aesop's fable "The Tortoise and the Hare," for example, uses supposed features of turtles and rabbits (slow but sure versus fast but arrogant) to make points about parallel traits in human beings. Many stories told among African American slaves used animals as codes for power relationships: Brer Bear has far more power than Brer Rabbit, but sometimes the latter outsmarts the former with his cunning—just as slaves could sometimes outwit their more powerful masters.

Illustration 5.3
Julius Lester, a specialist in Jewish and African American studies, has recently created lively retellings of the stories of Uncle Remus. (*The Last Tales of Uncle Remus* by Julius Lester. Illustrations copyright © 1994 by Jerry Pinkney. Used by permission of Dial Books for Young Readers, a division of Penguin Books USA, Inc.)

Trickster Tales. Tricksters are characters who try to get the better of others through cunning and guile. Brer Rabbit is a trickster. Another trickster of African origin is Anansi the Spider, hero of many tales told in the Caribbean and West Africa. In Native American tales, Coyote is a trickster. Trickster tales are popular with children, who like the idea of weak characters using their wits to get the better of more powerful characters.

Pourquoi Tales. Pourquoi tales—stories that explain "How come?"—came about to feed, in often delightful ways, children's insatiable thirst for explanations. Pourquoi tales range from the serious to the playful: from the seven days of creation in the book of Genesis to the Greek explanation for the seasons in the story of Demeter; to the beautiful Masai story, *The Orphan Boy* (1990), retold by Tololwa Mollel and illustrated by Paul Morin, which explains why the planet Venus appears in the east as the morning star but as the evening star in the west; to the Cuban story of *Medio pollito/Half-Chicken* (1995), a tongue-in-cheek account of the origin of the ornamental rooster that sits atop many a weather vane, retold in Spanish and English by Alma Flor Ada with illustrations by Kim Howard.

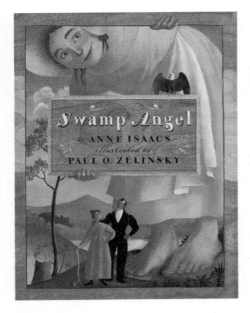

Illustration 5.4
Swamp Angel has all the hyperbole and swagger of the great American tall tales, but it is a contemporary story with a female hero. (*Swamp Angel* by Anne Isaacs. Illustration copyright © 1994 by Paul O. Zelinsky. Used by permission of Dutton Signet, a division of Penguin Books USA Inc.)

Tall Tales and Legends. Tall tales are greatly exaggerated accounts of the exploits of local heroes. Often these heroes are members of a vocational group. For example, New England sailors told the tale of Stormalong. Cowboys in the Old West told the exaggerated adventures of Pecos Bill. African American laborers had the story of John Henry, the steel-driving man. Even Japanese women had the wonderful tale of the Three Strong Women. After all, bragging is a way for members of a group to express who they are; when the bragging takes the form of a story, we have a tall tale. More recently, perhaps to add some balance to the gender ratio of these exaggerated heroes, Anne Isaacs has given us an original tall tale, *Swamp Angel* (1994).

Cumulative Tales. Cumulative tales are built up by repeating lines and adding to them. A Cuban folktale called *The Bossy Gallito* (1994), in a version retold by Lucia M. Gonzalez and illustrated by Lulu Delacre, is us a a good example: A rooster is dressed up and making his way to his uncle's wedding when he spies a kernel of corn lying in a mud puddle. Pecking it, he muddies his beak, so he commands the grass to clean his beak. The grass refuses, so he commands a lamb to frighten the grass; but the lamb refuses, so he commands a dog to frighten the lamb, and so on. Finally, some creature agrees and sets a whole sequence of coercion in motion until the rooster's beak is cleaned and he can proceed to the wedding. The structure of *The Bossy Gallito* closely parallels the English story of "The Old Lady and the Pig," collected by Joseph Jacobs, in which an old woman calls on a series of helpers to goad a pig who is stuck in a stile (a passageway through a fence). The Vietnamese story *Toad Is the Uncle of Heaven* (1985), retold and illustrated by Jeanne M. Lee, tells of an honorable toad who recuits other thirsty helpers as he makes his way to the palace of the King of Heaven to plead for rain. Each helper adds just the needed touch to achieve a solution, exactly as they do in the German tale "The Brementown Musicians." Songs such as "The Twelve Days of Christmas," "There Was an Old Woman Who Swallowed a Fly," and the Spanish song "Estaba la rana sentada cantando debajo del agua" follow cumulative patterns. The form of the cumulative tale was well suited to the oral tradition, since the repetition of lines gave the listeners plenty of chances to learn them. These tales are agreeable to children for the same reason.

Fairytales. Fairytales are folktales that involve magical possibilities. "Cinderella," "Snow White and the Seven Dwarfs," and "Rumpelstiltskin" fit the definition. So do the African tale "Mufaro's Beautiful Daughters" and the African American tale "The Talking Eggs." The plots of these stories stem from common drives and aspirations of ordinary people, and the magic often functions to lavish great rewards on the heroes for their goodness or steadfastness.

Apprenticeship Tales and Hero Tales. Apprenticeship tales and hero tales explain how a character rises from a lowly estate to a high one, or from being ignored or threatened to being recognized and rewarded for her or his qualities. Apprenticeship tales such as the English tale "Jack and the Beanstalk," the Iroquois "Bending Willow," the French "Beauty and the Beast," and the Russian "Ivan, the Grey Wolf, and the Firebird" are exciting, but they are also partly didactic: All teach lessons about qualities of character that are likely to be rewarded in the end.

Are tales of stereotyped strong men and wilting women still worth sharing with today's children?

You cannot read far in traditional folk stories without forming the unsettling impression that males are the active heroes and females are the passive prizes the heroes win in the end. Cinderella, Rapunzel, Sleeping Beauty—all of them act virtuously, look stunning, and wait (sometimes for excessive periods of time) for a prince to give them a future. As one third grader put it, "Boys get to do exciting things outside. All girls get to do is sit around and look beautiful."

Should we, as adults, simply avoid sharing with children traditional tales like "Cinderella" and "The Sleeping Beauty" that have limited roles for females? Should we share them anyway? Or should we invite children to question the roles males and females play? What do you think?

ISSUE TO CONSIDER

Illustration 5.5
First published by Charles Perrault during the reign of Louis XIV, "The Sleeping Beauty" undoubtedly has the most passive heroine in children's literature. (*The Sleeping Beauty* by Trina Schart Hyman. Used by permission of Little, Brown and Company.)

Numbskull Tales. Numbskull tales are stories of fools and idiots. We said earlier that in folktales, the simpleton is more likely to succeed than the sage. When he does, the story is of the type called the numbskull tale. Numbskull tales are popular the world around, from China to the Appalachian Mountains. Hans Christian Andersen's "Hans Clodhopper" tells of the numbskull brother who wins the hand of the princess when he speaks up stupidly but confidently in her presence. The success of the movie *Forrest Gump* shows that we still like to believe that a numbskull might just win the day.

Epics and Ballads

Epics and ballads are long narrative poems that tell of the heroic or tragic doings of a hero. In the many centuries before writing was widespread, long accounts that had to be remembered intact were highly structured and usually rhymed. Long rhymed accounts in traditional literature come to us in two main forms: epics and ballads.

Epics. Epics are extended accounts of the exploits of national heroes, often intended to provide the young with models to emulate and ideals to embrace. Their telling could carry over several days; in written form, they fill whole books. The ancient story of Odysseus is an epic; so are the early English tale of Beowulf and the Spanish *Poema de mio Cid*, about a medieval Christian hero in the reconquest of Spain from the Moors.

Ballads. Ballads are narratives in song, which were especially popular in England from the fourteenth century on. English and Scottish ballads are mostly built of four-line stanzas and can run from a half-dozen stanzas (the length of a modern popular song) to more than four hundred (a whole evening's entertainment, and then some). The ballad form was carried from the British Isles to North America, where in the nineteenth and early twentieth centuries, it had an even more robust following than in Europe. The Appalachian Mountains have a strong tradition of narrative songs, such as "Tom Dooley" and "Little Omie Wise." In the western United States, many cowboy ballads such as "The Streets of Laredo" and "The Colorado Trail" followed this tradition.

Folksongs and Poems

Songs and poems shorter than ballads but aimed at more mature listeners than nursery rhymes comprise another category of traditional literature. "I Been Working on the Railroad," "Cielito Lindo," and "I Wish I Was a Mole in the Ground" are folksongs that have been sung for generations. They were made up by unknown singers, and then verses were added by other singers. Folksongs appeal to children because their lyrics are often colorful and their melodies are catchy but accessible. Most folksongs can be sung easily *a capella* (without instrumental accompaniment) or with the aid of an autoharp or guitar. Many folksongs have been made into children's books.

Mother Goose Rhymes

Babies love to be bounced on grownups' knees, and the bouncers need rhythms and poems to sustain those rhythms. Perhaps that is how the nursery rhymes known as the Mother Goose rhymes were born. The name "Mother Goose" was first used by the Frenchman Charles Perrault in the seventeenth century, and Mother Goose rhymes were popularized in English by John Newbery,

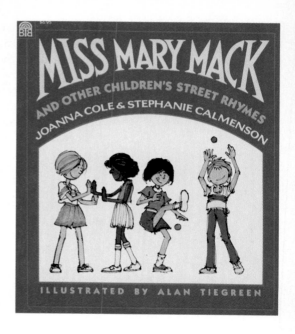

Illustration 5.6
The street rhymes collected in *Miss Mary Mack and Other Children's Street Rhymes* have an urban, colloquial, and African American flavor. Are such rhymes being published in books because children's oral culture is in danger of dying out? (*Miss Mary Mack and Other Children's Street Rhymes* by Joanna Cole and Stephanie Calmenson. Illustration copyright © 1990 by Alan Tiegreen. Used by permission of Morrow Junior Books, a division of William Morrow & Co., Inc.)

who published *The Original Mother Goose's Melody* in 1760. The rhymes that have come down to us under the name were recited by unknown nursery poets. (We will discuss these rhymes further in Chapter 7.)

Skipping Rhymes and Chants

Unlike Mother Goose rhymes, which were introduced to children by adults, skipping rhymes and other playground chants are recited by children themselves and passed on from child to child. Jump-rope and skipping rhymes are popular with children around the world. Here is one from Zambia:

IFULA INSA TWNAGALE NA
MAYIZA IFULA INSA INSA
TWANGALA NA MAYIZA.

"Rain come, rain come.
We want to play on the rain.
Rain come, rain come.
We want to play on the rain."

Skipping rhymes are highly rhythmic, and they often comment, however obliquely, on adult activities such as romancing. Consider this one from the United States:

Cinderella, dressed in yellow,
Went upstairs and kissed a fellow.

Riddles

Riddles are questions with clever, usually metaphorical, answers. Children in the United States have long amused each other with riddles. These classic ones have nearly fallen out of use:

A box without hinges, key, or lid
Yet golden treasure inside is hid.   (An egg)

> Round as an apple
> Deep as a cup
> All the king's horses
> Can't pull it up.   (A well)

But variations of the old riddles still survive among children:

> What has a head and can't think,
> Has legs and can't walk?   (A bed)

> What has four eyes and can't see?   (Mississippi)

And still more common in children's oral tradition are jokes made in the pattern of riddles (Bronner, 1988):

> What did the mother bullet say to the father bullet?
> We're going to have a BB.

HOW TRADITIONAL LITERATURE WORKS

With no system of recording but the human memory, traditional literature had to be, well, memorable—so it relied on catchy patterns of plot and language. Here we describe some of those devices, beginning with plots.

The Plot Structures of Folktales: Propp's Morphology

In the 1920s, a Russian critic named Vladimir Propp (1928) was struck by the similarity in the plots of the folktales told in his culture. He analyzed a collection of one hundred Russian folktales and found that all were built from a limited set of roles and actions.

Some of the stories fit the pattern of the victim-hero: Someone in the family leaves home, but before this happens, the hero is warned against doing something. The hero does it anyway. The villain comes spying, and finds out that the hero, or others in her care, are defenseless. The villain tries to trick the hero out of her person or her goods, and the hero falls for the trick. The villain hurts someone in the family, and so on.

Other stories Propp analyzed fit the pattern of the seeker-hero: Someone in the family needs something and makes that need known. The hero rises to the challenge to seek the desired thing, and leaves home. Along the way, the hero meets a test or challenge, which prepares him to receive the help of a magical helper, which he later receives. The hero is magically transported to the place where the desired object can be found, and enters direct combat with the villain. The hero might be branded (which leads to his recognition later). The villain is defeated, the threat is lifted, or the sought-for object is retrieved, and the hero leaves for home. The hero may be chased, and rescued from pursuit. The hero may return home unrecognized, to find that a false hero has presented claims in his absence. A further challenge is made to the hero, in which he triumphs, and is recognized. The false hero is unmasked and punished. The hero is married and crowned king.

The victim-hero pattern is found in a host of familiar stories, such as the Chinese tale "Lon Po Po," the English story "The Three Little Pigs," and the African American tale "Wiley and the Hairy Man." The seeker-hero pattern fits the West African story "Mufaro's Beautiful Daughters," as well as "Jack and the Beanstalk" and many others.

Why do so many stories follow these patterns? There are two possible explanations. One is that they all derived from the same geographical source—a common story told in one place and time. But such a common starting point for all folktales has not been found—and doesn't seem likely to be, since very similar stories (such as the 650 variants of the Cinderella story) have long been told in widely scattered parts of the globe. Another possibility is that the stories all come from the same *psychological* source: That is, they all stem from basic life experiences, hopes, and fears that are common to all people in all places and times. This is what Propp himself concluded at the end of his study.

Campbell's Hero Cycle

Noted scholar of mythology Joseph Campbell read the mythology, folktales, and religious literature of the world and concluded that one archetypal plot was repeated over and over. (*Archetype* means "old form," and an archetype is a device or a plot structure that is repeated in many stories.) Therefore, he named his book *The Hero with a Thousand Faces* (1968). The hero cycle unfolds in several episodes (see Figure 5.1).

- *Heroes at home.* In the beginning of the story, heroes are often the "lowest of the low," unrecognized but perhaps having a questioning nature or a quiet ambition to find out who they truly are.

- *The call to adventure.* Soon some problem arises that causes heroes to go on quests. In traditional literature, heroes often have to compete for the chance to go, as they are naturally overlooked in favor of their older or more glamorous siblings.

Figure 5.1
Campbell's hero cycle seems to tell many stories at once—a child's journey to adulthood, a rediscovery of meaning in mid-life, a summary of a whole life's journey.

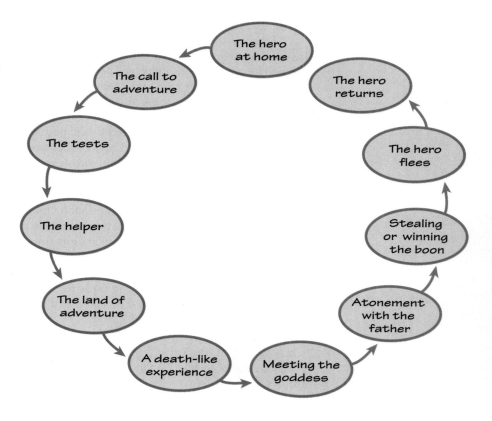

- *The tests.* Before they proceed very far on their adventure, heroes are faced with challenges or tests. If they meet them with cleverness, courage, or kindness, they often receive some magical help that enables them to proceed on their quest.

- *The helper.* The helper is a person or peculiar creature who provides the magical aid heroes need to cross the threshold into the place where the object of the quest is usually found. Sometimes the helper provides other miraculous equipment that enables heroes to succeed.

- *The land of adventure.* Quests lead heroes into what Campbell calls "the Land of Adventure." Like Never-Never Land, Narnia, or the land beyond the "wrinkle in time," this is often a magical place, impossible to reach without the aid the heroes received from the helper. Once there, heroes' adventures begin in earnest, but they find their true powers come to their aid, enabling them to rise to the challenges.

- *The "belly of the whale."* Once they arrive in the Land of Adventure, heroes usually have death and rebirth experiences: Their childish nature must die off, and their more mature, heroic nature must be born. Tomb imagery is very often used at this point.

- *The "goddess."* If heroes are male, they may encounter beautiful but formidable female figures who may challenge or love them, but in any case confirm them as worthy contenders.

- *Father atonement.* Heroes often come up against stern father figures who challenge them severely. Sometimes heroes overthrow these father figures. At the least, they force the father figures to recognize their worth and their status as heroes.

- *Elixir theft.* The object of the quest is often some magical gift or some boon, elixir, or remedy that is needed back at home. Heroes win this object, or steal it.

- *The flight.* If heroes steal the elixir or the object, they will run for their lives, pursued by powerful forces. It will take more trickery and bravery to get away.

- *The return.* When heroes return home, they bring what was needed to keep life going along comfortably. Sometimes they arrive in splendor and enter into royal marriage. Sometimes they slip into quiet reflection—changed people, more whole, more integrated, proven.

The hero cycle fits a host of stories—from the story of Hercules to the Russian tale "Ivan, the Grey Wolf, and the Firebird" to the Iroquois tale "The Boy Who Lived with the Bears" to the Lakota Sioux tale "The Orphan Boy and the Elk Dogs." In story after story, from culture after culture, a person of humble origins who is somehow special receives a challenge, is tested and receives special aid, crosses into a land of adventure, suffers a death and rebirth experience, meets and bests an authority, wins something of value, escapes with that boon, and returns home as a fully developed person.

That plot has been repeated so often that many have wondered if the plot itself might have symbolic meaning. Some say it is the story of growing up—of adolescents being tested and confirmed and taking their place in adult society. Others have said it applies to the psychic journey of middle-aged people seeking what the Swiss psychologist Carl Jung called "individuation"—a discovery and integration of the true powers they had unknowingly thrust aside in the strivings of adolescence and early adulthood (Jung, 1961). Of course, it can mean both these things, and more.

Lévi-Strauss's Structured Opposites

Hero versus villain, home-sweet-home versus land-of-adventure—folk literature is known for its stark contrasts. The French anthropologist Claude Lévi-Strauss (1957) asserted that these contrasts are not accidental. People orient themselves to the world by thinking in terms of opposites: hot and cold, up and down, light and dark, and male and female. Only after they establish the basic contrasts in experience do they look at the middle ground—the lukewarm, the shades of gray, the moderate.

In folk literature, stark contrasts are common. Lévi-Strauss noted that a set of contrasts in a story can stand for another set of contrasts in the real world, and often those contrasts deal with an issue that people find too painful or controversial to talk about directly. Thus, stories become a safe way of exploring and resolving issues that people can't or won't confront.

For example, what are the contrasts in "Jack and the Beanstalk"? There are many: Jack/the giant; the earth/the land in the sky; Jack's mother/the giant's wife; Jack at the beginning/Jack at the end; Jack as he seems to be/Jack as he really is.

When you contrast Jack and the giant, differences come tumbling out. Jack is young; the giant is old. Jack is small; the giant is huge. Jack has nothing but ambition; the giant has wealth and the fear of losing it. Jack is clever and confident; the giant is stupid and bullying. Jack seems insignificant but is really a hero; the giant is fierce, but his brutishness makes him vulnerable. Jack is on the way up; the giant is on the way down (pun intended!).

When Lévi-Strauss looks at opposing characters such as these, he treats them as interchangeable elements in fixed relation to each other—like subjects and objects in a sentence—and sees what other items would fit in their slots. For example, for the opposing characters in the story of "Jack and the Beanstalk," we have:

Jack	The Giant
young	old
small	huge
clever	stupid
seems weak	seems strong
needy	greedy
poor, questing	rich, holding on

Now, what other characters share those sets of features? Pairs that come to mind are David and Goliath, Juan Bobo and the devil, Taran and the Horned King, Gretel and the Witch, Hamlet and Claudius.

What do the stories about such pairs have in common? We might say that these stories stand for, among other things, the competition between young people on their way up, trying to win the freedom and recognition that come with maturity, and the older generation's struggle to hold onto those privileges.

Psychoanalytic Dynamics of Traditional Literature

Sigmund Freud (1923), the first great explorer of the human unconscious, made two large claims about human nature that shed light on the workings of folk literature. The first is that the most important preoccupations of people's lives—the most basic fears, secret lusts, and ambitions—follow patterns that were laid down in early childhood, in the drama of the relationships with parents and siblings. The second is that humans have an amazing capacity to symbolize and call on this capacity whenever they need a substitute for what they really want—especially if that is unattainable or inappropriate.

The first claim, about the power of the early drama of the family, suggests that since the preschool and early school years every adult has craved nurturance, control, romantic love, and recognition for his or her competence. The second claim, about the human capacity for symbolizing, led Freud to believe that dreams are symbolic (and therefore "safe") ways of exploring those basic urges and reducing some of the tension people feel because of them. Freud's followers, especially Carl Jung, decided that folktales and fairytales served a community the same way as dreams serve an individual—as symbolic and safe ways of working out deep-seated and powerful psychic material.

In 1975, the child therapist Bruno Bettelheim published the clearest application of psychoanalytic theory to children's reading of fairytales. Entitled *The Uses of Enchantment* (1975), Bettelheim's book is an extensive unpacking of the psychosexual symbols in the most familiar fairytales.

Many of Bettelheim's interpretations seem plausible. For example, he finds that "Hansel and Gretel" explores children's fears of having to separate from the family and make it in the world by their own wits. Hansel and Gretel rise to the challenge and are able to be reunited with their father as peers, rather than as dependents.

By locating so many symbols in each story, Bettelheim implies that most children understand fairytales in a certain way. But even setting aside the limits on understanding symbols imposed by children's cognitive development, it seems

Illustration 5.7
One of the most famous of the German tales collected by the Brothers Grimm, "Hansel and Gretel" is thought by some to have underlying meaning that relates to children's psychological challenges. (*Hansel and Gretel* by James Marshall. Copyright © 1990 by James Marshall. Used by permission of Dial Books for Young Readers, a division of Penguin Books USA Inc.)

unlikely that *all* children see these stories as Bettelheim does (Winner, 1982). Another psychoanalytic critic, Norman Holland (1975), observed that readers saw in stories what they wanted to see or were concerned about—or conversely, that they refused to see the elements of stories that reminded them of drives and urges they were afraid of. To Holland, a story is not so much a densely layered painting as a screen onto which readers project their own issues. Holland's observations are more in line with the reader response theory described in Chapter 3.

TRADITIONAL LITERATURE FROM MANY CULTURES

There is an abundance of outstanding examples of literature from traditional sources. A good number of the illustrated books that have won the Caldecott Medal have been traditional tales. When it comes to traditional tales from parallel cultures, the offerings are rich indeed.

Classic Myths and Legends

Some well-known myths originated in Egypt and in Scandinavia; myths told among the South American Indians continue to be reworked in Latin American literature; and the myths of Native Americans survive in folktales and inspire large new audiences of ecology-minded young people. Greek and Roman myths gave us the names of the planets: Mercury, Venus, Mars, Jupiter, Saturn, Uranus, Neptune, and Pluto. They gave us the names of the months and also one day of the week: January (named after Janus, the god who looks forward and backward), March (named for Mars), June (named for Juno), and Saturday (for Saturn). Norse mythology gave us the names for other days of the week: Tuesday (for Tiw, the Norse god of war), Wednesday (for Woden), Thursday (for Thor), and Friday (for Friga, Woden's wife, the goddess of love and the hearth).

The myths we still hear allusions to most often are the Greek and Roman myths. (Roman myths were Greek myths with the names changed.) The ancient Roman writer Ovid is the earliest source for these myths. His collection of tales, called *The Metamorphoses*, chronicles many of the old myths—with the theme of transformation loosely joining the fifteen books of what is otherwise a collection of separate stories.

The ancient Greeks personified the forces of nature as gods: heroes created in human form, with superhuman powers, but with human frailties, too. They could suffer anger, envy, pride, and lust.

Zeus, son of Chronos, was first among the twelve gods of the *pantheon* (Greek for "all gods," or the fellowship of the gods) and ruler of the universe. With the other eleven gods, he lived on Mount Olympus; from there, they could observe the goings-on of humans and sometimes meddle in them. Hera was Zeus's wife, the goddess of marriage. Hera was a jealous wife, and Zeus's dalliances with mortal women gave her reason to be. Poseidon, the god of the sea, was the brother of Zeus, and storms at sea were considered his making. Hestia was their sister, the goddess of the household. Hades, the lord of death, governed the underworld. A son of Zeus, Ares, was god of war. Another son, Apollo, the god of light, drove the sun chariot across the sky. He was the favorite god of the poets, since he was the maker of music. His twin sister, Artemis, was the moon goddess, the goddess of growing things and of the hunt. Athena was

Illustration 5.8
Greek myths have always fascinated young people. The D'Aulaires' versions are perhaps the most popular. Aliki's *The Gods and Goddesses of Olympus* is a brief "who's who" of the original superheroes. (*The Gods and Goddesses of Olympus* by Aliki. Copyright © 1992 by Aliki Brandenberg. Jacket art copyright © by Aliki Brandenberg.)

Zeus's favorite daughter, born from his forehead, so she was the goddess of wisdom. Another daughter, Aphrodite, was the goddess of love. Her brother, Hermes, was the messenger of the gods. Hephaestus, the god of fire, forged the armor of the gods and became the favorite of blacksmiths and craftspersons.

There were lesser gods, too. Dionysius, child of a union between Zeus and the mortal woman Semele, was the god of wine and vegetation—he came to represent people's animalistic and intuitive side, as opposed to their order and reason. Demeter was the goddess of grain. It was her daughter, Persephone, who was carried away by Hades to the underworld. The seasons of the year resulted from a bargain Demeter struck with Hades.

The Romans adopted the Greek gods but gave most of them new names:

Greek Name	Roman Name
Zeus (god of the universe)	Jupiter
Hera (goddess of marriage)	Juno
Poseidon (god of the sea)	Neptune
Hermes (messenger god)	Mercury
Aphrodite (goddess of love)	Venus
Hades (god of the underworld)	Pluto
Ares (god of war)	Mars
Apollo (sun god)	Apollo
Artemis (goddess of vegetation and the hunt)	Diana
Athena (goddess of wisdom)	Minerva
Hestia (goddess of the household)	Vesta
Hephaestus (god of fire)	Vulcan
Dionysius (god of wine)	Bacchus
Demeter (goddess of grain)	Ceres

Traditional Literature from the British Isles

England, Scotland, Wales, and Ireland are different nations within the British Isles. England is home to peoples who are descendants of the Angles and Saxons—Germanic stock—as well as of Vikings from Denmark and French from Normandy. Scotland, Ireland, and Wales are peopled by Celts—an ancient race from Central Europe—whose shaping influence on language and culture continues, especially with the various Celtic revival movements, to this day.

In Ireland and Wales, the oral tradition was highly organized, owing to the institution of the *bards*, professional poet/historians who were commissioned by the kings to learn and recite epic poems and genealogies. Bards were expected to know as many as four hundred epic poems, and they often studied for twenty years to learn them. Indeed, a bardic college was established in Tara, the ancient capital of Ireland, to pass on the old stories. In England, literacy was more widespread. Because literacy and the oral tradition are largely incompatible, the oral tradition in England was much more scattered than it was in Ireland.

Irish Folklore. In Ireland, everyone knows everyone, or so it seems—and even the folktales are likely to mention people with real names. Irish folklore tells of legendary Irish heroes—CuCulhain, Finn McCool, Cormac MacArt, and Saint

Patrick. There are stories of courageous and honorable acts, and there are stories of the struggle of Christianity to assert itself over the older Celtic religion of the Druid priests—stories that may go back sixteen hundred years.

There is often magic in the tales, usually centering around giants or the little people called fairies or leprechauns. The little people keep to themselves—though once in a lifetime some human may happen on a group of them. Then there is a chance of hearing ". . . the *fulparenee* and the *folparnee* and the *rap-lay hoota*, and the *roolya-boolya* . . ." (Jacobs, 1958) as the little people make merry. Fairies and leprechauns possess magical powers that humans can sometimes use, but they rarely allow this willingly. From time to time, fairies are said to steal a human baby and take it below ground to strengthen their stock—such a baby is called a strayaway child. If fairies steal a human child, they replace her or him with one of their own. These fairie babies—called changelings—look like the children they replace, but they have awful tempers and can never be taught good manners. So if your baby is especially difficult, the tradition advises, chances are it's a changeling.

Scottish Folklore. Scottish folklore has given us tales of Rob Roy, Robert Bruce, and other Scottish chiefs. These tales and many others were compiled in an extensive collection called ***The Scottish Tradition: A Collection of Scottish Folk Literature*** (1984), by David Buchan. The storytelling tradition has been kept alive to this day, especially by the tinkers, itinerant traders who live on the fringes of society, much as gypsies do. Duncan Williamson, author of a fine collection of Scottish folktales (***Tales of the Seal People: Scottish Folk Tales***, 1992), was a tinker in his younger days. His tales of the selchies, or seal people, tap an especially interesting vein of Scottish folklore.

Welsh Folklore. In Wales, much of the folklore recalls heroic legends, just as it does in Ireland. A fourteenth-century epic called *The Mabinogion* compiled the outstanding legends of Wales. The prolific children's author Lloyd Alexander traces his ancestry from Wales and credits the Welsh epics with the romantic adventurism of his own tales.

English Folklore. In England, the oral tradition included the epic of "Beowulf," a stirring tale of the hero's struggle against Grendel, the water monster. Probably composed in the eighth century, "Beowulf" was drawn from both the old Viking tradition and early Christian beliefs.

At the heart of the English oral tradition is the legend of King Arthur and the Knights of the Round Table. The legend has been traced back to the seventh century and seems to have derived from old Celtic hero tales. Arthur, illegitimate son of Uther Pendragon, shows his heroic qualities by pulling the sword from the stone. Merlin, the court magician, reveals Arthur's royal lineage. Arthur marries Guinevere, bears the great sword Excalibur, and is joined at the Round Table by the famous knights Sir Lancelot, Sir Gawain, Sir Galahad, and others.

Almost as central to the English oral tradition is the ballad of Robin Hood and his Merrie Men. Robin Hood has an uncertain historical basis, but the background to the ballad of the poacher-hero was real enough: It was the landowners' exluding people from hunting or fishing in vast expanses of countryside. (To this day in England, landowners own the fish in their streams and the deer in their woods.)

Other shaping events of the later Middle Ages were the Crusades—idealistic campaigns by English and other European Christians to drive the Moslems out of the Holy Land, which was considered to be the eastern Mediterranean city of Jerusalem and its surroundings. At the same time, Christian heroes sought the Holy Grail, the chalice with which Jesus Christ was said to have celebrated the

Last Supper. Even after centuries of striving, neither effort was successful, but both provided the grist for many tales and legends.

English folklore, as its great chronicler, Katherine Briggs, notes, is short on fairy tales: English folk characters are more likely to succeed on cunning and pluck than by magical aid. On the other hand, there may be other-worldly villains—giants, particularly, as in stories like "Jack the Giant-Killer" and "Jack and the Beanstalk." There are stories that make fun of both pretensions and silliness—especially the tale "The Three Sillies," in which a groom, on a bet, goes in search of three people sillier than his fiancée's family. "The Little Red Hen" and "The Three Little Pigs" both stress the virtue of industry. "The Old Woman Who Lived in a Vinegar Bottle" is a variation of "The Fisherman and His Wife"—both show the folly of wishing for more than you have. On the other hand, the hero of "The Pedlar of Swaffham" succeeds by following a dream.

German Traditional Literature

German traditional literature was ably chronicled, as we noted earlier in this chapter, by Jacob and Wilhelm Grimm. "Hansel and Gretel," "Rapunzel," "Rumplestiltskin," "The Brementown Musicians," "Snow White and the Seven Dwarfs"—a great number of favorite tales came from German sources. One tale, "Iron John," is not often told to children but has become the basis for a men's movement led by the prominent American poet Robert Bly (1992). The story tells of an ancient man who has lain for centuries beneath the moss at the bottom of a pond. The boy in the story drains the pond, resurrects Iron John, and learns the lessons of manhood from him. Bly believes the story stands for the importance of having manly things communicated from man to man—without this, he claims, the male spirit sickens.

Scandinavian Traditional Literature

The northernmost countries of Europe were home to seafaring folk who for centuries passed the time during the long, dark winters by telling stories. Those stories are so forceful and eloquent that they are known around the world. The Norse mythology told tales of Balder, the god of light; of Tiw, god of war; of Woden, the giver of order and creator of man and woman; of Thor, the god of thunder and might; and of Friga, Woden's wife and the goddess of love and domesticity—deities who gave us the names of days of the week.

The best-known collection of Scandinavian folktales is *Norwegian Folk Tales*, published in 1845 by Peter Christian Asbjorsen (1812–1885) and Jorgen Moe (1813–1882) and translated by the Englishman Sir George Webbe Dasent (1817–1896). The most famous of these tales is "East of the Sun and West of the Moon," a lively story that begins much like the French story "Beauty and the Beast" but goes on to include the mix of trolls, giants, witches, and hags that is typical of Norwegian folktales.

The Dane Hans Christian Andersen (1805–1875) ranks with the Grimms as a giant of world literature—and especially of literature for children. His work is difficult to categorize. Like the Frenchman Charles Perrault (whose work is discussed below), Andersen retold traditional tales to give them his particular twist; he also wrote scores of original tales in traditional form. His story "The Emperor's New Clothes" (retold from an old Spanish tale with Moorish origins) has become a worldwide metaphor for the dangers of believing in other people's pretensions. His original stories "The Ugly Duckling," "The Little Mermaid," and "The Steadfast Tin Soldier" are crystalline tales with gentle lessons for the young.

French Traditional Literature

"Little Red Riding Hood," "Cinderella," "Beauty and the Beast," "Puss in Boots," "Sleeping Beauty"—a startling number of the best-known fairytales came to us from French versions. That is not to say they originated in France: variations of most of them were told in other parts of the world, too. Cinderella was told from China to Persia to England to the sweat lodges of the Algonquin people. The British could have chosen a German tale called "Ashyputtel" or one in which the heroine had a black sheep for a fairy godmother. But it was the particular set of features in the French version that appealed to them, and they passed it on to North Americans.

Charles Perrault (1628–1703), a lawyer who worked for King Louis XIV, assembled the most popular collection of French fairytales, called *Histoires ou Contes du Temps Passé* ("Stories or Tales of Times Past"). The collection included "Cinderella," "The Sleeping Beauty in the Woods," "Little Red Riding Hood," "Puss in Boots," "The Foolish Wishes," and "Blue Beard."

If some of these tales wax excessively enthusiastic about glittering ballrooms, and if the heroines sometimes seem drawn like moths to candles by the gaiety of palace life, it helps to remember that the tales took their form during the long reign of the Sun King. His sumptuous courtly life has never been equaled, and he controlled the nobility by enmeshing them in countless social functions and keeping them guessing about who was in favor and who was out.

Russian Folktales

Russian folktales are a treasure trove of adventure stories, wonder tales, and anecdotes. Often playful, the tales abound in impossible quests, mysterious helpers, magical transformations, and dazzling rewards. Many of the structural features of other European tales are there: The old Tsar is dying, and he needs something. Three brothers are called on a quest, but the youngest and least significant—he may be a peasant or of noble birth—is the one who triumphs.

But Russian folktales are played out on a wider canvas than most. Heroes on their quests are propelled "through the thrice-ninth land to the thrice-ninth kingdom"—images that reflect the vastness of the Russian motherland. Russian folktales also have one of the great fixtures of world folklore, Baba Yaga ("Baba" means "Granny"). Baba Yaga lives in a hut perched on chicken feet that spins around three times and stops with the door facing you—provided you say the right words. Her nose grows down to her chin, and she flies around in a mortar, spurring it with a pestle, sweeping the way in front of her with a broom, and crying, "Foo! foo! foo! foo!" She is too exotic to be really frightening—and besides, although the young heroes are sometimes sorely tested by her, they always triumph.

The champion of Russian fairytales was Aleksandr Afanas'ev (1826–1871), an ethnographer who collected and published six hundred tales between 1855 and 1864. Unlike the Grimms, whom he sought to emulate, Afanas'ev got all but a dozen of his tales from other collectors.

Folklore from North America

Though folklore exists wherever people have established traditions, a few strands of North American folklore are especially well known: Native American, African American, Appalachian, pioneer, and Western. There are also the tall tales and historical legends. The oldest—by twenty thousand years—and perhaps the only American folklore that can truly claim to be original is that in the Native American tradition.

Native American Tales. Of course, Native American tales are as diverse as the hundreds of tribes in North America. Nonetheless, there are themes that are common to most Native American tribes as egalitarian tribal societies, just as there are themes that are common to most European nations as hierarchically arranged, power-and-ownership societies.

For example, many Native American tales speak of animals. But unlike European animal tales, in which animals are so often stand-ins for human characters, the point of the Native American tales is more often to help listeners better understand the animals' characteristics. Curiosity about the real powers of animals stems from the *totemic* tradition, in which traditional peoples identify with an animal in order to share its wisdom and prowess. Identifying with, rather than having control over, is a powerful dynamic in Native American folklore, and it has led to this folklore's being tied naturally to environmental education, as the warm reception of Joseph Bruchac's *Keepers of the Earth* (1988) and *Keepers of the Animals* (1991) has demonstrated.

Native American folklore also has many trickster stories, often featuring Coyote. There are creation stories, too—important because stories about beginnings explain a people's understanding of how things are ordered.

African American Folklore. The experience of slavery, faith, resistance, and solidarity has given a unique character to African American folklore. African Americans have a rich oral tradition that encompasses folk and gospel music as well as verbal games and stories.

The West African regions from which slaves were brought to the United States had trading settlements that were originally established by Europeans—primarily by the Portuguese, but also by the English and French. So *pidgin* or *patois*—mixtures of African languages and one of those three European languages—became the language of slaves in the New World. Pidgin English survived well into this century in rural Jamaica and the Bahamas and in the Gullah dialect of the Sea Islands of South Carolina and Georgia. In Haiti, Creole stands with French as one of the two official languages.

Along with their languages, Africans brought stories and proverbs (indeed, most West African languages are riddled with stories and proverbs). Many stories told of tricksters—usually a spider (sometimes called Anansi), a turtle, or a hare.

Slaves were taught the Christian religion, and their religious songs, known as spirituals, such as "Twelve Gates to the City," "Rock My Soul in the Bosom of Abraham," "Michael, Row the Boat Ashore," and "I Am a Poor Wayfaring Stranger," are some of the most stirring folk music we have. To the chagrin of the whites, slaves seized on the liberation message of Christianity—the story of the Hebrew children in bondage and their miraculous flight out of Egypt, led by Moses. Themes of liberation were reflected in many black spirituals, including "Go Down, Moses":

> When Israel was in Egypt land,
> Let my people go!
> Oppressed so hard, they could not stand,
> Let my people go!
>
> Go down, Moses, way down in Egypt land.
> Tell old Pharoah,
> Let my people go!

Some songs also contained coded encouragements for slaves to escape along the Underground Railroad. The best known is "Follow the Drinking Gourd," referring

ASK THE AUTHOR...

Patricia C. McKissack

Patricia C McKissack (signature)

Are you struck more by the universal qualities of African American folktales or by the particular insights they provide about the experiences of African Americans?

Favorite Books as a Child

Worldwide fairytales, myths, and legends are the kinds of reading materials I'd want with me on a desert island, but Hans Christian Andersen's "The Ugly Duckling" was my childhood favorite. The story helped me cope with the day-to-day humiliation I encountered growing up in the segregated South. *A Complete Collection of Poems* by Paul Laurence Dunbar was one of my favorite books, because I enjoyed Dunbar's ability to write using several language patterns. I loved scary stories, especially Edgar Allan Poe's "The Fall of the House of Usher."

"Children growing up without stories are adrift without an anchor," said Joseph Campbell. From fairytales, myths, and legends, children learn about their world and how to live with others in it. When I was growing up, however, my classroom literature anthologies didn't contain any folktales from the African American culture. I wasn't encouraged to read them either. And sadly, "plantation stories" recorded from our oral tradition were written in such an unfamiliar dialect that I felt ashamed and embarrassed when they were presented. Had it not been for my family, all of whom were master storytellers, I would have, indeed, been "adrift without an anchor."

Now, as a writer and storyteller, I am particularly proud of the way my slave ancestors salvaged West African story remnants, reshaped old folk heroes, and cast them in new tales. These stories were sometimes humorous, sometimes sad, and sometimes very scary, but each one recorded the unique experiences of African Americans—who used their lore to teach, to entertain, and to cope in a cruel and hostile environment. African American folktales have survived the horrors of slavery and have even transcended the adverse effects of racism and discrimination. I am pleased that today they are rightfully placed among the larger body of respected American folktales with universal appeal.

I guess that's why I am an advocate of *multicultural literacy*, because I believe it is important to expose children to a variety of story experiences. It broadens the pool of ideas from which to expand their problem-solving and decision-making skills. Actually, it takes nothing from one culture to appreciate another culture's stories. The results might be as exciting as a meeting between Br'er Rabbit and Peter Rabbit or between my Flossie and Little Red Riding Hood.

Patricia C. McKissack and her husband, Fredrick L. McKissack, have coauthored many award-winning nonfiction titles. However, Pat's solo picture books— Mirandy and Brother Wind, Flossie and the Fox, A Million Fish ... More or Less, *and* Nettie Jo's Friends—*have won the hearts of young readers all over the world. When Pat isn't writing, she enjoys traveling in search of new stories.*

to the Big Dipper, a beacon in the northern sky for slaves escaping from Southern plantations.

Appalachian Folklore. Settlers of Scotch, Irish, and English descent settled the mountains of the southeastern United States. Proudly self-reliant and somewhat isolated from the outside by their terrain, people of the Appalachian mountains nurtured a culture rich in stories, riddles, and folksongs. Much of the folklore is traceable to the British Isles—in fact, entire ballads from the seventeenth and eighteenth centuries were sung in the mountains well into this century. Stories of Jack abound, as do various stories of the wiles of the devil and the ways he can be tricked by clever people.

Tall Tales and Labor Stories. Wherever people worked hard and formed close-knit communities, folklore abounded. Lumberjacks lived long weeks and months in the woods—cutting trees to make lumber and harvesting logs to fire the steel mills that supported the early Industrial Revolution in North America. Felling the huge trees with axes and cutting them to length with handsaws was work so hard and thankless it is almost unimaginable now. When dark crept through the lonely woods, lumberjacks retired to rude and drafty shanties, where they took turns sitting in the "deacon's chair" and telling whoppers. The greatest whoppers of them all were those told about Paul Bunyan, with his two-headed axe that could cut trees "coming and going."

Cowboys lived almost the whole year out in the open, in every kind of weather. They had a wide repertoire of delightful songs, such as "Git Along, Little Dogies," "Red River Valley," "The Colorado Trail," and "Root, Hog, or Die," as well as a number of tall tales—the best known of which tells of the larger-than-life cowboy, Pecos Bill. Other folk stories have preserved the life and times of Mississippi riverboat people, of pioneers and settlers, of people along the Erie Canal, of railroad workers, and of farmers from all regions.

Legends and tales abound from every period of U.S. history. Revolutionary times, the Civil War, World War I, the Great Depression, the migration off the farm to the cities, the labor movement, World War II, the civil rights struggle, the women's movement—all of these and more have evoked tales that run the gamut from true accounts to far-fetched legends.

Hispanic Folklore

Americans with Hispanic backgrounds share a culture that was brought from Spain but mixed with the culture of the peoples the Spaniards encountered in the New World or imported as slaves: Indians from North, Central, and South America, and Africans, too. (A word or two on terms is in order. "Hispanic" refers to people of partly Spanish descent living in North or South America. "Latin American" refers to people of partly Spanish, Portuguese, or French descent from Central or South America or the Caribbean. People of partly Spanish descent who are living in the United States often refer to themselves as "Latinos" or "Latinas.")

Mexican and Mexican American folklore mixes stories of Christian saints with traditional beliefs that go back to the Aztecs and the Mayan. The folk medical practice known as *curanderismo*, still practiced among Hispanic peoples of Mexico and the Southwest, exemplifies this same mix. Spanish priests brought the belief that prayers to specific saints, as well as the use of plants and herbs, were effective against troubles of the body and spirit. Indigenous peoples grafted these beliefs onto local practices and expanded on them by applying their greater knowledge of local medicinal herbs. Spiritual medicine hasn't been taught by the Catholic church in Spain for centuries, but the practice of *curanderismo* continues in the New World to this day.

In Mexico, folk stories chronicle the magically curative exploits of Señor San Antonio, and San Miguel figures in local legends having to do with rain and drought. Among Mexican Americans in the Southwest, stories are still told of people's attempts to outwit the devil; many of these feature Pedro de Ordinales, a rough-and-ready lucky bumbler who was apparently imported from Spain. A character who plays a similar role in Mexican and Mexican American folklore is Juan Bobo.

Cuban, Puerto Rican, and Dominican folklore reflects influences from Africa as well as Spain; it also preserves some legends from the original peoples of those islands, who were driven to extinction within fifty years of the arrival of the Europeans in 1492. This folklore includes many animal stories. One of the oddest involves Ratóncito Pérez (also a Spanish import) and Cucarachita Martina. Cucarachita Martina is serious about marriage, but Ratóncito Pérez is apparently in it only for the wedding feast. In any case, his gluttony brings him to a bad end. Curiously, in Spain, Ratóncito Pérez is the tooth fairy.

African Folklore

In the thousand years before Europeans colonized Africa, the continent saw several great empires: Zimbabwe in the east and Mali, Ghana, and Songhai in the west. Moslem traders and missionaries linked much of Africa to Arabia and to Islamic culture. In the fifteenth century, when the Portuguese came to Benin (now in Nigeria), they were so impressed with the level of civilization that they opened diplomatic relations with that country.

Africa's long history was kept alive in poem and song. In West Africa, the *griots*, like the bards of Ireland, kept official histories. Some of their recitations could take twelve days. Poets, too, composed lays to praise kings or mourn them.

Africans who were not converted to Islam or Christianity (and these conversions began over a thousand years ago) shared beliefs that are collectively called *animism*. Many objects in nature are thought by animists to be endowed with spirits—so many that there is no real separation between religion and secular life. The tasks of daily living are carried out with the spirits in mind.

Storytelling was always popular in many parts of Africa, and stories deal with many themes. There are creation myths, stories of the gods, animal stories (especially the trickster tales featuring a turtle, hare, or spider), stories of arguments between neighbors or between men and women, and many proverbs that point out the proper way to live. Some stories are left for the hearers to finish. And some storytellers have the custom of inviting hearers to help tell their stories. (Typically, a person interrupts the teller and says, "I was there, and I saw _____"; whereupon the teller weaves this detail into the story.)

African stories, especially those from the lands in the west from which the slaves came, have greatly contributed to the African American folk tradition.

Asian Folklore

Asia is a big and diverse place; a fifth of humanity lives in China alone. It is hard to make generalizations about Asian folklore that would not also seem true for many other parts of the world. Nonetheless, China and Japan—to speak of two countries—had ancient cultures and written literature before the Europeans did. Japan has a highly developed contemporary literature for children.

Many Asian folktales seem almost parable-like. There is the Burmese story of the man who was so impatient that he pulled his rice plants up a little every day to make them as tall as his neighbors'. Of course, the plants withered and died. There is the Chinese story of a woman who is threatened by a monster, and who receives offers of help from a number of different strangers; together, they defeat the monster for good. Cultivate virtues, especially those of prudence, modesty, and a collaborative spirit, seems to be the message of many of these tales.

Folklore across Cultures

We have endeavored to show what *distinguishes* the folklore of many different cultural groups. Nonetheless, if you read widely in the folklore of the world, you're far more likely to be struck by similarities than by the differences.

In the earliest story known to humankind, the Mesopotamian hero Gilgamesh is bereft when a treasured friend dies. Gilgamesh tries to the limits of his being to understand where his friend has gone, and maybe even to bring him back. We've been there. Gilgamesh is our brother.

A father in a folktale from Burma—a place about as far from the United States as you can get—sends his son into the world. He wishes more than anything for his son to have a good life, but his son thinks that good life means enjoying many material things. Will the son learn real values in time? Do you know any parents who haven't fretted over that question as their child approached maturity?

Parents must leave home, and they warn their children not to let strangers in. A malicious stranger comes. The children are on their own to face the danger. Have you ever seen a child not shiver with anticipation at such a prospect?

As storytellers the world over know, the most important things are basic. The Greeks even made gods out of those basic qualities and concerns: power, wisdom, insight, reverie, love, mirth, skill, art, science, the earth, the sea, home, marriage, fate, war, death. For many of the same basic qualities and concerns, the Celts had *runes*, or symbols carved on bones and carried in a pouch, to be read at crucial points in people's lives. The Chinese considered roughly the same factors in the *I Ching: The Book of Changes*. As Vladimir Propp concluded many decades ago, all folktales have a common source—the human spirit.

DERIVATIVE LITERATURE

There are a host of books that are written in the form of, as embellishment on, or as a direct spoof of some traditional story.

Alma Flor Ada's **The Gold Coin** (1991), illustrated by Neil Waldman, is an original story with a folktale's simplicity, crafted by a reteller of Latin American folktales. Jane Yolen's **Greyling** (1991) is an original version of a selchie story; this noted U.S. author lives much of the time in Scotland, where such tales are part of the folklore.

Robin McKinley has rewritten the story "Beauty and the Beast" as a fantasy novel, called **Beauty** (1978). Nearly every nuance of the Arthurian legend is explored in a retelling by T. H. White in **The Once and Future King** (1939).

Jon Scieszka is a master at spoofs on folktales, and his hilarious books delight children who know the originals. **The True Story of the 3 Little Pigs!** (1989), illustrated by Lane Smith, tells the other side of the story, as narrated by A. Wolf from behind bars. (As Jerome Bruner has written, narrative was born with the first excuse!) Scieszka's **The Frog Prince, Continued** (1994) takes up the question "What happens after the 'happily ever after'?" And his ***The Stinky Cheese Man and Other Fairly Stupid Tales*** (1992) violates every imaginable convention of fairytale books.

Robert Munsch's ***The Paper Bag Princess*** (1980) is a popular modernist rejoinder to the active prince/passive princess syndrome. Jane Yolen's ***Sleeping Ugly*** (1984) explores what really counts in a relationship.

All of these books are interesting in their own right, and especially for the comparisons to traditional literature that they invite.

CRITERIA FOR SELECTING TRADITIONAL LITERATURE

Traditional tales have been favorite fare for children's literature as long as there has been children's literature. In choosing suitable traditional literature for children, several issues are brought into relief. Especially important to consider are stereotypical or even prejudicial treatment of characters of different sexes, races, and national groups and questions of fidelity to the source or the genre, including issues of violence and disagreeableness.

Avoiding Stereotypes and Prejudice

Traditional literature, as we said at the outset, is often strongly didactic: It exists to tell hearers who they are and how they should behave. The trouble is, these stories are usually based on the realities of many generations ago, and they may contain either overt teachings or covert attitudes that have no place in contemporary society.

Western society tolerated public expressions of racism and sexism until quite recently; so we don't have to go back very far in literature to find unwholesome stereotypes openly displayed. We discussed multicultural issues in Chapter 4. But what about gender stereotypes? Should adults still read "Cinderella," "Sleeping Beauty," "Beauty and the Beast," and the like to children? These stories show females as domestic "prizes" for charming princes to come and win. Some teachers and parents avoid these stories altogether; others read them with children but hold up their gender stereotypes for critical appraisal. Children have lively things to say about these issues if the discussion is truly open. We recommend that teachers who share these tales also offer stories that show strong female characters. Even in traditional literature these stories exist, as the collections *Tatterhood* (1978) and *The Maid of the North* (1981) have ably demonstrated. These books feature stories drawn from the folklore of the whole world and give girls and women strong roles.

Respecting Original Sources

Since folk literature conveys the values and beliefs of a people, teachers often use it to acquaint children with other cultures. Since even a small detail or a single saying can reveal something worth knowing about the people who originaged a story, it is desirable that folk material be true to the source from which it came. On the other hand, much folk material must be translated from other languages, and since most of these materials were shared by adults and speak of things unfamiliar to children living in North America, some degree of adaptation is unavoidable. Teachers will want to know, then, where the folk material came from; a responsible work will state its sources. Teachers also will want assurance that the adaptation was carefully done, so as to communicate the truth and spirit of the original material. One way of gaining this assurance is to seek stories from authors with reputations for careful treatment of the source material—authors such as Harold Courlander, Joseph Bruchac, Paul Goble, John Bierhorst, Rafe Martin, and Verna Aardema. Another way is to rely on expert reviews, such as those found in *The School Library Journal* and *The Horn Book*.

 ## TEACHING IDEAS

Discovering the Hero Cycle in Stories. After explaining the steps of the hero cycle, read the story of "Jack and the Beanstalk" to children (in third grade or higher), and ask them to see how many matches they can find between that story and the hero cycle. Read them the stories of Hercules and Orpheus (from the D'Aulaires' *Book of Greek Myths*, 1962), and ask them to do the same. Later, see if they can find parallels to the hero cycle in folktales such as "Hansel and Gretel," "The Orphan Boy and the Elk Dogs," and "Bending Willow."

Finding Lessons in Traditional Tales. Ask students in grades four through six to choose two or three main characters in a traditional tale. Have them jot down notes about the way these characters behave and the rewards or punishments they meet in the end. What do their findings tell about the ways the stories suggest boys and girls, or older people and younger people, *should* behave?

Contrasting Traditional Tales. Ask children in second grade or higher to examine two very different traditional tales and contrast the characters and the settings. Who else do these characters remind them of? What settings in other stories remind them of the settings in these stories? What do these differences remind them of in real life?

Describing Conflict in Fables. Rosemary Deen and Ann Marie Ponsot (1980) suggest an activity for writing fables that can work with children from second grade on. Give the children these instructions: Think of two very different characters (they can be people or animals). Make them argue. Keeping description to a minimum, write down their conversation, alternating between the two voices. Then, introduce an unexpected calamity (a tree falls on them, a wolf tries to gobble them up, etc.). Finally, resolve the argument. (The resolution could be a "last word" from one or both of them that "just goes to show you.")

Comparing and Contrasting Traditional Characters. Ask students in grades one and beyond to examine three trickster tales from African sources (stories about Anansi would be a good bet), three from European sources (stories about Jack would be appropriate), and three from Native American sources (stories about Coyote would be ideal). Ask them to note the ways the trickster characters are the same and different. Write their answers on a chart, for comparison. (See the suggestions for the language chart in Chapter 13.)

EXPERIENCES FOR YOUR LEARNING

1. Find as many variations as you can of the familiar European fairytales "Cinderella," "Hansel and Gretel," and "The Three Little Pigs." What do they have in common? What makes each one unique to its cultural setting?

2. Read four tales from the Grimms' collection and six from Mexico, Japan, or Africa. For each tale, describe the characteristics of the heroes, the situations they find themselves in, the kinds of solutions they try, and the message the story suggests.

Try to make statements about the sorts of issues that are important to each culture on the basis of these tales.

3. Analyze a familiar fairytale, such as "Sleeping Beauty," "Snow White and the Seven Dwarfs," or "Cinderella." Describe as explicitly as you can what the story seems to be saying to readers about *their* lives. What are the story's symbols, and what do they mean? Compare your analysis with the ones offered by Bruno Bettelheim, in *The Uses of Enchantment* (1975).

RECOMMENDED BOOKS

* indicates a picture book; **I** indicates interest level (P = preschool, YA = young adult)

Greek and Roman Myths

* Aliki. *The Gods and Goddesses of Olympus*. New York: HarperCollins, 1994. This book tells the story of how the gods and goddesses came to live at Olympus and provides a sketch of each of the twelve major gods and goddesses. (**I:** 6–10)

* ———. *The Olympians: Great Gods and Goddesses of Ancient Greece*. New York: Holiday House, 1984. Sketches of the key figures in the Pantheon. (**I:** 8–10)

* D'Aulaire, Ingri, and Edgar Parin D'Aulaire. *Book of Greek Myths*. New York: Doubleday, 1962. The stories of the major Greek gods and goddesses are intelligently told and beautifully illustrated. (**I:** 8–12)

Hutton, Warwick. *Persephone*. New York: McElderry, 1994. A beautiful retelling of the myth of the goddess who was spirited away to the underworld by Pluto. (**I:** 7–12)

* Orgel, Doris. *Ariadne, Awake!* Illustrated by Barry Moser. New York: Viking, 1994. The story focuses on Ariadne, who helped Theseus find his way through the Labyrinth to kill the Minotaur. It does a nice job of refocusing what is usually told as a male hero story. (**I:** 11–13)

* Wells, Rosemary. *Max and Ruby's First Greek Myth: Pandora's Box*. New York: Dial, 1993. The characters of Max and Ruby tell the story of Pandora's box as an object lesson. You probably won't find mythology made any more accessible to younger children than it is here. (**I:** 5–7)

North American Tales

Chase, Richard. *Grandfather Tales*. Boston: Houghton Mifflin, 1948. Twenty-five tales from the Appalachians are interspersed with the banter of the teller and his family. (**I:** 8–YA)

———. *The Jack Tales: Folk Tales from the Southern Appalachians*. Boston: Houghton Mifflin, 1943. Recently reissued in paperback, this is a collection of hair-raising stories featuring the plucky folk hero. (**I:** 8–YA)

* Haley, Gail E. *Jack and the Bean Tree*. New York: Crown, 1986. An Appalachian variant of the beanstalk tale. (**I:** 6–10)

———. *Mountain Jack Tales*. New York: Dutton, 1992. More tales of the Appalachian tricksters Jack and Mutsmag (Jack's female counterpart), by a storyteller and folklorist who is also a consummate illustrator. (**I:** 8–12)

* Hooks, William. *Moss Gown*. Illustrated by Donald Carrick. New York: Clarion, 1987. A Cinderella story from the author's native eastern North Carolina. (**I:** 7–10)

* Isaacs, Anne. *Swamp Angel*. Illustrated by Paul Zelinsky. New York: Dutton, 1994. An original tall tale with a female character. Zelinsky painted the illustrations for the book on wood veneers for an antique look. (**I:** 6–9)

* Kellogg, Steven. *Johnny Appleseed*. New York: Morrow, 1988. Active and expressive drawings illustrate this entry in Kellogg's tall tales series. (**I:** 6–10)

* ———. *Mike Fink: A Tall Tale*. New York: Morrow, 1992. Another colorful entry in Kellogg's American tall tales series. (**I:** 6–10)

* ———. *Paul Bunyan*. New York: Morrow, 1988. Kellogg's art brings this tall tale of a lumberjack to life. (**I:** 6–10)

* ———. *Pecos Bill*. New York: Mulberry, 1986. Lively and expressive drawings and clever details highlight this retelling of the Western tall tale of Pecos Bill and Slewfoot Sue. (**I:** 6–10)

Folktales from Great Britain

Briggs, Katherine, ed. *British Folktales*. New York: Pantheon, 1977. An adult collection of traditional tales as they were collected from folk storytellers, in interesting dialects. (**I:** YA)

Buchan, David. *Scottish Tradition: A Collection of Scottish Folk Literature*. New York: Routledge,

1984. An adult collection, but suitable for read-alouds. (**I:** YA)

* Chaucer, Geoffrey. *The Canterbury Tales.* Adapted by Barbara Cohen. Illustrated by Trina Schart Hyman. New York: Lothrop, Lee, & Shepard, 1988. A collection of four beautifully illustrated tales from Chaucer's story of a medieval English pilgrimage to Canterbury. (**I:** 11–YA)

* Galdone, Paul. *The Little Red Hen.* New York: Seabury, 1973. An old tale of industry and rewards that is good for acting out. (**I:** 5–7)

* ———. *What's in Fox's Sack?* New York: Clarion, 1982. A kidnap-minded fox is outsmarted by a clever old woman. (**I:** 5–8)

* Hodges, Margaret. *Saint George and the Dragon.* Illustrated by Trina Schart Hyman. Boston: Little, Brown, 1984. A Caldecott Honor Book with stunning illustrations. (**I:** 8–10)

Hodges, Margaret, and Margery Evernden. *Of Swords and Sorcerers: The Adventures of King Arthur and His Knights.* Illustrated by David Frampton. New York: Scribner's, 1993. The legend of Arthur's life is told, along with stories of Merlin, Guinevere, Percival, and Galahad. (**I:** 12–13)

Jacobs, Joseph. *Celtic Fairy Tales.* London: Frederick Muller, 1958. Jacobs, a noted collector, wrote these tales for children in 1890. (**I:** 9–12)

———. *English Fairy Tales.* Illustrated by John D. Batten. New York: Dover, 1967. (Originally published in 1898.) Well-told versions of stories familiar to Anglo-Saxon children. (**I:** 9–12)

Jones, Gwyn. *Welsh Legends and Folktales.* New York: Puffin, 1982. A collection of more than thirty active tales from Wales. (**I:** 11–13)

* Leeson, Robert. *The Story of Robin Hood.* Illustrated by Barbara Lofthouse. New York: Larousse Kingfisher, 1994. A retelling of the story from the ballads; well illustrated and with source notes. (**I:** 8–10)

* Marshall, James. *Goldilocks and the Three Bears.* New York: Dial, 1988. A humorous adaptation by the creator of *George and Martha.* (**I:** 5–8)

German Folktales

* Galdone, Paul. *Hansel and Gretel.* Illustrated by Paul Galdone. New York: McGraw-Hill, 1982. A version that will not horrify young children. (**I:** 7–9)

* Hyman, Trina Schart. *Little Red Riding Hood.* Illustrated by Trina Schart Hyman. New York: Holiday House, 1983. A beautiful adaptation by an award-winning artist. (**I:** 7–9)

* Kimmel, Eric. *Iron John.* Illustrated by Trina Schart Hyman. New York: Holiday House, 1994. The story of a prince who is trained in manly things by the wild man who lives in the woods. (**I:** 8–12)

* Rogasky, Barbara. *Rapunzel: From the Brothers Grimm.* Illustrated by Trina Schart Hyman. New York: Holiday House, 1982. A runaway ponytail leads to love. (**I:** 7–9)

* Zelinsky, Paul. *Rumplestiltskin.* Illustrated by Paul Zelinsky. New York: Dutton, 1986. A guess-my-name story. The English version is "Tom Tit Tot." (**I:** 7–9)

French Fairytales

* Mayer, Marianna. *Beauty and the Beast.* Illustrated by Mercer Mayer. New York: Macmillan, 1978. The ink and watercolor drawings are very expressive in this tale of love's redeeming powers. (**I:** 8–11)

Perrault, Charles. *Favorite Fairy Tales.* Ed. Jennifer Mulherin. New York: Grosset & Dunlap, 1983. This version has the original illustrations as they were published in England in the eighteenth century. (**I:** 10–12)

* ———. *The Glass Slipper: Charles Perrault's Tales of Times Past.* Trans. John Bierhorst. Illustrated by Mitchell Miller. New York: Four Winds, 1981. A translation of Perrault's tales by a careful reteller of world folk literature. (**I:** 8–10)

* ———. *Puss in Boots.* Illustrated by Marcia Brown. New York: Scribner's, 1952. A resourceful cat makes his master a rich man. As Joseph Campbell would say, this story stars the "magic helper." (**I:** 5–9)

* San Jose, Christine. *Cinderella.* Illustrated by Debra Santini. Homesale, PA: Boyds Mills Press, 1994. Set in New York City at the turn of the century, another period of elegant balls. (**I:** 8–11)

Russian Folktales

* Afanas'ev, Aleksandr. *Russian Folk Tales.* Trans. Robert Chandler. Illustrated by Ivan Bilibin. New York: Random House 1984. These seven tales are perfectly illustrated by Bilibin. Children will want to hear them again and again. (**I:** 7–12)

———. *Russian Folktales.* Trans. Norbert Guterman. New York: Pantheon, 1945. This is a collection of over two hundred tales, with commentary by Roman Jacokson. (**I:** 7–14)

* Gilchrist, Cherry. *Prince Ivan and the Firebird.* Illustrated by Andrei Troshkov. Boulder, CO: Barefoot, 1994. One of the most exciting of Afanas'ev's tales, richly illustrated. (**I:** 6–10)

* Mayer, Marianna. *Baba Yaga and Vasilisa the Brave.* Illustrated by K. Y. Craft. New York: Morrow, 1994. Two of children's favorite Russian characters in one story. Vasilisa succeeds with the help of the doll her dead mother gave her. (I: 6–10)

* Sherman, Josepha. *Vasilisa the Wise.* Illustrated by Robert D. San Souci. New York: Harcourt, 1988. "Mornings are wiser than evenings," says Vasilisa the Wise, and she saves her husband from peril. (I: 5–8)

African American Stories

* Bang, Molly Garrett. *Wiley and the Hairy Man.* New York: Macmillan, 1976. A spooky African American tale from Alabama, taken from Botkin's *Treasury of American Folklore.* (I: 6–9)

Hamilton, Virginia. *Her Stories: African American Folktales, Fairy Tales, and True Tales.* Illustrated by Leo and Diane Dillon. New York: Scholastic, 1995. Sixteen folktales and three true accounts from American black women. (I: 9–YA)

———. *The People Could Fly: American Black Folktales.* Illustrated by Leo and Diane Dillon. New York: Knopf, 1985. Twenty-four tales plus a bibliography. Includes "Wiley, His Mother, and the Hairy Man," and "Little Eight John." (I: 9–YA)

Harris, Joel Chandler. *The Tales of Uncle Remus, More Tales of Uncle Remus, Further Tales of Uncle Remus,* and *The Last Tales of Uncle Remus.* Adapted by Julius Lester and illustrated by Jerry Pinkney. New York: Dial, 1987, 1988, 1989. Lester's voice make these tales a joy to read aloud, and Pinkney's illustrations bring the characters to life. (I: 8–12)

* Jacquith, Priscilla. *Bo Rabbit Smart for True: Tall Tales from the Gullah.* Illustrated by Ed Young. New York: Philomel, 1981. These tales were collected from African Americans living in the Sea Islands of South Carolina and Georgia. (I: 9–12)

* Lester, Julius. *John Henry.* Illustrated by Jerry Pinkney. New York: Dial, 1994. A lively and careful retelling of this tall tale that pits man against machine. (I: 8–10)

* Temple, Frances. *Tiger Soup: An Anansi Story from Jamaica.* New York: Orchard, 1994. Anansi tricks Tiger, then teaches the monkeys a song that suggests they did it. (I: 5–8)

Turenne de Pres, François. *Children of Yayoute: Folktales of Haiti.* New York: Universe, 1994. Twelve tales originally published in Haiti in 1949, with colorful illustrations. (I: 7–10)

Native American Stories

Bruchac, Joseph. *Dog People: Native Dog Stories.* Illustrated by Murv Jacob. Golden, CO: Fulcrum Kids, 1995. Six stories told for thousands of years among the Abenaki people about dogs as companions of humans; complete with a glossary of terms. (I: 7–10)

* ———. *The First Strawberries: A Cherokee Story.* Illustrated by Anna Vojtech. New York: Dial, 1993. A touching and lyrical story about the first man and the first woman, the overcoming of anger, and the origin of strawberries. (I: 7–10)

* ———. *The Great Ball Game: A Muskogee Story.* Illustrated by Susan L. Roth. New York: Dial, 1994. In this pourquoi tale, the birds and the animals square off in a game of stickball to decide who will have dominion over the land; the bat sides with the animals and wins the game. (I: 7–10)

Bruchac, Joseph, and Gayle Ross. *The Girl Who Married the Moon.* Mahwah, NJ: Troll/BridgeWater, 1994. Tales with girl protagonists from sixteen Indian nations, with commentary. (I: 10–13)

* Cohen, Caron Lee. *The Mud Pony.* Illustrated by Shonto Begay. New York: Scholastic, 1988. A boy rises from his lowly origin to the position of chief with the aid of a magical pony in this Pawnee tale. The first children's book illustrated by Begay, a Navajo. (I: 7–10)

* Goble, Paul. *Dream Wolf.* New York: Bradbury, 1990. A brother and sister wander off from their family and spend the night on the mountainside. A wolf rescues them and leads them to safety. With illustrations inspired by traditional paintings of Plains tribes. (I: 7–10)

* ———. *Her Seven Bothers.* New York: Bradbury, 1988. In this Cheyenne pourquoi tale about the origin of the Big Dipper, an only child goes in search of brothers, after making beautiful clothing for them in the certainty that she will one day find them. (I: 8–11)

* ———. *Iktomi and the Buzzard: A Plains Indian Story.* New York: Orchard, 1994. Another in a series about Iktomi, the trickster of the Plains Indians. (I: 7–10)

* Luenn, Nancy. *Nessa's Fish.* Illustrated by Neil Waldman. New York: Atheneum, 1990. A brave Inuit girl defends her ailing grandmother and a cache of fish from marauding animals on the desolate ice. (I: 7–10)

* McDermott, Gerald. *Coyote: A Trickster Tale from the American Southwest.* New York: Harcourt, 1994. A Native American trickster tale from the Zuni people, presented by a master illustrator. (I: 6–9)

* Pollock, Penny. *The Turkey Girl: A Zuni Cinderella Story.* Illustrated by Ed Young. Boston: Little, Brown, 1996. This rich pourquoi tale with a moral

about keeping one's word is also a valuable take on the Cinderella story, with breathtaking illustrations. (I: 7–9)

* Rodanas, Kristina. *Dragonfly's Tale*. New York: Clarion Books, 1992. This Zuni tale with young protagonists promotes conservation and generosity and has a pourquoi twist, too. (I: 6–9)

Ross, Gayle. *How Rabbit Tricked Otter and Other Cherokee Stories*. Illustrated by Murv Jacob. New York: HarperCollins, 1994. Fifteen tales about the trickster Rabbit, by a master storyteller of Cherokee descent. (I: 8–12)

* ———. *How Turtle's Back Was Cracked: A Traditional Cherokee Tale*. Illustrated by Murv Jacob. New York: Dial, 1995. A pourquoi tale reminiscent of "Brer Rabbit and the Briar Patch," retold in a lively voice by a master storyteller. Students may want to compare this version with Tololwa Mollel's *The Flying Tortoise: An Igbo Tale*, which is based on a story from Southern Nigeria. (I: 6–9)

* Young, Ed. *Moon Mother: A Native American Creation Tale*. New York: HarperCollins, 1993. A beautiful creation story, with subtle pastel illustrations by an award-winning artist. (I: 7–10)

Tales from Africa

* Aardema, Verna. *Bringing the Rain to Kapiti Plain: A Nandi Tale*. Illustrated by Beatrice Vidal. New York: Dial, 1981. Can there be more rhythmic language than in this tale from Kenya? (I: 6–10)

———. *Misoso: Once Upon a Time Tales from Africa*. Illustrated by Reynold Ruffins. New York: Apple Soup, 1994. Twelve tales from many parts of Africa for young readers. (I: 6–10)

* ———. *Why Mosquitoes Buzz in People's Ears*. Illustrated by Leo and Diane Dillon. New York: Dial, 1978. A cumulative pourquoi tale. (I: 5–10)

* Bryan, Ashley. *Beat the Story-Drum, Pum-Pum*. New York: Atheneum, 1987. A collection of African tales to be read aloud—or, if you've ever heard Bryan read, you might say roared aloud. (I: 6–10)

* ———. *Turtle Knows Your Name*. New York: Atheneum, 1989. West Indian tales, good for oral reading and acting out. (I: 6–10)

Courlander, Harold. *The Crest and the Hide*. Illustrated by Monica Vachula. New York: Coward, McCann, 1982. One of our best folktale collectors presents twenty tales from across Africa, identified by society and region. (I: 10–YA)

* Gerson, Mary-Joan. *Why the Sky Is Far Away: A Nigerian Folktale*. Illustrated by Carla Golembe. Boston: Little, Brown, 1992. A lively pourquoi tale

whose theme is the importance of preventing waste. This pairs nicely with *The Dragonfly's Tale*, a Native American story. (I: 6–10)

* Haley, Gail E. *A Story, A Story*. New York: Atheneum, 1970. A traditional African tale about how Anansi won stories from the Sky God; a Caldecott winner. (I: 5–10)

* Knutson, Barbara. *Why the Crab Has No Head*. Minneapolis: Carolrhoda, 1987. A pourquoi tale from Zaire. (I: 5–9)

* Lester, Julius. *How Many Spots Does a Leopard Have?* Illustrated by David Shannon. New York: Scholastic, 1989. Folktales from Africa and from the Jewish tradition. (I: 9–12)

* McDermott, Gerald. *Anansi the Spider*. New York: Holt, 1972. A Caldecott-winning tale of the trickster from West Africa. (I: 7–10)

* Mollel, Tololwa. *The Flying Tortoise: An Igbo Tale*. Illustrated by Barbara Spurll. New York: Clarion, 1994. Greedy Tortoise persuades the birds to lend him feathers so that he can fly up to feast with the Skylanders. When he eats all the food himself, they repay him harshly and his shell is shattered. (I: 6–10)

* ———. *The Orphan Boy*. Illustrated by Paul Morin. New York: Clarion, 1990. A touching pourquoi tale from the Masai people of East Africa, about the tragic power of overweening curiosity and the reason for the transit of Venus. (I: 6–10)

* Steptoe, John. *Mufaro's Beautiful Daughters*. New York: Lothrop, Lee & Shepard, 1987. The humblest and kindest daughter gets the reward in this Caldecott winner. (I: 6–10)

Latin American Stories

* Ada, Alma Flor. *The Gold Coin*. Illustrated by Neil Waldman. New York: Aladdin, 1991. In this original folktale, a thief is made into an honest man in spite of himself, as he pursues a woman whose wealth turns out to be her generous spirit. (I: 5–11)

* ———. *The Great-Great-Granddaughter of Cucarachita Martina*. Illustrated by Ana Lopez Escriva. New York: Scholastic, 1993. A modern retelling of a Caribbean folktale. (I: 6–10)

* ———. *Medio pollito/Half-Chicken*. Illustrated by Kim Howard. New York: Doubleday, 1995. In Spanish and in English, this tongue-in-cheek pourquoi tale from Cuba explains the origin of the weather vane. (I: 6–10)

* ———. *The Rooster Who Went to His Uncle's Wedding*. Illustrated by Kathleen Kuchera. New York: Putnam, 1993. A cumulative tale from Cuba

(same as the bilingual story *The Bossy Gallito/El gallo de bodas*). (I: 6–10)

Aldana, Patricia, ed. *Jade and Iron: Latin American Tales from Two Cultures*. Trans. Hugh Hazleton. Illustrated by Luis Garay. Buffalo, NY: Douglas & McIntyre, 1996. The first group of seven stories comes from indigenous peoples of Central and South America; the second group of seven came to Central and South America from Spain. (I: 8–13)

* Arnold, Sandra. *Child of the Sun*. Illustrated by Dave Albers. Mahwah, NJ: Troll Associates, 1995. A Cuban creation story from the Ciboney people, a pre-Columbian tribe, which tells of the first man and woman and explains the origin of solar eclipses. (I: 7–11)

Campos, Anthony John. *Mexican Folktales*. Tucson: University of Arizona Press, 1977. The author learned these twenty-seven short tales from his family, who came to California from Jalisco, Mexico. (I: 8–12)

* de Paola, Tomie. *The Legend of the Poinsettia*. New York: Putnam, 1994. A Mexican legend of Christmas. (I: 7–10)

* Ehlert, Lois. *Moon Rope: A Peruvian Folktale/Un lazo a la luna: Una leyenda Peruana*. New York: Harcourt, 1992. A pourquoi tale in English and Spanish that explains why Mole lives in the ground and why we see Fox's likeness in the moon. (I: 6–8)

* Gonzalez, Lucia M. *The Bossy Gallito/El gallo de bodas*. Illustrated by Lulu Delacre. San Diego: Harcourt, 1994. A Spanish/English version of the cumulative tale of a rooster who wanted his beak cleaned (the same story as *The Rooster Who Went to His Uncle's Wedding*). (I: 7–10)

* Johnston, Tony. *The Tale of Rabbit and Coyote*. Illustrated by Tomie de Paola. New York: Putnam, 1994. A Zapotec pourquoi tale from the Oaxaca region of Mexico, told with some Spanish terms, explains why Coyote howls at the moon. (I: 6–9)

* Martinez, Alejandro Cruz. *The Woman Who Outshone the Sun/La mujer que brillaba aún más que el sol*. Illustrated by Fernando Olivera. San Francisco: Children's Book Press, 1991. With a touch of magical realism, this ancient Zapotec myth from Southern Mexico shares a message of the importance of accepting differences. (I: 6–10)

* Ober, Hal. *How Music Came to the World: An Ancient Mexican Myth*. Illustrated by Carol Ober. Boston: Houghton Mifflin, 1994. The sky god and the wind god cooperate to bring music to the earth in this ancient story. (I: 8–11)

* Reasoner, Charles. *Night Owl and the Rooster: A Haitian Legend*. Mahwah, NJ: Troll Associates, 1995. A touching tale of an owl who is helped to accept his odd looks by his true love. (I: 7–10)

* Rohmer, Harriet. *Uncle Nacho's Hat/El sombrero de Tio Nacho*. Illustrated by Mira Reisberg. San Francisco: Children's Book Press, 1989. Originally a play performed by the Puppet Workshop of Nicaraguan National Television, the story explores the difficulty of getting rid of an old hat (or an old habit) when given a new one. (I: 7–11)

Asian Folktales

* Ishii, Momoko. *The Tongue-Cut Sparrow*. Trans. Katherine Paterson. Illustrated by Suekichi Akaba. New York: Dutton/Lodestar, 1987. A kind old man and his greedy wife get their just deserts from a little sparrow. Comparable to "The Fisherman's Wife," "The Talking Eggs," "Mufaro's Beautiful Daughters," and "Three Perfect Peaches." (I: 7–10)

* Lee, Jeanne M. *Toad Is the Uncle of Heaven*. New York: Holt, 1985. Something of a cumulative tale, about a toad that asks the king of heaven to end a drought. The many helpers he recruits lend their aid at propitious moments, just as they do in the Grimms' "The Brementown Musicians" or in the Chinese tale "The Terrible Nung Gwama." (I: 7–10)

* McDermott, Gerald. *The Stonecutter*. New York: Puffin, 1975. Tasaku, a lowly stonecutter, wishes for increasing power. (I: 7–12)

* Morimoto, Junko. *The Inch Boy*. New York: Puffin, 1986. A Japanese Tom Thumb story. (I: 6–10)

Sakade, Florence, ed. *Japanese Children's Favorite Stories*. Illustrated by Yoshisuke Kurosaki. Boston: Tuttle, 1958. Here are twenty classic folktales of Japan, with authentic illustrations. (I: 10–12)

———. *Kintaro's Adventures and Other Japanese Children's Stories*. Illustrated by Yoshio Hayashi. Boston: Tuttle, 1958. These are stories well known among Japanese children, retold in traditional settings. (I: 10–12)

* San Souci, Robert D. *The Samurai's Daughter*. Illustrated by Stephen Johnson. New York: Dial, 1992. An exciting Japanese tale with a strong female hero. (I: 6–10)

* Uchida, Yoshiko. *The Two Foolish Cats*. New York: McElderry, 1987. Two cats quarrel foolishly over rice cakes until the wise old monkey unexpectedly stops their argument. (I: 5–9)

* ———. *The Wise Old Woman*. Illustrated by Martin Springett. New York: McElderry, 1994. A Japanese tale about a village that discriminates against old people. An old woman's wisdom saves the village from a marauding conqueror. (I: 6–10)

* Xiong, Blia. *Nine-in-One, Grr! Grr!* Adapted by Cathy Spagnoli. Illustrated by Nancy Hom. San Francisco: Children's Book Press, 1989. When the great god Shao tells First Tiger how many cubs she will have, Bird confuses her into believing she will have fewer—and so she does. A story from the Hmong people of Laos. (I: 6–10)

* Yacowitz, Caryn. *The Jade Stone: A Chinese Folktale.* Illustrated by Ju-Hong Chen. New York: Holiday House, 1992. In this thoughtful tale, a master stone-cutter listens to the rock and carves what it wants to be—a decision that causes him to defy the emperor and nearly costs his life. (I: 6–11)

* Yagawa, Sumiko. *The Crane Wife.* Trans. Katherine Peterson. Illustrated by Suekichi Akaba. New York: Morrow, 1987. In repayment for a kind deed, a crane changes a peasant into a beautiful woman who becomes his wife and weaves exquisite cloth to support them. (I: 8–10)

* Yep, Lawrence. *The Boy Who Swallowed Snakes.* Illustrated by Jean and Mou-sien Tseng. New York: Scholastic, 1994. In this original folktale in a Chinese setting, a boy swallows a poisonous snake as an act of heroism and flourishes in the end. (I: 8–10)

* ———. *The Ghost Fox.* Illustrated by Jean Tseng and Mou-sien Tseng. New York: Scholastic, 1994. For intermediate readers, a moving and ancient tale about a boy who rescues his mother's soul from a ghost fox. (I: 8–11)

* ———. *The Junior Thunder Lord.* Illustrated by Robert Van Nutt. Mahwah, NJ: Troll/BridgeWater, 1994. A seventeenth-century Chinese tale about a merchant's act of kindness, which is unexpectedly and magnificently rewarded. (I: 8–10)

RESOURCES

Bettelheim, Bruno. *The Uses of Enchantment.* New York: Vintage, 1975.

Bronner, Simon, ed. *American Children's Folklore.* Little Rock, AR: August House, 1988.

Luthi, Max. *The European Folktale: Form and Future.* Philadelphia: ISHI, 1981.

McGlathery, James, ed. *The Brothers Grimm and Folktale.* Urbana: University of Illinois Press, 1991.

Ong, Walter. *Orality and Literacy: The Technologizing of the Word.* New York: Methuen, 1985.

Von Franz, Marie Louise. *Interpretation of Fairy Tales.* Dallas: Spring Publications, 1970.

REFERENCES

Aarne, Antti. *The Types of the Folktale.* Trans. and rev. by Stith Thompson. Folklore Fellows Communication No. 184. Helsinki: Academia Scientiarum Fennica, 1961.

Bettelheim, Bruno. *The Uses of Enchantment.* New York: Vintage, 1975.

Bly, Robert. *Iron John: A Book about Men.* New York: Vintage, 1992.

Bronner, Simon, ed. *American Children's Folklore.* Little Rock, AR: August House, 1988.

Campbell, Joseph. *The Hero with a Thousand Faces.* Princeton, NJ: Bollingen, 1968.

Deen, Rosemary, and Ann Marie Ponsot. *Beat Not the Poor Desk.* Portsmouth, NH: Boynton-Cook, 1980.

Freud, Sigmund. *New Introductory Lectures on Psycho-analysis.* New York: Norton, 1923.

Holland, Norman. *Five Readers Reading.* New Haven: Yale University Press, 1975.

Jung, Carl, ed. *Man and His Symbols.* New York: Dell, 1961.

Lévi-Strauss, Claude. "The Structural Study of Myth." *Structural Anthropology.* Garden City, NY: Basic Books, 1957.

Lomax, Alan. *The Folksongs of North America.* New York: Dolphin, 1975.

Lonnrot, Elias, comp. *The Kalevala.* Trans. Francis Peabody Magoun, Jr. Cambridge, MA: Harvard University Press, 1963.

MacDonald, Margaret Read. *The StoryTeller's Sourcebook: A Subject, Title, and Motif-Index to Folklore Collections for Children.* Detroit: Neal-Schuman/Gale Research, 1982.

McGlathery, James M., ed. *The Brothers Grimm and Folktale.* Urbana: University of Illinois Press, 1991.

Miller, Jay. Introduction. *Coyote Stories,* by Mourning Dove. Lincoln: University of Nebraska Press, 1990.

Phelps, Ethel Johnston. *The Maid of the North: Feminist Folktales from Around the World.* New York: Holt, 1981.

Propp, Vladimir. *The Morphology of the Folktale.* 1928. Austin: The University of Texas Press, 1968.

White, T. H. *The Once and Future King.* New York: Putnam, 1939.

Winner, Ellen. *Invented Worlds: A Psychology of the Arts.* Cambridge, MA: Harvard University Press, 1982.

6 Picture Books

Alice was beginning to get very tired of sitting by her sister on the bank, and of having nothing to do; once or twice she had peeped into the book her sister was reading, but it had no pictures or conversations in it, "and what is the use of a book," thought Alice, "without pictures or conversation?"

from Alice's Adventures in Wonderland *(1865)*
by Lewis Carroll

PICTURE BOOKS DEFINED

Today's young readers share Alice's desire to see pictures in a book, and their wish is richly satisfied by contemporary children's literature. A picture book in the purest sense refers to a book that relies solely on illustrations to convey its message, but a broader definition includes books in which the illustrations combine with text to create a message. A picture book can take many forms. It can be a *wordless book*, which tells a story solely through illustrations. It can be an *illustrated book,* in which the words carry most of the message, but illustrations either depict what is stated in the text or decorate the page. It can be a *picture storybook,* in which a tale is told through a combination of illustrations and text, each amplifying the other in order to create a unified whole. Much of the discussion in this chapter focuses on the picture storybook.

THE EVOLUTION OF PICTURE BOOKS

Since the publication in 1658 of the first picture book, many factors have influenced the evolution of these books for children. Picture books have changed as their creators have explored the interplay of text and illustrations and refined their concepts of picture books. Developments in printing technology have influenced the technical as well as the artistic aspects of creating picture books.

The Development of the Concept of the Picture Book

What is generally considered the first picture book is **Orbis Sensualium Pictus** (**The Visible World in Pictures**), published in 1658 by John Amos Comenius (1592–1670), a visionary educator from what is now the Republic of Slovakia. Comenius believed that children should be taught about practical matters in the language they used daily, in addition to being taught the "dead" languages, history, and catechisms, as was popular at the time. He added illustrations to informational text to increase children's understanding and pleasure. Following the lead of Comenius, most picture books of the seventeenth and eighteenth centuries were created to educate children and guide their moral behavior.

Children's book publishing advanced dramatically under the leadership of John Newbery (1713–1767). In 1744, Newbery established a company in London dedicated almost exclusively to publishing beautiful children's books. He created books for children in attractive, playful formats, including the accordion book, which was a long strip folded accordion-like to form "pages." He was the first to introduce illustrations by accomplished artists, and his books had permanent, attractive bindings.

Picture books flourished in England during the nineteenth century. Much of the credit for changes in picture books is given to Edmund Evans, an artist, publisher, and printer. Evans advanced the development of picture books by recognizing the importance of the relationship between illustration and book design. In addition, using photographic techniques, he created copies that closely resembled the original illustrations in order to improve the color printing process. Evans persuaded artists such as Randolph Caldecott (1846–1886), Walter Crane (1845–1915), and Kate Greenaway (1846–1901) to create books for children (Kiefer, 1995).

Walter Crane is known for his careful attention to his books' designs and for synchronizing text and illustrations. He was among the first to attend to the overall effect of double-page spreads and to the use of color and beautifully designed pages. Some of the books Crane illustrated are still being reproduced, including his *Sing a Song of Sixpence* (1867) and *The House That Jack Built* (1865).

Another notable creator of picture books was Kate Greenaway, whose portrayal of an idealized childhood can be seen in *A—Apple Pie* (1886). Greenaway's enchantment with the Victorian world is evident in her illustrations, which are filled with flowers, gardens, and prettily dressed and happy children.

The picture book form made the greatest leap toward its modern manifestation in the hands of English illustrator Randolph Caldecott, of whom Maurice Sendak (1990) wrote:

> He devised an ingenious juxtaposition of picture and word, a counterpoint that never happened before. Words are left out—but the picture says it. Pictures are left out—but the word says it. In short, it is the invention of the picture book. (p. 21)

Caldecott built on Crane's ideas about book design, perfecting the unification of text and illustration and allowing illustrations to interpret and extend the text beyond what the words implied. Also, Caldecott created illustrations that were not contained within borders so that characters virtually bounced off the pages.

Later, another English illustrator, Beatrix Potter (1866–1943), recognized the need to consider the audience when creating children's books. She insisted that her books be appropriately sized for little hands. Potter's stories of woodland animals are endearing not only because of the well-written text, but also because of the meticulously drawn illustrations.

By the 1930s, the concept of the modern picture book had basically taken shape. The illustrations extended the text, the text and illustrations were interdependent, and the importance of the book's entire design was recognized (Schwartz, 1982).

Changes in Printing Technology

Improvements in printing technology over the years account for great changes in the appearance of picture books. Paper, the use of color, printing quality, and art styles have contributed to the evolution of the picture book.

Illustrations in early picture books were created using a relief method such as wood block printing. Artists carved illustrations on wood blocks by cutting away the background. The resulting images, which stood above the rest of the block, were inked and impressed on paper by printing machines. Comenius created *Orbis Pictus* on wood blocks and included elaborate illustrations and designs in the page borders, a carryover from the hand-decorated manuscripts created before the advent of the printing press. Each illustration had to be

painstakingly carved on a separate block. John Newbery, who was the first to produce books whose primary purpose was to amuse children, used *wood engravings* for most of his publications. Thomas Bewick perfected wood engraving in the late eighteenth century and is best known for being the first to add color to illustrations. Every book was colored by hand; ironically, some of those hands belonged to children who worked under sweatshop conditions.

William Blake used *etchings* on metal plates to illustrate his **Songs of Innocence** (1879). Walter Crane's illustrations in **Absurd ABC** (1874) were hand-colored, and the typography in that book was considered to be as excellent as the pictures. John Tenniel's illustrations of **Alice's Adventures in Wonderland** (1865) were printed by letterpress from metal engravings.

Lithography, a process invented in the late eighteenth century, allowed artists to work on flat stones that had a very hard, smoothly polished surface. Images were drawn on the stone with wax crayons or *touche*, a crayon-like liquid material. The ink adhered to the waxed portions of the stone; images were then printed on dampened paper using enormous pressure. Hans Fischer's illustrations for **Puss in Boots** (1958) were created by lithography.

The use of *photography* and *letterpress printing* revolutionized the printing of picture books in the early twentieth century. At first, colors had to be separated by hand, and the process was both tedious and expensive. It was not until illustrators could turn color separation over to machines that the number of full-color illustrations in picture books increased. Photography, and later, the laser scanner, made the greatest impact on the quality of art reproduction.

In the twentieth century, printing technology has improved, and art can be reproduced so that it closely resembles its original form. Picture books have become objects of great beauty. The use of computer technology to create picture books may lead to a new era of book illustration. Since the advent of the laser scanner, the printing process imposes few limitations on the artist. It is amazing what illustrators have been able to use: Imaginative picture books have been made with collages of cardboard, cereal, and plastic, as David Diaz did in illustrating Eve Bunting's **Smoky Night** (1994), or even wood veneers, which is what Paul O. Zelinsky used to illustrate Anne Isaacs's **Swamp Angel** (1994).

Computer technology itself offers illustrators a new medium. Artists have different reactions to the use of computers to create art. Some believe that children will not like art produced by computer. They suggest that technology separates the artist from the reader and that children will always prefer illustrations in which "the hand of the artist" is recognizable. On the other hand, Don and Audrey Wood, two highly regarded illustrators, have made such a complete transition to computer-generated art that they have given up paintbrushes entirely.

Authors and Illustrators Who Have Defined the Field

Before the 1930s, the picture books available to children in the United States were typically imported from England and other European countries. However, during the decades between 1930 and 1960, many authors and illustrators came from Europe and joined those working in the United States to establish a solid foundation of American picture books. Ludwig Bemelmans, Roger Duvoisin, Feodor Rojankovsky, and Tomi Ungerer were among those who emigrated from Europe. American picture book creators of that time were Robert

McCloskey, Wanda Gág, Robert Lawson, Virginia Lee Burton, Marie Hall Ets, and Margaret Wise Brown. Many of the books created during that era continue to be popular with children (Burns, 1995).

Wanda Gág's *Millions of Cats* (1929) still delights readers with the repeated phrases "Hundreds of cats, Thousands of cats, Millions and billions and trillions of cats." The lonely man who sets out to find a cat to keep him and his wife company simply cannot choose from among the millions of cats, each with unique qualities. The lines of the hills and roads in the black-and-white illustrations show the long distance the man travels in search of a cat and echo the long line of cats that follow him home.

Many adults today remember reading Virginia Lee Burton's story of *Mike Mulligan and His Steam Shovel* (1939) as they grew up. When new electric and diesel shovels take jobs away from steam shovels, Mike takes his steam shovel, Mary Anne, to Popperville and proves that she can dig "as much in one day as a hundred men could dig in a week." The house in Burton's *The Little House* (1942) was said to be so well built that the "great-great-grandchildren's great-great-grandchildren" would live there. Although both of these works are more than a half-century old, they meet contemporary criteria for good picture books.

Of the many books written by Margaret Wise Brown, the one cherished by millions of readers over the years is *Goodnight Moon* (1947). In this bedtime story, a little rabbit is in bed, saying goodnight to each item in the bedroom and outside the window. Gradually, the lights dim until it is dark in the room, and the rabbit falls asleep.

Robert McCloskey's Caldecott-winning *Make Way for Ducklings* (1941) made the Boston Public Garden famous all over the world to children who read and reread the endearing story of a duck family in search of a place to live. Among McCloskey's other books that continue to enjoy wide popularity are *Blueberries for Sal* (1948) and *Time of Wonder* (1957).

CATEGORIES OF PICTURE BOOKS

Picture books have a range of purposes, from introducing rhymes and serving as manipulative toys to helping children learn concepts. In this section, we organize picture books into four groups: early childhood books, wordless books, beginning readers' books, and picture storybooks. Early childhood books are those primarily intended for the youngest children and include board books, books of Mother Goose and nursery rhymes, concept books, alphabet books, counting books, and toy books. Wordless books vary more in intended age. Their primary purpose is to allow readers to create the text mentally while looking at the pictures. Beginning readers' books give children a start at reading independently. Picture storybooks comprise the largest subgroup of picture books. The stories are written specifically to be embellished by illustrations and are told through the marriage of text and illustrations.

Early Childhood Books

Many children enjoy books from the moment they are able to hold them. Some books are particularly appropriate for young children, because of both their form and their content. The novelty of toy books sustains children's curiosity, and the durable format of board books stands up to rough treatment from little hands (and teeth). The rhythmic rhymes of Mother Goose make it easy for little ones to chant along. Concept books introduce young children to informational books. Alphabet books help them explore the language in its written form, and counting books provide opportunities to practice math concepts.

Toy Books. Preschoolers can become acquainted with books very early—thanks to cloth, vinyl, and board books. What these books usually have in common are a sturdy or washable construction and simple pictures, showing one object per page. They are typically eight to ten pages long. If there are any words, they may simply label objects on the page. For slightly older children, pop-ups, pull-tabs, flaps to lift, half-pages, and other gadgets invite playful manipulation. Classic toy books include Dorothy Kunhardt's *Pat the Bunny* (1940), a tactile and participatory book still in print fifty years after its first edition, and *The Nutshell Library*, (1962) a boxed set of miniature books by Maurice Sendak that children have read for thirty-five years.

Among books for the very youngest are board books by noted author/illustrators such as Nancy Tafuri, Lucy Cousins, and Helen Oxenbury. Board books often come in series of three to four titles centered on topics of immediate interest to very young children, such as animals, things babies do, or family members. Tana Hoban created two books for newborns: *Black on White* (1993) and *White on Black* (1993). Both books show shadows of objects on solid backgrounds, creating high contrast between black and white. John Steptoe's *Baby Says* (1988) features African American babies, as do books by Eloise Greenfield and Angela Shelf Medearis. In another board book series, Rosemary Wells humorously chronicles the antics of Max. Other board books are reproductions of picture books originally published in hardback for older children, such as the board book version of Eric Carle's *The Very Busy Spider* (1985).

Some books, such as those in Cathryn Falwell's series about a toddler named Nicky, are not quite board books but books with pages that are thicker and glossier than usual. *Anno's Faces* (1989) offers pictures of vegetables on each page and two acetate bookmark-shaped pieces with happy and sad faces to be placed over the vegetables.

One particularly popular series is the lift-the-flap series by Eric Hill about a dog named Spot. In *Where's Spot?* (1980), children lift flaps to help mother dog Sally open the door, look inside a wardrobe, and peek under the bed, to search for her pup Spot.

Some pop-up books are fairly straightforward, with single-fold pop-ups; other "paper-engineered" pop-ups are more elaborate, often with moving parts. Children shiver with anticipation and delight as they turn each page of Jan Pienkowski's *Dinner Time* (1981) and a different creature's mouth pops up, declaring, "I'm going to eat you for my dinner."

Some books combine pop-ups with pull-tabs, flaps, and other parts to be manipulated. One example is Paul Zelinsky's *The Wheels on the Bus* (1990). In addition to wheels that turn, the book has a bus door that swings open, passengers that board, wipers that swish, babies who cry open-mouthed, and mothers who shake their fingers. In Mark Inkpen's *Where, Oh Where, Is Kipper's Bear?* (1995), Kipper the dog searches for his bear. Young readers delight in finding the bear under the covers, reading a book by flashlight—which turns on when they lift up the quilt. Cut-out shapes layer and unlayer on sixteen boldly colored pages to create various animal faces in *Color Zoo* (1989), by Lois Ehlert, which was a Caldecott Honor Book. She used the same method to create her *Color Farm* (1990).

Eric Carle's picture books have toy components that are integral to the story line. In *The Very Hungry Caterpillar* (1981), actual holes in a series of illustrations of food indicate where the caterpillar dined. *The Very Quiet Cricket* (1990) searches for a friend until he finally meets another cricket—at that point, readers hear the sound of a cricket (produced by a computer chip embedded in the book). The raised surface of the spider's web in *The Very Busy Spider* (1985) becomes increasingly larger as the spider continues to spin. When the firefly meets friends in *The Very Lonely Firefly* (1995), they light up.

Some books are toys themselves. *Maisy's Pop-Up Playhouse* (1995), by Lucy Cousins, looks like a book but opens up to create a doll house for Maisy the mouse. The house has a bedroom, a kitchen, and a bathroom and includes cutouts of dishes, pots and pans, and toys for the tub. Can *Sam's Sandwich* (Pelham, 1990) be called a book? Sam smirks as he creates an unusual sandwich for his sister—filled with the usual sandwich fillings as well as surprise creatures from the garden. Each page folds out in the shape of the filling and the covers are the bread. These toy books are artistic creations that stimulate children to create their own stories as they play with them.

Mother Goose and Nursery Rhymes. Children today still respond to the rhythmic rhyming verses of Mother Goose. Mother Goose selections are introductions to poetry and language play that invite participation. They encourage children to enjoy language and find pleasure in recognizing familiar rhymes.

The Frenchman Charles Perrault first used the name "Mother Goose" in the title of a collection of eight tales (not rhymes). His *Contes de ma Mere l'Ove (Tales of My Mother Goose),* published around 1697, contained favorite tales such as "Sleeping Beauty in the Woods" and "Little Red Riding Hood." In 1781, John Newbery's firm published the first English edition of *Mother Goose's Melody* as a collection of rhymes and jingles, which began the association of the name "Mother Goose" with highly rhythmic nursery rhymes. Since then, many of the very best illustrators of children's books have published editions of these familiar rhymes. Randolph Caldecott's *Hey Diddle Diddle Picture Book,* was probably published in the 1870s. In 1882, Kate Greenaway produced a beautiful version of *Mother Goose or the Old Nursery Rhymes.* Arthur Rackham's *Mother Goose: The Old Nursery Rhymes* was originally published around the turn of the century and reissued in 1978. Other classic versions were created by Tasha Tudor, Blanche Fisher Wright, and Feodor Rojankovsky. More recent editions include volumes by Jane Dyer, Arnold Lobel, James Marshall, Tomie de Paola, Rosemary Wells, and Brian Wildsmith. They vary from comprehensive, large editions to books focused on single rhymes. Lee Bennett Hopkins's *Animals from Mother Goose* (1989) and *People from Mother Goose* (1989) are interesting presentations of Mother Goose rhymes in guessing-game format, in toy books that fold out to reveal the answer.

Mother Goose equivalents and nursery rhymes are found in cultures around the world. They developed separately from the ones known in the Western world. Among books of Mother Goose and nursery rhymes from other cultures that have been published for English-speaking children are Robert Wyndham's *Chinese Mother Goose Rhymes* (1968), illustrated by Ed Young, and Lulu Delacre's *Arroz con leche: Popular Songs and Rhymes from Latin America* (1989). A bilingual Spanish/English book is *Tortillitas para Mama and Other Spanish Nursery Rhymes* (1981), selected and translated by Margot C. Griego, Betsy L. Bucks, Sharon S. Gilbert, and Laurel H. Kimball and illustrated by Barbara Cooney. Patricia Polacco's *Babushka's Mother Goose* (1995) includes Russian names and alludes to experiences from the Russian heritage.

Concept Books. Concept books convey knowledge, answering the question "What's that?" They cover a wide range of topics—the alphabet, numbers, colors, shapes, and opposites, to name a few. To appreciate the contribution of these picture books, you need only think about how difficult it sometimes is to describe and convey the meaning of concepts in words alone. Because of their significance and abundance, alphabet and counting books are discussed separately in this section.

Tana Hoban is perhaps the most prolific creator of concept books, and hers rely on photographs to relay information. One book, *26 Letters and 99 Cents* (1987), introduces the alphabet when it is read from one end and the concept of money when it is turned over and read from the other end. Bruce McMillan also creates photographic concept and information books. *One, Two, One Pair* (1991), shows objects that come in pairs—hands, feet, socks, mittens, boots, and skates. We see a child prepare to go skating and follow as pairs are introduced—but surprise! The child is also part of a pair, and a twin is introduced at the skating pond.

Two concept books that explore the primary colors and how colors mix are Ann Jonas's *Color Dance* (1989) and Ellen Stoll Walsh's *Mouse Paint* (1989). Both concepts are explored in the context of a story. In *Color Dance*, three girls dance with red, yellow, and blue sheets of sheer fabric. As they dance and their sheets cross, new colors are made. In *Mouse Paint*, three mice splash around in red, yellow, and blue paint. When they dance around in each other's puddles, new colors are made.

Donald Crews creates concept books such as his Caldecott Honor Book, *Freight Train* (1978), in which children are introduced to colors and the names of types of cars in a freight train. The book does much more than merely label objects, however. It shows the movement of the train in darkness and daylight by blurring the colors of the cars and introduces children to words such as "tunnel" and "trestle."

Alphabet Books. Alphabet books are one of the oldest and most popular varieties of concept books. Preschoolers are often first exposed to the alphabet through picture books, and such books are available in large numbers. A traditional alphabet book shows a one-to-one correspondence between a letter and an object whose name begins with that letter. Typically, there is one letter and one object per page. One example is Bert Kitchen's *Animal Alphabet* (1984). Each page of this book has a clearly printed letter and a picture of an animal—familiar or less familiar. More complex alphabet books show more objects per page to illustrate the featured letter, such as birds, bells, and beans for B in *Anno's Alphabet* (1975). Finally, some alphabet books challenge readers to discover as many objects as they can find hidden throughout a very busy illustration that includes numerous objects with names that begin with the featured letter. *Animalia* (1987) by Graeme Base is an example of such a book. The text on one page says, "Beautiful Blue Butterflies Basking by a Babbling Brook," and objects that begin with the letter B—baboon, bassoon, bee, beetle, book, bear, bonnet—are hidden on the page.

Many books play with the sounds of language while introducing the alphabet. A popular one is Bill Martin Jr. and John Archambault's *Chicka Chicka Boom Boom* (1989). Children especially enjoy the rhythmic, rhyming text that tells the story of alphabet letters vying to see which can climb to the top of the coconut tree first. A similar rhyming book featuring the letters of the alphabet is Jane Bayer's

A, My Name Is Alice (1984), whose alphabet rhymes are illustrated by Steven Kellogg. The rhymes are traditional accompaniments to playground games such as jump rope or ball games: "A, my name is Alice and my husband's name is Alex. We come from Alaska and we sell ants. Alice is an Ape. Alex is an Anteater."

A different way of playing with the sounds of language is through alliteration. Maurice Sendak's ***Alligators All Around*** (1962) has "Alligators all around / bursting balloons / catching colds / doing dishes." Crescent Dragonwagon's ***Alligator Arrived with Apples*** (1987), illustrated by José Aruego and Ariane Dewey, has various animals arriving for a Thanksgiving feast, each bringing foods beginning with the same letter as its name: "Bear Brought Banana Bread, Biscuits, and Butter."

A large variety of themed alphabet books are also available. One book with a food theme is ***Eating the Alphabet: Fruit & Vegetables from A to Z*** (1989) by Lois Ehlert, which shows a variety of fruits and vegetables in alphabetical order. Another alphabet book with a food theme is Arnold Lobel's ***On Market Street*** (1981), in which each page depicts a letter composed of fruits, vegetables, and other items found in markets that begin with that letter.

The alphabet is also used to organize all kinds of information at many conceptual levels; there is a rich array of alphabet books for all ages. ***Anno's Alphabet*** is subtitled "An Adventure in Imagination." For each letter, an intricate, unusual object beginning with that letter is pictured. For the beginner, these pictures are too sophisticated for simple letter-sound associations. This kind of book is for children who know the alphabet and are willing to extend their knowledge of its application. ***The Z Was Zapped*** (1987) by Chris Van Allsburg is an alphabet book that is suitable for intermediate-grade students. Each letter establishes a scene in a larger drama extending from A to Z. Leo and Diane Dillon won the Caldecott Medal for their illustrations for Margaret Musgrove's ***Ashanti to Zulu: African Traditions*** (1976), in which each letter introduces a paragraph of text about a tribe on the African continent. ***The Handmade Alphabet*** (1991), by Laura Rankin, introduces the hand and finger positions for the letters of the alphabet used by the American Sign Language Association. Each page also shows an object that begins with the featured letter.

Counting Books. Counting books introduce children to a mathematical concept. The most basic counting books clearly show a number and easily identifiable objects to count, without much background clutter to confuse children. Eric Carle's ***1, 2, 3 to the Zoo*** (1968) is about animals on their way to the zoo aboard a train. Each double-page spread shows a number on the upper left and a boxcar with the correct number of a particular animal on board. The eleventh page is a foldout in which children can see all the animals in their zoo home and the empty train.

Ten Black Dots (1986), by Donald Crews, shows dots placed in a child's world—"2/Two dots can make the eyes of a fox" or "5/Five dots can make buttons on a coat." The solid black dots are easy to find and count on all the backgrounds. Denise Fleming's ***Count!*** (1992) encourages children to count from one to ten vibrantly colored, action-oriented creatures. Then the book shows how to count by tens to fifty. Lois Ehlert's ***Fish Eyes: A Book You Can Count On*** (1990) encourages children to count the fish on a page, then add one more by counting the narrator fish. The illustrations have cut-out eyes for children to count.

Some counting books are more artistic than practical in their rendition of the concept of numbers. ***Numblers*** (1972), by Suse MacDonald and Bill Oakes, uses the shape of a number to create imaginary and real objects. The concepts covered include color, design, shapes, and numbers.

Wordless Books

The pictures tell all in wordless books, and it is an artistic feat to make the stories intriguing, understandable, and satisfying. The text resides in the mind of the reader, who must interpret the pictures to understand the story. Wordless books give children the opportunity to be flexible in their interpretation of a story: They can discuss possibilities for the text, look for clues in the illustrations, and practice storytelling.

Tuesday (1991) by David Wiesner won the Caldecott Medal in 1992. The only text is the notation about time of day on Tuesday. All the shades of green immerse the reader in the frog world. The hilarious exploits of this community of frogs who fly hither and yon on lily pads linger in readers' visual memory.

Pat Hutchins's *Changes, Changes* (1971) remains, after more than twenty-five years, one of the best wordless picture books. The characters and setting are established with images made from wood blocks. The story line is action-packed, and the theme is easily grasped yet thought-provoking. Emily Arnold McCully's *Picnic* (1984) tells the story of a mouse family whose picnic is interrupted when they realize that one child is missing. They drive back along the bumpy road and then continue their picnic once they have been reunited with the mouse who had gotten bumped out of the truck.

Wordless storybooks such as these offer children many opportunities to imagine what the text *could* be. Note, however, that not all wordless books contain stories. Some wordless books are simply a themed set of pictures.

Beginning Readers' Books

Children need books they can read independently as they practice their emerging reading abilities. Some books are more likely to be a success with beginning readers because of their predictable format. Other books are more likely to be accessible to beginning readers because of their controlled vocabulary.

Predictable Books. Predictable books have highly structured or repetitive texts that are easy for fledgling readers to read independently. For children, being able to predict what will happen serves as a motivation to read and provides great satisfaction. Predictable books often use rhythms and rhymes or simple story structures to make it easy for the young reader to perceive the pattern of the text and use it to guess upcoming words. Such factors encourage emerging readers to take risks—the reward is being in on what is happening.

As you recall from Chapter 5 (Traditional Literature), rhythms and rhymes and story structure are what helped people recite songs, poems, and folktales from memory before literacy was widespread. Predictable books use these devices from oral language to support beginning readers.

Predictable books have been available for many years. Some, like *Ask Mr. Bear* (Flack, 1960) and *It Looked Like Spilt Milk* (Shaw, 1947), have become classics. However, since the 1980s, there has been a tremendous increase in the availability of predictable books. This increase can be attributed in large part to the role these books play in beginning reading instruction in schools.

A pioneer writer in this format is children's author and educator Bill Martin, Jr. Three decades ago, Martin set out to write a series of books that would be easy for beginners to read. Of these *Instant Readers*, perhaps the best known is ***Brown Bear, Brown Bear, What Do You See?*** (1967). On one page, the text says, "Brown Bear, Brown Bear, what do you see?" The next page reads, "I see a yellow duck looking at me," and on that page readers find a yellow duck created by illustrator Eric Carle. The language pattern and illustrations work together so nicely that countless beginning readers have been able to recite/read the book after a brief introduction.

Uri Shulevitz's ***One Monday Morning*** (1967) uses a cumulative pattern and supportive illustrations to enumerate the important people who come to visit the young narrator in his urban apartment. ***The Napping House*** (1984), by Audrey and Don Wood, repeats the phrase "In a napping house, where everyone is sleeping" and builds a story by adding a new sleepy character on each page—along with an array of interesting words about sleeping, such as "dozing," "napping," and "snoring."

Though not all books that are enlarged are predictable books, many of the "big books" used for beginning reading instruction are three-foot-high versions of predictable books. Children can watch as the teacher points to the words as they are read. The numerous instructional possibilities that arise from allowing children to see the text make big books especially popular in primary classrooms (Holdaway, 1979). Teachers of young children often use them in front of a class or small group as students read in unison. Big books that are not predictable books are used in library storytimes or classroom read-aloud sessions. The advantage of big books in these situations is that the illustrations are large enough for all the children to see.

Easy Readers. Easy readers are often among the first books that children read independently. They typically have some kind of controlled vocabulary— that is, the number of words, the types of words, and the sentence structure and length are determined by a formula that estimates the relative reading level of a book. The controlled vocabulary can result in poor writing, and some easy reader books are reminiscent of basal readers of the past. However, many easy readers combine literary merit with an opportunity for beginning readers to read on their own successfully.

One of the most innovative and famous writers of easy reader books was Dr. Seuss (a pseudonym for Theodor Seuss Geisel). Dr. Seuss was the author of such children's books as ***The Five Hundred Hats of Bartholomew Cubbins*** (1938) and ***And to Think That I Saw It on Mulberry Street*** (1937). In 1957, convinced that beginning readers were being given uninteresting stories stifled by controlled vocabulary in basal readers of the time, Dr. Seuss changed the outlook on easy reader books when he published ***The Cat in the Hat***. With a limited number of words, he tells the story of a cat whose outlandish behavior stuns two well-behaved children who have been left alone in their house for a short while. Dr. Seuss went on to delight generations of beginning readers with more outrageous characters and out-of-the-ordinary events told in easy-reading verse in ***Hop on Pop*** (1963) and ***Green Eggs and Ham*** (1960), among others.

Henry and Mudge: The First Book of Their Adventures (1987), by Cynthia Rylant, is the first of a series of easy readers by this award-winning author. The text uses limited vocabulary yet has the qualities of poetry, as this excerpt about Mudge the dog shows:

> He couldn't smell Henry.
> He couldn't smell

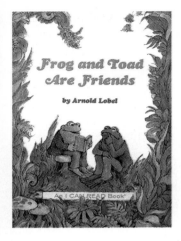

Illustration 6.2
Good stories, simple text, well-matched illustrations, and the effective use of line breaks and white space all combine to give beginning readers successful reading experiences. Arnold Lobel's *Frog and Toad Are Friends* is a good example of an inviting book for beginning readers. (*Frog and Toad Are Friends* by Arnold Lobel. Copyright © 1970 by Arnold Lobel. Used by permission of HarperCollins Publishers.)

his front porch.
He couldn't smell
the street he lived on.
Mudge looked all around
and didn't see anything
or anyone
he knew.

The friendly crayon line drawings by Sucie Stevenson enliven the text and encourage fledgling readers by giving visual clues to what the words must be.

Arnold Lobel is another writer who has written brilliantly within the constraints of limited numbers of words and simple sentence structures. In 1971, his *Frog and Toad Are Friends* (1970) was named a Caldecott Honor Book for its illustrations. And *Frog and Toad Together* (1972) was a 1973 Newbery Honor Book.

James Marshall's wit and creativity are evident in his many humorous easy-reading books. His text and illustrations are seemingly simple, yet the character and plot development are rich and complete. In *Three by the Sea* (1981) (written under the pseudonym Edward Marshall), readers meet Lolly, Spider, and Sam, who are having a picnic at the beach. Children are propelled to continue reading as they anticipate what will happen when a rat buys a cat to be his friend, or when a monster comes out of the sea and finds three children on a beach. Young readers are equally motivated to read about Fox attempting to make money at various jobs so that he can buy a new bike in *Fox on the Job* (1988).

Books like these fill a vital need. Many preschoolers have grown accustomed to having their parents and teachers read fascinating and eloquent books to them—and when children reach school age, although parents and teachers may continue to read to them, it will take much time and hard practice before they will be able to read such books for themselves. Easy readers, though, can be interesting and pithy books in highly readable language. Maintaining quality in a format in which simplicity is paramount can be difficult, but the efforts of young readers are rewarded when they are given interesting content in well-crafted language by authors such as Joanna Cole, Tomie de Paola, Jean Fritz, Arnold Lobel, James Marshall, and Dr. Seuss.

Picture Storybooks

There are more picture storybooks than any other type of picture book. As defined earlier, a picture storybook is one in which the text and the illustrations work together to amplify each other—in other words, part of the story is told through the illustrations and part is told through the text. Text and illustrations do not merely reflect each other—combined, they tell a story that goes beyond what one tells alone.

John Steptoe's *Mufaro's Beautiful Daughters* (1987) offers an example of the way text and illustration can work together in this way. In this African tale, the Great King is searching for a wife, and "The Most Worthy and Beautiful Daughters in the Land are invited to appear before the king." Mufaro sends both of his beautiful daughters: kind Nyasha and bad-tempered Manyara. As readers find out the sisters' true natures, the emotions are amplified through the illustrations. The text ends with the wedding preparations, but the final double-page illustration gives a glimpse ahead.

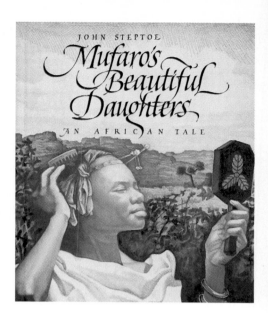

Illustration 6.3
Picture storybooks such as *Mufaro's Beautiful Daughters*, a Caldecott Honor Book, combine text and illustrations to create a story that could not be achieved with text or illustration alone. (*Mufaro's Beautiful Daughters* by John Steptoe. Copyright © 1987 by John Steptoe. Used by permission of Lothrop, Lee & Shepard Books, with the approval of the John Steptoe Literary Trust.)

APPRECIATING THE ARTISTIC CRAFT OF THE PICTURE BOOK

The illustrations in picture books for children have become increasingly sophisticated over the years as the picture book has developed. In addition, changes in printing technology have made it possible to reproduce a much greater range of artwork. This section focuses on two aspects of art in picture books: elements of design and artistic media.

Elements of Design

Artists rely on various elements of design to communicate with their audience. When artwork is done well, the reader can enjoy the aesthetics of the illustrations and appreciate the emotions conveyed through the manipulation of artistic elements. The elements of design are line, color, light, shape, and texture. The combination of line, color, light, shape, and texture is called composition.

Let's examine one book in some depth and look at the use of these elements. In ***The Paperboy*** (1996), Dav Pilkey presents the story of a paperboy's morning: As the story begins, the paperboy is asleep in his bed; readers see him rising, eating breakfast, folding papers, delivering on his route, returning home, and getting back into bed for some "time for dreaming." Throughout all of this, he is accompanied by his dog.

Line. Lines can be thin and light or heavy and bold, straight, jagged, or curved. Line is used effectively in ***The Paperboy*** to create the rolling shapes of the hills in the background, which give a sense of long distances. Line also conveys the sense of fast movement when the paperboy and his dog are returning home—the dog's tail is horizontal and the paperboy's empty bag is flying behind him.

Color. Color can range over the full spectrum, or it can be limited to a defined range—for example, black and white and the various shades of gray in between. One instance of dramatic use of color in ***The Paperboy*** is the single beam of the yellow headlight from the paperboy's bicycle, seen against the dark colors of the neighborhood before dawn.

And when the paperboy has delivered his last newspaper, he and his dog race home.

And his empty red bag flaps behind him in the cold morning air.

Light. Pilkey uses light to show the time of day in **The Paperboy**. When the lamp beside the boy's bed is turned on, his room lights up but it is dark outside. Only a nightlight gives light in the hallway when the paperboy is getting up in the morning. By the time he returns from his route, though, light is peeking from underneath his parents' door and the light in his sister's room can be seen beyond the doorway.

Shape. Shape is created when spaces are contained by a combination of lines. The triangular roof, the side-by-side arrangement of the rectangular doors in the hallway, the two square windows in the kitchen, and the big rectangular work table in the garage all combine with the center gutter of the book to give the house in **The Paperboy** a symmetrical feel—one that creates a sense of solid security in the paperboy's home. In the opening double-page spread, the predictable shapes of the houses give a sense of a solid community life. The rolling shapes of the land separate the houses and give a sense of distance between them, even though

And softly they step down the quiet hall past the door where the paperboy's father and mother are sleeping.

Past the door where his sister is asleep.

they are painted close together on the page. The sense of distance and spaciousness leads the reader to think that this is more a rural area than an urban one.

Texture. Texture is the illusion of a tactile surface created in an illustration. In *The Paperboy*, texture in the wood boards of the ceiling and floor is created through the use of lines and shading. The shading of the trees also contributes texture.

Artistic Media

The artists who create picture books rely on a number of media to express their visions of the stories. Some illustrators use a "signature" medium almost exclusively; others select different media depending on how they want to express their view of the particular story.

Painting: Watercolor, Gouache, Oil, and Other Paints. More children's books are illustrated with watercolor than with any other medium. Watercolors allow illustrators to convey many emotions. Watercolor paintings can be solidly intense or watery and fluid-looking, depending on the amount of water used.

Gouache is a type of watercolor paint that contains an added white powder to create a more opaque finished product. Artists who desire an opaque look may also use acrylic paints or oil paints.

Tomie de Paola has illustrated over a hundred books for children. His work is characteristically done in watercolor in a folk-art style. His book *Strega Nona* (1979) was named a Caldecott Honor Book. In it, an Italian "Grandma Witch" with a magical touch leaves her helper, Big Anthony, home alone. Big Anthony seizes this opportunity to prove to the townspeople that Strega Nona's magic pot can cook pasta by itself. He doesn't remember, however, how to get it to stop cooking. The punishment fits the crime—Big Anthony must eat all the pasta!

Allen Say is another noted illustrator who works in watercolor. In his Caldecott-winning book *Grandfather's Journey* (1993), Say tells the story of how his grandfather left Japan and made the United States his home. When the grandfather visited Japan years later, World War II prohibited him from returning to the United States. Now, his grandson has followed in his path and says, "The funny thing is, the moment I am in one country, I am homesick for the other." The natural beauty of each country is depicted in watercolor views of ocean, mountains, and greenery. The prequel to this story is Say's *Tree of Cranes* (1991).

Thomas Locker characteristically uses oil paintings that give viewers a sense of wide landscapes, such as in *The Boy Who Held Back the Sea* (1987). Paul Zelinsky's *Rumpelstiltskin* (1986) is also rendered in oil paint, an appropriate medium to complement the medieval setting. Floyd Cooper employs a variation on oil painting in which he applies a very thin layer of paint to a surface and, when it dries, creates areas of light by using an eraser; he then adds color at the end. He used this technique to create the illustrations in Jean Merrill's *The Girl Who Loved Caterpillars: A Twelfth-Century Tale from Japan* (1992), as well as those in all of his other works.

Pencil Drawing. Stephen Gammell uses pencils to convey a range of emotions, from the happy, nostalgic feel of *Song and Dance Man* (Ackerman, 1988) to the sinister, gory tone of Alvin Schwartz's *Scary Stories* series. Pencils can be used to create strong lines, shaded areas, smudged shadows, and fine details.

Illustration 6.6
The illustrations in *Strega Nona*, a Caldecott Honor Book, are excellent examples of Tomie de Paola's signature watercolor paintings. (*Strega Nona*, an old tale retold and illustrated by Tomie de Paola. Copyright © 1975 by Tomie de Paola. Used by permission of Simon & Schuster Books for Young Readers, an imprint of Simon & Schuster Children's Publishing Division.)

Readers sense the warmth of relationships in various books depicting family events that Gammell illustrated with colored pencils. For instance, in **Song and Dance Man,** pastel hues against the white background give a soft glow to the attic in which the grandfather and his grandchildren share a moment from the past, as the grandfather dances and reminisces about the times when he was a "song and dance man." Few areas are solidly shaded; rather, visible lines help guide the reader's eyes to areas of focus and give dimension to objects. Gammell's work in **Scary Stories to Tell in the Dark** (Schwartz, 1981) seems a far cry from that in **Song and Dance Man,** even though both are pencil illustrations. In the **Scary Stories** book, the black-and-white images have unfinished lines, supporting the sense of the haunted as being unpredictably present and only partially visible. Even without color, we can clearly visualize the blood dripping. The jagged lines create feelings of horror. Gammell shows the range of artistic expression possible with one medium.

Paper Crafts: Collage, Papermaking, Cut Paper. Various forms of paper crafts are used by illustrators of children's books. The most commonly used form is collage, in which, traditionally, various types of paper are cut or torn and pieced together onto a background to create a picture, as in the art of Ezra Jack Keats, Eric Carle, and Leo Lionni. The papers may be of varying weights and colors—anything from gift wrap to wallpaper to handmade paper.

Many illustrators do not limit themselves to paper when creating collages but employ a wide range of materials, including three-dimensional objects. For his Caldecott-winning book **Smoky Night** (1994), written by Eve Bunting, David Diaz used matches, plastic bags, hangers, cereal, bubble wrap, and shoe soles, in addition to a variety of papers, to create collage backgrounds to "frame" his acrylic paintings and the text on each page in this book depicting the 1992 Los Angeles riots. Lois Ehlert's **Snowballs** (1995) shows a family of snowpeople—complete with dog and cat—created with birdseed, a knit hat, seashells, a compass, a cinnamon stick, a pinecone, luggage claim checks, plastic forks, and toy fish, among other things. In another collage book about a sugar maple tree, **Red Leaf, Yellow Leaf** (1991), Ehlert used a kite, twine, ribbon, birdseed, burlap, twigs, and roots to create the illustrations.

Illustrator Denise Fleming creates vibrant illustrations by making a sheet of handmade paper for each illustration. She makes a pulp out of cotton rag fiber and water, adds color, and spreads the pulp out on a framed wire screen to create a background. The framed screen allows the excess water to drip out. Using plastic squeeze bottles filled with colored pulp, she pours shapes on the background or fills in stencils she has cut out. She adds various items such as hair from her horse's mane, pieces of plastic net bags, and coffee grounds to create interesting dimensions and textures. The completed piece is dried through a special process. Fleming's book **In the Small, Small Pond** (1993) was named a Caldecott Honor Book. The illustrations show the creatures of a small pond in their daily environment. Fleming captures their movements and activities with alliterative and rhyming phrases—for example, "lash, lunge, herons plunge" and "sweep, swoop, swallows scoop." She also created the book **Lunch** (1992), in which a mouse encounters foods of various colors—"crisp white turnip, crisp yellow corn." Meanwhile, readers are introduced to the foods by color names and adjectives that describe them.

Illustration 6.7
Denise Fleming uses vividly colored cotton pulp to create each picture in her books. (*In the Small, Small Pond* by Denise Fleming. Copyright © 1997 by Denise Fleming. Used by permission of Henry Holt & Co., Inc.)

David Wisniewski used cut paper to create the illustrations for his Caldecott Medal winner, *The Golem* (1996), as well as for his other books. He uses an X-Acto knife to cut intricate designs and layers pieces to achieve a three-dimensional effect.

Scratchboard. Brian Pinkney is known for using scratchboard as his signature medium. Scratchboard pictures are created by using sharp instruments to scratch away the top surface of a board, leaving precise lines on the surface. Pinkney believes that his passion for carving and painting come together in scratchboard—he both carves the pictures and paints them when creating his book illustrations. For Robert D. San Souci's *Sukey and the Mermaid* (1992), the story of how Sukey's luck changes when she meets a black mermaid, Pinkney created a black-and-white scratchboard. A photographic technique made it possible for him to add color to a print of the original scratchboard piece to attain the finished product. Pinkney used a similar technique to illustrate San Souci's *The Faithful Friend* (1995).

Woodcut. Woodcut illustrations were particularly common in books of the past but are still used today. Marcia Brown's *Once a Mouse* (1961), rendered in woodcut, was awarded a Caldecott Medal. Ed Emberley used woodcuts to illustrate Barbara Emberley's *Drummer Hoff* (1967), which also won a Caldecott Medal. Gail E. Haley's *A Story, a Story* (1970), another Caldecott winner, has illustrations carved on wood blocks. More recently, Barry Moser used a synthetic wood engraving medium to creating the illustrations for *Ever Heard of an Aardwolf?* (1996). The images were printed in black and white, laser-scanned and enlarged, then hand-colored with watercolors.

Keizaburo Tejima gives readers a sense of connection to the natural world through his use of woodcuts. *Swan Sky* (1988) tells the story of the migration of swans. One year, a swan, ill and unable to go to the summer home, is left behind by her family. The woodcut illustrations fully use the natural effect of the wood grain to illustrate the ripples in the lake, the reflections of the mountains, and the feathers of the swans.

Photography. Several children's book illustrators use photography to create visual images. Tana Hoban and Bruce McMillan create books with photographs that communicate a concept to young children. Hoban's *I Read Signs* (1983) includes photographs of signs that children see in their environment. In McMillan's *Counting Wildflowers* (1986), readers are presented with a numeral, the number word, and a photograph of the corresponding number of wildflowers. George Ancona relies on photographs to lend an air of immediacy to books focused on particular groups of people. For Maxine Rosenberg's *Being a Twin, Having a Twin* (1985), Ancona used photographs to capture an anecdotal sense of the special sibling relationship. Walter Dean Myers collected old photographs for *Brown Angels: An Album of Pictures and Verse* (1993) and for *Glorious Angels: A Celebration of Children* (1995). The photographs provided the impetus for poetry he created while imagining the lives of the people they portrayed.

Computer-Generated Art. A relative newcomer to the children's book field, J. Otto Siebold illustrated the *Mr. Lunch* books entirely with computer-generated art. Veteran illustrators Don Wood and Audrey Wood have given up their paintbrushes and turned completely to their computers to create drawings for their latest books. For his first work as a digital artist, Don Wood created the illustrations for *Bright and Early Thursday Evening: A Tangled Tale* (1996). Audrey Wood's first creation as a digital artist is *The Red Racer* (1996).

Mixed Media. Illustrators often combine different media in creating their work. Many illustrators combine pen and ink with watercolor washes. Patricia Polacco uses pencil to create initial sketches, then finishes them with watercolors, but the original pencil markings are often visible as part of the final product. Eric Carle paints on his tissue papers and pencils in details on his collages. Ruth Heller combines a large number of media—magic markers, paints, colored pencils, and others.

Illustration 6.10
Computers, scanners, and a stylus on a pad were used to create the images in *Bright and Early Thursday Evening*. (*Bright and Early Thursday Evening* by Audrey Wood. Illustration copyright © 1996 by Don Wood. Used by permission of Harcourt Brace & Company.)

HOW PICTURE BOOKS WORK

When we read a story that moves us deeply, we often speak of the setting, characters, plot, and other elements of the book that contributed to its effect. But if a picture moves us, most of us do not have a set of terms readily available for describing what caused the picture's effect. Picture books afford readers the opportunity to deepen their understanding of visual communication—their "visual literacy." Knowing some terms can help teachers and parents talk as knowledgeably about pictures as about texts and better appreciate the principles that govern how picture book illustrations communicate meaning. The following elements of visual communication will concern us here:

- Layout, including page turns, borders, and the number and placement of frames on a page
- Characterization, which refers to the consistent visual identity of the characters
- Perspective, settings, and other repeated phenomena
- Backgrounds
- Color, especially as it relates to mood

- Picture/text relationships, that is, which aspects of the communication are carried by the text and which are conveyed by the pictures and how the pictures and text interact

Clearly, much goes into the creating of picture books. Many people besides the author and illustrator are involved in creating the final product. Editors, art directors, and printers all have professional roles. Decisions about the book size, paper type, endpapers, and book jacket all contribute to the finished book.

The Layout of Picture Books

Children's books are printed in multiples of eight pages, and picture books are typically thirty-two pages long. One page is taken up by the title page, a second by the copyright information, and often another by the dedication—leaving the illustrator of most picture books a little less than thirty pages to work with. Within these few pages, the illustrator creates a visual world. By laying out the illustrations in a particular way, the illustrator controls the readers' journey through that world, much as a tour guide leads a group through a city or a landscape. Like a tour guide, the illustrator can move readers quickly from place to place and happening to happening or cause readers to pause in one spot and let impressions settle in.

Single Pages and Double-Page Spreads. As a rule, putting a picture on each page propels readers through the story at an even pace, whereas putting more than one picture on a page depicts a series of actions or the rapid occurance of actions. Spreading a single picture across two facing pages (a double-page spread) can signal a pause, a moment to ponder the events.

In *The Amazing Bone* (1983), written and illustrated by William Steig, a succession of one-page illustrations shows Pearl's quick progress through the bustle of town life. A double-page spread showing Pearl sitting on the ground in the woods under trees raining wild cherry blossoms conveys a sense of her being overwhelmed by the beauty (and the seeming innocence) of nature.

In *Working Cotton* (Williams, 1992), illustrator Carole Byard created a series of double-page spreads. These spreads communicate the boundless flatness of the migrant workers' world, where the child works from dark to dark in a field that appears to go on forever.

Philipe Dupasquier's book *Dear Daddy* (1988) has an unusual layout: pictures covering the lower half of the pages show the events in the girl's life, while the pictures across the top halves show her father's activities as a merchant seaman aboard a ship steaming around the world. Toward the end of the story, the pictures converge; finally, with Daddy's return, father and daughter occupy the visual space together.

Borders. Borders around pictures offer a means for the illustrator to control how intimately readers feel involved with the pictures. Some illustrators put decorative borders around four sides. These may put the action at some distance, sentimentalize it, or make it clear that the time period or place depicted is remote.

Trina Schart Hyman uses borders in an interesting way in *St. George and the Dragon* (1984). Each border

Illustration 6.11
Trina Schart Hyman's borders in *St. George and the Dragon* remind viewers of stained glass images on church windows. (*Saint George and the Dragon* by Margaret Hodges. Text Copyright © 1984 by Margaret Hodges. Illustrations Copyright © 1984 Trina Schart Hyman. Used by permission of Little, Brown and Company.)

suggests a stained glass window, and she reinforces this impression by sometimes drawing smaller images in the border panels in a way that embellishes the images in the center panel but that also makes it seem as if all of the images were painted on the glass, rather than seen through a window. On other pages, though, the images in the center intrude into the borders, and then we get the impression that we are looking not at static images in a stained glass window but through clear leaded glass at real figures just on the other side.

In *Where the Wild Things Are* (1963), author and illustrator Maurice Sendak uses borders in a striking way. The sizes of the borders wax and wane with the crescendo and decrescendo of Max's wild adventures. In the opening pages, plain white borders contain the relatively small pictures of Max. As his fantasy grows, though, so do the pictures—first filling a page, then spilling onto the opposite page, until the "wild rumpus" in the middle of the book pushes margins and words off the double-page spreads. As order returns, so do the borders—until on the last page, the pictures are gone, leaving nothing but text.

Page Turns. Page turns allow an illustrator to create and relieve suspense. William Moebius (1986) called this phenomenon "the drama of the turning page." Many illustrators make use of this technique to add dramatic interest. When Nancy Winslow Parker illustrated John Langstaff's text, *Oh, A-Hunting We Will Go* (1974), she broke up the verse of the folksong as follows:

> Oh, a-hunting we will go.
> A-hunting we will go.
> We'll catch a fox
> [page turn]
> And put him in a box,
> And then we'll let him go.

With each successive verse, children are implicitly challenged to guess where each animal will be "put" before they turn the page and read the completed rhyme.

The Last Page. The last page of a picture book is often used for something of an afterword. Many illustrators reserve this last page for an epilogue, a comment on what has gone before. Maurice Sendak used the last page of *Where the Wild Things Are* (1963) to tell the reader that Max's supper was still hot after he returned from his antics with the Wild Things. Dav Pilkey used the last page of *The Paperboy* (1996) to show readers that after finishing his route, the paperboy went back to bed and entered a dream world.

Characterization

Characterization refers to the way an illustrator makes readers identify a particular character and continue to recognize that character throughout the changes of scene or status in the whole book. This is not easy. Leonardo da Vinci painted only one Mona Lisa; but would we always recognize the Mona Lisa if da Vinci had had to depict her fifteen or twenty times, in different perspectives and in different circumstances? That is the challenge faced by the illustrator of virtually every picture book. To meet that challenge, some artists, like Ted Lewin, hire models to pose for their drawings in different settings. Others, like Jerry Pinkney, rely on family members to serve as models. When artists work purely from the imagination, though, they must decide on identifying features by which readers will immediately know their characters. When reading Arnold Lobel's books, for instance, we can keep Frog and Toad straight in our minds because Frog is always green and Toad is always brown.

Features of a character may become so recognizable that even a part of a character may serve to identify the whole. In James Marshall's **Fox and His Friends** (1982), for example, readers can recognize little sister Louise just from the tip of her tail hanging down into the frame from her perch atop a telephone pole. Similarly, in Mem Fox's **Hattie and the Fox** (1987), just the presence of a nose in the bushes signals that a fox is stalking the barnyard animals.

Rosemary Wells's rabbits are wonderfully endearing. She draws them with large faces, big eyes, and small mouths. Max seems to be passively suffering his plight; Ruby is manipulating things to her liking—either way, they evoke sympathy. A researcher of animal behavior, Iraneus Eibl-Eibesfeldt (1975), observed that among the higher animal species (including humans), adults are hereditarily conditioned to accept certain arrays of features as "cute"—and when they see this array, their nurturant behavior is triggered. The array includes a large head in proportion to the body, a large forehead, big eyes, and a small mouth. The pictures in **Max and Ruby's Midas: Another Greek Myth** (1995) by Rosemary Wells show many of these features.

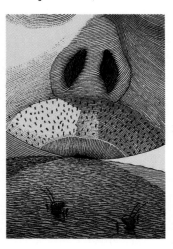

Illustration 6.12
Illustrations in Chris Van Allsburg's *Two Bad Ants* show the world as seen from an ant's-eye view. (*Two Bad Ants* by Chris Van Allsburg. Copyright © 1988 by Chris Van Allsburg. Used by permission of Houghton Mifflin Co. All rights reserved.)

Perspective

Illustrators use a variety of perspectives to give readers different vantage points from which to view the situation. In Chris Van Allsburg's **Two Bad Ants** (1988), two ants decide to stay behind in a kitchen when their fellow ants return to the colony with crystals requested by the queen. The two ants find themselves being scooped out of the bed of crystals, into a boiling lake of brown bitter water. Thus begins their dangerous adventure, which moves from coffee cup to toaster to garbage disposal to electrical outlet. Readers watch the ants' adventure from various perspectives—looking down to see the ants on the ground and up to see them on the kitchen counter. When the ants are in the coffee cup being rushed toward the mouth of the coffee drinker, the perspective is from directly behind the ants, and readers see the mouth just as they see it. Then the view is from inside the toaster, and the ants are seen sitting on top of the bread crust. The close-up view of the water faucet makes it is easy to see why the ants might mistake it for a waterfall.

Backgrounds

Characters are often identified by the objects that surround them. In **The Amazing Bone** (1976), Pearl seems most at home in the spring forest, gently

Illustration 6.13
The background of each illustration in *Where the Wild Things Are* sets the stage for the location of Max's story—his house, his room, the forest, the boat, and the land of the Wild Things. (*Where the Wild Things Are* by Maurice Sendak. Copyright © 1963 by Maurice Sendak. Used by permission of HarperCollins Publishers.)

showered by cherry blossoms. The loathsome wolf that accosts her, in spite of his dapper appearance, lives in a ramshackle cottage with the screen door hanging from one hinge and trash scattered about the overgrown front yard. His slovenly surroundings indicate an uncaring heart. In **Where the Wild Things Are** (1963), Max's room becomes overgrown with trees and bushes, as a signal that wildness is taking hold of him.

In *A New Coat for Anna* (1986), written by Harriet Ziefert and illustrated by Anita Lobel, piles of urban wreckage, peopled by maimed veterans with palms outstretched, dramatize the state of want, sadness, and shock in which Anna and her mother are living. The wilderness that surrounds Sylvester-turned-rock, in William Steig's *Sylvester and the Magic Pebble* (1969), conveys his terrible state of loneliness and isolation—a state that will surely last forever unless he finds some spectacular solution to his problem.

Color

Color is often used to reflect emotions and communicate moods. Both particular colors and their intensity are used to convey a mood to readers.

Arnold Lobel portrays Frog and Toad in greens and browns and uses the same colors for his backgrounds. This reminds readers of the natural camouflage of frogs and toads, whose skins blend into the landscape. The muted colors also prepare readers for plots that are more inwardly directed and thoughtful than overt and active.

James Marshall uses color symbolically even in the seemingly light cartoon-style illustrations of his *Hansel and Gretel* (1990). The sky looming beyond the trees that are disorienting the lost children and behind the witch's gingerbread house is pure black. The illustrations are completely free of this ominous color only when Hansel and Gretel cross the lake on a duck's back and arrive at home, where their father waits.

An especially skillful use of color is found in Anita Lobel's illustrations for *A New Coat for Anna* (1986). Set in a European city after World War II, the book tells of Anna's mother, apparently widowed, who barters family heirlooms to a shepherd, a weaver, a dye-maker, and a tailor—each of whom contributes something to making Anna a new coat. The story opens with the drab colors of a city in ruins, and the drabness is echoed by the bleak expression on the face of Anna's sad, exhausted mother. As each new character enters the story, a bit more color enters, too—until the story culminates in a festive Christmas celebration

Illustration 6.14
Color reflects the changing mood of the story in *A New Coat for Anna*. (*A New Coat for Anna* by Harriet Ziefert. Illustration copyright © 1986 by Anita Lobel. Used by permission of Alfred A. Knopf, Inc.)

with greenery and yellow candles and Anna at the center of things in her brand-new, bright-red coat. By giving up bits of her past and reaching out to others, Anna's mother has created a community, and she and her new friends have brought color and joy back into each other's lives.

Even though the most obvious difference between children's books of the early twentieth century and those of the present is the quality and quantity of color used, black and white still remains a viable alternative for book illustrations. Black-and-white illustrations communicate mood primarily through the intensity of black tones used in shading, the boldness of lines, and the placement of the illustration against the amount of white space. Cross-hatching, or criss-crossing of lines, can add texture and depth. Wanda Gág used black-and-white pen-and-ink drawings in her first book, *Millions of Cats* (1929). Chris Van Allsburg used a soft Conté pencil and Conté dust to create books that are entirely black and white: *The Garden of Abdul Gasazi* (1979), *The Mysteries of Harris Burdick* (1984), and *Jumanji* (1981) have all won awards. John Steptoe's black-and-white pencil drawings caused *The Story of Jumping Mouse: A Native American Legend* (1984) to be named a 1985 Caldecott Honor Book.

Picture/Text Relationships

If the relationship between the illustrations and the text is handled skillfully, the illustrations support the text, but not in a completely predictable way. Children will be more actively engaged if part of the meaning of the story is left for them to infer from the illustrations.

In *Where the Wild Things Are* (1963), the hand drawing of a Wild Thing "by Max" on the wall is a clue to the observant reader that the wild things Max encounters have been created out of his imagination. In the same vein, in Harry Allard's *Miss Nelson Is Missing!* (1977), artist James Marshall drew a box marked "wig" in upside-down letters next to an ugly black dress in the open closet next to Miss Nelson's bed. Observant readers will pick up this clue to the mystery of the disappearance of Miss Viola Swamp, Miss Nelson's harsh alter ego.

Author and illustrator Susan Meddaugh blurs the line between her two roles to produce interesting picture/text relationships in her recent works. In *Martha Speaks* (1992), Meddaugh tells the story of a family dog who gains the gift of speech after eating alphabet soup. Martha, the suddenly loquacious dog, spews language all over the page. The reader soon tires of reading it all, just as the family tires of hearing it. Meanwhile, the text of the story proceeds in the print on the bottom of the page. In *Hog-Eye* (1995), a story about a little piggie that outwits a mean but illiterate wolf, the piggie pretends to read from a book of magic spells. Those who can read can see what the hapless wolf cannot: The pig is reading from a tome entitled "Getting to Know Your Carburetor."

The 1996 Caldecott Medal winner, *Officer Buckle and Gloria* (1995) by Peggy Rathmann, tells of a police officer who makes tiresome speeches about home and school safety. Interest in his presentations

Illustration 6.15
Readers of *Officer Buckle and Gloria* must observe the illustrations to catch the humor of the story that is not told through text alone. (*Officer Buckle and Gloria* by Peggy Rathmann. Text and illustration copyright © 1995 by Peggy Rathmann. Used by permission of G. P. Putnam's Sons.)

suddenly increases a hundredfold, however, when he begins to take a police dog, Gloria, with him. Since Gloria stands just behind him, Officer Buckle doesn't see that the dog is pantomiming and generally cutting up while he gives his otherwise boring speech. The text doesn't mention Gloria's antics, either. We readers are in on a secret that Officer Buckle doesn't know, because we are informed by the pictures as well as the text.

CREATORS OF PICTURE BOOKS

Space limitations make it impossible to give a biographical sketch of every important picture book author or illustrator. We have chosen to highlight only a few; many others are mentioned in the discussions in this chapter, and still others are included as featured authors and illustrators in other chapters.

Mitsumasa Anno

Mitsumasa Anno, a Japanese author and illustrator, is a world-renowned contributor to the picture book field. He is best known for his wordless "journey" books, mathematical game books, and books with playful twists of visual perceptions. Anno's highly detailed and imaginative work appeals to all ages because his books offer multiple levels of humor and intrigue. His books combine technical sophistication with creative text, illustrations, and design. Many of his books also include detailed historic, scientific, or mathematical information for adult readers who share these books with children.

Anno delights in including mathematical and scientific details to make learning these ways of thinking enjoyable and interesting. *Anno's Counting House* (1982) shows ten children living in the house on the left side of the double-page spread and moving into the house on the right one by one. Children can see who has moved and what belongings the child has taken—but they can also note that the total number of children shown in both houses is always ten.

Anno also manipulates visual perception in a way that makes the physically impossible seem probable. For example, *Upside-Downers: More Pictures to Stretch the Imagination* (1971) is a book that bends the "rules" for enjoying books. A pair of jokers and the four kings leave a deck of cards, but nobody can tell what's up and what's down. In the author's postscript, Anno suggests that a child can sit opposite a parent and they can read the book to each other at the same time—or a child can read alone, turn the book around, and then read it from the other direction, upside down.

Anno's Journey (1978) begins a series of books that are filled with images of the countries he visits. Historical events, literary figures, and cultural markers fill the pages of the wordless books simply titled *Anno's U.S.A.* (1983), *Anno's Italy* (1980), and *Anno's Britain* (1982). On the double-page spread depicting New York City in *Anno's U.S.A.*, readers will delight in discovering the surprises embedded in the art: the Macy's Thanksgiving Day Parade with floats representing characters from *Where the Wild Things Are*, Tarzan, and the New York Public Library lions; Marilyn Monroe standing on a street corner with the wind sweeping her skirt up; and Native Americans selling Manhattan island.

Anno was born and raised in a small town in western Japan. He taught art at an elementary school in Tokyo for ten years before becoming a full-time artist. In addition to his numerous picture books, Anno creates many other works of art such as paintings, calendars, and stationery. In 1985, he was awarded the Hans Christian Andersen Award for Illustration, given by the International

Illustration 6.16
Knowledge of history and popular culture will enable readers to find many interesting details in this double-page picture of New York City by Anno. (*Anno's U.S.A.* by Mitsumasa Anno. Illustration by Mitsumasa Anno. Copyright © 1983 by Kuso-Kobo. Used by permission of Philomel Books.)

Board on Books for Young People to honor an illustrator who has made a significant contribution to children's literature worldwide.

Marcia Brown

Marcia Brown always knew that she wanted to create children's books. She worked as an English and drama teacher for three years, then became a librarian in the New York Public Library system for five years. All the while, she read and studied children's literature and took art classes. Brown's first book was published in 1946, and only one year later, she produced her first Caldecott Honor Book, *Stone Soup: An Old Tale* (1947). Her interest in folktales and fairytales continued in the many books that followed. She values the passing of stories down through generations and enjoys helping preserve traditional tales. In fact, all three of Brown's Caldecott Medal books are folktales or fairytales: *Cinderella* (1954), *Once a Mouse* (1961), and *Shadow* (1982). Each is illustrated with a different medium: *Cinderella* was created with watercolors; *Once a Mouse* has woodcut-style illustrations; *Shadow* mixes collage, paint, and print.

Eric Carle

Eric Carle spent his first six years in the United States and has happy memories of kindergarten, freely creating art on large sheets of paper with big brushes and bright colors. However, most of his childhood was spent in his parents' homeland, Germany, during World War II. Carle's introduction to the world of children's book illustration came when a pink lobster he had created for an advertising job caught the eye of author Bill Martin, Jr., who solicited Carle's work for a series of books he had written.

Eric Carle's many picture books are immediately recognizable because of his unique painted tissue-paper collages. Perhaps his best-known book is *The Very Hungry Caterpillar* (1981), in which a little egg hatches and the hungry caterpillar eats its way through various foods, spins a cocoon, and becomes a butterfly. This lesson on metamorphosis is accompanied by an introduction to numbers and the days of the week. Carle's many toy books, described earlier in this chapter, employ partial pages, holes, cutouts, pop-ups, sound chips, lights, and more. Carle tries to create books that combine heartfelt stories with opportunities for learning and play, and without a doubt, he has succeeded frequently. Among his well-known titles are *The Grouchy Ladybug* (1977), *The Very Busy Spider* (1985), and *The Very Quiet Cricket* (1990).

Leo and Diane Dillon

The artwork created by Leo and Diane Dillon is unique in that each piece is truly a work of collaboration, so much so that neither artist can identify who contributed which part to a finished product. They speak of a "third artist" who is a combination of both of them, yet different from each as individuals. The Dillons attribute their collaborative ability to their control of artistic techniques: They maintain that one of them could begin a line and the other could continue it without detectable interruption.

The first and second children's books the Dillons illustrated earned them the distinction of being the first (and only, so far) to receive the Caldecott Medal in two consecutive years. Verna Aardema's *Why Mosquitoes Buzz in People's Ears: A West African Tale* (1975) is told in cumulative verse format and has various animals passing along different versions of a rumor. For this book, the Dillons interpreted the text with stylized watercolor paintings that were influenced by batik art. Margaret Musgrove's *Ashanti to Zulu: African Traditions* (1976) uses an alphabet book format to describe aspects of daily life among the diverse cultures of Africa. For this book, the Dillons created art that was factually accurate as well as elegant and that captured both the commonality and diversity of human experiences. In Nancy White Carlstrom's *Northern Lullaby* (1992), they wove together the various native cultures of Alaska to present a unified image. This blending is seen by some critics as a worthy effort to make connections between different peoples but by others as a blurring together of cultural distinctions.

The Dillons have collaborated on some books with their son, Lee Dillon, a painter and sculptor. Lee and his parents created the artwork for *Pish, Posh, Said Hieronymus Bosch* (1991), a poem by Nancy Willard that describes the influence of the famous painter's imaginative creatures on his housekeeper. Lee carved a frame, incorporating some of these unusual creatures. Leo and Diane's paintings are centered in this frame, giving it the effect of being a "window" through which readers view the story. *Aida* (1990), by Leontyne Price, is another book on which the three Dillons have collaborated. Lee created a metal frame that was used as the border of each page. Leo and Diane's attention to detail is reflected in the design of this book. Of particular interest is their incorporation of marbelized paper and their creation of highly decorative endpapers.

In addition to illustrating picture books, the Dillons have created the art for many book jackets and for longer works of fiction. For the body of their work and the lasting contribution they have made to children's books, the United States Board of Books for Young People (USBBY) selected Leo and Diane Dillon as the 1996 U.S. nominees for the Hans Christian Andersen Award.

Kevin Henkes

Best known for his books portraying mice in real-life, childlike situations, Kevin Henkes enjoys wide popularity as a picture book author and illustrator. His cartoon-style drawings of mice done in pen and ink with watercolors, take

Illustration 6.17
Leo and Diane Dillon work so closely together that they attribute their finished products to the work of a "third artist" who is the combination of their individual talents. Their illustrations for *Why Mosquitoes Buzz in People's Ears* won the Caldecott Medal in 1976. (*Why Mosquitoes Buzz in People's Ears* by Verna Aardema. Pictures copyright © 1975 by Leo and Diane Dillon. Used by permission of Dial Books for Young Readers, a division of Penguin Books USA Inc.)

ASK THE ILLUSTRATOR . . .

Jerry Pinkney

Jerry Pinkney

> When any of the five members of your family collaborate in creating books for children, what effect do they have on each other's work?

I have always been interested in visual images and drew throughout my growing-up years. There were no artists in the family, nor visual artists in my neighborhood. I was fortunate to have had parents and teachers who recognized my talent and encouraged it.

In 1960, I began working as an illustrator for Rust Craft Greeting Card Company. Two years later, I began working for a small illustration studio; it was there that I illustrated my first book, which was a fully illustrated textbook. In 1963, I illustrated my first trade book, *The Adventures of Spider*. My career as a children's book artist had begun. I started freelancing and moved my studio into our home, where Gloria and I were raising a family of four.

Gloria talks about the effect of my working at home and how her innate talents had an effect on our children: "Jerry has been working at home for a very long time so the children have always been surrounded by art and bookmaking. I was a milliner and a silversmith before becoming an author. I also worked at home, so there has always been creative activity in the

household. And we always supplied the children with materials. They all had their own space, so they started creating at an early age."

Brian adds, "When we were growing up and went to museums or dance concerts, we always came home and made pictures. It was a family activity. We'd pull out the paper, and we'd all start drawing. It got to the point that it was just natural for me to draw."

Myles recalls, "We all attended the Elma Lewis Museum of the National Center of Afro-American Artists in Boston, Massachusetts, studying music, dance and drama." He says about his growing-up years and his interest in art, "A good part of it was growing up around art and going to different programs and presentations, all of the arts. Art is something that works on your senses, and I was always building my senses, by listening to music or observing through my eyes."

Gloria and I, from the beginning, wanted art to be part of their upbringing. When the children were growing up, what we wanted was for them to be able to make decisions about what

on personalities of typical children (and adults). Henkes depicts the personalities through facial expressions, the movements of the mice, and the poses they take. The predicaments the mice face—arrival of a new sibling, being teased by classmates, having an imaginary friend—are situations familiar to almost everyone.

Henkes's mice characters are memorable: Chrysanthemum, with whom we empathize over her agonies of being teased for her name; Sheila Rae, the bravest

would make them happy in terms of career choices. We recognized very early that they were all very talented. But we never put any form of pressure on them toward going into the arts. The first reason was that we wanted them to choose what they wanted to do. Secondly, Gloria and I have a love for art, music, and literature. We wanted them to have this, even if they didn't pursue it as a career—something else in their life that would give them that kind of joy.

It is quite amazing that all of us are involved in creative enterprises. Troy uses art therapy as a director of Child Life. Scott is a partner and designer in a direct advertising agency. Myles became interested in photography at an early age and joined a photo club in middle school. He remembers, "Dad got me a camera and I started taking pictures of different things. People told me that I had an eye for composition (which I suppose I developed through my early involvement in drawing). I continued taking pictures, and in high school my photos were used in the school yearbook." He has recently photographed Patricia McKissack for her autobiography, and he and poet Nikki Grimes are collaborating on a book, with Nikki creating poems inspired by his photos.

Brian illustrated over twenty books for children and wrote three himself. He married Andrea Davis in 1991. They have collaborated on five books, with more to come. Andrea Davis Pinkney is a children's book editor for Simon and Schuster, as well as an author who has written a novel, *Hold Fast to Dreams*.

Brian adds about their book collaboration, "It has to be something we're both excited about. Usually that means there is some aspect that adds something for me in terms of the visuals. Then we bounce it back and forth on the direction it may go in."

With my encouragement, Gloria Jean Pinkney started writing in 1989. We have collaborated on two books *Back Home* and *The Sunday Outing*. Gloria and I work in what would be considered a classic or traditional way, with Gloria writing the story first. My role as illustrator begins once she has finished. I do, however, see her work as it progresses. Therefore, I have a good sense of the history of her story as well as her vision of it. That experience of seeing the story develop becomes the inspiration for my visual interpretation.

There is a special quality in having a family that pursues and succeeds in the same careers. What comes to mind first is that we all have so much to share. Andrea adds, "It's an open exchange of ideas. It's just a very rich experience, and I think we're all very fortunate."

Jerry Pinkney has illustrated more than seventy-five books for children. He is the recipient of numerous awards, including three Caldecott Honor Books, four Coretta Scott King Awards, and the New York Times Best Illustrated Book for 1989 and for 1994. He has had one-man shows in museums and galleries across the United States and has been included in group shows in Europe, Japan, and Russia.

girl imaginable, who discovers that she needs her quiet little sister who has an inner strength that shines in times of distress; Chester and Wilson, who live predictable lives filled with routines and precautions until they encounter Lilly, the self-proclaimed "queen" who lives for thrilling moments of adventure.

Henkes has both written and illustrated most of his books. Among his many popular titles are **Chrysanthemum** (1991), *Julius, the Baby of the World*

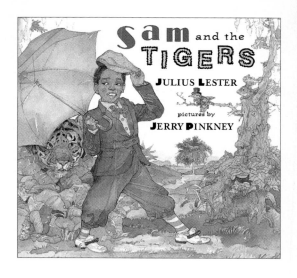

Illustration 6.18
Jerry Pinkney's illustrations and Julius Lester's text clearly set *Sam and the Tigers* within African American story-telling tradition. (*Sam and the Tigers* by Julius Lester. Illustrations copyright © 1996 by Jerry Pinkney. Used by permission of Dial Books for Young Readers, a division of Penguin Books USA Inc.)

(1990), **Sheila Rae, the Brave** (1987), **A Weekend with Wendell** (1987), and **Lilly's Purple Plastic Purse** (1996). In 1994, Henkes's **Owen** (1993) was named a Caldecott Honor Book. This book shows how one mouse family deals with a soon-to-be-kindergartener who refuses to give up a security blanket.

Ezra Jack Keats

Ezra Jack Keats is known for his distinctive collages and his depictions of the daily life of inner-city children. At first, he illustrated the work of others. Finding many of the texts to be contrived and not true to inner-city experiences of African American children, Keats decided to create his own text. **The Snowy Day** (1962) was his first book. This book was also pivotal in focusing Keats's attention on the use of collage. He used a variety of papers—gift wrap, wallpaper, and other printed papers—to add color and texture to his illustrations. In **The Snowy Day,** Peter wakes up one morning and finds a snowy scene outside his window. He bundles up in warm clothing and spends the day playing in the snow.

Keats continued to depict Peter's experiences in subsequent books. Although the experiences depicted are often universal—getting a new baby sister in **Peter's Chair** (1967) and playing in the neighborhood in **Apt. 3** (1971)—the details of the setting clearly place these stories in city neighborhoods. Keats's picture books are enjoyed in translations by children in many countries.

Leo Lionni

Leo Lionni began his career as a commercial artist. His career as a children's book author and illustrator began when he told a story to his grandchildren to pass the time while they were traveling together by train. Later published as a book, the story was about two children depicted as colors—blue and yellow—who hug and become green. **Little Blue and Little Yellow** (1959) was illustrated with torn paper collage, which portrayed an abstract representation of human emotions. Lionni continued to write and illustrate many books whose characters embodied concepts important in human relationships.

Inch by Inch (1962), Lionni's second book, was named a Caldecott Honor Book (one of three of his books to win that award). In this story, an inchworm outwits predators and survives by measuring them "inch by inch." For this book, Lionni mixed crayon with collage. In another story of survival, **Swimmy** (1963), a school of fish gathers into a formation resembling a large fish in order to fend off predators who have eaten Swimmy's family. The combination of sponge printing and watercolor in this book effectively depicts the underwater world.

Leo Lionni has created several books with mice as characters, all done in torn-paper collage style. *Frederick* (1967) is particularly well known, both for the artwork and for the story. As a family of mice gathers supplies to prepare for the coming winter, Frederick "stores up" stories and poetry as his contribution. Lionni's other books also focus on mice and other animals: *Let's Make Rabbits: A Fable* (1992), *Six Crows* (1988), *Frederick and His Friends* (1981), and *Matthew's Dream* (1991).

Beatrix Potter

Beatrix Potter spent a sheltered childhood in the home of her wealthy parents. She kept small pets such as rabbits and mice and, with her younger brother, Bertram, studied them carefully as she practiced drawing them. The siblings even brought dead animals home so that they could study them closely. This amateur scientific study paid off in later years in Potter's illustrations of various woodland animals in her books for children.

Potter first published her illustrations in 1893, in a book of children's verse entitled *A Happy Pair*. However, it is the 1902 publication of *The Tale of Peter Rabbit* that is celebrated as her debut as a creator of children's books. This story originally appeared in a series of letters in 1893 to Noel, the son of her former governess, intended to cheer him up when he was ill with scarlet fever. Potter included black-and-white drawings to accompany the story. Years later, after several publication rejections, she used her own funds to have the book published. Frederick Warne & Co. agreed to publish this "little book for little hands" on the condition that Potter provide color illustrations. More than twenty other books followed. The tales of such animal characters as Pigling Bland, Squirrel Nutkin, Jemima Puddleduck, Benjamin Bunny, Hunca Munca, and Jeremy Fisher are known by children all around the world.

Maurice Sendak

Maurice Sendak spent many of his childhood years sick in bed, reading comics, drawing, writing stories, and imagining the lives of the people in the houses in his neighborhood. From this beginning came a career devoted to the arts. Sendak is known for creating characters who are imaginative, strong-willed, and clever.

Sendak created *The Nutshell Library* (1962), a set of four two-by-four-inch books: *Chicken Soup with Rice: A Book of Months*; *One Was Johnny: A Counting Book*; *Alligators All Around: An Alphabet*; and *Pierre: A Cautionary Tale*. These stories remain popular today.

The publication of *Where the Wild Things Are* in 1963 brought much attention. Many adults feared that the Wild Things were too "frightening" for young children, but others applauded the central character's ability to deal with the strong emotions children face. The book was honored with the 1964 Caldecott Medal and today remains one of the most popular and well-known picture books for children.

Other Sendak books have also been the subject of controversy. *In the Night Kitchen* (1970) was criticized for the nudity of the central character and for the use of cartoon-style illustration. Some found the portrayal of babies' experiences in *Outside Over There* (1981) disturbing. Both books arose out of Sendak's own experiences, and he believes they are personally significant. More recently, *We*

ASK THE AUTHOR AND ILLUSTRATOR...

Jon Scieszka and Lane Smith

How do you come up with such imaginative and unique books?

I would love to describe how I get up before dawn every day, light my special candle of inspiration, and sit down to write for twelve hours. But I never do that. Then I could say I sit in a little shed and write on an old board I put across my lap, but Roald Dahl already said that. Maybe I used to work at an ad agency and someone challenged me to write a book for kids using only 100 different words. Nah. That was Dr. Seuss.

I don't know. Lane, how do we come up with such imaginative and unique books?

"I get up before dawn every day, light my special candle of inspiration, and sit down to paint and draw for twelve hours."

You do not.

"I go out to my little shed and draw on an old board I put across my lap?"

No.

"I used to work in an ad agency . . ."

Thanks for your help, Dr. Seuss.

I've never really given much thought to how we put our books together. I do the writing thing just like most other authors—writing, rewriting, reading the stuff to kids and teachers, then rewriting some more. And Lane does

---

Favorite Books as a Child

(Scieszka)	(Smith)
Green Eggs and Ham by Dr. Seuss	*The Carrot Seed* by Crockett Johnson
Grimms' Fairy Tales	*Treehorn x 3* by Florence Parry Heide, illustrated by E. Gorey
The Carrot Seed by Crockett Johnson	*How the Grinch Stole Christmas* by Dr. Seuss

---

Are All in the Dumps with Jack and Guy (1993) has disturbed some readers with the portrayal of homelessness.

In 1966, Maurice Sendak was the first American to be honored as a recipient of the International Board on Books for Young People's Hans Christian Andersen Award.

John Steptoe

John Steptoe knew from the time he was in high school that he wanted to write and illustrate books for African American children. He felt there was a great need for books these children could relate to. Immediately after high school, Steptoe published his first book, *Stevie* (1969). Although the theme—a boy's jealousy at having to share his mother's attention with a younger boy—is

the sketching, painting, and repainting thing like most other illustrators.

But, now that I think of it, we do have two secret ingredients that set us apart from those other Brand X books.

One, Lane and I are friends and work together. After I get a story to where I like it, I give it to Lane. He thinks about it, fools around with different ways to illustrate it; then we talk and goof around with changes in both the writing and the illustration to fit the new ideas. A lot of authors and illustrators never get this chance to work together.

Two, we have a secret weapon—our designer Molly Leach (who also happens to be Lane's wife and my wife's best friend and part of the reason Lane and I met and started working together and . . . that's a whole other story). As the designer, Molly is the one who takes the text and the illustrations and decides how to weave them together and present them on the page so everything works together.

So in *The Stinky Cheese Man,* it was Molly who came up with the idea to have the type grow and shrink to fit the page. And when Jack was telling his story endlessly over and over and over, I thought it would be funny if the text just ran off the page. Molly showed us how it would look better if the type got smaller and smaller.

For a book like *Math Curse,* the story stayed pretty close to the early finished draft. Lane came up with the idea to show the narrator under the spell of the curse. And we left it up to Molly to figure out how to cram all of the words, problems, and paintings into a picture book that looked kind of like a math book but not so ugly or so much like a math book that it would scare all of our readers away.

Our books look unique because we get to work in a unique way. Three people collaborate on getting the text, the illustration, and the design working to tell one story.

So, in conclusion, Lane and I make our imaginative and unique books by getting up before dawn every day, sitting in a little shed, working for an ad agency, and thanking our lucky stars that we get to work together and with Ace Designer, Molly Leach.

Jon Scieszka is the author of The True Story of the 3 Little Pigs!; The Frog Prince, Continued; The Stinky Cheese Man and Other Fairly Stupid Tales; The Book That Jack Wrote; Math Curse; *and the* Time Warp Trio *series. He's a lumberjack in his spare time. He once climbed Mount Everest in his bare feet. And he enjoys potato chips and making up lies. Lane Smith's bio is exactly the same as Jon's, except a couple of the book titles are different.*

universal and can be appreciated by all children, regardless of race, the book uses language to which African American children can relate directly. Steptoe continued to write and illustrate books that met his goal of providing for the literary needs of African American children, winning wide acclaim and numerous book awards, including the Coretta Scott King Award for illustrations.

In addition to illustrating his own books, Steptoe also illustrated works of other noted African American writers, including Lucille Clifton's **All Us Come Cross the Water** (1972), Eloise Greenfield's **She Come Bringing Me That Little Baby Girl** (1974), and Arnold Adoff's **OUTside/INside Poems** (1981), as well as Adoff's **All the Colors of the Race: Poems** (1982). Later in his career, John Steptoe created two books of ethnic folktales that became Caldecott Honor Books: **The Story of Jumping Mouse: A Native American Legend** (1984), and **Mufaro's Beautiful Daughters: An African Tale** (1987).

Illustration 6.19
Jon Scieszka's humorous text in *The True Story of the 3 Little Pigs!* is amplified through Lane Smith's illustrations and through the book's design. (*The True Story of the 3 Little Pigs!* by Jon Scieszka. Text copyright © 1989 by Jon Scieszka. Illustration copyright © 1989 by Lane Smith. Used by permission of Viking Penguin, a division of Penguin Books USA Inc.)

Chris Van Allsburg

Chris Van Allsburg's first book, ***The Garden of Abdul Gasazi,*** was published in 1979 and was a 1980 Caldecott Honor Book. Within a few years, he achieved notoriety as a remarkable creator of picture books and won two Caldecott Medals. The first was in 1982 for his second book, ***Jumanji*** (1981). This jungle adventure story is about two children playing a board game in which landing on particular squares has real consequences: Lions roar, monkeys create havoc, rhinos stampede, and a volcano erupts. The second Caldecott Medal was awarded in 1986 for ***The Polar Express*** (1985), in which children board a late-night "polar express" train and visit Santa at the North Pole. The book quickly became established as a Christmas classic.

Van Allsburg's early work was done in black pencil, but his later works are full-color paintings. His stories cross between reality and fantasy in ways that make fantasy believable and reality questionable; his illustrations have similar effects. One of his books that requires readers to let their imaginations fill in the unknown is ***The Mysteries of Harris Burdick*** (1984). It takes the form of a portfolio of paintings, each with only a title and a caption. Readers are to imagine the story behind each painting. Perhaps the appeal of Van Allsburg's books for children and adults alike lies in this lack of distinction between reality and fantasy—and in the subtlety of the interpretations allowed by his highly imaginative work.

More recently, Van Allsburg has created picture books with a social message. ***Just a Dream*** (1990) raises the issue of what happens when people don't take care of their environment. Walter abuses the environment until a nightmare reveals what his future will be like. Walter's attitude and behavior toward the environment make a complete turnaround when he awakes. Readers find a cautionary tale in ***The Sweetest Fig*** (1993), in which Monsieur Bibot is given two figs in payment for extracting a tooth—figs that can make his dream come true. An unexpected turn of events leaves readers pondering after they close the book, "How will Monsier Bibot's treatment of his dog and of others repay him in the future?"

Ed Young

Born and raised in China, Ed Young emigrated to the United States when he was twenty years old. His childhood years in China influence much of his

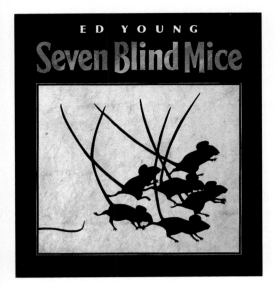

Illustration 6.20
The precision of paper-cut collage and dramatic use of color combine in the story of *The Seven Blind Mice*, a Caldecott Honor Book. (*Seven Blind Mice* by Ed Young. Illustration copyright © 1992 by Ed Young. Used by permission of Philomel Books.)

work as an artist. Early in his career, he primarily illustrated the writing of others. The most noted among his early illustrated books is Jane Yolen's ***The Emperor and the Kite*** (1967), which was a 1968 Caldecott Honor Book. Young illustrated several other texts with Chinese origins, including ***Chinese Mother Goose Rhymes*** (Wyndham, 1968), ***Yeh-Shen: A Cinderella Story from China*** (Louie, 1982), and ***White Wave: A Chinese Tale*** (Wolkstein, 1979).

Ed Young has both written and illustrated a number of books. For his 1989 book ***Lon Po Po: A Red Riding Hood Story from China***, Young was awarded the Caldecott Medal. In this version, the children make good decisions and outwit the wolf. A Caldecott Honor Book, ***Seven Blind Mice*** (1992), is the story of six blind mice who separately explore a mysterious "thing" and report a different interpretation to the others. The seventh mouse examines the whole "thing" more thoroughly and combines the other six interpretations to reveal what the "thing" is. The origin of the Chinese zodiac, a twelve-year cycle of years named for animals, is explained in ***Cat and Rat*** (1995). One of the most interesting aspects of Young's work is the diverse range of media he works with, from chalk, watercolor, and collage to mixed media.

CRITERIA FOR SELECTING PICTURE BOOKS

The plethora of picture books currently available makes the task of evaluation and selection complex. These days, picture books are enjoyed by readers of all ages—from infants to adults. Finding quality picture books to meet individual needs is quite possible. But two important questions must be answered first: How do teachers and librarians evaluate quality in picture books? What are the criteria for selecting particular picture books?

Evaluating Quality in Picture Books

When evaluating the quality of a picture book, it is important to consider the following:

- Text (literary elements)
- Illustrations (artistic elements)
- Integration of text and illustrations

Text. Is the storyline strong enough to be interesting without the pictures? Will the text alone hold children's attention? When a book is read to a group, some children may not be able to see the pictures. Some teachers prefer to read the story the first time through without showing the pictures. Under these circumstances, interesting text is essential.

Is the language of the text skillfully crafted? Children will want to hear and see a favorite picture book again and again. Skillfully crafted text can enhance children's understanding of language and expose them to the rich possibilities of language use.

Illustrations. Is the art accessible and interesting to the intended audience? Some books that may seem dazzling and creative to an adult may baffle a young viewer.

Does the art help children see things in a new way? Does it leave room for the child's imagination? Will children want to turn to it again and again? A book that children want to return to repeatedly is a better investment than one whose charms are quickly depleted. Do the illustrations communicate not just literally but symbolically through the use of colors, framing, shading, and the like?

Integration of Text and Illustrations. Do the pictures fit the text? Given that the text and the pictures may have been created independently, how well do they work together? Do the text and the pictures seem to be created to clarify, enhance, and extend each other?

Does the interplay between picture and text exercise the reader's imagination? Children don't need to be shown everything the text has said or told everything the pictures have shown. Children's imaginations are stretched when their senses fill in the gaps between pictures and text.

Are the illustrations well spaced and closely synchronized with the text? Earlier in this chapter, we noted how illustrators can employ the "drama of the turning page" and can speed or slow readers' progress through a text. Are these devices used in pleasing ways?

Will the pictures hold interest long enough for the text to be read? When children are being read to, they must focus their attention on the pictures while

Are picture books being designed more for adult buyers than for child readers?

ISSUE TO CONSIDER

Picture books are the biggest selling type of children's book. Are they purchased for their appeal to the adult buyers or for their appeal to child readers? Are the exquisite art and sophisticated humor of many picture books more appealing to parents than to children?

In the past, picture books were designed for preschoolers and young children. Decades ago, books such as those produced by Marie Hall Ets and Virginia Lee Burton were created for that audience. Today, picture books such as those by Eric Hill, Denise Fleming, and Mem Fox are still appropriate for young children. However, many picture books have reached a level of sophistication in both art and text that raises a question as to whom the books were created for.

Certainly, there are picture books today that appeal to all ages. Sally Lodge (1992) calls these sophisticated books "crossovers," books that are successful in both juvenile and adult markets. She believes that publishers cannot always predict which books will become crossover books. Celebrities such as Whoopie Goldberg, Carly Simon, Dolly Parton, and others have recently published picture books that publishers hope will appeal to adult buyers who may recognize such names. There are also picture books that have reprints of fine art from museums around the world or illustrations that reflect an adult sensibility in art appreciation. The text of some books seem to address issues that many children are not yet prepared to understand. Who, then, is the audience for these picture books?

What do you think?

the text is read. The balance between pictures and text is ideal when children have not lost interest in a picture long before the text is read or lost track of the story line while still engrossed in the details of a picture.

Picture Book Selection Criteria

In addition to determining the quality of a picture book, it is important to know whether a book is appropriate for particular children in particular situations. We can determine a book's appropriateness by considering the following:

- Intended audience
- Intended purpose
- Makeup of the collection

Intended Audience. Who is the intended audience? What are the needs of the children who will be reading the book? What level of sophistication is appropriate for the intended audience? What backgrounds do the children have, both experientially and as readers?

Intended Purpose. How will this book be used? How does it fit the children's needs? How does it match curricular or other purposes?

Makeup of the Collection. What other books are available to the children? How does this book fit in with other books to which children have access? Is there a good balance in the variety of books available for the purpose expressed?

Awards for Picture Books

Many awards honor high-quality picture books and their creators. Here, we highlight two of the most widely recognized awards: the Caldecott Medal and the Coretta Scott King Award for illustrations.

Caldecott Medal. The American Library Association's Association of Library Service to Children honored Randolph Caldecott in 1938 by giving his name to an annual award for the most distinguished picture book published in the previous year. Funds to establish the Caldecott Medal were donated to the ALA by Frederick Melcher, president of the Wilson Publishing Company. Books that have won the medal for their illustrations have a gold seal on the jackets, and honor books have a silver seal. A list of Caldecott winners appears in Appendix A.

Coretta Scott King Award. Each year, the American Library Association gives one Coretta Scott King Award for writing and one for illustrations, as well as honor book citations. The ALA's guidelines for the award state that "recipients are African American authors and illustrators whose distinguished books promote an understanding and appreciation of the culture and contribution of all people to the realization of the 'American dream.'" Appendix A lists all previous winners and honor books.

 TEACHING IDEAS

Observing Details in Wordless Books. The pictures in the wordless books by Mitsumasa Anno are full of detailed information, presented in a holistic, intricately woven artistic style. To hone children's visual observation skills, have them find as much pictorial information as they can in one of Anno's books. In

Anno's Alphabet (1975), younger children can look for items beginning with the featured alphabet letter; in *Anno's U.S.A.* (1983), older children can look for pictures of cultural artifacts, historical events, famous people, etc.

Comparing Mother Goose Books. Select Mother Goose books illustrated by a wide variety of illustrators, and show children illustrations of the same rhymes. What are the differences? Have children compare the artists' visual interpretations of the setting, meaning, and characters in the nursery rhymes.

Comparing Illustrations in Different Versions of the Same Story. Have children examine three or more illustrated versions of the fairytale "Puss in Boots." Some good illustrators of the tale are Fred Marcellino, Gail E. Haley, and Lorinda Bryan Cauley. Have children note differences that inform viewers of the illustrator's perspective on the time and place in which the story took place, on cats, on the character of this particular cat, on whether the story is humorous or not, and on the character of the would-be Prince.

EXPERIENCES FOR YOUR LEARNING

1. Compare and contrast some predictable books and some easy readers that have controlled vocabulary.

2. Select some books that appeal to you as an adult. Discuss with others the most appropriate audience for such books.

3. Select a book from an earlier era, such as the ones discussed in the section of this chapter entitled "Authors and Illustrators Who Have Defined the Field." Look at the illustrations in terms of elements of design. For example, how did Virginia Lee Burton use line, color, and shape to tell her story through the illustrations in *The Little House* (1942)?

4. Select some alphabet books for different audiences, such as preschoolers, elementary school children, and young adults. What makes each alphabet book appropriate for its level?

RECOMMENDED BOOKS

I indicates interest level (P = preschool, YA = young adult)

Mother Goose and Nursery Rhymes

Agard, John, and Grace Nichols. *No Hickory No Dickory No Dock: Caribbean Nursery Rhymes.* Illustrated by Cynthia Jabar. Cambridge, MA: Candlewick, 1991. Original and traditional rhymes enjoyed by children in the Caribbean are collected in this book. (I: P–6)

Delacre, Lulu, ed. *Arroz con leche: Popular Songs and Rhymes from Latin America.* Translated by Elena Paz. New York: Scholastic, 1989. This collection of folk rhymes, chants, and finger plays known throughout many Spanish-speaking countries is presented bilingually. (I: P–6)

Demi. *Dragon Kites and Dragonflies.* New York: Harcourt, 1986. This is a collection of twenty-two Chinese nursery rhymes. (I: P–8)

Dyer, Jane. *Animal Crackers: A Delectable Collection of Pictures, Poems, and Lullabies for the Very Young.* Boston: Little, Brown, 1996. This collection appeals to the very young and includes verses about animals, food, seasons, games, concepts (alphabet, numbers, shapes, colors) and nursery rhymes and lullabies. (I: P–6)

Griego, Margot C., Betsy L. Bucks, Sharon S. Gilbert, and Laurel H. Kimball. *Tortillitas para Mama and Other Spanish Nursery Rhymes.* Illustrated by Barbara Cooney. New York: Holt, 1981. Nursery rhymes are presented in Spanish and in English. (I: P–7)

Hale, Sara Josepha. *Mary Had a Little Lamb.* Illustrated by Tomie de Paola. New York: Holiday House, 1984. This traditional nursery rhyme and song is illustrated in Tomie de Paola's folk-art style. (I: P–6)

———. *Mary Had a Little Lamb.* Photographs by Bruce McMillan. New York: Scholastic, 1990. Photographs depict Mary as an African American girl in a modern setting. (I: P–6)

Hey Diddle Diddle and Other Mother Goose Rhymes. Illustrated by Tomie de Paola. New York: Putnam,

1985. Tomie de Paola created folk-art illustrations to accompany nearly fifty well-known Mother Goose rhymes. (**I:** P–7)

Hopkins, Lee Bennett. *Animals from Mother Goose.* Illustrated by Kathryn Hewitt. New York: Harcourt, 1989. This Mother Goose book presents familiar rhymes that include animals. The riddles are presented in a question format; each page unfolds to reveal the answer. A related title is *People from Mother Goose: A Question Book* (1989). (**I:** P)

Ivemey, John. *The Complete Story of the Three Blind Mice.* Illustrated by Paul Galdone. New York: Clarion, 1987. This popular song's verses are extended to tell a complete story. (**I:** P–7)

James Marshall's Mother Goose. Illustrated by James Marshall. New York: Farrar, 1979. This collection of thirty-five popular Mother Goose rhymes is accompanied by James Marshall's delightfully humorous illustrations. (**I:** P–7)

Larrick, Nancy. *Songs from Mother Goose with the Traditional Melody for Each.* Illustrated by Robin Spowart. New York: Harper & Row, 1989. This is a collection of fifty-six Mother Goose rhymes that are usually sung. Each rhyme is accompanied by an illustration and musical notation for the melody. (**I:** P–8)

The Little Dog Laughed. Illustrated by Lucy Cousins. New York: Dutton, 1990. Over fifty traditional nursery rhymes are illustrated with black lines and bold colors in simple, childlike style. (**I:** P–8)

Lobel, Arnold. *The Random House Book of Mother Goose.* Illustrated by Arnold Lobel. New York: Random House, 1986. This is an anthology of 306 nursery rhymes. (**I:** P–8)

Michael Foreman's Mother Goose. Illustrated by Michael Foreman. New York: Harcourt, 1991. This is a collection of over two hundred of the best-known Mother Goose rhymes. Each double-page spread has one background for rhymes that are thematically connected. (**I:** P–8)

Mother Goose. Illustrated by Brian Wildsmith. London: Oxford, 1964. Brian Wildsmith's water-color illustrations accompany eighty-six classic Mother Goose rhymes. (**I:** P–8)

Old Mother Hubbard and Her Wonderful Dog. Illustrated by James Marshall. New York: Farrar, 1991. The rhyme "Old Mother Hubbard" is accompanied by humorous illustrations as well as asides from the dog. (**I:** P–8)

Opie, Iona, ed. *My Very First Mother Goose.* Illustrated by Rosemary Wells. Cambridge, MA: Candlewick, 1996. The large print of the text and the appealing illustrations make this Mother Goose volume especially appropriate to share with the very young. (**I:** P–6)

Opie, Iona, and Peter Opie. *I Saw Esau: The School-child's Pocket Book.* Illustrated by Maurice Sendak. Cambridge, MA: Candlewick, 1992. Over 170 rhymes of childhood are included in this collection. Also included are end notes on the origins of and traditions associated with these rhymes. (**I:** all ages)

Polacco, Patricia. *Babushka's Mother Goose.* New York: Philomel, 1995. This collection of Mother Goose–inspired rhymes has a Russian theme. Three Babushkas live in their bed; Diadushka plants an enormous turnip; Matroishka is a nesting doll who greets other dolls inside her. (**I:** P–9)

Tomie de Paola's Mother Goose. Illustrated by Tomie de Paola. New York: Putnam, 1985. This large-format anthology of over two hundred traditional Mother Goose rhymes includes both well-known and lesser-known ones. Each rhyme is illustrated with de Paola's signature watercolor style. (**I:** P–8)

Tudor, Tasha. *Mother Goose.* New York: Walck, 1972. Seventy-seven well-known Mother Goose rhymes are included in this collection. (**I:** P–8)

Wyndham, Robert. *Chinese Mother Goose Rhymes/Ju tsu ko t'u.* 1968. Illustrated by Ed Young. New York: Philomel, 1989. Forty-one traditional Chinese nursery rhymes have been translated into English. Both the English and the Chinese text appear on each page, and the book is designed to be held vertically to give the appearance of a long Chinese scroll. (**I:** P–8)

Toy Books

Anno, Mitsumasa. *Anno's Faces.* New York: Philomel, 1989. Children can use plastic markers with a smiling face and a frowning face to add faces to fruits and vegetables. (**I:** P)

Brown, Marc. *One, Two, Buckle My Shoe.* New York: Dutton, 1989. This pop-up version of a familiar rhyme includes diagrams that show movements to accompany the rhyme. (**I:** P)

Campbell, Rod. *Dear Zoo.* New York: Four Winds, 1982. A boy writes to the zoo, requesting a pet. Lift-the-flap crates reveal various animals that the zoo sends him. (**I:** P)

Carle, Eric. *The Honeybee and the Robber.* Paper engineering by James Diaz, Tor Lokvig, and John Strejan. New York: Philomel, 1981. A little bee prevents a bear from stealing the honey. Children can make the book move by pulling tabs, lifting a flap, and opening a pop-up page. There are detailed facts for older readers at the end of the book. (**I:** 6–8)

Cousins, Lucy. *Country Animals*. New York: Penguin/ Tambourine, 1990. Simple, bold illustrations are accompanied by the name of each animal in this series of board books, which also includes *Farm Animals* (1990) and *Garden Animals* (1990). (I: P)

————*Maisy's Pop-Up Playhouse*. Cambridge, MA: Candlewick, 1995. Pages of this book fold down to create rooms in a playhouse. (I: P)

Ehlert, Lois. *Color Zoo*. New York: HarperCollins, 1989. As they turn the pages, children see various shapes that unlayer to reveal different animal faces. Shape names and animal names are included. A related title is *Color Farm* (1990). (I: P)

Falwell, Cathryn. *Nicky and Alex*. Boston: Houghton Mifflin, 1992. Collage-style illustrations on thick pages show two brothers playing together. Other books about Nicky are *Nicky and Grandpa* (1991) and *Nicky Loves Daddy* (1992). (I: P)

Hill, Eric. *Where's Spot?* New York: Putnam, 1980. Sally looks for Spot, who has not eaten his dinner. Children lift flaps to help search for the missing puppy. Over twenty other books about Spot (with Spanish versions of some titles) are available. (I: P)

Hoban, Tana. *Black on White*. New York: Greenwillow, 1993. This board book shows black shapes of familiar objects such as an elephant, a butterfly, and a leaf on a white background. Its companion book is *White on Black* (1993). (I: P)

————. *Look! Look! Look!* New York: Greenwillow, 1988. Children view part of an object through a hole on alternating pages and try to guess what the whole object may be. (I: P–7)

Inkpen, Mick. *Where, Oh Where, Is Kipper's Bear?* San Diego, CA: Red Wagon Books/Harcourt, 1995. Kipper the dog's teddy bear is missing, and flaps, pop-ups, and pull tabs help readers search for the missing bear. (I: P)

Kunhardt, Dorothy. *Pat the Bunny*. 1940. New York: Western, 1968. This interactive book invites children to touch, smell, look, and feel as they play with Paul and Judy. (I: P)

Oxenbury, Helen. *I Hear*. New York: Random House, 1986. This board book shows a child listening to sounds in the environment. A related title is *I See* (1986). (I: P)

Pelham, David. *Sam's Sandwich*. Illustrated by David Pelham and Harry Willock. New York: Dutton, 1990. Sam sneaks in creatures from the garden as his sister Samantha assembles her sandwich. The covers of the book are the bread and readers unfold pages that serve as the sandwich fillings. A related title is *Sam's Pizza* (1996). (I: P–7)

Pienkowski, Jan. *Dinner Time*. Text by Anne Carter. Paper engineering by Marcin Stajewski and James Roger Diaz. New York: Gallery Five, 1981. Pop-up mouths show how animals prey on one another for dinner. (I: P)

Rathmann, Peggy. *Good Night, Gorilla*. New York: Putnam, 1994. This is a board book with a nearly wordless story in which a zookeeper says good night to the animals in the zoo as the gorilla follows, unlocking their cages so the animals can follow the zookeeper home. (I: P)

Sendak, Maurice. *The Nutshell Library*. New York: Harper & Row, 1962. This set of four miniature books includes *Alligators All Around, Chicken Soup with Rice, One Was Johnny,* and *Pierre*. The first book is an alphabet book; the second is a series of poems about enjoying chicken soup all the months of the year; the third is a counting book; and the fourth is a cautionary tale. (I: P–7)

Steptoe, John. *Baby Says*. New York: Lothrop, Lee & Shepard, 1988. This nearly wordless picture book shows a young African American child learning to play with his baby brother. (I: P)

Watanabe, Shigeo. *Where's My Daddy?* Illustrated by Yasuo Ohtomo. New York: Philomel, 1979. The series *I Can Do It All By Myself* has the perspective of a child learning independence. In this book, a little bear looks for daddy all alone. (I: P)

Wells, Rosemary. *Max's First Word*. New York: Dial, 1979. Ruby works hard to expand Max's vocabulary from his one word—"bang." Other humorous stories in board book format about Max and Ruby are *Max's Bedtime* (1985), *Max's Birthday* (1985), and *Max's Breakfast* (1985). (I: P)

Wood, Audrey. *The Napping House Wakes Up*. Illustrated by Don Wood. New York: Harcourt, 1994. This is a pop-up version of the cumulative story about a group of nappers who are awakened by a flea. (I: P–7)

Zelinsky, Paul O. *The Wheels on the Bus*. New York: Dutton, 1990. This pop-up rendition of a popular action song shows movements for each verse as readers push, pull, or lift tabs on the pages. (I: P–6)

Alphabet Books

Agard, John. *The Calypso Alphabet*. Illustrated by Jennifer Bent. New York: Holt, 1989. This ABC book introduces words that have to do with the Caribbean islands. (I: P–7)

Anno, Mitsumasa. *Anno's Alphabet: An Adventure in Imagination*. New York: Harper, 1975. Individual letters are shown on one page, and a single object beginning with that letter is shown on the facing page. The imaginative drawings show wood letter shapes that could not possibly be cut as shown, and the items matching the letters are often unusual. (**I:** P–7)

Aylesworth, Jim. *The Folks in the Valley: A Pennsylvania Dutch ABC*. Illustrated by Stefano Vitale. New York: HarperCollins, 1992. Dutch motifs are used to present the alphabet. (**I:** P–7)

Base, Graeme. *Animalia*. New York: Abrams, 1987. For each letter of the alphabet, an alliterative phrase describes what various animals are doing. Illustrations are filled with items beginning with the featured letter. (**I:** all ages)

Bayer, Jane. *A, My Name Is Alice*. Illustrated by Steven Kellogg. New York: Dial, 1984. This familiar jump-rope and ball-bouncing chant has a verse for every letter of the alphabet. The animals and their names, the places they come from, and the things they sell all begin with the featured letter. (**I:** P–7)

Bowen, Betsy. *Antler, Bear, Canoe: A Northwoods Alphabet Year*. Boston: Little, Brown, 1991. Minnesota provides the theme for this alphabet book. (**I:** P–8)

Dragonwagon, Crescent. *Alligator Arrived with Apples: A Potluck Alphabet Feast*. Illustrated by José Aruego and Ariane Dewey. New York: Macmillan, 1987. Alliterative text describes various animals bringing food for a Thanksgiving feast. (**I:** P–7)

Ehlert, Lois. *Eating the Alphabet: Fruits and Vegetables from A to Z*. New York: Harcourt, 1989. Fruits and vegetables are displayed in alphabetical order. (**I:** P–7)

Feelings, Muriel. *Jambo Means Hello: A Swahili Alphabet Book*. New York: Dial, 1974. Readers are introduced, via the alphabet, to the Swahili culture. (**I:** P–9)

Greenaway, Kate. *A—Apple Pie*. London: Warne, 1886. A is an apple pie, and the words that tell what happens follow the alphabet letter by letter: "bit it," "cut it," "dealt it," etc. (**I:** P–6)

Hoban, Tana. *A, B, See!* New York: Greenwillow, 1982. Objects that begin with each letter of the alphabet are shown in photographs. (**I:** P)

Jonas, Ann. *Aardvarks, Disembark!* New York: Greenwillow, 1990. Extinct and endangered animals are seen departing from Noah's ark. (**I:** P–7)

Kitchen, Bert. *Animal Alphabet*. New York: Dial, 1984. Each letter of the alphabet is shown with an unusual animal whose name begins with the letter. (**I:** P–6)

Lear, Edward. *An Edward Lear Alphabet*. Illustrated by Carol Newsom. New York: Lothrop, Lee &

Shepard, 1983. Edward Lear's nonsense rhymes are newly illustrated. (**I:** P–7)

Lobel, Anita. *Alison's Zinnia*. New York: Greenwillow, 1990. This alphabet book has a gamelike format, using girls' names and flower names. (**I:** 6–8)

Lobel, Arnold. *On Market Street*. Illustrated by Anita Lobel. New York: Greenwillow, 1981. Alphabet letters are depicted as people whose bodies are made up of objects beginning with that letter. (**I:** P–7)

MacDonald, Suse. *Alphabatics*. New York: Bradbury, 1986. Each letter spins and changes into an object whose name begins with that letter. (**I:** P–7)

Martin, Bill, Jr., and John Archambault. *Chicka Chicka Boom Boom*. New York: Simon & Schuster, 1989. The alphabet letters race up a coconut tree in this rhythmic, rhyming verse. (**I:** P–7)

Musgrove, Margaret. *Ashanti to Zulu: African Traditions*. Illustrated by Leo and Diane Dillon. New York: Dial, 1976. Twenty-six African tribes are shown in alphabetical order, and their cultural traditions are described. (**I:** 7–11)

Provensen, Alice, and Martin Provensen. *A Peaceable Kingdom: The Shaker Abecedarius*. New York: Viking, 1978. The alphabet animal rhymes first published in the Shaker manifesto of July 1882 are newly illustrated in this edition. (**I:** P–7)

Rankin, Laura. *The Handmade Alphabet*. New York: Dial, 1991. The hand sign for each letter of the alphabet is shown along with an item whose name begins with the letter. (**I:** P–9)

Sendak, Maurice. *Alligators All Around*. New York: Harper, 1962. Part of *The Nutshell Library*. Alligators are described in many ways in alliterative phrases. (**I:** P–8)

Shannon, George. *Tomorrow's Alphabet*. Illustrated by Donald Crews. New York: Greenwillow, 1996. The concept of things changing over time is explored in this alphabet book. For example, "A is for seed—tomorrow's apple." (**I:** P–6)

Van Allsburg, Chris. *The Z Was Zapped*. Boston: Houghton Mifflin, 1987. Twenty-six one-act plays show what happens to each letter of the alphabet. (**I:** 8–10)

Counting Books

Anno, Mitsumasa. *Anno's Counting Book*. New York: Crowell, 1977. Illustrations of landscapes include objects that can be counted. (**I:** P)

———. *Anno's Counting House*. New York: Philomel, 1982. Cut-out windows of two houses show ten people who move from one house to the other. Readers will enjoy finding out who has moved and what items they have taken with them, adding to one house and subtracting from the other to count the ten people. (I: P–7)

Aylesworth, Jim. *One Crow: A Counting Rhyme.* Illustrated by Ruth Young. Philadelphia: Lippincott, 1988. Farm animals are counted twice in rhyming text, once in summer and the second time in winter. (I: P)

Bang, Molly. *Ten, Nine, Eight.* New York: Greenwillow, 1983. Objects are counted backwards in this bedtime story. (I: P)

Carle, Eric. *1, 2, 3 to the Zoo.* New York: Putnam, 1968. Beginning with one elephant and ending with ten birds, each car in the train has one more zoo animal than the one before it. At the end, readers unfold a page to see all the animals at their destination and an empty train along the bottom of the page. (I: P)

Christelow, Eileen. *Five Little Monkeys Jumping on the Bed.* New York: Clarion, 1989. Humorous illustrations accompany this familiar chant of what happens when one by one, the monkeys fall off and hit their heads. (I: P–7)

Crews, Donald. *Ten Black Dots.* New York: Greenwillow, 1986. Ten big, black dots are counted from one to ten and shown as parts of familiar objects. For example, "Three dots can make a snowman's face." (I: P–5)

Dunrea, Olivier. *Deep Down Under.* New York: Macmillan, 1989. Underground creatures are counted in this cumulative story. (I: P–7)

Ehlert, Lois. *Fish Eyes: A Book You Can Count On.* New York: Harcourt, 1990. The text is narrated in the voice of a young child who imagines touring the underwater world and seeing brightly colored fish. This counting book includes the concept of "one more" as the guide fish is added to the count on each page. (I: P–6)

Feelings, Muriel. *Moja Means One: A Swahili Counting Book.* Illustrated by Tom Feelings. New York: Dial, 1971. Scenes of Africa are shown in this counting book. (I: P and up)

Fleming, Denise. *Count!* New York: Holt, 1992. This vibrantly colored counting book shows one through ten animals to be counted. There are also small creatures to be counted by tens. (I: P)

Giganti, Paul, Jr. *Each Orange Had Eight Slices: A Counting Book.* Illustrated by Donald Crews. New York: Greenwillow, 1992. Mathematical concepts are shown in the illustrations. (I: P–8)

Haskins, Jim. *Count Your Way through Italy.* Illustrated by Beth Wright. Minneapolis, MN: Carolrhoda, 1990. This is one of a series of books that combine

an introduction to counting in various languages with information about the countries. (I: 6–9)

Kitchen, Bert. *Animal Numbers.* New York: Dial, 1987. Each page presents a large illustration of the featured number and that number of animals. (I: P–6)

MacDonald, Suse, and Bill Oakes. *Numblers.* New York: Bradbury, 1972. Objects take the shape of numbers and of other imaginary and real objects. The concepts covered include color, design, shapes, and numbers. (I: P–6)

Nikola-Lisa, W. *One Hole in the Road.* Illustrated by Dan Yaccarino. New York: Holt, 1996. The numbers 1 through 10 are introduced while showing how workers fix a hole in the road. (I: P–6)

Walsh, Ellen Stoll. *Mouse Count.* New York: Harcourt, 1991. A hungry snake counts mice. After they trick the snake into looking for more mice to fill up his jar, the mice tumble out as they "uncount" themselves. (I: P–7)

Wise, William. *Ten Sly Piranhas: A Counting Story in Reverse (A Tale of Wickedness—and Worse!).* Illustrated by Victoria Chess. New York: Dial, 1993. As the ten fish disappear, they are counted down. (I: P–6)

Concept Books

Carle, Eric. *My Very First Book of Colors.* New York: Crowell, 1974. Nine colors on half pages are matched to illustrations. (I: P)

———. *My Very First Book of Shapes.* New York: Crowell, 1974. Black shadows of shapes are matched with corresponding shapes in color illustrations. (I: P)

Crews, Donald. *Freight Train.* New York: Greenwillow, 1978. As a frieght train passes by, readers are introduced to colors, names of train cars, and the concepts of darkness and light. (I: P–7)

Falwell, Cathryn. *Shape Space.* New York: Clarion, 1992. A child plays gymnastically with various shapes. (I: P–7)

Hoban, Tana. *All About Where.* New York: Greenwillow, 1991. Words that describe "where" are listed on either side of an across-a-spread photograph. Readers use those words to tell where objects are found in the illustration. (I: P)

———. *Circles, Triangles, and Squares.* New York: Macmillan, 1974. Photographs show shapes in everyday objects. (I: P)

———. *I Read Signs.* New York: Greenwillow, 1983. Photographs of signs in the neighborhood encourage children to read them. (I: P–7)

———. *Over, Under, and Through and Other Spatial Concepts.* New York: Macmillan, 1973. Photographs show relationships of spatial concepts. (I: P)

———. *Push-Pull, Empty-Full: A Book of Opposites.* New York: Macmillan, 1972. Antonyms are shown through the photographs. (I: P)

———. *Shapes, Shapes, Shapes.* New York: Greenwillow, 1986. Shapes in the environment are shown in photographs. (I: P)

———. *26 Letters and 99 Cents.* New York: Greenwillow, 1987. Open the book one way, and find letters of the alphabet matched with objects whose names begin with each letter. Turn the book over and open it from the opposite end, and count money up to 99 cents. (I: P–8)

Jonas, Ann. *Color Dance.* New York: Greenwillow, 1989. Dancers with colored scarves introduce the primary colors. When their scarves overlap, the secondary colors are visible. (I: P–5)

McMillan, Bruce. *The Baby Zoo.* New York: Scholastic, 1992. A few lines of description accompany each photograph of baby animals. (I: P)

———. *Beach Ball—Left, Right.* New York: Holiday House, 1992. A beach ball on each page illustrates left or right. (I: P)

———. *Counting Wildflowers.* New York: Lothrop, Lee & Shepard, 1986. Colored photographs of wildflowers provide children with opportunities to count. (I: P)

———. *Fire Engine Shapes.* New York: Lothrop, Lee & Shepard, 1988. Photographs show the shapes found on various parts of a fire engine. (I: P)

———. *Here a Chick, There a Chick.* New York: Lothrop, Lee & Shepard, 1983. Photographs of a chick show opposites. (I: P)

———. *One, Two, One Pair.* New York: Scholastic, 1991. This counting book shows one item and a matching item to illustrate how the two together make one pair. (I: P)

Spier, Peter. *Fast-Slow, High-Low: A Book of Opposites.* Garden City, NY: Doubleday, 1972. Detailed pictures, typical of Spier's work, illustrate the concept of opposites. (I: P–7)

Walsh, Ellen Stoll. *Mouse Paint.* New York: Harcourt, 1989. Three white mice splash around in primary colored paint. When they dance in each other's colors, they make new colors. But when the cat comes around, they must find a way to keep from being seen. (I: P–5)

Wordless Books

Anno, Mitsumasa. *Anno's Journey.* New York: Philomel, 1978. The small towns and cities of Europe are shown, with cultural and historic details hidden throughout each page. Also by this author/illustrator are *Anno's Britain* (1982), *Anno's Italy* (1980), and *Anno's U.S.A.* (Putnam, 1983/1992). (I: 7 and up)

———. *Topsy-Turvies: Pictures to Stretch the Imagination.* New York: Weatherhill, 1970. These pictures of little elfish-looking men depict things that are impossible in the real world. They also stir the imagination of what might be. A sequel is *Upside-Downers: More Pictures to Stretch the Imagination* (1971). (I: 6–9)

Baker, Jeannie. *Window.* New York: Greenwillow, 1991. Collage illustrations show environmental changes as seen through a window of a house as the boy who lives there grows from babyhood to adulthood. (I: 6–9)

Bang, Molly. *The Grey Lady and the Strawberry Snatcher.* New York: Four Winds, 1980. The strawberry snatcher follows the Grey Lady through town and forest in hopes of snatching her strawberries, but instead comes across blackberries along the way. (I: P–6)

Carle, Eric. *Do You Want to Be My Friend?* New York: Crowell, 1971. A mouse asks, "Do you want to be my friend?" repeatedly as he looks for companionship. (I: P)

de Paola, Tomie. *Pancakes for Breakfast.* New York: Harcourt, 1978. This wordless book tells a story of how pancakes are made. (I: P–6)

Hutchins, Pat. *Changes, Changes.* New York: Macmillan, 1971. A story unfolds as two wooden dolls continuously change the things they create out of wooden blocks. (I: P–7)

McCully, Emily Arnold. *New Baby.* New York: Harper & Row, 1988. A mouse family adds a new baby. (I: P–8)

———. *Picnic.* New York: Harper & Row, 1984. When the family goes on a picnic, one mouse is bumped out of the car and left behind. The mice are also featured in *School* (1987). (I: P–8)

Spier, Peter. *Noah's Ark.* Garden City, NY: Doubleday, 1977. Humorous details illustrate the Biblical story in Jacobris Revius's poem "The Flood." (I: P–8)

Van Allsburg, Chris. *The Mysteries of Harris Burdick.* Boston: Houghton Mifflin, 1984. The book begins with an explanation of how Harris Burdick delivered a stack of pictures with titles and captions but mysteriously disappeared without delivering the accompanying stories. (I: 8–12)

Wiesner, David. *Tuesday.* New York: Clarion, 1991. On a mysterious Tuesday night, frogs float through the air on their lily pads. The mystery of this strange occurrence is complicated when the book closes with shadows of flying pigs. (**I:** P–9)

Easy Readers

Cole, Joanna, and Stephanie Calmenson. *Ready . . . Set . . . Read!* Garden City, NY: Doubleday, 1990. This is an anthology of short stories that are easy to read. (**I:** P–7)

Ehrlich, Amy. *Leo, Zack and Emmie.* New York: Dial, 1981. Stories of friendship among three children are told in easy-to-read format. (**I:** P–7)

Hoff, Syd. *Sammy the Seal.* New York: Harper & Row, 1959. Sammy wonders what life is like outside the zoo. (**I:** P–7)

Hopkins, Lee Bennett, ed. *Surprises.* Illustrated by Megan Lloyd. New York: Harper & Row, 1984. Lee Bennett Hopkins has compiled many poems that beginning readers can read easily. (**I:** 5–9)

Lobel, Arnold. *Frog and Toad Are Friends.* New York: Harper & Row, 1970. Five short stories tell of the friendship between Frog and Toad. Sequels are *Frog and Toad Together* (1972) and *Frog and Toad All Year* (1976). (**I:** P–8)

———. *Owl at Home.* New York: Harper & Row, 1975. Five short stories tell about Owl's adventures. (**I:** P–8)

Marshall, Edward. *Four on the Shore.* Illustrated by James Marshall. New York: Dial, 1985. Four boys take turns telling each other ghost stories. (**I:** P–8)

———. *Fox and His Friends.* Illustrated by James Marshall. New York: Dial, 1982. In this humorous story, Fox wishes his tag-along sister would not be with him when he plays with his friends. Other stories about Fox are *Fox in Love* (1982), *Fox at School* (1983), *Fox on Wheels* (1983), *Fox All Week* (1984), and *Fox on the Job* (1988). (**I:** 6–8)

———. *Three by the Sea.* Illustrated by James Marshall. New York: Dial, 1981. Lolly, Spider, and Sam go to the seashore and try to outdo each other in telling the most interesting story. (**I:** 6–8)

Rylant, Cynthia. *Henry and Mudge: The First Book of Their Adventures.* Illustrated by Sucie Stevenson. New York: Simon & Schuster/Aladdin, 1987. A lonely boy named Henry finds companionship with a big dog named Mudge. Other stories about Henry and Mudge include *Henry and Mudge and the Happy Cat* (Bradbury, 1990), *Henry and Mudge and the Bedtime Thump* (1991), *Henry and Mudge and the Long Weekend* (1992). (**I:** 6–8)

———. *Mr. Putter and Tabby Pour the Tea.* Illustrated by Arthur Howard. New York: Harcourt, 1994. An elderly man goes to the animal shelter to get a pet cat. A related title is *Mr. Putter and Tabby Walk the Dog* (1994). (**I:** 6–8)

Seuss, Dr. *The Cat in the Hat.* New York: Random House, 1957. One rainy day, when two children are home alone, an entertaining cat comes and creates chaos and wild fun. The sequel is *The Cat in the Hat Comes Back* (1958). (**I:** P–8)

———. *Green Eggs and Ham.* New York: Random House, 1960. Sam-I-Am insists on a favorable response from the cat to his offering of green eggs and ham, but the cat remains persistent in refusing. (**I:** P–8)

———. *Hop on Pop.* New York: Random House, 1963. Words with short *o* sounds tell a humorous story of creatures hopping on Pop. Other Seuss titles are *One Fish, Two Fish, Red Fish, Blue Fish* (1960) and *Fox in Socks* (1965). (**I:** P–7)

Van Leeuwen, Jean. *Tales of Oliver Pig.* Illustrated by Arnold Lobel. New York: Dial, 1979. This is a collection of five short stories about a pig named Oliver. Related titles are *More Tales of Oliver Pig* (1981), *Oliver Pig at School* (Dial, 1990), and *Oliver and Amanda's Halloween* (1992). (**I:** P–8)

Wiseman, Bernard. *Morris Goes to School.* New York: Harper & Row, 1970. Morris the moose decides to go to school to learn to count. A sequel is *Morris Has a Cold* (Dodd, Mead, 1978). (**I:** P–8)

Predictable Books

Flack, Marjorie. *Ask Mr. Bear.* New York: Macmillan, 1960. A little boy asks various animals what he should give his mother for her birthday. (**I:** P–7)

Fox, Mem. *Hattie and the Fox.* New York: Bradbury, 1987. As Hattie the hen tries to warn the barnyard animals of danger, more and more of a fox is revealed in the bushes. (**I:** P–7)

Langstaff, John. *Oh, A-Hunting We Will Go.* Illustrated by Nancy Winslow Parker. New York: Macmillan, 1974. Rhyming couplets in this folksong tell of a group of children who go hunting and find various animals they place somewhere temporarily—for example, "We'll catch a goat, and put him in a boat, and then we'll let him go." (**I:** 5–8)

Martin, Bill, Jr. *Brown Bear, Brown Bear, What Do You See?* 1967. Illustrated by Eric Carle. New York: Holt, 1983. Patterned, repetitive language is used to introduce colors and animal names. (**I:** P–7)

Numeroff, Laura Joffe. *If You Give a Mouse a Cookie.* Illustrated by Felicia Bond. New York: Harper, 1985. A circular story of cause and effect, beginning and ending with a mouse and a cookie. A related title is *If You Give a Moose a Muffin.* (**I:** P–8)

Shaw, Charles G. *It Looked Like Spilt Milk*. New York: Harper, 1947. Patterned language describes various objects that can be seen in clouds. (**I:** P–7)

Shulevitz, Uri. *One Monday Morning*. New York: Macmillan, 1967. Repetitive text depicts visitors on one Monday morning (**I:** P–6)

Wood, Audrey. *The Napping House*. Illustrated by Don Wood. New York: Harcourt, 1984. It is nap time, and the little boy, his granny, and various animals are piled on the bed. One wakeful flea causes everyone to spring up from naptime. (**I:** P–7)

Picture Storybooks

Aardema, Verna. *Who's in Rabbit's House?* 1969. Illustrated by Leo and Diane Dillon. New York: Dial, 1977. Someone is inside Rabbit's house and won't let her in. (**I:** P–9)

Ackerman, Karen. *Song and Dance Man*. Illustrated by Stephen Gammell. New York: Knopf, 1988. Grandpa reminisces about the bygone days when he danced in vaudeville. (**I:** 6–8)

Alexander, Lloyd. *The Fortune Tellers*. Illustrated by Trina Schart Hyman. New York: Dutton, 1992. This story, set in Central Africa, tells of a fortune teller who gives advice. (**I:** 8–11)

Aliki. *A Medieval Feast*. New York: Harper & Row, 1983. Preparations for a medieval feast at an English manor house are described. (**I:** 7–10)

Allard, Harry. *Miss Nelson Is Missing!* Illustrated by James Marshall. Boston: Houghton Mifflin, 1977. The children behave badly, and their sweet teacher, Miss Nelson, disappears. She is replaced by Miss Viola Swamp, who is out to set the children straight. Sequels are *Miss Nelson Is Back* (1982) and *Miss Nelson Has a Field Day* (1985). (**I:** 6–9)

Allison, Beverly. *Effie*. Illustrated by Barbara Reid. New York: Scholastic, 1991. Effie is an ant whose loud voice comes in handy. (**I:** 6–9)

Babbitt, Natalie. *BUB: Or the Very Best Thing*. New York: HarperCollins, 1994. A King and Queen search for the very best thing they can do for their son, who tells them it is "bub"—love. (**I:** 7–10)

Baer, Gene. *Thump, Thump, Rat-a-Tat-Tat*. Illustrated by Lois Ehlert. New York: Harper & Row, 1989. Bold illustrations show a marching band getting louder and larger as it approaches and then becoming softer and smaller as it continues down the street. (**I:** P–7)

Baker, Jeannie. *Where the Forest Meets the Sea*. New York: Greenwillow, 1988. Exquisitely detailed collage illustrations show an Australian forest. (**I:** 6–9)

Baker, Keith. *Who Is the Beast?* New York: Harcourt, 1990. A tiger points out similarities between him and the other jungle animals to show why he is not to be feared. (**I:** P–7)

Bang, Molly. *Goose*. New York: Blue Sky/Scholastic, 1996. A goose egg rolls out of its nest, and the baby goose is adopted by a woodchuck family. (**I:** P–7)

Baylor, Byrd. *The Best Town in the World*. Illustrated by Ronald Himler. New York: Scribner's, 1983. Small-town life is pictured with nostalgia. (**I:** 7–10)

Bemelmans, Ludwig. *Madeline*. 1939. New York: Viking, 1977. Madeline lives in Paris with eleven other little girls in a big brick house. This book tells about her appendectomy. A sequel is *Madeline's Rescue* (Viking, 1951/1981). (**I:** 7–10)

Birdseye, Tom. *Air Mail to the Moon*. Illustrated by Stephen Gammell. New York: Holiday House, 1992. Ora Mae Cotton dreams of what she'll do with the money from the tooth fairy, but before the tooth fairy can come, Ora Mae discovers that her tooth is missing. She vows to send the thief "airmail" to the moon—when she shoves her hands into pants pocket and feels something hard. (**I:** 6–9)

———. *Soap! Soap! Don't Forget the Soap!: An Appalachian Folktale*. Illustrated by Andrew Glass. New York: Holiday House, 1993. A boy has trouble remembering his errand when he repeats what the people he meets along the way say to him. (**I:** 6–9)

Blos, Joan W. *Old Henry*. Illustrated by Stephen Gammell. New York: Morrow/Mulberry, 1987. Henry is misunderstood by his neighbors and sent away. (**I:** 6–9)

Brett, Jan. *Annie and the Wild Animals*. Boston: Houghton Mifflin, 1985. Annie's cat is missing, and Annie tries to befriend various wild animals. (**I:** P–8)

———. *The Mitten*. New York: Putnam 1989. Nicki's lost mitten provides snug shelter for various animals until a bear sneezes. (**I:** P–8)

Brown, Craig. *My Barn*. New York: Greenwillow, 1991. Barnyard animals and the sounds they make are featured in this book. (**I:** P–8)

Brown, Marc. *Arthur's Eyes*. Boston: Little, Brown, 1979. Arthur needs glasses and must learn to cope with the teasing of others and adjust to wearing glasses. Eventually he is pleased to have new glasses. There are many other books about Arthur, his friends, and his sister, D.W. (**I:** 6–8)

Brown, Marcia. *Once a Mouse*. New York: Scribner's, 1961. This fable from India is illustrated with woodcuts. (**I:** 6–9)

Brown, Marcia, translator and illustrator. *Shadow*. New York: Macmillan, 1982. Brown's translation of a poem by a French poet Blaise Cendrars is about a dancing image, Shadow, that rises from ashes, brought to life by African storytellers. (**I:** 7–9)

Brown, Margaret Wise. *Goodnight Moon.* Illustrated by Clement Hurd. New York: Harper, 1947. A young rabbit says good night to various objects in the room and outside the window. (**I:** P)

Bunting, Eve. *Smoky Night.* Illustrated by David Diaz. San Diego, CA: Harcourt, 1994. The Los Angeles riots provided the impetus for the creation of this book. Families learn about acceptance and being good neighbors in order to survive difficult times. (**I:** 9–11)

———. *The Wednesday Surprise.* Illustrated by Donald Carrick. New York: Clarion, 1989. Every Wednesday, a seven-year-old girl and her grandmother practice reading and then surprise the family on Dad's birthday. (**I:** 6–9)

Burleigh, Robert. *Flight.* Illustrated by Mike Wimmer. New York: Philomel, 1991. Charles Lindbergh's 1927 nonstop solo flight from New York to Paris is described in this book. (**I:** 6–9)

Burningham, John. *Come Away from the Water, Shirley.* New York: Crowell, 1977. There are two stories in this family's trip to the beach: one is Shirley's daydreaming about pirate ships and gangplanks; the other is about the actual events and the parental warnings about how to behave at the beach. (**I:** P–8)

———. *Mr. Gumpy's Outing.* New York: Harper, 1976. Mr. Gumpy meets many animals that ask to go along on his boat outing. A related title is *Mr. Gumpy's Motor Car* (1976). (**I:** P–6)

Burton, Virginia Lee. *The Little House.* 1942. Boston: Houghton Mifflin, 1978. A house that was built in the countryside finds that as the years go by, it is becoming run down and is being surrounded by a city. (**I:** P–7)

———. *Mike Mulligan and His Steam Shovel.* Boston: Houghton Mifflin, 1939. Mike Mulligan and his steam shovel, Mary Anne, prove that they can dig more in one day than one hundred men can dig in a week. (**I:** P–7)

Carle, Eric. *The Grouchy Ladybug.* New York: Scholastic, 1977. Each hour of the day, a grouchy ladybug asks increasingly larger creatures if they want to fight. Ultimately, the ladybug learns a lesson. (**I:** P–7)

———. *A House for Hermit Crab.* Natick, MA: Picture Book Studio, 1987. A hermit crab outgrows its shell and seeks a larger home. (**I:** P–7)

———. *Rooster's Off to See the World.* Natick, MA: Picture Book Studio, 1972. A rooster sets off to see the world. In this book featuring mathematical concepts of addition and subtraction, Rooster is joined by others who return home when it gets dark. (**I:** P–7)

———. *The Secret Birthday Message.* New York: Harper & Row, 1986. A little boy receives a letter with a coded set of directions on how to find his birthday present. (**I:** P–7)

———. *The Tiny Seed.* Natick, MA: Picture Book Studio, 1991. In autumn, many seeds blow high in the wind and encounter various perils, but a surviving tiny seed grows into a flower. (**I:** P–7)

———. *Today Is Monday.* New York: Putnam, 1992. The illustrations for this familiar song about eating different kinds of food on each day of the week depict animals bringing foods to hungry children. (**I:** P–6)

———. *The Very Hungry Caterpillar.* New York: Philomel, 1981. A little caterpillar eats "holes" through the food on the pages, and the cycle of metamorphosis is explained when it emerges from a cocoon as a butterfly. (**I:** P–7)

———. *The Very Lonely Firefly.* New York: Philomel, 1995. A firefly is lonely and seeks company until it finds a group of fireflies. (**I:** P–7)

———. *The Very Quiet Cricket.* New York: Philomel, 1990. A quiet cricket learns to chirp upon meeting a friend. A computer chip in the book makes the sound. (**I:** P–7)

Carlstrom, Nancy White. *Jesse Bear, What Will You Wear?* Illustrated by Bruce Degen. New York: Macmillan, 1986. Rhythmic text of mother and Jesse Bear talking about what he will wear today. (**I:** P–6)

———. *Northern Lullaby.* Illustrated by Diane and Leo Dillon. New York: Putnam, 1992. A Native American voice bids goodnight to nature. (**I:** P–7)

Cherry, Lynne. *The Great Kapok Tree: A Tale of the Amazon Rain Forest.* New York: Harcourt, 1990. When a man takes a nap before cutting down the great kapok tree in the rain forest, the animals that depend on the tree for their survival appear in a dream and convince him not to chop down the tree. (**I:** 6–9)

Chetwin, Grace. *Box and Cox.* Illustrated by David Small. New York: Bradbury, 1990. A landlady tries to collect rent twice by renting a room out to two different boarders—one who works during the day and another who works at night—while trying to keep her scheme a secret from the two boarders. (**I:** 6–9)

Cole, Joanna. *The Magic School Bus on the Ocean Floor*. Illustrated by Bruce Degen. New York: Scholastic, 1992. In *The Magic School Bus* series, Ms. Frizzle takes her class on many field trips on the magic school bus. This time, they go to the ocean floor and explore ocean life there. (I: 6–8)

Conrad, Pam. *The Lost Sailor*. Illustrated by Richard Egielski. New York: HarperCollins, 1992. A sailor is shipwrecked on an island. When his makeshift home and all of his provisions are lost in a fire, his loss proves instead to be his good fortune. (I: 6–9)

Cowley, Joy. *Gracias the Thanksgiving Turkey*. Illustrated by Joe Cepeda. New York: Scholastic, 1996. Miguel becomes attached to the turkey that his father has sent home to be fattened up for Thanksgiving. (I: 6–9)

Cox, David. *Bossyboots*. New York: Crown, 1985. Abigail is bossy, and this makes her stagecoach companions angry. When an outlaw holds up the stagecoach, Abigail's bossy habits prove to be useful. (I: 6–9)

Cuyler, Margery. *That's Good! That's Bad!* Illustrated by David Catrow. New York: Holt, 1991. In alternating courses of good luck and bad luck, a little boy's balloon starts him on an adventure. (I: P–7)

de Brunhoff, Jean. *The Story of Babar*. 1933. New York: Random House, 1961. Babar becomes the king of the elephants. (I: P–7)

de Paola, Tomie. *The Cloud Book*. New York: Holiday House, 1975. This book describes the ten most common types of clouds and tells how weather predictions can be made by examining clouds. Also included are myths about cloud types. (I: 6–9)

———. *Strega Nona*. New York: Simon & Schuster, 1979. "Grandma Witch" hires a helper, Big Anthony, who thinks that he has found the secret of how to make the magic pot cook pasta. What he doesn't know is how to make it stop. Sequels are *Big Anthony and the Magic Ring* (1979), *Strega Nona's Magic Lessons* (1982), *Merry Christmas, Strega Nona* (1986), *Strega Nona Meets Her Match* (1993), and *Strega Nona: Her Story* (1996). (I: P–7)

Dupasquier, Philippe. *Dear Daddy*. New York: Puffin, 1988. A little girl's daily activities are depicted alongside the daily activities of her father, who is away at sea. (I: 6–8)

Duvoisin, Roger. *Petunia*. New York: Knopf, 1950. Petunia is a silly goose who thinks that all she has to do is carry a book in order to gain wisdom. (I: P–7)

Ehlert, Lois. *Feathers for Lunch*. New York: Harcourt, 1990. A housecat hopes to catch one of the birds in the backyard for lunch, but all get away safely and the cat ends up with only feathers. Bird descriptions are included. (I: P–7)

———. *Growing Vegetable Soup*. New York: Harcourt, 1987. Father and child plant seeds and sprouts and grow the vegetables that make a soup. A related title is *Planting a Rainbow* (1988). (I: P–5)

———. *Mole's Hill*. New York: Harcourt, 1994. A mole must think quickly in order to save his hill. (I: P–7)

———. *Moon Rope/Un lazo a la luna*. Translated into Spanish by Amy Prince. New York: Harcourt, 1992. This adaptation of a Peruvian folktale tells how Fox and Mole try to climb to the moon on a rope made of woven grass. (I: 6–9)

———. *Nuts to You!* New York: Harcourt, 1993. A squirrel gets into a city apartment, and the residents devise a plan to get it out. (I: P–7)

———. *Red Leaf, Yellow Leaf*. New York: Harcourt, 1991. The life cycle of a maple tree is shown through collage illustrations. (I: P–7)

———. *Snowballs*. New York: Harcourt, 1995. Children create a snow family, using a large variety of items they had saved—a luggage tag, a toy fish, popcorn, etc. (I: P–6)

Emberley, Barbara. *Drummer Hoff*. Illustrated by Ed Emberley. New York: Simon & Schuster, 1967. The story of how a cannon is fired is told through rhyming couplets in cumulative text. (I: 5–8)

Ericsson, Jennifer A. *No Milk!* Illustrated by Ora Eitan. New York: Tambourine, 1993. This is a humorous story, told in simple text, of a boy's attempt to milk a cow. (I: P–7)

Ernst, Lisa Campbell. *When Bluebell Sang*. New York: Macmillan, 1989. Bluebell is a cow who leads a peaceful life in the meadows until one day, fame takes her on the road and under the spotlights. (I: 5–8)

———. *Zinnia and Dot*. New York: Viking Penguin, 1992. Zinnia and Dot are two hens full of pride. When a weasel steals their eggs, they must learn to cooperate in order to save the one egg that is left behind. (I: 6–9)

Fleischman, Paul. *Rondo in C*. Illustrated by Janet Wentworth. New York: Harper & Row, 1988. During a piano student's recital performance of Rondo in C, the listeners are each reminded of experiences in their own past. (I: 6–8)

Fleming, Denise. *In the Small, Small Pond*. New York: Holt, 1993. Pond life is depicted with vividly colored illustrations. (I: P–6)

———. *In the Tall, Tall Grass*. New York: Holt, 1991. A young child finds a variety of creatures in the tall,

tall grass and describes their movements with rhyming, poetic text. (I: P–6)

———. *Lunch*. New York: Holt, 1992. A hungry mouse finds lunch, and readers are introduced to foods and colors. (I: P–6)

———. *Where Once There Was a Wood*. New York: Holt, 1996. Many kinds of wildlife lose their homes when housing developments are constructed. Endnotes invite readers to take action in creating wildlife habitats in their backyards and communities. (I: P–8)

Fleming, Virginia. *Be Good to Eddie Lee*. Illustrated by Floyd Cooper. New York: Philomel, 1993. Eddie Lee, a boy with Down syndrome, is considered a tag-along pest. But when he follows Christy into the woods, he is able to show her some special discoveries. (I: 6–9)

Flournoy, Valerie. *The Patchwork Quilt*. Illustrated by Jerry Pinkney. New York: Dial, 1985. Creating a quilt leads to collecting many family memories. (I: 6–9)

Fox, Mem. *Hattie and the Fox*. Illustrated by Patricia Mullins. New York: Bradbury, 1987. Hattie the hen tries to warn farm animals about the fox she sees in the bushes. (I: P–7)

———. *Koala Lou*. Illustrated by Pamela Lofts. New York: Harcourt, 1988. Koala Lou longs for the days before the other children came along, when her mother used to tell Koala Lou how much she loved her. Koala Lou enters a race in her attempt to win her mother's affections again. (I: P–7)

———. *Night Noises*. Illustrated by Terry Denton. New York: Harcourt, 1989. Lily Laceby, rumored to be ninety, dozes and dreams in her chair of years gone by. Her dog, Butch Aggie, hears strange noises outside—lots of relatives arriving for a surprise party! (I: P–7)

———. *Possum Magic*. Illustrated by Julie Vivas. New York: Harcourt, 1990. Grandma Poss turns Hush invisible and Hush enjoys many adventures because she can't be seen. But later, Grandma Poss and Hush must travel throughout Australian cities, eating Australian foods, in an attempt to remember the magic to make Hush visible again. (I: P–7)

———. *Wilfrid Gordon McDonald Partridge*. Illustrated by Julie Vivas. Brooklyn, NY: Kane/Miller, 1985. Wilfrid Gordon McDonald Partridge is worried because everyone is talking about Miss Nancy's lost memory. In his attempt to find out what "memory" is, he restores Miss Nancy's memory in an unusual way. (I: 6–9)

Gág, Wanda. *Millions of Cats*. New York: Coward, McCann, 1929. When a lonely old man cannot choose among hundreds of cats, thousands of cats, millions and billions and trillions of cats, the cats fight it out as each claims to be the prettiest. (I: P–7)

Gauch, Patricia Lee. *Christina Katerina and the Time She Quit the Family*. Illustrated by Elise Primavera. New York: Putnam, 1987. Christina Katerina decides to "quit" her family so that she can do things her own way. She discovers that being part of a family isn't so bad, after all. A sequel is *Christina Katerina and the Great Bear Train* (1990). (I: 6–9)

———. *Dance, Tanya*. Illustrated by Satomi Ichikawa. New York: Philomel, 1989. Tanya longs to be able to dance ballet on stage when she grows up. (I: P–7)

Ginsburg, Mirra. *Across the Stream*. Illustrated by Nancy Tafuri. New York: Greenwillow, 1982. A bad dream threatens a hen and her chicks, and they are saved by a duck and her ducklings. (I: P)

———. *Asleep, Asleep*. Illustrated by Nancy Tafuri. New York: Greenwillow, 1992. A mother tells her child about all that is asleep in nature, except the baby and the wind. (I: P)

Giovanni, Nikki. *The Genie in the Jar*. Illustrated by Chris Raschka. New York: Holt, 1996. A child's pursuit of dreams is supported by her family and community through metaphor-filled poetic text. (I: P–7)

Goble, Paul. *The Girl Who Loved Wild Horses*. New York: Macmillan, 1978. A girl finds that she communes with horses more easily than she does with her people and goes to join the wild horses. (I: P–7)

Greenfield, Eloise. *Grandpa's Face*. Illustrated by Floyd Cooper. New York: Philomel, 1988. A little girl is worried about losing her Grandfather's love when she sees her Grandfather making faces in the mirror. (I: 6–8)

———. *She Come Bringing Me That Little Baby Girl*. Illustrated by John Steptoe. New York: Harper, 1974. Keven had hoped for a baby brother. At first, he resents the attention that the baby sister is getting. (I: 5–7)

Griffith, Helen V. *Georgia Music*. Illustrated by James Stevenson. New York: Greenwillow, 1986. A grandfather and his granddaughter enjoy different types of music: his mouth organ and the birds and insects around his cabin. (I: 6–9)

Haley, Gail E. *A Story, a Story*. New York: Atheneum, 1970. This is an African tale in which Anansi the spider makes a bargain with the Sky God. (I: P–8)

Hall, Donald. *Ox-Cart Man*. Illustrated by Barbara Cooney. New York: Viking, 1979. In nineteenth-century New England, a family fills an ox cart with the extra things it has grown or made during the previous year. After everything in the cart is sold, the family purchases supplies and and goes through another year of growing things and making things to sell. (I: 6–8)

Henkes, Kevin. *Chester's Way*. New York: Greenwillow, 1988. Chester and Wilson, two inseparable friends, find room in their friendship for another when Lilly moves into the neighborhood and proves herself a true friend. (I: P–7)

———. *Chrysanthemum*. New York: Greenwillow, 1991. Chrysanthemum is pleased with her name until classmates tease her about it. With the help of the music teacher's affirmation, Chrysanthemum "blooms" as she regains pride in her name. (I: P–6)

———. *Julius, the Baby of the World*. New York: Greenwillow, 1990. Lilly cannot stand the attention showered on her new baby brother, Julius. She suddenly develops pride in him when a cousin makes unpleasant remarks about him. (I: P–8)

———. *Lilly's Purple Plastic Purse*. New York: Greenwillow, 1996. Lilly disrupts class to show off her new purple plastic purse and is devastated when Mr. Slinger, the teacher whom she idolizes, confiscates the purse until the end of the day. (I: P–8)

———. *Owen*. New York: Greenwillow, 1993. Owen is about to start school, and his nosy next-door neighbor is sure that there must be a way to get Owen to give up his security blanket. (I: P–7)

———. *Sheila Rae, the Brave*. New York: Greenwillow, 1987. Sheila Rae isn't afraid of anything, or so it seems, until she takes a wrong turn on the way home one day. It is little sister Louise—whom Sheila Rae refers to as the "scaredy cat"—who comes to the rescue. (I: P–6)

———. *A Weekend with Wendell*. New York: Greenwillow, 1987. Wendell is a weekend guest at Sophie's house, and he makes all the rules and demands they play by them. Sophie decides to stand up to Wendell's tyranny and makes him be the burning building while she plays the role of fire chief. (I: P–6)

Hoban, Russell. *A Baby Sister for Frances*. Illustrated by Lillian Hoban. New York: Harper & Row, 1964. Frances the badger tries to adjust to having a new baby sister around. A few of the other stories about Frances are *Bread and Jam for Frances* (1964), *Best Friends for Frances* (1969), and *A Bargain for Frances* (1970). (I: 6–8)

Hodges, Margaret. *St. George and the Dragon*. Illustrated by Trina Schart Hyman. Boston: Little, Brown, 1984. This adaptation of Edmund Spenser's *Faerie Queene* tells how the Red Cross Knight slays the dragon and ends its terrorizing of the English countryside. (I: 8–12)

Hoffman, Mary. *Amazing Grace*. New York: Dial, 1991. Illustrated by Caroline Binch. Grace has an amazing ability to act, but she is told by classmates that she cannot be Peter Pan in the class play because she is a girl and she is black. The sequel is *Boundless Grace* (1995). (I: P–7)

Hogrogian, Nonny. *One Fine Day*. New York: Macmillan, 1971. A thirsty fox drinks milk from an old woman's pail and she cuts off its tail. The woman will not return the tail until the fox returns her milk. Thus begins the circular tale in which the fox must ask for the help of many in order to retrieve its tail. Based on an Armenian folktale. (I: P–8)

Hort, Lenny. *The Boy Who Held Back the Sea*. Illustrated by Thomas Locker. New York: Dial, 1987. This is the story of a young, mischievous boy who saves his town from flooding by plugging a hole in the dike. (I: 7–9)

Houston, Gloria. *My Great-Aunt Arizona*. Illustrated by Susan Condie Lamb. New York: HarperCollins, 1992. A girl reflects on her great-aunt's teaching career in the Appalachian mountains. (I: 6–8)

———. *The Year of the Perfect Christmas Tree*. New York: Penguin, 1988. Set in Appalachia, this is the story of how Ruthie and her mother try to fulfill Papa's obligation to get the perfect Christmas tree to the town during his wartime absence. (I: 6–9)

Hughes, Shirley. *Alfie Gives a Hand*. New York: Lothrop, 1983. Alfie lends a helping hand to a friend and discovers that his security blanket is no longer a necessity. (I: P–6)

———. *Dogger*. 1977. New York: Lothrop, 1988. A favorite stuffed dog is missing, and the loss creates agony for the owner. (I: P–8)

Hutchins, Pat. *The Doorbell Rang*. New York: Greenwillow, 1986. Ma has baked cookies for Victoria and Sam, but every time the doorbell rings, more friends join them and there are fewer cookies to go around. (I: P–7)

———. *Tidy Titch*. New York: Greenwillow, 1991. Titch is supposedly helping his older brother and sister clean their rooms—but then, what does Titch's room look like? (I: P–7)

———. *The Wind Blew*. New York: Macmillan, 1974. When the wind blows, everyone loses something! The surprise is what they get back when the wind stops. (I: P–6)

———. *You'll Soon Grow into Them, Titch*. New York: Greenwillow, 1983. Titch is always getting his older siblings' hand-me-down clothes. (I: P–7)

Hyman, Trina Schart. *Little Red Riding Hood*. New York: Holiday House, 1983. The familiar tale of a little girl who is sent to visit her sick grandmother is illustrated with beautiful paintings in this Caldecott-winning version. (**I:** 6–9)

Innocenti, Roberto. *Rose Blanche*. New York: Stewart, Tabori & Chang, 1985. A young girl visits a German concentration camp with small gifts of food. (**I:** 9 and up)

Isaacs, Anne. *Swamp Angel*. New York: Dutton, 1994. Illustrated by Paul Zelinsky. A tall tale about a bear-wrestling heroine who helps settlers in Tennessee. (**I:** 6–9)

Isadora, Rachel. *Ben's Trumpet*. Greenwillow, 1979. Ben wants to learn to play a trumpet, and a night-club owner helps him realize his dream. (**I:** 6–9)

James, Simon. *Dear Mr. Blueberry*. New York: Macmillan, 1991. A little girl writes letters to Mr. Blueberry, telling him about the whale she insists lives in the pool in her yard. (**I:** P–6)

Johnson, Crockett. *Harold and the Purple Crayon*. New York: Harper & Row, 1958. Harold goes on a walk, drawing pictures with his purple crayon that create an adventure. Three sequels are *Harold's Trip to the Sky* (1957), *Harold's Circus* (1959), and *A Picture for Harold's Room* (1960). (**I:** P–7)

Johnston, Tony. *The Wagon*. Illustrated by James E. Ransome. New York: Tambourine/Morrow, 1996. A boy born into slavery builds a wagon for his master, imagining that it is the glorious chariot of freedom in the song "Swing Low, Sweet Chariot." (**I:** 6–9)

Jonas, Ann. *Round Trip*. New York: Greenwillow, 1983. The journey begins at dawn in a quiet neighborhood and passes through the countryside on the way to the city. Then readers turn the book upside down and see what the illustrations depict when viewed from the opposite direction, completing a round trip back to the neighborhood. (**I:** P–9)

Jorgensen, Gail. *Crocodile Beat*. Illustrated by Patricia Mullins. New York: Bradbury, 1989. Rhythmic, rhyming text tells of animals playing by the riverbank. When Crocodile awakens intending to have the animals for lunch, Lion puts an end to the crocodile's plan. (**I:** P–6)

Kasza, Keiko. *A Mother for Choco*. New York: Putnam, 1992. Choco goes in search of mother, only to find that nobody looks like he does. Instead, he meets a mother who asks what a mother would *do*. (**I:** P–7)

———. *The Rat and the Tiger*. New York: Putnam, 1993. Tiger always bullies his small friend Rat until one day, Rat decides to turn the tables. (**I:** P–7)

———. *Wolf's Chicken Stew*. New York: Putnam, 1987. Wolf is very hungry for chicken stew and finds the perfect chicken. While attempting to fatten her up, Wolf is surprised. (**I:** P–7)

Keats, Ezra Jack. *Goggles!* New York: Macmillan, 1969. Archie and Willie are met by bullies and must think quickly in order to return home safely. (**I:** P–7)

———. *A Letter to Amy*. New York: Harper & Row, 1968. Peter sends his friend Amy an invitation to a party. (**I:** P–8)

———. *Maggie and the Pirate*. 1979. New York: Macmillan, 1987. A "pirate" steals Maggie's pet cricket, Niki, and the cricket cage Maggie's father made. (**I:** 6–8)

———. *Peter's Chair*. New York: Harper, 1967. Peter is jealous of his new baby sister and refuses to give her his chair until he discovers that he has outgrown it. (**I:** P–7)

———. *Regards to the Man in the Moon*. New York: Four Winds, 1981. Two children find junk to build their spaceship. (**I:** P–8)

———. *The Snowy Day*. New York: Viking, 1962. Peter plays outside following a big snowfall. (**I:** P–7)

Keller, Holly. *Furry*. New York: Greenwillow, 1992. Laura wants a pet, but she is allergic to all things furry. (**I:** P–8)

———. *Harry and Tuck*. New York: Greenwillow, 1993. Harrison and Tucker are twins and do everything alike and together. When they are placed in different kindergarten classes, they begin to gain a sense of independence. (**I:** P–6)

Kellogg, Steven. *A Rose for Pinkerton*. New York: Dial, 1981. A family's Great Dane and a kitten are intended to be friends. (**I:** 6–9)

Kraus, Robert. *Leo the Late Bloomer*. Illustrated by Jose Aruego. New York: Windmill, 1971. Father tiger is anxious as his young son, Leo, seems unable to do anything yet. But in time, Leo finds that he has developed at his own rate. (**I:** P–6)

Leaf, Munro. *The Story of Ferdinand*. Illustrated by Robert Lawson. New York: Viking, 1936. Ferdinand grows to be a big strong bull, but he is only interested in sitting and smelling flowers. When he accidentally sits on a bumble bee, his resulting behavior causes him to be chosen for the bull fights in Madrid. (**I:** P–9)

Lionni, Leo. *Alexander and the Wind-Up Mouse*. New York: Knopf, 1969. Whenever Alexander, a real mouse, appears in Annie's house, he is unwelcome. Alexander wishes he could be like Willie, the wind-up toy mouse, who is loved and played with. (**I:** P–7)

———. *Frederick*. New York: Knopf, 1967. The field mice work hard to prepare for winter, and it appears that Frederick is shirking his responsibilities. However, when winter comes, he is able to entertain the other mice with his poems describing the warmth of the sun and the colors of the flowers. A sequel is *Frederick and His Friends* (1981). (**I:** P–7)

———. *Inch by Inch.* New York: Astor-Honor, 1962. In order to avoid being eaten by the birds who hold him captive, an inchworm cleverly sets off to measure the length of a nightingale's song. (**I:** P–7)

———. *Let's Make Rabbits: A Fable.* New York: Knopf, 1992. A pencil and a pair of scissors use wrapping paper to make two rabbits. (**I:** P–6)

———. *Little Blue and Little Yellow.* New York: Astor-Honor. 1959. Abstract shapes depict members of the blue family and the yellow family. When their children play and hug, they turn green. (**I:** P–6)

———. *Matthew's Dream.* New York: Knopf, 1991. Matthew lives in an attic without much decor. A trip to the art museum results in Matthew's having a dream and realizing that he wants to become an artist. (**I:** P–8)

———. *Six Crows.* New York: Knopf, 1988. Misunderstandings between a farmer and the crows are not cleared up until an owl steps in to arbitrate. (**I:** 6–8)

———. *Swimmy.* New York: Pantheon, 1963. A little fish comes up with a clever plan to protect the small fish in the school from being eaten by larger fish: They swim together in the formation of a giant fish. (**I:** P–7)

Lobel, Arnold. *Fables.* New York: Harper & Row, 1980. This collection has many fables told in the style of Aesop. (**I:** 7–9)

———. *The Rose in My Garden.* New York: Greenwillow, 1984. Illustrated by Anita Lobel. Cumulative text tells the story of a bee asleep on a rose in the garden—until a cat chases a mouse through the garden. (**I:** P–8)

Louie, Ai-Ling. *Yeh-Shen: A Cinderella Story from China.* Illustrated by Ed Young. New York: Putnam, 1982. This is a Chinese version of the Cinderella story. (**I:** 7–11)

Lyon, George Ella. *Come a Tide.* Illustrated by Stephen Gammell. New York: Orchard, 1990. High flood waters cause problems for a family. (**I:** P–8)

Macaulay, David. *Black and White.* Boston: Houghton, 1990. Here are four separate stories—or one intertwined story—about children, parents, trains, and cows. (**I:** 8–12)

———. *Why the Chicken Crossed the Road.* Boston: Houghton, 1987. This is a cause-and-effect story that starts and ends with a chicken crossing the road. (**I:** P–9)

Mahy, Margaret. *17 Kings and the 42 Elephants.* Illustrated by Patricia MacCarthy. New York: Dial, 1987. Rhythmic, rhyming text tells of kings and elephants romping through the jungle. Illustrations are silk batik. (**I:** P–8)

Marshall, James. *George and Martha.* Boston: Houghton, 1972. George and Martha are two hippos who share a fun-filled day. Other titles are *George and Martha Encore* (1973), *George and Martha Rise and Shine* (1976), *George and Martha One Fine Day* (1978), *George and Martha Back in Town* (1984), and *George and Martha 'Round and 'Round* (1988). (**I:** P–8)

———. *Hansel and Gretel.* New York: Dial, 1990. The well-known story of two children who are abandoned in the forest and who outsmart and escape from an evil witch is depicted with illustrations that are more light-hearted and humorous than those in many other versions. (**I:** 6–8)

Martin, Bill, Jr., and John Archambault. *The Ghost-Eye Tree.* Illustrated by Ted Rand. New York: Holt, 1985. When a brother and sister are sent to fetch a pail of milk one dark and spooky night, their imaginations run wild as they hurry past the Ghost-Eye Tree. (**I:** P–8)

———. *Up and Down on the Merry-Go-Round.* Illustrated by Ted Rand. New York: Holt, 1985. Rhythmic, rhyming text describes a delightful ride on a merry-go-round and all that can be seen from it. (**I:** P–6)

Martin, Rafe. *Will's Mammoth.* Illustrated by Stephen Gammell. New York: Putnam, 1989. While playing in the snow one day, a little boy lets his imagination take off. (**I:** P–8)

Maruki, Toshi. *Hiroshima No Pika.* New York: Lothrop, 1982. Expressionistic illustrations accompany the story that describes what happens to a family after the atomic bombing of Hiroshima in August 1945. (**I:** 10 and up)

Mayer, Mercer. *There's a Nightmare in My Closet.* New York: Dial, 1969. A boy is sure there is a nightmare living in his closet, but decides that he must confront the monster. (**I:** P–7)

McCloskey, Robert. *Blueberries for Sal.* New York: Viking, 1948. A little girl goes blueberry picking with her mother and a little bear follows its mother—but the two children get their mothers mixed up! (**I:** P–7)

———. *Make Way for Ducklings.* New York: Viking, 1941. Mr. and Mrs. Mallard set off in search of a perfect place to raise their family. They find that the

Boston Public Garden provides just the right home. (**I:** P–8)

———. *Time of Wonder*. New York: Viking, 1957. A family that lives on an island in Maine deals with a summer hurricane. (**I:** P–9)

McCully, Emily Arnold. *Mirette on the High Wire*. New York: Putnam, 1992. When a formerly great tightrope artist becomes fearful of walking the rope, it is a little girl, Mirette, who must help him overcome his fears. (**I:** 6–9)

McLerran, Alice. *Roxaboxen*. Illustrated by Barbara Cooney. New York: Lothrop, 1991. Marian and her sisters enjoy imaginary play with their friends as they create a community out of rocks on a hill. (**I:** 6–9)

McPhail, David. *Fix-It*. New York: Dutton, 1984. Emma Bear is distressed to find that the television won't turn on, until Mother Bear reads her a good book. (**I:** P–6)

———. *Pigs Aplenty, Pigs Galore!* New York: Dutton, 1993. Late one night, a man is reading when he discovers "pigs aplenty, pigs galore" in his house. More and more pigs arrive, wearing outrageous costumes and creating havoc. (**I:** P–8)

Meddaugh, Susan. *Hog-Eye*. Boston: Houghton, 1995. When the family demands an explanation for why little piggy missed school one day, she launches into a wild story of how she got on the wrong bus. She took a short cut through the forest, met a wolf who tied her up and made her teach him how to make soup. The piggy tells how she outwitted the wolf through the magic of "Hog-Eye." (**I:** 6–9)

———. *Martha Speaks*. Boston: Houghton, 1992. Martha the dog is able to speak after eating alphabet soup. Her family is thrilled to be able to communicate with her verbally and hear her thoughts on various subjects. Sequels are *Martha Calling* (1994), and *Martha Blah Blah* (1996). (**I:** 6–9)

Melmed, Laura Krass. *The First Song Ever Sung*. Illustrated by Ed Young. New York: Lothrop, 1993. When a Japanese boy repeatedly asks a question about the first song ever sung, different people and animals give their responses. (**I:** 6–8)

Merrill, Jean. *The Girl Who Loved Caterpillars: A Twelfth-Century Tale from Japan*. Illustrated by Floyd Cooper. New York: Putnam, 1992. Izumi is not interested in the traditional feminine arts as is expected of a Japanese woman of her background. Instead, she prefers to study caterpillars and prefers the company of boys who play with insects over that of nobleman who send her expensive gifts. (**I:** 10–14)

Moser, Madeline. *Ever Heard of an Aardwolf? A Miscellany of Uncommon Animals*. Illustrated by Barry Moser. New York: Harcourt, 1996. Twenty unusual animals such as the aardwolf, the loris, the pangolin, the viscacha, and the solenodon are introduced in a brief paragraph about each animal, and an appendix gives more detailed information. Illustrations are synthetic wood engravings. (**I:** 6–9)

Moss, Lloyd. *Zin! Zin! Zin! a Violin*. Illustrated by Marjorie Priceman. New York: Simon & Schuster, 1995. A trombone begins playing solo and is joined by the trumpet, french horn, cello, violin, flute, clarinet, oboe, bassoon, and harp. (**I:** P–8)

Most, Bernard. *My Very Own Octopus*. New York: Harcourt, 1980. A boy imagines all the fun he would have if only he had his very own octopus. (**I:** 6–8)

Narahashi, Keiko. *I Have a Friend*. New York: Macmillan, 1987. A little boy talks about his friend who goes everywhere with him—his shadow. (**I:** P–7)

Ness, Evaline. *Sam, Bangs and Moonshine*. New York: Holt, 1966. Sam always tells stories that her father calls "moonshine." One day, Sam's moonshine almost takes her friend Thomas's life. (**I:** 6–9)

Noble, Trinka Hakes. *The Day Jimmy's Boa Ate the Wash*. Illustrated by Steven Kellogg. New York: Dial, 1980. A little girl tells her mother an outrageous story of her class field trip to the farm in reverse cause-and-effect order. A sequel is *Jimmy's Boa Bounces Back* (1984). (**I:** 6–9)

Oakley, Graham. *The Church Mouse*. New York: Macmillan, 1972. This book begins a series of humorous stories of Arthur, a church mouse, and Samson, the church cat. Sequels are *The Church Mice and the Moon* (1974), *The Church Mice Spread Their Wings* (1976), and *The Church Mice in Action* (1983). (**I:** 7–9)

Oliver, Narelle. *The Best Beak in Boonaroo Bay*. Golden, CO: Fulcrum, 1995. In Australia's Boonaroo Bay, the birds try to decide whose beak is the best by holding a contest. (**I:** P–8)

Paxton, Tom. *Engelbert the Elephant*. Illustrated by Steven Kellogg. New York: Morrow, 1990. Everyone at the royal ball is surprised at Engelbert the Elephant's dancing skills. (**I:** P–8)

Peet, Bill. *Big Bad Bruce*. Boston: Houghton, 1977. Bruce has fun rolling boulders down the hill and scaring the small creatures of Forevergreen Forest. When he almost hits Roxy, a little fox who is a witch, Bruce is in for a surprise. (**I:** P–8)

Perrault, Charles. *Cinderella*. Illustrated by Marcia Brown. New York: Scribner's, 1954. This familiar French fairy tale has Caldecott-winning watercolor illustrations. (**I:** 6–9)

———. *Puss in Boots*. 1958. Illustrated by Hans Fischer. Translated by Anthea Bell. New York: North-South Books, 1996. This is the familiar tale of a clever cat that arranges for his poor master to marry into a royal family. The illustrations are lithographs. (I: 6–9)

———. *Puss in Boots*. Illustrated by Fred Marcellino. Translated by Malcolm Arthur. New York: Farrar, 1990. A miller's youngest son's inheritance is only a cat, but the cat proves to be clever and orchestrates a plan for his master to become the groom of the princess. (I: 6–9)

Pilkey, Dav. *The Paperboy*. New York: Orchard, 1996. Readers get a sense of ritual as a boy gets out of bed and begins his daily routine of delivering the newspaper. (I: P–8)

Pinkney, Gloria Jean. *Back Home*. Illustrated by Jerry Pinkney. New York: Dial, 1992. Eight-year-old Ernestine boards a train and goes to visit family members who still live on the farm in North Carolina where she was born. (I: 6–9)

Polacco, Patricia. *Applemando's Dreams*. New York: Philomel, 1991. Appelemando's dreams are vivid and entertaining, but only the children appreciate them at first. (I: 6–9)

———. *Babushka Baba Yaga*. New York: Philomel, 1990. Baba Yaga loves children, but disguises herself as a Babushka so the villagers won't be afraid of her. (I: 6–10)

———. *The Bee Tree*. New York: Philomel, 1993. A grandfather leads his daughter on a search for a bee tree. (I: 6–9)

———. *Thunder Cake*. New York: Philomel, 1993. Grandmother helps her granddaughter overcome her fear of thunder. (I: 6–9)

Potter, Beatrix. *The Tale of Peter Rabbit*. 1902. New York: Warne, 1986. This is the story of Peter, a naughty rabbit who disobeys his mother and ends up caught in Mr. McGregor's garden. (I: P–8)

Price, Leontyne. *Aida*. Illustrated by Leo Dillon and Diane Dillon. New York: Harcourt, 1990. This book tells the opera's famous love story in which a couple is united but the price is death. (I: 9–14)

Ransome, Arthur. *The Fool of the World and the Flying Ship*. Illustrated by Uri Shulevitz. New York: Farrar, 1968. A Russian boy of poor background marries the czar's daughter. (I: 7–10)

Raschka, Chris. *Yo! Yes?* New York: Orchard, 1993. Two boys use expressive body language to communicate. One is lonely, the other offers to be his friend. (I: P–8)

Rathmann, Peggy. *Officer Buckle and Gloria*. New York: Putnam, 1995. Officer Buckle makes school rounds, giving safety tips to children. His dog, Gloria, pantomimes the safety tips and is the one who actually keeps the children amused. (I: 6–9)

Rey, H. A. *Curious George*. Boston: Houghton, 1941. George is a monkey who leaves the jungle with the man with a yellow hat. His mischievousness and curiosity get him into trouble. There are other books about George: *Curious George Takes a Job* (1947), *Curious George Rides a Bike* (1952), *Curious George Gets a Medal* (1957); *Curious George Flies a Kite* (1973) and *Curious George Goes to the Hospital* (1973) were written by H. A. Rey's wife, Margaret Rey. (I: P–8)

Rosen, Michael. *We're Going on a Bear Hunt*. Illustrated by Helen Oxenbury. New York: Macmillan, 1989. A father takes his children on an imaginary bear hunt. They bravely go through various obstacles until they encounter the bear and make a mad dash home. Alternating full color and black-and-white illustrations depict what part of the story actually happens and what part is imagination. (I: P–6)

Rylant, Cynthia. *Mr. Griggs' Work*. Illustrated by Julie Downing. New York: Orchard, 1989. Mr. Griggs is a postal worker who loves his work so much that he cannot stop thinking about it. When he becomes ill, he cannot imagine that someone else is working at the post office in his place. (I: 6–8)

———. *When I Was Young in the Mountains*. Illustrated by Diane Goode. New York: Dutton, 1982. Through poetic text that repeatedly begins "When I was young in the mountains," the narrator reminisces about her childhood in the Appalachian mountains. (I: 6–9)

San Souci, Robert D. *The Faithful Friend*. Illustrated by Brian Pinkney. New York: Simon & Schuster, 1995. This is a retelling of a folktale from the Caribbean island of Martinique. The close bonds of friendship between Clement and Hippolyte break the spell cast by Monsieur Zabocat, a wizard, who opposes the marriage of his niece, Pauline, to Clement. (I: 7–10)

———. *Sukey and the Mermaid*. Illustrated by Brian Pinkney. New York: Four Winds, 1992. Sukey lives on an island off the coast of South Carolina. When she runs to her secret hiding place by the sea to escape from the hard work imposed by her new step-pa, she meets a black mermaid named Mama Jo, who changes her life forever. (I: 6–9)

Say, Allen. *Emma's Rug*. Boston: Houghton Mifflin, 1996. Emma learns that inspiration for art is in the world all around her and that she does not have to rely on the images she "sees" in her special rug. (I: 6–9)

————. *Grandfather's Journey*. Boston: Houghton, 1993. Say tells his own grandfather's story and expresses their mutual love for both Japan and America. (**I**: 8–10)

————. *Tree of Cranes*. Boston: Houghton, 1991. A Japanese woman brings a small pine tree indoors, folds origami cranes to decorate it, and shares memories with her son of spending her childhood Christmases in America. (**I**: P–8)

Schafer, Carole Lexa. *The Squiggle*. Illustrated by Pierr Morgan. New York: Crown, 1996. On an outing with her class, a little girl finds a rope that she imagines to be part of a dragon, the Great Wall of China, and various other things. (**I**: P–7)

Schroeder, Alan. *Minty: A Story of Young Harriet Tubman*. Illustrated by Jerry Pinkney. New York: Dial, 1996. Throughout Harriet Tubman's childhood, she dreamed and planned of escaping from slavery. (**I**: 6–9)

Schwartz, Amy. *Annabelle Swift, Kindergartner*. New York: Orchard, 1988. Before the beginning of kindergarten, Annabelle's older sister gives tips on what to do at school. (**I**: P–6)

Sendak, Maurice. *In the Night Kitchen*. New York: Harper, 1970. Mickey awakens to the noise of the night kitchen and embarks on a fantastic trip in which he falls through the night, out of his clothes, and into the bread dough where he creates an airplane to fly into the Milky Way and get the milk the bakers need. (**I**: P–8)

————. *Where the Wild Things Are*. New York: Harper & Row, 1963. When he is punished and sent to bed without supper, Max sails off to an imaginary world where he is the king of the Wild Things. (**I**: P–8)

Seuss, Dr. *And to Think That I Saw It on Mulberry Street*. New York: Vanguard, 1937. A little boy imagines what would happen if the horse and cart he sees on his street were transformed into a circus bandwagon. (**I**: P–8)

————. *The Five Hundred Hats of Bartholomew Cubbins*. New York: Random House, 1938. When Bartholomew tries to remove his hat in order to show respect to the king, another hat appears in its place. (**I**: P–8)

————. *Horton Hatches the Egg*. 1940. New York: Random House, 1968. Mayzie the bird leaves for a vacation and leaves Horton the elephant to sit on her nest and tend her egg. (**I**: P–8)

Steig, William. *The Amazing Bone*. New York: Farrar, 1983. Pearl, a pig, finds a talking bone in the forest and picks it up to take home. When she encounters danger in the forest, the bone does amazing things to keep them safe. (**I**: 6–9)

————. *Doctor De Soto*. New York: Farrar, 1982. A fox with a toothache tries to get a mouse dentist to work on the tooth—but the fox also has other plans for the mouse. A related title is *Doctor De Soto Goes to Africa* (HarperCollins, 1992). (**I**: 6–9)

————. *Spinky Sulks*. New York: Farrar, 1988. Spinky sulks about everything, but circumstances change his attitude and behavior. (**I**: 6–9)

————. *Sylvester and the Magic Pebble*. New York: Simon & Schuster, 1969. When Sylvester, a donkey, makes a wish while holding an extraordinary rock and turns *himself* into a rock, he finds that he is unable to turn himself back into a donkey. (**I**: 6–9)

Steptoe, John. *Stevie*. New York: Harper, 1969. A small boy resents having to share his mother with a little boy who is temporarily staying with them, until he realizes that the little boy is "kinda like a brother." (**I**: P–7)

————. *The Story of Jumping Mouse: A Native American Legend*. New York: Lothrop, 1984. An unselfish mouse gives away what other animals need. Ultimately, the mouse is transformed into an eagle as a reward for its generosity. (**I**: 6–9)

Stevenson, James. *Could Be Worse!* New York: Greenwillow, 1977 Grandpa tells his grandchildren a wild story. (**I**: 6–8)

Tafuri, Nancy. *Have You Seen My Duckling?* New York: Greenwillow, 1984. A mother duck leads her ducklings around the lake as they search for a missing duckling. (**I**: P)

Tejima, Keizaburo. *Swan Sky*. New York: Putnam, 1988. A young swan is unable to fly with the family when it is the season for migration. (**I**: P–8)

Van Allsburg, Chris. *The Garden of Abdul Gasazi*. Boston: Houghton, 1979. Alan chases Fritz the dog through the magician's garden and imagines that Fritz has been turned into a duck. (**I**: P–8)

————. *Jumanji*. Boston: Houghton, 1981. Peter and Judy find an unusual board game that comes alive and turns the house into a jungle. (**I**: 7–10)

————. *Just a Dream*. Boston: Houghton, 1990. Walter is careless about how he treats his environment. In a dream one night, he sees what the future will be like if everyone abuses the earth. He wakes up with a new determination. (**I**: P–8)

————. *The Polar Express* Boston: Houghton, 1985. Children board a night train headed for the North Pole. Santa grants the first wish of Christmas to a boy who asks for a bell from Santa's sleigh. (**I**: 6–9)

————. *The Sweetest Fig*. Boston: Houghton, 1993. A woman leaves two figs as payment for work on her teeth, telling Monsieur Bibot that the figs make dreams come true. (I: 7–10)

———. *Two Bad Ants*. Boston: Houghton, 1988. Two ants in search of sugar crystals for their queen divert from the path to seek adventure in the house. Their experiences prove terrifying. (I: 7–10)

Waber, Bernard. *Ira Sleeps Over*. Boston: Houghton, 1972. Two boys have a sleepover and each is relieved to find that the other still sleeps with a stuffed animal. (I: P–7)

Waddell, Martin. *Can't You Sleep, Little Bear?* Illustrated by Barbara Firth. Cambridge, MA: Candlewick, 1992. Little Bear's fear of the dark keeps him from falling asleep until Big Bear takes him outside to see the moon and the stars. (I: P–6)

———. *Farmer Duck*. Illustrated by Helen Oxenbury. Cambridge, MA: Candlewick, 1992. A duck is overworked by a lazy farmer, and the barnyard animals rescue the duck and keep his family intact. (I: P–7)

Ward, Lynd. *The Biggest Bear*. Boston: Houghton, 1952. When Johnny decides that he would like a bearskin on his wall, he goes out seeking the biggest bear. (I: 6–8).

Wells, Rosemary. *Max and Ruby's First Greek Myth: Pandora's Box*. New York: Dial, 1993. Ruby tells the story of Pandora's Box to her little brother Max. A sequel is *Max and Ruby's Midas: Another Greek Myth* (1995). (I: P–7)

Wiesner, David. *June 29, 1999*. New York: Clarion, 1992. Holly sends her science experiment vegetable seedlings high into the air. On June 29, 1999, a little over a month later, enormous vegetables appear all over earth, but when vegetables Holly did *not* send up begin to appear, everyone wonders where they came from. (I: 6–9)

Williams, Sherley Anne. *Working Cotton*. Illustrated by Carole Byard. New York: Harcourt, 1992. A migrant family works in the cotton fields. (I: P–8)

Williams, Vera B. *A Chair for My Mother*. New York: Greenwillow, 1982. When a fire destroys everything they own, a little girl saves money to buy Mother a comfortable chair in which to sit when she returns home from work. A sequel is *Something Special for Me*. (I: P–8)

———. *"More More More," Said the Baby: Three Love Stories*. New York: Greenwillow, 1990. Three love stories show the loving relationships between each child and his or her parent. (I: P)

Wisniewski, David. *The Golem*. New York: Clarion, 1996. A rabbi creates a clay giant, the golem, and brings it to life in order to help protect the Jews in Prague during the sixteenth century. (I: 9–12)

———. *Rain Player*. New York: Clarion, 1991. This Mayan tale is depicted with cut-paper illustrations. (I: 6–9)

Wolkstein, Diane *White Wave: A Chinese Tale*. Illustrated by Ed Young. New York: Philomel, 1979. A Chinese farmer who finds a snail and cares for it discovers that the snail is nurturing him by providing him with food. The snail turns into White Wave, a moon goddess, and returns to the sky. (I: 6–9)

Wood, Audrey. *King Bidgood's in the Bathtub*. Illustrated by Don Wood. New York: Harcourt, 1985. Throughout the day and into the night, King Bidgood entertains himself in his tub, to the great distress of his court. (I: P–8)

Yagawa, Sumiko. *The Crane Wife*. Illustrated by Suekichi Akaba. Translated by Katherine Paterson. New York: Morrow, 1981. This traditional Japanese tale tells of a lonely man whose curiosity over the identity of his lovely wife leads to her departure. (I: 6–10)

Yolen, Jane. *The Emperor and the Kite*. 1967. Illustrated by Ed Young. New York: Putnam, 1988. The diligence and loyalty of the emperor's smallest daughter allow him to rule the land again after being overthrown by evil plotters. The watercolor paintings are reminiscent of Chinese cut-paper art. (I: 6–9)

———. *Owl Moon*. Illustrated by John Schoenherr. New York: Philomel, 1987. A young boy goes "owling" with his father. (I: 7–9)

Yorinks, Arthur. *Hey, Al*. Illustrated by Richard Egielski. New York: Farrar, 1986. Al is a janitor who lives in an apartment with his dog, Eddie. A large bird, calling, "Hey, Al," offers them a new life in a place where they can be free of worries and cares. But Eddie and Al find their paradise back home. (I: 7–10)

Young, Ed. *Cat and Rat: The Legend of the Chinese Zodiac*. New York: Holt, 1995. The Jade Emperor invites all the animals to participate in a race. This story tells how the twelve animals became part of the zodiac, and why cat and rat will always remain enemies. (I: 6–9)

———. *Lon Po Po: A Red Riding Hood Story from China*. New York: Philomel, 1989. This Chinese variation of the Red Riding Hood story depicts three children left home alone when their mother goes to visit their grandmother. When the wolf enters the house, the children outsmart the wolf and get rid of it. (I: 6–10)

———. *Seven Blind Mice*. New York: Philomel, 1992. One by one, the blind mice feel the "thing" and describe various body parts they each feel. (I: P–9)

Zelinsky, Paul. *Rumpelstiltskin*. New York: Dutton, 1986. Zelinsky's oil paintings richly depict this familiar tale of a young woman who must either discover the name of the little man or give him her first-born child in exchange for assistance in weaving straw into gold. (**I:** 7–9)

Ziefert, Harriet. *A New Coat for Anna*. Illustrated by Anita Lobel. New York: Knopf, 1986. In Europe at the end of World War II, there is no money for a new coat. Anna's mother gives away her precious belongings in order to have a coat made for Anna. (**I:** P–8)

Zolotow, Charlotte. *William's Doll*. Illustrated by William Pene du Bois. New York: Harper & Row, 1972. William wants a doll, and various family members give differing responses to his request. (**I:** P–8)

RESOURCES

Bader, Barbara. *American Picturebooks from Noah's Ark to the Beast Within*. New York: Macmillan, 1976.

Bang, Molly. *Picture This: Perception and Composition*. Boston: Little, Brown, 1991.

Cianciolo, Patricia. *The Illustrations in Children's Books*. Dubuque, IA: William C. Brown, 1976.

———. *Picture Books for Children*. 3rd ed. Chicago: American Library Association, 1990.

Cummings, Pat, comp. and ed. *Talking with Artists*. 2 vols. New York: Bradbury, 1992.

Lacy, Lynn. *Art and Design in Children's Picture Books*. Chicago: American Library Association, 1986.

Nodleman, Perry. *Words about Pictures: The Narrative Art of Children's Picture Books*. Athens: University of Georgia Press, 1988.

Pitz, Henry C. *Illustrating Children's Books*. New York: Watson-Guptil, 1963.

Shulevitz, Uri. *Writing with Pictures: How to Write and Illustrate Children's Books*. New York: Watson-Guptill, 1985.

Stewig, John Warren. *Looking at Picture Books*. Fort Atkinson, WI: Highsmith, 1995.

REFERENCES

Eibl-Eibesfeldt, Iraneus. *Ethology: The Biology of Behavior*. 2nd ed. New York: Holt, 1975.

Holdaway, Don. *The Foundations of Literacy*. Sidney, Aust.: Ashton Scholastic, 1979.

Kiefer, Barbara Z. *The Potential of Picturebooks: From Visual Literacy to Aesthetic Understanding*. Englewood Cliffs, NJ: Merrill/Prentice-Hall, 1995.

Lodge, Sally. "The Making of a Crossover: One Book, Two Markets." *Publisher's Weekly* 239 (23 Nov. 1992): 39–42.

Moebius, William. "Introduction to Picturebook Codes." *Word & Image* 2.2 (1986): 141–52.

Schwartz, Joseph H. *Ways of the Illustrator: Visual Communication in Children's Literature*. Chicago: American Library Association, 1982.

Sendak, Maurice. *Caldecott and Co.* New York: Farrar, Straus, & Giroux. 1990.

7 Poetry for Children

What is poetry? Who knows?
Not a rose, but the scent of a rose;
Not the sky, but the light in the sky;
Not the fly, but the gleam of the fly;
Not the sea, but the sound of the sea;
Not myself, but what makes me
See, hear, and feel something that prose
Cannot: and what it is, who knows?

"Poetry" *(1951)*
by Eleanor Farjeon

WHAT IS POETRY?

It is impossible to coin a definition of poetry that some poem or other won't slither around. We might say poems are made of rhymed and rhythmic language—but poems like this one by Byrd Baylor (1981) are not:

Desert Tortoise

I am the *old* one here.

Mice
and snakes
and deer
and butterflies
and badgers
come and go.
Centipedes
and eagles
come and go.

But tortoises
grow old
and *stay* . . .

We might say poems are words arranged in a visually striking fashion that is different from the arrangement of prose—but some poems aren't. One example is "Football" by Walt Mason (in Prelutsky, 1983):

Football

The game was ended, and the noise at last had died away, and now they gathered up the boys where they in pieces lay. And one was hammered in the ground by many a jolt and jar; some fragments never have been found, they flew away so far. They found a stack of tawny hair, some fourteen cubits high; it was the halfback, lying there, where he had crawled to die. They placed the pieces on a door, and from the crimson field, that hero then they gently bore, like soldier on his shield. The surgeon toiled the livelong night above the gory wreck; he got the ribs adjusted right, the wishbone, and the neck. He soldered on the ears and toes, and got the spine in place, and fixed a gutta-percha nose upon the mangled face. And then he washed his hands and said: "I'm glad that task is done!" The halfback raised his fractured head, and cried: "I call this fun!"

Should we distinguish between "poems" and "rhymes"?

When Emily Dickinson spoke of poetry as writing that made her so cold no fire could ever warm her, presumably she didn't mean the likes of "Jack Sprat could eat no fat/His wife could eat no lean." Some authorities would say that this is not real poetry but rather should be called "verse" or "rhyme" (Lukens, 1992). According to that way of thinking, "poetry" is written expression that strikes readers in many ways at once—with sound, image, and meaning—and that repays careful rereading to savor the artistry and ponder the associations. Works that fall short—although perhaps very enjoyable—should be called "verse" or "rhymes."

The "Emily Dickinson test" might work with most nursery rhymes, but how would the Belle of Amherst's body temperature have responded to the poems of Shel Silverstein or Jack Prelutsky or David McCord or Eve Merriam? And if it could be proved—as some claim to have done—that many nursery rhymes contain cleverly encoded social and political messages, would we still be content to call these works mere rhymes?

The poem-versus-rhyme distinction is useful if it keeps us from expecting too much from every bit of verse we read. But the distinction is bound to lead to some unhappiness, as someone sniffs that one of your favorite poems is not a poem at all, but only a rhyme.

What do *you* think: Should we make a distinction between poems and rhymes?

We might say poems wed image and sound in especially pleasing ways—but good prose often does this, too. For example, consider this excerpt from *Charlotte's Web* (1952), by E. B. White:

> The barn was very large. It was very old. It smelled of hay and it smelled of manure. It smelled of perspiration of tired horses and the wonderful sweet breath of patient cows. It often had a sort of peaceful smell—as though nothing bad could happen ever again in the world. (p. 13)

Still, we usually know poetry when we see it. Poetry is a concise and memorable cast of language, with intense feeling, imagery, and qualities of sound that bounce pleasingly off the tongue, tickle the ear, and leave the mind something to ponder. Poetry, being the most memorable structure for language, has a particularly affecting honing of sound and meaning, giving it a special appeal to children—yet also inspiring the great American poet Emily Dickinson to exclaim, "If [writing] makes me so cold no fire can ever warm me, I know that it is poetry."

CATEGORIES OF POETRY FOR CHILDREN

Children enjoy several widely acknowledged kinds of poetry: nursery rhymes, jump-rope rhymes, folk poems, lyric poems, nonsense verse, and narrative poems. Poems can also be classified by their forms: sonnets, limericks, haiku, concrete poems, and others. Some poems, of course, resist easy categorization.

Nursery Rhymes

Nursery rhymes are verses by anonymous poets that are highly rhythmic, tightly rhymed, and popular with small children. Nursery rhymes have been recited to and by children since medieval times. Indeed, the associations in many nursery rhymes can be traced back several centuries.

> Baa, baa, black sheep, have you any wool?
> Yes, sir, yes, sir—three bags full.
> One for my master and one for my dame,
> And one for the little boy who lives down the lane.

This traditional rhyme dates from feudal times, when vassals paid shares of their produce to the powerful lords and ladies (masters and dames) who owned the lands of England.

> Ring around the roses,
> Pocket full of posies,
> Ashes, ashes,
> We all fall down.

This rhyme is said to refer to the Black Death, the bubonic plague, which killed a fourth of the population of England in the fourteenth century. The ring around the roses was a tell-tale rash of an infected person; the pocket full of posies was for protection against the "bad airs" that were believed to spread the sickness; and the ashes and falling down refer to the people who were stricken and died with dramatic suddenness (the disease ran its course in four days) and whose bodies were piled up and burned.

The most famous nursery rhymes, of course, are the Mother Goose rhymes. A popular version of Mother Goose rhymes, brought out by John Newbery's publishing house in the mid-eighteenth century, was one of the first children's books published in English. (There is more discussion of Mother Goose rhymes in Chapter 6, on picture books.)

Nursery rhymes have pleasing sounds. This one sends the tongue tapping around all parts of the mouth—perhaps that is why small children love to recite it:

> Polly put the kettle on,
> Polly put the kettle on,
> Polly put the kettle on,
> We'll all have tea.
>
> Sukey take it off again,
> Sukey take it off again,
> Sukey take it off again,
> They've all gone away.

Many traditional rhymes also have accompanying motions. This one is a favorite when bouncing small children on one's knees:

> This is the way the ladies ride,
> Tri, tre, tre, tree!
> Tri, tre, tre, tree!
> This is the way the ladies ride,
> Tri, tre, tre, tree!

And small children delight in having their toes wiggled to "This Little Piggie":

This little piggy went to market.
This little piggy stayed home.
This little piggy ate roast beef.
This little piggy ate none.
This little piggy cried "Wee! wee! wee!"
All the way home.

Jump-Rope and Counting-Out Rhymes

Unlike nursery rhymes, which are usually introduced to children by their parents or sitters, children's folk rhymes are anonymous verses passed on from child to child. Thus, they constitute, as the title of the well-known book by British experts Iona and Peter Opie suggests, *The Lore and Language of School Children* (1959)—an actual folklore that is the province of children themselves.

Hand-clapping rhymes such as this one often accompany children's play:

My boyfriend's name is Davy
He's in the U.S. Navy
With a pickle for his nose, cherries on his toes
That's the way my story goes.

Counting-out rhymes are perennially popular, too:

Bubble gum, bubble gum in a dish
How many pieces do you wish?
1, 2, 3 . . .

Children also enjoy rhythmic alphabet games such as this one:

A, my name is Annie,
And my husband's name is Al.
We come from Arkansas,
And we sell apples.

B, my name is Barbara,
And my husband's name is Bill . . .

And here's a popular jump-rope rhyme:

Cinderella
Dressed in yellow
Went upstairs
And kissed a fellow
Made a mistake and kissed a snake.
Came back down with a belly ache.
How many doctors does it take?
One . . . Two . . . Three . . . Four . . .

This rhyme may seem sexually suggestive. Note that Francelia Butler's *Skipping Around the World* (1989) has 350 skipping rhymes collected over forty years from seventy countries, and many of them turn out to have reworked adult themes, including historic military campaigns, politics, death, love, and even sex.

Several collections of children's folk rhymes are currently in print (see the Recommended Books list at the end of this chapter). That these rhymes have to be written down at all shows adults' recognition that children's oral traditions need some bolstering against the inroads of canned commercial media.

Illustration 7.1
Children get most of their poetry through songs, but commercial music is often hard to sing. Thus, a good collection of folksongs such as *Gonna Sing My Head Off!* is always welcome. (*Gonna Sing My Head Off!* by Kathleen Krull. Illustrations copyright © 1992 by Allen Garnes. Used by permission of Alfred A. Knopf, Inc.)

Folksongs Popular among Children

Another source of folk rhymes are folksongs that are popular with children. Some children's folksongs go back hundreds of years. "Oats, Peas, Beans, and Barley Grow" was sung in medieval times in England. Perhaps it's no coincidence that the plants in the song are mentioned in the order of proper crop rotation practiced by farmers for centuries.

Other folksongs popular with children are from more recent times. The song about the legendary John Henry, a mythical turn-of-the-century African American railroad worker, was recently made into a picture book by Julius Lester (1993). Here is a verse:

> When John Henry was a little baby
> Sittin' on his mama's knee,
> He picked up a hammer and a little piece of steel
> And said, "Hammerin's gonna be the death of me,
>   Lord, Lord,
> Hammerin's gonna be the death of me."

John Langstaff has made a number of excellent picture books of English folksongs over the years. Ashley Bryan and John Langstaff have collaborated on books of African American spirituals, such as *What a Morning!* (1987). An interesting collection of Appalachian riddles, rhymes, and folksongs for children is *Granny Will Your Dog Bite? and Other Mountain Rhymes* (1990), collected by Gerald Milnes and illustrated by Kimberly Bulcken Root (the book is available with a cassette recording).

Lyric or Expressive Poems

The original lyrics were Greek poems that were accompanied by the lyre, a small harp. Today's lyric or expressive poems are works of emotion, observation, or insight. The category includes a huge number of poems.

A good example of the genre are the poems in Eloise Greenfield's *Honey, I Love* (1978), which feature observations on life by an African American girl, narrated in a rich and distinctive voice. Here is the beginning of the title poem:

Honey, I Love

> I love
> I love a lot of things, a whole lot of things
> Like
> My cousin comes to visit and you know he's from the South
> 'Cause every word he says just kind of slides out of his mouth
> I like the way he whistles and I like the way he walks
> But honey, let me tell you that I LOVE the way he talks . . .

This anonymous reflection on the frog is a wonderful spoof of a lyric poem:

> What a wonderful bird the frog are—
> When he stand, he sit almost;
> When he hop, he fly almost.
> He ain't got no sense hardly;
> He ain't got no tail hardly either.
> When he sit, he sit on what he ain't got almost.

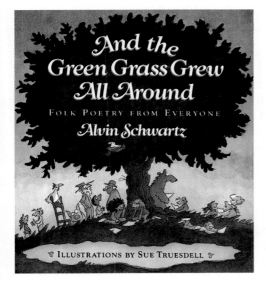

Illustration 7.2
Alvin Schwartz is known for his *Scary Stories to Tell in the Dark,* but his collection of folk poems, *And the Green Grass Grew All Around,* includes many appealing favorites and some less familiar ones. (*And the Green Grass Grew All Around: Folk Poetry from Everyone* by Alvin Schwartz. Illustration copyright © 1992 by Susan G. Truesdell. Used by permission of HarperCollins Publishers.)

Narrative Poems

Poems that tell stories are among the oldest of all poems, for at one time all stories that had wide currency were told in verse form. As you saw in Chapter 5, *The Odyssey, The Iliad, Beowulf,* and the *Poema de mio Cid* were all originally told in verse. In the Middle Ages, the ballads—long narrative poems—told the stories of Robin Hood, Lord Randall, and other heroes.

Narrative poetry written expressly for children began in the nineteenth century. Clement Clarke Moore's "A Visit from St. Nicholas, or 'Twas the Night before Christmas," published in 1822, not only helped establish the genre of narrative poetry for children but also contributed to the Santa Claus lore that is still widely circulated in North America. Robert Service's poems, such as "The Cremation of Sam McGee," have long been popular for their exciting plots involving tough men in wilderness settings.

One of the great American narrative poems is Ernest Lawrence Thayer's "Casey at the Bat" (1888), a favorite of generations of young people:

The outlook wasn't brilliant for the Mudville nine that day;
The score stood four to two with but one inning left to play . . .

Ludwig Bemelmans popularized rhyming narratives for modern children with his many books about Madeline, the feisty young resident of the convent school in Paris. And Roy Gerard continues to turn out imaginative contributions to the narrative poem genre: "Rosy and the Rustlers," "Sir Frances Drake," and others.

Nonsense Verse

In the middle of the last century, the English poet Edward Lear was the first to publish nonsense verse. Lear's "The Jumblies" (1846) is also known as "They Went to Sea in a Sieve":

They went to sea in a sieve, they did;
    In a sieve they went to sea;
In spite of all their friends would say,
On a winter's morn, on a stormy day,
    In a sieve they went to sea.

Nonsense poetry is alive and well among modern writers. Canadian poet Dennis Lee (1974) is a master of the art:

Alligator Pie

Alligator pie, alligator pie,
If I don't get some I think I'm gonna die.
Give away the green grass, give away the sky,
But don't give away my alligator pie . . .

Shel Silverstein's nonsense poetry is among the most popular these days. Here's a sample from ***Where the Sidewalk Ends*** (1974):

Chester

Chester come to school and said,
"Durn! I've growed another head!"

The teacher said, "It's time you knowed
The word is 'grew' instead of 'growed.'"

Form Poems: Limericks

Up until the beginning of this century, most poems in English had identifiable rhyme schemes and rhythmic patterns. Today, most poetry is more varied in
its structure and use of sounds. A few common forms of poetry persist, however.
The limerick is one of the most popular of the forms still current. Why? X. J. and
Dorothy Kennedy (1982) offer a poem by way of explanation:

> Well, it's partly the shape of the thing
> That makes the old limerick swing—
>   Its accordion pleats
>   Full of light, airy beats
> Take it up like a kite on the wing!

Limericks came into being in the early nineteenth century, but they found
an early champion at mid-century in the nonsense poet Edward Lear. Lear so
popularized the form that it is closely identified with him. Here is one of his limericks (1846):

> There was an Old Man who said, "Hush!
> I perceive a young bird in this bush!"
>   When they said, "Is it small?"
>   He replied, "Not at all;
> It is four times as big as the bush!"

Form Poems: Haiku

Another common form of poetry is the *haiku*, a three-line nonrhyming
poem developed in Japan. Haiku traditionally contain seventeen syllables, five in
the first line, seven in the middle, and five in the last (although English-language
haiku don't always follow that requirement). Most haiku make an observation
about nature in a particular moment and a particular place:

> Now at the black pond
>   twilight slowly abandons
> the lone blue heron.

Free Verse

Poetry that has no discernible form at all is *free verse*. Free verse has no
rhyme or particular rhythm but makes its impressions with an intensity of insight
or feeling, a clarity of vision, and sounds and rhythms that ebb and flow with the
intensity of the poet's feelings about the subject matter. Here is an example of
free verse (Worth, 1987):

Dog

Under a maple tree
The dog lies down,
Lolls his limp
Tongue, yawns,
Rests his long chin carefully between
Front paws:

Looks up, alert;
Chops, with heavy
Jaws, at a slow fly,
Blinks, rolls
On his side,
Sighs, closes
His eyes: sleeps
All afternoon
In his loose skin.

Here, with no meter or rhyme scheme to worry about, the poet can let the poem take its own shape. She sets out a series of images. She makes cadences in patterns and then suddenly breaks them, reflecting the erratic behavior of the poem's subject. She uses a series of sounds that echo each other (the *dog* lies *down* . . . *Lolls* his *limp* . . .), and then she shifts to other sounds.

THE EVOLUTION OF CHILDREN'S POETRY

Early Poetry for Children

Donald Hall, an American, and Iona and Peter Opie, both British, have put together historical collections of poems written in English for children. The early parts of both chronologically arranged collections make rather grim reading. Up until William Blake's *Songs of Innocence*, published in the late eighteenth century, the poems were cheerless, moralistic, didactic, and often downright mean-spirited. Here, for instance, is the beginning of an English alphabet poem from around 1700:

A was an Archer, and shot at a frog,
B was a Blindman, and led by a dog,
C was a Cutpurse, and lived in disgrace,
D was a Drunkard, and had a red face.
E was an Eater, a glutton was he,
F was a Fighter, and fought with a flea,
G was a Giant, and pulled down a house . . .

Early American poems for children were every bit as dour. Some poems exalted early death as the greatest aspiration of a young child—for by dying young, children reduced their chances of falling into sin. Other poems impressed on children the horrors of eternal damnation for their "original sin."

More Sympathetic Voices

The poems of the English poet William Blake (1757–1827), though, were something new. They appealed to children without preaching or sentimentalizing. In fact, in his *Songs of Innocence* (1789), Blake was the first to write with sympathy of the plight of child laborers:

The Chimney Sweeper

When my mother died I was very young,
And my father sold me while yet my tongue
Could scarcely cry "'weep! 'weep! 'weep! 'weep!"
So your chimneys I sweep, and in soot I sleep.

The better poets from Blake's time on left off the moralizing and wrote for children's enjoyment. The long narrative poems of Robert Browning (1812–1889) are imaginative and entertaining. Here is the beginning of "The Pied Piper of Hamelin" (1988):

Hamelin Town's in Brunswick,
    By famous Hanover city;
The river Weser, deep and wide,
Washes its wall by the southern side;
A pleasanter spot you never spied;
    But, when begins my ditty,
Almost five hundred years ago,
To see the townsfolk suffer so
    From vermin, was a pity.

    Rats!
They fought the dogs and killed the cats,
    And bit the babies in their cradles,
And ate the cheeses out of vats,
    And licked the soup from cooks' own ladles,
Split open kegs of salted sprats,
Made nests inside men's Sunday hats,
And even spoiled the women's chats
    By drowning their speaking
    With shrieking and squeaking
In fifty different sharps and flats . . .

From the mid-nineteenth century on, the poetry gets more and more delightful. We've already mentioned Edward Lear's nonsense verse—which plays with language and enlivens the imagination. In *Alice's Adventures in Wonderland* (1865), Lewis Carroll confidently spoofed the moralistic doggerel that was so prominent in poetry for children just a short time before:

Speak roughly to your little boy
And beat him if he sneezes!
He only does it to annoy,
And because he knows it teases.

Christina Rossetti (1830–1894) could be thoughtful and accessible at the same time, as in "The Wind" (1862):

Who has seen the wind?
    Neither you nor I;
But when the leaves hang trembling
    The wind is passing through.

Who has seen the wind?
    Neither you nor I;
But when the trees bow down their heads
    The wind is passing by.

Robert Louis Stevenson (1850–1894) gave us the great adventure novels *Treasure Island* and *Kidnapped*. His *A Child's Garden of Verses*, written at the end of the nineteenth century, is still much admired; through the middle of the twentieth century, it was among the most widely read of poetry collections. Stevenson (1885) could be gentle, yet savvy to a child's point of view:

Looking Forward

When I am grown to man's estate
I shall be very proud and great,
And tell the other girls and boys
Not to meddle with my toys.

At the turn of the century and after, Rudyard Kipling, A. A. Milne, T. S. Eliot and others appealed to children with exciting and delightful poems, with words and rhythms well suited to their themes.

Contemporary Poetry for Children

During the twentieth century, poetry for children has continued to evolve. One noticeable change has been freedom from formality: nonrhyming poems have become more common, and the language of poetry more "folksy." Another change is a greater inclusion of the minority experience in poetry for children, beginning with the poetry of Langston Hughes in the 1920s. Still another change is a more honest and direct voice in the poetry. As we have seen, in earlier centuries, the attitude of the poet could be aloof and punishing. Later, it became sentimental and reassuring. In the contemporary era, the voice of the poet becomes more honest and confiding—but poet and child both live in a troubled world, in which even adults often feel little power. Modern poets do not offer a naive reassurance they do not feel.

The voice of Langston Hughes's narrator in "Mother to Son" reflects the shift. The narrator is teaching a message of optimism, but the optimism is based on perseverance in grim circumstances. This world is a far cry from the cozy, sheltered world of the imagination constructed by poets in the nineteenth century. Note how Hughes (1986) uses a staircase in a slum dwelling as a metaphor for a hard life:

Illustration 7.3
The Dream Keeper is a well-loved collection of Langston Hughes's poems accessible to children. (*The Dream Keeper and Other Poems* by Langston Hughes. Illustration copyright © 1994 by J. Brian Pinkney. Used by permission of Alfred A. Knopf, Inc.)

Mother to Son

Well, son, I'll tell you:
Life for me ain't been no crystal stair.
It's had tacks in it,
And splinters,
And boards torn up,
And places with no carpet on the floor—
Bare.
But all the time
I'se been a-climbin' on,
And reachin' landin's,
And turnin' corners,
And sometimes goin' in the dark
Where there ain't been no light.
So, boy, don't you turn back.
Don't you set down on the steps
'Cause you finds it kinder hard.
Don't you fall now—
For I'se still goin', honey,
I'se still climbin',
And life for me ain't been no crystal stair.

The attitude of the honest and not superior voice is evident in the work of many modern poets who write for children—such as Eve Merriam, Myra Cohn

Livingston, Nikki Giovanni, and Gary Soto. The attitude is evident in Nikki Giovanni's "dance poem" (1985), in which the mother sounds almost desperate as she tries to cheer her children—or have them cheer her:

come nataki dance with me
bring your pablum dance with me
pull your plait and whirl around
come nataki dance with me

won't you tony dance with me
stop your crying dance with me
feel the rhythm of my arms
don't let's cry now dance with me

tommy stop your tearing up
don't you hear the music
don't you feel the happy beat
don't bite tony dance with me
mommy needs a partner . . .

Contemporary children's poets still write about the joys of childhood. But they also write about urban issues, about poverty and racism, about the dangers of environmental pollution, about the overmechanization and erosion of human values in our lives—as in this poem by Eve Merriam (1969):

Sing a Song of Subways

Sing a song of subways
Never see the sun;
Four-and-twenty people
In room for one.

When the doors are opened—
Everybody run.

The Many Voices of Children's Poetry

Many contemporary poets write to foster racial pride, as oppression has made pride hard to come by. Lucille Clifton writes eloquently to this end in "Listen Children" (in Adoff, 1994):

listen children
keep this in the place
you have for keeping
always
keep it all ways

we have never hated black

listen
we have been ashamed
hopeless   tired   mad

but always
all ways
we loved us

we have always loved each other

children   all ways

pass it on

Trinidad Sanchez, Jr. (1991) addresses the problem of finding pride in yourself when you don't look like the advertisements for beauty on billboards and in magazines (*mi'ja* means "my daughter"; a *Chicanita* is a young Chicana):

Why Am I So Brown?

A question Chicanitas sometimes ask
while others wonder: Why is the sky blue?
or the grass so green?

God made you brown, mi'ja,
color bronce—color of your raza, *your people*
connecting you to your raices, *your roots*
your story/historia
as you begin moving towards your future . . .

A breakthrough in contemporary literature for children is the publication of poetry from all quarters of American culture and from around the world as well. Poetry from the Caribbean is earthy and colorful, as this poem by Monica Gunning (1993) demonstrates:

The Corner Shop

"Chil', me stone broke," Grandma sighs.
"Not a copper penny in me house.
Go tell Maas Charles at the corner shop
I want to trust a pound of codfish
and two pounds of rice.
I'll pay him when the produce dealer
buys me dried pimento crop in season."

Maas Charles never says no.
He knows everyone in the village
by their first names.
He scoops from his bin, weighs and wraps,
adds to his credit sheet on the wall
a new amount under Grandma's name.

Illustration 7.4
Monica Gunning's poems and Frané Lessac's illustrations in *Not a Copper Penny in Me House* provide a child's-eye view of Caribbean village life. (*Not A Copper Penny in Me House* by Monica Gunning. Jacket illustration copyright © by Frané Lessac. Used by permission of Boyds Mills Press.)

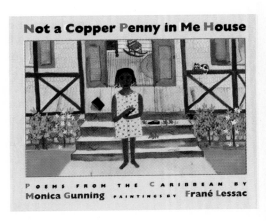

Grandma always says,
"Thank God for Maas Charles."

Poetry from Latin American communities can be worldly and upbeat, or wise and deep. Many collections are available in Spanish and English translations, like this poem from Mexico by Raul Banuelos (in Nye, 1995a):

Agua y tierra	**Water and Earth**
El agua	Water
es la luz	is the light
con raiz en la tierra.	with roots in the earth.
Beberla	To drink it
es echarse a caminar	is to journey
como un rio.	like a river.

Finally, though we mentioned that poetry for children continues to evolve, we should note that "evolution" in poetry for children is not the same thing as evolution in the design of automobiles. A Saturn is obviously a more sophisticated car than a Model T Ford, but a poem by Jack Prelutsky is not more sophisticated than a poem by A. A. Milne or one by Langston Hughes. As new poems are written, they add to the body of poetry available to children, without necessarily replacing it. Children today have access to exciting new poems that speak to contemporary realities; they can also read the best poems of the past.

ELEMENTS OF POETRY

Ask yourself this question: What do you like about a favorite poem? If you can't quite put your finger on it, consider the main features that critics agree make up a good poem: sounds, images, and forms.

Sounds

Most poetry for children is crafted with a keen ear for sound. That's why it is best read aloud. Sounds are the musical aspect of poetry. Just as music is said to speak the language of the emotions, so the sounds of poetry—rhythm, rhyme, alliteration and onomatopoeia—choreograph much of the listener's emotional experience.

Rhythm. Rhythm is the "beat" of a poem. Rhythm can be a direct route to the emotions. The rhythm of a slow heartbeat has a calming effect, even on a newborn, whereas the sound of a fast heartbeat causes anxiety. The pulse of a graduation march sweeps us along with dignity and pride; the pounding of a military drum keeps soldiers advancing in step with one another. The rhythm of a marching band makes us want to run to get a better look. Wallace Stevens captured the martial rhythm of a marching band in his poem "John Smith and His Son, John Smith" (in Kennedy and Kennedy, 1992):

John Smith and his son, John Smith,
    And his son's son John, and-a-one
    And-a-two and-a-three
And a rum-tum-tum, and-a
Lean John, and his son, lean John,
    And his lean son's John, and-a-one

And-a-two and-a-three
And a drum-rum-rum, and-a
Rich John, and his son, rich John,
    And his rich son's John, and-a-one
    And-a-two and-a-three . . .

The rhythm of this poem implicitly compares a proud parade of marchers to the passing of generations within a family.

Rhythm is prominent in many children's poems—and perhaps nowhere more so than in the work of NCTE award-winner David McCord. In his poem "The Pickety Fence" (1986), you can hear the rhythm of a stick dragging staccato across the pickets:

The pickety fence
The pickety fence
Give it a lick it's
The pickety fence
Give it a lick it's
A clickety fence
Give it a lick it's
A lickety fence
Give it a lick
Give it a lick
Give it a lick
With a rickety stick
Pickety
Pickety
Pickety
Pick

Children delight in clapping along to the rhythm of such poetry.

Rhyme. Along with rhythm, rhyme lends a musical quality to poetry by building patterns of repetition. Rhymes delight us—but they do more. Rhymes function in a poem to link words, to play them against each other, to build on their emotional content, as in this poem by Walter de la Mare (1923):

The Horseman

I heard a horseman
    Ride over the hill;
The moon shone clear,
The night was still;
His helm was silver,
    And pale was he;
And the horse he rode
    Was of ivory.

Rhymes are most pleasing when they surprise us. And poets can build up suspense by delaying rhymes when they are expected, as in this excerpt from "Train" (Temple, 1996):

The train stands trembling on the C&O *track,*
As the whistle puffs a warning, long and *low.*
Now the smoke starts chuffing from the short smoke*stack*
And the lights go sweeping

And the engine goes rumbling
And the wheels go squeaking kind of *slow*.

Of course, the rhyming words should suit the meaning of the poem, and not be included merely for the sake of sound. The rhymes in Christina Rossetti's "Caterpillar" (1862) are skillfully done:

Brown and furry
Caterpillar in a hurry,
Take your walk
To the shady leaf, or stalk,
Or what not,
Which may be the chosen spot.
No toad spy you,
Hovering bird of prey pass by you;
Spin and die,
To live again a butterfly.

Alliteration. Poems also may have repeated sounds that are more subtle than rhymes. These are *consonance*, the stringing together of similar consonant sounds, and *assonance*, the making of a series of similar vowel sounds. Together, consonance and assonance are known as *alliteration*.

Listen to this line from a poem by Rowena Bennett: "There once was a witch of Willowby Wood. . . ." A series of similar consonant sounds ties her words together; this is an example of consonance. No matter that "once" begins with *o*; the initial *w* sounds knit Bennett's words into a sonorous fabric.

Consonance doesn't have to be smooth, though. A succession of percussive consonants can sound like feet walking on dry sticks, as in this anonymous Welsh poem translated by Gwyn Williams (in Heaney and Hughes, 1982):

Dinogad's speckled petticoat
was made of skins and speckled stoat:
whip whip whipalong
eight times we'll sing the song.

The succession of consonant clusters in Alfred, Lord Tennyson's "The Eagle" (1851) helps us see and feel the bird's harsh, desolate perch; when the consonants give way to smoother sounds, they suggest the expansive beauty of the landscape below:

He clasps the crag with crooked hands;
Close to the sun in lonely lands,
Ringed with the azure world, he stands . . .

Assonance, the use of a series of similar vowel sounds, also ties the words in a line together. Note the repeated short vowel sounds in "clasps," "crag," and "hands" in Tennyson's poem. Carl Sandburg also used assonance skillfully in "Splinter" (1928):

The voice of the last cricket
across the first frost
is one kind of goodbye.
It is so thin a splinter of singing.

Note the high thin "ih" sounds in the last line, holding out against the more ponderous "ah" sounds in the second.

Onomatopoeia. When words in a poem imitate actual sounds of things (such as "moo," "oink," "bam"), the poet is using *onomatopoeia*. Hilaire Belloc gave us some fine examples of onomatopoeia as he described Spanish dancers in these lines from "Tarantella" (in Heaney and Hughes, 1982):

> . . . And the *Hip*! *Hop*! *Hap*!
> Of the clap
> Of the hands . . .
> . . . And the *Ting, Tong, Tang* of the Guitar . . .

In sum, poets use sounds deliberately to approximate the emotional qualities of their subjects and to weave words together into tight compositions. Good poets blend sounds so skillfully that we feel the effects without being aware of the devices they have used. Note how Rodney Bennet has employed rhythm, rhyme, alliteration, and onomatopoeia in this poem (in Kennedy and Kennedy, 1982):

Windy Nights

> Rumbling in the chimneys,
>   Rattling at the doors,
> Round the roofs and round the roads
>   The rude wind roars;
> Raging through the darkness,
>   Raving through the trees
> Racing off again across
>   The great grey seas.

Images

Imagery is an appeal to the senses. It results from a poem's sensory details that enable us to imagine how things look, sound, feel, smell, or taste.

In "The Child on Top of a Greenhouse" (1946), Theodore Roethke first anchors our impressions in the narrator's point of view, by reporting what the narrator sees, hears, and feels:

> The wind billowing out the seat of my britches,
> My feet crackling splinters of glass and dried putty,
> The half-grown chrysanthemums staring up like accusers,
> Up through the streaked glass, flashing with sunlight,
> A few white clouds all rushing eastward,
> A line of elms plunging and tossing like horses,
> And everyone, everyone pointing up and shouting!

By the end of the poem, the danger of the narrator's plight sinks in. We realize that the child's absorption in sensory details, in which we have shared, has made him oblivious to the perils of climbing on top of a greenhouse.

Mary O'Neill's poem "My Fingers" (1969) about the sense of touch is full of tactile imagery:

> My fingers are antennae.
> Whatever they touch:
> Bud, rose, apple,
> Cellophane, crutch—
> They race the feel
> Into my brain,
> Plant it there and

Begin again.
This is how I knew
Hot from cold
Before I was even
Two years old.

Imagery is one of poetry's great contributions to human awareness. With imagery, poems name sensations and expand people's consciousness of their minute-to-minute experiences.

Likenesses, or Figures of Speech. Toddlers have the wonderful power to put words together in new ways: A naked child spread his arms and proclaimed, "I'm barefoot all over!" Making words do new work is one of the poet's greatest talents, too. Poets often use language in fresh ways by making comparisons: similes and metaphors and personifications.

The definitions of these terms never do justice to their power. A *simile* is defined as an explicit comparison, using the word "like" or "as." A *metaphor* lacks either of those two words and is a direct comparison in which one thing is described as if it were another. *Personification* is a sort of metaphor in which an inanimate thing is described as if it were human (or, at least, had sensations and will). But look what writers do with these literary devices. Practically all mythology is built on personification. The ancient Norse myths, for example, personified the reckless forces of nature in the character of Thor. Most religious writing is built around metaphor and simile: Having no direct experience of any world but this one, religious writers use familar terms to speak of things beyond.

The Mexican poet Alberto Forcada compares a belly button to the knot in a balloon in this translated poem (in Nye, 1995b), making a simile:

Ombligo

Como los globos
que flotan en las fiestas,
tengo, para no desinflarme,
un nudo en el estomago.

Belly Button

Like the balloons
that float at parties,
I have a knot on my belly
so I won't go flat.

Illustration 7.5
Poet Naomi Shihab Nye is of Palestinian ancestry, but she enjoys introducing poetry from many cultures to American children. Her book *The Tree Is Older Than You Are* is a collection of poems and stories from Mexico. (*The Tree Is Older Than You Are* by Naomi Shihab Nye. Illustration copyright © Leticia Tarragó. Oil on canvas. Used by permission of Leticia Tarragó.)

In "Mirrorment" (in de Regniers et al., 1988) A. R. Ammons equates flowers and birds, making a metaphor:

Birds are flowers flying
and flowers perched birds.

Dorothy Aldis slips an almost unnoticed metaphor into her poem "When I Was Lost" (1928):

Underneath my belt
My stomach was a stone.
Sinking was the way I felt.
And hollow.
And alone.

Roethke's young narrator in "The Child on Top of a Greenhouse" said the half-grown chrysanthemums were ". . . staring up at him like accusers." This comparison gave the flowers human senses and motives—it *personified* them.

Langston Hughes personified rain in his "April Rain Song" (1986):

Let the rain kiss you.
Let the rain beat upon your head with silver liquid drops.
Let the rain sing you a lullaby.
The rain makes running pools in the gutter.
The rain plays a little sleep-song on our roof at night.
And I love the rain.

In summary, all of these ways of making likenesses—similes, metaphors, and personification—expand the power of language. In so doing, they expand our perceptions, too: They make us, the readers and hearers, experience the world in new ways.

Forms

The arrangement of words on the page affects their look, readers' progress through them, and the emphasis given to some of the words.

Shel Silverstein uses a columnar arrangement in his poem "Valentine" (1974):

I got a valentine from Timmy
               Jimmy
               Tillie
               Billy
               Nicky
               Micky
               Ricky
               Dicky
               Laura
               Nora
               Cora
               Flora
               Donnie
               Ronnie
               Lonnie
               Connie
               Eva even sent me two
               But I didn't get *none* from you.

This poem is a list. Its arrangement invites reading one name at a time, as if a child were keeping track of who her friends are.

Sometimes poets arrange their words to look like their topic. Consider Bobbi Katz's "Spring Is" (in Prelutsky, 1983):

Spring is when
     the morning sputters like
bacon
   and
       your
          sneakers
             run
                down
                   the
                      stairs
so fast you can hardly keep up with them
and
spring is when
   your scrambled eggs
      jump
         off
           the
              plate
and turn into a million daffodils
trembling in the sunshine.

In this poem, the progressively indented lines resemble the staircase that the sneakers run down.

Insight

Above and beyond the effects of particular literary devices, poems often startle us with *insight*—a noticing of things that makes us say, "Yes—that's it! But I never thought of mentioning it before." Some insights are simple but still surprising, like this one in Philip Whalen's poem "Early Spring" (1969):

The dog writes on the window with his nose.

Some insights are more complicated, such as those in this poem by Naomi Shihab Nye (1995a):

Famous

The river is famous to the fish.

The loud voice is famous to silence,
which knew it would inherit the earth
before anybody said so.

The cat sleeping on the fence is famous to the birds
watching him from the birdhouse.

The tear is famous, briefly, to the cheek.

The idea you carry close to your bosom
is famous to your bosom.

The boot is famous to the earth,

more famous than the dress shoe,
which is famous only to floors.

The bent photograph is famous to the one who carries it
and not at all famous to the one who is pictured.

I want to be famous to shuffling men
who smile while crossing streets,
sticky children in grocery lines,
famous as the one who smiled back.

I want to be famous the way a pulley is famous,
or a buttonhole, not because it did anything spectacular,
but because it never forgot what it could do.

Imagery is one of poetry's great values, but insight is even greater. Good poems are often noteworthy for their concentrated clarity of understanding. The insight expressed in Naomi Shihab Nye's poem might well have been elaborated by another writer into a book-length manuscript.

CHOOSING POETRY FOR CHILDREN

When we are choosing good poetry for children, we face two issues right off: What are the criteria that define good poetry? What kinds of poetry do children like? Although there are many fine poems that children like, the answers to these two questions, as we shall see, are not always in easy balance.

Criteria for Good Poetry for Children

Good poems for children must satisfy the same criteria for quality as any other form of children's literature—except that their shorter form puts a special emphasis on qualities such as skilled use of language, imagery, and insight.

Sounds. Poems don't have to rhyme. Among those that do, though, the better ones have exact rhymes (they don't try to pass off near misses, like "alone" and "home"). Better poems also have fresh rhymes: Readers cannot predict with boring certainty what the words at the ends of the lines will be. Above all, the rhymes don't get in the way of the poem's images and meanings.

Poems do not have to have fixed rhythms. But if they do, the rhythms should be consistent enough for children to discern them, yet not so consistent as to become monotonous.

It is a very tall order to mix rhymes with exact word choices and to use clear rhythms that aren't cloying. No wonder so many modern poets avoid rhymes and fixed rhythms altogether. If a poet opts for blank verse, though, we still expect a careful handling of sound and meter. If their poems don't rhyme, poets must match the sounds of their words to the emotional tone of their topics. If their poems don't have a fixed rhythm throughout, poets must write in syllables that match the pace of the reading to the meaning of the poem.

Images. Good poems bring clear images to the mind's eye. Whether they use language denotatively with precise word choices or connotatively with metaphors, similes, and symbols—good poems serve as models of the ways in which language can name experiences and even as vehicles that take readers beyond experience.

ASK THE AUTHOR...
Myra Cohn Livingston

Myra Cohn Livingston

As a poet who does not write "down" to children, what advice do you have for teachers who want to help children appreciate poetry that isn't necessarily playful?

Perhaps our television age has spawned this need for easy entertainment, instantaneous laughter which announces to the adult, parent, or teacher that a child is happy! While laughter is certainly a positive disposition—we have a number of versifiers who are playful, who entertain splendidly and know their craft—it is also true that *no one laughs all the time.* Certainly one of the most telling and important hallmarks of real poetry is that it touches other emotions, including wonder, hope, fear, anger, and sorrow. Fine poetry lets a

child know that others not only laugh but experience moments of serious and deep emotion, finding in poetry a new way of looking at the world.

There are a number of ways by which we may judge the difference between verse and poetry. Keen observation, vision, judicious use of figurative language, and form distinguish the poet from the versifier. It is a leap of the imagination that enables Shakespeare to turn a bush into a bear and James Reeves to identify a snail as a "toppling caravan." Such moments enrich the child's world and

Insight. Finally, good poems surprise us with fresh or wise observations. In so doing, they expand our awareness and raise our spirits.

These features summarize what adult readers look for in good poetry. But are these the features children like?

Children's Preferences in Poetry

Young children have an affinity for poetry. Unfortunately, children's pleasure in poetry does not always survive middle childhood, when poetry for the young moves beyond the merely playful, to more ambitious uses of language.

What sorts of poetry *do* elementary school children like? Studies of children's poetry preferences over the past quarter-century have yielded fairly consistent answers. A study by Kutiper and Wilson (1993) reached findings very similar to those of a landmark study done by Terry (1974) twenty years earlier. Kutiper and Wilson summarized their findings as follows (pp. 28–35):

1. The narrative form of poetry is popular with readers of all ages, while free verse and haiku are the most disliked forms.

2. Students prefer poems that contain rhyme, rhythm, and sound.

make possible, in the midst of stark reality, a space in which to dream.

One sure way in which teachers may foster appreciation of poetry is to begin by digging into some serious anthologies and reading poems of all moods aloud. There is no need for young children to analyze the work, to discuss punctuation or line breaks or parts of speech (no more than one would lecture about key signatures, clef signs, dotted quarters, or six-teenths when children learn to sing a song). The poem, like the song, is sim-ply there to enjoy—to hear. A few weeks of reading and a pattern emerges; one or two of the children enjoy a certain poem. Why? A dis-cussion may or may not ensue, but eventually it will and the children themselves begin to search for more than the instant laughter of verse.

But like all knowledge, children's appreciation of the difference is not gained by swallowing some magical pill, but by being immersed in poetry, thus activating a curiosity which will lead them to taking the first steps of this discovery for themselves.

Myra Cohn Livingston wrote or edited over eighty books and anthologies of poetry and books about the writing of poetry, as well as articles for profes-sional journals on children and creative writing. Her awards include the NCTE poetry award for 1980, an award from the Texas Institute of Letters, the Kerlan Award from the University of Minnesota in 1994, and a Grammy award in 1996. She lived in Los Angeles, California, where she taught in the UCLA Extension Writer's Program until her death in 1996.

3. Children most enjoy poetry that contains humor, familiar experi-ences—and animals.

4. Younger students (elementary and middle school and junior high age) prefer contemporary poems.

5. Students dislike poems that contain (extensive) visual imagery or figurative language.

In terms of particular poets, according to the same study, elementary-grade students prefer the light and funny poetry of Jack Prelutsky and Shel Silverstein far above any other. Poetry deemed by critics to have greater literary merit has nowhere near the circulation of the works of these two poets.

How Can We Expand Children's Taste in Poetry? Of course, findings like those above don't settle anything. If worth were reducible to popularity, all children's fiction would come from *The Babysitter's Club* series and all their food would be chosen from McDonald's menu. Since what children enjoy is largely synonymous with whatever is most familiar to them, our task as advocates of lit-erature is to expand the range of poetry children know and, eventually, the range that they consider enjoyable.

There are three main ways to enhance children's appreciation of poetry. One way is to share poetry informally with children every chance you get. Children will appreciate poems if you offer them for their content—for the insights and feelings they communicate—rather than as complex objects to be analyzed. A second way to promote poetry is to have children practice choral speaking and performance. Most poetry is best read aloud, and the variations possible with a voice choir can make poems sound magnificent. A third way to encourage appreciation of poetry is to encourage children to write it. Writing poetry gives children a connection to what poets are trying to do.

How can we keep children's liking for poetry alive?

ISSUE TO CONSIDER

Jack Prelutsky, a very popular poet among North American children, explains the problem this way (1983, p. 18):

> For very young children, poetry is as natural as breathing. . . . But then something happens to this early love affair with poetry. At some point during their school careers, many children seem to lose their interest and enthusiasm for poetry and their easygoing pleasure in its sounds and images.

What is to be done? What kinds of poems will keep children's interest alive? Here is Prelutsky's answer (1983, p. 18):

> . . . poems that evoke laughter and delight, poems that cause a palpable ripple of surprise by the unexpected comparisons they make, poems that paint pictures with words that are as vivid as brushstrokes, poems that reawaken pleasure in the sounds and meanings of language.

A contrasting opinion was expressed by Myra Cohn Livingston (1992, p. 9):

> [Poetry] is now pouring from the publishers, but much of it is little more than prose arranged as poetry, overblown metaphors, tired clichés, and light verse that caters to many of the baser emotions, calculated to give children a quick laugh. It has, in many instances, no sign of helping children evolve, but on the contrary [allows them to] remain in the same old place.

Prelutsky and Livingston have written very different poetry. Prelutsky creates rhymed and rhythmic poems that are noted for their humor and surprising twists. Livingston's poems take more varied forms, including blank verse, and most of them explore serious themes. One has the feeling, reading their comments, that each might consider the other's poetry part of the problem.

What do you think? In order to keep children's interest in poetry alive, should we offer them mostly poems that are enjoyable? Or should we offer them mostly poems that take their inner complexities seriously? Should the poems be immediately rewarding? Or should they challenge children to ponder their meanings and associations? Or is there some middle ground?

MAJOR CHILDREN'S POETS AND THEIR WORKS

Hundreds of poets have written for children, but we will look closely at only a handful who are especially noteworthy, both for their insight and literary skill and for their acceptance by children over the years. We will begin with contemporary poets and work backwards. The first ten poets have won the National Council of Teachers of English (NCTE) Award for Excellence in Poetry for Children, which goes to a living poet for exceptional quality in a body of work (not just one book or poem) for children ages three to thirteen.

David McCord

David McCord was the first recipient of the NCTE poetry award in 1977. His books of poems include *All Small: Poems by David McCord* (1986), *Always and Ago: Rhymes of the Never Was and Always Is* (1975), *Every Time I Climb a Tree* (1987), *One at a Time* (1986), and *The Star in the Pail* (1975).

One of McCord's poems that delights most preschoolers is "I Want You to Meet . . ." (in de Regniers, 1988):

> . . . Meet Ladybug
> her little sister Sadiebug,
> her mother, Mrs. Gradybug,

Illustration 7.6
Bernice Cullinan donated the funds that established the NCTE poetry award, so it is fitting that she edited this collection, *A Jar of Tiny Stars: Poems by NCTE Award–Winning Poets.*
(*A Jar of Tiny Stars* edited by Bernice E. Cullinan. Illustration by Andi MacLeod. Copyright © 1996 by Boyds Mills Press. Used by permission of Boyds Mills Press.)

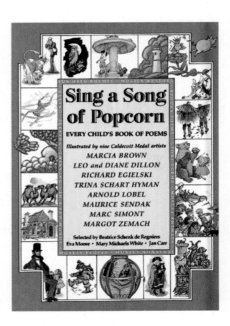

Illustration 7.7
Beatrice Schenk de Regniers put together a modern classic in the poetry collection *Sing a Song of Popcorn,* with illustrations by nine Caldecott-winning artists. (*Sing a Song of Popcorn* selected by Beatrice Schenk de Regniers. Copyright © 1988 by Scholastic Inc. Used by permission of Scholastic Inc.)

her aunt, that nice oldmaidybug,
and Baby—she's a fraidybug.

Another of his poems, "The Pickety Fence," was highlighted earlier in this chapter for its brilliant use of rhythm.

Aileen Fisher

Aileen Fisher won the NCTE poetry award in 1978. She has written more than a half-dozen books of poems for children, including **Out in the Dark and Daylight** (1980), illustrated by Gail Owens, and **Always Wondering: Some Favorite Poems of Aileen Fisher** (1991), illustrated by Joan Sandin. Her poems bounce with rhythm and rhyme, but they always offer children a glimmer of insight. Here's an example (Fisher, 1980):

Noises

We play we are soldiers:
Tramp! Tramp! Tramp!
We play we are horses:
Stamp! Stamp! Stamp!
We play we have boots on:
Scuff! Scuff! Scuff!
Till Mother tells us, "Quiet!
        Enough's enough."

We play we know secrets:
Sh! Sh! Sh!
We play that we are whispers:
Sp! Sp! Sp!
We play that we are sleepy:
Yawn! Yawn! Yawn!
Till Mother says, "I wonder
        where everybody's gone?"

Karla Kuskin

Of her poem "I Have a Friend" (1975), Karla Kuskin wrote: "The smallest observation can be the start of a poem. I thought of [this one] as I tried to talk to my daughter Julia (then about seven years old) while she endlessly practiced standing on her hands":

I have a friend who keeps standing on her hands.
That's fine,
Except I find it very difficult to talk to her
Unless I stand on mine.

Kuskin's poems are delightfully absurd, and she punches her ideas home with a splendid variety of rhythms and rhyme schemes. Her books of poetry include **Any Me I Want to Be** (1972) and **Dogs and Dragons, Trees and Dreams** (1980). She won the NCTE poetry award in 1979. Ironically, Kuskin, who is also an illustrator, had designed the medallion for the award three years earlier!

Myra Cohn Livingston

Myra Cohn Livingston published more than a dozen books of her own poems and edited nearly a dozen collections of other people's poetry for children before her death in 1996. Her poems show her empathy with all children in their joys and private hurts—for example, "Circles" (1988) alludes sensitively to how it feels to come from a broken home:

> I am speaking of circles.
>
> The circle we made around the table,
> our hands brushing as we passed the potatoes.
> The circle we made in our potatoes
> to pour in gravy, whirling in its round bowl.
> The circle we made every evening
> finding our own place at the table
> with its own napkin in its own ring.
>
> I am speaking of circles broken.

Livingston often used blank verse; when she used rhymes, the bitterness of her themes could clash with the prettiness of the forms, as in this poem (Livingston, 1988):

His Girlfriend

> She smiles a lot.
> She's pretty, I guess.
> She tries to be nice,
>   but it's really a mess
>
>   to go out and have fun,
>   pretending you care,
>   laughing at jokes,
>   when your real mom's not there.

Myra Cohn Livingston's collections of poems include *Birthday Poems* (1989), illustrated by Margot Tomes, *Earth Songs* (1986), illustrated by Leonard Everett Fisher, and *There Was a Place and Other Poems* (1988). She won the NCTE poetry award in 1980.

Arnold Adoff

Children are often inspired by Arnold Adoff's poems to play with the arrangement of words on the page. Consider this poem (Adoff, 1979):

My Mouth

> stays shut
>   but
> food just
> finds
>   a way
>   my tongue says
> we are
>   full today
>   but
>   teeth just
>   grin
>   and
>   say

Illustration 7.8
Arnold Adoff's powerful collection *My Black Me* brings well-known black poets, as well as powerful but lesser-known ones, into classrooms. (*My Black Me* by Arnold Adoff, editor. Illustration copyright © 1974 by Tyrone Geter. Used by permission of Dutton Signet, a division of Penguin Books USA Inc.)

come in
i am always hungry.

Adoff taught in the city schools of New York for many years. Though he is white, he has been a champion of the poetry of the African American community—see, for example his edited collection, *My Black Me: A Beginning Book of Black Poetry* (1994). His book *All the Colors of the Race* (1982) celebrates the experiences of biracial children. Adoff won the NCTE poetry award in 1988. (See Chapter 4 for more information about Arnold Adoff.)

Eve Merriam

Few writers for children have been more adventurous with language than Eve Merriam, who died in 1992. She could rhyme, but she could also imitate the sound of her topic almost perfectly, as in this poem (1989):

Windshield Wiper

fog smear	fog smear
tissue paper	tissue paper
clear the blear	clear the smear
fog more	fog more
splat splat	downpour
rubber scraper	rubber scraper
overshoes	macintosh
bumbershoot	muddle on
slosh through	slosh through
drying up	drying up
sky lighter	sky lighter
nearly clear	nearly clear

clearing clearing veer
clear here clear

Merriam published more than a half-dozen books of poems. Some of her titles are *Blackberry Ink* (1985), *Chortles: New and Selected Wordplay Poems* (1989), and *You Be Good and I'll Be Night: Jump-on-the-Bed Poems* (1988). Poems by her have also been included in most contemporary anthologies of poetry for children. She won the NCTE poetry award in 1981.

John Ciardi

John Ciardi (pronounced "CHARdee") could be wonderfully subversive in his poems. Just look at this verse from "The Happy Family" (1961):

Before the children say goodnight,
    Mother, Father, stop and think:
Have you screwed their heads on tight?
    Have you washed their ears with ink?

Or these two couplets from "What Did You Learn at the Zoo?" (1981):

Gorillas are good, gorillas are bad,
But all of them look a lot like Dad.

Some do one thing, some another,
But all of them scream a lot like Mother.

Ciardi won the NCTE poetry award in 1982 and died in 1986. A popular book of his poems is **You Read to Me, I'll Read to You** (1962). Several of his works from the 1960s have been reissued, including **The Monster Den: or Look What Happened at My House** (1991), illustrated by Edward Gorey, and **The Reason for the Pelican** (1994), illustrated by Dominic Catalano.

Lilian Moore

The poems of Lilian Moore can be cheerful, but all of them make children notice things. Her poem "Construction" (1969), for instance, puts a human being back into the superhuman undertaking of skyscraper construction:

> The giant mouth
> chews
> rocks
> spews them
> and is back for
> more.
>
> The giant arm
> swings up
> with a girder
> for
> the fourteenth floor.
>
> Down there,
> a tiny man
> is
> telling them
> where
> to put a skyscraper.

Moore's books of poetry include **I Feel the Same Way** (1976), illustrated by Robert Quackenbush, **Something New Begins** (1982), illustrated by Mary J. Dunton, and **Think of Shadows** (1980), illustrated by Deborah Robinson. She won the NCTE poetry award in 1985.

Valerie Worth

Known for her "small poems," five volumes of which were illustrated by Natalie Babbitt, Valerie Worth found things to celebrate in the everyday objects, large and small. Consider "safety pin" (1987):

> Closed, it sleeps
> On its side
> Quietly,
> The silver
> image
> Of some
> Small fish;
>
> Opened, it snaps
> Its tail out
> Like a thin
> Shrimp, and looks
> At the sharp

Point with a
Surprised eye.

Worth won the NCTE poetry award in 1991. She died in 1994. Her books of poems include *All the Small Poems* (1987) and *Small Poems Again* (1985), both illustrated by Natalie Babbitt.

Barbara Juster Esbensen

Barbara Juster Esbensen's poems flash with insight. Many of them are rhymed and rhythmical. "Snake" (1992) moves playfully from one level of reality to another:

The word begins to
hiss as soon as the first
letter
goes on   S
s-s-s-s-s-s   forked tongue flickers
Hard eyes stare
Already the rest of the poem
shrinks back from
his narrow speed   The paper
draws in its breath   SNAKE
loops around the pencil
slides
among the typewriter keys   slips
like a silk shoelace
away

Esbensen's books of poems include *Echoes for the Eye: Poems to Celebrate Patterns in Nature* (1996), illustrated by Helen K. Davie; *Dance with Me* (1995), illustrated by Megan Lloyd; and *Who Shrank My Grandmother's House? Poems of Discovery* (1992), illustrated by Eric Beddows. Esbensen won the NCTE poetry award in 1994. She died in 1996.

Lee Bennett Hopkins

Lee Bennett Hopkins deserves grateful mention here simply for his work compiling dozens of anthologies of poems for children and his enthusiastic advice to teachers and parents on ways to help children enjoy poetry. Hopkins is also a skilled poet who celebrates the exuberance and ironies of contemporary childhood with colorful language and apt phrasing. Consider "This Tooth" (1970), for example:

I jiggled it
        jaggled it
        jerked it.

I pushed
        and pulled
        and poked it.
But—
As soon as I stopped
and left it alone,
This tooth came out
on its very own!

Hopkins's own poems can be found in ***Been to Yesterdays: Poems of a Life*** (1995) and ***Charlie's World: A Book of Poems*** (1972).

Jack Prelutsky

A popular poet, Jack Prelutsky has produced a prodigious amount of poetry for the young over the past two decades. His poems are funny, ironic, and lively, and they address the challenges and joys of modern childhood. An example is "No Girls Allowed" (1980):

. . . We play hide-and-go-seek
and the girls wander near.
They say, "Please let us hide."
We pretend not to hear.

We don't care for girls
so we don't let them in,
we think that they're dumb—
and besides, they might win.

Prelutsky has produced many books of poems, including ***The Baby Uggs Are Hatching*** (1982), illustrated by James Stevenson; ***Beneath a Blue Umbrella*** (1990), illustrated by Garth Williams; ***The New Kid on the Block*** (1984), illustrated by James Stevenson; and ***The Dragons Are Singing Tonight*** (1993), illustrated by Peter Sis. He has also edited many popular anthologies, including ***For Laughing Out Loud*** (1991) and the ***Random House Book of Poetry for Children*** (1983), illustrated by Arnold Lobel.

Shel Silverstein

In the 1970s, Shel Silverstein was to children's poetry what Judy Blume was to children's novels—a fresh and irreverent voice that projected a mischievous take on life and utterly resisted the sentimentality that was long associated with children's literature. Silverstein's books of poetry, ***Where the Sidewalk Ends*** (1974) and ***A Light in the Attic*** (1981), are eminently popular with children, if not always with critics.

Nikki Giovanni

Nikki Giovanni's "tell it like it is" poems speak in the voice of African American children and their parents. Without rhyme, other obvious formalities, or sentimentalism, her poems magically evoke the anxieties, joys, and frustrations of real people in real situations. Reading her poems reminds all her listeners, no matter how small or downtrodden they feel, that their point of view is important, too. Consider this lyric poem (1972):

Winter Poem

once a snowflake fell
on my brow and i loved
it so much and i kissed
it and it was happy and called its cousins
and brothers and a web
of snow engulfed me then
i reached to love them all
and i squeezed them and they became

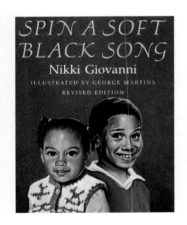

Illustration 7.9
In *Spin a Soft Black Song,* Nikki Giovanni presents poems describing the African American experience. Her poems, unfettered by rhyme or other formalities, flash with insight. (*Spin a Soft Black Song* by Nikki Giovanni. Jacket design copyright © 1985 by George Martins. Used by permission of Farrar, Straus & Giroux, Inc.)

a spring rain and i stood perfectly
still and was a flower

Langston Hughes

Langston Hughes (1902–1967) was the first African American poet to be widely read by children. Born in Joplin, Missouri, Hughes became a prominent member of the literary and artistic movement known as the Harlem Renaissance. Hughes's poems explore the sounds and rhythms of the urban black experience before mid-century, as well as describing an idealized vision of Africa. Although he wrote most of his poetry before the civil rights movement of the 1960s, poems such as "Dream Deferred" (1951) speak eloquently and powerfully of the injustices African Americans have endured in this country:

What happens to a dream deferred?

Does it dry up
like a raisin in the sun?
Or fester like a sore—
And then run?
Does it stink like rotten meat?
Or crust and sugar over—
like a syrupy sweet?

Maybe it just sags
like a heavy load.

Or does it explode?

With its experimental style and its solid grounding in the voice and realities of the city, Hughes's poetry has lost none of its freshness or urgency over the decades. (This fact is a sad commentary on the nation's lack of genuine social progress.)

A. A. Milne

Alan Alexander Milne (1882–1956) created the famous Winnie-the-Pooh stories using his son, Christopher Robin, as the model for the human character. Milne's volumes of poetry for children, **When We Were Very Young** (1924) and **Now We Are Six** (1927), perfectly portray the importance of the young child *to* the young child. Long before people understood what the psychologist Jean Piaget meant by "egocentrism," they had seen the concept demonstrated eloquently in verses such as "Buckingham Palace" (1924):

They're changing the guard at Buckingham Palace—
Christopher Robin went down with Alice.
A face looked out, but it wasn't the King's.
"He's much too busy a-signing things,"
                     Says Alice.

They're changing the guard at Buckingham Palace—
Christopher Robin went down with Alice.
"Do you think the King knows all about *me*?"
"Sure to, dear, but it's time for tea,"
                     Says Alice.

Milne's poems use sounds and rhythms perfectly (here, his rhythm catches the cadence of a regimental drumbeat). Since young children like to respond to poetry with movement, Milne's poems are good choices for reading aloud and moving to.

Walter de la Mare

Walter de la Mare (1873–1956) was a master of weaving sensory details into the sounds and rhythms of poetry. "Some One" (1923) begs to be read aloud for its air of mystery—and it invites children to focus their attention on sensory details:

Some One

Some one came knocking
    At my wee, small door;
Some one came knocking,
    I'm sure—sure—sure;
I listened, I opened,
    I looked to left and right,
But nought there was a-stirring
    In the still dark night;
Only the busy beetle
    Tap-tapping in the wall,
Only from the forest,
    The screech-owl's call,
Only the cricket whistling
    While the dew drops fall,
So I know not who came knocking,
    At all, at all, at all.

Walter de la Mare's poems are still published as picture books and included in poetry anthologies, because children still find wonder and mystery in his images.

Robert Louis Stevenson

Robert Louis Stevenson's lyrics from *A Child's Garden of Verses* (1885) have been household staples for over a century—and with good reason. The poet had a keen insight into the wonders and frustrations experienced by young children, and he skillfully matched those ideas with direct and sonorous language. Some of Stevenson's poems seem overly flowery for today's young readers, but many poems in his repertoire still speak to the issues of young life and offer strong examples of language beautifully used. Consider "At the Seaside" (1885):

When I was down beside the sea,
A wooden spade they gave to me
To dig the sandy shore.

My holes were hollow like a cup,
In every hole the sea came up,
Till it could hold no more.

 TEACHING IDEAS

Choral Reading. Read a dozen poems aloud. Choose three that would sound good if read chorally. "Script" them to be read by a chorus of five or six voices, allowing for different solo and choral parts, as well as for the dynamics of loud and soft, fast and slow, staccato and glissando. Try these arrangements out with children. After the children have rehearsed several times, tape record them.

Creating Metaphors. Mary O'Neill's poem "My Fingers" on pages 241–242 is really a list of tactile sensations. Using her poem as a model, ask a group of children to write a list of tastes, or sounds, or shapes, or colors. Remind them to think metaphorically; for example, "round" can refer to a wheel or to the consequences of a bad deed.

Creating a Poem Collage. Have children make a poem collage. Pass out copies of a lyric or expressive poem. Have the children read it aloud, with each child taking a line. Then go around the room, having each child chant out a line or phrase he or she found especially striking. Finally, invite them to cut the poems apart and reassemble the lines or phrases as they see fit. If they want, they may repeat a line or phrase, for special emphasis.

EXPERIENCES FOR YOUR LEARNING

1. Compile your own anthology of poems for children. Organize it around a theme or an issue—for example, poems for choral reading, poems from many cultures, or poems to celebrate holidays. So that you can become acquainted with contemporary poetry, use ten different sources, choose no more than two poems per source, and make sure they were published within the last fifteen years. (Thanks to Linnea Henderson for this suggestion.)

2. A good poem may sound natural, but on examination it is likely to turn out to have been very carefully crafted. Take a poem such as A. A. Milne's "Happiness." Try substituting other words for any of Milne's. Does the poem sound as good?

3. Put together a collection of rhymes that accompany activities—jump-rope rhymes and the like. Ask for examples from friends and fellow students. Be especially attuned to rhymes from different cultures—Mexican American, Asian American, African American, and Appalachian.

4. Since singing folksongs is an excellent way to participate in poetry and rhyme, learn to play a musical instrument—one that lets you play and sing at the same time. The easiest is the autoharp—all you do is press the button marked with the letter of the chord (most song books include guitar chords). A guitar is not too hard, once your fingers get adjusted—and there are four-string versions, to make the chording simpler to learn.

RECOMMENDED BOOKS

* indicates a picture book; I indicates interest level (P = preschool, YA = young adult)

Adoff, Arnold. *All the Colors of the Race.* Illustrated by John Steptoe. New York: Lothrop, Lee, & Shepard, 1982. Drawing on the experience of the poet's own family, these are poems about the experiences of mixed-race children. (**I**: 5–9).

———. *In for Winter, Out for Spring.* New York: Harcourt, 1991. Collected poems by the NCTE award–winning urban poet. (**I**: 5–8).

———. *My Black Me: A Beginning Book of Black Poetry.* Rev. ed. New York: Dutton, 1994. Adoff includes poems by Imamu Amiri Baraka, Lucille Clifton, Nikki Giovanni, Langston Hughes, and a dozen others who are better known to adults than to children but who all celebrate the black experience. (**I**: 9–12).

Aldis, Dorothy. *All Together.* 1928. New York: Putnam, 1952. Insightful poems from a child's-eye view, in casual rhyme. (**I**: 7–11).

Axelrod, Alan, and Dan Fox, eds. *Songs of the Wild West.* New York: Metropolitan Museum of Art/Simon & Schuster, 1991. Some favorite songs from the Old West, illustrated with fine Western art. (**I**: all ages)

Baylor, Byrd. *Desert Voices.* New York: Scribner's, 1981. Unrhymed poems on desert topics by the author of *I'm In Charge of Celebrations.* (**I**: 8–11)

Berry, James, ed. *Classic Poems to Read Aloud.* New York: Larousse Kingfisher, 1995. An excellent collection of poems from many cultures. (**I**: 10–YA)

Brooks, Gwendolyn. *Bronzeville Boys and Girls*. New York: HarperCollins, 1967. Poems for children by the first African American woman to win a Pulitzer Prize. (I: 8–11)

* Bruchac, Joseph. *The Earth under Sky Bear's Feet: Native American Poems of the Land*. Illustrated by Thomas Locker. New York: Putnam, 1995. Most of these poems are reflections on the Sky Bear constellation, also known as the Big Dipper. Some of Locker's rich oil paintings are magnificent. (I: 7–11).

Bryan, Ashley. *Sing to the Sun*. New York: Harper-Collins, 1992. Bryan's Caribbean background comes through in his lively poems—some with choruses—and his bright palette. (I: 7–10)

* Burgie, Irving. *Caribbean Carnival: Songs of the West Indies*. Illustrated by Frané Lessac. New York: Morrow/Tambourine, 1992. Thirteen songs include the familiar "Day-O," "Yellow Bird," "Michael Row the Boat Ashore," and "Jamaica Farewell." Also includes one song in Spanish, "Que bonita bandera!" from Puerto Rico. (I: 6–12)

Ciardi, John. *Doodle Soup*. Illustrated by Merle Nacht. Boston: Houghton Mifflin, 1985. Funny poems by a master of the genre. (I: 6–8)

———. *You Read to Me, I'll Read to You*. New York: Harper Trophy, 1987. Favorite poems for children by a much-loved poet. (I: 7–11)

Cole, Joanna, and Stephanie Calmenson. *Miss Mary Mack and Other Children's Street Rhymes*. Illustrated by Alan Tiegreen. New York: Morrow/Beech Tree, 1990. Jump-rope rhymes and more from city streets. (I: 4–8)

Cole, William, ed. *Poem Stew*. Illustrated by Karen Ann Weinhaus. New York: Harper Trophy, 1981. This Reading Rainbow book contains fifty-seven humorous poems by the likes of Shel Silverstein, Dennis Lee, John Ciardi, X. J. Kennedy, and William Cole. (I: 6–10)

———. *A Zooful of Animals*. Illustrated by Lynn Munsinger. Boston: Houghton Mifflin, 1992. Forty-five poems about animals by John Ciardi, Theodore Roethke, Jack Prelutsky, and others. (I: 5–7)

Cullinan, Bernice, ed. *A Jar of Tiny Stars: Poems from NCTE Award-Winning Poets*. Honesdale, PA: Wordsong/Boyds Mills Press, 1996. 3,500 children chose their five favorite poems from the works of each of the poets who won the NCTE poetry award through 1994. (I: 6–13)

Dahl, Roald. *Revolting Rhymes*. New York: Bantam, 1983. If you like Roald Dahl, you'll like this hilarious collection of poems—some of which are in dubious taste. (I: 9–12)

Delacre, Lulu. *Arroz con leche: Popular Songs and Rhythms from Latin America*. New York: Scholastic, 1989. Twelve poems from Puerto Rico, Mexico, and Argentina are first presented as verses in English and Spanish; the musical scores, with simple guitar chords, are provided in the back. (I: 6–11)

Demi. *In the Eyes of the Cat: Japanese Poetry for All Seasons*. Illustrated by Tze-si Huang. New York: Holt, 1992. Some of these short poems are four hundred years old, and some are recent. All crackle with keen observation and insight. (I: 7–12)

* de Paola, Tomie. *The Friendly Beasts*. New York: Putnam, 1981. This lovely old English carol of the Christmas story is a favorite of many children. With music for piano. (I: 5–6)

———. *Tomie de Paola's Book of Poems*. New York: Putnam, 1988. These eighty-six poems, many well known, range from works by contemporary poets such as Aileen Fisher, Valerie Worth, and Jack Prelutsky to poems by Emily Dickinson, Robert Louis Stevenson, and William Blake. (I: 5–12)

de Regniers, Beatrice Schenk, Eva Moore, Mary Michaels White, and Jan Carr, eds. *Sing a Song of Popcorn: Every Child's Book of Poems*. New York: Scholastic, 1988. A beautifully illustrated large-format collection (all of the illustrators are Caldecott winners). (I: 7–12)

Dunn, Sonja. *Butterscotch Dreams*. Portsmouth, NH: Heinemann, 1987. Lively chants and games by a popular Canadian performer and educator. (I: 6–10)

Esbensen, Barbara Juster. *Dance with Me*. Illustrated by Megan Lloyd. New York: HarperCollins, 1995. Fifteen poems by an award-winning poet. (I: 5–12)

* ———. *Echoes for the Eyes: Poems about Patterns in Nature*. Illustrated by Helen K. Davie. New York: HarperCollins, 1996. These poems celebrate visual patterns in nature: spirals, branches, polygons, meanders, and circles. (I: 7–11)

———. *Words with Wrinkled Knees*. New York: HarperCollins, 1987. More poems by the NCTE award–winning poet. (I: 6–12)

Farjeon, Eleanor. *Eleanor Farjeon's Poems for Children*. Philadelphia: Lippincott, 1951. Farjeon won the first Hans Christian Andersen Award for her contribution to children's literature of the world. The poems are touching, funny, and insightful. (I: 7–11)

Farrell, Kate, and Kenneth Koch, eds. *Talking to the Sun: An Illustrated Anthology of Poems for Young People*. New York: Holt, 1985. A beautifully illustrated collection of poems old and new from international sources. Many won't strike you as "children's poems" on a first reading, but there is much to ponder in them. (I: 11–YA)

Fleischman, Paul. *I Am Phoenix: Poems for Two Voices.* Illustrated by Ken Nutt. New York: Harper Trophy, 1989. Poems about birds, set for two voices. (I: 9–12)

———. *Joyful Noise: Poems for Two Voices.* New York: Harper, 1988. This book of poems about insects won a Newbery Medal. (I: 9–12)

Fox, Dan. *Go In and Out the Window: An Illustrated Songbook for Young People.* New York: Holt, 1987. Whether sung or read chorally, these are fine poems, illustrated with classic art. (I: 10–12)

Giovanni, Nikki. *Spin a Soft Black Song.* New York: Farrar, 1985. Fine poems for children by a noted African American poet. (I: 8–12)

Greenfield, Eloise. *Honey, I Love.* Illustrated by Leo and Diane Dillon. New York: Harper Trophy, 1978. Poems for young people by a highly esteemed African American poet. (I: 6–10)

* ———. *Nathaniel Talking.* Illustrated by Joanna Spivey Gilchrist. New York: Writers & Readers/ Black Butterfly, 1988. Fifteen poems from the point of view of Nathaniel, an urban African American boy. (I: 7–11)

* ———. *Night on Neighborhood Street.* Illustrated by Joanna Spivey Gilchrist. New York: Puffin, 1991. Seventeen poems depicting lives of urban African American children. (I: 6–10)

* Gunning, Monica. *Not a Copper Penny in Me House.* Illustrated by Frané Lessac. Honesdale, PA: Wordsong/Boyds Mills, 1993. A dozen poems and naive illustrations celebrate rural life in Jamaica. (I: 6–10)

Harrison, Michael, and Christopher Stuart-Clark, eds. *The Oxford Treasury of Children's Poems.* New York: Oxford University Press, 1988. A lively collection, mostly by English poets, with classics from such authors as Robert Louis Stevenson and Edward Lear. (I: 6–11)

Heaney, Seamus, and Ted Hughes, eds. *The Rattle Bag.* London: Faber & Faber, 1982. Available in paperback in Canada (and elsewhere), an extensive collection of poems from the oral tradition and from poets writing in English. (I: all ages)

Hoban, Russell. *Egg Thoughts and Other Frances Songs.* New York: Harper, 1972. Children who like Hoban's *Frances* books will love these poems, which are Frances's musings on everything from fickle friends to Lorna Doone cookies ("You are plain and you are square/And your flavor's only fair"). (I: 6–9)

Hopkins, Lee Bennett, ed. *Best Friends.* Illustrated by James Watts. New York: Harper, 1986. Poems about friends by Gwendolyn Brooks, Judith Viorst, Langston Hughes, and others. (I: 10–12)

———. *Good Books, Good Times.* New York: Trumpet Club, 1990. Poems about books by a favorite children's poet and anthologist. (I: 8–10)

* ———. *Side by Side: Poems to Read Together.* New York: Simon & Schuster, 1988. Another fine collection by a noted children's poet and anthologist. (I: 7–10)

Hudson, Wade, ed. *Pass It On: African American Poetry for Children.* Illustrated by Floyd Cooper. New York: Scholastic, 1993. Poems by Eloise Greenfield, Lucille Clifton, Gwendolyn Brooks, Langston Hughes, and others. (I: 8–12)

* Hughes, Langston. *The Book of Rhythms.* Introduction by Wynton Marsalis. New York: Oxford University Press, 1995. Hughes wrote this lively illustrated text to make children aware of rhythm in all things—not just in poetry, but in music, art, and life. (I: 7–11)

———. *The Dream Keeper and Other Poems.* New York: Knopf, 1986. Poems suitable for young people by one of American's greatest poets, who was a leader of the Harlem Renaissance. (I: 8–YA)

Janeczko, Paul B., ed. *The Place My Words Are Looking For: What Poets Say About and Through Their Work.* New York: Bradbury, 1990. Poems by Cynthia Rylant, Gary Soto, Gwendolyn Brooks, Myra Cohn Livingston, Naomi Shihab Nye, and others, with comments by the poets. (I: 12–YA)

———. *Poetry from A to Z: A Guide for Young Writers.* New York: Bradbury, 1994. Poems by Naomi Shihab Nye, Lilian Moore, Patricia Hubbell, and Myra Cohn Livingston are given, along with comments by the poets and suggestions for writing poems. (I: 11–YA)

———. *This Delicious Day.* New York: Orchard, 1987. Sixty-five thoughtful poems, presented with a minimum of editorial comment to invite meditation. (I: 12–YA)

Johnson, James Weldon. *The Creation.* Illustrated by James E. Ransome. New York: Holiday House, 1994. Johnson composed "Lift Every Voice and Sing," considered by many to be the African American national anthem. His long poem "The Creation" recalls the oratory of Southern black preachers of the last century. (I: 7–13)

Kennedy, X. J., and Dorothy Kennedy, eds. *Knock at a Star.* Boston: Little, Brown, 1982. An exquisite collection of poems with comments on their literary devices and notes for teachers by two noted American poets. (I: 9–YA)

———. *Talking Like the Rain.* Illustrated by Jane Dyer. Boston: Little, Brown, 1992. A large-format, illustrated collection of poems for children, drawn from many sources by these noted poets. (I: 7–12)

Krull, Kathleen. *Gonna Sing My Head Off! American Folk Songs for Children*. Illustrated by Allen Garnes. New York: Knopf, 1992. With piano arrangements and guitar chords, these sixty-three songs are the best of the old and not-so-old songs that "folkies" in the United States have been singing for years. (I: P–12)

* Langstaff, John. *What a Morning! The Christmas Story in Black Spirituals*. Illustrated by Ashley Bryan. New York: Simon & Schuster/McElderry, 1987. Five spirituals with glorious illustrations, background notes, and stirring musical arrangements. (I: all ages)

Larrick, Nancy, ed. *Piping Down the Valleys Wild*. Illustrated by Ellen Raskin. New York: Dell, 1968. A most useful collection of pleasing poems suitable for children, drawn from a range of contemporary and classic poets. (I: 9–YA)

Lear, Edward. *The Complete Book of Nonsense*. 1846. New York: Dodd, Mead, 1946. A complete collection of poems by the world's most influential nonsense poet. Includes "The Jumblies," or "They Went to Sea in a Sieve," and "The Owl and the Pussycat." (I: 5–9)

Lee, Dennis. *Alligator Pie*. Illustrated by Frank Newfield. Boston: Houghton Mifflin, 1974. These memorable poems on nonsensical subjects are as tightly rhymed and rhythmical as jump-rope rhymes. (I: 7–10)

———. *Garbage Delight*. Illustrated by Frank Newfield. Boston: Houghton Mifflin, 1977. A good source for the nonsense poems of this award-winning Canadian poet. (I: 7–10)

* Lester, Julius. *John Henry*. Illustrated by Jerry Pinkney. New York: Dial, 1994. An African American folksong that pits the "steel-driving man" against a steam drill. (I: 8–10)

Livingston, Myra Cohn. *There Was a Place and Other Poems*. New York: Simon & Schuster/McElderry, 1988. Poems about sadnesses children bear, particularly as families have been broken apart. (I: 10–YA)

———. *Valentine Poems*. New York: Holiday House, 1987. This well-known poet manages to do fresh things with a well-worn topic in this collection of poems for Valentine's Day. (I: 8–12)

McCord, David. *One at a Time*. Illustrated by Henry B. Kane. Boston: Little, Brown, 1986. McCord's poems include "The Pickety Fence," a percussive and rhythmic poem. (I: 8–12)

Merriam, Eve. *Chortles*. New York: Morrow, 1989. The late Eve Merriam was a master experimenter with words. (I: 9–YA)

———. *The Inner City Mother Goose*. New York: Simon & Schuster, 1969. Poems on urban themes patterned on older forms and with an ironic flavor. (I: 9–YA)

Milnes, Gerald. *Granny Will Your Dog Bite? and Other Mountain Rhymes*. Illustrated by Kimberly Bulcken Root. New York: Knopf, 1990. Milnes learned these songs from his West Virginia neighbors. Root's illustrations evoke the mountain setting from which the songs came. (I: 6–12)

Moore, Lilian. *Go with the Poem*. New York: McGraw-Hill, 1979. Ninety lively poems for children by modern poets. (I: 8–12)

Nye, Naomi Shihab. *Words under the Words*. Portland, OR: Eighth Mountain Press, 1995a. This is not really a children's collection, but Nye is so insightful, so generous of spirit, and so clear that many of these poems will appeal to middle-grade students. (I: 12–YA)

Nye, Naomi Shihab, ed. *This Same Sky: A Collection of Poems from Around the World*. New York: Macmillan, 1992. English translations of more than one hundred poems from all of the continents except North America. (I: 8–YA)

———. *The Tree Is Older Than You: Bilingual Poems from Mexico*. New York: Simon & Schuster, 1995b. A wonderfully illustrated collection of poems from Mexico, in Spanish with side-by-side translation. (I: 8–YA)

O'Neill, Mary. *My Fingers Are Always Bringing Me News*. New York: Doubleday, 1969. Poems celebrating the sense of touch, by the author of *Hailstones and Halibut Bones*. (I: 6–10)

Patterson, Annie, and Peter Blood. *Rise Up Singing!* Bethlehem, PA: Sing Out!, 1990. Hundreds of folksongs, some with music and all with guitar chords. Tape recordings of the songs are available. (I: all ages)

Phillip, Neil. *Singing America: Poems That Define a Nation*. Illustrated by Michael McCurdy. New York: Viking, 1995. Containing famous and should-be-famous poems from every period of U.S. history, the book is a wonderful source book of basic American poetry. (I: 8–YA)

Prelutsky, Jack. *The New Kid on the Block*. Illustrated by James Stevenson. New York: Greenwillow, 1984. The new kid in this collection who is intimidating the boys in the neighborhood is a girl, of course. (I: 5–12)

———. *Something Big Has Been Here*. Illustrated by James Stevenson. New York: Greenwillow, 1990. These lively poems range from the hilarious to the serious. (I: 5–12)

Prelutsky, Jack, ed. *The Random House Book of Poetry for Children*. Illustrated by Arnold Lobel. New York: Random House, 1983. An extensive anthology collected by one of America's favorite children's poets. (I: 7–12)

Roethke, Theodore. *The Collected Poems of Theodore Roethke*. New York: Doubleday, 1946. Not all of these poems were written for children; nonetheless, they are full of rich imagery and sometimes startling insights. (I: 10–YA).

Rosen, Michael, ed. *The Kingfisher Book of Children's Poetry*. New York: Larousse Kingfisher, 1993. This thick collection comes from England. Not illustrated, but a good classroom resource. (I: 7–YA)

Rylant, Cynthia. *But I'll Be Back Again: An Album*. New York: Orchard, 1989. Poems describing the difficult Appalachian childhood of a Newbery award–winning author and poet. (I: 12–YA)

Sanchez, Trinidad, Jr. *Why Am I So Brown?* Chicago: MARCH/Abrazo, 1991. Poems describing the Latino experience, for middle school and high school students. (I: 12–YA)

Sandburg, Carl. *Good Morning, America*. New York: Harcourt, 1928. Poems for young and old by one of America's outstanding poets. (I: 10–YA)

———. *Rainbows Are Made: Poems*. New York: Harcourt, 1982. A good source of poems for children by one of America's great poets. (I: 9–12)

Schwartz, Alvin. *And the Green Grass Grew All Around: Folk Poetry for Children*. Illustrated by Sue Truesdell. New York: HarperCollins, 1992. You'll probably remember many of these poems from your childhood. All are suitable for children and make lively choral reading. Nice illustrations, too. (I: 6–YA)

Seeger, Ruth Crawford. *American Folksongs for Children*. New York: Doubleday, 1976. A fine collection of folksongs with accompanying games. Music and guitar chords are included. (I: all ages)

Silverstein, Shel. *Where the Sidewalk Ends*. New York: HarperCollins, 1974. Funny and irreverent poems by one of the most popular of children's poets. (I: 5–12)

Sneve, Virginia Driving Hawk. *Dancing Teepee*. Illustrated by Stephen Gammell. New York: Holiday House, 1989. Traditional poems still popular among Native American young people, these are mostly brief, lyrical observations on various topics. (I: 8–12)

Strickland, Dorothy, and Michael Strickland. *Families: Poems Celebrating the African American Experience*. Honesdale, PA: Wordsong/Boyds Mills, 1994. An upbeat collection by outstanding African American poets, including Gwendolyn Brooks, Nikki Giovanni, Lucille Clifton, Langston Hughes—and also Arnold Adoff. (I: 7–12)

* Temple, Charles. *Train*. Illustrated by Larry Johnson. Boston: Houghton Mifflin, 1996. A rhymed picture book evokes a train ride that lasts from early morning to late at night. (I: 6–9)

* Thayer, Ernest L. *Casey at the Bat*. 1888. Illustrated by Patricia Polacco. New York: Putnam, 1992. A classic American baseball story set to verse. (I: 8–YA)

Viorst, Judith. *If I Were in Charge of the World and Other Worries*. Illustrated by Lynn Cherry. New York: Atheneum, 1981. Viorst penetrates to the heart of the foibles of children and their parents. (I: 12–YA)

Watson, Clyde. *Father Fox's Pennyrhymes*. Illustrated by Wendy Watson. New York: HarperCollins, 1987. Watson has an uncanny ability to create poems that sound fresh off the playground. His sister's illustrations are full of fascinating details and conversations in balloons. (I: P–9)

Worth, Valerie. *All the Small Poems*. Illustrated by Natalie Babbitt. New York: Farrar, 1987. Worth is a master at finding wonder in small and everyday things: a magnet, a cricket, a sleeping dog. (I: 8 and up)

Yolen, Jane. *Best Witches: Poems for Halloween*. New York: Putnam, 1983. Yolen's assemblage of witches has a contemporary flair. (I: 6–10)

———. *Dinosaur Dances*. Illustrated by Bruce Degen. New York: Putnam, 1990. Yolen's poems invoke the unlikely spectacle of dinosaurs dancing the whole gamut of dances. (I: 7–9)

RESOURCES

Butler, Francelia. *Skipping Around the World: The Ritual Nature of Folk Rhymes*. New York: Ballantine, 1989.

Copeland, Jeffrey S., ed. *Speaking of Poets: Interviews with Poets Who Write for Children and Young Adults*. Urbana, IL: National Council of Teachers of English, 1993.

Esbensen, Barbara. *A Celebration of Bees*. New York: HarperCollins, 1987.

Hopkins, Lee Bennett. *Pass the Poetry, Please!* New York: HarperCollins, 1987.

Janeczko, Paul B. *Poetspeak: In Their Work, About Their Work: A Special Kind of Poetry Anthology*. New York: Simon & Schuster, 1991.

Larrick, Nancy. *Let's Do a Poem.* New York: Delacorte, 1991.

Livingston, Myra Cohn. *Poem-Making: Ways to Begin Writing Poetry.* New York: HarperCollins, 1991.

McClure, Amy, et al. *Sunrises and Songs: Reading and Writing Poetry in an Elementary Classroom.* Portsmouth, NH: Heinemann, 1990.

Opie, Iona, and Peter Opie. *The Lore and Language of School Children.* New York: Oxford University Press, 1959.

Wolf, Alan. *It's Show Time! Poetry from Page to Stage.* Asheville, NC: Poetry Alive!, 1993.

REFERENCES

Browning, Robert. *The Pied Piper of Hamelin.* London: Routledge, 1888.

Ciardi, John. *The Man Who Sang the Softies.* Illustrated by Edward Gorey. New York: HarperCollins, 1981.

de la Mare, Walter. *Peacock Pie.* New York: Holt, 1923.

Hall, Donald, ed. *The Oxford Book of Children's Verse in America.* New York: Oxford University Press, 1985.

Hopkins, Lee Bennett. "This Tooth." *Me!* Philadelphia: Curtis Brown, 1970.

Janeczko, Paul B. "Sparks and Wonder: Poetry for Children in the Nineties." *Fanfare: The Christopher-Gordon Children's Literature Annual.* Ed. Joel Taxel. Norwood, MA: Christopher-Gordon, 1992.

Janeczko, Paul B., ed. *The Place My Words Are Looking For: What Poets Say About and Through Their Work.* New York: Bradbury, 1990.

Kutiper, Karen, and Patricia Wilson. "Updating Poetry Preferences: A Look at the Poetry Children Like." *The Reading Teacher* 47. 1 (September, 1993): 28–35.

Livingston, Myra Cohn. "Poetry and the Self." *Fanfare: The Christopher-Gordon Children's Literature Annual.* Ed. Joel Taxel. Norwood, MA: Christopher-Gordon, 1992.

Lukens, Rebecca J. *A Critical Handbook of Children's Literature.* 4th ed. New York: HarperCollins, 1992.

Mason, Walt. "Football." *The Random House Book of Poetry for Children.* Ed. Jack Prelutsky. Illustrated by Arnold Lobel. New York: Random House, 1983.

Merriam, Eve. "The World outside My Skin." *Fanfare: The Christopher-Gordon Children's Literature Annual.* Ed. Joel Taxel. Norwood, MA: Christopher-Gordon, 1992.

Moore, Lilian. *I Thought I Heard the City.* New York: Macmillan, 1967.

Stevenson, Robet Louis. *A Child's Garden of Verses.* London: Longman's, 1885.

Tennyson, Alfred. "The Eagle." 1851. *Poems of Tennyson 1830–1870.* Ed. T. Herbert Warren. New York: Oxford University Press, 1912.

Terry, Ann. *Children's Poetry Preferences: A National Survey of the Upper Elementary Grades.* Urbana, IL: National Council of Teachers of English, 1974.

White, E. B. *Charlotte's Web.* New York: Harper Trophy, 1952.

8 Realistic Fiction

Met Sadrak had taught the school two whole years with only smiles for pay, Grann said. A good man, though plenty strict. But last week the *macoutes* had come, yelling about how Met Sadrak was "La-valas," and dragged him out of the school shed. One man wasn't in uniform, but he had a gun anyway, and an armband that said FRAPH. Paulie saw him beat Met Sadrak with twin slaps on the face, making his head jerk back again and again. All the children were crying. The *macoutes* fired guns in the air. She and the other children ran home, and when they came back again, they found a sign on the school shed saying, THIS SCHOOL IS CLOSED DOWN BY ORDER OF THE PROVISIONAL GOVERNMENT OF HAITI.

from Tonight, By Sea *(1995)*
by Frances Temple

WHAT IS REALISTIC FICTION?

All fiction bears *some* relation to life as we know it. Kenneth Grahame's fanciful animal story **The Wind in the Willows** (1933) tells much about friendship. C. S. Lewis's allegorical fantasy **The Lion, the Witch, and the Wardrobe** (1950) warns that youthful selfishness can lead to corruption. Nonetheless, the trappings of such books are fanciful: We wouldn't think of learning about the driving habits of toads from reading **The Wind in the Willows**; nor would we expect to find a trapdoor in the back of our closet after reading **The Lion, the Witch, and the Wardrobe** (although some of us might check, just to be sure!).

Realistic fiction, however, is a different story. Although the particular characters and plots are made up, the trappings of realistic novels are drawn from the world as it is. Haiti, the setting of Frances Temple's **Tonight, By Sea** (1995), is a real place, where people have suffered political oppression in recent years. Many of the victims of that oppression were young people, and some of them made it to the United States and are students in American classrooms today. Salamanca, the protagonist of Sharon Creech's **Walk Two Moons** (1994), is a made-up character. But there are untold thousands of children in the United States who are parents themselves. These children struggle to have a childhood while taking responsibility for holding their lives together.

Realistic fiction, then, brings the same moral challenges as any fiction does. But it presents those challenges in a here-and-now setting and in a way that says "Hey—this is happening. You or somebody near you could be going through these very experiences."

Realistic Fiction Defined

Realistic fiction is derived from actual circumstances, with realistic settings and characters who face problems and possibilities that are within the range of what is possible in real life. In addition, the events portrayed in realistic fiction raise moral questions that a reader might face in real life. Characters in realistic fiction for children usually have certain characteristics:

- They resemble real people.
- They live in a place that is or could be real.
- They participate in a plausible, if not probable, series of events.

- They are presented with a dilemma that is of interest to children.
- They discover a realistic solution.

Realistic fiction is not exaggeration or fantasy. There are no animals who talk, no anthropomorphized machines, no ghosts, giants, or supernatural happenings. Of course, works of realistic fiction do not literally recount real life, either. Works that do that are considered biographies or informational books.

The Value of Realistic Fiction

Of all the genres of children's literature, realistic fiction is the one that most closely approaches the reality of children's own lives. Reading realistic fiction can benefit children in several ways:

- They may come to feel that they are not alone.
- They may learn to reflect on the choices in their own lives.
- They may learn empathy for other people.
- They may see beyond the limitations of their own experiences.

Illustration 8.1
Maniac Magee was sure he could untie Cobble's knot—but it took a lot of running to untangle the town's social divisions marked by Hector Street. Jerry Spinelli's book won the Newbery Medal in 1991. (*Maniac Magee* by Jerry Spinelli. Used by permission of Little, Brown and Company.)

When child readers recognize in a story something similar to their own feelings or thoughts, they realize they are not alone. For example, Jerry Spinelli's *Maniac Magee* (1990) recounts Jeffrey ("Maniac") Magee's search for a home after the death of his parents. After living with relatives and a succession of surrogate families, Maniac finds himself again without a home. This time he loses hope:

> He . . . put himself up in one of the cabins. It was scarcely bigger than a large doghouse. The floor was dirt. There was a doorway, but no door. . . .
> The second evening came and went. Maniac never stirred. Knowing it would not be fast or easy, and wanting, deserving nothing less, grimly, patiently, he waited for death. (p. 96)

Most children in the middle elementary grades have had feelings of desolation from time to time. They can empathize with a fictional character who passes through such feelings and back into constructive engagement with life.

When children read realistic fiction, they may reflect on the choices they face in their own lives. Characters in books make choices that encourage young readers to think about their own dilemmas. In discussions of *Maniac Magee*, for instance, children like to talk about one of Maniac's decisions:

> He held up the candy bar, an inch from Maniac's lips. "Wanna bite?"
> Maniac couldn't figure. "You sure?"
> "Yeah, go ahead. Take a bite."
> Maniac shrugged, took the Mars Bar, bit off a chunk, and handed it back. "Thanks."
> Dead silence along the street. The kid had done the unthinkable, he had chomped on one of Mars's own bars. Not only that, but white kids just didn't put their mouths where black kids had had theirs. . . . (pp. 34–35)

Not every child reader would have taken a bite of that Mars Bar—but nearly every reader stops to think about the choice after reading this passage.

Realistic fiction helps readers empathize with other people. In *Tonight, By Sea* (1995), Paulie and her family become so harassed by government-backed thugs that they take their chances on the ocean in a small boat. That boat eventually brings Paulie to the United States. Though they are unlikely to get to know any of the many thousands of real "boat people" whom they have seen flicker across the television screen, young readers get to know Paulie's story. They know what happened to her and how she felt about it. They know why she sailed in that boat. They believe that in her place, they might have made the same choice.

Realistic fiction helps readers see beyond the limitations of their own experience. Many American readers don't know what it's like to be a member of a minority group, trying to get along in a setting that is dominated by the majority. After reading Jacqueline Woodson's *Maizon at Blue Hill* (1992), they will at least have an idea. Most young people have longed at one time or another to be a popular young musician with thousands of fans. After reading Katherine Paterson's *Come Sing, Jimmie Jo* (1985), however, they will understand the perils of having too much success too early. Most young readers, thank goodness, will never have to sell their bodies for the sake of their family's survival. But after reading Gary Paulsen's *Sisters/Hermanas* (1993), they will understand something about that awful decision—both by walking in the shoes of a young prostitute and because the book is built on a thoughtful analogy: Paulsen compares child prostitution to the awkward predicament of a daughter who is a star cheerleader to fulfill her mother's excessive ambitions.

THE EVOLUTION OF REALISTIC FICTION

Realistic fiction has been available for children for a surprisingly long time. The first title read by children that might be called realistic fiction was *Robinson Crusoe,* published in 1719. Though written for the general reader, this book became associated with children in the mid-eighteenth century, when it was recommended for them by the philosopher Jean Jacques Rousseau. Rousseau's recommendation was timely, because publishers had begun to make the transition from publishing books for children about dying and repentance to publishing new forms of writing, including realistic fiction.

The Nineteenth Century

The first significant works of realistic fiction written expressly for children appeared in the mid-nineteenth century in England. Hannah More began writing fictionalized religious lessons that were more pleasing to children than the then-popular didactic tracts. At the same time, Anna Laetitia Barbauld wrote accessible and realistic nature stories. In *Hymns of Prose for Children* (1797), Barbauld wrote in carefully phrased sentences:

> I will show you what is strong. The lion is strong when he raiseth himself from his lair, when he shaketh his mane. . . . The lion is strong but
> He who made the lion is stronger than he.

Meanwhile, on the other side of the Atlantic, Americans developed strong nationalistic feelings after the War of 1812—and as a by-product, they created their own distinctive literature for children. The break from the influence of British literature meant that fewer instructional and sectarian books but more books that could be called entertaining realistic fiction were published.

The adventure story, a blending of the extraordinary with the possible, came into being with the works of James Fenimore Cooper. His *The Last of the*

Mohicans, set on the frontier of New York State and published in 1826, is considered the first American novel. Louisa May Alcott's *Little Women* appeared in 1868. Alcott's work, based on her own family experiences, was the first to present the dilemma facing young women—how to balance interests inside and outside of the home. *Little Women* was enormously popular on both sides of the Atlantic with readers of all ages.

For boys, Horatio Alger's books such as *Ragged Dick* (1897) provided strong fictional images of the American dream of getting rich through determination, cleverness—and impressing powerful people. Alger's tales of lowly urban heroes going from "rags to riches" became lasting pieces of American culture.

Mark Twain's *The Adventures of Tom Sawyer* (1876) and *The Adventures of Huckleberry Finn* (1885) are considered two of the best American novels of any period. Both develop a strong sense of place—the Mississippi river towns of Mark Twain's childhood (Mark Twain was the penname of Samuel Clemens). They are also quintessentially American novels, complete with issues of race and the conflict between overpious religion and the boisterous spirits of real people, all salted with the rich, gamy flavors of the frontier. Like other books of the period, Twain's works exalted "boys will be boys" naughtiness but restricted girls to strait-laced behavior. The double standard was alive and well in books for children.

The first of the great horse stories, Anna Sewell's *Black Beauty,* was published in 1877 and paved the way for the continuing popularity of realistic animal stories. Although *Black Beauty* is still read today, new editions have expurgated the elements of racism found in the original.

Also in the nineteenth century, when U.S. industry grew increasingly involved in international trade, the first realistic fiction about contemporary life in other countries became available. Mary Mapes Dodge's *Hans Brinker, or the Silver Skates* (1865) was based on that American author's careful research about Holland; Johanna Spyri's *Heidi* (1884) was written from the childhood reminiscences of a Swiss author and translated into English. Both works informed American children about life in other lands, and both are still read today.

Toward the end of the century, shortly after the Indian Wars drew to a close and the great cattle drives ended, many adventurers from the West, such as Buffalo Bill Cody, went East to glamorize the cowboy's and cowgirl's life in "Wild West Shows." The mass-produced dime novel appeared at the same time, and scores of these were written about the wild West.

The end of the nineteenth century saw a resurgence of sentimentalism toward the child. Frances Hodgson Burnett published *Little Lord Fauntleroy* in 1886, and its somewhat saccharine plot involving a good and gentle boy who loves everyone and solves everyone's problems was a runaway success. After she moved to the United States, Burnett wrote *The Secret Garden* (1910), a book with a more believable theme of children's redemptive effects on each other. This book is still popular with children.

The Twentieth Century

At the dawn of the twentieth century, writers continued to romanticize the innocence and beauty of children. The domestic novel flourished and was epitomized by *Pollyanna* (1912) by Eleanor Porter. Never having met her bitter and cross Aunt Polly before, Pollyanna exclaims, "Oh, I'm so glad, glad, GLAD to see you . . ." (p. 16). Pollyanna gains power over difficulties by following her father's advice to face each hardship by finding something to be glad about. "Glad" clubs formed all over the United States, their members emulating Pollyanna's unquenchably optimistic view of the world.

A prolific writer and ingenious entrepreneur named Edward Stratemeyer began a "fiction factory" shortly after the turn of the century. Stratemeyer generated brief plot summaries and handed them to hack writers who completed the books under fictitious names. Hundreds of series books about the Rover Boys, the Hardy Boys, Tom Swift, the Bobbsey Twins, and others were products of Stratemeyer's fertile imagination, if not his typewriter.

Edward Stratemeyer had produced thirteen hundred of his plot summaries by the time he died, a rich man, in 1930. His daughter Harriet Stratemeyer Adams began churning out the *Nancy Drew* series under the penname Carolyn Keene. She is said to have written three hundred titles in the series; and two hundred million copies of them had been sold by the time she died in 1982, at age 89.

The *Hardy Boys* and *Nancy Drew* books are still being updated and marketed to new generations. But today books from the Stratemeyer Syndicate compete with series such as *The Babysitters Club, Encyclopedia Brown, Goosebumps,* and others—which crowd the shelves of bookstores and worry some teachers, parents, and librarians because of their sheer predictability and scant literary quality. (In fact, seventy years ago, adults' objections to the same short comings in the original Stratemeyer books were much more strident, with teachers often speaking out against the books—and most libraries refusing to stock them.)

Between the two world wars, a host of now-classic writers and illustrators began their work. Robert McCloskey wrote and illustrated nature stories for younger children and humorous ones for older children, the most famous of which are **Make Way for Ducklings** (1941) and **Homer Price** (1943). A large crop of still-popular realistic fiction was published for the mid-elementary school reader, such as **The Box Car Children** (1950), by Gertrude Warner, and **The Moffats** (1941), by Eleanor Estes, both of which were followed by more books about the same characters.

From New Realism to Diverse Perspectives

Until the eve of World War II, most of the protagonists and settings in children's realistic fiction were white and middle class. Then Florence Crannell Means, herself white, wrote several books about children of color: **Shuttered Windows** (1938), about an African American girl in an all-white school, and **The Moved Outers** (1945), about the World War II internment of Japanese Americans. Jesse Jasper Jackson wrote **Call Me Charley** (1945), the first children's book by an African American to openly introduce the subject of racism. The character Charley was the only person of color in an all-white school.

Sexuality appeared in girls' books before the subject was addressed for boys. **Seventeenth Summer** (1942) by Maureen Daly introduced awakening sexuality and the teenage romance novel. The book was enormously popular up to the mid-1960s. In the 1970s, Judy Blume's **Are You There God? It's Me, Margaret** (1970) and **Forever** (1975) caused loud protests from censors because of their open discussion of sexuality. A rather tame view of teenage male sexual fantasies is the theme of Kin Platt's very funny and highly acclaimed book, **The Terrible Love Life of Dudley Cornflower** (1976). In his fantasies, Dudley is continually devising ways to have his first sexual encounter—he even considers the housekeeper who vacuums the floor—but it is his developing friendship with Kelly Lake that finally takes him out of fantasy and into reality.

Illustration 8.2
Margaret talked to God "without even moving her lips," and asked if He could hurry her growing up. (*Are You There God? It's Me Margaret* by Judy Blume. Copyright © 1970 by Judy Blume. Used by permission of Dell Books, a division of Bantam Doubleday Dell Publishing Group, Inc.)

In the 1970s, Shelton Root (1977) described the unvarnished picture of children's life that was emerging in realistic fiction as "New Realism." Old realism depicted children's lives in more protected terms, glossing over circumstances that lead children to feel helpless or hopeless. New Realism looked at the downside of life: children suffering from poverty, racism, sexism, war, economic upheavals, and parental irresponsibility. Characters often faced unsolvable problems or moral dilemmas. New Realism focused on adolescents as a distinct social group—not just extensions of their parents. Writing about problems became a way of describing life.

Since the 1970s, more writers of different races, nationalities, income groups, and sexual preferences have appeared on the children's book scene, to write about life as they know it. Their themes go beyond New Realism, in that differences and hardships may be background factors in works that focus on the development of character or the pursuit of a worthwhile life. In her 1995 book, **_Like Sisters on the Homefront_**, Rita Williams-Garcia does not dwell on teenage sexuality and abortion but uses these as background issues against which her characters grow from naiveté to knowledge. Contemporary authors of the young adult novel such as John Donovan, M. E. Kerr, Judy Blume, Richard Peck, Norma Klein, Paula Danzinger, Ron Koertge, Harry Mazer, Paul Zindel, Robert Cormier, Walter Dean Myers, and Norma Mazer sympathetically depict the cul-

Are contemporary books *too* realistic?

ISSUE TO CONSIDER

"New" or not, realism is still a dominant element in fiction for children. Truly disturbing social problems are depicted even in books that win critical acclaim. For example, of the four 1996 Newbery Honor Books, three are works of realistic fiction. Of these, one, *What Jamie Saw* (1995) by Carolyn Coman, is about child abuse; another, *The Watsons Go to Birmingham—1963* (1995) by Christopher Paul Curtis, is about racism and violence; the third, *Yolonda's Genius* (1995) by Carol Fenner, portrays drug abuse, racism, and obesity. The winner of the Newbery Medal, Karen Cushman's *The Midwife's Apprentice* (1995), is a work of historical fiction, but even its protagonist is a homeless girl who sleeps in dung heaps and never experiences home or family. The winning books in the previous few years aren't much different. You might wonder whether such books are robbing children of the joy of reading about happy childhood. And is the continuing popularity of "gentler" books, such as Laura Ingalls Wilder's *Little House* series, or *The Boxcar Children*, or the many titles by E. Nesbit, an indication that many children, parents, and teachers do not appreciate the stronger contemporary fare?

On the other hand, Katherine Paterson was probably correct when she wrote, "Children who have never felt the sting of prejudice, who laugh freely and bring their parents joy are a tiny minority of all the children in the world" (1993, p. 67). Surely, as teachers and parents, we have some obligation to expose children to the realities of life as other people live it.

What do you think? Would you advocate choosing works of contemporary realism for reading in school?

ture of adolescents and their social and personal problems, as well as the new possibilities they face.

The broader range of topics in contemporary realistic fiction certainly expands young readers' awareness of the varieties of possible experience. But it also gives rise to disagreements between those who would shelter children from such material and those who believe it is healthy for young people to explore difficult real-life issues in books.

CATEGORIES OF REALISTIC FICTION

Over the generations, when children have been asked what topics they enjoy in realistic fiction, their preferences have remained fairly constant. Barbara Elleman's (1986) retrospective bibliographies in *Booklist*, a publication of the American Library Association, are arranged by genres most requested by children. The most popular categories of realistic fiction are humor, mystery, and stories about survival. Hurley (1970) found in a summary of research that ". . . there is an amazing consistency in patterns of reading interest, beginning in preschool" (p. 96).

It is surprising how many of these topics writers can get into one book. *Yolonda's Genius* (1995) by Carol Fenner, a Newbery Honor Book, works in the topics of school and friendship—as well as size and appearance, music, drugs, and life in a single-parent family. In *Dancing Carl* (1983), author Gary Paulsen covers sports (ice skating), school, and the meaning of love. Betsy Byars has humor, school, romance, writing, and moving away in her popular *The Burning Questions of Bingo Brown* (1988).

Teachers also choose realistic fiction to introduce curriculum topics and invite children to learn. The following categories are broad ones, but they are the topics of the books that children, teachers, and parents regularly seek out.

Books about Self-Discovery and Growing Up

Many works of realistic fiction enable children to explore their own thoughts, feelings, and predispositions and to compare their inner experiences with those of others. Good books about self-discovery are even available for preschoolers. *"More More More" Said the Baby* (1990), a Caldecott Honor Book by Vera Williams, promotes self-discovery by having the baby the center of play and loving attention from a father, a grandmother, and a mother. Bernard Waber created the now-classic *Ira Sleeps Over* (1972), in which he answered unasked questions of young children, such as "Am I the only person who sleeps with a teddy?" (Ira, of course, discovers he is not.)

The complex plot of *Where the Lilies Bloom* (1969), by Bill and Vera Cleaver, is underpinned by the issue of discovering one's self. Mary Call must make decisions for herself when she discovers that the advice her father gave her before he died doesn't work for her or for her sister.

Another way to discover one's self is to find one's own talents and passions. Although there are scores of titles about becoming good at sports (these will be treated in a later section), *The Facts and Fictions of Minna Pratt* (1988), by Patricia MacLachlan, is one of a few books that feature a child developing abilities in another area—in this case, playing the cello. Zilpha Keatley Snyder's main character in *Libby on Wednesday* (1990) is a writer who forms a writers' club. Leigh Botts, in Beverly Cleary's *Dear Mr. Henshaw* (1983), is forced by teachers to write to an author and soon he is writing for writing's sake. Tomie de Paola's

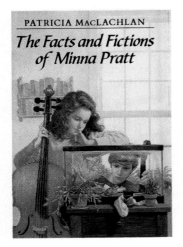

Illustration 8.3
The young cellist Minna Pratt works to match the skill of her brother Lucas, who can already play a cello with vibrato. (*The Facts and Fictions of Minna Pratt* by Patricia MacLachlan. Jacket art copyright © 1988 by Ruth Sanderson. Jacket copyright © 1988 by HarperCollins Publishers. Used by permission of HarperCollins Publishers.)

The Art Lesson (1989) tells about a child eager to become an artist. Nonetheless, given the importance of children's developing a sense of industry and competence during their early school years (an issue discussed in Chapter 1), it seems lamentable that there are not more books celebrating children's development of their various talents.

Having navigated the sometimes arduous path to maturity, many adults have an impulse to share what they have learned with young people. So they write. For their part, children often say they "can't wait" to grow up. So they enjoy reading about the process of maturing and learning. No wonder growing up is a popular theme in children's literature.

In *Class Pictures* (1980) by Marilyn Sachs, Pat and Lolly chronicle the crucial events in their lives from kindergarten through high school and how they felt about each other and themselves. For younger children, *Just Us Women* (1982), by Jeannette Caines, describes a child traveling with her aunt and learning how to create daily routines to make life more interesting. *Baseball in April and Other Stories* (1990), by Gary Soto, shows Mexican American young people on both sides of the mysterious threshhold of adolescence striving to get by in a California neighborhood where people make do with high hopes and limited means.

Books about Families

Family stories abound in realistic fiction. They take as many twists and turns as do families in the real world. In *Shiloh* (1991), Phyllis Reynolds Naylor has created a stable nuclear family in which each member cares about the others. Marty expresses that sense of belonging when he says, "You ask *me* the best place to live, I'd say right where we are, a little four-room house with hills on three sides."

In a different kind of family, Margot schemes gently and caringly to help her obese mother to walk down five flights from their apartment to the outside in *The Law of Gravity* (1978), by Johanna Hurwitz. Getting acquainted with past generations of her African American family is important to Emily in *Toning the Sweep* (1993) by Angela Johnson. Emily videotapes the storytelling that goes on while she helps her grandmother prepare for chemotherapy and eventual death. James Stevenson also extends the reach of family through generations in his short, illustrated chapter books. In *Higher on the Door* (1987), Stevenson creates a warm and lasting connection between a child and a grandparent who gently and humorously offers lessons from his own past.

Divorce, broken homes, alcoholism, child abuse, and same-sex relationships—all nearly absent from books written thirty years ago—are now widely treated in children's realistic fiction. Barbara Seabrooke has her character in *Judy Scuppernong* (1990) tell imagined stories about her alcoholic mother to her friends until it is time to move again. Foster homes, and wondering where and to whom one belongs, are the themes of Betsy Byars's *The Pinballs* (1977) and Katherine Paterson's *The Great Gilly Hopkins* (1978). The stress between family members of different generations disturbs the youngest member in Sharon Bell Mathis's novel, *The Hundred Penny Box* (1975). *Heather Has Two Mommies* (1989), by Leslea Newman, and *Daddy's Roommate* (1990), by Michael Willhoite, both rather stiffly introduce the topic of same-sex parents. In *My Two Uncles* (1995), however, Judith Vigna has created a realistic and interesting plot about a grandfather's initial antagonism toward Elly's uncle and his partner. In *From the Notebooks of Melanin Sun* (1995), Jacqueline Woodson treats very sensitively the issue of a young teenage boy's discovery that his mother is a lesbian.

Homelessness is also a subject in increasing numbers of children's books. Theresa Nelson's ***The Beggar's Ride*** (1992) tells of a twelve-year-old girl who runs away from home to the streets of Atlantic City, where she is befriended by other homeless people and learns to survive. The search for a home and an address is the unifying theme of ***Maniac Magee*** (1990). Maniac cannot go to school, he says, because going to school requires going home after school. ***Secret City*** (1990) by Felice Holman describes homeless children taking over an abandoned house in a city. Paula Fox's ***Monkey Island*** (1991) is a haunting story of a boy who lives in a hotel room with his mother, until she leaves and never comes back. Frances Temple's ***Grab Hands and Run*** (1993) was fictionalized from a true account of the flight of the surviving members of a Salvadoran family from their homeland and their search for a permanent home in the North, after the father has been assassinated.

Books about School and Society

The school day is a source of constant drama for young people. School is their stage, their proving ground, their source of social contacts. There are many good works of realistic fiction that explore the pushes and tugs of schooling.

Young children just entering school worry about what the experience will be like. Amy Schwartz's ***Annabelle Swift, Kindergartner*** (1988) helps answer that question for children. Annabelle's sister informs her about what she needs to know to begin kindergarten. Annabelle, however, prefers to make her own way. Schwartz creates a believable kindergarten setting in this reassuring book.

No one has succeeded better at helping children see the teacher's point of view than Harry Allard, in ***Miss Nelson Is Missing!*** (1977) and ***Miss Nelson Is Back*** (1982) (both illustrated by James Marshall). In the first, the children's bad behavior comes abruptly to an end when kind and gentle Miss Nelson appears to go on leave, to be replaced by a terrible disciplinarian, Miss Viola Swamp.

The pitfalls of school for older children is the subject of Louis Sachar's thoughtful ***There's a Boy in the Girls' Bathroom*** (1987), which provides telling details about an eleven-year-old bungler who learns to fit in. Barthe DeClements touches the right note for each grade in ***Nothing's Fair in Fifth Grade*** (1981) and ***Sixth Grade Can Really Kill You*** (1995).

Illustration 8.4
Annabelle's sister has overprepared her for kindergarten, and Annabelle's knowledge astounds the whole class. (*Annabelle Swift, Kindergartner* by Amy Schwartz. Copyright © 1988 by Amy Schwartz. Used by permission of the Publisher, Orchard Books, New York.)

Illustration 8.5
It was one thing for Lucas to be a clown when he felt like it; another when he was assigned to the role of clown. (*Class Clown* by Johanna Hurwitz. Illustration copyright © 1987 by Sheila Hamanaka. Used by permission of Morrow Junior Books, a division of William Morrow and Company, Inc.)

Illustration 8.6
Vernon finds himself by accepting friendship from the neighborhood crazy lady and her mentally challenged son. (*Crazy Lady!* by Jane Leslie Conly. Jacket art copyright © 1993 by Elena Pavlov. Jacket copyright © 1993 by HarperCollins Publishers. Used by permission of HarperCollins Publishers.)

Getting along in the community beyond the school is the subject of many books written for young people. In *Scooter* (1993), written and illustrated by the Caldecott-winning author and illustrator Vera B. Williams, Elana Rose Rosen is literally pushed into the neighborhood by her mother. The main character in *Queenie Peavy* (1966) by Robert Burch identifies herself only as the daughter of a father in prison; she has to find an identity in her school and community other than the prisoner's daughter. Eleven-year-old Libby offers the school writing club her tree house as a place to meet on Wednesday in *Libby on Wednesday* (1990), by Zilpha Keatley Snyder.

Books about Interpersonal Relations

Some useful works of realistic fiction revolve around the problems of getting along with others. In this area, a work of fiction can do what real life cannot do—allow us to experience the perspectives of more than one character. Charlotte Zolotow is a master at authoring books about relationships. *The Hating Book* (1969), *The Quarreling Book* (1963), and others of her works are about learning to get along with another person. Johanna Hurwitz addresses a common peer group problem in *Class Clown* (1987), in which third grader Lucas Cott decides to turn over a new leaf, only to discover that changing one's role in the group turns out to be more difficult than he thought.

The protagonist of *Harriet the Spy* (1964), by Louise Fitzhugh, believes she can become a writer by spying on her friends and neighbors and writing up her unflattering observations. However, after her friends see what she has written about them, she discovers that she needs friends more than she needs the aloofness she had associated with being a writer.

In *Crazy Lady!* (1993), a Newbery Honor Book by Jane Leslie Conly, Vernon's mother has died, and his kindly but barely literate father is unable to assist Vernon in his troubled efforts to read. Maxine, the neighborhood alcoholic (commonly called the "Crazy Lady"), and her mentally challenged, mute son help Vernon come to terms with his learning disability as well as the loss of his mother.

Books about Mental and Physical Challenges

People in real life can flourish in spite of challenging mental and physical conditions. The limiting factors they face are not only the challenging conditions, but their own sense of the possible and the limited expectations of those around them. The trick for authors is to create characters who can achieve success without having the disability seem to give them special powers.

In 1971, author Betsy Byars won a Newbery Medal for *The Summer of the Swans* (1970), in which protagonist Sara's brother is mentally retarded. Sara feels awkward and self-conscious about her brother's condition and just about everything else in her life. When her brother is lost, Sara struggles to determine what really counts about herself and her relationships with others.

The Alfred Summer (1980) by Jan Slepian is distinguished for being one of the first books with a main character who is physically challenged. Cerebral palsy does not stop Lester from helping his friends build a boat in their basement—but it takes some doing to overcome his own and his mother's doubts about what he can accomplish.

Berneice Rabe has written several books about characters with physical limitations. In *Margaret's Moves* (1987), the nine-year-old hero is confined to a wheelchair because of spina bifida, but she is not confined *by* the wheelchair. Her favorite activity is playing ball. The first-grade protagonist of *The Balancing*

Girl (1986), normally confined to a wheelchair, performs a balancing act on crutches for a school carnival.

Several authors have created good stories about mentally challenged children. Carrie, in *The Language of Goldfish* (1980) by Zibby O'Neal, has every material, intellectual, and artistic advantage, but she suffers from mental illness. She fears discrimination by her peers but eventually makes friends. The situation is the opposite for Adam in *Pictures of Adam* (1986), by Myron Levoy. Adam is abused and has multiple learning disabilities, but gains self-acceptance when Lisa makes friends with him, drawn to him partially through her love of photography. M.E. is overjoyed to have Polly as a best friend in Sylvia Cassidy's *M.E. and Morton* (1987), but she learns from Polly that her neighbor—mentally retarded Morton—can be a good friend, too. In *Where's Chimp?* (1988), Misty has Down syndrome. Her father talks to her about events of the day, including a lost stuffed monkey. For younger children, *Be Good to Eddie Lee* (1993), by Violet Fleming, and *Thumbs Up, Rico* (1994), by Maria Testa, have characters with Down syndrome. Eddie Lee is able to see flowers and frog's eggs better than other children; in one of three stories about Rico, he can't shoot a slam dunk, but he can draw an imaginative picture of one. In *Fire in the Wind* (1995) by Betty Levin, the protagonist protects her mentally challenged cousin but learns from him as well.

Books about Romance and Sexuality

Works of realistic fiction that focus on romance cover topics that run the gamut from girl-boy friendships to explicit aspects of sexuality to the true meaning of love. In Bette Greene's *Philip Hall Likes Me, I Reckon Maybe* (1974), a Newbery Honor Book, Beth enjoys a competitive friendship with Philip Hall and experiences unspoken feelings of sexual awakening. In *Forever* (1975) by Judy Blume (a book you still won't find on many school library shelves), there is an explicit step-by-step depiction of sexual intercourse. On the other hand, readers enticed by the title of Jenny Davis's *Sex Education: A Novel* (1988) will be surprised to find a complex and powerful plot involving all aspects of human love.

It is often said that the experience of falling in love is indescribable, but several authors of realistic fiction have succeeded in finding apt words for intense feelings. Going to a movie with a boy and receiving a first kiss is explored in Sharon Creech's *Absolutely Normal Chaos* (1995). In *Jason and Marceline* (1986), by Jerry Spinelli, Jason reflects on his feelings of physical attraction to Marceline. *Anastasia at This Address* (1992), one of a series of books by Lois Lowry about Anastasia growing up, lets the reader share the heroine's experience of falling in love. Robert Newton Peck's *Soup in Love* (1992) describes how Valentine's Day stirs Soup to try his first kiss. In *A Hand Full of Stars* (1990), set in modern Syria, a young boy's romantic intentions are interrupted by his involvement in publishing an underground opposition newspaper.

Books about Moral Dilemmas and Moral Responsibility

Like *Shiloh* (1991) and *Maniac Magee* (1990), many works of realistic fiction for young people pose moral dilemmas that confront people in the real world. Some are personal dilemmas that characters cannot avoid; others have to do with social issues in which characters can choose to become involved or to stand on the sidelines.

A good example of the first kind of dilemma is Sharon Bell Mathis's Newbery Honor Book, *The Hundred Penny Box* (1975), in which Michael, the

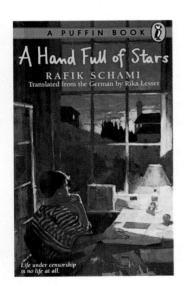

Illustration 8.7
A fourteen-year-old Syrian boy who loves to write starts a newspaper to oppose the policies of the government. (*A Hand Full of Stars* by Rafik Schami, translated by Rika Lesser. Copyright © 1987 by Beltz Verlag, Weinheim und Basel. English translation copyright © 1990 by Rika Lesser. Used by permission of Dutton Children's Books, a division of Penguin Books USA Inc.)

young protagonist, is caught in the middle of a conflict between his mother and a one-hundred-year-old aunt: Does he obey his mother's rules, or does he protect Aunt Dew's memories and dignity?

A story about a character caught up in a moral dilemma of his own making is Avi's ***Nothing But the Truth: A Documentary Novel*** (1991), in which high school student Phillip Malloy falsely reports that his English teacher refused to let him sing the national anthem. The book has no narrator, but rather uses diaries, newspaper clippings, memos, letters, dialogues, and radio talk-show scripts to recount the disastrous consequences of a distortion of the truth.

An example of a book in which a character involves herself in a social issue is Sharon Bell Mathis's ***Sidewalk Story*** (1971). A family is evicted from their home. The book's protagonist, Lilly Etta, befriends the family, calls a newspaper reporter who exposes the injustice, and eventually saves the day.

In some recent books, young protagonists go up against injustices of historic proportions. The characters in Christopher Paul Curtis's Newbery Honor Book ***The Watsons Go to Birmingham—1963*** (1995) witness the most shameful event of the civil rights era, when Klansmen bomb a Sunday school and kill four African American children. The family in Rachel Isadora's ***At the Crossroads*** (1994), living in a South Africa still in the grip of apartheid, is split apart by the father's long separation from home as he goes off to work in the diamond mines.

Books about Survival

Many characters in realistic fiction are severely tested by challenges and struggle to find ways to survive. Some must overcome their own self-doubts or limitations. Some must overcome prejudice and societal oppression. And some must overcome natural challenges.

Overcoming Self-Doubts. Jackie worked to ***Keep Ms. Sugarman in the Fourth Grade*** (1992) (a book by Elizabeth Levy), because Ms. Sugarman was the first teacher who helped her overcome self-doubt and reduce the number of her visits to the principal's office. When Ms. Sugarman is promoted to principal, Jackie chains herself to a desk in protest. The teacher compares Jackie's efforts to great social protests in history, and Jackie learns to value her independence of thought rather than condemning herself for it.

Mikey is good at all sports except swimming in ***When the Water Closes Over My Head*** (1994), by Donna Jo Napoli. After much family torment, he finally identifies the exact moment when his fear arises, and his mother suggests he concentrate on just that moment to overcome his fear successfully. It works. ***The Hundred Dresses*** (1944), by Eleanor Estes, is a now classic story about overcoming the cruelty of prejudice. Wanda Petronski is belittled by Peggy and Maddie for wearing the same dress every day, though she claims to have one hundred dresses at home. When Wanda's family moves away because of the prejudices they face, Wanda mails Peggy and Maddie drawings of themselves, each pictured in one of the hundred dresses she has designed. Maddie's and Peggy's consciences are pricked by Wanda's responding to malevolence with kindness.

In a similar plot, the main character in ***Blubber*** (1974), by Judy Blume, must cope with the cruel treatment her peers direct at her because she is overweight. Then the table turns; one of her tormentors becomes the one being tormented—leaving most readers feeling uncomfortable about Blubber's lack of kindness.

Overcoming Prejudice. The eight children in ***Mayfield Crossing*** (1993), by Vaunda Micheaux Nelson, are excited about two things—baseball and going

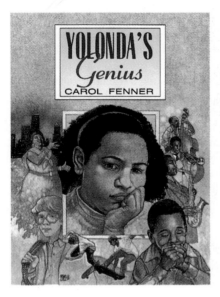

Illustration 8.8
Yolonda's genius is devoted to devising schemes to get her brother Andrew recognized for his musical talent. This book was a 1996 Newbery Honor Book. (*Yolonda's Genius* by Carol Fenner. Illustration copyright © Stephen Marchesi. Used by permission of Stephen Marchesi.)

Illustration 8.9
Marisol grows one sunflower on a neglected New York City block, and her efforts lead to a flowering community. (*The Garden of Happiness* by Erika Tamar. Illustration copyright © 1996 by Barbara Lambase. Used by permission of Harcourt Brace & Company.)

to a new, integrated school in the fall. The children at the new school, however, are unwilling to accept African American children on their ball team. The possibility of changing racist traditions opens up when blond and friendly Ivy accepts Meg's invitation to become the ninth player on the Mayfield Crossing team.

The hero of *Somewhere in the Darkness* (1992) by Walter Dean Myers is a very bright African American tenth grader, for whom life seems to be falling apart. The school counselor doesn't help, his deceased mother's friend who cares for him can't help, and then his father returns unexpectedly (and illegally) from prison to convince Jimmy that he was not guilty of the crime for which he was convicted. In the end, the reader feels that Jimmy will be able to find strength to put his own life together.

There can be no stronger hero than Yolonda in *Yolonda's Genius* (1995), who overcomes discrimination and the evil intentions of some of her classmates. In *The Garden of Happiness* (1996), Marisol plants a sunflower seed in her New York City block and finds that she is not alone in wanting to make the multiethnic community more beautiful.

Overcoming Natural Challenges. In some books for children, nature is presented as a harsh adversary; in others, nature helps characters survive. In some books, nature is portrayed as both harsh and helpful. Brian, in Gary Paulsen's Newbery Honor Book, *Hatchet* (1987), finds himself alone in the wilderness after an airplane crash, and he must come to understand nature in order to find food and shelter to stay alive. In *Julie of the Wolves* (1972), a Newbery Medal winner by Jean George, Julie escapes from an arranged marriage in her Inuit village to survive in the desolate Alaskan tundra by living with wolves. In order to be accepted by the wolves, she observes and mimics the intricacies of their behavior.

The sibling protagonists in *Toughboy and Sister* (1990), by Kirkpatrick Hill, are eleven- and eight-year-old Athabascans who are stranded in a Yukon River camp after their father dies of alcoholism. The children struggle for food and shelter until they are rescued by a neighbor, Natasha. In the sequel, *Winter Camp* (1993), Natasha takes the children camping "like in the old days." A sled driver is injured, Natasha has to leave to get help, and the children must run the camp, all the time wishing for modern conveniences as nature threatens them with cruel cold, unsafe ice, and potentially dangerous fire.

Nature provides solace in *Blue Heron* (1992) by Avi. Maggie and Tucker, both facing severe family problems, meet at the water's edge, where Maggie gains spiritual renewal from the peaceful heron while Tucker tries to kill it with a bow and arrow. Both characters are assisted in dealing with their family struggles by their observations and discussions of the heron.

Mystery Books

Mysteries have long been favorite recreational reading for adults, ever since Edgar Allan Poe published "The Murders in the Rue Morgue" in 1841. Although very few are considered serious literature, mystery stories nonetheless enjoy wide appeal, especially among those readers who enjoy the challenge of following the author's hints and diversions as they seek a solution to the mystery. Young people can enjoy mystery stories for the same reasons; thus, many teachers prize the genre for the practice it provides young readers in looking for meaning.

Mystery books for young readers have as much variety as adult mysteries. In *The Westing Game* (1978), a Newbery Honor Book by Ellen Raskin, the characters are involved in a battle of wits to inherit a million dollars. E. L. Konigsburg, in her adventure-mystery *From the Mixed-Up Files of Mrs. Basil E. Frankweiler* (1967), writes of a set of youthful protagonists who run away from home. Being knowledgeable New Yorkers, they figure out how to spend nights in the Metropolitan Museum of Art without being detected.

In *The Secret of Gumbo Grove* (1987), author Elnora Tate incorporates African American community history, into which the protagonist delves to solve a mystery. Virginia Hamilton does much the same thing in *The House of Dies Drear* (1968), which uses the history of the Underground Railroad and a huge old house with secret passages as background to a mystery plot. (Hamilton is well known for her writing in other genres as well.)

In one of Eve Bunting's several forays into mystery writing (she is another author well known for writing in a number of genres), twelve-year-old Henry takes over his father's detective agency, and Lily enters the door looking for help to find her mother in *Coffin on a Case* (1992). Another well-known children's author and illustrator, Natalie Babbitt, wrote a mystery entitled *Goody Hall* (1971), in which a tutor finds that the situation at her new school is not what it seems.

John Bellairs has written many popular mysteries. In *The Mummy, the Will, and the Crypt* (1983), Johnny and the professor look for a will hidden by an eccentric cereal tycoon who wished to make life difficult for his heirs. David Adler has penned a series of mysteries, one of which is *Cam Jansen and the Mystery of the Gold Coins* (1982). Cam uses her photographic memory to find her missing science fair project. Each book in the *Encyclopedia Brown* series (1990) by Donald Sobol calls for readers to get involved in solving cases along with the son of a police chief.

Lois Duncan, author of many compelling mysteries, wrote *The Gift of Magic* (1971), in which the character has extrasensory perception. Willa Davis

Roberts also writes effective mystery stories. Sitting on a limb in *A View from the Cherry Tree* (1975), the protagonist sees a murder in progress. In *Babysitting Is a Dangerous Job* (1987), Darcy and her three charges are kidnapped. With the help of the children and a wasp's nest, Darcy devises ways to outwit the kidnappers. Plausible realism is minimal in some of these mysteries; events happen too fast, and some are on the edge of believability. However, the characters' efforts to solve problems provide good models of tenacity and good sense.

Books about Sports

Sports enthusiasts enjoy reading play-by-play accounts of athletic contests. *Shoot for the Hoop* (1995), by Matt Christopher, satisfies this craving. Beyond merely describing basketball action, however, the author creates a hero who is not only a good basketball player but also struggles with diabetes. Christopher writes voluminously—he has published over fifty sports titles—and is the focus of a fan club. *The Year Mom Won the Pennant* (1968) is a favorite with children.

Better sports books like Christopher's go beyond simply describing games and offer imaginative twists, well-developed characters, and a wide range of settings. *There's a Girl in My Hammerlock* (1991), by Jerry Spinelli, chronicles a wrestling team that comes unglued when a girl joins the team. His *Crash* (1996) places a middle school sports hero in conflict with a mild-mannered vegetarian neighbor. Robert Lipsyte has written over a dozen excellent sports books. *The Contender* (1967) tells of Alfred's desire to be a boxer; his coach teaches him the difference between being a contender (one who finds the effort its own reward) and being a champion (one who stands by truth and principles). Alfred becomes both. Chris Lynch has written excellent sports stories about teenage boys, in which sports serve as a metaphor for the development of the characters. Like his earlier books *Shadow Boxer* (1993) and *Iceman* (1994) (both about hockey), *Slot Machine* (1995) has plenty of "play-by-play" to please the enthusiast, as well as an excellent thematic thread on friendship and wrestling with one's own identity—or finding one's "slot," as the story has it. Bruce Brooks's *The Moves Make the Man* (1984), a story in which basketball provides metaphors for living in the world, was named a Newbery Honor Book.

Thank You, Jackie Robinson (1974), by Barbara Cohen, shows how baseball unites a young boy and an old man. Avi's *S.O.R. Losers* (1984), in which an unlikely soccer team strives for a winless season, is a hilarious antidote to the "winning is everything" ethos of too many school sports teams.

Books about Nature

Authors who write animal and nature stories for children provide information about the natural world; they also help children build commitments to the living things with which they share the world.

The Wheel on the School (1954), by Meindert DeJong, tells of Dutch schoolchildren who place a wheel on the roof of their schoolhouse to entice storks to make their nest there. The excitement of the school children and townspeople is contagious, and readers effortlessly become informed about the habits of storks as well as those of the people in this Dutch community. The book won the Newbery Medal; the author won the Hans Christian Andersen Award for his contribution to world children's literature.

A good number of Gary Paulsen's books celebrate animal life and the wilderness, especially in the cold northern lands. His *Dogsong* (1985) takes readers on a dog sled ride with Inuit boy Russell Susskit, introducing them to the

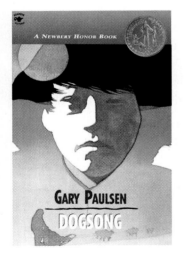

Illustration 8.10
Inuit culture teaches that every living thing has its own unique song, and through his dogsledding experiences, Russell is able to learn his, too. (*Dogsong* by Gary Paulsen. Copyright © 1985 Bradbury Press. Jacket painting by Neil Waldman. Used by permission of Simon and Schuster Books for Young Readers.)

interactions of dogs and humans. Another Paulsen nature story is *The Island* (1990), in which Will decides to live on a Northern Wisconsin island by himself.

Many realistic fiction books for younger children explore the multifaceted wonders of nature. *Play with Me* (1955), written and illustrated by Marie Hall Ets, demonstrates in pictures and text that communion with small animals requires a child to sit quietly. *Time of Wonder* (1957), winner of a Caldecott Medal, and *One Morning in Maine* (1966), both written and illustrated by Robert McCloskey, tell stories about living on an island and experiencing rough weather on the New England coast. *Come a Tide* (1990), by George Ella Lyon, shows an Appalachian community undergoing a storm and flooding.

Many children, especially girls, go through a horse-story phase. Why? Perhaps the association with horses gives girls a sense of freedom and power, as Poll (1961) suggests. Horse stories by Marguerite Henry and Walter Farley are perennial favorites. Both wrote about horses and other animals for over thirty years. Henry's *Misty of Chincoteague* (1947), a Newbery Honor Book, and Farley's series of books about *The Black Stallion* (1941) remain justifiably popular.

Bill Wallace is a contemporary prolific writer of animal stories. *Beauty* (1988) tells of an eleven-year-old's attachment to a horse, and *Ferret in the Bedroom, Lizards in the Fridge* (1986) is about the many animals that interfere with the political ambitions at school of the daughter of a zoologist.

Humorous Books

In much realistic fiction, humorous incidents serve as a release from the more serious topical themes explored by an author. For example, one could easily laugh all the way through *Maniac Magee* (1990), despite the seriousness of the theme.

Authors who write chiefly humor for children are careful not to poke fun at the natural surprises children experience—and often, their ineptness—as they learn about life. The challenge to authors of realistic fiction is to help children empathize with others and to see the humor in the plight of characters whose first stabs at life's opportunities fail. Leigh Botts's letters in *Dear Mr. Henshaw* (1983), by Beverly Cleary, are a good example. The letters began when Leigh was in the second grade, so his growth up to sixth grade is clear, and it is okay to laugh about what he didn't know earlier.

Adults often either function as the butt of the humor or buffer the pain of characters who are being laughed at. In Paula Danziger's *Make Like a Tree and Leave* (1990) the humor includes puns, such as the title, and "bathroom" humor. For several pages the characters argue about who is responsible for putting on a new toilet paper roll. Mrs. Martin tells her children about "making out" when she was young, and the children are horrified at the thought—and at the thought that Mr. and Mrs. Martin still make out—giving expression to the exact thoughts of many a child. Danziger has published a long list of amusing books for young and older children.

Beverly Cleary's characters, including Ramona and Henry Huggins, are strong, admirable children who can carry on in spite of mistakes and goofs. Readers laugh at the misunderstandings. Throughout *Ramona the Brave* (1975), Ramona assumes her teacher thinks she is a nuisance. The misconception motivates her to compensate and try to win approval, and all the time the reader is enjoying her mistake.

Betsy Byars's humor is often based on characters taking themselves more seriously than the reader thinks necessary. Byars wrote several books about Bingo Brown. This situation, from *The Burning Questions of Bingo Brown* (1988), is typical:

> Bingo Brown fell in love three times during English classes.
>
> Bingo had never been in love before. He had never even worried about falling in love. He thought love couldn't start until a person had zits, so he had plenty of time. Bingo was worried about being called on. (p. 3)

Sheila Greenwald's heroine, Rosy Cole, provides amusing adventures for younger readers. In *Rosy Cole: She Walks in Beauty* (1994), Rosy tries to become a model, giving the author the opportunity to point out some of the absurdities of the modeling profession. Dean Hughes wrote *Nutty for President* (1981), in which fifth-grade boys run Nutty's outrageous campaign. The humor is in the campaign and is not directed at Nutty.

Judy Blume's stories about sibling rivalry and parental approval are favorites among children—*Tales of a Fourth Grade Nothing* (1972) and *Superfudge* (1980), especially. In the former, Peter Hatcher is annoyed at his little brother's antics, but to the reader they are funny. Peter's unnecessary concern about his own status in the family will ring true to many young readers. In *Superfudge,* when Fudge swallows Peter's pet turtle, readers can feel Peter's pain and laugh at the same time.

Jamie Gilson is a popular writer of humorous stories. In *Hello, My Name Is Scrambled Eggs* (1985), Tuan Nguyen's family moves in with the Trumbles. Harvey Trumble's attempt to teach Tuan English and American ways provides laughs for other American readers. Gilson pokes enlightening fun at vegetarian cooking, the captivating influence of television, and horoscopes in *Can't Catch Me, I'm the Gingerbread Man* (1981). Endangered Animal Month sets Richard and Ben in competition with Dawn Marie and troublesome Patrick over the real story about bats in *It Goes Eeeeeeeeeeeee!* (1994).

Books about Death and Dying

Realistic fiction examines many aspects of death and dying: the natural process of aging; caring for the sick; grieving for lost loved ones; and the stages that lead from grief to acceptance. The death of an animal or pet is often a child's first experience with death, although books for children describe the deaths of peers, siblings, parents, and grandparents.

In *The Accident* (1976), by Carol Carrick with beautiful illustrations by Donald Carrick, Christopher is overcome by feelings of guilt and sadness when his dog is hit by a truck. In Judith Viorst's *The Tenth Good Thing about Barney* (1977), the protagonist's mother suggests that he think of ten good things about the cat Barney, for the family to recite at its funeral. Edith Stull deals more matter-of-factly with the death of a turtle in *My Turtle Died Today* (1964).

Edie Jo's sadness over the death of a Cherokee friend is combined with her sadness over the prejudice that her friend suffered in *Music from a Place Called Half Moon* (1995) by Jerrie Oughton. *A Taste of Blackberries* (1973) is Doris Buchanan Smith's excellent contribution to understanding the stages of grief over loss of a friend. In *Breadsticks and Blessing Places* (1985), Candy Dawson Boyd has Maddie enlist the help of a sympathetic neighbor, Mrs. Stamp, in performing a ritual to mourn her friend, killed by a drunken driver. The Newbery winner *Bridge to Terabithia* (1977), by Katherine Paterson, gives the reader a rich character in Leslie, who can be remembered long after her accidental death.

For older children, Fran Arrick wrote *Tunnel Vision* (1980), which describes the feelings of responsibility that a variety of people experience after a high school student they know commits suicide. Richard Peck writes about the pressure to succeed that drives teenager Trav to consider suicide in *Remembering the Good Times* (1985).

The death of a grandparent is a theme that allows authors to write of death as a natural phenomenon associated with age. In *My Grandson Lew* (1974), by Charlotte Zolotow, a child wakes up in the middle of the night wondering why he hasn't seen his grandfather for some time. *Blackberries in the Dark* (1985), by Mavis Jukes, shows a child and her grandmother going through rituals as a way of remembering the grandfather.

The death of parents is most difficult for children to endure. In Cynthia Rylant's *Missing May* (1992), it is an aunt who has raised Sumer, but her loss is doubly hard because Sumer has already lost her mother and father. For younger children, Lucille Clifton's *Everett Anderson's Goodbye* (1983) is a poetic account of the grief felt on the death of a father. Paula Fox, in *The Eagle Kite* (1995), describes Liam's anger, which arises not only because his father died of AIDS but also because he had not known of his father's homosexuality.

Books with Multicultural and International Themes

Books set in countries other than the United States and Canada also treat the range of themes we have been discussing. Nonetheless, many books highlight foreign settings, with the clear intention of expanding readers' awareness of life in other places.

Lyll Becerra de Jenkins wrote *The Honorable Prison* (1988) about her home country, Colombia. Her *Celebrating the Hero* (1993) tells of an American girl who goes back to Colombia to learn about her grandfather.

A moving book written jointly by a Cambodian woman, You Yang, and an American, Pegi Deitz (with illustrations by Anita Riggio), *The Whispering Cloth* (1995) shows in pictures and text the pathos of having to leave one's native land. *A Boat to Nowhere* (1980), by Maureen Crane Wartski, is one of two books about two war orphans who emigrate from Vietnam to a less-than-hospitable United States.

Frances Temple published her first book in 1992 and died in 1995, but in her brief career she broke new ground with her realistic works with political themes, set in other countries. Two of her books are set in Haiti and explore young people's struggles against political oppression: *Taste of Salt: A Story of Modern Haiti* (1992) won the Jane Addams Peace Award and *Tonight, By Sea* (1995) won the Américas Award (for the best book on a Latin American subject).

Books that portray the real-life experiences of people growing up in parallel cultures in North America are now plentiful. In *Child of the Owl* (1977) and later in *Thief of Hearts* (1995), Laurence Yep explores how Chinese American girls struggle to come to terms with their own identities. The title character in *Julie* (1996), by Jean Craighead George, is an Inuit who learns to accommodate to both old and new cultures in Alaska. In *When the Nightingale Sings* (1992) by Joyce Carol Thomas, Marigold, who was born in a Southern swamp, finds her origins and a home in the African American community of which she is a part.

For more authors and titles of international books and a discussion of books from parallel cultures, see Chapter 4.

Illustration 8.11
For Casey, San Francisco's Chinatown was home, the earth that made her strong—and not the impediment to fulfillment she had once thought it was. (*Child of the Owl* by Laurence Yep. Jacket art by Allen Say. Used by permission of HarperCollins Publishers.)

Series Books

Series books are popular with children because they take the guesswork out of choosing something to read. Their very sameness, however, means that these books do less to expand a child's awareness of and appreciation for literature than one-of-a-kind books. Nonetheless, parents and teachers eager to foster the reading habit often forgive the shortcomings of series books in the hope that once children are "hooked on books," they may move beyond series books to more substantial reading. Teachers are also aware that reading series books may be something of an elementary school status symbol.

Series books have been available to children for most of this century, at least since the time of the fiction-writing syndicate of Edward Stratemeyer, the prolific producer of the books about Tom Swift, the Bobbsey Twins, the Hardy Boys, and Nancy Drew. Nowadays, series books are more popular than ever, and virtually all publishers welcome authors who can and will write engaging books in series. Indeed, in the 1990s R. L. Stine outsold all other authors of children's books with his *Goosebumps* series.

Just as with any other books, the quality of series books varies. The worst are plagued by thin description, flat characters, and plots that pull readers from one suspenseful moment to another. The best—those by authors who have established themselves for their individual books—can be funny, upbeat, and full of delightful language play. Fourth grader Amber Brown appears in a series of funny stories by Paula Danziger. Phyllis Reynolds Naylor writes a series about Alice—a thirteen-year-old whose mother's death means that she must become the "woman of the house" for her father and much older brother. Jerry Spinelli has created the character Tooter Pepperday, who has reluctantly moved to the country with her family. Many of her hilarious adventures are based on her lack of familiarity with farm life. Johanna Hurwitz's Aldo finds just about everything "interesting." His becoming a vegetarian earns him various nicknames in **Aldo Applesauce** (1989). His puppies are named Peanut and Butter in **Aldo Peanut Butter** (1990). All of these series books use good language, engaging themes, and well-rounded characters to give substance to the plots.

HOW REALISTIC FICTION WORKS

The term "realistic fiction" implies something of a paradox. A work of fiction is contrived, yet readers are meant to believe that a work of realistic fiction is real, at least while they are engrossed in reading it. But this paradox contains some other seeming contradictions as well. Exploring two of them will clarify how realistic fiction "works."

An effective work of realistic fiction makes us believe that what it describes might really have happened. Yet because it is fiction, the work is organized into a plot—and that makes it quite different from real life, in which the lion's share of our days is made of meaningless details: minutes spent waiting for traffic lights to change, minutes spent searching for lost papers or misplaced keys, minutes spent half-listening to uninteresting conversations. In contrast, just about every detail in a work of fiction is meaningful. Why aren't we aware of the difference right off?

Although realistic fiction does not much resemble day-to-day reality, it *does* resemble the ways we represent that reality to ourselves and others. Fiction is not like life—but it *is* like our stories of our lives. By taking events from life and giving them meaning, fiction shows us how we find significance and purpose in our lives.

ASK THE AUTHOR . . .

Katherine Paterson

Katherine Paterson

Favorite Books as a Child

Winnie-the-Pooh by A. A. Milne

The Secret Garden by Frances Hodgson Burnett

The Yearling by Marjorie Kinnan Rawlings

How do you decide how far to go in the direction of social realism when writing for young people?

I think the short answer to the question is: I don't write about ethics or problems, I write about people. My first responsibility in writing a novel is not to an abstract concept of virtue or to some desire to tackle the sins of society, but to the people of the story. The truth of a novel is to be found in the truth of the characters who people its pages. If they do not ring true, then the novel is a lie, no matter how worthy the motives of the writer.

Of course, my allegiance to my characters gets me into trouble. Neither the "right-thinkers" of the right or those of the left wholly approve of my work, and I've been challenged and banned from both directions. Gilly Hopkins is a case in point. Some folks have asked that all the antisocial behavior and inappropriate language be removed. If the author would do this, they declare, Gilly Hopkins would be a beautiful book. Others are willing for her to misbehave initially, but lament the fact that on the last page she is still cussing and that she has never actually apologized for her thieving, bullying, racist behavior. I have some sympathy for my critics. Gilly doesn't behave well, but then, I never intended for her to be a role model, only a real child.

I may be Gilly's creator, but I am not her manipulator. I owe her respect for the person she is. Nor do I want the young reader who has fallen in love with her story to feel betrayed by a last-page fake-sounding conversion. Yes, Gilly does change, but on her own terms, not those of all of us right-minded adult moralists who think if we don't spell it out in bold type, our children won't get the message that they're not supposed to speak and behave like Gilly Hopkins.

Take, for example, the characters in Phyllis Reynolds Naylor's *Shiloh* (1991). Judd Travers, a man without awareness who acts violently in the world, unthinkingly recreates the violence with which he was raised. The boy Marty makes a commitment to protect the dog Shiloh and, in so doing, goes beyond blind obedience to his father and also beyond his mother's unexamined code of ethics. Marty is aware of what he is doing. He gradually comes to understand the reasons behind his father's demands, his mother's pure but insufficient morality, and Judd Travers's brutish nature—after which he reaches his own conclusions about what he should do. Then there is the reader. Thanks to Naylor's narrative, the reader is privileged to see these several ways of thinking through the moral issues in *Shiloh* and is allowed to make a personal judgment about them. It is not too great a step for readers to think of the issues in their lives in the complex ways Naylor reveals as they read *Shiloh.*

No wonder scholars who have studied the effects of literacy have claimed that reading expands awareness (Luria, 1976; Postman, 1994; Stanovich, 1992).

I have chosen to write about people who do not live protected, comfortable lives. That, of course, is my choice. But a writer's choice is a complicated matter. Her whole intellectual, emotional, and spiritual life, her ancestry, the circumstances of her birth and growing up, her education, play, and interest—in short, all she is forms her artistic choices. This happens in such a way that often what is looked on by the outsider as a conscious choice feels much more like an inevitable consequence to the writer herself.

People often tell me that they have an idea for me. I have never yet been able to turn someone else's idea into a novel. It's his or her idea, not mine. I can only write out of myself—and that self has been evolving since the Creation. So when I'm asked if there are some things I have been unwilling to write about, well, yes, there are. For a long time, I was unwilling to write about foot-binding, which made it impossible for me to write historical fiction set in China. Then, suddenly, one day, for no reason that I can explain, I knew I had to write about the land of my birth. I notice that in *Rebels of the Heavenly Kingdom,* I've set the foot-binding scene off-stage, but it is there, and I've seldom written a more painful chapter in my life.

I know that I write for the young, and I am sure the young person I write for is the child that I was, rather than some statistically created mannequin of a modern child. This will keep me from writing some things because I know that the child who still lives inside of me could not bear to read them. I could put down on this page what some of those unbearable scenes are, but, like foot-binding, they may change. A day may well come when a story I feel compelled to write will demand of me something I could not bear to write about today. Like Gilly, I'm still growing.

Katherine Paterson is the author of twelve novels for young readers, including Bridge to Terabithia *and* Jacob Have I Loved *(both Newbery Medal winners),* The Great Gilly Hopkins *(a Newbery Honor Book and National Book Award winner), and* The Master Puppeteer *(also a winner of the National Book Award). She and her husband, a Presbyterian minister, have four grown children and two grandchildren.*

Over time, the habit of reading allows children to see patterns in their lives, to look into their own motives and those of others, and to see possibilities for independent action.

A second contradiction of realistic fiction is the fact that it encourages one way of seeing events more than others, even as it presents a lifelike description of them. A story may seem to tell "what happened," but it almost invariably makes a point about what happened and makes readers see the events in a certain way, with a "slant." The slant of *Shiloh* vindicates Marty's opposition to the adults around him as he chooses to care for the dog. But the story might have been told differently: If Judd Travers had narrated the story, he might have stressed Marty's theft, his disobedience of his parents, and his violation of community norms. Because stories tend to emphasize one way of seeing events, in discussions about literature it can be revealing to ask, "How would the events in this story have looked from a different character's point of view?"

MAJOR WRITERS OF REALISTIC FICTION AND THEIR WORKS

The writers discussed in the following sections are all from the United States. Of course, there are stellar writers who come from other English-speaking countries and others whose books have been translated into English. Some of those are discussed earlier in this chapter and in Chapter 4.

Avi

After a publisher accepted his first book, Avi Wortis was asked how he wanted his name to appear on the book. He answered "Avi"—and his books have appeared without his last name ever since. As a child, Avi had problems with both reading and writing; now, he likes to show his manuscripts covered with red pencil marks to special students in schools he visits. His desire to write novels followed attempts at playwriting and many years of working as a librarian and, he claims, grew out of a stubborn wish to prove something to those who had criticized his writing.

Avi writes historical as well as realistic fiction. In 1991, he won the Boston Globe–Horn Book Award for a historical novel, *The True Confessions of Charlotte Doyle* (1990), which was also a Newbery Honor Book. The next year he won the same awards for a work of realistic fiction, *Nothing But the Truth* (1991). Among Avi's other popular and award-winning novels are *Romeo and Juliet, Together (and Alive) at Last* (1987) and *Who Was That Masked Man Anyway?* (1992). His strength as a writer lies mainly in his respect for children, but his books are also notable for gripping first chapters, terse action-filled writing, thematic richness, and imaginative variety in format.

Marion Dane Bauer

The characters in Marion Dane Bauer's books face traumatic events but manage to make choices to resolve their dilemmas honorably. In *On My Honor*, a 1986 Newbery Honor Book, Joel is wracked with feelings of guilt about his best friend's drowning and about having broken a promise to his father. Bauer's stories are tightly told, maintaining the voice of the characters and building unusual suspense around moral issues. Among her other books are *A Question of Trust* (1994), in which a mother leaves home, and *Shelter from the Wind* (1976), about a runaway girl who finds solace with an old woman living in the desert. Bauer's latest book is an edited collection of short stories for middle school children about homosexuality, *Am I Blue? Coming Out from the Silence* (1994).

Judy Blume

In 1996, Judy Blume received the Margaret Edwards Award for her lifetime contribution to literature for young adults. With books selling in the millions, she is one of the most popular children's authors of all time, and also one of the most controversial. Blume took the world of children's books by storm during the 1970s with stories on subjects—such as the viciousness of peer groups, sexuality, and hypocrisy—that were of intense concern to children but difficult for many adults to explore with them. That her works have struck a chord with children is obvious by their popularity, but their frankness, and perhaps the absence of any helpful or caring adult figures in many of them, has made them the most consistently controversial children's books ever. Judy Blume has stood up to her critics forthrightly and has long been active in the fight against those who would limit children's access to her books or those by other authors.

Blume's first book, *The One in the Middle Is the Green Kangaroo* (1969/1981), remains a favorite for younger children. *Tales of a Fourth Grade Nothing* (1972) and its sequels are hugely popular with those in the middle elementary grades.

For young adolescents, *Are You There God? It's Me, Margaret* (1970) openly discusses menstruation and emerging female sexuality. Blume has said she considers *Blubber* (1974), a book about a group of children victimizing an overweight peer, her most important work, because children must be told about their own cruelty if they are to raise their level of moral behavior. *Forever* (1975) is the target of the most censorship because it describes a sexual encounter explicitly, and *Starring Sally J. Freedman as Herself* (1977) is the most autobiographical, according to Blume. Naylor and Wintercorn (1986) quote Blume as saying, "If parents talked to their children, I wouldn't have to write books."

Eve Bunting

Eve Bunting's early life in Northern Ireland, an area long beset by intergroup strife, nurtured her concern for the underdog and an interest in social issues. She has written more than 150 books in several genres, for all ages of children. Her works of realistic fiction cover topics such as illness, drunken drivers, the environment, aging, the Holocaust, war, and literacy. Bunting's characters are of a variety of class and ethnic groups. In 1994, the Caldecott Medal went to David Diaz for his illustration of Bunting's *Smoky Night* (1994), which depicts people of different ethnic backgrounds coming together during the Los Angeles riots. *Fly Away Home* (1991) is a picture book about a homeless father and child who live in an airport. Bunting uses dialogue extensively in her books and centers issues in the everyday lives of her child characters.

Betsy Byars

Betsy Byars is one of the foremost writers of realistic fiction for children. Malcolm Usrey (1995) praises this prolific writer for creating books with an authentic Southern regional style, a sense of irony and humor, a charming and optimistic tone, and daring. Byars tackles painful situations in children's lives for which solutions are not always at hand. Another of Byars's strengths is her ability to create memorable adult characters.

Byars won the Newbery Medal in 1971 for *The Summer of the Swans* (1970), which tells of a young girl who learns about herself as she searches for her retarded brother, who is lost. Byars has created two series of books. She introduced an indomitable twelve-year-old, Bingo Brown, in *Bingo Brown and the Language of Love* (1989) and has followed his antics through three other books. The other series comprises five books about a not-too-ordinary family, the Blossoms. This vivacious and close-knit family is headed by Mother Blossom, who rides in a rodeo. Her children—Junior, Maggie, and Vern—are cared for by Pap, the grandfather, when she is absent.

Beverly Cleary

Beverly Cleary was a school librarian for a brief period, and she says in her autobiographies, *Beverly Cleary, a Girl from Yamhill: A Memoir* (1988) and *My Own Two Feet: A Memoir* (1995), that she wrote books she sensed school children wanted and needed. She certainly succeeded: The characters in Beverly Cleary's books—Henry Huggins, Beezus, the dog Ribsy, Otis Spofford, but above all, Ramona—are as familiar to most middle elementary school children as their classmates. The seven books about Ramona span a twenty-nine-year writing period. Ramona starts as a four-year-old and progresses through the seven books to third grade. *Ramona Quimby, Age 8* (1981) and *Ramona and Her Father* (1977) were Newbery Honor Books.

Cleary won the Newbery Medal for *Dear Mr. Henshaw* (1983), a story related through the correspondence between an elementary school boy and a children's author. Her books are marked by their strong character delineation, humor, and joyfulness. In 1975, Cleary won the Laura Ingalls Wilder Medal, for lifetime achievement in children's literature.

Brock Cole

Brock Cole left academia and a career as a philosophy professor to write children's books. He wrote first, he says, for his own children. As they grew older, Cole's stories changed from picture books to adolescent novels.

Cole illustrated his own picture books, among them *Alpha and the Dirty Baby* (1991). His adolescent novels, *The Goats* (1987) and *Celine* (1989), are treasured by connoisseurs of fine writing. *The Goats* are two twelve-year-old campers who are left on a deserted island—naked—by their fellow campers. Celine and the young child next door become close friends as they work to survive their parents' divorces and remarriages. *Celine* is rich in humor and insights into young people's views of adults' imperfections.

Paula Fox

Paula Fox has written over two dozen books for children, all with unusual settings, engaging characters, and multilayered plots. Fox's strengths are the verisimilitude of her settings, her writing style, and her unforgettable characters.

Maurice's Room (1966) is about a boy fascinated with collecting "things" and their names. *Monkey Island* (1991) is about a homeless child, and *The One-Eyed Cat* (1984), a Newbery Honor Book, is a captivating story about a boy whose feelings of guilt make him wonder if he is responsible for having shot a cat. Fox won the Newbery Medal in 1974 for *The Slave Dancer* (1973), a book about a young white boy's horrifying time playing the flute to provide music while African slaves are forced to exercise during the long ocean voyage to the United States.

E. L. Konigsburg

E. L. Konigsburg was a wife and mother when she began writing in secret during the hours waiting for children, doctors, and shoe salesmen. Her stories emerged out of these very experiences. She wrote novels about city children, baseball, and relationships between Jews and gentiles.

Konigsburg published two books in the same year, 1967: *From the Mixed-Up Files of Mrs. Basil E. Frankweiler* and *Jennifer, Hecate, Macbeth, William McKinley, and Me, Elizabeth.* The first won the Newbery Medal, and the second was a Newbery Honor Book. (The books also started a temporary trend toward long titles!) Thirty years later, Konigsburg won the Newbery Medal again, for *The View from Saturday* (1996), a book about precocious sixth graders.

Lois Lowry

Lois Lowry treats the large and small troubles of childhood gently but seriously in her realistic fiction. Her characters all manage to assume some responsibility for solving their own problems. *A Summer to Die* (1977), about sisters, life, and death, was her first novel. Lowry remains one of the most frequently read of children's authors. She has written seven books about the character Anastasia, beginning with *Anastasia Krupnik* (1979); the latest one is *Anastasia at This Address* (1992). The humor in the Anastasia books is in the language play and the hilarious descriptions of the best-laid plans going awry. In addition, Lowry portrays sympathetic adults who always come to the rescue of child characters.

Patricia MacLachlan

Patricia MacLachlan writes in several genres. Her realistic fiction features atypical, introspective characters. The protagonist in *The Facts and Fictions of Minna Pratt* (1988) is an eleven-year-old cellist who ponders her parents' facts and fictions and learns the technique of vibrato in playing Mozart. In *Journey* (1991), children learn to accept that their mother's life journey does not include them. In *Arthur, for the Very First Time* (1980) MacLachlan maintains the character's point of view, even though the reader is clued in to Arthur's insecurity. MacLachlan has said that she came to realize that "basically character and plot are the same thing." This belief is reflected in her powerful characterizations.

Phyllis Reynolds Naylor

Before writing for children, Phyllis Naylor studied to be a clinical psychologist. Her plots are designed to reveal interpersonal relationships but are laced with humor rather than didacticism. Her Newbery Medal winner, *Shiloh* (1991), demonstrates her ability to suggest to young readers the larger moral issues that emerge from everyday, ordinary personal problems. Topics of her novels are varied. *Send No Blessings* (1990) is about a teenager whose needs can't be met because of her poverty; *The Keeper* (1986) explores the mental illness of a middle schooler's father; and *Josie's Troubles* (1992), for younger children, is about a girl who has to pay for damaging a friend's piano bench. The title of *Beetles, Lightly Toasted* (1987) alludes to a recipe concocted by the protagonist, Andy, for a cooking contest.

Naylor's eight books about Alice are set in the household of this upbeat, assertive middle school girl. Her mother is dead, and she lives with her father and her much older brother. The stories are at once funny, wise, and convincing. *Alice in Rapture, Sort of* (1989) tells of Alice's first boyfriend. In *Reluctantly Alice* (1991), Alice tries to advise her father and brother about their love lives. In *Alice in April* (1993), she practices being the "woman of the house," and in *All But Alice* (1992), she discovers the dangers of wanting to be a part of the "in" crowd.

Katherine Paterson

As the daughter of missionaries, Katherine Paterson learned Chinese as her first language. Later, she became a missionary herself and learned Japanese. Today, even when she is writing about an American setting, Paterson is able to show insight into the lives of an unusually broad range of characters. *The Great Gilly Hopkins* (1978) lets readers get to know a foster child who is learning about love; *Come Sing, Jimmy Jo* (1985) explores the music and the aspirations of Appalachian people; and Newbery Medal winner *Bridge to Terabithia* (1977) brings together children of different social classes.

Paterson's stories are notable for the richness of their philosophical and religious underpinnings. *Jacob Have I Loved* (1980) won the Newbery Medal for its sense of place and the depth with which Paterson explores the rivalry between twin sisters. Paterson uses an afterword as a device to help the reader reflect on the themes.

Paterson's writing weaves together multiple plot strands, each maintained through symbols and strong imagery. Her stories often reflect happenings or emotions in her own life. For example, her son lost a close friend—a tragedy that is portrayed in *Bridge to Terabithia*. It is Paterson's ability to place her own feelings into her writing and characters that gives her books their power.

Gary Paulsen

Gary Paulsen had a rough childhood and an equally rough and varied adulthood before finding success as a children's author. He has more than fifty books to his credit, and many have won awards. His works are informed by his range of experiences—as a truck driver, construction worker, and lumberjack, and in other physically demanding jobs—and are permeated by the theme of survival. Paulsen has a passionate tie to nature and the wilderness, evident in his poetic, vivid writing about protagonists learning from nature as they set out on their own life journeys.

The brighter side of Paulsen's own childhood is reflected in the hilarious episodes of *Harris and Me* (1993); some of the less happy moments are recounted in *Eastern Sun, Western Moon: an Autobiographical Odyssey* (1993). *Hatchet* (1987), a Newbery Honor Book, is an immensely popular story of a boy's survival in the Canadian wilderness. Paulsen wrote two sequels in response to popular demand: *The River* (1993), in which his protagonist returns to collect data on survival for scientists, and *Brian's Winter* (1996), in which the original story is extended.

The Winter Room (1989), another Newbery Honor Book, is a descriptive piece about a Minnesota logging cabin and the people in it. The Iditarod, a cross-Alaska dogsled race in which Paulsen has participated, figures in two of his books, *Winterdance* (1994) and *Woodsong* (1990). Paulsen's realistic fiction is intense and emotion-packed.

Cynthia Rylant

The works of versatile and prolific Appalachian writer Cynthia Rylant range from poetry to easy readers to young adult novels to picture books about the city. Her books have been enhanced by a variety of illustrators. Her Newbery Medal–winner is *Missing May* (1992), mentioned earlier. *A Fine White Dust* (1986), about religious choice, was a Newbery Honor Book. Other memorable books for older readers include *Soda Jerk* (1990), poetic reflections on small-town life from the perspective of a teenage boy, and *A Kindness* (1988), which chronicles a young boy's adjustment to his mother's romantic involvement.

Rylant has also produced fourteen Henry and Mudge stories, all easy readers for younger children. First and second graders go from one emotional trauma to another with Henry and his dog Mudge. *Henry and Mudge and the Careful Cousin* (1994) is the most recent in the series.

Among Rylant's Appalachian stories for middle grades is *Miss Maggie* (1983), which relates a gripping moral dilemma. *A Blue-Eyed Daisy* (1987) and *But I'll Be Back Again* (1989) are set in the coal mine country of West Virginia. Topics covered in other books by Rylant are old age, animal life, and nature. Her own childhood experiences in West Virginia, living with her grandparents, led to *The Relatives Came* (1985), *When I Was Young in the Mountains* (1982), and *Appalachia: The Voices of Singing Birds* (1990).

Jerry Spinelli

Jerry Spinelli claims he always knew he wanted to be a writer but he didn't know he was going to write for children until his own got involved in antics worth writing about. Spinelli's child dialogue rings with authenticity and vitality. Readers enter a world in which children are portrayed without nostalgia or condescension; rather, Spinelli's books offer substance, affection, respect, wisdom, and good humor.

Jason, the hero of Spinelli's first book, *Space Station Seventh Grade* (1982), builds a space station with help from his family and school class. Jason also appears in *Jason and Marceline* (1986), in which he is divided between pleasing Marceline and pleasing his peers. For younger children, Spinelli has written *The Bathwater Gang* (1990), the first in a series in which Grandmother gives good advice for a nonsexist summertime "gang" activity. In *Fourth Grade Rats* (1991), third graders eventually find that they don't have to give up baloney sandwiches in fourth grade, as their child mentors would have them believe. *Maniac Magee* (1990) won the Newbery Medal for its flowing language and child's view of the seemingly unfathomable nature of racism. Maniac was a character in an earlier book, *Dump Days* (1988).

Cynthia Voigt

Cynthia Voigt won a Newbery Medal for *The Homecoming* (1991), about a teenage girl who takes her brothers and sisters on a difficult journey to make a home with their estranged grandmother when their mother proves too incompetent to keep them. Voigt wrote five other books about the Tillerman family. *Dicey's Song* (1982) relates Dicey's hard work in making a family with her emotionally aloof grandmother on the Eastern Shore of Maryland. In *Sons from Afar* (1987) the two younger boys, now grown, go in search of their father. In *Seventeen against the Dealer* (1988) Dicey experiences her first romance.

Voigt provides rich and complex plots about siblings making their way in the world against great odds, often without strong adult guidance, but with courage and family loyalty. *David and Jonathan* (1992) concerns a survivor of the Holocaust. Making a life after a car accident and an amputation is the subject of *Izzy, Willy-Nilly* (1986). Voigt has written about sports in *The Runner* (1985) and about divorce in *A Solitary Blue* (1983), a Newbery Honor Book. *When She Hollers* (1994) is a story about child abuse. Rich in imagery and undercurrents of emotion, and with a strong sense of place, Voigt's stories are unforgettable.

Vera Williams

The artist in Vera Williams preceded the writer, but since she began writing, Williams has written and illustrated lasting realistic fiction for young readers. Williams's stories are typically about the poor, women, and/or people of color. They have tranquil plots rather than conflicts. *A Chair for My Mother* (1982), *Music, Music for Everyone* (1984), and *Something Special for Me* (1983) all revolve around one member of a family wanting to do something nice for another; the dilemmas usually involve financing the favor. *Cherries and Cherry Pits* (1986) is a dreamy story about a child who draws pictures and tells tales to go with them. Adjusting to a move and her parents' divorce is the task that faces *Scooter* (1993), who accomplishes it with the help of her no-nonsense mother. Books that celebrate the power of ordinary people to help each other—a theme all too rare in American children's literature—are Williams's considerable contribution to children's literature.

Charlotte Zolotow

Charlotte Zolotow has said, "We are not different from the children we were, only more experienced, better able to disguise our feelings from others, if not from ourselves." From her books we know that Zolotow has not lost touch with childhood. Her books show unusual sensitivity in exploring children's relationships with family and other children. Several of her books are concerned with children's views of parents and grandparents. *A Father Like That* (1971) is a boy's description of what he would like in a father. *My Grandson Lew* (1974) is a tender book about remembering a grandfather's words after his death. *May I Visit?* (1976) expresses a child's fear that she won't be able to return home when she grows up. *Say It!* (1980) is a loving conversation between a mother and daughter as they take a walk. In *William's Doll* (1972), a father becomes convinced that dolls help boys learn how to be fathers.

Other stories develop an understanding of communication among children. *The Unfriendly Book* (1975) is about jealousy; *The Hating Book* (1969) and *The Quarreling Book* (1963) are about what the titles suggest. *The Old Dog* (1995) is about grief. Zolotow's poetic prose and hopeful tone reveal the possibilities of the real world for young children.

CRITERIA FOR EVALUATING AND SELECTING REALISTIC FICTION

Adults write realistic fiction for children in order to provide a view of the world and to pass on some of the wisdom they may have gained by having lived longer. Their hope is that their books leave children with something to reflect on about their own lives or those of others. It is not surprising that even the best of writers succumb once in a while to "teaching and preaching" in realistic fiction, especially when they feel child readers might need a little help in getting at an important idea. Twelve-year-old Pamela in Phyllis Naylor's *Alice in April* (1993) says, "You know what? When you come right down to it, all we can do is just try to be the best friends to each other that we can and hope it's enough." Somehow that sounds more like an adult than the character Pamela. A little nudging toward an insight isn't objectionable, but if it's overdone, the writing may seem didactic.

In evaluating realistic fiction, we should remain wary of statements and attitudes that seem to condescend to children, implying that children wouldn't be capable of making their own moral judgments or of understanding the consequences of a character's actions. We adults can ask ourselves some questions in an effort to identify books with the "teaching and preaching" tendency—a tendency that doesn't contribute to the telling or reading of a good story. These questions help identify the honesty of a book and an author's willingness to trust the reader to understand.

* Do the characters resemble real people you know?

* Are events plausible? Will children believe that they could happen?

* Will children readily grasp the insights offered by the book? Are children led to those insights by the flow of the action, rather than by the author's explicit instruction?

When selecting realistic fiction, teachers and librarians often focus on the topic of the book. Just because the book is said to address a topic, however, does not guarantee that it has a good story, or even accurate or appropriate information on the topic. Therefore, teachers and librarians might want to consider the following questions before selecting a book.

- Are the descriptions of people accurate, given the historical and social setting?
- Does the plot avoid the manipulative devices of sentimentality and sensationalism?
- Is the style of writing (the vocabulary and sentence structure) pleasing, engaging, and suited to the time and place of the story?
- Is the plot resolution believable—not contrived to end in a certain way?
- Is the story imaginative or original so that it engages children's interest?

Authors express their attitudes toward children by the breadth of their inclusion of characters and perspectives.

- Do events, descriptions, or styles of speech demean classes of people or individuals?
- Does the author avoid condescending to children?

Finally, a book should add up to more than entertainment. Worthwhile realistic fiction leaves children with something to reflect on about their own lives or those of others.

TEACHING IDEAS

Real Life versus Fiction. Ask students in grades three through six to record in a diary all the events that happen to them in a single day—just the facts, without embellishment. Then, have them exchange diaries with a friend and write up the friend's account as if it were a chapter in a work of realistic fiction. Afterwards, ask the students to compare the two versions. What was added to make the fictionalized version? What was left out? How did the *dramatic contour* (that is, the pattern of building suspense and its resolution) of the diary version compare with that of the fictionalized version? What was made clearer about the events of the day when they were fictionalized? What was distorted?

Capturing an Author's Voice. Repeat the above exercise, but this time have the students write the fictionalized version in the voice of (that is, have them imitate the style of) an author such as Jerry Spinelli, Walter Dean Myers, Beverly Cleary, or Judy Blume. Afterwards, have students read the fictionalized versions to others. Can the others identify which author is being imitated? How? What is it about the author's style that has been captured?

Playing the Role of "the Implied Reader." Sometimes, as students read realistic fiction, their loyalties are stretched. That is, books tacitly invite them to identify with the protagonist—the main character—and in the process condone the character's overall behavior. As we said in Chapter 2, a book invites readers to take the role of "the implied reader"—the ideal reader whom the author had in mind when he or she shaped the work. Sometimes taking this role is only mildly difficult, as when a character does risky or controversial things that go only slightly beyond what the reader would do in real life. But sometimes taking the role of the implied reader becomes close to impossible, as when the protagonist does things the reader would never do. What is unacceptable differs for different readers, of course. Most children become moderately tense in response to the actions of the protagonist in Phyllis Reynolds Naylor's *Shiloh* (1991), but the actions of the character in Judy Blume's *Blubber* (1974) make them extremely tense. Have students in third through sixth grade read both books, and identify the points in each where they were made the most uncomfortable. Why were they uncomfortable? Did they feel more at ease at the end of the book? Why? Explain what identifying with a character means. What have they learned from identifying with the protagonist in *Shiloh*? What have they learned from identifying with the protagonist in *Blubber*?

Realistic Fiction versus Other Genres. Both realistic fiction and fantasy often treat serious themes. William Steig's *The Real Thief* (1976) and Avi's *Nothing But the Truth* (1991) both deal with false accusations. But the first is a fantasy, with animal characters, whereas the second is realistic fiction, made up of newspaper clippings and memoranda. Have students in fourth through sixth grade read both books, and then ask them: What did you learn from reading *The Real Thief*? What did you learn from reading *Nothing But the Truth*? Is one book any more true than the other? In what ways? What, really, is the difference between them?

Censorship and Propriety. This chapter referred to the struggle between some adults who defend books that contain controversial material and others who want to put such books out of the reach of children. But what do children say? Ask a group of children in grades two through six what things they think should or should not be written about in the books they read. What disagreements emerge among them? How do the children think such disagreements should be resolved? Should the books be banned? Should they be made available only to those whose parents give permission for them to read them? Made available to all students, no matter what their parents think?

EXPERIENCES FOR YOUR LEARNING

1. Read a book by M. E. Kerr or Ron Koertge and identify references to the real world that a reader would have to know to understand the book better. An example is on page 75 of *The Arizona Kid* (1988) by Koertge: "I'll bet," he said, "It isn't the Welcome Wagon." If readers don't know what the Welcome Wagon is in the real world, how is their understanding of the passage affected?

2. The moral dilemma in the 1953 Newbery Medal winner, *The Secret of the Andes* (1952) by Ann Nolan Clark, has been described as too difficult for children to comprehend. Read the book yourself to determine the moral dilemma. Decide whether children in the 1990s may be able to comprehend it more than their parents did as children. Do you agree that today's children are more aware of Third World countries (in this case, Peru) and are better able to understand a child's moral commitment to his or her culture? Why or why not?

3. Find editions of the same Hardy Boys or Nancy Drew title published before 1940, between 1945 and the 1950s, and after 1969. Examine changes in character descriptions, especially descriptions of the "good guys" and the "bad guys," that were made because of changes in social consciousness and political philosophy. (The books are often available in used book stores or historical collections in libraries.)

4. Read at least four books by one of the major authors discussed in this chapter. In spite of differences in topic and grade level, what clues do you have as to the world view of the author

and/or the context in which he or she writes? Read the work of an author who lives in a context totally different from your own—a different country, say, or a different kind of place. For example, if you are a Southerner, read Gary Paulsen. If you live in an urban area, read Cynthia Rylant. Look for comments from adult characters or descriptive passages that show you how the author reflects on character, setting, and moral issues.

RECOMMENDED BOOKS

* indicates a picture book; I indicates interest level (P = preschool, YA = young adult)

Self-Discovery and Growing Up

Blume, Judy. *Are You There God? It's Me, Margaret.* New York: Dell, 1970. Margaret and her friends learn about puberty and search for truths to live by. (I: 10–12)

* Caines, Jeannette. *Just Us Women.* Illustrated by Pat Cummings. New York: Harper & Row, 1982. A young girl and her Aunt go on an automobile trip to North Carolina and create their own adventures. (I: P–8)

Cleary, Beverly. *Beezus and Ramona.* New York: Morrow, 1955. The first of a series about the indomitable and spirited Ramona and her older sister; here Ramona is a preschooler. (I: 8–10)

———. *Dear Mr. Henshaw.* New York: Morrow, 1983. Writing to an author helps a young boy accept his father's absence and lack of concern. (I: 10–12)

———. *Ramona Quimby, Age 8.* New York: Morrow, 1981. As a third grader, Ramona's life changes drastically when her father loses his job and goes back to school. (I: 7–9)

Cleaver, Bill, and Vera Cleaver. *Where the Lilies Bloom.* New York: New American Library, 1969. Mary Call acts on her father's advice until she discovers it doesn't work for her or her sister. (I: 9–12)

* de Paola, Tomie. *The Art Lesson.* New York: Putnam, 1989. A little boy looks forward to taking a real art lesson at school. (I: 6–9)

Fox, Paula. *Maurice's Room.* New York: Macmillan, 1966. Maurice collects so many things that his parents decide to move to the country. (I: 8–10)

Hurwitz, Johanna. *The Adventures of Ali Baba Bernstein.* New York, Scholastic, 1985. Eight-year-old David is convinced that his life will be more adventurous when he changes his name to Ali Baba. (I: 8–10)

Lowry, Lois. *A Summer to Die.* Boston: Houghton Mifflin, 1977. A thirteen-year-old gives up feelings of envy when she learns her beautiful sister is fatally ill. (I: 10–YA)

MacLachlan, Patricia. *The Facts and Fictions of Minna Pratt.* New York: HarperTrophy, 1988. Minna plays the cello and learns about life and passions from her family, friends, and Mozart. (I: 10–YA)

Myers, Walter Dean. *Darnell Rock Reporting.* New York: Delacorte, 1994. A thirteen-year-old's family and friends doubt that Darnell will make it as a writer for the school newspaper. (I: 11–YA)

Neville, Emily. *It's Like This, Cat.* New York: Harper & Row, 1963. A boy learns about friendship with the help of a stray tomcat. (I: 11–YA)

Paulsen, Gary. *Dancing Carl.* New York: Bradbury, 1983. Two school boys learn about the many kinds of love from Carl the town drunk, their teachers, and their parents. (I: 10–12)

———. *Harris and Me: A Summer Remembered.* San Diego, CA: Harcourt, 1993. A city boy goes to live with his distant cousin on a farm, where he finds love and hilarious adventures. (I: 9–12)

* Rylant, Cynthia. *Birthday Presents.* Illustrated by Sucie Stevenson. New York: Orchard, 1987. A recounting of a child's birthdays, as she progresses from only receiving presents to giving them when she is older. (I: P–7)

Snyder, Zilpha Keatley. *Libby on Wednesday.* New York: Delacorte, 1990. Libby invites the writing club to meet in her tree house, where they experience unexpected revelations. (I: 10–YA)

Soto, Gary. *Baseball in April and Other Stories.* San Diego, CA: Harcourt, 1990. Tender stories of children fitting into families and of the Latino culture of California. (I: 10–YA)

* Waber, Bernard. *Ira Says Goodbye.* Boston: Houghton Mifflin, 1988. The story deals with the recognition of sadness that a child feels when a friend moves. (I: P–7)

* ———. *Ira Sleeps Over.* Boston: Houghton Mifflin, 1972. Ira is relieved to learn that he isn't the only one sleeping with a teddy. (I: P–7)

* Williams, Vera. *"More, More, More" Said the Baby.* New York: Greenwillow, 1990. A father, mother, and grandmother follow playful rituals with a baby. (I: P–K)

* Zolotow, Charlotte. *The Old Dog*. New York: Harper-Collins, 1995. A boy remembers the fun he had with his dog. (I: P–K)

* ———. *The Quarreling Book*. Illustrated by Arnold Lobel. New York: Harper & Row, 1963. Youngsters learn about appropriate ways to communicate. (I: P–7)

* ———. *William's Doll*. Illustrated by William Pene du Bois. New York: Harper & Row, 1972. A boy and his father disagree about playing with dolls. (I: P–7)

Families

Bauer, Marion Dane. *A Question of Trust*. New York: Scholastic, 1994. After his mother leaves the family, Brad involves his younger brother in a plan to bring her back. (I: 10–YA)

Blume, Judy. *Fudge-a-Mania*. New York: Dutton, 1990. The antics of Pete's little brother Fudge make the family vacation memorable. (I: 7–9)

———. *The One in the Middle Is the Green Kangaroo*. 1969. Scarsdale, NY: Bradbury, 1981. A middle child gains self-confidence by being in a school play. (I: 7–9)

Boyd, Candy Dawson. *Charlie Pippin*. New York: Macmillan, 1987. Charlie earns money to help in her search for clues about her father's Vietnam War experience. (I: 10–12)

———. *Chevrolet Saturdays*. New York: Macmillan, 1993. When he enters fifth grade after his mother's remarriage, Joey has difficulty with his teacher and stepfather. (I: 9–11)

Brooks, Bruce. *Midnight Hour Encores*. New York: Harper & Row, 1986. A sixteen-year-old travels cross country with her father to meet the mother who abandoned her as a baby. (I: 12–YA)

———. *What Hearts*. New York: HarperCollins, 1992. A boy learns to forgive after his parents' divorce and his mother's remarriage. (I: 11–YA)

Bunting, Eve. *Fly Away Home*. Illustrated by Ronald Himler. New York: Clarion, 1991. A homeless boy finds hope in the freedom of a bird. (I: 7–9)

Byars, Betsy. *The Pinballs*. New York: Harper & Row, 1977. Three lonely foster children learn to care for each other and their foster parents. (I: 9–12)

Cole, Brock. *Celine*. New York: Farrar, 1989. A high school girl copes with divorced parents along with a young child next door. (I: 11–YA)

Coman, Carolyn. *What Jamie Saw*. Arden, NC: Front Street, 1995. Jamie witnesses his sister being abused by his mother's boyfriend. (I: 9–12)

Creech, Sharon. *Walk Two Moons*. New York: Harper-Collins, 1994. A thirteen-year-old girl and her grandparents follow the journey of her mother after she leaves them. (I: 10–YA)

* de Paola, Tomie. *Tom*. New York: Putnam, 1993. A boy and his grandfather have a special relationship. (I: P–7)

Ellis, Sarah. *Baby Project*. New York: McElderry, 1986. A young girl and her family eagerly prepare for the changes that will occur with the birth of a new baby. (I: 10–YA)

Fitzhugh, Louise. *Sport*. New York: Delacorte, 1979. A boy's life is disrupted when his ruthless mother suddenly wants custody of him. (I: 10–12)

Fox, Paula. *Blowfish Live in the Sea*. New York: Bradbury, 1970. On a strange visit to Boston, Ben discovers that his father needs him. (I: 11–YA)

———. *Monkey Island*. New York: Orchard, 1991. Two men help a homeless boy after his mother abandons him. (I: 10–12)

* Griffith, Helen V. *Georgia Music*. Illustrated by James Stevenson. New York: Greenwillow, 1986. A little girl and her grandfather enjoy making music and listening to the music of Mother Nature. (I: 6–10)

* ———. *Grandaddy and Janetta*. Illustrated by James Stevenson. New York: Greenwillow, 1993. Grandaddy tells stories that help Janetta learn about new things. (I: P–7)

* ———. *Grandaddy's Place*. Illustrated by James Stevenson. New York: Greenwillow, 1987. A little girl learns to enjoy her grandfather's rural home. (I: P–7)

Hamilton, Virginia. *Cousins*. New York: Philomel, 1990. Cammy is not prepared for the accidental death of a relative. (I: 9–12)

Henkes, Kevin. *Protecting Marie*. New York: Greenwillow, 1995. A twelve-year-old has a love/hate relationship with her father. (I: 10–YA)

Hurwitz, Johanna. *The Law of Gravity*. New York: Morrow, 1978. A young girl helps her overweight mother overcome fear of going outside. (I: 9–11)

Johnson, Angela. *Toning the Sweep*. New York: Orchard, 1993. Three generations come together when a dying grandmother prepares to move. (I: 11–YA)

Jukes, Mavis. *Like Jake and Me*. New York: Knopf, 1984. A spider brings Alex and his stepfather closer together. (I: 8–10)

Lowry, Lois. *Rabble Starkey*. Boston: Houghton Mifflin, 1987. Ten-year-old Rabble moves in with another family and changes everyone's life. (I: 9–12)

MacLachlan, Patricia. *Baby*. New York: Delacorte, 1993. Taking care of a baby left by a stranger helps a family come to terms with the death of an infant child. (I: 10–YA)

———. *Journey*. New York: Delacorte, 1991. When two children are left by their mother, the grandparents make a home for them. (I: 9–12)

Mathis, Sharon Bell. *The Hundred Penny Box*. New York: Viking Press, 1975. Michael intercedes when his mother tries to toss out Aunt Dew's memorabilia. (I: 8–10)

Myers, Walter Dean. *Me, Mop, and the Moondance Kid*. New York: Delacorte, 1988. Two adopted boys remain friends with an orphan girl who seeks to be adopted, too. (I: 9–12)

Naylor, Phyllis Reynolds. *Alice in April*. New York: Atheneum, 1993. Thirteen-year-old Alice demands more appreciation from her father and older brother. (I: 10–13)

———. *Shiloh*. New York: Atheneum/Maxwell Macmillan International, 1991. Marty wants to keep a mistreated beagle that he found in the hills surrounding his West Virginia home. (I: 9–12)

Nelson, Theresa. *The Beggar's Ride*. New York: Orchard, 1992. A twelve-year-old girl looks for someone to make a home for her and gets help from other homeless children. (I: 10–YA)

Paterson, Katherine. *Flip-Flop Girl*. New York: Dutton, 1994. A young girl finds it difficult to accept that her father has died. (I: 10–YA)

———. *The Great Gilly Hopkins*. New York: Crowell, 1978. A foster child tries to avoid her own fears by plotting against those who are trying to help. (I: 10–12)

Seabrooke, Barbara. *Judy Scuppernong*. New York: Dutton, 1990. Judy covers up her mother's alcoholism with made-up stories, and then it's time to move again. (I: 9–12)

Spinelli, Jerry. *Maniac Magee*. Boston: Little, Brown, 1990. Maniac is an orphan who discovers that a real home is difficult to find. (I: 9–12)

Temple, Frances. *Grab Hands and Run*. New York: Orchard, 1993. A Salvadoran family struggles to escape oppression and go to Canada. (I: 10–YA)

Thesman, Jean. *When the Road Ends*. Boston: Houghton Mifflin, 1992. Three foster children and an elderly invalid are abandoned by a cruel caretaker. (I: 10–12)

Voigt, Cynthia. *Dicey's Song*. New York: Fawcett/Ballantine, 1982. Dicey and her siblings are left by their mother and try to adjust to life with grandmother. (I: 10–YA)

———. *A Solitary Blue*. New York: Atheneum, 1983. A mother re-enters the life of her abandoned son, causing pain as well as joy. (I: 12–YA)

———. *When She Hollers*. New York: Scholastic, 1994. A teenage girl decides to take action against her abusive stepfather. (I: 11–YA)

Wier, Ester. *The Loner*. New York: Scholastic, 1991. A homeless boy works as a migrant laborer and finds friends. (I: 10–YA)

* Williams, Vera. *A Chair for My Mother*. New York: Greenwillow, 1982. After all their furniture is lost in a fire, the family saves their spare change to buy a chair for mother. (I: P–8)

* ———. *Cherries and Cherry Pits*. New York: Greenwillow, 1986. Bidemmi draws pictures and tells stories about cherries. (I: P–7)

Williams-Garcia, Rita. *Like Sisters on the Home Front*. New York: Lodestar, 1995. A troubled teenager is sent South to live with relatives and experiences the healing power of family roots. (I: 12–YA)

Woodson, Jacqueline. *From the Notebooks of Melanin Sun*. New York: Blue Sky, 1995. A teenage boy copes with the news that his mother is in love with another woman. (I: YA)

School and Society

* Allard, Harry. *Miss Nelson Is Missing!* Illustrated by James Marshall. Boston: Houghton Mifflin, 1977. The strange substitute teacher, Viola Swamp, has the class worried. (I: 7–10)

Burch, Robert. *Queenie Peavy*. New York: Viking, 1966. A girl must bear the burden of her father's being in prison. (I: 9–12)

Byars, Betsy. *Bingo Brown and the Language of Love*. New York: Viking/Kestrel, 1989. Bingo discovers that he has much to learn about expressing how he feels to others. (I: 10–12)

Cole, Brock. *The Goats*. New York: Farrar, 1990. Two summer campers are picked on by other campers, and they develop a deep understanding of themselves and each other. (I: 10–YA)

Danziger, Paula. *The Cat Ate My Gymsuit*. New York: Delacorte, 1974. A junior high student leads the campaign to reinstate an unconventional teacher who was fired. (I: 11–YA)

Davis, Jenny. *Checking on the Moon*. New York: Orchard, 1991. A country girl learns about working-class city folks by working in her grandmother's restaurant. (I: 11–YA)

Hurwitz, Johanna. *Class President*. New York: Scholastic, 1990. Julio hides his ambitions to help another candidate win the nomination for class president. (I: 10–12)

Jukes, Mavis. *Getting Even*. New York: Knopf, 1988. Maggie receives conflicting advice on how to handle an obnoxious classmate. (I: 10–12)

Neville, Emily. *The Bridge*. New York: Harper & Row, 1988. A young boy delights in watching the replacement of a fallen bridge. (I: 10–12)

Sachar, Louis. *There's a Boy in the Girls' Bathroom*. New York: Knopf, 1987. An inept, troublesome fifth grader finds a friend in the school counselor. (I: 10–12)

* Schwartz, Amy. *Annabelle Swift, Kindergartner*. New York: Orchard, 1988. Annabelle believes what her sister tells her about kindergarten, until she gets there. (I: P–7)

Smith, Janice Lee. *The Show-and-Tell War*. New York: Harper & Row, 1988. Five short stories about the misadventures of insecure Adam Joshua. (I: 7–9)

Spinelli, Jerry. *The Bathwater Gang*. Boston: Little, Brown, 1990. An all-girl gang gets into a harmless but heartfelt war directed by a grandmother. (I: 7–9)

———. *Fourth Grade Rats*. New York: Scholastic, 1991. Suds learns that being tough is not what is required in fourth grade, in spite of rumors. (I: 7–9)

* Williams, Vera. *Scooter*. New York: Greenwillow, 1993. A child's scooter helps her adjust to her new home. (I: 8–11)

Wolff, Virginia Euwer. *Make Lemonade*. New York: Holt, 1993. Two young girls, one with a baby of her own, help each other with parenting and education. (I: 11–YA)

* Zolotow, Charlotte. *I Know a Lady*. New York: Greenwillow, 1984. A woman spreads cheer to the young people in her neighborhood by growing flowers and making cookies. (I: P–8)

Interpersonal Relationships

Bunting, Eve. *The Happy Funeral*. New York: Harper & Row, 1982. A Chinese American girl pays tribute to her grandfather as she helps with preparations for his funeral. (I: 10–YA)

Carey, Valerie Scho. *Tsugele's Broom*. New York: HarperCollins, 1993. A young Polish girl insists that she will never marry until she finds a man as reliable as her broom. (I: 10–12)

Clark, Ann Nolan. *Secret of the Andes*. New York: Viking, 1952. An Inca boy learns how the traditions and secrets of his ancestors shape his own life. (I: 10–12)

Conly, Jane Leslie. *Crazy Lady!* New York: Harper-Collins, 1993. A teenage boy copes with the death of his mother by befriending an alcoholic neighbor and her retarded son. (I: 10–12)

Fitzhugh, Louise. *Harriet the Spy*. New York: Harper & Row, 1964. Harriet learns that writing down everything you think can get you in trouble with your friends. (I: 9–11)

———. *The Long Secret*. New York: Harper & Row, 1965. More about Harriet as she becomes more mature and ponders issues of religion and friendships. (I: 10–12)

———. *Nobody's Family Is Going to Change*. New York: Farrar, 1974. Emma wants to be a lawyer and her brother a tap dancer, but their father will not hear of it. (I: 10–12)

Hamilton, Virginia. *M. C. Higgins, the Great*. New York: Macmillan, 1974. M.C. has to reconcile his love for his mountain home with its pending destruction by a slag heap. (I: 10–12)

Hurwitz, Johanna. *Class Clown*. New York: Morrow, 1987. Lucas Cott tries to overcome his need to attract attention to himself and finds it difficult. (I: 10–12)

Konigsburg, E. L. *Jennifer, Hecate, Macbeth, William McKinley, and Me, Elizabeth*. New York: Atheneum, 1968. A girl becomes an apprentice to a witch in this story about interracial friendships. (I: 9–11)

Mohr, Nicholasa. *Felita*. New York: Dial, 1979. The everyday experiences of an eight-year-old Puerto Rican girl growing up in a close-knit urban community. (I: 7–9)

———. *Going Home*. Needham, MA: Silver Burdett Ginn, 1986. An eleven-year-old girl learns to embrace her heritage in Puerto Rico. (I: 10–12)

Namioka, Lensey. *April and the Dragon Lady*. San Diego, CA: Browndeer, 1994. A sixteen-year-old Chinese American is torn between her needs and those of her grandmother. (I: 10–YA)

* ———. *Yang the Youngest and His Terrible Ear*. Boston: Little, Brown, 1992. A young Chinese immigrant prefers baseball to playing the violin. (I: 8–10)

Paterson, Katherine. *Come Sing, Jimmie Jo*. New York: Dutton, 1985. Young Jimmie Jo becomes famous as a singer, but fame doesn't last. (I: 10–12)

Platt, Kin. *The Boy Who Could Make Himself Disappear*. Philadelphia: Chilton, 1968. Harsh parents cause a boy to develop a speech defect and eventually withdraw totally. (I: 10–12)

Soto, Gary. *Boys at Work*. New York: Delacorte, 1995. Rudy and Alex take on many jobs to pay for a broken toy. (I: 9–10)

———. *Summer on Wheels*. New York: Scholastic, 1995. Two boys go on a biking adventure in California. (I: 11–YA)

———. *Taking Sides*. San Diego, CA: Harcourt, 1991. Lincoln Mendoza moves to a white neighborhood and has to take sides on the basketball court. (I: 12–YA)

* Thiele, Colin. *Farmer Schulz's Ducks*. New York: Harper & Row, 1986. A young girl solves a disastrous problem on her family's Australian farm. (I: 6–9)

Woodson, Jacqueline. *Maizon at Blue Hill*. New York: Delacorte, 1992. Winning a scholarship at a boarding school does not ensure Maizon's acceptance by the almost all-white student body. (I: 12–YA)

* Zolotow, Charlotte. *The Hating Book*. New York: Harper & Row, 1969. Two little girls think they hate each other until they talk about it. (I: P–7)

Mental and Physical Challenges

Byars, Betsy. *Just One Friend*. New York: Scribner's, 1985. A learning disabled teenager faces the loss of a friendship as she is mainstreamed into a regular school. (I: 10–YA).

———. *The Summer of the Swans*. New York: Avon, 1970. A mentally handicapped boy searches for the wild swans that return each year. (I: 10–YA)

Kerr, M. E. *Dinky Hocker Shoots Smack*. New York: Harper & Row, 1972. A teenage boy's life changes in many ways when he meets the unusual, overweight girl who gives his cat a home. (I: 11–YA)

———. *Little Little*. New York: Harper & Row, 1981. Two dwarf friends compete for the affection of a dwarf heiress. (I: 12–YA)

Levin, Betty. *Fire in the Wind*. New York: Greenwillow, 1995. Sparks from a chainsaw start a fire that changes the lives of Meg Yeadon, her cousin Orin, and her half-brother Paul, who has just started first grade. (I: 11–YA)

Lipsyte, Robert. *One Fat Summer*. New York: Harper & Row, 1977. An overweight teenage boy learns to stand up for himself. (I: 10–12)

Mathis, Sharon Bell. *Listen for the Fig Tree*. New York: Viking, 1974. A teenager celebrates her first Kwanzaa and gains the strength to deal with her blindness. (I: 12–YA)

———. *Teacup Full of Roses*. New York: Viking, 1975. A teenager leaves home when he realizes his mother will never learn to deal with his brother's drug addiction. (I: 12–YA)

Platt, Kin. *Hey, Dummy*. New York: Dell, 1971. Despite the opposition of his friends and family, Neil befriends his brain-damaged neighbor. (I: 10–12)

Slepian, Jan. *The Alfred Summer*. New York: Macmillan, 1980. Lester and Alfred are strongly developed characters with physical disabilities who together build a boat in the basement. (I: 9–12)

Romance and Sexuality

Bauer, Marion Dane, ed. *Am I Blue? Coming Out from the Silence*. New York: HarperCollins, 1994. Short stories about homosexuality by such authors as Jane Yolen and M. E. Kerr. (I: 12–YA)

Creech, Sharon. *Absolutely Normal Chaos*. New York: HarperCollins, 1995. Mary Lou Finney is wrapped up in family and school affairs, but manages to have Alex come visit in the midst of the chaos. (I: 10–12)

Daly, Maureen. *Seventeenth Summer*. New York: Dodd, Mead, 1942. A first love doesn't last but provides a beautiful memory. (I: 12–YA)

Davis, Jenny. *Sex Education: A Novel*. New York: Orchard, 1988. A tragic end results when two teenagers befriend an abused, pregnant neighbor. (I: 12–YA)

Greene, Bette. *Philip Hall Likes Me, I Reckon Maybe*. New York: Dial, 1974. An eleven-year-old girl has an on-again, off-again relationship with a boy at school. (I: 10–12)

Kerr, M. E. *Gentlehands*. New York: HarperCollins, 1978. A teenage boy faces the pain of love and loss in one summer. (I: 12–YA)

Koertge, Ronald. *The Arizona Kid*. Boston: Joy Street, 1988. A sixteen-year-old boy visits his gay uncle for the summer and falls in love with a girl at a racetrack. (I: 12–YA)

Lowry, Lois. *Anastasia at This Address*. Boston: Houghton Mifflin, 1992. Anastasia answers an ad in a singles column of the newspaper. (I: 9–12)

———. *Anastasia Krupnik*. Boston: Houghton Mifflin, 1979. A ten-year-old girl faces her first love and the news that she will soon have a baby brother. (I: 9–12)

Naylor, Phyllis. *Alice in Rapture, Sort of*. New York: Atheneum, 1989. The summer before entering seventh grade becomes one of turmoil as Alice discovers that falling in love is not what she thought it would be. (I: 10–12)

Platt, Kin. *The Terrible Love Life of Dudley Cornflower*. New York: Bradbury, 1976. Dudley believes all his friends know more about sex than he does. His fumbling fantasies are painful and hilarious. (**I**: YA)

Rylant, Cynthia. *Henry and Mudge and the Careful Cousin*. New York: Bradbury, 1994. Henry's neat cousin learns to enjoy her visit, even Mudge's slobbery kisses. (**I**: 6–8)

———. *A Kindness*. New York: Orchard, 1988. A fifteen-year-old faces the prospect of his unmarried mother's having a baby. (**I**: YA)

Schami, Rafik. *A Hand Full of Stars*. New York: Dutton, 1990. A teenage boy is torn between protesting governmental oppression and spending time with his beloved Nadia. (**I**: 12–YA)

Spinelli, Jerry. *Jason and Marceline*. Boston: Little, Brown, 1986. In this sequel to *Space Station Seventh Grade*, Jason is surprised by his own feelings of affection for Marceline. (**I**: 12–YA)

Woodson, Jacqueline. *I Hadn't Meant to Tell You This*. New York: Delacorte, 1994. Racial barriers are overcome as two girls face a horrible secret. (**I**: 12–YA)

Moral Dilemmas and Moral Responsibility

Avi. *Nothing But the Truth*. New York: Orchard, 1991. A ninth grader's suspension for singing "The Star Spangled Banner" becomes a political football. (**I**: 12–YA)

Boyd, Candy Dawson. *Circle of Gold*. New York: Scholastic, 1984. A young girl copes with her father's death and her mother's struggle to support the family. (**I**: 9–11)

* Bunting, Eve. *The Wednesday Surprise*. New York: Clarion, 1989. Anna secretly teaches her grandmother to read. (**I**: 7–9)

Cunningham, Julia. *Dorp Dead*. New York: Pantheon, 1965. An orphan boy learns about good and evil while working as a carpenter's apprentice. (**I**: 9–12)

Curtis, Christopher Paul. *The Watsons Go to Birmingham—1963*. New York: Delacorte, 1995. A family from the North participates in the civil rights struggles of 1963. (**I**: 10–12)

Davis, Jenny. *Goodbye and Keep Cold*. New York: Orchard, 1987. Edda's mother is courted by the man responsible for her father's death in a mining accident. (**I**: 10–YA)

Fox, Paula. *One-Eyed Cat*. New York: Dell, 1984. An eleven-year-old boy deals with his guilt feelings after shooting a gun he is not supposed to handle. (**I**: 10–YA)

Isadora, Rachel. *At the Crossroads*. New York: Mulberry, 1994. Families in South Africa maintain connection in spite of the separation caused by apartheid. (**I**: 11–YA)

Mathis, Sharon Bell. *Sidewalk Story*. New York: Viking, 1971. A nine-year-old girl decides to do something about her neighbor's eviction. (**I**: 8–10)

Neville, Emily. *Berries Goodman*. New York: Harper & Row, 1965. Anti-Semitic actions move students to rally to support the value of a diverse neighborhood. (**I**: 9–12)

———. *Garden of Broken Glass*. New York: Dell, 1975. Martha acts on her own and Brian's behalf against great odds. (**I**: 9–12)

Rylant, Cynthia. *A Fine White Dust*. New York: Bradbury, 1986. A young boy struggles to reconcile his own religious beliefs with those of family and community. (**I**: 10–YA)

* ———. *Miss Maggie*. New York: Dutton, 1983. A young boy unexpectedly overcomes his fears of an old lady and the rumors he has heard about her. (**I**: 9–11)

Slepian, Jan. *Risk 'n' Roses*. New York: Philomel, 1990. Eleven-year-old Skip wants to relinquish her responsibility to her mentally handicapped sister so that she will have time to make new friends. (**I**: 10–12)

Survival

Bauer, Marion Dane. *Rain of Fire*. New York: Clarion, 1983. Steve's brother, a World War II vet, refuses to tell any stories of the war, making Steve's friends doubt that his brother is a hero. (**I**: 12–YA)

Benary-Isbert, Margot. *The Ark*. New York: Harcourt, 1953. A German family tries to reestablish itself after World War II. (**I**: 10–YA)

Blume, Judy. *Blubber*. New York: Bradbury, 1974. The tables are turned on the tormentor of an overweight classmate. (**I**: 9–12)

Coman, Carolyn. *Tell Me Everything*. New York: Farrar, 1993. Roz talks to God and to the boy her mother gave her life to save. (**I**: 9–12)

* Estes, Eleanor. *The Hundred Dresses*. New York: Harcourt, 1944. Wanda acts with kindness toward those who ridiculed her. (**I**: 7–10)

Fenner, Carol. *Yolonda's Genius*. New York: McElderry, 1995. Yolonda's genius is in discovering not only her own but also her brother's talent. (**I**: 10–YA)

George, Jean Craighead. *Julie of the Wolves*. New York: Harper & Row, 1972. Running away from home means learning to live with wolves to survive. (**I**: 9–12)

Henkes, Kevin. *Words of Stone*. New York: Greenwillow, 1992. A ten-year-old boy struggles to cope with the death of his mother, until he meets boisterous Joselle. (I: 10–12)

Hesse, Karen. *Phoenix Rising*. New York: Holt, 1994. A thirteen-year-old girl learns about relationships and death when Ezra, who was exposed to a radiation leak, comes to live at her grandmother's home. (I: 12–YA)

Hill, Kirkpatrick. *Toughboy and Sister*. New York: McElderry, 1990. Siblings lose their parents and are stranded in a Yukon River camp. (I: 9–11)

Levy, Elizabeth. *Keep Ms. Sugarman in the Fourth Grade*. New York: HarperCollins, 1992. Jackie needs the support of her teacher and doesn't think she can survive when Ms. S. is promoted. (I: 8–10)

Myers, Walter Dean. *Somewhere in the Darkness*. New York: Scholastic, 1992. Jimmy learns that the truth isn't always what it seems on the surface. (I: 12–YA)

Nelson, Vaunda Micheaux. *Mayfield Crossing*. New York: Putnam, 1993. The children in an all-white school gradually learn to accept their African American counterparts. (I: 9–12)

Paulsen, Gary. *Hatchet*. New York: Viking, 1987. Surviving fifty-three days in the wilderness helps Brian cope with his parents' divorce. (I: 9–12)

Tamar, Erika. *The Garden of Happiness*. Illustrated by Barbara Lambase. New York: Harcourt, 1996. Marisol found a seed, which she planted in a small piece of ground on her neglected neighborhood block. The sunflower that grew changed the neighborhood. (I: P–7)

Mystery Books

Adler, David. *Cam Jansen and the Mystery of the Gold Coins*. New York: Viking, 1982. A photographic memory helps Cam solve this mystery. (I: 9–12)

Babbitt, Natalie. *Goody Hall*. New York: Farrar, 1971. A tutor likes his charges, but there is something strange about the household. (I: 9–12)

Bellairs, John. *The Mummy, the Will, and the Crypt*. New York: Dial, 1983. One of several books about Johnny and the professor who solve mysteries, in this case about a cereal tycoon's will. (I: 10–12)

Bunting, Eve. *Coffin on a Case*. New York: HarperCollins, 1992. Henry, the son of a detective, becomes one himself in the mystery of a young client's missing mother. (I: 10–12)

Duncan, Lois. *The Gift of Magic*. Boston: Little, Brown, 1971. Extrasensory perception is hard to handle until it helps solve a mystery. (I: 11–YA)

Hamilton, Virginia. *The House of Dies Drear*. Needham, MA: Silver Burdett Ginn, 1968. A black family moves into an old house where slaves used to be harbored and they find themselves dealing with a number of "ghosts." (I: 10–YA)

Konigsburg, E. L. *From the Mixed-Up Files of Mrs. Basil E. Frankweiler*. New York: Atheneum, 1967. Teenagers learn some important life lessons from an elderly woman. (I: 9–11)

Raskin, Ellen. *The Westing Game*. New York: Dutton, 1978. Sixteen heirs to a fortune work out an intricate riddle and solve a mystery. (I: 9–12)

Sobol, Donald. *Encylopedia Brown Finds the Clues*. New York: Bantam, 1968. One of a series of detective stories starring Encyclopedia Brown and his partner Sally. (I: 9–12)

Tate, Elnora. *The Secret of Gumbo Grove*. New York: Watts, 1987. Snooping around a cemetery reveals interesting stories about an African American community. (I: 9–12)

Sports

Avi. *S.O.R. Losers*. New York: Bradbury, 1984. A humorous account of basketball devotees. (I: 12–YA)

Brooks, Bruce. *The Moves Make the Man*. New York: Harper & Row, 1984. Boys of two races, at first distrustful of one another, become friends through basketball. (I: 12–YA)

Christopher, Matt. *Shoot for the Hoop*. Boston: Little, Brown, 1995. The main character thinks that diabetes will prevent him from playing, but it actually teaches him discipline. (I: 10–12)

———. *The Year Mom Won the Pennant*. Boston: Little, Brown, 1968. Mom not only suffices as a coach—she does quite well. (I: 10–12)

Cohen, Barbara. *Thank You, Jackie Robinson*. New York: Lothrop, 1974. Baseball helps a fatherless boy become close friends with a hotel cook. (I: 9–11)

Lipsyte, Robert. *The Brave*. New York: HarperCollins, 1991. A seventeen-year-old Native American boy learns to control his anger by training with a retired boxer. (I: YA)

———. *The Contender*. New York: Harper & Row, 1967. A young boy finds he can be a survivor in boxing and in life. (I: 10–YA)

Lynch, Chris. *Iceman*. New York: HarperCollins, 1994. An ice hockey player transfers his anger at his parents to players on the ice. (I: 12–YA)

———. *Shadow Boxer*. New York: HarperCollins, 1993. A fourteen-year-old boy struggles to protect his younger brother from the dangers of the inner city. (I: 12–YA)

———. *Slot Machine*. New York: HarperCollins, 1995. High school boys visit a college and find that they must have a sports slot in order to belong. (I: 12–YA)

Slote, Alfred. *Finding Buck McHenry*. New York: HarperCollins, 1991. A boy believes the school janitor is a former famous baseball player. (I: 12–YA)

———. *Hang Tough, Paul Mather*. Philadelphia: Lippincott, 1973. A boy deals with his illness by involving himself in sports. (I: 10–YA)

Spinelli, Jerry. *Crash*. New York: Knopf, 1996. Crash earned his name by being a star athlete from babyhood to middle school, but he earned friendship through different behaviors. (I: 10–YA)

———. *There's a Girl in My Hammerlock*. New York: Simon & Schuster, 1991. A girl is determined to be a wrestler; the boys are disturbed by the idea. (I: 10–YA)

Voigt, Cynthia. *The Runner*. New York: Atheneum, 1985. A dedicated runner, who has always been a loner, learns the value of giving and receiving. (I: 12–YA)

Nature and Animal Stories

Burnford, Sheila Every. *The Incredible Journey*. Boston: Little, Brown, 1961. Three domesticated animals travel through the Canadian wilderness to find their family. (I: 10–YA)

DeJong, Meindert. *The Wheel on the School*. New York: Harper & Row, 1954. Dutch children become absorbed in watching the storks nesting on their schoolhouse roof. (I: 8–12)

* Ets, Marie Hall. *Play with Me*. New York: Viking, 1955. A small child learns to sit still so that animals will come close. (I: P–6)

Farley, Walter. *The Black Stallion*. New York: Random House, 1969. The first of a series about a wild horse found by a seventeen-year-old, who trains him to race. (I: 9–12)

George, Jean Craighead. *My Side of the Mountain*. New York: Dutton, 1959. An old, hollow tree becomes a boy's home. (I: 10–12)

George, John Lothar. *Vulpes, the Red Fox*. New York: Dutton, 1948. A realistic, suspenseful tale of how a fox survives in natural surroundings. (I: 9–12)

Hall, Lynn. *The Boy with the Off-White Hat*. New York: Scribner's, 1984. A thirteen-year-old girl faces a crisis on her summer job at a horse ranch. (I: 12–YA)

Henry, Marguerite. *Misty of Chincoteague*. New York: Checkerboard, 1975. Two youngsters buy a wild colt on the island of Chincoteague, off the eastern shore of Virginia. (I: 9–11)

* Lyon, George Ella. *Come a Tide*. Illustrated by Steven Gammell. New York: Orchard, 1990. A girl provides an account of the spring floods at her rural homeplace. (I: P–8)

* McCloskey, Robert. *One Morning in Maine*. New York: Viking, 1966. Sal and her family live by the sea, catch clams, and travel by boat for other food. (I: P–8)

* ———. *Time of Wonder*. New York: Viking, 1957. Islanders prepare for a big nor'easter. (I: P–8)

Paulsen, Gary. *Brian's Winter*. New York: Delacorte, 1996. Brian faces winter in the wilderness before being rescued, in this continuation of the story that begins in *Hatchet*. (I: 10–YA)

———. *Dogsong*. New York: Bradbury, 1985. The cold and mysteries of the wilderness are made real to readers of this story of a journey on a dog sled. (I: 10–YA)

———. *Woodsong*. New York: Bradbury, 1990. A family in the wilds of northern Minnesota recount their first dealings with sled dogs and the Iditarod race. (I: 12–YA)

Peck, Robert Newton. *A Day No Pigs Would Die*. New York: Knopf, 1972. A thirteen-year-old Vermont farm boy faces the slaughter of his pet pig. (I: 10–12)

———. *Wild Cat*. New York: Holiday House, 1975. Follows the life of a city cat and shows her survival tactics. (I: 10–12)

Wallace, Bill. *Beauty*. New York: Holiday House, 1988. Caring for his grandfather's horse Beauty helps Luke cope with his parents' divorce. (I: 10–12)

———. *Ferret in the Bedroom, Lizards in the Fridge*. New York: Holiday House, 1986. Liz thinks all her father's animals interfere with her political ambitions in school. (I: 10–12)

Humor

Bauer, Joan. *Squashed*. New York: Delacorte, 1992. A humorous story about a girl competing in a pumpkin-growing contest. (I: 10–12)

Blume, Judy. *Tales of a Fourth Grade Nothing*. New York: Dutton, 1972. Readers will sympathize and laugh at Peter's embarrassment over and envy of his little brother, Fudge. (I: 7–9)

Bunting, Eve. *Sixth Grade Sugar Babies*. New York: Lippincott, 1990. Students are learning to care for babies by taking care of bags of sugar. (I: 10–12)

————. *The Burning Questions of Bingo Brown*. New York: Viking, 1988. Bingo takes to heart the questions of love and right actions. (I: 10–12)

Chetwin, Grace. *Box and Cox*. New York: Bradbury, 1990. Two men rent one room and are in it at different times of the day, and the results are hilarious. (I: 12–YA)

Cleary, Beverly. *Ramona the Brave*. New York: Morrow, 1975. This Ramona story has some of the funniest episodes in the series, including Ramona's breaking a raw egg on her head. (I: 12–YA)

Danziger, Paula. *Make Like a Tree and Leave*. New York: Delacorte, 1990. An inside view of the adults and children in the Martin family as they learn about love and life. (I: 12–YA)

Hughes, Dean. *Nutty for President*. New York: Atheneum, 1981. The campaign manager for a candidate for fifth-grade class president tries to manipulate the voters in unusual ways. (I: 10–12)

Hurwitz, Johanna. *Aldo Applesauce*. New York: Morrow, 1989. Aldo becomes a vegetarian and takes a ribbing from his classmates. (I: 8–10)

Robinson, Barbara. *The Best Christmas Pageant Ever*. Wheaton, IL: Tyndale House, 1972. Six rowdy siblings find themselves in the community Christmas pageant. (I: 8–12)

————. *The Worst Best School Year Ever*. New York: HarperCollins, 1994. The rowdy Herdman kids create havoc throughout a school year. This is the sequel to *The Best Christmas Pageant Ever*. (I: 8–12)

Death and Dying

Arrick, Fran. *Tunnel Vision*. New York: Bradbury, 1980. This book reveals the feelings and memoires of each member of the family and of the friends of a boy who commits suicide. (I: 12–YA)

Bauer, Marion Dane. *On My Honor*. New York: Clarion, 1986. Having promised his father he will not go swimming, a boy feels responsible for his friend's drowning when they break the promise. (I: 10–YA)

Boyd, Candy Dawson. *Breadsticks and Blessing Places*. New York: Macmillan, 1985. Maddie's best friend is killed by a drunk driver. (I: 9–12)

* Carrick, Carol. *The Accident*. Illustrated by Donald Carrick. New York: Seabury, 1976. A truck kills Christopher's dog and he feels responsible. (I: 7–9)

* Clifton, Lucille. *Everett Anderson's Goodbye*. Illustrated by Ann Grifalconi. New York: Holt, 1983. The story, in rhyme, of Everett's grief at losing his father. (I: P–7)

Fox, Paula. *The Eagle Kite*. New York: Orchard, 1995. Liam must face his father's dying of AIDS. (I: 10–YA)

Kennedy, Richard. *Oliver's Dishcloth Concert*. Boston: Little, Brown, 1977. Oliver wants to cover his face forever after the death of his wife. (I: 8–12)

Oughton, Jerrie. *Music from a Place Called Half Moon*. Boston: Houghton Mifflin, 1995. Edie faces the death of a friend and her own prejudices. (I: 11–YA)

Paterson, Katherine. *Bridge to Terabithia*. New York: Crowell, 1977. Jess and Leslie form an unusual friendship, which ends in tragedy. (I: 9–12)

Peck, Richard. *Remembering the Good Times*. New York: Delacorte, 1985. Trav considers suicide as a solution to his worries. (I: YA).

Rylant, Cynthia. *Missing May*. New York: Dell, 1992. A child and her uncle search for ways to overcome grief after Aunt May's death. (I: 10–YA)

Smith, Doris Buchanan. *A Taste of Blackberries*. New York: Crowell, 1973. A young boy dies of a bee sting and his best friend grieves. (I: 8–10)

* Zolotow, Charlotte. *My Grandson Lew*. Illustrated by William Pene du Bois. New York: Harper & Row, 1974. Lew wakes up in the night wondering where his grandfather has gone. (I: P–9)

Books with Multicultural and International Themes

George, Jean Craighead. *Julie*. New York: HarperCollins, 1996. Julie joins in efforts to save wolves from extinction. This is a sequel to *Julie of the Wolves*. (I: 11–YA)

Guback, Georgia. *Luka's Quilt*. New York: Greenwillow, 1994. Beautiful illustrations by the author. The setting is Hawaii, and Luka is learning how to make a traditional quilt. (I: 6–9)

Jenkins, Lyll Beccerra de. *Celebrating the Hero*. New York: Lodestar, 1993. Camila learns there is more to her grandfather's life than legend had made her believe. (I: YA).

————. *The Honorable Prison*. New York: Dutton, 1988. Marta's father, a newspaper editor in Colombia, is imprisoned with his family in their own house. (I: YA)

Quinn, Patrick J. *Signs of Spring*. Prior Lake, MN: Eagle Creek, 1995. Eddie prefers city life to moving into the forest and living like his Native American ancestors. (I: 10–12)

Thomas, Joyce Carol. *When the Nightingale Sings*. New York: HarperCollins, 1992. An orphan finds refuge from a mean foster mother by joining a church choir. (I: 9–12)

Temple, Frances. *Taste of Salt: A Story of Modern Haiti*. New York: Orchard, 1992. Djo tells his story of suffering under the Haitian military dictatorship and the countermovement led by Aristide. (I: 12–YA)

———. *Tonight, By Sea*. New York: Orchard, 1995. A Haitian family and friends finally complete the construction of a boat, which helps them escape the tyranny of the government before Aristide returns. (I: 11–YA)

Yep, Laurence. *Child of the Owl*. New York: Harper & Row, 1977. A twelve-year-old girl living with her grandmother in San Francisco learns about her Chinese heritage. (I: 10–12)

———. *Thief of Hearts*. New York: HarperCollins, 1995. Stacey has to decide whether to report a theft or to be loyal to another Chinese American girl. (I: 11–YA)

RESOURCES

Asher, Sandy. ed. *But That's Another Story*. New York: Walker, 1996.

Barbauld, Anna Letitia. *The Works of Anna Letitia Barbauld. With a Memoir by Lucy Aikin*. London: Longman, Hurst, Rees, & Green, 1825.

Billman, Carol. *The Secret of the Stratemeyer Syndicate: Nancy Drew, the Hardy Boys, and the Million Dollar Fiction Factory*. New York: Ungar, 1986.

Blume, Judy. *Letters to Judy: What Your Kids Wish They Could Tell You*. New York: Putnam, 1986.

Coles, Robert. *The Moral Life of Children*. Boston: Atlantic Monthly, 1986.

England, Claire. *Childview: Evaluating and Reviewing Materials for Children*. Englewood, CO: Libraries Unlimited, 1987.

Hunt, Peter, ed. *Children's Literature: An Illustrated History*. New York: Oxford University Press, 1995.

Langer, Judith. *Envisioning Literature*. New York: Teachers' College Press, 1995.

REFERENCES

Alcott, Louisa May. *Little Women*. 1868. New York: MacMillan, 1962.

Aldrich, Thomas Bailey. *The Story of a Bad Boy*. New York: Grosset & Dunlap, 1928.

Alger, Horatio. *Frank and Fearless: Or the Fortunes of Jasper Kent*. Leyden, MA: Aenoian, 1897.

———. *Ragged Dick, and Mark, the Match Boy*. 1897. New York: Collier, 1962.

Allard, Harry. *Miss Nelson Is Back*. Illustrated by James Marshall. Boston: Houghton Mifflin, 1982.

Avi. *Blue Heron*. New York: Bradbury, 1992.

———. *Romeo and Juliet, Together (and Alive!) at Last*. New York: Orchard, 1987.

———. *The True Confessions of Charlotte Doyle*. New York: Orchard, 1990.

———. *Who Was That Masked Man Anyway?* New York: Orchard, 1992.

Babbitt, Natalie. *Tuck Everlasting*. New York: Farrar, 1975.

Barbauld, Anna Laetitia. *Hymns of Prose for Children*. Boston: Spotswood, 1797.

Bauer, Marion Dane. *Shelter from the Wind*. New York: Seabury, 1976.

Blume, Judy. *Forever*. Scarsdale, NY: Bradbury, 1975.

———. *Starring Sally J. Freedman as Herself*. New York: Bradbury, 1977.

———. *Superfudge*. New York: Dutton, 1980.

Brooks, Bruce. *No Kidding*. New York: Harper & Row, 1989.

Bunting, Eve. *Nasty Stinky Sneakers*. New York: HarperCollins, 1994.

———. *Sixth Grade Sleepover*. New York: Scholastic, 1987.

———. *Smoky Night*. San Diego, CA: Harcourt Brace, 1994.

Burgess, Gelett. *Goops and How to Be Them: A Manual for Polite Infants Inculcating Many Juvenile Virtues Both by Precept and Example with Ninety Drawings*. London: Frederick A. Stokes, 1900.

Burnett, Frances Hodgson. *Little Lord Fauntleroy*. New York: Garland, 1976.

———. *The Secret Garden*. 1910. Philadelphia: Lippincott, 1962.

Byars, Betsy. *The Blossoms and the Green Phantom*. New York: Delacorte, 1987.

Caseley, Judith. *Harry and Willy and Carrothead*. New York: Greenwillow, 1992.

Cleary, Beverly. *Ellen Tibbitts*. New York: Morrow, 1951.

———. *A Girl from Yamhill: A Memoir*. New York: Morrow, 1988.

———. *Henry Huggins*. New York: Morrow, 1950.

———. *My Own Two Feet: A Memoir*. New York: Morrow, 1995.

———. *Ramona and Her Father*. New York: Morrow, 1977.

———. *Ramona Forever*. New York: Morrow, 1984.

Cole, Brock. *Alpha and the Dirty Baby*. New York: Farrar, 1991.

Cooper, James Fenimore. *The Last of the Mohicans*. 1826. Chicago: Scott, Foresman, 1950.

Cormier, Robert. *I Am the Cheese: A Novel*. New York: Pantheon, 1977.

———. *In the Middle of the Night*. New York: Delacorte, 1995.

Danziger, Paula. *Amber Brown*. New York: Putnam, 1994.

———. *Earth to Matthew*. New York: Delacorte, 1995.

DeClements, Barthe. *Nothing's Fair in Fifth Grade*. Viking, 1981.

———. *Sixth Grade Can Really Kill You*. New York: Puffin, 1995.

Defoe, Daniel. *The Life and Surprising Adventures of the Renowned Robinson Crusoe*. 1719. Massachusetts: printed and sold by Herman Mann, 1800.

Dodge, Mary Mapes. *Hans Brinker, or the Silver Skates*. 1865. New York: Garden City, 1932.

Donovan, John. *I'll Get There. It Better Be Worth the Trip*. New York: Harper, 1969.

Doyle, Arthur Conan. *The Adventures of Sherlock Holmes*. New York: Airmont, 1966.

Duncan, Lois. *Stranger with My Face*. Boston: Little, Brown, 1981.

———. *They Never Came Home*. New York: Dell, 1990.

Elleman, Barbara. "Introduction." *Popular Reading for Children, II*. Chicago: American Library Association, 1986. v–vi.

Estes, Eleanor. *The Moffats*. New York: Harcourt, 1941.

Finley, Martha. *Elsie Dinsmore*. 1896. New York: Arno, 1974. (1896)

Fleming, Violet. *Be Good to Eddie Lee*. New York: Philomel, 1993.

Fox, Paula. *The Slave Dancer*. New York: Dell, 1973.

George, Jean Craighead. *Dear Rebecca, Winter Is Here*. New York: HarperCollins, 1993.

———. *Fire Bug Connection: An Ecological Mystery*. New York: HarperCollins, 1993.

———. *Missing Gator of Gumbo Limbo: An Ecological Mystery*. New York: HarperCollins, 1992.

———. *On the Far Side of the Mountain*. New York: HarperCollins, 1990.

———. *To Climb a Waterfall*. New York: Philomel, 1995

Gilson, Jamie. *Can't Catch Me, I'm the Gingerbread Man*. New York: Lothrop, 1981.

———. *Hello, My Name Is Scrambled Eggs*. New York: Lothrop, 1985.

———. *It Goes Eeeeeeeeeeee!* Boston: Houghton Mifflin, 1994.

Grahame, Kenneth. *Wind in the Willows*. New York: Scribner's, 1933.

Greenwald, Sheila. *Give Us a Great Big Smile, Rosy Cole*. Boston: Little, Brown, 1981.

———. *Rosy Cole: She Walks in Beauty*. Boston: Little, Brown, 1994.

———. *Write on, Rosy!* Boston: Joy Street, 1988.

Grey, Zane. *Riders of the Purple Sage*. New York: Grosset & Dunlap, 1912.

Hamilton, Virginia. *Zeely*. New York: MacMillan, 1967.

Haywood, Carolyn. *B Is for Betsy*. New York: Harcourt, 1939.

Henkes, Kevin. *Chester's Way*. New York: Greenwillow, 1988.

———. *Chrysanthemum*. New York: Greenwillow, 1991.

———. *Julius, Baby of the World*. New York: Greenwillow, 1990.

Hill, Kirkpatrick. *Winter Camp*. New York: Maxwell Macmillan International, 1993.

Holman, Felice. *Secret City*. New York: Scribner's, 1990.

Hurley, Richard J. "Reading Patterns of Children: What and Why They Read." *Reading Interests of Children and Young Adults*. Ed. Jean Kujoth. Metuchen, NJ: Scarecrow, 1970. 96–97.

Hurwitz, Johanna. *Aldo Peanut Butter*. New York: Morrow, 1990.

Jackson, Jesse. *Call Me Charley*. New York: Harper, 1945.

James, Will. *Smoky the Cow Horse*. New York: Scribner's, 1929.

Jukes, Mavis. *Blackberries in the Dark*. New York: Knopf, 1985.

Kastner, Erich. *Emil and the Detectives*. Garden City, NY: Doubleday, Doran, 1930.

Keene, Carolyn. *The Bungalow Mystery*. New York: Grosset & Dunlap, 1988.

Kerr, M. E. *Love Is a Missing Person*. New York: Harper & Row, 1975.

———. *Me, Me, Me, Me, Me: Not a Novel*. New York: Harper & Row, 1983.

Klein, Norma. *Mom, the Wolfman, and Me*. New York: Pantheon, 1972.

Krumgold, Joseph. . . . *And Now Miguel*. New York: Crowell, 1953.

———. *Henry 3*. New York: Atheneum, 1968.

———. *Onion John*. New York: Crowell, 1959.

Luria, A. R. *Cognitive Development: Its Cultural and Social Foundations*. Cambridge, MA: Harvard University Press, 1976.

Levoy, Myron. *Pictures of Adam*. New York: Harper & Row, 1986.

Lewis, C. S. *The Lion, the Witch, and the Wardrobe: A Story for Children*. New York: Macmillan, 1950.

MacLachlan, Patricia. *Arthur, for the Very First Time*. New York: Harper & Row, 1980.

Mazer, Norma. *Heartbeat*. New York: Bantam, 1989.

McCloskey, Robert. *Homer Price*. New York: Viking, 1943.

———. *Make Way for Ducklings*. New York: Viking, 1941.

Means, Florence. *The Moved Outers*. Boston: Houghton Mifflin, 1945.

———. *Shuttered Windows*. Boston: Houghton Mifflin, 1938.

Murphy, Jill. *Five Minutes' Peace*. New York: Putnam, 1986.

Napoli, Donna Jo. *When the Water Closes Over My Head*. New York: Dutton, 1994.

Naylor, Alice Phoebe, and Carol Wintercorn. "Judy Blume." *Dictionary of Literary Biography: American Writers for Children Since 1960: Fiction*. Volume 52. Detroit: Gale Research, 1986. 30–38.

Naylor, Phyllis Reynolds. *All But Alice*. New York: Maxwell Macmillan International, 1992.

———. *Beetles, Lightly Toasted*. New York: Atheneum, 1987.

———. *Josie's Troubles*. New York: Atheneum, 1992.

———. *The Keeper*. New York: Atheneum, 1986.

———. *Reluctantly Alice*. New York: Atheneum, 1991.

———. *Send No Blessings*. New York: Atheneum, 1990.

Newman, Leslea. *Heather Has Two Mommies*. Boston: Alyson Wonderland, 1989.

Nostlinger, Christine. *Marrying Off Mother*. San Diego, CA: Harcourt, 1978.

O'Neal, Zibby. *Language of Goldfish*. New York: Viking, 1980.

Pascal, Francine. *Best Friends* (Sweet Valley Twins Series). Lakeville, CT: Grey Castle, 1990.

Paterson, Katherine. *Jacob Have I Loved*. New York: Crowell, 1980.

———. *The Zena Sutherland Lectures: 1983–1992*. Edited by Betsy Hearne. New York: Clarion, 1993.

Paulsen, Gary. *Eastern Sun, Winter Moon: An Autobiographical Odyssey*. San Diego, CA: Harcourt, 1993.

———. *The Island*. New York: Dell, 1990.

———. *The River*. New York: Dell, 1993.

———. *Sisters/Hermanas*. San Diego, CA: Harcourt, 1993.

———. *Tracker*. New York: Bradbury, 1984.

———. *The Winter Room*. New York: Orchard, 1989.

———. *Winterdance: The Fine Madness of Running the Iditarod*. San Diego, CA: Harcourt, 1994.

Peck, George Wibur. *Peck's Bad Boy*. Upper Saddle River, NJ: Literature House, 1970.

Peck, Richard. *The Last Safe Place on Earth*. New York: Delacorte, 1995.

———. *Princess Ashley*. New York: Delacorte, 1987.

Peck, Robert Newton. *Soup for President*. New York: Knopf, 1978.

———. *Soup in Love*. New York: Delacorte, 1992.

———. *Soup on Fire*. New York: Delacorte, 1987.

———. *Soup on Wheels*. New York: Knopf, 1981.

———. *Trig*. Boston: Little, Brown, 1977.

Poe, Edgar Allan. *Prose Romances: Murders in the Rue Morgue and the Man Who Was Used Up*. Edina, MN: St. John's University Press, 1968.

Poll, Bernard. "Why Children Like Horse Stories." *Elementary Education*, 38 (November, 1961): 473–74.

Porter, Eleanor. *Pollyanna*. Boston: L.C. Page, 1913.

Postman, Neil. *The Disappearance of Childhood*. New York: Delacorte, 1994.

Rabe, Berniece. *The Balancing Girl*. New York: Dutton, 1986.

———. *Margaret's Moves*. New York: Dutton, 1987.

———. *Where's Chimp*. Morton Grove, IL: Albert Whitman, 1988.

Reuter, Bjarne. *Buster's World*. New York: Dutton, 1989.

Roberts, Willa Davis. *Babysitting Is a Dangerous Job*. New York: Fawcett, 1987.

———. *View from the Cherry Tree*. New York: Atheneum, 1975.

Root, Shelton. "The New Realism: Some Personal Reflections." *Language Arts* 54.1 (1977): 19–24.

Rylant, Cynthia. *Appalachia: The Voices of Sleeping Birds*. San Diego, CA: Harcourt, 1990.

———. *A Blue-Eyed Daisy*. New York: Dell, 1987.

———. *But I'll Be Back Again: An Album*. New York: Orchard, 1989.

———. *The Relatives Came*. New York: Bradbury, 1985.

———. *Soda Jerk*. New York: Orchard, 1990.

———. *When I Was Young in the Mountains*. New York: Dutton, 1982.

Sachs, Marilyn. *Class Pictures*. New York: Dutton, 1980.

Seligson, Susan, and Howie Schneider. *Amos: The Story of an Old Dog and His Couch*. Boston: Little, Brown, 1987.

Sewell, Anna. *Black Beauty: The Autobiography of a Horse*. 1877. New York: Dodd, Mead, 1941.

Shea, Pegi Deitz. *The Whispering Cloth: A Refugee's Story*. Illustrated by Anita Riggio. Stitched by You Yang. Honesdale, PA: Boyds Mill, 1994.

Sidney, Margaret. *Five Little Peppers and How They Grew*. New York: Grosset, 1948.

Slepian, Jan. *Lester's Turn*. New York: Macmillan, 1981.

Sobol, Donald. *Encyclopedia Brown and the Case of the Disgusting Sneakers*. New York: Morrow, 1990.

Something About the Author, 78. Detroit: Gale Research, 1994, p. 261.

Spinelli, Jerry. *Dump Days*. New York: Dell, 1988.

———. *Space Station Seventh Grade*. Boston: Little, Brown, 1982.

———. *Tooter Pepperday*. New York: Random House, 1995.

Spyri, Joanna. *Heidi*. 1884. New York: Scribner's, 1946.

Stanovich, Keith. "Are We Overselling Literacy?" *Stories and Readers: New Perspectives on Literature in the Elementary Classroom*. Eds. Charles Temple and Patrick Collins. Norwood, MA: Christopher-Gordon, 1992. 217.

Steig, William. *Sylvester and the Magic Pebble*. New York: Windmill, 1969.

Stevenson, James. *Higher on the Door*. New York: Greenwillow, 1987.

Stevenson, Robert Louis. *Treasure Island*. 1883. New York: Macmillan, 1963.

Stull, Edith Gilbert. *My Turtle Died Today*. New York: Holt, 1964.

Tarkington, Booth. *Penrod*. Garden City, NY: Doubleday, Page, 1914.

Taylor, Sydney. *All-of-a-Kind Family*. Chicago: Wilcox & Follett, 1951.

Testa, Maria. *Thumbs Up, Rico!* Morton Grove, IL: Albert Whitman, 1994.

Twain, Mark. *The Adventures of Huckleberry Finn*. 1885. New York: Chanticleer, 1950.

———. *The Adventures of Tom Sawyer*. 1876. Chicago: Scott, Foresman, 1949.

Usrey, Malcolm. *Betsy Byars*. Old Tappan, NJ: Twayne, 1995.

Vigna, Judith. *My Two Uncles*. Morton Grove, IL: Albert Whitman, 1995.

Voigt, Cynthia. *David and Jonathan*. New York: Scholastic, 1992.

———. *The Homecoming*. New York: Atheneum, 1991.

———. *Izzy, Willy-Nilly*. New York: Atheneum, 1986.

———. *Seventeen against the Dealer*. New York: Atheneum, 1988.

———. *Sons from Afar*. New York: Atheneum, 1987.

Warner, Gertrude Chandler. *The Boxcar Children*. Chicago: Scott, Foresman, 1950.

Wartski, Maureen Crane. *A Boat to Nowhere*. Philadelphia: Westminster, 1980.

Willhoite, Michael. *Daddy's Roommate*. Boston: Alyson Wonderland, 1990.

Williams, Vera. *Music, Music, for Everyone*. New York: Greenwillow, 1984.

———. *Something Special For Me*. New York: Greenwillow, 1983.

Zindel, Paul. *David and Della*. New York: HarperCollins, 1993.

Zolotow, Charlotte. *A Father Like That*. New York: Harper & Row, 1971.

———. *May I Visit?* New York: Harper & Row, 1976.

———. *Say It!* New York: Greenwillow, 1980.

———. *The Unfriendly Book*. New York: Harper & Row, 1975.

9 Historical Fiction

Today I chased a rat about the hall with a broom and set the broom afire, ruined my embroidery, threw it in the privy, ate too much for dinner, hid in the barnyard and sulked, teased the littlest kitchen boy until he cried, turned the mattresses, took the linen outside for airing, hid from Morwenna and her endless chores, ate supper, brought in the forgotten linen now wet with dew, endured scolding and slapping from Morwenna, pinched Perkin, and went to bed. And having writ this, Edward, I feel no less childish or more learned than I was.

from Catherine, Called Birdy *(1994)*
by Karen Cushman

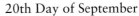

Illustration 9.1
Readers of *Catherine, Called Birdy* (a Newbery Honor Book) enter into the medieval world through the rich details woven into the main character's journal entries. (*Catherine, Called Birdy* by Karen Cushman. Cover art copyright © 1995 by Bryan Leister. Cover design by Stefanie Rosenfield. Cover copyright © 1995 by HarperCollins. Used by permission of HarperCollins Publishers.)

Karen Cushman set her story about Birdy in 1290, a time far removed from our own. The details of our lives are vastly different from those of Birdy's. When (if ever) did you last use a privy? And yet it is easy to empathize with Birdy. Who hasn't had a day when nothing went right? Writers of fine historical fiction are able to help readers feel connected to people and situations from the past, which is what makes historical fiction an important tool in the classroom.

HISTORICAL FICTION DEFINED

Historical fiction is widely viewed as a work of fiction set in a time prior to when it was written. How far in the past must a story be set to qualify as historical fiction? Some say twenty-five years; others say fifty. The precise number of years doesn't matter. Perhaps what matters most is the child's perspective. To a child, a story set fifteen years ago qualifies as being about "the good old days." So, a book like Christopher Paul Curtis's *The Watsons Go to Birmingham—1963* (1995) falls in the realm of historical fiction, even though many adults view the civil rights movement of the 1960s as something that happened "just yesterday."

Yet even the general definition given above may sometimes be too limiting. Some books feature events that were contemporary at the time they were written, but with the passing of time the events have gained historical significance. One such book is Beverly Naidoo's *Journey to Jo'burg* (1986), which details the jour-

Illustration 9.2
The tragic events leading up to the civil rights movement intrude on a family's trip in *The Watsons Go to Birmingham—1963*, both a Newbery Honor Book and a winner of the Coretta Scott King Award. (*The Watsons Go to Birmingham—1963* by Christopher Paul Curtis. Used by permission of Delacorte Press, a division of Bantam Doubleday Dell Publishing Group, Inc.)

ney of two black South African children who experience the harsh realities of apartheid as they travel from their homeland to Johannesburg. At the time of its publication, the book described contemporary conditions in South Africa. However, the apartheid system has since been dismantled, and so the events in Naidoo's book are significant from an historical perspective. Books like this one can be considered historical fiction rather than contemporary realistic fiction.

Value of Historical Fiction

Why should teachers introduce children to historical fiction? First, many works of historical fiction present wonderful stories that children can "step into" for a rich aesthetic experience. After all, who can read Patricia Mac-Lachlan's *Sarah, Plain and Tall* (1985) and not be touched by Anna and Caleb's fervent hope that Sarah will choose to stay on the prairie and become their mother? Readers of Minfong Ho's *The Clay Marble* (1991) will be moved by young Dara's determination to reunite her family after it is separated by war along the border of Cambodia and Thailand.

Teachers also want children to read historical fiction because children are naturally curious about the past, and historical fiction offers answers to some of their questions. Historical fiction has another special value: The genre may help readers develop consciousness of how time and place influence who they are. That is, by better understanding the past, children better understand themselves, their community, their culture, and the world. In fact, the problems of today can often be understood only in light of times past.

You may wonder why we are recommending turning to historical fiction to help children learn about the past. Why not turn exclusively to textbooks and informational books written for children? Textbooks and informational books are important as sources of background for readers. However, historical fiction offers something that textbooks do not. Through historical fiction, children "encounter the complexities of historical events, where facts from the past become living, breathing drama, significant beyond their own time" (Levstik, 1989, p. 136). Although this dramatic element can be found in informational books by fine writers such as Milton Meltzer and Russell Freedman, it is too often missing from textbooks. According to Carl M. Tomlinson, Michael O. Tunnell, and Donald J. Richgels (1993), readers need "historical empathy" in order to develop historical understanding. That is, readers "must be able to perceive past events and issues as they were experienced by the people at the time" (p. 54). Helping readers develop historical empathy is what historical fiction does best, by emphasizing human motives and ordinary people.

Tomlinson and his colleagues also note that historical coverage in textbooks and works of historical fiction differs dramatically. Writers of textbooks aim for broad coverage, whereas writers of historical fiction focus on a single subject and examine it in depth. Certainly, readers need the broad view to place the story situation in proper perspective, but the broad view alone is not sufficient.

THE EVOLUTION OF HISTORICAL FICTION

It is not possible to identify a single creator for most literary genres, but that is not the case with historical fiction. Sir Walter Scott is generally believed to be the first person to write a work of what we now call historical fiction (Blos, 1993). *Waverly*, Scott's first piece of historical fiction, was published in 1810 and was followed by others, including *Ivanhoe*. Though Scott didn't write specifically for children, his books were read by young and old.

Early historical fiction consisted primarily of adventure stories and contained lengthy descriptive passages and many inaccuracies. Early writers who wrote historical fiction specifically for children had their own agenda—teaching students historical information. By the 1930s and 1940s, many of these works were romantic, highly idealized views of the past that contained an overwhelming amount of information (Tomlinson, Tunnell, and Richgels, 1993).

Fortunately, historical fiction has changed considerably in recent decades. The genre is no longer viewed simply as a vehicle for conveying historical information. Rather, writers strive to tell stories—stories that show how living in a particular time and place in the past shaped the lives of people, especially ordinary people. And though ordinary people sometimes become caught up in major historical events, historical fiction is not primarily about those events. For example, Laura Ingalls Wilder's books were inspired by her own experiences. These were among the early works of historical fiction for children that had stories to tell rather than information to convey. **Little House in the Big Woods,** published in 1932, was the first of the *Little House* books. Like the others in the series, it is a warm story full of the everyday experiences of a close-knit frontier family. This shift to storytelling, however, does not mean that historical accuracy is unimportant. In fact, writers of historical fiction should be held accountable to standards of historical accuracy.

Style

The style of writing used in historical fiction has also changed. The ornate descriptions, the sometimes archaic language, and the lengthy factual passages are gone. The language of today's historical fiction is likely to be accessible to children. Consider the opening passage from Patricia MacLachlan's **Sarah Plain and Tall** (1985):

> "Did Mama sing every day?" asked Caleb. "Every-single-day?" He sat close to the fire, his chin in his hand. It was dusk, and the dogs lay beside him on the warm hearthstones.
>
> "Every-single-day," I told him for the second time this week. For the twentieth time this month. The hundredth time this year? And the past few years? (p. 1)

It is the simplicity and immediacy of MacLachlan's language that pulls the reader into the story.

Historical Perspective

One of the most striking changes in historical fiction for children is the perspective from which stories are told. Today's writers are less likely to assume idealized views of the past. Joel Taxel (1983) analyzed thirty-two pieces of historical fiction about the American Revolution written between 1899 and 1976; he discussed two of these books at length. The first, Esther Forbes's **Johnny Tremain,** which was published in 1943, encapsulates an idealized view of the American Revolution: The American patriots are viewed as a united people involved in a divinely inspired struggle for freedom and equality. The perspective in James and Christopher Collier's **My Brother Sam Is Dead** (1974) stands in marked contrast: The colonists are a divided people; many of them remain loyal to the king of England. Tim Meeker, the book's protagonist, questions the values of the revolution, eventually choosing not to become part of the revolutionary fervor. Differing perspectives can be explained in large part by the times in which authors live and write. Esther Forbes wrote **Johnny Tremain** in the midst of the patriotic fervor of World War II, whereas **My Brother Sam Is Dead** was published in 1974, when the United States was waging an unpopular war in Vietnam.

Recent historical fiction for children has seen the emergence of many new perspectives. In **Encounter** (1992), Jane Yolen used a picture book format to show Columbus through the eyes of a Taino child who tries to warn his people of the coming destruction he has seen in a dream. Perspectives on pioneer times have also changed in historical fiction for children. Until recently, the common perspective on pioneer life was of the sort seen in the *Little House* books:

Illustration 9.3
A quiet undercurrent of suspense runs through this Newbery Medal–winning story of pioneer life. (*Sarah, Plain and Tall* by Patricia MacLachlan. Jacket art copyright © 1985 by Marcia Sewall. Jacket copyright © 1985 by HarperCollins Publishers, Inc. Used by permission of HarperCollins Publishers.)

Though times were hard, a warm, united family was an ever-present, sustaining force. More recent books, such as, Pamela Conrad's *Prairie Songs* (1985) and Eve Bunting's *Dandelions* (1995), explore the loneliness and isolation of pioneer life from a woman's perspective.

Subject Matter

The subject matter of historical fiction for children has changed as well. Authors of historical fiction set in the United States are writing about less well-known historical events and periods. Candace Christiansen's *Calico and Tin Horns* (1992) focuses on sharecroppers' rebellion against wealthy landowners in the Hudson River Valley in the 1840s. Eve Bunting's *Train to Somewhere* (1996) is about the "Orphan Trains" that transported children to the West for adoption from the 1850s to the 1920s.

Writers of earlier times adhered to an unspoken code that children needed to be protected from the less savory aspects of the past (Tunnell, 1993). This is no longer true. Mildred Taylor and other writers have written about the senseless prejudice and violence that African Americans have faced. Yoshiko Uchida in *Journey to Topaz* (1985) wrote movingly about the experiences of Japanese Americans in internment camps during World War II. And in *The Island on Bird Street* (1984), Uri Orlev wrote about the suffering of Jews during World War II.

Historical fiction about other parts of the world, especially Third World countries, is increasingly available to American audiences. In writing *The Year of Impossible Goodbyes* (1991), Korean writer Sook Nyul Choi drew on her family's experiences under Japanese occupation during World War II and their subsequent struggle to escape communist rule in what became North Korea. In *The Clay Marble* (1991), set in war-torn Cambodia during the early 1980s, twelve-year-old Dara and her family seek refuge in a camp on the border of Cambodia and Thailand. In *The Bomb* (1995), Theodore Taylor tells a story about the Bikini islanders who were forced to evacuate their homes to make way for nuclear testing by the United States. There is still too little historical fiction about other countries and cultures available to young American readers, but this situation is beginning to turn around.

Illustration 9.4
A young orphan riding a train westward fears that no family will choose her. (*Train to Somewhere* by Eve Bunting. Jacket illustration copyright © 1996 by Ronald Himler. Used by permission of Clarion Books/Houghton Mifflin Company. All rights reserved.)

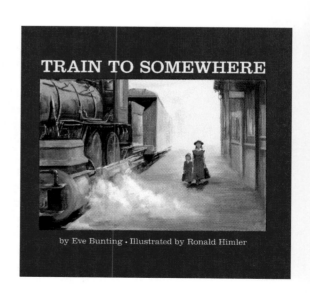

TRAIN TO SOMEWHERE

by Eve Bunting · Illustrated by Ronald Himler

What is appropriate historical subject matter for young children?

History doesn't always wear a pretty face, and increasing numbers of authors of historical fiction for children are writing about some of the more disturbing episodes from the past and using a picture book format to tell these stories. This trend places teachers of young children in the position of having to decide whether such picture books are appropriate for their students.

One picture book with potentially disturbing historical subject matter is Toshi Maruki's *Hiroshima No Pika* (1980). The author recounts the dropping of the first atomic bomb from the perspective of a young girl and her family, who live in Hiroshima. Graphic textual details and illustrations depict the devastation caused by the bomb. The Holocaust is another subject that a number of writers have explored in picture book format. Margaret Wild's *Let the Celebrations Begin!* (1991) is about a group of women who are imprisoned in a Nazi concentration camp and who collaborate to make stuffed toys for the children in the camp. In *Rose Blanche* (1985), a young German girl discovers a concentration camp outside her own town. *Baseball Saved Us* (1993) and *The Bracelet* (1993) are about Japanese Americans' internment in camps in their own country during World War II. Readers of *The Whispering Cloth* (1995) learn about a Hmong refugee's experiences, including the brutal murder of her parents.

Are picture books with such strong subject matter appropriate for elementary school children? Some educators fear that children may be frightened by these negative aspects of history. They argue that children should not be introduced to such books until they more fully understand the historical contexts in which the stories are set, for only then will they be able to place the stories in proper perspective. Others argue that by coming to understand the past at an early age, children will be less likely to repeat the mistakes of past generations. Those on this side of the issue maintain that if a story has a theme that is hopeful and uplifting, then the book is appropriate even for younger children.

What do you think?

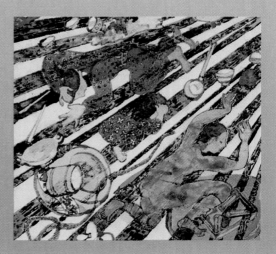

Illustration 9.5
The devastation caused by the first atomic bomb is depicted through graphic textual details and illustrations in *Hiroshima No Pika*. (*Hiroshima No Pika* by Toshi Maruki. Text copyright © 1980 by Toshi Maruki. Used by permission of Lothrop, Lee and Shepard, a division of William Morrow & Co., Inc.)

Picture Books

The emergence, in recent years, of many works of historical fiction in picture book format is another noteworthy change. Some of these stories, such as Riki Levinson's *I Go with My Family to Grandma's* (1986), are appropriate for children as young as five to eight, whereas stories such as Karen Ackerman's *The Tin Heart* (1990) are better suited for children in the upper elementary grades.

Many readers especially enjoy the picture book format because illustrations can bring sometimes hard-to-imagine settings to life. Illustrations often help readers to develop a feel for bygone eras that words alone may not convey. In *Baseball Saved Us* (1993), Dom Lee's scenes depicting vast expanses of desert enclosed by barbed-wire fences and guard towers capture the desolation that Japanese Americans must surely have felt when imprisoned in their own country during World War II. Illustrations play another important role as well: They frequently convey information about the past that adds to, supports, or clarifies textual information. Through Thomas Locker's illustrations in *The Ice House* (1993), readers discover how ice was "harvested" from rivers at the turn of the century, and the illustrations in *Sami and the Time of the Troubles* (1992) reveal Beirut's destruction in the Lebanese civil war.

All the changes in the genre in recent decades make for a bright future for children's historical fiction. Certainly books in this genre have been awarded an impressive number of Newbery Medals and Honors in recent years: Patricia MacLachlan's *Sarah, Plain and Tall* (1985), Lois Lowry's *Number the Stars* (1989), Avi's *The True Confessions of Charlotte Doyle* (1990), Karen Cushman's *Catherine, Called Birdy* (1994), Christopher Curtis's *The Watsons Go to Birmingham—1963* (1995), and Karen Cushman's *The Midwife's Apprentice* (1995). Given the special values of historical fiction, many teachers look forward to even more books of this caliber.

CATEGORIES OF HISTORICAL FICTION

Joan Blos (1993) identifies three types of historical fiction: (1) fictionalized memoirs, (2) fictionalized family history, and (3) fiction based on research. She notes that the author's relationship to the material is different for each type.

Fictionalized Memoirs

Because writers of fictionalized memoirs have lived through the bygone era about which they write, they are able to draw on their own experiences in crafting their stories. The result is often a story that is full of extraordinarily rich details about daily life and holds a special sense of immediacy for the reader. It is easy to imagine, for example, how in writing *Little House on the Prairie* (1935) Laura Ingalls Wilder drew on personal memories to describe the family's first Christmas on the prairie:

> For Christmas dinner there was the tender, juicy, roasted turkey. There were the sweet potatoes, baked in the ashes and carefully wiped so that you could eat the good skins, too. There was a loaf of salt-rising bread made from the last of the white flour.
> And after all that there were stewed dried blackberries and little cakes. But these little cakes were made with brown sugar and they did not have white sugar sprinkled over their tops.

Then Pa and Ma and Mr. Edwards sat by the fire and talked about Christmas times back in Tennessee and up north in the Big Woods. But Mary and Laura looked at their beautiful cakes and played with their pennies and drank their water out of their new cups. And little by little they licked and sucked their sticks of candy, till each stick was sharp-pointed on one end.

That was a happy Christmas. (pp. 251–252)

If personal experiences serve as the inspiration of fictionalized memoirs, you may wonder why such books are not considered biography. The reason is, quite simply, that the writers fictionalize their personal experiences. For example, in the first paragraph of *Little House on the Prairie,* Ingalls says that Baby Carrie made the trip from the Big Woods, but her real sister Carrie had not yet been born when the family left their home in Wisconsin (Frey and Griffith, 1987).

Writers of fictionalized memoirs may draw on personal memories, but these memoirs are seen from an historical perspective—for the time about which the authors write may be vastly different from the time in which they are writing. Once again, Laura Ingalls Wilder is a good example. She was born in 1867 but did not publish *The Little House in the Big Woods,* the first of the *Little House* books, until 1932. Between 1867 (just two years after the Civil War ended) and 1932, the world changed enormously. People no longer crossed the country in covered wagons as Wilder's own family had done; instead, they relied on trains, cars, and sometimes even airplanes. Thus, the passage of time allows a writer to achieve historical perspective.

Fictionalized Family History

Many families treasure a tradition of passing family stories from one generation to the next, and family stories have fed the historical fiction of many writers. Sometimes historical fiction develops from only the barest snippet of a family story. Such was the case for writer Ann Turner. As Turner and her aunt looked at an old trunk together, her aunt remembered another old trunk (Turner, 1993):

> "You know, there used to be a VERY old trunk in Grandpa's house, in the basement. . . . It was an eighteenth-century trunk . . . a big, black domed thing covered with leather. . . . And there were two stories about it. One was that during the early period of settlement some of our ancestors escaped from an Indian attack in that trunk. The other story is that when the rebels came, some children were hidden in that trunk and escaped the rebels."
>
> "You mean we were TORIES?" . . .
>
> "Oh, yes, some were . . . Anyway, I wonder what happened to that trunk." (p. 11)

From this fleeting exchange grew *Katie's Trunk* (1992), the story of a Tory child who hid in the family trunk when a band of Patriots came to her home.

In other instances, relatively well developed stories are passed down, stories that writers can use with only a little fleshing out. According to Patricia Polacco, *Pink and Say* (1994), her story of the friendship between two Union soldiers, was passed down through her family from her great-great-grandfather, who happened to be the white soldier in the story.

Mildred Taylor's historical fiction is also fictionalized family history. Reviewers and critics have long marveled that someone who did not live

Illustration 9.6
This picture book about the American Revolution is told from a Tory perspective. (*Katie's Trunk* by Ann Turner. Illustration copyright © 1993 Ron Himler. Used by permission of Simon & Schuster Books for Young Readers.)

KATIE'S TRUNK
by Ann Turner

illustrations by Ron Himler

through the Depression era can write about that period of American history with such authenticity. The answer lies, at least in part, in the family stories that Taylor listened to as a child. She was born in Mississippi, but her family moved to Toledo, Ohio, while she was still a baby. Though Taylor grew up in the North, she was connected to the South through the stories her father told about his own childhood in rural Mississippi. Also, each summer the Taylors traveled to Mississippi to visit their extended family. Family stories were woven into the fabric of those summer visits with the Taylor clan, and many of the events narrated in those stories became events in the stories Taylor has written.

Fiction Based on Research

Probably the bulk of historical fiction for children fits into the third type—fiction that is based on research. Writers who set their stories in eras about which they have no firsthand knowledge must perform research to ensure authenticity. Occasionally, a writer does the research after writing the story. This is how Pam Conrad worked when writing *Prairie Songs* (1985). Conrad (1993) says that she had read so much historical fiction and so many journals written in pioneer times that she was confident that she could write her story without doing research first—though she did research some details after the fact to verify their accuracy.

The amount of information that is available to writers can vary extensively. Writers who feature cultures with no writing systems frequently have only scant anthropological evidence to draw on. Michael Dorris faced this situation when writing *Morning Girl* (1992). Set on a Bahamian island in 1492, the book centers around a sister and brother of the Taino tribe. The story ends as Morning Girl greets the white visitors who paddle to shore—men from Columbus's ship. Dorris (1992) notes that the Tainos had no writing system, and within a generation or two the tribe was wiped out by disease. The only written reference to these people was one Columbus included his journal.

In contrast, writers who focus on literate societies often have a wealth of original sources as well as extensive reference material from which to draw their information. Frances Temple (1994) described the research she did in writing *The Ramsay Scallop* (1994), a story about a couple's religious pilgrimage, set in Europe in 1300:

> More than seventy books turn up cited in my notes for *The Ramsay Scallop*, some in English, some in French or Spanish, some in medieval French. . . . One source led to another: art books; religious meditations; playscripts; a guidebook written in 1190 by a priest, with tips on where to find clean water and what to use to discourage fleas; histories, where I found a picture of Nana Sybille in her wheelbarrow; and song books. (p. 18)

Research can take other forms as well. For example, Temple described how her research for *The Ramsay Scallop* also involved walking along dusty paths, wading in streams, and kneeling in ancient chapels.

HOW HISTORICAL FICTION WORKS

Historical fiction differs—at least in some ways—from other genres. Let's consider some of these critical aspects of historical fiction, which affect how it is written and read.

Setting

Because historical fiction takes place in a time removed from that of the reader, setting is an especially important element. The writer's obligation is to bring place and time to life for the reader by providing details that are neither romanticized nor distorted but as authentic as possible, given what is known about the era in which the story is set. Extensive research is the most likely means by which the writer obtains these rich details, especially if a story is about a literate culture that left extensive records. But when writers set stories in times about which little is known, they must rely on their imaginations to construct details of time and place that are consistent with whatever little is known about the period.

The importance of rich details of setting is evident in Gary Bowen's *Stranded at Plimoth Plantation 1626* (1994). The story is told in journal format by a thirteen-year-old orphan named Christopher Sears. The ship that Christopher and others sailed to Jamestown on wrecked, and the group was stranded at Plimoth Plantation. Young Christopher records his arrival at Plimoth in his journal:

> On our tenth day here, we were transported to Plimoth and will remain here until a ship can sail us 700 miles south to Jamestown. My leg became too swollen to walk on, and I had to be lifted into the shallop.
>
> The soldiers said New Plimoth was established on the site of an abandoned Indian village 35 miles north of where our ship wrecked. Within an eight-foot paling I saw a fort and 30 houses arranged neatly on streets, as in England.
>
> Lodging has been found for each of us, and I am staying with the Elder William Brewster family. Their house has only one room and a fireplace, but here is a wooden floor that is warmer than the clay we had in London. The Elder says only gentry can afford such floors back home, due to the scarcity of timber. (pp. 2–3)

Illustration 9.7
A boy's journal entries bring an early period of American history to life. (*Stranded at Plimoth Plantation 1626* by Gary Bowen. Copyright © 1994 by Gary Bowen. Used by permission of HarperCollins Publishers.)

The details Bowen includes make it easy for the reader to envision how very small the Plimoth of 1626 was and how very basic life must have been in the simple homes found in the village. Details about setting are crucial—though it is equally crucial not to include so many as to overwhelm the story. Illustrated works of historical fiction provide additional details about setting through illustrations. In *Stranded at Plimoth Plantation 1626*, the main character is learning wood engraving, and his engravings provide even more information about Plimoth in 1626.

The time and place in which a writer situates a story must be integral to the story. How can a reader judge whether this is the case? If the story could just as easily have been set in another era, then the setting is not essential to the story. The setting of *Journey to Jo'burg* (1986) is integral to the story. Naidoo's story is set in South Africa during the time when apartheid was officially sanctioned, and apartheid shapes every aspect of the main characters' experiences as they journey from their homeland to the white-controlled city of Johannesburg.

Plot

According to Jean Fritz (1986), a writer of many works of historical fiction for children, the original sense of the word "history" is "to ask questions," and Fritz says that this is just what she does as she delves into another time and place in order to craft a work of historical fiction. It is easy to imagine Karen Hesse,

Illustration 9.8
Strong characterization marks
Letters from Rifka, the story of a
young immigrant girl who journeys
to the United States on her own.
(*Letters from Rifka* by Karen Hesse.
Illustration copyright © 1992 by Diana
Zelvin. Used by permission of Puffin
Books, a division of Penguin Books
USA Inc.)

author of *Letters from Rifka* (1992), doing just this. The book is about a young Jewish girl who sets out from Russia with her family but is not allowed by officials to cross the Atlantic with her family because she has contracted ringworm. Left behind in the care of strangers, Rifka eventually makes the journey alone. In creating this dramatic emigration story, Hesse might have asked questions like these: What was it like to cross the ocean in search of a new life in a new land? Who were the people who made those journeys? Why did they do it? What uncertainties did they face? Questions like these suggest possibilities for story conflict and the events that culminate in an eventual resolution of the conflict. The answers to those questions may be found through historical research, from knowledge of family events, and in the writer's own knowledge of humanity.

Jean Fritz hopes that readers of historical fiction will also ask questions as they read a book—questions that may be quite similar to those asked by the writer. However, Violet Harris (1995) warns that young readers may not have sufficient historical knowledge of a period about which they are reading to ask questions, and she suggests that they be given opportunities to read informational books to gain the background that may be needed to read historical fiction.

In historical fiction, the writer creates a conflict that grows out of the time in which the story is set. Events must unfold plausibly, and the conflict must be resolved in a manner that is consistent with the historical context in which the story is situated. Mildred Taylor achieves all this in *Roll of Thunder, Hear My Cry* (1976). The Logans' struggle against the Wallaces and Harlan Granger reflects the broader struggle of African Americans in the racist society of rural Mississippi in the 1930s. The indignities the Logan children face typify the times—being splashed with mud by the white children's school bus, having to use worn-out school books discarded by whites. The resolution of *Roll of Thunder, Hear My Cry* is also in keeping with the times. The threat of violent confrontation between the whites and David Logan and Mr. Morrison is not realized, but the Logans pay a high price: They lose a quarter of their cotton crop—cotton they needed to sell in order to pay their taxes. T. J. Avery is not lynched in the middle of the night, but the story ends with the very real threat that T. J. will be convicted of a crime he did not commit and executed, all because he is an African American.

Characters

More often than not, the characters in historical fiction are ordinary people rather than figures of historical importance. Sometimes, they are swept up in great historical events of their time, as are the Kurdish characters in Elizabeth Laird's *Kiss the Dust* (1991), who are driven out of Iraq and forced to become refugees in Iran. As often as not, though, the characters in historical fiction are living what can best be described as ordinary lives. For example, the children in Avi's frontier story, *The Barn* (1994), must carry on with all the tasks of daily life when their father is crippled by a massive stroke.

At times, though, major historical figures do enter into works of historical fiction. Sometimes they play only a minor role. For example, in Donald Hall's *When Willard Met Babe Ruth* (1996), a family is held together by a love of baseball and an interest in Babe Ruth, but the Babe himself plays only the briefest role in the story. In other books, historical figures play more prominent roles. In Ann Rinaldi's *Finishing Becca* (1994), the protagonist is employed in the home of General Benedict Arnold and is able to observe the general's treason firsthand.

Whether their characters are ordinary people or important historical figures, writers of historical fiction strive to create authentic characters who behave in ways consistent with the period. Windrider, a Chinese immigrant in Laurence Yep's *Dragonwings* (1975), longs to build and fly an airplane. His dream is believable, for the story is set at the time when the Wright brothers had just flown the first airplane and when visionaries understood the revolutionizing potential of airplanes. Equally believable, though, are the reactions of Windrider's relatives. Like many others, they are convinced the Wright brothers never flew, and so they try to persuade Windrider to abandon his dream.

Theme

We can discern a great deal about life by learning about our past, and writers of historical fiction frequently explore themes that are significant not only for the historical period of the story but also for the present. In a listing of the themes she explored in her Newbery Medal winner, *A Gathering of Days: A New England Girl's Journal, 1830–1832* (1979), Joan Blos (1993) includes "parent loss, death, remarriage, teacher accountability, community control, civil rights, moral responsibility versus personal loyalty" (p. 14). All are still relevant today.

The themes found in historical fiction are diverse and significant—the senselessness of prejudice and violence, the importance of family and community, the destructiveness of oppression, the need for freedom and independence, the importance of loyalty, faith and honor, the need to reach out to others. Kathy Broderick (1994) observed that "we learn about the present from studying the past. Though some of the problems of the past have been solved, there are questions that the characters in . . . [books] ask that we are still asking today" (p. 19).

MAJOR WRITERS OF HISTORICAL FICTION AND THEIR WORKS

This section is organized into major historical periods and topics. Many writers write about more than one historical era. Such writers are discussed in the section on the period about which they have written most extensively. An author who has written a landmark book about a particular period is discussed in the section on that period.

Ancient Times through the Medieval Period

Not many writers have chosen to write about ancient times. Perhaps writers assume that children are less likely to be interested in times far removed from their own; perhaps the difficulties of researching ancient times deter some writers. Fortunately, there are some notable exceptions.

Karen Cushman. To date, Karen Cushman has published three books, all historical fiction. She has established a remarkable record. Her first book, *Catherine, Called Birdy* (1994) was named a 1995 Newbery Honor Book, and the second, *The Midwife's Apprentice* (1995), was awarded the 1996 Newbery Medal. These two books are set in the Middle Ages. Her third book, *The Ballad of Lucy Whipple* (1996), is set in the California gold rush of 1848.

Cushman says that she turned long ago from an interest in queens and kings and princesses and princes to an interest in ordinary people. That interest led her to do extensive research on the lives of ordinary people in medieval England, the setting of two of her three books. The protagonist of *Catherine, Called Birdy* is a strong-willed young lady who is determined not to marry the man her father has selected for her. In her journal, Birdy records with frequent humor her ongoing battle with her father, her changing perspectives on life, and her many everyday occurrences. In *The Midwife's Apprentice,* a homeless and nameless girl is literally pulled from the dung heap where she is sleeping and given the opportunity to become a midwife's apprentice. Cushman chronicles the girl's transformation from a nameless waif to a person with a name, a place in the world, and a vision of who she can become.

Marguerite de Angeli. Marguerite de Angeli began her career in publishing as an illustrator in 1922. It was not until 1948 that she turned her attention to historical fiction. Her research on English castles and a long-dreamed-of trip to England culminated in her best-known work, *A Door in the Wall* (1949), which is set in medieval England and earned de Angeli a Newbery Medal. Robin, the book's protagonist, is destined to be trained as a knight. His plans are turned topsy-turvy when he is stricken by a mysterious paralysis, but he eventually discovers that there are many different ways of being a hero. The story is memorable for both its strength of characterization and its details about medieval life.

In addition to the Newbery Medal, Marguerite de Angeli received the Lewis Carroll Shelf Award and the Regina Medal. She died in 1987 at the age of 98.

Rosemary Sutcliff. Rosemary Sutcliff has repeatedly demonstrated that historical fiction set in ancient times can appeal to children. She is most widely recognized for her works set in England, most especially for her trilogy about the days of the Roman occupation there. *The Eagle of the Ninth* (1954), the first in the trilogy, is the story of a young Roman centurion who is beginning his military career in second-century England. *The Silver Branch* (1957) focuses on a junior surgeon caught up in the turbulent politics of third-century England. The third book in the trilogy, *The Lantern Bearers* (1959), is set in the midst of the decline of Roman rule in England. Sutcliff's wide-ranging historical interests are also evident in books about the Iceni tribe of ancient Britain (*Sun Horse, Moon Horse,* 1977), the people of the Bronze Age (*Warrior Scarlet,* 1958), and the Saxon invasion of Britain (*Dawn Wind,* 1961).

Rosemary Sutcliff received numerous awards for her contributions to children's literature, including the Carnegie Medal and the Lewis Carroll Shelf Award. She died in 1992.

The New World

Although children's authors have told stories of early explorers and settlers throughout the Americas, the bulk of children's historical fiction about the New World has focused on what happened in what is now the United States, and most of these stories have been told from the perspective of white people. However, diverse perspectives are increasingly being represented in stories set in the Americas in the sixteenth and seventeenth centuries.

Scott O'Dell. Scott O'Dell was a prolific writer of historical fiction for children. Although his stories are set in a variety of periods, his work is discussed at this point because he is one of the few children's writers to have written about the period of the Spanish conquest and exploration of the New World.

O'Dell wrote a number of books about early America and its conquest by Spain. *The King's Fifth* (1966), a Newbery Honor Book, is about a group of Spaniards who travel through Mexico and what is now the southwestern United States in search of gold—which brings only grief when they find it. *The Captive* (1979) is the first book in a trilogy about the conquests of the Mayan, Aztec, and Incan civilizations. In this book, Julian Escobar, a young seminarian, views his journey to the Americas as an opportunity to save the souls of the Indians, but the New World, filled with slavery and exploitation, is not what he imagined. O'Dell continued the story of New World greed and corruption in *The Feathered Serpent* (1981) and *The Amethyst Ring* (1983).

Scott O'Dell won the 1961 Newbery Medal for *Island of the Blue Dolphins* (1960), a story about Karana, a young Native American girl who survived alone on an island off the coast of California for eighteen years. *Sing Down the Moon* (1970), a Newbery Honor Book, is the story of the forced resettlement of the Navajos and of the young Navajo girl who determined to return to the home of her ancestors. O'Dell died in 1989 at the age of 91.

Elizabeth George Speare. Elizabeth George Speare always intended to be a writer; however, she was nearly fifty before she turned to professional writing. Born in 1908, Speare began her writing career in 1955 with magazine articles about family life. Not until 1957 did she publish her first historical fiction for children.

That first novel was *The Witch of Blackbird Pond* (1958), the book for which Speare is best known. The story is set in colonial America. Kit, the protagonist, travels from her home in Barbados to live with her aunt's family in Puritan Connecticut. Kit's values and beliefs soon clash with those of members of the rigid Puritan community, and the clash culminates in Kit's being tried for witchcraft. *The Witch of Blackbird Pond* was awarded the Newbery Medal in 1959 by a unanimous vote—a very rare occurrence.

Speare has written other historical fiction as well: *Calico Captive* (1957), set in the early nineteenth century; *The Bronze Bow* (1961), set in Biblical Palestine; and *The Sign of the Beaver* (1983), set on the western frontier. Speare has received two Newbery Medals and the Laura Ingalls Wilder Award for her distinguished contribution to children's literature.

American Revolution

The American Revolution was a pivotal point in the history of the United States, and many writers have written about it. Quite a few of the writers highlighted in this section have also produced historical fiction about other periods, but they are discussed here because of the way they have helped to shape children's understanding of this era.

James Lincoln Collier and Christopher Collier. Brothers James and Christopher Collier come from a family of writers, but what makes their journey along the writing pathway unusual is that they have teamed up to write historical fiction for children. Each brother brings particular talents to the team. Before their collaboration, James was an established writer of fiction and nonfiction for children as well as adults. Christopher was a renowned historian, teacher, and scholarly writer. Their partnership began when Christopher, discouraged by dry history textbooks, approached his brother with a proposal: He would fashion the concept and provide the necessary historical information while James would develop the characters and story line. Their first collaborative effort, *My Brother Sam Is Dead* (1974), was named a Newbery Honor Book.

The Colliers' treatment of issues related to the American Revolution was unlike that found in most other children's books about the war. Rather than presenting the war primarily as a conflict between the Americans and their British oppressors, the Colliers chose an alternative perspective: They presented it as an internal conflict that divided communities and even families.

Other pieces of historical fiction on which the Colliers have collaborated include *Jump Ship to Freedom* (1981), the story of a runaway slave, and *War Comes to Willy Freeman* (1983), about a young African American girl who must cope with the loss of her parents.

Esther Forbes. Esther Forbes was highly regarded both as an historian and as a novelist. She was awarded a Pulitzer Prize in history, and she received the Newbery Medal in 1944 for *Johnny Tremain* (1943). This story is situated in the very midst of the American Revolution. Major figures such as Samuel Adams and Benjamin Franklin are part of the backdrop of the story, and the protagonist, Johnny Tremain, is apprenticed to Paul Revere. Johnny becomes caught up in the political issues of the times, and he and his compatriots rally in opposition to what they perceive as oppression from the British crown. Critics have praised Forbes for probing issues related to the war in far greater depth than was typical of earlier books for young people. However, in recent years the book has come under criticism for having been written from what many regard as a simplistic "good guy versus bad guy" perspective that revealed more about attitudes of the World War II era in which it was written than about the American Revolution.

Civil War and Slavery

From the founding of the United States to President Lincoln's Emancipation Proclamation in 1863, slavery was legal in the United States. This odious institution was one of the conditions that led to the tragedy of the Civil War, which tore the country apart. Some outstanding children's writers have written about this era of U.S. history.

Paul Fleischman. Paul Fleischman's work extends across genres, and his historical fiction extends across eras. His novel *Bull Run* (1993), about the first battle of the Civil War, is of note for its original format. Sixteen characters—each with a distinctive voice—step forward to tell their stories in one- and two-page segments. Whether Northerner or Southerner, each character's early naiveté quickly changes to disillusionment with this first battle of the Civil War.

Fleischman has also written about changes in the Ohio frontier in *The Borning Room* (1991); and in *Saturnalia* (1990), he wrote about a Native American boy in colonial times who had been raised by white men but who longed to understand his true ancestry. *Saturnalia* was a Boston Globe–Horn Book Honor Book, and *The Borning Room* was named a Golden Kite Honor Book.

Irene Hunt. Irene Hunt's *Across Five Aprils* (1964) is one of the finest books about the Civil War written for children. Hunt chronicles the experiences of the Creighton family during the five springs the war was fought. This family of Union sympathizers is torn apart when one of the sons joins the Confederate army. Hunt weaves detailed historical information into her novel. *Across Five Aprils* brings home one of the greatest tragedies of this devastating war—the tragedy of families and communities torn apart. *Across Five Aprils* was a Newbery Honor Book in 1965.

Settling and Building the United States

Most children are intrigued by stories of the Western frontier, and there is a wealth of books about this topic from which to choose. Many stories have been written about the arduous journeys west and the determination and dreams of those who dared to undertake those journeys. Still other stories focus on life on the frontier. Many of these stories emphasize the importance of strong family bonds and evoke the strength of spirit nurtured by life on the frontier. In recent years, a number of books have explored the isolation and loneliness of frontier life. And, of course, there is a downside to the Western expansion: This continuous push meant that the Native Americans' way of life was constantly threatened.

Patricia MacLachlan. Patricia MacLachlan writes both picture books and novels in different genres, but she is best known for *Sarah, Plain and Tall* (1985). This Newbery Medal winner is set in the nineteenth century on the Nebraska prairie, where MacLachlan has her family roots. Anna and Caleb's father places an ad in an Eastern newspaper for a wife, and Sarah, who lives by the sea in Maine, answers the ad and comes west on a trial basis. Anna and Caleb come to love Sarah, but knowing how much Sarah misses the sea, they fear she will leave. Gradually, though, Sarah comes to love Anna, Caleb, and their father and discovers how like the sea the prairie can be. The tone of *Sarah, Plain and Tall* is quiet, and in its simplicity the book simultaneously captures the loneliness of life on the prairie and the remarkable beauty of the land. In *Skylark* (1994), a sequel to *Sarah, Plain and Tall,* MacLachlan writes about a devastating drought on the prairie that forces Sarah and the children to go to Maine. In addition to the Newbery Medal, MacLachlan received the Scott O'Dell Historical Fiction Award and the Christopher Award for *Sarah, Plain and Tall.*

Laura Ingalls Wilder. Since the publication of her first book in 1932, *Little House in the Big Woods,* Laura Ingalls Wilder has been a favorite with children. Wilder was born in 1867 in Wisconsin and spent her early years there. During the rest of her childhood, she moved throughout the West with her family. These moves provided a wealth of material for the *Little House* books. The early stories feature the Ingalls family—Ma, Pa, Laura, older sister Mary, and younger sisters Carrie and Grace. In *These Happy Golden Years* (1953), Laura becomes a teacher and meets her husband-to-be; *The First Four Years* (1971) is about the early years of their marriage. Narrated by Laura, the stories are told from a child's perspective, and the writing is noteworthy for its characterization, rich use of language, and descriptions of the joys and challenges of frontier life.

Though remembered as a writer, Wilder actually spent most of her adult life as a farm wife. Under the tutelage of her daughter Rose, she began to write later in life; she published *Little House in the Big Woods* when she was sixty-five. *On the Banks of Plum Creek* (1937) and *The Long Winter* (1940) were both Newbery Honor Books. She was the first recipient of the Laura Ingalls Wilder Award, an award which is now presented every five years in her honor by the American Library Association to an outstanding author or illustrator of children's books whose body of work has made a significant contribution to children's literature.

Early Twentieth Century in the United States

The early twentieth century was a period of upheaval in the United States. With the industrialization of American society, massive social changes occurred as people left rural areas to find work in urban centers. Immigration reached a peak during this period. The United States became embroiled in World War I, and for most of the 1930s, the Great Depression brought widespread suffering to the nation.

Margaret Rostkowski. As a writer of historical fiction, Margaret Rostkowski ventures into territory not often frequented by other writers. In *After the Dancing Days* (1986), she wrote about the period immediately following World

War I. The book, she says, began with a question: What must it have been like for soldiers returning from the war so badly wounded that others turned away from them in horror? In developing the story, Rostkowski drew heavily on family history. Her mother's uncles were gassed in World War I. Family photos also supplied material for *After the Dancing Days,* especially a photo showing a great-aunt's fear as she sees her brothers off to war and another photo revealing Rostkowski's mother's and aunt's joy as they sit between their uncles who have just returned from the fighting. *After the Dancing Days* portrays a sensitive young girl with the strength and compassion to reach out to severely wounded soldiers who were shunned by others. Rostkowski received the Golden Kite Award and the Children's Book Award of the International Reading Association for *After the Dancing Days.*

Mildred Taylor. Mildred Taylor has given a special gift to children's literature, the gift of the Logan family, an African American family living in rural Mississippi during the Depression. Readers met the Logan family in Taylor's first book, *Song of the Trees* (1975). For *Roll of Thunder, Hear My Cry* (1976), her second novel about the Logans, Taylor was awarded the Newbery Medal. The family's determination to keep their land and the necessity of surviving the racism directed at African Americans in rural Mississippi of the 1930s create the central tensions in *Roll of Thunder, Hear My Cry.*

The characters Taylor introduced in *Roll of Thunder, Hear My Cry* appear in many of her subsequent books. She also continued to explore the themes of that book in those works, which include *Let the Circle Be Unbroken* (1981), *The Friendship* (1987), *The Gold Cadillac* (1987), *Mississippi Bridge* (1990), and *The Well* (1995).

World War II and After

World War II was a war of appalling magnitude and destructiveness. Millions of soldiers around the world died. Six million Jews died in Europe. The war ended with the detonation of two atomic bombs in Japan, which changed the world forever. A majority of the books about this period focus on the war in Europe, but there are also outstanding books about the war in the Pacific and about the wartime era in the United States.

Lois Lowry. Most of Lois Lowry's extensive writing for children has been realistic fiction set in the present day. However, with *Number the Stars* (1989), she made a major contribution to historical fiction. The story is based on the work of the Danish Resistance, whose members shuttled numerous Jews to safety in neutral Sweden during World War II. This suspenseful story is told from the perspective of Annemarie, whose family agrees to shelter her best friend; eventually they lead the friend to safety. The story is a tribute to the bravery of the Danish people in World War II.

Lowry won the first of her two Newbery Medals for *Number the Stars.* She also received the National Jewish Book Award and the Sidney Taylor Award for this book.

Uri Orlev. Uri Orlev, now an Israeli citizen, was born in Warsaw, Poland, in 1931. World War II broke out when he was six and lasted until he was fourteen. Orlev has said that the Holocaust was his childhood, and he has written about that tragic time for children. *The Island on Bird Street* (1984) tells the story of a Jewish boy who hides in a bombed-out building in the ghetto. In this island, he struggles with terror, loneliness, and near starvation as he waits for his father to return. The story ends on a hopeful note as the boy and his father join the partisans who are resisting the Nazis. In *The Man from the Other Side* (1991), a Polish boy and his father risk their lives to help the Jews who are confined to the Warsaw ghetto.

All of Orlev's books have been translated into English. He has been recognized internationally for his writing for children, and a number of his books have won the Mildred L. Batchelder Award given annually by the American Library Association for the most outstanding book published originally in a foreign language. In recognition of his body of work, Orlev received the Hans Christian Andersen Award in 1996.

Yoshiko Uchida. During her lifetime, Yoshiko Uchida was a prolific writer whose stories included folktales, contemporary realistic fiction, and historical fiction about the experiences of Japanese Americans during World War II. In *Journey to Topaz* (1971), Uchida tells the story of Yuri and her family, who, like all Japanese Americans living on the west coast of the United States at the outbreak of World War II, were incarcerated in internment camps. Despite the limited freedom and poor conditions in which the prisoners lived at Topaz, the camp to which Yuri's family was sent, the strength of family and community make the story a hopeful one. Uchida based much of *Journey to Topaz* on her own family's experiences during World War II. In *Journey Home* (1978), sequel to *Journey to Topaz,* Uchida tells of the difficulties that Yuri's family had in rebuilding their lives in the face of continued racism.

Uchida received a citation from the Contra Costa Chapter of the Japanese American Citizens League for her contribution to the cultural development of society. *Journey Home* was selected as a Children's Choices book by the International Reading Association and as a Notable Children's Trade Book in the Field of Social Studies by the National Council for Social Studies and the Children's Book Council.

CRITERIA FOR SELECTING HISTORICAL FICTION

In evaluating historical fiction, teachers and librarians need to look for many of the same things as in other genres. Yet because historical fiction has distinct qualities, it's also necessary to use some genre-specific selection and evaluation criteria that have to do with authenticity.

Historical Authenticity

The writer (and the illustrator, if there is one) of historical fiction must make the work historically authentic. Writers must know the period about which they are writing so well that every detail, small or large, is accurate.

Setting. It should go without saying that the setting of a work of historical fiction must be authentic. It is also important for the writer to include rich details that will bring the setting to life for the reader, but these details must be carefully integrated into the story. Serious writers of historical fiction do their homework. That is, they do the background research necessary to develop authentic settings. However, writers sometimes yield to the temptation to include more information about the time period than is necessary—and in the process they obscure their story with historical information.

ASK THE AUTHOR . . .

Karen Cushman

Karen Cushman signature

How do you strike a balance between maintaining historical accuracy and creating a "good read" for young people?

When we are speaking of historical fiction, part of what makes a book a "good read" *is* historical accuracy. As a reader, I want to believe what I'm reading—that some is true, the rest could be true, and it all *seems* true. As a writer, I research enough to be able to stand firmly and say, "I know this place and these people." I probably use 10 percent of what I find, but it is that other 90 percent that allows me to say, "This is how it was."

Rosemary Sutcliff referred to "the Truth of Fact and the Truth of the Spirit." For historical fiction, both are essential; all the boiled eels and kirtles and "Corpus bones!" in the world would not make a good medieval novel if the characters thought, believed, and reacted in modern ways, not true to the spirit and values of the time. There is, of course, no way to be completely exact about a long-ago time. Sometimes I have to make things up; that is when the Truth of the Spirit comes in. Does it seem right? Does it sound and smell right? If so, it is the best I can do.

I write by making a trip backwards in time and seeing a place and people from the inside in order to bring them to life as convincingly as possible. I cannot ask "How would this boy feel in this situation?" but "How would I feel?" or, even better, "Here *I* am. How *do* I feel?"

I personally have felt no pressure to include more detail, for that is how I make my stories come alive, how I try to breathe life into the bare bones of history. Without historical accuracy, my books would be fantasy. With *only* historical accuracy, they would be textbooks. For historical fiction, there must be a story, accurate in detail but brought to life through imagination and creativity.

Characters. Characters in historical fiction must think and behave in ways that are believable given the time period in which they live. For example, Puritan New England, the setting of **The Witch of Blackbird Pond** (1958), was an era in which women did not often assert themselves. Yet Kit, Elizabeth George

Speare's protagonist, is a strong-willed young woman, who leaves her grandfather's home in Barbados after he dies to live with her aunt and uncle in New England. Speare legitimizes Kit's behavior and makes her a believable character by allowing readers to discover, as the story unfolds, that the culture of Barbados was one in which young women were allowed far more independence than they were in Puritan New England.

The need to create characters who behave in ways that are believable for the time period can create a quandary for the author who must also develop a character with whom today's readers can identify. Some argue that Karen Cushman's character Birdy, in *Catherine, Called Birdy,* was created with more attention to the present-day reader than to the ways in which young girls behaved in medieval times. Yet Birdy is an immensely popular character with young readers. If Cushman had opted for total historical accuracy about a period in which girls did very little, the story would have offered little to hold modern readers' interest—with the result that many of them might never have gotten a taste of life in the medieval period.

Conflict. Authors of historical fiction strive to create conflicts that could arise given conditions of the time period in which the story is set and to develop those conflicts in ways that are plausible. Mildred Taylor did this in *Roll of Thunder, Hear My Cry.* Mississippi in the 1930s was a place in which racial tensions that had existed for decades were exacerbated by the grim economic realities of the Depression. So the violence that erupts as a consequence of the boycott organized by the Logans is in keeping with the story's setting.

Awards for Historical Fiction

A lot of historical fiction for children is available today, and teachers and librarians will want to choose the best to offer to young readers. Looking for award-winning books is one way to be assured of selecting high-quality books. As you've seen from earlier sections of this chapter, historical fiction is well represented among Newbery Medal winners and Honor Books. In addition, the Scott O'Dell Award for Historical Fiction was established in 1981 to encourage the writing and reading of historical fiction. The National Council for Social Studies annually identifies Notable Children's Trade Books in the Field of Social Studies, and historical fiction is frequently included among these books.

 TEACHING IDEAS

Getting Ready to Read Historical Fiction. Use Donna Ogle's (1986) K-W-L strategy when reading historical fiction with children. To use this comprehension strategy, ask students before they read a story what they know (K) about the time period in which the story is set and what they want (W) to know. Then, once they have read the story, ask them what they learned (L) about the time period. Try this strategy with a story such as Laurence Yep's *Dragonwings* (1975), about Chinese immigrants to the United States in the early twentieth century.

Exploring Family Stories. Share with children works of historical fiction that are fictionalized family stories—such as *Pink and Say* (1994) or *Katie's Trunk* (1992). Discuss with the children how the writers came up with ideas for their stories. Invite them to ask their grandparents, parents, or other older relatives and friends to talk about childhood memories. Ask children to share the stories they collect and decide which, if any, might make interesting material for a fictionalized family story.

Exploring Different Perspectives. Have children read two works of historical fiction set in the same period—such as Pamela Conrad's *Prairie Songs* (1985) and Patricia MacLachlan's *Sarah, Plain and Tall* (1985), both of which explore life on the western frontier. Discuss with the children how the authors' perspectives differ.

Discovering How Authors Bring the Past to Life. Invite students to reread a work of historical fiction to find examples of writing that bring the past to life for them. Encourage students to pay particular attention to story events, what characters say and do, and the ways in which the author describes the story's setting. Have students start with a work of historical fiction in picture book format—such as Candace Christiansen's *Calico and Tin Horns* (1992)—before moving on to chapter books.

EXPERIENCES FOR YOUR LEARNING

1. Read two books set in the same period and discuss with a classmate how the authors' perspectives on the period seem to differ. If you are interested in the medieval period, you may want to choose *The Ramsay Scallop* (1994) and *Catherine, Called Birdy* (1994).

2. After reading Mildred Taylor's *Roll of Thunder, Hear My Cry* (1976), read a fifth-grade social studies textbook to see what information it includes about race relations in the South during the 1930s and about the Depression. Discuss with a fellow student the differences in the way the textbook authors and Mildred Taylor handled these two topics.

3. Choose a piece of historical fiction to read aloud to a group of students. Consider relatively short chapter books like Mildred Taylor's *Mississippi Bridge* (1990) or Marguerite de Angeli's *The Door in the Wall* (1949). Before reading the book to the group, talk with them to find out what

they know about the time period in which the story is set. Once you have finished reading the story aloud, talk to the students once again to find out what they have discovered about the time period. Based on your conversations with the students, discuss with a group of peers what you have learned about the values of historical fiction for children.

4. More and more historical fiction is being published in picture book format, and some of these picture books explore potentially disturbing subject matter. (See Issue to Consider on page 313.) Teachers must make judgments about the appropriate audience for these books. Read a sampling of historical fiction picture books, and discuss with your classmates the most appropriate audience for these books. You might want to read *Let the Celebrations Begin!* (1991), by Margaret Wild; *The Whispering Cloth* (1995), by Pegi Shea; and *Baseball Saved Us* (1993), by Ken Mochizuki.

RECOMMENDED BOOKS

* indicates a picture book; I indicates interest level (P = preschool, YA = young adult)

Ancient Times through the Medieval Period

Cushman, Karen. *Catherine, Called Birdy*. New York: Clarion, 1994. Through her journal, a young girl chronicles her daily life in medieval England. (**I**: 11–YA)

———. *The Midwife's Apprentice*. New York: Clarion, 1995. A homeless waif in medieval England is given the opportunity to become a midwife's apprentice. (**I**: 9–12)

de Angeli, Marguerite. *A Door in the Wall*. New York: Doubleday, 1949. A young boy loses the use of his legs and is still able to save the town and serve the king. (**I**: 8–12)

Paterson, Katherine. *The Master Puppeteer*. Illustrated by Haru Wells. New York: Harper, 1975. A youth describes life as a puppeteer in eighteenth-century Japan. (I: YA)

————. *The Sign of the Chrysanthemum*. Illustrated by Peter Landa. New York: Crowell, 1973. During troubled times in the Heian period in Japan, a boy searches for his father. (I: 11–YA)

Speare, Elizabeth George. *The Bronze Bow*. New York: Houghton Mifflin, 1961. Consumed by his hatred of the Roman occupiers of Palestine, a boy discovers the teachings of Jesus. (I: 11-YA)

Sutcliff, Rosemary. *Dawn Wind*. Illustrated by Charles Keeping. London: Oxford University Press, 1961. A boy is sold into slavery by the Saxons, who have destroyed his people. (I: YA)

————. *The Eagle of the Ninth*. Illustrated by C. Walter Hodges. London: Oxford University Press, 1954. The story of a young Roman centurion in second-century England. (I: YA)

————. *The Lantern Bearers*. Illustrated by Charles Keeping. London: Oxford University Press, 1959. As the Roman Empire declines and Roman soldiers are leaving their former outpost in Britain, the protagonist chooses to remain behind. (I: YA)

————. *The Silver Branch*. Illustrated by Charles Keeping. London: Oxford University Press, 1957. A junior surgeon is caught up in the turbulent politics of third-century England. (I: YA)

————. *Sun Horse, Moon Horse*. Illustrated by Shirley Felts. London: Oxford University Press, 1977. A boy in pre-Roman Britain saves his people from slavery. (I: YA)

————. *Warrior Scarlet*. Illustrated by Charles Keeping. London: Oxford University Press, 1958. A boy comes of age in the Bronze Age of Britain. (I: YA)

Temple, Frances. *The Ramsay Scallop*. New York: Orchard, 1994. A young couple's pilgrimage from England to Spain transforms their views of the world and one another. (I: 11–YA)

The New World

Bowen, Gary. *Stranded at Plimoth Plantation 1626*. New York: HarperCollins, 1994. An orphan stranded in Plimoth Plantation documents his life in the village. (I: 10–12)

Clapp, Patricia. *Constance: A Story of Early Plymouth*. New York: Lothrop, 1968. A girl details her life in the early days of the Plymouth settlement. (I: 11–YA)

————. *Witches' Children: A Story of Salem*. New York: Lothrop, 1982. The story of the Salem witch trials is narrated by one of the young girls claiming to be possessed. (I: 10–YA)

Dorris, Michael. *Guests*. New York: Hyperion, 1994. This story of a young Native American boy's coming of age is entwined with the story of the first Thanksgiving. (I: 8–12)

————. *Morning Girl*. New York: Hyperion, 1992. Life on an island is described by two Taino children prior to and on the day that Columbus lands. (I: 8–12)

Koller, Jackie French. *The Primrose Way*. New York: Harcourt, 1992. A young girl in the New World becomes an interpreter between the Puritans and the Pawtuckets. (I: 9–12)

O'Dell, Scott. *The Amethyst Ring*. Boston: Houghton Mifflin, 1983. Cortez and Pizarro bring about the fall of the Mayan and Incan civilizations. (I: 11–YA)

————. *The Captive*. Boston: Houghton Mifflin, 1979. In the New World, a Jesuit priest journeys with a Spanish expedition and witnesses the enslavement and exploitation of the Mayans. (I: 11–YA)

————. *The Feathered Serpent*. Boston: Houghton Mifflin, 1981. A Spanish seminarian witnesses Cortez's capture of Tenochtitlan. (I: 11–YA)

————. *The King's Fifth*. Boston: Houghton Mifflin, 1966. Estaban de Sandoval is waiting to be tried for not turning over to the King of Spain a fifth of the treasure he found on his expedition through Mexico. (I: 11–YA)

Petry, Ann Lane. *Tituba of Salem Village*. New York: Crowell, 1964. Tituba becomes one of the first "witches" to be tried in Salem. (I: 10–YA)

Rinaldi, Ann. *A Break with Charity: A Story about the Salem Witch Trials*. New York: Harcourt, 1992. A young girl struggles to find the courage to tell the truth about the Salem witch hunt. (I: YA)

Speare, Elizabeth George. *The Witch of Blackbird Pond*. Boston: Houghton Mifflin, 1958. A girl is accused of witchcraft in colonial New England. (I: 10–YA)

* Yolen, Jane. *Encounter*. Illustrated by David Shannon. New York: Harcourt, 1992. A Taino boy tries to warn his people of coming destruction when Columbus arrives on their island. (I: 8–12)

American Revolution

Collier, James Lincoln, and Christopher Collier. *My Brother Sam Is Dead*. Portland, OR: Four Winds, 1974. A family is torn apart as members take different sides during the American Revolution. (I: 10–YA)

Forbes, Esther. *Johnny Tremain*. Boston: Houghton Mifflin, 1943. A silversmith's apprentice becomes part of the Sons of Liberty. (I: 10–YA)

Rinaldi, Ann. *The Fifth of March: A Story of the Boston Massacre*. New York: Harcourt, 1993. A fourteen-year-old indentured servant is caught between the rebelling colonists and loyal Tories. (I: YA)

———. *Finishing Becca*. New York: Harcourt, 1994. Becca, sent to work for a wealthy family in Philadelphia, finds herself caught up in the intrigues of the American Revolution. (I: YA)

* Turner, Ann. *Katie's Trunk*. Illustrated by Ron Himler. New York: Macmillan, 1992. A Tory child hides in a trunk when Patriots come to her home. (I: 5–9)

Civil War and Slavery

* Ackerman, Karen. *The Tin Heart*. Illustrated by Michael Hays. New York: Atheneum, 1990. Best friends Mahaley and Flora live on opposite sides of the Ohio River, but when the Civil War breaks out, the ferry stops running. (I: 8–12)

Collier, James, and Christopher Collier. *Jump Ship to Freedom*. New York: Delacorte, 1981. A fourteen-year-old boy runs away to escape slavery. (I: 10–12)

———. *War Comes to Willy Freeman*. New York: Delacorte, 1983. A free African American girl strives to maintain her freedom during the era of the American Revolution. (I: 10–12)

Fleischman, Paul. *Bull Run*. New York: HarperCollins, 1993. The first battle of the Civil War is described from sixteen different perspectives. (I: 10–YA)

* Hopkinson, Deborah. *Sweet Clara and the Freedom Quilt*. Illustrated by James Ransome. New York: Knopf, 1993. Determined to escape from slavery, Clara sews a quilt that maps the way to freedom. (I: 8–12)

Hunt, Irene. *Across Five Aprils*. Chicago: Follett, 1964. Jethro grows up during the Civil War in the midst of a family and a community divided by that war. (I: 10–YA)

* Polacco, Patricia. *Pink and Say*. New York: Philomel, 1994. During the Civil War, an African American Union soldier befriends a white one. (I: 8–12)

Rosen, Michael J. *A School For Pompey Walker*. Illustrated by Aminah Brenda Lynn Robinson. New York: Harcourt, 1995. A former slave remembers how he raised money to build a school for all children. (I: 9–12)

* Turner, Ann. *Nettie's Trip South*. Illustrated by Ron Himler. New York: Macmillan, 1987. A girl travels into the South and sees slavery for the first time. (I: 6–9)

Settling and Building the United States

Armstrong, Jennifer. *Black-Eyed Susan*. Illustrated by Emily Martindale. New York: Crown, 1995. A little girl and her father love their new home in the Dakota territory but long to find a way of helping their mother and wife pull out of her depression. (I: 6–9)

Avi. *The Barn*. New York: Orchard, 1994. Set in the Oregon territory, this story tells of three children who build a barn in the vain attempt to keep a promise to their dying father. (I: 10–12)

———. *The True Confessions of Charlotte Doyle*. New York: Orchard, 1990. The story of a young girl's misadventures on board a ship traveling from England to Providence. (I: YA)

Blos, Joan. *A Gathering of Days: A New England Girl's Journal, 1830–1832*. New York: Scribner's. 1979. A thirteen-year-old girl chronicles her life on the family farm. (I: 10–12)

Brink, Carol Ryrie. *Caddie Woodlawn*. Illustrated by Trina Schart Hyman. New York: Macmillan, 1973. Adventures of an eleven-year-old tomboy growing up on the Wisconsin frontier. (I: 8–11)

* Bunting, Eve. *Dandelions*. Illustrated by Greg Shed. New York: Harcourt, 1995. A family experiences mixed emotions as they travel across the prairie to settle in the Nebraska territory. (I: 8–12)

* ———. *Train to Somewhere*. Illustrated by Ronald Himler. New York: Clarion, 1996. The story of New York orphans taken out West to be placed with families. (I: 9–11)

* Christiansen, Candace. *Calico and Tin Horns*. Illustrated by Thomas Locker. New York: Dial, 1992. A little girl aids sharecroppers who are rebelling against the wealthy landowners in the Hudson River Valley in the 1840s. (I: 7–11)

Conrad, Pamela. *Prairie Songs*. New York: Harper, 1985. Louisa sees her neighbor driven mad by the loneliness she endures on the prairie. (I: 9–12)

Cushman, Karen. *The Ballad of Lucy Whipple*. New York: Clarion, 1996. When Lucy, her mother, and siblings arrive in California in the midst of the gold rush, Lucy directs every waking thought to how she will get back home to Massachusetts. (I: 10–12)

Fleischman, Paul. *The Borning Room*. New York: HarperCollins, 1991. Georgina Lott, her life nearly over, reminisces about all that has happened to her. (I: 11–YA)

———. *Saturnalia*. New York: HarperCollins, 1990. A Narraganset boy, captured by whites at age eight, works as a printer's apprentice until he begins his search for his past. (I: 9-12)

* Hall, Donald. *Ox-Cart Man*. Illustrated by Barbara Cooney. New York: Viking, 1979. Life on a New England farm throughout a year. (I: P–9)

Hudson, Jan. *Sweetgrass*. New York: Philomel, 1989. Sweetgrass must help her people survive smallpox in the winter of 1838. (I: 9–12)

Keehn, Sally M. *I Am Regina*. New York: Philomel, 1991. A young girl is captured by Native Americans and must learn to live as they do to survive. (I: 10–YA)

* Kinsey-Warnock, Natalie. *Wilderness Cat*. Illustrated by Mark Graham. New York: Dutton, 1992. A family fears it won't survive the first winter in the Canadian wilderness. (I: 5–9)

MacLachlan, Patricia. *Sarah, Plain and Tall*. New York: Harper, 1985. A brother and sister hope that Sarah will choose to stay on the prairie and become their mother. (I: 9–12)

———. *Skylark*. New York: HarperCollins, 1994. The sequel to *Sarah, Plain and Tall,* in which a severe drought forces Sarah and the children to journey to Maine. (I: 9–12)

* McCully, Emily Arnold. *The Bobbin Girl*. New York: Dial, 1996. This story about the injustices suffered by the women who worked in the cotton mills in Lowell, Massachusetts, is told from the perspective of a ten-year-old mill worker. (I: 8–12)

Meyer, Carolyn. *Where the Broken Heart Still Beats*. New York: Harcourt, 1992. Cynthia is kidnapped by the Comanches, recaptured by the Rangers, and returned to her "home." (I: 10–YA)

O'Dell, Scott. *Island of the Blue Dolphins*. New York: Dell, 1960. When her people leave their island home, Karana is left to survive on her own. (I: 10–YA)

———. *Sing Down the Moon*. Boston: Houghton Mifflin, 1970. A Navajo girl recounts her journey to Fort Sumner as an Army prisoner. (I: 10–YA)

Paterson, Katherine. *Lyddie*. New York: Dutton, 1991. After losing her parents and being separated from her brother and sister, Lyddie works in the textile mills to earn money to reunite her siblings. (I: 10–YA)

Speare, Elizabeth George. *Calico Captive*. Illustrated by W. T. Mars. Boston: Houghton Mifflin, 1957. Cap-

tured by Native Americans, a family is eventually sold as slaves in Montreal. (I: 10–12)

———. *The Sign of the Beaver*. Boston: Houghton Mifflin, 1983. A Native American boy teaches his white friend how to survive in his frontier cabin. (I: 9–12)

* Turner, Ann. *Dakota Dugout*. Illustrated by Ron Himler. New York: Macmillan, 1985. A historical poem in which a grandmother tells her granddaughter about her earlier life in a sod house on the Dakota prairie. (I: 5–8)

———. *Grasshopper Summer*. New York: Macmillan, 1989. A boy and his family leave their farm in Kentucky to begin life anew on the Dakota prairie. (I: 10–12)

Whelan, Gloria. *Once on This Island*. New York: HarperCollins, 1995. When the War of 1812 breaks out and the British take control of Mackinac Island, a young girl watches as the world she knows changes. (I: 10–YA)

* Wilder, Laura Ingalls. *Christmas in the Big Woods*. Adapted from the *Little House* books. Illustrated by Renee Graef. New York: HarperCollins, 1995. Christmas day is full of good times for the Ingalls. Other adaptations in the series include *Dance at Grandpa's* (1994), *The Deer in the Woods* (1995), *Going to Town* (1995), and *Winter Days in the Big Woods* (1994). (I: P–8)

———. *The Little House in the Big Woods*. Illustrated by Garth Williams. New York: Harper, 1932. This first book about the Ingalls family details their life in the Big Woods of Wisconsin. Other books in the series include *The First Four Years* (1971), *Little House on the Prairie* (1935), *The Long Winter* (1940), and *These Happy Golden Years* (1953). (I: 7–11)

Yep, Laurence. *Dragon's Gate*. New York: HarperCollins, 1993. A Chinese boy joins his father in America where he works under dire conditions to build the transcontinental railroad. (I: 10–YA)

Early Twentieth Century in the United States

Armstrong, William H. *Sounder*. New York: Harper, 1969. The story of an African American's life in the rural South. (I: 10–12)

* Christiansen, Candace. *The Ice House*. Illustrated by Thomas Locker. New York: Dial, 1993. Before refrigerators, men harvested blocks of ice from the rivers to be used all year round. (I: 5–10)

* Hall, Donald. *When Willard Met Babe Ruth*. Illustrated by Barry Moser. New York: Harcourt, 1996. Babe Ruth touches the lives of three generations of the Babson family. (I: 6–10)

Hesse, Karen. *Letters from Rifka*. New York: Holt, 1992. Rifka writes about fleeing Russia and having to stay behind in Belgium when her family goes on to the United States. (I: 9–12)

Houston, Gloria. *Littlejim*. Illustrated by Thomas B. Allen. New York: Philomel, 1990. Conflict arises as Littlejim chooses reading and writing over working the fields and hunting. (I: 8–12)

* ———. *The Year of the Perfect Christmas Tree*. Illustrated by Barbara Cooney. New York: Dial, 1988. Because her father is away at war, Ruthie and her mom deliver the Christmas tree to the church. (I: 5–9)

* Johnston, Tony. *Amber on the Mountain*. Illustrated by Robert Duncan. New York: Dial, 1994. A mountain girl learns to read and write with the help of a friend. (I: 5–10)

* Levinson, Riki. *I Go with My Family to Grandma's*. Illustrated by Diane Goode. New York: Dutton, 1986. An extended family living near New York City at the turn of the century uses many different modes of transportation to gather at the grandparents' home. (I: P–8)

Mayerson, Evelyn Wilde. *The Cat Who Escaped from Steerage*. New York: Scribner's, 1990. A Polish girl smuggles a cat on board a ship headed for the United States. (I: 9–12)

Rostkowski, Margaret. *After the Dancing Days*. New York: Harper, 1986. The story of a young girl's friendship with a wounded World War I veteran. (I: 10–YA)

* Rylant, Cynthia. *When I Was Young in the Mountains*. Illustrated by Diane Goode. New York: Dutton, 1982. The memories of a young girl growing up in the Appalachian mountains. (I: 5–9)

Taylor, Mildred D. *The Friendship*. Illustrated by Max Ginsburg. New York: Dial, 1987. At the local store, children witness a confrontation between an elderly African American man and the white storekeeper. (I: 9–YA)

———. *Let the Circle Be Unbroken*. New York: Dial, 1981. During the Great Depression, Cassie and her family must overcome racism in the South. (I: 10–12)

———. *Mississippi Bridge*. Illustrated by Max Ginsburg. New York: Dial, 1990. Jeremy witnesses racism as a bus driver orders all African Americans off the bus to make room for white passengers. (I: 9–12)

———. *Roll of Thunder, Hear My Cry*. Illustrated by Jerry Pinkney. New York: Dial, 1976. An African American family faces prejudice and discrimination in the South. (I: 10–12)

———. *Song of the Trees*. Illustrated by Jerry Pinkney. New York: Dial, 1975. An African American family tries to save their forest from being logged during the Depression. (I: 9–12)

———. *The Well*. New York: Dial, 1995. Racial tensions escalate between boys when the only water comes from the Logan's well. (I: 10–12)

Thesman, Jean. *Rachel Chance*. Boston: Houghton Mifflin, 1990. Baby Rider has disappeared, and it is up to Rachel and her grandfather to rescue him. (I: 10–YA)

Yep, Laurence. *Dragonwings*. New York: Harper, 1975. The story of a Chinese boy immigrating to San Francisco to join his father. (I: YA)

World War II and After

* Adler, David A. *One Yellow Daffodil: A Hanukkah Story*. Illustrated by Lloyd Bloom. New York: Harcourt, 1995. After many years, a survivor of the Holocaust begins to value his religion again. (I: 6–12)

Choi, Sook Nyul. *The Year of Impossible Goodbyes*. New York: Dell, 1991. When the war ends in Korea, the Russians take over the northern half of the country, forcing Sookan and her family to flee to the south. (I: 10–YA)

Coerr, Eleanor. *Sadako and the Thousand Paper Cranes*. New York: Putnam, 1977. The story of a survivor of the Hiroshima bombing who tries to make a thousand paper cranes to make her wish for health come true. (I: 10–12)

Curtis, Christopher Paul. *The Watsons Go to Birmingham—1963*. New York: Delacorte, 1995. An African American family from Detroit visits in Birmingham in 1963, the summer of the fateful church bombing that set the civil rights movement in motion. (I: 10–12)

Hahn, Mary Downing. *Stepping on the Cracks*. New York: Clarion, 1991. While her brother is away at war, Elizabeth befriends an army deserter. (I: 10–12)

* Heide, Florence Parry and Judith Heide Gilliland. *Sami and the Time of the Troubles*. Illustrated by Ted Lewin. New York: Clarion, 1992. Sami recounts his daily life in war-torn Beirut. (I: 7–11)

Ho, Minfong. *The Clay Marble*. New York: Farrar, 1991. Dara's family is forced from their home in war-torn Cambodia only to be again embroiled in war in a refugee camp on the Thai border. (I: 10–12)

* Howard, Elizabeth Fitzgerald. *Aunt Flossie's Hats (and Crab Cakes Later)*. Illustrated by James Ransome. New York: Clarion, 1991. Sunday afternoons meant a day full of tea, cookies, and stories with Aunt Flossie. (I: 5–9)

* Innocenti, Roberto, and Christophe Gallaz. *Rose Blanche*. Translated by Martha Coventry and Richard Graglia. Chicago: Creative Education, 1985. The story of a young German girl's life during World War II after she discovers a nearby concentration camp. (I: YA)

Kerr, Judith. *When Hitler Stole Pink Rabbit*. New York: Coward, McCann, 1972. A family's life is changed forever as they escape Hitler's Germany. (I: 9–12)

Laird, Elizabeth. *Kiss the Dust*. New York: Puffin, 1991. A Kurd family is driven from their home in Iraq to a harsh life in a refugee camp in Iran. (I: 10–YA)

Levitin, Sonia. *Annie's Promise*. New York: Atheneum, 1993. A young girl enjoys the experience of summer camp away from an overprotective German Jewish family. (I: YA)

Lowry, Lois. *Number the Stars*. Boston: Houghton Mifflin, 1989. A story of how the Danes aid Jews in their flight to freedom. (I: 10–12)

* Maruki, Toshi. *Hiroshima No Pika*. New York: Lothrop, 1980. The poignant story of one family's experiences on the day Hiroshima was bombed. (I: 8–12)

* Mochizuki, Ken. *Baseball Saved Us*. Illustrated by Dom Lee. New York: Lee & Low, 1993. A Japanese American boy's memories of life in an internment camp. (I: 8–12)

Naidoo, Beverley. *Journey to Jo'Burg: A South African Story*. Illustrated by Eric Velasquez. New York: HarperTrophy, 1986. A brother and sister are caught up in the cruelty of apartheid when they journey to Johannesburg to find their mother. (I: 10–12)

* Oppenheim, Shulamith Levey. *The Lily Cupboard*. Illustrated by Ronald Himler. New York: HarperCollins, 1992. A little girl hides from the Nazis on the farm of a sympathetic Dutch family. (I: 6–10)

Orlev, Uri. *The Island on Bird Street*. Translated by Hillel Halkin. Boston: Houghton Mifflin, 1984. A boy struggles to survive in the Warsaw ghetto as he waits for his father to return. (I: 11–YA)

———. *The Man from the Other Side*. Translated by Hillel Halkin. Boston: Houghton Mifflin, 1991. A man and his son risk their own lives to help the Jews in the Warsaw ghetto. (I: YA)

Sacks, Margaret. *Themba*. Illustrated by Wil Clay. New York: Lodestar, 1985. Themba goes to the city to find his father, who has failed to return from working in the South African gold mines. (I: 6–9)

* Shea, Pegi Deitz. *The Whispering Cloth: A Refugee's Story*. Illustrated by Anita Riggio. Stitched by You Yang. Honesdale, PA: Boyds Mill Press, 1994. A young Hmong refugee stitches her own story on her first "story cloth." (I: 7–11)

Taylor, Mildred. *The Gold Cadillac*. Illustrated by Michael Hays. New York: Dial, 1987. An African American family from the North experiences prejudice when they visit the South. (I: 9–12)

Taylor, Theodore. *The Bomb*. New York: Harcourt, 1995. Nuclear bombs are to be tested on Bikini Atoll, and Sorry and his people must move off the island. (I: YA)

* Uchida, Yoshiko. *The Bracelet*. Illustrated by Joanna Yardley. New York: Philomel, 1993. Sent away to an internment camp during World War II, a young Japanese American girl discovers the power of memory. (I: 7–11)

———. *Journey Home*. Illustrated by Charles Robinson. New York: Atheneum, 1978. A Japanese American family returns from an internment camp to try and rebuild their lives in California. (I: 10–12)

———. *Journey to Topaz*. Illustrated by Donald Carrick. New York: Scribner's, 1971. A Japanese American family is sent away to an internment camp when World War II breaks out. (I: 10–12)

Vos, Ida. *Hide and Seek*. Translated by Terese Edelstein and Inez Smidt. Boston: Houghton Mifflin, 1981. The story of a family of Dutch Jews who are separated as they hide during the Nazi occupation. (I: 11–YA)

* Wild, Margaret. *Let the Celebrations Begin*! Illustrated by Julie Vivas. New York: Orchard, 1991. A young girl in a Nazi concentration camp makes toys for the children in the camp. (I: 9–12)

Yep, Laurence. *Hiroshima*. New York: Scholastic, 1995. The story of Sachi and the day the atomic bomb was dropped on her city of Hiroshima. (I: 10–12)

RESOURCES

Chatton, Barbara. "The Civil War, Part I: Update." *Book Links* 5.1 (1995): 42–50.

Chatton, Barbara, and Judy Parks. "The Colonial Period." *Book Links* 4.3 (1995): 44–53.

Chatton, Barbara, and Shirley Tastad. "The Depression Years." *Book Links* 2.3 (1993): 31–37.

———. "1900–1919." *Book Links* 3.4 (1994): 50–56.

Elleman, Barbara. "The Columbus Encounter—Update." *Book Links* 2.1 (1992): 31–34.

Hopkins, Lee Bennett, ed. *More Books by More People*. New York: Citation, 1974.

Steiner, Stanley, and Linda Marie Zaerr. "The Middle Ages." *Book Links* 4.2 (November, 1994): 11–15.

Tunnell, Michael O., and Richard Ammon, eds. *The Story of Ourselves: Teaching History through Children's Literature*. Portsmouth, NH: Heinemann, 1993.

REFERENCES

Blos, Joan W. "Perspectives on Historical Fiction." *The Story of Ourselves: Teaching History through Children's Literature*. Eds. Michael O. Tunnell and Richard Ammon. Portsmouth, NH: Heinemann, 1993. 11–17.

Broderick, Kathy. "*The Ramsay Scallop* by Frances Temple." *Book Links* 4.2 (November 1994): 19.

Conrad, Pam. "Finding Ourselves in History." *The Story of Ourselves: Teaching History through Children's Literature*. Eds. Michael O. Tunnell and Richard Ammon. Portsmouth, NH: Heinemann, 1993. 33–38.

Dorris, Michael. "On Writing *Morning Girl*." *Book Links* 4.1 (September 1992): 32–33.

Frey, Charles, and John Griffith. *The Literary Heritage of Childhood: An Appraisal of Children's Classics in the Western Tradition*. New York: Greenwood, 1987.

Fritz, Jean. "There Once Was." *The Horn Book Magazine* (July/August 1986): 432–35.

Harris, Violet. "Historical Fact and Fiction: Using Informational Books to Provide Background for Using Multicultural Literature." *Teaching for Lifelong Learning,* 85th Annual Convention of the National Council of Teachers of English, San Diego, November, 1995.

Levstik, Linda. "A Gift of Time: Children's Historical Fiction." *Children's Literature in the Classroom:*

Weaving Charlotte's Web. Eds. Janet Hickman and Bernice E. Cullinan. Norwood, MA: Christopher-Gordon, 1989. 135–45.

Ogle, Donna. "K-W-L: A Teaching Model that Develops Active Reading of Expository Text." *The Reading Teacher* 39 (1986): 564–70.

Taxel, Joel. "The American Revolution in Children's Fiction." *Research in the Teaching of English* 17 (1983): 61–83.

Temple, Frances. "Researching *The Ramsay Scallop*." *Book Links* 4.2 (November 1994): 18.

Tomlinson, Carl M., Michael O. Tunnell, and Donald J. Richgels. "The Content and Writing of History in Textbooks and Trade Books." *The Story of Ourselves: Teaching History through Children's Literature*. Eds. Michael O. Tunnell and Richard Ammon. Portsmouth, NH: Heinemann, 1993. 51–62.

Tunnell, Michael O. "Unmasking the Fiction of History: Children's Historical Literature Begins to Come of Age." *The Story of Ourselves: Teaching History through Children's Literature*. Eds. Michael O. Tunnell and Richard Ammon. Portsmouth, NH: Heinemann, 1993. 79–90.

Turner, Ann. "On Writing *Katie's Trunk*." *Book Links* 2.5 (May 1993): 11.

10 Modern Fantasy and Science Fiction

She [Kate] said, "Watch," and she dipped the funnel into the dish and blew through it, and out of the funnel grew the most magnificent bubble I have ever seen, iridescent, gleaming.

"Look at it from here," said Kate, intent. "Just look at the light!" And in the sunlight, all the colors in the world were swimming over that glimmering sphere—swirling, glowing, achingly beautiful. Like a dancing rainbow the bubble hung there for a long moment; then it was gone.

I thought: *That's* fantasy.

I said: "I wish they didn't have to vanish so soon."

"But you can always blow another," Kate said.

from Dreams and Wishes *(1996)*
by Susan Cooper

This bubble metaphor comes from fantasy writer Susan Cooper, who was sitting in her study, contemplating a description of "fantasy," when her daughter Kate entered the room. It provides a visual image that shows how fantasy takes shape when a believer makes a new creation possible. Writers of fantasy do just that—they create magnificent bubbles that are so achingly beautiful that readers can only marvel and enjoy.

MODERN FANTASY AND SCIENCE FICTION DEFINED

Definition of Modern Fantasy

Fantasy literature has unexplainable magic—and it is this element that captures the minds and hearts of children. According to Lynn (1989),

Fantasy has been variously described as imaginative, fanciful, visionary, strange, otherworldly, supernatural, mysterious, frightening, magical, inexplicable, wondrous, dreamlike, and, paradoxically, realistic. It has been termed an awareness of the inexplicable existence of "magic" in the everyday world, a yearning for a sudden glimpse of something strange and wonderful, and a different and perhaps truer version of reality. (p. xxi)

Jean Greenlaw (1995a) adds that fantasy literature goes beyond the known world and imaginatively creates a new or transformed world. "Nonrational phenomena" have a significant role in fantasy, as do events, settings, and creatures that don't exist in the real world. The imaginative creation must be so well crafted that readers accept the fantasy through a "willing suspension of disbelief," though this happens only when story details are totally consistent with the fantastic elements.

Fantasy extends reality into the unknown. It gives readers a way of understanding the world they live in by going beyond it for a wider, imaginative vision. Sometimes people mistakenly think that fantasy is merely an escape from the complexity of reality to a simplistic world. Rather, the world created by fantasy can "refresh . . . delight . . . give a new vision," as it artfully presents rich characters and engaging and complex plots that are woven with fantastic elements.

(Alexander, 1971). For some readers, the strength and depth of emotion they experience as they triumph and despair along with characters reaches a height beyond what they could experience from a simplistic world.

Modern fantasy falls into two major classifications: low fantasy and high fantasy. Low fantasy occurs in the world we live in, in settings we recognize, but the magical elements of fantasy make the story impossible. All authors who write fantasy draw on the here and now, what Lloyd Alexander calls the "primary world"—people's knowledge and experience of real life—for "raw material" (Alexander, p. 164). Projecting this information, they create images and situations of a "secondary world." Authors of high fantasy create a secondary world whose concrete elements are impossible according to the logic of the primary world but consistent with its own laws. Some high fantasy stories remain totally in the created world, and some travel between that world and the primary world. Others involve a world within the primary world, marked by boundaries that keep the magic inside the created world (Tymn, Zahorski, and Boyer, 1979).

Definition of Science Fiction

Science fiction is a variety of fantasy in which an author, inspired by real developments in science, has conceived a version of reality different from the one we inhabit. Science fiction writers weave into stories and make plausible scientific concepts that are extrapolations of current scientific understandings (Greenlaw, 1995b). In short, they make readers believe the unbelievable because they convince them it is *possible*.

Because works of science fiction make readers entertain possibilities that go well beyond the everyday, they have a useful role to play in educating the imagination—to borrow a phrase from the literary critic Northrop Frye (1957). The imagination, as Frye points out, is the source of all human invention. For example, people told stories about human flight for thousands of years before the Wright Brothers' plane flew off a sand dune at Kitty Hawk. Humans would never have gotten off the ground if they hadn't long imagined the wonders of flight. Such imagining can be nourished by stories.

Distinction between Fantasy and Science Fiction

Greenlaw (1982) describes the distinction between modern fantasy and science fiction this way: "Fantasy never could be. Science fiction has the possibility of being—maybe not in our time or on our planet, but the possibility of happening within some time and in some place" (p. 64). In other words, a story that is clearly *impossible* is called fantasy; a story with aspects of the *improbable* is called science fiction. The possibility that someday an invention or new knowledge could make the seemingly improbable possible distinguishes science fiction from other forms of fantasy. Jules Verne wrote *Twenty Thousand Leagues Under the Sea* (1869) in the nineteenth century. The *idea* of a submarine obviously existed in Verne's imagination, but no real submarine had yet been built. A submarine may have seemed improbable at the time, but as it turned out, it was very possible.

At times it is difficult to make a clear distinction between science fiction and fantasy because certain books have characteristics of both genres. These "hybrid" books may present details purported to have scientific bases, yet they also include elements that make the story clearly impossible. The result is a type of science fiction called "science fantasy." Science fantasy includes elements previously considered traditional in high fantasy (such as dragons, wizards, fairies) as well as elements traditional in science fiction (space travel or interplanetary exploration). Science fantasy begins with an extrapolation based on scientific understanding, but the story is predominantly a fantasy.

We'll discuss modern fantasy in the first half of this chapter and science fiction in the second half. This parallel structure will allow a more focused look at each genre.

THE EVOLUTION OF MODERN FANTASY

Myths, legends, and folktales are predecessors of the modern genres of fantasy and science fiction. For centuries, the oral tradition of storytelling passed along many tales of magical beings, fantastic occurrences, and imaginative places. The beginning of modern fantasy as a genre is traced to the nineteenth century when stories that later became known as "literary fairytales" were created in the style of stories from the oral tradition. These literary fairytales included features of works from traditional folklore: generic settings in kingdoms far away, in a distant time "long, long ago," one-dimensional stock characters, magical elements, and, quite often, happy endings. Unlike stories from the oral tradition, however, literary fairytales have known authors. Notable examples are the works created by Hans Christian Andersen in the mid-nineteenth century. For example, in Andersen's "The Princess and the Pea," these elements of folklore are present: the setting in a time period described simply as "there once was . . .," the stock characters of a prince seeking a princess for a wife, the magical way in which the princess felt the pea through layers and layers of mattresses, and the "lived happily ever after" ending.

Some nineteenth-century British writers also turned their attention to creating fantasy for children. Many of these early works are now considered classics and are still enjoyed by today's children. *Alice's Adventures in Wonderland* (1865), written by Charles Lutwidge Dodgson under the pseudonym Lewis Carroll, was regarded as a turning point in writing for children, because it was written with humor and imagination rather than with a didactic purpose. In the story, Alice falls into a rabbit hole and enters a fantastic world—a world that demands a sense of humor and an imaginative mind. Another early work of fantasy is George MacDonald's *At the Back of the North Wind* (1871), about a boy swept off to an imaginary land where he has adventures with a cab-horse. Published in 1894, Rudyard Kipling's *The Jungle Book* is the story of Mowgli, a human child left in the jungle, raised by wolves, and nurtured by the wisdom of a bear, a python, and a panther.

At the turn of the century, the publication of the play *Peter and Wendy* (1904) made a large impact on fantasy for children; it was later published as *Peter Pan* (1911). The story of how Peter teaches three children how to fly to Never Never Land so that they will never have to grow up is still well-known and loved among children. Beatrix Potter is another early genius of the fantasy genre. Her childhood study of animals led to a thorough understanding of them and enabled her to draw and write imaginative stories that somehow seemed true to the animals' natures. Beginning in 1902 with the publication of *The Tale of Peter Rabbit,* Potter created a series of "little books," each featuring a different animal character. Another milestone book about personified animals, the *Wind in the Willows,* was created in 1908 by British writer Kenneth Grahame. In this series of stories about day-to-day events, woodland animals bond in complex friendships that reflect the various trials and rewards human beings experience.

Illustration 10.1
The personalities of the toys in *Winnie-the-Pooh* are well developed and embody recognizable human attributes. (From *Winnie-the-Pooh* by A. A. Milne, illustrated by E. H. Shepard. Copyright © 1926 by E. P. Dutton, renewed 1954 by A. A. Milne. Used by permission of Dutton Children's Books, a division of Penguin Books USA Inc.)

In 1926, A. A. Milne created *Winnie-the-Pooh*, a classic story of personified toy animals. Milne gave clear descriptions of the personalities of each character—Pooh, Eeyore, Tigger, Piglet, Owl, Kanga, and Roo—and young readers find the predictability of their words and actions in various circumstances reassuring.

Other light-hearted fantasies written in the first half of this century include Hugh Lofting's *The Story of Doctor Dolittle* (1920) and P. L. Travers's *Mary Poppins* (1934). Doctor Dolittle is an animal doctor who sets off with his dog, duck, pig, parrot, and owl to cure monkeys in Africa of a disease. In Travers's book, a seemingly prim and proper nanny named Mary Poppins enters the Banks household, and her arrival "on the East Wind" foreshadows the magical adventures ahead for the two children.

Fantasy literature was also published in other European countries. Carlo Collodi's personified toy story *The Adventures of Pinocchio* was published in Italy in 1881. Children are still intrigued by this story of a lonely man who carves a marionette that comes alive and becomes his little boy. Young readers can relate to the choices that Pinocchio must learn to make: to do what is expected by parents, not to be enticed by strangers who offer tempting alternatives, and to tell the truth. The two-volume edition of *The Wonderful Adventures of Nils* (1906–1907) by Selma Lagerlöf was originally published as a geography primer for Swedish children. The story became a classic when it was translated into other languages; children around the world were enchanted by the story of how Nils Holgersson became elf-sized and traveled all over Sweden on the back of a goose. In 1937, France's Jean de Brunhoff began a series of stories recounting the adventures of an elephant named Babar and his family. Tove Jansson's *Finn Family Moomintroll* marked the beginning of a series of humorous books published during the 1940s and 1950s in Finland about the Moomins, imaginary troll-like creatures living amidst magical powers. In Sweden in 1945, Astrid Lindgren published *Pippi Longstocking*, a fantasy featuring an eccentric protagonist: a little girl who lives her life in such an uncharacteristic way that children who read of her adventures are fascinated by the possibility that a child like that might exist. Pippi is a nine-year-old who does as she pleases whenever she wants to because she lives alone and there are no adults to supervise her activities. Mary Norton's *The Borrowers* (1953), a story of a family of "little people" who live by borrowing everyday objects from humans, was published in England. This popular book was the start of a series about the Borrowers.

The first modern fantasy for children published in the United States was *The Wonderful Wizard of Oz*, created by Frank Baum in 1900. Baum created thirteen more volumes about Oz. They were so immensely popular that, following his death in 1919, his publisher hired Ruth Plumly Thompson to write nineteen more stories to satiate the appetite of readers who loved the world of Oz.

Robert Lawson won the Newbery Medal for his personified animal story *Rabbit Hill* (1944). The story centers around animals in the Connecticut countryside where Father and Mother Rabbit and Little Georgie live. The rumor is that new folks are coming to live in the big house, and all the animals who live in the surrounding area wonder what this will mean to them—how will they be treated?

A few years later, E. B. White published a book that was to become a much-loved favorite of children in the United States and in other countries. *Charlotte's Web* (1952), tells the story of Wilbur, a runt pig who is rescued from being slaughtered and is then catapulted into fame by Charlotte, a kind spider who spins words of praise for Wilbur in her web.

Low fantasy stories are particularly prevalent in picture book format. Currently, authors such as Kevin Henkes, Rosemary Wells, Susan Meddaugh, and Lisa Campbell Ernst are producing high-quality picture book fantasies. Their work is discussed in more detail later in this chapter.

The mid-twentieth century marked the beginning of the publication of high fantasy series for children. J. R. R. Tolkien published *The Hobbit,* the first book in his popular series, in 1937. The *Chronicles of Narnia* is a seven-volume series published between 1950 and 1956 by C. S. Lewis, who wove Christian allegories throughout his stories set in the fantasy world of Narnia. The *Chronicles of Prydain*, a high fantasy series by Lloyd Alexander, began in 1964 with the publication of *The Book of Three*. Robin McKinley's quest fantasy *The Hero and the Crown* was published in 1984 and won the Newbery Medal in 1985. It was almost unique among high fantasy books because it featured a female protagonist. One of the newer high fantasy series is Brian Jacques's *Redwall* series, whose first volume was published in England in 1987. Philip Pullman's *The Golden Compass,* published in 1996, is the beginning of a trilogy.

CATEGORIES OF MODERN FANTASY

This section examines several categories of fantasy. However, Egoff (1988) has pointed out that good literature "can never be fitted into one sterile slot." Some books fit into multiple genres. For example, Jane Yolen's *The Devil's Arithmetic* (1988) can be considered historical fiction because it is set mainly during the Holocaust; yet it might also be considered modern fantasy because the book's protagonist travels through time. William Steig's *Doctor De Soto* (1982) is a picture book, but it also fits in the personified animal category of modern fantasy. Even within the genre of fantasy, books can be placed in more than one category. For example, in Jon Scieszka's *Time Warp Trio* series, each story concerns a "time slip," yet each one begins with an object of magical power—a book. Further, authors are increasingly including elements of science fiction with fantasy. For example, works of T. A. Barron use elements of science fiction, mythology, and fantasy. Although it is hard to put books into neat categories, trying to do so allows for interesting comparisons.

Low Fantasy

Low fantasy features nonrational events that occur without explanation in the real world. Low fantasy is also known as light fantasy, for the tone is usually rather lighthearted, often humorous. Children typically read low fantasy at a younger age and tend to read more low fantasy than high fantasy overall. The forms of low fantasy include stories about personified animals, personified toys, outlandish characters and humorous situations, magical powers, extraordinary worlds, supernatural elements, and time slips. These forms are discussed here in the order in which children are likely to be introduced to them—which roughly corresponds to young readers' increasingly higher levels of engagement in the fantasy elements.

Personified Animals. Stories with animals talking and behaving as humans do are often called *personified animal fantasies*. Animal characters who behave like humans are said to be *anthropomorphic*. Typically, this is the first type of fantasy book that young children encounter. There are many picture books and even a number of novels about personified animals.

Beatrix Potter's many personified animals may be among the first fantasy characters children are introduced to. In *The Tale of Peter Rabbit* (1902), Potter

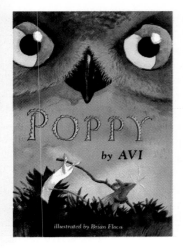

Illustration 10.2

The situations in which the characters in *Poppy* find themselves are set in the animal world, but the solutions arise out of thoughts and behaviors that are quite human. (*Poppy* by Avi. Jacket illustration copyright © 1995 by Brian Floca. Used by permission of Orchard Books, New York.)

mixes behaviors typical of rabbits with behaviors of humans. Peter and his family live in a sand bank underneath the roots of a tree, play in the fields, eat garden vegetables, and hop away from danger—all rabbit-like behaviors. But Mrs. Rabbit talks to her children using words, the rabbits wear clothing, and they drink chamomile tea—all human behaviors.

Kevin Henkes has written and illustrated many stories about personified mice. Sheila Rae, the brave older sister who suddenly panics and relies on the wits of her younger sister in *Sheila Rae, the Brave* (1987), and Chester and Wilson, whose particular ways of doing things are disrupted by Lilly's move into the neighborhood in *Chester's Way* (1988), are mice. However, they not only *behave* like people but think like them, too. As children get older, they may encounter William Steig's personified animals. In *Doctor De Soto* (1982), a fox gets a toothache and seeks the help of a dentist who is a mouse. In Avi's book of personified animals, *Poppy* (1995), a deer mouse, tries to convince her family to move close to a large cornfield because it could provide food for them forever. This move is thwarted when the tyrannical great horned owl, Mr. Ocax, refuses to give his consent.

An unlikely group of personified animals interacts in Cynthia Rylant's *Gooseberry Park* (1995). A Labrador retriever named Kona befriends Stumpy, a squirrel in Gooseberry Park. When Stumpy is separated from her babies during an ice storm, a bat named Murray and a hermit crab named Gwendolyn team up with Kona to reunite the newborns with their mother.

Several popular stories about personified animals center around a community of animals. *Charlotte's Web* by E. B. White is one immensely popular example. British writer Dick King-Smith created the fantasy stories *Pigs Might Fly* (1982), *Babe: The Gallant Pig* (1985), and *Ace: The Very Important Pig* (1988). As in E. B. White's books, the barnyard animals in King-Smith's stories become the community within which the story takes place. *The Wind in the Willows* (1908), by Kenneth Grahame, also features a community of animals. The four good friends—Ratty, Mole, Badger, and Toad—are animals with strong personal characteristics that define their roles. George Selden's *The Cricket in Times Square* (1960) is about a community of city-dwelling animals; other books in the series center around the same animals' visits to the country.

Personified Toys. Another type of fantasy enjoyed by very young children features personified toys (as well as other inanimate objects) that come to life. In these books, toys are able to talk and behave like humans. The toys that come to life are typically stuffed animals or dolls. The reason may be that when children play, they frequently pretend that stuffed animals and dolls have human attributes.

Perhaps the best-known personified toy story is A. A. Milne's classic work *Winnie-the-Pooh* (1926). The story was inspired by Milne's son, Christopher Robin, and his collection of stuffed animals.

The Castle in the Attic (1985) is a personified toy story in which a finger-high knight in a model castle comes alive when William, the young protagonist, picks him up. The sequel to this tale by Elizabeth Winthrop is *The Battle for the Castle* (1993). Lynne Reid Banks's *The Indian in the Cupboard* (1981) and its sequels are popular among children. A toy Indian and other toys come alive when Omri puts them in a magical cupboard. Having toys come alive, seeing the unfolding adventure as the toys engage in lifelike situations, and realizing what responsibility means are all part of the drama Omri and his friend Patrick experience. Although these popular books sensitively answer the question "What if toys came alive?" the toy people in them do not rise above stereotypes of Indians and cowboys.

Pam Conrad's picture books about the escapades of a family of bathtub toys—consisting of Father, Mother, Grandmother, Grandfather, Child, and Dog—are quite believable. The events that the toy family experiences in **The Tub People** (1989) and **The Tub Grandfather** (1993)—Tub Child being lost down the drain when the bathwater is let out, Tub Grandfather being discovered under the radiator with layers of dust from having been lost a long time—are likely events in toys' "lives." The toys' thoughts, actions, and speech in these realistic situations are believable because they reflect how humans under similar circumstances might think, act, and speak. Richard Egielski's illustrations depict the tub people as realistic wooden dolls, extending the believability of the story. Although the dolls maintain stiff poses, they clearly express the emotions of the characters.

Outlandish Characters and Humorous Situations. Stories that appear to be realistic fiction but have characters that behave in outrageous, highly exaggerated ways are classified as *fantasy with outlandish characters*. These characters may possess abilities that are outside the range of normal human behavior or act in eccentric ways.

P. L. Travers created a series of stories about a character with magical abilities. The first of these was **Mary Poppins** (1934), in which the unusual nanny arrives at the home of Jane and Michael Banks by way of an umbrella that carries her airborne on a gust of wind.

Swedish writer Astrid Lindgren is known around the world as the creator of **Pippi Longstocking** (1950) and two sequels, as well as more than a hundred other books. Pippi lives alone—without any adult supervision—and displays outrageous and eccentric behavior that constantly keeps the neighborhood children amused.

Magical Powers. The notion that magic might exist is an intriguing thought to children: Could there be sayings that make magical things happen, objects that hold magical powers, or other ways of bringing about magical events?

Natalie Babbitt's **Tuck Everlasting** (1975) has the ultimate magic in it—a spring that gives eternal life to those who drink from it. The source of this water is not explained, nor does the story offer an explanation of how it gives eternal life. All readers know are the consequences of drinking from the spring.

Donna Jo Napoli has continued her frog-turned-prince story, **Prince of the Pond** (1992), in **Jimmy, the Pickpocket of the Palace** (1995). When Jimmy, the frog son of a frog prince, shows up at the palace with a hurt leg, a princess kisses it. In keeping with the fairytale story of the frog prince, Jimmy turns into a human. His search for a magic ring that will convert him into a frog again so that he can save his pond from an evil hag, leaves him open to accusations of theft.

In **Lizard Music** (1976), Daniel Pinkwater tells a humorous story of Victor, who discovers a mysterious band of lizards playing outrageous music on television late at night. A mysterious Chicken Man and his hen named Claudia guide Victor to an invisible island—past the force field, under a deep-water barrier—to meet the music-playing lizards.

Extraordinary Worlds. The first task of an author who creates a world very different from the one in which we live is to make it believable to readers. Sometimes a story begins with convincing characters in the known world who then move into an extraordinary world through various devices. For example, when Milo enters the mysterious tollbooth in Norton Juster's popular novel **The Phantom Tollbooth** (1961), he finds an extraordinary world. In Roald Dahl's

Charlie and the Chocolate Factory (1964), the search for gold tickets hidden in chocolate bars takes place in the real world, but an invitation to enter a mysterious chocolate factory leads a selected few into an extraordinary world. Alice, a seemingly ordinary child, falls into a rabbit hole and finds an extraordinary world at the other end in *Alice's Adventures in Wonderland* (1865).

Other stories are set entirely in an extraordinary world. What makes the extraordinary world believable in Mary Norton's *The Borrowers* (1953) is the author's careful attention to the smallest of details when describing how the tiny Borrowers adapt various everyday human-size objects to their own uses.

Supernatural Elements. Scary stories with supernatural elements— ghosts, haunted houses, and the like—intrigue children. Margaret Mahy tells the story of a family with psychic powers in *The Haunting* (1982). The family members struggle with what these powers do to their relationships with one another. Pam Conrad's *Stonewords* (1990) tells about Zoe, who is visited by the ghost of Zoe Louise. Zoe realizes that she must prevent Zoe Louise's untimely death, and to do so, she must go back in time and change the course of events. In Mary Downing Hahn's *Wait Till Helen Comes* (1986), the ghost of Helen, who died years ago, waits by the pond to drown other children her age in hopes of getting a playmate. Molly must save her new stepsister from joining Helen.

Among the most popular books among children today are stories that can be classified as fantasies with supernatural elements. Many children eagerly seek out these "horror stories" and "scary stories." The most popular series of the 1990s is R. L. Stine's *Goosebumps* which has over fifty titles. Though they vary, typically, most such books are of questionable literary quality.

Time Slips. In time slip stories, characters move from one time period to another. This element of time travel allows the author to explore themes in ways that are not possible in stories that take place in a single time period. Typically, the time slips allow the characters to develop an understanding of situations that enhance their development. Barbara Elleman (1985, p. 1407) notes that "time-slip plots often center on a particular historical period, a mystery that needs to be solved, or a common problem shared across generations." Going back in time allows characters to gain firsthand experience that deepens understanding of how historical events influence the present. Time slips in mysteries allow characters to find the clues to solve the mysteries. Sometimes, issues span generations, and in some time slip stories, the protagonist finds ways to cope with such issues by meeting others who have faced them in an earlier time. In *Tom's Midnight Garden* (1984), Philippa Pearce tells the story of a boy who is bored with his summer until he discovers that when the grandfather clock strikes thirteen, he can enter the garden and play with a child from the past.

Jon Scieszka has written a series of books about three boys who comprise the Time Warp Trio: *Knights of the Kitchen Table* (1991), *The Not-So-Jolly Roger* (1991), *The Good, the Bad, and the Goofy* (1992), *Your Mother Was a Neanderthal* (1993), *2095* (1995), and *Tut, Tut* (1996). The device that allows the boys to travel in time is a magical object—"The Book," which Joe receives as a birthday present from his uncle, a magician. When Joe and his two friends, Fred and Sam, open the book, they are whisked off to a different place and time—the medieval days of King Arthur, the days of pirates and buried treasure, the nineteenth century in the Old West, the Stone Age, the twenty-first century, or ancient Egypt.

Belinda Hurmence's *A Girl Called Boy* (1982) and Jane Yolen's *The Devil's Arithmetic* (1988) are both time slip stories and works of historical fiction as well. In both, the protagonists question what they believe to be excessive pride in heritage and almost obsessive need to remember the past. In *A Girl Called Boy,* Blanche ("Boy") is transported back into the days of African American slavery. In *The Devil's Arithmetic,* Hannah is transported to the time of the Holocaust. Both return to the present with a deepened understanding of themselves as descendants of a particular heritage and a commitment not to forget the past.

Two other books have protagonists whose travel back in time allows them to explore their relationships with their parents. In Cynthia Voigt's *Building Blocks* (1984), Brann is frustrated with his father and cannot understand him. When Brann creates a fortress with his father's childhood building blocks and enters into it, he finds himself transported to the time of his father's childhood. In Canadian author Kit Pearson's *A Handful of Time* (1988) a twelve-year-old girl finds an old watch under the floor while visiting her cousins. The watch takes her back to the time when her mother was the same age.

High Fantasy

As we mentioned earlier, high fantasy takes place in a created "secondary world." Much high fantasy is enjoyed by young adults. However, many middle school students and some elementary school readers are attracted to works of high fantasy. There are various categories of high fantasy: myth fantasy, gothic fantasy, epic/heroic fantasy, and sword and sorcery fantasy. Myth fantasy can be retellings of old myths, modern adaptations of old myths, or new inventions. Gothic fantasy includes elements such as the fear of the unknown and the unnatural. Epic/heroic fantasy tries to recreate the world of the medieval epic and romance. Such fantasies are grand in their design and often have a strong emotional impact on readers. Heroic actions stem from the protagonist's commitment to serve "the common good." In many ways closely related to legends from the oral tradition, epic/hero fantasies often contain components of Arthurian, Welsh, Scandinavian, or other myths and legends. Sword and sorcery fantasy is similar to heroic fantasy. However, sword and sorcery fantasy is *not* to be mistaken with the "sword and sinew subgenre," which violates many of the characteristics of high fantasy. This subgenre includes a barbarian superhero, has much action, lacks thematic substance, uses a colloquial style of language, and sensationalizes violence (Egoff, 1988; Tymn, Zahorski, and Boyer, 1979).

Heroic romance is a form of high fantasy that draws from mythology and includes stories of heroes and worlds of great power. Alexander (1971) has called heroic romance a "cauldron of story" in which is found a "mythological minestrone" that combines real history with imaginary history. Included is an array of characters, events, and situations—quests, tasks, swords, dragons, and other elements of heroic romance. Because fantasy is written on many levels, Alexander suggests that readers may "ladle up whatever suits (their) taste," and "digest it, assimilate it" as thoroughly as possible.

Tymn, Zahorski, and Boyer (1979) characterize high fantasy as having "noble characters, archetypes, and elevated style." The focus on morality in high fantasy requires a hero who is compassionate, courageous, and humane and who accomplishes many good deeds. The hero is often a representative human being, "Everyman," who may be a commoner-hero or a morally ambivalent hero. The commoner-hero is at first reluctant to become involved in the events that are unfolding but proves courageous, loyal, and generous. The morally ambivalent hero is basically good but is more concerned with maintaining independence and individuality. The imagery for the created world is often supported by the elevated speaking style of noble characters. The themes explored in high fantasies usually give a sense of being unrelated to personal concerns. They are generally universal and focus on an all-out struggle between good and evil in which entire worlds are at stake. These other worlds tend to be reminiscent of medieval worlds—Tolkien's Middle-Earth, Alexander's Prydain, and Lewis's Narnia are just a few. Authors of high fantasy often provide readers with a detailed map of the lands in the secondary world.

Lloyd Alexander (1978, p. 442) classifies the plots in high fantasy into five categories:

- Tests of identity, endurance, and character
- Tasks, imposed or undertaken voluntarily
- Quests for marvelous objects or animals
- Escapes from death, through disguise or substitution or with help
- Journeys to other lands or worlds

Sometimes authors combine two or more of the five plot categories, either in one book or in a series of books. Although a work of high fantasy presents an impossible world, the "undercurrent of rationality" makes the story believable. The universal vitality of fantasy is timeless and eternal (Alexander, 1971).

HOW FANTASY WORKS

Asked why anyone reads or writes fantasy, author Susan Cooper (1981) explained that fantasy goes one stage beyond realism in requiring complete intellectual surrender. Fantasy asks more of readers, and the best works of fantasy may offer readers more. She argues that the escape so often attributed to fantasy is indeed offered, but it is an inward rather than an outward escape, as readers learn to discover themselves. Cooper suggests that by going beyond the time and space of the known world, readers allow themselves to enter a dreamlike world containing accumulated images and emotions of the human race.

Although different authors have their own thoughts on what makes a work fantasy, a number of generalizations can be made. First, fantasy includes literary elements characteristic of good literature but one or more of these elements is transformed by the author into something magical or not possible in the known world. Fantasy is made believable by the consistent use of logic or laws of the created world and descriptive detail. The fantasy element cannot be suddenly brought out to magically solve problems. Whatever element makes the story a fantasy must be an integral part of the story and all details must be consistent with that element. Fantasy is not an escape from reality, but a mirror in which reality is reflected and extended in the imagination. Finally, fantasy occurs in a secondary world created by the author or in the real world (the primary world) but with changed rules of logic, or sometimes in both worlds.

When reading fantasy, we accept the impossible by *suspending disbelief*. We know donkeys cannot turn into rocks, little people do not live under the floor, and inquisitive girls do not go down rabbit holes. Those things simply don't happen—but if the author has done a good job, the power of story is such that we suspend disbelief in order to find out what happens next. If at any time the author misses a detail and leaves the reader wondering about the inconsistency, the reader is apt to drop out, losing interest in what happens because he or she hasn't been convinced that the story *could* happen. Authors engage readers in fantasy by anchoring stories in plausibility.

According to Shapiro (1996), authors use a combination of devices in making the fantasy elements of a story believable to readers:

1. Many authors firmly ground a story in reality before gradually moving into fantasy. In other words, they begin the story in the primary world and move into the secondary world.

2. Authors have one of the characters mirror the disbelief of the reader. The narrator or protagonist reassures readers that the fantastic events are normal or real. When a believable character who initially doubted the fantasy is convinced, readers are likewise convinced.

3. Details of setting are an integral part of the story. Good authors make details so vivid that readers may be able to see, hear, and feel the setting as they read the description.

4. Authors use language that is consistent and distinct for each character or group.

Can reading fantasy be inappropriate for children?

Fantasy literature has often been the subject of controversy. Some adults do not consider children capable of distinguishing between reality and fantasy, even though school curricula often state (and psychological studies hold) that children in the primary grades should be able to make that distinction. Others worry that fantasy is a genre that allows an escape from reality and that reading works of fantasy takes time away from more important kinds of reading that children need to be doing. Still others complain that fantasy literature is inappropriate for children because it refers to the supernatural.

In recent years, parents and others in some communities have opposed the reading of fantasy literature in schools and have called for censor of certain types of books. In his experiences with such groups, school administrator Rick Traw (1996) found that the presence of magic, witchcraft, and animism caused the most concern. Traw found that even the slightest hint of the supernatural made a book appear on the list of censored materials. For example, a reference to Halloween or a story about a city witch and a country witch might get the work into trouble.

Tunnell (1994) writes about fantasy and censorship as the "double-edged sword." He believes that "fantasy is fundamentally the most important kind of story to share with [children]." He also believes that "children vicariously vent frustrations in healthy ways by subconsciously identifying with . . . heroes." In addition, Tunnell believes that fantasy gives children "a sense of hope about their ultimate abilities to succeed in the world."

What do you think?

ISSUE TO CONSIDER

5. In some stories, something from the fantastic world is brought back to the real world in order to make a connection between the two worlds.

6. The plot has internal consistency and logic.

In *Tuck Everlasting* (1975), Natalie Babbitt grounds the story in reality by first introducing a setting, a character, and a mood that are perfectly normal in the real world. Winnie Foster, the protagonist, has lost patience with the rules of all the adults in her life and considers running away from home. She is frustrated and wants more adventure. When the plot steps into the realm of the fantastic, Winnie tries to understand how people who drink special water could possibly live forever. As Winnie struggles with the decision she must make, readers are also convinced of the power of the water. They become intrigued with Winnie's dilemma and suspend disbelief in what they rationally know is not possible; they have followed Winnie into the fantasy. The author has created a story with internal consistency, and the intertwining of details about characters and plot development leave no loose threads or contradictions.

MAJOR WRITERS OF FANTASY AND THEIR WORKS

Many writers of fantasy and their works have already been mentioned in this chapter. Here, we highlight a few authors who have made significant contributions to the genre.

Lloyd Alexander

Lloyd Alexander knew he wanted to write from a young age. He claims that the seeds of his stories were planted by the extensive reading he did as a child as well as the military assignments that allowed him to travel and live in Wales, Germany, and France. Alexander began his career as a writer for adults, but his fantasy stories for children have been his major literary contribution. *The Chronicles of Prydain* is among the most widely read fantasy series for children and young adults. *The Book of Three* (1964) sets the story in the created world of Prydain, in which readers meet Taran, the Assistant Pig-Keeper, who is in search of an oracular pig named Hen Wen. The evil Arawn uses inhumane tactics to fight the nobility in Prydain, and Taran leads the expedition to fight against the evil. The series continues with *The Black Cauldron* (1965), *The Castle of Llyr* (1966), *Taran Wanderer* (1967), and *The High King* (1968). *The Black Cauldron* was named a Newbery Honor Book in 1966, and *The High King* was awarded the Newbery Medal in 1969.

Natalie Babbitt

At age nine, Natalie Babbitt saw the illustrations in *Alice in Wonderland* and decided to become a children's book illustrator. She did so, but is best known for her writing. Babbitt's book *The Search for Delicious* (1969) shows elements of mythology and fantasy, as a twelve-year-old is sent out to seek the true meaning of the word "delicious," following a disagreement among members of the court. *Tuck Everlasting* (1975) asks whether it's desirable to have eternal life. The Tuck family drank out of a magical spring and will live forever—but they do not want to and are forced to guard the secret from normal humans by living the life of drifters. Babbitt's *The Devil's Storybook* (1974) and *The Devil's Other*

Storybook (1987) are collections of short stories about the devil's efforts to recruit more members for his world.

T. A. Barron

Growing up in the Colorado mountains imbued T. A. Barron with a love of nature, which is apparent in his writing. He has traveled around the world, backpacking and experiencing a variety of lifestyles. Barron's travel experiences and his varied formal studies fuel the imagination from which he writes.

Heartlight (1990) is Barron's first book in a series about thirteen-year-old Kate. Kate searches for her grandfather, who has disappeared after inventing the means of traveling faster than light. His mission is to save the sun from extinction, and Kate's mission is to save her grandfather from evil forces that have captured him. In the second book of the series, *The Ancient One* (1992), Kate goes with her grandfather's sister, Aunt Kate, to protest the cutting of redwood trees in Oregon. Barron creates an eerie environment that prepares readers for Kate's falling into a time tunnel that takes her back five centuries to when the trees were young but still threatened by human greed.

Barron has written several books about Merlin. In *The Merlin Effect* (1994), Kate joins her father on a scientific expedition off the coast of Baja, California. One day at dusk, Kate disobeys her father and takes a kayak out too far; her forbidden expedition leads to an encounter with a whale and the discovery of forgotten legends involving Merlin. In *The Lost Years of Merlin* (1996), Merlin is a young boy who has lost his memory and is searching for his identity. His journey to discover his past shows readers how he gained his magical sight and became a wizard. The story of Merlin is to continue in two upcoming sequels: *The Seven Songs of Merlin* and *The Wings of Merlin*.

Grace Chetwin

Grace Chetwin was born in England, lived in New Zealand for a time, and now resides on Long Island. Her works of fantasy often include science fiction elements and are greatly influenced by European folktales—she incorporates folktale motifs and elaborates on their meaning in the course of the stories.

Chetwin's saga *Tales of Gom in the Legends of Ulm* comprises four of her best fantasies. The saga begins with *Gom on Windy Mountain* (1986). Gom's mother is sent away by her husband after she gives birth to Gom, the youngest of many children. She knows that Gom is the "chosen one" of the current generation, who will carry on the magic, so she leaves the rune (a charm) with him. When he grows up, Gom is sent off to seek his fortune, because nobody wants him—an example of a folktale motif. In the second book, *The Riddle and the Rune* (1987), the rune provides the clue to the riddle of Gom's missing mother. Gom becomes a wizard in *The Crystal Stair* (1988), and in the final book, *The Starstone* (1989), he seeks and finds a mate.

In *Jason's Seven Magical Night Rides* (1994), Jason longs for a father. A mysterious stranger offers him rides on mythical horses, including Pegasus, Chiron the Centaur, and the Trojan Horse. This stranger serves as a teacher, who helps Jason gain the strength to accept his circumstances, overcome his feelings of inadequacy, and become whole by assuming responsibility for himself.

In 1995, Chetwin broadened her involvement in children's book publishing by starting a publishing house of her own, Feral Press. Her first book under this imprint, *Rufus* (1996), is a work of realistic fiction.

Susan Cooper

Susan Cooper is the author of the acclaimed high fantasy series *The Dark Is Rising*. She was an established writer when she began this series, inspired by a contest. The first book in the series is *Over Sea, Under Stone* (1965). In the second book, *The Dark Is Rising* (1973), eleven-year-old Will Stanton discovers that he is the last of the "Old Ones" and a servant of the Light. It is his destiny to fight evil and to protect the Light in this story that draws on the legend of King Arthur and other British legends and myths. *The Dark Is Rising* was named a Newbery Honor Book in 1974. The series continues as Will searches for the remaining "Things of Power" needed to fight the final rising of the Dark in *Greenwitch* (1974), *The Grey King* (1975), for which Cooper received the Newbery Medal in 1976, and *Silver on the Tree* (1977). Born and educated in England, Cooper's first marriage to an American brought her to the United States, where she began her writing career. She believes that her imagination was as lonely and homesick as she was and therefore turned to fantasy as a home.

Roald Dahl

Roald Dahl's work is tremendously popular among children. Children who discover his work find themselves compelled to read one book after the other. They are delighted by his stories' irreverent voice and zany events. His portrayals of truly detestable characters—usually adults but sometimes children—powerfully engage children's emotions. For example, Dahl sometimes sets up a character, such as the grandmother in *George's Marvelous Medicine* (1982), or a whole class of characters, such as the witches in *The Witches* (1983), and invites readers to hate them without remorse. Not all teachers and critics are convinced that this is a healthy practice, however.

Some say that Roald Dahl's childhood influenced his writings. Born to Norwegian parents in South Wales, Dahl moved to England with his mother upon the death of his father. He entered boarding school at age eight and was subjected to disciplinary measures bordering on torture. Dahl's early life is recounted in his book *Boy* (1984). Perhaps his best-known book is *Charlie and the Chocolate Factory* (1964), in which a poor boy finds a lucky golden ticket that allows him to visit Willy Wonka's Chocolate Factory and earn a chance to be Willy Wonka's successor.

Mollie Hunter

Mollie Hunter, whose full name is Maureen Mollie Hunter McIlwraith, received only the legally required minimum of formal education in her native Scotland. But her great-grandmother's songs and stories of Scottish history and Hunter's own informal study of original historical source materials added to her learning. Her love of words and natural storytelling ability, combined with her young sons' requests to create a book out of her stories, initiated her writing career. Her lifetime interest in Celtic folklore and Scottish history fueled her imagination. In Hunter's book of essays about writing for children, *Talent Is Not Enough* (1976), she states her belief that talent is only the beginning of becoming a writer, that it is life's experiences that fully develop the voice behind the story. Hunter's much-acclaimed works of fantasy include *A Stranger Came Ashore* (1975) and *The Kelpie's Pearls* (1966).

Brian Jacques

Born in Liverpool, England, Brian Jacques became a sailor at age fifteen. After working as a radio broadcaster, comedian, and truck driver, Jacques wrote

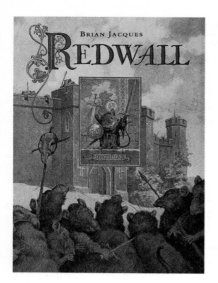

Illustration 10.3

Animals engage in high fantasy quests and battles in the *Redwall* series. (*Redwall* by Brian Jacques. Illustration copyright © 1996 by Troy Howell. Used by permission of Philomel Books.)

his first book to entertain students at a school for the blind. The publication of *Redwall* (1987) began a series of fantasies about the animals living at Redwall Abbey. Since then, many other books in the *Redwall* series have been published, and they have a following of readers anxious to hear more about the rats and other field animals engaged in classic fantasy quests. The series includes *Mossflower* (1988), *Mattimeo* (1990), *Mariel of Redwall* (1991), *Salamandastron* (1993), *Martin the Warrior* (1994), *The Bellmaker* (1994), and *Outcast of Redwall* (1996).

Diana Wynne Jones

About her creation of fantasy for children, Diana Wynne Jones observes: "What I am after is an exciting and exacting wisdom, in which contemporary life and potent myth are intricately involved and superimposed" (Olendorf and Telgen, 1993, p. 116). Jones succeeds in producing not only exciting, diverse, and wise stories but humorous ones as well. She says that as a child she "suffered from perpetual book starvation" and began to write. It was not until she had her own children, however, that Jones began writing for children.

While studying at Oxford, Jones attended lectures given by C. S. Lewis and J. R. R. Tolkien, and her classmates included Penelope Lively and Jill Paton Walsh, who also went on to become writers of fantasy literature for children.

Three of Jones's books won Carnegie commendations. *Dogsbody* (1975) is about Sirius the Dog Star, who is reborn on earth as a puppy and fulfills a mission to find the murder weapon of the stars. *Power of Three* (1976) is about a curse threatening the English moors and how three children and some strange creatures work together to save them. *A Charmed Life* (1977) is based on Jones's own unusual childhood and is the first volume in the *Chrestomanci* cycle of linked novels. The protagonist is a young boy magician who is manipulated by his sister. The other titles in the series are *The Magicians of Caprona* (1980), in which the children of two feuding families make magical peace; *Witch Week* (1982), which takes place in a school where the teacher suspects someone in class is a witch (1982); and *The Lives of Christopher Chant* (1988), which recounts the training of the next Chrestomanci, or controller of magic.

Some of Jones's other books are *A Sudden Wild Magic* (1992), which is about witchcraft; *Stopping for a Spell: Three Fantasies* (1993), which has three humorous stories set in England; and *Aunt Maria* (1991), in which Mig and Chris discover that their poor old great-aunt possesses unnatural powers.

C. S. Lewis

As children in Northern Ireland, Clive Staples Lewis and his brother read many books that probably influenced their creation of books about imaginary lands. As a child, Lewis made animals for a created world of Animal-Land, and they proved to be the predecessors to the talking animals in Narnia. At the age of fifty-two, Lewis published the first of the seven *Narnia* books, *The Lion, the Witch, and the Wardrobe* (1950). This book, awarded the Lewis Carroll Shelf Award in 1962, tells the story of four siblings who play in a wardrobe and find that it becomes their entryway into a magical land called Narnia. The children encounter the lion Aslan, whose purpose is to free Narnia from the spell cast by the White Witch. The Narnia stories continue in *Prince Caspian, the Return to Narnia* (1951), *The Voyage of the Dawn Treader* (1952), *The Silver Chair* (1953), *The Horse and His Boy* (1954), and *The Magician's Nephew* (1955).

The end of Narnia is depicted in *The Last Battle* (1956), which won the Carnegie Medal. Lewis's Christian beliefs are embodied throughout his writing in the form of symbolism that reflects Christian allegories.

A. A. Milne

Alan Alexander Milne created personified toy stories based on the stuffed animals of his son, Christopher Robin. Children around the world have come to adore the stories in *Winnie-the-Pooh* (1926) and *The House at Pooh Corner* (1928), which feature Winnie-the-Pooh, Piglet, Eeyore, Tigger, Kanga, Roo, and Owl, who live in the Hundred Acre Woods. The interactions among the characters range from silly to serious while addressing the events of daily life in the woods from a child's perspective. The illustrations by Ernest H. Shepard in the Pooh books contribute to their charm.

Milne credits his own childhood wanderings outdoors with his brother as the source of his inspiration for the adventures these animals have. Interestingly, Milne's son, Christopher, resented being considered a storybook character; he felt that, contrary to the image of the storytelling father that readers meet in the books, Milne was more of an observer than a participant in his son's growing up.

William Steig

William Steig is an illustrator and author whose accomplishments are laudable in both areas. He spent his childhood years in the Bronx, and the Depression forced him to work to support his family. He sold cartoons to magazines such as *The New Yorker*. Steig's entry into the children's book field came at the age of sixty, at the instigation of a colleague at *The New Yorker,* children's book author Robert Kraus. Steig's illustrations have a doodling quality to them; they show movement and spontaneity in their lines.

Sylvester and the Magic Pebble (1969) was awarded the Caldecott Medal in 1970. It is the story of a donkey whose parents miss him after he is turned into a rock. *The Amazing Bone* (1976) was a Caldecott Honor Book. The magical powers of the amazing bone save Pearl the Pig from being gobbled up by the wolf. Steig's Newbery Honor Books are *Abel's Island* (1976) and *Doctor De Soto* (1982). In *Abel's Island,* Abel is a happily married mouse living in style and comfort until a storm leaves him marooned all alone on an island with barely the necessities of life. In *Doctor De Soto,* a mouse dentist is asked to remove a bothersome tooth from a fox patient—leading readers to ponder who the clever one is in this story.

J. R. R. Tolkien

John Ronald Reuel Tolkien, a professor of medieval studies at Oxford, is known as one of the foremost creators of fantasy literature. Read by millions of children and adults and translated into over twenty-five languages, *The Hobbit* (1937) is among the most popular of twentieth-century fantasy works written for children. For years, fans clamored for more stories about the Hobbits, and in 1954 and 1955 Tolkien produced a trilogy titled *The Lord of the Rings,* which includes *The Fellowship of the Ring*, *The Two Towers*, and *The Return of the King*. Based on Tolkien's thorough understanding of mythology, these books allow readers to follow the protagonist, Bilbo Baggins, on a quest.

Rosemary Wells

Rosemary Wells creates humorous stories about animals who are caught in situations and relationships much like those children find themselves in with their friends and siblings. She cites events in her own and her children's lives as the models for many of her situations. Wells believes that her animal characters are able to convey deeply felt emotions that are familiar to children and adults alike. In many of her books, the dialogue is succinct but is supplemented by a narrator's voice that offers humorous explanations of what thoughts are going through the characters' heads and what the characters are doing.

Perhaps the best known of Wells's works are her stories about Max, a rabbit. The interactions between little brother Max and big sister Ruby reflect ways in which human siblings often interact. In a board book series about this brother-sister pair, readers find Ruby giving instructions that Max pretends not to understand—the humor comes in Ruby's exasperation as Max revels in his responses to her edicts. In *Max's Breakfast* (1985), Ruby tries repeatedly to convince Max to eat his egg. The joke is on Ruby when Max announces, "All Gone," as Ruby finishes the egg in her attempt to show Max how yummy it is.

E. B. White

E. B. White wrote extensively all of his life, particularly essays and humorous adult fiction. He was a regular contributor to *The New Yorker,* as well as to numerous other magazines. Perhaps his best-known children's book is *Charlotte's Web* (1952). This book has gained such wide popularity over the years that it is considered a classic fantasy of personified animals. Although the tone of the book is lighthearted, the themes of relationships, friendship, death, and legacy are very serious. White wrote two other books for children. *Stuart Little*, published in 1945, was his first. It is the story of a mouse, based on bedtime stories that White told his nieces and nephews. *The Trumpet of the Swan* (1970) is about a friendship between a mute swan and a young boy.

Patricia Wrede

Patricia Wrede began writing in the seventh grade and immediately had the support of her family. She would write her stories out by hand, her mother would type them, her father would read them and praise her efforts, and her four younger siblings would listen to them read aloud. Although she continued writing, Wrede believed her efforts would never amount to more than a hobby. She attributes her early growth as a writer to the Scribblies, a group of friends who formed a critique group.

Wrede's entry into the world of published writers began in 1986 with an invitation to write a short story for an anthology edited by Jane Yolen. Yolen suggested that Wrede expand the story into a novel; it eventually became *Talking to Dragons* (1993), the fourth book in the *Chronicles of the Enchanted Forest.* series. In this story, Queen Cimorene sends her sixteen-year-old son to stave off evil magic in the Enchanted Forest. The *Chronicles of the Enchanted Forest* series begins with *Dealing with Dragons* (1990), in which Princess Cimorene, bored with palace life, becomes a warrior in a fight with wizards. Next is *Searching for Dragons* (1991), and this time Princess Cimorene teams up with Mendanbar, King of the Enchanted Forest, to try to save the forest. In *Calling on Dragons* (1992) now-Queen Cimorene calls on friends and dragons to help her once again save the Enchanted Forest from wizards who are soaking up its magic.

Other Notable Writers of Modern Fantasy

There is no way to include every noteworthy author in a section on major authors and illustrators of modern fantasy. Some noted writers of fantasy are dis-

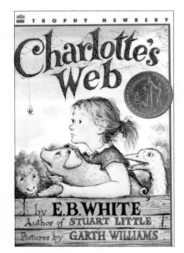

Illustration 10.4
Charlotte's Web is one of the most popular fantasy books for children. (*Charlotte's Web* by E. B. White. Illustration copyright renewed © 1980 Garth Williams. Used by permission of HarperCollins Publishers.)

ASK THE AUTHOR . . . *Jane Yolen*

What do you say to those who criticize your choice to write and publish fantasy books for children?

I think that fantasy books speak to reality heart to heart. They are metaphoric shorthand. No one reading them—children or adults—is fooled into believing them word for word; that is, the reader does not believe in the actuality of dragons, unicorns, flying horses. But these stories are like points on a map, acting as a guide to life as we actually live it by showing us life as it *could* be lived.

For those folks who are afraid of fantasy books, seeing Satan where none exists, I tell them that they do not understand the role of metaphor in literature. But if they persist in seeing devils and the hand of hell in these stories, I cannot change their minds. And I do not try to.

What I look for in fantasy books is a strong storyline, a character who changes and grows, and wonderful chewy prose. I am not interested in generic sword and sorcery, but in invention, imagination, and a prose style that sings. I have read a lot of

fantasy novels in my life. So I want to be surprised, delighted, and have the little hairs on the back of my neck stand up with recognition, just as I do when I read a poem by Emily Dickinson. A fantasy book should force me to confront my real world with the imagined world.

Jane Yolen, who has been referred to as "America's Hans Christian Andersen" and the "Twentieth-Century Aesop" because of her many fairytales and fantasy stories, is the author of over 170 books for children and adults. Her fantasy and science fiction imprint, Jane Yolen Books, part of Harcourt Brace & Company, published books by such authors as Bruce Coville (Jeremy Thatcher, Dragon Hatcher, 1991), Patricia C. Wrede (Dealing with Dragons, 1990), Vivian Vande Velde (Companions of the Night, 1995) and Caroline Stevermer (River Rats, 1992).

Favorite Books as a Child

The Andrew Lang Color Fairy Books

The Sword in the Stone by T. H. White

The Jungle Book by Rudyard Kipling

---

cussed in other chapters: For example, Kevin Henkes, Beatrix Potter, Maurice Sendak, and Chris Van Allsburg are featured in Chapter 6; Laurence Yep and Virginia Hamilton are included in Chapter 4. Other writers of fantasy who are very popular among children include Bruce Coville, Lois Duncan, Tom Mc-Gowen, Tamora Pierce, and Meredith Pierce, but much of their work is intended for and read predominantly by young adults.

CRITERIA FOR SELECTING FANTASY

What makes a good fantasy? The same qualities that make a good story of any kind are necessary. The author has to engage the reader with beautiful language, encourage the reader to continue to the end, and never let the reader down with a broken or unbelievable plot thread. Fantasy writers must try harder to keep a story believable because of the imaginary elements.

When evaluating works of fantasy, teachers and parents should keep the following points in mind:

- Is the story well written, according to generally accepted literary standards?

- How consistent and well developed are the fantasy elements?

- Are the elements that make this story a fantasy convincing? Does the story allow readers to "suspend disbelief"?

- Does the author maintain a sense of logic and order within the created world?

THE EVOLUTION OF SCIENCE FICTION

The first work of science fiction may have been English author Mary Wollstonecraft Shelley's best-seller, *Frankenstein*, published in 1811. It used medical science as the point of departure from reality, and anticipated by over a century and a half the possibility of inventing new life forms and of transplanting organs.

In the mid-nineteenth century, the Frenchman Jules Verne was inspired by rapidly advancing technology to publish works of science fiction. Some of his stories anticipated later inventions. The submarine was featured in *Twenty Thousand Leagues under the Sea* (1869), and rocket travel was part of *From the Earth to the Moon* (1865).

At the turn of the century, a biology teacher named H. G. Wells wrote the first book about an invasion from outer space. Later, on Halloween of 1938, Orson Welles's broadcast of *The War of the Worlds* as a radio play caused thousands of people to panic. Although the announcer indicated throughout the broadcast that it was a work of science fiction, the genre was so new to American audiences that many believed the earth was under attack from aliens in spaceships.

At about the same time, pulp magazines published stories with science fiction themes. The term "science fiction" was coined by Hugo Gernsback, who began *Amazing Stories* in 1926; Gernsback later published *Science Wonder Stories*. Many notable science fiction writers got their start in those pages, including Edgar Rice Burroughs, Isaac Asimov, and Robert A. Heinlein.

Both Heinlein and Asimov owe the early nurturing of their careers to *Amazing Stories* editor John W. Campbell, who later began the magazine *Astounding Science Fiction*. Campbell helped to launch the careers of many science fiction writers of the time. Robert Heinlein is credited with transforming the way science fiction stories are told. Rather than relying on pure fantasy, he researched contemporary scientific discoveries and made careful extrapolations on which he based the plots of his novels and short stories. Heinlein's 1947 book **Rocket Ship Galileo** and the twelve junior novels that were published in the succeeding years are considered to be the first children's science fiction published in the United States. Isaac Asimov coined the term "robotics" in his prolific writings about robots. He formally outlined the "Three Laws of Robotics" that have guided the way robots have been portrayed in science fiction ever since.

In 1957, the Soviet Union launched Sputnik, the first satellite, and spurred not only the U.S. space initiative but also a competition among authors to provide children with imaginative stories set in outer space. Several authors wrote "space fantasies" in the 1950s. Ellen MacGregor wrote the *Miss Pickerell* series.

Jay Williams wrote a series of space fantasy stories such as **Danny Dunn and the Anti-Gravity Paint** (1956). Louis Slobodkin's **The Space Ship under the Apple Tree** was published in 1952 and followed ten years later by **The Three-Seated Space Ship: The Latest Model of the Space Ship under the Apple Tree.** Although the limited scientific information in these books is accurate, the premises of the stories are based on imagination.

In the 1960s, the movie *2001: A Space Odyssey* and the television program "Star Trek" enlarged the audience of young devotees of space fiction. In 1969 came the actual landing on the moon by manned spacecraft—a true space adventures—and in the following decade a few well-made movies, especially *Star Wars* and *E.T.,* continued to enhance the popularity of science fiction.

Madeleine L'Engle's **A Wrinkle in Time** (1962) was the first science fiction book to be named a winner of the Newbery Medal. Along with the prestige of the award came the recognition that science fiction would have a wider readership among children than in years past.

Today, serious themes abound in science fiction for young people. Many authors of science fiction say that they choose to write in this genre because "other world" settings help readers explore serious questions about their own world from a distance, and thus with clearer vision. Madeleine L'Engle, for example, explores ethical and theological questions in her books. When, in **Invitation to the Game** (1990), Monica Hughes creates a futuristic society in which educated and talented young people find no employment and are instead invited to play a game that turns out to be a fight for survival in a new world, she is asking her readers to question whether society today is guilty of similarly wasting the talents of young people. Nancy Farmer creates a horrendous community living under the garbage heaps of a city in **The Ear, the Eye and the Arm** (1994). With a little imagination, a reader can visualize the local landfill producing characters like the vlei people. In the same book, readers enter a controlled, militaristic society in which buildings are hundreds of stories high and no one is safe. Readers are forced to ask themselves how this future could be prevented from becoming reality. Readers of **The Giver** (1993), by Lois Lowry, find a society in which memory of the past is erased and all matters of family, work, and pleasure are determined by an unknown few who control the society. When one child is chosen to receive the memory for the whole society from the Giver of memories, he questions what is important in order to remain human. Good science fiction is entertaining, addictive, and inevitably thought-provoking.

Illustration 10.5
Readers of Lois Lowry's *The Giver* will ponder whether a utopian society can truly exist and whether a controlled society is a desirable goal. The book won the Newbery Medal in 1994. (*The Giver* by Lois Lowry. Copyright © 1993 by Lois Lowry. Used by permission of Houghton Mifflin Co. All rights reserved.)

CATEGORIES OF SCIENCE FICTION

Some would prefer the plural term "science fictions" for this genre of literature, for the many works labeled science fiction provide very different reading experiences. Let's look at the most common varieties.

Projecting Scientific Principles

One kind of science fiction takes one or more principles known to science, makes extrapolations of what the principles might lead to, and plays the possibilities out in a narrative, often in an everyday setting not unlike the real world. Peter Dickinson's **Eva** (1989) is an example of a book in which a scientific principle is explored in a story about a possible future. Following an accident, a young girl's body is destroyed but her brain survives and is transplanted into a chimpanzee's body. The story probes who Eva will be—the human Eva in a chimpanzee's body, or the chimpanzee Kelly with a human mind? How will she live—as a human or as a chimpanzee? *Eva* is a gripping work that questions human feelings of superiority to animals.

In *Anna to the Infinite Power* (1981) by Mildred Ames, twelve-year-old Anna discovers that she is a clone. The idea of creating a clone has fascinated people for years and is also explored in other books for young readers. William Sleator explores the idea of multiple clones in *The Duplicate* (1988). At first, sixteen-year-old David thinks it would be convenient to have a clone, but by the time he realizes the difficulties involved in living with Duplicate A, the experiment has gotten out of hand and Duplicate B arrives.

Utopian and Dystopian Societies

Societies different from the one we live in have been explored in adult literature for thousands of years. The Biblical Eden was one of several detailed versions of ideal societies, or utopias: Plato's *Republic* (in the fourth century B.C.) and St. Augustine's *The City of God* (in the fourth century A.D.). Dante's *Inferno* (written between 1307 and 1321), a detailed account of what hell is like, provided an early example of a dystopia, a terrible place to live.

The Ear, the Eye and the Arm (1994), by Nancy Farmer, explores a futuristic society in Zambia. What may appear intially as utopian—a highly efficient, technologically managed society—soon shows its dystopian side as readers are introduced to the vlei people who live in what was a city dump. Likewise, what appears to be a utopia at the beginning of Lois Lowry's *The Giver* (1993) is a supposedly ideal society whose people are free from all hardship—but also lack freedom of choice. The revealed dystopia highlights the implications of social planning. Lowry's book makes readers stop to consider whether an ideal society is possible—or desirable.

Monica Hughes's *Invitation to the Game* (1990) introduces a group of teenagers who are told on the day they graduate from high school, "Congratulations on graduating with honors! Enjoy your leisure years!" Ironically, the educated, eager-to-work protagonists are sent to a community for the unemployed to play "the game"—not a game at all, but a master plan to dispose of excess population. Hughes reports that the situation for the book was suggested by a friend from Liverpool, England, where unemployment has been so entrenched for so long that many teachers see their greatest challenge to be preparing young people for a life without work. Reading about this situation in the genre of science fiction frees readers from making associations with particular social classes and historical moments and helps them see the larger point of the work: That individual opportunities for a meaningful life may depend on the sort of social and economic system a person lives in.

Surviving Environmental Catastrophes

Some science fiction deals with survival in the future, following some kind of environmental catastrophe. This catastrophe could be a nuclear holocaust, overpollution, overcrowding, or destruction of other aspects of the earth's environment.

Louise Lawrence's *Children of the Dust* (1985) tells of three generations of an English family following a nuclear holocaust. The lives of those who live in a sheltered but restricted bunker are compared with the lives of those who live outside and suffer from mutations.

Illustration 10.6
When the children of General Matsika are kidnapped while on an outing, they face a bizarre world outside their controlled environment. Nancy Farmer's *The Ear, the Eye and the Arm* was a Newbery Honor Book in 1995. (*The Ear, the Eye and the Arm* by Nancy Farmer. Jacket painting © 1994 by Charles A. Bibbs. Used by permission of the Publisher, Orchard Books, New York.)

Illustration 10.7

Karen Hesse explores what life following a nuclear catastrophe might be like in *Phoenix Rising*. (*Phoenix Rising* by Karen Hesse. Copyright © 1994 Karen Hesse. Used by permission of Henry Holt & Co., Inc.)

Phoenix Rising (1994), by Karen Hesse, deals with the issue of survival following an accident at a nuclear power plant. Nyle's life on a Vermont sheep farm changes as she, and others in her family and community, attempt to survive the effects of the fallout. She must learn to deal with contamination, illnesses, and death.

Science Fantasies

Books that include extrapolations of scientific understandings yet are predominantly based on imagination are classified as *science fantasy*. What some have previously called *space fantasy*—books about space travel, interplanetary exploration, alien visitors—are also included in this category. Arthur Yorinks writes about a spaceship whose alien passengers are invited for dinner in **Company's Coming** (1988). Edward Marshall's extraterrestrial creature in **Space Case** (1980) is mistaken for a Halloween trick-or-treater. Pamela Service's **Stinker from Space** (1988) and **Stinker's Return** (1993) are about an agent from outer space, Tsynq Yr, who, not knowing the nature of the beast, enters the body of an earthly skunk for camouflage.

Paula Danziger's **This Place Has No Atmosphere** (1987) is a humorous story about a family's move from the earth to the moon in the twenty-first century. Daniel Pinkwater's science fantasies are based on the foibles of people on earth. In **Fat Men from Space** (1977), invaders attempt to steal all the junk food on earth.

William Sleator's **Interstellar Pig** (1984) is another example of science fantasy. Barney, the hero of Sleator's book, gradually discovers that his new neighbors in an isolated Cape Cod beach setting are shape-shifting aliens, involved in a deadly game of keep-away that has been going on for over a century. As the tale of the aliens' game unfolds, readers are led to imagine the many possibile consequences of contact between humans and creatures with a far greater variety of body forms, a larger territorial range, and more complex relationships to time.

HOW SCIENCE FICTION WORKS

One of the questions readers ask themselves when they encounter a new book is what genre it belongs to. Some works of science fiction identify their genre right off. Because Monica Hughes's **The Keeper of the Isis Light** (1981), for example, occurs on a remote planet, readers know from the beginning that they are reading science fiction. Other works plant ambiguous clues. William Sleator's **The Boy Who Reversed Himself** (1986) raises readers' curiosity when the protagonist creates mirror writing, but they don't discover until further into the book that through some scientific process, the boy has reversed himself and can go into the fourth dimension. Like others of Sleator's works, this book gives readers an extra taste of suspense before the genre is made clear, making them wonder not only about the explanations behind events but about the kind of reality those explanations belong to—the logic of daily life or the more imaginative realm of fantasy or science fiction?

It is easy for an author of science fiction to get caught up in the adventure of the plot or the setting and give insufficient thought to developing the characters. The best works of science fiction, then, are those that draw believable characters—with complex but understandable feelings and perceptions—even when those characters are members of some invented species. Good science fiction makes its premises plausible: There is a logic to the setting, the characters, and the situation that is accessible to young readers, so that they can "think their way around" in the work just as they could in any other sort of fiction. Finally, good science fiction does not merely dazzle the reader with bizarre details but plants clues and invites the reader to guess and predict what is happening or what will happen.

Once a work has opened up the possibility of the fantastic—scientific or otherwise—readers interpret events in the work within that realm of possibility and even reconstruct the parts of the work they read earlier in light of fantastic explanations. But even fantasy or science fiction is based on reality. Readers must have some points of identification with a work—something they find familiar and understandable—or they are not likely to be able to comprehend what they read.

Understanding the remote and strange in terms of the familiar is a challenge readers face not only in science fiction, but to some degree in all literature. Authors often begin with familar details and lead readers gradually into the unfamiliar. Pamela Sargent begins *Alien Child* (1988) this way:

> Nita's earliest memory was of the day she had nearly drowned in the pool. She was toddling down the wide, lighted hall of her home; but her short legs could not keep pace with her guardian's long strides. Llipel suddenly retracted her claws, picked Nita up as the door to the garden slid open, and carried her outside. (p. 1)

Is Llipel Nita's dog or cat? If so, who is the guardian? Or is Llipel a guardian with claws? The questioning begins after the reader steps into what appears to be a human child's memory. Science fiction plays on the wonderful human capacity to project from real experiences to other-worldly ones: At its best, it allows us to touch the stars from our own living rooms.

MAJOR WRITERS OF SCIENCE FICTION AND THEIR WORKS

Some authors of science fiction and their major works were mentioned earlier in this chapter. Also, many writers who are major contributors to the genre are not listed in this section because their books are predominantly read by young adults rather than by children.

Isaac Asimov

One of the world's most prolific writers until his death in 1992, Isaac Asimov wrote over three hundred books on a wide range of topics, spanning such genres as science fiction, history, hard science, and mysteries. His works of science fiction are carefully researched, and readers—children and adults alike—can gain clear understandings of scientific and technical concepts from them.

Asimov had made his first tries at writing science fiction by the age of eleven and his first published works were short stories that benefited from the guidance of the noted editor of *Astounding Science Fiction*, John W. Campbell. Much of Asimov's work appears in story collections which he himself edited, such as *Fantastic Reading: Stories and Activities for Grades 5–8* (1984). Many of his children's books were co-authored by Janet Asimov, his psychiatrist wife who also wrote under the pseudonym J. D. Jeppson. Together they wrote a series about Norby, a robot. In *Norby and the Invaders* (1985), Norby helps solve a mystery on earth, and in *Norby and the Court Jester* (1991), Norby travels to the planet Izz.

John Christopher

Christopher Samuel Youd is a British author who writes for adults and young people under six pseudonyms. But his books for young people written under the name John Christopher are his most successful. Christopher was asked by his publisher to write science fiction for boys, and he now prefers to write for young people. His first book for young readers was *The White Mountains,* which was published in 1967 and became the first volume of the *Tripod* trilogy. *The White Mountains* is about the earth's being conquered by alien Tripods who cap humans' heads to control them by making them docile and enslaved. Henry, Beanpole, and Will embark on a perilous journey to free the humans and rescue the earth from destruction. *The City of Gold and Lead* (1967) takes the three boys into the Tripod secret city in order to learn more about the Tripods. In *The Pool of Fire* (1968), Will and a group of free people carry out a plan to intercede in the interplanetary war between the Tripods and the Masters. *When the Tripods Came,* about aliens landing on earth, was published in 1988, as a prequel to the *Tripod* trilogy.

As a student in a chemistry lab, Christopher first began experimenting with possibilities that went far beyond his textbooks. He has said that that experience set the stage for his becoming a writer of science fiction. Christopher has written other science fiction in addition to the *Tripod* trilogy. The *Swords of the Spirit* trilogy was published in the 1970s and a *Fireball* trilogy was published in the 1980s.

Peter Dickinson

Peter Dickinson was born in Zambia, spent his early years there, and eventually moved to England and attended Eton College. After serving in the army and then graduating from Oxford University, he was a crime novel reviewer for a British humor magazine. It was not until he was in his forties that Dickinson turned to writing as a career. He writes for both children and adults.

Dickinson's first book for children was *The Weathermonger* (1968). It later became part of *The Changes* trilogy, in which Geoffrey and his sister Sally are among those in England who fear the impact of technology and machines that destroy nature; they seek instead to recreate the culture of the Dark Age. The trilogy was written and published in reverse chronological order. The first book of the trilogy is *The Devil's Children* (1986), in which the siblings are abandoned and homeless; the second book is *Heartsease* (1969). In *The Weathermonger* (1968), Geoffrey controls the weather, but when his power is gone, technology again invades their world.

Robert Heinlein

Robert Heinlein began his writing career in 1939 when his need for money prompted him to answer an ad in a science fiction magazine. He wrote so many short stories for *Astounding Science Fiction* magazine that the editor asked him to use a variety of pseudonyms—so Heinlein wrote as Anson MacDonald, Lyle Monroe, John Riverside, Caleb Saunders, and Simon York. Heinlein created highly believable characters as his way of persuading readers to accept what would otherwise be unbelievable actions. His stories appeal to young people as well as to adults because of their fast-paced plots, clear style, and respectful tone that is never condescending. In fact, some of his stories have been published for both audiences.

Heinlein's stories feature characters who use reason to solve problems and escape ills of the earth and other planets or galaxies. In *Farmer in the Sky* (1950), a family settles on another planet to find better resources for living. *Citizen of the Galaxy* (1957) is about a slave who is rescued by an unusual beggar so that he can help fulfill a mission. In *Rocket Ship Galileo* (1948), a scientist and three teenagers build a rocket ship and set off into outer space. Heinlein won the Hugo Award four times and the Locus Award twice and was the first to win the Nebula Grand Master Award, in 1975. Some of Heinlein's books have become the basis of adaptations in other media. For example, *Space Cadet* (1948) was transformed into a television series in the 1950s, and *Starship Troopers* (1959) became the basis of a board game. Over 40 million copies of Heinlein's books have sold in thirty languages. Robert Heinlein died in 1988.

H. M. Hoover

The topics of Helen Mary Hoover's many books are varied, her vision is original and powerful, and her writing style is impressive. Her first short stories were published by Scholastic and led to her writing novels. In *Orvis* (1987), two children find an outmoded robot with artificial intelligence in a dump and learn to care about it. In *The Delikon* (1977), an alien race has conquered earth, and Varina, a Delikon, has been assigned to teach two youngsters who revolt against the aliens. The twenty-fourth century is the setting of *Away Is a Strange Place to Be* (1990), in which two children are kidnapped to work in space. A theme in many of Hoover's books is the negative aspects of colonization of one society by another.

Monica Hughes

Although she was born in England and lived in Egypt, Monica Hughes is now known as one of Canada's finest writers for children. Hughes's early interest in science fiction was sparked by her mother and father, who taught her about astronomy and science. In addition, she read all of Jules Verne's science fiction books that had been translated into English, then proceeded to read the rest in French.

Hughes began writing after her own children started school. Her settings are always in the not-too-distant future, so they seem logical extensions of contemporary real life. Hughes does not make up the scientific elements of her stories, but always bases them on laws of physics.

Her plots, especially in books such as *The Keeper of the Isis Light* (1981) in her trilogy about a colony on the planet Isis, combine her interest in the emergence of new cultures and the isolation an individual feels in searching for identity. In *The Dream Catcher* (1987), Ruth feels an isolation and a sense of not belonging in the domed city, so she embarks on a dangerous journey with her companions.

Louise Lawrence

Louise Lawrence's grandfather told stories to her as a child and developed in her a sense of storytelling. It was not until adulthood, when she was living in an isolated farmhouse with her young children, that the fear of mental stagnation compelled Lawrence to begin writing. Her first book, *Andra* (1971), is set two thousand years in the future and is about a girl who receives a brain graft from a boy who died in the 1980s.

In *Star Lord* (1978), Erlich crashes on the mountain Mawrrhyn, not unlike the mountains of Wales, and explains to the children he meets that he comes from eleven light years across space. The brother and sister protect him from the military on earth until he escapes. The story reflects on nature and contrasts the values by which people on earth live with those of people in a future world.

In *The Warriors of Taan* (1988), Khian comes to the planet Taan as a warrior but is intrigued with the nonviolent ways of the Stonewraiths. In this book, Lawrence explores the differences between genders with regard to violence and community.

Madeleine L'Engle

In the 1980s, Madeleine L'Engle was among the top six best-selling authors of children's books (*Dictionary of Literary Biography*, 1986), and her popularity continues today. She won the Newbery Medal in 1963 for *A Wrinkle in Time* (1962), in which three children go to the planet of Camazotz to find Meg and Charles Wallace's father. Ironically, the story was rejected by twenty-six publishers before being accepted, yet it continues to be L'Engle's most popular novel. In this first book of a trilogy, L'Engle clearly defines the good and evil forces that help or impede the children's search. *A Wind in the Door* (1973) expands the story: Meg must save Charles Wallace from the evil in the cosmos as well as from the evil within himself. *A Swiftly Tilting Planet* (1978) continues the plot in a fast-moving story involving time shifts and moral dilemmas facing the characters.

In 1981, L'Engle's *A Ring of Endless Light* (1980) was a Newbery Honor Book. It explores issues of death, a common theme in L'Engle's books. It also features members of the Austin family, who were first introduced in *Meet the Austins* (1960). Often characters from one of L'Engle's books appear in others written later.

Madeleine L'Engle says that you can't write science fiction out of your own experience, so you have to search for something deeper than that. She states that her books are about the clash between good and evil on a cosmic level. L'Engle was the runner-up for the 1964 Hans Christian Andersen Award for the body of her work, and she received the 1984 Catholic Library Association's Regina Award for consistent, sustained quality of work.

Andre Norton

Andre Norton is a pseudonym used by Alice Mary Norton. It is actually a combination of two other pseudonyms that Norton has also used: Andrew North and Allen Weston. Norton's use of pseudonyms arose from her conviction that masculine names would give her works credibility with male readers. At the start of her writing career in the 1930s, Norton had to convince publishers—who believed that girls would not read science fiction and that boys would not read about female protagonists in a science fiction story—to accept her work.

Often, Norton's stories are based on English folklore, mythology, or history. For example, in *Outside* (1974), a Pied Piper figure leads children living in an enclosed city where the air has become foul to the outside, where the formerly hazardous air is now free of nuclear fallout. Norton is also known for her inclusion of various ethnic characters. The heroine of *The Beast Master* (1987) is a Navajo. She survives the destruction of the planet and travels to another. Native American culture underpins *The Sioux Spacemen* (1974) as well.

Norton most often writes about interplanetary adventures but is also the author of the *Time Travel* series. In *The Time Traders* (1958), the protagonist,

Ross Murdock, is rescued from going to jail. Instead, he is sent across several periods of time and finds alien spaceships in the Bronze Age.

Author of over a hundred books, Norton was first published at the age of twenty. She was awarded the 1984 Nebula Grand Master Award for lifetime achievement in science fiction.

Pamela Sargent

Pamela Sargent's interest in writing was evident from the time she was a young child. During the elementary grades, she wrote plays for her classmates and told stories to her siblings and campmates; as an adolescent, she wrote autobiographical short stories; in prep school, she contributed to the literary magazine; as a college student, she had her first story published. Once, as a teenager, Sargent received a science fiction book by accident with a paperback book order. From that time, she has been an avid reader of the genre. Sargent has published over forty science fiction short stories and over a dozen novels and is a distinguished anthologist of science fiction by women writers. Her books invariably have good character development, especially of strong female protagonists, and explore complex issues of relationships.

Sargent's first book, *Cloned Lives* (1976), features beings with the capacity for immortality; *The Sudden Star* (1979) tells of survivors of a nuclear holocaust. Her first young adult book, *Earthseed* (1983), explores the subject of evil in a story about genetic engineering. In *Alien Child* (1988), Nita and Sven are raised by guardians in a futuristic society. They discover that they were left as embryos by their parents until a time when earth's inhabitants overcome the violent and destructive side of their nature.

William Sleator

William Sleator comes from a family of scientists, which may have led to his early interest in science. He feels that his hobbies of playing the piano, reading, and writing allow him to explore his interest in expressing his feelings about the supernatural. After spending many years as an accompanist for ballet companies, he turned to full-time writing. Sleator now lives in Thailand and the United States. He likens his life in an exotic foreign country to being on another planet because he has had to learn a new language and a new lifestyle.

Interstellar Pig (1984) begins with characters playing an unusual board game and then reveals that some of the players are aliens. In *Strange Attractors* (1990), Max finds himself having to protect a time travel device from its inventor and his alter ego from another time warp.

CRITERIA FOR SELECTING SCIENCE FICTION

When evaluating science fiction, teachers and parents should keep the following questions in mind:

- Has the author made clear how characters (whether invented species or otherwise) feel about their world and their dilemmas?

- Are there clear plot threads for the reader to follow in the invented world?

- Are there familiar guideposts that serve as jumping-off places from reality to imagination for the reader?

- Does the author allow the reader to feel a sense of delight (even if it is tinged with fear and suspense) that encourages him or her to continue reading about an imaginary place?

AWARDS FOR FANTASY AND SCIENCE FICTION

There are few awards specifically for children's books of fantasy or science fiction, although fantasy and science fiction books qualify for general awards such as the Newbery Medal. There are, however, some general science fiction awards that have categories for juvenile literature. The Hugo Award is named after Hugo Gernsback, the founding editor of *Amazing Stories* magazine and the person who coined the term "science fiction." This award, known officially as the Science Fiction Achievement Award, is given annually for outstanding achievement in the writing of science fiction. Several winners of this award have written science fiction for both adults and children. The Nebula Award is awarded by members of Science Fiction and Fantasy Writers of America. Nebula Awards are given in several categories, one of which is juvenile fiction.

 ## TEACHING IDEAS

Stepping Into and Out of Fantasy Worlds. Have students conduct a literary treasure hunt to identify exactly where in their favorite works of fantasy the author steps out of reality into fantasy and back again. Usually, there is such a place at the beginning and at the end of a story. For example, E. B. White writes on page 16 of *Charlotte's Web* (1952): ". . . and it made Wilbur happy to know that she was sitting there, right outside his pen. But he never had any fun—no walks, no rides, no swims." That seems to be the point at which Wilbur becomes a character and no longer just a pig. In some books, the author steps in and out of the created world a number of times.

Examining Ourselves in Science Fiction. In Nancy Farmer's *The Ear, the Eye and the Arm* (1994), the author is clearly pointing a finger at current ills of society. The same is true of Daniel Pinkwater's *Fat Men from Space* (1977). Have students list familiar aspects of society that the authors of one or both of these books have chosen to parody and exaggerate. Groups of students can discuss three different questions: (1) What aspects of society did the authors choose to exaggerate, and how did they accomplish their purpose? For example, what significance did Pinkwater give to junk food? (2) What is the current reality concerning those aspects of society? For example, have students read about the problems of landfills in or near their community as a way of understanding Farmer's book. (3) How did the authors make readers laugh about serious problems and at the same time help them to understand the problems with a clearer vision?

EXPERIENCES FOR YOUR LEARNING

1. Many books in the fantasy genre have been censored. (See Issue to Consider on page 346.) Read a book that has been censored, and discuss with a classmate or colleague your response to the book. Does the possibility of censorship determine the kinds of books you choose to have in your classroom? The books you have students select for reading and literature discussion? The books you read aloud? Is there a difference in the criteria you use to choose books for these separate activities?

2. In time slip books, the author uses a specific device to move readers from one time into another. Determine what devices are used in books you have read, and discuss how they are different and why each device is appropriate to the particular story in which it is used. For example, why is the door appropriate as the time slip device in Jane Yolen's *The Devil's Arithmetic* (1988)?

3. Read several science fiction books, such as Heinlein's *Citizen of the Galaxy* (1957), Lowry's *The Giver* (1993), L'Engle's *A Wrinkle in Time* (1962), or others in which authors portray controlled societies, the institution of slavery, or victorious evil forces. See if you can identify hints from the authors in the stories that help explain the existence of these negative conditions in the future. Do you think the authors are pessimistic about the future or about the present? What clues from the books support your position?

4. Science fiction centers on concepts of science and positive or negative views of the human future or present. After reading several science fiction titles, such as *Stinker from Space* (1988) by Pamela Service and *The Giver* (1993) by Lois Lowry, think about the developmental stages of childhood described in Chapter 1 in relation to the age levels given for these books. Does the enjoyment of science fiction require the ability to think abstractly? Do particular writers do better than others in creating concrete settings that younger children can understand?

RECOMMENDED BOOKS

* indicates a picture book; **I** indicates interest level (P = preschool, YA = young adult)

Personified Animals

Avi. *Poppy*. Illustrated by Brian Floca. New York: Orchard, 1995. Poppy the deer mouse tries to convince her family to move closer to a large cornfield that could provide plentiful food forever. The frightening king of the forest, a great horned owl named Mr. Ocax, denies them permission to make the move. (**I:** 9–12)

Bond, Michael. *A Bear Called Paddington*. Illustrated by Peggy Fortnum. Boston: Houghton Mifflin, 1960. This is the first of a series of more than twenty books about the adventures of a bear found at Paddington train station and adopted by the Brown family. Other books in the series include *Paddington Helps Out* (1961), *More about Paddington* (1962), *Paddington at Large* (1963), *Paddington Marches On* (1965), *Paddington's Lucky Day* (1974), and *Paddington on Screen* (1982). (**I:** 7–9)

Cleary, Beverly. *The Mouse and the Motorcycle*. Illustrated by Louis Darling. New York: Morrow, 1965. A boy named Keith shows Ralph, a mouse, how to ride a toy motorcycle. Other books in the series include *Runaway Ralph* (1970) and *Ralph S. Mouse* (1982). (**I:** 7–9)

Grahame, Kenneth. *The Wind in the Willows*. 1908. Illustrated by E. H. Shepard. New York: Scribner's, 1933. Rat, Mole, Badger, and Toad of Toad Hall, a group of loyal friends with very distinct personalities, enjoy various adventures in the outdoors. (**I:** 7–11)

* Henkes, Kevin. *Chester's Way*. New York: Greenwillow, 1988. Chester and Wilson are very particular about how things are done, and they never vary from their routines. One day, Lilly moves into the neighborhood and she is full of surprises. (**I:** P–8)

* ———. *Lilly's Purple Plastic Purse*. New York: Greenwillow, 1996. When her teacher catches Lilly playing with her new plastic purple purse and confiscates it, Lilly is devastated. (**I:** P–8)

* ———. *Sheila Rae, the Brave*. New York: Greenwillow, 1987. Sheila Rae is very brave, and quite proud of how brave she is. One day, she gets lost and finds that she is not as brave and fearless as she thought. (**I:** P–8)

Howe, James, and Deborah Howe. *Bunnicula*. Illustrated by Leslie Morrill. New York: Atheneum, 1979. This humorous fantasy is about the belief of two family pets that the newest arrival, a rabbit, is actually a vampire bunny. Other books in the series include *Howliday Inn* (1982), *The Celery Stalks at Midnight* (1983), and *Nighty-Nightmare* (1987). (**I:** 8–10)

* Keller, Holly. *Horace*. New York: Greenwillow, 1991. Horace is a leopard whose dots don't match the stripes of his adoptive tiger family. They constantly reassure him about how much they like his spots and how much they wanted to adopt him when he lost his first family. (**I:** P–8)

King-Smith, Dick. *Ace: The Very Important Pig*. Illustrated by Mary Rayner. New York: Crown, 1988. Ace is a pig who is born with an ace of clubs mark on his thigh and the exceptional ability to understand human speech. (**I:** 9–11)

————. *Babe: The Gallant Pig*. Illustrated by Mary Rayner. New York: Crown, 1985. This story is about a barnyard community and how Babe, a pig, learns to be a champion sheepherder. (I: 8–11)

————. *Martin's Mice*. Illustrated by Jez Alborough. New York: Crown, 1989. Martin the cat keeps Drusilla the mouse as his pet. He helps with her babies and protects them from mice-eating cats. (I: 8–11)

————. *The Mouse Butcher*. Illustrated by Margot Apple. New York: Viking, 1982. A wealthy Persian cat family hires a cat to be their "mouse butcher" but trouble arises when a killer cat arrives on the scene. (I: 9–11)

————. *Pigs Might Fly*. Illustrated by Mary Rayner. New York: Viking, 1982. Daggie, the runt, rescues his fellow pigs by learning to swim during a flash flood. (I: 9–11)

Lawson, Robert. *Ben & Me: A New and Astonishing Life of Benjamin Franklin as Written by His Good Mouse, Amos*. 1939. Boston: Little, Brown, 1988. A mouse named Amos takes credit for the ideas behind most of Benjamin Franklin's inventions and describes various adventures they had together. (I: 9–12)

————. *Rabbit Hill*. New York: Viking, 1944. The animals on Rabbit Hill anxiously await the arrival of the new folks—will they bring traps and guns? (I: 7–10)

* Meddaugh, Susan. *Martha Speaks*. Boston: Houghton Mifflin, 1992. When Martha, the family dog, eats alphabet soup, she is suddenly able to speak and express her thoughts to her family. Other stories about Martha are *Martha Calling* (1994) and *Martha Blah, Blah* (1996). (I: 7–9)

* Potter, Beatrix. *The Tale of Peter Rabbit*. London: Warne, 1902. This is the classic story of a rabbit who finds himself in trouble when sneaking into Mr. McGregor's garden. It is the first of a number of stories about animals. (I: P–7)

Rylant, Cynthia. *Gooseberry Park*. Illustrated by Arthur Howard. San Diego, CA: Harcourt, 1995. A Labrador retriever, a hermit crab, and a bat must work together to come to the aid of their friend, a squirrel, who has become separated from her babies during an ice storm. (I: 7–10)

Selden, George. *The Cricket in Times Square*. Illustrated by Garth Williams. New York: Farrar, 1960. Chester the cricket finds himself transported from the country to the city in a picnic basket. With new friends, he finds a home in a newspaper stand in a subway station below Times Square. Other books in the series include *Tucker's Countryside* (1969), *Chester Cricket's Pigeon Ride* (1981), and *The Old Meadow* (1987). (I: 7–11)

Sharp, Margery. *The Rescuers*. Illustrated by Garth Williams. Boston: Little, Brown, 1959. Miss Bianca and friends go on a dangerous journey to save a poet from imprisonment. Other books in the series include *Miss Bianca* (1962) and *Bernard the Brave*, 1977. (I: 8–11)

Steig, William. *Abel's Island*. New York: Farrar, 1976. A gentrified town mouse named Abel is swept away from his bride, Amanda, in a storm and learns to survive the elements for a year on a deserted island. (I: 8–10)

* ————. *The Amazing Bone*. New York: Farrar, 1976. The amazing bone can talk—and this magical ability saves a piglet from being eaten by a fox. (I: P–7)

* ————. *Doctor De Soto*. New York: Farrar, 1982. A fox visits a mouse dentist with the hope of having the dentist for dinner after his tooth has been fixed. (I: P–8)

* ————. *Sylvester and the Magic Pebble*. New York: Simon & Schuster, 1969. Sylvester, a donkey, comes across a special pebble for his pebble collection—one that grants wishes. The problem arises when Sylvester wishes to turn into a rock temporarily to escape trouble but cannot revert back to being a donkey. (I: P–8)

* Wells, Rosemary. *Max's Breakfast*. New York: Dial, 1985. Ruby tries repeatedly to convince her little brother, Max, to eat his eggs, but he refuses. (I: P)

* ————. *Max's Dragon Shirt*. New York: Dial, 1991. Ruby takes Max on a shopping excursion for new pants, but as usual, Max and Ruby's ideas differ—Max wants a dragon shirt instead. (I: P–7)

White, E. B. *Charlotte's Web*. Illustrated by Garth Williams. New York: Harper & Row, 1952. A runt pig named Wilbur is saved by Fern, who wants to show him at the fair. Meanwhile, Charlotte the spider enlists the barnyard animals in a campaign to keep Wilbur alive. (I: 7–11)

————. *Stuart Little*. Illustrated by Garth Williams. New York: Harper & Row, 1945. An otherwise normal family has an abnormal experience—their second son is a mouse. This book describes the humorous adventures of the son, Stuart. (I: 8–11)

————. *The Trumpet of the Swan*. Illustrated by Edward Frascino. New York: Harper & Row, 1970. Louis is a mute swan. Unable to trumpet, he is unable to attract the attention of Serena. (I: 9–11)

Personified Toys

Collodi, Carlo. *The Adventures of Pinocchio*. 1881 Translated by M. L. Rosenthal. Illustrated by Troy Howell. New York: Lothrop, Lee & Shepard, 1983. This classic story is about a wooden puppet named

Pinocchio whose creator is lonely and longs for company. When Pinocchio comes alive, his naiveté lands him in an adventure that forces him to learn about truthfulness. The story has been published in many other editions. (I: 9–12)

* Conrad, Pam. *The Tub Grandfather.* Illustrated by Richard Egielski. New York: HarperCollins, 1993. Tub Child finds Tub Grandfather covered in dust under a radiator, where he has been lost for a long time. (I: P–8)

* ———. *The Tub People.* Illustrated by Richard Egielski. New York: HarperCollins, 1989. The wooden tub toy family stays lined up at the edge of the bathtub every day except at bathtime. One day, Tub Child disappears down the drain. (I: P–8)

Godden, Rumer. *The Doll's House.* 1947. Illustrated by Tasha Tudor. New York: Penguin, 1976. The arrival of a new doll upsets the resident dolls of a Victorian dollhouse. (I: 7–10)

———. *Four Dolls.* Illustrated by Pauline Baynes. New York: Greenwillow, 1984. These four stories about four spirited dolls and their owners were originally published as separate books: *Impunity Jane* (1954), *The Fairy Doll* (1956), *The Story of Holly and Ivy* (1958), and *Candy Floss* (1960). (I: 8–10)

Hoffmann, E. T. A. *The Nutcracker.* 1816. Illustrated by Maurice Sendak. New York: Crown, 1984. Clara dreams on Christmas Eve that her toy nutcracker comes to life and takes her to a magical world filled with music and dancing flowers and candy. The story has been published in other editions with various illustrators. (I: 8–11)

Kennedy, Richard. *Amy's Eyes.* Illustrated by Richard Egielski. New York: Harper & Row, 1985. Amy is an orphan who loves her sailor doll. When Captain comes to life, he runs away from the Home for Girls and promises to return for Amy as soon as he has made his fortune. (I: 11–YA)

Milne, A. A. *Winnie-the-Pooh.* Illustrated by Ernest H. Shepard. New York: Dutton, 1926. Christopher Robin and his friends Winnie-the-Pooh, Eeyore, Piglet, Owl, Tigger, Kanga, and Roo share many adventures in the Hundred Acre Woods. A sequel is *The House at Pooh Corner* (1928). (I: P–10)

Williams, Margery. *The Velveteen Rabbit.* 1922. Illustrated by Michael Hague. New York: Holt, 1983. A well-loved toy rabbit is discarded but then transformed into a real rabbit. Several other editions have been published with various illustrators. (I: 6–9)

Winthrop, Elizabeth. *The Castle in the Attic.* Illustrated by Donna Green. New York: Holiday House, 1985. William receives a wooden model of a castle and discovers that the silver knight comes alive in his hands.

Sir Simon leads William on an adventure in which they battle a fiery dragon and an evil wizard. The sequel is *The Battle for the Castle* (1993). (I: 9–11)

Outlandish Characters and Humorous Situations

Babbitt, Natalie. *The Devil's Storybook.* New York: Farrar, 1974. This is a collection of short stories about the devil's attempts to recruit more members to his world. A sequel is *The Devil's Other Storybook* (1987). (I: 9–12)

———. *The Search for Delicious.* New York: Farrar, 1969. Twelve-year-old Gaylen is sent out to seek the true meaning of the word "delicious" when there is disagreement among members of the court. What he discovers is a secret plot for the queen's brother to take over the kingdom. (I: 8–11)

Dahl, Roald. *Matilda.* Illustrated by Quentin Blake. New York: Viking, 1988. Matilda uses her intellectual genius and psychic abilities to bestow a childlike interpretation of justice on the good and the bad. (I: 9–11)

Le Guin, Ursula K. *Catwings.* Illustrated by S. D. Schindler. Danbury, CT: Franklin Watts, 1988. Mrs. Jane Tabby is pleased that her kittens have wings, for they can escape the dangers of the city—only to meet with the dangers of the woods. Sequels are *Catwings Return* (1989) and *Wonderful Alexander and the Catwings* (1994) (I: 7–10)

Lindgren, Astrid. *Pippi Longstocking.* 1945. Illustrated by Louis S. Glanzman. New York: Viking, 1950. Pippi Longstocking lives without adult supervision in a town in Sweden. She leads an outrageous lifestyle and keeps the neighborhood children entertained. A sequel is *Pippi in the South Seas* (1959) (I: 7–11)

Travers, Pamela L. *Mary Poppins.* 1934. Illustrated by Mary Shepard. New York: Harcourt, 1962. Mary Poppins arrives with the East Wind to care for the Banks children. The nanny's unusual ways surprise and delight the children. Other books in the series include *Mary Poppins Comes Back* (1935) and *Mary Poppins in Cherry Tree Lane* (1982). (I: 7–11)

Magical Powers

Babbitt, Natalie. *Tuck Everlasting.* New York: Farrar, 1975. Winnie discovers that the Tuck family drank from a spring that has given them eternal life. When the Tucks reveal their feelings about having eternal life, an enterprising man overhears the secret and attempts to capitalize on it by selling the water. (I: 8–12)

Barrie, Sir James Matthew. *Peter Pan.* 1911. Peter Pan teaches three children how to fly to Never Never

Land where they will never have to grow up, but a fairy intervenes and leads them astray to danger on Captain Hook's pirate ship. The story has been published in many editions. (I: 8–12)

Brittain, Bill. *The Wish Giver: Three Tales of Coventry.* Illustrated by Andrew Glass. New York: Harper & Row, 1983. A stranger appears, granting the wishes of a few children who are surprised at the result. Related titles are *The Devil's Donkey* (1981) and *Dr. Dredd's Wagon of Wonders* (1987). (I: 9–12)

Coville, Bruce. *Jennifer Murdley's Toad.* Illustrated by Gary A. Lippincott. San Diego, CA: Harcourt, 1992. When Jennifer buys a mysterious toad, Bufo, at a discount store, she finds that it leads her into many adventures. (I: 8–10)

———. *Jeremy Thatcher, Dragon Hatcher.* San Diego, CA: Harcourt, 1991. Jeremy stumbles upon Mr. Eilve's Magic Shop, which mysteriously appears. A beautiful ball from the store turns out to be a dragon's egg, and many adventures follow as the dragon grows larger and larger. (I: 9–12)

Duncan, Lois. *Gift of Magic.* Illustrated by Arvis Stewart. Boston: Little, Brown, 1971. Grandmother has ESP, and she predicts the gifts that her grandchildren will have: Kirby's is dance, Nancy's is magic, and Brendon's is music. (I: 10–12)

Jones, Diana Wynne. *Aunt Maria.* Greenwillow, 1991. Aunt Marie Mig and Chris discover that their poor old great-aunt possesses unnatural powers. (I: 11–YA)

———. *A Charmed Life.* New York: Greenwillow, 1977. Witchcraft enables Gwen to trade places with a twentieth-century girl in this time travel story. This is the first volume in a series about a young boy magician who is manipulated by his sister. The prequel is *The Lives of Christopher Chant* (1988), about a Chrestomanci-in-training who will become the next controller of magic. The other titles in the *Chrestomanci* series are *The Magicians of Caprona* (1980), in which the children of two feuding families make magical peace, and *Witch Week* (1982), which takes place in a school where the teacher suspects someone in class is a witch. Short stories about Chrestomanci are found in *Warlock at the Wheel* (1985) and *Dragons and Dreams* (Harper, 1986). (I: 11–YA)

———. *Stopping for a Spell: Three Fantasies.* Illustrated by Joseph A. Smith. New York: Greenwillow, 1993. Unusual visitors is the theme of three humorous short stories. In one, an Auntie turns up with a conjurer's kit; in another, a little girl gets turned into a teddy bear when four Grannies come to babysit; and in a third story, pieces of furniture work together to get rid of an unwelcome visitor who has offended them. (I: 8–11)

McGowen, Tom. *The Magician's Apprentice.* New York: Lodestar, 1987. The magician's apprentice is a street urchin chosen by the magician for his courage and intelligence. Together with some talking animal friends, they manage to overcome danger and separation to get to the Wild Lands, where the secrets of magic reside. Other books in the trilogy are *The Magician's Company* (1988) and *The Magician's Challenge* (1989). (I: 10–13)

* Mendez, Phil. *The Black Snowman.* Illustrated by Carole Byard. New York: Scholastic, 1989. Jacob must overcome his anger about being poor and black. A black snowman uses the magical power of an old Ashanti kente cloth to show Jacob why he should be proud of his heritage. (I: 6–9)

Napoli, Donna Jo. *Jimmy, the Pickpocket of the Palace.* Illustrated by Judith Byron Schachner. New York: Dutton, 1995. When a princess kisses a frog with a hurt leg, he turns into a human boy. In order to revert back into a frog, he must somehow obtain a ring that does not belong to him. A related title is *Prince of the Pond* (1992). (I: 9–12)

Pinkwater, D. Manus. *Lizard Music.* New York: Dodd, Mead, 1976. Victor finds a mysterious band of lizards playing amazing music late at night on television. The Chicken Man and his hen guide Victor to an invisible island to meet the lizards. (I: 9–12)

* Ringgold, Faith. *Aunt Harriet's Underground Railroad in the Sky.* New York: Crown, 1992. When flying around one day, Cassie and her brother Be Be find a train in the sky. The woman conductor is Harriet Tubman, and she leads Cassie on the Underground Railroad so that Cassie will never forget the experiences of her ancestors. (I: 6–9)

* ———. *Dinner at Aunt Connie's House.* New York: Hyperion, 1993. While playing hide-and-go-seek at Aunt Connie's house, Melody and Lonnie find a dozen portraits of African American women. The paintings speak and tell the women's historically significant stories. (I: 7–10)

* Van Allsburg, Chris. *Jumanji.* Boston: Houghton Mifflin, 1981. Peter and Judy begin the jungle adventure board game of Jumanji, only to find that with each play, real parts of the jungle appear—monkeys tear up the kitchen, rhinos stampede through the house, and a monsoon begins in the living room. (I: 6–10)

Wrede, Patricia C. *Dealing with Dragons.* New York: Scholastic, 1990. Princess Cimorene, bored with palace life, becomes a warrior in a fight with wizards. Other books in the *Enchanted Forest Chronicles* series are *Searching for Dragons* (1991), *Calling on Dragons* (1992), and *Talking to Dragons* (1993). (I: 12–YA)

Yep, Laurence. *Dragon of the Lost Sea*. New York: HarperCollins, 1982. Shimmer is a dragon princess on a quest to find the lost sea that is her home. Although she dismisses the human Thorn as unable to help, she realizes that, being homeless, they have common bonds. Related titles are *Dragon Steel* (1985) and *Dragon Cauldron* (1991). (I: 12–YA)

Extraordinary Worlds

Baum, L. Frank. *The Wonderful Wizard of Oz*. 1900. Illustrated by Michael Hague. New York: Holt, 1982. Dorothy is transported from her home in Kansas to the Land of Oz by way of a tornado. In her search for a way home, she meets a tin man who wants a heart, a lion who wants courage, and a scarecrow who wants a brain. To get their wishes, they must kill the Wicked Witch of the West. There are many other editions with various illustrators, as well as forty-seven sequels, of which Baum wrote the first thirteen. (I: 9–12)

Carroll, Lewis. *Alice's Adventures in Wonderland*. 1865. Alice follows a rabbit down a rabbit hole and finds herself in an extraordinary world. Many different editions with various illustrators are available. (I: 10–YA)

———. *Through the Looking Glass and What Alice Found There*. 1899. When Alice steps through a mirror, she finds herself in a backwards world. Many different editions with various illustrators are available. (I: 11–YA)

Dahl, Roald. *Charlie and the Chocolate Factory*. Illustrated by John Schindelman. New York: Knopf, 1964. Charlie is one of five lucky winners who find a golden ticket that allows them to tour Willy Wonka's mysterious chocolate factory. Inside the factory are imaginative processes for creating Wonka chocolate. (I: 8–10)

———. *James and the Giant Peach*. 1961. New York: Knopf, 1996. James's unhappy life takes a turn when the magical contents of a bag makes a peach grow large enough to enter and garden insects grow large enough to be his friends. (I: 7–11)

Juster, Norton. *The Phantom Tollbooth*. Illustrated by Jules Feiffer. New York: Random House, 1961. Milo thinks that learning is a waste of time and there's never anything to do. Entering a tollbooth, he finds himself in the Kingdom of Wisdom where he learns to jump to Conclusions and seek Rhyme and Reason; Tock teaches Milo not to waste time. (I: 9–11)

Norton, Mary. *The Borrowers*. Illustrated by Beth and Joe Krush. New York: Harcourt, 1953. Pod, Homily, and Arietty Clock are a family of little people who borrow everyday items from a human family and use them in ways that suit people their size. When

Arietty befriends a human boy, the family fears for their safety. There are several more books in the series: *The Borrowers Afield* (1955), *The Borrowers Afloat* (1959), *The Borrowers Aloft* (1961), *Poor Stainless* (1971), and *The Borrowers Avenged* (1982). (I: 8–11)

Supernatural Elements

Belden, Wilanne Schneider. *Mind-Hold*. San Diego: Harcourt, 1987. Carson and his sister, who has ESP, seek new friends in a desert as they try to survive following an earthquake. (I: 11–13)

Bellairs, John. *The House with a Clock in Its Walls*. Illustrated by Edward Gorey. New York: Dial, 1973. Lewis's uncle has magical abilities that Lewis tries to imitate, but when he does, he unexpectedly creates a wicked ghost. The sequels are *The Figure in the Shadows* (1975) and *The Letter, the Witch and the Ring* (1977). (I: 10–12)

Cameron, Eleanor. *The Court of the Stone Children*. New York: Dutton, 1973. The ghost of a French girl from the nineteenth century appears to a contemporary girl. The ghost's father was executed for treason and now she wants Nina to help prove his innocence. (I: 10–12)

Conrad, Pam. *Stonewords: A Ghost Story*. New York: HarperCollins, 1990. Zoe is visited by the ghost of Zoe Louise, a person from the past. When Zoe realizes that she must prevent Zoe Louise's untimely death, she goes back in time to the 1850s. (I: 10–12)

Hahn, Mary Downing. *Wait Till Helen Comes*. New York: Clarion, 1986. Helen is a ghost from the nineteenth century who is trying to convince another child to drown in the same lake she did so that they can be playmates. (I: 8–12)

Jacques, Brian. *Seven Strange & Ghostly Tales*. New York: Putnam, 1991. This is a collection of seven scary stories that include humorous as well as frightening elements. (I: 9–12)

Lively, Penelope. *The Ghost of Thomas Kempe*. Illustrated by Antony Maitland. New York: Dutton, 1973. James and his family move into an old house in an English village. When the resident ghost begins to act out, James gets blamed. (I: 10–12)

Mahy, Margaret. *The Changeover*. New York: Atheneum, 1984. A girl's supernatural abilities save her brother. (I: 10–13)

———. *The Haunting*. New York: Macmillan, 1982. Barry, an eight-year-old, begins receiving mental messages from an uncle who was presumed dead. (I: 10–12)

Peck, Richard. *The Ghost Belonged to Me*. New York: Viking, 1975. Richard tries to solve the mystery of a missing girl and ends up unwillingly receiving the assistance of Blossom Culp, his nemesis. Sequels are *Ghosts I Have Been* (1977) and *The Dreadful Future of Blossom Culp* (1983). (I: 10–YA)

Walsh, Jill Paton. *Birdy and the Ghosties*. Illustrated by Alan Marks. New York: Farrar, 1989. Birdy is able to see ghosties although her father, who is being pestered by them, cannot. (I: 6–9)

Wright, Betty Ren. *Christina's Ghost*. New York: Holiday House, 1985. When Christina finds that she must spend the summer with Uncle Ralph in his old Victorian house, she is unhappy about it. When she discovers that there is a ghost in the house, she is even more distraught. (I: 9–12)

———. *The Dollhouse Murders*. New York: Holiday, 1983. The dolls in a dollhouse come to life and try to help resolve the mysteries of murders that happened long ago. (I: 9–12)

Yep, Laurence. *The Ghost Fox*. Illustrated by Jean and Mou-sien Tseng. New York: Scholastic, 1994. While Little Lee's father is away at sea, Little Lee is responsible for taking care of his mother, including getting rid of the ghost that is trying to take over her soul. This is an adaptation of a story taken from the ancient Chinese tradition of ghost storytelling. (I: 7–10)

Time Slips

Barron, T. A. *The Ancient One*. New York: Philomel, 1992. Thirteen-year-old Kate goes with her grandfather's sister, Aunt Kate, to protest the cutting of redwood trees in Oregon. Kate falls into a time tunnel that takes her back five centuries when the trees were young but still threatened by human greed. (I: 12–YA)

Boston, L. M. *The Children of Green Knowe*. Illustrated by Peter Boston. New York: Harcourt, 1989. A lonely boy moves to an old English house, only to find that various children who played in the house over the years reappear to be his playmates. There are several sequels: *The Treasure of Green Knowe* (1989), *A Stranger at Green Knowe* (1989), *An Enemy at Green Knowe* (1989), and *The River at Green Knowe* (1989). (I: 9–11)

Dexter, Catherine. *Mazemaker*. New York: Morrow, 1989. Winnie enters a maze and finds herself in the nineteenth century. She must solve the mystery of the maze in order to return to her own time. (I: 10–12)

Fleischman, Sid. *The 13th Floor: A Ghost Story*. Illustrated by Peter Sis. New York: Greenwillow, 1995. Buddy Stebbins steps off an elevator on the thirteenth floor of an old building and follows his sister three hundred years back in time. They end up on a pirate ship captained by one of their own ancestors. (I: 9–12)

Hurmence, Belinda. *A Girl Called Boy*. Boston: Houghton Mifflin, 1982. Blanche goes back in time to 1853 in North Carolina and experiences slavery when she becomes one of her ancestors. (I: 10–12)

Lunn, Janet. *The Root Cellar*. New York: Scribner's, 1983. Rose goes to live with her relatives when she is orphaned. While hiding in a root cellar, she is transported back to 1860 and helps a young woman seek out her loved one who is missing as a result of the Civil War. (I: 10–12)

Park, Ruth. *Playing Beatie Bow*. New York: Atheneum, 1982. A contemporary Australian girl finds that she has traveled back in time to the nineteenth century. (I: 10–12)

Pearce, Philippa. *Tom's Midnight Garden*. Illustrated by Susan Einzig. New York: Harper, 1984. Tom is bored with his summer until he finds that he can visit a garden that appears only when the grandfather clock strikes thirteen every night. There he develops a special friendship with a mysterious girl named Hatty. (I: 10–12)

Pearson, Kit. *A Handful of Time*. New York: Viking, 1988. A twelve-year-old finds a watch under the floor while visiting her cousins one unhappy summer. The watch takes her back to the time her mother was the same age and allows her to gain insights about her mother. (I: 11–13)

Scieszka, Jon. *Knights of the Kitchen Table*. Illustrated by Lane Smith. New York: Viking, 1991. Joe, Fred, and Sam, the Time Warp Trio, travel back to the days of King Arthur when they open "The Book" that a magician uncle sent Joe for a birthday present. Other Time Warp stories include *The Not-So-Jolly Roger* (1991), *The Good, the Bad, and the Goofy* (1992), *Your Mother Was a Neanderthal* (1993), *2095* (1995), and *Tut, Tut* (1996). (I: 8–11)

Voigt, Cynthia. *Building Blocks*. New York: Atheneum, 1984. A boy's journey back into the time of his father's childhood helps him to understand his father better. (I: 9–11)

Wiseman, David. *Jeremy Visick*. Boston: Houghton Mifflin, 1981. A contemporary Cornish boy goes back in time to try to discover the location of a boy named Jeremy who was lost in a mine accident in 1852. (I: 10–12)

———. *Thimbles*. Boston: Houghton Mifflin, 1982. Two thimbles found in an old family trunk prove important as Cathy goes back to the year 1819. She alternately becomes two girls who are involved in a dangerous right-to-vote demonstration. (I: 10–12)

Yolen, Jane. *The Devil's Arithmetic*. New York: Viking, 1988. Hannah finds herself transported as Chaya back to the days of the Holocaust. (I: 9–12)

High Fantasy

Alexander, Lloyd. *The Arkadians*. New York: Dutton, 1995. An unlikely group of unusual creatures travel together. (I: 11–13)

———. *The Book of Three*. New York: Holt, 1964. The Chronicles of Prydain tell of the struggle between the people of Prydain and the Lord of the Land of Death. Other books in the series are *The Black Cauldron* (1965), *The Castle of Llyr* (1966), *Taran Wanderer* (1967), and *The High King* (1968). (I: 10–13)

———. *The Remarkable Journey of Prince Jen*. New York: Dutton, 1991. In this coming-of-age story, brave Prince Jen embarks on a dangerous journey, bearing six unusual gifts. (I: 10–13)

Barron, T. A. *The Lost Years of Merlin*. New York: Philomel, 1996. Merlin as a young boy searches for his identity. He has lost his memory and doesn't trust that the woman he is with is really his mother. His journey to discover his past introduces the reader to how Merlin gained magical sight and became a wizard. (I: 11–YA)

———. *The Merlin Effect*. New York: Philomel, 1994. Kate joins her father on a scientific expedition off the coast of Baja, California. At dusk Kate takes a kayak out too far and finds her forbidden expedition leads to an encounter with a whale and the discovery of forgotten legends involving Merlin. (I: 11–YA)

Chetwin, Grace. *Gom on Windy Mountain*. New York: Lothrop, Lee & Shepard, 1986. Gom's mother leaves him a rune with magical powers when his father, Stig, sends his strange wife away. Chetwin's saga, Tales of Gom in the Legends of Ulm, includes *The Riddle and the Rune* (1987), *The Crystal Stair* (Bradbury, 1988), and *The Starstone* (1989). (I: 10–YA)

———. *Jason's Seven Magical Night Rides*. New York: Bradbury, 1994. A mysterious stranger offers Jason rides on mythical horses, including Pegasus, Chiron the Centaur, and the Trojan Horse, and helps Jason overcome feelings of inadequacy and become whole by accepting responsibility for himself. (I: 11–YA)

Cooper, Susan. *Over Sea, Under Stone*. Illustrated by Alan E. Cover. New York: Atheneum, 1965. A search for King Arthur's grail begins this story of fighting evil and protecting Light. The series continues in *The Dark Is Rising* (1973), *Greenwitch* (1974), *The Grey King* (1975), and *Silver on the Tree* (1977). (I: 10–13)

Jacques, Brian. *Redwall*. New York: Philomel, 1987. Rats and other field animals living at Redwall Abbey engage in a classic quest fantasy. The series includes *Mossflower* (1988), *Mattimeo* (1990), *Mariel of Redwall* (1991), *Salamandastron* (1993), *Martin the Warrior* (1994), *The Bellmaker* (1994), and *Outcast of Redwall* (1996). (I: 11–13)

Jones, Diana Wynne. *The Crown of Dalemark*. New York: Greenwillow, 1993. This final book in a quartet about the mythical kingdom of Dalemark continues the story of Mitt, who is joined by Moril and Maewen in their quest to reunite Dalemark with Adon's gifts—the ring, the sword, and the cup. Earlier books in the quartet are *Cart and Cwidder* (1977), *Drowned Ammet* (1978), and *The Spellcoats* (1979). (I: 12–YA)

———. *Dogsbody*. New York: Morrow, 1988. Sirius, the Dog Star, is reborn on earth as a puppy and fulfills a mission to find the murder weapon of the stars. (I: YA)

Le Guin, Ursula K. *A Wizard of Earthsea*. Illustrated by Ruth Robbins. Hyannis, MA: Parnassus, 1968. This first book in a series describes how Ged studies wizardry, becomes a wizard, and confronts evil. Other books in the series are *Tombs of Atuan* (Atheneum, 1971/1985), *The Farthest Shore* (Atheneum, 1972/1985), and *Tehanu: The Last Book of Earthsea* (Atheneum, 1990). (I: 13–YA)

Lewis, C. S. *The Lion, the Witch and the Wardrobe*. Illustrated by Pauline Baynes. New York: Macmillan, 1950. Four children discover that they can go through the back of a wardrobe to enter the magical world of Narnia. There, they meet the lion Aslan, who is trying to free Narnia of the evil spell cast by the White Witch. The Narnia stories continue in *Prince Caspian, the Return to Narnia* (1951), *The Voyage of the Dawn Treader* (1952), *The Silver Chair* (1953), *The Horse and His Boy* (1954), *The Magician's Nephew* (1955), and *The Last Battle* (1956). (I: 9–13)

McKinley, Robin. *The Blue Sword*. New York: Greenwillow, 1982. Princess Aerin's mysterious powers help her slay dragons as she fights to save her kingdom. The prequel is *The Hero and the Crown* (1984). (I: 12–YA)

Pierce, Meredith Ann. *Dark Moon*. Boston: Joy Street, 1992. Book 2 of the *Firebringer* trilogy. The protagonist, Jan, is prince of the unicorns and he journeys to obtain fire from two-footed creatures to save the unicorns from enemies. Book 1 is *Birth of the Firebringer* (1985). Book 3 is *The Son of Summer Stars* (Little, Brown, 1996). (I: 13–YA)

———. *The Darkangel*, Boston: Little, Brown, 1982. This is the first book in Pierce's *Darkangel* trilogy. Other titles are *A Gathering of Gargoyles* (1984) and *The Pearl of the Soul of the World* (1990). (I: 13–YA)

Pierce, Tamora. *Wild Magic*. New York: Atheneum, 1992. This is the first book in a series called *The*

Immortals. Thirteen-year-old Daine faces battle with dreadful immortal creatures. (**I:** 12–YA)

Pullman, Philip. *The Golden Compass.* New York: Knopf, 1996. In this first book of a trilogy, Lyra realizes that she must find a way to prevent kidnapped children from being victimized as scientific experiments. (**I:** 11–YA)

Shetterly, Wil. *Elsewhere.* San Diego: Harcourt, 1991. A runaway teenager finds himself in Bordertown, a magic world peopled by punk elves. The sequel is *Nevernever* (1993). (**I:** 13–YA)

Smith, Sherwood. *Wren to the Rescue.* San Diego: Harcourt, 1990. Wren rescues a Princess from a wicked king in this second book about Wren. Other books in the series are *Wren's Quest* (1993) and *Wren's War* (1995). (**I:** 13–YA)

Sutcliff, Rosemary. *The Sword and the Circle: King Arthur and the Knights of the Round Table.* New York: Dutton, 1981. These stories about King Arthur, Merlin, and Sir Lancelot are mostly drawn from *Le Morte d'Arthur* by Sir Thomas Malory (1485). Sutcliff's rendition of The Arthurian trilogy continues with *The Light beyond the Forest: The Quest for the Holy Grail* (1980) and *The Road to Camlann* (1982). (**I:** 11–YA)

Tolkien, J. R. R. *The Fellowship of the Ring.* 1955. Boston: Houghton Mifflin, 1967. This is the first part of the *Lord of the Rings* trilogy in which Frodo Baggins inherits a magic ring from his Uncle Bilbo (hero of *The Hobbit)* and must eventually take the ring to Mount Doom where it will be destroyed in order to help the good force win against the Dark Lord. Other volumes in the trilogy are *The Two Towers* (1967) and *The Return of the King* (1967). (**I:** 12–YA)

Tolkien, J. R. R. *The Hobbit.* Boston: Houghton Mifflin, 1937. Bilbo Baggins, a peaceful Hobbit, is tricked by a wizard into going on a dangerous quest to retrieve stolen dwarf treasure from a dragon. The story of Middle Earth continues in the *Lord of the Rings* trilogy. (**I:** 11–YA)

Yolen, Jane. *Merlin and the Dragons.* Illustrated by Li Ming. New York: Cobblehill/Dutton, 1995. Young King Arthur has troublesome dreams and visits Merlin, where he hears stories of Merlin's childhood. Upon hearing tales of dragons, King Vortigern, and Uther Pendragon, Arthur is reassured of his right to the crown. (**I:** 8–11)

Projecting Scientific Principles

Ames, Mildred. *Anna to the Infinite Power.* New York: Macmillan, 1981. A twelve-year-old discovers that she is a clone. (**I:** 11–13)

Cross, Gillian. *New World.* New York: Holiday House, 1994. Gillian and Stuart agree to test out a new top secret virtual reality computer game. The frightening experience turns out to be more than they expected. (**I:** YA)

Dickinson, Peter. *Eva.* New York: Delacorte, 1989. Following an accident, a young girl's body is destroyed but her brain survives and is transplanted into a chimpanzee's body. (**I:** 12–YA)

Heinlein, Robert. *Red Planet.* New York: Ballantine, 1981. A robot helps earthlings as they make their first exploration on Mars. (**I:** 12–YA)

———. *Rocket Ship Galileo.* New York: Macmillan, 1948. Mystery surrounds efforts to build the first rocket ship. (**I:** 12–YA)

Verne, Jules. *Twenty Thousand Leagues under the Sea.* New York: Washington Square Press, 1976. An eccentric captain successfully makes an electric submarine. (**I:** YA)

Utopian and Dystopian Societies

Auer, Martin. *The Blue Boy.* Illustrated by Simone Klages. New York: Macmillan, 1992. A boy leaves the earth to find a planet safe from violent weapons. (**I:** 8–11)

Christopher, John. *When the Tripods Came.* New York: Dutton, 1988. The Tripods arrive on earth and brainwash earthlings with hypnotic caps. The *White Mountains* series continues in *The White Mountains* (Macmillan, 1967), *The City of Gold and Lead* (1967), and *The Pool of Fire* (1968). (**I:** 10–13)

———. *Wild Jack.* New York: Macmillan. 1991. In London in the twenty-third century, after being ostracized from society, Clive meets up with a Robin Hood–like character named Wild Jack. (**I:** 10–13)

Farmer, Nancy. *The Ear, the Eye and the Arm.* New York: Orchard, 1994. In Zimbabwe in the year 2194, three mutants—the Ear, the Eye, the Arm—form a detective agency and are hired to find the kidnapped children of General Matsika. (**I:** 11–YA)

Heinlein, Robert. *Citizen of the Galaxy.* New York: Macmillan, 1957. A young boy is able to leave slavery in order to fulfill a mission and learns there is more to the galaxy than he knew. (**I:** 11–13)

Hoover, H. M. *Away Is a Strange Place to Be.* New York: Dutton, 1990. Kidnapped from earth in 2349 to serve as a worker on a construction project, Abby plans her escape. (**I:** 11–13)

———. *The Delikon.* New York: Penguin, 1977. The Delikon is an alien race whose control of the earth is destroyed by two children and their teacher. (I: 12–YA)

———. *Only Child.* New York: Dutton, 1992. A young member of a colonizing group, Cody, works to save intelligent insect-like creatures whose lives are threatened by the settlers. (I: 10–13)

———. *Orvis.* New York: Viking, 1987. An outdated robot named Orvis, found in a dump, accompanies twelve-year-old Toby as she runs away from home. (I: 11–13)

Hughes, Monica. *The Dream Catcher.* New York: Macmillan, 1987. Ruth does not fit into life in her domed city and decides to leave on a dangerous journey along with her companions. A related title is *Devil on My Back* (1985). (I: 10–YA)

———. *Invitation to the Game.* New York: Simon & Schuster, 1990. Recent high school graduates, unemployed in an overpopulated world, find themselves playing a mysterious game of survival in a different world. (I: 11–YA)

———. *The Keeper of the Isis Light.* New York: Macmillan, 1981. Olwen lives with a robot on a barren planet until another human lands. (I: 12–YA)

Lowry, Lois. *The Giver.* Boston: Houghton Mifflin, 1993. Knowledge is controlled in a futuristic society and Jonah must grapple with the right to make choices when he begins to receive memories. (I: 11–YA)

Norton, Andre. *The Beast Master.* New York: Ballantine, 1987. A Navajo, Hosteem Storm, survives the destruction of her planet and is able to settle on the planet of Arzor. (I: 12–YA)

———. *Outside.* New York: Avon, 1974. When the air in the protected city turns foul, a Pied Piper figure leads the children to the outside where the air, previously contaminated by nuclear fallout, has regenerated. (I: 11–13)

———. *The Sioux Spacemen.* Boston: Gregg, 1978. Kade Whitehawk is a descendent of Sioux warriors and is able to use his knowledge to defend himself and others. (I: 12–YA)

Surviving Environmental Catastrophes

Hesse, Karen. *Phoenix Rising.* New York: Holt, 1994. An accident at a nuclear power plant changes Nyle's life on a Vermont sheep farm as she and others in her family and community attempt to survive the effects of the fallout. (I: 12–YA)

Hughes, Monica. *The Crystal Drop.* New York: Silver Burdett Ginn, 1992. Megan and her younger brother have a harrowing journey to find a semblance of life as it was before a drought. (I: 12–YA)

Karl, Jean. *Strange Tomorrow.* New York: Dell, 1985. This book includes two stories about survival: one about survival on earth when all living things are destroyed, and the other about rebuilding a society that has been destroyed. A related title is *The Turning Place* (1976). (I: 10–13)

Lawrence, Louise. *Children of the Dust.* New York: Harper, 1985. Earth is devastated by a nuclear war, and a small group of people in England struggle to survive through three generations in a new world where children are born with mutations. (I: 12–YA)

Macdonald, Caroline. *The Lake at the End of the World.* New York: Dial, 1989. When a boy climbs out of a cave, Diana realizes that someone other than her family has survived the environmental holocaust. (I: 12–YA)

O'Brien, Robert. *Z for Zachariah.* New York: Atheneum, 1975. Ann Burden believes that she is the only person left after a nuclear holocaust, until Mr. Loomis arrives. (I: 12–YA)

Strieber, Whitley. *Wolf of Shadows.* New York: Knopf, 1985. After a nuclear holocaust, a wolf and a woman find a mysterious bond that brings them closer to the spirits of the destroyed earth. (I: 12–YA)

Swinells, Robert. *Brother in the Land.* New York: Holiday House, 1985. England is hit by nuclear war, and Danny and his brother fight for survival in the aftermath. (I: 12–YA)

Walsh, Jill Paton. *The Green Book.* Illustrated by Lloyd Bloom. New York: Farrar, 1982. A group of colonists try to grow food on a hostile new planet called Shine, when the dying planet of earth can no longer sustain life. (I: 9–12)

Science Fantasies

Alcock, Vivien. *The Monster Garden.* New York: Delacorte, 1988. Frankie plays with her father's genetic experiments and creates a monster. (I: 9–12)

Asimov, Janet, and Isaac Asimov. *Norby and the Court Jester.* New York: Walker, 1991. Jeff and robot Norby travel to planet Izz. (I: 10–13)

———. *Norby and the Invaders.* New York: Walker, 1985. Norby is a robot who helps solve a mystery on earth. (I: 10–13)

———. *Norby and the Oldest Dragon.* New York: Walker, 1990. Jeff faces a mysterious phenomonon on planet Jamyn. (I: 10–13)

Barron, T. A. *Heartlight.* New York: Philomel, 1990. Kate travels to a distant star in search of her astrophysicist grandfather who has disappeared after inventing the means of traveling faster than light. His mission is to save the sun from extinction;

Kate's mission is to save her grandfather from evil forces that have captured him. (I: 12–YA)

Bechard, Margaret. *Star Hatchling*. New York: Viking, 1995. Shem witnesses the arrival of a "star" on his planet, and views the "hatchling" with fear. He does not know that this is a human girl who has been separated from her family. (I: 8–12)

Chetwin, Grace. *On All Hallows' Eve*. New York: Macmillan, 1992. Characters are transported to a different world on the eve of Halloween. (I: 9–11)

Coville, Bruce. *Aliens Ate My Homework*. New York: Pocket Books, 1993. Aliens interested in interplanetary justice cause Rod Allbright no end of trouble and joy. (I: 8–11)

———. *My Teacher Is an Alien*. New York: Pocket Books 1991. A teacher comes from outer space to study the human brain, which is believed to be defective, since humans kill one another. This theme is carried on in a series of other titles. (I: 8–11)

Danziger, Paula. *This Place Has No Atmosphere*. New York: Dell, 1987. Humorous story of a move to the moon by reluctant Aurora and her family. (I: 11–YA)

Dickinson, Peter. *The Devil's Children*. New York: Delacorte, 1986. Abandoned and homeless, Geoffrey and his sister Sally are among those in England who fear the impact of technology and instead re-create the culture of the Dark Age. The *Changes* trilogy continues in *Heartsease* (1969) and *The Weathermonger* (1968). (I: 12–YA)

* Etra, Jonathan, and Stephanie Spinner. *Aliens for Lunch*. Illustrated by Steve Bjorkman. New York: Random House, 1991. Aliens appear out of the microwave and desserts are at risk in the universe. (I: 7–9)

Gormley, Beatrice. *Wanted: UFO*. Illustrated by Emily Arnold McCully. New York: Dutton, 1990. Elise is surprised at the intention of two aliens that appear in Nick's backyard. (I: 8–11)

Griffin, Peni R. *Otto from Otherwhere*. New York: Macmillan, 1990. A boy from another world lands on earth. (I: 9–11)

Klause, Annette. *Alien Secrets*. New York. Delacorte, 1993. Puck befriends a troubled alien while traveling to another planet. (I: 10–YA)

Lawrence, Louise. *Star Lord*. New York: Harper & Row, 1978. Erlich crashes on the mountain Mawr-rhyn, not unlike the mountains of Wales, and explains he comes from eleven light years across space. A brother and sister protect him from the military on earth until he escapes. (I: 12–YA)

———. *The Warriors of Taan*. New York: Harper & Row, 1988. Khian, or Carl Simonson as he was

called on earth, comes to the planet Taan as a warrior but is intrigued with the nonviolent ways of the Stonewraiths. (I: 12–YA)

L'Engle, Madeleine. *A Wrinkle in Time*. New York: Farrar, 1962. Meg and Charles Wallace go to the planet Camazotz to search for their scientist father. The sequels are *A Wind in the Door* (1973) and *A Swiftly Tilting Planet* (1978). (I: 10–YA)

Lively, Penelope. *Uninvited Ghosts and Other Stories*. New York: Dutton, 1985. This book of short stories features both science fiction and fantasy, including "A Martian Comes to Stay," "Uninvited Ghosts," and "A Flock of Gryphons." (I: 9–11)

Mahy, Margaret. *Raging Robots and Unruly Uncles*. Woodstock, NY: Overlook, 1993. Two fathers find that robots behave worse than children. (I: 9–11)

O'Brien, Robert C. *Mrs. Frisby and the Rats of NIMH*. Illustrated by Zena Bernstein. New York: Atheneum, 1971. Laboratory rats who have been made superintelligent escape and help a field mouse, Mrs. Frisby, who in turn helps them get away. O'Brien's daughter, Jane Leslie Conly, has written two sequels, illustrated by Leonard Lubin: *Racso and the Rats of NIMH* (Harper, 1986) and *R-T, Margaret, and the Rats of NIMH* (Harper, 1990). (I: 10–12)

Pinkwater, Daniel. *Fat Men from Space*. New York: Dodd, Mead, 1977. The men from space are most interested in the earth's junk food. (I: 8–11)

———. *Alan Mendelsohn, the Boy from Mars*. New York: Dutton, 1979. Alan makes friends with a junior high boy from earth. (I: 10–12)

Sargent, Pamela. *Alien Child*. New York: Harper-Collins, 1988. Nita and Sven are raised by guardians in an alien society. They discover they were left as embryos by their parents until a time when earth's inhabitants could overcome the violent and destructive side of their nature. (I: YA)

Service, Pamela. *Stinker from Space*. New York: Scribner's, 1988. A secret agent from space enters the body of a skunk. (I: 9–12)

———. *Stinker's Return*. New York: Scribner's, 1993. Tsynq Yr returns to earth, still in the skunk's body. (I: 9–12)

Sleator, William. *Interstellar Pig*. New York: Dutton, 1984. As Barney plays a strange board game, it becomes real. (I: 11–YA)

* Yorinks, Arthur. *Company's Coming*. New York: Crown, 1988. When a space ship lands, Shirley invites two visitors from outer space to dinner, to Moe's chagrin. (I: 6–8)

RESOURCES

Asimov, Isaac. *Asimov on Science Fiction*. New York: Garden City, 1981.

Barron, Neil, ed. *Anatomy of Wonder 4: A Critical Guide to Science Fiction*. New Providence, NJ: R.R. Bowker, 1995.

Cameron, Eleanor. *The Green and Burning Tree: On the Writing and Enjoyment of Children's Books*. Boston: Little, Brown, 1969.

Cook, Elizabeth. *The Ordinary and the Fabulous: An Introduction to Myths, Legends, and Fairy Tales*. New York: Cambridge University Press, 1976.

Egoff, Sheila A. *Thursday's Child: Trends and Patterns in Contemporary Children's Literature*. Chicago: American Library Association, 1981.

Greenlaw, M. Jean. "Fantasy." *Children's Books and Their Creators*. Ed. Anita Silvey. Boston: Houghton Mifflin, 1995a.

———. "Science Fiction." *Children's Books and Their Creators*. Ed. Anita Silvey. Boston: Houghton Mifflin, 1995b.

———. "Science Fiction: Images of the Future, Shadows of the Past." *Top of the News* 39 (1982): 64–71.

Knight, Damon Francis. *In Search of Wonder: Essays on Modern Science Fiction*. Chicago: Advent, 1967.

Lagerlöf, Selma. *The Wonderful Adventures of Nils*. 1906–07. New York: Dover, 1995.

Le Guin, Ursula K. *The Language of the Night: Essays on Fantasy and Science Fiction*. Rev. ed. New York: HarperCollins, 1992.

Lynn, Ruth Nadelman. *Fantasy Literature for Children and Young Adults: An Annotated Bibliography*. 3rd ed. New Providence, NJ: R.R. Bowker, 1989.

Sullivan, C. W. III, ed. *Science Fiction for Young Readers*. Westport, CT: Greenwood, 1993.

Tymn, Marshall B., Kenneth J. Zahorski, and Robert H. Boyer. *Fantasy Literature: A Core Collection and Reference Guide*. New Providence, NJ: R.R. Bowker, 1979.

Yolen, Jane. *Touch Magic: Fantasy, Faerie and Folklore in the Literature of Childhood*. New York: Philomel, 1981.

REFERENCES

Alexander, Lloyd. "Future Conditional." *Children's Literature Quarterly* 10.4 (Winter 1986): 164.

———. "Fantasy as Images: A Literary View." *Language Arts* 55 (1978): 440–46.

———. "High Fantasy and Heroic Romance." *The Horn Book* 47 (December 1971): 577–94.

Andersen, Hans Christian. *The Princess and the Pea*. 1840. Boston: Houghton Mifflin, 1979.

Chetwin, Grace. *Rufus*. New York: Feral Press, 1995.

Cooper, Susan. "Escaping into Ourselves." *Celebrating Children's Books: Essays on Children's Literature in Honor of Zena Sutherland*. Eds. Betsy Hearne and Marily Kaye. New York: Lothrop, Lee & Shepard, 1981. 14–23.

Dahl, Roald. *Boy: Tales of a Childhood*. New York: Farrar, 1984.

———. *George's Marvelous Medicine*. Illustrated by Quentin Blake. New York: Knopf, 1982.

———. *Matilda*. Illustrated by Quentin Blake. New York: Viking, 1988.

———. *The Witches*. Illustrated by Quentin Blake. New York: Farrar, 1983.

de Brunhoff, Jean. *Babar*. New York: Random House, 1937.

Dictionary of Literary Biography. "American Writers for Children since 1960: Fiction." Vol. 52. Detroit: Gale Research, 1986. 249.

Dupasquier, Philippe. *Dear Daddy*. New York: Puffin, 1985. 31.

Eibl-Eibesfeldt, Iraneus. *Ethology: The Biology of Behavior*. 2nd ed. New York: Aldine de Gruyter, 1989.

Egoff, Sheila A. *Worlds Within: Children's Fantasy from the Middle Ages to Today*. Chicago: American Library Association, 1988.

Elleman, Barbara. "Popular Reading—Time Fantasy Update." *Booklist* 81.19 (1985): 1407–08.

Frye, Northrop. *The Educated Imagination*. Bloomington: Indiana UP, 1957.

Greenlaw, M. Jean. "Fantasy." *Children's Books and Their Creators*. Ed. Anita Silvey. Boston: Houghton Mifflin, 1995.

———. "Science Fiction: Images of the Future, Shadows of the Past." *Top of the News* (Fall 1982): 64.

Hunter, Mollie. *Talent Is Not Enough: Mollie Hunter on Writing for Children*. New York: Harper, 1976.

Lynn, Ruth Nadelman. *Fantasy Literature for Children and Young Adults: An Annotated Bibliography*. 3rd ed. New Providence, NJ: R.R. Bowker, 1989.

Olendorf, D., and D. Telgen, eds. "Diana Wynne Jones." *Something about the Author*. Vol. 70. Detroit: Gale Research, 1993. 116–17.

MacDonald, George. *At the Back of the North Wind*. 1871. Illustrated by Charles Mozley. New York: Penguin, 1985.

Shapiro, Lesley. Unpublished manuscript, 1996.

Shelley, Mary Wollstonecraft. *Frankenstein*. 1818. New York: Dutton, 1963.

Traw, Rick. "Beware! Here There Be Beasties: Responding to Fundamentalist Censors." *The New Advocate* 9.1 (1996): 35–56.

Tunnell, Michael O. "The Double-Edged Sword: Fantasy and Censorship." *Language Arts* 71 (1994): 606–12.

Tymn, Marshall B., Kenneth J. Zahorski, and Robert H. Boyer. *Fantasy Literature: A Core Collection and Reference Guide*. New Providence, NJ: R.R. Bowker, 1979.

Wells, H. G. *War of the Worlds*. 1898. New York: Random House, 1960.

11 Informational Books and Biography

After crossing the Chicago River for a second time and invading the North Division, the fire widened its front. Tens of thousands of people scrambled for their lives, became trapped and confused; most figured out how to escape, but scores of people perished in dead-end streets. Hundreds of people near the shores of Lake Michigan had no other choice but to wade into the cold water. They would stand there for hours, the water to their shoulders, with a panoramic view of their city in flames.

from The Great Fire *(1995)*
by Jim Murphy

Informational books and biographies offer endless possibilities for use in the classroom. Children may select them for independent reading and teachers may choose them for class read-alouds. These books provide material for readers theater and process drama. They support content area and integrated theme study by fostering a spirit of inquiry as well as by supplying facts, concepts, and ideas for children's own investigations and projects. Informational books and biographies also serve as strong models for children's own expository writing.

INFORMATIONAL BOOKS DEFINED

The Great Fire (1995), by Jim Murphy, is an example of an informational book, one of a genre created mainly to inform readers about a particular subject, issue, or idea. *Informational books*, sometimes referred to as the *literature of fact*, convey factual information about the world. A good informational book, however, not only informs, it also excites. Russell Freedman has written many wonderful informational books and biographies for children, including the Newbery Medal–winner **Lincoln: A Photobiography** (1987). Here is how he describes his mission: "Certainly the basic purpose of nonfiction is to inform, to instruct, hopefully to enlighten. But that's not enough. An effective nonfiction book must animate its subject, infuse it with life. It must create a vivid and believable world that the reader will enter willingly and leave only with reluctance" (Freedman, 1992, p. 3).

Although biographies and informational books are generally classified as nonfiction, many writers of informational books prefer not to refer to their works as "nonfiction." They take exception to the term because it identifies their genre by what it isn't rather than what it is.

Why should informational books be included in a literature program? First, children are naturally curious about their world and informational books satisfy their desire to know. Books such as **Summer Ice: Life along the Antarctic Peninsula** (1995), by Bruce McMillan, enable children to travel to distant places; books such as **Many Thousand Gone: African Americans from Slavery to Freedom** (1993), by Virginia Hamilton, allow them to experience the past and reward their curiosity about their ancestors as well as their nation's history. Informational books help children understand the natural world, explore science topics, learn how things work, play a game, or do a craft.

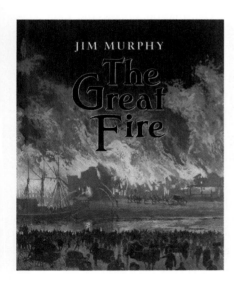

Illustration 11.1
Jim Murphy's riveting account of the 1871 Chicago fire has received many awards. (*The Great Fire* by Jim Murphy. Copyright © 1995 by Jim Murphy. Used by permission of Scholastic Inc.)

Yet, even when children don't seek the answer to a question, a good informational book may hook children's attention with a colorful cover or catchy title, then draw them in and deepen their curiosity about a topic while also informing them about science, social studies, mathematics, the arts, or sports.

Both of these reasons lead to a third reason for making informational books readily available: As psychologists since Jean Piaget have pointed out, knowing a little bit about a topic gives a child a basis for learning more about it. When children read an informational book, they establish a framework or schema to assist them in reading more complex material about the topic in the future. Therefore, providing interesting informational books has the promise of making children more engaged learners.

It is no small achievement to write a book that will nurture young readers' curiosity at the same time as it informs them. Although people tend to reserve the word "creative" to describe writing that creates fictional worlds, a considerable amount of creativity also goes into producing a successful informational book. Works of fiction can count on plots—narrative structures—to engage their readers' curiosity and pull them into and through a work. Writers of informational books rely on expository structures to do the same thing. The writer of an informational book does not create a fictional world, but he or she must use words (and perhaps illustrations) carefully to create a unique vision of a portion of the actual world and draw readers into wondering about it, observing it, and understanding it. The expository text structures that are used to do this may take the form of asking a question about an effect and then answering it by tracing a cause, following a chronological sequence of events, or comparing and contrasting the members of a species.

Readers benefit in several ways by becoming accustomed to the structures of informational books. In the same way that coming to know story structure enables students to read various stories more successfully, learning to follow expository text enables readers to comprehend informational books more successfully. Wise teachers say, "Children learn to read by reading." It is particularly true that children learn to read informational books by reading informational books. Moreover, studies have shown that unless children have experience with informational books prior to the third and fourth grades, they may be unable to cope with the sudden increase in informational reading that school curricula impose.

Another advantage of reading informational books is that they draw children into the patterns of inquiry used by specialists in the fields in which the books are written. Reading James Cross Giblin's *Chimney Sweeps* (1982) not only informs readers but allows them to think along with a gifted writer doing historical inquiry. Reading *Volcano: The Eruption and Healing of Mount St. Helens* (1986), by Patricia Lauber, shows young readers how a person with geological and ecological training investigates the cause and effect and environmental succession of a volcanic eruption and its aftermath. Studying Steven Beisty's illustrations in *Cross Sections: Man-of-War* (1993) or David Macaulay's *Castle* (1977) lends young readers an architect's eye for delineating structure and detail.

THE EVOLUTION OF INFORMATIONAL BOOKS

Orbis Sensualium Pictus ("The Visible World in Pictures," usually referred to as *Orbis Pictus*) was written by Moravian bishop John Amos Comenius and published in 1657. Considered the first informational book for children, it was a picture dictionary whose content was in Latin and focused mainly on natural history. It was illustrated with woodcuts and used as a textbook throughout Europe until the late eighteenth century. In the nineteenth century, travel books emerged as the dominant type of informational book for children. Evelyn L. Wenzel (1982) describes the format of these books: "A family or an adult escorting a group of children takes a series of trips to a foreign land (usually several countries of Europe); the children are instructed by the adult, who, of course, attends to morals as well as to mind" (p. 18).

In 1922, the first Newbery Medal was awarded to an informational book, *The Story of Mankind*, by Hendrik Willem van Loon. Twenty years later, a book that broke new ground by informing through lavish illustrations was named a Caldecott Honor Book. The author and illustrator was Holling C. Holling. The book, *Paddle-to-the-Sea* (1941), was a fictionalized but geographically accurate account of an expedition through the Great Lakes to the Atlantic Ocean.

Is it acceptable to fictionalize informational books?

ISSUE TO CONSIDER

A relatively new issue with regard to informational books is the value of a hybrid type often referred to as an *informational storybook*. Although the primary purpose of these books is to inform, they also contain fictionalized elements. The popular *Magic School Bus* books written by Joanna Cole and illustrated by Bruce Degen fit in this category. In these books, Ms. Frizzle and her class experience a fantasy adventure while they learn about the subject of the book, such as the waterworks, dinosaurs, or hurricanes. Because accuracy and authenticity are critical criteria when selecting informational books, this mixing of genres has become a controversial issue. Sayers (1982) stated: "The outstanding tenet of writing for children . . . is the insistence on first-hand authenticity in science, the arts, history, biography, and travel" (p. 97).

The blurring of the lines between fact and fiction is not a new issue. Margery Fisher (1982) has written that "the distinction between fiction and nonfiction is blurred and constantly shifting, but we still use it and need it" (p. 13). Mixed-genre books are the focus of debate because of their popularity with children on the one hand and their potential to mislead and confuse children on the other.

On the positive side, Leal (1993) points out some benefits of informational storybooks. They enable readers to "become involved in an engaging story" (pp. 63–64), identify with a main character, activate prior knowledge about the topic, generate interest for further content study, participate in discussion, and experience a model of process writing. Leal's research has confirmed children's positive responses to informational storybooks. On the other hand, Zarnowski (1995) believes that informational storybooks "introduce irrelevant, distracting, and potentially confusing 'information'" (p. 185). According to this view, students may have difficulty distinguishing fact from fiction in the story and thus may come away confused or with inaccurate information on the subject.

Supporters and detractors of informational storybooks present compelling arguments. What do you think?

Edwin Tunis was a pioneering author/illustrator of informational books whose passion for American history is evident in his works. Tunis's finely detailed black-and-white line drawings present a visual representation of the social history of the United States. One of his many books on colonial life and early American history, *Frontier Living* (1961), was a Newbery Honor Book in 1962.

Informational science books for children have been strongly influenced by the work of Millicent Selsam and Herbert Zim. With a strong background in biology and botany, Selsam published her first book, *Egg to Chick*, in 1946. Herbert Zim, an elementary science teacher, initiated the "single species" title, writing focused accounts of individual species, including *Snakes* (1949), *Sharks* (1966), and *Golden Hamsters* (1951).

The photo essay format made its debut in the world of children's informational books in the 1970s and remains very popular today. In 1976, photographer Jill Krementz published *A Very Young Dancer*, which became the first in a series of photo essays about individual children engaged in various activities. Also during the 1970s, David Macaulay began crafting informational picture books in which text and illustrations formed a unified whole. Macaulay's specialty is oversized books about architecture illustrated with intricate pen-and-ink drawings. Two books he created in this format were named Caldecott Honor Books: *Cathedral* in 1974 and *Castle* in 1978.

Even though informational books for children have a long history, they have often been relegated to a second-class status. For much of its history, the genre had the reputation of being boring, best used mainly for report work, and unpleasantly difficult for children to read. In other words, applying the term "nonfiction" to a book was like adding "unsweetened" to chocolate—like as not, synonymous with "disappointment."

Since the 1980s, however, informational books have gained momentum and established a place as a popular and important genre in children's literature. During the 1980s, several nonfiction titles were named Newbery Honor Books: *Sugaring Time* (1983) by Kathryn Lasky, *Volcano: The Eruption and Healing of Mount St. Helens* (1986) by Patricia Lauber, and *Commodore Perry in the Land of Shogun* (1985) by Rhoda Blumberg. *The Glorious Flight: Across the Channel with Louis Blériot* (1983), by Alice and Martin Provensen, received the Caldecott Medal in 1984. This book's carefully researched paintings recreate France in the early twentieth century, the flying machines developed by Blériot, and his dramatic flight across the English Channel in 1909. Today, informational books abound—they cover a myriad of topics and have exciting, aesthetically appealing formats and strong writing.

CATEGORIES OF INFORMATIONAL BOOKS

Informational books examine all kinds of topics and appear in many types of formats. Some informational books present a comprehensive view of their subject; others discuss one facet in depth. Let's look at the variety of informational books that are currently available.

History

Some informational books help readers travel back in time to find out about people, places, and events of long ago. Through such books, children can catch a glimpse of the past.

Children of the Dust Bowl: The True Story of the School at Weedpatch Camp (1992), by Jerry Stanley, recounts the work of a dedicated California educator, Leo Hart, who inspired the creation of a school for Okie children in 1940. "Okie" was the term used to describe poor Oklahoma farmers who moved to California during the Depression, when high winds and poor farming practices had made a dustbowl out of once fertile Midwestern farmland. Stanley, a history professor in California, establishes the reasons for the Okies' mass migration to California and describes the prejudice and discrimination they faced.

Flight (1991), by Robert Burleigh, takes readers across the Atlantic Ocean with Charles Lindbergh on the *Spirit of St. Louis*. Magnificent, vibrant paintings by Mike Wimmer contribute to the excitement and tension. Every detail of this transatlantic flight is described, including the strategies that Lindbergh used to stay awake, the critical importance of staying on course, and the means that Lindbergh used to lighten the plane. Lindbergh's diary is quoted as a primary source throughout the book.

Employing an alphabet book format, Jonathan Hunt provides information about the Middle Ages in *Illuminations* (1989). Each letter represents a term from the Middle Ages, such as *Excalibur, grail,* or *troubadour.* Hunt explicates each term with text and carefully rendered watercolors that resemble an illuminated manuscript page of the time.

Understanding Peoples and Cultures

Some informational books introduce young readers to children like themselves who live in other parts of the world or other areas of the United States. These books help children understand the concept of culture and appreciate similarities and differences among peoples around the world. A recent trend in photo essays is to feature a child who lives in another part of the world or in a particular cultural group in the United States. By focusing on the life of one child, these books enable young readers to identify with that child while learning about another culture.

Award-winning photojournalist Jan Reynolds has traveled the globe to photograph and write books about "vanishing cultures." In *Sahara* (1991, n.pag.), readers meet Manda, a young boy from the nomadic Tuareg tribe of the Sahara desert. Reynolds points out: "Although the Tuareg may appear different from us because of the way they spend their days, we all share the same feelings and basic needs." The text and color photographs allows readers to follow Manda and his

Illustration 11.2
Photographer Jan Reynolds lived with the Tuareg people to research his book about the Sahara. (*Sahara* by Jan Reynolds. Used by permission of Jan Reynolds/Vanishing Cultures with Harcourt Brace & Company.)

father as they travel across the desert to the camel festival. Reynolds has also written *Mongolia* (1994), *The Amazon Basin* (1993), and *Frozen Land* (1988) (about the Arctic region).

Children from various cultures within the United States are the subjects of books by Diane Hoyt-Goldsmith, who has teamed with photographer Lawrence Migdale to portray each culture through a child's eyes. David introduces the Tsmishian tribe of the Pacific Northwest in *Totem Pole* (1990); Bridget tells about the Cherokee Nation in *Cherokee Summer* (1993); and Axucena and Ximena explain the *Day of the Dead: A Mexican-American Celebration* (1994).

Nature

Many informational books explore the natural world and lead children to discoveries about animals, plants, geology, geography, and the human body. National Geographic photographer Jim Brandenburg travels *To the Top of the World: Adventures with Arctic Wolves* (1993). This firsthand account describes the author's experiences on Ellesmere Island, several hundred miles further north than Alaska in Canada's Northwest Territories, as he carefully observed and photographed the wolves. Another book on the same subject, *Wolves* (1993) by Seymour Simon, explodes many myths and stereotypes about wolves. Simon asks: "Are wolves savage and destructive hunters of people and livestock? Or are they one of nature's most misunderstood creatures? It is possible that people don't like wolves because they don't know very much about them" (n.pag.).

For an exciting underwater adventure, children can read *Safari beneath the Sea: The Wonder World of the North Pacific Coast* (1994) by Diane Swanson, with breathtaking underwater photographs from the Royal British Columbia Museum. Descriptive language entices young readers to continue turning the pages and relish the underwater sights. Swanson begins the book by asking readers to "imagine fish that tie themselves in knots, plants that flash lights in the dark, sea stars that turn their stomach inside out and mammals that hammer their food. Life in the sea is bizarre, beautiful, funny, and fabulous" (p. 1).

Informational books even offer adventures inside the human body. In *The Magic School Bus inside the Human Body* (1989), written by Joanna Cole and illustrated by Bruce Degen, Ms. Frizzle and her class go on a tour of cells and systems of the human body. Cole and Degen have collaborated to present information in multiple formats within the book: text, dialogue between Ms. Frizzle and her students, and short explanations by students on notebook paper, charts, and diagrams.

The Arts

Art, music, drama, and dance enrich people's lives; through the arts, children creatively express thoughts and feelings, tell stories, and celebrate life. Children are introduced to the art world through books such as *The Sculptor's Eye: Looking at Contemporary American Art* (1993), by Jan Greenberg and Sandra Jordan, and *Take a Look: An Introduction to the Experience of Art* (1993), by Rosemary Davidson. Davidson's book invites readers to participate in activities and experiments as they discover how art is part of everyday life. Similarly, Greenberg and Jordan connect sculpture to children's personal experiences and involve readers in the text.

Music, opera, and marionettes combine in *The Magic of Mozart: Mozart, the Magic Flute, and the Salzburg Marionettes* (1995), by Ellen Switzer. In this three-part book, readers learn about Mozart's life; the story of his opera the

Magic Flute, as performed by the Salzburg Marionettes; and about the Salzburg Marionettes. Primary school children can experience ballet in Susan Kuklin's photo essay, **Going to My Ballet Class** (1989).

How Things Work

Children are naturally curious about how things work. They ask the proverbial "why?" as they search for answers. David Macaulay's **The Way Things Work** (1988) provides a comprehensive introduction to the mechanics of movement, the elements, waves, electricity, automation, and the invention of machines. The book is heavily illustrated with Macaulay's intricate drawings that both convey and clarify information. After reading Macaulay's brief introduction to robots, children may want to pursue the topic in more depth in Gloria Skurzynski's **Robots: Your High-Tech World** (1990). Illustrated with color photographs, this book explains how robots move and are controlled and describes their many uses and their history.

Activity, Craft, and How-to Books

Informational books can help children to develop and pursue hobbies. Children who want to improve their culinary talents might consult **The Little House Cookbook** (1979) by Barbara M. Walker, which includes recipes for foods that are mentioned in various *Little House* books and also gives fascinating information about food and cooking during Laura Ingalls Wilder's time. The book includes recipes for johnny-cake, codfish balls, and salt-rising bread. Another children's cookbook, **The Wild, Wild Cookbook: A Guide for Young Wild-Food Foragers** (1982), by Jean Craighead George, instructs children on gathering and preparing wild plants such as bracken fern, dandelion, acorns, and grass seeds.

To find out how to transform their faces for a Chinese opera or the Japanese form of theater called *kabuki*, children can consult **Painting Faces** (1988), by Suzanne Haldane. Haldane explains why people in all parts of the world decorate their faces, includes full-color pictures of people with painted faces from every continent, and gives children instructions on painting their own faces. Photographs of children illustrate the various types of face painting.

Children can find directions in informational books for playing a game or enjoying a recreational activity. Mary Lankford provides directions for nineteen variants of **Hopscotch around the World** (1992). A descriptive paragraph tells how each variant is played in the country where it originates, and a diagram accompanies step-by-step directions. George Sullivan instructs children on **In-Line Skating: A Complete Guide for Beginners** (1993). Color photographs illustrate chapters that reveal how to stop and teach about swizzling, crossovers, and skating backwards.

Series Books

Series books are developed by publishers to provide groups of works about related topics. The books have a specified format, which means that every book in the series is organized in the same way. One popular series, the *Eyewitness Books*, published by Dorling Kindersley, presents information on many different topics with extensive color photographs. Another series, *Let's Read-and-Find-Out Science*, from HarperCollins, was initiated by Dr. Franklyn M. Branley, an astronomer and former chairman of the American Museum–Hayden Planetarium. This series introduces primary school children to science by providing them with material for independent reading. Well-known children's authors have contributed—notably Patricia Lauber with *Be a Friend to Trees* (1994) and Aliki with *Dinosaurs Are Different* (1985).

HOW INFORMATIONAL BOOKS WORK

What distinguishes informational books from other literary genres? Writers of informational books face the challenging task of compiling all their research on a topic and selecting facts, concepts, and ideas to include in their books. Further, they must decide how to organize this information in a way that is interesting and accessible to their readers. Authors of informational books employ an expository style of writing to explain, inform, and describe. Expository writing uses various organizational patterns to present information, such as description, chronological sequencing, explanation, comparison/contrast, defining with examples, and problem/solution. For example, Jim Murphy organizes *Across America on an Emigrant Train* (1993) sequentially, as readers follow Robert Louis Stevenson's travels from Scotland to San Francisco in search of his true love. Vicki Cobb explains and defines terms with examples in *The Secret Life of Cosmetics* (1985): "There has been an almost endless list of *dentifrices*, substances used for cleaning the teeth. These included, at one time or another: ground chalk, ground charcoal, powdered pumice stone, soap, lemon juice, ashes, tobacoo mixed with honey, a mixture of cinnamon and cream of tartar (ugh!) to name a few" (p. 25).

Authors of informational books must also generate and maintain readers' interest. The beginning chapters of James Cross Giblin's books pique readers' interest. Note, for example, this first paragraph from *Chimney Sweeps* (1982):

> On a sunny October morning, a van pulls up in front of a ranch-style house in an American suburb. Out jump a young man and woman dressed in black tailcoats and top hats. They are both professional chimney sweeps, and are wearing the costume that has been the trademark of chimney sweeps for almost four hundred years. (p. 1)

An author's enthusiasm for the topic is usually evident in a good informational book. Writers use various literary techniques to engage the reader: posing a question, writing in the first person, addressing the reader directly as "you," and using highly descriptive language and imagery. Informational books need not be serious, and many writers incorporate humor to sustain the reader's involvement. A good example is *If You Made a Million* (1989) by David M. Schwartz, with its exaggerated, colorful illustrations by Steven Kellogg.

Graphics play an important role in informational books. They can help clarify abstract concepts that may be unknown to readers or difficult to understand. They can convey specific facts and specialized vocabulary or present a realistic visual rendering of a concept. They can help provide the background knowledge necessary for readers' understanding. Graphics take many forms: photographs, paintings, drawings, charts, maps, copies of documents, and so on.

Authors of informational books may provide readers with other aids for locating and understanding material, such as an index, glossary, table of contents, or list of additional facts. A reference list or an acknowledgment of the sources or experts consulted is usually included.

Informational books require readers to engage in critical thinking, as they are called on to distinguish fact from opinion and theory. Readers consider the author's spirit of inquiry and what kind of research and investigation went into the book. Authors have their own points of view and perspectives, and readers must decide if an author has presented a balanced discussion or if it is biased in some way. After gleaning all the information in the book, readers draw inferences and reach their own conclusions.

MAJOR WRITERS OF INFORMATIONAL BOOKS AND THEIR WORKS

Many authors write informational books for children. Several who have received recognition for their significant contributions to the genre are discussed in this section.

Aliki

Aliki, a much loved author and illustrator of informational picture books and biographies for children, wrote her first book, *The Story of William Tell*, in 1960. Since that time, her informational books have spanned a wide range of topics from dinosaurs to the Middle Ages. Aliki presents complex, detailed subject matter to young children in a clear, accessible manner. Many of her books are appropriate for the early primary grades. Her illustrations make concepts clear and visible to children. Aliki's books often include humorous elements that are complemented by a comic strip format with dialogue balloons.

In *How a Book Is Made* (1986), selected for the PBS television program "Reading Rainbow," Aliki traces the steps in a book's development and describes the kinds of occupations involved in the process. Using cats instead of people as the characters and a comic strip format, Aliki begins with the role of the author and concludes with the salespeople who sell the book. In another book, Aliki leads readers on a fascinating journey to ancient Egypt, presenting a comprehensive view of mummification in *Mummies Made in Egypt* (1979). Her finely detailed illustrations are accompanied by labels, captions, and longer explanations.

Joanna Cole

Joanna Cole has been writing informational science books for children since the 1971 publication of *Cockroaches*. In recent years, she has teamed with Bruce Degen to create the popular *Magic School Bus* series, which emphasizes the joy of science and shows that complex information can be conveyed with humor and enthusiasm. *The Magic School Bus at the Waterworks* (1986) was named a *Boston Globe–Horn Book* Honor Book, and *The Magic School Bus inside the Earth* (1987) was chosen as a "Reading Rainbow" feature selection.

Cole collaborated with photographer Jerome Wexler on several books introducing young children to the anatomy of animals and amphibians: *A Cat's Body* (1982), *A Frog's Body* (1980), and *A Horse's Body* (1981). In clear, lucid prose, Cole explains technical vocabulary and presents the animal's anatomy to primary-grade readers. Cole's books have been selected as American Library Association Notable Books and as Outstanding Science Trade Books for Children by the National Science Teachers Association. Her contribution to nonfiction literature for children was recognized in 1991 by the *Washington Post*–Children's Book Guild Nonfiction Award.

Gail Gibbons

As an author and illustrator of more than fifty informational picture books, Gail Gibbons has introduced primary-grade children to a range of topics. After receiving an undergraduate degree in fine arts, she pursued a career as a staff artist for a New York television station. Gibbons has the special ability to explain complicated information lucidly and concisely for young children. Her illustrations help introduce concepts and show children a visual representation of them.

Through watercolor illustrations and text, *The Great St. Lawrence Seaway* (1992) gives the seaway's history, explains important vocabulary associated with it, such as "lock" and "canal," and describes how locks work. The book contains many helpful aids for readers, such as labeled illustrations, maps, and a concluding page of additional information. If young children wish to satisfy their curiosity about spiders, Gibbons's *Spiders* (1993) will answer their questions. Gibbons explains that spiders are not insects and shows young readers the difference between the two in detailed, labeled diagrams of a spider's body and an insect's body.

Gail Gibbons's work has been widely recognized. Two of her books, *The Milk Makers* (1985) and *Sunken Treasure* (1988), were selected for "Reading Rainbow." Gibbons received the *Washington Post*–Children's Book Guild Award for her contribution to children's nonfiction.

James Cross Giblin

James Cross Giblin had a successful career as a children's book editor before he began writing nonfiction for children. After majoring in English and dramatic arts at Case Western Reserve University, he earned a master's degree in playwriting from Columbia University. As a writer of children's informational books, he is known for his imaginative and engaging treatment of unusual topics. For example, *From Hand to Mouth or, How We Invented Knives, Forks, Spoons, and Chopsticks and the Table Manners to Go with Them* (1987) traces the history of eating utensils in great detail.

Giblin does careful research, not only for his books' text but also for the illustrations, which are carefully selected photographs, prints, and drawings. In *The Riddle of the Rosetta Stone: Key to Ancient Egypt* (1990), Giblin uses illustrations from the British Museum and the Metropolitan Museum of Art. His books have received many honors: *Chimney Sweeps: Yesterday and Today* (1982) was awarded the 1983 American Book Award for Children's Nonfiction, and *The Truth about Santa Claus* (1985) was named a *Boston Globe–Horn Book* Nonfiction Honor Book in 1986.

James Haskins

As a child living in racially segregated Demopolis, Alabama, James Haskins (who also writes as Jim Haskins) was prevented from using the public library. His mother purchased an encyclopedia set, volume by volume, from the grocery store, and Jim had read every volume by the time he was fourteen. He taught special education in New York City and currently is an English professor. Haskins has written over one hundred books on social science topics, many of which have focused on the African American experience. In addition to informational books, Haskins also writes biographies for children. He has developed the popular *Count Your Way* series, which uses a counting format to present information about various cultures.

In *The March on Washington* (1993), Haskins recounts the events of August 28, 1963, when 250,000 people marched in support of racial equality; the book highlights the courageous individuals who made the march happen and describes the planning that was needed. The history of the Underground Railroad is told in **Get on Board: The Story of the Underground Railroad** (1993). Readers visit the "stations" of the railroad and learn about the remarkable courage of the slaves and those who assisted them.

Kathryn Lasky

A versatile writer who skillfully writes both fiction and nonfiction for children, Kathryn Lasky has commented, "People often ask me how and why I do both fiction and nonfiction. I am equally attracted to both kinds of writing because for me the most important thing is if a story is real. Real stories can be either fiction or nonfiction" (Scribner's, 1985). In 1981, Lasky received the *Boston Globe–Horn Book* Award for Nonfiction for **The Weaver's Gift** (1980), a collaboration with her husband, photographer Christopher Knight. Another collaboration, **Sugaring Time** (1982), was named a Newbery Honor Book in 1983. Lasky received the 1986 *Washington Post*–Children's Book Guild Award for her body of work in children's nonfiction.

Lasky and Knight experience firsthand the subjects they write about and photograph. They traveled to Iceland to research **Surtsey: The Newest Place on Earth** (1992), about the creation of an island by a volcanic eruption in the Atlantic Ocean south of Iceland in 1963. Each chapter of the book begins with a selection from the Icelandic creation myth, the *Edda*, as Lasky intertwines Icelandic folklore with a description of the island's creation. Her descriptive language, rich in imagery, engages readers in this amazing event of the natural world.

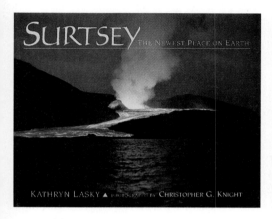

Illustration 11.3
Kathryn Lasky and her husband Christopher Knight received special permission to visit the new island of Surtsey so that they could write all about it. (*Surtsey: The Newest Place on Earth* by Kathryn Lasky. Text © 1992 by Kathryn Lasky. Jacket photo © 1992 Sigurgeir Jonasson. Used by permission of Hyperion Books for Children.)

Patricia Lauber

Patricia Lauber has written more than sixty informational books on science topics for children. She writes: "Overall, my aims are to help children understand how the earth (or its parts) works and to try to imbue them with some of my own sense of wonderment, in the hope that they will grow up to be good stewards, who will take care of the earth, not just use (or abuse) it" (1992, pp. 14–15).

Lauber's books have received much critical acclaim: **Volcano: The Eruption and Healing of Mt. St. Helens** (1986) was named a 1987 Newbery Honor Book, and **Seeing Earth from Space** (1990) was a 1991 Orbis Pictus Honor Book. Lauber was recognized for her contribution to children's nonfiction with the 1983 *Washington Post*–Children's Book Guild Award.

In **The News about Dinosaurs** (1989), Lauber promotes the spirit of inquiry as she points out that previously accepted "facts" about dinosaurs are being altered by new discoveries. She juxtaposes what scientists used to think with "The News Is," which presents the most current scientific knowledge. For example, although "scientists used to think dinosaurs did not take care of their young. . . . The News Is: At least some dinosaurs do seem to have cared for their young" (p. 26).

Milton Meltzer

Milton Meltzer has been writing outstanding informational books and biographies for children for almost forty years. His books focus on history, social issues, and underrepresented groups in society. Meltzer features the authentic voices of people about whom he writes and primary source materials. On writing history for children, Meltzer (1981) says: "The writing of history is as much an

ASK THE AUTHOR...

Milton Meltzer

Milton Meltzer

Favorite Books as a Child

An omnivorous reader as a child, I read everything from junk to classics. A few of the best I remember most fondly are *Arabian Nights*, Jonathan Swift's *Gulliver's Travels*, and Mark Twain's *Huckleberrry Finn*.

What are you trying to do in your informational books?

I do not call what I write "informational books." Together with other nonfiction writers, I have been struggling long and hard to break down that stereotype that plagues our work. Yes, my books are full of facts, but they are also, I hope, far more than merely "informational." The same quality of imagination required for the creation of good fiction is just as essential for the writing of good nonfiction. Whether an author is dealing with history or biography, the events, the personalities, and the selection and shaping of them are influenced strongly by the imagination. Of course, the documents and other sources must be treated honestly, but what you do with them, the emphasis you give this element as against that, the words you choose, the tone, the voice, the structure of the narrative—all are acts of creation. Are imagination, invention, selection, form, and language any less important in the making of a good work of history or biography than in the making of fiction?

What I try to do in my writing is to help young readers understand the world they live in, to see the events and people in all their rich complexity, to find links between themselves and the experience of others. My readers face a world they will inevitably influence, whether by action or by inaction. I hope to raise questions in their minds that will help them think more clearly, help them make sense of their world, help them act fairly and decently in their relations with their family, their friends, and their community, and help them bring about a more just and peaceful tomorrow.

Milton Meltzer, historian and biographer, is the author of more than ninety books for young people and adults, which have earned numerous honors and awards. He and his wife live in New York City.

art as the writing of poetry or fiction. The writer tries to express his vision of history and to communicate it to the reader. As historian he does not invent that past, but he must give it artistic shape if he is to connect with the reader" (p. 96).

Meltzer's books have received wide recognition and have appeared on various notable book lists. ***All Times, All Peoples: A World History of Slavery*** (1980) was awarded the 1980 Christopher Award; ***Never to Forget: The Jews of the Holocaust*** (1976) was designated as a 1976 *Boston Globe–Horn Book* Award Nonfiction Honor Book; and ***The Jewish Americans: A History in Their Own Words, 1650–1950*** (1982) was named a 1983 *Boston Globe–Horn Book* Award Honor Book.

In *The Amazing Potato: A Story in Which the Incas, Conquistadors, Marie Antoinette, Thomas Jefferson, Wars, Famines, Immigrants and French Fries All Play a Part* (1992), Meltzer provides a fascinating, thoroughly researched social history of the potato. In the foreword, Meltzer points out that he wanted young readers to see "how such an everyday object, one we scarcely notice except perhaps when we have a hankering for french fries, can be of such vast significance in the history of humankind" (n.pag.).

Laurence Pringle

Former editor of *Nature and Society*, published by the American Museum of Natural History, Laurence Pringle has contributed significantly to informational science books for children. Drawing on his degrees in wildlife biology, Pringle has written more than seventy books that focus primarily on nature, wildlife, and ecology and environmental issues. In discussing what it means to "do science," Pringle (1981) wrote: "Doing science means being curious, asking questions. It means having a healthy skepticism toward authority and announced truths. It is both a way of looking at the world and a way of thinking. It values both fantasy and reality, and provides a framework for telling the difference" (p. 110).

In *Antarctica: The Last Unspoiled Continent* (1992), Pringle presents an in-depth look at this fascinating continent, including its history, climate, plant and animal life, and political and environmental issues. Pringle selected color photographs from many sources for the book, which includes a glossary of terms and an index. In *Fire in the Forest: A Cycle of Growth and Renewal* (1995), Pringle helps young people take a different perspective on the fires in Yellowstone National Park: "To ecologists, fire is a normal and even welcome force in nature . . . fire brings change, diversity, and new life. The Yellowstone fires of 1988 were no exception" (p. 6).

Seymour Simon

Seymour Simon, a prolific writer of more than 125 informational science books for children, attended the Bronx High School of Science. After receiving a bachelor's degree, he began teaching science in New York City schools. His first children's book, *Animals in Field and Laboratory: Projects in Animal Behavior*, was published in 1968. In 1979, after more than twenty years, Simon stopped teaching to pursue writing full-time. He received the Eva L. Gordon Award from the American Nature Society, and many of his books have been named Outstanding Science Trade Books by the National Science Teachers Association.

Simon's conversational, clear, and direct writing style enables children to understand a host of science topics. He immediately creates interest among his readers, as the beginning of *Sharks* (1995, n.pag.) exemplifies: "It never fails. You're at the ocean, swimming in the surf, and someone pretends to be a shark. They sing ominous music and then lunge at you." Full-page color photographs support the text that attempts to convey "the truth about sharks" so readers will "see them as the fascinating creatures they are, instead of the monsters of myth."

Illustration 11.4
Are sharks fascinating creatures or monsters of the sea? Seymour Simon uses factual information to answer this question. (*Sharks* by Seymour Simon. Jacket photo copyright © 1995 by David B. Fleetham. Jacket copyright © 1995 by HarperCollins Publishers. Used by permission of HarperCollins Publishers.)

CRITERIA FOR SELECTING INFORMATIONAL BOOKS

Informational books have many unique characteristics that distinguish them from other genres of children's literature. Although children's needs and interests should always be foremost in your mind as you choose informational books, there are other specific criteria to consider as well. These are discussed below.

Accuracy and Authenticity

An informational book must be accurate in conveying factual, documented material. To determine accuracy if you are not knowledgable about the subject yourself, consider the author's credentials and qualifications. Often authors credit experts in the field who have assisted them or reviewed the manuscript for accuracy. Has the author provided a reference list or cited sources for the information?

Another indication of accuracy is the copyright date: When was the book published? Is the information outdated? Sometimes world events happen so rapidly that an otherwise outstanding book may become quickly outdated. For example, don't necessarily eliminate all books about the Soviet Union even though that country has been disbanded. Instead, supplement the inaccurate information with current articles from newspapers and magazines that will update the one outdated section of the book. On the other hand, if the essence of the book is completely outdated, it's better not to select it.

Some other aspects of accuracy include whether the author makes a clear distinction between known fact and theory or speculation and whether the book offers a balanced presentation of the topic. If there is more than one interpretation or theory about the topic, have they all been fairly presented? Another important consideration is whether the author has avoided stereotypes about race, ethnicity, gender, disabilities, lifestyle, and socioeconomic class.

Organization

A second selection criterion concerns the book's overall organization and the way the author has developed ideas and content. Authors have many options regarding how to organize material. One way to organize information is sequentially, or chronologically—that is, in the order in which events or activities occur. Authors may also choose to arrange material by key concepts, main ideas, or distinguishing characteristics. The author may develop ideas by beginning with generalizations and then becoming more specific. Or the author may begin with a simple aspect of the topic and then gradually become more complex. Often, authors compare a new concept to something already familiar to readers.

If the book is lengthy, has it been divided into chapters? Does the text have headings and subheadings to assist readers to clearly understand the book's organization? Has the author connected ideas and shown the interrelationships among them? Think about the audience for the book, too. Given the age range of the intended audience, is the scope and organization of content appropriate?

Format and Design

A book's appearance affects children's interest in it. Is the book visually attractive and appealing? How big is the book? Does it have an unusual format? What is the size and style of the type? Can children read it easily? What are the nature and quality of the illustrations—photographs, paintings, drawings, reproductions of realia, graphs, maps, charts? Do illustrations complement, clarify, and extend the text? What kinds of information are they conveying? In thinking about the format, consider whether the placement of illustrations on the page contributes to the overall design.

Writing Style

As you would in evaluating any genre, consider the author's writing style in selecting informational books. How has the author generated interest and enthusiasm for the topic? Does the author invoke a spirit of wonder and inquiry in the reader? Has technical vocabulary been introduced within a context meaningful to the reader? Does the author's writing include descriptive and figurative language? Is the writing clear and interesting?

BIOGRAPHY DEFINED

Some of the oldest books for children are biographies—works that describe and discuss the lives of real individuals. In earlier periods, it was common to expose children to the (sometimes idealized) lives of national and cultural heroes. That practice still exists, but in a somewhat altered form. For one thing, in the United States, there is growing recognition that the society is made up of more than one culture—so the goal of many writers of biography has become promoting a more inclusive view of noteworthy Americans. For another thing, the trend toward exposure-oriented journalism—journalism that delves below the surface—has become steadily stronger since the Vietnam War era. Thus, even children are less likely than they were in previous generations to believe larger-than-life accounts of heroes. Third, the study of history has become less preoccupied with great people and great events and more focused on the common people and the ambience of earlier times. Thus, even though a biography may have a well-known person as its subject, the author is more likely to explain that person in the context of his or her time, and the concerns, available choices, and social movements of the day.

How does biography differ from historical fiction? Biographies that focus on famous individuals from the past offer insight into historical times just as historical fiction does. However, the information presented in a biography is based on known facts about the individual and her or his time period. Incidents, dialogue, and people are not fictionalized as they are in historical fiction. Autobiographies differ from biographies in that their authors are writing about themselves.

Biographies have some unique features that justify their inclusion in a literature program. First, they help children learn from the lives of others. In a biography, after all, children can see how choices a person makes early in life can bear fruit later on, or how inauspicious beginnings can lead to a good outcome. Reading biographies can also encourage children to recognize links between people's lives and the social and historical times in which they lived. For instance, Jean Fritz, in her biography *You Want Women to Vote, Lizzie Stanton?* (1995) writes: "Yes, Elizabeth Cady Stanton did want women to vote. It was an outlandish idea, but that's what she wanted. Not at first. As a child, she knew that girls didn't count for much, but she didn't expect to change that. First she had to grow up" (p. 1). This biography of Stanton, who dedicated her life to women's suffrage in the United States, describes gender roles during the nineteenth century and reasons for people's beliefs about women's suffrage. Through biographies, children come to understand the people who have shaped history, created inventions, discovered scientific principles, composed music, crafted works of art, and

Illustration 11.5
With humor and insight, Jean Fritz recounts the life of the famous suffragette Elizabeth Cady Stanton. (*You Want Women to Vote, Lizzie Stanton?* by Jean Fritz. Illustration copyright © 1995 by DyAnne DiSalvo-Ryan. Used by permission of G. P. Putnam's Sons.)

contributed to their local communities. Children realize that they, too, can make a difference in the world.

THE EVOLUTION OF BIOGRAPHY

In the past, biographies for children were criticized for poor writing, invented details, and exaggerations of the positive sides of their subjects. Moreover, in the first half of this century, the subjects of biographies were mostly limited to white males who were political leaders or who made some other historic contribution to society. The prevailing thought—alive and well since ancient times—was that children should hear or read biographies of individuals who displayed admirable virtues and thus could serve as role models for children to emulate. These individuals were idealized—presented as being morally perfect. Because societal norms dictated that children should not be exposed to the less savory realities of life, such as discrimination, violence, or abuse, early biographies were bland and unrealistic.

Fictionalization was also an accepted practice in earlier children's biographies. For instance, authors routinely invented conversations and scenes for which there was no historic basis. True, authors had good motives for these distortions. In explaining why he fictionalized biography for children, F. N. Monjo (1982) pointed out that he used a child associated with the "great figure" as the narrator because it "makes possible a casual intimacy which, I believe, young readers find congenial" (p. 99). Author Robert Lawson included fantastic elements in his fictionalized biographies. His study of Christopher Columbus, *I Discover Columbus* (1941), was narrated by Aurelio, a parrot; his biography of Benjamin Franklin, *Ben & Me* (1939), was told by a mouse named Amos. Although these books were very popular with children, they raised the question of whether it was necessary to fictionalize biographies to such an extent to make them palatable to young readers. The answer was decades away.

As with informational books in general, critical recognition of biographies for children was slow in coming. The first Newbery Medal for a work of biography was awarded in 1934 to *Invincible Louisa* (1933), a biography of Louisa May Alcott, written by Corneila Meigs. In 1940, James Daugherty received the Newbery Medal for *Daniel Boone* (1939). (Contemporary readers, though, may be appalled at the book's portrayal of Native Americans.) In the same year, the Caldecott Medal for the best illustrated book of the year went to a biography, *Abraham Lincoln* (1939), by Edgar Parin D'Aulaire and Ingri D'Aulaire. This book is said to have "established the picture-book biography for younger children as a valued staple of library-book collections" (Hoke, 1995, p. 188). Still, biographies for children had a long way to go.

The 1970s were a turning point for children's biographies. With the publication of *And Then What Happened, Paul Revere?* in 1973, author Jean Fritz set a new standard. Fritz created an authentic biography for children without any invented dialogue; she also included "Notes from the Author," containing additional facts keyed to various pages of the book. Fritz did not rely on the fictionalizing of earlier days to make her books congenial to young readers. Her writing style—conversational, humorous, and easily accessible—as well as her focus on one or two interesting events were and are what draw readers to her works.

Since the early 1970s, biographies have advanced further, to give children a wider representation of noteworthy people. Biographies written in the past three decades have featured men, women, and children of many ethnic and racial backgrounds engaging in a variety of occupations and contributing in many different ways to society. For example, *Sequoyah's Gift* (1993), by Janet Klausner, describes the Cherokee leader who developed the writing system for the Cherokee language; *Cleopatra* (1994), by Diane Stanley and Peter Vennema, highlights the life of the famous Egyptian queen. Contemporary authors handle their subjects with a "new realism," presenting them as human beings with vulnerabilities and weaknesses.

In 1988, Russell Freedman received the Newbery Medal for ***Lincoln: A Photobiography*** (1987), establishing a new era of prestige and recognition for authentic biography for children. James Cross Giblin, himself a distinguished author of informational books as well as an editor, explains that the significance of *Lincoln* in the evolution of children's biography is that it offers a "fresh approach to familiar material, demythologizing Lincoln without debunking him," telling "a dramatic true story," emphasizing the visual with its photo essay format, and providing an "accessible yet literate text" (1992, p. 25).

CATEGORIES OF BIOGRAPHY

Biographies for children feature contemporary people, historical figures, athletes, and entertainers—as well as young people similar to those reading the biographies. A current trend in children's biographies is the publication of series biographies. These biographies follow a specified format and include the same types of information for each individual. Carolrhoda Books has several biography series: *Creative Minds*, targeted for children in grades 3 through 6, includes biographies of Hans Christian Andersen and Milton Hershey; *Trailblazers, Achievers, and Sports Achievers*, for grades 4 and above, features biographies of Zora Neale Hurston, Jackie Kennedy Onassis, and Shaquille O'Neal. Little, Brown touts its *Sports Illustrated for Kids* biographies, which include books about Steffi Graf and Michael Jordan. For primary grades, Random House offers *Step-Up Biographies*, with such titles as ***Meet Thomas Jefferson*** (1989) and ***Meet Christopher Columbus*** (1989); Holiday House offers its *Picture Book Biographies* by David Adler.

Partial Biographies

Instead of presenting an entire life, a writer may create a more interesting work by selecting one segment from a person's life and exploring it in depth and detail. Jean Fritz's biographies of famous early Americans are good examples of partial biographies. For example, in ***Why Don't You Get a Horse, Sam Adams?*** (1974), Fritz recounts how patriot Samuel Adams walked the streets of pre-Revolutionary Boston promoting independence from England. (Was he earth-bound out of fear of horses, or because he wanted to stay closer to the people?) Another example of a partial biography is ***Coming Home: From the Life of Langston Hughes*** (1994), by Floyd Cooper, which limits its coverage to the ground-breaking poet's childhood.

Collective Biographies

A *collective biography* is a book that describes the lives of several people who share something in common. In ***Indian Chiefs*** (1987), Russell Freedman chronicles the lives of six famous Native American leaders: Red Cloud of the Oglala Sioux, Santanta of the Kiowa, Quanah Parker of the Comanche, Washakie of the Shoshoni, Joseph of the Nez Perce, and Sitting Bull of the Hunkpapa

Sioux. Freedman points out that "the six chiefs whose stories are told here were called upon to lead their people at a time of crisis" (p. 9).

Another approach to collective biography is seen in the collaborative work of author Kathleen Krull and illustrator Kathryn Hewitt. They have produced three collective biographies: *Lives of the Musicians: Good Times, Bad Times (and What the Neighbors Thought)* (1993), *Lives of the Writers: Comedies, Tragedies (and What the Neighbors Thought)* (1994), and *Lives of the Artists: Masterpieces, Messes (and What the Neighbors Thought)* (1995). The format of these appealing and humorous books includes biographical sketches of the individuals accompanied by watercolor illustrations. Krull has carefully researched each musician, writer, and artist, discovering little-known information that will fascinate readers.

Biographies of Explorers of Earth and Space

Discovery and exploration enable civilizations to move forward, as individuals continue taking risks to tackle the unknown. Maria Mitchell discovered a comet—her life is described in *Maria Mitchell: The Soul of an Astronomer* (1995) by Beatrice Gormley. Eratosthenes figured out how to measure the earth's circumference—Kathryn Lasky tells his story in *The Librarian Who Measured the Earth* (1994). Modern-day discoverer Dr. Robert Ballard uncovered the *Titanic*'s sunken remains—his life is described by Rick Archbold in *Deep-Sea Explorer: The Story of Robert Ballard, Discoverer of the Titanic* (1994). Astronaut Judith Resnik lost her life on the space shuttle *Challenger*—her life is portrayed in *Judith Resnik: Challenger Astronaut* (1990), by Joanne E. Bernstein and Rose Blue.

Biographies of Social and Political Activists

Political leaders have always been a popular subject for biographies. Numerous political biographies of the U.S. presidents, and of many of their wives, have been written for children over the years. Authors have also focused on courageous individuals in other parts of the world who have led their people to freedom. For example, Leonard Everett Fisher's *Gandhi* (1995) chronicles the life of the man whose nonviolent approach to resistance paved the way for India's independence from Great Britain in 1947. Social reformers are dedicated to the betterment of people's lives. In *Mother Jones: One Woman's Fight for Labor* (1995), Betsy Harvey Kraft provides an insightful look at the story of Mary Harris Jones, an Irish immigrant, who helped organize labor unions among coal miners in the early twentieth century. Another great woman reformer, Jane Addams, founded the community center called Hull House community center in an impoverished area of Chicago in 1889. She is featured in *Peace and Bread: The Story of Jane Addams* (1993), by Stephanie Sammartino McPherson.

Biographies of Artists and Authors

Many biographies feature individuals who have contributed to the arts through music, art, dance, drama, and writing. *Anna Pavlova: Genius of the Dance* (1995), by Ellen Levine, tells the story of the world-famous ballerina. Martha Graham, choreographer and modern dance innovator, is described in Trudy Garfunkel's *Letter to the World: The Life and Dances of Martha Graham* (1995). The life of artist John James Audubon is recounted in *Capturing Nature: The Writings and Art of John James Audubon* (1993) by Peter and Connie Roop. Audubon's paintings of birds helped people gain awareness of the natural world, and the Roops rely on the artist's own journals to convey his life. The literary contribution of African American writer and anthropologist Zora Neale Hurston is chronicled in *Sorrow's Kitchen: The Life and Folklore of Zora Neale Hurston* (1990), by Mary E. Lyons. Children's authors have been the subject of many biographers. Notable books are *Nothing Is Impossible: The Story of Beatrix Potter* (1980), by Dorothy Aldis, and *Louisa May: The World and Works of Louisa May Alcott* (1991), by Norma Johnston.

Biographies of People Who Persevered

Throughout history, people in cultures and nations throughout the world have faced persecution because of their religion or ethnicity or have endured terrible economic or political conditions. The stories of how people have persevered against what seem insurmountable obstacles provide inspiration and teach valuable lessons.

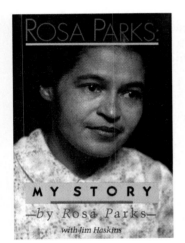

Illustration 11.6
Rosa Parks, the courageous woman whose action helped begin the civil rights movement, tells her story with the help of Jim Haskins. (*Rosa Parks: My Story* by Rosa Parks with Jim Haskins. Copyright © 1992 by Rosa Parks. Used by permission of Dial Books for Young Readers, a division of Penguin Books USA Inc.)

Religious and ethnic persecution in Europe has provided the backdrop for many biographies in this category. In *The Road from Home: The Story of an Armenian Girl* (1979), David Kherdian describes the life of his mother, who, as a child in Turkey, survived the Turkish persecution of Armenians during the early years of the twentieth century. Not all children survived the Holocaust of World War II; David Adler describes the life of *Hilde and Eli* (1994), two children who perished at the hands of the Nazis. Probably the most well-known child of the Holocaust, Anne Frank, is remembered in *Anne Frank: Beyond the Diary* (1993), by Ruud van der Rol and Rian Verhoeven.

African Americans' quest for freedom began during slavery, and their quest for equal treatment progressed through the civil rights movement and continues today. Those who have been part of this struggle have been featured in many biographies: Martin Luther King, Jr., Harriet Tubman, Frederick Douglass, Sojourner Truth. Rosa Parks became famous for refusing to sit in the back of a Montgomery, Alabama, bus in 1955. Jim Haskins collaborated with Parks to tell her life story in *Rosa Parks: My Story* (1992).

Autobiographies

In an autobiography, a person writes about his or her own life. Many children's authors have written their autobiographies. Children who delight in these authors' books enjoy reading about their childhoods and how they became writers. Laurence Yep penned *The Lost Garden* (1991), Yoshiko Uchida provided her memoirs in *The Invisible Thread* (1991), illustrator Ted Lewin described his early years in *I Was a Teenage Professional Wrestler* (1993), and Beverly Cleary wrote *A Girl from Yamhill: A Memoir* (1988).

Ordinary individuals often experience extraordinary events or inspire others with their courage and determination. Nelly S. Toll gives readers a glimpse into her childhood in *Behind the Secret Window: A Memoir of a Hidden Childhood during World War Two* (1993). Nelly and her mother lived for more than a year hiding in a Gentile couple's home in Lwów, Poland, where Nelly kept a diary and painted pictures. Ryan White, the teenager who contracted AIDS from blood products he needed because he was a hemophiliac, recounted his life with Ann Marie Cunningham's help in *Ryan White: My Own Story* (1991).

HOW BIOGRAPHIES WORK

Biographies are stories about real people. Like the writer of any good story, the biographer must create a main character about whom children care and want to learn more. Biographers develop their subjects' personalities and recreate their lives by describing their actions and their interactions with others, what they say, and the ways others talk about them. Descriptive language creates visual pictures in readers' minds, which help readers put themselves in the time and place of the biography's subject. Although biographers present lives of real people based on careful research, they must also interpret facts and events. Zarnowski (1990) points out:

> While biographers do gather all the information they can, they also filter that information through their minds. Biographers are active decision makers, deciding what to include and what to omit, what to highlight, and what to place in the background, and what to claim as truth and what to suggest as informed speculation. Biographers are interpreters of the information they collect. (p. 9)

Just as biographers interpret information, readers must interpret critically what they are reading. They must decide if the portrait of the person is balanced, if any aspects of the person's life have been fictionalized, if dialogue is authentic, and if the person is believable.

MAJOR WRITERS OF BIOGRAPHIES AND THEIR WORKS

A number of authors have established themselves as writers of biographies for children. Four who have influenced the nature and evolution of this genre are discussed in this section.

David Adler

David Adler, a former math teacher, has written books for children since 1972. A prolific writer of more than one hundred books, he pens novels and informational books as well as biographies. Adler is known for picture book biographies that primary school children can read independently. He notes that "the picture book biographies must be short, but that makes them very difficult to write" (Olendorf and Telgen, 1993, p. 4). Many of his biographies and informational books focus on Jewish persons or topics.

Our Golda: The Story of Golda Meir (1984), named a Carter G. Woodson Award Honor Book by the National Council of the Social Studies, traces Golda Meir's life from her childhood in Russia to her immigration to Milwaukee in 1906, her marriage and move to Palestine, her participation in the shaping of Israel, and her election in 1969 as Israel's Prime Minister.

In *Jackie Robinson: He Was the First* (1989), Adler follows Robinson's life from his birth in 1919 to his death in 1972. This complete biography is easily accessible to elementary students and includes a table of contents, an index, and a time line of Robinson's life.

Edgar Parin D'Aulaire and Ingri D'Aulaire

This husband and wife were both artists when they met and married in Paris in 1925. Ingri was born in Norway and Edgar in Germany. They immigrated to the United States in 1929 and began writing and illustrating children's books. Most of their more than twenty books are biographies of famous Americans and books about Norwegian culture. Ingri died in 1980 and Edgar in 1986.

Their biography *Abraham Lincoln* (1939) received the Caldecott Medal in 1940. The oversized picture book format of this book is typical of their other biographies: *Benjamin Franklin* (1950), *Columbus* (1955), and *George Washington* (1936). Hoke (1995) comments that "the style of their large, colorful, impressionistic illustrations was intended to appeal to a child's eye. The figures have a large paper-doll quality, resembling folk art" (p. 188).

Russell Freedman

Russell Freedman graduated from the University of California at Berkeley and worked for the Associated Press and on several television shows before becoming a writer of books for children in 1961. He has distinguished himself as an authentic biographer, conducting meticulous research in order to craft insightful portraits of real people. His biographies are illustrated with carefully selected photographs and include indexes, references, and lists of places to visit if one wants to learn more about the subjects. Freedman's biographies have received many awards and recognitions: *Franklin Delano Roosevelt* (1990) received the 1991 Orbis Pictus Award; *The Wright Brothers: How They Invented the Airplane* (1991) was named a Newbery Honor Book in 1992; and *Eleanor Roosevelt: A Life of Discovery* (1993) was a 1994 Newbery Honor Book.

Lincoln: A Photobiography (1987), which received the Newbery Medal in 1988, includes carefully researched illustrations to support and complement the text. In reflecting about this book, Freedman (1992) has pointed out: "The more I studied Lincoln, the more I came to appreciate his subtleties and complexities. The man himself turned out to be vastly more interesting than the myth" (p. 9).

Illustration 11.7
Winner of the Newbery Medal, Russell Freedman's photobiography provides a sympathetic, yet realistic picture of one of the most compelling of the U.S. Presidents. (*Lincoln: A Photobiography.* Copyright © 1987 by Russell Freedman. Reprinted by permission of Clarion Books/Houghton Mifflin Company. All rights reserved.)

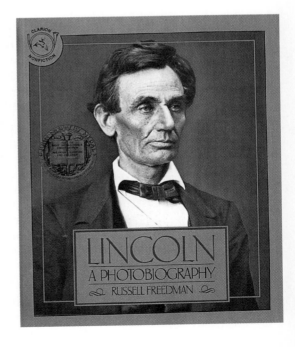

Jean Fritz

Jean Fritz has shaped and directed the genre of children's biography for more than twenty years. In addition to writing biography, Fritz also writes historical fiction and informational books. An attention to detail, the use of humor, and the ability to present historical figures in an interesting, appealing way are characteristic of her work. Fritz (1995) has commented: "I like to think of a historian or a biographer as an artist who has made a compact with the past to be true to it. As an artist, the historian has to use his or her imagination to penetrate the record, to dig deep into the past to the place where life emerges" (p. 257).

Several of Fritz's biographies have received prestigious awards: *Stonewall* (1979) and *Will You Sign Here, John Hancock?* (1974) were *Boston Globe–Horn Book* Honor Books; *The Great Little Madison* (1989) was named both the Orbis Pictus Award winner and the *Boston Globe–Horn Book* Nonfiction Award recipient in 1990; and *Where Do You Think You're Going, Christopher Columbus?* (1980) was an American Book Award Honor Book. For her significant contributions to children's literature, Fritz received the Laura Ingalls Wilder Award of the American Library Association in 1986.

CRITERIA FOR SELECTING BIOGRAPHIES

Like informational books, biographies have many unique characteristics that distinguish them from other genres of children's literature. As when choosing informational books, keep children's needs and interests foremost in your mind as you choose biographies. In addition, consider the following specific selection criteria.

Choice of Subject

The first criterion to think about in evaluating a biography is the subject of the work. Is the person someone whose life will be of interest to young readers? Has the individual contributed in a positive way to society? Controversial figures and people who have had a negative impact on society are also appropriate subjects for biographies because children's perspectives are broadened by reading about them—children can practice critical thinking by examining the individual's impact on society. The biography's subject may not be someone famous but rather an ordinary individual whose life inspires and/or interests readers.

Characterization

In writing a biography, an author must develop the subject so that readers identify with him or her as an authentic, believable human being. Notice how the author handles characterization and what details about the person's life the author includes. Readers learn about characters through their actions and interactions with others, through their thoughts and feelings, and through the things that others say about them. It is important for the author to avoid stereotyping the individual in any way. Another aspect of good characterization is balanced treatment of the subject. Is the individual's life presented honestly? Has the author avoided idealizing the individual and creating a superhuman personality?

Accuracy and Authenticity

A biography needs to reflect careful research about the individual's life so that the information presented is accurate. Generally, authors try to consult primary source material, such as the subject's personal journal or letters to others. If photographs are used as illustrations, they should be carefully selected to support the biography. In addition, what kinds of information has the author selected to include? Has any important information been omitted? The author should include a bibliography that lists the sources of information. An author's note may add an explanation about the type of research that was conducted or describe background material.

Writing Style

The author's writing style influences readers' interest and enjoyment of a biography. Has the author written in an engaging style that maintains readers' attention? Has the author created a story line that will involve the reader without sacrificing accuracy? What is the author's tone? It may be serious, humorous, or neutral. From whose point of view is the biography being told?

AWARDS FOR INFORMATIONAL BOOKS AND BIOGRAPHIES

Although many awards, such as the Newbery Medal and the Caldecott Medal, may be given to a children's book of any genre, certain awards focus exclusively on nonfiction. Many of these awards are indicated on the book in some way—for example, by seals that appear on the book jacket. The National Council of Teachers of English annually bestows the Orbis Pictus Award for Outstanding Nonfiction for Children, with one book receiving the award and several being cited as Honor Books. The *Boston Globe–Horn Book* Award, which has a separate category for nonfiction, is given annually to one book, with up to three books being designated as Honor Books. The National Council for the Social Studies sponsors the Carter G. Woodson Book Award to honor children's books that sensitively and accurately deal with ethnic minorities and race relations. The Washington D.C. Children's Book Guild, in conjunction with the *Washington Post,* annually presents the *Washington Post*–Children's Book Guild Nonfiction Award to an author in recognition of his or her contribution to children's nonfiction. The American Nature Society honors an author for his or her contribution to science writing for children with the Eva L. Gordon Award for Children's Science Literature. The Golden Kite Award of the Society for Children's Book Writers has a nonfiction category, which includes one winner and one Honor Book annually. The Jefferson Cup Award, sponsored by the Virginia Library Association, is presented to one book of fiction or nonfiction that deals with U.S. history or biography. In addition, the Children's Book Council, in cooperation with both the National Council of the Social Studies and the National Science Teachers Association, develops annual lists of outstanding books from all genres: *Notable Children's Trade Books in the Field of Social Studies* and *Outstanding Science Trade Books for Children.*

 TEACHING IDEAS

Writing in a Comparison/Contrast Format. Introduce children to books whose purpose is to compare and contrast two animals or concepts—for example, *Toad or Frog, Swamp or Bog?* (1994) by Lynda Graham-Barber, *A Wasp Is*

Not a Bee (1995) by Marilyn Singer, and *What's the Difference?* (1993) by Elizabeth Lacey. After discussing the techniques the author used to make the comparisons, ask children to write their own comparison of two animals, plants, or items.

Studying an Author in Depth. Involve a group of children in an in-depth study of one particular author of informational books or biographies. Have children read several books by the author and respond to these books in various ways, such as with discussion, writing, art, and drama. Small groups of students can create projects such as murals, mobiles, dioramas, and skits to represent the books and the author.

Critically Reviewing Books on the Same Topic. Ask children to select a topic and read at least two books about it. For example, students can compare *Wildlife Rescue: The Work of Dr. Kathleen Ramsay* (1994), by Jennifer Owings Dewey, with *Raptor Rescue: An Eagle Flies Free* (1995), by Sylvia Johnson. Have children develop categories for comparison, and chart the similarities and differences in the books. This idea can also be applied to biographies. Ask children to read two or more biographies about an individual and chart their similarities and differences.

Readers Theater. Have groups of three or four children read the same biography (for example, *Kate Shelley: Bound for Legend*, 1995, by Robert D. San Souci) and create a readers theater script of the biography. After writing the script, the group can present it to the entire class.

EXPERIENCES FOR YOUR LEARNING

1. Review an award-winning informational book such as *Volcano: The Eruption and Healing of Mount St. Helens* (1986), by Patricia Lauber, and an award-winning biography such as *Eleanor Roosevelt: A Life of Discovery* (1993), by Russell Freedman. Critique each book according to the criteria in this chapter. Would you agree that the books are worthy of the awards they received? What do you see as their strengths and weaknesses?

2. Select a topic that interests you, say wolves. Compare the treatment of the topic in an informational book (such as *To the Top of the World: Adventures with Arctic Wolves*, 1993, by Jim Brandenburg) to its treatment in other genres such as novels (for example, *Julie of the Wolves*, 1972, by Jean Craighead George), picture books (*Wolf's Favor*, 1986, by Fulvio Testa), and folktales (*Peter and the Wolf*, 1990, retold by Selina Hastings). How do different genres contribute to your understanding of the topic?

3. Select three informational books on the same topic (for example, for the Negro Baseball Leagues, you could use *Black Diamond: The Story of the Negro Baseball Leagues*, 1994, by Patricia C. McKissack and Fredrick McKissack, Jr.; *Shadow Ball: The History of the Negro Leagues*, 1994, by Geoffrey C. Ward and Ken Burns; and *Leagues Apart: The Men and Times of the Negro Baseball Leagues*, 1995, by Lawrence S. Ritter). Review the illustrations in each book. How do the illustrations convey information? What kind of information is presented? What types of illustrations are included—photographs, paintings, drawings, diagrams, charts? Are some illustrations more effective than others? What makes them more effective? Compare the illustrations on a chart with a column for each book. Share your findings with classmates.

4. Compare the scope, content, and presentation of material about a science topic in an informational book and a textbook. How are the books alike? How are they different? Which type of book do you think is more effective in conveying information? Why? Discuss these issues with your classmates.

RECOMMENDED BOOKS

History

Blumberg, Rhoda. *Commodore Perry in the Land of the Shogun*. New York: Lothrop, Lee & Shepard, 1985. Describes Matthew Perry's important voyage to Japan to open trade and whaling ports to America. (**I:** 10–YA)

——. *Full Steam Ahead: The Race to Build a Transcontinental Railroad*. Washington, D.C.: National Geographic Society, 1996. A fascinating account of the race between the Central Pacific and the Union Pacific to finish laying the tracks for the transcontinental railroad. (**I:** 10–YA)

——. *The Great American Gold Rush*. New York: Bradbury, 1989. The discovery of gold in California in 1848 caused "gold fever" and mass emigration. (**I:** 10–YA)

Burleigh, Robert. *Flight*. New York: Philomel, 1991. Chronicles Charles Lindbergh's 1927 solo flight across the Atlantic from New York to Paris. (**I:** 8–12)

Colman, Penny. *Rosie the Riveter: Women Working on the Home Front during World War II*. New York: Crown, 1995. Details the role of women in the wartime workforce. (**I:** 9–YA)

Fraser, Mary Ann. *In Search of the Grand Canyon*. New York: Holt, 1995. Describes the journey of John Wesley Powell and his nine-man crew as they explored the Colorado River in 1869. (**I:** 8–12)

* Gibbons, Gail. *Sunken Treasure*. New York: Crowell, 1988. Full-color illustrations help describe the sinking of an ancient Spanish galleon and the discovery of its treasures. (**I:** 6–10)

Giblin, James Cross. *From Hand to Mouth or, How We Invented Knives, Forks, Spoons, and Chopsticks and the Table Manners to Go with Them*. New York: Crowell, 1987. Presents the history of eating utensils and the social customs surrounding their use. (**I:** 8–12)

——. *The Riddle of the Rosetta Stone: Key to Ancient Egypt*. New York: Crowell, 1990. The story of the discovery of the ancient Rosetta Stone and the deciphering of its hieroglyphics. (**I:** 8–12)

Hamilton, Virginia. *Many Thousand Gone: African Americans from Slavery to Freedom*. Illustrated by Leo and Diane Dillon. New York: Knopf, 1993. Tells thirty-five stories of African Americans during slavery and in the Underground Railroad. (**I:** 8–YA)

Haskins, James. *Get on Board: The Story of the Underground Railroad*. New York: Scholastic, 1993. Chronicles the Underground Railroad, which shepherded slaves to freedom in the North. (**I:** 8–12)

——. *The March on Washington*. New York: HarperCollins, 1993. Describes the planning and consequences of the historic 1963 March on Washington for Jobs and Freedom. (**I:** 9–12)

Hunt, Jonathan. *Illuminations*. New York: Bradbury, 1989. This book uses an alphabet format to discuss the Middle Ages. (**I:** 8–12)

Jacobs, Francine. *The Tainos: The People Who Welcomed Columbus*. Illustrated by Patrick Collins. New York: Putnam. 1992. A history of the Taino people who lived in the Caribbean when Christopher Columbus arrived there. (**I:** 9–YA)

Lawrence, Jacob. *The Great Migration: An American Story*. New York: HarperCollins, 1993. A narrative sequence of vibrant paintings help tell the story of African Americans' migration from the South to the North around World War I. (**I:** 8–12)

McKissack, Patricia C., and Fredrick L. McKissack. *Christmas in the Big House, Christmas in the Quarters*. New York: Scholastic, 1994. A fascinating and insightful comparison of life in a Virginia plantation house and in the slave quarters around Christmas time in 1859. (**I:** 8–12)

Murphy, Jim. *Across America on an Emigrant Train*. New York: Clarion, 1993. The story of Robert Louis Stevenson's trip from Scotland to San Francisco in 1879 in search of his true love is combined with a history of the railroad. (**I:** 10–YA)

——. *The Great Fire*. New York: Scholastic, 1995. Describes the Chicago fire of 1871 and its effects on individual people and the city. (**I:** 10–YA)

——. *The Long Road to Gettysburg*. New York: Clarion, 1992. Two perspectives on the 1863 battle of Gettysburg, one from a Confederate soldier and the other from a Union one. (**I:** 10–YA)

Myers, Walter Dean. *Now Is Your Time! The African-American Struggle for Freedom*. New York: HarperCollins, 1991. Provides a history of African Americans from slavery to modern times. (**I:** 10–YA)

Rounds, Glen. *Sod Houses of the Great Plains*. New York: Holiday House, 1995. Explanation of how homesteaders on the Great Plains built houses from prairie sod. (**I:** 5–9)

Stanley, Jerry. *Children of the Dust Bowl: The True Story of the School at Weedpatch Camp*. New York: Crown, 1992. The inspirational story of how educator Leo Hart and Okie children built their own school during the depression in California. (**I**: 10–YA)

———. *I Am an American: A True Story of Japanese Internment*. New York: Crown, 1994. Discusses the relocation of Japanese Americans from 1942 to 1945. (**I**: 10–YA)

Warren, A. *Orphan Train Rider: One Boy's True Story*. Boston: Houghton Mifflin, 1996. The story of Lee Nailling, who rode the "Orphan Train" in 1926, provides the framework for discussing this train, which transported orphaned and abandoned children from the East Coast to the Midwest from 1854 to 1929. (**I**: 9–12)

Understanding Peoples and Cultures

* Aliki. *Mummies Made in Egypt*. New York: Harper-Collins, 1979. Details the reasons for mummification and explains how it was done. (**I**: 7–12)

Anderson, Joan. *The American Family Farm*. Photographs by George Ancona. San Diego, CA: Harcourt, 1989. Describes the daily farm life of three families who live in Georgia, Iowa, and Massachusetts. (**I**: 8–12)

Cha, Dia. *Dia's Story Cloth: The Hmong People's Journey of Freedom*. Stitched by Chue and Nhia Thao Cha. New York: Lee & Low, 1996. A hand-embroidered story cloth recounts the story of the Hmong people of ancient China and Laos and their emigration to the United States. (**I**: 8–12)

Giblin, James Cross. *Chimney Sweeps: Yesterday and Today*. Illustrated by Margot Tomes. New York: HarperCollins, 1982. An examination of the job of chimney sweeps from the fifteenth century to modern times. (**I**: 9–12)

———. *When Plague Strikes: The Black Death, Smallpox, AIDS*. New York: HarperCollins, 1995. Discusses epidemic diseases and their political, social, religious, and cultural consequences. (**I**: 10–YA)

Hoyt-Goldsmith, Diane. *Cherokee Summer*. Photographs by Lawrence Migdale. New York: Holiday House, 1993. Ten-year-old Bridget shares information about her life and the Cherokee Nation. (**I**: 7–12)

———. *Day of the Dead: A Mexican-American Celebration*. Photographs by Lawrence Migdale. New York: Holiday House,1994. Twin sisters in California describe the Day of the Dead celebration. (**I**: 7–12)

———. *Totem Pole*. Photographs by Lawrence Migdale. New York: Holiday House, 1990. David, a Tsimshian boy, describes how his father carved a ceremonial totem pole for the tribe. (**I**: 7–12)

Meltzer, Milton. *The Amazing Potato*. New York: HarperCollins, 1992. A fascinating discussion of the history and social aspects of the potato. (**I**: 8–12)

———. *Cheap Raw Material: How Our Youngest Workers Are Exploited and Abused*. New York: Viking, 1994. A compelling account of child labor from long ago to the present. (**I**: 10–YA)

Onyefulu, I. *Ogbo: Sharing Life in an African Village*. San Diego, CA: Harcourt, 1996. Six-year-old Obioma explains the Nigerian tradition of *ogbo*, or age group, in this photo essay. (**I**: 7–11)

Osborne, Mary Pope, *One World, Many Religions: The Ways We Worship*. New York: Knopf, 1996. Photographs and text describe the world's major religions: Judaism, Christianity, Islam, Hinduism, Buddhism, Confucianism, and Taoism. (**I**: 8–YA)

Reynolds, Jan. *Amazon Basin*. San Diego, CA: Harcourt, 1993. A photo essay on the Yanomama people of the Amazon Basin. (**I**: 7–12)

———. *Frozen Land*. San Diego, CA: Harcourt, 1988. Description of the Inuit culture of the Arctic. (**I**: 7–12)

———. *Mongolia*. San Diego, CA: Harcourt, 1994. The nomadic way of life in Mongolia is described in this photo essay. (**I**: 8–12)

———. *Sahara*. San Diego, CA: Harcourt, 1991. The Tuareg tribe who live in the Sahara desert are featured in this photo essay. (**I**: 7–12)

Rylant, Cynthia. *Appalachia: The Voices of Sleeping Birds*. Illustrated by Barry Moser. San Diego, CA: Harcourt, 1991. Watercolor paintings complement this description of social life and customs in the Appalachian region. (**I**: 8–12)

Science and Nature

Bash, Barbara. *Ancient Ones: The World of the Old-Growth Douglas Fir*. San Francisco: Sierra Club, 1994. Watercolor paintings enhance this discussion of the life cycle of the Douglas fir and the ecology of the forest. (**I**: 6–12)

———. *Shadows of Night: The Hidden World of the Little Brown Bat*. San Francisco: Sierra Club, 1993. Describes the life of the brown bat in text and illustrations. (**I**: 6–12)

———. *Urban Roosts: Where Birds Nest in the City*. San Francisco: Sierra Club, 1990. Watercolor illustrations complement this discussion of the many birds who have adapted to urban life. (**I**: 6–12)

Brandenburg, Jim. *To the Top of the World: Adventures with Arctic Wolves*. New York: Walker, 1993.

Magnificent color photographs enhance this personal account of the author's observations of a wolf pack. (I: 6–12)

Brooks, Bruce. *Making Sense: Animal Perception and Communication*. New York: Farrar, 1993. An insightful examination of animals' six senses and how they use them to communicate. (I: 8–12)

Cherry, Lynne. *A River Ran Wild*. San Diego, CA: Harcourt, 1992. This history of the Nashua River in New England explores humans' influence on nature. (I: 6–12)

Cole, Joanna. *The Magic School Bus inside the Earth*. Illustrated by Bruce Degen. New York: Scholastic, 1987. Ms. Frizzle and her class investigate geology on a field trip to the center of earth. (I: 5–8)

Cone, Molly. *Come Back, Salmon*. Photographs by Sidnee Wheelwright. San Francisco: Sierra Club, 1992. The inspiring story of the students at Jackson Elementary School in Everett, Washington, who adopted the stream by their school and brought it back to life. (I: 7–12)

Dewey, Jennifer Owings. *Wildlife Rescue: The Work of Dr. Kathleen Ramsay*. Photographs by Don MacCarter. Honesdale, PA: Boyds Mills, 1994. Describes the wildlife center in rural New Mexico founded by veterinarian Ramsay, who takes care of injured and sick animals. (I: 7–12)

George, Jean Craighead. *Animals Who Have Won Our Hearts*. Illustrated by Christine Herman Merrill. New York: HarperCollins, 1994. Portraits of ten famous animals including Balto the sled dog and Koko the signing gorilla. (I: 5–12)

* Gibbons, Gail. *The Milk Makers*. New York: Macmillan, 1985. Describes how dairy cows produce milk and the steps it follows to get to the store. (I: P–8)

* ———. *Spiders*. New York: Holiday House, 1993. A picture book examination of different kinds of spiders and their characteristics. (I: P–8)

Johnson, Sylvia. *Raptor Rescue! An Eagle Flies Free*. Photographs by Ron Winch. New York: Dutton, 1995. Describes the work of the Gabbert Raptor Center at the University of Minnesota, which cares for and rehabilitates injured birds. (I: 7–12)

Keeler, Patricia A., and Francis X. McCall, Jr. *Unraveling Fibers*. New York: Atheneum, 1995. Illustrated with color photographs, this book explores fibers from plants and animals as well as synthetic fibers. (I: 8–12)

Lasky, Kathryn. *Sugaring Time*. Photographs by Christopher Knight. New York: Macmillan, 1983. Describes maple sugar time on a Vermont family farm. (I: 8–12)

———. *Surtsey: The Newest Place on Earth*. New York: Hyperion, 1992. Describes the creation of Surtsey, a volcanic island off the coast of Iceland. (I: 8–12)

Lauber, Patricia. *The News about Dinosaurs*. New York: Bradbury, 1989. Examines new discoveries about dinosaurs that challenge what scientists previously believed. (I: 6–12)

———. *Seeing Earth from Space*. New York: Orchard, 1990. NASA photographs complement the text, which provides a unique perspective on the earth. (I: 10–YA)

———. *Summer of Fire: Yellowstone 1988*. New York: Orchard, 1991. Describes the 1988 Yellowstone fire and the return of plants and animals to the forest ecology. (I: 8–12)

———. *Volcano: The Eruption and Healing of Mount St. Helens*. New York: Bradbury, 1986. Illustrated with color photographs, this book describes the 1980 eruption of Mount St. Helens and its aftermath. (I: 8–12)

Markle, Sandra. *Science to the Rescue*. New York: Atheneum, 1994. Describes contemporary problems and discusses ways that science is solving them. (I: 8–12)

McMillan, Bruce. *Summer Ice: Life along the Antarctic Peninsula*. Boston: Houghton Mifflin, 1995. A photo essay about the plants and animals of the Antarctic. (I: 7–12)

Pringle, Laurence. *Antarctica*. New York: Simon and Schuster, 1992. A comprehensive discussion of the continent of Antarctica. (I: 8–12)

———. *Fire in the Forest: A Cycle of Growth and Renewal*. Illustrated by Bob Marstall. New York: Atheneum, 1995. An explanation of the fire cycle and its relationship to the forest ecology. (I: 6–12)

Simon, Seymour. *Earthquakes*. New York: Morrow, 1991. Photographs help explain the nature of earthquakes. (I: 5–12)

———. *Sharks*. New York: HarperCollins, 1995. With full-page photographs, this book dispels many myths about these fascinating creatures. (I: 7–12)

———. *Wolves*. New York: HarperCollins, 1993. Color photographs enhance the discussion of characteristics and habits of wolves. (I: 5–12)

Swanson, Diane. *Safari beneath the Sea: The Wonder World of the North Pacific Coast*. San Francisco: Sierra Club, 1994. Underwater color photographs from the Royal British Columbia Museum introduce readers to the plants and animals of the North Pacific coast. (I: 7–12)

The Arts

Davidson, Rosemary. *Take a Look: An Introduction to the Experience of Art*. New York: Viking, 1993. Experiments and activities introduce children to the history, techniques, and functions of art. (I: 10–YA)

Greenberg, Jan, and Sandra Jordan. *Sculptor's Eye: Looking at Contemporary American Art*. New York: Delacorte, 1993. Explores modern sculpture—its subject matter and techniques—and important artists. (I: 10–YA)

Haldane, Suzanne. *Painting Faces*. New York: Dutton, 1988. Explains different kinds of face painting around the world, with directions on how to do each kind. (I: 7–12)

* Kuklin, Susan. *Going to My Ballet Class*. New York: Bradbury, 1989. A photo essay takes readers to a young girl's ballet class. (I: P–8)

Sullivan, Charles, ed. *Children of Promise: African-American Literature and Art for Young People*. New York: Abrams, 1991. African American history is chronicled through art, literary excerpts, and poems. (I: 8–YA)

Switzer, Ellen. *The Magic of Mozart: Mozart, the Magic Flute, and the Salzburg Marionettes*. Photos by Costas. New York: Atheneum, 1995. A book with three interrelated sections that describe the life of Mozart, his opera the *Magic Flute*, and the Salzburg Marionettes that perform it. (I: 9–12)

How Things Work

* Aliki. *How a Book Is Made*. New York: Crowell, 1986. Details the steps in book production from the author's idea to when the book is finally in the hands of salespeople in the store. (I: 7–12)

Cobb, Vicki. *The Secret Life of Cosmetics*. Illustrated by Theo Cobb. Philadelphia: Lippincott, 1985. Science experiments provide understanding of how shampoo, toothpaste, soap, and nail polish work. (I: 10–YA)

Cole, Joanna. *The Magic School Bus at the Waterworks*. Illustrated by Bruce Degen. New York: Scholastic, 1987. Ms. Frizzle and her class visit a water treatment plant. (I: 5–8)

———. *The Magic School Bus inside the Human Body*. Illustrated by Bruce Degen. New York: Scholastic, 1989. Ms. Frizzle and her class discover how the human body and its systems work. (I: 5–8)

* Gibbons, Gail. *The Great St. Lawrence Seaway*. New York: Morrow, 1992. Explains how this inland waterway system works and permits ships to travel from the ocean to the Great Lakes through canals, locks, and gates. (I: 6–10)

Giblin, James Cross. *Be Seated: A Book about Chairs*. New York: HarperCollins, 1993. This book explores the changing technology and design of chairs as well as their social functions. (I: 8–12)

Harris, Robie H. *It's Perfectly Normal: Changing Bodies, Growing Up, Sex, and Sexual Health*. Illustrated by Michael Emberley. Cambridge, MA: Candlewick, 1994. A detailed description of how the reproductive system works, including a section on staying healthy. (I: 10–YA)

Macaulay, David. *Castle*. Boston: Houghton Mifflin, 1977. Detailed description of how a thirteenth-century Welsh castle was constructed. (I: 9–YA)

———. *Cathedral: The Story of Its Construction*. Boston: Houghton Mifflin, 1973. Explains the intricate process of building a Gothic cathedral. (I: 9–YA)

———. *The Way Things Work*. Boston: Houghton Mifflin, 1988. A tribute to technology, this book explains how all kinds of machines work. (I: 10–YA)

Moser, Barry. *Fly: A Brief History of Flight Illustrated*. New York: HarperCollins, 1993. Through illustrations and text, readers learn about various methods of flying that have been tried throughout history. (I: 8–12)

* Platt, Richard. *Cross Sections: Man-of-War*. Illustrated by Steven Beisty. New York: Dorling Kindersley, 1993. Intricate, detailed drawings take readers aboard an eighteenth-century British warship. (I: 8–12)

* Schwartz, David M. *If You Made a Million*. Illustrated by Steven Kellogg. New York: Lothrop, Lee & Shepard, 1989. This informational picture book introduces readers to various forms of money and personal finance. (I: 6–12)

Skurzynski, Gloria. *Robots: Your High-Tech World*. New York: Bradbury, 1990. A comprehensive discussion of robots and robotics technology. (I: 8–12)

Activity, Craft, and How-to Books

Hansen-Smith, Bradford. *The Hands-On Marvelous Ball Book*. New York: Scientific American, 1995. Using paper plates, masking tape, and bobby pins, readers follow directions to explore three-dimensional geometry and the unity of shapes and patterns. (I: 8–12)

Lankford, Mary D. *Hopscotch around the World*. Illustrated by Karen Milone. New York: Morrow, 1992. Illustrated directions for playing nineteen variants of hopscotch. (I: 5–10)

Sachar, Louis. *Sideways Arithmetic from Wayside School*. New York: Scholastic, 1989. Logical problem-solving is emphasized in this humorous book, which links puzzle-type math to other school subjects. (I: 8–12)

Sullivan, George. *In-Line Skating: A Complete Guide for Beginners*. New York: Dutton, 1993. Explains rollerblading and includes information on safety and how to take care of skates. (I: 8–12)

Walker, Barbara M. *The Little House Cookbook: Frontier Food from Laura Ingalls Wilder's Classic Stories*. New York: HarperCollins, 1979. Each of the more than one hundred recipes is accompanied by a short introduction and is featured in one of Wilder's books. (I: 6–12)

U.S. Political Leaders

Freedman, Russell. *Eleanor Roosevelt: A Life of Discovery*. New York: Clarion, 1993. The life of a famous first lady, wife of President Franklin Delano Roosevelt, who devoted herself to public service and worked on behalf of human rights. (I: 9–YA)

———. *Franklin Delano Roosevelt*. New York: Clarion, 1990. The life of Franklin Delano Roosevelt, who was President during the Depression and World War II. (I: 10–YA)

———. *Lincoln: A Photobiography*. New York: Clarion, 1987. The biography of Abraham Lincoln, who was President during the Civil War. (I: 9–YA)

Fritz, Jean. *And Then What Happened, Paul Revere?* Illustrated by Margot Tomes. New York: Coward McCann, 1973. A humorous biography of patriot Paul Revere. (I: 7–12)

———. *Bully for You, Teddy Roosevelt!* Illustrated by Mike Wimmer. New York: Putnam, 1991. A biography of the twenty-sixth President who was also a conservationist. (I: 9–12)

———. *The Great Little Madison*. New York: Putnam, 1989. A biography of James Madison, fourth President of the United States and the father of the Constitution. (I: 9–12)

———. *Why Don't You Get a Horse, Sam Adams?* Illustrated by Trina Schart Hyman. New York: Coward McCann, 1974. Describes the reluctance of Sam Adams to ride a horse. (I: 7–12)

———. *Will You Sign Here, John Hancock?* Illustrated by Trina Schart Hyman. New York: Coward McCann, 1974. A biography of the famous signer of the Declaration of Independence. (I: 7–12)

———. *You Want Women to Vote, Lizzie Stanton?* Illustrated by DyAnne DiSalvo-Ryan. New York: Putnam, 1995. A biography of Elizabeth Cady Stanton, a pioneer in the women's suffrage movement. (I: 8–12)

Harrison, Barbara, and Daniel Terris. *A Twilight Struggle: The Life of John Fitzgerald Kennedy*. New York: Lothrop, Lee & Shepard, 1992. The biography of President John Fitzgerald Kennedy, who was assassinated while in office in 1963. (I: 11–YA)

* Marzollo, Jean. *Happy Birthday, Martin Luther King*. Illustrated by Brian Pinkney. New York: Scholastic, 1993. A picture book biography of the famous civil rights leader. (I: 5–9)

Myers, Walter Dean. *Malcolm X: By Any Means Necessary*. New York: Scholastic, 1993. The life of the black leader who was assassinated in 1965. (I: 10–YA)

U.S. Historical Figures

Conrad, Pam. *Prairie Visions: The Life and Times of Solomon Butcher*. New York: HarperCollins, 1991. A biography of Solomon Butcher, a photographer in Nebraska in the late nineteenth century. (I: 9–12)

Freedman, Russell. *Indian Chiefs*. New York: Holiday House, 1987. A collective biography of six famous Native American leaders. (I: 10–YA)

———. *Kids at Work: Lewis Hine and the Crusade against Child Labor*. New York: Clarion, 1994. The biography of photographer and social reformer Lewis Hine, whose photographs helped ensure the passage of child labor laws. (I: 9–YA)

Fritz, Jean. *Stonewall*. Illustrated by Stephen Gammell. New York: Putnam, 1979. A biography of Thomas J. Jackson, the Confederate Civil War general. (I: 10–YA)

———. *Where Do You Think You're Going, Christopher Columbus?* Illustrated by Margot Tomes. New York: Putnam, 1980. A biography of explorer Christopher Columbus. (I: 7–12)

Klausner, Janet. *Sequoyah's Gift: A Portrait of the Cherokee Leader*. New York: HarperCollins, 1993. A biography of the Cherokee leader who developed the system of writing the Cherokee language. (I: 9–12)

Kraft, Betsy Harvey. *Mother Jones: One Woman's Fight for Labor*. New York: Clarion, 1995. A biography of the courageous woman labor leader who worked on behalf of coal miners and child laborers during the nineteenth and early twentieth centuries. (I: 8–12)

Marrin, Albert. *Unconditional Surrender: U. S. Grant and the Civil War*. New York: Atheneum, 1994. This biography describes the role of Ulysses S. Grant as a military leader during the Civil War. (I: 10–YA)

McPherson, Stephanie Sammartino. *Peace and Bread: The Story of Jane Addams*. Minneapolis: Carolrhoda, 1993. A biography of the woman who founded Hull

House in Chicago and was active in the Women's International League for Peace and Freedom. (I: 9–12)

San Souci, Robert D. *Kate Shelley: Bound for Legend.* Illustrated by Max Ginsburg. New York: Dial. 1995. The courage of a fifteen-year-old prevents a train disaster in Iowa in 1881. (I: 8–12)

World Leaders

Adler, David A. *Our Golda: The Story of Golda Meir.* Illlustrated by Donna Ruff. New York: Puffin, 1986. Biography of the first female prime minister of Israel. (I: 7–11)

Cooper, Floyd. *Mandela: From the Life of the South African Statesman.* New York: Philomel, 1996. Describes the life of Nelson Mandela from his birth in a tiny South African village in 1918 to his release from prison in 1990. (I: 8–12)

Fisher, Leonard Everett. *Gandhi.* New York: Atheneum, 1995. The biography of Mohandas K. Gandhi, who developed the practice of nonviolent resistance as he led India to independence from England. (I: 9–12)

Stanley, Diane, and Peter Vennema. *Cleopatra.* New York: Morrow, 1994. Full-page paintings complement the story of the famous Egyptian queen. (I:10–YA)

Explorers of Earth and Space

Archbold, Rick. *Deep-Sea Explorer: The Story of Robert Ballard, Discoverer of the Titantic.* New York: Scholastic, 1994. The life of Dr. Robert Ballard, the oceanographer who discovered the wreck of the *Titanic* in 1986. (I: 8–YA)

Freedman, Russell. *The Wright Brothers: How They Invented the Airplane.* New York: Holiday House, 1991. The lives of Wilbur and Orville Wright. (I: 9–YA)

Gormley, Beatrice. *Maria Mitchell: The Soul of an Astronomer.* Grand Rapids, MI: William B. Eerdmans, 1995. The story of the first female professional astronomer in the United States, who discovered a comet. (I: 10–YA)

* Lasky, Kathryn. *The Librarian Who Measured the Earth.* Illustrated by Kevin Hawkes. New York: Little, Brown, 1994. A picture book biography of Eratosthenes, the Greek astronomer who measured the circumference of the earth. (I: 6–12)

Meltzer, Milton. *Columbus and the World around Him.* Danbury, CT: Franklin Watts, 1990. A provocative biography of Christopher Columbus, the Italian explorer who sailed for the Orient and landed in America. (I: 10–YA)

Provensen, Alice, and Martin Provensen. *The Glorious Flight: Across the Channel with Louis Blériot.* New York: Viking, 1983. A Frenchman builds a flying machine to cross the English Channel in 1909. (I: 6–12)

Sis, Peter. *Starry Messenger.* New York: Farrar, 1996. Exquisite illustrations help recount the life of astronomer Galileo Galilei. (I: 7–11)

Towle, Wendy. *The Real McCoy: The Life of an African-American Inventor.* Illustrated by Wil Clay. New York: Scholastic, 1993. The life of Elijah McCoy, who patented over fifty inventions. (I: 6–12)

Artists and Authors

Ada, Alma Flor. *Where the Flame Trees Bloom.* Illustrated by Antonio Martorell. New York: Atheneum, 1994. A children's author shares stories about her family and growing up in Cuba. (I: 8–12)

* Cooper, Floyd. *Coming Home: From the Life of Langston Hughes.* New York: Philomel, 1994. This picture book biography focuses on the childhood of the well-known African American poet. (I: 6–12)

* Cummings, Pat. *Talking with Artists.* New York: Bradbury, 1992. Biographical interviews with fourteen well-known children's book illustrators. (I: 5–12)

Garfunkel, Trudy. *Letter to the World: The Life and Dances of Martha Graham.* New York: Little, Brown, 1995. The biography of the dancer and choreographer who pioneered modern dance. (I: 8–12)

Johnston, Norma. *Louisa May: The World and Works of Louisa May Alcott.* New York: Macmillan, 1991. A carefully researched biography of the beloved author of *Little Women.* (I: 10–YA)

Krull, Kathleen. *Lives of the Artists: Masterpieces, Messes (and What the Neighbors Thought).* Illustrated by Kathryn Hewitt. San Diego, CA: Harcourt, 1995. Biographical sketches of sixteen artists including Georgia O'Keefe, Diego Rivera, and Frida Kahlo. (I: 8–12)

———. *Lives of the Musicians: Good Times, Bad Times (and What the Neighbors Thought).* Illustrated by Kathryn Hewitt. San Diego, CA: Harcourt, 1993. Biographical sketches of twenty musicians and composers including Bach, Scott Joplin, and Woody Guthrie. (I: 8–12)

———. *Lives of the Writers: Comedies, Tragedies (and What the Neighbors Thought).* Illustrated by Kathryn Hewitt. San Diego, CA: Harcourt, 1994. Biographical sketches of sixteen writers, including Langston Hughes, Zora Neale Hurston, and E. B. White. (I: 8–12)

Levine, Ellen. *Anna Pavlova: Genius of the Dance.* New York: Scholastic, 1995. A complete biography of the famous Russian ballet dancer. (I: 8–12)

Lewin, Ted. *I Was a Teenage Professional Wrestler.* New York: Orchard, 1993. An autobiography of children's author-illustrator Ted Lewin, who supported himself through art school as a wrestler. (I: 10–YA)

Lyons, Mary E. *Sorrow's Kitchen: The Life and Folklore of Zora Neale Hurston.* New York: Scribner's, 1990. A biography of the African American folklorist, who lived during the Harlem Renaissance. (I: 10–YA)

Mohr, Nicholasa. *In My Own Words: Growing Up inside the Sanctuary of My Imagination.* New York: Julian Messner, 1994. A children's author describes her own childhood until she was almost fifteen, when her mother died. (I: 8–12)

Monceaux, Morgan. *Jazz: My Music, My People.* New York: Knopf, 1994. Biographical sketches of jazz musicians from the early years to bebop and modern jazz. (I: 8–12)

Roop, Peter, and Connie Roop. *Capturing Nature: The Writings and Art of John James Audubon.* Illustrated by Rick Farley. New York: Walker, 1993. The life and work of this naturalist and artist are conveyed through his journals. (I: 8–12)

Sills, Leslie. *Visions: Stories about Women Artists.* Morton Grove, IL: Whitman, 1993. Biographies of four visionary women artists: Mary Cassatt, Leonora Carrington, Betye Saar, and Mary Frank. (I: 10–YA)

* Stanley, Diane, and Peter Vennema. *The Bard of Avon: The Story of William Shakespeare.* New York: Morrow, 1992. A picture book biography of the most famous British playwright. (I: 10–YA)

Uchida, Yoshiko. *The Invisible Thread.* New York: Julian Messner, 1991. An autobiography of a Japanese American children's author whose family spent World War II in an internment camp. (I: 9–12)

Yep, Laurence. *The Lost Garden.* New York: Julian Messner, 1991. A memoir by the award-winning children's author. (I: 8–12)

People Who Persevered

Adler, David A. *Hilde and Eli: Children of the Holocaust.* Illustrated by Karen Ritz. New York: Holiday House, 1994. The story of two Jewish children killed by the Nazis during World War II. (I: 8–12)

———. *Jackie Robinson: He Was the First.* Illustrated by Robert Casilla. New York: Holiday House, 1989. The biography of the first African American to play major league baseball. (I: 5–9)

Hamilton, Virginia. *Anthony Burns: The Defeat and Triumph of a Fugitive Slave.* New York: Knopf. 1988. In 1854, Anthony Burns escaped from a Virginia plantation and came to Boston, where he was arrested, and tried under the Fugitive Slave Act. (I: 10–YA)

Krull, Kathleen. *Wilma Unlimited: How Wilma Rudolph Became the World's Fastest Woman.* Illustrated by David Diaz. San Diego, CA: Harcourt, 1996. Striking paintings help tell the story of Wilma Rudolph, who overcame childhood polio to win three gold medals for track at the 1960 Olympics. (I: 6–12)

Littlefield, Bill. *Champions: Stories of Ten Remarkable Athletes.* Illustrated by Bernie Fuchs. New York: Little, Brown, 1993. Ten athletes, including Satchel Paige and Roberto Clemente, are featured in this biographical collection of athletes who persevered to become champions in their sports. (I: 8–YA)

Parks, Rosa, with Jim Haskins. *Rosa Parks: My Story.* New York: Dial, 1992. The biography of the courageous woman whose refusal to give up her seat on a Montgomery, Alabama, bus in 1955 led to a boycott. (I: 10–YA)

Toll, Nelly S. *Behind the Secret Window: A Memoir of a Hidden Childhood during World War Two.* New York: Dial, 1993. In this autobiography, Nelly Toll describes her life in hiding with a Polish family during World War II. (I: 10–YA)

van der Rol, Ruud, and Rian Verhoeven. *Anne Frank: Beyond the Diary.* New York: Viking, 1993. Heavily illustrated with photographs, this book describes Anne Frank's life before, during, and after her family went into hiding in Holland during World War II. (I: 10–YA)

White, Ryan, and Ann Marie Cunningham. *Ryan White: My Own Story.* New York: Dial, 1991. After being infected with AIDS from a blood transfusion, Ryan shared his story about living with the disease that eventually killed him. (I: 10–YA)

RESOURCES

Burke, Eileen M., and Susan Mandel Glazer. *Using Nonfiction in the Classroom.* New York: Scholastic, 1994.

Cullinan, Bernice E., ed. *Fact and Fiction: Literature across the Curriculum.* Newark, DE: International Reading Association, 1993.

Freeman, Evelyn B., and Diane Goetz Person, eds. *Using Nonfiction Trade Books in the Elementary Classroom: From Ants to Zeppelins.* Urbana, IL: National Council of Teachers of English, 1992

Graves, Donald. *Investigate Nonfiction*. Portsmouth, NH: Heinemann, 1989.

Kobrin, Beverly. *Eyeopeners II*. New York: Scholastic, 1995.

Meltzer, M. "Where Do All the Prizes Go? The Case for Nonfiction." *Horn Book* 52 (1976): 17–23.

Teale, William H. "Nonfiction, Language Learning, and Language Teaching." *Language Arts* 68.6 (1991): Entire isssue.

Tunnell, Michael O., and Richard Ammon. eds. *The Story of Ourselves: Teaching History through Children's Literature*. Portsmouth, NH: Heinemann, 1993.

Whitin, David J., and Sandra Wilde. *It's the Story That Counts: More Children's Books for Mathematical Learning, K–6*. Portsmouth, NH: Heinemann, 1995.

———. *Read Any Good Math Lately? Children's Books for Mathematical Learning, K–6*. Portsmouth, NH: Heinemann, 1992.

Zarnowski, Myra. *Learning about Biographies: A Reading-and-Writing Approach for Children*. Urbana, IL: National Council of Teachers of English, 1990.

REFERENCES

Aldis, Dorothy, *Nothing is Impossible: The Story of Beatrix Potter*. Drawings by Richard Cuffari. New York: Atheneum, 1980.

Aliki. *Dinosaurs are Different*. New York: HarperCollins, 1985.

———. *The Story of William Tell*. New York: A.S. Barnes, 1960.

Bernstein, Joanne E., and Rose Blue. *Judith Resnick: Challenger Astronaut*. New York: Dutton, 1990.

Cleary, Beverly. *A Girl from Yamhill: A Memoir*. New York: Morrow, 1988.

Cole, Joanna. *A Cat's Body*. Photographs by Jerome Wexler. New York: Morrow, 1982.

———. *Cockroaches*. New York: Morrow, 1971.

———. *A Frog's Body*. Photographs by Jerome Wexler. New York: Morrow, 1980.

———. *A Horse's Body*. Photographs by Jerome Wexler. New York: Morrow, 1981.

Daugherty, James. *Daniel Boone*. New York: Viking, 1939.

D'Aulaire, Ingri, and Edgar Parin D'Aulaire. *Abraham Lincoln*. New York: Doubleday, 1939.

———. *Benjamin Franklin*. New York: Doubleday, 1950.

———. *Columbus*. New York: Doubleday, 1955.

———. *George Washington*. New York: Doubleday, 1936.

Fisher, M. Introduction to *Matters of Fact. Beyond Fact: Nonfiction for Children and Young People*. Ed. J. Carr. Chicago: American Library Association, 1982. 12–16.

Freedman, R. "Fact or fiction?" *Using Nonfiction Trade Books in the Elementary Classroom: From Ants to Zeppelins*. Eds. E. B. Freeman and D. G. Person. Urbana, IL: National Council of Teachers of English, 1992. 2–10.

Fritz, J. "Voices of the Creators." *Children's Books and Their Creators*. Ed. A. Silvey. Boston: Houghton Mifflin, 1995. 257.

George, Jean Craighead. *The Wild, Wild Cookbook: A Guide for Young Wild-Food Foragers*. Illustrated by Walter Kessell. New York: Crowell, 1982.

Giblin, J. C. "The Rise and Fall and Rise of Juvenile Nonfiction, 1961–1988." *Using Nonfiction Trade Books in the Elementary Classroom: From Ants to Zeppelins*.

Eds. E. B. Freeman and D. G. Person. Urbana, IL: National Council of Teachers of English, 1992. 17–25.

———. *The Truth about Santa Claus*. New York: Crowell, 1985.

Hoke, E. C. "Edgar Parin D'Aulaire and Ingri D'Aulaire." *Children's Books and Their Creators*. Ed. A. Silvey. Boston: Houghton Mifflin, 1995. 188–89.

Holling, Holling Clancy. *Paddle-to-the-Sea*. Boston: Houghton Mifflin, 1941.

Kherdian, David. *The Road from Home: The Story of an Armenian Girl*. New York: Greenwillow, 1979.

Krementz, Jill. *A Very Young Dancer*. New York: Knopf, 1976.

Lasky, Kathryn. *The Weaver's Gift*. Photographs by Christopher Knight. New York: F. Warne, 1980.

Lauber, Patricia. *Be a Friend to Trees*. Illustrated by Holly Keller. New York: HarperCollins, 1994.

———. "The Evolution of a Science Writer." *Using Nonfiction Trade Books in the Elementary Classroom: From Ants to Zeppelins*. Eds. E. B. Freeman and D. G. Person. Urbana, IL: National Council of Teachers of English, 1992. 11–16.

Lawson, Robert. *Ben & Me*. Boston: Little, Brown, 1939.

———. *I Discover Columbus*. Boston: Little, Brown, 1941.

Leal, D. (1993). "Storybooks, Information Books and Informational Storybooks: An Explication of an Ambiguous Grey Genre." *The New Advocate* 6 (1993) 61–70.

Macaulay, David. *Castle*. Boston: Houghton Mifflin, 1977.

Meigs, Cornelia. *Invincible Louisa*. Boston: Little, Brown, 1933.

Meltzer, Milton. *All Times, All Peoples: A World History of Slavery*. Illustrated by Leonard Everett Fisher. New York: Harper and Row, 1980.

———. "Beyond the Span of a Single Life." *Celebrating Children's Books: Essays on Children's Literature in Honor of Zena Sutherland*. Eds. B. Hearne and M. Kaye. New York: Lothrop, Lee and Shepard, 1981. 87–96.

———. *The Jewish Americans: A History in Their Own Words, 1650–1950*. New York: Crowell, 1982.

———. *Never to Forget: The Jews of the Holocaust*. New York: HarperCollins, 1976.

Monjo, F. N. "The Ten Bad Things about History." *Beyond Fact: Nonfiction for Children and Young People*. Ed. J. Carr. Chicago: American Library Association, 1982. 99–103.

Olendorf, D., and D. Telgen. "David Adler." *Something About the Author*. Vol. 70. Detroit: Gale Research, 1993. 1–4.

Pringle, L. "Science Done Here." *Celebrating Children's Books: Essays on Children's Literature in Honor of Zena Sutherland*. Eds. B. Hearne and M. Kaye. New York: Lothrop, Lee and Shepard, 1981. 108–15.

Sayers, F. C. "History Books for Children." *Beyond Fact: Nonfiction for Children and Young People*. Ed. J. Carr. Chicago: American Library Association, 1982. 95–98.

Selsam, Millicent. *Egg to Chick*. Illustrated by Barbara Wolff. New York: Harper and Row, 1946.

Scribner's. Promotional pamphlet about Kathryn Lasky. New York: 1985.

Simon, Seymour. *Animals in Field and Laboratory: Projects in Animal Behavior*. New York: McGraw-Hill, 1968.

Tunis, Edwin. *Frontier Living*. New York: World, 1961.

van Loon, Hendrik Willem. *The Story of Mankind*. New York: Boni & Liveright, 1921.

Wenzel, E. L. "Historical Backgrounds." *Beyond Fact: Nonfiction for Children and Young People*. Ed. J. Carr. Chicago: American Library Association, 1982. 16–26.

Zarnowski, M. *Learning about Biographies: A Reading-and-Writing Approach for Children*. Urbana, IL: National Council of Teachers of English, 1990.

———. "Learning History with Informational Storybooks: A Social Studies Educator's Perspective." *The New Advocate* 8 (1995): 183–96.

Zim, Herbert. *Golden Hamsters*. Illustrated by Herschel Wartik. New York: Morrow, 1951.

———. *Sharks*. Illustrated by Stephen Howe. New York: Morrow, 1966.

———. *Snakes*. Illustrated by James Gordon Irving. New York: Morrow, 1949.

Part Three

Creating the Literature-Based Classroom

12 Inviting Children into Literature

Grandpa took Mary Ellen inside away from the crowd. "Now, child I am going to show you what my father showed me, and his father before him," he said quietly.

He spooned the honey onto the cover of one of her books. "Taste," he said, almost in a whisper.

Mary Ellen savored the honey on her book.

"There is such sweetness inside of that book too!" he said thoughtfully. "Such things . . . adventure, knowledge and wisdom. But these things do not come easily. You have to pursue them. Just like we ran after the bees to find their tree, so you must also chase these things through the pages of a book!"

from The Bee Tree *(1993)*
by Patricia Polacco

Illustration 12.1

A spirit of joyous adventure marks a romp through the countryside in search of a bee tree. (*The Bee Tree* by Patricia Polacco. Copyright © 1993 by Patricia Polacco. Used by permission of Philomel Books.)

Patricia Polacco's wonderful book **The Bee Tree** begins when Mary Ellen announces she is tired of reading. So her grandfather invites her to go on an adventure—a hunt for a bee tree. In preparation, Grandpa captures several bees in a jar, and soon Mary Ellen and Grandpa are off and running, following the first bee released from the jar. Before long, the twosome grows into a motley crew as friends and neighbors join the merry chase that ends at the bee tree. Back at Grandpa's, everyone enjoys biscuits, tea, and sweet honey. It is then that Grandpa reminds Mary Ellen that joys as sweet as honey can also be found in books.

Mary Ellen's grandfather knew the importance of motivating children to become readers. As important as it is to teach children how to read, that isn't enough to ensure that they will *choose* to read. If anything, the evidence indicates that too many children do not read. Linda Fielding, Paul T. Wilson, and Richard C. Anderson (1986) found that 50 percent of fifth graders read voluntarily for four minutes a day or less, 30 percent read for two minutes a day or less, and almost 10 percent reported never reading any books during their leisure time. It's little wonder that 45 percent of adult Americans don't read books either (Cole and Gold, 1979).

Mary Ellen's Grandpa was a wonderful teacher, and the lesson he taught Mary Ellen is one you'll want to pass on to your students: Inside the pages of a book, readers can find adventure, knowledge, and wisdom. You probably won't be able to take your students on romps through the countryside in search of bee trees. How then will you help them discover the joys of reading? We believe you can best accomplish this by carefully designing your classroom, by reading aloud, by telling stories, by inviting students to dramatize stories, and by demonstrating your enthusiasm for literature.

THE CLASSROOM LIBRARY

A good classroom library is a focal area where children can go to read quality children's literature. Is it really necessary to have a library in the classroom, especially if your school has a well-stocked central library? We think it is essential. Children in classrooms containing literature collections read 50 percent more than children in classrooms where literature is not available (Bissett, 1969). What a difference!

Designing the Classroom Library Center

Not all library centers are equally appealing. Children beg to visit some library centers, but others stand unused. Research by Lesley Morrow (1982) has shown how to create classroom libraries that children *choose* to use. There are a number of design features that make such libraries appealing. These features are summarized in Table 12.1.

The Center Is the Focal Area of the Classroom. Often, when you step into a classroom, your eye is drawn to one area of the room; that eye-catching part is what is meant by "the focal area." It isn't easy to define what makes a library center a focal area; in fact, it may be all the design features taken together that do this. Whatever the explanation, it's important to create an eye-catching center that announces to students, "Literature matters in this classroom." In one school, teachers created centers built around themes. One teacher built a seven-foot-high papier-mache apple tree and printed a banner that read "Don't Sit under the Apple Tree without a Good Book to Read." The apple motif was reflected throughout the center—for example, red bean bag chairs looked just like big apples. Another teacher used a sidewalk cafe theme and called her center "Cafe Escape." It was a perfect invitation to escape into a good book.

The Library Is Partitioned Off. Children prefer to read in areas away from lots of hustle and bustle. So it makes sense to use something—for example, bookshelves or old sofas—to partition the library off from the rest of the classroom. One teacher turned the library center into the "O.K. Corral," using mesquite posts to build a fence around it. The possibilities are limited only by your imagination.

The Seating Area Is Large Enough. To make the seating area large enough, you will have to devote a chunk of floor space to the library center. Why not just store the books in a bookcase instead, and let students read at their desks? Many children don't find it comfortable to read at their desks, preferring instead to lounge around in a library center. Besides, there are many times when reading becomes a social activity. Children may choose to read with a buddy or

---

Table 12.1 *Characteristics of an Appealing Library Center*

- The library center is a focal area of the classroom.
- The library center is partitioned off from the rest of the room.
- The library center is large enough to seat five or six children comfortably.
- The library center has two types of bookshelves, some that display the spines of books and others that display the covers of books.
- The library center offers comfortable seating.
- The library center offers a variety of other materials—literature-related displays, stuffed animals, and the like.
- The library center has an organizational system.
- The library center has *books, books, and more books!*

The classroom library center gives children a convenient place to share a book.

to share something they're reading. Imagine reading a riddle book without trying to stump someone! And the optical illusions in Kathleen Westray's **Picture Puzzler** (1994) simply must be shared.

The Shelving Displays Both Spines of Books and Covers. Bookshelves that display the spines of books are necessary because they hold a lot of books. But the spines of books don't make for interesting viewing—so it's also necessary to display book covers. This may be the single most important way of enticing children into selecting books, for many have exquisite covers (which is why most booksellers try to display as many book covers as possible).

Bookshelves designed to display the covers of books are expensive, and many schools can't stretch their budgets to buy these shelves. So you'll need to use your creativity. Slightly open books can stand alone on standard shelves or on a window ledge. To display paperbacks, visit a home supply center and buy plastic chain and clothespins. Hang the chain in an accessible spot and attach the paperbacks to it with the clothespins.

The Seating Is Comfortable. It is pretty obvious why comfortable seating is important in a library center. After all, where do *you* read for pleasure? Sofas and upholstered chairs are far more appealing than straight-back chairs. Carpeting, bean bags, pillows, and cushions are also comfortable and make the library center cozy.

The Center Uses a Variety of Materials. Materials that highlight literature are assets in the library center. Posters showing the covers of featured books can be obtained from publishers. Displays of book jackets catch children's attention, as do children's own artistic responses to literature. For example, children might make masks for the library center after listening to Lulu Delacre's **Vejigante/ Masquerader** (1993). Younger children enjoy cuddling up with stuffed animals when they read or using flannel boards or puppets to act out stories.

The Center Uses an Organizational System. Children like organizational systems in their libraries for the same reason adults do: Organizational systems help them find books. No one particular system is best. In fact, some teachers nurture "ownership" of the classroom library by inviting students to create their own system. Systems that classify books based on their difficulty level can be good, especially for beginning readers. Teachers can even set up systems to reinforce the literary language they want students to acquire—for example, books can be grouped by genre. In determining the best system for your classroom, consider the interests and abilities of your students as well as your instructional goals.

The Center Has Books, Books, and More Books! Unless the library center is well stocked with a rich variety of quality books, children will not use it. Jann Fractor, Marjorie Woodruff, Miriam G. Martinez, and William H. Teale (1993) recommend having from four to eight books per child. In fact, the more books you have, the richer the literature context you create in your classroom. Unfortunately, school budgets rarely stretch far enough to allow teachers to buy books for classroom libraries. However, some teachers persuade their administrators to let them order children's literature instead of reading workbooks. Even if your school provides monetary assistance for purchasing books, you'll probably still have to find creative ways of supplementing the collection. Many public libraries allow teachers to check out large numbers of books for extended periods of time. Checking books out of the school library is another alternative. If your students have the financial means to order books from book clubs, the class can earn bonus points that can be cashed in for books. Secondhand book stores can sometimes be a good source of inexpensive copies of worthwhile books.

Stocking the Classroom Library with Books

Which books the classroom library holds is even more important than how many books there are.

Illustration 12.2
An unusual blend of humor and wonder permeates this fantasy about a boy chosen to hatch a dragon. (*Jeremy Thatcher, Dragon Hatcher* by Bruce Coville. Illustration copyright © 1991 by Gary A. Lippincott. Used by permission of Harcourt Brace & Company.)

Quality Literature. You owe it to your students to stock the classroom library with the highest-quality literature. Take care to choose books for your center that have distinctly crafted literary elements. Consider books such as Mary Hoffman's *Amazing Grace* (1991) for its wonderful characterization and Jean Craighead George's *My Side of the Mountain* (1959) for its distinctive setting. Include books with significant themes, such as Barbara Cooney's *Miss Rumphius* (1982), and don't forget books with exquisite language, such as Cynthia Rylant's *When I Was Young in the Mountains* (1982). But, when selecting books to motivate voluntary reading, pay special attention to the story line. A strong story line sells itself. Well-paced, action-oriented stories, such as Kasza Keiko's *The Wolf's Chicken Stew* (1987) for younger children and Bruce Coville's *Jeremy Thatcher, Dragon Hatcher* (1991) for older children, are especially popular. Children also love books with humorous and unusual story lines, such as Judi Barrett's *Cloudy with a Chance of Meatballs* (1978) and Judy Blume's *Tales of a Fourth Grade Nothing* (1972). Stories with unusual formats make good additions to the library center—books such as Jon Scieszka's *The Stinky Cheese Man and Other Fairly Stupid Tales* (1992) and Sally Grindley's *Shhh!* (1991). Finally, children will rush to choose books with distinctive illustrations—books such as Audrey and Don Wood's *The Napping House* (1984). A useful resource for identifying books with "kid appeal" is the Children's Choice list that appears annually in the October issue of *The Reading Teacher,* a journal published by the International Reading Association.

A Variety of Genres. Be sure to include as many genres as possible in your library center—fantasy, folktales, contemporary realistic fiction, historical fiction, informational books, and poetry. Also find room for those odds and ends for which there is no apparent genre niche—predictable books, joke books and riddle books, and lift-the-flap and pop-up books. The more choices you provide students, the more they'll read.

Student Interests. Just as you have particular reading preferences and reading interests, so will your students. Take the time to discover those interests. Talk to students about the books they're reading. Have them keep logs of their voluntary reading, in which they record the author and title of each book they read. Monitor those logs, and fill the classroom library with books related to student's reading interests. Table 12.2 suggests some typical interests of students in different grades.

A Variety of Reading Levels. If a child believes a book will be too challenging to read, in all likelihood the child won't give it a try. To motivate children

Table 12.2 Children's Interests at Different Grade Levels

Grades	Interests
Grades 1 and 2	Animals, nature, fantasy, child characters, general and science informational materials, history
Grades 3 and 4	Nature, animals, adventure, familiar experiences
Grades 5 and 6	History, science, mystery, adventure, travel, animal stories, fairytales
Grades 7 and 8	Science fiction, mystery, adventure, biography, history, animals, sports, romance, religion, career stories, comedy, biography

to do lots of reading, it's critical that you provide books they feel comfortable reading. Anticipate a wide range of reading levels in your classroom. A typical second-grade classroom may have some students who are nonreaders and others reading at a sixth-grade reading level. The mythical classroom of "grade-level readers" is just that—a myth. By watching students, you can discover if they are comfortable with the books in your classroom library.

Should children's preferences for "nonliterary" works be accommodated in the classroom literature program?

ISSUE TO CONSIDER

Imagine this scenario: You consistently strive to introduce your students to quality literature. Yet on their book club orders, many select only series books—*Goosebumps, The Babysitters Club, Sweet Valley Kids.* Series books have been popular with children for generations—probably since the Horatio Alger series began in 1868. Throughout this book, however, we have emphasized the importance of using quality literature with children, and too many series books are characterized by shallow, formulaic writing.

So what do teachers do in the face of students' seemingly insatiable appetite for series books? Is it enough, as some assert, to continue to use quality literature for read-alouds and in literature study, in the hope that sufficient exposure will eventually cause children to recognize and choose quality books for themselves (Gonzalez, Fry, Lopez, Jordan, Sloan, and McAdams, 1995)? Or should teachers take a more active role in shaping children's literary choices by inviting them to talk about the differences they see between series books and other types of books in order to help them develop their own evaluation criteria? Or perhaps there's a middle ground as Carolyn Bauer and LaVonne Sanborn (1981) suggest? Perhaps teachers need to guide students actively toward books that represent the "best of both worlds"—books that have been chosen by children as favorites and also recognized by adults for their literary merit.

What do you think?

Illustration 12.3
Who can resist joining in the fun of an exciting bear hunt? (*We're Going on a Bear Hunt* by Michael Rosen. Illustration copyright © 1989 Helen Oxenbury. Used by permission of Margaret K. McElderry Books, an imprint of Simon & Schuster Children's Publishing Division.)

Illustration 12.4
Moon Rope, a lively pourquoi tale from Peru, is told in English and Spanish. (*Moon Rope: A Peruvian Folktale* by Lois Ehlert. Text and illustration © 1992 by Lois Ehlert. Used by permission of Harcourt Brace & Company.)

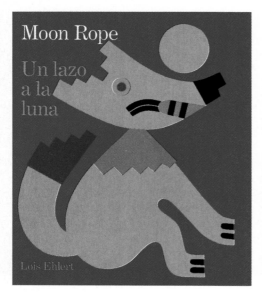

Even kindergartners who have not yet learned to read conventionally need books they can feel comfortable with. Kindergartners are far more likely to "pretend read" predictable books, such as Bill Martin, Jr.'s **Brown Bear, Brown Bear, What Do You See?** (1967) and Michael Rosen's **We're Going on a Bear Hunt** (1989).

Beginning readers—whether they are in first grade or higher grades—also respond well to predictable books. In addition, they need picture books with limited text and lots of illustration cues, such as Dick Gackenbach's **Harry and the Terrible Whatzit** (1977) and Gerald McDermott's **Anansi the Spider** (1972). Beginning readers soon graduate to very easy-to-read chapter books, such as Cynthia Rylant's *Henry and Mudge* series or James Marshall's comical series about Fox.

More challenging picture books for developing readers include Harry Allard's **The Stupids Step Out** (1974) and Lois Ehlert's **Moon Rope** (1992). When children have made the jump into chapter books, supply them with easier ones—those with fifty to one hundred pages that contain simple vocabulary. Books that fit this bill include Margaret Sacks's **Themba** (1985) and Betsy Byars's **The Seven Treasure Hunts** (1991).

Read-Alouds. Observing in literature-rich classrooms, Janet Hickman (1981) found that children are especially likely to select books for independent reading that have been introduced or read to them. Children are likely to feel more confident picking up a book they have heard read aloud.

Thematic Units. The library center can be a tool to support and extend children's learning in other areas. For example, if you are doing a unit on slavery, stock the library with books such as Patricia and Fredrick McKissack's **Christmas in the Big House, Christmas in the Quarters** (1994) and Michael J. Rosen's **A School for Pompey Walker** (1995). Just as special collections within the library center support students' learning in the content areas, so too do students' content studies support their voluntary reading, by building background and interest. (See Chapter 14 for a detailed discussion of thematic units.)

Multicultural Books. Including multicultural literature in the library is important for all children but especially for those from diverse backgrounds, who need to see themselves in the books they read. An Hispanic American child once said to one of us, "They don't have people like us in books." Fortunately, more and more multicultural literature is available, and it is the responsibility of every teacher to ensure that students have ample opportunities to meet characters like themselves in literature.

Some teachers assume that it is not necessary to bring multicultural literature into their classrooms because none of their students are children of color. Nothing could be further from the truth. It is important for children of the mainstream culture to see children different from themselves involved in situations both similar to and different from their own. Schools are preparing children to live in a diverse society, and it is important for them to understand this society. (See Chapter 4 for a complete discussion of these issues.)

READING ALOUD TO CHILDREN

In its report *Becoming a Nation of Readers*, the Commission on Reading declared, "There is no substitute for a teacher who reads children good stories" (Anderson, Hiebert, Scott, and Wilkinson, 1984). That is our sentiment exactly! Research indicates that reading to children has many positive outcomes. First, it whets their appetite for reading. Young children who are read to discover the rewards of reading and are motivated to learn to read. Literature also nurtures children's language development and comprehension abilities. Through read-alouds, children become acquainted with the cadences of written language and discover how print functions, especially if the adult reader draws attention to print conventions. Finally, through read-alouds, children acquire the real-world knowledge that is so critical for success in school.

Read-alouds support children's literary development: Children are introduced to conventional story openers ("Once upon a time"); they discover literary motifs such as the transformation motif; they meet stock characters like the sly fox and the tricky coyote. Read-alouds are the ideal vehicle for encouraging children to think in response to literature, and when discussion is a part of the read-aloud experience, children learn how to participate in literary conversations.

Like the Commission on Reading, we believe that read-alouds should be an essential instructional activity for children of all ages. Although older children may have acquired basic understandings of how print functions and how stories are structured, their language, reading, and literary development must continue. Also, there are many books that developing readers do not have the skill to read on their own but will delight in if read aloud to them. In fact, by the time children are able to read many books on their own, the books are no longer age-appropriate.

Research on Read-Aloud Programs

The most recent and comprehensive study on read-aloud programs was done by James V. Hoffman, Nancy L. Roser, and Jennifer Battle (1993). Reports from 537 classrooms across the United States revealed that 74 percent of teachers read to their students on a given day. However, there was a steady decline in the percentage of teachers reading aloud as grade levels rose. In kindergarten, 84 percent of the teachers read to their students, but in fifth grade only 64 percent did so. There is room for improvement. Teachers at every grade level should read aloud at least once a day. All too often, teachers at upper grade levels believe that their students should be reading books on their own—which is true, of course. However, this is not an either/or situation. We hope that teachers will recognize the special value of read-alouds. Another argument made by some intermediate-level teachers is that they have too much content to cover to devote time to reading aloud to students. One way of dealing with this time restriciton is "double dipping"—that is, using read-alouds to achieve both literary goals and curricular goals. If students are studying the American Revolution, then read aloud James and Christopher Collier's *My Brother Sam Is Dead* (1974). Patricia Polacco's *Pink and Say* (1994) and Karen Ackerman's *The Tin Heart* (1990) are perfect read-alouds when a class is studying the Civil War.

Hoffman and his colleagues also looked at the books chosen for read-alouds and at the organization of the read-aloud programs. Well-known authors—Bill Martin, Jr., Maurice Sendak, Roald Dahl, E. B. White, and Judy Blume—were at the top of the list of books most frequently read. Included among the frequently read titles were *Brown Bear, Brown Bear, What Do You See?* (1967), *Where the Wild Things Are* (1964), *Charlotte's Web* (1952), *James and the Giant Peach* (1961), and *The Indian in the Cupboard* (1981). It is heartening that the quality of these authors and titles is widely recognized, but it is discouraging to note that not a single multicultural author or title appeared at the top of the list. In fact, one of the titles, *The Indian in the Cupboard* by Lynne Reid Banks, has received criticism for its stereotypical portrayal of Native Americans.

Hoffman, Roser, and Battle found that the typical read-aloud session had a number of distinctive characteristics:

- A length of ten to twenty minutes
- A literature selection unrelated to a unit of study
- Discussion that took less than five minutes
- No response activity following the read-aloud

A read-aloud becomes a special time for young children when they can gather close to the adult who is sharing the story.

They cautioned that this "typical read-aloud" was not a model, arguing that a daily read-aloud of at least twenty minutes should be scheduled in a specific time slot. Instead of unrelated literature selections, Hoffman and his colleagues call for organizing read-aloud programs around units. Mature readers often read books related in some way to others that they have read, and literature units encourage students to do this. Hoffman, Roser, and Battle also questioned the adequacy of five minutes of literature discussion. Sustained conversation that can enrich the understanding of all participants does not occur in five minutes.

The Read-Aloud Experience

The read-aloud experience is one of the highlights of the school day for most children. This is especially likely to be true when the teacher carefully selects each book and spends time preparing to read it aloud.

When to Read Aloud. Read-alouds shouldn't be used merely to fill time between activities. By scheduling a read-aloud each day, you communicate to students that this is a valued activity. Besides, there is the all-too-real danger that on many days there won't be any extra time between activities.

Illustration 12.5
Many readers are likely to identify with the strong female character in *The Girl Who Loved Caterpillars,* a retelling of an ancient Japanese story. (*The Girl Who Loved Caterpillars* by Jean Merrill. Illustration copyright © 1992 by Floyd Cooper. Used by permission of Philomel Books.)

At lower grade levels, teachers should read aloud several times a day, especially if their students have had only limited experiences with stories before entering school. Some children enter school having listened to thousands of storybook readings, others have not been read to at all. These children especially deserve a rich read-aloud program.

Selecting Books for Read-Alouds. Much of what was said about selecting books for the classroom library also applies to selecting read-aloud stories. First and foremost, select high-quality books. We especially encourage you to choose books that deal with significant themes, for these books have the potential to evoke insightful discussions. A book such as *The Shimmershine Queens* (1989) fits this bill, as do Patricia Polacco's *Chicken Sunday* (1992) and Jean Merrill's *The Girl Who Loved Caterpillars* (1992).

It is important to read books from a variety of genres, including poetry and informational books. Remember, your preferences may not be the same as those of your students. One first-grade teacher decided to let her students select the daily read-aloud books. The girls selected the same kinds of books their teacher had been selecting—picture storybooks, but much to her surprise, the boys overwhelmingly favored informational books, a genre from which she had never read aloud.

Select age-appropriate books. There are no firm and fast guidelines about which books are appropriate for particular grade levels. In fact, many books appeal to students across grade levels. Nonetheless, as a general rule, simpler, shorter books are more appropriate for younger children and those with limited literature experience. However, this does not mean that picture books are for younger children and chapter books are for older ones. Many picture books, such as Chris Van Allsburg's *The Widow's Broom* (1992), Michael J. Rosen's *Elijah's Angel* (1992), and Barbara Bash's *Tree of Life: The World of the African Baobab* (1989), are wonderful for older children. Conversely, many younger children enjoy listening to chapter books such as Ann Cameron's *The Stories Julian Tells* (1981) and E. B. White's *Charlotte's Web* (1952).

Preparing to Read Aloud. To make read-alouds a success, there is one cardinal rule to remember: *Never* read aloud a book that you have not previously

Illustration 12.6
The distinctive folk art illustrations in *Elijah's Angel* enhance this sensitive story of cross-cultural understanding. (*Elijah's Angel: A Story for Chanukah and Christmas* by Michael Rosen. Illustration copyright © 1992 by Aminah Brenda Lynn Robinson. Used by permission of Harcourt Brace and Company.)

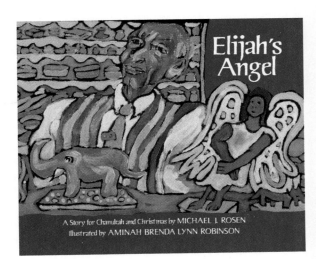

ASK THE AUTHOR . . .

Bill Martin, Jr.

How is it that you are able to craft such wonderful read-alouds?

I never learned to read until I was in college. Throughout all of my elementary and high school years, I was dependent upon having someone read aloud to me since I couldn't read myself. This caused me to rely on my hearing as a substitute for the visual experience of reading. I was always asking teachers, librarians, friends, and parents to read to me. Consequently, I learned language in the oral tradition and far more abundantly than my classmates.

To my good fortune, the Kansas State Teacher's College at Emporia, where I received my B.S. degree in education, offered many oral language courses that featured poetry, drama, and native languages. All of which are reflected in my writing of children's books. When I finally learned to read, during my college years, I became and still am an avid reader. But I also continue to feed my appetite for language used in the oral tradition.

Bill Martin, Jr. is the author of many highly acclaimed children's books, including Brown Bear, Brown Bear, What Do You See? *and* Chicka Chicka Boom Boom. *He is also the author of the* Sounds of Language *series of readers for kindergarten through sixth grade. Bill lives in the small Texas town of Campbell.*

Favorite Books as a Child

Treasure Island by Robert Louis Stevenson

The Letters of Robert Frost

Mother Goose Nursery Rhymes

---

read. In fact, you really should read a book out loud to yourself or someone else before reading it to children, because sometimes a book you loved when you read it silently just doesn't flow when it is read aloud. If you plan to read a book with unfamiliar words or language—Gary Soto's **Chato's Kitchen** (1995), for example—it is especially important to practice pronunciations prior to reading it aloud.

In preparing for a read-aloud, thoughtfully read the book you select (see Table 12.3). Look for difficulties the story presents that might interfere with comprehension. Be alert to stopping points at which you might invite predictions or discussion. Also, be sure and monitor your own responses to the story. The things you notice or wonder about are worth remembering because these spontaneous responses can become conversation starters following the reading.

If you have never read a story aloud before, it makes good sense to practice pacing and expression before reading it to an audience. What feelings and moods

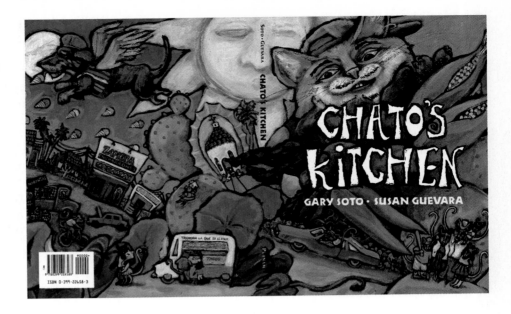

can you convey with your voice? Is a character surprised? Does a character become angry? Is a character especially wise or silly or confused? Get to know the characters so that you can bring them to life. Don't be shy. Try out different voices and even facial expressions or gestures. And don't forget to practice holding the book so the children can see the illustrations as you read. The end result of all this preparation is likely to be an engaging read-aloud experience for your students.

Introducing the Story. Before introducing the story, gather the students together for the read-aloud. If there is room, pull chairs into a circle, and if a picture book is to be read aloud, situate everyone so that they can see the illustrations. Keep your introduction to the book in proper perspective: Time and attention should be devoted primarily to the read-aloud and to subsequent discussion. Nonetheless, an introduction offers an opportunity to help children

Table 12.3 *How to Prepare for a Read-Aloud*

- Anticipate difficulties the story may present to students, and prepare to help them through those difficulties.
- Watch for interesting places to stop reading and invite children's predictions or discussion.
- Heed your own responses to the story as one basis for after-reading discussion.
- Practice varying your reading pace to highlight particular portions of the story.
- Become acquainted with the characters and changing moods of the story so that you can read with appropriate expression.
- Try out different voices for different characters.

Pictures are an important source of the support young children need for their first story experiences.

expand their store of literary understandings and allows you to "prime" them for the book.

In addition to introducing the story (or poem) by title, remember to mention the name of the author (and, when appropriate, the illustrator). This is an excellent way of helping students begin to develop a sense of author. Also mention other books written by the same author, especially those the children are likely to be familiar with. Mentioning the book's genre is a way of gently introducing children to some of the language of literature. Be sure to choose literary terminology appropriate for the age level. Young children may respond better to the terms "pretend" stories and "real" stories than to "fantasy" and "realism" or "fiction" and "nonfiction."

Before starting to read the story, you may need to build background. This may be especially important for an informational book. If some concepts important to understanding the book are not adequately explained within the book, then pay some attention to these concepts in your introduction. To set expectations for the book, you may want to invite children to make predictions based on the title or the cover illustration. Finally, if the book is being read as part of a literature unit, mention books you have read previously.

Reading the Story. When you finally read the story, use everything you tried out in preparing for the read-aloud. Vary your reading pace to reflect changes in mood and emotion, read expressively, and use different voices when appropriate.

Some teachers believe that stories should be read straight through without any interruptions so as not to distract from the story line. However, we encourage you to feel free to interrupt the reading of a story to talk with your students, especially younger ones. Older children are able to hold back with their responses until the read-aloud is complete, but younger children often forget their observations if they are forced to wait. So if a child interrupts to ask a question or share a response, honor that interruption. Children are also likely to interrupt when you reach a point in the story that begs for predictions. Or there may be times when you need to guide students through a tricky part of the story or briefly fill in information important to understanding the story. Finally, when you read predictable books, children enjoy joining in on repeated phrases.

After Reading. The read-aloud experience should not be over as soon as you've read the final page of the story. The literary transaction will continue if you provide ample opportunity after the reading for children to discuss the story. Chapter 13 focuses on literary discussion.

STORIES AND STORYTELLING

Children's literature starts with the telling of stories. For thousands of years before the first story was written down, humans told stories and recited poems. The thousands of years of human experience with stories (compared to a little over a century of mass literacy) surely adapted the human mind to storytelling in a special way and nourished an art of storytelling that still moves hearers deeply. This is why teachers must make storytelling a regular feature in the classroom.

Storytelling: The Tenacious Art

Many cultures have specific storytelling styles and rituals. In Jamaica today, a storyteller still begins a session by asking, "Creek?" This means, "Do you want a story?" If the people want one, they answer, "Creek," and the storyteller begins. But if they say "Crack," the storyteller passes on to find others willing to hear the tale. Japanese storytellers use *kamishibai*, a large set of pictures with text on the back; these pictures are presented in a box that looks like a traditional theater. Whatever the style, storytelling has never passed out of vogue, even with the proliferation of books.

Because storytelling is so active—from the point of view of both tellers *and* listeners—it is an especially appropriate activity to do with younger children. Because it offers a bridge to literature, storytelling is also appropriate with reluctant readers. A wise teacher used to advocate telling stories to students. "Most children," said Edmund Henderson, "will come running when you read a story. But if one does not, tell the story instead. The told story is the older form. Hence it will have more appeal." Telling a story allows you to look your students in the eye and invite them to help you bring the story to life.

Storytelling exercises the often neglected art of using the voice. The teller must provide the excitement, drama, and cadences that pull listeners in and play their emotions like a violin. To tell a story well, the storyteller must decide how the characters sound, where the suspenseful parts are, and what parts should be slow or fast, loud or soft.

Children enjoy telling stories, too, and there are many good reasons why they should. In this section, we will present ways to choose, practice, and tell stories, and most of our advice will apply to both the adult and the child storyteller.

Common Story Types: Personal Tales to Tall Tales

Stories differ in the amount of effort they require for learning or for improvising. They also differ in the kind of attention they require of listeners and the sorts of participation they invite. These points will be made clear as we talk about different types of stories.

Story types vary from personal tales, which usually evoke more inventiveness from the teller but offer less form for guidance, to already-heard stories, which offer more form but pose a challenge because they must be learned—they cannot be improvised.

Personal Stories. Personal stories are anecdotes from your own experience—about a camping trip, about being lost, about raising a pet. They can be rambling, especially if you haven't honed them down through practice. That's okay—especially when you're giving an example for children to copy when they do the telling. You can work with personal stories over time to give them more shape.

Family Stories. Family stories are true (well, maybe slightly embellished) stories about someone in your family. Because these stories may have been passed along through several generations, they are usually better formed than personal stories. Family stories often portray what people think is funniest about themselves and their relatives. They can be a lot like stories that are written down—the Ramona Quimby stories come to mind. After all, writers come from families, right?

Friend-of-a-Friend Stories. Friend-of-a-friend stories, or "urban legends," are accounts of bizarre events in a community told by people who believe they might have happened. When you try to check them out, though, it always turns out they happened to someone the teller almost knows—"a friend of a friend."

Friend-of-a-friend stories are close to the folktale tradition. In his fascinating collections, the folklorist Jan de Brunvard has compiled urban legends from newspaper, radio, and personal accounts of hundreds of people. Though the tales are often recounted breathlessly, as if they just happened last week, de Brunvard (1981) is often able to find variations that are hundreds of years old. For example, the story of the "vanishing hitchhiker," told in contemporary Georgia, has a song version, "The Phantom 409." Some years ago in West Africa, Frances Temple heard a version of the story from a nervous nun who claimed to have been in the jeep when the hitchhiker disappeared.

Ghost Stories. Ghost stories usually lie somewhere in between "friend-of-a-friend" stories and folktales. Alvin Schwartz's popular collection *Scary Stories to Tell in the Dark* (1985) was collected from folktale sources. Some teachers find ghost stories good fare to tell to middle-grade children, or for them to learn and tell. If the children are to do the telling, prepare to screen their choices.

Jokes and Riddles. Jokes and riddles aren't stories, exactly, but they are so engaging that telling them in front of a group is good practice for children. Also, they are short enough that many children can participate in a single storytelling session.

Folktales and Fables. Folktales, the traditional stories we discussed in Chapter 5, provide excellent fare for storytelling. Because they were passed down orally, folktales have been pared down to their essentials, which makes them well formed and memorable but also leaves room for embellishments by the storyteller. Fables, those brief instructive tales that end with a moral, can also be fun to tell, especially when you stop and ask students to guess the moral.

Myths. Myths range from serious creation stories, such as the Iroquois tale of Da-Ga-Na-We-Da, to the lighter pourquoi tales that explain various natural phenomena, such as the African tale *Why Mosquitoes Buzz in People's Ears* (1975). Teachers should have no trouble finding collections from many cultures that offer abundant suitable fare for storytelling.

Legends and Tall Tales. Legends are stories about famous cultural heroes that usually have a core of truth to them. The characters may be real—George Washington is the subject of a number of legends. Or the events—like those in the story of John Henry—may portray qualities people like to claim for themselves. Legends make good fare for oral telling—especially in conjunction with social studies units.

One or two steps removed from legends are tall tales, which tell about exaggerated fictitious characters. These characters usually also show qualities that real people like to claim for themselves. For example, Paul Bunyan didn't exist, but lumberjacks liked to be thought of as tough.

Learning Stories to Tell

As Margaret Read MacDonald (1993) says, it is certainly easiest to learn a story from another teller. A story well told is so much more than the words—it's the voices of the characters, the pauses and dramatic flourishes, the joy and sorrow and excitement and dread, all communicated by the storyteller. If you have a chance to listen to a storyteller who can show you all those things, you're way ahead. If you can't find a live storyteller, you can watch videotapes of live performances.

Learning the story is the first task of the storyteller. Most storytellers agree that the way to prepare a story is not to memorize it. Memorizing will make a story sound flat or set the teller up for a mental block during the telling. Besides, the beauty of a told story is that it is forever invented.

But a story is not random, either: A well-told story is crisp, with the beginnings, endings, and repeated parts told just so. How does a storyteller achieve this crispness without memorizing the story? Here's one way.

Get some index cards, and read through the story four times, each time with a different purpose:

1. On the first pass, read for the sense of the whole tale.

2. Next time, pay close attention to the different events in the story. Jot down each event in a few words on a separate card.

3. On the third read-through, pay close attention to the characters. On a separate card, name each character and make notes about the way she or he should sound and move. Note any gestures you want to associate with each character.

4. Read through the story again and jot down the beginning and ending, as well as any repeated phrases. This is important: If you know exactly how a story begins, you can launch into it more confidently. If you know exactly how the story ends, you can wrap it up crisply. So memorize both. In between, pay attention to repeated phrases (such as "Little pig, little pig, let me in. Not by the hair on my chinny-chin-chin.") or any repeated pattern of actions.

Practice the Story. Once you have the cards prepared and arranged in the order you find most useful, tell the story repeatedly (to yourself, to a friend, to your cat) until you can tell it confidently without looking at the cards. Later, when you tell the story, keep the cards unobtrusively in your lap—but have them handy in case you begin to forget.

If children are learning stories, have them pair up and tell their stories to each other. Also, have them tell the story at home a set number of times as they learn it (say, three times a day).

Refine the Story. Once you have the gist of the story down, the fun part begins. This is where you refine the characterization, the gestures, the pauses and other dynamics of narration.

Determine appropriate language. Determine the sort of word choices appropriate to the story you're telling. A story in a traditional setting requires the teller to say "a certain boy" or "There was an old woman who" instead of "this guy" or "this old lady." If your story is an Old English folktale, perhaps you want to sound modest and precise. If it's a Western tale from Texas, your language will be relaxed, expansive, and given to exaggeration.

Visualize the characters. You don't need to describe the characters fully to the audience, but you should still have a clear idea of what they are like, so that your voice and gestures will fit. You should decide the following for each main character in your story:

• How short or tall is she or he? How heavy? How does the character's size make her or him move?

- Is this character dignified? Sly? Lazy? Vain? How do these traits affect the way he or she talks?

- What is the character's usual mood?

If you're helping children learn storytelling, ask these questions and follow them up with activities that will give the children practice in developing their characters. Have each child "get into" one of his or her characters as they all parade around the room. Call on several characters to introduce themselves in their own voices—and say what's on their minds.

Visualize the setting. When Jack steps out onto the clouds at the top of the beanstalk, how is his footing? How does he step? When he gets to the giant's castle, how big is the door? How does Jack knock on it? Having thought through details like this will enable you to use voices and gestures that help the audience visualize—and believe—the setting.

Practice gestures. As a storyteller says the wolf's lines in "The Three Little Pigs," she or he probably makes a fist and pounds on an imaginary door. When the storyteller says a pig's lines, she or he pulls at the imaginary chin whiskers. A few gestures like these help the story, but too many will distract. Use only such gestures as will give a hint of the setting of a scene, provide the signature of a character, or display a strong emotion.

Practice facial expressions. Boston storyteller Jay O'Callahan says storytelling is the theater of the face. Gestures are important, but facial expressions and voices convey most of the story's meaning. Storytellers must learn to make facial expressions that project the way their characters feel: innocent, cunning, frightened, and so on.

If you're working with children, have them stand in a circle. One student decides on a facial expression and, without identifying the expression, "passes" it to the next, who duplicates it and passes it on in turn. This continues until the expression has gone completely around. Take time out to debrief: Were the students understanding the expression correctly? Then another student "passes" a different expression.

Practice the voice. The storyteller's voice must be both loud enough to carry to the back of the audience and expressive enough to portray the characters in the tale. For practice, say the line "Twinkle, twinkle, little star" in the voice of each of these characters:

- A pitiful child with a big problem, who wants to make an important wish

- A mean giant, who is *demanding* that the star twinkle

- A crafty wizard, who is making a magic charm

Many stories are told in the dialect of a region or of an ethnic group. And after watching storytellers on television, you may believe that using dialect is an important part of the storyteller's art. As a general rule, though, if a dialect is not yours, don't use it. It is very easy to insult other people if you appear to make fun of their speech.

Once children have learned stories, they should tell them before audiences that have not heard them practice—such as children in other classes or parents on Parents Night. They will make many friends and bring good cheer if they perform their stories at a Head Start Center or a senior citizens' activity center. You might even arrange a story swap: Senior citizens can tell stories of their own in exchange for the children's stories.

DRAMATIZING STORIES

Dramatization takes many forms, but in any form, it is an especially engaging way of inviting children into literature. In story dramatizations, children become story characters (at least for a little while) and look at the world through their eyes. In this section, we'll look at four different forms of literature-based dramatizations.

Story Theater

Story theater is a form of drama in which participants mime a story as it is read aloud. Because no dialogue is required, it is probably the simplest form of drama and is especially well suited for use with very young children. Also, because groups of participants (or all participants, for that matter) can play the same role in story theater, it is a good introduction to drama for students who feel shy about participating.

Typically, story theater is not performed for an audience. It's the acting out itself that is important for young children. Sometimes children won't be satisfied with playing the story only once and may ask to act the story out again immediately.

What the Player Does in Story Theater. Although the players in story theater don't have to worry about dialogue, they do assume an active part. First, players must listen to the narrator in order to act out the story line appropriately. Even more important, the players need to attend to characterization, and the teacher may want to encourage discussion about what the characters are like.

Selecting Stories for Story Theater. For story theater, look for stories that rely on extensive narration, have plenty of action, and use minimal dialogue. Esphyr Slobodkina's *Caps for Sale* (1940) works well. The main character is a peddler of hats who carries his wares on his head. One day the peddler goes for a walk in the country. (Imagine how carefully you would have to walk with hats piled high on your head.) When the peddler gets tired, he sits down (very carefully) and leans (very slowly) against a tree to nap; upon waking, he reaches up (slowly and carefully) to make sure his hats are still in place. They're gone! (Imagine the peddler's reactions!) After a great deal of looking to the left, right, and all around, the peddler finally looks up into the tree, and on every branch of the tree there is a monkey wearing a cap. (What a surprise!) The peddler is upset; so he shakes his fist at the monkeys, and what happens? You've heard the saying "Monkey see, monkey do." Well, that is just what happens. The monkeys shake their fists right back at the peddler, and each of the peddler's subsequent expressions of frustration is repeated precisely by the monkeys. Children will insist on playing this story repeatedly.

Readers Theater

In readers theater, students don't act out stories; they read (not memorize) scripted versions of stories and rely on their voices to convey the characters' emotions. Audiences can add to the success of readers theater because students are likely to be motivated to practice and refine their readings in order to do well.

What the Player Does in Readers Theater. Readers theater is more formal than story theater because the aim is for the players to present as polished a reading as possible. Usually, readers need to practice reading a script repeatedly in order to learn to read their parts fluently and to interpret them with sensitivity.

Although the players in a readers theater presentation don't have to worry about how to act out the story, they do have to be concerned with character interpretation. What is the character like? How does he or she react to the events in the story? How (if at all) does the character change over the course of the story? What changes in speaking tone, volume, speed, or pitch might convey particular emotions? Both the teacher and fellow students can offer feedback after each practice reading, sharing what they especially liked about the interpretations and offering suggestions for improvement.

Selecting Stories and Creating Scripts for Readers Theater. Both picture books and chapter books can be used for readers theater. Books containing extensive dialogue are the best choices, and some picture books are perfect for readers theater. These "ready-to-use" picture books are written in dialogue form without dialogue tags ("he said" or "she replied") and contain no narration. Angela Johnson's ***Tell Me a Story, Mama*** (1989) is a dialogue between a little girl and her mother; Chris Raschka's ***Yo! Yes?*** (1993) is a simple dialogue between two little boys. Picture books that contain some narration and a great deal of dialogue with dialogue tags can be made into readers theater scripts quite easily. A few picture books, such as Richard and Roni Schotter's ***There's a Dragon About: A Winter's Revel*** (1994), are actually written as scripts, and the inside of the dust jacket of Frances Temple's ***Tiger Soup*** (1994) offers a scripted version of this Jamaican folktale. In looking for portions of chapter books to turn into readers theater scripts, look for the same features you would look for in picture books—minimal narration and extensive dialogue.

Older students can help create scripts. You may want to use teacher-created scripts initially, but once students gain some experience with readers theater, show them how you select text and turn it into scripts. Students will soon be reading stories with an ear toward whether they can be readily made into scripts.

Creative Dramatics

In creative dramatics, players act out the story. However, unlike staged productions of plays, there are no sets, few if any props, and usually no audience. And instead of having a script, the players improvise dialogue.

What Is Required of the Player. Creative dramatics can be challenging, especially when students first try their hands at it. Because no one reads the story (unlike story theater), the students must remember the story line. Also, because there is no script (unlike readers theater), students are on their own in creating

Stories can be brought to life via classroom dramatizations.

dialogue. And, of course, the players in a creative dramatics activity must be as attuned to characterization as the players in story theater and readers theater.

Teacher Support in Creative Dramatics. Teacher support in creative dramatics is important. Geraldine Siks (1958) recommends that teachers support students in creative dramatics in the following ways:

1. *Motivate children into a specific mood.* Preparing children for a creative dramatics experience begins prior to reading the story aloud as the teacher sets an appropriate mood for the story.

2. *Share the story.* The teacher's reading of the story should help the students with their interpretation of it.

3. *Guide children in making a plan for playing.* The teacher and students need to collaborate to review and list the characters in the story to ensure that all important story roles are filled. They should also review and list the scenes in the story. This will help students remember the order of story events; if only part of the story is to be reenacted, then the students can use the list of scenes to select the one(s) they want to recreate. The teacher and students should also talk about the staging of the story. What parts of the staging area will be used for which scenes? How will tricky staging problems be handled? And once students have chosen or been assigned parts, the most valuable support a teacher can provide is to help them reflect on characterization.

4. *Guide children into creating while they play.* Children may need support while reenacting stories, especially if they have had little or no experience with creative dramatics. The teacher should lend a helping hand as a coach rather than a director. Teachers can provide support from within the story or from without. They provide support from within by playing the part of one of the characters. As a character, the teacher can create dialogue that signals what happens next in a story or how another character might respond to a situation. For example, if the teacher is playing the part of Petunia in Roger Duvoisin's *Petunia* (1950), she might signal the

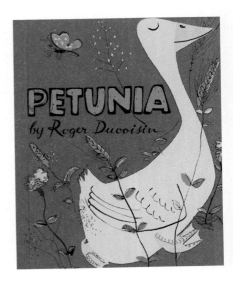

Illustration 12.8
The story of *Petunia,* a silly goose who creates pandemonium in the barnyard, has become a classic. (*Petunia* by Roger Duvoisin. Copyright © 1950 and renewed 1978 by Roger Duvoisin. Used by permission of Random House, Inc.)

upcoming scene (assuming the students need a signal) by saying, "I see Straw the horse, and by the way he's holding his mouth, I bet he has a toothache." With a cue like that, Straw will know what comes next. The teacher can provide support from outside of the story simply by being available to whisper lines to students who get stuck.

5. *Praise and guide children to evaluate the playing.* After playing a story, students need to reflect on how the playing went. What did they especially like? What might have been done differently? And the teacher shouldn't be the only one giving feedback. Eventually, the students should take over the praising and evaluating.

Selecting Stories for Creative Dramatics. The same sorts of stories that are great for storytelling work well for creative dramatics. In particular, stories with strong action sequences, lots of dialogue, and minimal narration work well—stories such as *Petunia* or "The Three Billy Goats Gruff." Vivian Paley (1981) found that her kindergartners enjoyed playing the longer and more complex fairytales over and over because the stories had enough depth to challenge the players in their interpretations.

Improvisational Drama

Literature-based improvisational drama is quite different from the other forms of dramatization we have discussed. The players do not recreate a story, but they do become story characters. As the characters, they respond to issues, themes, and situations suggested by the story (Booth, 1985). That is, the teacher creates a situation inspired by the story that students are to explore through dramatic improvisation. The situation should be one that helps the students gain insights into a story theme.

An example can clarify how improvisational drama might work. In Matt Novak's *Mouse TV* (1994), a mouse family loves to watch television. Then, one night the television doesn't work; so the mice turn to other activities—exploring, making things, playing games, singing songs, making scary faces, conducting experiments, reading stories. Stylistically, the story is a light-hearted fantasy, but it explores a substantial theme that children can explore further through improvisational drama. After listening to the story, they can become members of the mouse household on the following evening, when the television is working once again. How will the mice choose to spend their time this evening?

What Is Required of the Player? In improvisational drama, players must create their own dialogue and action. Although the dialogue and action can move in different directions, they must remain within the confines created by the teacher. Further, if the players have taken on the roles of characters from the story, they must act in ways consistent with those characters. This may sound like an especially demanding form of drama, and in some ways it is. Yet, in many ways, it resembles the way children play when they are on their own: They define the play situation and create action and dialogue within that situation. In fact, educators such as Brian Edmiston (1993) have successfully used improvisational drama even with primary-grade students.

Teacher Support in Improvisational Drama. In improvisational drama, the teacher must carefully structure a context that will enable the children to explore issues raised by a story. For example, in Chapter 18 of *The Giver* (1993),

Jonas and The Giver talk about the possibility of Jonas's being lost and all the memories he has received being released on the society that has always been protected from memories. This chapter could easily be used to create a context for improvisational drama, in which the players become members of Jonas's society and receive memories for the first time.

Having introduced the dramatic context to the students, the teacher must help them select the roles they will play. Then, as in creative dramatics, the teacher can support students' playing from within or from outside of the improvisational context. If the improvisation is based on *The Giver*, the teacher can become one of the people receiving memories. As a player, she might express joy or pain in response to the memories she receives. If the memories are joyful ones, the teacher might suggest that all the people go to The Giver to demand still more memories. Or the teacher might take a more neutral role that would allow her to question other players in such a way as to suggest directions in which they might move the drama: "I have received none of these memories you speak of. Tell me what they are like!"

Finally, the teacher can join the students in reflecting on the completed improvisation. Participants can talk about why they did and said particular things.

ENGAGING CHILDREN IN POETRY

In this section of the chapter, we share ideas for engaging children in poetry. There are several ways of doing this: surrounding children with poetry, encouraging children's responses to poetry, encouraging public performances of poems, and helping children write poetry.

Making Songs and Poems a Part of the School Day

Songs and poems fit into the school day in a surprising number of ways— and the more children get used to them, the more they will enjoy them. Poems should be shared often in read-aloud time. They should be read with an expressive voice for pure enjoyment and reflection. Topical poems can be posted around the room as comments on the seasons, on holidays, or on science or social studies. You can find poems appropriate to nearly any occasion in anthologies such as *The Random House Book of Poetry* (1983), edited by Jack Prelutsky, which indexes poems by topic. Children's own poems should be shared and posted along with those of published poets. Poetry can also be included along with other literary works in the readings for a thematic or a literary unit (see Chapter 14).

Here are some further ideas for sharing poetry with children and young people.

Songs and Poems in the Reading Circle. Poems and songs make excellent fare for beginning reading instruction. Their catchy rhythms and rhymes give children support and alleviate some of the burden of word recognition. You may introduce kindergartners and first graders to a short poem or song lyric, with the words written on a large chart. Make smaller versions for them to keep in a growing notebook of verses.

Two reliable sources of song lyrics for children are Kathleen Krull's *Gonna Sing My Head Off!* (1992), illustrated by Allen Garns, and the collection by Peter Blood and Annie Paterson entitled *Rise Up Singing* (1992). Some sources of poems for children are given in the Recommended Books list at the end of Chapter 7.

"Poetry and Tell." For older children, we especially like the suggestion that teachers initiate "Poetry and Tell" sessions (Wolf, 1993). Children are invited to choose a poem (with guidance from the teacher, as necessary) and share it with the class.

With younger children, you can extend this idea and invite them to bring in single words that intrigue them, a particularly vivid description, or a funny or interesting way of saying things they've heard someone use—fragments of intriguing language to celebrate with the class. After all, the idea is to encourage—really, to keep alive—the fascination with language that all children are born with.

Poetry Break. Another worthwhile suggestion is having a "Poetry Break" every day or so (Wolf, 1993). A "Poemster of the Day" (the principal, a custodian, a parent—or, certainly, one or more children) is elected to go from class to class reading or reciting a poem—perhaps the same poem in each class. The teacher holds up a big sign that reads "Poetry Break!" and the poemster delivers!

Poetry Caravan. When the students have learned poems and interesting ways to present them, the whole class may go from room to room throughout the school, "serenading" the other classes with poetry.

Encouraging Responses to Poetry

For years, teachers believed that the most reasonble way to have children respond to a poem was to have them say what it meant and to analyze its parts. But poetry speaks to us on many levels besides the intellectual one—and to assume that it is possible to summarize in so many words what a poem "is really saying" usually misses the point. The issue is often not what the poem says or means, but what it does and how it does it.

Often the best way to respond to a poem is not analytical but expressive. Invite children to draw as you read a poem to them. Invite them to invent sound effects or movements to accompany the verses. Invite them to act the poem out. Invite them to shout out the phrases they like best.

Choral Reading and Reciting

Most poetry is anchored in sound and is intended to be read or recited aloud. This section offers some suggestions for making an event out of oral reading and reciting. Choral reading and reciting—the reading and reciting of poems by a chorus or "voice choir"—can be great fun, as children explore the dramatic possibilities of poems and of their own voices.

Whole Chorus Presentations. The trick to having a whole chorus of children recite is to keep all the voices animated, not "sing-song." Children learn to focus on their sound if they are challenged to make a poem sound a certain way.

Say you ask children to recite the traditional poem "The Grand Old Duke of York":

The Grand Old Duke of York
He had ten thousand men.
He always marched them up the hill
Then he marched them down again.

And when they were up they were up.
And when they were down they were down.
And when they were only halfway up
They were neither up nor down.

To focus their attention on the sound they want to make, tell them the poem is about a group of soldiers marching along. Ask them, "Are the soldiers wounded and weary, or are they marching snappily in a Fourth of July parade? Which? Okay, then how should they sound? Do they sound one way as they are marching proudly to battle, and another way when they're dragging themselves painfully home again?"

Poems in Dialogue. Many poems can be effectively divided between two voices. When children recite Milne's (1924) poem "Happiness" in two voices—one child taking every other line—they can bring out the plodding, two-step gait of a small child in big boots and a raincoat:

John had
        Great Big
Waterproof
        Boots on;
John had a
        Great Big
Waterproof
        Hat;
John had a
        Great Big
Waterproof
        Mackintosh—
And that
        (Said John)
Is
        That.

The trick with more than one voice is to keep the poem moving on the beat. Pairs of children can take parts and practice the poem until they can recite it smoothly. You may need to clap out the beat for them the first time through. (You may also have to tell children that in England a raincoat is called a "mackintosh.")

Poems in dialogue can achieve a dramatic effect. Harold Monro's (1953) "Overheard in a Salt Marsh" is written for two voices. The performers will need to answer some questions about it: Where is this taking place? Who are the characters and what are they like? How does each one feel? How does each one's voice sound? When does one speak quickly? When slowly and musically?

Nymph, nymph, what are your beads?
        Green glass, goblin. Why do you stare at them?
Give them me.
        No.
Give them me. Give them me.
        No.
Then I will howl all night in the reeds,
Lie in the mud and howl for them.
        Goblin, why do you love them so?

They are better than stars or water,
Better than voices of wind that sing,
Better than any man's fair daughter,
Your green glass beads on a silver ring.

Hush, I stole them out of the moon.
Give me your beads, I desire them.
No.
I will howl in a deep lagoon
For your green glass beads. I love them so.
Give them me. Give them.
No.

Poems as Rounds. As children, many of us sang rounds like "Row, Row, Row Your Boat." Some poems can work very well as rounds, when they are recited—not sung—by small groups repeating the same verse and starting at staggered intervals.

The traditional poem "Can You Dig That Crazy Music?" can be recited by two or three groups. If you want to use three groups, start by having all the children say the verse through as a single group. Then have Group A read the first line alone. As Group A begins the second line, Group B begins the first. When Group A starts in on the third line, Group C begins the first, and Group B begins the second. The third time through, Group A gets to the last line and keeps repeating it until Group B and then Group C reach and recite that line—then the poem is over. The results are amazing! Here is the poem with the accented syllables marked:

Can	you	dig	that	crazy	music?	
Can	you	dig	it?	Can you dig it?	Can you dig it?	Can you dig it?
Can	you	dig	that	crazy	music?	
Can	you	dig	it?	Can you dig it?	Can you dig it?	Can you dig it?
Oh,	look.	There's a chicken on a	barbed wire	fence.		
Now,	now.	There's another one,	coming down the	road.		
	Ma-	ma,	ma-	ma,		
	Get that	son-of-a-gun	off my	porch!		

You may want to try out other poems as rounds. Many nursery rhymes are well suited to this technique. Try "Diddle, Diddle, Dumpling, My Son John," or "The Grand Old Duke of York."

Inviting Children to Write Poetry

Here's a paradox: Surveys show that children prefer to listen to and read rhymed and rhythmic poetry. Yet they have great difficulty writing rhymed and rhythmic poems, at least ones that make good sense. When teachers help children write poems, they often share techniques that will lead the children to write unrhymed poems. Not only is this the most likely way of ensuring successful poetry-writing sessions, it also broadens children's appreciation for modern poetry, since most poets these days—particularly those writing for adults—do not write rhyming poems. The following are suggestions for writing poems that are expressive but that do not rhyme.

Making Metaphors. Ask students to think of a person they believe has some particular quality—say, a lively personality. (Have them hold off writing the person's name.) They should write the answer to each of the following questions on a line by itself:

- If this person were a stage of a fire, what stage (a tiny spark, roaring flames, glowing embers)?
- If this person were a season of the year, what season?
- If this person were weather, what sort of weather?
- If this person were a bird, what kind of bird?
- If this person were landscape, what landscape?
- If this person were music, what kind of music?
- If this person were footwear, what kind of footwear?
- If this person were a car, what kind of car?
- If this person were a time of day, what time of day?

On the line below their answers, have the children write the person's name. Now they tinker with these lines—move them around, add or take away words, let the poem speak itself in the best way it can.

List Poems. Throughout the ages, many fine poems have been developed around the idea of lists. Take this medieval prayer, for example:

From Ghoulies
And Ghosties
And long-legged Beasties
And Things that go bump in the night:
Good Lord, deliver us.

You can use the idea of listing by asking students to list all of the things they know that are dark, or lonely, or round, or scary. The effect is heightened when they include both concrete and abstract things in their lists, for example, all of these are round:

- Ripples in a pond when a pebble is thrown in
- A policeman's beat
- The moon's halo
- Subway tokens
- Surprised eyes
- A ghost's mouth
- The world
- Life

It's best if children free-write the lists first, then arrange them for best effect.

Incantations. From oldest times, the power of poetry has been used to summon energy and spirit and marshall concentration to a particular end. (Some call this magic.) In the eighth century, Saint Patrick of Ireland wrote a prayer that is part enchantment (Kennelly, 1981):

St. Patrick's Rune

I bind unto myself today
The virtues of the starlit heaven,
The glorious sun's life-giving ray,
The whiteness of the moon at even;
The flashing of the lightning free,
The howling wind's tempestuous shocks,
The stable earth, the deep salt sea
And all the old eternal rocks.

Ask students to write an incantation to make someone brave, tough, fast, lucky, or smart. Here is a format they can follow:

May the _____ of the _____ ,
The _____ of the _____ ,
The _____ of the _____ , and
The _____ of the _____
Be with me this day.

The Cinquain. A cinquain is a five-line poem tightly focused on one topic. Writing cinquains is a way for children to explore a character in a story they are reading. Here's an example, based on the hero of "Jack and the Beanstalk":

Jack
young, wily
believing, climbing, winning
brave, or just reckless?
Giant-killer

Cinquains are written according to this formula:

1. The first line names the subject in one word.
2. The second line gives two words describing the subject.
3. The third gives three action words related to the subject and ending in -*ing*.
4. The fourth line has four words, which can be a four-word phrase, related to the subject.
5. The fifth line is one word, a synonym for the subject.

In spite of the use of a formula, the results can be striking.

The Diamante. Diamantes are a variation on the cinquain form. Whereas a cinquain describes a character as she or he is now, a diamante describes how a character (or some other aspect of a story) changes over time. Let's look at the character "Jack" again:

Boy
young, simpleton
loafing, goofing, grinning
naive child/plucky hero
"Fetch the axe!"
proven man
Jack

The first half of a diamante relates to the character in the beginning of the story. Then, midway through the poem, the descriptions change and relate to the character at the end of the story.

The pattern of a diamante is as follows:

1. The first line is a one-word name for the character as he or she was in the beginning of the story.

2. The second line gives two words describing the character in the beginning.

3. The third line is three action words (*-ing* words) describing the character in the beginning.

4. In the fourth line, the first two words describe the character in the beginning. Then there is a slash, followed by two words that describe the character at the end of the story.

5. The fifth line has three action words related to the character at the end of the story.

6. The sixth line has two words that describe the character at the end of the story.

7. The seventh line is a one-word name for the character at the end of the story.

Of course, there are many more ways to help children write poems, but space won't permit us to describe them here. Please consult the list of Resources at the end of Chapter 7.

OTHER DIMENSIONS OF THE LITERATURE-RICH CLASSROOM

If teachers wish to foster a love of literature, then they must devote ample time to reading, listening, and responding to literature. This is time above and beyond that devoted to teaching reading skills.

DEAR Time

Sometimes teachers tell students they can read "once their work is done." That works fine for the strong students who consistently finish their work early, but many students *never* finish their work early. To ensure that *all* students get to read every day, many teachers build in a block of time during which all the children in the classroom stop what they are doing and choose books, magazines, or newspapers to read. These blocks of reading time are known as DEAR (Drop Everything And Read), SSR (Sustained Silent Reading), or USSR (Uninterrupted Sustained Silent Reading).

Students need to realize that their teacher values DEAR time. Teachers can demonstrate this commitment by scheduling DEAR time *daily,* beginning with the first day of school, and by spending the DEAR time reading with their students. Students may need to read for shorter blocks of time at the beginning of the year (ten to fifteen minutes) and then work up to longer stretches (thirty to forty-five minutes). DEAR time is for all students; even those not yet reading conventionally can engage in "pretend reading." And because silent reading may

Table 12.4 How to Make DEAR a Success

- Make DEAR time a part of students' daily routine.
- Let students choose their own reading materials for DEAR time.
- Ensure that everyone, including the teacher, reads during DEAR time.
- For students who have a difficult time reading for long stretches, begin with a few minutes of reading time (perhaps ten minutes) and build to longer blocks of time (thirty to forty-five minutes).
- For younger readers, don't require that the reading time be silent; beginning readers frequently need to hear themselves read aloud.
- Let kindergartners participate in DEAR time by "pretend reading" stories.

not be appropriate for beginning readers who may need to hear themselves read aloud, there is no reason they can't read their books out loud. (See Table 12.4.)

Author Visits

There is probably no better way to bring both literature *and* the process of creating literature to life for children than through a visit by a recognized children's author (or illustrator). Such a visit can usually be arranged by contacting the children's marketing department of the author's publisher.

A visit by an author should be viewed as an opportunity to celebrate literature and literacy. Some schools do this by hosting a Young Author's Conference in conjunction with the author's visit. Presentations by the visiting author typically get top billing at the conference. Ideally, the author will be able to present to small groups of students. Visiting authors often have wonderful stories to share with students about the inspiration for their work, and illustrators frequently offer fascinating demonstrations of their art. If time permits, it is ideal to organize more informal sessions in which small groups can really talk to the visitor. The author or illustrator is the celebrity of the Young Author's Conference, but this doesn't mean other important things aren't happening. Students who attend the conference should be authors or illustrators themselves and should come to the conference prepared to join peer groups to share stories and illustrations they have created. A third type of conference event can center around children's literature selections. Students can attend sessions offered by teachers or members of the community in which they listen to a story read aloud and participate in a response activity based on that story.

Teachers need to prepare students for an upcoming author visit. First, they must ensure that students know the featured author's work. In the weeks preceding the visit, the teacher should read the visiting author's stories aloud. Children should have the opportunity to respond to the author's work through writing and artwork. Their responses can be displayed throughout the classroom or school. If students will have the opportunity to interview the visiting author, the teacher needs to help them generate questions that will yield insights into how writers (or illustrators) go about their work—where they get ideas, how they budget their time to ensure their work gets finished, what special techniques they use, and what advice they might offer young writers (or artists).

TEACHING IDEAS

Preparing a Read-Aloud. Prepare to read aloud *The Ghost-Eye Tree* (1985) by Bill Martin, Jr. In the story, a mother asks her son and daughter to walk at night to the end of the town to fetch a bucket of milk. The trip to town is uneventful, even though the children must pass the dreaded ghost-eye tree. However, on the walk home, the children, loaded down with a full bucket of milk, are certain they see the ghost eye. Then, to complicate matters, the children discover that the brother has dropped his much-loved hat by the ghost-eye tree. This story is full of drama, tense moments, and changing emotions. Practice reading it aloud. Because there is so much dialogue between the siblings, you may want to try out different voices for the brother and sister. Vary the pace of your reading. As the children approach the tree, try reading faster. When they see the ghost eye, pick up your pace even more. There are ample opportunities to vary your expression. How might the children sound as they exchange good-natured jibes with one another? How do they feel when they spot the ghost eye? What emotions does the brother experience when his sister announces that she will retrieve his hat? Now try reading the story to a group of children.

Setting Up a Student Book Referral Service. You can set up a student book referral service by inviting students to record the books they have read and their responses to those books in a database maintained on the classroom computer. The entry for each book should include title, author/illustrator, genre, summary, response to book. A computerized database will give students great flexibility in selecting books. If they want to find a good fantasy to read, they simply call up the category "Fantasy." If they want recommendations for books by a particular author, the computer will sort books by authors' names.

Stocking the Classroom Library. Although you will probably want a set of core books to remain in your library center all year, you will want to rotate additional books through regularly (probably every month or so). When you rotate new books into the library center, don't just place them there without fanfare. Introduce the books one by one, helping students make connections between the new books and ones with which they are already familiar: "Here's Sid Hite's latest book; I thought you might enjoy it since we read *It's Nothing to a Mountain* (1994)" or "We've been reading and writing a lot of trickster tales. So I've brought in *Tops and Bottoms* (1995) by Janet Stevens. You'll love the way you read the book from top to bottom—just like the title says."

EXPERIENCES FOR YOUR LEARNING

1. Develop an improvisational drama based on *The Giver* (1993). Often, the ending of a book suggests a situation for improvising. Present the improvisational situation you create for *The Giver* to a group of peers and ask them to join you in the improvisation.

2. Visit a classroom library center. Which of the design features identified by Morrow (on page 414) were evident in the center? Given what you saw, how would you rate the library center—basic, good, or excellent? Why?

3. Interview at least five of your peers to determine how they feel about storytelling. Discuss some of the storytelling activities described in this chapter. Afterwards, talk to the same five people to see if their attitudes toward storytelling have changed.

RECOMMENDED BOOKS

* indicates a picture book; I indicates interest level
(P = preschool, YA = young adult)

Read-Alouds and the Classroom Library Collection

* Aardema, Verna. *Why Mosquitoes Buzz in People's Ears*. Illustrated by Leo and Diane Dillon. New York: Dial, 1975. In this African pourquoi tale, an unexpected chain of events explains why mosquitoes buzz in people's ears. (I: P–8)

* Ackerman, Karen. *The Tin Heart*. Illustrated by Michael Hays. New York: Atheneum, 1990. Best friends Mahaley and Flora live on opposite sides of the Ohio River, and when the Civil War breaks out, the ferry stops running. (I: 8–12)

* Aliki. *Wild and Woolly Mammoths*. New York: HarperCollins, 1977. This is a fascinating account of the woolly mammoth and its relationship to cave dwellers. (I: 6–10)

* Allard, Harry. *Miss Nelson Is Missing!* Illustrated by James Marshall. Boston: Houghton Mifflin, 1977. When Viola Swamp becomes the sub in Room 207, the children are desperate to find their missing teacher. (I: P–8)

* ———. *The Stupids Step Out*. Boston: Houghton Mifflin, 1974. An outrageous family is involved in hilarious antics. (I: P–8)

* Ancona, George. *Fiesta U.S.A.* New York: Dutton, 1995. Through text and photographs, Ancona introduces readers to some of the many fiestas celebrated by Spanish-speaking people in the United States. (I: 6–10)

* Barrett, Judi. *Cloudy with a Chance of Meatballs*. Illustrated by Ron Barrett. New York: Atheneum, 1978. Storms of food fall from the sky in the town of Chew-and-Swallow. (I: P–8)

* Bash, Barbara. *Tree of Life: The World of the African Baobab*. San Francisco: Sierra Club, 1989. With lyrical language, the author documents the rich ecosystem of the African baobab tree. (I: 6–10)

* ———. *Urban Roosts*. San Francisco: Sierra Club, 1990. The author explores how birds that live in the city have adapted their nest building habits to their urban environment. (I: 6–11)

Blume, Judy. *Tales of a Fourth Grade Nothing*. New York: Dutton, 1972. Peter's little brother causes endless (and funny) complications in his life. (I: 6–10)

Bond, Michael *A Bear Called Paddington*. Illustrated by Peggy Fortnum. Boston: Houghton Mifflin, 1958. Paddington Bear becomes a member of the Brown family. (I: P–7)

Byars, Betsy. *The Seven Treasure Hunts*. Illustrated by Jennifer Barrett. New York: HarperCollins, 1991. Two friends design treasure hunts that do not go quite as planned. (I: 6–10)

Cameron, Ann. *The Stories Julian Tells*. Illustrated by Ann Strugness. New York: Knopf, 1981. Julian relates humorous stories about everyday experiences. (I: 5–8)

Cleary, Beverly. *Ramona the Pest*. New York: Morrow, 1968. Ramona makes mischief when she enters kindergarten. (I: 6–10)

Collier, James Lincoln, and Christopher Collier. *My Brother Sam Is Dead*. New York: Scholastic, 1974. A family is torn apart as father and son take different sides in the American Revolution. (I: 9–12)

* Cooney, Barbara. *Miss Rumphius*. New York: Puffin, 1982. Miss Rumphius finds ways of achieving her three life-long goals. (I: 6–10)

Coville, Bruce. *Jeremy Thatcher, Dragon Hatcher*. Illustrated by Gary A. Lippincott. San Diego, CA: Harcourt, 1991. Being selected as a dragon hatcher opens up a world of adventure for Jeremy Thatcher. (I: 8–11)

Dahl, Roald. *James and the Giant Peach*. Illustrated by Nancy Ekholm Burkert. New York: Knopf, 1961. A boy leaves his misery behind when a giant peach, inhabited by magical characters, grows in his backyard. (I: 6–10)

* Delacre, Lulu. *Vejigante/Masquerader*. New York: Scholastic, 1993. A Puerto Rican boy dreams of joining in the play of the masqueraders. (I: 5–9)

* de Paola, Tomie. *Strega Nona*. New York: Prentice-Hall, 1975. Big Anthony and the townspeople face disaster when Big Anthony can't make the magic pasta pot stop cooking. (I: P–8)

* Ehlert, Lois. *Moon Rope/Un lazo a la luna*. San Diego, CA: Harcourt, 1992. In this pourquoi tale, fox convinces mole to climb to the moon on a rope woven of grass. (I: P–8)

Fleischman, Sid. *The Whipping Boy*. New York: Greenwillow, 1986. A whipping boy changes places with a prince. (I: 9–12)

* Fleming, Denise. *In the Tall, Tall Grass*. New York: Holt, 1991. A caterpillar munches its way through the tall, tall grass in the midst of lively activities. (I: P–7)

* Gackenbach, Dick. *Harry and the Terrible Whatzit*. New York: Clarion, 1977. To save his mother, Harry must face the terrible Whatzit that lives in the cellar. (I: P–7)

* ———. *Mighty Tree.* San Diego, CA: Harcourt, 1992. Three seeds grow into trees. One provides pleasure; another provides products, and the third offers shelter. (I: 4–8)

George, Jean Craighead. *My Side of the Mountain.* New York: Dutton, 1959. A boy survives alone in the wilds of upper New York State. (I: 10–YA)

* Grindley, Sally. *Shhh!* Illustrated by Peter Utton. New York: Little, Brown. 1991. The reader is invited to join in a trek through the giant's castle, and must try all the while to avoid waking the giant. (I: P–8)

Hite, Sid. *It's Nothing to a Mountain.* New York: Holt, 1994. A brother and sister find adventure and friendship in the Blue Ridge Mountains of Virginia. (I: 10–12)

* Hoffman, Mary. *Amazing Grace.* Illustrated by Caroline Binch. New York: Dial, 1991. A little girl's grandmother helps her realize that she can achieve anything she sets her mind to. (I: 6–10)

* Howard, Elizabeth Fitzgerald. *Aunt Flossie's Hats (and Crab Cakes Later).* Illustrated by James Ransome. New York: Clarion, 1991. Stories that accompany the old hats in Aunt Flossie's collection make Sunday visits memorable. (I: P–8)

Howe, Deborah, and James Howe. *Bunnicula: A Rabbit Tale of Mystery.* Illustrated by Alan Daniel. New York: Atheneum, 1979. The family pets are certain the new bunny is a vampire rabbit. (I: 6–10)

* Hutchins, Pat. *Rosie's Walk.* New York: Macmillan, 1968. Rosie the hen takes a stroll around the barnyard, oblivious to the danger that is stalking her. (I: P–7)

* Johnson, Angela. *Tell Me a Story, Mama.* Illustrated by David Soman. New York: Orchard, 1989. A little girl ends up being the storyteller when she asks her mother for a story. (I: P–8)

* Keiko, Kasza. *The Wolf's Chicken Stew.* New York: Putnam, 1987. A chicken outsmarts the wolf who wants her for his dinner. (I: P–8)

* Kellogg, Steven. *The Mysterious Tadpole.* New York: Dial, 1972. A boy must find a home for his pet tadpole, which grows to an outrageous size. (I: P–8)

* Kimmel, Eric A. *Anansi Goes Fishing.* Illustrated by Janet Stevens. New York: Holiday, 1992. The tables are turned when Anansi sets out to trick his friend into doing all the work. (I: P–8)

* Kitchen, Bert. *And So They Build.* Cambridge, MA: Candlewick, 1993. Using a distinctive format, the author provides information about the nesting habits of a variety of animals. (I: 6–10)

Konigsburg, E. L. *From the Mixed-up Files of Mrs. Basil E. Frankweiler.* New York: Dell, 1987. Claudia and her younger brother run away to live in the Metropolitan Museum of Art. (I: 9–12)

* Krull, Kathleen. *Wilma Unlimited.* Illustrated by David Diaz. San Diego, CA: Harcourt, 1996. This is the story of how Wilma Rudolph became the world's fastest woman runner. (I: 7–11)

Lindgren, Astrid. *Pippi Longstocking.* Trans. by Florence Lamborn. Illustrated by Louis S. Glanzman. New York: Viking, 1950. Living all alone, Pippi—the strongest girl in the world—is free to engage in hilarious antics. (I: 5–9)

Lowry, Lois. *The Giver.* Boston: Houghton Mifflin, 1993. Living in a controlled society, a boy is given access to the dark secrets that lie beneath the order. (I: 11–YA)

MacLachlan, Patricia. *Sarah, Plain and Tall.* New York: Harper, 1985. In this stroy set in pioneer times, two children long for someone to fill the empty place left by the death of their own mother. (I: 8–12)

* Martin, Bill, Jr., and John Archambault. *Barn Dance.* Illustrated by Ted Rand. New York: Holt, 1986. A boy joins in the animals' square dance. (I: P–8)

* ———. *The Ghost-Eye Tree.* Illustrated by Ted Rand. New York: Holt, 1985. This story about a brother and sister's scary experience with a haunted tree can easily be adapted for readers theater. (I: P–9)

* Mayer, Mercer. *Liza Lou and the Yeller Belly Swamp.* New York: Macmillan, 1976. Liza Lou proves to be too clever for the witches, haunts, and gobblygooks of the Yeller Belly Swamp. (I: P–8)

* McCloskey, Robert. *Make Way for Ducklings.* New York: Viking, 1941. Mrs. Mallard seeks the perfect home for her ducklings. (I: P–7)

* McDermott, Gerald. *Anansi the Spider.* New York: Holt, 1972. Anansi's sons use their special abilities to rescue their father. (I: P–8)

* McKissack, Patricia. *Flossie and the Fox.* Illustrated by Rachel Isadora. New York: Dial, 1986. Flossie turns the tables on Mr. Fox when he tries to get her basket of eggs. (I: 5–10)

* ———. *A Million Fish . . . More or Less.* Illustrated by Dena Schutzer. New York: Knopf, 1992. Visits to the bayou inspire unforgettable yarns. (I: 6–10)

McKissack, Patricia C., and Fredrick L. McKissack. *Christmas in the Big House, Christmas in the Quarters.* Illustrated by John Thompson. New York: Scholastic, 1994. A comparison of Christmas in the big house and in the slave quarters the year before the Civil War breaks out. (I: 9–12)

* McNaughton, Colin. *Suddenly.* San Digeo: Harcourt, 1994. Oblivious to the danger that looms over him,

a little pig saunters through town on his round of errands. (I: P–7)

* Merrill, Jean. *The Girl Who Loved Caterpillars.* Illustrated by Floyd Cooper. New York: Philomel, 1992. A young woman in twelfth-century Japan follows her heart rather than the dictates of her culture. (I: 8–12)

Milne, A. A. *Winnie-the-Pooh.* Illustrated by Ernest H. Shepard. New York: Dutton, 1924. Winnie-the-Pooh has marvelous adventures in the Hundred Acre Wood with his host of friends—all stuffed animals like him. (I: P–8)

* Mitchell, Margaree King. *Uncle Jed's Barbershop.* Illustrated by James Ransome. New York: Simon & Schuster, 1993. Uncle Jed refuses to let racial prejudice and economic setbacks keep him from realizing his dream. (I: 10–YA)

* Mora, Pat. *A Birthday Basket for Tia.* Illustrated by Cecily Lang. New York: Macmillan, 1992. A little girl puts together the perfect birthday basket for her great-aunt. (I: P–7)

* Mosel, Arlene. *Tikki Tikki Tembo.* Illustrated by Blair Lent. New York: Scholastic, 1968. This Chinese folktale explains why Chinese children are now given short names. (I: P–8)

Naylor, Phyllis Reynolds. *The Grand Escape.* Illustrated by Alan Daniel. New York: Atheneum, 1993. Two house cats make a grand escape to the outside world where challenges and opportunities abound. (I: 6–10)

———. *Shiloh.* New York: Atheneum, 1991. A boy determines to save the dog Shiloh from his abusive owner. (I: 8 and up)

Paterson, Katherine. *Bridge to Terabithia.* New York: Crowell, 1977. Jesse's friendship with a new girl in his rural neighborhood extends the boundaries of his life. (I: 10–12)

Paulsen, Gary. *Hatchet.* New York: Bradbury, 1987. The survivor of a plane crash, a boy struggles to survive in the wilderness. (I: 10–YA)

* Polacco, Patricia. *The Bee Tree.* New York: Philomel, 1993. A little girl and her grandfather are joined by friends in a merry chase through the countryside in search of a bee tree. (I: 5–10)

* ———. *Chicken Sunday.* New York: Philomel, 1992. A group of friends extend a hand of friendship across cultural boundaries. (I: 6–10)

* ———. *Pink and Say.* New York: Philomel, 1994. During the Civil War, an African American Union soldier befriends a white Union soldier. (I: 8–YA)

Robinson, Barbara. *The Best Christmas Pageant Ever.* New York: Harper, 1972. Everyone anticipates dis-

aster when the Herdmans participate in the church's Christmas pageant, but much to everyone's surprise, it's the best Christmas pageant ever. (I: 6–10)

Rosen, Michael J. *Elijah's Angel.* Illustrated by Aminah Brenda Lynn Robinson. San Diego, CA: Harcourt, 1992. A boy's parents help him reach across cultural boundaries. (I: 8–YA)

* ———. *A School for Pompey Walker.* Illustrated by Aminah Brenda Lynn Robinson. San Diego, CA: Harcourt, 1995. Bought out of slavery, Pompey Walker willingly faces personal dangers in order to achieve his goal of founding a school for black children. (I: 8–12)

Rylant, Cynthia. *Gooseberry Park.* Illustrated by Arthur Howard. San Diego, CA: Harcourt, 1995. When disaster strikes Gooseberry Park, Kona, a Labrador retriever, proves himself a hero and true friend of Stumpy the squirrel. (I: 5–9)

———. *The Van Gogh Cafe.* San Diego, CA: Harcourt, 1995. The magic in the walls of the Van Gogh Cafe spills out into the lives of its patrons. (I: 8–12)

* ———. *When I Was Young in the Mountains.* Illustrated by Diane Goode. New York: Dutton, 1982. In lyrical language, a girl tells of her life in the mountains. (I: 5–10)

Sacks, Margaret. *Themba.* Illustrated by Wil Clay. New York: Dutton, 1985. A South African boy waits for his father to return from the mines. (I: 7–10)

* San Souci, Robert D. *The Talking Eggs.* Illustrated by Jerry Pinkney. New York: Dial, 1989. An African American variant of Cinderella. (I: 5–10)

* Say, Allan. *Tree of Cranes.* Boston: Houghton Mifflin, 1991. A Japanese boy is introduced to Christmas by his mother. (I: P–8)

* Scieszka, Jon. *The Stinky Cheese Man and Other Fairly Stupid Tales.* Illustrated by Lane Smith. New York: Viking, 1992. A collection of wacky folktale spin-offs. (I: 5–10)

Selden, George. *The Cricket in Times Square.* Illustrated by Garth Williams. New York: Dell, 1960. Chester the cricket must make a life for himself in the alien world of the Times Square subway station. (I: 6–10)

* Sendak, Maurice. *Chicken Soup with Rice.* New York: Harper, 1962. This is a celebration of the virtues of chicken soup. (I: 4–7)

* ———. *Where the Wild Things Are.* New York: Harper, 1964. Sent to his room, Max travels to where the Wild Things are and becomes king of all Wild Things. (I: P–8)

Shelton, Rick. *Hoggle's Christmas.* Illustrated by Donald Gates. New York: Dutton, 1993. When

Isabel and Richard's friend moves away, he doesn't forget them. (**I:** 6–10)

Soto, Gary. *Baseball in April*. San Diego, CA: Harcourt, 1990. A collection of short stories about everyday experiences of young Mexican Americans. (**I:** 11–YA)

* ———. *Chato's Kitchen*. Illustrated by Susan Guevara. New York: Knopf, 1995. Chato, the coolest cat in East L.A., can't believe his luck when a family of mice moves in next door. (**I:** P–8)

* ———. *Too Many Tamales*. Illustrated by Ed Martinez. New York: Putnam, 1993. A little girl fears she has lost her mother's diamond ring in the tamale masa. (**I:** P–8)

* Steig, William. *Doctor De Soto*. New York: Farrar, 1982. When a mouse dentist and his wife agree to treat a fox's toothache, only their cleverness saves them from becoming the fox's dinner. (**I:** P–9)

* Stevens, Janet. *How the Manx Cat Lost Its Tail*. San Diego, CA: Harcourt, 1990. The Manx cat almost misses the last call to board Noah's ark. (**I:** P–8)

* ———. *Tops and Bottoms*. San Diego, CA: Harcourt, 1995. Hare tricks lazy Bear by wheeling and dealing in the tops and bottoms of vegetables. (**I:** P–8)

* Van Allsburg, Chris. *Two Bad Ants*. Boston: Houghton Mifflin, 1988. A visit to a kitchen spells near disaster for two bad ants. (**I:** P–9)

* ———. *The Widow's Broom*. Boston: Houghton Mifflin, 1992. A broom with special powers brings out the prejudices of the widow's neighbors. (**I:** 8–12)

* Viorst, Judith. *Alexander and the Terrible, Horrible, No Good, Very Bad Day*. Illustrated by Ray Cruz. New York: Atheneum, 1972. Alexander tells about all the things that have gone wrong in a single day. (**I:** P–8)

* Wahl, Jan. *Tailypo!* Illustrated by Wil Clay. New York: Holt, 1991. A man cuts off the tail of a night visitor and it comes back to haunt him. (**I:** P–8)

* Wallace, Karen. *Think of a Beaver*. Cambridge, MA: Candlewick, 1993. Using lyrical language, the author gives a firsthand account of a beaver's life. Additional facts are interwoven in the form of hand-lettered notes. (**I:** 6–10)

* Westray, Kathleen. *Picture Puzzler*. New York: Ticknor & Fields, 1994. A collection of optical illusions accompanied by explanations. (**I:** 8 and up)

White, E. B. *Charlotte's Web*. Illustrated by Garth Williams. New York: Harper, 1952. Charlotte the spider proves herself the truest of friends by saving the life of Wilbur the pig. (**I:** 5–10)

* Wild, Margaret. *Our Granny*. Illustrated by Julie Vivas. New York: Ticknor & Fields, 1994. A celebration of all kinds of grannies. (**I:** P–8)

* Willard, Nancy. *The High Rise Glorious Skittle Skat Roarious Sky Pie Angel Food Cake*. Illustrated by Richard Jesse Watson. San Diego, CA: Harcourt, 1990. A girl gets angelic help in making her mother a heavenly birthday cake. (**I:** 8–12)

* Williams, Shirley Anne. *Working Cotton*. Illustrated by C. Byard. San Diego, CA: Harcourt, 1992. Readers experience a day in the cotton fields with a migrant family. (**I:** 6–10)

* Wood, A. J. *Egg!* New York: Little, Brown, 1993. Information about the eggs of different animals is presented in riddles. (**I:** 5–10)

* Wood, Audrey. *King Bidgood's in the Bathtub*. Illustrated by Don Wood. San Diego, CA: Harcourt, 1985. Throughout the day and into the night, King Bidgood entertains himself in his tub, much to the distress of the court. (**I:** P–8)

* ———. *The Napping House*. Illustrated by Don Wood. San Diego, CA: Harcourt, 1984. Animals and humans snooze away a rainy day—until a flea wakes up. (**I:** P–8)

* ———. *Weird Parents*. New York: Dial, 1990. A boy describes his weird parents. (**I:** 8–12)

Yarbrough, Camille. *The Shimmershine Queens*. New York: Putnam, 1989. Angie loves to dream about her future, but her dreams begin to fade in the face of peer pressure. (**I:** 10–YA)

* Yolen, Jane. *Owl Moon*. Illustrated by John Schoenherr. New York: Philomel, 1987. A parent and child share a special time when they go out in search of an owl on a winter's night. (**I:** P–8)

* Young, Ed. *Lon Po Po*. New York: Philomel, 1989. Sisters outwit the evil wolf in this Chinese variant of "Little Red Riding Hood." (**I:** 5–9)

Storytelling

Afanas'ev, Aleksandr. *Russian Fairy Tales*. New York: Pantheon, 1973. A collection of fine tales, most without illustrations. (**I:** 7–14)

Briggs, Katherine. *British Folktales*. New York: Pantheon, 1977. Some familiar tales presented in the form in which they were traditionally told. The book also includes new tales. (**I:** YA)

Bruchac, Joseph. *Iroquois Tales*. Freedom, CA: Crossing Press, 1988. A collection of tales told by Native Americans in what is now New York State. (**I:** 8–11)

Courlander, Harold. *The Tiger's Whisker, and Other Tales from Asia and the Pacific*. New York: Holt, 1987. Short, pristine tales, written to be read aloud. (**I:** 8–11)

Erdoes, Richard, and Alfonso Ortiz. *American Indian Myths and Legends*. New York: Pantheon, 1984. A collection of Native American tales and lore, written for adults but good for read-alouds. (**I:** 10–YA)

Forest, Heather. *Wonder Tales from Around the World*. Little Rock, AR: August House, 1995. An international collection of fairy tales of enchantment. (**I:** 8–11)

Hamilton, Virginia. *In the Beginning: Creation Stories from Around the World*. New York: Harcourt, 1988. With beautiful illustrations, this collection places the Biblical story of Adam and Eve and the Greek myth of Pandora alongside creation myths from peoples around the world. (**I:** 8–YA)

———. *Her Stories: African American Folktales, Fairy Tales, and True Tales*. New York: Scholastic, 1995. With illustrations by Leo and Diane Dillon, these stories celebrate African American women. (**I:** 9–YA)

———. *The People Could Fly: American Black Folktales*. New York: Knopf, 1985. With illustrations by Leo and Diane Dillon, this collection has favorites such as "Brer Rabbit and the Tar Baby" and "Wiley and the Hairy Man." (**I:** 9–YA)

Haskins, James. *The Headless Haunt, and Other African American Ghost Stories*. New York: HarperCollins, 1994. With lively black-and-white illustrations, this collection was compiled for middle elementary grades and up. (**I:** 8–13)

Hearne, Betsy. *Beauties and Beasts*. Phoenix, AZ: Oryx, 1993. A fascinating collection of stories from around the world based on the beauty and the beast motif. (**I:** 9–YA)

MacDonald, Margaret Read. *Twenty Tellable Tales: Audience Participation Folktales for the Beginning Story-Teller*. Bronx, NY: H.W. Wilson, 1986. These tales have been honed by repeated telling to library groups. (**I:** 9–YA)

Mayo, Margaret. *Magical Tales from Many Lands*. New York: Dutton, 1993. The tales were collected for adult tellers but are quite suitable for children. (**I:** 9–YA)

Mourning Dove. *Coyote Stories*. Lincoln: University of Nebraska Press, 1990. Stories of the trickster, Coyote, collected in the 1930s by an Okanogan teller. (**I:** 9–YA)

National Association for the Preservation and Perpetuation of Storytelling. *More Best-Loved Stories Told at the National Storytelling Festival*. Little Rock, AR: August House, 1992. A collection of Native American and African American tales in the voices of their tellers. (**I:** 9–YA)

National Storytelling Association. *True Tales from America's Past*. Little Rock, AR: National Storytelling Press, 1995. These tales of pioneers, civil

rights activists, scientists, women factory workers bring the social studies curriculum to life. (**I:** 9–YA)

Perdue, Charles, ed. *Outwitting the Devil: Jack Tales from Wise County, Virginia*. Santa Fe, NM: Ancient City Press, 1987. Jack is a trickster in these tales from the Appalachian Mountains, and the devil is his favorite adversary. (**I:** 9–YA)

Phelps, Ethel Johnston. *Tatterhood and Other Tales*. New York: Feminist Press, 1978. Tales from around the world with strong female protagonists. (**I:** 9–YA)

Reneaux, J. J. *Cajun Folktales*. Little Rock, AR: August House, 1992. Animal tales, fairytales, funny folktales, and ghost stories from the Cajun people of the Louisiana bayou country. (**I:** 9–YA)

Schwartz, Alvin. *Scary Stories to Tell in the Dark*. New York: HarperCollins, 1985. Stories for middle elementary grade students and up, collected by a serious folklore collector. (**I:** 8–13)

Shannon, George. *A Knock at the Door: An International Collection*. Phoenix, AZ: Oryx, 1992. An international collection of intruder tales, like "The Three Little Pigs" and "Lon Po Po." (**I:** 9–YA)

Sierra, Judith. *Cinderella: An International Collection*. Phoenix, AZ: Oryx, 1992. Two dozen of the 650 variants of the Cinderella tale. (**I:** 9–YA)

———. *Hansel and Gretel: An International Collection*. Phoenix, AZ: Oryx, 1994. Stories from around the world about children who are forced out on their own. (**I:** 9–YA)

Stoutenburg, Adrien. *American Tall Tales*. New York: Viking, 1966. A paperback reprint of an older collection; includes "Stormalong," "Pecos Bill," "Johnny Appleseed," and others. (**I:** 8–13)

Van Etten, Teresa Pijoan de. *Spanish American Folktales*. Little Rock, AR: August House, 1990. Twenty-eight tales collected by the author, mostly in New Mexico. (**I:** 9–YA)

Dramatic Activities

* Ambrus, Victor G. *The Seven Skinny Goats*. San Diego: Harcourt, 1969. Creatures can't resist dancing when a boy plays his flute. Good for story theater. (**I:** P–8)

* Brown, Marc. *Arthur's Pet Business*. New York: Little, Brown, 1990. Arthur is in for surprises when he sets up a pet business. This and the many other books about Arthur are easily adapted for readers theater. (**I:** 6–9)

* Cuyler, Margery. *That's Good! That's Bad!* Illustrated by David Catrow. New York: Holt, 1991. A little boy has some hair-raising adventures on his trip to the zoo. Can be used, as written, as a two-part readers theater script. (I: 5–9)

* Duvoisin, Roger. *Petunia*. New York: Knopf, 1950. The barnyard will never again be the same once the silly goose Petunia finds a book and acquires "wisdom." Excellent for creative dramatics. (I: P–8)

* Fox, Mem. *Hattie and the Fox*. Illustrated by Patricia Mullins. New York: Bradbury, 1987. Hattie spots danger on the farm. Can be easily adapted for readers theater or creative dramatics. (I: P–8)

* Gray, Libba Moore. *Small Green Snake*. Illustrated by Holly Meade. New York: Orchard, 1994. A small green snake has too adventurous a spirit to heed his mother's warnings. (I: P–7)

* Jorgensen, Gail. *Crocodile Beat*. Illustrated by Patricia Mullins. New York: Macmillan, 1988. The animals' celebration is interrupted when crocodile arrives for dinner. Good for story theater. (I: P–7)

* Kroll, Virginia. *The Seasons and Someone*. Illustrated by Tatsuro Kiuchi. San Diego, CA: Harcourt, 1994. Through a series of questions and answers, the reader discovers how the seasons change for an Inuit child. Can be used, as written, as a two-part readers theater script. (I: 6–10)

* Lionni, Leo. *Frederick*. New York: Pantheon, 1967 A mouse family discovers how a poet can contribute to their community. Offers interesting opportunities for improvisational drama. (I: 6–10)

* Martin, Bill, Jr., *Brown Bear, Brown Bear, What Do You See?* Illustrated by Eric Carle. New York: Holt, 1967. A series of rhythmical questions and answers reveal what all sorts of animals see. Can be used, as written, for readers theater. (I: P–8)

* ———. *White Dynamite and Curly Kidd*. Illustrated by Ted Rand. New York: Holt, 1986. A dialogue between child and father about an upcoming rodeo event. Can be used, as written, for readers theater. (I: 6–10)

* Mazer, Anne. *The Salamander Room*. Illustrated by Steve Johnson. New York: Knopf, 1991. A mother and child discuss the feasibility of bringing a salamander indoors to live. Can be used, as is, as a two-part readers theater script. (I: 5-8)

* Noble, Trinka Hakes. *The Day Jimmy's Boa Ate the Wash*. Illustrated by Steven Kellogg. New York: Dial, 1980. A child recounts her class's out-of-control field trip to a farm. Can be used, as written, as a two-part readers theater script. (I: 5–8)

* Novak, Matt. *Mouse TV*. New York: Orchard, 1994. When their TV set breaks down, a mouse family discovers new ways to pass the evening. Offers opportunities for creative dramatics and improvisational drama. (I: P–8)

* Raschka, Chris. *Yo! Yes?* New York: Scholastic, 1993. A simple dialogue between two boys is the beginning of a friendship. Can be used, as written, as a two-part readers theater script. (I: P–8)

* Rosen, Michael. *We're Going on a Bear Hunt*. Illustrated by Helen Oxenbury. New York: Macmillan, 1989 A surprise awaits a family that goes on a bear hunt. Perfect for use in story theater. (I: P–8)

* Schotter, Richard, and Roni Schotter. *There's a Dragon About: A Winter's Revel*. Illustrated by R. W. Alley. New York: Orchard, 1994. A group of children set out to perform a play about a fierce dragon, brave damsels and lads, and a gallant knight. Written in script form. (I: 6–10)

* Scieszka, Jon. *The True Story of the 3 Little Pigs!* Illustrated by Lane Smith. New York: Viking, 1989. The wolf tells his side of the story in this spin-off of "The Three Little Pigs." Students will enjoy conducting an improvised trial of the wolf. (I: all ages)

* Slobodkina, Esphyr. *Caps for Sale*. New York: W.R. Scott, 1940. A peddler loses his caps to a group of monkeys. Good for story theater or creative dramatics. (I: P–7)

Taylor, Mildred. *Roll of Thunder, Hear My Cry*. New York: Dial, 1976. In the face of racism, an African American family struggles to save the family farm. (I: 10–YA)

* Temple, Frances. *Tiger Soup*. New York: Orchard, 1994. This Jamaican Anansi tale explains why monkeys live high up in trees. A scripted version of the tale appears on the inside of the dust jacket. (I: P–8)

Voight, Cynthia. *Homecoming*. New York: Atheneum, 1981. When their mother disappears, Dicey and her siblings seek a place to call their home. (I: 10–YA)

RESOURCES

Hamilton, Martha, and Mitch Weiss. *Children Tell Stories: A Teaching Guide*. Katonah, NY: Richard C. Owen, 1990.

Jensen, Julie M., and Nancy L. Roser, eds. *Adventuring with Books: A Booklist for Pre-K–Grade 6*. 10th ed. Urbana, IL: National Council of Teachers of English, 1993.

Lipson, Eden Ross. *The New York Times Parent's Guide to the Best Books for Children*. New York: Random House, 1991.

Martinez, Miriam, and William H. Teale. "Reading in a Kindergarten Library Center." *The Reading Teacher* 41 (l988): 568–72.

Morgan, Norah, and Juliana Saxton. *Teaching Drama: A Mind of Many Wonders*. Portsmouth, NH: Heinemann, 1987.

Prelutsky, Jack, ed. *The Random House Book of Poetry*. New York: Random House, 1983.

Sawyer, Ruth. *The Way of the Storyteller*. New York: Viking, 1942.

Trelease, Jim. *The Read-Aloud Handbook*. 4th ed. New York: Penguin, 1995.

REFERENCES

Anderson, Richard C., Elfrieda H. Hiebert, Judith A. Scott, and Ian A. G. Wilkinson. *Becoming a Nation of Readers: The Report of the Commission on Reading*. Washington, DC: National Institute of Education, 1984.

Banks, Lynne Reid, *The Indian in the Cupboard*. Illustrated by Brock Cole. New York: Doubleday, 1981.

Bauer, Carolyn J., and LaVonne H. Sanborn. "The Best of Both Worlds: Children's Books Acclaimed by Adults and Young Readers." *Top of the World* 38 (Fall 1981): 53–56.

Bissett, D. "The Amount and Effect of Recreational Reading in Selected Fifth Grade Classes." Diss. Syracuse University, 1969.

Blood, Peter, and Annie Paterson. *Rise Up Singing*. Bethlehem, PA: Sing Out! Publications, 1992.

Booth, David. "Imaginary Gardens with Real Toads: Reading and Drama in Education." *Theory into Practice* 24 (1985): 193–98.

Cole, J. Y., and C. S. Gold, eds. *Reading in America 1978: Selected Findings of the Book Industry Study Group's 1978 Study of American Book-Reading and Book-Buying Habits and Discussion of Those Findings at the Library of Congress on October 25 and 26, 1978*. Washington, DC: Library of Congress, 1979.

de Brunvard, Jan. *The Vanishing Hitchhiker and Other Urban Legends*. New York: Norton, 1981.

Edmiston, Brian. "Going Up the Beanstalk: Discovering Giant Possibilities for Responding to Literature through Drama." *Journeying: Children Responding to Literature*. Eds. Kathleen E. Holland, Rachael A. Hungerford, and Shirley B. Ernst. Portsmouth, NH: Heinemann, 1993. 250–66.

Fielding, Linda G., Paul T. Wilson, and Richard C. Anderson. "A New Focus on Free Reading: The Role of Trade Books in Reading Instruction." *Contexts of Literacy*. Eds. Taffy Raphael and Ralph Reynolds. New York: Longman, 1986.

Fractor, Jann Sorrell, Marjorie Ciruti Woodruff, Miriam G. Martinez, and William H. Teale. "Let's Not Miss Opportunities to Promote Voluntary Reading: Classroom Libraries in the Elementary School." *The Reading Teacher* 46 (1993): 476–84.

Gonzalez, Veronica, Linda D. Fry, Sylvia Lopez, Julie V. Jordan, Cynthia L. Sloan, and Diane McAdams. "Our Journey toward Better Conversations about Books." *Book Talk and Beyond: Children and Teachers Respond to Literature*. Eds. Nancy L. Roser and Miriam G. Martinez. Newark, DE: International Reading Association, 1995. 168–78.

Hickman, Janet. "A New Perspective on Response to Literature: Research in an Elementary School Setting." *Research in the Teaching of English* 15 (1981): 343–54.

Hoffman, James V., Nancy L. Roser, and Jennifer Battle. "Reading Aloud in Classrooms: From the Modal toward a 'Model.'" *The Reading Teacher* 46 (1993): 496–503.

Kennelly, Brendan. *The Penguin Book of Irish Verse*. 2nd ed. New York: Penguin, 1981.

Krull, Kathleen. *Gonna Sing My Head Off!* Illustrated by Allen Garns. New York: Knopf, 1992.

MacDonald, Margaret Read. *The Story-Teller's Start-Up Book*. Little Rock, AR: August House, 1993.

Milne, A. A. "Happiness." *When We Were Very Young*. New York: Dutton, 1924.

Morrow, Lesley Mandel. "Relationships between Literature Program, Library Corner Designs, and Children's Use of Literature." *Journal of Educational Research* 75 (1982): 339–44.

Munro, Harold. "Overheard in a Saltmarsh." *Collected Poems*. London: Duckworth, 1953.

Paley, Vivian. *Wally's Stories: Conversations in the Kindergarten*. Cambridge, MA: Harvard University Press, 1981.

Siks, Geraldine Brain. *Creative Dramatics: An Art for Children*. New York: Harper & Row, 1958.

Wolf, Alan. *It's Show Time! Poetry from Page to Stage*. Asheville, NC: Poetry Alive!, 1993.

13 Encouraging Response to Literature
Literary Discussion

Our two families, the Logans and the Simmses, had never much gotten along. What with the Simmses living less than a mile or so from us on that forty-acre spot of land they tenant-farmed, and we sitting on our own two hundred acres, there was always likely to be trouble, and there was. Now this was back before my papa went and bought that second two hundred acres; but still that two hundred acres we had then, that was a lot, and the Simmses didn't like it—that we had when they didn't. They didn't like it one bit. That was part of the trouble between us. Other part of the trouble was that we were colored and they were white. Fact of the matter was we ain't never had much use for the Simmses, and they ain't never had much use for us either; but seeing that we couldn't hardly afford trouble with them, Papa said best thing to do was try and stay out of their way much as we could. He said it was better to mind our business, let them mind theirs, and just walk away if they tried to start something.

I heeded his words. My brother Hammer didn't.

from The Well *(1995)*
by Mildred D. Taylor

WHAT IS A BOOK CLUB?

The Well (1995) is written in a forthright matter and deals with substantive issues that are not easy for readers of any age to forget once they've read about them. Fortunately, more and more classroom teachers are recognizing the importance of creating opportunities for children to come together to grapple with the issues they encounter in books like **The Well.** Book clubs are one vehicle for organizing literature discussion in classrooms. In fact, educational circles are abuzz with talk about book clubs and creating "interpretive communities" in elementary classrooms. Such talk may be startling to some. It might seem more likely that adults would belong to book clubs and literature majors and scholars would belong to "interpretive communities"—but such is not the case. Many children belong to book clubs or have been part of interpretive communities, for an interpretive community is simply a group of people (perhaps only two) who get together to talk about a book.

Strategies for engaging students in book clubs are highlighted in this chapter. Some of the examples focus on **Shiloh** (1991) and **Maniac Magee** (1990), books you may want to read if you have not yet done so.

An Interpretive Community

Reading can be an intensely satisfying solitary experience, but it can be even more meaningful when shared with others. Think of times when you've done just that. Perhaps you finished a wonderful book and discovered that a friend had also read it. No doubt you were off and talking. Or perhaps you were in the midst of a story and simply had to stop reading to tell a friend about a hilarious scene. You may even have explored books with peers in more formal settings, such as a book club at your local library. Whatever the context—informal or formal—the odds are you have been a part of an interpretive community.

Compare notes with your peers about some of the book discussions you've enjoyed. There are likely to be some common features. First, these discussions

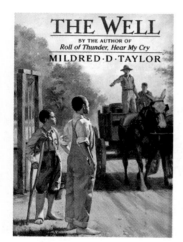

Illustration 13.1
In *The Well,* racial conflict erupts in the midst of a drought in Mississippi in the late nineteenth century. (*The Well: David's Story* by Mildred D. Taylor. Jacket painting copyright © 1995 by Max Ginsburg. Used by permission of Dial Books for Young Readers, a division of Penguin Books USA Inc.)

were probably conversational in nature: People have compared book discussions to the kind of stimulating conversations they engage in at a memorable dinner party. You may remember many of these conversations as being lively: Perhaps those involved in the conversations had diverse perspectives on the book that led to some informal debate. These conversations probably moved in different directions: Sometimes, you may have been caught up in the story world—talking about what characters did, why they did those things, and the likely outcomes of their actions. At other times, your talk may have moved out of the realm of the story world to discuss the ways the story related to your own life or to explore the author's craft. Perhaps there have been times when you came away from a book discussion with deeper insights gained from others. In short, the members of an interpretive community share impressions, wonder together, challenge ideas, and explore together.

Children in elementary classrooms also form interpretive communities. Sometimes, the entire class talks about a book; at other times, smaller groups of students come together for literature discussion. These interpretive communities are known by various names: book clubs (Raphael, Goatley, McMahon, and Woodman, 1995), literature circles (Harste, Short, and Burke, 1988), literature study groups (Eeds and Wells, 1989), or conversational discussion groups (Wiencek and O'Flahavan, 1994). We have chosen to use the term "book club" to describe the interpretive communities at work in classrooms.

An Opportunity for "Grand Conversations"

To get a feel for the type of book club talk that can occur in classrooms, we'll look in on a literature conversation in Ms. Gonzalez's second-grade classroom. Not long before this conversation, Ms. Gonzalez had finished reading aloud Elizabeth Winthrop's *Castle in the Attic* (1985). This book is a fantasy in which a young boy named William travels back in time to medieval England where he confronts a wicked wizard, Alastor, who has taken over the good Sir Simon's kingdom and turned much of the populace to stone. Currently, Ms. Gonzalez is reading Phyllis Naylor's *Shiloh* (1991), the Newbery Medal–winning story of Marty, who secretly harbors the dog Shiloh to protect it from abuse by its owner. Ms. Gonzalez has just finished reading the first two chapters, and the class has stopped to talk:

MS. GONZALEZ: Reread what you wrote in your journals about Chapters 1 and 2. What were your thoughts and wonderings? Matthew?

MATTHEW: William reminds me of Marty.

ANNA: Marty IS sorta like William because he's so nice to the dog and stuff.

MS. GONZALEZ: Paul, did you want to bring out somebody else you're reminded of?

PAUL: William and Marty both found something wonderful. Marty found a dog, and in *Castle in the Attic,* William found the half of the token.

BEN: He didn't find it.

PAUL: I mean when the soldier [knight] dropped it. He was looking at William, and he found it.

MS. GONZALEZ:	Albert?
ALBERT:	Judd is like Alastor.
MS GONZALEZ:	How is he like him?
ALBERT:	Because Judd was mean to everybody just like him. And Alastor didn't like anybody either. He froze them. And Judd hurts them.
ADAM:	Judd's like Alastor. The dogs are [like] the people, and get turned to stone. The dogs are sort of like that.
MS. GONZALEZ:	Why do you see them like that?
ADAM:	Cause he [Judd] . . . instead of turning them into stone, he is mean to them.
PAUL:	I disagree. I think Marty is like Tolliver.
MS. GONZALEZ:	You're saying he's more like Tolliver, the young boy in *Castle in the Attic*.
LINDSAY:	I think William and Marty are more alike because they each had to make a choice in the story.
ALEX:	. . . Yeah, because Shiloh has to leave and Mrs. Williams . . .
MS. GONZALEZ:	Excuse me, Alex, I think you mean Mrs. Phillips. Not Mrs. Williams.
ALEX:	Right, Mrs. Phillips. He don't want Mrs. Phillips to go, and Marty don't want Shiloh to go. So, it's kind of like the other.
AMANDA:	When William didn't want Mrs. Phillips to go and Marty didn't want Shiloh to go, because there's two different reasons. . . .

These children were engaged in the work of an interpretive community. Their lively exchange was conversational in nature; it was the children, not Ms. Gonzalez, who initiated the topics of discussion. The children did some impressive thinking as they compared the two books, arrived at and defended their own insights, and worked together to build meaning. This discussion had all the marks of what Maryann Eeds and Deborah Wells (1989) have called a "grand conversation."

Eeds and Wells have contrasted grand conversations with what has been described as "gentle inquisitions," those question-and-answer sessions in which the teacher quizzes students with comprehension questions. Researchers such as Courtney Cazden (1988) and Hugh Mehan (1979) have described the pattern of interaction in these "gentle inquisitions." They found that the teacher initiates a topic by asking a question, the student responds to the question, and the teacher evaluates the student's response—a pattern of interaction called I-R-E (Initiate-Respond-Evaluate). As Taffy E. Raphael, Virginia J. Goatley, Susan I. McMahon, and Deborah A. Woodman (1995) have observed, an over-reliance on the I-R-E pattern means "students have little opportunity to raise topics of interest, pursue lines of thinking, or collaborate in critical problem solving" (p. 67).

ORGANIZING BOOK CLUBS

How can teachers ensure that their students have the opportunity to participate in interpretive communities? We believe there are five key factors that affect the workings of book clubs: the books chosen, group size, length and frequency of sessions, who leads discussions, and whether responses are free or guided. There is no single "right" decision with regard to each factor that will ensure that children will engage in lively and thoughtful book conversations. However, it is important to understand how each factor affects the workings of a book club and to consider thoughtfully the possible decisions you can make. We will discuss the factors in this and the next sections.

Selecting Books for Use in Book Clubs

Selecting books is one of the most important book club decisions you'll make. Not every book has the same potential to engage children in rich discussion. In their investigation of literature discussion groups, Eeds and Wells (1989) involved groups of fifth and sixth graders in reading and discussing one of four books—*Harriet the Spy* (1964), *After the Goat Man* (1974), *The Darkangel* (1982), and *Tuck Everlasting* (1975)—each of which is recognized as a quality piece of literature. Although the group leaders in all four groups proved to be equally skillful in facilitating discussions, Eeds and Wells found that the students in the group reading *Tuck Everlasting* shared the most insightful responses. They concluded that differences in the books accounted for differences in the quality of talk. Of the four books, only *Tuck Everlasting* had the power to launch the children into discussions of issues touching the very essence of the human experience.

Thematic Discussions. Books like *Tuck Everlasting* that focus on important issues tend to evoke talk at a thematic level. Other books likely to engender thematic-level talk include Mildred Taylor's powerful books about the Logan family, which explore racism as well as the sustaining power of family love and unity, and Lois Lowry's *The Giver* (1993), an exploration of a society designed to control the pain and sorrow of life as well its joys.

Discussions about Story Line. Other types of books are likely to move children's talk in other directions (Martinez and Roser, 1995). When children read books with strong story lines, they tend to "step into the story" (Langer, 1992), and their talk reflects their engagement with its characters, conflicts, and events. In particular, books engender lively talk when they center around problems with which the students can easily identify and whose solutions are not readily apparent. Examples of such books are Phyllis Naylor's *Shiloh* (1991) and its sequel, *Shiloh Season* (1996), Cynthia Voigt's *Homecoming* (1981), E. L. Konigsburg's *From the Mixed-Up Files of Mrs. Basil E. Frankweiler* (1967), and Nancy Farmer's *The Ear, the Eye and the Arm* (1994).

Discussions of Craft. Children are most likely to talk about a book as the creation of a particular author or artist when they read distinctively crafted books such as Chris Van Allsburg's *Jumanji* (1981), or David Macaulay's *Black and White* (1990), in which four plot lines are intertwined, or Jon Scieszka's *The Stinky Cheese Man and Other Fairly Stupid Tales* (1992), with its many violations of standard format.

Illustration 13.2
Readers of Chris Van Allsburg's books expect to encounter the fantastic and bizarre. *Jumanji* (winner of the 1982 Caldecott Medal) is no exception. (*Jumanji* by Chris Van Allsburg. Copyright © 1981 by Chris Van Allsburg. Used by permission of Houghton Mifflin Company. All rights reserved.)

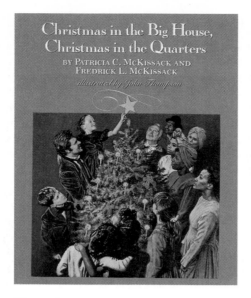

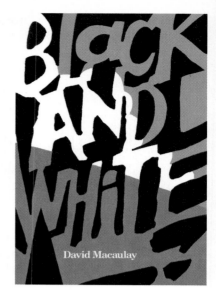

Illustration 13.3
The celebration in the "big house" is juxtaposed against that in the slave quarters during the last Christmas season before the outbreak of the Civil War. (*Christmas in the Big House, Christmas in the Quarters* by Patricia C. McKissack and Fredrick L. McKissack. Jacket art copyright © 1994 by John Thompson. Used by permission of Scholastic Inc.)

Illustration 13.4
Readers will wonder if they are reading a single story or four different stories in this exquisitely designed Caldecott Medal winner. (*Black and White* by David Macaulay. Copyright © 1990 by David Macaulay. Used by permission of Houghton Mifflin Company. All rights reserved.)

Likewise, children are likely to talk about craft when they read books with distinctive patterns of organization, such as Audrey Wood's predictable book *The Napping House* (1984), Paul Fleischman's *Joyful Noise* (1988), which is a collection of poems for two voices, or Patricia and Fredrick McKissack's *Christmas in the Big House, Christmas in the Quarters* (1994), with its strong comparison/contrast structure. Exquisitely illustrated books, such as Nancy Willard's *Pish, Posh, Said Hieronymus Bosch* (1991), and books with tantalizing language, such as Libba Moore Gray's *Small Green Snake* (1994), also encourage children to examine books as crafted objects.

So, to encourage diverse talk during book club conversations, it makes sense to use a variety of types of literature—literature with strong story lines, literature that develops significant themes, and distinctly crafted literature.

Discussions across the Curriculum. You will want to consider other factors as well in selecting literature to use in book clubs. Perhaps the class is studying a topic in science or social studies that lends itself to further exploration in a book club. A teacher whose students are studying the weather might select Patricia MacLachlan's *Skylark* (1994) for book club use. This sequel to the Newbery Medal winner *Sarah, Plain and Tall* (1985) is set in the prairie in the nineteenth century and explores the impact on those living there of a devastating drought. Virginia Hamilton's *Drylongso* (1992) also shows the ravaging effects of drought, and the drama of Mildred Taylor's *The Well* (1995) unfolds in the context of a drought. Informational books about drought could also be used in

Illustration 13.5
Strikingly bizarre creatures inhabit the pages of this distinctively crafted fantasy. (*Pish, Posh, Said Hieronymus Bosch* by Nancy Willard. Illustration copyright © 1991 by Leo, Diane, and Lee Dillon. Used by permission of Harcourt Brace & Company.)

the book club. In fact, many of the books you choose to support cross-curricular studies are likely to be informational books, and discussions about informational books can be as lively as discussions of fiction.

Discussions of Genre. Genre is yet another consideration when choosing books. Joyce Wiencek and John O'Flahavan (1994) note the importance of bringing in books from various genres so that students develop a repertoire of appropriate interpretive strategies. Although variety is important, particular genres do have the potential to offer students rich issues and ideas to explore. Many works of realistic and historical fiction, high fantasy, and poetry are especially likely to evoke students' best insights because of the significant themes they explore.

Student Participation in Book Selection. This discussion has implied that the teacher is the one who selects the books for use in book clubs. However, Louise Rosenblatt (1938) reminds us that the ultimate aim is to prepare students to select their own books wisely. Therefore, teachers must ensure that students have some voice in book selection. This can be accomplished by inviting students to suggest themes, authors, or particular titles they would like to read for book club. Or, if a single title is to be used, the teacher can nominate a number of titles as possible candidates and let the students make the final selection. Yet another alternative is to have several small groups, each focusing on a different book, and give students the opportunity to decide which group to join after listening to introductions of the several books and browsing through them.

Forming the Discussion Groups

How many students should belong to a book club? How should students be selected for membership in a book club? Experienced teachers have found book clubs of widely varying sizes to be successful. Some teachers advocate whole-class book clubs (Gonzalez, Fry, Lopez, Jordan, Sloan, and McAdams, 1995); others believe that small groups are ideal (Short and Kauffman, 1995). There is no "best" size. It may, in fact, be a good idea to vary the sizes of book clubs, depending on the children's previous experience. If you find at the beginning of

ASK THE AUTHOR . . . *Eve Bunting*

How do you decide what is an appropriate issue to address in a book for children?

Eve Bunting

I believe that children are smarter, more intuitive, and more sensitive and have more common sense than we give them credit for. They are an important part, perhaps the most important part, of the world we share.

I have never had difficulty in my writing, or my thinking, in putting myself into the mind of the child, interested in everything around me—the animals, the trees, the funny things that happen, the sad things, the things that are inexplicable.

As a child in Northern Ireland I'd ask, "Won't someone tell me why Catholics are not as good as Protestants?" No use assuring me that they were. I could see who had the poorest housing. I could see who wasn't allowed to go to my school. Or play tennis in the tennis club with us. No use telling me to wait, I'd understand some day. I wanted to know now. I wanted to talk about it. If we had talked, if we, as children, had been helped to see clearly, would Northern Ireland be the way it is now, sixty years later?

"Why do we have homeless people?" the child asks. The child wants an answer. Do we think our children are blind and don't notice the misery in our parks or on our street corners?

The questions are there.

"Why does grandma have to go into a nursing home?" Does her grandchild not hear her weep?

"Why do we have riots that scare people? Why are they burning those stores? I see it on TV after cartoons. I see it on TV news. I know you turn it off when I come in but I saw it. I want to know why those people are doing those things."

A boy wrote to me from Baltimore: "We have had no riots yet. But maybe we will someday." What that child knows intuitively is that while he may be here and they may be there, they could be here and he could be one of them.

Are these kinds of subjects appropriate for small children? Is it appropriate *not* to address them? I don't have answers. But sometimes I can help my readers see both sides.

One child had read my book *Fly Away Home*. She wrote: "We have a homeless girl in our class. She is dirty. I will not laugh at her anymore."

One thing I know. Prejudice, injustice, and ignorance fester in the dark of silence.

Eve Bunting is married and has three grown children and four grandchildren, all living in California. She was born and educated in Northern Ireland and has written more than 160 books for children and young adults.

the school year that most of your students have previously participated in literature discussions, they may be ready to launch immediately into small-group book clubs. If, however, you work with very young children or your students initially appear to be more at ease with traditional "gentle inquisitions," you may want to begin with whole-class literature discussion following read-aloud sessions. Then, once they feel comfortable with this format, students can begin working in small groups of five to seven students.

What factors should be taken into account by teachers before bringing children together in these smaller book clubs? First, consider whether all students in the class will be reading the same book or whether small groups will be reading different books. If each group will be reading a different book, it makes sense to let students listen to book introductions and then choose the group that they want to join. Also, consider group dynamics. Aim for a group that is balanced in terms of the students' leadership, communication, and social skills (Raphael, McMahon, Goatley, Bentley, Boyd, Pardo, and Woodman, 1992).

Length and Frequency of Book Club Sessions

The length of book club conversations will vary. Early in the school year, sessions may be relatively short—ten or fifteen minutes (in addition to the time you may need to read the story to the students). Once children gain book club experience, they are likely to talk a lot more about engaging books—perhaps thirty or forty minutes, though twenty minutes is a typical length for a book club conversation.

The frequency with which book clubs meet will probably depend on other decisions you make. Book clubs may be part of your read-aloud program—especially if your students do not yet have the reading skills needed to independently read books that have enough "meat" to engender good discussions. If this is the case, then you'll certainly be reading aloud to your students each day, and daily literature discussion will naturally go hand-in-hand with the read-aloud. Even if your students are able to read "meaty" books independently, there may still be times when you want to make book club part of the daily read-aloud, especially at the beginning of the year before students are skilled in participating in book conversations. Even after your students have acquired experience as members of an interpretive community, you may sometimes want to make discussion an integral part of the read-aloud experience, especially when reading aloud a challenging chapter book. Some of the most interesting book club conversations occur when students are in the midst of a chapter book rather than at the end, and little wonder, for then students are caught up in a web of events and very naturally have questions and predictions about how that web of events is likely to be sorted out (Martinez and Roser, 1994).

When your students do their own reading in preparation for book club, you'll need to schedule reading time for them. Some teachers give students opportunities to touch base with one another while they are reading the book, even though more focused discussion is scheduled to take place when everyone has finished the book. By meeting briefly every three days or so, students can help one another clarify any questions they may have about the book they are reading.

Some teachers set up a pacing guide for students' reading and then gather students together for book club only after all of them have finished the book. When a schedule guides the book club, it's best to have students jot down their thoughts about the book each day, either during or immediately after completing a daily reading assignment. They can bring these notes to book club.

Once students have finished reading a book, they'll be ready to get together for more focused talk. You may want to devote more than a single day to discussion. The first day may be devoted to sharing responses and even reading journal entries. At the end of the first session, you might ask students to generate a list of ideas for more intensive literature study on subsequent days. As a group, they can choose a topic (or two) from the list and prepare to talk about that topic at their next meeting. Preparation might include rereading relevant portions of the book to find support for their opinions. For example, after reading and sharing impressions about *Maniac Magee* (1990), Mr. Lee's class decided to spend their second book club meeting exploring all of the diverse images of home found throughout the book. Such focused explorations of a book are especially likely to lead to in-depth discussion of theme and craft.

THE ROLES OF THE TEACHER IN LITERARY DISCUSSIONS

What roles do teachers play during book club? Again, there is no simple answer to this question. The one thing that educators agree on is that the teacher should not assume the role of sole leader, whose job is to ask the questions. Beyond that, recommendations vary widely. Opinion is even divided on the question of whether the teacher should be present during book club discussions. Some educators argue that if teachers want students to learn to participate in book club conversations in much the same way more mature readers do, they must give students the opportunity to do so by bowing out of the picture (Raphael, McMahon, Goatley, Bentley, Boyd, Pardo, and Woodman, 1992). Others argue that students have the best opportunity to learn these skills by talking about books with experienced adult readers who model the appropriate conversational roles (McGee, 1992). Adherents of both positions make valid points; so reducing the question to an either/or proposition (the teacher either is or is not present) may be too simplistic. Perhaps the best question to ask is this: Under what circumstances should the teacher participate in book club conversations? We will address this question after taking a closer look at the roles that the teacher may choose to play during book club.

As participants in book clubs, teachers may, at various times, want to assume any of four roles: (1) modeling response-based discussion, (2) helping children learn new discussion roles, (3) moving discussion forward, and (4) supporting literary learning as opportunities arise.

Modeling Response-Based Discussion

On arriving in your classroom, many of your students are likely to feel comfortable only when the teacher is in charge of book talk. The typical question-and-answer session that results when students have these expectations is similar to what occurred after Mrs. McDougal read *Arthur's Prize Reader* (Hoban, 1978) to her second graders:

MRS. McDOUGAL:	Okay, Michelle, can you give us our title?
MICHELLE:	*Arthur's Prize Reader.*
MRS. McDOUGAL:	Oh, great. Thank you. Okay, Josh, characters. Give me the major characters first.
JOSH:	Arthur.
MRS. McDOUGAL:	Arthur and who else?
JOSH:	Violet.

MRS. McDOUGAL: Okay, we should consider them major characters. Were there any other characters in the book that we would consider minor, Josh?

This is not literature discussion, and students who have only participated in question-and-answer sessions like this one are reticent when first invited to share their personal thoughts about stories. Yet genuine talk about stories occurs as participants share and reflect on their own responses to them. The best way for students to learn how to do this is by seeing others share their thinking about stories. So it's important for teachers to model response-based meaning making—that is, share their own responses to stories. Students who see their teachers doing this are much more likely to realize that their responses will be valued. As students gain confidence, book club talk will arise entirely from their responses.

Teachers can also model diverse kinds of thinking about books. Ms. Gonzalez found that her students were not asking the questions they had about books. So she decided to model this type of thinking when she and her students were discussing Diane Stanley's *Captain Whiz-Bang* (1987), a story in which a little girl named Annie names her new kitten Captain Whiz-Bang. At first, Annie and Captain Whiz-Bang are inseparable, but, as Annie grows up, her interests turn to other things. Finally, she leaves home and marries, leaving Captain Whiz-Bang behind with her parents. But she doesn't forget Captain Whiz-Bang and one day returns with her own child so that the little girl can meet the aged cat.

MS. GONZALEZ: I wonder what kind of things Captain Whiz-Bang will do with Annie's little girl. He can't run and jump and play as fast as he did before. So I wonder what kinds of things they did when they played together. Since he wasn't so active.

Ms. Gonzalez found that it wasn't long before her students were sharing their own wonderings about the stories they read.

Helping Children Learn New Roles during Book Clubs

Book clubs are different from traditional book discussions. Unlike traditional book discussions, in which students typically answer questions, no one participant is "in charge" in a book club. Rather, all participants can initiate topics for discussion, and discussion proceeds as a conversation. How do you engage students in such conversations about books if they come to your classroom expecting to answer questions? As Kathy G. Short and Gloria Kauffman (1995) point out, students have plenty of experience participating in conversations in other situations, and they can draw on these experiences in book clubs. Teachers can introduce students to book conversations by inviting them to think about all the times they've talked with their friends about movies or TV shows.

Since no one person is "in charge" during book club, you may want to establish simple guidelines for group behavior. Lea M. McGee (1995, p. 13) suggests the following:

- Sit in a circle so that everyone can see each other.
- Only one person talks at a time.
- Listen to each other.
- Stay on the topic.

One of the most important (and difficult) expectations to establish is that book club is a time for conversation—thus, it is okay for students to talk directly with one another. Many of the teachers with whom we work find it helpful to remind students of this explicitly. By seating students in a circle so that they can talk to each other directly and occasionally reminding them that it makes sense to address their thoughts to peers, you will encourage them to engage in real conversations about literature.

Moving Conversation Forward

Teachers make an important contribution to book clubs when they move a flagging conversation forward. Earlier in the chapter, we pointed out that teachers do not "direct" book clubs by asking question after question, but that does not mean a teacher should never ask a question. An occasional, well-placed question can get a conversation moving forward. Lea McGee (1995) suggests that when preparing to meet with a book club, a teacher develop one or two interpretive questions that focus on "the significance of the story as a whole" (p. 111). Wendy Saul (1989) calls such questions "literary questions" and observes that they are connected to the story but never have a single correct answer. A teacher may not need to ask these planned questions, depending on the direction in which the students move the conversation. However, if the students do not discuss an aspect of a story the teacher feels is important, then the teacher may choose to pose a literary question before the book club concludes. The preparation of literary questions is discussed later in this chapter.

Louise Rosenblatt reminds us that not all responses are equally valid; rather, their value is determined by the extent to which readers make use of the text to defend and support their ideas (Farrell and Squire, 1990). This point suggests yet another way in which teachers can help to move conversations forward—by encouraging students to reflect on and return to the text to find support for their ideas, as Ms. Gonzalez did when her students discussed *Castle in the Attic* (1985):

CHRIS: I think that [the reason] Calendar didn't want to get the spells that turned the lead people into humans again is because all the guards would probably tell Alastor, and she'd be [turned] into lead.

MS. GONZALEZ: What makes you think that?

CHRIS: Remember the guards wanted to get away. It was against their will to be a guard. They didn't know that anyone was coming and they were obeying Alastor. And if Alastor found out that they didn't tell him, then they would all be turned into lead.

Supporting Literary Learning

Supporting students' literary learning is perhaps the single most important contribution a teacher can make during book club discussions. Literary works are distinctive because of the ways in which writers structure and craft them, and like Ralph L. Peterson and Maryann Eeds (1990), we believe that awareness of literary elements and the writer's craft can add a new dimension to students' experiences of stories. But it's important to proceed carefully in helping students learn about literary elements. Teaching about literature in a decontextualized manner—that is, without reference to a particular story—is the surest way to squelch students' love of literature. Lecturing about literature and asking students to memorize the definitions of literary terms have no place in the classroom. Yet, we want children to understand how stories work, and the most appropriate way of doing this is by taking advantage of opportunities to foster awareness that arise naturally as students share their observations during book clubs. For example, the student who noticed "all the changes that keep happening in 'Cinderella'" had become aware of the transformation motif that is so prevalent in folklore. This student, who had a concept but not the literary language to name that concept, gave her teacher the perfect opening to introduce the term "transformation." The student's observation provided the teacher with an opportunity to "shoot a literary arrow" (Peterson and Eeds, 1990). Such an opportunity occurs as students struggle to talk about the author's crafting and when their talk indicates that they have grasped a concept even though they do not have the literary language to talk about the element, device, or structure. Observing in elementary classrooms for extended periods of time, both Hickman (1979, 1981) and Kiefer (1983) found that children's talk about stories became more sophisticated when their teachers used the specialized language of art and literature with them during conversations about books.

We began this section with a question: What roles do teachers play during book club? The four roles we have described point toward the answer to that question. At the beginning of the school year, many if not all of your students are likely to have no experience with book clubs and to expect you to pose questions for them to answer. If this happens, you should initially join in as a book club participant. Then, as book club discussions become more conversational, you can let students work independently. However, we do not recommend pulling

ISSUE TO CONSIDER

Is it necessary to attend to comprehension before moving on to critical discussions of a story?

Story comprehension is not the same as literary response, but the two are not unrelated. Readers respond to stories they understand differently than they do to those they find confusing. Therefore, it's important to attend to children's story comprehension. However, what is the best way to ensure that children comprehend literature?

Some believe that it is best to ask children comprehension questions before moving on to more critical discussions. The use of comprehension questions allows teachers to move students systematically through a story, talking about information important to the story's development.

Others argue that teachers are more likely to ensure students' comprehension by launching them right into grand conversations. The rationale for this position is that when students participate in interpretive communities on an equal footing with their peers (and sometimes their teacher as well), more likely than not they will choose to ask their peers for help in working through parts of a story they found to be confusing (Almasi, 1995).

What do you think?

entirely out of book club sessions, for opportunities to help students learn about literary crafting can occur at any time.

RESPONSE STRATEGIES

Teachers often ask whether book club discussions should center around the children's free responses or if they should use instructional strategies to guide the conversation. Once again, this is not an either/or issue. It makes more sense to think about *when* each approach is appropriate.

Invite Students to Share and Reflect

It is critical to begin discussion of a book or poem by inviting students to share and reflect on their own responses to the work. Rosenblatt (1938) has pointed out the problems that may emerge when teachers rely too heavily on strategies for guiding students' discussion. Once, she had become totally drawn into a poem she was reading, only to find herself rudely torn away from that web of emotion and reflection when she turned the page to find questions posed by the textbook editor asking her to identify the formal characteristics of the poem. The magic of what Rosenblatt has called the "lived through experience" was destroyed by those questions. By beginning discussions with students' ideas, teachers can avoid trivializing literary works by overinspection (Cianciolo, 1982; Babbitt, 1990).

Although it is ideal for discussions to emerge from students' own responses to stories, this does not mean that the teacher should never guide their talk. There are many times when it may be necessary to move talk in a particular direction in order to reach an instructional goal. For example, assume that one of your goals in a unit entitled "Giants in Stories" is to help students explore the ways giants are typically characterized in literature. If students' responses do not focus on characterization, it may be necessary to use an appropriate instructional strategy to ensure that talk eventually moves in that direction.

In this section, we present instructional strategies designed to foster students' free responses as well as strategies for guiding responses.

Have Children Use Journals for Recording Thoughts

By responding to a story in their literature journals, children have the opportunity to consider it more thoughtfully.

How do teachers ensure that book club discussion initially emerges from students' own responses to literature? One especially effective strategy is to have children keep journals and bring them to book club to share. The use of journals in book club announces to participants the legitimacy and value of each individual's independent reaction to stories. Margaret Anzul (1993) suggests that students read with pen in hand so that they can record their immediate thoughts and feelings in their journal entries.

Teachers can use a number of different kinds of journals to support book club discussions, including free response journals, prompted response journals, literary journals, and dialogue journals.

Free Response Journals. In free response journals, students are encouraged to write about anything they choose in response to a story. The purpose of writing is to record thoughts, feelings, questions, and interpretations.

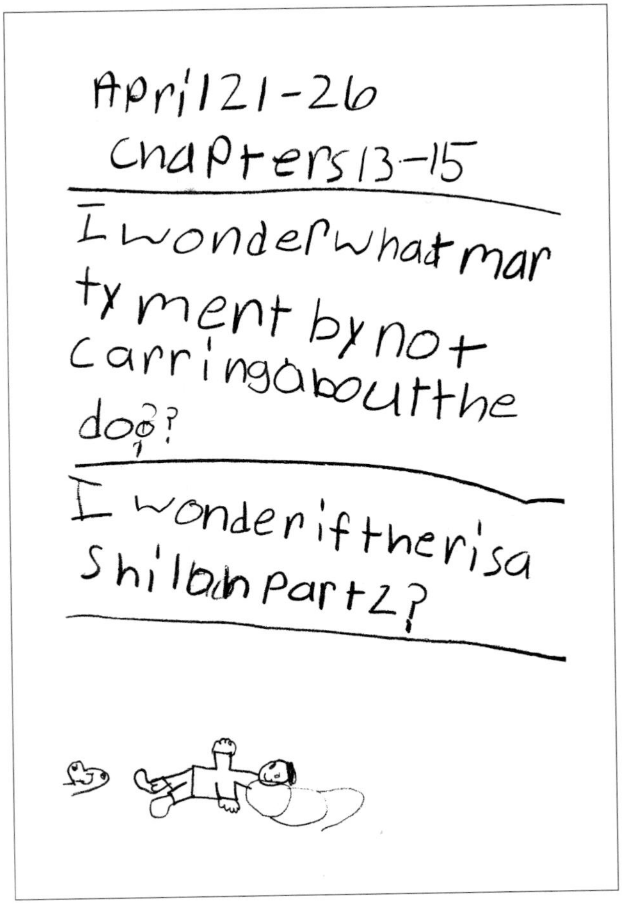

I wonder what marty ment by not carring about the dog?

I wonder if there is a Shiloh Part 2?

April 21-26
Chapters 13-15

Figure 13.1
The ideas students record in their journals can serve as starters for literature discussion.

If students are reading a book independently in preparation for book club, they can be asked to write in their journals periodically, perhaps after completing each chapter. Then, in book club, they may share entries to initiate discussion.

Miriam Martinez, Nancy Roser, James Hoffman, and Jennifer Battle (1992) have found that free response journals can also be used effectively when the teacher reads a story aloud. Students simply spend a few minutes writing in response to the just completed chapter or story. Even kindergartners can respond with drawings. These few minutes of writing time can give students an opportunity to record their thoughts and feelings before they are lost in the midst of discussion. Free response journal entries can serve as wonderful conversation starters. Writing in her journal about the final chapters of *Shiloh* (1991), Ana, a second grader, recorded her "wonderings" (see Figure 13.1). When shared aloud, questions like Ana's offer rich material for conversation.

When students first start to write in journals, especially free response journals, they may not be very comfortable recording their thoughts and feelings; instead, they may look for an easy way out by writing stock responses: "I like this book" or "My favorite part was when Maniac McGee runs across the football field." Teachers can keep their own journals so that when students fall into "writing ruts," they share their entries, thereby modeling new ways of thinking about literature.

Prompted Response Journals. Some teachers use prompted response journals. That is, they give their students a prompt to respond to, or they may provide a number of prompts and encourage the students to choose one or more to use. The prompts may be generic ones that appply to almost any story:

- Select your favorite character and tell what she or he is like.
- Choose a character you think is changing and growing in this story. Write about the ways in which the character is changing and the reasons for these changes.
- How is the setting important in this story?
- Write about some of the tensest moments in the story. How does the author make those moments tense?

Prompts can also be specific to a story:

- In Chapter 19 of *The Giver*, Jonas learns what "release" means. How do you think this knowledge will affect him?
- Do you think that Marty did the right thing in Chapter 14 of *Shiloh* when he made his bargain with Judd?

Students who initially lack confidence in writing personal responses to a story may benefit from prompts. Specific prompts are also a means of encouraging students to respond to literature in more diverse ways.

Literary Journals. Pamela J. Farris (1989) has described the use of literary journals. In this type of journal, students assume the persona of one of the characters in the story and write journal entries as that character. For example, students reading *Shiloh* (1991) might become Marty and write in their journals about all their experiences with and feelings for the dog they found. Writing in a literary journal requires the reader to try and step into the shoes of the character and see story events and conflicts as that character might. Thus, literary journals are more appropriate for older students than for younger ones, who still view the world from a very egocentric perspective.

Dialogue Journals. In a dialogue journal, a student and the teacher maintain a written dialogue about a story. (Students can also be assigned partners and write to one another.) The other types of journals we have discussed can readily be shared in book club sessions to spark group discussion. Dialogue journals are more often used to extend discussion beyond book club. Marcia Nash (1995) has found that dialogue journals allow teachers to gain insights into how their students respond to literature, to model their own responses to literature, and to foster growth in students' responses. For example, through written dialogue with a fifth grader, one teacher was able to encourage her student to reflect on what constitutes strong plot development (Nash, 1995, p. 222):

STUDENT: *Dolphin Adventure* was a Good Book But it was missing some Good "stuff" I look for. I probably wouldent chose this Bok on my own.

TEACHER: Can you tell me what good stuff you look for in a book that *Dolphin Adventure* didn't have?

STUDENT: I can't relly desribe the "stuff" I look for. [and later] I also read *Mandie and the Cherokee Ledgend*. I thought that was good but it neaded more of that "stuff" I like.

TEACHER: If we could only figure out what that "stuff" is that makes a book good, we would probably become famous. People have been trying to come up with a definition of what makes good literature for centuries. Still, I think it is interesting to think and talk about. For instance, what was it about Joan Carris's style that you liked enough to make you want to read another book by her after you read *Just a Little Ham*?

STUDENT: What a Great Book! [*Aunt Morbelia and the Screaming Skull*, 1990, the other Joan Carris book referred to in the previous entry] "stuff" poped out every where! I can define "stuff": comedy mixed in with adventuere and drama = Good Book!

Ask Open-Ended Discussion Questions

Open-ended discussion frameworks can help ensure that book club discussion is based on students' own thinking. Margaret Anzul recommends beginning discussion with a simple invitation: "Talk about what touched you the most" (Anzul, 1993, p. 190). Miriam Martinez, Nancy Roser, James Hoffman, and

Jennifer Battle (1992) have used a three-pronged invitation to encourage children to talk about a piece of literature. This open-ended framework, based on the work of Aidan Chambers (1985), invites students to share their (1) observations, (2) unanswered questions or wonderings, and (3) anything they were reminded of by the story. Frequently, students' observations are so insightful that lively conversations ensue. And students' wonderings, which are legitimate questions, are especially likely to evoke interesting discussions. Such was the case when Eric, a fourth grader, shared one of his questions about C. S. Lewis's *The Lion, the Witch, and the Wardrobe* (1951) with his classmates:

ERIC: I wonder why Edmund wasn't mentioned in the last three chapters?

MS. FRY: Good question. Who wants to respond to that? Why hasn't the author mentioned Edmund in the last three chapters?

CARLO: Probably because they, they could think that Edmund might be like in the special place, like where the witch has them. Except he was a traitor, and they don't want to talk about him. They want to save him, and they talk about the other kids so that . . .

CAROL: And then like they're having the battles, and whoever wins the battle gets Edmund or . . .

JACKIE: 'Cause if they kill the witch, then all the animals . . . she probably created most of her enemies. And then the witch dies; then all of her creatures die, and Edmund isn't a traitor anymore, and they can get him back.

MS. FRY: Boy, you got an answer to the question, I can tell! But the bottom line was that you think the author has some special purpose for holding Edmund aside for these last three chapters. Does anybody else have something to respond about Aslan, I mean keeping Edmund out of it so far?

MICHELLE: Maybe the witch can turn [inaudible] can turn one of those stone beasts into another animal, and then he could be a spy.

MS. FRY: Maybe Edmund . . . that is an excellent idea. Maybe Edmund isn't what Edmund used to be anymore. That is a possibility.

When students are invited to share their own connections to a story, they sometimes offer personal experiences related to the story, or they connect the story with others they have read. We find that children frequently share some of their most insightful thinking when they compare stories. When her teacher read *Captain Whiz-Bang* (1987) aloud, Kim was reminded of E. B. White's *Charlotte's Web* (1952):

KIM: This book reminds me of *Charlotte's Web* because Fern had Wilbur and the little girl had the cat. And as Fern and the little girl got older, they didn't pay much attention to their animals.

An open-ended discussion framework can give students interesting alternatives for responding to a story without rigidly prescribing acceptable ways in which to respond. An added benefit of using this discussion framework is that it also works well as an invitation to journal writing, thereby integrating writing and discussion.

Pose Literary Questions for Discussion

As we noted earlier, there are times during book club discussions when teachers may want to pose questions. For example, if the teacher believes the students have not discussed an important aspect of a story, she or he may try to move discussion forward by asking a literary question. Carefully crafted questions can encourage students to think more insightfully about a story. According to Wendy Saul (1989), literary questions require interpretation and are the "key to literary comprehension, conversation, and enjoyment." She has identified some distinctive features of literary questions, which are listed in Table 13.1. Not every literary question will have all these features, but questions with one or more of them have the potential to "lead children into the story and help them consider the work as a human construction where craft and effect are taken seriously" (p. 297).

Lea McGee (1995) recommends that in preparing literary questions, teachers read the story thoughtfully, staying in tune with their own responses to the story and noting conclusions they draw from it or any noteworthy elements they discover in it. She further notes the importance of focusing on "the significance of the story as a whole" (p. 111).

Saul (1989) describes a strategy, called "diagramming stories," that helps teachers to ". . . focus on the structural peculiarities of a text, to comment on what in the book or story looms largest to the reader, and to describe, in something close to metaphorical terms, the essence of the book" (p. 297). Figure 13.2 shows a story diagram of Jerry Spinelli's *Maniac Magee* (1990). The teacher who created the diagram explained what she was trying to do in this way:

> At the beginning of the book, there was a "wall" between the West End and the East End that was never supposed to be crossed, and everyone knew there was a wall there—that is, everyone except Maniac. He just went back and forth between the West End and the East End as though there was no wall at all. Then, all of a sudden, on the day everyone was playing in the water from the fire hydrant and the man called Maniac "Whitey," Maniac finally saw the wall, and it

Table 13.1 *How to Ask Good Literary Questions*

- Ask questions that go beyond what is in the story but that always come back to the story.
- Ask questions that help readers better understand the story.
- Ask questions that have at least two good answers, either of which can help the reader with the story.
- Ask questions whose answers can be argued intelligently in different ways.
- Ask some questions that deal with issues of craft.

Adapted from Saul, 1989, p. 301.

Figure 13.2
Teachers can prepare to lead literature discussions by creating story diagrams.

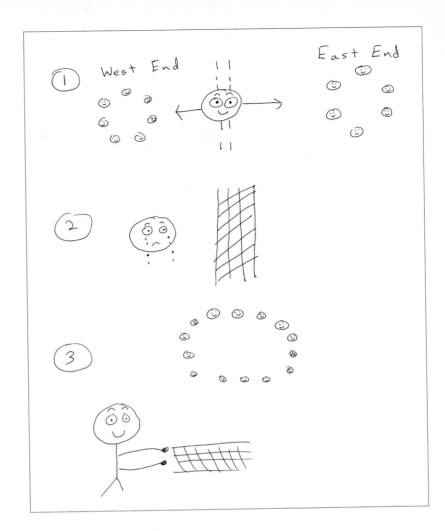

almost broke his heart. But finally, Maniac found a way to bring that wall down, and doing that meant he was finally able to have the home and happiness he wanted so much.

Literary questions based on this story diagram might include:

- Why wasn't Maniac able to see the "wall" between the East End and the West End?
- Why did it hurt Maniac so much when he finally saw the wall?
- How did Maniac help bring down the wall?
- What other walls did the author include in the book that had an impact on Maniac?

Each of these questions goes beyond the text, but the answers (and there will be more than one answer to each question) naturally come back to the text. The questions should help readers understand the story better, and the final question treats the story as a crafted object. Grand conversations may well be sparked when students are invited to respond to the kind of literary questions that Saul advocates.

Prepare Language Charts

Language charts function much as literary questions do: They focus students' thinking about literature. Developed by Nancy Roser, James V. Hoffman, and Cynthia Farest (1990), language charts are designed for use primarily with related sets of books. These large charts, intended to be displayed on a classroom wall, are ruled into a matrix. The titles (and perhaps authors and illustrators) of each book in the set are recorded along one axis of the matrix. Questions devised to stimulate connections among the books are recorded along the other axis. These questions might focus attention on particular aspects of the story worlds in the featured books or on themes that emerge from the books or on the crafting of the stories or illustrations. Students' responses to the questions are recorded on the matrix as each book is read and discussed.

A language chart designed for use with a unit entitled "Cumulative Tales" appears in Figure 13.3. The questions on this chart encourage students to focus on the structural commonalities in the cumulative tales included in the unit. The chart in Figure 13.4 focuses students' attention on the style of Chris Van Allsburg, for a unit on that author/illustrator.

Some teachers report that a language chart can become a "worksheet on the wall" if the class begins to complete the chart too soon after reading. These charts are not meant to displace conversations about books. Rather, teachers and students should turn to the language chart only after having fully discussed a book. Teachers who have used language charts in this way report that they can be effective tools for fostering literary understandings. In fact, many teachers change the design of their language charts throughout the school year in order to help students continue to explore different aspects of literature. For example, the questions that Ms. Coker, a kindergarten teacher, uses on her language charts at the beginning of the year are designed to help her students learn basic literary language: Who are the characters? What is the setting? What was the problem in the story? Once students have made this terminology their own, she changes the chart questions to focus on other literary understandings.

Figure 13.3
This language chart encourages students to think about the structure of cumulative tales.

Title	Author	What starts the add-on?	What things are added on?	What problem is solved by the add-on?
One Fine Day	Nonny Hogrogian			
The Great Big Enormous Turnip	Aleksey N. Tolstoy			
Bringing the Rain to Kapiti Plain	Verna Aardema			

Books by Chris Van Allsburg	What strange things happened in the story?	What surprise did the ending hold?	What did we notice about the illustrations?
Jumanji			
The Wreck of the Zephyr			
The Sweetest Fig			

Develop Story Webs

Story webs are visual displays that show how categories of information are related; the name arose because they often look like the webs spiders build. Teachers use story webs to achieve different purposes, but Karen Bromley (1991) believes that all too often they overlook the potential of webs to foster responses to literature. Story webs, like literary questions, focus students' thinking about literature. According to Bromley (1995), webs can be used to support and extend students' literary understanding in many ways:

- Webs can help students identify important issues in stories.
- Webs can be used to focus attention on connections between books.

Book webs can support children's thinking about the information or stories they read.

- Webs can help students understand how literary and artistic elements work.
- Webs can help students explore characteristics of different genres.
- Webs can help students explore the literary devices authors use (perspective, metaphor, and so on).

Story webs can emerge from children's responses. This happened in Ms. Alducin's class when her students were discussing *Beethoven Lives Upstairs* (1993). Ms. Alducin introduced the web that appears in Figure 13.5 by saying, "Someone said earlier that Christoph's feelings about Beethoven changed a lot in the book, and I want us to explore that idea a little more." However, just as teachers sometimes create literary questions for possible use during book club

Figure 13.5
Character development can be explored with a web.

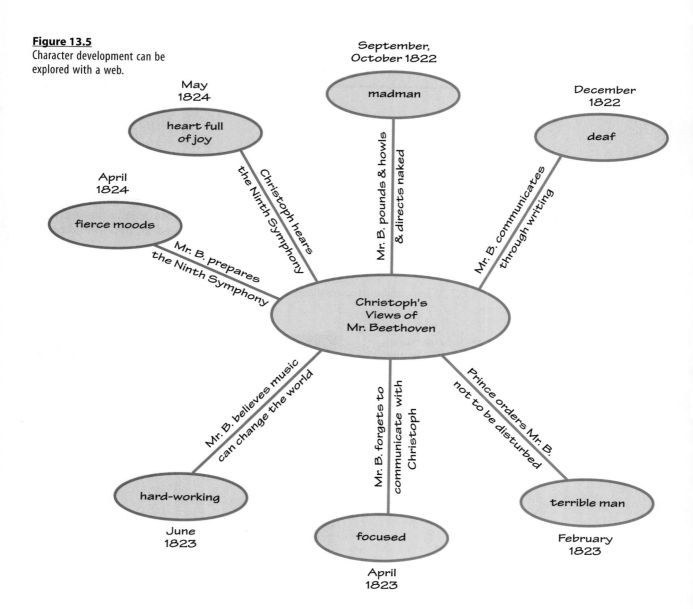

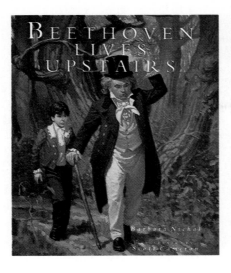

discussions, they may design webs that will help students explore a particular aspect of a story. We recommend introducing a story web only after students have engaged in free-ranging discussion about the story.

Barbara Nichol's **Beethoven Lives Upstairs** (1993) is told almost exclusively through the correspondence of the young Christoph and his uncle Karl. To make a living following the death of Christoph's father, his mother has rented the upstairs portion of their house to Beethoven. Mistaking the famous composer's eccentric behavior for madness, Christoph is appalled. During a period of two years, Christoph keeps his uncle updated on the happenings upstairs, and his uncle's letters gently help Christoph develop compassion for his neighbor. The web in Figure 13.5 chronologically records Christoph's feelings toward Beethoven and the story details related to those feelings. Christoph's increasingly mature understanding of Beethoven reveals his own growth as a character.

The story web in Figure 13.6 is based on **Maniac Magee** (1990). In Jerry Spinelli's Newbery Medal–winning book, a boy who began life as Jeffrey Magee becomes a legend nicknamed Maniac. The web shows some of the incidents that led to Maniac's acquiring his nickname.

Figure 13.6
This web reveals how Maniac Magee emerges as a legendary figure in Jerry Spinelli's Newbery Medal–winning book.

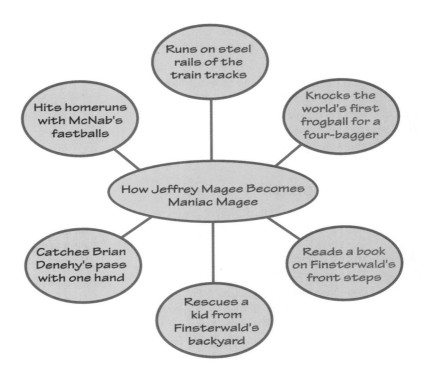

 **TEACHING IDEAS**

Responses to Books. As you engage children in book club discussions, try modeling a particular type of response. For example, you might repeatedly share the things you wonder about when reading a story or talk about how the book connects to other books you have read. Watch and see if children begin to share similar responses during book club.

Children's Picks versus Teacher's Picks. Both teachers and students can select books for use in book clubs. Try comparing book club conversations when students discuss books you've chosen with those when they discuss books they've chosen. How do the discussions differ? What are the advantages (if any) of involving students in selecting books for literature discussion?

Journal Writing. Try engaging students in literature discussion without having them keep journals. Once they are feeling comfortable as members of a book club, encourage the students to record their responses in journals. You can then use the students' journal entries as conversation starters. How does literature discussion change with the use of journals?

Character Development. Marty's development as a character in *Shiloh* (1991) is particularly interesting. To help your students see Marty's growth, create a character web with the students. Make discussion an integral part of the process.

EXPERIENCES FOR YOUR LEARNING

1. Questions can be tools for "gentle inquisitions" or tools that foster "grand conversations." Select a book and develop questions you think are likely to promote grand conversations. Which features identified by Saul (1989) do your literary questions have?

2. Reflect on literature discussions in which you've participated. Which were grand conversations? Describe one of these discussions to a fellow student, and explain why you consider it to have been a grand conversation.

3. One way teachers can support literary learning is by helping students become aware of the writer's craft. Distinctively crafted books offer teachers opportunities to talk about different aspects of craft (mood, voice, tension, and so on). Select some well-crafted children's books and identify the aspects of craft in each book that you would like to discuss with students.

RECOMMENDED BOOKS

* indicates a picture book; I indicates interest level
  (P = preschool, YA = young adult)

Books with Strong Themes

* Ackerman, Karen. *The Tin Heart.* Illustrated by Michael Hays. New York: Atheneum, 1990. Two friends are separated by the American Civil War, but their friendship remains as strong as ever. (**I:** 8–11)

Babbitt, Natalie. *Tuck Everlasting.* New York: Farrar, 1975. A young girl is given the opportunity to drink from a spring that offers eternal life. (**I:** 10–YA)

* Blos, Joan. *Old Henry.* Illustrated by Stephen Gammell. New York: Morrow, 1987. A neighborhood discovers that there is room for all kinds of people. (**I:** 6–9)

* Bunting, Eve. *A Day's Work.* Illustrated by Ronald Himler. New York: Clarion, 1994. Francisco is so anxious to find work for his non–English-speaking grandfather that he lies about the man's qualifications for a gardening job. When the boss discovers the work has been botched, Francisco's *abuelito* teaches him a valuable lesson. (**I:** 6–10)

* ———. *The Wall.* Illustrated by Ronald Himler. New York: Clarion, 1992. A boy and his father visit the Vietnam Memorial searching for the name of the boy's grandfather. (**I:** 7–10)

* ———. *The Wednesday Surprise.* Illustrated by Donald Carrick. New York: Clarion, 1989. A little girl surprises her family by teaching her grandmother to read. (**I:** 6–10)

Coerr, Eleanor. *Sadako and the Thousand Paper Cranes.* New York: Dell, 1977. A victim of leukemia resulting from the atomic bomb dropped on Hiroshima, Sadako determines to fight for her life by folding a thousand paper cranes. (**I:** 9–12)

Cole, Norma. *The Final Tide.* New York: McElderry, 1990. Geneva Haw knows that when the Wolf Creek Dam is completed, her family's valley will be flooded and the world she knows will change forever. (**I:** YA)

* Cooney, Barbara. *Miss Rumphius.* New York: Puffin, 1982. A woman achieves her life's goals, including the most important one of making the world more beautiful. (**I:** 6–10)

* Daly, Niki. *My Dad.* New York: McElderry, 1995. A brother and sister discover that their father is an alcoholic. (**I:** 8–11)

* Everitt, Betsy. *Mean Soup.* San Diego, CA: Harcourt, 1992. When Horace has a bad day at school, his mother shows him how to get rid of his anger. (**I:** P–7)

* Garland, Sherry. *The Lotus Seed.* Illustrated by Tatsuro Kiuchi. San Diego, CA: Harcourt, 1993. When the emperor in Vietnam loses his throne, a young girl sees him cry and takes a lotus seed from the pond to remember that moment. Throughout the war in her country and her relocation to the United Sates, the girl holds on to the lotus seed as a symbol of life and hope. (**I:** 6–12)

* Gerstein, Mordicai. *The Seal Mother.* New York: Dial, 1986. A fisherman steals a seal's skin, forcing her to live as a human. (**I:** 5–9)

* Golenbock, Peter. *Teammates.* Illustrated by Paul Bacon. San Diego, CA: Harcourt, 1990. When Jackie Robinson becomes the first African American to play major league baseball, only one man stands by him—his teammate Pee Wee Reese. (**I:** 9–12)

* Harshman, Marc. *Uncle James.* Illustrated by Michael Dooling. New York: Dutton, 1993. Uncle James promises his sister's family the world, but when he finally comes, he brings his own problems. (**I:** 10–YA)

* Heide, Florence Parry, and Judith Heide Gilliland. *Sami and the Time of the Troubles.* Illustrated by Ted Lewin. New York: Clarion, 1992. Sami lives in war-torn Beirut with his mother, sister, and grandfather. He describes the bad days and the good days in his life. (**I:** 6–10)

* Hesse, Karen. *Lester's Dog.* Illustrated by Nancy Carpenter. New York: Crown, 1993. A young boy lives on the same street as a vicious and frightening dog that belongs to Lester. The boy is afraid to walk past Lester's dog, but one day he has to in order to save a kitten. (**I:** P–8)

Hobbie, W. D. *Bloodroot.* Illustrated by Holly Hobbie. New York: Crown, 1991. Lizzie and her grandmother join forces to save the rural New England land they love from the developers who threaten it. (**I:** 9–12)

* Hoffman, Mary. *Amazing Grace.* Illustrated by Caroline Binch. New York: Dial, 1991. With the support of her grandmother and mother, a young girl discovers she can be anything she wants to be. (**I:** 5–10)

* Houston, Gloria. *My Great-Aunt Arizona.* Illustrated by Susan Condie Lamb. New York: HarperCollins, 1991. Arizona was born in a small community in the Blue Ridge Mountains, where she dreamed of traveling to faraway places. She never left the area but became a teacher who touched the lives of many children by teaching them about the world. (**I:** 6–10)

* Johnston, Tony. *Amber on the Mountain.* Illustrated by Robert Duncan. New York: Dial, 1994. Amber's lonely mountain life opens up when a friend teaches her to read. (**I:** 6–10)

L'Engle, Madeleine. *A Wrinkle in Time.* New York: Dell, 1962. When Meg's father mysteriously disappears during some experiments with the Fifth Dimension, Meg, her friend, and her brother must face evil forces to rescue him. (**I:** 10–YA)

* Levine, Arthur A. *Pearl Moscowitz's Last Stand.* Illustrated by Robert Roth. New York: Morrow/Tambourine, 1993. Over the years, Pearl Moscowitz watches her neighborhood change in both good and bad ways. (**I:** 7–11)

Lewis, C. S. *The Lion, the Witch, and the Wardrobe.* New York: Macmillan, 1951. Four siblings enter the magical kingdom of Narnia, where they become embroiled in a struggle between good and evil. (**I:** 8–11)

Lowry, Lois. *The Giver.* Boston: Houghton Mifflin, 1993. A boy discovers the secrets behind the controlled society in which he lives. (**I:** YA)

MacLachlan, Patricia. *Journey.* New York: Delacorte, 1991. Journey spends the summer trying to find out why his mother has abandoned him and his sister. (**I:** 9–12)

Mazer, Anne. *The Oxboy*. New York: Knopf, 1993. The Oxboy faces prejudice because he is the son of a human and an ox. (I: 9–12)

* McCully, Emily Arnold. *Mirette on the High Wire*. New York: Putnam, 1992. A young girl helps a tightrope walker rediscover his courage. (I: 5–9)

* Merrill, Jean. *The Girl Who Loved Caterpillars*. Illustrated by Floyd Cooper. New York: Philomel, 1992. A twelfth-century Japanese tale in which a young girl pursues her own dreams rather than those of her parents. (I: 10–YA)

* Mitchell, Margaree King. *Uncle Jed's Barbershop*. Illustrated by James Ransome. New York: Simon & Schuster, 1993. Despite all the adversity he encounters in the segregated South of the 1920s, Uncle Jed never gives up his dream of opening his own barbershop. (I: 9–12)

* Mochizuki, Ken. *Baseball Saved Us*. Illustrated by Dom Lee. New York: Lee and Low, 1993. Living in an internment camp during World War II, a young Japanese American boy finds a way to gain dignity and self-respect. (I: 8–12)

* Nye, Naomi Shihab. *Sitti's Secrets*. Illustrated by Nancy Carpenter. New York: Four Winds, 1994. When Mona visits her grandmother in a Palestinian village on the West Bank, she discovers many connections between her world and her grandmother's, even though their homes are separated by thousands of miles. (I: 6–10)

Paterson, Katherine. *Lyddie*. New York: Penguin/Lodestar, 1991. Lyddie struggles against injustices in the fabric mills of Massachusetts in the 1840s. (I: 11–YA)

* Polacco, Patricia. *Chicken Sunday*. New York: Philomel, 1992. When three children are falsely accused of throwing eggs at a shopkeeper's window, they discover a way of reaching across a cultural gap to solve a problem. (I: 7–11)

* ———. *Pink and Say*. New York: Philomel, 1994. When a young Union soldier of fifteen is wounded in the Civil War, a young black soldier reaches out his hand in friendship and takes the white soldier to his home. (I: 8–YA)

* Provensen, Alice, and Martin Provensen. *Shaker Lane*. New York: Puffin, 1987. When the county decides to build a dam, the neighborhood that has grown up along Shaker Lane becomes the victim of progress. (I: 6–10)

* Rylant, Cynthia. *This Year's Garden*. New York: Bradbury, 1984. A descriptive story about planting the family garden. (I: P–8)

* Stanley, Diane. *Captain Whiz-Bang*. New York: Morrow, 1987. A little girl grows up and in the process seems to forget her beloved cat. (I: P–8)

* Steig, William. *Amos and Boris*. New York: Farrar, 1971. A mouse and a whale form a deep friendship. (I: 6–9)

* ———. *Sylvester and the Magic Pebble*. New York: Simon & Schuster, 1969. After making a wish on a magic pebble and being transformed into a rock, Sylvester comes to realize what's important in life. (I: 6–9)

Talbert, Marc. *A Sunburned Prayer*. New York: Simon & Schuster, 1995. Eloy is determined to make the long pilgrimage to Chimayo in hopes of saving his grandmother, who is dying from cancer. (I: YA)

Taylor, Mildred D. *Song of the Trees*. New York: Dial, 1975. In this first book about the Logans, an African American family living in rural Mississippi during the Depression, a white man tries to buy from the Logans trees that he has already claimed as his own and sold for lumber. (I: 10–YA)

——— . *Roll of Thunder, Hear My Cry*. New York: Dial, 1976. The Logans stand strong in the face of discrimination when a white man tries to cheat them out of their land. (I: 10–YA)

* Van Allsburg, Chris. *The Polar Express*. Boston: Houghton Mifflin, 1985. A young boy boards a train that takes him to the North Pole, where Santa offers him any gift he would like. (I: P–8)

* ———. *The Wretched Stone*. Boston: Houghton Mifflin, 1991. The crew on a sailing ship discovers an uncharted island with an unusual glowing rock on it. They take the rock on board, where it soon consumes the attention of the crew and causes all of them except the captain to regress into apes. (I: 8–12)

Voigt, Cynthia. *Dicey's Song*. New York: Atheneum, 1983. Dicey and her siblings learn to build a new life with the grandmother they had never known before. (I: 10–YA)

* Weller, Frances Ward. *Matthew Wheelock's Wall*. Illustrated by Ted Lewin. New York: Macmillan, 1992. Matthew Wheelock builds a wall that becomes a gift for the generations that follow. (I: 6–10)

* Wild, Margaret. *Let the Celebrations BEGIN!* Illustrated by Julie Vivas. New York: Orchard, 1991. Inmates in a Nazi concentration camp maintain their hope by making toys for the children. (I: 10–YA)

* ———. *The Very Best of Friends*. Illustrated by Julie Vivas. San Diego, CA: Harcourt, 1989. When her husband dies, Jessie's cat helps her overcome her grief. (I: 10–YA)

* Yolen, Jane. *Encounter*. Illustrated by David Shannon. San Diego, CA: Harcourt, 1992. Columbus's first landing in America is told through the eyes of a Taino boy. (**I:** 10–YA)

Strong Story Lines

* Alexander, Sally Hobart. *Maggie's Whopper*. Illustrated by Deborah Kogan Ray. New York: Macmillan, 1992. Sally loves fishing with her great-uncle Ezra. Determined to catch a whopper of a fish this time, she does so just in time to save her uncle from a threatening black bear. (**I:** P–8)

* Bunting, Eve. *The In-Between Days*. Illustrated by Alexander Pertzoff. New York: HarperCollins, 1994. When his father decides to remarry, George must come to terms with this change in his life. (**I:** 8–11)

———. *Summer Wheels*. San Diego, CA: Harcourt, 1992. The Bicycle Man helps two boys learn a lesson about the importance of giving instead of blaming. (**I:** 7–10)

* de Paola, Tomie. *Helga's Dowry: A Troll Love Story*. New York: Harcourt, 1977. A troll maiden discovers it is more important to be loved for who she is than for what she has. (**I:** 7–12)

Dorris, Michael. *Guests*. New York: Hyperion, 1994. Frustrated that white people are to join the village for the harvest meal, Moss leaves for some "away time" in hopes of finding answers to his questions. (**I:** 9–12)

Farmer, Nancy. *The Ear, the Eye and the Arm*. New York: Orchard, 1994. Set in a futuristic Africa, this imaginative science fiction work explores where the world may be heading. (**I:** YA)

Fitzhugh, Louise. *Harriet the Spy*. New York: Harper, 1964. Harriet documents her observations of the people around her in her journal. (**I:** 8–11)

Fox, Mem. *Wilford Gordon McDonald Partridge*. Illustrated by Julie Vivas. Brooklyn, NY: Kane/Miller, 1984. Through his gifts, a little boy helps an elderly friend find memories. (**I:** P–8)

* Gackenbach, Dick. *Harry and the Terrible Whatzit*. New York: Clarion, 1977. Sure that his mother has come to harm, a boy dares to confront the Terrible Whatzit living in his basement. (**I:** P–7)

George, Jean Craighead. *Julie of the Wolves*. New York: Harper, 1972. Lost on the tundra, Julie must depend on a wolf pack for survival. (**I:** 10–YA)

———. *My Side of the Mountain*. New York: Dutton, 1959. A young boy relies on his knowledge of nature to survive on his own for a year in the wilderness of upper New York State. (**I:** 10–YA)

Hamilton, Virginia. *Drylongso*. Illustrated by Jerry Pinkney. San Diego, CA: Harcourt, 1992. An African American family, victimized by a severe drought, is helped by an unknown boy. (**I:** 8–11)

Ho, Minfong. *The Clay Marble*. New York: Farrar, 1991. Forced from their war-torn village in Cambodia, Dara and her family are separated in the chaos of war. (**I:** 10–YA)

Hodge, Merle. *For the Life of Laetitia*. New York: Farrar, 1993. Having grown up with her grandparents in their rural Caribbean home, Laetitia discovers a new and not always happy world when she moves to the city to attend the government secondary school. (**I:** YA)

Konigsburg, E. L. *From the Mixed-Up Files of Mrs. Basil E. Frankweiler*. New York: Atheneum, 1967. Claudia and her brother run away from home and live in the Metropolitan Museum of Art. (**I:** 9–12)

* Lionni, Leo. *Alexander and the Wind-Up Mouse*. New York: Pantheon, 1969. A real mouse longs to be like his friend the wind-up mouse. (**I:** P–7)

Lord, Bette Bao. *In the Year of the Boar and Jackie Robinson*. New York: Harper, 1984. When a young girl comes to the United States, she has trouble adjusting to her new life and language. She becomes interested in baseball and Jackie Robinson and is inspired by all that he had to overcome to reach his dreams. (**I:** 8–12)

* Luenn, Nancy. *Nessa's Fish*. Illustrated by Neil Waldman. New York: Macmillan, 1990. Nessa and her grandmother walk half a day from their home in the far north to catch fish for the village. When Nessa's grandmother becomes ill, Nessa must take care of her and keep the fish safe. (**I:** P–8)

MacLachlan, Patricia. *Sarah, Plain and Tall*. New York: Harper, 1985. A brother and sister hope that Sarah will choose to stay on the prairie and become their mother. (**I:** 9–12)

* McKissack, Patricia. *Flossie and the Fox*. New York: Dial, 1986. Flossie outfoxes the fox who tries to steal her eggs. (**I:** 5–10)

* Naylor, Phyllis Reynolds. *King of the Playground*. Illustrated by Nola Langner Malone. New York: Atheneum, 1991. When Kevin can't play at the playground because of Sammy's threats, his father helps him learn to handle a difficult situation. (**I:** P–8)

———. *Shiloh*. New York: Atheneum, 1991. A boy determines to save the dog he loves from further abuse by its owner. (**I:** 7–11)

———. *Shiloh Season*. New York: Atheneum, 1996. Having saved the dog Shiloh from Judd, the dog's abusive owner, Marty must now deal with Judd's anger. (I: 7–11)

* Ness, Evaline. *Sam, Bangs & Moonshine*. New York: Holt, 1966. A fisherman's daughter named Sam has a great imagination filled with chariots, dragons, and a mermaid mother, but one day she is forced to learn the difference between real and make-believe when one of her stories places a friend in danger. (I: 6–9)

* Novak, Matt. *Mouse TV*. New York: Orchard, 1994. When the TV stops working, a mouse family discovers a host of wonderful alternative activities. (I: P–8)

Paulsen, Gary. *Hatchet*. New York: Bradbury, 1987. A boy stranded in the wilderness has only his hatchet and his wits to help him survive. (I: 10–YA)

* San Souci, Robert D. *The Talking Eggs*. Illustrated by Jerry Pinkney. New York: Dial, 1989. Adapted from a Creole folktale, this is the story of two sisters— one is lazy and bad-tempered and the other is sweet and kind. (I: 6–10)

Speare, Elizabeth. *Sign of the Beaver*. New York: Dell, 1983. Alone in the wilderness, a white boy survives with the help of his Native American friend. (I: 9–12)

———. *The Witch of Blackbird Pond*. New York: Dell, 1958. Kit Tyler becomes the focus of a witch hunt when she goes to live in a Puritan community in the Connecticut colony. (I: YA)

Spinelli, Jerry. *Maniac Magee*. Boston: Little, Brown, 1990. A homeless boy brings together the segregated sides of his adopted town and in the process becomes a legend. (I: 10–YA)

Taylor, Mildred D. *The Gold Cadillac*. New York: Dial, 1987. When an African American family tries to drive their new car into the deep South, they find themselves the victims of racial prejudice. (I: 10–YA)

———. *The Friendship*. Illustrated by Max Ginsburg. New York: Dial, 1987. An old black man is shot when he insists on his right to call a white man by his first name. (I: 10–YA)

———. *Mississippi Bridge*. Illustrated by Max Ginsburg. New York: Dial, 1990. In this story set in Mississippi in the 1930s, African American passengers on a bus are displaced by white passengers. (I: 10–YA)

Taylor, Theodore. *The Cay*. New York: Doubleday, 1969. During World War II, a blind boy is stranded on an island with a West Indian. (I: YA)

Temple, Frances. *Grab Hands and Run*. New York: Harper, 1993. When his father disappears in El Salvador, Felipe and his family set out on a dangerous trek to Canada. (I: 9–12)

* Van Allsburg, Chris. *Jumanji*. Boston: Houghton Mifflin, 1981. A brother and sister find unexpected adventure in a board game they play. (I: 6–10)

* ———. *The Stranger*. Boston: Houghton Mifflin, 1986. The stranger who stays on the Bailey's farm seems to be accompanied by mysterious changes in the weather. (I: 7–12)

* ———. *The Widow's Broom*. Boston: Houghton Mifflin, 1992. When a widow comes into possession of a witch's broom, the broom begins to help out around the house, which raises the ire of the neighbors. (I: 8–YA)

* ———. *The Wreck of the Zephyr*. Boston: Houghton Mifflin, 1983. The wreck of the Zephyr is on a high cliff above the sea. Did a storm with unusually high waves throw it there, or did a boy sailor use magic sails to sail it through the sky? (I: 8–12)

Voigt, Cynthia. *Homecoming*. New York: Atheneum, 1981. When their mother abandons them, Dicey and her siblings seek out the grandmother they have never met. (I: 10–YA)

* Waber, Bernard. *Ira Sleeps Over*. Boston: Houghton Mifflin, 1972. Ira has been invited to sleep over at his best friend's house and must decide whether to risk being laughed at by taking his teddy bear. (I: P–8)

White, E. B. *Charlotte's Web*. Illustrated by Garth Williams. New York: Harper, 1952. Charlotte the spider befriends Wilbur the pig and saves his life. (I: 6–10)

* Willard, Nancy. *The High Rise Glorious Skittle Skat Roarious Sky Pie Angel Food Cake*. Illustrated by Richard Jesse Watson. San Diego, CA: Harcourt, 1990. A girl discovers her grandmother's secret recipe and with some heavenly help makes her mother the birthday present she longs for. (I: 8–11)

Winthrop, Elizabeth. *Castle in the Attic*. New York: Holiday House, 1985. A boy travels back to medieval times and confronts an evil wizard. (I: 7–11)

* Wood, Audrey. *Elbert's Bad Word*. Illustrated by Audrey and Don Wood. San Diego, CA: Harcourt, 1988. When Elbert blurts out a bad word at an elegant garden party, the wizard gardener helps Elbert discover strong descriptive words to use instead. (I: P–8)

Yolen, Jane. *The Devil's Arithmetic*. New York: Puffin, 1988. A time travel fantasy in which Hannah finds herself caught up in the Holocaust. (I: 10–YA)

* Yorinks, Arthur. *Hey, Al!* Illustrated by Richard Egielski. New York: Farrar, 1986. The paradise promised by a bird does not live up to the expectations of Al and his dog. (I: 6–12)

* Zolotow, Charlotte. *Mr. Rabbit and the Lovely Present*. Illustrated by Maurice Sendak. New York: Harper, 1962. A rabbit helps a little girl choose the perfect present for her mother. (I: 4–7)

Distinctive Crafting

* Browne, Anthony. *Changes*. New York: Knopf, 1990. Mysterious things begin to happen around the house after a father tells his son that things are going to change. (I: P–8)

* Bunting, Eve. *Smoky Night*. Illustrated by David Diaz. San Diego, CA: Harcourt, 1994. In the midst of the violence of the L.A. riots, Daniel and his mother make a new friend. (I: 6–12)

* Burton, Virginia Lee. *The Little House*. 1942. Boston: Houghton Mifflin, 1969. As the city grows up around a little house, the house longs to be in the country again. (I: P–8)

* Carle, Eric. *The Very Busy Spider*. New York: Philomel, 1984. In this carefully crafted predictable book, the very busy spider is too busy to take time for the other animals. (I: P–8)

* Cherry, Lynne. *A River Ran Wild*. San Diego, CA: Harcourt, 1992. Six centuries of change and development are depicted in this story of the Nashua River. (I: 6–12)

Creech, Sharon. *Walk Two Moons*. New York: HarperCollins, 1994. Salamanca Tree Hiddle travels from Ohio to Idaho with her eccentric grandparents in an attempt to understand why her mother left her. (I: YA)

Fleischman, Paul. *Joyful Noise*. Illustrated by E. Beddows. New York: HarperCollins, 1988. This distinctive collection of poems for two voices focuses on insects. (I: 8–YA)

* Fleming, Denise. *In the Tall, Tall Grass*. New York: Holt, 1991. From caterpillars and ants to rabbits and bats, a boy explores the world of the animals who live in the tall grass in his backyard. (I: P–7)

* Gray, Libba Moore. *Small Green Snake*. Illustrated by Holly Meade. New York: Orchard, 1994. This story of a lively little snake is told in equally lively language. (I: P–7)

* Grifalconi, Ann. *Osa's Pride*. Boston: Little, Brown, 1990. Osa lives in an African village and has a special relationship with her grandmother. When Osa starts acting a little too proud for her own good, her grandmother decides to gently teach her a lesson. (I: 6–10)

* Heide, Florence Parry, and Judith Heide Gilliland. *The Day of Ahmed's Secret*. Illustrated by Ted Lewin. New York: Lothrop, 1990. All day young Ahmed drives his cart through the streets of Cairo, looking forward to the time he can share his secret with his family. (I: 7–10)

* Johnston, Deborah. *Mathew Michael's Beastly Day*. Illustrated by Seymour Chwast. San Diego, CA: Harcourt, 1992. Over the course of the day, a boy feels like various animals. (I: P–7)

* Kroll, Virginia. *Masai and I*. Illustrated by Nancy Carpenter. New York: Four Winds, 1992. An African American girl discovers the similarities and differences between her life and the life of a Masai girl. (I: 7–10)

* Lyon, George Ella. *Who Came Down That Road?* Illustrated by Peter Catalonotto. New York: Orchard, 1992. While on a walk, a boy asks his mother, "Who came down this path?" She tells the history of the path, tracing it back through his grandparents, Union soldiers, elk, pioneer settlers, Native Americans, Ice Age animals, to the beginning of time. (I: P–8)

* Macaulay, David. *Black and White*. Boston: Houghton Mifflin, 1990. Four stories are intertwined in one in this cleverly crafted book. (I: 6–10)

MacLachlan, Patricia. *Skylark*. New York: HarperCollins, 1994. A sequel to *Sarah, Plain and Tall*, in which a severe drought forces Sarah and the children to journey to Maine. (I: 9–12)

* Mazer, Anne. *The Salamander Room*. Illustrated by Steve Johnson. New York: Knopf, 1991. A little boy tells his mother how he will turn his room into the perfect home for the little orange salamander he wants to keep for a pet. (I: P–8)

McKissack, Patricia C., and Fredrick L. McKissack. *Christmas in the Big House, Christmas in the Quarters*. New York: Scholastic, 1994. Christmas in the big house is compared to Christmas in the slave quarters in the year before the Civil War breaks out. (I: 9–12)

* Nichol, Barbara. *Beethoven Lives Upstairs*. Illustrated by Scott Cameron. New York: Orchard, 1993. Through the exchange of letters with his uncle, a young boy comes to see Beethoven, his upstairs neighbor, in a new light. (I: 8–11)

* Polacco, Patricia. *The Keeping Quilt*. New York: Simon & Schuster, 1988. An immigrant family makes a quilt that is used for celebrations in subsequent generations. (I: 6–10)

* Rosen, Michael J. *Elijah's Angel*. Illustrated by Aminah Brenda Lynn Robinson. San Diego: Harcourt, 1992. Michael's family helps him to understand that the gifts of friendship transcend cultural gaps. (I: 8–12)

* Say, Allen. *Grandfather's Journey*. Boston: Houghton Mifflin, 1993. A young man recounts the unique

cross-cultural experience his family had living in Japan and America. (I: 6–10)

* Scieszka, Jon. *The Stinky Cheese Man and Other Fairly Stupid Tales*. Illustrated by Lane Smith. New York: Viking, 1992. A wacky collection of folktale spin-offs. (I: 6–10)

Sebestyen, Ouida. *Out of Nowhere*. New York: Orchard, 1994. Abandoned by his mother, a boy finds a way to build a new family. (I: 10–YA)

* Seymour, Tres. *Hunting the White Cow*. Illustrated by Wendy Anderson Halperin. New York: Orchard, 1993. A young girl living on a farm in Kentucky tries to catch the white cow that her daddy, her uncles, and their friends have been unable to catch. (I: P–8)

* Shulevitz, Uri. *One Monday Morning*. New York: Scribner's, 1967. A little boy in a tenement house imagines the members of a royal court coming to visit him each day in an otherwise dull week. (I: P–8)

* Willard, Nancy. *Pish, Posh, Said Hieronymus Bosch*. Illustrated by Leo, Diane, and Lee Dillon. San Diego, CA: Harcourt, 1991. Strange creatures haunt Hieronymus Bosch's housekeeper. (I: 5–9)

* Wood, Audrey. *King Bidgood's in the Bathtub*. Illustrated by Don Wood. New York: Harcourt, 1984. The members of the royal court try unsuccessfully all day to get the king out of the bathtub. (I: P–8)

* ———. *The Napping House*. Illustrated by Don Wood. New York: Harcourt, 1984. A child and her grandmother take a peaceful nap along with the family dog, cat, and a mouse—until a wakeful flea stirs things up. (I: P–8)

RESOURCES

Bromley, Karen D. *Webbing with Literature: Creating Story Maps with Children's Books*. Boston: Allyn & Bacon, 1991.

Harste, Jerome C., and Kathy G. Short, with Carolyn Burke. *Creating Classrooms for Authors: The Reading Writing Connection*. Portsmouth, NH: Heinemann, 1988.

Hill, Bonnie C., Nancy J. Johnson, and Katherine L. Schlick Noe. *Literature Circles and Response*. Norwood, MA: Christopher-Gordon, 1995.

Holland, Kathleen E., Rachel A. Hungerford, and Shirley B. Ernst, eds. *Journeying: Children Responding to Literature*. Portsmouth, NH: Heinemann, 1993.

Literature Study: Karen Smith's Classroom. Dirs. Maryann Eeds, Carole Edelsky, Karen Smith, C. Penka, and B. Love. Tempe, AZ: Center for Establishing Dialogue in Teaching and Learning, 1990.

Peterson, Ralph, and Maryann Eeds. *Grand Conversations: Literature Groups in Action*. Toronto: Scholastic–TAB, 1990.

Raphael, Taffy E., Susan I. McMahon, Virginia J. Goatley, J. L. Bentley, F. B. Boyd, Laura S. Pardo, and Deborah A. Woodman. "Research Directions: Literature and Discussion in the Reading Program." *Language Arts* 69 (1992): 54–61.

Roser, Nancy L., and Miriam G. Martinez, eds. *Book Talk and Beyond: Children and Teachers Respond to Literature*. Newark, DE: International Reading Association, 1995.

Wiencek, Joyce, and John F. O'Flahavan. "From Teacher-Led to Peer Discussions about Literature: Suggestions for Making the Shift." *Language Arts* 71 (1994): 488–98.

REFERENCES

Almasi, Janice. "The Nature of Fourth Graders' Sociocognitive Conflicts in Peer-led and Teacher-led Discussions of Literature." *Reading Research Quarterly* 30 (1995): 314–51.

Anzul, Margaret. "Exploring Literature with Children within a Transactional Framework." *Journeying: Children Responding to Literature*. Eds. Kathleen E. Holland, Rachel A. Hungerford, and Shirley B. Ernst. Portsmouth, NH: Heinemann, 1993. 187–203.

Babbitt, Natalie. "Protecting Children's Literature." *Horn Book* 66 (1990): 696–703.

Bromley, Karen D. "Enriching Responses to Literature with Webbing." *Book Talk and Beyond: Children and Teachers Respond to Literature*. Eds. Nancy L. Roser and Miriam G. Martinez. Newark, DE: International Reading Association, 1995. 90–101.

———. *Webbing with Literature: Creating Story Maps with Children's Books*. Boston: Allyn & Bacon, 1991.

Byars, Betsy. *After the Goat Man*. Illustrated by Ron Himler. New York: Viking, 1974.

Carris, Joan. *Aunt Morbelia and the Screaming Skull*. Boston: Little, Brown, 1990.

———. *Just a Little Ham*. Boston: Little, Brown, 1989.

Cazden, Courtney. *Classroom Discourse: The Language of Teaching and Learning*. Portsmouth, NH: Heinemann, 1988.

Cianciolo, Patricia J. "Responding to Literature as a Work of Art—An Aesthetic Literary Experience." *Language Arts* 59 (1982): 259–64.

Chambers, Aidan. *Booktalk: Occasional Writing on Literature and Children.* New York: Harper, 1985.

Eeds, Maryann, and Deborah Wells. "Grand Conversations: An Exploration of Meaning Construction in Literature Study Groups." *Research in the Teaching of English* 23 (1989): 4–29.

Farrell, Edmund J., and James R. Squire. *Transactions with Literature: A Fifty-Year Perspective.* Urbana, IL: National Council of Teachers of English, 1990.

Farris, Pamela J. "Story Time and Story Journals: Linking Literature and Writing." *The New Advocate* 2 (1989): 179–85.

Gonzalez, Veronica, Linda Fry, Sylvia Lopez, Julie Jordan, Cindy Sloan, and Diane McAdams. "Our Journey toward Better Coversations about Books." *Book Talk and Beyond: Children and Teachers Respond to Literature.* Eds. Nancy L. Roser and Miriam G. Martinez. Newark, DE: International Reading Association, 1995. 168–78.

Grover, W. *Dolphin Adventure.* New York: Greenwillow, 1990.

Harste, Jerome C., and Kathy G. Short, with Carolyn Burke. *Creating Classrooms for Authors: The Reading Writing Connection.* Portsmouth, NH: Heinemann, 1988.

Hickman, Janet. "A New Perspective on Response to Literature: Research in an Elementary School Setting." *Research in the Teaching of English* 15 (1981): 343–54.

———. "Response to Literature in a School Environment, Grades K through 5." Diss. Ohio State University, 1979.

Hoban, Lillian. *Arthur's Prize Reader.* New York: Harper, 1978.

Kiefer, Barbara. "The Responses of Children in a Combination First/Second Grade Classroom to Picture Books in a Variety of Artistic Styles." *Journal of Research and Development in Education* 16 (1983): 14–20.

Langer, Judith. "Rethinking Literature." *Literature Instruction: A Focus on Students' Response.* Ed. Judith A. Langer. Urbana, IL: National Council of Teachers of English, 1992. 35–53.

Leppard, L. *Mandie and the Cherokee Legend.* New York: Bethany House, 1983.

Martinez, Miriam, and Nancy L. Roser. "The Books Make a Difference in Story Talk." *Book Talk and Beyond: Children and Teachers Respond to Literature.* Eds. Nancy L. Roser and Miriam G. Martinez. Newark, DE: International Reading Association, 1995. 32–41.

———. "Children's Responses to a Chapter Book across Grade Levels: Implications for Sustained Text." *Multidimensional Aspects of Literacy Research, Theory and Practice.* Eds. Charles K. Kinzer and Donald J. Leu. Chicago: National Reading Conference, 1994. 317–24.

Martinez, Miriam, Nancy L. Roser, James V. Hoffman, and Jennifer Battle. "Fostering Better Book Discussions through Response Logs and a Response Framework: A Case Description." *Literacy Research, Theory and Practice: Views from Many Perspectives.* Eds. Charles

K. Kinzer and Donald J. Leu. Chicago: National Reading Conference, 1992. 303–11.

McGee, Lea M. "An Exploration of Meaning Construction in First Graders' Grand Conversations." *Literacy Research, Theory, and Practice: Views from Many Perspectives.* Eds. Charles K. Kinzer and Donald J. Leu. Chicago: National Reading Conference, 1992. 177–86.

———. "Talking about Books with Young Children." *Book Talk and Beyond: Children and Teachers Respond to Literature.* Eds. Nancy L. Roser and Miriam G. Martinez. Newark, DE: International Reading Association, 1995. 105–16.

Mehan, Hugh. *Learning Lessons: Social Organization in the Classroom.* Cambridge, MA: Harvard University Press, 1979.

Nash, Marcia. "'Leading from Behind': Dialogue Response Journals." *Book Talk and Beyond: Children and Teachers Respond to Literature.* Eds. Nancy L. Roser and Miriam G. Martinez. Newark, DE: International Reading Association, 1995. 217–25.

Peterson, Ralph, and Maryann Eeds. *Grand Conversations: Literature Groups in Action.* Toronto: Scholastic–TAB, 1990.

Pierce, Meredith. *The Darkangel.* New York: Atlantic Monthly, 1982.

Raphael, Taffy E., Virginia J. Goatley, Susan I. McMahon, and Deborah A. Woodman. "Teaching Literacy through Student Book Clubs: Promoting Meaningful Conversations about Books." *Book Talk and Beyond: Children and Teachers Respond to Literature.* Eds. Nancy L. Roser and Miriam G. Martinez. Newark, DE: International Reading Association, 1995. 66–79.

Raphael, Taffy E., Susan I. McMahon, Virginia J. Goatley, J. L. Bentley, F. B. Boyd, Laura S. Pardo, and Deborah A. Woodman. "Research Directions: Literature and Discussion in the Reading Program." *Language Arts* 69 (1992): 54–61.

Rosenblatt, Louise M. *Literature as Exploration.* 3rd ed. New York: Noble & Noble, 1938.

Roser, Nancy L., James V. Hoffman, and Cynthia Farest. "Language, Literature, and At-risk Children." *The Reading Teacher* 43 (1990): 554–59.

Saul, Wendy. "'What Did Leo Feed the Turtle?' and Other Nonliterary Questions." *Language Arts* 66 (1989): 295–303.

Short, Kathy G., and Gloria Kauffman. "'So What Do I Do?' The Role of the Teacher in Literature Circles." *Book Talk and Beyond: Children and Teachers Respond to Literature.* Eds. Nancy L. Roser and Miriam G. Martinez. Newark, DE: International Reading Association, 1995. 140–49.

Wells, Deborah. "Leading Grand Conversations." *Book Talk and Beyond: Children and Teachers Respond to Literature.* Eds. Nancy L. Roser and Miriam G. Martinez. Newark, DE: International Reading Association, 1995. 132–39.

Wiencek, Joyce, and John F. O'Flahavan. "From Teacher-Led to Peer Discussions about Literature: Suggestions for Making the Shift." *Language Arts* 71 (1994): 488–98.

14 Literature Units in the Curriculum

Once on a time when wishes were aplenty, a fisherman and his wife lived by the side of the sea. All that they ate came out of the sea. Their hut was covered with the finest mosses that kept them cool in the summer and warm in the winter. And there was nothing they needed or wanted except a child.

from Greyling *(1968)*
by Jane Yolen

WHAT IS A LITERATURE UNIT?

The opening lines of *Greyling* (1968) generated a discussion about conventions and recurring motifs in folktales and fairytales in the context of a literature unit for fourth-grade students. This unit, structured around sea tales, will be described in some detail later in this chapter to illustrate the study of literature in the classroom. At this point, it is important to address the question "What is a literature unit?"

A *literature unit* is an instructional framework in which children are given opportunities to experience, enjoy, and study literature in the classroom. Each literature unit has a central focus that guides the selection of related texts that are used to develop a cumulative literary experience. This cumulative literary experience takes advantage of the connections between diverse literary texts, between literature and other areas of the curriculum, and between literature and life. As students of literature, children explore these connections and engage in inquiry and discovery, collaborative reasoning and learning, and self-initiated study.

The literature unit described in this chapter is grounded in a reader-response theory of literature. (See Chapter 3 for a discussion of reader-response perspectives.) Students are invited to "live through" each story as a unique personal experience, to reflect on this experience, and to articulate their feelings, responses, understandings, and interpretations in the social context of the group discussions that are a central feature of the unit (Rosenblatt, 1938, 1978). After reflecting on their "lived through" experiences, students are invited to stand back from the text and to respond to it as a literary work.

Literature units promote exploration of the interconnections between fiction, poetry, and nonfiction and diverse areas of the curriculum.

Informational books offer windows through which young readers can see beyond their own experience and learn about nature and the physical world, history and culture, the arts, hobbies and crafts, and sports, as well as about human nature and the lives of others. On the other hand, fiction and poetry offer doors that allow young readers to enter into other lives and view the world through other eyes. Literature is the language of the heart; it has the power to touch minds and hearts by allowing readers to walk in the shoes of fictional characters, respond with empathy and compassion, and make emotional connections. Readers of literature who enter worlds beyond the boundaries of their own experience have opportunities to gain new perspectives and insights about what it means to be human, about the universality of human experience, and about the uniqueness of each human being. Reading literature is also a learning experience when readers stand back and explore the text as a rich source of ideas and information about the world as well as about literature and the craft of writers and artists.

The term "thematic unit" is often used synonymously with the term "literature unit" to describe a multitext, cumulative learning experience that is structured around literature and that is designed to bring literature into the lives of children. In this chapter, we differentiate between literature units and thematic units structured around informational texts that serve as the primary resources for studying a particular topic or problem. That is, when informational books are used as the core of a thematic unit into which fiction and poetry may or may not be integrated, that unit is not the same as a literature unit. In this chapter, the term "literature unit" is used to highlight a *focus on literature*. A literature unit provides a context for aesthetic response to literature as well as opportunities to explore and study literature. Fiction and poetry serve as the core of a literature unit; informational books may or may not be integrated into the unit, and cross-curricular study may or may not be an integral part of the unit. (For more information about thematic units, see the Resources list at the end of this chapter.)

DISTINGUISHING FEATURES OF A LITERATURE UNIT

Research carried out over the past twenty-five years has provided significant insights into literacy and literary learning. These insights serve as a theoretical foundation for the literature unit described in this chapter.

Literature Units Include Many Genres

Literature units are designed to include diverse genres: traditional folktales, fables, nursery rhymes, myths, legends, and epics; modern fantasy; poetry; contemporary and historical realistic fiction; short stories; biography and autobiography; informational books; and picture books. Exposure to a range of genres helps students discover the distinguishing features of each genre, what to expect of each, and the relationships between traditional and modern literature. Students' knowledge of genre is a critical factor in their ability to generate meaning as readers and writers. In addition, each genre makes a distinctive contribution to students' total experience of the particular topic selected as the focus for the literature unit.

Children's experiences with literature trigger questions that serve as springboards for inquiry and exploration.

For example, in a third-grade classroom, a literature unit focusing on birds began with an introduction to a variety of traditional and modern stories and poems featuring birds. The focus for this unit was selected for several reasons: the children's fascination with these creatures, the wealth of quality literature available for developing this unit, and the potential for integrating a study of birds in literature with a study of birds in nature. As the children listened to and read traditional tales in the first segment of this unit, they discovered that birds have been part of folklore since ancient times: the ibis of Egypt; the crows, storks, and cranes in the fables of Aesop; the phoenix in Greek mythology; the crane in Japanese tales; the raven in Native American legends; and the firebird in Russian tales. They discovered that some storytellers used birds as symbols of the soul, peace, and hope; others used birds as symbols of evil and misfortune. They

Illustration 14.1

Trickster characters, found in folklore around the world, are clever and crafty beings who can be mischief-makers or helpers. Gerald McDermott's *Raven*, a 1994 Caldecott Honor Book, is a trickster tale from the Pacific Northwest. (*Raven: A Trickster Tale from the Pacific Northwest* by Gerald McDermott. Illustration copyright © 1993 by Gerald McDermott. Used by permission of Harcourt Brace & Company.)

discovered recurring patterns and literary themes in these traditional tales and learned to recognize the distinguishing features of various genres in the oral tradition.

The second segment of this literature unit explored modern stories and poems featuring birds. The children were able to identify the roots of the modern stories and poems in traditional literature by examining form, motifs, themes, character types, plot patterns, language, and symbolism. They also began to make connections between birds in literature and birds in nature. They found evidence that ancient storytellers and modern writers had observed birds in nature and had used these observations to create stories.

The children's literary experiences triggered questions about bird habits, habitats, and different species. Their questions served as springboards for inquiry and exploration and as the starting point for the third segment of the unit, in which the children consulted informational books and studied birds in nature.

In the final segment of the unit, the children moved from nonfiction back to fiction. They focused on literary themes and patterns and on the craft of authors and artists who incorporated facts about birds into their stories and poems; the next step was to create their own stories and poems about birds. Two of the literary selections used in this unit were **Raven: A Trickster Tale from the Pacific Northwest** (1993), by Gerald McDermott, and **Firebird** (1994), by Rachel Isadora, one of the many Russian tales about this remarkable mythical bird. Other titles can be found in the Recommended Books list at the end of this chapter.

Literature Units Provide Cumulative Experiences

A literature unit provides a cumulative experience, in which students listen to or read and respond to a series of related texts and search for connections between them and between the texts and their own lives. "Learning and understanding are processes of making connections. We are able to understand what we read only because of the connections we make between the current book and our past experiences, which include books we have read or written" (Harste, Short, and Burke, 1988, p. 358). In the cumulative experience of the literature unit, listening to or reading one text serves as a preparation for understanding other texts, and students are encouraged to draw on their own literary histories to enrich each new literary experience and to use intertextual links to generate meaning.

Reading research carried out over the past twenty-five years has generated some important insights about the impact of *prior knowledge* on comprehension. According to Frank Smith, "the meaning that readers comprehend from text is always relative to what they already know and what they want to know" (1988, p. 154). The cumulative literary experiences at the core of literature units provide opportunities for children to engage in the extensive reading that is necessary to (1) build a rich background of prior knowledge about literature, language, the human experience, and the world and (2) bring this enriched background to transactions with new texts.

Literature and Language Arts Are Integrated

In the context of a literature unit, literature and the language arts are integrated. Students listen to, read, and discuss literary texts. In addition, they write about their experiences with and responses to literature and compose their own narratives and poems. Reading and writing are complementary processes of meaning making and communication. According to Sandra Stotsky, "reading experience may be as critical a factor in developing writing ability as writing instruction itself" (1983, p. 637). Frank Smith (1984) emphasizes that learning to write involves learning to read like a writer. Certain knowledge that writers require—such as the knowledge of genres, narrative elements, literary techniques, and linguistic features—resides in texts; so reading like a writer helps students build a background of writers' knowledge. In the context of the literature unit, students are encouraged to study authors' craft to enrich their experiences as readers and as writers. In her book *The Art of Teaching Writing* (1994), Lucy Calkins suggests that authors can serve as mentors when children discover that authors use diverse techniques to elicit reader response. She applies the term "touchstone text" to any book that has the potential to assist young writers: "Any single wonderful text can teach students about dialogue, language, drama, detail, and everything else there is to learn about literature" (p. 278).

In the context of the literature unit, students are invited to engage in other forms of meaning making and communication in addition to the language arts. They are given opportunities to respond to and interpret literature through art, drama, music, and dance (see Chapter 12). They learn to explore and share literary concepts and connections using graphic displays such as language charts and story webs (see Chapter 13).

Student Journals Are Used throughout a Literature Unit

Throughout a literature unit, students write their personal responses in journals. As students experience and respond to literary texts, they record their understandings and questions, their insights and interpretations, their thoughts and feelings in their journals. Journal writing provides a vehicle through which children can respond to literature, and it enables teachers to observe and learn about reader response. A student journal can also take the form of a dialogue journal, in which the teacher responds to student entries and invites the student to engage in a written interchange (Atwell, 1987; Bode, 1989; Staton, 1980, 1989). This ongoing written conversation enables students to participate in both sides of the communication process and helps to reinforce their grasp of the connections between reading and writing (see Chapter 13).

Literature units provide wide-ranging opportunities for independent reading and "book talk" in the social context of a literature-rich curriculum.

The Study of Literature Evolves in a Social Context

The study of literature in a literature unit evolves in a social context. Susan Hepler and Janet Hickman (1982) used the term "community of readers" to describe children who are working together to become readers of literature and to explore and build meanings. A literature unit should provide diverse opportunities for "book talk" (Roser and Martinez, 1995) in whole-group discussions, book clubs, dialogue journals, and other contexts in which children talk about their experiences as readers and writers (see Chapter 13).

A LITERATURE UNIT FEATURING THE SEA: THEORY INTO PRACTICE

In this section, we will give a detailed description of a literature unit to illustrate the translation of the theoretical background into practice. A literature unit featuring the sea was developed for a fourth-grade class. Most of the children in this class had, at some point in their lives, discovered the power of the sea firsthand, and many had expressed a fascination with the sea. The sea was selected as the central topic for this unit in large part in response to the students' expressed interest. Another consideration was the wide variety of traditional and modern stories and poems as well as informational books that could be incorporated into this unit. A third important consideration was the curriculum as a whole and the teacher's goals for students' literary and literacy learning during the school year.

The unit began with literature created by storytellers and writers from around the world who have been moved to interpret the dual nature of the sea through themes of good and evil, fascination and dread, love and hate, life and death. These tales reflect people's ambivalence about the sea: Its power and mystery inspire feelings of awe and wonder as well as terror and hatred.

The eleven whole-group sessions outlined below were developed to provide a cumulative literary experience that gives students an opportunity to find connections between diverse literary texts featuring the sea and between literature and life. This series of sessions was designed to progress naturally from a focus on traditional and modern sea tales and poetry to a focus on realistic fiction and informational books about the sea. In general, the number and content of the whole-group sessions for literature units will vary depending on the nature of the literature selected for the unit, the goals of the teacher, and the needs, interests, and experiences of the students.

Session One: Introducing the Content and Components of the Sea Unit

The unit was introduced in the first whole-group session with the question "What do you know about the sea?" After the students shared their knowledge and experiences, the teacher recorded key words drawn from their comments about the sea on a wall chart and invited them to add to the chart in the course of their study of the sea.

Greyling (1968), written by Jane Yolen and illustrated by William Stobbs, was selected for this first *shared-text experience* to introduce some of the mythical creatures of the sea found in traditional and modern literature. Before reading aloud, the teacher held up the picture book and asked the students to examine and discuss the cover. (See Benedict and Carlisle, 1992.) Many students recognized the author and mentioned some of her other stories they had heard or read. They also talked about the picture of the boy and the seal on the cover and used the cover illustration to make predictions about the story. Most of the students predicted that the story would be about a friendship between a boy and a seal. A few observed that the boy and the seal had similar eyes and wondered why the illustrator created this connection. One student shared some of his own knowledge about seals and concluded, "I think, in a lot of ways, they're sort of like humans." Finally, the teacher explained that this story is rooted in the ancient legends told on the Scottish island of Shetland and made a few comments about the legend as a literary genre. This preliminary discussion set the stage for the literary experience.

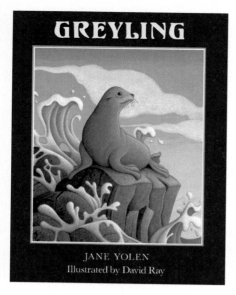

GREYLING

JANE YOLEN
Illustrated by David Ray

Illustration 14.2
For the cover of the 1991 edition of Jane Yolen's *Greyling*, David Ray portrayed Greyling alone after his return to the sea as a seal. (*Greyling* by Jane Yolen. Illustration copyright © 1991 by David Ray. Used by permission of Philomel Books.)

Illustration 14.3
After saving his father, Greyling returns to the sea. Illustrator Ray extends Yolen's text in his interpretation of this bittersweet moment of rescue and farewell. (*Greyling* by Jane Yolen. Illustration copyright © 1991 by David Ray. Used by permission of Philomel Books.)

Greyling is the story of a fisherman and his wife who long for a child of their own. One day, the fisherman finds a small grey seal stranded on a sand bar. When he brings it home, it becomes a human child. The couple love him as a son, but they know he is a Selchie—"men upon the land and seals in the sea." They try to keep him away from the sea, but when the fisherman is about to drown during a terrible storm, Greyling dives into the sea to save him. After listening to the story, the students shared their own thoughts and feelings and returned to their original predictions and questions that had been prompted by the book cover. For example, "Oh . . . now I see why the artist made them [the boy and the seal] look alike . . . the boy *is* the seal!"

As this discussion came to an end, the teacher invited the students to compare the original 1968 edition of *Greyling,* illustrated by William Stobbs, with the 1991 edition, illustrated by David Ray. Most of them expressed a preference for Stobbs's cover: "This one shows the seal and the boy together, and it seems more mysterious. . . . But in this one [David Ray's cover] it's just the seal . . . it looks sort of like a nonfiction book." However, Ray's scenes recording Greyling's rescue of the fisherman generated special interest: "Here, it's more like close-up pictures . . . in the other book you can hardly see Greyling dive into the sea to save his dad." "I like this one because you can see the transformation . . . when the boy changes into a seal." "My favorite one is this one with the seal holding his father in the sea. He's saving him from drowning, but he's also saying goodbye."

At the conclusion of this session, some of the students expressed an interest in reading other stories about selchies; others wanted to read about seals. At this point, the teacher called attention to two display tables set up in a corner of the classroom: one held a collection of traditional and modern sea stories and poems; the other displayed a collection of informational books about the sea. The students were encouraged to browse and to select at least two books from each table for independent reading. Each student was given a notebook to use as a journal for recording personal responses to the books read aloud or independently during the Sea Unit. The journals sometimes became dialogue journals when the teacher wrote responses to students' comments and questions or initiated ongoing conversations with individual students. Small discussion groups, or book clubs, were formed to allow students to talk about and compare their independent reading selections and the works that were read aloud. Students shared selected journal entries in these small book clubs. Thus, the dialogue initiated in the whole-group sessions extended into other interactions in this "community of readers."

To assist the students in choosing books for their independent reading, the teacher or the school librarian provided brief "book talks" about selected titles at the end of each session. For example, at the end of the first session, the teacher highlighted several stories about mythical sea creatures and transformations (see the Recommended Books list at the end of this chapter).

The teacher invited students who had expressed a special interest in seals to work together to gather information from nonfiction texts and other resources in the classroom collection and in the school or local library. Thus, the first research committee was established. When the students in this group had gathered information about seals, they organized it into an illustrated booklet about seals and later shared what they had learned with their classmates.

Session Two: Setting the Stage for Comparative Analysis of Sea Tales

When the teacher held up the book *Sukey and the Mermaid* (1992), retold by Robert San Souci, several African American students expressed surprise and delight: "Look, it's a *black* mermaid! I thought all the mermaids were white!" In response, the teacher read the author's note at the back of the book about the history of this tale and its roots in American and African folklore. This note generated a conversation about the nature of the oral tradition and "retold tales." The dialogue extended the discussion in the previous session about the legend as a traditional literary genre often revived in modern literature.

Sukey lives in a rickety cabin with her mother and stepfather on a little island off the coast of South Carolina. When she escapes from her stepfather's harsh treatment and goes to her secret hideaway by the sea, Sukey encounters a "beautiful, brown-skinned, black-eyed mermaid," who treats her with kindness and takes her to live beneath the sea. In the end, Sukey returns to her home and marries a fisherman selected by the mermaid.

After sharing their personal responses to this story, the students were invited to compare it with *Greyling* and other stories they had selected for independent reading. Excerpts from this comparative analysis reveal some of the connections they discovered: "In both stories, the sea world and the human world are connected." "I read two stories about seal women who married humans and then, later, went back to being seals, like Greyling . . . but they never forgot their human families." "In the selchie stories I read, they were kidnapped . . . their sealskins were stolen. . . . In *Greyling* the fisherman just wanted to help the baby seal." "I read *A Stranger Came Ashore*. The stranger was a selchie . . . but he was an *evil* character!" "I saw this movie with my mom and dad . . . *The Secret of Roan Inish* . . . it's hard to understand unless you know about the selchie legends."

At the conclusion of the session, many of the children were anxious to read some of the stories recommended by their classmates. Several students expressed an interest in writing their own sea legends and/or drawing sea-world pictures. In response, the teacher invited them to form a special author/artist group to create an illustrated collection of original sea legends.

Session Three: Identifying Recurring Literary Themes in Sea Tales

"The Sea of Gold" (1988), adapted by Yoshiko Uchida, is about Hikoichi, a cook on a fishing boat, who feeds the fish every evening for many long years and is rewarded for his kindness by the King of the Sea. After listening to this folktale, the children continued their comparative analysis of the stories they had

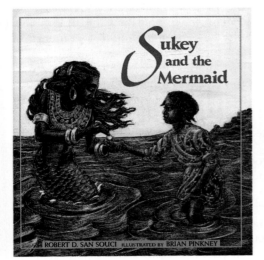

Illustration 14.4
The cover of *Sukey and the Mermaid* reflects the origins of the story in African American as well as African folklore. The book was named a Coretta Scott King Award Honor Book in 1993 for its illustrations. (*Sukey and the Mermaid* by Robert D. San Souci. Jacket illustration copyright © 1992 Brian Pinkney. Used by permission of Simon & Schuster Books for Young Readers, an imprint of Simon & Schuster Children's Publishing Division.)

heard read aloud and read independently for this unit and drew from their knowledge about traditional and modern literature to respond to this tale. "It's an old story that was written down . . . it says it was 'adapted'." "I read 'Urashima' [in Lafcadio Hearn's *The Boy Who Drew Cats* (1963)]. He helps a tortoise, and the Dragon King of the Sea rewards him. It's the rewarding kindness theme, and both storytellers believed in a kingdom under the sea." "I read that story in a poem[*Urashima and the Kingdom Beneath the Sea* (1993), retold by Ralph McCarthy]." "In *Taro and the Sea Turtles: A Tale of Japan* [by Arnold Dobrin 1966], a boy saves the sea turtles, and they save him from pirates." "But in some of the stories people get punished . . . *The Fisherwoman* [a modern fairy-tale by Louise Brierley, 1991] is like that one about the fisherman and his wife [a Grimm tale] when the wife lost everything because she was so greedy."

Having identified this recurring literary theme of reward and punishment in both traditional and modern stories, the students discussed various hypotheses regarding the widespread use of this theme by storytellers and writers across the centuries and throughout the world. They concluded that the value of kindness and the consequences of greed and cruelty have been highlighted in literature from ancient days to modern times.

At the end of this session, members of the special author/artist group shared their original sea legends. Their work inspired others to form another special writing group to create illustrated stories about kingdoms under the sea. Two more research committees were established to study shells and sea turtles. A student who had read Gail Gibbons's *Sea Turtles* (1995) recommended this book to the new Sea Turtle Committee.

By the end of the third whole-group session, the group dialogue had become a cumulative experience in which students made connections and used prior literary experiences to enrich current ones. Initially, the teacher introduced questions to stimulate discussion, guide literary response, and demonstrate for students the kinds of questions they could initiate and use to guide their own explorations of literature. As students gained confidence and became more involved, the literature unit became more student-directed. Students became less dependent on the teacher as a guide in these literary explorations and more involved in student-initiated and collaborative literary response and analysis. The teacher's role gradually changed: Instead of guiding literary response and prompting reluctant participants, the teacher was often able to enter into the collaborative process of literary response and analysis as a student of literature. As more students brought independent reading selections to the group sessions, student-initiated "book talks" began to replace the ones originally initiated by the teacher and the librarian to assist students in selecting books for independent reading.

Illustration 14.5
This cover illustration invites the reader to wonder what the girl hears as she holds the nautilus shell to her ear. (*Prince Nautilus* by Laura Krauss Melmed. Illustration copyright © 1994 by Henri Sorensen. Used by permission of Lothrop, Lee and Shepard Books, a division of William Morrow and Company, Inc.)

Session Four: Comparing Traditional and Modern Sea Tales

When the teacher introduced *Prince Nautilus* (1994) by Laura Krauss Melmed to the group, a member of the Shell Committee shared what she had learned about the many-chambered spiral shell called the nautilus. Most of the children interpreted the picture of the girl on the cover based on their own experiences at the beach: "She's holding the shell up to her ear, so she's listening to the sea." Some of the children predicted that the title character would be a merman who would marry the girl. This original fairytale is about a fisherman's two daughters: Columbine, who is beautiful but vain, cold, and lazy, and Fiona, who is generous, kind, and courageous. Their quest is to save a prince who has been imprisoned in a seashell by an evil wizard. It is Fiona who finally breaks the spell and frees Prince Nautilus from his lonely prison.

After listening to this story, the students initiated a comparative analysis: "This starts out just like Cinderella . . . with the vain sister . . . and Fiona does all the work. . . . But it doesn't end with a wedding!" "When the prince asks Fiona to marry him . . . she refuses him because she wants to go on adventures!" "I know! This author doesn't use the old *stereotype* of a girl . . . Fiona plans to have an interesting life!" "This has the kindness rewarded theme. Fiona helps the fish and the seabird and the sea turtle . . . and then they helped her." "I read . . . *The Children of Lir* [by Sheila MacGill-Callahan, 1993] . . . it's from an Irish legend . . . it's like that story of the seven brothers that were changed into swans. In this story, the king's children are changed into swans, and sea creatures save them." "A lot of the stories have sea creatures that help people . . . like in *Arion and the Dolphins* [by Lonzo Anderson, 1978]. Dolphins save the boy from drowning." "But sea creatures can be dangerous, too . . . like the sea monster in *Prince Nautilus*." "The sea can be good *and* bad. You can go surfing . . . but you can also drown."

At the end of this session, three more research committees were established to study whales, dolphins, and tides and tidal waves.

Session Five: Finding Ancient Roots in Modern Sea Tales

The teacher introduced *The Jolly Mon* (1988), by songwriter and musician Jimmy Buffett and his daughter, Savannah Jane, by reading the dedication included in the book and the "Storytellers' Note" that precedes the story. The first lines of this note provide interesting background for those who read or listen to this tale of a fisherman and his magic guitar:

> It seems that pirates have been throwing musicians into the ocean since the beginning of time, and thankfully dolphins have been around just as long to pluck us out so that we can continue to sing. . . . The poet and musician Arion seems to be the first musician to have gotten the proverbial "hook" as he was traveling and singing his way through Italy around 625 B.C. He was saved by a dolphin who liked music a lot more than the pirates. (n.pag.)

The students responded spontaneously with predictions about the story line as well as relevant information about pirates, dolphins, Caribbean islands, and the constellation Orion. As they listened to the story, they were eager to confirm or revise their initial predictions and to generate new predictions about subsequent events. At the conclusion of the story, the students' comments focused on the mystery of the magical guitar, the dolphin painted on the back, the words inscribed in gold, and the diamond stars forming the constellation Orion. The discovery that the dolphin on the guitar was the very one that saved the Jolly Mon when the pirates pushed him into the sea reminded many of the children of Japanese folktales they had read during a previous literature unit. They identified a number of ancient Japanese tales in which an animal had left the surface on which it had been painted and had come to life—for example, "Kogi" and "The Boy Who Drew Cats" in *Mysterious Tales of Japan* (1996) by Rafe Martin. Those who had selected Lonzo Anderson's *Arion and the Dolphins* (1978) or Vikram Seth's *Arion and the Dolphin* (1995) for independent reading were anxious to compare *The Jolly Mon* with these retellings of an ancient Greek legend: "These stories are about friendship between humans and dolphins, and the dolphins save them." "Here it is again—that theme about the two sides of the sea. It's just like I said . . . you can swim and sail, but you can also drown like the Jolly Mon and Arion almost drowned." "There are friendly dolphins, but in *The Black Horse* [by Marianna Mayer, 1984] the Sea King is evil!" "*The Wave* [a Japanese tale retold by Margaret Hodges, 1964] is about a tidal wave. The sea is the *villain*." "But the sea is good for fishermen!"

This session concluded with the establishment of new research committees on pirates and sunken treasure, islands and lighthouses, and constellations.

Session Six: Exploring Literary Connections and Authors' Craft

When the teacher introduced *The Wreck of the Zephyr* (1983) by Chris Van Allsburg, many of the students identified other titles by this popular author. One student predicted: "This one will probably have something mysterious in it, too!" The story begins with a question about how the wreck of a small sailing boat happened to be at the edge of some cliffs high above the sea. The answer is revealed in a story within a story. The students' responses to this story reflected their willingness and ability to stretch their minds and imaginations to construct meaning, to use their literary histories to enrich their response to this text, and to analyze the text in terms of literary connections and author's craft: "The boy in the story is like that guy who tried to ride Pegasus to Mount Olympus." "He's like Icarus, too." ". . . and the kid who rode too high in the sun chariot! I think this author probably read the Greek myths in fourth grade, too!" "And they all had *warnings* . . . that goddess *warned* him not to ride Pegasus too high. In the Zephyr story, the warning was hidden in that song about Samuel Blue." "A lot of stories have warnings like 'Don't open that door' and you *know* they're going to do it."

Illustration 14.6
Chris Van Allsburg's ominous sky and rolling waves foreshadow the fate of the small boat named *Zephyr*. (*The Wreck of the Zephyr* by Chris Van Allsburg. Copyright © 1983 by Chris Van Allsburg. Used by permission of Houghton Mifflin Company. All rights reserved.)

"But if they *did* obey the warnings, it wouldn't be a very good story . . . nothing much would happen!" "The Zephyr story is like the fables we read last year about pride goes before the fall." "I knew this would have a mystery in it . . . like that the old man is *really* the boy in the story. . . . It's a *flashback*!" "It's also like two stories . . . a 'story in a story.' . . . The traveler asks about the wrecked boat, and then the old man tells the story about it."

This dialogue in response to *The Wreck of the Zephyr* shows that the students seemed to have developed an awareness of authors' craft as well as of the fundamental unity of world literature and the way modern writers have drawn from traditional literature to compose new stories.

At the end of this session, two new research committees were formed to study boats and coral reefs.

Session Seven: Finding Facts in Realistic Fiction about the Sea

In this and several subsequent sessions, the teacher introduced examples of realistic fiction. Before reading aloud *A Thousand Pails of Water* (1978) by Ronald Roy, the teacher reviewed the students' knowledge about tides and whales, since this would be important for understanding this story. Members of the Tides and Whale Research Committees contributed relevant information to this discussion.

Yukio, the central character in Roy's story, is distressed that his father is a whale hunter. When Yukio finds a whale lodged between some rocks on the beach, he realizes that it has been left behind when the tide went out and will not survive out of the sea. Although Yukio makes a valiant attempt to keep the whale alive by himself, it is his father who helps him save the whale's life.

This moving story elicited thoughtful comments about the conflict between the father and son and about the father's decision to help Yukio save the whale. The teacher's question about the possible effect of this episode on the father's and son's attitudes and their relationship stimulated hypothetical statements as the students explored possibilities beyond the text. The author concludes the story at the point when the whale swims out to sea. The students had their own opinions about what would happen next in the lives of the characters. Several chose to write a sequel.

Another question initiated by the teacher—"What factual information do you think the author used to compose this story?"—prompted the students to draw from their knowledge about the patterns of tides and about what whales need to survive. They concluded that the author's use of factual information helped make the story realistic. At this point, the teacher shared a brief news item that had appeared in a newspaper *before* the publication of *A Thousand Pails of Water*. Under the headline "Bucket Brigade Saves Whale," the story from Clacton, England, began with this sentence: "More than 60 children and their parents organized a bucket brigade to save the life of a whale that ran aground at nearby St. Osyth." Since this is exactly what happened in Ronald Roy's story of Yukio, the students concluded that the author had probably based his story on an actual incident and that it could definitely be classified as realistic fiction.

Session Eight: Comparing Nonfiction and Fiction about the Sea

In this session, the teacher introduced a nonfiction account about whales. She showed students the cover of *The Story of Three Whales* (1989) by Giles Whittell. The teacher also drew students' attention to the pages that preceded the title page, which showed reports and photos from several different newspapers about whales trapped in the ice in Alaska. In 1988, the plight of these whales became world news; millions of people followed reports of the rescue attempts that continued for twenty days, until finally a huge Russian ice-breaker was able to free the whales from their ice prison. After reading aloud this brief, illustrated story of an event that had been watched by millions of people, the teacher showed students the last two pages of the book, which contained information about organizations dedicated to saving whales and other wildlife, a list of fiction and nonfiction books about whales, and a list of words about the sea. Several students decided to establish a Save the Whales Committee and to write to some of the organizations listed at the back of the book to learn more about this issue and how they could participate in wildlife preservation.

In the discussion of this story, the students explored differences between nonfiction, realistic fiction, and fantasy and the role of facts in each genre. At the end of this session, the teacher shared examples of fictional accounts of actual events as well as some related informational books. For example, *Ibis: A True Whale Story* (1990), by John Himmelman, is the story of a humpback whale calf that becomes entangled in a fishing net and is freed by a group of whale watchers. In the afterword, the author explained that he saw Ibis in 1985 when he was on a whale-watching boat and heard the story of her rescue. *I Wonder If I'll See a*

Whale (1991) by Frances Weller is a first-person account of a young girl's encounter with a humpback whale during a whale-watching trip, based on the author's experiences with her family. *Harry's Wrong Turn* (1989) by Harriet Ziefert is also about a humpback whale that swims into New York harbor instead of out into the ocean. The author includes a copy of an item in the *New York Daily News* of June 18, 1988, recording the actual incident. "The Three Gray Whales: Persevering Captives of the Ice" is included in a collection of true stories called *Animals Who Have Won Our Hearts* (1994), by Jean Craighead George. The teacher also introduced *Dolphin Adventure: A True Story* (1990), by Wayne Grover, a nonfiction book written by a scuba diver and naturalist about his own remarkable experience eighty feet below the ocean's surface. In eight chapters, he tells the story of his encounter with a family of dolphins and how he saved the life of a baby dolphin that had been caught in a fishing line.

Session Nine: Focusing on the Craft of the Author and Artist

The Boy Who Held Back the Sea (1987), illustrated by Thomas Locker, is an unusual retelling by Lenny Hort of the famous legend of the Dutch boy who held his finger in the dike to stop a leak and protect his village from a flood. This new version of the story is illustrated with striking paintings that reflect the influence of the great Dutch masters. The teacher brought in a book of Dutch paintings so that the students could see the works of Rembrandt and Vermeer, two of the artists who apparently inspired Locker as he created the realistic illustrations for this picture book. Before reading the book aloud, the teacher asked if anyone was familiar with the legend, first told by Mary Mapes Dodge more than a century ago. Quite a few students had heard the story. One boy volunteered to retell it; another explained the purpose of the dikes in Holland and the threat of flooding of land that is below sea level. This discussion provided important background information for understanding Hort's retelling.

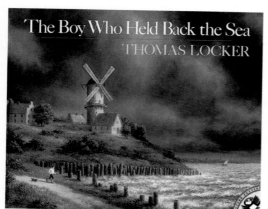

Illustration 14.7

Thomas Locker's stunning oil paintings of landscapes and interiors in *The Boy Who Held Back the Sea* are suggestive of the early Dutch masters. (*The Boy Who Held Back the Sea* by Thomas Locker. Copyright © 1987 by Thomas Locker. Used by permission of Dial Books for Young Readers, a division of Penguin Books USA Inc.)

The students responded to this book with observations about the writer's craft. They noted that Hort had created a story within a story and that the Dutch boy in this retelling was a more richly developed, dynamic character than the original one. They also compared this author with other writers who used facts to create realistic fiction. They found thematic connections with other stories in which a single individual had made a difference in the lives of others.

Session Ten: Connecting Literary Themes about the Sea to Current Social Issues

Jack, the Seal and the Sea (1988) by Gerald Aschenbrenner, adapted by Joanne Fink, is a contemporary story about pollution and an example of a blending of fantasy and realism. Jack, a fisherman, finds a half-dead seal covered with an oily film in his net. He takes care of the seal until its health returns and is rewarded for his kindness. In a dream, Jack hears a voice from the sea pleading for help, and he decides to devote his life to the fight against pollution.

Students drew from their previous encounters with sea tales as well as their experiences with the language of literary analysis to respond to this story. They noticed that the author used traditional folktale themes to create a story about a current issue. They also discovered a third perspective for exploring the relationship between humans and the sea: "In some stories, the sea is an enemy, and in some stories, it's a friend . . . but in this story, *people* are the enemy of the sea because they pollute it, and the sea is the *victim*!"

A new committee was established in response to this story. The Pollution Committee set up a bulletin board to display newspaper and magazine clippings about this problem facing the global community. They produced posters to call attention to the different kinds of pollution, the causes and tragic consequences of pollution, and possible ways to prevent further pollution.

As the students became immersed in the literary experiences that evolved in the course of this literature unit, they developed the habit of responding to each new text in light of texts they had experienced previously. By making connections between diverse texts, they moved beyond each immediate literary experience to generate new meanings and build new understandings. The excerpts drawn from the whole-group sessions in this literature unit reflect and illustrate the cumulative nature of the students' literary experience and the quality of their literary responses as they explored related texts, engaged in inquiry and discovery, and made use of their growing literary and conceptual background to generate meaning.

Session Eleven: Moving from Analysis to Synthesis

Students reviewed the literary themes and concepts discovered in the course of the sea unit to move from analysis toward synthesis. They identified threads that seemed to weave through and interconnect these diverse tales and link them to the literature of the world. Their review highlighted recurring literary themes such as "kindness rewarded" and "greed and pride punished" and motifs such as warnings, helpful animals, transformations, and supernatural characters. They discovered that storytellers around the world have interpreted the dual nature of the sea through themes of good and evil, love and hate, and life and death. In the context of this review, students discussed the literary genres represented in the works used in the unit and the techniques and styles of diverse writers and artists. They explored contemporary writers' use of literary themes and patterns from traditional literature as well as symbolism and allusions to myths, legends, biblical tales, and folktales. Thus, these students began to read like writers and to discover what writers do to create a literary text (Smith, 1984).

These fourth-grade students were learning to bring relevant personal, conceptual, and literary knowledge to each new text to generate meaning. Besides developing this important reading strategy, the students learned to consider each text from the viewpoint of its author: What literary and factual knowledge did the author bring to the composition process?

As a class project, the students produced an illustrated dictionary: "The Sea Dictionary: Fact and Fantasy." They composed definitions and sketches for each word, beginning with *anemone* and ending with *zephyr*. They included words from folklore and legends and from nonfiction about the sea. Members of each research committee contributed key words so that the final product represented a synthesis of the students' diverse explorations and discoveries about the sea.

Final Sessions: Sharing Research Findings

Several class meetings were scheduled to allow the research committees to share what they had discovered and learned. Members of each committee had worked together to study their area of interest and to decide the form in which

Students can share the results of their study of a favorite author or other subject of special interest.

they would present the results of their study to the rest of the class. Committees made murals, seascapes, and treasure maps; wrote plays about pirates, floods, undersea worlds, and heroic deeds; put together booklets about whales, dolphins, sharks, tides, and islands; set up displays of shells and other gifts from the sea; made charts to classify fish and boats; drew posters about pollution and saving the whales; and wrote stories and poems and songs that reflected their study of the sea, their growing background of literary motifs, themes, and techniques, their concerns about the future of the sea, and their ability to integrate fact and fiction.

DEVELOPING A LITERATURE UNIT: AN OVERVIEW

Although the content of literature units varies in accord with students' interests, the school's curriculum, and the teacher's instructional goals, the form of a literature unit is defined by its basic components. Teachers can apply these basic components to the development of diverse units.

Selecting a Focus for the Unit

The first step in developing a literature unit is selecting a focus that has the potential for generating rich and meaningful literary experiences. The selection process is influenced by students' interests and learning needs, by the teacher's instructional goals, by curricular considerations, and by the availability of quality literature that reflects this focus.

Literature units can be structured around (1) *topics,* such as birds or the sea; (2) *literary genres,* such as fables, folktales, or historical fiction; (3) *literary motifs,* such as transformations or magic objects; (4) *literary themes* or significant truths, such as the triumph of the human spirit or the power of love, mercy, and kindness; (5) *character types,* such as tricksters or folk heroes or heroines; or (6) *the craft of authors and artists,* such as the use of viewpoint or the story-within-a-story technique.

Selecting Literary Texts

After determining a focus for the literature unit, the next step is to select a variety of related literary texts that reflect that focus. This book collection should be kept in the classroom for easy access, and students should be invited to add to the collection in the course of the unit. The collection serves as the literary core of the unit and, when appropriate, should include diverse literary genres. By selecting literary texts relating to the focus of the unit, the teacher sets the stage for students to discover unifying literary themes or significant truths embedded in these texts. But the teacher's plans must not impose limits on the students' critical and creative thinking or their imaginative explorations. During the course of most units, students tend to generate meanings, insights, interpretations, and truths that the teacher had not considered during his or her preparations for this cumulative learning experience. In addition to the titles included in the Recommended Books list at the end of this chapter, Appendix D at the end of the book includes a list of professional resources that will assist teachers in the selection process.

Shared-Text Experiences

A literature unit is developed around a series of shared-text experiences in which the teacher reads aloud selected texts and invites the students to discuss these shared texts. This series of whole-class sessions is planned to generate a cumulative dialogue: The text introduced in one session prepares students to explore subsequent texts; responses to each new text are informed by prior literary experiences. The teacher introduces questions that call attention to literary elements and authors' craft and that invite students to engage in literary analysis and to search for connections among texts and between literature and their own lives. Students are encouraged to share personal responses to each text and to articulate and defend opinions and interpretations. Teacher-initiated questions are employed as *teaching tools* to enrich the literary experience and students' responses and to help students learn to generate their own questions as they read and write. Students use their own questions as *learning tools* to guide their own literary transactions and explorations. For example, in the sea unit, the teacher asked students to compare and contrast the shared text **Greyling** (1968) with other stories about mythical sea creatures. Students found similarities in plot patterns, character types, motifs, symbols, and themes—as well as significant differences. In subsequent discussions, the students *initiated* comparative analyses that reflected their own questions about literary connections and patterns as well as differences between related stories.

Independent Reading

The shared-text experiences set the stage for independent reading. Students select one or more of the books in the classroom collection to read independently. These independent reading experiences are informed by the discussions of the shared texts in whole-group sessions, and the students are encouraged to discover connections between the texts they read independently and the shared texts.

Response Journals

Students record their responses to the shared texts and their independent reading in their journals. They are invited to record personal feelings, opinions, interpretations, insights, understandings, and questions; discoveries of connections among literary texts and between literature and life; and responses to teacher-initiated or student-initiated questions about literary elements, genres, and authors' craft. These journals serve as ongoing records of reader response and meaning making as well as vehicles for teachers to learn about their students as readers and writers.

Book Clubs

Students who select the same title, books by the same author, or texts with a common theme form small book clubs to share and discuss their independent reading experiences. Entries from response journals are often used to initiate or enhance the conversation in these book clubs. These student-led groups extend the cumulative dialogue begun in the shared-text sessions. (See Chapter 13 for further discussion of response journals and book clubs.)

Extensions

Throughout the literature unit, students' literary experiences are extended with drama, art, dance, storytelling, and research activities, in which they turn to informational texts to explore areas of interest and to answer questions generated by the literary texts.

Synthesis

At the conclusion of each literature unit, students are given an opportunity to work together toward a synthesis of the ideas and insights derived from their exploration of the related texts introduced in the unit. They review discoveries, insights and understandings, concepts, connections, and knowledge. As they consider each group of stories *as a whole*, students can begin to formulate more comprehensive ideas and insights about literature and life.

For example, as the students explored the shared texts in the sea unit, they discovered recurring literary themes, such as the value of kindness and generosity and the consequences of cruelty and greed. Reflecting on this discovery, they began to move beyond the limits of the unit to explore the significance of this theme in the wider world of literature and in human experience. As they reflected on their discovery of another recurring theme—the dual nature of the sea—their discussion led to a consideration of the potential for other forces of nature—and humans as well—to be good or evil and to bring life or death, beauty or terror.

DEVELOPING LITERATURE UNITS: OTHER POSSIBLITIES

Available texts and the lives of children suggest an almost limitless number of possibilities for developing literature units. For example, the idea for the sea unit initially emerged in response to the students' expressed interests. Two other possibilities for literature units in elementary school classrooms are discussed below. The Resources list at the end of this chapter also suggests possibilities.

Friendship

In response to students' concerns about peer relationships, many teachers have developed units that focus on friendship. For example, one teacher structured a friendship unit for the primary grades around a series of stories about establishing, building, and maintaining friendships. The stories selected for this

Illustration 14.8
Examining this cover, a young reader observed: "The artist tells you how *much* that boy loves to play his violin!" (*Sing to the Stars* by Mary Barrett. Used by permission of Little, Brown and Company.)

literature unit had characters who represented diverse ethnic, racial, and religious backgrounds and who differed from one another in terms of lifestyle, gender, age, culture, physical or cognitive capability, and family structure. Some of the stories' characters lived in urban neighborhoods, others in rural areas; a few were homeless. Some lived in contemporary settings, others in historical settings. For example, a friendship that crosses generations is featured in *Sing to the Stars* (1994), by Mary Brigid Barrett. Other examples of friendship stories can be found in the Recommended Books list at the end of this chapter.

Selecting stories with diversity of characters offers students opportunities to encounter a wide variety of people and to broaden their perspective on the human experience. The friendship unit invited children to make connections between the fictional worlds and their own world and to explore significant themes about social relationships and the nature of friendship.

Literary Genres

Literature units can be structured around literary genres. For example, units featuring fables or legends can introduce children to these forms of traditional literature and help them discover their distinguishing characteristics. Units can be designed to introduce folktales and fairytales from a particular country or from different parts of the world. Units can be developed around giants, dragons, tricksters, or other familiar characters found in traditional literature from various

ASK THE EDITOR . . .

Barbara Elleman

Barbara Elleman

What is your theoretical rationale for developing annotated lists of thematically linked books for classroom use?

Children read, see, remember, and learn in a variety of ways, and in order to become confident learners, they need to have many kinds of materials available. Just as children's bodies vary in height, weight, and shape, so their minds differ in how and what they comprehend. Today's classrooms must be grounded in respect for differences in human growth and development; differences in ethnic, social, and economic backgrounds; and variations in individual tastes, interests, and needs. This concern parallels the need to have many books within arms' reach of young readers. Children need informational books that will take them from where they are in the learning process and propel them toward new horizons, but they also need storybooks, picture books, biographies, and poems that will extend and illuminate facts and statistics. Learning, researchers have found, is more effective when children are energized by their own interests as well as those of concerned and knowledgeable adults working with them. Bringing new and old books together in a thematically linked format and providing annotations and grade ranges can help teachers give children the tools they need to be successful learners.

When approaching a particular subject unit, teachers should consult with their school library media specialist to plan a course of action. Then, working together, they could identify

cultures. Literary motifs such as transformation, magical objects, supernatural helpers, or wishes can also serve as the focus for literature units. Variants of a single type of tale found in diverse cultures around the world can be used to create units that provide opportunities for cross-cultural study and contribute to students' multicultural perspective. Literature units can also be structured around specific categories of stories, such as those about survival, sports, or coming of age or those categorized as mystery or humor.

THE LITERATURE UNIT AND LITERACY AND LITERARY LEARNING

As discussed and illustrated in this chapter, a literature unit creates a learning environment in which students engage in all aspects of the language arts as they respond to literature and in which teachers and students work collaboratively to make connections and generate meaning. The excerpts of students' dialogues from the sea unit, included in earlier sections of this chapter, reflect their active involvement in the unit and the quality of their thinking and problem solving.

a range of books that would bring focus and meaning to the teacher's intended subject. Having a variety of books available allows teachers and students to choose books with appeal and with wide-ranging viewpoints to meet the needs of today's highly diverse classrooms. A work of fiction or a picture book, depending on the grade level, might be chosen for a read-aloud to introduce the unit, but a well-written nonfiction title or a poem, biography, or folktale could work as well. Teachers should introduce the various books to the students, pointing out the different genres and talking about how the students might use the books in their exploration of the topic. Students might then read the books together or individually, discuss the books in groups, or use the books for research projects (or some combination of the three). Drawing from a recommended, thematically linked list can not only save teachers time but, more importantly, can motivate them to tap into their own resources. The ultimate goal, of course, is to help children become lifelong readers and develop lifelong learning patterns.

Favorite Books as a Child

A Child's Garden of Verses
by Robert Louis Stevenson

Make Way for Ducklings
by Robert McCloskey

Caddie Woodlawn
by Carol Brink

Barbara Elleman, former editor of Book Links: Connecting Books, Libraries and Classrooms *and of the Children's Section of* Booklist, *both published by the American Library Association, has been named Distinguished Scholar of Children's Literature at Marquette University. She writes and speaks extensively about children's literature and serves on several advisory boards including those for* The New Advocate, Cobblestone Publishing, *and* Reading Rainbow. *In 1996, she won the Hope S. Dean Award, given by the Foundation for Children's Literature.*

Literature builds bridges between the known and the new; a literature unit invites students to cross these bridges and to make connections between their prior knowledge and new discoveries. A well-planned literature unit provides experiences that stretch students' minds and imaginations and touch their hearts. It creates a social context in which students become actively involved as thinkers, problem solvers, and learners as they explore literary texts that have personal meaning for them.

Judith Langer (1995) describes the role of literature in our lives:

> All literature . . . provides us with a way to imagine human potential. In its best sense, literature is intellectually provocative as well as humanizing, allowing us to use various angles of vision to examine thoughts, beliefs, and actions. (p. 5)

Literature units provide a context for literacy learning and for developing habits and attitudes associated with becoming lifelong readers, writers, and students of literature. With literature units, teachers can introduce literature into the lives of young people so that they can discover for themselves its power and joy.

TEACHING IDEAS

Planning a Literature Unit. Plan a literature unit around traditional tales from diverse cultures that feature characters with opposite traits. Begin with *Mufaro's Beautiful Daughters* (1987), retold by John Steptoe, and select at least four other traditional tales to read aloud in consecutive whole-group sessions. (For example, you may want to use *Toads and Diamonds*, 1995, retold by Robert Bender; *The Stone Lion*, 1994, retold by Alan Schroeder; *The Luminous Pearl*, 1990, retold by Bette Torre; *The Talking Eggs*, 1989, retold by Robert D. San Souci; *Adopted by the Eagles*, 1994, retold by Paul Goble; and/or *Papa Gatto*, 1995, retold by Ruth Sanderson.) What questions would you ask to help your students discover recurring patterns that link these tales and point to clues about human nature? What questions might reveal differences among the stories that point to clues about a particular culture or reflect the influence of a time and place on the storyteller?

Comparative Analysis: Student Discoveries versus Teacher Discoveries. Select four of the following transformation tales to read aloud to your students: *Greyling* (1991), by Jane Yolen; *Selkie Girl* (1986), by Susan Cooper; *The Seal Mother* (1986), by Mordicai Gerstein; *The Mermaid's Cape* (1981), by Margaret Wetterer; *The Seal Prince* (1995) or *The Children of Lir* (1993), by Sheila MacGill-Callahan; *The Swan Children* (1991), by David Day; and *The Black Horse* (1984), by Marianna Mayer. What recurring motifs and themes do the students discover? As you help the students compare the four tales, record discoveries *they* articulate that you had not noticed when you prepared for this literary experience.

Author/Artist Unit. Discuss authors and illustrators with your students. Invite them to identify their favorites and to vote for one author/illustrator team (or an author who illustrates his or her own stories) to study in a literature unit. Use your own knowledge of literature units to develop and implement a unit *with* your students.

EXPERIENCES FOR YOUR LEARNING

1. Read *Snow-White and the Seven Dwarfs* (1972), a tale from the Brothers Grimm translated by Randall Jarrell and illustrated by Nancy Ekholm Burkert, and *Rimonah of the Flashing Sword* (1995), adapted by Eric A. Kimmel and illustrated by Omar Rayyan. Compare these two variants of a single type of traditional tale, noting the similarities and differences between them. Then read *Snow White in New York* (1986), by Fiona French, and note the relationship between this modern revision and the traditional tales. Analyze the craft of this author/illustrator.

2. Prior knowledge enables readers to make predictions as they interact with a text. Select a picture book, and make predictions about the story by looking at the cover. As you read the book, revise or confirm your initial predictions and make new predictions. What prior knowledge from your personal experiences and literary history enabled you to make these predictions?

3. In the context of a literature unit, students are encouraged to study authors' craft to enrich their experiences as readers and writers. Study the author's craft in several children's books. How did your awareness of the techniques used by a specific author enrich your experience as a reader? Select one of these books to use as a "touchstone text" and write your own narrative.

RECOMMENDED BOOKS

* indicates a picture book; **I** indicates interest level
(P = preschool, YA = young adult)

Bird Tales: A Literature Unit for Grade 3

Andersen, Hans Christian. *The Nightingale*. Illustrated by Nancy Ekholm Burkert. New York: Harper & Row, 1965. This is a modern fairytale about an emperor who learns wisdom from a small nightingale. (**I**: 7–10)

* Arnosky, Jim. *All About Owls*. New York: Scholastic, 1995. An informational book with watercolor illustrations of North American owls. (**I**: 5–8)

* Bash, Barbara. *Urban Roosts: Where Birds Nest in the City*. San Francisco: Sierra Club, 1990. An informational book that documents the urban roosts of birds that have adapted to city life. (**I**: 6–9)

Brown, Mary Barrett. *Wings along the Waterway*. New York: Orchard, 1992. An informational book that offers pictures of waterbirds in a style similar to the paintings of John James Audubon. (**I**: 8–11)

Cole, Joanna. *A New Treasury of Children's Poetry*. Garden City, NY: Doubleday, 1984. "The Eagle" by Alfred, Lord Tennyson, and "The Wren" by Issa are suited for use in a unit on birds. (**I**: 8–10)

Esbensen, Barbara. *Tiger with Wings: The Great Horned Owl*. Illustrated by Mary Barrett Brown. New York: Orchard, 1991. Describes the hunting technique, physical characteristics, mating ritual, nesting and child-rearing practices of the great horned owl. (**I**: 7–10)

George, Jean. *The Cry of the Crow*. New York: Crown, 1980. A realistic novel about a girl who tames a wild crow. (**I**: 8–10)

Gibbons, Gail. *The Puffins Are Back!* New York: HarperCollins, 1991. An informational book about the yearly pilgrimage of Atlantic puffins to the coast of Maine to lay eggs and raise their young. (**I**: 7–9)

* Haley, Gail. *Birdsong*. New York: Crown, 1984. A modern fantasy about a girl whose kindness is rewarded by the birds she has freed. (**I**: 7–10)

Hirschi, Ron. *The Mountain Bluebird*. Photographs by Galen Burrell. New York: Penguin/Cobblehill, 1989. Provides detailed information about every aspect of the life of the mountain bluebird. (**I**: 7–11)

* Isadora, Rachel. *Firebird*. New York: Putnam, 1994. A Russian folktale featuring the firebird, a famous mythical bird. (**I**: 7–10)

Johnson, Sylvia. *Raptor Rescue! An Eagle Flies Free*. Photographs by Ron Winch. New York: Dutton, 1995. An informational book about the animal rescue work at the Gabbert Raptor Center in St. Paul, Minnesota. (**I**: 5–8)

* Laurin, Anne. *Perfect Crane*. Illustrated by Charles Mikolaycak. New York: Harper & Row, 1981. A modern fairytale in which a magician brings to life an origami crane he created. (**I**: 7–10)

* McDermott, Gerald. *Raven: A Trickster Tale from the Pacific Northwest*. New York: Oxford University Press, 1993. Raven wants to give people the gift of light, so he sets out to find the sun in this Native American legend. (**I**: 7–10)

* McMillan, Bruce. *Nights of the Pufflings*. Boston: Houghton Mifflin, 1995. An informational book with color photographs about a group of Icelandic children who help young pufflings get safely to the ocean. (**I**: 5–8)

Patent, Dorothy Hinshaw. *The Whooping Crane: A Comeback Story*. Photographs by William Munoz. New York: Clarion, 1988. This book traces the decades-long attempt to save the endangered whooping crane from extinction. (**I**: 8–12)

* Politi, Leo. *Song of the Swallows*. Illustrated by Leo Politi. New York: Scribner's, 1949. A realistic story about a young boy who waits for the swallows to return to his small town. (**I**: 6–8)

Ryder, Joanne. *Dancers in the Garden*. Illustrated by Judith Lopez. San Francisco: Sierra Club, 1992. An informational book about hummingbirds. (**I**: 6–10)

Sattler, Helen Roney. *The Book of Eagles*. Illustrated by Jean Day Zallinger. New York: Lothrop, Lee & Shepard, 1989. An informational book with carefully detailed color drawings on every page. The author discusses the physical characteristics, behavior, and life cycle of eagles and describes individual species such as the African fish eagle, the bald eagle, and the harpy eagle. (**I**: 8–10)

———. *The Book of North American Owls*. Illustrated by Jean Day Zallinger. New York: Clarion, 1995. This informational book follows the same pattern as other Sattler-Zallinger collaborations. (**I**: 8–10)

* Toye, William. *The Loon's Necklace*. Illustrated by Elizabeth Cleaver. New York: Oxford University Press, 1977. A Native American nature myth about the origin of the loon's markings. (**I**: 6–10)

Voeller, Edward. *The Red-Crowned Crane*. Parsippany, NJ: Dillon, 1989. This informational book combines text and color photographs to describe the appearance, behavior, habitat, and current status of the Japanese red-crowned crane. (**I**: 8–10)

White, E. B. *The Trumpet of the Swan.* Illustrated by Edward Frascino. New York: Harper & Row, 1970. This animal fantasy by the author of *Charlotte's Web* has an interesting blend of fantasy and realism. (I: 8–10)

* Wise, William. *The Black Falcon: A Tale from the Decameron.* Illustrated by Gillian Barlow. New York: Philomel, 1990. Because of his love for the beautiful widow Lady Elena, the impoverished knight Federigo sacrifices his single treasure: a peregrine falcon. This is a retelling of a story by the fourteenth-century Italian author Giovanni Boccaccio. (I: 8–10)

* Yagawa, Sumiko. *The Crane Wife.* Illustrated by Suekichi Akaba. New York: Morrow, 1981. A retelling of a traditional transformation tale from Japan. (I: 8–10)

Yolen, Jane. *Bird Watch.* Illustrated by Ted Lewin. New York: Philomel, 1990. An illustrated collection of bird poems. (I: all ages)

———. *The Hundredth Dove and Other Tales.* Illustrated by David Palladini. New York: Crowell, 1977. A collection of original stories rooted in the tradition of the classical folktale. "The Hundredth Dove" features a mysterious connection between the king's bride-to-be and a small white dove. (I: 8–11)

* ———. *Owl Moon.* Illustrated by John Schoenherr. New York: Philomel, 1987. A realistic story of a young girl and her father who share a magical moment one snowy night. (I: 5–9)

Sea Tales: A Literature Unit for Grade 4

Tales of Mythical Sea Creatures and Transformations

Andersen, Hans Christian. "The Little Mermaid." Andersen's modern fairy tale can be found in a wide variety of collections and illustrated editions. (I: 7–11)

* Cooper, Susan. *Selkie Girl.* Illustrated by Warwick Hutton. New York: McElderry, 1986. A seal woman is captured by a human man who wishes to marry her. But she eventually returns to the sea. (I: 7–9)

* Deuchar, Ian. *The Prince and the Mermaid.* New York: Dial, 1990. The prince and the mermaid's happy marriage is threatened when a witch casts an evil spell. (I: 7–9)

* Esterl, Arnica. *Okino and the Whales.* Illustrated by Marek Zawadzki. San Diego, CA: Harcourt Brace, 1995. In this Japanese story, a mother weaves a coat for a whale to gain her daughter's release from the palace of the whales under the sea. (I: 7–9)

* Gerstein, Mordicai. *The Seal Mother.* New York: Dial, 1986. Based on a Scottish folktale, this is the story of a seal who sheds her skin and becomes a beautiful woman. She marries the fisherman who steals her skin, but years later her son finds the sealskin. He knows he should help her return to her seal family in the sea, but he is afraid of losing her forever. (I: 7–10)

* Haley, Gail. *Sea Tale.* New York: Dutton, 1990. When a sea captain falls in love with a mermaid, he goes into the sea to live with her. (I: 7–9)

Hunter, Mollie. *A Stranger Came Ashore.* New York: Harper & Row, 1975. The stranger who comes ashore is a Selchie. In this modern novel, the Selchie is an evil character. (I: 8–12)

* MacGill-Callahan, Sheila. *The Children of Lir.* Illustrated by Gennady Spirin. New York: Dial, 1993. This story is from an Irish legend about the four children of a king, who are transformed into swans by their wicked stepmother. (I: 7–10)

* ———. *The Seal Prince.* Illustrated by: Kris Waldherr. New York: Dial, 1995. A seal man and a human girl fall in love and get married. They live for a while on land and then make their home in the sea. (I: 7–10)

* Martin, Rafe. *The Boy Who Lived with Seals.* Illustrated by David Shannon. New York: Putnam, 1993. A Chinook legend about a lost boy who has grown up with the seals and returns to his tribe. (I: 7–9)

———. *Mysterious Tales of Japan.* Illustrated by Tatsuro Kiuchi. New York: Putnam, 1996. A collection of traditional tales from Japan. The author includes notes about his principal source and inspiration, Lafcadio Hearn. (I: 8–12)

* Noble, Trinka. *Hansy's Mermaid.* New York: Dial, 1983. Hansy's kindness to a mermaid is rewarded in this fantasy tale set in Holland. (I: 6–8)

* Nones, Eric Jon. *Caleb's Friend.* New York: Farrar, 1993. A boy on a fishing boat develops a friendship with a merboy. (I: 7–9)

Osborne, Mary Pope. *Mermaid Tales from Around the World.* Illustrated by Troy Howell. New York: Scholastic, 1993. A collection of twelve mermaid tales from around the world. (I: 8–12)

Peck, Sylvia. *Seal Child.* New York: Bantam, 1991. While visiting at her family's cottage in Maine, Molly becomes friends with a mysterious child. (I: 8–10)

* San Souci, Robert D. *Sukey and the Mermaid.* Illustrated by Brian Pinkney. New York: Four Winds, 1992. When Sukey escapes from the harsh treatment of her stepfather to her secret hideaway by the sea, she encounters a "beautiful, brown-skinned, black-eyed mermaid" who treats her with kindness. (I: 7–10)

Untermeyer, Louis. *The Golden Treasury of Poetry.* 1959. New York: Golden, 1966. See "The Mermaid" and "The Merman" by Alfred, Lord Tennyson. (I: 8–10)

Walsh, Jill Paton. *Matthew and the Sea Singer.* Illustrated by Alan Marks. New York: Farrar, 1992. A seal queen kidnaps a human boy because she likes the sound of his voice. (I: 7–9)

Wetterer, Margaret. *The Mermaid's Cape.* Illustrated by Elise Primavera. New York: Atheneum, 1981. When a fisherman steals a mermaid's cape, she can no longer live in the sea. Although she marries the fisherman, she waits for the day her cape is returned to her. (I: 7–9)

* Yolen, Jane. *Greyling.* Illustrated by William Stobbs. Cleveland: Collins-World, 1968. It is interesting to compare the illustrations in this first edition of Yolen's story with those in the second edition, illustrated by David Ray. (I: 7–10)

* ———. *Greyling.* Illustrated by David Ray. New York: Philomel, 1991. When a fisherman finds an orphaned grey seal pup and takes it home, the seal becomes a human baby. Greyling is a Selchie—"men upon the land and seals in the sea." (I: 7–10)

———. *The Mermaid's Three Wisdoms.* Illustrated by Laura Rader. Cleveland: World, 1978. Fantasy and realism are blended in this story about a girl who has a mermaid for a friend. (I: 8–12)

Recurring Themes: Rewards and Punishments

* Anderson, Lonzo. *Arion and the Dolphins.* Illustrated by Adrienne Adams. New York: Scribner's, 1978. This story of Arion and the dolphins who save him from drowning can be compared with *The Jolly Mon* by Jimmy Buffett. (I: 6–9)

* Brierly, Louise. *The Fisherwoman.* New York: Lothrop, Lee & Shepard, 1991. A woman is punished for her greed after she receives a gift from the sea. (I: 7–9)

* Dobrin, Arnold. *Taro and the Sea Turtles: A Tale of Japan.* New York: Coward-McCann, 1966. After a young boy frees two sea turtles, they save him from pirates. (I: 7–10)

Hearn, Lafcadio. *The Boy Who Drew Cats and Other Tales of Lafcadio Hearn.* New York: Macmillan, 1963. This collection of Japanese tales includes "Urashima," the story of the fisherman who frees a tortoise and is rewarded by the Dragon King of the Sea. (I: 7–10)

* McCarthy, Ralph. *Urashima and the Kingdom Beneath the Sea.* Illustrated by Shiro Kasamatsa. New York: Kodansha, 1993. The story of Urashima is retold in verse. (I: 7–10)

* Moodie, Fiona. *The Boy and the Giants.* New York: Farrar, 1993. Based on a Scottish folktale, this story

is about a boy who goes to a kingdom under the sea to rescue his friend from a giant. (I: 6–9)

* Seth, Vikram. *Arion and the Dolphin.* Illustrated by Jane Ray. New York: Dutton, 1995. This story can be compared with Lonzo Anderson's version listed above. (I: 6–9)

Uchida, Yoshiko. *The Sea of Gold and Other Tales from Japan.* 1965. Illustrated by Marianne Yamaguchi. Berkeley, CA: Creative Arts, 1988. In "The Sea of Gold," the Dragon King of the sea rewards a cook on a fishing boat for his kindness to the fish. (I: 7–10)

Recurring Patterns: Dual Nature of the Sea

* Hodges, Margaret. *The Wave.* Illustrated by Blair Lent. Boston: Houghton Mifflin, 1964. An old man saves the villagers from a tidal wave in this old tale from Japan. (I: 7–10)

* Mayer, Marianna. *The Black Horse.* Illustrated by Katie Thamer. New York: Dial, 1984. A young man challenges the power of the evil Sea King with the help of an enchanted horse. (I: 7–10)

* San Souci, Robert D. *The Samurai's Daughter: A Japanese Legend.* Illustrated by Stephen Johnson. New York: Dial, 1992. Tokoyo, the daughter of a samurai nobleman, sets out on a quest to rescue her exiled father. She encounters bandits, a ghost ship, and a monstrous sea serpent. (I: 8–10)

Yolen, Jane. *The Hundredth Dove.* Illustrated by David Palladini. New York: Crowell, 1977. This collection of original stories includes "The Wind Cap," the story of Jon, who saves the life of a tiny green turtle and is rewarded with a magic cap full of wind—"the kind that sailors most desire." (I: 8–10)

Modern Sea Tales: Fantasy and Realism

* Aschenbrenner, Gerald. *Jack, the Seal, and the Sea.* Adapted by Joanne Fink. Englewood Cliffs, NJ: Silver Burdett, 1988. Jack, a fisherman, finds a seal covered with oil in his net. When he frees the seal, he is rewarded for his kindness. This contemporary story is about pollution, but the author blends realism with traditional folktale patterns. (I: 6–9)

* Buffett, Jimmy, and Savannah Jane Buffett. *The Jolly Mon.* Illustrated by Lambert Davis. San Diego, CA: Harcourt, 1988. This story is about a magical guitar and a dolphin that saves the Jolly Mon from drowning after pirates push him overboard. (I: 7–9)

* Cooney, Barbara. *Island Boy.* New York: Viking/Kestrel, 1988. Matthias grows from a little boy to a grandfather on a small island out in the bay. It is known as Tibbetts Island for the family that first made a home there. (I: 6–8)

Grover, Wayne. *Dolphin Treasure.* Illustrated by Jim Fowler. New York: Greenwillow, 1996. In a sequel to *Dolphin Adventure,* the author weaves fact and fiction together. In this story, he is searching for buried treasure sunk with a Spanish galleon off the Florida coast when a storm arises and his dolphin comes to his rescue. (I: 7–10)

* Himmelman, John. *Ibis: A True Whale Story.* New York: Scholastic, 1990. A humpback whale calf that becomes entangled in a fishing net is freed by a group of whale watchers. (I: 6–8)

* Hort, Lenny. *The Boy Who Held Back the Sea.* Illustrated by Thomas Locker. New York: Dial, 1987. The author uses a story-within-a-story device in this unusual retelling of the story of the Dutch boy who held his finger in the dike to stop a leak and protect his village from a flood. (I: 6–9)

* Lasky, Kathryn. *My Island Grandma.* Illustrated by Emily McCully. New York: Warne, 1979. Abbey describes all the things she does with her grandmother during the summers they spend on an island off the coast of Maine. (I: 6–8)

* Lent, Blair. *Bayberry Bluff.* Boston: Houghton Mifflin, 1987. A real village with houses grows up on an island where people first spent summers in tents. (I: 6–8)

* Martin, Charles. *Island Winter.* New York: Greenwillow, 1984. Staying behind on an island after the summer people have left, Heather wonders what there will be to do. (I: 6–8)

* Melmed, Laura Krauss. *Prince Nautilus.* Illustrated by Henri Sorensen. New York: Lothrop, Lee & Shepard, 1994. This is an original fairytale about a fisherman's daughter who frees Prince Nautilus, who has been imprisoned in a seashell by an evil wizard. (I: 6–9)

* Orr, Katherine. *Story of a Dolphin.* Minneapolis, MN: Carolrhoda, 1993. This is a story of a friendship between a man and a dolphin. (I: 6–9)

* Radcliffe, Theresa. *Cimru the Seal.* Illustrated by John Butler. New York: Viking, 1996. This is a true-to-life story of seals' struggle for survival in the waters off Scotland's Shetland Islands. (I: 6–8)

* Rand, Gloria. *Prince William.* Illustrated by Ted Rand. New York: Holt, 1992. On Prince William Sound in Alaska, Denny rescues a baby seal hurt by an oil spill and watches it recover in a nearby animal hospital. (I: 6–9)

* Roy, Ronald. *A Thousand Pails of Water.* Illustrated by Vo-Dinh Mai. New York: Knopf, 1978. Yukio finds a whale lodged between some rocks on the beach. He makes a valiant attempt to keep the whale alive by himself until his father and the villagers arrive to help him save its life. (I: 6–9)

* Van Allsburg, Chris. *The Wreck of the Zephyr.* Boston: Houghton Mifflin, 1983. An old man explains the mystery of a small sailing boat that is on the edge of some cliffs high above the sea. (I: 7–10)

* Weller, Frances Ward. *I Wonder If I'll See a Whale.* New York: Philomel, 1991. A first-person account of a young girl's encounter with a humpback whale. (I: 6–8)

* Ziefert, Harriet. *Harry's Wrong Turn.* Boston: Little, Brown, 1989. A humpback whale swims into New York harbor instead of out to sea. (I: 6–8)

Informational Books about the Sea

Bender, Lionel. *Island.* New York: Watts, 1989. Color photographs and drawings are used along with the text to offer a geological explanation of the formation, characteristics, and properties of islands and a discussion of their historical importance. From *The Story of the Earth* series. (I: 8–10)

George, Jean Craighead. *Animals Who Have Won Our Hearts.* New York: HarperCollins, 1994. This collection of true stories includes the story of three whales rescued from their ice prison. (I: 6–9)

Gibbons, Gail. *Beacons of Light: Lighthouses.* New York: Morrow, 1990. A survey of lighthouses and how they work with simple text and pictures. (I: 6–8)

———. *Pirates: Robbers on the High Seas.* Boston: Little, Brown, 1993. Gibbons chronicles the world of pirates including the exploits of famous villains such as Captain Kidd and Blackbeard. (I: 6–8)

———. *Sea Turtles.* New York: Holiday House, 1995. Gibbons's colorful drawings and text introduce young readers to a variety of sea turtle species and point out their similarities and differences. She has also written and illustrated books about whales and sharks for young readers. (I: 5–8)

———. *Sunken Treasure.* New York: Crowell, 1988. Gibbons describes the long search for the treasure that went down with the *Atocha,* a Spanish galleon sunk off the Florida coast in a hurricane in 1622. Students may want to read this with Wayne Grover's *Dolphin Treasure.* (I: 6–9)

Grover, Wayne. *Dolphin Adventure: A True Story.* New York: Greenwillow, 1990. A scuba diver and naturalist tells his own story of saving a baby dolphin caught in a fishing line. (I: 7–10)

Mallory, Kenneth, and Andrea Conley. *Rescue of the Stranded Whales.* New York: Simon & Schuster, 1989. Students may want to read other stories of this rescue mission along with this informational book with color photographs. (I: 7–9)

* McMillan, Bruce. *Going on a Whale Watch*. New York: Scholastic, 1992. A photo guide about whales and whale-watching. (I: 6–8)

McWilliams, Karen. *Pirates*. New York: Watts, 1989. Describes the ships, social conditions, rules, and behavior of pirates and includes stories from the lives of famous pirates such as Blackbeard and Anne Bonny. (I: 6–9)

Milton, Joyce. *Whales, the Gentle Giants*. Illustrated by Alton Langford. New York: Random House, 1989. This informational book, part of the *Step-into-Reading* series, describes how whales live and some different types of whales. (I: 6–8)

Simon, Seymour. *Sharks*. New York: HarperCollins, 1995. In this photo essay, Simon explains that sharks have been around for tens of thousands of years and offers other interesting information that helps to overcome the view of sharks as monsters. (I: 5–8)

———. *Whales*. New York: Crowell, 1989. Color photographs accompany the text in this informative book about the physical characteristics, habits, and natural environment of various species of whales. (I: 6–9)

White, Sandra, and Micheal Filisky. *Sterling: The Rescue of a Baby Harbor Seal*. New York: Crown, 1989. Text and photographs follow the story of an abandoned harbor seal pup that is rescued and cared for at the New England Aquarium until she is strong enough to return to her natural environment. (I: 6–9)

* Whittell, Giles. *The Story of Three Whales*. Milwaukee: Gareth Stevens, 1989. This is the story of the remarkable rescue of three whales trapped in the ice in Alaska in 1988. (I: 6–9)

Friendship Tales: A Literature Unit for the Primary Grades

* Ackerman, Karen. *The Tin Heart*. Illustrated by Michael Hayes. New York: Atheneum, 1990. The story of best friends whose families are on opposing sides during the Civil War. (I: 7–10)

* Barrett, Mary. *Sing to the Stars*. Illustrated by Sandra Speidel. Boston: Little, Brown, 1994. A friendship that crosses generations. (I: 7–10)

Bulla, Clyde. *The Chalk Box Kid*. New York: Random House, 1987. A chapter book about a friendship between a boy and a girl who share an interest in art. (I: 8–11)

Bunting, Eve. *Summer Wheels*. Illustrated by Thomas Allen. San Diego, CA: Harcourt, 1992. A chapter book about friendships that cross lines of race and age. (I: 8–11)

* Clifton, Lucille. *Three Wishes*. Illustrated by Michael Hayes. New York: Delacorte, 1992. A picture book about a boy-girl friendship. (I: 6–8)

* Grimes, Nikki. *Meet Danitra Brown*. Illustrated by Floyd Cooper. New York: Lothrop, Lee & Shepard, 1994. An African American girl uses poetry to express her ideas of friendship. (I: 7–10)

* Havill, Juanita. *Jamaica and Brianna*. Illustrated by Anne Sibley O'Brien. Boston: Houghton Mifflin, 1993. This friendship survives a misunderstanding. (I: 5–7)

* Hesse, Karen. *Lester's Dog*. Illustrated by Nancy Carpenter. New York: Crown, 1993. One of the friends in this picture book is a child with a physical disability. (I: 6–10)

* Johnston, Tony. *Amber on the Mountain*. Illustrated by Robert Duncan. New York: Dial, 1994. This picture book tells the story of a friendship between a girl whose home is on an isolated mountain and a girl whose home is in the city. (I: 6–9)

* Jones, Rebecca. *Matthew and Tilly*. Illustrated by Beth Peck. New York: Dutton, 1991. A picture book about a friendship that crosses lines of gender and race. (I: 5–8)

* Kroll, Virginia. *Pink Paper Swans*. Illustrated by Nancy Clouse. Grand Rapids, MI: Eerdmans, 1994. The friendship in this picture book crosses lines of age and culture. (I: 7–10)

* Polacco, Patricia. *Mrs. Katz and Tush*. New York: Bantam, 1992. The friendship in this picture book is between two people of different ages, religions, races, and genders. (I: 6–9)

* Russo, Marisabina. *Alex Is My Friend*. New York: Greenwillow, 1992. Alex's physical handicap is not a barrier for the best friends featured in this picture book. (I: 7–9)

Soto, Gary. *The Skirt*. Illustrated by Eric Velasquez. New York: Delacorte, 1992. This book for transitional readers features a Mexican American girl. (I: 7–10)

* Weisman, Joan. *The Storyteller*. Illustrated by David Bradley. New York: Rizzoli, 1993. This story features an intergenerational friendship. (I: 8–11)

Survival Tales: A Literature Unit for Grades 4–6

Survival in Nature

George, Jean Craighead. *Julie of the Wolves*. New York: Harper & Row, 1972. Thirteen-year-old Julie manages to survive alone on the Alaskan tundra with the help of a pack of Arctic wolves who come to accept her as a friend as she learns to communicate with them. (I: 9–12)

———. *My Side of the Mountain*. New York: Dutton, 1959. This is the story of the survival of a city boy who chooses to spend the winter alone in the Catskill Mountains. (I: 8–12)

Mazer, Harry. *Snowbound*. New York: Delacorte, 1973. Two teenagers are stranded during a blizzard in a desolate area far from the main highway in New York State. (I: 9–12)

O'Dell, Scott. *Island of the Blue Dolphins*. Boston: Houghton Mifflin, 1960. Based on actual events, this is the story of Karana, who survived alone on an island off the coast of California for eighteen years. (I: 9–12)

Paulsen, Gary. *Hatchet*. New York: Bradbury, 1987. Thirteen-year-old Brian Robeson is on his way to visit his father in the Canadian wilderness when the pilot of the small plane in which he is the only passenger suffers a fatal heart attack. Brian manages to crash-land the plane in an isolated lake and then survives for fifty-four days on his own in the wilds. (I: 9–12)

Southall, Ivan. *Ash Road*. New York: Greenwillow, 1965. A group of children, cut off from adult help, struggle to survive a raging bush fire in Australia. (I: 9–12)

Survival in the City

Fox, Paula. *Monkey Island*. New York: Orchard, 1991. Eleven-year-old Clay Garrity is forced to live on the streets of New York City when his mother disappears from their room in a welfare hotel. (I: 9–12)

Hamilton, Virginia. *The Planet of Junior Brown*. New York: Macmillan, 1971. The story of homeless children struggling to survive in the inner city in a complex network of secret underground shelters, called "planets." (I: 9–13)

Holman, Felice. *Slake's Limbo*. 1974. New York: Scribner's, 1986. Thirteen-year-old Aremis Slake is an orphan who escapes from the cruelty and degradation that mark his existence and finds refuge in a cave-like room hidden in New York City's subway system. (I: 9–13)

Paterson, Katherine. *Lyddie*. New York: Dutton, 1991. This is an historical novel set in New England in the nineteenth century. Thirteen-year-old Lyddie is on her own, working in a textile mill in Lowell, Massachusetts. (I: 9–13)

Paulsen, Gary. *The Crossing*. New York: Dell, 1987. Fourteen-year-old Manuel Bustos is a Mexican orphan fighting to survive alone on the streets of Juarez. His only hope for survival is to cross through the shallows of the Rio Grande to get to Texas. (I: 9–14)

Voigt, Cynthia. *Homecoming*. New York: Atheneum, 1981. Four children, abandoned by their parents, walk the length of the Connecticut coastline along Route 1 to find a home. (I: 9–14)

Survival during War and Revolution

Choi, Sook Nyul. *Year of Impossible Goodbyes*. Boston: Houghton Mifflin, 1991. This is the story of a North Korean girl's escape to freedom in the 1940s. (I: 9–14)

Hautzig, Esther. *The Endless Steppe*. New York: Harper & Row, 1968. The author describes her experiences in a slave labor camp in Siberia during World War II. (I: 9–14)

Ho, Minfong. *The Clay Marble*. New York: Farrar, 1991. A moving account of refugees in war-torn Cambodia during the 1980s. (I: 9–14)

Holman, Felice. *The Wild Children*. New York: Scribner's, 1983. Set in Russia during the period following the Bolshevik Revolution, this is the story of children left homeless because their parents were dead or imprisoned. They banded together in packs to survive in Moscow on their own without adults. (I: 9–14)

Houston, Jeanne Wakatsuki. *Farewell to Manzanar*. Boston: Houghton Mifflin, 1973. The Japanese American narrator tells her own story of life behind barbed wire in an internment camp in World War II. (I: 9–14)

Laird, Christa. *Shadow of the Wall*. New York: Greenwillow, 1989. The central character is a young boy living in the Warsaw ghetto as the Nazis tighten their control and intensify their brutality against the Jews in 1942. (I: 9–14)

Matas, Carol. *Daniel's Story*. New York: Scholastic, 1993. This is the story of one Jewish boy's journey during the late 1930s. He and his family were forced out of their home in Frankfurt by the Nazis. They were first sent to the Lodz ghetto in Poland and then to Auschwitz, the Nazi death camp. (I: 9–14)

O'Dell, Scott. *Sarah Bishop*. Boston: Houghton Mifflin, 1980. This is a fictionalized biography of a young girl caught in the middle of the conflict between the rebels and the redcoats during the American Revolution. She flees the British and the killing into the Connecticut wilderness. (I: 9–14)

Orlev, Uri. *The Island on Bird Street*. Boston: Houghton Mifflin, 1984. An eleven-year-old Jewish boy hides in a deserted Polish ghetto during World War II. (I: 9–14)

Watkins, Yoko Kawashima. *My Brother, My Sister, and I*. New York: Bradbury, 1994. Sequel to *So Far from the Bamboo Grove*. (I: YA)

———. *So Far from the Bamboo Grove*. New York: Lothrop, Lee & Shepard, 1986. Chronicles the flight of a Japanese family from Korea during World War II. (I: YA)

William Steig, Author and Illustrator: A Literature Unit for the Primary Grades

* Steig, William. *The Amazing Bone*. New York: Farrar, 1976. A magical bone saves Pearl from the villain. (I: 5–8)

* ———. *Amos and Boris*. New York: Farrar, 1971. A modern counterpart of Aesop's fable "The Lion and the Mouse." (I: 5–8)

* ———. *Caleb and Kate*. New York: Farrar, 1977. A witch changes Caleb into a dog, so he cannot tell his wife, Kate, who he is. (I: 5–8)

* ———. *Doctor De Soto*. New York: Farrar, 1982. A mouse dentist and his wife/assistant outwit a fox. (I: 5–8)

* ———. *Roland the Minstrel Pig*. New York: Harper & Row, 1968. Roland's quest-journey is interrupted by a hungry fox. (I: 5–8)

* ———. *Solomon the Rusty Nail*. New York: Farrar, 1985. Solomon discovers that magic can be danger-ous. (I: 5–8)

* ———. *Sylvester and the Magic Pebble*. 1969: New York: Simon & Schuster, 1979. To escape from a lion, Sylvester uses his magic pebble to become a rock. But how will he change back into himself? (I: 5–8)

* ———. *Zeke Pippin*. New York: HarperCollins, 1994. Zeke discovers that the harmonica he finds in the street has magical powers. (I: 5–8)

Magic Object Tales: A Literature Unit for Grades K–4

* Demi. *Chen Ping and His Magic Axe*. New York: Dodd Mead, 1987. Chen Ping's honesty earns him a magic axe. (I: 6–8)

* ———. *Liang and the Magic Paintbrush*. New York: Holt, 1980. When Liang uses his magic paintbrush his pictures come alive. (I: 6–9)

* de Paola, Tomie. *Strega Nona*. Englewood Cliffs, NJ: Prentice-Hall, 1975. When Strega Nona is away, Big Anthony loses control of the magic pasta pot. (I: 6–8)

* Galdone, Paul. *The Magic Porridge Pot*. Boston: Houghton Mifflin, 1976. Without the specific words, the magic pot won't stop making porridge. (I: 5–8)

* Haviland, Virginia. *The Talking Pot: A Danish Folk-tale*. Illustrated by Melissa Sweet. Boston: Little, Brown, 1990. A poor man sells his only cow for a three-legged pot that skips to the rich man's house

and returns with food and riches for the poor family. (I: 5–8)

* Kimmel, Eric. *Anansi and the Moss-Covered Rock*. Illustrated by Janet Stevens. New York: Holiday House, 1988. Anansi, the trickster, uses the magic rock to trick the other animals, until little Bush Deer teaches him a lesson. (I: 5–8)

* ———. *The Tale of Aladdin and His Wonderful Lamp: A Story from the Arabian Nights*. Illustrated by Ju-Hong Chen. New York: Holiday House, 1992. Children can compare this edition with other illus-trated editions of the Aladdin tale. (I: 6–9)

* Lionni, Leo. *Alexander and the Wind-Up Mouse*. New York: Pantheon, 1969. Alexander the mouse makes a wish with a magical purple pebble. (I: 5–8)

* Scott, Sally. *The Magic Horse*. New York: Greenwillow, 1985. This story from *The Arabian Nights* is about a Persian prince who uses a life-size ebony horse to outwit an evil wizard and to marry the princess he loves. (I: 7–9)

* Towle, Faith. *The Magic Cooking Pot*. Boston: Hough-ton Mifflin, 1975. Towle uses batik to retell this tale of ancient India about a poor man whose magic cooking pot is stolen by a greedy innkeeper. (I: 7–9)

American Folk Heroes and Heroines: A Literature Unit for Grades 1–6

Brooke, William. *A Telling of the Tales: Five Stories*. Illustrated by Richard Egielski. New York: Harper-Collins, 1990. This collection of nontraditional re-tellings of traditional tales includes the story of an encounter between Paul Bunyan, the logger, and Johnny Appleseed, the environmentalist. (I: 8–12)

* Cohen, Caron Lee. *Sally Ann Thunder Ann Whirlwind Crockett*. Illustrated by Ariane Dewey. New York: Greenwillow, 1985. This tall tale heroine, the fic-tional wife of Davy Crockett, wore a snake for a belt and used a bowie knife for a toothpick. (I: 7–9)

Hamilton, Virginia. *The People Could Fly: American Black Folktales*. Illustrated by Leo and Diane Dil-lon. New York: Knopf, 1985. In this collection of twenty-four tales, Hamilton tells the stories of slaves and fugitives that are part of her own heritage as an African American. (I: 8–14)

* Kellogg, Steven. *Johnny Appleseed*. New York: Morrow, 1988. Kellogg presents the life of John Chapman, better known as Johnny Appleseed, who distributed apple seeds and trees across the Midwest. (I: 6–9)

* ———. *Mike Fink*. New York: Morrow, 1992. Mike Fink is the legendary keel-boat operator and fron-tiersman who wrestled bears to become the strongest man on the Mississippi River. (I: 7–9)

* ———. *Paul Bunyan*. New York: Morrow, 1984. This is one of the many stories of this mythical giant folk hero. (I: 7–9)

* ———. *Pecos Bill*. New York: Morrow, 1986. This story of the tall tale hero who became the first cattle rancher begins with his childhood among the coyotes and ends with his wedding day. (I: 7–9)

* ———. *Sally Ann Thunder Ann Whirlwind Crockett*. New York: Morrow, 1995. Compare this edition with the illustrated retelling by Cohen and Dewey. (I: 7–9)

* Lester, Julius. *John Henry*. Illustrated by Jerry Pinkney. New York: Dial, 1994. This is the legendary African American hero who raced against a steam drill to cut through a mountain. (I: 7–9)

Osborne, Mary Pope. *American Tall Tales*. Illustrated by Michael McCurdy. New York: Knopf, 1991. A collection of nine tall tales about American folk heroes such as Davy Crockett and Paul Bunyan and the folk heroine Sally Ann Thunder Ann Whirlwind Crockett. (I: 8–12)

San Souci, Robert D. *Cut from the Same Cloth: American Women of Myth, Legend, and Tall Tale*. Illustrated by Brian Pinkney. New York: Philomel, 1993. This collection of stories about legendary American heroines includes two about female giant slayers. (I: 8–12)

Sanfield, Steven. *The Adventures of High John the Conquerer*. Illustrated by John Ward. New York: Orchard, 1989. Sixteen retellings of stories about High John, the nineteenth-century African American trickster hero. (I: 9–14)

Stoutenberg, Adrien. *American Tall Tales*. Illustrated by Richard Powers. New York: Penguin, 1976. The stories in this collection have fitting titles such as "Sky-bright Axe" (about Paul Bunyan) and "Hammerman" (about John Henry). (I: 8–12)

Stories from China or about Chinese Americans: A Literature Unit for Grades 1–6

Chang, Heidi. *Elaine, Mary Lewis, and the Frogs*. New York: Crown, 1988. This contemporary realistic novel for transitional readers is about a Chinese American girl who feels like an outsider in her new school until she meets Mary Lewis. (I: 7–9)

* Demi. *The Empty Pot*. New York: Holt, 1990. The Emperor rewards Ping for his honesty. (I: 6–8)

* ———. *The Magic Boat*. New York: Holt, 1990. When Chang rescues an old man from a river, he is rewarded with a small magical dragon boat. (I: 6–8)

* Heyer, Marilee. *The Weaving of the Dream: A Chinese Folktale*. New York: Viking, 1986. After a woman weaves a magnificent tapestry, it blows away. The youngest of her three sons perseveres in his quest to retrieve it for her. (I: 8–12)

* Leaf, Margaret. *Eyes of the Dragon*. Illustrated by Ed Young. New York: Lothrop, Lee & Shepard, 1987. An artist agrees to paint a dragon on the wall of a village, but the magistrate's demand that he paint the eyes on the dragon has surprising results! (I: 7–9)

Lord, Bette Bao. *In the Year of the Boar and Jackie Robinson*. Illustrated by Marc Simont. New York: Harper & Row, 1984. An autobiographical novel about a Chinese girl who learns to love baseball as she adjusts to her new life in the United States. (I: 9–12)

* Louie, Ai-Ling. *Yeh-Shen: A Cinderella Story from China*. Illustrated by Ed Young. New York: Philomel, 1982. A young girl is rewarded for her kindness to her pet fish. (I: 8–12)

* Mahy, Margaret. *The Seven Chinese Brothers*. Illustrated by Jean and Mou-sien Tseng. New York: Scholastic, 1990. Seven brothers use their special powers to help others and to escape the cruelty of the emperor. (I: 7–9)

Namioka, Lensey. *Yang the Third and Her Impossible Family*. Boston: Little, Brown, 1995. This sequel to Namioka's earlier book features Third Sister. (I: 8–10)

———. *Yang the Youngest and His Terrible Ear*. Illustrated by Kees de Kiefte. Boston: Little, Brown, 1992. This humorous contemporary realistic novel is about nine-year-old Yingtao, who moves with his musical family from China to Seattle. (I: 8–12)

* Rappaport, Doreen. *The Long-Haired Girl: A Chinese Legend*. Illustrated by Yang Ming-Yi. New York: Dial, 1995. A young girl risks her life to bring water to the villagers. (I: 8–12)

Sadler, Catherine. *Treasure Mountain: Folktales from Southern China*. Illustrated by Chen Mung Yun. New York: Atheneum, 1982. Six tales about peasants who suffer under the rule of evil officials. (I: 8–12)

* Say, Allen. *El Chino*. Boston: Houghton Mifflin, 1990. A biography of Bill Wong, a Chinese American who became a famous bullfighter in Spain. (I: 8–10)

* Torre, Bette. *The Luminous Pearl: A Chinese Folktale*. Illustrated by Carol Inouye. New York: Orchard, 1990. Two brothers set out on a quest to prove their honesty and bravery in order to win the hand of the Dragon King's daughter. (I: 8–10)

* Wang, Rosalind. *The Fourth Question: A Chinese Tale*. Illustrated by Ju-Hong Chen. New York: Holiday House, 1991. A young man is rewarded for keeping his promise to those who entrusted him with their questions for the wise man. (I: 8–10)

* Wilson, Barbara Ker. *Wishbones: A Folktale from China*. Illustrated by Meilo So. New York: Bradbury, 1993. Compare this story of Yeh Hsein with the version retold by Louie and illustrated by Young. (I: 8–10)

Yee, Paul. *Tales from Gold Mountain: Stories of the Chinese in the New World*. Illustrated by Simon Ng. New York: Macmillan, 1990. Eight original stories based on the experiences of Chinese immigrants. (I: 9–12)

Yep, Laurence. *Child of the Owl*. New York: Harper & Row, 1977. A contemporary realistic novel about a Chinese American girl who discovers her roots in San Francisco's Chinatown. (I: 9–13)

———. *Dragonwings*. New York: Harper, 1977. This historical novel portrays Chinese immigrants in San Francisco after 1900. (I: 9–13)

* ———. *The Man Who Tricked a Ghost*. Illustrated by Isadore Seltzer. Mahwah, NJ: Troll/Bridgewater, 1993. Sung encounters a ghost on a dark, deserted road. (I: 7–10)

———. *The Rainbow People*. Illustrated by David Wiesner. New York: Harper, 1989. Twenty folktales brought to the United States by Chinese immigrants. (I: 8–12)

* ———. *The Shell Woman and the King: A Chinese Folktale*. Illustrated by Yang Ming-Yi. New York: Dial, 1993. A young woman agrees to bring an evil king three wonders in order to save her husband and herself. (I: 8–10)

———. *The Star Fisher*. New York: Morrow, 1991. This historical novel portrays the challenges faced by a Chinese American family who move to West Virginia in 1927. (I: 9–14)

———. *Tongues of Jade*. Illustrated by David Wiesner. New York: Harper, 1991. Seventeen folktales brought to the United States by Chinese immigrants. (I: 9–14)

Young, Ed. *High on a Hill: A Book of Chinese Riddles*. New York: Collins, 1980. These riddles are printed in Chinese and in English. (I: 6–9)

* ———. *Little Plum*. New York: Philomel, 1994. A Chinese variant of "Tom Thumb." (I: 7–9)

* ———. *Lon Po Po: A Red Riding Hood Story from China*. New York: Philomel, 1989. Like the Grimm tale, the wolf is disguised as the grandmother, but in this ancient Chinese tale, three sisters outwit the wolf. (I: 7–10)

Picture Books about King Arthur and His Knights: A Literature Unit for Grades 3–6

* Hastings, Selina. *Sir Gawain and the Green Knight*. Illustrated by Juan Wijngaard. New York: Lothrop, Lee & Shepard, 1981. The story of the contest between Sir Gawain, the noblest of King Arthur's knights, and the Green Knight, a huge warrior who challenges him. (I: 9–12)

* ———. *Sir Gawain and the Loathly Lady*. Illustrated by Juan Wijngaard. New York: Lothrop, Lee & Shepard, 1985. Sir Gawain must agree to marry the Loathly Lady in order to get the answer to a riddle for King Arthur. (I: 9–12)

* Heyer, Carol. *Excalibur*. Nashville, TN: Ideals, 1991. King Arthur loses his sword in battle with the Black Knight and receives a new one, Excalibur, from the Lady of the Lake. (I: 8–12)

* Hodges, Margaret. *The Kitchen Knight: A Tale of King Arthur*. Illustrated by Trina Schart Hyman. New York: Holiday House, 1990. Gareth, the nephew of King Arthur, fights the fierce Red Knight and rescues the fair Linesse. (I: 8–12)

* San Souci, Robert D. *Young Guinevere*. Illustrated by Jamichael Henterly. New York: Doubleday, 1993. Presents the life of Guinevere from her childhood and youth to her betrothal to King Arthur. (I: 8–12)

———. *Young Merlin*. Illustrated by Daniel Horne. New York: Doubleday, 1990. The story of Merlin the magician from his miraculous birth through the age of seventeen prior to his meeting King Arthur. (I: 8–12)

* Talbott, Hudson. *Excalibur*. New York: Morrow, 1996. Compare this retelling with Carol Heyer's retelling. (I: 8–12)

* ———. *King Arthur and the Round Table*. New York: Morrow, 1995. The story of Arthur's early days and how he became the King of all Britain and assembled the Knights of the Round Table. (I: 8–12)

* ———. *King Arthur: The Sword in the Stone*. New York: Morrow, 1991. As a young boy, Arthur proves that he is to succeed to the throne of Britain when he draws a sword from an anvil. (I: 8–12)

* Yolen, Jane. *Merlin and the Dragons*. Illustrated by Li Ming. New York: Dutton, 1995. Yolen draws from the legends of King Arthur to create this story of young Arthur, who turns to Merlin when he is troubled by dreams. (I: 8–12)

Traditional Trickster Tales: A Literature Unit for Grades K–6

Chase, Richard. *The Jack Tales*. 1943. Illustrated by Berkley Williams, Jr. Boston: Houghton Mifflin, 1971. A collection of folktales from the Southern Appalachians. (I: 8–12)

* Faulkner, William. *Brer Tiger and the Big Wind*. Illustrated by Roberta Wilson. New York: Morrow,

1995. In this African American tale, Brer Rabbit tricks Brer Tiger and helps the other animals during a famine. (**I:** 5–8)

* Galdone, Paul. *The Monkey and the Crocodile: A Jataka Tale from India*. New York: Seabury, 1969. Monkey uses his wits to escape from the crocodile. (**I:** 5–8)

———. *Puss in Boots*. New York: Seabury, 1976. Resourceful and dashing Puss in Boots outwits the Giant and helps the miller's youngest son gain wealth and the hand of the king's daughter. (**I:** 7–9)

* Goble, Paul. *Iktomi and the Berries: A Plains Indian Story*. New York: Orchard, 1989. Alongside the story of Iktomi the trickster, Goble provides sample responses that listeners might insert as it unfolds. Goble has also retold and illustrated several other Iktomi tales. (**I:** 5–8)

* Haley, Gail. *A Story, A Story: An African Tale*. New York: Atheneum, 1970. In order to buy the golden box of stories from Nyame the Sky God, Anansi the Spider has to use his wits to pay the price. (**I:** 6–9)

* Han, Suzanne Crowder. *The Rabbit's Escape*. Illustrated by Yumi Heo. New York: Holt, 1995. In this bilingual adaptation of a Korean folktale, a turtle seeks a rabbit whose liver will cure the Dragon King's illness. (**I:** 5–8)

Harris, Joel Chandler. *Jump! The Adventures of Brer Rabbit*. Adapted by Van Dyke Parks and Malcolm Jones. Illustrated by Barry Moser. New York: Harcourt, 1986. Brer Rabbit tales from the American South adapted for children. (**I:** all ages)

* Hastings, Selina. *Reynard the Fox*. Illustrated by Graham Percy. New York: Tambourine, 1990. Retells various adventures and schemes of the legendary trickster Reynard. (**I:** 7–9)

Hayes, Sarah. *Robin Hood*. Illustrated by Patrick Benson. New York: Holt, 1989. In thirteen chapters, Hayes retells the adventures of Robin Hood and his band of outlaws in Sherwood forest in their quest to fight injustice. (**I:** 8–12)

Janisch, Heinz. *Till Eulenspiegel's Merry Pranks*. Illustrated by Lizbeth Zwerger. Translated by Anthea Bell. Saxonville, MA: Picture Books, 1990. A series of tales of Till's life and adventures from his infancy to his final prank at his own funeral. (**I:** 8–10)

* Johnston, Tony. *The Tale of Rabbit and Coyote*. Illustrated by Tomie de Paola. New York: Putnam, 1994. This Zapotec legend tells how rabbit outwits coyote and why coyotes howl at the moon. (**I:** 5–8)

* Kimmel, Eric. *Anansi and the Talking Melon*. Illustrated by Janet Stevens. New York: Holiday House, 1994. Anansi tricks Elephant and other animals into thinking the melon he's hiding in can talk. (**I:** 5–8)

* Knutson, Barbara. *Sungura and Leopard: A Swahili Trickster Tale*. Boston: Little, Brown, 1993. A small but clever hare and a fierce leopard agree to share a house. (**I:** 5–8)

Lester, Julius. *The Tales of Uncle Remus: The Adventures of Brer Rabbit*. Illustrated by Jerry Pinkney. New York: Dial, 1987. Uncle Remus classics retold in African American dialect. (**I:** all ages)

Mayo, Gretchen Will. *The Tricky Coyote: Native American Trickster Tales*. New York: Walker, 1993. A collection of legends about a cunning trickster who never seems to learn from his mistakes. (**I:** 6–8)

* McDermott, Gerald. *Anansi the Spider: A Tale from the Ashanti*. New York: Holt, 1972. Whenever Anansi is in danger, one of his six sons saves him. (**I:** 5–8)

* ———. *Zomo the Rabbit: A Trickster Tale from West Africa*. New York: Harcourt, 1992. Zomo the Rabbit is portrayed here wearing an African dashiki. (**I:** 5–8)

* Shetterly, Susan Hand. *Muwin and the Magic Hare*. Illustrated by Robert Shetterly. New York: Atheneum, 1993. A Passamaquoddy tale about Muwin the bear and the trickster, the Great Magic Hare of the Woods. (**I:** 6–8)

* Snyder, Dianne. *The Boy of the Three-Year Nap*. Illustrated by Allan Say. Boston: Houghton Mifflin, 1988. In this Japanese tale, a lazy boy gains wealth by tricking his rich neighbor, but the boy's mother proves she is an even more cunning trickster. (**I:** 6–9)

* Stevens, Janet. *Tops and Bottoms*. San Diego, CA: Harcourt, 1995. An African American tale about clever Hare who makes a bargain with rich and lazy Bear. (**I:** 5–8)

* Temple, Frances. *Tiger Soup: An Anansi Story from Jamaica*. New York: Orchard, 1994. When Anansi eats Tiger's soup, he manages to put the blame on the monkeys. (**I:** 5–8)

RESOURCES

Bosma, Bette, and Nancy Guth. *Children's Literature in an Integrated Curriculum: The Authentic Voice*. New York: Teachers College Press, 1995.

Bromley, Karen D'Angelo. *Webbing with Literature: Creating Story Maps with Children's Books*. Boston: Allyn & Bacon, 1996.

Meinbach, Anita Meyer, Liz Rothlein, and Anthony Fredericks. *The Complete Guide to Thematic Units: Creating the Integrated Curriculum*. Norwood, MA: Christopher-Gordon, 1995.

Moss, Joy F. *Focus on Literature: A Context for Literacy Learning*. Katonah, NY: Richard C. Owen, 1990.

———. *Teaching Literature in the Elementary School: A Thematic Approach*. Norwood, MA: Christopher-Gordon, 1996.

———. *Using Literature in the Middle Grades: A Thematic Approach*. Norwood, MA: Christopher-Gordon, 1994.

Walmsley, Sean. *Children Exploring Their World: Theme Teaching in Elementary School*. Portsmouth, NH: Heinemann, 1994.

REFERENCES

Atwell, Nancie. *In the Middle: Writing, Reading, and Learning with Adolescents*. Portsmouth, NH: Boynton/Cook, 1987.

Benedict, Susan, and Lenore Carlisle. *Beyond Words: Picture Books for Older Readers and Writers*. Portsmouth, NH: Heinemann, 1992.

Bode, Barbara. "Dialogue Journal Writing." *The Reading Teacher* 42 (1989): 568–71.

Calkins, Lucy McCormick. *The Art of Teaching Writing*. Portsmouth, NH: Heinemann, 1994.

Harste, Jerome, Kathy Short, and Carolyn Burke. *Creating Classrooms for Authors: The Reading-Writing Connection*. Portsmouth, NH: Heinemann, 1988.

Hepler, Susan I., and Janet Hickman. "'The Book Was Okay. I Love You'—Social Aspects of Response to Literature." *Theory into Practice* 21 (1982): 278–83.

Langer, Judith A. *Envisioning Literature: Literary Understanding and Literature Instruction*. New York: Teachers College Press, 1995.

Rosenblatt, Louise M. *Literature as Exploration*. New York: Appleton-Century, 1938.

———. *The Reader, the Text, and the Poem*. Carbondale, IL: Southern Illinois University Press, 1978.

Roser, Nancy L., and Miriam Martinez. *Book Talk and Beyond: Children and Teachers Respond to Literature*. Newark, DE: International Reading Association, 1995.

Smith, Frank. "Reading Like a Writer." *Composing and Comprehending*. Ed. Julie Jensen. Urbana, IL: National Conference on Research in English, 1984. ERIC Clearinghouse on Reading and Communication Skills.

———. *Understanding Reading: A Psycholinguistic Analysis of Reading and Learning to Read*. 4th ed. Hillsdale, NJ: Lawrence Erlbaum Associates, 1988.

Staton, Jana. "An Introduction to Dialogue Journal Communication." *Dialogue Journal Communication*. Ed. Jana Staton et al. Norwood, NJ: Ablex, 1989.

———. "Writing and Counseling: Using a Dialogue Journal." *Language Arts* 75 (1980): 514–18.

Stotsky, Sandra. "Research on Reading/Writing Relationships: A Synthesis and Suggested Directions." *Language Arts* 60 (1983): 627–42.

Temple, Charles, and Patrick Collins. *Stories and Readers: New Perspectives on Literature in the Elementary Classroom*. Norwood, MA: Christopher-Gordon, 1992.

Appendix A
Children's Book Awards

There are many more awards and prizes for children's books than are described in this appendix. In some states, children vote for books that are nominated for awards. Information about awards from children can be obtained from various state libraries. Other awards are given in specific genres, such as the Nebula Award for science fiction and the Edgar Allan Poe Award for mystery. Many cultural and ethnic organizations give awards to authors of children's books that contribute to understanding and appreciation of the many cultures within the United States.

HANS CHRISTIAN ANDERSEN AWARD

The International Board on Books for Young People has given the Hans Christian Andersen Award biennially since 1956 (since 1966 for the illustrator award). It is awarded to one author and one illustrator in recognition of his or her entire body of work.

1956
Eleanor Farjeon, Great Britain

1958
Astrid Lindgren, Sweden

1960
Erich Kästner, Federal Republic of Germany

1962
Meindert DeJong, United States

1964
René Guillot, France

1966
Author: Tove Jansson, Finland
Illustrator: Alois Carigiet, Switzerland

1968
Authors: James Krüss, Federal Republic of Germany
   José Maria Sanchez-Silva, Spain
Illustrator: Jǐrí Trnka, Czechoslovakia

1970
Author: Gianni Rodari, Italy
Illustrator: Maurice Sendak, United States

1972
Author: Scott O'Dell, United States
Illustrator: Ib Spang Olsen, Denmark

1974
Author: Maria Gripe, Sweden
Illustrator: Farshid Mesghali, Iran

1976
Author: Cecil Bødker, Denmark
Illustrator: Tatjana Mawrina, Soviet Union

1978
Author: Paula Fox, United States
Illustrator: Svend Otto S., Denmark

1980
Author: Bohumil Ríha, Czechoslovakia
Illustrator: Suekichi Akaba, Japan

1982
Author: Lygia Bojunga Nunes, Brazil
Illustrator: Zbigniew Rychlicki, Poland

1984
Author: Christine Nöstlinger, Austria
Illustrator: Mitsumasa Anno, Japan

1986
Author: Patricia Wrightson, Australia
Illustrator: Robert Ingpen, Australia

1988
Author: Annie M. G. Schmidt, Holland
Illustrator: Dǔsan Kállay, Czechoslovakia

1990
Author: Tormod Haugen (Norway)
Illustrator: Lisbeth Zwerger, Austria

1992
Author: Virginia Hamilton, United States
Illustrator: Květá Pacovská, Czechoslovakia

1994
Author: Michio Mado, Japan
Illustrator: Jorg Müller, Switzerland

1996
Author: Uri Orlev, Israel
Illustrator: Klaus Ensikat, Germany

MILDRED L. BATCHELDER AWARD

This award honors the former executive director of the Association for Library Service to Children (ALSC), a division of the American Library Association (ALA). The citation is given annually to a U.S. publisher for a children's book (defined as any trade book for children from pre–nursery school age through eighth grade) deemed the most outstanding book originally published in a foreign language in a foreign country, and then published in the United States. (From 1968 through 1977, the award was given for a book published in the previous two years; since 1979, the award has been given to a book published in the preceding year.)

1968
The Little Man by Erich Kästner, translated from German by James Krikup (Knopf)

1969
Don't Take Teddy by Babbis Friis-Baastad, translated from Norwegian by Lise Sømme McKinnon (Scribner's)

1970
Wildcat under Glass by Alki Zei, translated from Greek by Edward Fenton (Holt)

1971
In the Land of Ur, the Discovery of Ancient Mesopotamia by Hans Baumann, translated from German by Stella Humphries (Pantheon)

1972
Friedrich by Hans Peter Richter, translated from German by Edite Kroll (Holt)

1973
Pulga by S. R. Van Iterson, translated from Dutch by Alexander and Alison Gode (Morrow)

1974
Petro's War by Alki Zei, translated from Greek by Edward Fenton (Dutton)

1975
An Old Tale Carved Out of Stone by A. Linevski, translated from Russian by Maria Polushkin (Crown)

1976
The Cat and Mouse Who Shared a House by Ruth Hürlimann, translated from German by Anthea Bell (Walck)

1977
The Leopard by Cecil Bødker, translated from Danish by Gunnar Poulsen (Atheneum)

1978
No award

1979
Konrad by Christine Nöstlinger (published 1977), translated from German by Anthea Bell (Watts)
Rabbit Island by Jörg Steiner (published 1978), translated from German by Ann Conrad Lammers (Harcourt)

1980
The Sound of the Dragon's Feet by Alki Zei, translated from Greek by Edward Fenton (Dutton)

1981
The Winter When Time Was Frozen by Els Pelgrom, translated from Dutch by Maryka and Raphael Rudnik (Morrow)

1982
The Battle Horse by Harry Kullman, translated from Swedish by George Blecher and Lone Thygesen Blecher (Bradbury)

1983
Hiroshima No Pika by Toshi Maruki, translated from Japanese through Kurita-Bando Literary Agency (Lothrop)

1984
Ronia, the Robber's Daughter by Astrid Lindgren, translated from Swedish by Patricia Crampton (Viking)
The Island on Bird Street by Uri Orlev, translated from Hebrew by Hillel Halkin (Houghton Mifflin)

1986
Rose Blanche by Christophe Gallaz and Robert Innocenti, translated from Italian by Martha Coventry and Richard Craglia (Creative Education)

1987
No Hero for the Kaiser by Rudolf Frank, translated from German by Patricia Crampton (Lothrop)

1988
If You Didn't Have Me by Ulf Nilsson, translated from Swedish by Lone Thygesen Blecher and George Blecher (McElderry)

1989
Crutches by Peter Härtling, translated from Danish by Anthea Bell (Dutton)

1991
A Hand Full of Stars by Rafik Schami, translated from German by Rika Lesser (Dutton)

1992
The Man from the Other Side by Uri Orlev, translated from Hebrew by Hillel Halkin (Houghton Mifflin)

1993
No award

1994
The Apprentice by Pilar M. Llorente, translated from Spanish by Robin Longshaw (Farrar)

1995
Boys from St. Petri by Bjarne Reuter, translated from Danish by Anthea Bell (Dutton)

1996
The Lady with the Hat by Uri Orlev, translated from Hebrew by Hillel Halkin (Houghton Mifflin)
Honor Books
Star of Fear, Star of Hope by Jo Hoestlandt, translated from French by Mark Polizzotti (Walker)
Damned Strong Love: The True Story of Willi G. and Stephan K. by Lutz van Dijk, translated from German by Elizabeth D. Crawford (Holt)

1997
The Friends by Kazumi Yumoto, translated from Japanese by Cathy Hirano (Farrar)

BOSTON GLOBE–HORN BOOK AWARD

This award, which was established in 1967, is cosponsored by the *Boston Globe* and the *Horn Book Magazine*. Originally, the award was given for text and illustration, but in 1976, the categories were changed. Currently, the award goes to one outstanding example of fiction, nonfiction, and illustration each year. The recipients of the awards need not be U.S. citizens; however, the books must have been published in the United States.

1967
Text: The Little Fishes by Erik Christian Haugaard (Houghton Mifflin)
Illustration: London Bridge Is Falling Down by Peter Spier (Doubleday)

1968
Text: The Spring Rider by John Lawson (Crowell)
Illustration: Tikki Tikki Tembo by Arlene Mosel, illustrated by Blair Lent (Holt)

1969
Text: A Wizard of Earthsea by Ursula K. Le Guin (Houghton Mifflin)
Illustration: The Adventures of Paddy Pork by John S. Goodall (Harcourt)

1970
Text: The Intruder by John Rowe Townsend (Lippincott)
Illustration: Hi, Cat! by Ezra Jack Keats (Macmillan)

1971
Text: A Room Made of Windows by Eleanor Cameron (Atlantic/Little, Brown)
Illustration: If I Built a Village by Kazue Mizumura (Crowell)

1972
Text: Tristan and Iseult by Rosemary Sutcliff (Dutton)
Illustration: Mr. Gumpy's Outing by John Burningham (Holt)

1973
Text: The Dark Is Rising by Susan Cooper (Atheneum/McElderry)
Illustration: King Stork by Trina Schart Hyman (Little, Brown)

1974
Text: M. C. Higgins, the Great by Virginia Hamilton (Macmillan)
Illustration: Jambo Means Hello by Muriel Feelings, illustrated by Tom Feelings (Dial)

1975
Text: Transport 7-41-R by T. Degens (Viking)
Illustration: Anno's Alphabet by Mitsumasa Anno (Crowell)

1976
Fiction: Unleaving by Jill Paton Walsh (Farrar)
Nonfiction: Voyaging to Cathay: Americans in the China Trade by Alfred Tamarin and Shirley Glubok (Viking)
Illustration: Thirteen by Remy Charlip and Jerry Joyner (Parents)

1977
Fiction: Child of the Owl by Laurence Yep (Harper)
Nonfiction: Chance, Luck and Density by Peter Dickinson (Atlantic/Little, Brown)
Illustration: Granfa' Grig Had a Pig and Other Rhymes by Wallace Tripp (Little, Brown)

1978
Fiction: The Westing Game by Ellen Raskin (Dutton)
Nonfiction: Mischling, Second Degree: My Childhood in Nazi Germany by Ilse Koehn (Greenwillow)
Illustration: Anno's Journey by Mitsumasa Anno (Philomel)

1979
Fiction: Humbug Mountain by Sid Fleischman (Atlantic/Little, Brown)
Nonfiction: The Road from Home: The Story of an Armenian Girl by David Kherdian (Greenwillow)
Illustration: The Snowman by Raymond Briggs (Random House)

1980
Fiction: Conrad's War by Andrew Davies (Crown)
Nonfiction: Building: The Fight against Gravity by Mario Salvadori (Atheneum/McElderry)
Illustration: The Garden of Abdul Gasazi by Chris Van Allsburg (Houghton Mifflin)

1981
Fiction: The Leaving by Lynn Hall (Scribner's)
Nonfiction: The Weaver's Gift by Kathryn Lasky (Warne)
Illustration: Outside Over There by Maurice Sendak (Harper)

1982
Fiction: Playing Beatie Bow by Ruth Park (Atheneum)
Nonfiction: Upon the Head of the Goat: A Childhood in Hungary, 1939–1944 by Aranka Siegal (Farrar)
Illustration: A Visit to William Blake's Inn: Poems for Innocent and Experienced Travelers by Nancy Willard, illustrated by Alice and Martin Provensen (Harcourt)

1983
Fiction: Sweet Whispers, Brother Rush by Virginia Hamilton (Philomel)
Nonfiction: Behind Barbed Wire: The Imprisonment of Japanese Americans during World War II by Daniel S. Davis (Dutton)
Illustration: A Chair for My Mother by Vera B. Williams (Greenwillow)

1984
Fiction: A Little Fear by Patricia Wrightson (McElderry/Atheneum)
Nonfiction: The Double Life of Pocahontas by Jean Fritz (Putnam)
Illustration: Jonah and the Great Fish, retold and illustrated by Warwick Hutton (McElderry/Atheneum)

1985
Fiction: The Moves Make the Man by Bruce Brooks (Harper)
Nonfiction: Commodore Perry in the Land of the Shogun by Rhoda Blumberg (Lothrop)
Illustration: Mama Don't Allow by Thatcher Hurd (Harper)

1986
Fiction: In Summer Light by Zibby O'Neal (Viking)
Nonfiction: Auks, Rocks, and the Odd Dinosaur:

Inside Stories from the Smithsonian Museum of Natural History by Peggy Thomson (Crowell)
Illustration: Paper Crane by Molly Bang (Greenwillow)

1987
Fiction: Rabble Starkey by Lois Lowry (Houghton Mifflin)
Nonfiction: Pilgrims of Plimoth by Marcia Sewall (Atheneum)
Illustration: Mufaro's Beautiful Daughters: An African Tale by John Steptoe (Lothrop)

1988
Fiction: The Friendship by Mildred D. Taylor (Dial)
Nonfiction: Anthony Burns: The Defeat and Triumph of a Fugitive Slave by Virginia Hamilton (Knopf)
Illustration: The Boy of the Three-Year Nap by Dianne Snyder, illustrated by Allen Say (Houghton Mifflin)

1989
Fiction: Village by the Sea by Paula Fox (Orchard)
Nonfiction: The Way Things Work by David Macaulay (Houghton Mifflin)
Illustration: Shy Charles by Rosemary Wells (Dial)

1990
Fiction: Maniac Magee by Jerry Spinelli (Little, Brown)
Nonfiction: Great Little Madison by Jean Fritz (Putnam)
Illustration: Lon Po Po: A Red Riding Hood Story from China by Ed Young (Philomel)

1991
Fiction: True Confessions of Charlotte Doyle by Avi (Orchard)
Nonfiction: Appalachia: The Voices of Sleeping Birds by Cynthia Rylant (Harcourt)
Illustration: Tale of the Mandarin Ducks by Katherine Paterson, illustrated by Leo and Diane Dillon (Lodestar)

1992
Fiction: Missing May by Cynthia Rylant (Orchard)
Nonfiction: Talking with Artists by Pat Cummings (Bradbury)
Illustration: Seven Blind Mice by Ed Young (Philomel)

1993
Fiction: Ajeemah and His Son by James Berry (Harper)
Nonfiction: Sojourner Truth: Ain't I a Woman? by Patricia and Fredrick McKissack (Scholastic)
Illustration: Fortune Tellers by Lloyd Alexander, illustrated by Trina Schart Hyman (Dutton)

1994
Fiction: Scooter by Vera Williams (Greenwillow)
Nonfiction: Eleanor Roosevelt: A Life of Discovery by Russell Freedman (Houghton Mifflin)
Illustration: Grandfather's Journey by Allen Say (Houghton Mifflin)

1995

*Fiction: **Some of the Kinder Planets*** by Tim Wynne-Jones (Orchard)

*Nonfiction: **Abigail Adams: Witness to a Revolution*** by Natalie S. Bober (Atheneum)

*Illustration: **John Henry*** by Julius Lester, illustrated by Jerry Pinkney (Dial)

1996

*Fiction: **Poppy*** by Avi, illustrated by Brian Floca (Jackson/Orchard)

*Nonfiction: **Orphan Train Rider: One Boy's True Story*** by Andrea Warren (Houghton Mifflin)

*Illustration: **In the Rain with Baby Duck*** by Amy Hest, illustrated by Jill Baron (Candlewick)

1997

*Fiction: **The Friends*** by Kazumi Yumoto (Farrar)

*Nonfiction: **A Drop of Water: A Book of Science and Wonder*** by Walter Wick (Scholastic)

*Illustration: **The Adventures of Sparrowboy*** by Brian Pinkney (Simon & Schuster)

RANDOLPH CALDECOTT MEDAL

The Randolph Caldecott Medal, named in honor of the nineteenth-century illustrator of children's books, is awarded annually under the supervision of the Association for Library Service to Children of the American Library Association. It is awarded to the illustrator of the most distinguished children's book published in the United States in the previous year. Usually, one or more Honor Books are also chosen. The award is limited to residents or citizens of the United States.

1938

Animals of the Bible by Helen Dean Fish, illustrated by Dorothy P. Lathrop (Lippincott)

Honor Books

Four and Twenty Blackbirds by Helen Dean Fish, illustrated by Robert Lawson (Stokes)

Seven Simeons by Boris Artzybasheff (Viking)

1939

Mei Li by Thomas Handforth (Doubleday)

Honor Books

Andy and the Lion by James Daugherty (Viking)

Barkis by Clare Newberry (Harper)

The Forest Pool by Laura Adams Armer (Longman)

Snow White and the Seven Dwarfs by Wanda Gág (Coward)

Wee Gillis by Munro Leaf, illustrated by Robert Lawson (Viking)

1940

Abraham Lincoln by Ingri and Edgar Parin D'Aulaire (Doubleday)

Honor Books

The Ageless Story by Lauren Ford (Dodd)

Cock-a-Doodle Doo by Berta and Elmer Hader (Macmillan)

Madeline by Ludwig Bemelmans (Viking)

1941

They Were Strong and Good by Robert Lawson (Viking)

Honor Book

April's Kittens by Clare Newberry (Harper)

1942

Make Way for Ducklings by Robert McCloskey (Viking)

Honor Books

An American ABC by Maud and Miska Petersham (Macmillan)

In My Mother's House by Ann Nolan Clark, illustrated by Velino Herrera (Viking)

Nothing at All by Wanda Gág (Coward)

Paddle-to-the-Sea by Holling C. Holling (Houghton Mifflin)

1943

The Little House by Virginia Lee Burton (Houghton Mifflin)

Honor Books

Dash and Dart by Mary and Conrad Buff (Viking)

Marshmallow by Clare Newberry (Harper)

1944

Many Moons by James Thurber, illustrated by Louis Slobodkin (Harcourt)

Honor Books

A Child's Good Night Book by Margaret Wise Brown, illustrated by Jean Charlot (Scott)

Good Luck Horse by Chin-Yi Chan, illustrated by Plao Chan (Whittlesey)

The Mighty Hunter by Berta and Elmer Hader (Macmillan)

Pierre Pigeon by Lee Kingman, illustrated by Arnold E. Bare (Houghton Mifflin)

Small Rain: Verses from the Bible selected by Jessie Orton Jones, illustrated by Elizabeth Orton Jones (Viking)

1945

Prayer for a Child by Rachel Field, illustrated by Elizabeth Orton Jones (Macmillan)

Honor Books
The Christmas Anna Angel by Ruth Sawyer, illustrated by Kate Seredy (Viking)
In the Forest by Marie Hall Ets (Viking)
Mother Goose illustrated by Tasha Tudor (Walck)
Yonie Wondernose by Marguerite de Angeli (Doubleday)

1946
The Rooster Crows (traditional Mother Goose) illustrated by Maud and Miska Petersham (Macmillan)

Honor Books
Little Lost Lamb by Golden MacDonald, illustrated by Leonard Weisgard (Doubleday)
My Mother Is the Most Beautiful Woman in the World by Becky Reyher, illustrated by Ruth C. Gannett (Lothrop)
Sing Mother Goose by Opal Wheeler, illustrated by Marjorie Torrey (Dutton)
You Can Write Chinese by Kurt Wiese (Viking)

1947
The Little Island by Golden MacDonald, illustrated by Leonard Weisgard (Doubleday)

Honor Books
Boats on the River by Marjorie Flack, illustrated by Jay Hyde Barnum (Viking)
Pedro, the Angel of Olvera Street by Leo Politi (Scribner's)
Rain Drop Splash by Alvin Tresselt, illustrated by Leonard Weisgard (Lothrop)
Sing in Praise: A Collection of the Best Loved Hymns by Opal Wheeler, illustrated by Marjorie Torrey (Dutton)
Timothy Turtle by Al Graham, illustrated by Tony Palazzo (Welch)

1948
White Snow, Bright Snow by Alvin Tresselt, illustrated by Roger Duvoisin (Lothrop)

Honor Books
Bambino the Clown by George Schreiber (Viking)
McElligot's Pool by Dr. Seuss (Random House)
Roger and the Fox by Lavinia Davis, illustrated by Hildegard Woodward (Doubleday)
Song of Robin Hood edited by Anne Malcolmson, illustrated by Virginia Lee Burton (Houghton Mifflin)
Stone Soup by Marcia Brown (Scribner's)

1949
The Big Snow by Berta and Elmer Hader (Macmillan)

Honor Books
All Around the Town by Phyllis McGinley, illustrated by Helen Stone (Lippincott)
Blueberries for Sal by Robert McCloskey (Viking)
Fish in the Air by Kurt Wiese (Viking)
Juanita by Leo Politi (Scribner's)

1950
Song of the Swallows by Leo Politi (Scribner's)

Honor Books
America's Ethan Allen by Stewart Holbrook, illustrated by Lynd Ward (Houghton Mifflin)
Bartholomew and the Oobleck by Dr. Seuss (Random House)
The Happy Day by Ruth Krauss, illustrated by Marc Simont (Harper)
Henry Fisherman by Marcia Brown (Scribner's)
The Wild Birthday Cake by Lavinia Davis, illustrated by Hildegard Woodward (Doubleday)

1951
The Egg Tree by Katherine Milhous (Scribner's)

Honor Books
Dick Whittington and His Cat by Marcia Brown (Scribner's)
If I Ran the Zoo by Dr. Seuss (Random House)
The Most Wonderful Doll in the World by Phyllis McGinley, illustrated by Helen Stone (Lippincott)
T-Bone, the Baby Sitter by Clare Newberry (Harper)
The Two Reds by Will, illustrated by Nicolas (Harcourt)

1952
Finders Keepers by Will, illustrated by Nicolas (Harcourt)

Honor Books
All Falling Down by Gene Zion, illustrated by Margaret Bloy Graham (Harper)
Bear Party by William Pène du Bois (Viking)
Feather Mountain by Elizabeth Olds (Houghton Mifflin)
Mr. T. W. Anthony Woo by Marie Hall Ets (Viking)
Skipper John's Cook by Marcia Brown (Scribner's)

1953
The Biggest Bear by Lynd Ward (Houghton Mifflin)

Honor Books
Ape in a Cape by Fritz Eichenberg (Harcourt)
Five Little Monkeys by Juliet Kepes (Houghton Mifflin)
One Morning in Maine by Robert McCloskey (Viking)
Puss in Boots by Charles Perrault, illustrated by Marcia Brown (Scribner's)
The Storm Book by Charlotte Zolotow, illustrated by Margaret Bloy Graham (Harper)

1954
Madeline's Rescue by Ludwig Bemelmans (Viking)

Honor Books
A Very Special House by Ruth Krauss, illustrated by Maurice Sendak (Harper)
Green Eyes by A. Birnbaum (Capitol)
Journey Cake, Ho! by Ruth Sawyer, illustrated by Robert McCloskey (Viking)
The Steadfast Tin Soldier by Hans Christian Andersen, illustrated by Marcia Brown (Scribner's)

When Will the World Be Mine? by Miriam Schlein, illustrated by Jean Charlot (Scott)

1955
Cinderella, or the Little Glass Slipper by Charles Perrault, illustrated by Marcia Brown (Scribner's)
Honor Books
Book of Nursery and Mother Goose Rhymes, illustrated by Marguerite de Angeli (Doubleday)
The Thanksgiving Story by Alice Dalgliesh, illustrated by Helen Sewell (Scribner's)
Wheel on the Chimney by Margaret Wise Brown, illustrated by Tibor Gergely (Lippincott)

1956
Frog Went A-Courtin' retold by John Langstaff, illustrated by Feodor Rojankovsky (Harcourt)
Honor Books
Crow Boy by Taro Yashima (Viking)
Play with Me by Marie Hall Ets (Viking)

1957
A Tree Is Nice by Janice May Udry, illustrated by Marc Simont (Harper)
Honor Books
Anatole by Eve Titus, illustrated by Paul Galdone (McGraw-Hill)
Gillespie and the Guards by Benjamin Elkin, illustrated by James Daugherty (Viking)
Lion by William Pène du Bois (Viking)
Mr. Penny's Race Horse by Marie Hall Ets (Viking)
1 Is One by Tasha Tudor (Walck)

1958
Time of Wonder by Robert McCloskey (Viking)
Honor Books
Anatole and the Cat by Eve Titus, illustrated by Paul Galdone (McGraw-Hill)
Fly High, Fly Low by Don Freeman (Viking)

1959
Chanticleer and the Fox adapted from Chaucer, illustrated by Barbara Cooney (Crowell)
Honor Books
The House That Jack Built by Antonio Frasconi (Harcourt)
Umbrella by Taro Yashima (Viking)
What Do You Say, Dear? by Sesyle Joslin, illustrated by Maurice Sendak (Scott)

1960
Nine Days to Christmas by Marie Hall Ets and Aurora Labastida, illustrated by Marie Hall Ets (Viking)
Honor Books
Houses from the Sea by Alice E. Goudey, illustrated by Adrienne Adams (Scribner's)

The Moon Jumpers by Janice May Udry, illustrated by Maurice Sendak (Harper)

1961
Baboushka and the Three Kings by Ruth Robbins, illustrated by Nicholas Sidjakov (Parnassus)
Honor Book
Inch by Inch by Leo Lionni (Astor-Honor)

1962
Once a Mouse by Marcia Brown (Scribner's)
Honor Books
The Day We Saw the Sun Come Up by Alice E. Goudey, illustrated by Adrienne Adams (Scribner's)
The Fox Went Out on a Chilly Night, illustrated by Peter Spier (Doubleday)
Little Bear's Visit by Else Holmelund Minarik, illustrated by Maurice Sendak (Harper)

1963
The Snowy Day by Ezra Jack Keats (Viking)
Honor Books
Mr. Rabbit and the Lovely Present by Charlotte Zolotow, illustrated by Maurice Sendak (Harper)
The Sun Is a Golden Earring by Natalia M. Belting, illustrated by Bernarda Bryson (Holt)

1964
Where the Wild Things Are by Maurice Sendak (Harper)
Honor Books
All in the Morning Early by Sorche Nic Leodhas, illustrated by Evaline Ness (Holt)
Mother Goose and Nursery Rhymes, illustrated by Philip Reed (Atheneum)
Swimmy by Leo Lionni (Pantheon)

1965
May I Bring a Friend? by Beatrice Schenk de Regniers, illustrated by Beni Montresor (Atheneum)
Honor Books
A Pocketful of Cricket by Rebecca Caudill, illustrated by Evaline Ness (Holt)
Rain Makes Applesauce by Julian Scheer, illustrated by Marvin Bileck (Holiday House)
The Wave by Margaret Hodges, illustrated by Blair Lent (Houghton Mifflin)

1966
Always Room for One More by Sorche Nic Leodhas, illustrated by Nonny Hogrogian (Holt)
Honor Books
Hide and Seek Fog by Alvin Tresselt, illustrated by Roger Duvoisin (Lothrop)
Just Me by Marie Hall Ets (Viking)
Tom Tit Tot by Evaline Ness (Scribner's)

1967
Sam, Bangs & Moonshine by Evaline Ness (Holt)

Honor Book
One Wide River to Cross by Barbara Emberley, illustrated by Ed Emberley (Prentice-Hall)

1968
Drummer Hoff by Barbara Emberley, illustrated by Ed Emberley (Prentice-Hall)

Honor Books
The Emperor and the Kite by Jane Yolen, illustrated by Ed Young (World)
Frederick by Leo Lionni (Pantheon)
Seashore Story by Taro Yashima (Viking)

1969
The Fool of the World and the Flying Ship retold by Arthur Ransome, illustrated by Uri Shulevitz (Farrar)

Honor Book
Why the Sun and the Moon Live in the Sky by Elphinstone Dayrell, illustrated by Blair Lent (Houghton Mifflin)

1970
Sylvester and the Magic Pebble by William Steig (Windmill/Simon & Schuster)

Honor Books
Alexander and the Wind-Up Mouse by Leo Lionni (Pantheon)
Goggles! by Ezra Jack Keats (Macmillan)
The Judge by Harve Zemach, illustrated by Margot Zemach (Farrar)
Pop Corn & Ma Goodness by Edna Mitchell Preston, illustrated by Robert Andrew Parker (Viking)
Thy Friend, Obadiah by Brinton Turkle (Viking)

1971
A Story, a Story by Gail E. Haley (Atheneum)

Honor Books
The Angry Moon by William Sleator, illustrated by Blair Lent (Atlantic/Little, Brown)
Frog and Toad Are Friends by Arnold Lobel (Harper)
In the Night Kitchen by Maurice Sendak (Harper)

1972
One Fine Day by Nonny Hogrogian (Macmillan)

Honor Books
Hildilid's Night by Cheli Durán Ryan, illustrated by Arnold Lobel (Macmillan)
If All the Seas Were One Sea by Janina Domanska (Macmillan)
Moja Means One by Muriel Feelings, illustrated by Tom Feelings (Dial)

1973
The Funny Little Woman retold by Arlene Mosel, illustrated by Blair Lent (Dutton)

Honor Books
Anansi the Spider adapted and illustrated by Gerald McDermott (Holt)
Hosie's Alphabet by Hosea, Tobias, and Lisa Baskin, illustrated by Leonard Baskin (Viking)
Snow White and the Seven Dwarfs, illustrated by Nancy Eckholm Burkert (Farrar)
When Clay Sings by Byrd Baylor, illustrated by Tom Bahti (Scribner's)

1974
Duffy and the Devil retold by Harve Zemach, illustrated by Margot Zemach (Farrar)

Honor Books
Cathedral by David Macaulay (Houghton Mifflin)
Three Jovial Huntsmen by Susan Jeffers (Bradbury)

1975
Arrow to the Sun by Gerald McDermott (Viking)

Honor Book
Jambo Means Hello by Muriel Feelings, illustrated by Tom Feelings (Dial)

1976
Why Mosquitoes Buzz in People's Ears by Verna Aardema, illustrated by Leo and Diane Dillon (Dial)

Honor Books
The Desert Is Theirs by Byrd Baylor, illustrated by Peter Parnall (Scribner's)
Strega Nona retold and illustrated by Tomie de Paola (Prentice)

1977
Ashanti to Zulu: African Traditions by Margaret Musgrove, illustrated by Leo and Diane Dillon (Dial)

Honor Books
The Amazing Bone by William Steig (Farrar)
The Contest retold and illustrated by Nonny Hogrogian (Greenwillow)
Fish for Supper by M. B. Goffstein (Dial)
The Golem by Beverly Brodsky McDermott (Lippincott)
Hawk, I'm Your Brother by Byrd Baylor, illustrated by Peter Parnall (Scribner's)

1978
Noah's Ark illustrated by Peter Spier (Doubleday)

Honor Books
Castle by David Macaulay (Houghton Mifflin)
It Could Always Be Worse by Margot Zemach (Farrar)

1979
The Girl Who Loved Wild Horses by Paul Goble (Bradbury)

Honor Books
Freight Train by Donald Crews (Greenwillow)
The Way to Start a Day by Byrd Baylor, illustrated by Peter Parnall (Scribner's)

1980

Ox-Cart Man by Donald Hall, illustrated by Barbara Cooney (Viking)

Honor Books
Ben's Trumpet by Rachel Isadora (Greenwillow)
The Garden of Abdul Gasazi by Chris Van Allsburg (Houghton Mifflin)
The Treasure by Uri Shulevitz (Farrar)

1981

Fables by Arnold Lobel (Harper)

Honor Books
The Bremen Town Musicians retold and illustrated by Ilse Plume (Doubleday)
The Grey Lady and the Strawberry Snatcher by Molly Bang (Four Winds)
Mice Twice by Joseph Low (McElderry)
Truck by Donald Crews (Greenwillow)

1982

Jumanji by Chris Van Allsburg (Houghton Mifflin)

Honor Books
On Market Street by Arnold Lobel, illustrated by Anita Lobel (Greenwillow)
Outside Over There by Maurice Sendak (Harper)
A Visit to William Blake's Inn: Poems for Innocent and Experienced Travelers by Nancy Willard, illustrated by Alice and Martin Provensen (Harcourt)
Where the Buffaloes Begin by Olaf Baker, illustrated by Stephen Gammell (Warne)

1983

Shadow by Blaise Cendrars, illustrated by Marcia Brown (Scribner's)

Honor Books
A Chair for My Mother by Vera B. Williams (Greenwillow)
When I Was Young in the Mountains by Cynthia Rylant, illustrated by Diane Goode (Dutton)

1984

The Glorious Flight: Across the Channel with Louis Blériot by Alice and Martin Provensen (Viking)

Honor Books
Little Red Riding Hood retold and illustrated by Trina Schart Hyman (Holiday House)
Ten, Nine, Eight by Molly Bang (Greenwillow)

1985

Saint George and the Dragon by Margaret Hodges, illustrated by Trina Schart Hyman (Little, Brown)

Honor Books
Hansel and Gretel retold by Rika Lesser, illustrated by Paul O. Zelinsky (Dodd)
Have You Seen My Duckling? by Nancy Tafuri (Greenwillow)

The Story of Jumping Mouse retold and illustrated by John Steptoe (Lothrop)

1986

The Polar Express by Chris Van Allsburg (Houghton Mifflin)

Honor Books
King Bidgood's in the Bathtub by Audrey Wood, illustrated by Don Wood (Harcourt)
The Relatives Came by Cynthia Rylant, illustrated by Stephen Gammell (Bradbury)

1987

Hey, Al by Arthur Yorinks, illustrated by Richard Egielski (Farrar)

Honor Books
Alphabatics by Suse MacDonald (Bradbury)
Rumpelstiltskin by Paul O. Zelinsky (Dutton)
The Village of Round and Square Houses by Ann Grifalconi (Little, Brown)

1988

Owl Moon by Jane Yolen, illustrated by John Schoenherr (Philomel)

Honor Book
Mufaro's Beautiful Daughters: An African Tale by John Steptoe (Lothrop)

1989

Song and Dance Man by Karen Ackerman, illustrated by Stephen Gammell (Knopf)

Honor Books
The Boy of the Three-Year Nap by Dianne Snyder, illustrated by Allen Say (Houghton Mifflin)
Free-Fall by David Wiesner (Lothrop)
Goldilocks and the Three Bears by James Marshall (Dial)
Mirandy and Brother Wind by Patricia C. McKissack, illustrated by Jerry Pinkney (Knopf)

1990

Lon Po Po: A Red-Riding Hood Story from China translated and illustrated by Ed Young (Philomel)

Honor Books
Bill Peet: An Autobiography by Bill Peet (Houghton Mifflin)
Color Zoo by Lois Ehlert (Lippincott)
Hershel and the Hanukkah Goblins by Eric Kimmel, illustrated by Trina Schart Hyman (Holiday House)
The Talking Eggs by Robert D. San Souci, illustrated by Jerry Pinkney (Dial)

1991

Black and White by David Macaulay (Houghton Mifflin)

Honor Books
"More More More," Said the Baby: 3 Love Stories by Vera B. Williams (Greenwillow)
Puss in Boots by Charles Perrault, translated by Malcolm Arthur, illustrated by Fred Marcellino (Farrar)

1992
Tuesday by David Wiesner (Clarion)
Honor Book
Tar Beach by Faith Ringgold (Crown)

1993
Mirette on the High Wire by Emily Arnold McCully (Putnam)
Honor Books
Seven Blind Mice by Ed Young (Philomel)
The Stinky Cheese Man and Other Fairly Stupid Tales by Jon Scieszka, illustrated by Lane Smith (Viking)
Working Cotton by Sherley Anne Williams, illustrated by Carole Byard (Harcourt)

1994
Grandfather's Journey by Allen Say (Houghton Mifflin)
Honor Books
Owen by Kevin Henkes (Greenwillow)
Peppe, the Lamplighter by Elisa Bartone (Lothrop)
Raven by Gerald McDermott (Harcourt)
In the Small, Small Pond by Denise Fleming (Holt)
Yo! Yes? by Chris Raschka (Orchard)

1995
Smoky Night by Eve Bunting, illustrated by David Diaz (Harcourt)

Honor Books
Swamp Angel by Anne Isaacs, illustrated by Paul O. Zelinsky (Dutton)
John Henry by Julius Lester, illustrated by Jerry Pinkney (Dial)
Time Flies by Eric Rohmann (Crown)

1996
Officer Buckle and Gloria by Peggy Rathmann (Putnam)
Honor Books
Alphabet City by Stephen T. Johnson (Viking)
Zin! Zin! Zin! A Violin by Lloyd Moss (Simon & Schuster)
The Faithful Friend by Robert D. San Souci, illustrated by Brian Pinkney (Simon & Schuster)
Tops & Bottoms adapted and illustrated by Janet Stevens (Harcourt)

1997
Golem by David Wisniewski (Clarion)
Honor Books
Hush! A Thai Lullaby by Minfong Ho, illustrated by Holly Meade (Kroupa/Orchard)
The Graphic Alphabet by Neal Porter, illustrated by David Pelletier (Orchard)
The Paperboy by Dav Pilkey (Jackson/Orchard)
Starry Messenger by Peter Sis (Foster/Farrar)

INTERNATIONAL READING ASSOCIATION CHILDREN'S BOOK AWARD

This award is given annually to honor new talent in children's literature. Publishers worldwide are invited to suggest candidates. Since 1987, an award has been given to one author who writes for older readers and one author who writes for younger readers. In 1995, a third award was added for an author of an informational book.

1975
Transport 7-41-R by T. Degens (Viking, United States)

1976
Dragonwings by Laurence Yep (Harper, United States)

1977
A String in the Harp by Nancy Bond (McElderry, United States)

1978
A Summer to Die by Lois Lowry (Houghton Mifflin, United States)

1979
Reserved for Mark Anthony Crowder by Alison Smith (Dutton, United States)

1980
Words by Heart by Ouida Sebestyen (Atlantic/Little, Brown, United States)

1981
My Own Private Sky by Delores Beckman (Dutton, United States)

1982
Goodnight, Mister Tom by Michelle Magorian (Kestrel, Great Britain)

1983
The Darkangel by Meredith Ann Pierce (Atlantic/Little, Brown, United States)

1984
Ratha's Creature by Clare Bell (McElderry, United States)

1985
Badger on the Barge by Janni Howker (Julia MacRae, Great Britain)

1986
Prairie Songs by Pam Conrad (Harper, United States)

1987
Older Readers: After the Dancing Days by Margaret I. Rostkowski (Harper, United States)
Younger Readers: The Line-Up Book by Marisabina Russo (Greenwillow, United States)

1988
Older Readers: **The Ruby in the Smoke** and **Shadow in the North** by Philip Pullman (Oxford, Great Britain)
Younger Readers: **The Third-Story Cat** by Leslie Baker (Little, Brown, United States)

1989
Older Readers: **Probably Still Nick Swansen** by Virginia Euwer Wolff (Holt, United States)
Younger Readers: **Rechenka's Eggs** by Patricia Polacco (Philomel, United States)

1990
Older Readers: **Children of the River** by Linda Crew (Delacorte, United States)
Younger Readers: **No Star Nights** by Anna Egan Smucker, illustrated by Steve Johnson (Knopf, United States)

1991
Older Readers: **Under the Hawthorn Tree** by Marita Conlon-McKenna (O'Brien Press, Ireland)
Younger Readers: **Is This a House for Hermit Crab?** by Megan McDonald, illustrated by S. D. Schindler (Orchard, United States)

1992
Older Readers: **Rescue Josh McGuire** by Ben Mikaelsen (Hyperion, United States)
Younger Readers: **Ten Little Rabbits** by Virginia Grossman, illustrated by Sylvia Long (Chronicle, United States)

1993
Older Readers: **Letters from Rifka** by Karen Hesse (Holt, United States)
Younger Readers: **Old Turtle** by Douglas Wood, illustrated by Cheng-Khee Chee (Pfeifer-Hamilton, United States)

1994
Older Readers: **Behind the Secret Window: A Memoir of a Hidden Childhood** by Nelly S. Toll (Dutton, United States)
Younger Readers: **Sweet Clara and the Freedom Quilt** by Deborah Hopkinson, illustrated by James E. Ransome (Knopf, United States)

1995
Older Readers: **Spite Fences** by Trudy Krisher (Bantam, United States)
Younger Readers: **The Ledgerbook of Thomas Blue Eagle** by Gay Matthaei and Jewel Grutman, illustrated by Adam Cvijanovic (Thomasson-Grant, United States)
Informational Book: **Stranded at Plimoth Plantation 1626** by Gary Bowen (HarperCollins, United States)

1996
Older Readers: **The King's Shadow** by Elizabeth Adler (Farrar, United States)
Younger Readers: **More Than Anything Else** by Marie Bradby, illustrated by Chris K. Soentpiet
Informational Book: **The Case of the Mummified Pigs and Other Mysteries in Nature** by Susan E. Quinland (Boyds Mills, United States)

1997
Older Readers: **Don't You Dare Read This Mrs. Dunphrey** by Margaret Peterson Haddix (Simon & Schuster, United States)
Younger Readers: **The Fabulous Flying Fandinis** by Ingrid Slyder (Cobblehill, United States)
Informational Book: **Brooklyn Bridge** by Elizabeth Mann (Mikaya Press, United States)

EZRA JACK KEATS NEW WRITERS AWARD

Ezra Jack Keats (1919–1983) was a prolific illustrator of children's picture books who won the Caldecott Medal in 1963 for **The Snowy Day**. The Ezra Jack Keats award is funded by the Ezra Jack Keats Foundation and is given to a promising writer who has had six or fewer children's books published. The writer need not be the illustrator. The books must "reflect the tradition of Ezra Jack Keats," whose books portrayed strong family relationships and universal qualities of childhood; the books must also appeal to children nine years old or younger. The award is presented at two-year intervals and is administered by the Early Childhood Resources and Information Center of the New York Public Library.

1987
The Patchwork Quilt by Valerie Flournoy, illustrated by Jerry Pinkney (Dial)

1989
Jamaica's Find by Juanita Havill, illustrated by Anne Sibley O'Brien (Houghton Mifflin)

1991
Tell Me a Story, Mama by Angela Johnson (Orchard)

1993
Tar Beach by Faith Ringgold (Crown)

1995
Taxi, Taxi by Carrie Best, illustrated by Dale Gottlieb (Little, Brown)

1997
Calling the Doves/El canto de las palomas by Juan Felipé Herrera (Children's Book Press)

The Coretta Scott King Award is presented annually by the Coretta Scott King Task Force of the American Library Association's Social Responsibilities Round Table. It has been awarded to African American authors since 1970 and also to African American illustrators since 1974 for books that encourage understanding and appreciation of people of all cultures and their pursuit of the "American dream." The award celebrates the life of Martin Luther King, Jr., and honors his widow, Coretta Scott King, for her strength and dedication in continuing the fight for racial equity and universal peace. One or more Honor Books may also be chosen each year.

1970
Author Award: **Dr. Martin Luther King, Jr., Man of Peace** by Lillie Patterson (Garrard)

1971
Author Award: **Black Troubadour: Langston Hughes** by Charlemae Rollins (Rand McNally)
Honor Books
I Know Why the Caged Bird Sings by Maya Angelou (Random House)
Unbought and Unbossed by Shirley Chisholm (Houghton Mifflin)
I Am a Black Woman by Mari Evans (Morrow)
Every Man Heart Lay Down by Lorenz Graham (Crowell)
The Voice of the Children by June Jordan and Terri Bush (Holt)
Black Means by Gladys Groom and Bonnie Grossman (Hill & Wang)
Ebony Book of Black Achievement by Margaret W. Peters (Johnson)
Mary Jo's Grandmother by Janice May Udry (Whitman)

1972
Author Award: **17 Black Artists** by Elton C. Fax (Dodd)

1973
Author Award: **I Never Had It Made: The Autobiography of Jackie Robinson** by Alfred Duckett (Putnam),

1974
Author Award: **Ray Charles** by Sharon Bell Mathis (Crowell)
Honor Books
A Hero Ain't Nothin' but a Sandwich by Alice Childress (Coward-McCann)
Don't You Remember? by Lucille Clifton (Dutton)
Ms. Africa: Profiles of Modern African Women by Louise Crane (Lippincott)
Guest in the Promised Land by Kristin Hunter (Scribner's)
Mukasa by John Nagenda (Macmillan)

Illustrator Award: **Ray Charles** by Sharon Bell Mathis, illustrated by George Ford (Crowell)

1975
Author Award: **The Legend of Africana** by Dorothy Robinson (Johnson)

1976
Author Award: **Duey's Tale** by Pearl Bailey (Harcourt)
Honor Books
Julius K. Nyerere: Teacher of Africa by Shirley Graham (Messner)
Paul Robeson by Eloise Greenfield (Crowell)
Fast Sam, Cool Clyde and Stuff by Walter Dean Myers (Viking)
Song of the Trees by Mildred Taylor (Dial)

1977
Author Award: **The Story of Stevie Wonder** by James Haskins (Lothrop)
Honor Books
Everett Anderson's Friend by Lucille Clifton (Holt)
Roll of Thunder, Hear My Cry by Mildred D. Taylor (Dial)
Quiz Book on Black America by Clarence N. Blake and Donald F. Martin (Houghton Mifflin)

1978
Author Award: **Africa Dreams** by Eloise Greenfield (Crowell)
Honor Books
The Days When the Animals Talked: Black Folk Tales and How They Came to Be by William J. Faulkner (Follett)
Marvin and Tige by Frankcina Glass (St. Martin's)
Mary McCleod Bethune by Eloise Greenfield (Crowell)
Barbara Jordan by James Haskins (Dial)
Coretta Scott King by Lillie Patterson (Garrard)
Portia: The Life of Portia Washington Pittman, the Daughter of Booker T. Washington by Ruth Ann Stewart (Doubleday)

1979
Author Award: **Escape to Freedom: A Play about Young Frederick Douglass** by Ossie Davis (Viking)
Honor Books
Skates of Uncle Richard by Carol Fenner (Random House)
Justice and Her Brothers by Virginia Hamilton (Greenwillow)
Benjamin Banneker by Lillie Patterson (Abingdon)
I Have a Sister, My Sister Is Deaf by Jeanne W. Peterson (Harper)
Illustrator Award: **Something on My Mind** by Nikki Grimes, illustrated by Tom Feelings (Dial)

1980

Author Award: **The Young Landlords** by Walter Dean Myers (Viking)

Honor Books
Movin' Up by Berry Gordy (Harper)
Childtimes: A Three-Generation Memoir by Eloise Greenfield and Leslie Jones Little (Harper)
Andrew Young: Young Man with a Mission by James Haskins (Lothrop)
James Van Der Zee: The Picture Takin' Man by James Haskins (Dodd)
Let the Lion Eat Straw by Ellease Southerland (Scribner's)

Illustrator Award: **Cornrows** by Camille Yarbrough, illustrated by Carole Byard (Coward-McCann)

1981

Author Award: **This Life** by Sidney Poitier (Knopf)

Honor Books
Don't Explain: A Song of Billie Holiday by Alexis De Veaux (Harper)

Illustrator Award: **Beat the Story Drum, Pum-Pum** by Ashley Bryan (Atheneum)

Honor Books
Grandmama's Joy by Eloise Greenfield, illustrated by Carole Byard (Philomel)
Count on Your Fingers African Style by Claudia Zaslavsky, illustrated by Jerry Pinkney (Crowell)

1982

Author Award: **Let the Circle Be Unbroken** by Mildred D. Taylor (Dial)

Honor Books
Rainbow Jordan by Alice Childress (Coward-McCann)
Lou in the Limelight by Kristin Hunter (Scribner's)
Mary: An Autobiography by Mary E. Mebane (Viking)

Illustrator Award: **Mother Crocodile: An Uncle Amadou Tale from Senegal** translated by Rosa Guy, illustrated by John Steptoe (Delacorte)

Honor Book
Daydreamers by Eloise Greenfield, illustrated by Tom Feelings (Dial)

1983

Author Award: **Sweet Whispers, Brother Rush** by Virginia Hamilton (Philomel)

Honor Book
This Strange New Feeling by Julius Lester (Dial)

Illustrator Award: **Black Child** by Peter Magubane (Knopf)

Honor Books
All the Colors of the Race by Arnold Adoff, illustrated by John Steptoe (Lothrop)
Just Us Women by Jeannette Caines, illustrated by Pat Cummings (Harper)

1984

Author Award: **Everett Anderson's Goodbye** by Lucille Clifton (Holt)

Special Citation
The Words of Martin Luther King, Jr. compiled by Coretta Scott King (Newmarket)

Honor Books
The Magical Adventures of Pretty Pearl by Virginia Hamilton (Harper)
Lena Horne by James Haskins (Coward-McCann)
Bright Shadow by Joyce Carol Thomas (Avon)
Because We Are by Mildred Pitts Walter (Lothrop)

Illustrator Award: **My Mama Needs Me** by Mildred Pitts Walter, illustrated by Pat Cummings (Lothrop)

1985

Author Award: **Motown and Didi** by Walter Dean Myers (Viking)

Honor Books
Circle of Gold by Candy Dawson Boyd (Apple/Scholastic)
A Little Love by Virginia Hamilton (Philomel)

1986

Author Award: **The People Could Fly: American Black Folktales** by Virginia Hamilton (Knopf)

Honor Books
Junius Over Far by Virginia Hamilton (Harper)
Trouble's Child by Mildred Pitts Walter (Lothrop)

Illustrator Award: **The Patchwork Quilt** by Valerie Flournoy, illustrated by Jerry Pinkney (Dial)

Honor Book
The People Could Fly: American Black Folktales retold by Virginia Hamilton, illustrated by Leo and Diane Dillon (Knopf)

1987

Author Award: **Justin and the Best Biscuits in the World** by Mildred Pitts Walter (Lothrop)

Honor Books
Lion and the Ostrich Chicks and Other African Folk Tales by Ashley Bryan (Atheneum)
Which Way Freedom? by Joyce Hansen (Walker)

Illustrator Award: **Half a Moon and One Whole Star** by Crescent Dragonwagon, illustrated by Jerry Pinkney (Macmillan)

Honor Books
Lion and the Ostrich Chicks and Other African Folk Tales by Ashley Bryan (Atheneum)
C.L.O.U.D.S. by Pat Cummings (Lothrop)

1988

Author Award: **The Friendship** by Mildred D. Taylor (Dial)

Honor Books
An Enchanted Hair Tale by Alexis De Veaux (Harper)

The Tales of Uncle Remus: The Adventures of Brer Rabbit by Julius Lester (Dial)

Illustrator Award: Mufaro's Beautiful Daughters by John Steptoe

Honor Books
What a Morning! The Christmas Story in Black Spirituals selected by John Langstaff, illustrated by Ashley Bryan (Macmillan)
The Invisible Hunters: A Legend from the Miskito Indians of Nicaragua compiled by Harriet Rohmer et al., illustrated by Joe Sam (Children's Book Press)

1989
Author Award: Fallen Angels by Walter Dean Myers (Scholastic)

Honor Books
A Thief in the Village and Other Stories by James Berry (Orchard)
Anthony Burns: The Defeat and Triumph of a Fugitive Slave by Virginia Hamilton (Knopf)

Illustrator Award: Mirandy and Brother Wind by Patricia C. McKissack, illustrated by Jerry Pinkney (Knopf)

Honor Books
Under the Sunday Tree by Eloise Greenfield, illustrated by Amos Ferguson (Harper)
Storm in the Night by Mary Stolz, illustrated by Pat Cummings (Harper)

1990
Author Award: A Long Hard Journey: The Story of the Pullman Porter by Patricia C. McKissack and Fredrick McKissack (Walker)

Honor Books
Nathaniel Talking by Eloise Greenfield (Black Butterfly)
The Bells of Christmas by Virginia Hamilton (Harcourt)
Martin Luther King, Jr. & the Freedom Movement by Lillie Patterson (Facts on File)

Illustrator Award: Nathaniel Talking by Eloise Greenfield, illustrated by Jan Spivey Gilchrist (Black Butterfly)

Honor Book
The Talking Eggs by Robert D. San Souci, illustrated by Jerry Pinkney (Dial)

1991
Author Award: The Road to Memphis by Mildred D. Taylor (Dial)

Honor Books
Black Dance in America by James Haskins (Crowell)
When I Am Old with You by Angela Johnson (Orchard)

Illustrator Award: Aida by Leontyne Price, illustrated by Leo Dillon and Diane Dillon (Harcourt)

1992
Author Award: Now Is Your Time: The African American Struggle for Freedom by Walter Dean Myers (HarperCollins)

Honor Book
Night on Neighborhood Street by Eloise Greenfield (Dial)

Illustrator Award: Tar Beach by Faith Ringgold (Crown)

Honor Books
All Night, All Day! A Child's First Book of African American Spirituals selected by Ashley Bryan (Atheneum)
Night on Neighborhood Street by Eloise Greenfield, illustrated by Jan Spivey Gilchrist (Dial)

1993
Author Award: The Dark-Thirty: Southern Tales of the Supernatural by Patricia C. McKissack (Knopf)

Honor Books
Mississippi Challenge by Mildred Pitts Walter (Bradbury)
Sojourner Truth: Ain't I a Woman? by Patricia C. McKissack and Fredrick McKissack (Scholastic)
Somewhere in the Darkness by Walter Dean Myers (Scholastic)

Illustrator Award: The Origin of Life on Earth: An African Creation Myth retold by David A. Anderson, illustrated by Kathleen Atkins Wilson (Sights)

Honor Books
Little Eight John by Jan Wahl, illustrated by Wil Clay (Lodestar)
Sukey and the Mermaid by Robert D. San Souci, illustrated by Brian Pinkney (Four Winds)
Working Cotton by Sherley Anne Williams, illustrated by Carole Byard (Harcourt)

1994
Author Award: Toning the Sweep by Angela Johnson (Orchard)

Honor Books
Brown Honey in Broomwheat Tea by Joyce Carol Thomas (HarperCollins)
Malcolm X: By Any Means Necessary by Walter Dean Myers (Scholastic)

Illustrator Award: Soul Looks Back in Wonder: Collection of African American Poets edited by Phyllis Fogelman, illustrated by Tom Feelings (Dial)

Honor Books
Brown Honey in Broomwheat Tea by Joyce Carol Thomas, illustrated by Floyd Cooper (HarperCollins)
Uncle Jed's Barbershop by Margaret King Mitchell, illustrated by James Ransome (Simon & Schuster)

1995
Author Award: Christmas in the Big House, Christmas in the Quarters by Patricia C. and Fredrick L. McKissack (Scholastic)

Honor Books

Black Diamond: The Story of the Negro Baseball Leagues by Patricia C. and Fredrick L. McKissack (Scholastic)

I Hadn't Meant to Tell You This by Jacqueline Woodson (Delacorte)

The Captive by Joyce Hansen (Scholastic)

Illustrator Award: **The Creation** by James Weldon Johnson, illustrated by James Ransome (Holiday House)

Honor Books

Meet Danitra Brown by Nikki Grimes, illustrated by Floyd Cooper (Lothrop)

The Singing Man by Angela Shelf, illustrated by Terea Shaffer (Holiday House)

1996

Author Award: **Her Stories** by Virginia Hamilton, (Blue Sky Press)

Honor Books

The Watsons Go to Birmingham—1963 by Christopher Paul Curtis (Delacorte)

Like Sisters on the Homefront by Rita Williams-Garcia (Lodestar)

From the Notebooks of Melanin Sun by Jacqueline Woodson (Blue Sky)

Illustrator Award: **The Middle Passage: White Ships, Black Cargo** by Tom Feelings (Dial)

Honor Books

Her Stories by Virginia Hamilton, illustrated by Leo and Diane Dillon (Blue Sky)

The Faithful Friend by Robert D. San Souci, illustrated by Brian Pinkney (Simon & Schuster)

1997

Author Award: **Slam!** by Walter Dean Myers (Scholastic)

Honor Book

Rebels against Slavery: American Slave Revolts by Patricia C. McKissack and Fredrick McKissack (Scholastic)

Illustrator Award: **Minty: A Story of Young Harriet Tubman** by Alan Schroeder, illustrated by Jerry Pinkney (Dial)

Honor Books

The Palm of My Heart: Poetry by African American Children by Davida Adedjouma, illustrated by Gregory Christie (Lee & Low)

Running the Road to ABC by Denize Lauture, illustrated by Reynold Ruffins (Simon & Schuster)

Neeny Coming, Neeny Going by Karen English, illustrated by Synthia Saint James (Bridgewater)

NATIONAL COUNCIL OF TEACHERS OF ENGLISH (NCTE) AWARD FOR EXCELLENCE IN POETRY FOR CHILDREN

This award was given annually from 1977 to 1982 and every three years after that to a living American poet in recognition of his or her entire body of work for children ages three through thirteen.

1977   David McCord

1978   Aileen Fisher

1979   Karla Kuskin

1980   Myra Cohn Livingston

1981   Eve Merriam

1982   John Ciardi

1985   Lilian Moore

1988   Arnold Adoff

1991   Valerie Worth

1994   Barbara Esbensen

1997   Eloise Greenfield

JOHN NEWBERY MEDAL

The John Newbery Medal has been awarded annually since 1922 under the supervision of the ALA's Association for Library Service to Children. It is presented to the author of the work judged to be the most distinguished contribution to literature for children published in the United States during the previous year. One or more Honor Books are also chosen. Winners must be residents or citizens of the United States.

1922

The Story of Mankind by Hendrik Willem van Loon (Liveright)

Honor Books

Cedric the Forester by Bernard Marshall (Appleton)

The Golden Fleece and the Heroes Who Lived before Achilles by Padraic Colum (Macmillan)

The Great Quest by Charles Hawes (Little, Brown)

The Old Tobacco Shop by William Bowen (Macmillan)
Windy Hill by Cornelia Meigs (Macmillan)

1923
The Voyages of Doctor Dolittle by Hugh Lofting (Lippincott)
Honor Book
No record

1924
The Dark Frigate by Charles Hawes (Atlantic/Little, Brown)
Honor Book
No record

1925
Tales from Silver Lands by Charles Finger (Doubleday)
Honor Books
Dream Coach by Anne Parrish (Macmillan)
Nicholas by Anne Carroll Moore (Putnam)

1926
Shen of the Sea by Arthur Bowie Chrisman (Dutton)
Honor Book
Voyagers by Padraic Colum (Macmillan)

1927
Smoky, the Cowhorse by Will James (Scribner's)
Honor Book
No record

1928
Gayneck, the Story of a Pigeon by Dhan Gopal Mukerji (Dutton)
Honor Books
Downright Dencey by Caroline Snedeker (Doubleday)
The Wonder Smith and His Son by Ella Young (Longmans)

1929
The Trumpeter of Krakow by Eric P. Kelly (Macmillan)
Honor Books
The Boy Who Was by Grace Hallock (Dutton)
Clearing Weather by Cornelia Meigs (Little, Brown)
Millions of Cats by Wanda Gág (Coward)
Pigtail of Ah Lee Ben Loo by John Bennett (Longmans)
Runaway Papoose by Grace Moon (Doubleday)
Tod of the Fens by Elinor Whitney (Macmillan)

1930
Hitty, Her First Hundred Years by Rachel Field (Macmillan)
Honor Books
Daughter of the Seine by Jeanette Eaton (Harper)
Jumping-Off Place by Marian Hurd McNeely (Longmans)
Little Blacknose by Hildegarde Swift (Harcourt)
Pran of Albania by Elizabeth Miller (Doubleday)

Tangle-Coated Horse and Other Tales by Ella Young (Longmans)
Vaino by Julia Davis Adams (Dutton)

1931
The Cat Who Went to Heaven by Elizabeth Coatsworth (Macmillan)
Honor Books
The Dark Star of Itza by Alida Malkus (Harcourt)
Floating Island by Anne Parrish (Harper)
Garram the Hunter by Herbert Best (Doubleday)
Meggy Macintosh by Elizabeth Janet Gray (Doubleday)
Mountains Are Free by Julia Davis Adams (Dutton)
Ood-Le-Uk the Wanderer by Alice Lide and Margaret Johansen (Little, Brown)
Queer Person by Ralph Hubbard (Doubleday)
Spice and the Devil's Cake by Agnes Hewes (Knopf)

1932
Waterless Mountain by Laura Adams Armer (Longmans)
Honor Books
Boy of the South Seas by Eunice Tietjens (Coward)
Calico Bush by Rachel Field (Macmillan)
The Fairy Circus by Dorothy P. Lathrop (Macmillan)
Jane's Island by Marjorie Allee (Houghton Mifflin)
Out of the Flames by Eloise Lownsbery (Longmans)
Truce of the Wolf and Other Tales of Old Italy by Mary Gould Davis (Harcourt)

1933
Young Fu of the Upper Yangtze by Elizabeth Lewis (Winston)
Honor Books
Children of the Soil by Nora Burglon (Doubleday)
The Railroad to Freedom by Hildegarde Swift (Harcourt)
Swift Rivers by Cornelia Meigs (Little, Brown)

1934
Invincible Louisa by Cornelia Meigs (Little, Brown)
Honor Books
ABC Bunny by Wanda Gág (Coward)
Apprentice of Florence by Anne Kyle (Houghton Mifflin)
Big Tree of Bunlaby by Padraic Colum (Macmillan)
The Forgotten Daughter by Caroline Snedeker (Doubleday)
Glory of the Seas by Agnes Hewes (Knopf)
New Land by Sarah Schmidt (McBride)
Swords of Steel by Elsie Singmaster (Houghton Mifflin)
Winged Girl of Knossos by Erik Berry (Appleton)

1935
Dobry by Monica Shannon (Viking)
Honor Books
Davy Crockett by Constance Rourke (Harcourt)
Day on Skates by Hilda Van Stockum (Harper)
Pageant of Chinese History by Elizabeth Seeger (Longmans)

1936

Caddie Woodlawn by Carol Ryrie Brink (Macmillan)

Honor Books
All Sail Set by Armstrong Sperry (Winston)
The Good Master by Kate Seredy (Viking)
Honk, the Moose by Phil Strong (Dodd)
Young Walter Scott by Elizabeth Janet Gray (Viking)

1937

Roller Skates by Ruth Sawyer (Viking)

Honor Books
Audubon by Constance Rourke (Harcourt)
The Codfish Musket by Agnes Hewes (Doubleday)
Golden Basket by Ludwig Bemelmans (Viking)
Phebe Fairchild: Her Book by Lois Lenski (Stokes)
Whistler's Van by Idwal Jones (Viking)
Winterbound by Margery Bianco (Viking)

1938

The White Stag by Kate Seredy (Viking)

Honor Books
Bright Island by Mabel Robinson (Random House)
On the Banks of Plum Creek by Laura Ingalls Wilder (Harper)
Pecos Bill by James Cloyd Bowman (Little, Brown)

1939

Thimble Summer by Elizabeth Enright (Rinehart)

Honor Books
Hello the Boat! by Phyllis Crawford (Holt)
Leader by Destiny: George Washington, Man and Patriot by Jeanette Eaton (Harcourt)
Mr. Popper's Penguins by Richard and Florence Atwater (Little, Brown)
Nino by Valenti Angelo (Viking)
Penn by Elizabeth Janet Gray (Viking)

1940

Daniel Boone by James Daugherty (Viking)

Honor Books
Boy with a Pack by Stephen W. Meader (Harcourt)
By the Shores of Silver Lake by Laura Ingalls Wilder (Harper)
Runner of the Mountain Tops by Mabel Robinson (Random House)
The Singing Tree by Kate Seredy (Viking)

1941

Call It Courage by Armstrong Sperry (Macmillan)

Honor Books
Blue Willow by Doris Gates (Viking)
The Long Winter by Laura Ingalls Wilder (Harper)
Nansen by Anna Gertrude Hall (Viking)
Young Mac of Fort Vancouver by Mary Jane Carr (Crowell)

1942

The Matchlock Gun by Walter D. Edmonds (Dodd)

Honor Books
Down Ryton Water by Eva Roe Gaggin (Viking)
George Washington's World by Genevieve Foster (Scribner's)
Indian Captive: The Story of Mary Jemison by Lois Lenski (Lippincott)
Little Town on the Prairie by Laura Ingalls Wilder (Harper)

1943

Adam of the Road by Elizabeth Janet Gray (Viking)

Honor Books
Have You Seen Tom Thumb? by Mabel Leigh Hunt (Lippincott)
The Middle Moffat by Eleanor Estes (Harcourt)

1944

Johnny Tremain by Esther Forbes (Houghton Mifflin)

Honor Books
Fog Magic by Julia Sauer (Viking)
Mountain Born by Elizabeth Yates (Coward)
Rufus M. by Eleanor Estes (Harcourt)
These Happy Golden Years by Laura Ingalls Wilder (Harper)

1945

Rabbit Hill by Robert Lawson (Viking)

Honor Books
Abraham Lincoln's World by Genevieve Foster (Scribner's)
The Hundred Dresses by Eleanor Estes (Harcourt)
Lone Journey: The Life of Roger Williams by Jeanette Eaton (Harcourt)
The Silver Pencil by Alice Dalgliesh (Scribner's)

1946

Strawberry Girl by Lois Lenski (Lippincott)

Honor Books
Bhimsa, the Dancing Bear by Christine Weston (Scribner's)
Justin Morgan Had a Horse by Marguerite Henry (Rand McNally)
The Moved-Outers by Florence Crannell Means (Houghton Mifflin)
New Found World by Katherine Shippen (Viking)

1947

Miss Hickory by Carolyn Sherwin Bailey (Viking)

Honor Books
The Avion My Uncle Flew by Cyrus Fisher (Appleton)
Big Tree by Mary and Conrad Buff (Viking)
The Heavenly Tenants by William Maxwell (Harper)
The Hidden Treasure of Glaston by Eleanore Jewett (Viking)

Wonderful Year by Nancy Barnes (Messner)

1948
The Twenty-One Balloons by William Pène du Bois
(Viking)

Honor Books
The Cow-Tail Switch and Other West African Stories
by Harold Courlander (Holt)
Li Lun, Lad of Courage by Carolyn Treffinger
(Abingdon)
Misty of Chincoteague by Marguerite Henry (Rand
McNally)
Pancakes—Paris by Claire Huchet Bishop (Viking)
The Quaint and Curious Quest of Johnny Longfoot by
Catherine Besterman (Bobbs)

1949
King of the Wind by Marguerite Henry (Rand McNally)

Honor Books
Daughter of the Mountains by Louise Rankin (Viking)
My Father's Dragon by Ruth S. Gannett (Random
House)
Seabird by Holling C. Holling (Houghton Mifflin)
Story of the Negro by Arna Bontemps (Knopf)

1950
A Door in the Wall by Marguerite de Angeli
(Doubleday)

Honor Books
The Blue Cat of Castle Town by Catherine Coblentz
(Longmans)
George Washington by Genevieve Foster (Scribner's)
Kildee House by Rutherford Montgomery (Doubleday)
Song of the Pines by Walter and Marion Havighurst
(Winston)
Tree of Freedom by Rebecca Caudill (Viking)

1951
Amos Fortune, Free Man by Elizabeth Yates (Dutton)

Honor Books
Abraham Lincoln, Friend of the People by Clara
Ingram Judson (Follett)
Better Known as Johnny Appleseed by Mabel Leigh
Hunt (Lippincott)
Gandhi, Fighter without a Sword by Jeanette Eaton
(Morrow)
The Story of Appleby Capple by Anne Parrish (Harper)

1952
Ginger Pye by Eleanor Estes (Harcourt)

Honor Books
Americans before Columbus by Elizabeth Baity (Viking)
The Apple and the Arrow by Mary and Conrad Buff
(Houghton Mifflin)
The Defender by Nicholas Kalashnikoff (Scribner's)
The Light at Tern Rocks by Julia Sauer (Viking)

Minn of the Mississippi by Holling C. Holling
(Houghton Mifflin)

1953
Secret of the Andes by Ann Nolan Clark (Viking)

Honor Books
The Bears of Hemlock Mountain by Alice Dalgliesh
(Scribner's)
Birthdays of Freedom, Vol. 1 by Genevieve Foster
(Scribner's)
Charlotte's Web by E. B. White (Harper)
Moccasin Trail by Eloise McGraw (Coward)
Red Sails to Capri by Ann Weil (Viking)

1954
. . . And Now Miguel by Joseph Krumgold (Crowell)

Honor Books
All Alone by Claire Huchet Bishop (Viking)
Hurry Home Candy by Meindert DeJong (Harper)
Magic Maize by Mary and Conrad Buff (Houghton
Mifflin)
Shadrach by Meindert DeJong (Harper)
Theodore Roosevelt, Fighting Patriot by Clara Ingram
Judson (Follett)

1955
The Wheel on the School by Meindert DeJong (Harper)

Honor Books
Banner in the Sky by James Ullman (Lippincott)
Courage of Sarah Noble by Alice Dalgliesh (Scribner's)

1956
Carry On, Mr. Bowditch by Jean Lee Latham (Houghton Mifflin)

Honor Books
The Golden Name Day by Jennie Lindquist (Harper)
Men, Microscopes, and Living Things by Katherine
Shippen (Viking)
The Secret River by Marjorie Kinnan Rawlings
(Scribner's)

1957
Miracles on Maple Hill by Virginia Sorensen (Harcourt)

Honor Books
Black Fox of Lorne by Marguerite de Angeli (Doubleday)
The Corn Grows Ripe by Dorothy Rhoads (Viking)
The House of Sixty Fathers by Meindert DeJong
(Harper)
Mr. Justice Holmes by Clara Ingram Judson (Follett)
Old Yeller by Fred Gipson (Harper)

1958
Rifles for Watie by Harold Keith (Crowell)

Honor Books
Gone-Away Lake by Elizabeth Enright (Harcourt)
The Great Wheel by Robert Lawson (Viking)
The Horse Catcher by Mari Sandoz (Westminster)

Tom Paine, Freedom's Apostle by Leo Gurko (Crowell)

1959

The Witch of Blackbird Pond by Elizabeth George Speare (Houghton Mifflin)

Honor Books
Along Came a Dog by Meindert DeJong (Harper)
Chucaro: Wild Pony of the Pampa by Francis Kalnay (Harcourt)
The Family under the Bridge by Natalie Savage Carlson (Harper)
The Perilous Road by William O. Steele (Harcourt)

1960

Onion John by Joseph Krumgold (Crowell)

Honor Books
America Is Born by Gerald W. Johnson (Morrow)
The Gammage Cup by Carol Kendall (Harcourt)
My Side of the Mountain by Jean Craighead George (Dutton)

1961

Island of the Blue Dolphins by Scott O'Dell (Houghton Mifflin)

Honor Books
America Moves Forward by Gerald W. Johnson (Morrow)
The Cricket in Times Square by George Selden (Farrar)
Old Ramon by Jack Schaefer (Houghton Mifflin)

1962

The Bronze Bow by Elizabeth George Speare (Houghton Mifflin)

Honor Books
Belling the Tiger by Mary Stolz (Harper)
Frontier Living by Edwin Tunis (World)
The Golden Goblet by Eloise McGraw (Coward)

1963

A Wrinkle in Time by Madeleine L'Engle (Farrar)
Honor Books
Men of Athens by Olivia Coolidge (Houghton Mifflin)
Thistle and Thyme by Sorche Nic Leodhas (Holt)

1964

It's Like This, Cat by Emily Cheney Neville (Harper)
Honor Books
The Loner by Ester Wier (McKay)
Rascal by Sterling North (Dutton)

1965

Shadow of a Bull by Maia Wojciechowska (Atheneum)
Honor Books
Across Five Aprils by Irene Hunt (Follett)

1966

I, Juan de Pareja by Elizabeth Borten de Trevino (Farrar)

Honor Books
The Animal Family by Randall Jarrell (Pantheon)
The Black Cauldron by Lloyd Alexander (Holt)
The Noonday Friends by Mary Stolz (Harper)

1967

Up a Road Slowly by Irene Hunt (Follett)
Honor Books
The Jazz Man by Mary H. Weik (Atheneum)
The King's Fifth by Scott O'Dell (Houghton)
Zlateh the Goat and Other Stories by Isaac Bashevis Singer (Harper)

1968

From the Mixed-Up Files of Mrs. Basil E. Frankweiler by E. L. Konigsburg (Atheneum)

Honor Books
The Black Pearl by Scott O'Dell (Houghton Mifflin)
The Egypt Game by Zilpha Keatley Snyder (Atheneum)
The Fearsome Inn by Isaac Bashevis Singer (Scribner's)
Jennifer, Hecate, Macbeth, William McKinley, and Me, Elizabeth by E. L. Konigsburg (Atheneum)

1969

The High King by Lloyd Alexander (Holt)
Honor Books
To Be a Slave by Julius Lester (Dial)
When Sheemiel Went to Warsaw and Other Stories by Isaac Bashevis Singer (Farrar)

1970

Sounder by William H. Armstrong (Harper)
Honor Books
Journey Outside by Mary Q. Steele (Viking)
The Many Ways of Seeing: An Introduction to the Pleasures of Art by Janet Gaylord Moore (World)
Our Eddie by Sulamith Ish-Kishor (Pantheon)

1971

Summer of the Swans by Betsy Byars (Viking)
Honor Books
Enchantress from the Stars by Sylvia Louise Engdahl (Atheneum)
Knee-Knock Rise by Natalie Babbitt (Farrar)
Sing Down the Moon by Scott O'Dell (Houghton Mifflin)

1972

Mrs. Frisby and the Rats of NIMH by Robert C. O'Brien (Atheneum)
Honor Books
Annie and the Old One by Miska Miles (Atlantic/Little, Brown)
The Headless Cupid by Zilpha Keatley Snyder (Atheneum)
Incident at Hawk's Hill by Allan W. Eckert (Little, Brown)

The Planet of Junior Brown by Virginia Hamilton
(Macmillan)
The Tombs of Atuan by Ursula K. Le Guin (Atheneum)

1973
Julie of the Wolves by Jean Craighead George (Harper)
Honor Books
Frog and Toad Together by Arnold Lobel (Harper)
The Upstairs Room by Johanna Reiss (Crowell)
The Witches of Worm by Zilpha Keatley Snyder
(Atheneum)

1974
The Slave Dancer by Paula Fox (Bradbury)
Honor Book
The Dark Is Rising by Susan Cooper (McElderry)

1975
M. C. Higgins, the Great by Virginia Hamilton
(Macmillan)
Honor Books
Figgs and Phantoms by Ellen Raskin (Dutton)
My Brother Sam Is Dead by James Lincoln Collier and
Christopher Collier (Four Winds)
The Perilous Gard by Elizabeth Marie Pope (Hough-
ton Mifflin)
Philip Hall Likes Me, I Reckon Maybe by Bette Greene
(Dial)

1976
The Grey King by Susan Cooper (McElderry)
Honor Books
Dragonwings by Laurence Yep (Harper)
The Hundred Penny Box by Sharon Bell Mathis (Viking)

1977
Roll of Thunder, Hear My Cry by Mildred D. Taylor
(Dial)
Honor Books
Abel's Island by William Steig (Farrar)
A String in the Harp by Nancy Bond (McElderry)

1978
Bridge to Terabithia by Katherine Paterson (Crowell)
Honor Books
Anpao: An American Indian Odyssey by Jamake
Highwater (Lippincott)
Ramona and Her Father by Beverly Cleary (Morrow)

1979
The Westing Game by Ellen Raskin (Dutton)
Honor Books
The Great Gilly Hopkins by Katherine Paterson
(Crowell)

1980
*A Gathering of Days: A New England Girl's Journal,
1830–32* by Joan W. Blos (Scribner's)

Honor Book
The Road from Home: The Story of an Armenian Girl
by David Kherdian (Greenwillow)

1981
Jacob Have I Loved by Katherine Paterson (Crowell)
Honor Books
The Fledgling by Jane Langton (Harper)
A Ring of Endless Light by Madeleine L'Engle (Farrar)

1982
*A Visit to William Blake's Inn: Poems for Innocent and
Experienced Travelers* by Nancy Willard (Harcourt)
Honor Books
Ramona Quimby, Age 8 by Beverly Cleary (Morrow)
*Upon the Head of the Goat: A Childhood in Hungary,
1939–1944* by Aranka Siegal (Farrar)

1983
Dicey's Song by Cynthia Voigt (Atheneum)
Honor Books
The Blue Sword by Robin McKinley (Greenwillow)
Doctor De Soto by William Steig (Farrar)
Graven Images by Paul Fleischman (Harper)
Homesick: My Own Story by Jean Fritz (Putnam)
Sweet Whispers, Brother Rush by Virginia Hamilton
(Philomel)

1984
Dear Mr. Henshaw by Beverly Cleary (Morrow)
Honor Books
The Sign of the Beaver by Elizabeth George Speare
(Houghton Mifflin)
A Solitary Blue by Cynthia Voigt (Atheneum)
Sugaring Time by Kathryn Lasky (Macmillan)
The Wish Giver by Bill Brittain (Harper)

1985
The Hero and the Crown by Robin McKinley
(Greenwillow)
Honor Books
Like Jake and Me by Mavis Jukes (Knopf)
The Moves Make the Man by Bruce Brooks (Harper)
One-Eyed Cat by Paula Fox (Bradbury)

1986
Sarah, Plain and Tall by Patricia MacLachlan (Harper)
Honor Books
Commodore Perry in the Land of the Shogun by Rhoda
Blumberg (Lothrop)
Dogsong by Gary Paulsen (Bradbury)

1987
The Whipping Boy by Sid Fleischman (Greenwillow)
Honor Books
A Fine White Dust by Cynthia Rylant (Bradbury)
On My Honor by Marion Dane Bauer (Clarion)

Volcano: The Eruption and Healing of Mount St. Helens by Patricia Lauber (Bradbury)

1988
Lincoln: A Photobiography by Russell Freedman (Clarion)
Honor Books
After the Rain by Norma Fox Mazer (Morrow)
Hatchet by Gary Paulsen (Bradbury)

1989
Joyful Noise: Poems for Two Voices by Paul Fleischman (Harper)
Honor Books
In the Beginning: Creation Stories from Around the World by Virginia Hamilton (Harcourt)
Scorpions by Walter Dean Myers (Harper)

1990
Number the Stars by Lois Lowry (Houghton Mifflin)
Honor Books
Afternoon of the Elves by Janet Taylor Lisle (Orchard)
Shabanu: Daughter of the Wind by Suzanne Fisher Staples (Knopf)
The Winter Room by Gary Paulsen (Orchard)

1991
Maniac Magee by Jerry Spinelli (Little, Brown)
Honor Book
The True Confessions of Charlotte Doyle by Avi (Orchard)

1992
Shiloh by Phyllis Reynolds Naylor (Atheneum)
Honor Books
Nothing but the Truth: A Documentary Novel by Avi (Orchard)
The Wright Brothers: How They Invented the Airplane by Russell Freedman (Holiday House)

1993
Missing May by Cynthia Rylant (Orchard)

Honor Books
The Dark-Thirty: Southern Tales of the Supernatural by Patricia McKissack (Knopf)
Somewhere in the Darkness by Walter Dean Myers (Scholastic)
What Hearts by Bruce Brooks (HarperCollins)

1994
The Giver by Lois Lowry (Houghton Mifflin)
Honor Books
Crazy Lady! by Jane Leslie Conly (HarperCollins)
Dragon's Gate by Laurence Yep (HarperCollins)
Eleanor Roosevelt: A Life of Discovery by Russell Freedman (Clarion)

1995
Walk Two Moons by Sharon Creech (HarperCollins)
Honor Books
Catherine, Called Birdy by Karen Cushman (Clarion)
The Ear, the Eye and the Arm by Nancy Farmer (Orchard/Richard Jackson)

1996
The Midwife's Apprentice by Karen Cushman (Clarion)
Honor Books
What Jamie Saw by Carolyn Coman (Front Street)
The Watsons Go to Birmingham—1963 by Christopher Paul Curtis (Delacorte)
Yolonda's Genius by Carol Fenner (McElderry/Simon & Schuster)
The Great Fire by Jim Murphy (Scholastic)

1997
The View from Saturday by E. L. Konigsburg (Jean Karl/Atheneum)
Honor Books
A Girl Named Disaster by Nancy Farmer (Richard Jackson/Orchard)
Moorchild by Elois McGraw (McElderry)
The Thief by Megan Whalen Turner (Greenwillow)
Belle Prater's Boy by Ruth White (Farrar)

ORBIS PICTUS AWARD FOR OUTSTANDING NONFICTION FOR CHILDREN

The National Council of Teachers of English (NCTE) established the Orbis Pictus Award in 1990 to recognize outstanding nonfiction for children. The annual award is named for *Orbis Pictus (The World in Pictures)*, a 1657 work by John Amos Comenius, believed to be the first book written expressly for children.

1990
The Great Little Madison by Jean Fritz (Putnam)

Honor Books
The Great American Gold Rush by Rhoda Blumberg (Bradbury)
The News about Dinosaurs by Patricia Lauber (Bradbury)

1991
Franklin Delano Roosevelt by Russell Freedman (Clarion)

Honor Books
Arctic Memories by Normee Ekoomiak (Holt)
Seeing Earth from Space by Patricia Lauber (Orchard)

1992
Flight: The Journey of Charles Lindbergh by Robert Burleigh and Mike Wimmer (Philomel)

Honor Books
Now Is Your Time! The African American Struggle for Freedom by Walter Dean Myers (HarperCollins)
Prairie Visions: The Life and Times of Solomon Butcher by Pam Conrad (HarperCollins)

1993
Children of the Dust Bowl: The True Story of the School of Weedpatch Camp by Jerry Stanley (Crown)

Honor Books
Talking with Artists by Pat Cummings (Bradbury)
Come Back, Salmon by Molly Cone (Sierra Club)

1994
Across America on an Emigrant Train by Jim Murphy (Clarion)

Honor Books
To the Top of the World: Adventures with Arctic Wolves by Jim Brandenburg (Walker)
Making Sense: Animal Perception and Communication by Bruce Brooks (Farrar)

1995
Safari Beneath the Sea: The Wonder World of the North Pacific Coast by Diane Swanson (Sierra Club)

Honor Books
Wildlife Rescue: The Work of Dr. Kathleen Ramsay by Jennifer Owings Dewey (Boyds Mills)
Kids at Work: Lewis Hine and the Crusade against Child Labor by Russell Freedman (Clarion)
Christmas in the Big House, Christmas in the Quarters by Patricia and Fredrick McKissack (Scholastic)

1996
The Great Fire by Jim Murphy (Scholastic)

Honor Books
Dolphin Man: Exploring the World of Dolphins by Laurence Pringle, photos by Randall S. Wells (Atheneum)
Rosie the Riveter: Women Working on the Home Front in World War II by Penny Colman (Crown)

1997
Leonardo da Vinci by Diane Stanley (Morrow)

Honor Books
Full Steam Ahead: The Race to Build a Transcontinental Railroad by Rhoda Blumberg (National Geographic)
The Life and Death of Crazy Horse by Russell Freedman (Holiday House)
One World, Many Religions: The Ways We Worship by Mary Pope Osborne (Knopf)

LAURA INGALLS WILDER AWARD

The Laura Ingalls Wilder Award is presented to an author or an illustrator whose books are published in the United States and have made a substantial and lasting contribution to literature for children over a period of years. The award was first presented in 1954 and was given every five years from 1960 to 1980; since then, it has been given every three years.

1954 Laura Ingalls Wilder

1960 Clara Ingram Judson

1965 Ruth Sawyer

1970 E. B. White

1975 Beverly Cleary

1980 Dr. Seuss (Theodor Seuss Geisel)

1983 Maurice B. Sendak

1986 Jean Fritz

1989 Elizabeth George Speare

1992 Marcia Brown

1995 Virginia Hamilton

American Library Association
50 E. Huron Street
Chicago, IL 60611-2795
    The Association of Library Service to Children
    (ALSC), the Office of Intellectual Freedom, and the
    Young Adult Library Services Association are also at
    this address.

Children's Book Council
568 Broadway
New York, NY 10012
Order Center:
350 Scotland Road
Orange, NJ 07050

Children's Literature Association
22 Harvest Lake
Battle Creek, MI 49017

Cooperative Children's Book Center of the University
    of Wisconsin
600 North Park Street
Madison, WI 53706
Orders:
P.O. Box 5288
Madison, WI 53705

International Reading Association
800 Barksdale Road
Box 8139
Newark, DE 19714-8139

National Council of Teachers of English
1111 Kenyon Road
Urbana, IL 61801
    The Assembly on Literature for Adolescents and the
    Children's Literature Assembly are also at this
    address.

USBBY (United States Board on Books for Youth)
434 West Downer Place
Aurora, IL 60506
    (IBBY is the International Board on Books for
    Young People.)

Whole Language Umbrella
P.O. Box 2029
Bloomington, IN 47402-2029

Abingdon Press
Division of The United Methodist
 Publishing House
201 Eighth Avenue South
Nashville, TN 37202

Addison-Wesley Publishing
One Jacob Way
Reading, MA 01867

Arcade & Bulfinch
Imprint of Little, Brown & Co.

Atheneum
Imprint of Simon & Schuster

Avon Books
Division of The Hearst Corp.
1350 Avenue of the Americas
New York, NY 10019

Bantam Books
Division of Bantam Doubleday Dell

Bantam Doubleday Dell
1540 Broadway
New York, NY 10036

Barron's Educational Series
250 Wireless Boulevard
Hauppauge, NY 11788

Beech Tree Books
Division of William Morrow & Co.

Bellerophon Books
36 Anacapa Street
Santa Barbara, CA 93101

Berkley Publishing Group
Subsidiary of The Putnam Berkley
 Group

The Blue Sky Press
Imprint of Scholastic Books

Boyds Mills Press
815 Church Street
Honesdale, PA 18431

Browndeer Press
Imprint of Harcourt Brace & Co.

Candlewick Press
2067 Massachusetts Avenue
Cambridge, MA 02140

Carolrhoda Books
241 First Avenue North
Minneapolis, MN 55401

Chelsea House Publishers
Division of Main Line Book Co.
95 Madison Avenue
New York, NY 10016

Children's Book Press
6400 Hollis Street, Suite 4
Emeryville, CA 94608

Children's Press
Subsidiary of Grolier Inc.

Chronicle Books
275 Fifth Street
San Francisco, CA 94103

Clarion Books
Division of Houghton Mifflin

Cobblehill Books
Imprint of Penguin USA

Creative Arts Book Co.
833 Bancroft Way
Berkeley, CA 94710

Creative Education
Box 227
123 South Broad Street
Mankato, MN 56001

Crown Publishers
Imprint of Random House

Delacorte Press
666 Fifth Avenue
New York, NY 10013

Dell Publishing
Division of Bantam Doubleday Dell

Dial Books for Young Readers
Imprint of Penguin USA

Dorling Kindersley Publishing
95 Madison Avenue
New York, NY 10016

Doubleday
Division of Bantam Doubleday Dell

Dutton Children's Books
Imprint of Penguin USA

Farrar, Straus & Giroux
19 Union Square West
New York, NY 10003

Franklin Watts
Subsidiary of Grolier Inc.

Frederick Warne & Co.
Imprint of Penguin USA

Funk & Wagnalls
Field Publications, Suite 44
One International Boulevard
Mahwah, NJ 07495

Gareth Stevens
River Center Building, Suite 201
1555 North River Center Drive
Milwaukee, WI 53212

Golden Books
Division of Western Publishing

Green Tiger Press
Subsidiary of WJT Enterprises
435 Carmel Street
San Marcos, CA 92069

Greenwillow Books
Division of William Morrow & Co.

Grolier Inc.
Sherman Turnpike
Danbury, CT 06816

Grosset & Dunlap
Member of The Putnam Berkley
 Group

Gulliver Books
Imprint of Harcourt Brace & Co.

Harcourt Brace & Company
525 B Street, Suite 1900
San Diego, CA 92101

HarperCollins
10 East 53rd Street
New York, NY 10022

Henry Holt
115 West 18th Street
New York, NY 10011

Hill & Wang
Division of Farrar, Straus & Giroux

Holiday House
425 Madison Avenue
New York, NY 10017

Holt, Rinehart and Winston
Subsidiary of Harcourt Brace & Co.

Houghton Mifflin Company
222 Berkeley Street
Boston, MA 02116

Hyperion Books for Children
114 Fifth Avenue
New York, NY 10011

Alfred A. Knopf
Subsidiary of Random House

Lee & Low Books
95 Madison Avenue
New York, NY 10016

Lerner Publications
241 First Avenue North
Minneapolis, MN 55401

Libros Colibri
Imprint of Simon & Schuster

J. B. Lippincott Co.
227 East Washington Square
Philadelphia, PA 19106

Little, Brown & Company
34 Beacon Street
Boston, MA 02108

Lodestar Publishing
Imprint of Penguin USA

Lothrop, Lee & Shepard
Division of William Morrow & Co.

Macmillan
Imprint of Simon & Schuster

Margaret K. McElderry Books
Imprint of Simon & Schuster

McGraw-Hill Book Co.
Division of McGraw-Hill
1221 Avenue of the Americas
New York, NY 10020

William Morrow & Co.
1350 Avenue of the Americas
New York, NY 10019

Morrow Junior Books
Division of William Morrow & Co.

Mulberry Books
Division of William Morrow & Co.

National Geographic Society
1145 17th Street N.W.
Washington, DC 20036

North-South Books
1133 Broadway, Suite 1016
New York, NY 10010

Orchard Books
Division of Grolier Inc.

Oxford University Press
200 Madison Avenue
New York, NY 10016

Parents Magazine Press
Division of Gruner & Jahr USA,
   Publishing
685 Third Avenue
New York, NY 10017

Penguin USA
375 Hudson Street
New York, NY 10014

Philomel Books
Member of The Putnam Berkley
   Group

Platt & Munk
Division of The Putnam Berkley
   Group

Puffin Books
Imprint of Penguin USA

The Putnam Berkley Group
200 Madison Avenue
New York, NY 10016

G. P. Putnam's Sons
Member of The Putnam Berkley
   Group

Random House
201 East 50th Street
New York, NY 10022

Scholastic
555 Broadway
New York, NY 10012

Charles Scribner's
Imprint of Simon & Schuster

The Shoe String Press
Box 4327
925 Sherman Avenue
Hamden, CN 06514

Sierra Club Books for Children
Imprint of Little, Brown & Co.

Simon & Schuster
1230 Avenue of the Americas
New York, NY 10020

Tambourine Books
Division of William Morrow & Co.

Troll Communications/BridgeWater
100 Corporate Drive
Mahwah, NJ 07430

Tupelo Books
Division of William Morrow & Co.

Charles E. Tuttle Co.
77 Central Street at McKinley Sq.
Boston, MA 02109

Viking
Imprint of Penguin USA

Walker and Company
435 Hudson Street
New York, NY 10014

Warner Books
1271 Avenue of the Americas
New York, NY 10020

Western Publishing
1220 Mound Avenue
Racine, WI 53404

Albert Whitman & Company
6340 Oakton Street
Morton Grove, IL 60053

William Morrow Children's Books
Division of William Morrow & Co.

Wordsong
Imprint of Boyds Mills Press

Appendix D
Book Selection Aids

The school library/media center, district resource center, and community public library will have many aids to book selection. Some of the books listed below provide author biographies or literary criticism; others give suggestions for finding the best of new books, choosing the right book or books to meet individual children's needs, and developing literature-based curriculum units.

BOOKS

Adventuring with Books: A Booklist for Pre-K–Grade 6. 10th ed. Edited by Julie M. Jensen and Nancy L. Roser. Urbana, IL: NCTE, 1996. Provides summaries of nearly 1,800 books written between 1993 and 1996.

American Indian Reference Books for Children and Young Adults. By Barbara J. Kuipers. Englewood, CO: Libraries Unlimited, 1991. Includes detailed evaluation criteria.

American Writers for Children before 1900. Edited by Glenn E. Estes. Detroit: Gale Research, 1985. Each volume in this series contains a biography, with photographs, and literary criticism of each major American writer of the specified period.

American Writers for Children since 1960: Fiction. Edited by Glenn E. Estes. Detroit: Gale Research, 1986.

American Writers for Children since 1960: Poets, Illustrators, and Nonfiction Authors. Edited by Glenn E. Estes. Detroit: Gale Research, 1987.

The Antic Art: Enhancing Children's Literary Experiences through Film and Video. Edited by Lucy Rollin. Fort Atkinson, WI: Highsmith, 1993. Essays on improving literary appreciation.

Battling Dragons: Issues and Controversy in Children's Literature. Edited by Susan Lehr. Portsmouth, NH: Heinemann, 1995. Essays on censorship, family values, and more.

Behind the Covers: Interviews with Authors and Illustrators of Books for Children and Young Adults. By James W. Roginski. Littleton, CO: Libraries Unlimited, 1985.

Best Books for Children: Preschool through Grade 6. 5th ed. By John T. Gillespie and Corinne J. Naden. New Providence, NJ: R.R. Bowker, 1994. Lists 15,500 titles recommended by at least two reviewers; arranged by subject, with extensive index.

The Best: High/Low Books for Reluctant Readers. By Marianne Laino Pilla. Englewood, CO: Libraries Unlimited, 1990. The "high" refers to interest, the "low" to difficulty of reading.

Best of the Bookfinder: A Guide to Children's Literature about the Interests and Concerns of Youth Aged 2–18. By Sharon Spredemann Dreyer. Circle Pines, MN: American Guidance Service, 1992. Fully annotated entries for over 600 titles about psychological and sociological issues facing children.

The Bookfinder: A Guide to Children's Literature about the Needs and Problems of Youth Aged 2–15. By Sharon Spredemann Dreyer. Circle Pines, MN: American Guidance Service, annual. Three volumes of fully annotated entries.

Books by African-American Authors and Illustrators for Children and Young Adults. By Helen E. Williams. Chicago: ALA, 1991. Books with an African American perspective published in the twentieth century.

Books That Heal: A Whole Language Approach. By Carolyn Mohr, Dorothy Nixon, and Shirley Vickers. Illustrated by Linda East. Englewood, CO: Teacher Ideas, 1991. Bibliotherapy methods and bibliography.

Books to Help Children Cope with Separation and Loss: An Annotated Bibliography. 4th ed. By Masha K. Rudman et al. New Providence, NJ: R.R. Bowker, 1994. Over 700 titles useful for bibliotherapy and counseling.

British Children's Writers, 1800–1880. Edited by Meena Khorana. Detroit: Gale Research, 1996. Each volume in this series contains a biography, with photographs, and literary criticism of each major British writer of the specified period.

British Children's Writers, 1880–1914. Edited by Laura M. Zaidman. Detroit: Gale Research, 1994.

British Children's Writers, 1914–1960. Edited by Donald Hettinga and Gary D. Schmidt. Detroit: Gale Research, 1996.

British Children's Writers since 1960. First Series. Edited by Caroline C. Hunt. Detroit: Gale Research, 1996.

But That's Another Story: Famous Authors Introduce Popular Genres. Edited by Sandy Asher. New York: Walker, 1996. Stories that illustrate the characteristics of various genres.

Children Talking about Books. By Sarah Borders and Alice Phoebe Naylor. Phoenix, AZ: Oryx, 1993.

Children's Authors and Illustrators: An Index to Biographical Dictionaries. 5th ed. By Joyce Nakamura. Detroit: Gale Research, 1995.

Children's Book Awards International: A Directory of Awards and Winners, from Inception through 1990. By Laura J. Smith. Jefferson, NC: McFarland, 1992.

Children's Book Review Index. Detroit: Gale Research. Annual. Cites sources of reviews of children's and young adult literature, reference books, and professional resources.

Children's Books: Awards and Prizes. Rev. ed. New York: Children's Book Council, 1996. Information about awards from the United States, the United Kingdom, and other countries.

Children's Books and Their Creators. Edited by Anita Silvey. Boston: Houghton Mifflin, 1995. An illustrated encyclopedia of twentieth-century works and authors.

Children's Books in Print. New Providence, NJ: R.R. Bowker. Annual.

Children's Books 1911–1986: Favorite Children's Books from the Branch Collections of the New York Public Library. New York: Office of Children's Services, New York Public Library, 1986.

Children's Catalog. 17th ed. Bronx, NY: Wilson, 1996. Main volume plus four annual supplements. Over 6,000 titles described; includes critical annotations, grade levels, and subject headings.

Children's Literature: Criticism and the Fictional Child. By Karin Lesnik-Oberstein. New York: Oxford UP, 1994. A history of literary criticism of children's literature and its relationship to criticism of adult literature.

Children's Literature: A Guide to the Criticism. By Linnea Henderson. Boston: G. K. Hall, 1987. An annotated bibliography arranged by author or illustrator and covering subjects, themes, and genres.

Children's Literature: Theory, Research, and Teaching. By Kay E. Vandergrift. Englewood, CO: Libraries Unlimited, 1990. Provides theoretical background and practical ideas on how to teach children's literature.

Children's Literature and Critical Theory: Reading and Writing for Understanding. By Jill P. May. New York: Oxford UP, 1995. Demonstrates the importance of a knowledge of critical theory to understanding and writing about children's books.

Children's Literature in an Integrated Curriculum: The Authentic Voice. Edited by Bette Bosma and Nancy DeVries. Newark, DE: International Reading Association, 1995. Case studies of interdisciplinary approaches to teaching.

Children's Literature in Canada. By Elizabeth Waterston. New York: Twayne, 1992. Critical history of Canadian children's books, arranged by genre.

Connecting Cultures: A Guide to Multicultural Literature for Children. By Rebecca L. Thomas. New Providence, NJ: R.R. Bowker, 1996. An extensive bibliography indexed by grade level, title, subject, culture, and author.

Criticism, Theory, and Children's Literature. By Peter Hunt. Cambridge, MA: Blackwell, 1991. Describes new ways of reading texts that help readers gain a deeper understanding of meaning.

Dealing with Censorship. Edited by James E. Davis. Urbana, IL: National Council of Teachers of English, 1979. A still valuable discussion of censorship issues, with suggestions for how to respond to would-be censors.

E for Environment: An Annotated Bibliography of Children's Books with Environmental Themes. By Patti K. Sinclair. New Providence, NJ: R.R. Bowker, 1992.

The Elementary School Library Collection: A Guide to Books and Other Media. Phases 1-2-3. 20th ed. Edited by Lauren K. Lee. Williamsport, PA: Brodart, 1996. Designed to aid in development of school library collections. Includes over 12,000 print and nonprint materials, with evaluative comments and annotations.

Every Teacher's Thematic Booklist. By William J. Devers III and James Cipielewski. New York: Scholastic, 1993. More than 500 annotated descriptions of children's books.

Exploring the United States through Literature. Edited by Kathy Howard Latrobe. Phoenix, AZ: Oryx, 1994. Citations include literature, media, and professional materials for K–8 curriculum planning, listed by region.

Fantasy Literature for Children and Young Adults: An Annotated Bibliography. 4th ed. By Ruth Nadelman Lynn. New Providence, NJ: R.R. Bowker, 1995. All books recommended by at least two review sources. Topics include witchcraft, time travel, alternate worlds, allegorical fantasy, and others.

From Dr. Mather to Dr. Seuss: 200 Years of American Books for Children. By Mary H. Lystad. Boston: G. K. Hall, 1980. A discussion of how changes in attitudes toward childhood are reflected in children's books.

From Page to Screen: Children's and Young Adult Books on Film and Video. By Joy Moss and George Wilson. Detroit: Gale Research, 1992. Evaluates 1,400 P–12 films for their adherence to the book and their quality.

Gender Positive! A Teachers' and Librarians' Guide to Nonstereotyped Children's Literature. By Patricia L. Roberts et al. Jefferson, NC: McFarland, 1993. Lists over 200 titles in which gender roles are portrayed nonstereotypically. Activities for use are indicated.

High/Low Handbook: Encouraging Literacy in the 1990s. 3rd ed. By Ellen V. LiBretto. New Providence, NJ: R.R. Bowker, 1990. Annotated entries for over 300 titles, dedicated to the eradication of illiteracy in the 1990s.

Infant Tongues: The Voices of the Child in Literature. Edited by Elizabeth Goodenough, Mark A. Beberle, and Naomi Sokoloff. Foreword by Robert Coles. Detroit: Wayne State University, 1994.

Intellectual Freedom Manual. 4th ed. Chicago: Office of Intellectual Freedom, ALA, 1992.

International Companion Encyclopedia of Children's Literature. Edited by Peter Hunt. New York: Routledge, 1996.

It's the Story That Counts: More Children's Books for Mathematical Learning, K–6. By David J. Whitin

and Sandra Wilde. Portsmouth, NH: Heinemann, 1995. Recommends titles and suggests activities.

Kaleidoscope: A Multicultural Booklist for Grades K–8. Edited by Rudine Sims Bishop. Urbana, IL: NCTE, 1994. Includes over 400 titles published during 1990–1992, arranged by genre and indexed by subject.

Language and Ideology in Children's Fiction. By John Stephens. New York: Longman, 1992. An interdisciplinary discussion of how language and its ideological bases affect reading for meaning.

Literature-Based Reading Activities. By Ruth Helen Yopp and Hallie Kay Yopp. Boston: Allyn & Bacon, 1992. A series of activities that can be used with a wide variety of literature selections.

Literature-Based Science: Children's Books and Activities to Enrich the K–5 Curriculum. Phoenix, AZ: Oryx, 1995. Activities and readings teachers can use to integrate science and literature.

Literature for Children: Contemporary Criticism. Edited by Peter Hunt. New York: Routledge, 1992. Elucidates the links between literary criticism and education, psychology, history, and scientific theory.

Literature for Children about Asians and Asian Americans: Analysis and Annotated Bibliography with Additional Readings for Adults. By Esther C. Jenkins and Mary C. Austin. Westport, CT: Greenwood, 1987.

The Literature of Delight: A Critical Guide to Humorous Books for Children. By Kimberly Olson Fakih. New Providence, NJ: R.R. Bowker, 1993. Includes books on a wide range of humorous topics.

Magazines for Children. Edited by Donald R. Stoll. Glassboro, NJ: Educational Press Association of America. Newark, DE: International Reading Association, 1990.

Math through Children's Literature: Making the NCTM Standards Come Alive. By Kathryn L. Braddon et al. Englewood, CO: Libraries Unlimited, 1993.

McElmeel Booknotes: Literature across the Curriculum. Englewood, CO: Teacher Ideas, 1993. Information on how fiction and nonfiction works can foster learning across the curriculum.

Mirrors of American Culture: Children's Fiction Series in the Twentieth Century. By Paul Dean. Metuchen, NJ: Scarecrow, 1991.

More Exciting, Funny, Scary, Short, Different, and Sad Books Kids Like about Animals, Science, Sports, Families, Songs, and Other Things. By Frances

Laverne Carroll and Mary Meacham. Chicago: ALA, 1992. Lists books for grades 2 through 5.

More Kids' Favorite Books: A Compilation of Children's Choices, 1992–1994. New York: Children's Book Council/IRA, 1995. Annotated entries on three years' worth of children's favorites.

Music through Children's Literature: Theme and Variations. Englewood, CO: Teacher Ideas, 1993. Brings together children's musical knowledge and literature with musical qualities.

Newbery and Caldecott Medal and Honor Books in Other Media. By Paulette B. Sharkey and James W. Roginski. New York: Neal-Schuman, 1992. Formats include filmstrip, video, large print, audio, Braille, and others.

Newbery and Caldecott Medalists and Honor Book Winners: Bibliographies and Resource Material through 1991. Compiled by Muriel W. Brown and Rita Schooch Foudray. Edited by Jim Roginski. Littleton, CO: Libraries Unlimited, 1992.

Our Family, Our Friends, Our World: An Annotated Guide to Significant Multicultural Books for Children and Teenagers. By Lyn Miller-Lachmann. New Providence, NJ: R.R. Bowker, 1992. Lists over 1,000 titles about ethnic groups in several countries and suggests selection criteria.

The Oxford Companion to Children's Literature. By Humphrey Carpenter and Mari Prichard. New York: Oxford University Press, 1984. Contains nearly 2,000 entries, of which more than 900 are biographical sketches of authors, illustrators, printers, and publishers.

Pipers at the Gates of Dawn: The Wisdom of Children's Literature. By Jonathan Cott. New York: Random House, 1983.

The Pleasures of Children's Literature. 2nd ed. By Perry Nodelman. White Plains, NY: Longman, 1992. A guide to exploring children's literature.

Popular Reading for Children III: A Collection of Booklist Columns. Edited by Sally Estes. Chicago: American Library Association, 1992. The books recommended in these lists cover a wide range of topics; includes author and title index.

Portraying Persons with Disabilities: An Annotated Bibliography of Fiction for Children and Teenagers. By Debra Robertson. New Providence, NJ: R.R. Bowker, 1992. Critical annotations of over 600 titles about health, physical impairments, emotional disturbances, and learning disabilities.

Read Any Good Math Lately? Children's Books for Mathematical Learning. K–6. By David J. Whitin and Sandra Wilde. Portsmouth, NH: Heinemann, 1992. Lists titles and activities related to fractions, estimation, geometry, and the like.

Reading Rainbow Guide to Children's Books: The 101 Best Titles. By Twila C. Liggett and Cynthia Mayer Benfield. Secaucus, NJ: Citadel, 1994. Lists the most popular titles from the PBS television program.

Reading Response Logs: Inviting Students to Explore Novels, Short Stories, Plays, Poetry, and More. By Mary Kooy and Jan Wells. Portsmouth, NH: Heinemann, 1996. Suggest ways to incorporate interactive response-based approaches into the classroom.

Recreating the Past: A Guide to American and World Historical Fiction for Children and Young Adults. By Lynda G. Adamson. Westport, CT: Greenwood, 1994. About 70 percent of the nearly 1,000 titles listed are about the United States and England.

The Right Book, The Right Time: Helping Children Cope. By Martha C. Grindler, Beverly D. Stratton, and Michael C. McKenna. Boston: Allyn & Bacon, 1997. This book provides a uniquely broad and usable approach to bibliotherapy. Its accompanying database disk, available in either Mac or IBM-compatible format, suggests over 2,000 titles.

Rip-Roaring Reads for Reluctant Teen Readers. By Gale W. Sherman. Englewood, CO: Libraries Unlimited, 1993.

Science and Technology in Fact and Fiction: A Guide to Children's Books. By DayAnn M. Kennedy et al. New Providence, NJ: R.R. Bowker, 1990. Gives critical evaluations of recommended titles for pre-K to grade 6; includes subject index.

Sensitive Issues: An Annotated Guide to Children's Literature K–6. By Timothy V. Rasinski and Cindy S. Gillespie. Annotated list of titles on divorce, substance abuse, moving, discrimination, and other topics; includes teaching strategies. Phoenix, AZ: Oryx, 1992.

Sketching Stories, Stretching Minds: Responding Visually to Literature. By Phyllis Whitin. Foreword by Jerome C. Harste. Portsmouth, NH: Heinemann, 1996. Captures the power of young people's visual responses to literature.

Something about the Author: Facts and Pictures about Contemporary Authors and Illustrators of Books for Young People. Detroit: Gale Research, 1971 to date, several volumes each year.

Special Collections in Children's Literature: An International Directory. 3rd ed. Chicago: Association for Library Service to Children, 1995. Holdings of 300 institutions in the United States whose collections have materials pertinent to the study of children's and young adult literature.

Survival Themes in Fiction for Children and Young People. 2nd ed. By Binnie Tate Wilkin. Metuchen, NJ: Scarecrow, 1993. Commentary and description of 300 titles on personal and social pressures experienced by children.

Talking about Books: Creating Literate Communities. Edited by Kathy G. Short and Kathryn Mitchell Pierce. Portsmouth, NH: Heinemann, 1990. Practical strategies for creating a literature-based, integrated-curriculum classroom.

Teachers' Favorite Books for Kids. Teachers' Choices, 1989–1993. Newark, DE: International Reading Association, 1994. A compilation of columns from *The Reading Teacher* that describe outstanding trade books for children K–8.

This Land Is Our Land: A Guide to Multicultural Literature for Children and Young Adults. By Althea K. Helbig and Agnes Regan Perkins. Westport, CT: Greenwood, 1994. Over 600 titles published since 1985 on African, Native American, Asian, and Hispanic cultures within the United States.

Touchstones: Reflections on the Best in Children's Literature. 3 vols. Edited by Perry Nodelman. West Lafayette, IN: Children's Literature Association, 1985, 1987, 1989. Distributed by Scarecrow Press, Metuchen, NJ. Lengthy essays on titles selected by the CLA.

Twentieth-Century Children's Writers. 4th ed. Edited by Laura Standley. Chicago: St. James, 1995. Provides biographical, bibliographical, and critical information on more than 400 authors.

Venture into Cultures: A Resource Book of Multicultural Materials and Programs. Edited by Carla D. Hayden. Chicago: ALA, 1992. Activities and titles representing Arabic, Jewish, Persian, Asian, African, Hispanic, and Native American cultures. Some titles are in languages other than English.

War and Peace Literature for Children and Young Adults: A Resource Guide to Significant Issues. By Virginia A. Walter. Phoenix, AZ: Oryx, 1993. Titles for pre-K through grade 9 offer fiction and nonfiction examples of conflict resolution.

Webbing with Literature: Creating Story Maps with Children's Books. 2nd ed. By Karen D'Angelo Bromley. Boston: Allyn & Bacon, 1996. Introduces webbing and describes how to use it creatively.

What Do Children Read Next? A Reader's Guide to Fiction for Children. Edited by Candy Colborn. Detroit: Gale Research, 1994. "If you've read this book, here's a similar one" is the basis of this annotated list of 2,000 titles.

Wordless/Almost Wordless Picture Books: A Guide. By Virginia H. Richey and Katharyn E. Puckett. Englewood, CO: Libraries Unlimited, 1992. Plot, characters, format, and illustrations are described for each title.

Yesterday's Authors of Books for Children: Facts and Pictures about Authors and Illustrators of Books for Young People, from Early Times to 1960. 2 vols. Detroit: Gale Research, 1977–1978.

Young Adult Literature and Nonprint Materials: Resources for Selection. By Millicent Lenz. Metuchen, NJ: Scarecrow, 1994. Comprehensive listing of sources useful for selecting books for young adults and answering reference questions.

The Young Reader's Companion. By Gorton Carruth. New Providence, NJ: R.R. Bowker, 1993. A one-volume encyclopedia of characters, plots, themes, and so forth in children's books.

The Zena Sutherland Lectures, 1983–1992. Edited by Betsy Hearne. New York: Clarion, 1993. Speeches by authors of children's books on their craft.

PROFESSIONAL JOURNALS

ALAN Review
Assembly on Literature for Adolescents
National Council of Teachers of English
1111 Kenyon Road
Urbana, IL 60611
> Three issues per year. Offers articles and reviews of new books for middle and high school students.

Appraisal
Children's Science Book Review Committee
Department of Science Education
Boston University School of Education
605 Commonwealth Avenue
Boston, MA 02215
> Quarterly. Reviews of children's science books.

Book Links: Connecting Books, Libraries and Classrooms
American Library Association
50 East Huron Street
Chicago, IL 60611

> Six issues per year. Well-researched articles that contain thematic bibliographies on curriculum topics.

Bookbird: World of Children's Books
P.O. Box 3156
West Lafayette, IN 47906

> Quarterly. Published by the International Board of Books for Young People (IBBY). Articles on authors and trends in book publishing from around the world. Reviews of books from many countries.

Booklist and Reference Books Bulletin
American Library Association
50 East Huron Street
Chicago, IL 60611

> Twenty-two issues per year. A regular section is devoted to reviews of new children's books.

Bulletin of the Center for Children's Books
Center for Children's Books
University of Illinois at Chicago
University of Illinois Press
1325 South Oak Street
Champagne, IL 61820

> Eleven issues per year. Dependable reviews of approximately 75 new children's titles in each issue.

Canadian Children's Literature
Canadian Children's Press/Canadian Children's Literature Association
Department of English
University of Guelph
Guelph, Ontario, NIG 2W Canada

> Quarterly. Book reviews and critical essays about literature written for Canadian children.

CBC Features
The Children's Book Council
350 Scotland Road
Orange, NJ 07050

> Two issues per year. A newsletter of primarily free and inexpensive display and bulletin board materials available from publishers. Author interviews included.

Children's Literature in Education
Human Sciences Press
P.O. Box 735
Canal Street Station
New York, NY 10013

> Quarterly. Scholarly and practical articles for teachers, plus interviews with authors.

[handwritten: Bob Darnowski 212 620 8000]

Dragon Lode
Children's Literature Section, International Reading Association
12147 Wycliff Lane
Austin, TX 78727

> Three issues per year. Requires membership in Children's Literature Section. Articles on all phases of children's literature, plus book reviews.

Horn Book Magazine
Horn Book Inc.
11 Beacon Street
Suite 1000
Boston, MA 02108-3704

> Six issues per year.

Journal of Children's Literature
Children's Literature Assembly of the National Council of Teachers of English
1111 Kenyon Road
Urbana, IL 61801

> Two issues per year. Requires membership in Children's Literature Assembly. Includes articles, literature criticism, and new book reviews.

Journal of Youth Services in Libraries (JOYS)
Association of Library Service to Children and Young Adult Services Division
American Library Association
50 East Huron Street
Chicago, IL 60611

> Quarterly. Contains articles, reviews of professional materials, and speeches by authors of Newbery, Caldecott, and other award-winning books.

Language Arts
National Council of Teachers of English
Elementary Section
1111 Kenyon Road
Urbana, IL 61611

> Eight issues per year. Articles and reviews of current children's literature publications with occasional author profiles. One issue annually is devoted exclusively to literature.

The Lion and the Unicorn
Johns Hopkins University Press
2715 West Charles Street
Baltimore, MD 21218-4319

> Two issues per year. Each issue is on a theme related to children's literature, with lengthy analyses of books and interviews with authors.

New Advocate
Christopher-Gordon Publishers, Inc.
480 Washington Street
Norwood, MA 02062

Quarterly. Articles and book reviews by teachers and scholars in education in the field of children's literature.

New York Times Book Review
New York Times
229 West 43rd Street
New York, NY 10036

Fifty-two issues per year. Reviews selected new children's books in each issue. Two issues a year have extensive coverage of new publications.

The Reading Teacher
International Reading Association and International Council for the Improvement of Reading
800 Barksdale Road
Box 8139
Newark, DE 19714-8139

Eight issues per year. Contains applications of research and teaching strategies for elementary school teachers, plus a column of reviews of children's books.

School Library Journal
P.O. Box 2606
Boulder, CO 80322-2606

Twelve issues per year. Articles plus reviews of a large number of new publications listed by grade and subject. Reviews are short and offer one reviewer's opinion.

Teaching and Learning Literature with Children and Young Adults (TALL)
Essmont Publishing
P.O. Box 186
Brandon, VT 03733

Five issues per year. Suggests activities using books to integrate curriculum and literature studies in the classroom.

Voice of Youth Advocates (VOYA)
Scarecrow Press
4720 Boston Way
Lanham, MD 20706

Six issues per year. Articles and extensive reviews of new books for middle and high school students.

Children's Magazines with Literary Content

Boomerang
Listen and Learn Home Education, Inc.
13366 Pescadero Road
Box 261
La Honda, CA 94020
> Twelve issues per year. An audiomagazine on cassette with an insert of games, articles on current events, children's book reviews, and recommended reading.

Boys' Life
Boy Scouts of America
1325 Walnut Hill Lane
P.O. Box 15079
Irving, TX 75015-2079
> Twelve issues per year. Entertaining games, crafts, outdoor activities, and fiction.

Calliope: World History for Young People
Cobblestone Publishing, Inc.
7 School Street
Peterborough, NH 03458
> Five issues per year. Full-length articles and stories with an emphasis on history and related topics.

Chickadee (The French edition is entitled **Coulicou**.)
The Canadian Magazine for Young Children
Young Naturalist Foundation
255 Great Arrow Avenue
Buffalo, NY 14207-3082
> Ten issues per year. A magazine with a science and nature emphasis that includes related fiction and poetry.

Children's Digest
Children's Better Health Institute
P.O. Box 7133
Red Oak, IA 51591
> Eight issues per year. Contemporary fiction in all genres for pre-teens, with emphasis on health.

Children's Playmate
Children's Better Health Institute
P.O. Box 7133
Red Oak, IA 51591
> Eight issues per year. Includes illustrated fiction and nonfiction that helps beginning readers learn to make healthy life choices.

Cobblestone: The History Magazine for Young People
Cobblestone Publishing, Inc.
7 School Street
Peterborough, NH 03458
> Ten issues per year. Well-researched articles with artwork, puzzles, and activities that stimulate creative ways to learn history.

Creative Kids
Prufrock Press
P.O. Box 8813
Waco, TX 76714-8813
> Four issues per year. A magazine of quality writing by children. Does not contain sexist or racist material or violent expressions.

Cricket: The Magazine for Children
Carus Publishing
P.O. Box 593
Mt. Morris, IL 61054-0593
> Twelve issues per year. Encourages a love of reading by introducing literature and art from many countries.

Faces
Cobblestone Publishing, Inc.
7 School Street
Peterborough, NH 03458
> Nine issues per year. Theme-related issues that explore human diversity and different lifestyles and customs worldwide.

Harambee
Just Us Books, Inc.
301 Main Street
Orange, NJ 07050
> Six issues per year. Fosters understanding of African and African American culture and history.

Hopscotch: The Magazine for Young Girls
Bluffton News Publishing and Printing Company
P.O. Box 164
Bluffton, OH 45817-0164
> Six issues per year. Celebrates childhood with imaginative and inspiring activities and articles.

Jack and Jill
Children's Better Health Institute
P.O. Box 10003
Des Moines, IA 50340

Eight issues per year. Illustrated stories, articles, poems, and comic strip features.

Kid City
Children's Television Workshop
200 Watt Street
P.O. Box 2924
Boulder, CO 80322
Ten issues per year. Specifically designed to encourage reading and writing; includes fiction, poetry, articles.

Kids Copy
Kids Copy, Inc.
P.O. Box 42
Wyncote, PA 19095
Ten issues per year. A children's newspaper that encourages integrated classroom activities.

Ladybug: The Magazine for Young Children
Carus Publishing
P.O. Box 593
Mt. Morris, IL 61054-0593
Twelve issues per year. Read-aloud poetry, songs, and stories for preschoolers. Includes games.

Letterbug
Research for Better Schools
444 North Third Street
Philadelphia, PA 19123
Eight issues per year. Also available in boxed sets of 30 copies. A whole-language newsletter that highlights various literary genres in each issue.

New Moon
P.O. Box 3587
Duluth, MN 55803
Six issues per year. Thematic issues designed for girls to read and discuss with their parents.

Nineteenth Avenue
The Humphrey Forum
301 19th Avenue South
Minneapolis, MN 55455
Six issues per year. Encourages an interest in politics, the arts, and community activities.

Odyssey
Cobblestone Publishing, Inc.
7 School Street
Peterborough, NH 03458
Ten issues per year. Quality science magazine that explores topics and professions in the sciences.

Owl (The French edition is entitled Hibou.)
Young Naturalist Foundation
255 Great Arrow Avenue
Buffalo, NY 14207
Ten issues per year. A Canadian magazine that presents science topics to young children.

Plays: The Drama Magazine for Young People
120 Boylston Street
Boston, MA 02116
Seven issues per year. Royalty-free plays and programs for children.

Ranger Rick
National Wildlife Federation
8925 Leesburg Pike
Vienna, VA 22184-0001
Twelve issues per year. All articles, stories, and poems are about nature.

Scienceland
Scienceland, Inc.
501 Fifth Avenue
Suite 2108
New York, NY 10017-6102
Eight issues per year. A picture book format that integrates science and language activities.

Seedling Series
Short Story International
P.O. Box 405
Great Neck, NY 11022
Four issues per year. Short stories from all over the world for a wide range of readers.

Skipping Stones: A Multicultural Children's Quarterly
Skipping Stones
P.O. Box 3939
Eugene, OR 97403
Four issues per year. Designed as a forum for children to share multilingual and multicultural information and stories. Accepts children's writing and pen pals.

Spark!
F & W Publications, Inc.
P.O. Box 5028
Harlan, IA 51593-4528
Nine issues per year. Suggests creative, literary, and artistic activities that children can do at home.

Spider: The Magazine for Children
Carus Publishing
P.O. Box 593
Mt. Morris, IL 61054-0593
Twelve issues per year. Highlights fiction by well-known authors.

Stone Soup: A Magazine for Children
Children's Art Foundation
P.O. Box 83
Santa Cruz, CA 95063
Five issues per year. Stories, poems, book reviews, and art work, all by children.

Appendix F
Children's Literature
Web Sites

Worl Wide Web resources in the following list are organized into three groups: web guides, which primarily catalog other materials available on the web and provide a convenient starting point from which to explore; on-line resources, which provide direct access to electronic texts and critical and pedagogic materials that can be downloaded to your computer; and writing by children, sites that offer children opportunities to publish their own writing electronically. Within each category, sites have been listed roughly according to the amount and usefulness of material they contain, beginning with the best/most useful site.

WEB GUIDES

Children's Literature Web Guide
http://www.ucalgary.ca/~dkbrown/index.html
Includes links to children's publishers and booksellers, conferences and book events, children's writing, children's literature discussion groups, journals, book reviews, and resources for storytellers, parents, teachers, writers, and illustrators.

Kids' Web
http://www.npac.syr.edu/textbook/kidsweb/
A web guide specifically for children, with links to a variety of sites relating to literature, the arts, science, social studies, games, and sports, among others.

Young Adult Librarians' Help/Home Page
http://www.acpl.lib.in.us/young_adult_lib_ass
/yaweb.html

Fairly large web guide focusing on areas of potential interest to young adult librarians; updated twice a month to eliminate "dead" links and add new materials.

Teacher Resource Page
http://grove.ufl.edu:80/~klesyk/
Small site with a user-friendly organization; particularly helpful for elementary teachers beginning to use World Wide Web resources in the classroom.

Story Resources on the Web
http://www.cc.swarthmore.edu/~sjohnson/stories/
Specialized web guide providing links to on-line stories, professional storytellers, and storytelling organizations; useful for teachers using storytelling in the classroom or library.

ON-LINE RESOURCES

Children's Literature Gopher
gopher://lib.nmsu.edu:70/11/.subjects/Education/.childlit
Access to information on authors, book awards, conferences and events, on-line texts and journals, other Internet resources, college course syllabi, and more.

Children's Literature: A Guide to the Criticism
http://www.unm.edu/~lhendr/
On-line version of Linnea Hendrickson's invaluable reference work by the same title; offers an extensive annotated bibliography of criticism.

Fairossa Cyber Library: Children's Literature
http://www.users.interport.net/~fairrosa/

Interesting collection of children's literature resources, including background materials, critical exchanges from electronic discussion lists, and a gateway to the New York Public library's list of child-friendly Internet sites (directly accessible at <http://www.users.interport.net/~fairrosa/nypl/index.html>).

Kay Vandergrift's Home Page
http://www.scils.rutgers.edu/special/kay/kayhp2.html
Offers extensive materials on connecting literature to learning across the curriculum and a collection of bibliographies and on-line resources related to the history of children's literature.

Carol Hurst's Children's Literature Site
http://www.crocker.com/~rebotis/
 Compilation of articles and sections from Hurst's books for teachers and librarians, including book reviews, suggestions for using books, and a variety of thematic lists of books and activities.

Children's Literature Sampler
http://funnelweb.utcc.utk.edu/~estes/estes2.html
 Lists of critical reading thoughtfully organized into thematic groups, suggested curricular connections on various themes, and miscellaneous materials.

Children's Literature Authors and Illustrators
http://www.ucet.ufl.edu/~jbrown/chauth.html
 A highly specialized web site providing direct links to pages of information about contemporary and historic children's authors.

Ask the Author
http://ipl.sils.umich.edu/youth/AskAuthor/
 Part of the Internet Public Library, offering biographies and interviews with well-known children's authors and illustrators.

Book Nook
http://i-site.on.ca/isite/education/bk_report/booknook/
 Compilation of book reviews written by children themselves; children can see what other children have said about a particular book, post their own reviews, or select titles from a list of books awaiting review.

Children's Book Council
http://www.cbcbooks.org/
 Information about Children's Book Week, selected articles from CBC publications, and links to a large number of children's book publishers.

The Storytelling Home Page
http://members.aol.com/storypage/
 A list of electronic and other resources for storytelling and puppetry, including schedules of storytelling events around the country and on-line sources of stories to tell.

Tales of Wonder
http://www.ece.ucdavis.edu/~darsie/tales.html
 Archive of folktales and fairytales from around the world, arranged according to the country or region of origin, along with print sources of tales.

ALAN Review
http://scholar.kib.vt.edu/ejournals/ALAN/alan-review.html
 Regularly updated electronic version of the quarterly journal of the Assembly on Literature for Adolescents, with full texts of scholarly articles and back issues.

Bulletin of the Center for Children's Books
http://edfu.lis.uiuc.edu/puboff/bccb/
 On-line version of the CCB's print newsletter, with samples of reviews and back issues and news about the CCB's activities.

Children's Literature Service Collection
http://www.nlc-bnc.ca/services/eclse.htm
 Site maintained by the National Library of Canada, with an emphasis on Canadian works in the library's research collection; also provides information on the Canadian *Read Up on It* program and various other materials produced by the library.

Reading Rainbow Home Page
http://www.pbs.org:80/readingrainbow/rr.html
 Brief descriptions of the books featured during the PBS show's current season, along with full publication information and recommended activities to accompany the books.

Cinderella Project and Little Red Riding Hood Project
http://www.usm.edu/usmhburg/lib_arts/english/cinderella/cinderella.html
http://www-dept.usm.edu/~engdept/lrrh/lrrhhome.htm
 Both provide direct access to on-line texts and reproductions of pages from various print versions of these two fairytales contained in the DeGrummond Collection at the University of Southern Mississippi.

WRITING BY CHILDREN

KidPub
http://www.en-garde.com/kidpub/
 A place for children to publish stories on the World Wide Web and to read stories published by others, with an ongoing collaborative story to which children are invited to contribute. Be warned, however, that the sheer volume of stories can be overwhelming.

Kidopedia
http://rdz.stjohns.edu/kidopedia/
 An on-line encyclopedia written entirely by children from around the world, with instructions for posting entries and for creating local kidopedias.

Cyberkids' Home
http://www.woodwind.com:80/cyberkids/
 A electronic magazine written by (though apparently not edited by) children; offers children opportunities for creativity in music and art and a children's writing contest.

Name/Title Index

Subject Index

Accommodation, 15
Accuracy
  in biography, 398–399
  in informational books, 379, 390
Action, rising, 38
Activists, biographies of, 394
Activity, craft, and how-to books, 383,
  404–405
Adolescents
  problems of, 23
  in realistic fiction, 269, 270–271
Adult literature, 113
Aesthetic judgments, 59
Aesthetic reading, 61
African Americans
  folklore of, 157–159
  literature portraying, 86, 87, 91, 93, 94,
    95–97, 98–99, 100, 116–121, 166
  as readers, 86, 90
  stereotyped images of, 90
African culture
  folklore of, 160, 167
  literature portraying, 92–93, 94,
    116–121
Alliteration, 240
Alphabet books, 177–178, 208–209
American folk heroes and heroines, litera-
  ture unit on, 507–508
American Revolution, historical fiction
  about, 321–322, 329–330
Animals, personified, in fantasy, 340–341,
  364–365
Animism, 160
Antagonist, 37
Appalachian Americans
  folklore of, 159
  literature portraying, 91–92
Apprenticeship tales, 144
Archetype, 148
Art, computer-generated, 187
Art projects, as response to literature, 69
Artistic license, 89
Artists, biographies of, 394–395, 406–407.
  See also Illustrators
Arts, informational books on, 382–383,
  404
Asian Americans, 86, 87, 91, 121–124. *See*
  also Chinese Americans; Japanese
  Americans
Asian folklore, 160–161, 168–169
Assimilation, 15
Assonance, 49, 240
Attitudes, social, reading for, 59, 60
Authenticity
  in biography, 398–399
  cultural, 87, 88, 89
  and cultural details, accuracy of,
    102–103
  in historical fiction, 325–327
  in informational books, 379, 390
Authors. *See also* Poets
  biographies of, 394–395, 406–407

craft of, 31, 453–545, 460–461, 490,
  492
  of multicultural literature, 92–102
  perspective of (insider versus outsider),
    88–90
  social responsibility of, 83
  visits to schools by, 440
Autobiographies, 395
Autonomy versus shame (Erikson's second
  stage of personality development), 21
Awards, 512–533. *See also names of spe-*
  cific awards
  for biographies, 399
  for fantasy, 363
  for informational books, 399
  for international literature, 107–109
  for multicultural literature, 107–109
  for picture books, 205
  for science fiction, 363

Background, in illustrations, 190–191
Ballads, 145
Bards, 153
Beginning readers, books for, 418. *See also*
  Easy readers; Picture storybooks;
  Predictable books
Being in and moving through, 63–64
Being in and stepping out, 64
Being out and stepping in , 62–63
Bettelheim's theory, on traditional literature, 151
Big books, 180
Biographies
  of activists, 394
  of artists and authors, 394–395,
    406–407
  awards for, 399
  benefits of, 391–392
  characterization in, 398
  collective, 393–394
  criteria for selecting, 398–399
  definition of, 391–392
  evolution of, 392–393
  of explorers, 394, 406
  fictionalization of, 392
  versus historical fiction, 315, 391
  major authors of, 396–398
  partial, 393
  theory of, 395–396
  of U.S. historical figures, 405–406
  of U.S. political leaders, 405
  of world leaders, 406
Birds, literature unit on, 482–483,
  501–502
Blacks. *See* African Americans
Board books, 175
Book clubs. *See also* Literature units
  definition of, 450, 451
  factors affecting, 453
  and group size, 455–457
  journal use in, 462–464
  and language charts, 468

response strategies for, 462–472
  role of teacher in, 458–461
  roles of children in, 459–460
  selecting books for use in, 453–455
  sessions, length and frequency of,
    457–458
  and story webs, 469–471
  teacher's use of questions in, 460,
    464–467
Book Links, 499
Book selection aids, 537–543
Bookbird, 26
Booklist, 26, 271, 499
Borders, 188–189
Boston Globe–Horn Book Award, 96,
  514–516
British Isles, traditional literature of,
  153–154, 164–165
*Bulletin of the Center for Children's
  Books, The,* 10

Caldecott Medal, 96, 107, 109, 152, 197,
  205, 516–521
Campbell's hero cycle, 148–150
Censorship, 14–15
  and fantasy literature, 346
  and realistic fiction, 269, 270, 294
Chants, 146
Chapbooks, 12
Characterization, 35–37, 54. *See also*
  Characters
  in biography, 398
  through illustrations, 189–190
Characters. *See also* Characterization
  in folktales, 37
  in historical fiction, 318–319, 326–327
  identifying with, 45
  outlandish, in fantasy, 342, 366
  questions about, 43–44
  types of, 37
Childhood, historical views of, 11–15
Children
  egocentrism of, 16, 19, 20
  intellectual development of, 15–18
  magazines for, 544–545
  moral development of, 18–20
  personality development of, 20–23
  reading interests of, at different grade
    levels, 417
  responses to literature of, 67. *See also*
    Reader response
  roles of, in book clubs, 459–460
  sentimentalism toward, 268
  as storytellers, 427, 428
  and writing of poetry, 436–439
Children's literature. *See also specific genres*
  appropriate issues in, 456
  benefits of, 6–7
  and children's intellectual development,
    17–18
  and children's moral development,
    19–20

Children's literature (*continued*)
and children's personality development, 20, 21, 22, 23
definition of, 7–8
evaluating, 7, 10, 34
genres of, 25–26
qualities of, 8–11
resources for, 26–27
social issues in, 269, 270, 271, 272–273, 276. *See also* Realistic fiction
web sites about, 546–547
Children's magazines, 545–546
Chinese Americans
literature portraying, 90, 100–101
literature unit on, 508–509
as readers, 75, 90
Cinquain, 438
Civil War, historical fiction about, 322, 330
Classroom library
characteristics of, 414–416
multicultural books in, 419
"nonliterary" works in, 417
stocking of, 416–419, 441, 442–445
Climax, 38
Cloth books, 175
Collage, 185
Collective biographies, 393–394
Color, in illustrations, 182, 191–192
Communication, visual, 187–191
Complication, in plot, 38
Composition, in artwork, 182
Comprehension, reading, 24–25, 58–59, 66, 461
Computer-generated art, 187
Concept books, 177, 210–211
Concrete operational period, 16, 66
Conflict, 38
in historical fiction, 327
Consonance, 49, 240
Constructivist theory, 74
Content, reading for, 58–59, 61
Contour, dramatic, 293
Controlled vocabulary, 180
Conversations, grand, 71, 452
Coretta Scott King Award, 86, 107, 108, 197, 205, 523–526
Council for Interracial Books for Children, 86, 87
Counting books, 178–179, 209–210
Counting-out rhymes, 229
Craft books, 383, 404–405
Creative dramatics, 430–432
Cultural authenticity, 87, 88, 89
Cultural details, accuracy of, 102–103
Cultural groups. *See also names of specific groups*
identification of, 91–92
informational books about, 381–382, 402
literature portraying, 127–129
multidimensional portrayal of, 102
Cultural markers, 115
Cultural perspective on reader response, 71–74
Culturally generic, neutral, and specific books, 85–86
Cultures, parallel, 84
Cumulative tales, 143–144

Curriculum
literary discussion in, 454–455
and multicultural books, 104
Cut paper, as artistic medium, 185–186

DEAR time, 439–440
Death, realistic fiction on, 281–282, 303
Denouement, 38
Developmental perspective on reader response, 65–67
Dialogue journals, 464
Diamante, 438–439
Disbelief, suspension of, 345–347
Discussion groups. *See also* Book clubs
with older elementary students, 70–71
open-ended questions in, 464–466
peer-led versus teacher-led, 71
teacher roles in, 71
with younger elementary students, 71
Diversity, 111–112. *See also* Multiple perspectives
in literature units, 497
in realistic fiction, 269–271
in United States, 82–84
Drama. *See also* Creative dramatics; Readers theater; Story theater
as response to literature, 69
improvisational, 432–433
Dramatic contour, 293
Dramatizing stories, 429, 446–447. *See also* Creative dramatics; Readers theater; Story theater
Drawing, pencil, 184–185
Dying, realistic fiction on, 281–282, 303
Dystopian societies, in science fiction, 356, 371–372

Early childhood books, 174–179
Easy readers, 180–181, 212
Efferent reading, 61
Egocentrism, of children, 16, 19, 20
English folklore, 154–155, 164–165
Environmental catastrophes, in science fiction, 356–357, 372
Envisionment building, 62
Epics, 145
Episodes, 39
Erikson's theory of personality development, 20–23
Ethnic groups in United States, books about, 84. *See also names of specific groups*
European Americans, literature portraying, 92
Exceptionalities, literature portraying, 112–113, 130–131
Experiential perspective on reader response, 62–65
Explicit themes, 42
Explorers, biographies of, 394, 406
Expository writing, 384
Extraordinary worlds, in fantasy, 342–343, 368
Ezra Jack Keats New Writers Award, 522

Fables, 141–142, 426
Fairytales, 144. *See also* Folktales; Traditional literature
setting in, 32

Families, realistic fiction on, 272–273, 296–297
Family history, 315–316, 327–328
Fantasy
appropriateness of, for children, 346
awards for, 363
criteria for selecting, 353–354
definition of, 336–337
distinguished from science fiction, 337–338
evolution of, 338–340
extraordinary worlds in, 342–343, 368
high, 337, 344–345, 370–371
low, 337, 340–344
magical powers in, 342, 366–368
major authors of, 347–353
outlandish characters in, 342, 366
personified animals in, 340–341, 364–365
personified toys in, 341–342, 365–366
versus realistic fiction, 294
supernatural elements in, 343–344, 368–369
theory of, 345–347
time slips in, 343–344, 369
Fictionalization
of biography, 392
of informational books, 379
of memoirs, 314–315
First-person point of view, 46–47
Flashbacks, 39
Folklore, 140–141. *See also* Folktales; Traditional literature
African, 160, 167
African American, 157–159
Appalachian, 159
Asian, 160–161, 168–169
English, 154–155
Hispanic, 159
Irish, 153–154
Latin American, 159–160, 167–168
Native American, 156–157
original sources of, 162–163
Russian, 156
Scandinavian, 155
Scottish, 154
similarities of, across cultures, 161
Welsh, 154
Folksongs, 145
as poetry, 230
Folktales, 138. *See also* Folklore; Traditional literature
characters in, 37
collections of, 139–140, 141
contrasts in, 150
French, 156, 165
German, 155, 165
North American, 156–157
plot in, 38–39, 41, 147–148
Russian, 156, 165–166
setting in, 32, 52
stereotyping in, 144
for storytelling, 426
types of, 142–145
Form, in poetry, 243–244
Formal operations period, 16, 17
Free response journals, 462–463
Free verse, 232–233
French folktales, 156, 165

Freud's theory, 35, 50–51, 151
Friendship, literature unit on, 497, 505
Frontier, western, historical fiction about, 322–323, 330–331

Gender equity, literature portraying, 109–111
Gender issues
  double standard in early realistic fiction, 268
  literature portraying, 129–130
Gender roles
  in books published in the past, 114
  criteria for evaluating, 110
  literature portraying, 109–111
Genres, 25–26. *See also specific genres*
  in book clubs, 454
  in collections of books, 104
  and cultural groups, 115
  in literature units, 482–483, 497–498
German folktales, 155, 165
Gouache, 184
Grand conversations, 71, 452. *See also*
  Book clubs; Literary discussion
Graphics, in informational books, 384
Greek myths, 152–153, 164
Grimms' fairytales, 138–139, 155
Griots, 160
Growing up, realistic fiction on, 271–272, 295–296
Guides, web, 546
Guilt, in Erikson's third stage of personality development, 21

Haiku, 232
Hans Christian Andersen Award, 107, 108–109, 512–513
Hero cycle (of Campbell), 148–150
Hero tales, 144, 148–149, 163
High fantasy, 337, 344–345, 370–371
Hispanic folklore, 159
Historical fiction
  about the American Revolution, 321–322, 329–330
  about ancient times through the medieval period, 319–320, 328–329
  versus biography, 315, 391
  characters in, 318–319, 326–327
  about the Civil War and slavery, 322, 330
  conflict in, 327
  definition of, 309
  about the early twentieth century, 323–324, 331–332
  evolution of, 310–314
  family history as, 315–316, 327–328
  fictionalized memoirs as, 314–315
  historical authenticity of, 325–327
  historical perspective in, 311–312
  versus informational books and textbooks, 310
  about the New World, 320–321, 329
  picture books as, 314
  plot in, 317–318
  research for, 316
  setting in, 317, 325
  style in, 311
  subject matter of, 312–313
  theme in, 319

value of, 309–310
  about the Western frontier, 322–323, 330–331
  about World War II and after, 324–325, 332–333
History, family, 315–316, 327–328
History, informational books on, 380–381, 401–402
Homosexuality, literature portraying, 111
Horn Book Magazine, The, 10, 26, 34, 163
Hornbooks, 12
How-to books, 383, 404–405
Humor, in realistic fiction, 280–281, 302–303

Identification, of reader with characters, 45
Identity versus role confusion (Erikson's fifth stage of personality development), 23
Illustrations. *See also* Picture books
  in early picture books, 172–173
  in multicultural literature, 101–102
Illustrators
  and artistic license, 89
  defining, of American picture books, 173–174
  media used by, 184–187
  of multicultural literature, 92–101
  of picture books, 193–203
  visual communication and, 188–192
Imagery, 42–43
Images, 48–49
  in poetry, 241–243, 245
Implicit themes, 42
Implied reader, 44–46, 53, 293–294
Imprints, 8
Improvisational drama, 432–433
Independent reading, 496
Industry versus inferiority (Erikson's fourth stage of personality development), 21–23
Informational books
  accuracy and authenticity in, 379, 390
  activity, craft, and how-to books, 383, 404–405
  on the arts, 382–383, 404
  awards for, 399
  benefits of, 377–378
  classroom uses for, 377
  criteria for selecting, 390–391
  definition of, 377–378
  evolution of, 378–380
  fictionalization of, 379
  graphics in, 384
  and historical fiction, 310, 318
  on history, 380–381, 401–402
  on how things work, 383, 404
  literary features of, 51–52
  major authors of, 385–389
  on nature, 382, 402–403
  on other cultures, 381–382, 402
  photo essay format in, 380
  series books, 383–384
  as support for literary discussion, 454–455
  text structures in, 378
  in thematic units, 482

theory of, 384–385, 388
  as vehicles for promoting understanding of other cultures, 83
Informational storybook, 379
Initiation stories, 40–41
Initiative versus guilt (Erikson's third stage of personality development), 21
Insider perspective, 88–90, 96, 101–102. *See also* Outsider perspective
Insight, in poetry, 244–245, 246
Intellectual development, of children, 15–18
International literature, 84
  awards for, 107–109
  definition of, 104–105
  evaluating quality of, 105–107
  translation of, 106–107
International Reading Association Children's Book Award, 521–522
Internet sites. *See* Web sites
Interpersonal relations, realistic fiction on, 274, 298–299
Interpretive community, 450–451. *See also* Book clubs
Intertextuality, 76
Irish folklore, 153–154

Japanese Americans, 97–98, 99–100
Jewish Americans, 91
John Newbery Medal. *See* Newbery Medal
Journals
  classroom use of, 462–464, 484, 496
  dialogue, 464
  free response, 462–463
  literary, 464
  professional, 26, 541–543
  prompted response, 463
Journey, as plot form, 41
Jump-rope rhymes, 229
Jung's theory, 141, 150, 151

King Arthur, literature unit on, 509

Labor stories, 159
Language
  authentic use of, 103
  sounds of, 49–50
Language Arts, 26
Language arts, in literature units, 483–484
Language charts, 468
Latin Americans
  folklore of, 159–160, 167–168
  literature portraying, 86, 87, 90, 91, 93, 124–125
  stereotyped images of, 90
Laura Ingalls Wilder Award, 533
Layout, 188–189
Learning, Vygotsky's theory of, 17. *See also* Intellectual development
Legends, 138, 143
  classic, 152–153
  for storytelling, 426
Lévi-Strauss's structured opposites, 150–151
Librarians
  and censorship, 14
  compilation of book collections by, 103–104
  professional journals for, 541–543
  selection of realistic fiction by, 293

Library. *See* Classroom library
Life-to-text transaction, 65
Lift-the-flap books, 175
Light, as element of design, 183
Limericks, 232
Line, as element of design, 182
Literacy
    lifelong, 498–499
    multicultural, 158
Literary craft
    elements of, 31, 453–454, 460–461,
        490, 492
    examples of, 477–478
Literary discussion. *See also* Book clubs;
        Literature units
    related to curriculum, 454–455
    role of teacher in, 458–461
Literary features, of informational books,
    51–52
Literary journals, 464
Literary learning
    and literature units, 498–499
    teacher support for, 460–461
Literary meaning making, 58–60, 65, 67.
    See also Reader response
Literary response. *See also* Reader response
    cumulative nature of, 483, 493
    dynamics of, 25
    and intellectual development, 17–18
Literary voice, 50–51
Literature of fact. *See* Informational books
Literature unit(s). *See also* Book clubs;
        Literary discussion
    on birds, 482–483
    on Chinese Americans, 508–509
    and comparative analysis, 487
    comparison of fiction and nonfiction in,
        491–492
    comparison of traditional and modern
        tales in, 488–490
    content of, 485–487
    contrasted to thematic unit, 482
    definition of, 481–482
    distinguishing features of, 482–484
    diversity in, 497
    explorations of author's craft in, 490, 492
    focus for, 494
    on friendship, 497, 505
    genres in, 482–483, 497–498
    independent reading in, 496
    on King Arthur, 509
    literacy and literary learning and,
        498–499
    on magical objects, 507
    realistic fiction in, 490–491
    response journals in, 496
    role of teacher in, 488
    selecting books for, 494–495
    as shared-text experience, 495–496
    student research in, 493–494
    on survival, 505–507
    synthesis in, 493, 496–497
    themes in, 487–488, 492–493
    on William Steig, 507
Low fantasy, 337, 340–344
Lyrics (expressive poems), 230

Magazines, for children, 544–545
Magical objects, literature unit on, 507

Magical powers, in fantasy, 342, 366–368
Margaret A. Edwards Award, 97
Media, for illustrations, 184-187
Medieval period, historical fiction about,
    319–320, 328–329
Memoirs, and historical fiction, 314–315
Mental challenges, realistic fiction on,
    274–275, 299
Mental schemes, 15
Metaphor, 49, 242, 437
Mexican Americans
    literature portraying, 98
    as readers, 88
Mildred Batchelder Award, 107, 109,
    513–514
Mistrust (in Erikson's first stage of person-
    ality development), 21
Mixed media, 187
Moral development, of children, 18–20
Moral dilemmas, realistic fiction on,
    275–276, 300
Moral stance, of reader, 45–46
Morphology, Propp's, 147–148
Mother Goose rhymes, 145–146, 176–177,
    206–207, 228
Motif, 141
Motives, children's assessment of, 19
Multicultural education, 82
Multicultural literacy, 158
Multicultural literature
    awards for, 107–109
    in the classroom library, 419
    criteria for evaluating and selecting,
        101–104
    and cultural authenticity, 87, 88, 89
    definition of, 84
    ensuring balance in collections of,
        103–104
    evolution of, 86–87
    and identification of cultural groups,
        91–92
    major authors and illustrators of,
        92–101, 282, 303–304
    and stereotyping, 90–91
    types of, 85–86
    value of, 84–85
Multiple perspectives
    role of literature in influencing, 83–84
    role of schools in presenting, 83
    role of teachers in presenting, 113–114
Mysteries, 39
    plot in, 41
    as realistic fiction, 278–279, 301
Myths, 138, 141
    classic, 152–152
    for storytelling, 426

Narrative poems, 231
National Council of Teachers of English
    (NCTE) Award for Excellence in Poetry
    for Children, 249, 526
Native Americans, 87
    folklore of, 156–157
    literature portraying, 86, 87, 89, 90, 91,
        93–94, 95, 125–127, 166–167
    stereotyped images of, 90
    traditional stories of, 139
Nature
    informational books on, 382, 402–403

realistic fiction on, 279–280, 302
New Advocate, The, 26, 34
New Realism, 270, 393
New World, historical fiction about,
    320–321, 329
Newbery Medal, 13, 34, 96, 107, 109,
    526–532
Nonsense verse, 231–232
North American folktales, 156–157, 164
Numbskull tales, 145
Nursery rhymes, 176, 206–207
    contrasted to poetry, 227
    as form of poetry, 228–229

Oil painting, 184
On-line resources, 546–547
Onomatopoeia, 241
Open-ended questions, 464–466
Opposites, structured, 150–151
Orbis Pictus Award for Outstanding
    Nonfiction for Children, 532–533
Outlandish characters, in fantasy, 342, 366
Outsider perspective, 87, 88–90. *See also*
    Insider perspective

Page turns, 189
Painting, 184
Pantheon, 152
Paper crafts, as artistic media, 185–186
Papermaking, 185
Parallel cultures, 84
Partial biographies, 393
Patois, 157
Peer-led discussions, 71
Pencil drawing, as artistic medium,
    184–185
Personal stories, 72
Personality development, of children,
    20–23
Personification, 49, 242
    of animals, 340–341, 364–365
    of toys, 341–342, 365–366
Perspective(s)
    of author, 87, 88–90, 96, 101–102
    in illustrations, 190
    multiple, 83–84, 113–114
Photographs, as illustrations, 187, 380
Physical challenges, realistic fiction on,
    274–275, 299
Piaget's developmental theory, 15–17,
    18–19
Picture books
    audience for, 204, 205
    awards for, 205
    categories of, 174–181
    and changes in printing technology,
        172–173
    definition of, 171
    design elements of, 182–184
    evaluating quality in, 203–205
    evolution of, 171–174
    historical fiction in, 314
    illustrators of, 193–203
    on King Arthur, literature unit using,
        509
    media used in, 184–187
    picture/text relationships in, 192–193
    for readers theater, 430
    selection criteria for, 205

theory of. *See* Visual communication
Picture storybooks, 171, 181, 182, 213–224
Picture/text relationships, 192–193
Pidgin, 157
Plot, 9, 38–42, 54–55, 453, 475–477
  and character development, 37
  episodes in, 39
  in folktales, 38–39, 41, 147–148
  in historical fiction, 317–318
  recurring, 40–41
  structure of, 52
Pluralism, 82. *See also* Diversity
Poetry. *See also names of specific poetic forms*
  categories of, 227–233
  children's preferences in, 246–248
  children's writing of, 436–439
  choral reading of, 248, 257–258, 434–436
  contemporary, 235–238
  contrasted to verse and rhyme, 227, 246
  criteria for choosing, 245–248
  definition of, 226–227
  encouraging responses to, 434
  evolution of, 233–235
  folksongs as, 230
  form in, 243–244
  images in, 241–243, 245
  incorporating into school day, 433–434
  insight in, 244–245, 246
  literary features of, 52
  sounds in, 238–241, 245
  as traditional literature, 145
Poets, 249–257
Point of view, 46–47
Pop-up books, 175
Pourquoi tales, 143
Predictable books, 179–180, 212–213
Preoperational period, 16, 18, 66
Prior knowledge, 483
Professional journals, 26, 541–543
Professional organizations, addresses of, 534
Prompted response journals, 463
Propp's morphology, 147–148
Protagonist, 37
Proverb, 141
Psychoanalytic dynamics, of traditional literature, 151–152
Publishers, addresses of, 535–536

Randolph Caldecott Medal. *See* Caldecott Medal
Read-alouds. *See* Reading aloud
Reader response
  in book clubs, 462–472
  and comprehension, 461
  cultural perspective on, 71–74
  developmental perspective on, 65–67
  experiential perspective on, 62–65
  and language charts, 468
  and personal stories, 72
  psychoanalytic dynamic of, 152
  social perspective on, 68–71
  and story webs, 469–471
  textual perspective on, 74–77
  theory of, 60
Reader(s)
  filling in the gaps by, 46

  implied, 44–46, 53, 293–294
  role of, in aesthetic reading, 61
  stances of, while reading, 62–65
Readers theater, 429–430
Reading
  for aesthetic judgments, 59, 61
  against the grain, 43–44
  components of skills for, 24–25
  for content, 58–59, 61
  as a continuum, 61
  efferent, 61
  for social attitudes, 59, 60
  by textual structures, 59
  theory of, 23–25
  as a transaction, 59, 60
Reading aloud, 418
  benefits of, 20
  and book club sessions, 457
  preparing for, 421–423
  research on, 419–420
  scheduling, 420–421
  selecting books for, 421, 442–445
  techniques for, 423–424
Reading comprehension, 24–25, 58–59, 66, 461
Reading Teacher, The, 416
Realistic fiction
  adolescents in, 269, 270–271
  characters in, 37
  on death and dying, 281–282, 303
  definition of, 265–266
  disagreements about, 270, 271
  diversity in, 269–271
  evaluating, 292–293
  evolution of, 267–271
  on families, 272–273, 296–297
  versus fantasy, 294
  humor in, 280–281, 302–303
  on interpersonal relations, 274, 298–299
  in literature unit on the sea, 490–491
  major authors of, 286–292
  on mental and physical challenges, 274–275, 299
  on moral dilemmas, 275–276, 300
  with multicultural and international themes, 282
  mysteries in, 278–279, 301
  on nature, 279–280, 302
  on romance and sexuality, 275, 299–300
  on school and society, 273–274, 297–298
  on self-discovery and growing up, 271–272, 295–296
  setting in, 32–33
  on sports, 279, 301–302
  on survival, 276–278, 300–301
  theory of, 283–285
  value of, 266–267
Recurring plots, 40–41
Religious stories, 141
Repetition, as factor in encouraging responses to literature, 68–69, 77
Research
  for historical fiction, 316
  on reading aloud, 419–420
  by students, 493–494
Resolution, 38
Response-based discussion, role of teacher in modeling, 458–459
Response journals, 462–463, 496

Response to literature, 25. *See also* Book clubs; Journals; Reader response theory
  and children's intellectual development, 17–18
  and children's moral development, 19–20
Rhyme(s), 239–240, 245. *See also* Mother Goose rhymes; Nursery rhymes
  counting-out, 229
  jump-rope, 229
Rhythm, in poetry, 238–239, 245
Riddles, 146–147
Rising action, 38
Role confusion (in Erikson's fifth stage of personality development), 23
Roman myths, 152–153, 164
Romance, realistic fiction on, 275, 299–300
Runes, 161
Russian folktales, 156, 165–166

Scaffolding, 71
Scandinavian folktales, 155
Schemes, mental, 15
School, realistic fiction on, 273–274, 297–298
School Library Journal, 26, 34, 163
Science fantasy, 337–338, 357, 372–373. *See also* Fantasy; Science fiction
Science fiction
  awards for, 363
  criteria for selecting, 362–363
  definition of, 337
  distinguished from fantasy, 337–338
  about environmental catastrophes, 356–357, 372
  evolution of, 354–355
  major authors of, 358–362
  scientific principles as basis for, 355–356, 371
  themes in, 355
  theory of, 357–358
  about utopian and dystopian societies, 356, 371–372
Scientific principles, as basis for science fiction, 355–356, 371
Scottish folklore, 154
Scratchboard, 186
Sea, literature unit on, 502–505
Selection aids, 538–541
Self-discovery, realistic fiction on, 271–272, 295–296
Sensorimotor period, 16
Series books, 269, 283
  biographies as, 393
  in the classroom library, 417
  informational books as, 383–384
Setting, 31–35, 53
  in folktales, 32, 52
  in historical fiction, 317, 325
  as literary feature, 33–35
Sexuality, realistic fiction on, 275, 299–300
Shame versus autonomy (Erikson's second stage of personality development), 21
Shape, as element of design, 183–184
Shared-text experience, 485
Sight vocabulary, 24
Simile, 49, 242
Skipping rhymes, 146

Slavery, historical fiction about, 322, 330
Social issues, 114–115, 129–130, 269, 270, 271, 272–273, 276
realistic fiction on, 273–274, 297–298
Social perspective on reader response, 68–71
Sounds, in poetry, 238–239, 245
Space fantasy, 357. *See also* Fantasy; Science fiction
Sports, realistic fiction on, 279, 301–302
Stage theories of child development, 15–18, 20–23
Stances, of readers, 62–65
Steig, William, literature unit on, 507
Stepping out and objectifying the (reading) experience, 64–65
Stereotyping, 90–91
of cultural groups, 102
of gender roles, 144
of people with exceptionalities, 112
in traditional literature, 144, 162
Stories
dramatizing of, 429–433
religious, 141
learning, for storytelling, 426–428
types, for storytelling, 425–426
Story line. *See* Plot
Story theater, 429
Story webs, 469–471
Storytellers, children as, 427, 428
Storytelling, 139, 424, 445–446
benefits of, 425
folktales for, 426
learning stories for, 426–428
and story types, 425–426
Style, 47–51. *See also* Writing style
Supernatural elements, in fantasy, 343–344, 368–369
Survival
literature unit on, 505–507
realistic fiction on, 276–278, 300–301
Survival stories, 22, 23
Suspension of disbelief, 345–347

Tale type, 141
Tall tales, 143, 159, 426
Teachers
and adult reading, 113–114
and author visits to schools, 440
and censorship, 14
compilation of book collections by, 103–104
demonstration of commitment to reading by, 439–440
and evaluation of international literature, 105–106
professional journals for, 541–543

and professional literature, 114
role of, in book club discussions, 458–461
role of, in creative dramatics, 431–432
role of, in encouraging responses to reading, 67, 68
role of, in improvisational drama, 433
role of, in literature units, 488
role of, in presenting multiple perspectives, 113–114, 419
role of, in shaping children's reading choices, 417
selection of realistic fiction by, 293
Text structures, in informational books, 378
Text-to-life transaction, 65, 77
Textbooks, versus historical fiction, 310
Textual perspective on reader response, 74–77
Textual structures, reading by, 59
Texture, as element of design, 184
Thematic unit, contrasted to literature unit, 482
Theme(s), 42–44, 55–56, 453, 472–475
explicit, 42
in historical fiction, 319
implicit, 42
linking of books by, 498–499
in literature unit on the sea, 487–488, 492–493
multicultural and international, in realistic fiction, 282
in science fiction, 355
Third-person (omniscient) point of view, 47
Time slips, in fantasy literature, 343–344, 369
Time variations, 39
Totemic tradition, 157
Toy books, 175–176, 207–208
Toys, personified, in fantasy, 341–342
Traditional literature. *See also specific types of stories*
from the British Isles, 153–154
categories of, 141–147
criteria for selecting, 162–163
definition of, 137
derivatives of, 161–162
evolution of, 137–141
French, 156
German, 155
psychoanalytic dynamics of, 151–152
qualities of, 138
Scandinavian, 155
theory of, 147–152
Transaction, reading as, 59, 60
life-to-text, 65
perspectives on, 61–77
text-to-life, 65, 77

Transitional objects, books as, 21
Translation, of international books, 106–107
Trickster tales, 143, 157, 163, 509–510
Trust versus mistrust (Erikson's first stage of personality development), 21

Underground Railroad, 84, 157
United States
diversity in, 82–84
historical figures, biographies of, 405–406
political leaders, biographies of, 405
Utopian societies, in science fiction, 356, 371–372

Verse. *See also* Poetry
free, 232–233
nonsense, 231–232
Vinyl books, 175
Visual communication
backgrounds in, 190–191
characterization in, 189–190
color in, 191–192
elements of, 187–188
layout in, 188–189
perspective in, 190
Vocabulary
controlled, 180
sight, 24
Voice, literary, 50–51
Vygotsky's learning theory, 17

Watercolor painting, as artistic medium, 184
Web sites on children's literature, 546–547
Webs, story, 469–471
Welsh folklore, 154
Western frontier, historical fiction about, 322–323, 330–331
Wood block printing, 172–173
Woodcut illustrations, 186
Word choice, 48
Wordless books, 171, 179, 205–206, 211–212
World leaders, biographies of, 406
World War II, historical fiction about, 324–325, 332–333
Writers. *See* Authors
Writing. *See also* Journals
expository, 384
as response to literature, 69
web sites on, 547
Writing style
in biography, 399
in historical fiction, 311
in informational books, 391

Credits